Preface

It is perhaps natural to ask whether a book that covers this many topics is unavoidably superficial. For example, 2D Canvas, a topic that sometimes takes an entire book to teach, is fully covered in just 9 pages here. Having envisioned and designed this book from scratch, I am compelled to clarify that it is not my intention to sacrifice depth for breadth. Instead, this book is meant to be concise, comprehensive and comprehensible. The careful reader will find that this book includes many 'tricks' that have hardly been documented at all. The goal of this book is to allow any reader to become sufficiently proficient in web development to be able to undertake almost any web mission with ease.

Condensing so much content into just one book is itself a Herculean task. However, given the ubiquity of the Internet, it is also a worthwhile one. There have already been many books that teach a single topic, but hardly has any book covered so many topics.

The first five chapters establish the foundation of the book, and are meant to be read in sequence. The other chapters may be read in any order. Those who wish to set up their own servers early may choose to read Chapter 13 first.

This is not to say the topics were selected without discretion. The proliferation of server technologies, for instance, often confuses a newcomer. Instead of covering all server technologies which serve similar purposes, I have chosen to focus on PHP, which is the dominant server technology presently. What can be achieved by other competing server technologies can generally be achieved by PHP. Some languages, like Java, are also covered partially, because a full coverage of their extensive libraries is apparently well beyond the scope of a book such as this.

'Give a man a fish and you feed him for a day. Teach a man to fish and you feed him for a lifetime'. This book is not so much about top-down designs, algorithms and best practices. Rather, this book focuses exclusively on the technical fundamentals of web technologies. Each tag, function, or keyword is usually accompanied by an illustrating example. Readers are encouraged to exercise their imagination in devising various programs, which can take on infinite forms.

Out of the numerous illustrations, where permitted, a few were adopted directly, with references to the sources. Sometimes it is very difficult, if not impossible, to exceed the skill with which a concept is explained. There is little point in making slight modifications to the original examples and pretending they are my own. Instead, I have tried to acknowledge the original teachers' works. This will also serve to guide the reader to some good external sources, should the reader need any further study on a topic.

Given the availability of free information in the Internet, the rationality of buying a book on a similar subject is questionable. For one thing, a book is easy to carry about, and can be read in places like a bus. Having all the materials nicely packed into one book will save the learner the troubles of searching different sources and consulting other professionals. The contents are carefully chosen and succinctly written, so that they cover all essential concepts, without diverting the reader's attention to complex, unimportant information. The book is split into parts, chapters, sections, subsections and tables, and the functions are grouped by their functional similarities instead of listed by the alphabetical order. The high level of organization means that the reader will know how various technologies relate to one another. After knowing their proper places in web development, the reader will obtain a clear, holistic view on this complex field.

When writing a programming book, the writer always finds it a challenge to try to suit readers of varying knowledge background. While a beginner may prefer detailed explanations with many examples, an expert seeking a good reference may find a lengthy writing to be boring and inefficient. Bear in mind that this is an accelerated course. The explanations tend to be brief and curt, but just adequate. Although previous programming experience is not strictly a requirement, those already savvy in programming will find this book easier to read. A novice is urged to stay focused, slowly digest the concepts, and study the examples carefully. Soon the novice will find the learning to be enjoyable, and the reading a rewarding session.

Acknowledgements

The author expresses his gratitude for the following contributors' assistance in the completion of this book:

Freelancer AnnaWinn (Dr. Paul McArthur, United States) for an excellent exposition on SEO.

Freelancer invictos (Mujtaba Aslam, Pakistan) for co-writing a chapter on Java Applet.

Freelancer ekklisis (Fotinee Economou, Greece) for a draft on SQL.

Freelancer icq (India) for his direct-login scripts in PHP.

Freelancer YiamiYo (Greece) for his WebGL script on stencil shadow volume.

Freelancer ITExpert78 (India) for helping to setup the Red5 media server.

Freelancer vano101 (Ukraine) for helping to compile a libcURL program.

Freelancer richwales75 (United States) for proofreading a chapter.

Freelancer louiz920 (United States) for helping to set up a home server.

Dr. Michael Kay (United Kingdom) for his answers to XML-related questions in StackOverflow.

About the Author

Chong Lip Phang was born in Kota Kinabalu, Malaysia in 1982. He was educated in SJK(C) Chung Hwa Likas and briefly in Sabah Tshung Tsin Secondary School. Later, he studied in Singapore in The Chinese High School under the ASEAN Scholarship and Hwa Chong Junior College.

Chong Lip Phang has been involved in programming since 1993. He graduated with a degree in Computer Science from the National University of Singapore, the top university in Asia. Being a web developer and a freelancer himself, he has been coding many websites.

An advocator of concise technical writing, he has been planning to publish a programming manual since he was in university.

List of Chapters

Table of Contents

8. 2D Canvas

9. WebGL Canvas

10. Java Applet

11. Flash ActionScript

12. Translated Text & Video Chat

13. Servers

14. .htaccess

18. Search Engine Optimization

1. Hyper Text Markup Language

A webpage that one sees when browsing the Internet is composed of tags organized into a hierarchical fashion. Conceptually each tag, enclosed within <>, can be regarded as a node in a tree that branches out to form more nodes.

Notpad++ is the recommended editor when working with HTML, CSS, JavaScript, PHP, XML etc. The names of HTML files end with a .html or .htm extension. "index.html" can be retrieved by specifying only the directory in the address bar.

basic.html : A simple html file for the browser.

```
<!DOCTYPE html>
<html>
   <head>
      <title> A Simple HTML Document </title>
   </head>
   <body>
     <p  id="s1"> This example outlines the typical structure
                  of an HTML document.</p>
     <p  id="s2"> This p node has the attribute id. There
                  should be one &lt;html&gt;, one
                  &lt;head&gt; and one &lt;body&gt;
                  nodes.</p>
   </body>
</html>
```

This example outlines the typical structure of an HTML document.

This p node has the attribute id. There should be one <html>, one <head> and one <body> nodes.

An opening tag usually needs to be closed by the corresponding closing tag. Each kind of tag can be associated with specific *attributes*. These are extra descriptions that exist in the opening tags before '>'. Some tags can also be associated with *events* (1.5.2). Prefixed with 'on', events specify what Javascript code to run upon an incident such as a mouse click or the pressing of a key. In the following sections, the word after ...... is an *attribute* or *event*. The tags that are underlined here do not need to be closed with a separate closing tag.

1.1. Structural Elements

1.1.1 Declaration

<!DOCTYPE> declares the version of HTML used. It must precede <html>. (1.5.3)
Use <!DOCTYPE html> for HTML 5.

<html> marks the start of a html document, which can be divided into the head and the body.
...... manifest=*url*: relates to the application cache file that specifies what to be loaded into the cache for fast and offline browsing (1.6.3).
...... xmlns=*uri*: specifies the namespace if XHTML is to be conformed to. Although any string can be specified here, a URI (Uniform Resource Identifier) such as 'http://www.example.com' is generally used. No connection will be made to the site. Its use is meant to prevent the clash of names in the child elements with those of other XML tags (Chapter 6).

As a side note, it is worthwhile to mention that an IRI (International Resource Identifier) differs from a URI (Uniform Resource Identifier) in that IRI supports international characters, whereas URI supports only ASCII encoding. On the other hand, a URL (Uniform Resource Locator) is a type of URI that identifies its resource using the representation of its network access.

1.1.2 Head

<head> defines the head section, which contains general information about the document and relates to external files. It can contain the following tags in this subsection (1.1.2).

<title> is meant to be displayed by the browser tab, favorite folder and search engines.

<script> defines a client-side script (Chapter 3).
...... async: asynchronous execution
...... defer: execution of an external script after parsing
...... type= MIME_type (1.5.7)
...... charset= charset (1.5.4)
...... src=url

<noscript> defines the content when the client-side script cannot be loaded. (Chapter 3)

<style> defines style information (Chapter 2).
...... type=MIME_type (1.5.7)
...... media=media-query (1.5.8)
...... disabled: disable the style rules
...... scoped: apply to the parent only

<link> defines the relationship with an external file.
...... href=url
...... hreflang = two_letter_language_code (1.5.5)
...... media = media-query (1.5.8)
...... sizes = heightxwidth (eg. sizes="32x32")
...... type = MIME_type (1.5.7)
...... crossorigin = {anonymous | use-credentials}
...... rel= { alternate | archives | author | bookmark | external | first | help | icon | index | last | license | next | nofollow | noreferrer | pingback | prefetch | prev | profile | search | stylesheet | sidebar | tag | up }

<base> specifies the base URL for all relative URLs
...... href=URL
...... target= {_blank: new window or tab |
_parent: in the parent frame |
_self: in the current frame |
_top: in the full body |
framename: in the frame}

<meta> defines metadata such as page information, authors, keywords and modification dates. It is not displayed but can be parsed by machines and search engines (Chapter 18).
...... http-equiv= {default-style: preferred CSS |
refresh: no. of seconds to refresh}
...... name={application-name |
author |
description |
generator |
keywords}
...... content=description
...... charset=charset(1.5.4)

If the 'url' part in the <meta> tag is omitted, the webpage simply refreshes itself.

Setting the 'charset' to be 'UTF-8' allows Chinese characters etc. to be displayed.

```
<!DOCTYPE html>
<html manifest="cache.appcache">
<head>
  <title>HTML Header Tags</title>
  <meta name="author" content="Phillip" />
  <meta name="keywords" content="HTML, head " />
  <meta name="description" content="for SEO." />
  <meta http-equiv="refresh"
        content="30; url=http://www.google.com" />
  <meta charset="UTF-8" />
  <base href="http://www.youtube.com" />
</head>
<body>
  Wait 30 seconds to be redirected to Google.
  谢谢。
</body>
</html>
```

1.1.3 Division

<body> defines the body section. All subsequent tags in this chapter go into the body section.

<hr /> displays a horizontal line.

**
** inserts a line break.

<!-- --> define a comment. A comment is used to explain a piece of code.

The following tags in this subsection (1.1.3) allow the document to be modified using CSS. Correctly using an element type makes the code more readable.

<p> denotes a paragraph on a new line.

<div> divides the body into blocks of content. It can be used to set styles with CSS and format the document layout into rows and columns (2.7.1).

<section> denotes a section.

<main> defines the main content.

<span> provides a hook to group inline elements and format the text within with CSS, without starting a new line.

<article> contains an article. The self-contained content could exist independently of the rest of the content.

<aside> defines a section that does not belong to the main flow. It contains side information like an explanation box or an advertisement.

<details> represents a widget from which the user can obtain additional information or controls.
......open: makes the details visible
<summary> specifies a summary inside <details>.

<blockquote> indents a section that is quoted from another source.
...... cite=URL

<nav> groups navigation links.

<header> and **<footer>** define the header and footer respectively.

```
<!DOCTYPE html> <!-- HTML5 -->
<html>
<head>
  <title>HTML Sectioning</title>
</head>
<body>
  <header>
     About HTML. <hr />
  </header>
  <section>
    <h1> Tags </h1>
    <p> There are over 100 kinds of HTML tags. </p>
    <p> Comments are not displayed. </p>
  </section> <hr />
  <section>
    <h1> Articles </h1>
    <article>Here is my article.</article>
    <blockquote>  I have a dream that one day this nation
will rise up and live out the true meaning of its creed:  "We
hold these truths to be self-evident: that  all men are created
equal." </blockquote>
  </section> <hr />
  <aside>
    Ad: Buy Web Coding Bible at Amazon now!
  </aside> <hr />
  <footer>
     This is the footer. <br /> <br /> <br /> <br /> The end.
  </footer>
</body>
</html>
```

About HTML.

Tags

There are over 100 kinds of HTML tags.

Comments are not displayed.

Articles

Here is my article.

> I have a dream that one day this nation will rise up and live out the true meaning of its creed: "We hold these truths to be self-evident: that all men are created equal."

Ad: Buy Web Coding Bible at Amazon now!

This is the footer.

The end.

1.1.4 iframe

<iframe> loads an external HTML file within. Between the opening and closing tags is the alternative content if iframe is not supported

...... src=url
...... height=pixels
...... width=pixels
...... name=text
...... allowfullscreen
...... sandbox={"":allows all options below |
allow-forms |
allow-same-origin |
allow-scripts |
allow-top-navigation |
allow-popups |
allow-pointer-lock}
...... seamless
...... srcdoc=HTML_code

You can embed a YouTube video using an iframe. All you have to do is note the video id.

```
<!DOCTYPE html>
<html>
<head>
  <title>YouTube iframe</title>
  <base href="http://www.youtube.com"/>
</head>
<body>
  <iframe width="420" height="345" seamless allowfullscreen
       name="youtubeframe" src="/embed/RRvJ9ff0TUs">
    <p>Your browser does not support iframes.</p>
  </iframe>
</body>
</html>
```

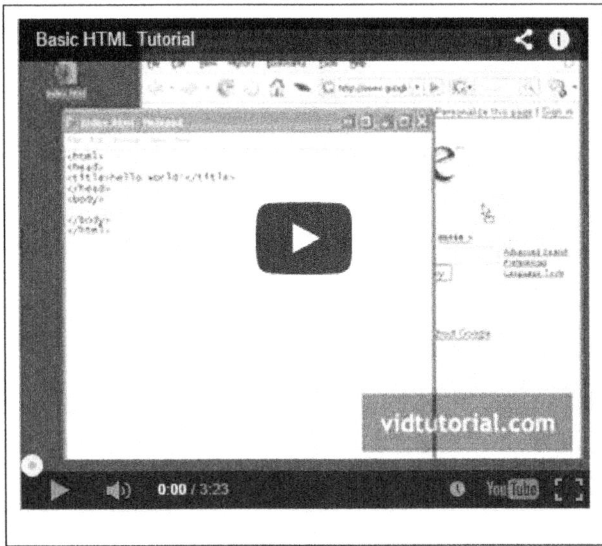

1.2 Text Elements

1.2.1 Hyperlink

<a> specifies a hyperlink to an external HTML file

...... href=URL#tag_id
...... hreflang=two_letter_language_code(1.5.5)
...... media=media_query (1.5.8)
...... type=MIME_type(1.5.7).
...... download
...... ping
...... target= {_blank: in a new window or tab |
_parent: in the parent frame |
_self: in the current frame |
_top: in the full body |
framename: in the named frame}
...... rel={ alternate|
author|
bookmark|
help|
license: copyright information|
next|
nofollow: tells search engines not to follow|
noreferrer: no HTTP referrer header|
prefetch: to be cached|
prev|
search: links to a search tool|
tag}

```
<!DOCTYPE html>
<html>
<head>
  <title>Hyperlinking</title>
</head>
<body>
Click <a href="http://www.w3.org/TR/2012/WD-html5-diff-
20120329/#abstract" rel="help">here</a> for more
information.

<p>You can send an email like
  <a href="mailto:testing@example.com?Subject=Hi">
  this</a>.
</p>

<p>You can download a file like
  <a href="testing.gif" download>this</a>.
</p>
</body>
</html>
```

Click here for more information.

You can send an email like this.

You can download a file like this.

1.2.2 Formatting

<h1> ,<h2>,<h3>,<h4>,<h5> and **<h6>** define headings, with h1 being the biggest. Using headings allows engines to produce smarter search results. **<hgroup>** groups heading tags.

<b>:bold. **<i>**:italic **<u>:**underline
<sub>: subscript **<sup>**:superscript
<mark>: highlights **<small>**:small font
<s>:strikethrough

<q>:quotes
...... cite=URL

<del>:deleted text
...... cite=URL
...... datetime=datetime

<ins>: inserted text
...... cite=URL
...... datetime=datetime

<pre>: preformatted text, ie. fixed-width font. The space inside the content here does not collapse, which can be important when there is a need to indent or space out the text.

```
<!DOCTYPE html>
<html>
<head>
  <title>Formatting</title>
</head>
<body>
  <hgroup>
    <h1>Formatting</h1>
           <h2>-- Sizing, Decoration, and Spacing</h2>
  </hgroup>
  <b>bold</b> <br/>
  <i>italic</i> <br/>
  <u>underline</u> <br/>
  X<sub>1</sub> <br/>
  X<sup>2</sup> <br/>
  <mark>mark</mark> <br/>
  <small>small</small> <br/>
  <q>quotes</q> <br/>
  <s>strikethrough</s> <br/>
  <del>deleted text</del> <br/>
  <ins>inserted text</ins> <br/>
  <pre>   See ?
   Space   does      not
           collapse    here.
  </pre>
</body>
</html>
```

Formatting

-- Sizing, Decoration, and Spacing

bold
italic
underline
X_1
X^2
mark
small
"quotes"
~~strikethrough~~
~~deleted text~~
inserted text

```
   See ?
     Space   does         not
         collapse    here.
```

1.2.3 Orientation

<ruby> writes some text directly above some other text. **<rt>** is used within <ruby> to describe the text above.**<rp>** is used within <ruby> to instruct what to show if <ruby> annotations are not supported.

<bdi> isolates text that might be formatted differently from the text outside. **<bdo>:** bidirectional override......dir={lrt:left-to-right| rtl:right-to-left}
<wbr> says where is fine to add a line-break.

```
<!DOCTYPE html>
<html>
<head>
  <title>Orientation</title>
  <meta charset="UTF-8"/>
</head>
<body>
The <b>&#60ruby&#62</b> tag can be used to show
the pronunciation of an East-<wbr/>Asian word.
For example:
<ruby>网<rt>wang3</rt>上<rt>shang4</rt></ruby>
This is <bdo dir="rtl">inverted</bdo>.
</body>
</html>
```

The **<ruby>** tag can be used to show the pronunciation of an East-Asian word. For example: 网(wang3) 上(shang4) This is detrevni.

1.2.4 Special Meanings

The 7 phrase tags below can be used to achieve richer effects with CSS. **<em>** renders as emphasized text. **<strong>** means important text. **<abbr>** contains an abbreviation. **<samp>** defines a sample output. **<kbd>** defines keyboard input. **<var>** defines a variable. **<address>** defines a physical address related to the website. **<cite>** contains the title of a piece of work.

<time> defines time.
...... datetime=datetime

```
<!DOCTYPE html>
<html>
<head>
  <title>Information</title>
</head>
<body>
  This is <em>emphasized</em>.<br/>
  This is <strong>important</strong>.<br/>
  Made in the <abbr>UK</abbr>.<br/>
  Command:<code>alert("Hello");</code>.<br/>
  Key:<kdb>CTRL+S</kdb>.<br/>
  Variable:<var>i</var>.<br/>
  More information can be found at
  <cite>W3C Recommendation for HTML</cite>.<br/>
  Written at
  <time datetime="2014-10-13 12:47">
   12:47pm</time>.<br/>
  In <address>Tanjung Aru Beach,
  Kota Kinabalu, Malaysia.</address><br/>
</body>
</html>
```

This is *emphasized*.
This is **important**.
Made in the UK.
Command:`alert("Hello");`.
Key:CTRL+S.
Variable:*i*.
More information can be found at *W3C Recommendation for HTML*.
Written at 12:47pm.
In
Tanjung Aru Beach, Kota Kinabalu, Malaysia.

1.3 Figure Elements

1.3.1 List

<ol>: ordered list.
...... reversed
...... start= number
...... type= {1|A|a|I|i}

<ul>: unordered list.

<li>:used within <ol> and <ul> to list items.
...... value=number

<dl>:definition list.
<dt>:definition term, used within <dl>.
<dfn>: defining instance of a term.
<dd>:definition description, used within <dl>.

```
<!DOCTYPE html>
<html>
<head>
  <title> Lists </title>
</head>
<body>
  <ol reversed>
    <li> An ordered list has a number in front of each item.
       </li>
    <li> There are five types of ordered list. </li>
    <li> The order can be reversed. </li>
  </ol><br />
  <ul>
    <li> An unordered list does not show any number. </li>
    <li> A list can be controlled in more ways with CSS. </li>
    <li> The order can be changed. </li>
  </ul><br />
  <dl>
  <dt><dfn>dl</dfn></dt><dd>definition list</dd>
  <dt><dfn>dt</dfn></dt><dd>definition term</dd>
  <dt><dfn>dd</dfn></dt><dd>definition description</dd>
  </dl><br />
</body>
</html>
```

3. An ordered list has a number in front of each item.
2. There are five types of ordered list.
1. The order can be reversed.

- An unordered list does not show any number.
- A list can be controlled in more ways with CSS.
- The order can be changed.

dl
    definition list
dt
    definition term
dd
    definition description

1.3.2 Progress and Meter

<progress> defines progress.
...... max=number: the total amount of work
...... value=number: amount of work done.

<meter> defines a scalar measurement.
...... form=form_id
...... high= number
...... low= number
...... max= number
...... min= number
...... optimum= number
...... value= number

The meter bar changes its colour when the value is less than 'low' or more than 'high'.

```
<!DOCTYPE>
<html>
<head>
  <title>Fraction Display</title>
</head>
<body>
  Progress:
  <progress max="100" value="80">
   80% complete</progress>
  <br/><br/>
  Meter:
  <meter min="200" max="500" value="400"
            low="250" high="350">400C</meter>
</body>
</html>
```

Progress:

Meter:

1.3.3 Table

<table> defines a table.

<tr> defines a table row, used within <table>.
<th> defines a table header cell, used within <tr>.
...... colspan=number
...... rowspan=number
...... headers=headers_ids : the related header cells
...... scope={col |
colgroup |
row |
rowgroup}
<td> defines a table cell, used within <tr>.
...... colspan=number
...... rowspan=number
...... headers=headers_ids cells

<caption> defines a caption immediately after <table>.

<col> specifies the properties for the entire columns, used within <colgroup>.
...... span=number

<colgroup> groups <col>, used within <table>.
......span=number

<thead> <tfoot> <tbody> optionally group the <tr> tags, used within <table>, and represents the first, last, and central rows respectively.

```
<!DOCTYPE html>
<html>
<head>
  <title> Table </title>
</head>
<body>
<table>
  <caption> HTML Table </caption>
  <colgroup>
    <col style="background-color:grey" />
    <col span="2" style="background-color:yellow" />
    <col style="background-color:orange" />
  </colgroup>
  <thead>
    <tr><th>Name</th>
          <td>Wins</td>
          <td>Losses</td>
          <td>Score</td>
    </tr>
  </thead>
  <tfoot>
    <tr><th colspan=3>Total score:</th>
          <td>17</td>
    </tr>
  </tfoot>
  <tbody>
    <tr><th>George</th>
          <td>20</td>
          <td>15</td>
          <td>5</td>
    </tr>
    <tr><th>Bill</th>
          <td>15</td>
          <td>3</td>
          <td>12</td>
    </tr>
  </tbody>
</table><br />
</body>
</html>
```

HTML Table

Name	Wins	Losses	Score
George	20	15	5
Bill	15	3	12
Total score:			17

1.3.4 Image

<img> shows an image file. (tip: Use the Magic Wand Tool in Paint.NET to delete any transparent regions.)
...... src= URL
...... alt=text: alternative text
...... height=pixels
...... width= pixels
...... ismap: server-side image map
...... usemap=mapname: client-side image map
...... crossorigin={ anonymous | use-credentials }

<map> defines an image-map that splits an image into clickable sections, with the <area> tags.
......name=text

<area> defines a part on an image-map that can be clicked, used within <map>.
...... alt= alternate_text
...... shape={rect| circle| poly}
...... coords= commas_ separated_coords
    _rect (x1,y1,x2,y2)
    _circle (x1,y1,rad)
    _poly (x1,y1,x2,y2,x3,y3......)
...... download
...... {href ...... hreflang ...... media ...... rel...... target...... type }→ as in <a>.

<figure> can contain a <img> and a <figcaption> tags. **<figcaption>** specifies a caption for <figure>, used within <figure>.

Include a '#' when referencing an image map. Here a circular region is carved out of the image, so that only the circle can be clicked to link to Google.

```
<!DOCTYPE html>
<html>
<head>
  <title> Image </title>
</head>
<body>
<map name="planet">
  <area shape="circle" coords="50,50,44" alt="planet"
        href= "http://google.com" />
</map>
<figure>
  <figcaption> HTML Image </figcaption> <br />
  <img src="neptune.jpg" alt="neptune"
        usemap="#planet" height="100" width="100" />
</figure><br />

</body>
</html>
```

HTML Image

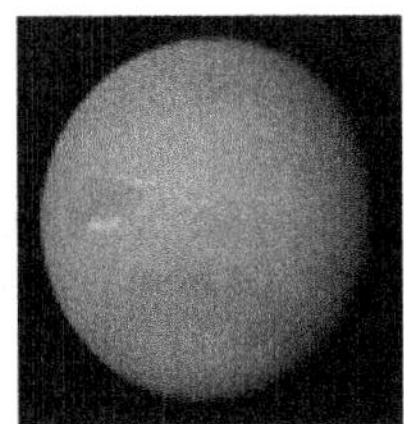

1.3.5 Multimedia

<audio> plays a sound file; contains the alternative text.
...... src=URL
...... volume= 0.0 to 1.0
...... autoplay: plays as soon as it is ready
...... buffered: a TimeRanges object
...... played: a TimeRanges object
...... muted: initially silenced?
...... controls: displays controls
...... loop: repeats again after finishing
...... preload= {auto: entire file |
        metadata: only meta data|
        "":nothing }

<video> plays a movie; contains the alternative text.
...... {src=URL...... autoplay.......buffered......controls...... loop......muted......played......preload} → as in <audio>
...... crossorigin = {anonymous | use-credentials}
...... height=pixels
...... width=pixels
...... poster=URL: the image to show while the video is downloading

<source> is used within <audio> and <video>, specifies alternative files which the browser may choose from.
...... src=URL
...... media= media_query(1.5.8)
...... type= MIME_type(1.5.7)

<track> is used within <audio> and <video>, specifies subtitles and other text that should be visible when playing.
...... src=URL
...... label=text
...... srclang= two_ letter_ language _code
...... kind= {captions| chapters |descriptions|
        metadata| subtitles}
...... default: specifies that the track is the default among all tracks

<object> produces an embedded object such as an image, audio, video, applet (Chapter 10), ActiveX, PDF, Flash (Chapter 11) etc. <img>,<audio> and <video> should be used instead where appropriate. The text contained by the <object> tags is the alternative text to be displayed when the plug-in is not supported.
...... data=URL
...... height=pixels
...... width=pixels
...... name=text
...... type=MIME_type(1.5.7)
...... form=form_id
...... usemap=mapname
...... typemustmatch

<param> used within <object>, passes parameters to the plugin.
...... name=text
...... value=value

<embed> defines an external application or plug-in. This tag shares some similarities with <object> and used to be better supported by Netscape.
.......src=URL
...... height=pixels
...... width=pixels
...... type=MIME_type (1.5.7)

<canvas> reserves a region for a script to draw. (Chapter 8,9)
...... height=pixels
...... width= pixels

A multimedia file can be played in different ways. For instance, to play a movie file, we can use:

```
<embed src="movie.swf" height="300" width="300"/>
                    OR
<object data="movie.swf" height="300" width="300"/>
                    OR
<video src="movie.mp4" width="300" height="300">
                    OR
<video width="300" height="300" controls="controls">
  <source src="movie.mp4" type="video/mp4" />
  <source src="movie.ogg" type="video/ogg" />
  <source src="movie.webm" type="video/webm" />
  <object data="movie.mp4" width="300" height="300">
    <embed src="movie.swf" width="300" height="300">
      Your browser does not support video.
    </embed>
  </object>
</video>
```

In the last example, the browser first tries the mp4, ogg, or webm format. If all these fail, it tries the <object> element. The <embed> element will be tried if everything else fails.

1.4 Form Elements

Form elements are used to obtain input from a visitor, allowing more interactivity in the browser. The input can also be submitted to the server. Until you have learned JavaScript (Chapter 3) and PHP (Chapter 4), everything here probably doesn't make much sense.

1.4.1 Basics

<form> can contain all the subsequent elements in this section (1.4).

...... name=text
This specifies the name of the form.

...... action=URL
This specifies the URI of the processing script.

...... method= { get | post }
'get' appends input data to the URL so that everything can be bookmarked. 'post' sends input data as a HTTP transaction, is secure, and has no size limitation.

...... accept-charset=charset
This specifies a space-or-comma-separated list of character encodings that the server accepts.

...... autocomplete={on|off}
This specifies whether to complete the form automatically based on previous results as the user types.

...... enctype= {application/x-www-form-urlencoded |
multipart/form-data |
text/plain }

This MIME type is only applicable when the method is 'post'. The first value converts spaces to '+' and special characters to ASCII HEX. The second value encodes no characters. The third converts spaces to '+'.

...... novalidate
If present, this boolean attribute indicates that the form is not to be validated.

...... target= {_blank| _self | _parent| _top| framename}→ as in <a>.

<fieldset> draws a box around the related elements, used within <form>.
...... name=text
...... form=form_ids
...... disabled

<legend> defines the caption for the form, used within <fieldset>.

<button> creates a clickable button. Text and images can be inserted within.
...... name=text
...... form=form_ids
...... type={button | reset | submit}
...... value=text
...... autofocus
...... disabled
...... {formaction......formenctype...... formmethod...... formnovalidate......formtarget}→ as in <form>, for type="submit".

<select> makes a drop-down list with <option> .
...... name=text
...... form=form_ids
...... autofocus
...... disabled
...... multiple: multiple options can be selected
...... size=number: the number of visible options.
<option> defines the options within <select> and <datalist>.
...... label=text: to be shown
...... value=text
...... disabled
...... selected
<optgroup> groups the <option> tags within <select>.
...... label=text: to be shown
...... disabled

<textarea> creates a multiline textbox
...... name=text
...... form=form_ids
...... autofocus
...... disabled
...... readonly
...... required
...... cols=number
...... rows=number
...... maxlength=number
...... placeholder=text: initial hinting text
...... wrap={off : lines do not break |
soft : default |
hard : contains newlines when submitted,
'cols' must be specified }

```
<!DOCTYPE html>
<html>
<head>
  <title>Form Basics</title>
</head>
<body>
  <form id="frm" method="get" action="action.php"
        style="width:280px"><fieldset>
    <legend>Make A Report</legend>
    <br />Type:<br/>
    <select name="type" size="8">
      <optgroup label="Normal">
        <option>Money Received</option>
        <option>Employee Off</option>
        <option selected>New Employee</option>
      </optgroup>
      <optgroup label="Urgent">
        <option>Money Lost</option>
        <option>Server Down</option>
        <option>Insufficient Stock</option>
      </optgroup>
    </select>
    <br /><br />Message:<br />
    <textarea name="message" rows="4" cols="30"
              autofocus wrap="no">Here is the report.
    </textarea>
    <button type="submit">SUBMIT</button>
  </fieldset></form>
</body>
</html>
```

1.4.2 Generic <input>

<input> creates a generic input control
...... name=text
...... form= form_ids
...... type= {button | submit | image | reset |
text | password | search | hidden |
number | email | tel | url |
checkbox | color | file | radio | range
date | datetime | datetime-local |
month | week | time }

The first line defines buttons. 'image' submits. (4.3.2)
The second line defines text types.
The third line defines text validated upon submission.
The fourth line defines special graphical selectors.
The last two lines define datetime graphical selectors.

...... value= text
...... autofocus
...... autocomplete={on|off}
...... autosave=unique_value
...... disabled
...... readonly
...... required
...... multiple
...... pattern=regexp
...... placeholder= text : initial hinting text
...... minlength=number : permissible input length
...... maxlength=number : permissible input length
...... size= number : width of the control

...... max= number_or_date: for datetime and range
...... min= number_or_date: for datetime and range
...... step= number: for datetime and range
...... list=datalist_id: for 'text' etc.
...... checked: for 'checkbox' or 'radio'
...... accept= {audio/*| video/*| image/*| MIME_type} for 'file'
{...... height= pixels ...... width= pixels
......alt= text ...... src= URL} → for 'image'

...... {formaction...... formenctype ...... formmethod ...... formnovalidate ......formtarget}→ as in <form>, for 'submit' and 'image', override the corresponding attributes in <form>.

<datalist> used with <input> , displays a text box with an autocomplete feature when entering text. It contains the <option> tags.

<label> displays a label for a check box, a radio option etc. Clicking the label toggles the control.
...... for=element_id
...... form=form_ids.

There can only be one checked input for radio controls with the same name. Here, the submission will fail if the 'Name' contains invalid characters or if the 'Email' is invalid.

```
<!DOCTYPE html>
<html>
<head>
  <title>Generic Input Types</title>
</head>
<body><form action="process.asp">
  Name:
  <input type="text" name="name" autofocus
          placeholder="Enter your name here"
          autosave="123" pattern="[A-Za-z ]*"/>
  <br/><br/>

  Date:
  <input type="date" name="dt" value="2014-11-25";/>
  <br/><br/>

  Time:
  <input type="time" name="tm" value="17:00:00";/>
  <br/><br/>

  Department:
  <input list="departments" name="department"
          spellcheck="true"/>
  <datalist id="departments">
    <option value="Finance"></option>
    <option value="Management"></option>
    <option value="Marketing"></option>
    <option value="Public Relations"></option>
    <option value="Research"></option>
  </datalist>
  <br/><br/>

  Email:
  <input type="email" name="em" maxlength="30"/>
  <br/><br/>

  Sex:
  <input type="radio" name="sex" id="f" />
  <label for="f">female</label>
  <input type="radio" name="sex" id="m"/>
  <label for="m">male</label>
  <br /><br/>
  Rating:
  <input type="range" min="0" max="100"
         step="1" value="90"/>
  <br/><br/>
  <input type="checkbox" id="confirm" name="conditions"/>
  <label for="confirm">
    I have read the conditions.
  </label>

  <input type="submit"/>
</form></body>
</html>
```

Name: [Enter your name here]

Date: 11/25/2014

Time: 05:00 PM

Department:

Email:

Sex: female male

Rating:

I have read the conditions. Submit

1.4.3 Others

<output> marks the result of a calculation.

...... name=text

...... form=form_ids

...... for=element_ids

```
<!DOCTYPE html>
<html>
<head>
  <title>Output</title>
</head>
<body>
  <form oninput=
        "result.value=parseInt(a.value)+parseInt(b.value)">
    <input type="range" id="b" name="b" value="50" /> +
    <input type="number" id="a" name="a" value="10" /> =
    <output for="a b" name="result"></output>
  </form>
</body>
</html>
```

+ 10 = 60

<keygen> creates a key-pair generator field, with the private key stored locally, and the public key sent to the server

...... name= text

...... form= form_ids

...... challenge=string

...... keytype= {rsa|dsa|ec}

...... autofocus

...... disabled

1.5 Other References

1.5.1 Global Attributes

These global attributes can be used on almost any element:

......accesskey=key: the shortcut to activate a tag

......class=text: for style sheets and microformats

......contenteditable: whether it can be edited

......contextmenu=text: appears on a right click

......dir={rtl | ltr}:the direction of content

......draggable={ true | false | auto }: draggable?

......dropzone={ copy | move | link }:when dragged

......hidden: disables the element

......id=text: the element identification

......lang=two_letter_language_code: language(1.5.5)

......spellcheck={"true"|"false"}: checks the spelling

......style=CSS_style: an inline style

......tabindex=number: the tabbing order

......title=text: information to display on mouse over

```
<!DOCTYPE html>
<html>
<body>
  <p contenteditable
  title="Click to edit">
  Hello World!</p>
</body>
</html>
```

Hello World!

See? This can be edited. Click to edit

This example illustrates the drag-and-drop events. More about CSS, DOM and JavaScript will be described in the later chapters.

```
<!DOCTYPE HTML>
<html>
<head>
  <style type="text/css">
    #div1 {width:70px;height:70px;padding:3px;
           border:1px solid #aaaaaa;}
  </style>
  <script type="text/javascript">
    function allowDrop(ev){
      ev.preventDefault();
    }
    function drag(ev){
      ev.dataTransfer.setData("Text",ev.target.id);
    }
    function drop(ev){
      ev.preventDefault();
      var data=ev.dataTransfer.getData("Text");
      ev.target.appendChild(
                          document.getElementById(data));
    }
  </script>
</head>
<body>
  <p>Drag the image into the square:</p>
  <div id="div1" ondrop="drop(event)"
               ondragover="allowDrop(event)"></div>
  <br />
  <img id="drag1" src="neptune.jpg" draggable="true"
    ondragstart="drag(event)" width="69" height="69" />
</body>
</html>
```

Drag the image into the square:

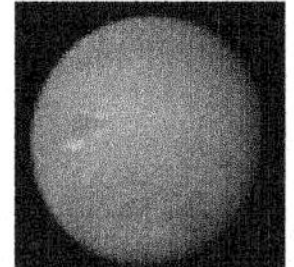

1.5.2 Events

Window events that trigger a script :
......onafterprint...... onbeforeprint...... onbeforeunload...... onblur...... onerror...... onfocus...... onhaschange...... onload...... onmessage...... onoffline...... ononline...... onpagehide...... onpageshow...... onpopstate...... onredo...... onresize...... onstorage...... onundo...... onunload

Form events that trigger a script:
......onblur...... onchange...... oncontextmenu...... onfocus...... onformchange...... onforminput...... oninput...... oninvalid...... onselect...... onsubmit

Keyboad events that trigger a script:
...... onkeydown......onkeypress......onkeyup

Mouse events that trigger a script:
......onclick......ondblclick......ondrag......ondragend...... ondragenter...... ondragleave...... ondragover...... ondragstart...... ondrop...... onmousedown...... onmousemove...... onmouseout...... onmouseover...... onmouseup...... onmousewheel...... onscroll

Media events that trigger a script:
......onabort...... oncanplay...... oncanplaythrough...... ondurationchange...... onemptied...... onended...... onerror...... onloadeddata...... onloadedmetadata...... onloadstart...... onpause...... onplay...... onplaying...... onprogress...... onratechange...... onreadystatechange ......onseeked...... onseeking...... onstalled...... onsuspend...... ontimeupdate...... onvolumechange...... onwaiting

```
<!DOCTYPE>
<html>
<head>
  <script>
    function showMouseP(event){
      document.getElementsByTagName("p")[0].innerHTML=
        "mouse at("+event.clientX+","+event.clientY+")\n";
    }
  </script>
</head>

<body onscroll="alert(document.body.scrollTop)"
        onkeydown="alert(event.keyCode)"
        onmousemove="showMouseP(event)"
        onbeforeunload="alert('Sad to see you leave!')">
  <button onclick="scrollBy(0,300)">
            Scroll down</button>
  <p></p>
  <pre>
            asided
            asd
            addressad
            addressadda
            datada
            sda
            sdaasd
            ......
  </pre>
</body>
</html>
```

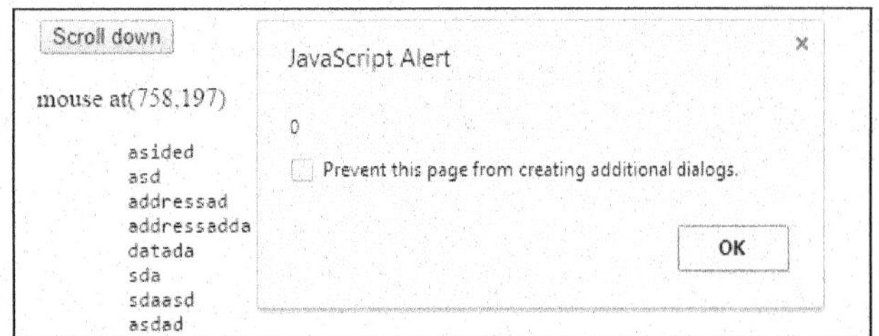

1.5.3 DOCTYPE

A. HTML5 (2012)
<!DOCTYPE html>
declares the document as HTML5. The deprecated tags include: <acronym>, <applet>, <bgsound>, <basefont>, <big>, <blink> <center>, <dir>, <font>, <fn>, <frame>, <frameset>, <ilayer>,<isindex>,<layer>,<listing> <marquee>, <nobr>, <noembed>, <noframes>, <nolayer>, <plaintext>, <strike>, <tt>, <xml> and <xmp>.

B. HTML 4.01 and XHTML 1.0 Strict(2000)
<!DOCTYPE html PUBLIC "-//W3C//DTD HTML 4.01//EN" "http://www.w3.org/TR/html4/strict.dtd">
<!DOCTYPE html PUBLIC "-//W3C//DTD XHTML 1.0 Strict//EN" "http://www.w3.org/TR/xhtml1/DTD/xhtml1-strict.dtd">
exclude presentational or deprecated elements like <font>. Framesets are not allowed. The second declaration must conform to XML.

C. HTML 4.01 and XHTML 1.0 Transitional (2000)
<!DOCTYPE html PUBLIC "-//W3C//DTD HTML 4.01 Transitional//EN" "http://www.w3.org/TR/html4/loose.dtd">
<!DOCTYPE html PUBLIC "-//W3C//DTD XHTML 1.0 Transitional//EN" "http://www.w3.org/TR/xhtml1/DTD/xhtml1-transitional.dtd">
include all elements but framesets are not allowed. The second declaration must conform to XML.

D. HTML 4.01 and XHTML 1.0 Frameset (2000)
<!DOCTYPE html PUBLIC "-//W3C//DTD HTML 4.01 Frameset//EN" "http://www.w3.org/TR/html4/frameset.dtd">
<!DOCTYPE html PUBLIC "-//W3C//DTD XHTML 1.0 Frameset//EN" "http://www.w3.org/TR/xhtml1/DTD/xhtml1-frameset.dtd">
include all elements and allow the use of framesets. The second declaration must conform to XML.

E. XHTML 1.1(2001)
<!DOCTYPE html PUBLIC "-//W3C//DTD XHTML 1.1//EN" "http://www.w3.org/TR/xhtml11/DTD/xhtml11.dtd">
is about the same as XHTML 1.0 Strict, but allows modularization.

F. HTML 3.2 (1997)
<!DOCTYPE HTML PUBLIC "-//W3C//DTD HTML 3.2 Final//EN">

G. HTML 3.0 (1995)
<!DOCTYPE HTML PUBLIC "-//IETF//DTD HTML 3.0//EN">

H. HTML 2.0 (1995)
<!DOCTYPE HTML PUBLIC "-//IETF//DTD HTML 2.0 Level 2//EN">

Extensible HyperText Markup Language (XHTML) is a stricter version of HTML in the sense that: 1) <DOCTYPE>, <html>, <head>, <title> and <body> are mandatory. 2) The XML namespace ie. the xmlns attribute in <html> is mandatory. 3) The elements must be closed, properly nested and in lowercase. (eg.
 is not closed.) 4) The attributes must have names in lower case and values quoted. 5) Attribute minimization is not allowed. For example, <textarea readonly> must be replaced with <textarea readonly="readonly">.

1.5.4 Character Sets

'charset' can assume any of the values below:

ISO-8859-1: Latin 1 (default) ISO-8859-2: Latin 2 Eastern Europe
ISO-8859-3: Latin 3 SEE,Esp. ISO-8859-4: Latin 4 Scandi, Baltics
ISO-8859-5: Latin/Cyrillic 5 ISO-8859-6: Latin/Arabic 6
ISO-8859-7: Latin/Greek 7 ISO-8859-8: Latin/Hebrew 8
ISO-8859-9: Latin 5/Turkish 9 ISO-8859-15: Latin 9/0
ISO-8859-10: Latin 6 Lappish, Nordic, Eskimo
ISO-2022-JP: Latin/Japanese 1 ISO-2022-JP-2: Latin/Japanese 2
ISO-2022-KR: Latin/Korean 1
UTF-8: 1 to 4 bytes long, first 256 covers ISO-8859-1
UTF-16: variable length, first 256 covers ISO-8859-1

The first 128 characters of ISO-8859-1 is the same as the original ASCII. The higher part of ISO-8859-1 contains some commonly used special characters, which can be implemented in the html document by entities as shown below. The use of   (non-breaking space) allows spaces to be displayed without being truncated by the browser.

"	"	"	Í	Í	Í
'	'	'	Î	Î	Î
&	&	&	Ï	Ï	Ï
<	<	<	Ð	Ð	Ð
>	>	>	Ñ	Ñ	Ñ
			Ò	Ò	Ò
¡	¡	¡	Ó	Ó	Ó
¢	¢	¢	Ô	Ô	Ô
£	£	£	Õ	Õ	Õ
¤	¤	¤	Ö	Ö	Ö
¥	¥	¥	×	×	×
¦	¦	¦	Ø	Ø	Ø
§	§	§	Ù	Ù	Ù
¨	¨	¨	Ú	Ú	Ú
©	©	©	Û	Û	Û
ª	ª	ª	Ü	Ü	Ü
«	«	«	Ý	Ý	Ý
¬	¬	¬	Þ	Þ	Þ
			ß	ß	ß
®	®	®	à	à	à
¯	¯	¯	á	á	á
°	°	°	â	â	â
±	±	±	ã	ã	ã
²	²	²	ä	ä	ä
³	³	³	å	å	å
´	´	´	æ	æ	æ
µ	µ	µ	ç	ç	ç
¶	¶	¶	è	è	è
·	·	·	é	é	é
¸	¸	¸	ê	ê	ê
¹	¹	¹	ë	ë	ë
º	º	º	ì	ì	ì
»	»	»	í	í	í
¼	¼	¼	î	î	î
½	½	½	ï	ï	ï
¾	¾	¾	ð	ð	ð
¿	¿	¿	ñ	ñ	ñ
À	À	À	ò	ò	ò
Á	Á	Á	ó	ó	ó
Â	Â	Â	ô	ô	ô
Ã	Ã	Ã	õ	õ	õ
Ä	Ä	Ä	ö	ö	ö
Å	Å	Å	÷	÷	÷

Æ	Æ	Æ	Ø	ø	ø
Ç	Ç	Ç	Ù	ù	ù
È	È	È	Ú	ú	ú
É	É	É	Û	û	û
Ê	Ê	Ê	Ü	ü	ü
Ë	Ë	Ë	Ý	ý	ý
Ì	Ì	Ì	Þ	þ	þ
			Ÿ	ÿ	ÿ

1.5.5 Language

'lang' and 'hreflang' can assume any of the values below:
ab:Abkhazian, aa:Afar, af:Afrikaans, sq:Albanian, am:Amharic, ar:Arabic, an:Aragonese, hy:Armenian, as:Assamese, ay:Aymara, az:Azerbaijani, ba:Bashkir, eu:Basque, bn:Bengali (Bangla), dz:Bhutani, bh:Bihari, bi:Bislama, br:Breton, bg:Bulgarian, my:Burmese, be:Byelorussian (Belarusian), km:Cambodian, ca:Catalan, zh:Chinese (Simplified), zh:Chinese (Traditional), co:Corsican, hr:Croatian, cs:Czech, da:Danish, nl:Dutch, en:English, eo:Esperanto, et:Estonian, fo:Faeroese, fa:Farsi, fj:Fiji, fi:Finnish, ??:Flemish, fr:French, fy:Frisian, ??:Fulfulde, gl:Galician, gd:Gaelic (Scottish), gv:Gaelic (Manx), ka:Georgian, de:German, el:Greek, kl:Greenlandic, gn:Guarani, gu:Gujarati, ht:Haitian Creole, ha:Hausa, ??:Hawaiian, he/iw:Hebrew, hi:Hindi, hu:Hungarian, ??:Ibibio, is:Icelandic, io:Ido, ??:Igbo, id/in: Indonesian, ia:Interlingua, ie:Interlingue, iu:Inuktitut, ik:Inupiak, ga:Irish, it:Italian, ja:Japanese, jv:Javanese, kn:Kannada, ??:Kanuri, ks:Kashmiri, kk:Kazakh, rw:Kinyarwanda (Ruanda), ky:Kirghiz, rn:Kirundi (Rundi), ??:Konkani, ko:Korean, ku:Kurdish, lo:Laothian, la:Latin, lv:Latvian (Lettish), li:Limburgish (Limburger), ln:Lingala, lt:Lithuanian, mk:Macedonian, mg:Malagasy, ms:Malay, ml:Malayalam, mt:Maltese, mi:Maori, mr:Marathi, mo:Moldavian, mn:Mongolian, na:Nauru, ne:Nepali, no:Norwegian, oc:Occitan, or:Oriya, om:Oromo (Afan, Galla), ??:Papiamentu, ps:Pashto Pushto), pl:Polish, pt:Portuguese, pa:Punjabi, qu:Quechua, rm:Rhaeto-Romance, ro:Romanian, ru:Russian, ??:Sami (Lappish), sm:Samoan, sg:Sangro, sa:Sanskrit, sr:Serbian, sh:Serbo-Croatian, st:Sesotho, tn:Setswana, sn:Shona, ii:Sichuan Yi, sd:Sindhi, si:Sinhalese, ss:Siswati, sk:Slovak, sl:Slovenian, o:Somali, es:Spanish, su:Sundanese, sw:Swahili (Kiswahili), sv:Swedish, ??:Syriac, tl:Tagalog, tg:Tajik, ??:Tamazight, ta:Tamil, tt:Tatar, te:Telugu, th:Thai, bo:Tibetan, ti:Tigrinya, to:Tonga, ts:Tsonga, tr:Turkish, tk:Turkmen, tw:Twi, ug:Uighur, uk:Ukrainian, ur:Urdu, uz:Uzbek, ??:Venda, vi:Vietnamese, vo:Volapük, wa:Wallon, cy:Welsh, wo:Wolof, xh:Xhosa, ??:Yi, yi/ji:Yiddish, yo:Yoruba, zu:Zulu,

1.5.6 URL Encoding

Some characters cannot be sent in the URL directly. These unsafe ASCII characters are encoded with a "%" followed by two hexadecimal digits. URL encoding sometimes replaces a space with a + sign.

spc	%20	X	%58		%90	È	%C8
!	%21	Y	%59	‘	%91	É	%C9
"	%22	Z	%5A	’	%92	Ê	%CA
#	%23	[	%5B	“	%93	Ë	%CB
$	%24	\	%5C	”	%94	Ì	%CC
%	%25	]	%5D	•	%95	Í	%CD
&	%26	^	%5E	–	%96	Î	%CE
'	%27	_	%5F	—	%97	Ï	%CF
(	%28	`	%60	˜	%98	Ð	%D0
)	%29	a	%61	™	%99	Ñ	%D1
*	%2A	b	%62	š	%9A	Ò	%D2
+	%2B	c	%63	›	%9B	Ó	%D3
,	%2C	d	%64	œ	%9C	Ô	%D4
-	%2D	e	%65		%9D	Õ	%D5
.	%2E	f	%66	ž	%9E	Ö	%D6
/	%2F	g	%67	Ÿ	%9F		%D7

0	%30	h	%68		%A0	Ø	%D8
1	%31	i	%69	¡	%A1	Ù	%D9
2	%32	j	%6A	¢	%A2	Ú	%DA
3	%33	k	%6B	£	%A3	Û	%DB
4	%34	l	%6C		%A4	Ü	%DC
5	%35	m	%6D	¥	%A5	Ý	%DD
6	%36	n	%6E	|	%A6	Þ	%DE
7	%37	o	%6F	§	%A7	ß	%DF
8	%38	p	%70	¨	%A8	à	%E0
9	%39	q	%71	©	%A9	á	%E1
:	%3A	r	%72	ª	%AA	â	%E2
;	%3B	s	%73	«	%AB	ã	%E3
<	%3C	t	%74	¬	%AC	ä	%E4
=	%3D	u	%75	¯	%AD	å	%E5
>	%3E	v	%76	®	%AE	æ	%E6
?	%3F	w	%77	¯	%AF	ç	%E7
@	%40	x	%78	°	%B0	è	%E8
A	%41	y	%79	±	%B1	é	%E9
B	%42	z	%7A	²	%B2	ê	%EA
C	%43	{	%7B	³	%B3	ë	%EB
D	%44	|	%7C	´	%B4	ì	%EC
E	%45	}	%7D	µ	%B5	í	%ED
F	%46	~	%7E	¶	%B6	î	%EE
G	%47		%7F	·	%B7	ï	%EF
H	%48	€	%80	¸	%B8	ð	%F0
I	%49		%81	¹	%B9	ñ	%F1
J	%4A	‚	%82	º	%BA	ò	%F2
K	%4B	ƒ	%83	»	%BB	ó	%F3
L	%4C	„	%84	¼	%BC	ô	%F4
M	%4D	…	%85	½	%BD	õ	%F5
N	%4E	†	%86	¾	%BE	ö	%F6
O	%4F	‡	%87	¿	%BF	÷	%F7
P	%50	ˆ	%88	À	%C0	ø	%F8
Q	%51	‰	%89	Á	%C1	ù	%F9
R	%52	Š	%8A	Â	%C2	ú	%FA
S	%53	‹	%8B	Ã	%C3	û	%FB
T	%54	Œ	%8C	Ä	%C4	ü	%FC
U	%55		%8D	Å	%C5	ý	%FD
V	%56	Ž	%8E	Æ	%C6	þ	%FE
W	%57		%8F	Ç	%C7	ÿ	%FF

1.5.7 MIME Types

A Multipurpose Internet Mail Extensions(MIME) type refers to a standard defined for a file. Some common examples are:

application/ecmascript
application/javascript
application/x-shockwave-flash
text/javascript (default scripting language)
text/ecmascript
text/vbscript
text/css (used in<style>and<link>to define CSS)

A complete list can be found at:
http://www.iana.org/assignments/media-types/media-types.xhtml

1.5.8 Media-Query

Used in <script>, <link>, <a>, <area>, <source>, a media-query specifies what devices the resource is optimized for. It assumes the following format:

[not|only]*device* [and ([min-|max-]*vname*:*value*)]

which can be repeated any number of times, separated by commas. 'device' can be:

- all: all devices
- aural: speech synthesizers
- braille: Braille feedback devices
- embossed : embossed devices
- handheld: handheld devices
- print: printer
- projection: projectors
- screen: computer screens
- tty: teletypes
- tv: television

'vname' can be: width, height, device-width, device-height, orientation(portrait|landscape), aspect-ratio, device-aspect-ratio, color:bits per color, color-index: number of colors, monochrome: bits per pixel, resolution, scan(progressive| interlace), and grid(1|0). For example:

```
<link media="handheld,
             screen and (min-width:500px),
             tv and (scan:interlace),
             print and (resolution:300dpi),
             not screen and (monochrome:2),
             handheld and (grid:1)">
```

1.6 Miscellaneous Techniques

This section describes some useful and important techniques of web design. No knowledge of JavaScript or PHP is required.

1.6.1 Favicon

A favicon is a small image displayed besides the website address and the title. To include a favicon for your website:

Step 1: Prepare a 16*16-pixels image.

Step 2: Convert the image type to '.ico'. This can be done at http://favicon-generator.org/.
Step 3: Name the file 'favicon.ico'.
Step 4: Upload the icon file to the root directory.

Placing the favicon in the root directory of the domain causes the icon to be displayed for all pages of the domain, including those in the subdirectories.

To use different favicons for different pages, include the following in the <head> section of the webpages:

```
<link rel="shortcut icon" type="image/x-icon"
      href="/favicon.ico">
```

where 'href' specifies the location of the favicon.

Note that Internet Explorer caches the favicon. In order for a new favicon to be displayed in Internet Explorer, you must delete the browsing history.

1.6.2 Google Map

To embed a Google Map into a HTML document, first enter the name of the place in the Google search engine. A map will appear at the side of the screen. Click on the map.

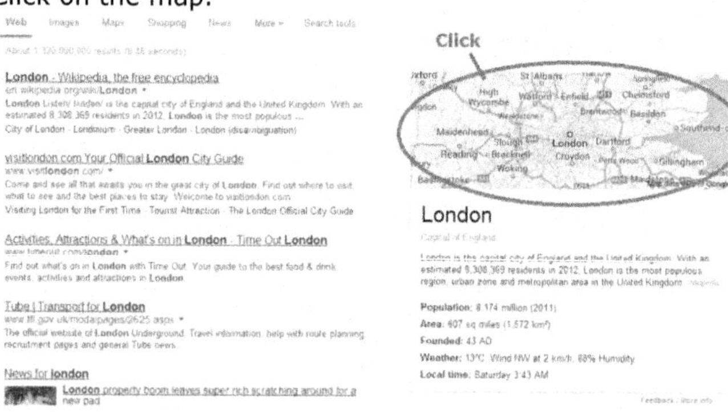

In the next screen, search for the link button and click on it.

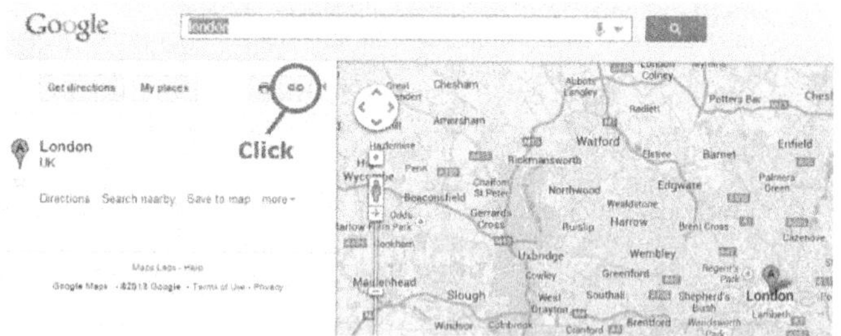

From the box that pops up, copy the content of the second textbox and paste it to any place in the HTML document where you want to display the map.

```
<iframe width="425" height="350" frameborder="0"
scrolling="no" marginheight="0" marginwidth="0"
src="https://maps.google.com/maps?q=london&amp;ie=UTF8
&amp;hq=&amp;hnear=London,+United+Kingdom&amp;ll=5
1.511214,-0.119824&amp;spn=0.484855,1.352692&amp;
t=m&amp;z=10&amp;output=embed"></iframe>
<br />

<small><a
href="https://maps.google.com/maps?q=london&amp;ie=UTF
8&amp;hq=&amp;hnear=London,+United+Kingdom&amp;ll=
51.511214,-0.119824&amp;spn=0.484855,1.352692&amp
;t=m&amp;z=10 &amp;source=embed"
style="color:#0000FF; text-align:left">View Larger
Map</a></small>
```

1.6.3 Application Cache

cache.appcache: This manifest loads the first 3 files into the cache for fast and offline browsing. "login.asp" will never be cached by the browser and will always require an internet connection. "fail-safe.html" will be loaded whenever an internet connection to /html5/ cannot be established. The first line is required. The comment symbol # can be used to update the cache by changing the manifest file. The asterisk * indicates that all other files require an internet connection.

```
<!DOCTYPE html>
<html manifest="cache.appcache">
...
</html>
```

```
CACHE MANIFEST
# cache.appcache
background.css
/banner.gif
http://example.com/functions.js

NETWORK:
login.asp
*

FALLBACK:
/html5/ /fail-safe.html
```

1.6.4 Code Compression

You can minify your HTML, CSS and JavaScript files so that they load fast and become hard to copy. Sites that allow you to do so include:

http://skalman.github.io/UglifyJS-online/
http://www.willpeavy.com/minifier/
http://compressmycode.com/

1.7 Microformats

Microformats attach meaningful semantics to HTML tags so that engines can produce smarter search results and process metadata more easily. The 'class', 'rel', and 'rev' attributes are used within tags of microformats.

1.7.1 hCalendar

This describes events.
class=vcalendar(vevent(dtstart, summary, location, url, dtend, duration, rdate, rrule, category, description, uid, geo(latitude, longitude), attendee, contact, organizer, attach, status)). eg.:

```
<div class="vcalendar">
  <p class="vevent">
    Tentative event:
    <span class="summary">Golf Competition</span>
    <span class="location">Kuala Lumpur</span>,
    Friday 6th Feb,
   <abbr class="dtstart" title="20080206F0900">9am</abbr> -
   <abbr class="dtend" title="20080206F1100">11am</abbr>
  </p>
</div>
```

1.7.2 hCard

This describes contact information.
class=vcard(fn:full name, n:structured name(honorific-prefix,given-name, additional-name, family-name, honorific suffix), nickname, org, photo, url, email, tel, adr(post-office-box, extended-address, street-address, locality, region, postal-code, country-name), bday, category, note) . eg.:

```
<div class="vcard"> <span class="fn">Roxanne Chai</span>
 <span class="n">
   <span class="honorific-prefix">Dr.</span>
   <span class="given-name">Roxanne</span>
   <abbr class="additional-name">K.</abbr>
   <span class="family-name">Chai</span>
   <span class="honorific-suffix">Ph.D.</span></span>
<span class="nickname">Rosy</span> (IRC)
 <div class="org">Rosy Science</div>
 <img class="photo" src="http://example.com/sk.jpg"/>
<a class="url" href="http://rosy.example.com">w</a>,
<a class="email" href="mailto:rosy@example.com">e</a>
<div class="tel">+1.818.555.1212</div>
 <div class="adr">
  <div class="street-address">123 Main st.</div>
  <span class="locality">Los Angeles</span>,
  <abbr class="region" title="California">CA</abbr>,
  <span class="postal-code">91316</span>
  <div class="country-name">U.S.A</div></div>
 <time class="bday">1953-08-31</time> birthday
 <div class="category">physicist</div>
 <div class="note">The woman in space.</div>
 </div>
```

1.7.3 rel-license

This describes a copyright license.
rel=license. eg.:

```
<a href="http://creativecommons.org/licenses/by/2.0/"
rel="license">cc by 2.0</a>
```

1.7.4 rel-nofollow

This prevents searching by engines.
rel=nofollow. eg.:

```
<a href="http://example.com/tag/tech"
rel="nofollow">lorry</a>
```

1.7.5 rel-tag

This designates a tag for the current section.
rel=tag. eg.:

```
<a href="http://technorati.com/tag/tech" rel="tag">ocean</a>
```

1.7.6 VoteLinks

This describes a voting system.
rev=vote-for, vote-abstain, vote-against. eg.:

```
<a rev="vote-for" href="http://example.com/housevote.html"
  title="Build a house!">Agree!</a>
<a rev="vote-against"
href="http://example.com/housevote.html"
  title="Don't build a house!">Against!</a>
```

1.7.7 XFN

This describes XHTML Friends Network.
rel=[space separated quote]contact, acquaintance, friend, met, co-worker, colleague, co-resident, neighbor, child, parent, sibling, spouse, kin, muse, crush, date, sweetheart, me. eg.:

```
<a href="http://june-blog.example.org/"
   rel="sweetheart date  met">June</a>
<a href="http://steven-blog.example.org/"
   rel="friend met">Steven</a>
<a href="http://james-blog.example.com/"
   rel="met">James Wong</a>
<a href="http://catherine.example.com/"
   rel="met acquaintance">Catherine</a>
<a href="http://mary.example.com/"
   rel="co-worker friend met">Mary</a>
<a href="http://nicholas.example.com/">Nicholas</a>
```

1.7.8 XMDP

This describes XHTML Meta Data Profiles.
rel=profile. eg.:

```
<head>
  <link rel="profile" href=
                    "http://microformats.org/profile/hcard"/>
  <link rel="profile" href="http://gmpg.org/xfn/11" />
...
```

This tells engines to define microformats based on the two human-readable URLs.

class=profile. eg.:

```
<dl class="profile">
  <dt id="title">Work Title</dt>
  <dd>Work Name.</dd>
</dl>
```

This defines the profile for a piece of work.

1.7.9. XOXO

This defines lists and outlines.
class=xoxo. eg.:

```
<ol class="xoxo">
  <li>Subject 1
    <ol>
      <li>objective A</li>
      <li>objective B</li>
    </ol>
  </li>
  <li>Subject 2
    <ol compact>
      <li>objective C</li>
      <li>objective D</li>
    </ol>
  </li>
  <li>Subject 3
    <ol>
      <li>objective E</li>
    </ol>
  </li>
</ol>
```

1.7.10 Others

Other microformats include:

- **hAtom**: for marking up Atom feeds from within standard HTML.
- **hMedia**: for audio/video content.
- **hAudio**: for audio content.
- **hNews**: for news content.
- **hProduct**: for products.
- **hRecipe**: for recipes and foodstuffs.
- **hResume**: for resumes of CVs.
- **rel-directory**: for distributed directory creation and inclusion.
- **rel-enclosure**: for multimedia attachments to web pages.
- **xFolk**: for tagged links.

2. Cascading Style Sheet

A CSS describes the look and format of elements. It can exist as a separate file, in the head section of a html file, or within the opening tag in the body section.

A. An external CSS with <link>

```
......
<head>
 <link rel="stylesheet" type="text/css"
       href="mystylesheet.css" />
< /head>
......
```

```
/* mystylesheet.css */

hr {color:green;}
table.mytable {text-decoration:underline;
                    border-collapse:separate;
                    border-spacing:9px 9px;}
body {background: url("images/bg.gif");}
```

B. An internal CSS with <style>

```
......
<head>
<style type="text/css">
  hr {color:green;}
  p#p1 {margin-top:20px;}
  div {background: url("images/bg.gif");}
< /style>
< /head>
......
```

C. An inline style with ......style

```
<!DOCTYPE html>
<html>
<head>
</head>
<body>
  <p style="letter-spacing:9px;">
    This is <span style="font-size=40px">big</span>.
  </p>
</body>
</html>
```

T h i s i s b i g .

An inline style has the highest priority and will overwrite any repeated styles defined in the head section. The external CSS will overwrite the internal CSS if <link> appears after <style>.

The 'class' attribute is often used to control the CSS properties of an element. Note that you can't start a class name with a numeric digit or one of other special symbols. Read the example at the end of 2.4.5 for an example.

Sometimes only the prefixed variations of a new property are supported by a browser. The prefixes are -ms- for Internet Explorer, -moz- for Firefox, -O- for Opera, and -webkit- for Safari and Chrome. To make sure a new property is supported by all browsers, simply include all variations when using the property. See the code section at 2.7.4 for an example.

Sass (Syntactically Awesome Stylesheets), an extension of CSS, is beyond the scope of this book. It adds features like nested rules, variables and mixins

2.1 Values

2.1.1 Colours

A CSS colour can be specified in several ways:

1) By #RGB HEX, eg. #0F0
2) By #RRGGBB HEX, eg. #00FF00
3) By decimal RGB, eg. rgb(0,255,0)
4) By decimal RGBA, eg. rgba(0,255,0,0.3)
   (a=1.0 means fully opaque)
5) By % RGB, eg. rgb(0%,100%,0%)
6) By % RGBA, eg. rgba(0,100%,0,0.3)
   (a=1.0 means fully opaque)
7) By Name, eg. green:

AliceBlue, AntiqueWhite, Aqua, Aquamarine, Azure, Beige, Bisque ,Black, BlanchedAlmond ,Blue, BlueViolet , Brown ,BurlyWood, CadetBlue ,Chartreuse, Chocolate, Coral, CornflowerBlue, Cornsilk, Crimson, Cyan, DarkBlue, DarkCyan, DarkGoldenRod, DarkGray, DarkGrey, DarkGreen, DarkKhaki, DarkMagenta, DarkOliveGreen, Darkorange, DarkOrchid, DarkRed, DarkSalmon, DarkSeaGreen, DarkSlateBlue, DarkSlateGray, DarkSlateGrey, DarkTurquoise, DarkViolet, DeepPink, DeepSkyBlue, DimGray, DimGrey, DodgerBlue, FireBrick, FloralWhite, ForestGreen, Fuchsia, Gainsboro, GhostWhite, Gold, GoldenRod, Gray, Grey, Green, GreenYellow, HoneyDew, HotPink, IndianRed, Indigo, Ivory, Khaki, Lavender, LavenderBlush, LawnGreen, LemonChiffon, LightBlue, LightCoral, LightCyan, LightGoldenRodYellow, LightGray, LightGrey ,LightGreen, LightPink, LightSalmon, LightSeaGreen, LightSkyBlue, LightSlateGray, LightSlateGrey, LightSteelBlue, LightYellow, Lime, LimeGreen, Linen, Magenta, Maroon, MediumAquaMarine, MediumBlue, MediumOrchid, MediumPurple, MediumSeaGreen, MediumSlateBlue, MediumSpringGreen, MediumTurquoise, MediumVioletRed, MidnightBlue, MintCream, MistyRose, Moccasin, NavajoWhite, Navy, OldLace, Olive, OliveDrab, Orange, OrangeRed, Orchid, PaleGoldenRod, PaleGreen, PaleTurquoise, PaleVioletRed, PapayaWhip, PeachPuff, Peru, Pink, Plum, PowderBlue, Purple, Red, RosyBrown, RoyalBlue, SaddleBrown, Salmon, SandyBrown, SeaGreen, SeaShell, Sienna, Silver, SkyBlue, SlateBlue, SlateGray, SlateGrey, Snow, SpringGreen, SteelBlue, Tan, Teal, Thistle, Tomato, Turquoise, Violet, Wheat, White, WhiteSmoke, Yellow, YellowGreen

2.1.2 Lengths

A CSS length can be specified in several ways:
1) 30% --- percent
2) 1in --- inch
3) 2cm --- centimeter
4) 25mm --- millimeter
5) 1em --- font size
6) 1ex --- about half-the font size
7) 12pt --- 1 point equals 1/72 inch
8) 5pc --- 1 pica equals 12 points
9) 100px --- 100 pixels
10) 80vh --- 80% of the viewport height
11) 80vw --- 80% of the viewport width
12) 1vmin --- smallest of 1vh and 1vw
13) 1vmax --- largest of 1vh and 1vw

2.2 Selectors

Elements can be selected in various ways for definition. The selectors can be combined when used.**:**

p: all <p> elements
:not(p): all elements that are not <p>
:root: the document's root element
.cn: all elements with class="cn"
p.cn: all <p> elements with class="cn"
#id: the element with id="id"
ul#id: all <ul> elements with id="id"
*****: all elements

div,p: all <div> and all <p> elements
div p: all <p> elements inside <div> elements
.cn p: all <p> elements inside elements with class="cn"
div>p: all <p>elements where the parent is <div>
div+p: all <p>elements immediately after <div>
ul~p: all <p> elements that are preceded by <ul>

[target]: all elements with a target attribute
[target=_blank]: all elements with target="_blank"
[title~=car]: all elements with title <u>containing</u> "car" as one of the space-separated values.
[lang|=en]: all elements with lang <u>starting with</u> "en" in a hyphen-separated list
a[href^="https"]: all <a> with href <u>starting with</u>"https"
a[href$=".html"]: all <a> with href <u>ending with</u> ".html"
a[href*="world"]: all <a> with href <u>containing</u> "world"
p:lang(ms): all <p> elements with lang <u>starting with</u>"ms"
p:id(meta): all <p> elements with id <u>starting with</u> "meta"

a:link: all unvisited links
a:visited: all visited links
a:hover: links on mouse over (after :link and :visited)
a:active: the active link (must come after :hover)
#anc:target: the element containing the clicked anchor
::selection: the portion that is selected by the user

input:focus: the <input> element which has focus
input:enabled: all enabled <input> elements
input:disabled: all disabled <input> elements
input:checked: all checked <input> elements

p:first-child: every <p> that is the first child
p:last-child: every <p> that is the last child
p:only-child: every <p> that is the only child
p:nth-child(3): every <p> that is the third child
p:nth-child(2n): every <p> child at even locations
p:nth-child(even): every <p> child at even locations
p:nth-child(odd): every <p> child at odd locations
p:nth-last-child(3): every <p> that is the third last child

p:first-of-type: every first <p> of its parent
p:last-of-type: every last <p> of its parent
p:only-of-type: every <p> that is the only <p> element of its parent
p:nth-of-type(3): every third <p> of its parent
p:nth-of-type(3n+1): every <p> of its parent at multiple-of-three locations with 1 offset
p:nth-last-of-type(3): every third last <p> of its parent
p:empty: every <p> that has no children

p:first-letter: the first letter of <p> elements
p:first-line: the first line of <p> elements
p:before: inserts content before every <p> content (2.8)
p:after: inserts content after every <p> element (2.8)

@font-face...: defines a font-family(2.4.6)
@**page...:** sets properties for printing
@**support...:** support conditions
@keyframe kf...: defines an animation named kf (2.9.2)
@import url("base.css")**:** imports an external css file (must appear first)
@**charset 'UTF-8':** defines the character set (must appear first)
@media print......: sets the style for printers (2.4.3). Other acceptable values besides 'print' are:
'all', for all devices
'aural', for speech and sound synthesizers
'braille', for braille tactile feedback devices
'embossed', for paged braille printers
'handheld', for small or handheld devices
'projection', for projectors
'screen', for computer monitors
'tty', for fixed-pitch-grid devices, such as teletypes
'tv', for televisions

Fixing the <body> width prevents the elements from shifting around as the browser window is resized.

Setting the 'height' of <body> and <html> to 100% allows a <div> inside to extend 100% vertically over the entire page.

'!important' prevents a property from being overridden if it is declared again (not much of a use here).

```
<!DOCTYPE html>
<html>
<head>
  <style type="text/css">
    html, body {height: 100%}
    p:nth-child(2){text-decoration:underline;}
    p:nth-of-type(2){font-weight:bold !important;}
  </style>
</head>
<body style="width:1440px; margin:0px;">
  <div style="background:orange; height:100%;">
    <div><p>Hello World!</p>
          <div>Hello World!</div>
          <p>Hello World!</p></div>
    <div><p>Hello World!</p>
          <p>Hello World!</p>
          <p>Hello World!</p></div>
  </div>
</body>
</html>
```

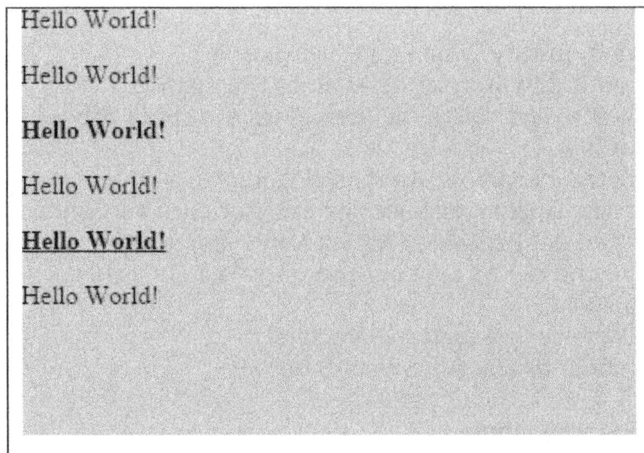

2.3 Background Properties

Note that some browsers also support gradient background colours. For more information about this experimental technology, visit:
https://developer.mozilla.org/en-US/docs/Web/Guide/CSS/Using_CSS_gradients

background (all-in-one declaration) eg.:
body {background: #ff0000 url('a.gif') scroll repeat-x right}

background-color
:#ff0000: sets the background color to be red
:rgb(255,0,0) : sets the background color to be red
:red: sets the background color to be red
:transparent: no color; default
:inherit: inherits the value from the parent element

background-image
:url('a.gif'): sets 'a.gif' to be the background image
:inherit: inherits the value from the parent element

background-attachment
:scroll: scrolls the background image with the page
:fixed: fixes the background image
:inherit: inherits the value from the parent element

background-position
:left top: sets the image at top left
:bottom center: sets the image at bottom center
:right: sets the image at center right
:30% 50%: sets the image at x=30%,y=50%
:100px 120px: sets the image at x=100px,y=120px
:inherit: inherits the value from the parent element

background-repeat
:repeat: repeats the image horizontally and vertically. Default.
:repeat-x: repeats the image horizontally
:repeat-y: repeats the image vertically
:no-repeat: does not repeat the image
:inherit: inherits the value from the parent element

background-clip
:border-box: paints the image on the border box(2.6)
:padding-box: paints the image on the padding box(2.6)
:content-box: paints the image on the content box(2.6)

background-origin
:border-box: starts the image at the border box(2.6)
:padding-box: starts the image at the padding box(2.6)
:content-box: starts image at the content box(2.6)

background-size
:cover: scales until the image contains the region
:contain: scales until the region just contains the image
:50px 80px: scales the width=50px, the height=80px
:50% 80%: scales the width=50%, the height=80% of the region

The use of negative x and y positions shifts the image up and left. This allows the right and bottom parts of the image to be displayed. Note the use of 'display'.

```
<!DOCTYPE html>
<html>
<head>
  <style>
     #spriteslist {list-style:none;}
     #spriteslist li, #spriteslist  a{height:60px;display:block;}
     #star{left:0px;width:60px;}
     #star{background:url('sprites.gif') 0 0;}
     #star a:hover{background: url('sprites.gif') 0 -65px;}
     #heart{left:63px;width:67px;}
     #heart{background:url('sprites.gif') -65px 0;}
     #heart a:hover
            {background: url('sprites.gif') -65px -65px;}
     #hexagon{left:129px;width:60px;}
     #hexagon{background:url('sprites.gif') -135px 0;}
     #hexagon a:hover
            {background: url('sprites.gif') -135px -65px;}
  </style>
</head>
<body>
  Whole Image: <br /><img src="sprites.gif"/>
               <br /><br /><br />
  Sprites:
  <ul id="spriteslist">
    <li id="star"><a href="a.html"></a></li>
    <li id="heart"><a href="b.html"></a></li>
    <li id="hexagon"><a href="c.html"></a></li>
  </ul>
  <p style="float:none;">
    Pointing the mouse at a shape changes its colour to black.
  </p>
</body>
</html>
```

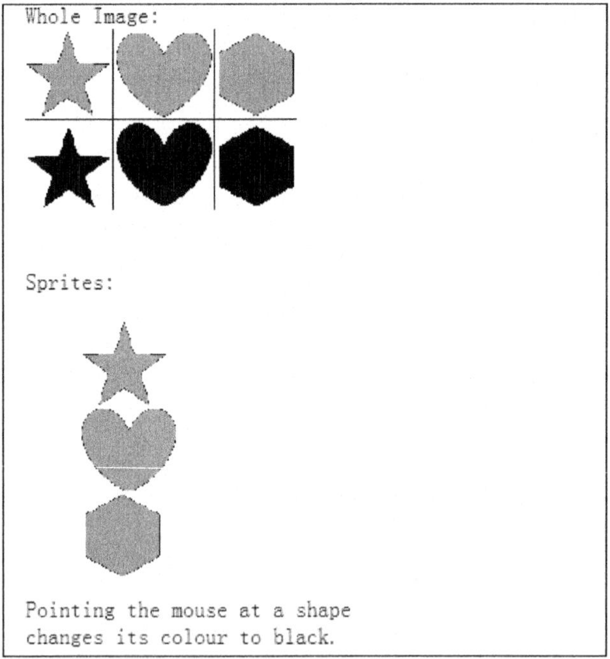
Whole Image:
Sprites:
Pointing the mouse at a shape
changes its colour to black.

2.4 Text Properties

2.4.1 Alignment

direction
:ltr: aligns the text to the left. Default.
:rtl: aligns the text to the right
:inherit: inherits the value from the parent element

Unicode-bidi (bidirectional text)
:normal: does not open an embedding level. Implicit Unicode ordering is obeyed.
:embed: opens an embedding level with direction determined by 'direction'. Implicit Unicode ordering is obeyed.
:bidi-override: opens an embedding level with direction determined ONLY by 'direction'. Implicit Unicode ordering is not obeyed.
:inherit: inherits the value from the parent element

text-align
:left: aligns the text to the left
:right: aligns the text to the right
:center: aligns the text to the center
:justify: stretches each line to have equal width
:inherit: inherits the value from the parent element

text-align-last
:left: aligns the last line to the left
:right: aligns the last line to the right
:center: aligns the last line to the center
:justify: stretches the last line to both edges
:start: left-aligns if 'direction' is ltr, right-aligns otherwise
:end: right-aligns if 'direction' is ltr, left-aligns otherwise
:auto: uses the default value
:inherit: inherits the value from the parent element

text-justify (when text-align:justify)
:auto: the browser determines the method
:inter-word: increases/decreases the space between words
:inter-ideograph: justifies ideographic text
:inter-cluster: justifies content that does not contain inter-word spacing such as Asian languages
:distribute: as in newspaper. The last line is not justified.
:kashida: elongates characters
:none: disables the justification

vertical-align
:baseline: aligns the baseline with the parent. Default.
:sub: aligns the text as subscript
:super: aligns the text as superscript
:top: aligns the top with the tallest element
:text-top: aligns the top with the parent's font
:middle: aligns with the middle of the parent
:bottom: aligns the bottom with the lowest element
:text-bottom: aligns the bottom with the parent's font
:-3px: lowers an element by 3px
:10%: raises an element by 10% the line-height.
:inherit: inherits the value from the parent element

```
<!DOCTYPE html>
<html>
<body>
  <img src="interchain.jpg" width="100" height="100"
       style="vertical-align:middle"/>
  Text along the middle line.
</body>
</html>
```

 Text along the middle line.

2.4.2 Spacing

letter-spacing
:normal: no extra space. Default.
:-3px: removes 3px of space between characters
:inherit: inherits the value from the parent element

line-height
:normal: normal line height. Default.
:3: 3 times the font height to the next line
:3px: 3px between lines
:50%:50% font height to the next line
:inherit: inherits the value from the parent element

text-indent
:15px: indents 15px at the start of the first line
:10%: indents 10% parent's width at the first line
:inherit: inherits the value from the parent element

word-spacing
:normal: normal space between words. Default.
:3px: leaves 3px between words.
:inherit: inherits the value from the parent element.

```
font:12px/18px;
        is the same as:
font-size: 12px;
line-height: 18px;
```

2.4.3 Wrapping

white-space
:normal: white spaces collapse. Text wraps. Default.
:nowrap: white spaces collapse. Text continues.
:pre-line: white spaces collapse. Text wraps.
:pre: white spaces are preserved. Text continues.
:pre-wrap: white spaces are preserved. Text wraps.
:inherit: inherits the value from the parent element.

text-overflow
:clip: cuts away any overflowed text
:ellipsis: shows "..." to represent any overflowed text

text-wrap
:normal: lines may break at allowed points only
:none: lines may not break.
:unrestricted: lines may break between any characters
:suppress: lines may break only if there are no other valid break points

word-break (line breaking for non-Chinese-Japanese-and-Korean scripts)
:normal: lines may break at allowed points only
:break-all: lines may break between any characters
:hyphenate: words may break at a hyphenate

word-wrap
:normal: lines may break at allowed points only
:break-word: lines may break between any characters

hanging-punctuation
:none: no punctuation may hang outside the line box
:first: punctuation may hang outside the start edge of the first line
:last: punctuation may hang outside the end edge of the last line
:allow-end: punctuation may hang outside the end edge of all lines.
:force-end: punctuation may hang outside the end edge of all lines. It will force it to hang if justification is enabled.

punctuation-trim
:none: does not trim punctuation
:start: trims opening punctuation at the start of each line
:end: trims closing punctuation at the end of each line
:allow-end: trims closing punctuation at the end of each line if it does not otherwise fit prior to justification
:adjacent: trims opening punctuation if its previous adjacent character is a fullwidth opening, middle, or closing punctuation, or ideographic space. It trims closing punctuation if its next adjacent character is a fullwidth closing or middle dot punctuation, or ideographic space.

page-break-{before|after|inside}
:auto: the browser inserts the page break
:always: always inserts a page break
:avoid: avoids inserting a page break
:left: inserts a page break until a blank left page
:right: inserts a page break until a blank right page
:inherit: inherits the value from the parent element

This example shows a portion of a html file that defines properties for printers and handheld devices.

```
......
<head>
<style>
  @media print, handheld {
     table {page-break-inside:avoid}
     p     {font-weight:bold;}
  }
</style>
< /head>
......
```

2.4.4 Outlook

color
:red: sets the text color to be red
:inherit: inherits the value from the parent element

text-decoration
:none: normal text. Default.
:underline: draws a line below
:overline: draws a line above
:line-through: draws a line through
:blink: blinks the text
:inherit: inherits the value from the parent element

text-transform
:none: no capitalization. Default.
:capitalize: capitalize the first character of each word
:uppercase: transforms all characters to uppercase
:lowercase: transforms all characters to lowercase
:inherit: inherits the value from the parent element

text-outline
:2px 1px red: outlines the text with 2px thickness, 1px blur, and a red color

text-shadow
:2px 3px 4px green: displays a shadow for the text at 2px right, 3px down, 4px blur, and in green color

user-select
:none: can't be selected
:text: can be selected
:all: selects highest ancestor
:element: contained by the bounds of the element

```
<!DOCTYPE html>
<html>
<head>
<style type="text/css">
  .noselect {
     -webkit-touch-callout: none;
     -webkit-user-select: none;
     -khtml-user-select: none;
     -moz-user-select: none;
     -ms-user-select: none;
     user-select: none;
  }
</style>
</head>
<body>
  <p>Selectable text.</p>
  <p class="noselect">
    Unselectable text.
  </p>
</body>
</html>
```

Selectable text.

Unselectable text.

2.4.5 Font

font(all-in-one declaration) eg.:
p{font: 15px italic bold "Times New Roman", sans-serif;}

font-family
:"Courier New",Verdana,Arial,Serif: tries to use the font "Courier New". If the font cannot be found, it tries Verdana. Arial is tried next. Let the browser choose a font from the generic family Serif if everything else fails. Generic font families include: Serif, Sans-serif, Cursive, Fantasy, Monospace.
:inherits: inherits the value from the parent element.

font-size
:xx-small: uses a very small size
:x-small: uses an extra small size
:small: uses a small size
:medium: uses a medium size
:large: uses a large size
:x-large: uses an extra large size
:xx-large: uses a very large size
:smaller: uses a size smaller than the parent
:larger: uses a size larger than the parent
:10px:sets the size to be 10px
:80%:sets the size to be 80% of the parent's size
:inherit: inherits the value from the parent element

font-size-adjust
:0.49: adjusts the font size such that the size difference between 'x' and 'X' is 0.49. This allows sizes to be standardized across fallback fonts.
:none: no adjustment
:inherit: inherits the value from the parent element

font-style
:normal: uses the default font style
:italic: uses the italic font style
:oblique: uses the oblique font style
:inherit: inherits the value from the parent element

font-variant
:normal: uses a normal font
:small-caps: uses a small, capitalized font
:inherit: inherits the value from the parent element

font-weight
:normal: uses a normal weight
:bold: uses a thick weight
:bolder: uses a thicker weight
:lighter: uses a lighter weight
:800: uses a weight as bold as 800. The normal weight is 400. The bold weight is 700.
:inherit: inherits the value from the parent element

font-stretch
:wider: displays wider text
:narrower: displays narrower text
:ultra-condensed: displays the narrowest text
:extra-condensed: displays narrower text
:condensed: displays narrow text
:semi-condensed: displays slightly narrow text
:normal: displays normal text
:semi-expanded: displays slightly wide text
:expanded: displays wide text
:extra-expanded: displays wider text
:ultra-expanded: displays the widest text
:inherit: inherits the value from the parent element

A 'class' attribute can be given more than one values. Fixing the 'width' of <body> prevents the content from shifting around as the visitor resizes the window. Setting the 'margin' to zero in <body> allows the content to stick to the border without any space in between.

```
<!DOCTYPE html>
<html>
<head>
  <style type="text/css">
    div {background:orange;}
    .i {font-style:italic;}
    .b {font-weight:bold;}
    .u {text-decoration:underline;}
  </style>
</head>
<body style="width:1440px; margin:0px;">
  <div class="i b u">Hello World! Hello World!
                     Hello World! Hello World!
                     Hello World! Hello World!
                     Hello World! Hello World!
                     Hello World! Hello World!</div>
</body>
</html>
```

Hello World! Hello World! Hello World! Hello World! Hello

2.4.6 @font-face

A font name can be defined to be used by font-family.

font-family (required)
src (required)
font-stretch (see 2.4.5)
font-style (see 2.4.5)
font-weight (see 2.4.5)
unicode-range (the range of Unicode characters supported. Default:' U+0-10FFFF')

This example shows a portion of a html file that defines and uses a font. The font is tried one by one downwards. local() uses a font on the visitor's local computer.

```
......
<head>
<style type="text/css">
  @font-face{
      font-family: newfont;
      src: local('Green Web'),
          url('Gabriola.ttf'),
          url(' http://www.example.com/Gabriola.eot');
      font-style:italic;
    }
  p{ font-family:newfont; }
</style>
</head>
......
```

2.5 List and Table Properties

2.5.1 List

list-style (all-in-one declaration) eg.:
ul {list-style: circle inside;}

list-style-type
:none: no bullet
:circle: a circle bullet
:disc: a disc bullet
:square: a square bullet
:decimal: a numeric marker
:decimal-leading-zero: a numeric marker from 0
:lower-alpha: alphabets in lowercase
:lower-greek: greek characters in lowercase
:lower-latin: latin characters in lowercase
:lower-roman: roman characters in lowercase
:upper-alpha: alphabets in uppercase
:upper-latin: latin characters in uppercase
:upper-roman: roman characters in uppercase
:armenian: Armenian numbering
:cjk-ideographic: ideograhic numbering
:georgian: Georgian numbering
:hebrew: Hebrew numbering
:hiragana: Hiragana numbering
:hiragana-iroha: Hiragana-iroha numbering
:katakana: Katakana numbering
:katakana-iroha: Katakana-iroha numbering
:inherit: inherits the value from the parent element

list-style-position
:inside: displays the bullet inside the content flow
:outside: displays the bullet outside the content flow
:inherit: inherits the value from the parent element

list-style-image
:url('spade.gif'): uses spade.gif as the bullet

This changes the colour of the list bullets.

```
<!DOCTYPE html>
<html>
<head>
<meta charset="UTF-8"/>
<style type="text/css">
  ul {list-style: none;
      padding:0;
      margin:0;}
  li {padding-left: 1em;
      text-indent: -.7em;}
  li:before {
    content: "• ";
    color: red;}
</style>
</head>
<body>
  <ul><li>Cat</li>
       <li>Dog</li>
       <li>Fish</li></ul>
</body>
</html>
```

• Cat
• Dog
• Fish

2.5.2 Table

border-collapse
:collapse: a border is a single line
:separate: reserves some space around each cell
:inherit: inherits the value from the parent element

border-spacing
:10px: leaves 10px space between cells
:10px 20px: leaves 10px space between cells horizontally and 20px space between cells vertically
:inherit: inherits the value from the parent element

caption-side
:top: displays the caption above the table
:bottom: displays the caption below the table
:inherit: inherits the value from the parent element

empty-cells
:hide: empty cells show no background or borders
:show: empty cells show background and borders
:inherit: inherits the value from the parent element

table-layout
:auto: the longest unbreakable content determines the column width
:fixed: the column width is fixed
:inherit: inherits the value from the parent element

Setting the margin to 'auto' centralizes the table horizontally in the webpage.

```
<!DOCTYPE html>
<html>
<head>
  <style type="text/css">
  table {margin: auto;
         border-collapse:collapse;
         table-layout:fixed;
         width:200px;
         word-wrap:break-word;}
  td {border: solid 1px;}
  tr:nth-child(odd) {background:grey;}
  tr:nth-child(even){background:white;}
  </style>
</head>
<body>
  <table>
    <tr><td>Mike</td><td>90</td></tr>
    <tr><td>Catherine</td><td>82</td></tr>
    <tr><td>Lee</td><td>73</td></tr>
    <tr><td>TengkuAhmadIskandarShah</td>
        <td>80</td></tr>
    <tr><td>Alice</td><td>95</td></tr>
  </table>
</body>
</html>
```

Mike	90
Catherine	82
Lee	73
TengkuAhmad IskandarShah	80
Alice	95

2.6 Box Model Properties

Some CSS properties are not supported in some browsers.

Margin with an outline on it
Border
Padding
Content

2.6.1 Sizing

[min-|max-]{height|width} (the content box does not include the margin, border and padding)
:80px: sets the dimension to be 80px
:90%: sets the dimension to be 90%
:auto: sets the dimension automatically
:inherit: inherits the value from the parent element

box-sizing (with height, width)
:content-box: applies the width and height to the content box (excluding the padding and border)
:border-box: applies the width and height to the border box (including the padding and border)
:inherit: inherits the value from the parent element

resize
:none: cannot be resized
:both: both the width and height can be resized
:horizontal: the width can be resized
:vertical: the height can be resized

{margin|padding}[-top|-right|-bottom|-left]
(note the all-in-one declarations of 'margin' and 'padding', which can take 1 to 4 values. Negative values may be used for the margin to crop a section out.)
:20px: reserves 20px for the margin or padding
:10% 30px: reserves 10% vertically and 30px horizontally for the margin or padding
:auto: sets the dimension automatically (center)
:inherit: inherits the value from the parent element

outline[-color| -style| -width](note the all-in-one declaration of outline. An outline is a line outside the border on the margin.)

border[-top|-right|-bottom|-left] [-color|-style|-width] (note the all-in-one declarations such as border, border-bottom and border-color)

...-color
:red: draws a red line
:invert: color inversion

...-style
:none: no border
:hidden: no border
:dotted: dotted border
:dashed: dashed border
:solid: solid border
:double: double border
:groove: grooved border
:ridge: ridged border
:inset: inset border
:outset: outset border
:inherit: inherits the value from the parent element

...-width
:thin: a thin line
:medium: a medium line
:thick: a thick line
:30px: a line that is 30px thick
:inherit: inherits the value from the parent element

outline-offset
:15px: draws the outline 15px beyond the border

Setting one of the two dimensions to 'auto' scales an image proportionally. Placing a <div> inside <a> makes it a clickable link. Also note the use of calc().

```
<!DOCTYPE html>
<html>
<head>
<style type="text/css">
  img, div, a{
    display: inline-block;}
  img {
    width: calc(20% - 170px);
    height: auto;}
  #triangle {
    width: 0;
    height: 0;
    border-left: 50px solid transparent;
    border-right: 50px solid transparent;
    border-bottom: 100px solid red;
  }
  #circle {
    width: 100px;
    height: 100px;
    border-radius: 50px;
    border: 2px solid;
    background: url('interchain.jpg');   }
</style>
</head>
<body>
  <img src="leaves.jpg"/>
  <div id="triangle"></div>
  <a href="http://google.com"><div id="circle"></div></a>
</body>
</html>
```

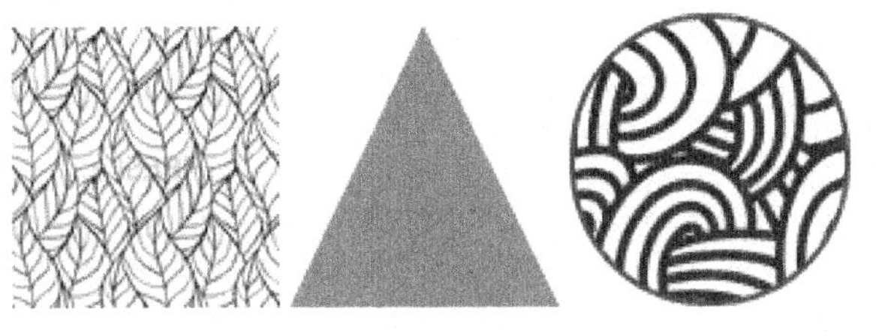

2.6.2 Border Image

border-image {source} {slice} / [width] [outset] [repeat];
(all-in-one declaration)

border-image-source
:"url(a.gif)": uses a.gif as the border

border-image-slice (1 to 4 values)
:75: slices 75px from the edge
:30%: slices 30% from the edge

border-image-width (1 to 4 values)
:75px 50px 30px: sets the top width to be 75px, the right and left widths to be 50px, and the bottom width to be 30px
:10%:sets the width to be 10% of the image area
:auto: uses the value of the image slice

border-image-outset (1 to 4 values)
:10px: the image extends 10px beyond the border
:5: the image extends beyond 5 times the width

border-image-repeat (1 to 2 values)
:stretch: the image is stretched
:repeat: the image is repeated
:round: the image is repeated and scaled to fit a whole number

```
<!DOCTYPE html>
<html>
<head>
<style type="text/css">
  div{
    border-width:15px;
    width:160px;
    padding:10px 20px;
  }
  #round{
    border-image:url("border image.gif")
    75 75/30px 70px round;
  }
  #stretch{
    border-image:url("border image.gif")
    75 75/30px stretch;
  }
</style>
</head>
<body>
<p>The image used:</p>
<img src="border image.gif" /><br /><br /><br />
<div id="round">repeated border image</div><br />
<div id="stretch">stretched border image</div>
</body>
</html>
```

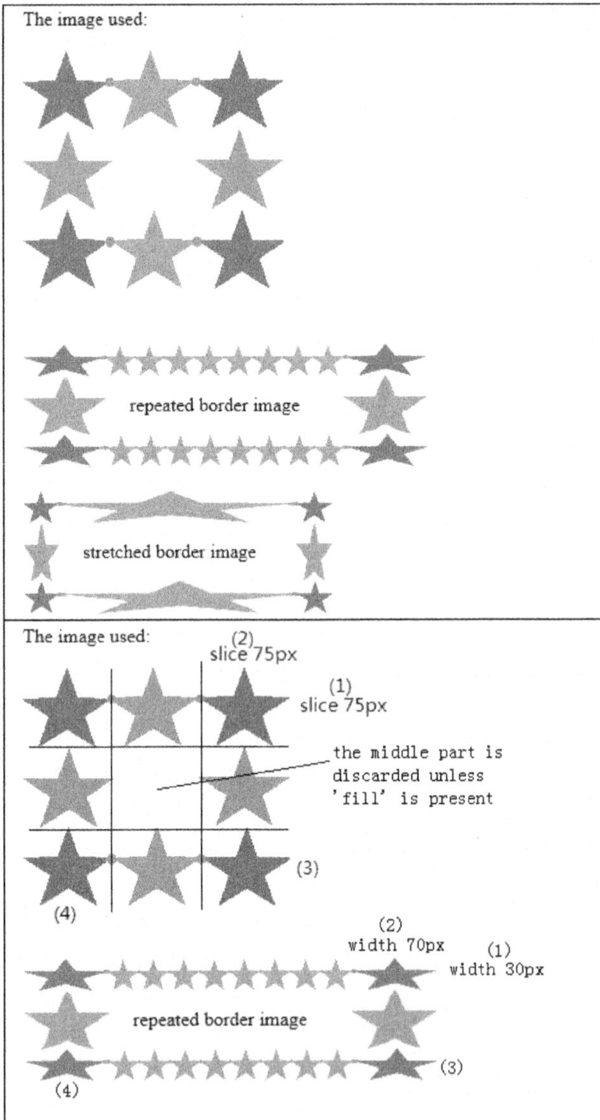

2.6.3 Radius, Shadow and Wrapping

border[-bottom-left|-bottom-right|top-left|top-right]-radius (note the all-in-one declaration of border-radius)
:50px: rounds off the corner with a radius of 50px
:50%: rounds off 50% of the element at the corner

box-shadow (2 to 6 values)
:10px 20px 30px black: renders for the border box an external overlapped shadow that is 10px to the right, 20px to the bottom, 30px blur, and black in colour
:10px 20px 30px 40px black inset: renders for the border box an internal overlapping shadow that is 10px to the right, 20px to the bottom, 30px blur, 40px in spread, and black in colour

box-decoration-break
:clone: at a page break, column break, or line break, box fragments are individually wrapped. The border, padding, border image, radius, shadow and background are redrawn at each box fragment.
:slice: at a page break, column break, or line break, box fragments are sliced. No border, padding, border image, radius, shadow, and background is redrawn at the adjoining edges.

```
<!DOCTYPE html>
<html>
<head>
  <style type="text/css">
  div {
    box-shadow: 10px 10px 30px inset;
    width: 70px;
    height: 70px;
    background : lightgreen;}
  button {
    box-shadow: 10px 10px 30px;
    border-radius: 30px;}
  </style>
</head>
<body>
  <div></div>
  <button>Click Me</button>
</body>
</html>
```

2.6.4 Flexible Box (for <div>)

box-align
:start: aligns the children to the top of the box
:end: aligns the children to the bottom of the box
:center: centers the children in the box
:baseline: aligns the baselines of all children
:stretch: stretches the children to fill the box

box-pack
:start: aligns the children to the left
:end: aligns the children to the right
:center: centers the children
:justify: divides the extra space equally among the children

box-direction
:normal: displays the children from left to right, top to bottom
:reverse: displays the children from right to left, bottom to top
:inherit: inherits the value from the parent element

box-flex
:2.0: specifies that the element has a flexibility of 2.0. A flexible element stretches or shrinks with the containing box.

box-flex-group
:3: assigns the element to flexible group 3

box-lines
:single: all children are placed in a single line
:multiple: the box expands to accommodate all the child elements

box-ordinal-group
:2: specifies the display order to be 2. Elements with a lower display order will be displayed before elements with a higher display order.

box-orient
:horizontal: displays from left to right
:vertical: displays from top to bottom
:inline-axis: displays along the inline (x-)axis
:block-axis: displays along the block (y-)axis
:inherit: inherits the value from the parent element

```
<!DOCTYPE html>
<html>
<head>
  <style>
  .box { display:-moz-box; /* Firefox */
         display:box;
         width:200px;
         height:200px;
         border:1px solid black;
         -moz-box-align:center;
         -moz-box-pack:center;
         -moz-box-direction:reverse;
         -moz-box-orient:vertical;
    }
  .o1 { margin:5px;
        -moz-box-ordinal-group:1;
        box-ordinal-group:1;
    }
  .o2 { margin:5px;
        -moz-box-ordinal-group:2;
        box-ordinal-group:2;
    }
  </style>
</head>
<body>
  <div class="box">
    <div class="o2">One</div>
    <div class="o1">Two</div>
    <div class="o1">Three</div>
    <div class="o1">Four</div>
    <div class="o1">Five</div>
  </div>
</body>
</html>
```

One
Five
Four
Three
Two

2.6.5 Multiple Columns

columns (all-in-one declaration for column-width and column-count) eg.:
div{columns:300px 3}

column-width
:auto: the browser determines the column width
:200px: sets the column width to be 200px thick
column-count
:auto: sets the number of columns by other means such as column-width
:3: sets the number of columns to be 3

column-fill
:auto: columns can have different lengths
:balance: columns have equal lengths

column-gap
:normal: normal gap width
:100px: columns are 100px apart

column-span
:all: the element spans across all columns
:2: the element spans across 2 columns

column-rule (all-in-one declaration) eg.**:**
div {column-rule:3px outset #ff00ff;}

column-rule-color
:green: displays a green columns dividing line

column-rule-style
:none: no dividing line
:hidden: hidden dividing line
:dotted: dotted dividing line
:dashed: dashed dividing line
:solid: solid dividing line
:double: double dividing lines
:groove: grooved dividing line
:ridge: ridged dividing line
:inset: inset dividing line
:outset: outset dividing line

column-rule-width
:thin: thin dividing line
:medium: medium dividing line
:thick: thick dividing line
:10px: a dividing line that is 10px thick

```
<!DOCTYPE html>
<html>
<head>
  <title>Multi-columms</title>
  <style>
    div {background-color:yellow;
         width:400px;
         columns:3 auto;
         column-gap: 70px;
         column-rule: 4px dotted red;
       }
  </style>
</head>
<body>
  <div>
    This is some text. This is some text. This is some text.
This is some text. This is some text. This is some text. This is
some text. This is some text.
  </div>
</body>
</html>
```

This is some text. This is some text. This is some	text. This is some text. This is some text. This is	some text. This is some text. This is some text.

2.7 Positioning Properties

2.7.1 General Positioning

{bottom|left|right|top}
:auto: the browser sets the position
:30px: sets the position of the element
:30%: sets the position of the element
:inherit: inherits the value from the parent element

position (with bottom, left, right, top)
:static: elements are displayed in order
:absolute: relative to the nearest positioned ancestor
:fixed: relative to the browser window
:relative: relative to the original position
:inherit: inherits the value from the parent element

float
:none: begins at a new line
:left: mixes with the content above at the left
:right: mixes with the content above at the right
:inherit: inherits the value from the parent element

clear
:left: no float object is allowed on the left
:right: no float object is allowed on the right
:both: no float object is allowed on the left and right
:none: objects are allowed to float
:inherit: inherits the value from the parent element

This example illustrates how to design document layout in HTML and CSS using <div> and 'float'. Note the use of the length unit 'vw'.

```
<!DOCTYPE html>
<html>
<body style="margin:0">
  <div id="container" style="width:100vw">
    <div id="header" style="background-color:#FFA555;">
      <span>Header</span>
    </div>
    <div id="menu"
         style="background-color:#22D700;
                height:250px;width:100px;float:left;">
      <h3 style="margin:20px; width:45px;
                 border:black dotted 5px;
                 outline: dashed 3px grey">Menu</h3>
    </div>
    <div id="content"
         style="background-color:#EEEEEE;
                height:250px;width:300px;float:left;
                position:relative;">
      <h3>Content</h3>
      <h3 style="position:absolute; bottom:5px">
        The End</h3>
    </div>
    <div id="footer"
         style="background-color:#FFA555;clear:both;">
      <h3>Footer</h3>
    </div>
  </div>
</body>
</html>
```

Header
Menu
Content
The End
Footer

2.7.2 Visibility

visibility
:visible: the object is visible
:hidden: the object is invisible but takes up space
:collapse: a table column or row is removed
:inherit: inherits the value from the parent element

display
:none: no space is used to display the object
:block: displays as a block element
:inline: displays as an inline element
:inline-block: displays as an inline block
:inline-table: displays as an inline table
:list-item: displays as a list item
:table: displays as a table
:table-caption: displays as a table caption
:table-cell: displays as a table cell
:table-column: displays as a table column
:table-column-group: displays as a column group
:table-footer-group: displays as a footer group
:table-header-group: displays as a header group
:table-row: displays as a table row
:table-row-group: displays as a row group
:inherit: inherits the value from the parent element

z-index
:auto: the stack order equals that of the parent
:-3: sets the stack order to be -3. A larger stack order causes the object to appear in front, overlapping objects with a smaller stack order.
:inherit: inherits the value from the parent element

opacity (for <img>)
:0.5: sets the opacity to 0.5. A value of 0 means fully transparent while 1.0 means fully opaque
:inherit: inherits the value from the parent element

clip
:auto: the browser handles any clipping
:rect(10px,20px,30px,40px): shows only the rectangular portion defined by the coordinates (40,10) at the upper left and (20,30) at the lower right
:inherit: inherits the value from the parent element

overflow[-x|-y]
:visible: the content flows out of the element
:hidden: any overflowed content is clipped
:scroll: a scroll bar is added
:auto: a scroll bar is added if the content overflows
:no-display: removes the whole element if it overflows
:no-content: hides the whole element if it overflows
:inherit: inherits the value from the parent element

overflow-style
:auto: the browser determines the style
:scrollbar: add scrollbars if the content overflows
:panner: add a panner if the content overflows
:move: the user moves the content by mouse drag
:marquee: the content moves by itself

This shrinks-to-fit the <div> element. Setting "overflow:hidden;" in <body> hides the scrollbars of the webpage. Setting 'wrap' to 'off' allows the line to continue without breaking.

```
<!DOCTYPE html>
<html>
<body style="overflow:hidden;">
  <div style="background:orange; display:inline-block;">
    <textarea style="overflow:auto; resize:none"
              wrap="off"></textarea>
  </div>
</body>
</html>
```

2.7.3 Interface

cursor (sets the appearance of the cursor when the mouse pointer is on the element)
:crosshair: displays a crosshair (t)
:help: displays a help sign (?)
:move: displays a move sign (four-arrows)
:pointer: displays a pointer (hand finger)
:progress: displays a progress sign
:text: displays a text sign (I)
:wait: displays a waiting sign
:e-resize: displays a right-resize sign
:w-resize: displays a left-resize sign
:n-resize: displays a top-resize sign
:s-resize: displays a bottom-resize sign
:ne-resize: displays a top-right-resize sign
:se-resize: displays a bottom-right resize sign
:nw-resize: displays a top-left-resize sign
:sw-resize: displays a bottom-left resize sign
:auto: the browser sets the cursor
:default: uses the default cursor
:url('a.gif'),url('b.cur'),auto; tries a.gif, then b.cur if that fails. Use the generic cursor auto if everything fails.
:inherit: inherits the value from the parent element

pointer-events
auto: the default
none: the element is never the target of mouse events

nav-index
:auto: the browser sets the tabbing order
:3: sets the tabbing order to be 3
:inherit: inherits the value from the parent element

nav-{left|right|up|down}
:auto: the browser determines how to navigate
:#target: when an arrow navigational key is pressed, navigates to the element with id="target"
:inherit: inherits the value from the parent element

This illustrates how to place something right at the center. If you wish to centralize something horizontally only, then you should use:

margin: 0 auto;

As the visitor resizes the window, the dialog box remains at the center, shrinking or expanding along with the text. The dialog box is closed by clicking the 'X' at the upper right corner.

Note that two background images are used simultaneously.

```
<!DOCTYPE html>
<html>
<head>
  <style type="text/css">
  .center {  margin:auto;
             position: absolute;
             top:0; left:0; bottom:0; right:0; }
  .dialogBox { height: 50%;
               width: 50%;
               outline: 3px dotted;
               font-size: 5vw;
               background: rgba(200,200,0,0.8);}
  #close { position: absolute;
           left:91%;}
  #close:hover { font-weight: bold;
                 cursor: pointer;}
  .boxMsg { width:90%;
            height:5vw;}
  </style>
</head>
<body style="background:url('interchain.jpg') repeat-x,
                         url('leaves.jpg') repeat;
             background-size:100px 100px,
                             120px 120px;">
  <a href="http://google.com"
     style="cursor:default; pointer-events:none;">
        Disabled Link</a>
  <span style="background:black; color:white"
        onclick="document.getElementsByTagName('div')[0].
                style.display='block';">
     Show Dialog Box</span>
  <div class="center dialogBox">
    <span id="close"
        onclick="document.getElementsByTagName('div')[0].
                style.display='none';">X</span>
    <p class="center boxMsg">An error has occurred.</p>
  </div>
</body>
</html>
```

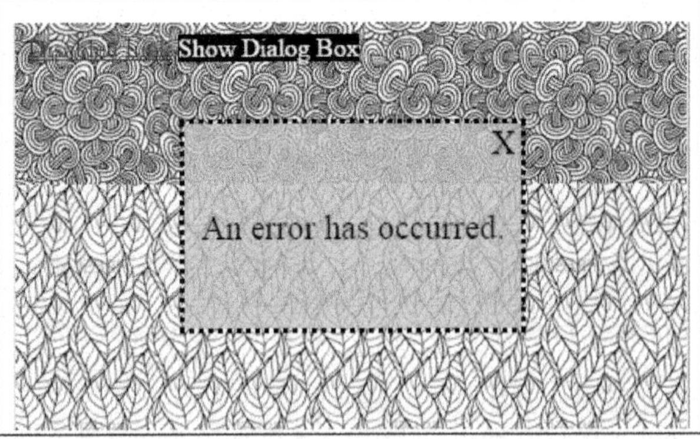

2.7.4 Transformation

rotation-point (with **rotation**)
:[left|right|center] [top|bottom|center]: rotates around a fixed point
:30% 50%: rotates around a point 30% from the left of the border box, 50% from its top

rotation (with **rotation-point**)
:300deg: rotates 300 degree counterclockwise

transform
:none: no transformation
:matrix(1,2,3,4,5,6):2D matrix transformation
:matrix3d(1,2,3,4,5,6,7,8,9,10,11,12,13,14,15,16): 3D matrix transformation
:perspective(100): the perspective view
:translate(10px,-20px): 2D translation
:translate3d(10px,-20px,30px): 3D translation
:translateX(10px): translation along the X-axis
:translateY(20px): translation along the Y-axis
:translateZ(-10px):translation along the Z-axis
:scale(1,2): 2D scaling
:scale3d(1,2,3): 3D scaling
:scaleX(3): scaling along the X-axis
:scaleY(3): scaling along the Y-axis
:scaleZ(3): scaling along the Z-axis
:rotate(10deg): 2D rotation
:rotate3d(1,2,3,10deg): 3D rotation around (1,2,3)
:rotateX(10deg): rotation around the X-axis
:rotateY(10deg): rotation around the Y-axis
:rotateZ(10deg): rotation around the Z-axis
:skew(10deg,20deg): 2D skewing
:skewX(10deg): skewing along the X-axis
:skewY(10deg): skewing along the Y-axis

transform-origin(with the transform property)
Syntax:{left|center|right|length|%} {top |center|bottom|length|%} [length]
Examples:
:left 20px: changes the origin of transformation
:10% bottom 10px: changes the origin of transformation

transform-style(with the transform property)
:flat: does not preserve the 3D positions of the child elements
:preserve-3d: preserves the 3D positions of the child elements

perspective
:none: no perspective view set
:100: places 100 pixels from the view

perspective-origin(with the perspective property)
Syntax:{left|center|right|length|%} {top |center|bottom|length|%}
Examples:
:30% bottom: changes the origin of the perspective

backface-visibility
:visible: the backside is visible(after rotation)
:hidden: the backside is invisible(after rotation)

```
<!DOCTYPE html>
<html>
<head>
  <style>
    div {left:100px;
          padding:30px;
          position: absolute;
          border: 1px solid black;
          background-color: yellow;
          transform: rotate(25deg);
          transform-origin:20% 20%;
          -ms-transform: rotate(25deg);
          -ms-transform-origin:20% 20%;
          -moz-transform: rotate(25deg);
          -moz-transform-origin:20% 20%;
          -o-transform: rotate(25deg);
          -o-transform-origin:20% 20%;
          -webkit-transform: rotate(25deg);
          -webkit-transform-origin:20% 20%;
        }
  </style>
</head>
<body>
  <div id="div1">
    <div id="div2">
      Testing
    </div>
  </div>
</body>
</html>
```

Testing

2.8 Generated Content Properties

content (with the selectors :before and :after)
:none: inserts nothing
:normal: inserts nothing
:open-quote: inserts "
:close-quote: inserts "
:no-open-quote: removes "
:no-close-quote: removes "
:"hello": inserts the word "hello"
:attr(class): inserts the content of the class attribute
:url('a.gif'): inserts the image a.gif
:counter(cnt): inserts a counter named cnt (A counter is a number that increases when counter-increment is called.)
:inherit: inherits the value from the parent element

counter-reset
:none: no counter is set
:cnt 5: creates a counter named cnt and sets it to 5
:inherit: inherits the value from the parent element

counter-increment (with the selectors :before and :after, and counter-reset)
:none: no counter is incremented
:cnt 2: increment the counter called cnt by 2
:inherit: inherits the value from the parent element

quotes (for <q> and embedded quotations)
:none:_use no quotes
:"<<" ">>" "'" "'": sets the symbols for the first-level quotations to be << and >>, the second-level quotations to be ' and '. More symbols may ensue.
:inherit: inherits the value from the parent element

```
<!DOCTYPE html>
<html>
<head>
<style type="text/css">
  body {counter-reset:section;}
  h1 {counter-reset:subsection;}
  h1:before{ counter-increment:section;
    content:"Identity " counter(section) ". (" attr(class) ")";
  }
  h2:before { counter-increment:subsection;
     content:counter(section) "."  counter(subsection) " ";
  }
  q {quotes: "<" ">" "'" "'";}
</style>
</head>
<body>
  <h1 class="R"><q><q>Main</q> Race</q></h1>
  <h2>Dutch</h2>
  <h2>American</h2>
  <h2>Indian</h2>
  <h1 class="P"><q>Place</q></h1>
  <h2>London</h2>
  <h2>Beijing</h2>
  <h1 class="S"><q>Sex</q></h1>
  <h2>Male</h2>
  <h2>Female</h2>
</body>
</html>
```

Identity 1. (R)〈'Main' Race〉

1.1 Dutch

1.2 American

1.3 Indian

Identity 2. (P)〈Place〉

2.1 London

2.2 Beijing

Identity 3. (S)〈Sex〉

3.1 Male

3.2 Female

2.9 Animation Properties

2.9.1 Transition

transition {css property} {duration} [function] [delay] (all-in-one declaration) eg.:
div {transition: width 3s linear 4s}: changes the width linearly for 3s after a delay of 4s

transition-property {css properties list}
:none: no transition
:all: changes all properties
:height, width: changes the height and width

transition-duration
:5s: the transition lasts 5 seconds

transition-timing-function
:linear: same speed from the start to the end
:ease: slow start and end
:ease-in: slow start
:ease-out: slow end
:ease-in-out: slow start and end
:cubic-bezier(0,0.5,0.25,0.3): custom speed function

transition-delay
:5s: delays 5 seconds before the animation

As the mouse leaves the enlarged box, the box gradually shrinks to its original size and fades-in, after a 2s delay.

```
<!DOCTYPE html>
<html>
<head>
  <title>Transition</title>
  <style>
    div {width:150px;
         height:150px;
         position:fixed;
         background:yellow;
         opacity:1.0;
         transition:width 5s linear,
                    height 5s cubic-bezier(0,0.3,0.5,0.1),
                    opacity 5s;
         transition-delay:2s; }
    div:hover{
        width:300px;
        height:300px;
        opacity:0.0; }
  </style>
</head>
<body>
  <div>Pointing at this box with the mouse gradually enlarges it and fades it out.</div>
</body>
</html>
```

Pointing at this box with the mouse gradually enlarges it and fades it out.

2.9.2 @keyframes

animation (all-in-one declaration) eg.
div { animation: anm 3s 4s 3 alternate;}

animation-name
:none: no animation
:kfn: uses the defined keyframe kfn

animation-duration
:3s: each cycle of animation lasts 3 seconds

animation-timing-function
:linear: same speed from start to end
:ease: slow start and end
:ease-in: slow start
:ease-out: slow end
:ease-in-out: slow start and end
:cubic-bezier(0,0.5,0.25,0.3): custom speed function

animation-delay
:4s: delays 4 seconds before starting the animation

animation-iteration-count
:3: plays the animation 3 times
:infinite: plays the animation infinitely

animation-direction
:normal: restarts after each cycle
:alternate: reverses on alternate cycles, smoothing the animation during a cycle change

animation-play-state
:paused: pauses the animation
:running: continues the animation

Include the vendor-specific prefix if a browser doesn't support this.

```
<!DOCTYPE html>
<html>
<head>
  <style>
    @keyframes kf{
      from {left:0px; background:yellow;}
       25% {left:100px; background:green;}
       50% {left:50px; background:white;}
       75% {left:200px; background:blue;}
        to {left:300px; background:yellow;}
    }
    div {width:100px;
        height:100px;
        position:relative;
        background:yellow;
        animation: kf 5s 3s alternate infinite;
    }
  </style>
</head>
<body>
  <div>A moving box that changes its colour.</div>
</body>
</html>
```

A moving box that changes its colour.

3. Javascript

Javascript is a lightweight yet powerful programming language that commonly runs on the client's browser instead of the server. By embedding some Javascript code within an HTML file, you can react to events and process data. Some browsers have a web console which allows you to enter simple Javascript commands.

Use the <script> tag to include a Javascript. The script can exist as a separate file, in the head section, or in the body section. Multiple scripts may be used and scripts may exist multiple times in an HTML document.

An external Javascript

```
<!DOCTYPE html>
<html>
  <body>
    <script src="myScript.js"></script>
    <noscript>
      <p>Your browser does not support Javascript.</p>
    </noscript>
  < /body>
< /html>
```

Because Javascript has become a standard for HTML 5, the attribute type="text/javascript" can be omitted within <script>. If you wish to unminify a compressed Javascript file, consider using tools such as:
http://jsbeautifier.org/

3.1 Basic Syntax

Letters in Javascript are case-sensitive. Statements are separated by '**;**'. Inline comments are denoted by **//** while block comments are denoted by **/*** ... ***/**.

3.1.1 Variables and Constants

Variables can be declared with the '**var**' keyword:

```
var a; var b,c;
```

When declaring variables, data types can be assigned with '**new**':

```
var a=new Number;
var b=new Boolean;
var c=new String;
```

There are many other data types. The type of a piece of data o can be returned as a string by the function **typeof(o)** or **typeof o**. Values can be passed directly to the variables during declaration.:

```
var n1=new Number(3.0), n2=3141e-3;
var n3=0454,n3=0x3AF; //octal and hex numbers
var b1=true, b2=false,c3=null; // booleans
var s1="a string"; var s2='a "string"'; //strings
var s3="\"Special\" Characters\n" // escaped string
```

Empty variables can be declared with **null**. To remove a variable, use **delete:**

```
delete n1; delete n2;
```

Special characters can be inserted into a string with the \ symbol: **\'** (single quote), **\"**(double quote), ****(backslash),**\n**(new line), **\r**(carriage return), **\t**(horizontal tab), **\v**(vertical tab), **\b**(backspace), **\f** (form feed), \ddd(octal sequence), \xdd (hexadecimal sequence) and \udddd(Unicode sequence). A string can also be broken into multiple lines with the **** symbol.

```
document.write("\251Hi   \
    There");
        // valid syntax, \251 is the copyright symbol
```

Assinging a value to a variable without the 'var' keyword declares a global variable.

Some browsers allow block-scope variables to be declared with '**let**', which is an experimental syntax. The values of these variables persist only within {}, which can be an 'if', a 'switch', a 'do', a 'while', or a 'for' block.

```
<!DOCTYPE html>
<html>
<body>
  <script>
  var a;
  if (10>5){
    let a=10;
    alert(a); // 10
  }
  alert(a); // undefined
  </script>
</body>
</html>
```

Constants can be declared with the '**const**' keyword. The value of a constant does not change.

```
<!DOCTYPE html>
<html>
<body>
<script>
  const a = 100;
  alert(a); // 100
  a=10;
  alert(a); // 100
</script>
</body>
</html>
```

3.1.2 Operators

The operators, in order of decreasing precedence, are:

. [] {} new ()	field, array, object, function, group
++ -- (at the front, such as ++a;)	pre-increment, pre-decrement
~ ! delete typeof	unary, delete, typeof
* / %	multiplication, division, remainder
+ -	addition, subtraction
<< >> >>>	bit shift
< <= > >= instanceof in	comparison, objects
&	bitwise AND
^	bitwise XOR
|	bitwise OR
&&	logical and

<table>
<tr><td>||</td><td>logical or</td></tr>
<tr><td>?:</td><td>conditional</td></tr>
<tr><td>= *= /= %= += -= &= ^= |= <<= >>= >>>=</td><td>assignment</td></tr>
<tr><td>,</td><td>multiple evaluation</td></tr>
<tr><td>++ -- (at the back, such as a++;)</td><td>post-increment/ post-decrement</td></tr>
</table>

Placing ++ at the back of a variable increases its value by one, after the whole statement has been executed. Placing it in front of a variable increases its value by one before the statement is executed.

An assignment may be regarded as an expression that evaluates to the value of assignment. For example: 'a=(b=5);' assigns 5 to 'a' because 'b=5' evaluates to 5. There exist shorthand notations for assignment operations. For example: 'a%=b' is the same as 'a=a%b', which renews the value of 'a' with 'a%b'.

The comma operator evaluates both operands but returns only the value of the right operand. For instance, 'alert((1,2,3));' shows 3.

Strings may be concatenated with **+**. For example: {var s="5"+5;} gives {s=="55"}.

The comparison operators are:

- == equals in value
- === equals in value and type
- != does not equal
- !== equals in neither value nor type
- > is strictly greater than
- < is strictly less than
- >= is greater than or equal to
- <= is less than or equal to

Strings may be compared with comparison operators. Applying < or > to strings compares the character codes of the first characters of the strings. If they are the same, the second characters will be compared, and so on. For example: "ACD">"ABD" is true.

The logical operators are:

- **&&** and
- **||** or
- **!** not

Eg.:

```
if (a>b+c && !d) x="correct"; // not d
var b=("5"==5) ;  //true
var d=("5"===5);  //false
```

For bitwise operators:

- **a & b:** 1 for which both corresponding bits are 1s
- **a | b:** 1 for which either corresponding bit is 1
- **a ^ b:** 1 for which either but not both bit is 1
- **~a:** inverts the bits
- **a >> b:** shifts the binary form b bits to the right
- **a << b:** shifts the binary form b bits to the left shifting in zeros from the right
- **a >>> b:** shifts the binary form b bits to the right, shifting in zeros from the left

3.1.3 Conditionals

The execution flow of statements may be controlled by **if**:

if (*condition*) *statement1*; [**else** *statement2*;]

If (condition) evaluates to true, statement1 will be executed; otherwise statement2 will be executed. Notice that the **else** part is optional. If there are more than one *statements*, they must be contained by {...}:

if (*condition*){*statements1*;}[**else** {*statements2*;}]

Sometimes conditional statements can be shortened with **switch**:

switch(*expression*){
  case *value1*: *statements1;* **break**;
  case *value2*: *statements2;* **break**;
  case *value3*: *statements3;* **break**;
  ......
  default: *statements4;*
}

The *expression*, usually a variable, will be evaluated once only. The use of **break** prevents the execution from flowing into the next block. The statements after **default** are executed if the expression does not match any of the values specified by **case**.

These two code segments do the same thing roughly.

```
if (a+b==c)  x="car";
else if (a+b==d)  x="bus";
else {x="nothing"; v="restart";}
```

```
switch (a+b){
  case c: x="car"; break;
  case d: x="bus"; break;
  default:  x="nothing"; v="restart";
}
```

There exists a shorthand notation for conditional expressions:

```
<!DOCTYPE html>
<html>
<body>
  <div id="result"></div>
  <script>
    document.write( (50>100)?"Greater than 100"
                   :(50>80)?"Greater than 80"
                   :(50>30)?"Greater than 30"
                   :"Smaller than 30"
             );
</script>
</body>
</html>
```

Greater than 30

3.1.4 Loops

Statements can be run repeatedly in several ways:

while(*cycle condition*){*statements*;}
do {*statements*;} **while**(*cycle condition*);
for (*pre-loop statements*;
  cycle condition;
  cycle statements;){*statements*;}
for (*property* **in** *object*){*statements;*}
for (*element* **of** *array*){*statements;*}

Each of these code segments calculates the sum of 0 to 9.

```
var i=0,sum=0;
while (i<10) {sum+=i; i++;}
```

```
var i=0,sum=0;
do {sum+=i++;} while (i<10);
```

```
for (var i=0,sum=0; i<10; i++) sum+=i;
```

for...**in** loops through the properties of an object or elements of an array. Notice here that x is a string that contains the property name.

```
<!DOCTYPE html>
<html>
<head>
</head>
<body>
  <script>
    var s="";
    var obj={firstName:"John",lastName:"Brooks",age:30}
    for (x in obj) s+=obj[x];
    document.write(s);
  </script>
</body>
</html>
```

JohnBrooks30

This illustrates some differences between **for...in** and **for...of**.

```
<!DOCTYPE html>
<html><body><script>
  arr = [ 3, 5, 7 ];
  arr.foo = "hello";
  for (i in arr) {
    alert(i); // 0, 1, 2, foo
  }
  for (i of arr) {
    alert(i); // 3, 5, 7
  }
</script></body></html>
```

break; gets one out of the innermost loop instantly. **continue;** ends the current cycle of the innermost loop and continues with the next cycle. If used with a label, these two keywords also allow outer loops to be controlled at once.

```
<!DOCTYPE html>
<html>
<head></head>
<body>
<script>
var m;
outerloop:
for (var i=0; i<10; i++){
  for (var j=0; j<10; j++){
    m=i*j;
    if (j>8) continue;
    if (m>50) break outerloop;
  }
}
document.write(i+"*"+j+"="+m);
</script>
</body>
</html>
```

7*8=56

3.1.5 Functions and Objects

A **function** is a block of code that can be run repeatedly by calling its name. It can take in values and **return** a value. When triggered, an HTML event usually pass the execution to a function. Variables and functions declared within a function cannot be used outside the function.

```
<!DOCTYPE html>
<html>
<head></head>
<body>
  <script>
    function sum(a,b){return a+b;}
    document.write(sum(10,20));
  </script>
</body>
</html>
```

30

Functions can be nested or recursive. There are various ways to create and use a function. A function that accesses variables outside its lexical scope in an outer function is called a *closure*.

```
<!DOCTYPE html>
<html><body><script>
function f(num){
  // 1. Function Declaration
  function a(){num++; return num;}

  // 2. Function Expression / Anonymous Function
  var b = function(){num++; return num;};

  // 3. Recursive Function Expression
  var c = function d(n){if (n==1) return 1;
                        else return n+d(n-1));};

  // 4. Function Constructor
  var e = new Function('a','b','return (a+b);');
  alert (a());          // 2
  alert (b());          // 3
  alert (c(4));         // 10
  alert (typeof(c));    // function
  alert (typeof(d));    // undefined
  alert (e(2,3));       // 5
  alert ((function (n){return n;})(100)); // 100

  return e;
}
alert(f(1)(3,4));    // 7
var g = f(1);
alert(g(5,6));       // 11
</script></body></html>
```

A function can be used as a constructor for a new user-defined data type. Methods of the data type can be declared within the function. Use **instanceof** to test if an object belongs to an object. Use **in** to test if a property, method or array index belongs to an object.

```
<!DOCTYPE html>
<html>
<head></head>
<body>
<script>
function rectangle(a,b){
  this.width=a;
  this.height=b;
  this.area=function(){
    return this.width*this.height;
  }
}
var r=new rectangle(10,20);
r.height=30;
document.write(r.area()+"<br />");
document.write((r instanceof rectangle)+"<br />");
document.write((r instanceof Object)+"<br />");
document.write(("width" in r)+"<br />");
document.write(("width" in rectangle)+"<br />");
document.write(("PI" in Math)+"<br />");
</script>
</body>
</html>
```

```
300
true
true
true
false
true
```

Creating functions within other functions unnecessarily will decrease processing speed and increase memory consumption. However, one may choose to use closures to simulate object-oriented paradigm, in which some members of an object are hidden from the outside(private), while some others are exposed (public). Read 3.2.5 for more information about objects.

```
<!DOCTYPE html>
<html><body><script>
var makeCounter = function() {
  var privateCounter = 0;
  function changeBy(val) {
    privateCounter += val;
  }
  return {
    increment: function() {
      changeBy(1);
    },
    decrement: function() {
      changeBy(-1);
    },
    value: function() {
      return privateCounter;
    }
  }
};
var x = makeCounter();
alert(x.value()); // 0
x.increment();
x.increment();
alert(x.value()); // 2
x.decrement();
alert(x.value()); // 1

</script></body></html>
```

Function parameters are passed-by-value or passed-by-reference.

```
<!DOCTYPE html>
<html>
<body>
<script>
function changeStuff(num, obj1, obj2){
  num = num * 10;
  obj1.item = "changed";
  obj2 = {item: "changed"};
}
var num = 10;
var obj1 = {item: "unchanged"};
var obj2 = {item: "unchanged"};
changeStuff(num, obj1, obj2);
alert(num);        // 10
alert(obj1.item);  // changed
alert(obj2.item);  // unchanged
function myobject(){
  this.value = 5;
}
myobject.prototype.add = function(){
  this.value++;
}
function objectchanger(fnc){
  fnc();
}
var o = new myobject();
alert(o.value);         // 5
o.add();
alert(o.value);         // 6
objectchanger(o.add);
alert(o.value);         // 6

</script>
</body>
</html>
```

Some browsers may support generator functions, which can be exited and re-entered without losing context information. Generator functions are at an experimental stage at the time of writing.

```
<!DOCTYPE html>
<html>
<body>
  <script>
  function* idMaker(){
    var index = 0;
    while(true) yield index++;
  }
  var gen = idMaker();
  alert(gen.next().value); // 0
  alert(gen.next().value); // 1
  alert(gen.next().value); // 2
  </script>
</body>
</html>
```

3.1.6 Error Handling

Errors are caught within **try**{...} and handled in **catch**(e){...}. The **finally**{...} clause will always be executed, even if there is no error:

This example tries to call a function that is not defined. The resulting error is captured by the error object err.

```
<!DOCTYPE html>
<html>
<head></head>
<body>
  <script>
    try {
      asdd(5);
    } catch(err){
      document.write(err.message);
    } finally {
      document.write("***");
    }
  </script>
</body>
</html>
```

The value of the property 'asdd' is null or undefined, not a Function object ***

We can **throw** our own exceptions:

```
<!DOCTYPE html>
<html>
<head></head>
<body>
  <script>
    try {
      var a=0;
      if (a==0) throw "Division by zero.";
      document.write(5/a);
    } catch(err){
      document.write(err);
    }
  </script>
</body>
</html>
```

Division by zero.

3.1.7 Embedding in HTML

Where there is supposed to be a URL traditionally, JavaScript code can be run instead by prepending the string 'javascript:'. 'void' prevents a value from being returned.

```
<!DOCTYPE html>
<html>
<body>
  <script>
    function a(){alert('Hello');  }
  </script>
  <form action="javascript:a()">
    Form   <button>SUBMIT</button>
  </form>
  <a href="javascript:void(a())">Link</a>
</body>
</html>
```

Form SUBMIT
Link

JavaScript Alert ×

Hello

OK

You can use 'this' to pass an element object, 'value' to pass a value, and 'name' to pass a name.

```
<!DOCTYPE html><html><body>
  <button name="BTN"  onclick="alert(this.name)">
  Click</button>
</body></html>
```

When combined with the 'form' property, 'this' can refer to the parent form.

```
<form name="myForm">
Form name:
<input type="text" name="text1" value="Hello"/>
<input name="button1" type="button"
       value="Show Form Name"
       onclick="this.form.text1.value = this.form.name;"/>
</form>
```

3.1.8 Strict Mode

Javascript may be run as a restricted variant called 'strict mode'. To invoke strict mode, execute the following statement:

```
"use strict";
```

Executing the above statement within a function limits strict mode to the body of the function.
Among other things, strict mode causes:

- some originally-accepted mistakes to become errors.
- assignments which would silently fail to throw an exception.
- deletions of undeletable properties to throw.
- duplicate property names in an object literal to throw.
- duplicate function argument names to throw.
- octal syntax to become a syntax error.
- the use of 'with' to be forbidden.
- 'eval' of strict-mode code from introducing new variables into the surrounding scope.
- deletions of plain names to become a syntax error.
- assignments of 'eval' and 'arguments' to become syntax errors.
- properties aliasing of 'arguments' object created within it to fail.
- 'arguments.callee' to be undefined.
- non-object value of 'this' passed to a function to be allowed.
- it to become impossible to walk the stack via commonly-implemented extensions to ECMAScript.
- the function arguments to be inaccessible with 'arguments'.
- 'implements', 'interface', 'let', 'package', 'private', 'protected', 'public', 'static', and 'yield' to become reserved keywords.
- function statements not at the top level of a script or function to be prohibited.

3.1.9 Reserved Words

Besides the keywords and names of global variables and functions, the following words must not be used as names of variables or functions. Some of them are reserved for future use: **class, debugger, enum, export, extends, import, super, void.**

3.2 Core Objects

You can define the *constructor* and *prototype* properties of the core objects. ***constructor*** is a special string that contains the type name. ***prototype*** can be used to add functions to the data type. Some of these core objects also have the methods **toString**() , which converts the value to a string automatically, and **valueOf**(), which returns the intrinsic value.

The **Intl** object, which is the namespace for internationalization API, is beyond the scope of this book. Among other things, it provides language-sensitive string comparison, number formatting, and date-time formatting.

```
<!DOCTYPE html>
<html>
<head></head>
<body>
<script>
Number.prototype.square=function(){
  this.s=this.valueOf()*this.valueOf();
}
Number.prototype.toString=function(){
  return 'eleven';
}
var n=new Number(11);
n.square();
alert(n.s); // 121
alert(n); // eleven
alert(n.constructor); // function Number(){[native code]}
</script></body></html>
```

3.2.1 Boolean

Remember that 'undefined', 'null', 0, 'NaN', and the empty string "" evaluate to false in a Boolean context.

```
// No alert at all
var b2 = new Boolean;
b2 = false;
if (b2) alert(100);
if (undefined) alert(1);
if (null) alert(1);
if (0) alert(1);
if (NaN) alert(1);
if (false) alert(1);

// Alerts 100 as b1 is not a primitive value
var b1 = new Boolean(false);
if (b1) alert(100);
```

3.2.2 Function

The Function object/constructor has been described in (3.1.5). A function object is evaluated each time it is used, which is less efficient than calling pre-compiled function declarations.

Properties:

length returns the number of parameters expected by a function. Within the function body, you can use the **arguments** array to access a variable number of parameters.

```
<!DOCTYPE html>
<html>
<body>
  <script>
  function S(){
    var sum=0;
    for (i=0; i<arguments.length; i++){
      sum+=arguments[i];
    }
    alert(arguments.callee); // shows the function definition
    return sum;
  }
  alert(S(10,20,30));                   // 60
  alert((function(a,b,c){}).length); // 3
  </script>
</body>
</html>
```

Methods:

call(o1[,o2......]) calls the function by passing o1 as the 'this' value, and subsequent arguments as the parameters. **apply(o[,arr])** is similar to call() but passes the arguments as an array instead.

```
<!DOCTYPE html>
<html>
<body>
  <script>
  // 1. Chaining constructors
  function Product(name, price) {
    this.name = name;
    this.price = price;
    return this;
  }
  function Food(name, price) {
    Product.call(this, name, price);
    this.category = 'food';
  }
  Food.prototype = Object.create(Product.prototype);
  var cheese = new Food('feta', 5);

  // 2. Anonymous function
  var animals = [ { species: 'Lion', name: 'King' },
                  { species: 'Whale', name: 'Willy' }];
  for (var i = 0; i < animals.length; i++) {
    (function(i) {
      alert('#' + i + ' ' + this.species + ': ' + this.name);
    }).call(animals[i], i);
  }
  </script>
</body>
</html>
```

bind(o1[,o2......]) creates a new function by passing o1 as the 'this' value, and subsequent arguments as the parameters.

```
<!DOCTYPE html>
<html>
<body>
  <script>
  function sum(){
    var sum=0;
    for (i=0; i<arguments.length; i++){
            sum+=arguments[i];
          }
          return sum;
  }
  alert(sum(10,20,30)); // 60
  sum1000 = sum.bind(null,1000);
  alert(sum1000(10,20,30)); // 1060
  </script>
</body>
</html>
```

3.2.3 Number

Properties:

MAX_VALUE and **MIN_VALUE** store the largest and smallest possible values in Javascript respectively. **NEGATIVE_INFINITY** and **POSITIVE_INFINITY** store negative infinity and positive infinity respectively, and are resulted by overflowed operations. **NaN** represents an undefined number (not a number).

Methods:

toExponential([i]) switches a number to exponential form. **toFixed(i)** rounds off a number to one with i digits after the decimal point. **toPrecision(i)** rounds off a number to one with i digits altogether.

```
<!DOCTYPE html>
<html>
<head></head>
<body>
<script>
var pi=3.14159;
document.write(
  Number.MAX_VALUE + "</br>"+
  Number.MIN_VALUE + "</br>"+
  Number.NEGATIVE_INFINITY + "</br>"+
  Number.POSITIVE_INFINITY + "</br>"+
  Number.NaN + "</br>"+
  pi + "</br>"+
  pi.toExponential() + "</br>"+
  pi.toExponential(3) + "</br>"+
  pi.toFixed(3) + "</br>"+
  pi.toPrecision(3)
);
</script>
</body>
</html>
```

```
1.7976931348623157e+308
5e-324
-Infinity
Infinity
NaN
3.14159
3.14159e+0
3.142e+0
3.142
3.14
```

3.2.4 String

properties:

length stores the number of characters in the string.

methods:

charAt(i) returns the character at position i. **indexOf(s[,i])** returns the first found position of the string s after position i. **lastIndexOf (s[,i])** returns the last found position of the string s before position i. -1 is returned if the string cannot be found.

charCodeAt(i) returns the Unicode of the character at position i. **fromCharCode (i1[,i2,i3....])** returns a string from the Unicodes i1,i2,i3...

concat(s1[,s2......]) returns a new string formed by two or more strings joined together. **split(s[,i])** splits a string into an array of substrings by breaking at s, and returns an array of the first i strings. **substr (i1[,i2])** returns a substring from position i1 to the end (or i2 characters). **substring (i1[,i2])** or **slice(i1[,i2])** returns a substring from position i1 to the end (or to i2-1). Use a negative integer to select from the end.

trim() removes spaces at the front and the end. **trimLeft()** removes spaces at the front. **trimRight()** removes spaces at the end.

toLowerCase() converts the string to lowercase. **toUpperCase()** converts the string to uppercasae.

```
var s="abcdabcd";
alert(s.charAt(2));                      // c
alert(s.indexOf('ab',3));                // 4
alert(s.indexOf('AB'));                  // -1
alert(s.lastIndexOf('abc',2));           // 0
alert(s.charCodeAt(0));                  // 97
alert(String.fromCharCode(97,98,99)); // abc
alert(s.concat('XXX','YYY'));            // abcdabcdXXXYYY
alert(s.split('b',3));                   // a,cda,cda
alert(s.substr(3));                      // dabcd
alert(s.substr(3,4));                    // dabc
alert(s.substr(-3,2));                   // bc
alert(s.substring(3,4));                 // d
alert(s.slice(3,4));                     // d
alert(s.slice(-3,8));                    // bcd
alert('('+'  abc  '.trim()+')');         // (abc)
alert(s.toUpperCase().toLowerCase()); // abcdabcd
```

match(r) returns an array of strings which are the matches of a regular expression r. **search(r)** returns the position of the matched regular expression r. **replace(r,s)** returns a new string formed by replacing the substrings matched by the regular expression r with s. (3.2.9)

```
var s="abcdabcd";
alert(s.match(/abcd/));        // abcd
alert(s.match(/ABcd/gi));       // abcd,abcd
alert(s.search(/b.d/gi));      // 1
alert(s.replace(/ABc/gi,'X')); // XdXd
```

big(), blink(), bold(), fixed(), italics(), small(), strike(), sub(), sup(), anchor(s) and **link(s)** create HTML-formatted strings.

```
var s="abc";

// <big>abc</big>
alert(s.big());

// <a name="myLink">abc</a>
alert(s.anchor('myLink'));

//<a href="http://google.com">abc</a>
alert(s.link('http://google.com'));
```

Some browsers support the experimental **startsWith()** function, which returns a Boolean value.

```
var str = "To be, or not to be, that is the question.";
alert(str.startsWith("To be"));          // true
alert(str.startsWith("not to be"));      // false
alert(str.startsWith("not to be", 10)); // true
```

(Courtesy of https://developer.mozilla.org/en-US/docs/Web/JavaScript/Reference/Global_Objects/String/startsWith)

Some browsers support string generics, which means that String methods can be applied to other objects.

```
alert(String.replace(15, /5/, '2'));
```

3.2.5 Object

An object literal can be initialized by passing a value to each property name inside **{...}**:

var o={p1:5,"p2":"Ali"}; // optional "" for p2

is the same as

var o=new Object();

o.p1=5; o.p2="Ali";

A property of an object can be accessed in two ways: o.p1 or o["p1"]. Using **with**, the object name can be omitted.

```
var o={p1:5,"p2":"Ali"};
alert(o.p2);                   // Ali
alert(o instanceof Object);    // true
alert('p1' in o);              // true
alert('PI' in Math);           // true
with (o){alert(p1);}           // 5
with (Math){alert(cos(PI));} // -1
delete o.p1;
alert('p1' in o);              // false
```

Non-string property names can be used.

```
var obj = { 1.5: "a",
            ""  : "b",
            "!" :"c"
            "q q" :"d"};
```

Some browsers may support object destructuring, which is an experimental syntax at the time of writing.

```
var o = {p: 42, q: true};
var {p, q} = o;
alert(p); // 42
alert(q); // true

var {p: foo, q: bar} = o;
alert (foo); // 42
alert (bar); // true
```

methods:

is(o1,o2) checks if o1 and o2 are the same.

```
alert(Object.is(NaN,NaN)); // true
```

create(o1[,o2]) creates a new object, with o1 as the prototype object, and o2 as the properties object. o2 corresponds to the second argument of defineProperties().

This illustrates classical inheritance in JavaScript.

```
function Shape() {
  this.x = 0;
  this.y = 0;
}
Shape.prototype.move = function(x, y) {
  this.x += x;
  this.y += y;
  alert('Shape moved.');
};
function Rectangle() {
  Shape.call(this);
}
Rectangle.prototype = Object.create(Shape.prototype);
Rectangle.prototype.constructor = Rectangle;
var rect = new Rectangle();
rect instanceof Rectangle; // true
rect instanceof Shape; // true
rect.move(1, 1);
```

(Courtesy of https://developer.mozilla.org/en-US/docs/Web/JavaScript/Reference/Global_Objects/Object/create)

defineProperty(o1,s,o2) defines a property s for object o1 with the descriptor o2. **defineProperties(o1, o2)** defines multiple properties for the object o1 using the property-descriptor object o2. **getOwnPropertyDescriptor(o1,s)** returns the descriptor for the property s on object o1.

Property Descriptor
configurable: true if the property may be deleted and the type of this property descriptor may be changed. Defaults to false.
enumerable: true if this property shows up during enumeration. Defaults to false.
writable: true if the value may be changed. Defaults to false.
value: the value associated with the property.
get: the getter function.
set: the setter function.

```
<!DOCTYPE html>
<html>
<body>
  <script>
  var o1 = {};
  var o1v=100;
  Object.defineProperty(o1,'a',
    {configurable:true,
     enumerable:true,
     get: function(){return o1v;},
     set: function(v){o1v=v;}});
  alert(o1.a); // 100
  o1.a=200;
  alert(o1.a); // 200

  var o2 = {};
  Object.defineProperties(o2,{
    b:{value: 'hello', enumerable:true},
    c:{value: 1000, writable:true}});
  alert(o2.propertyIsEnumerable('b')); // true
  alert(o2.propertyIsEnumerable('c')); // false
  alert('b' in o2); // true
  alert('c' in o2); // true
  for (var p in o2) {alert(p);} // b
  o2.b='world'; alert(o2.b);    // hello
  o2.c=10     ; alert(o2.c);    // 10
  alert(Object.getOwnPropertyDescriptor(o2,'b'));
  </script>
</body>
</html>
```

There is an alternative syntax for getters and setters.

```
<!DOCTYPE html>
<html><body><script>
var obj = {
  get foo(){
    return this.___foo___
  },
  set foo(value){
    this.___foo___ = value*value;
  }
}
obj.foo = 10;
alert (obj.foo);  // alert 100
</script></body></html>
```

keys() returns an array of enumerable properties. **getOwnPropertyNames()** returns an array of all properties.

```
<!DOCTYPE html>
<html>
<body>
  <script>
  var obj={'a':10,'b':20};
  alert(Object.keys(obj)); // a,b
  alert(Object.getOwnPropertyNames(obj));  // a,b

  var arr=['a','b','c'];
  alert(Object.keys(arr));  // 0,1,2
  alert(Object.getOwnPropertyNames(arr));  // 0,1,2,length
  </script>
</body>
</html>
```

preventExtensions(o) prevents new properties from being added to the object o. **isExtensible(o)** returns true if new objects can be added to the object o.

seal(o) prevents new properties from being added to the object o, and marks all properties as non-configurable. **isSealed(o)** returns true if the object o is sealed.

freeze(o) prevents new properties from being added to the object o, and prevents existing properties from being removed or changed. **isFrozen(o)** returns true if the object o is frozen.

```
<!DOCTYPE html>
<html>
<body>
  <script>
  var o={'a':10,'b':20};
  Object.preventExtensions(o);
  alert(Object.isExtensible(o)); // false
  o.c=30; alert(o.c); // undefined
  o.b=200; alert(o.b); // 200
  Object.freeze(o);
  o.b=2000; alert(o.b); // 200
  </script>
</body>
</html>
```

3.2.6 Array

An **Array** in Javascript is an object that stores a series of values. These values can be of different data types. Among a few ways, it can be initialized with [...].

The following rows all result in the same 'data' array.
var data=["Sophia",25,myFunction];
var data=new Array("Sophia",25, myFunction);
var data=Array("Sophia",25, myFunction);

var data=[];
data[0]="Sophia";
data[1]=25;
data[2]=myFunction;

var data=new Array(); // 'new' is optional
data[0]="Sophia";
data[1]=25;
data[2]=myFunction;

var data=Array(3); // reserves 3 elements
data[0]="Sophia";
data[1]=25;
data[2]=myFunction;

Arrays can contain objects and be associated with properties. Properties are not counted as elements.

```
var arr=[3];   // an element
arr.p = {x:1}; // an object as a property
arr[1] = 5;    // an element
arr[1.5] = 6;  // a property
alert(arr[0]);       // 3
alert(arr[1]);       // 5
alert(arr.p);        // [object Object]
alert(arr.length); // 2
alert(arr.hasOwnProperty(1.5));  // true
arr[30] = {y:2};     // an object as an element
alert(arr['length']);  // 31
alert(arr[1.5]);        // 6
arr.length = 3;         // truncates the array
alert(arr[30]);         // undefined
```

Elements in an array literal can be skipped, in which case the values for the elements will be 'undefined'.

```
var a = [0,,2,3,,,6,,];
```

Multi-dimensional arrays can be created by nesting arrays.

```
var ma = [[1,2,3],['a','b','c']];
alert(ma[1][2]);  // c
```

If your array consists of only DOM (3.4.1) nodes, you can iterate through the nodes efficiently like this:

```
var divs = document.getElementsByTagName('div');
for (var i=0, div; div = divs[i]; i++){
  // Process div
}
```

properties:
length stores the number of elements.

methods:
isArray(o) returns true if o is an array.

indexOf(o[,i]) returns the index of the first found object o after the ith element. **lastIndexOf(o[,i])** returns the index of the last found object o before the ith item. -1 is returned if the item cannot be found.

join([s]) returns a string made by joining up of all the items joined together, separated by the string s. **concat(a1[,a2,a3......])** returns an array made up of all the arrays a,a1,a2,a3...... joined together. **reverse()** reverses the order of the items.

```
var arr = [10,20,30,40,10];

alert(Array.isArray([]));       // true

alert(arr.indexOf(30));         // 2
alert(arr.indexOf(60));         // -1
alert(arr.indexOf(10,2));       // 4
alert(arr.lastIndexOf(10));     // 4
alert(arr.lastIndexOf(10,2));   // 0

alert(arr.join('-'));           // 10-20-30-40-10
alert(arr.concat([5,6],[7]));   // 10,20,30,40,10,5,6,7
alert(arr.reverse());           // 10,40,30,20,10
```

pop() removes and returns the last item. **push (o1[,o2,o3......])** adds items to the end and returns the new length. **shift()** removes and returns the first element. **unshift(o1[,o2,o3......])** adds elements to the start and returns the new length. **slice (i1[,i2])** returns an array made up of items from index i1 to the end (or to i2-1). **splice (i1,i2[,o1,o2......])** removes i2 items from index i1 onwards, add o1,o2... to that location, and returns an array containing the removed items. Negative i1 counts the position backwards from the end.

```
var arr = [10,20,30,40];
alert(arr.pop());                     // 40
alert(arr.push(1,2));                 // 5
alert(arr);                           // 10,20,30,1,2
alert(arr.shift());                   // 10
alert(arr.unshift(5,6,7));            // 7
alert(arr);                           // 5,6,7,20,30,1,2
alert(arr.slice(2,7));                // 7,20,30,1,2
alert(arr.splice(2,2,100,200));       // 7,20
alert(arr);                           // 5,6,100,200,30,1,2
```

forEach(f(o)) executes the function f on every element. **map(f(o))** returns a new array of the return value from executing the callback function f on every array item. **filter(f(o))** returns a new array containing the items for which the callback function f returned true. **every(f(o))** returns true if callback f returns true for every item in the array. **some(f(o))** returns true if callback f returns true for at least one item in the array.

```
var arr = [10,20,30,40];
arr.forEach(alert);  // (alerting 10,20,30,40)
alert(arr.map(function (x){return x+1;}));       // 11,21,31,41
alert(arr.filter(function (x){return (x>20);})); //30,40
alert(arr.some(function (x){return (x>20);})); // true
alert(arr.every(function (x){return (x>20);})); // false
```

sort([f(o1,o2)]) sorts the elements with function f. f is a function that takes in two items. It returns a negative number if the first argument precedes the second argument, and zero if the two items have the same precedence. **reduce(f(o1,o2)[,o3])** applies f to reduce the list of items down to a single value using the initial value o3. **reduceRight(f(o1,o2)[,o3])** works like reduce() but starts with the last element.

```
function sortByLength(a,b){
  return a.length > b.length;
}
var reduceByJoining = function (a,b){
  return a.concat(b);
}
arr = ['fish','cat',,,'dolphin'];
alert(arr.sort());                              // cat,dolphin,fish,,
alert(arr.sort(sortByLength));                  // cat,fish,dolphin,,
alert(arr.reduce(reduceByJoining));;            // catfishdolphin
alert(arr.reduceRight(reduceByJoining,'ant'));
                                                // antdolphinfishcat
```

If your browser supports JavaScript 1.7, *array comprehensions* may be used in place of map() and filter().

```
  arr=[1,2,3,4,5];
  alert([i*i for (i of arr)]); // 1,4,9,16,25
  alert([i*i for (i of arr) if (i%2==0)]); // 4,16
```

Some objects, such as:

- HTMLCollection returned by document.getElementsByTagName()
- the 'arguments' object made available within the body of a function
- strings

look and behave like arrays but do not share all their methods. You can run generic 'Array.' methods on these array-like objects in browsers that support this.

```
// (alerting a,b,c)
Array.prototype.forEach.call('abc',function (c){alert(c);});

// This is not supported by some browsers.
Array.forEach('abc',function (c){alert(c);});
```

Some browsers support arrays destructuring, which is an experimental syntax.

```
var arr=[10,20,30];
var [a,b,c] = arr;
                          IS THE SAME AS
var arr=[10,20,30];
var a = arr[0];
var b = arr[1];
var c = arr[2];
```

3.2.7 Date

A **Date()** can be initialized in several ways.:

var d = new Date();
var d = new Date(*milliseconds*);
var d = new Date(*dateString*);
var d = new Date(*year*, *month*, *day*, *hours*, *minutes*, *seconds*, *milliseconds*);

Some parameters in the last form of initialization are optional. For example:

```
var today = new Date()
var d1 = new Date("July 14, 1997 10:30:00");
var d2 = new Date(97,7,14);
var d3 = new Date(97,7,14,10,30,0);
```

Calling Date without the new keyword simply converts the provided date to a string.

```
// Tue Oct 21 2014 16:53:17 GMT+0800
// (Malay Peninsula Standard Time)
alert(Date());
```

methods:
Date and time parameters can be accessed and modified with the 'get-' and 'set-' functions. If present, UTC represents Universal Time.:

{get|set} [UTC]FullYear(<i>)......a number
{get|set} [UTC]Month(<i>)......0 to 11
{get|set}[UTC]Date(<i>)......1 to 31
get[UTC]Day()......0 to 6
{get|set} [UTC]Hours(<i>)......0 to 23
{get|set} [UTC]Minutes(<i>)......0 to 59
{get|set} [UTC]Seconds(<i>)......0 to 59
{get|set} [UTC]Milliseconds(<i>)......0 to 999

{get|set}Time(<i>) gets or sets the number of milliseconds elapsed since midnight 1 Jan, 1970. **parse(ds)** takes in a date string and returns the number of milliseconds elapsed since midnight 1 Jan,1970. **UTC(y,n,d[,h,m,s,ms])** returns the number of milliseconds between a specified datetime and midnight 1 Jan 1970. **getTimezoneOffset()** returns the difference between UTC time and local time in minutes.

A Date() can be converted to different formats: **toDateString(), toTimeString(), toISOString(), toJSON(), toLocaleDateString(), toLocaleTimeString(), toLocaleString(), toUTCString()**

```
<!DOCTYPE html>
<html>
<head></head>
<body>
<script>
var d=new Date();  // current datetime
document.write(d+"<br />"); // calls .toString()
d.setMonth(0);
d.setFullYear(2010);
document.write(d.toDateString()+" "+d.getDay()+"<br />");
document.write(d.getHours()+"<br />");
document.write(d.getUTCHours()+"<br />");
document.write(d.getTimezoneOffset()+"<br />");

var d2=Date.parse("January 05,2012");
document.write(d2+"<br />");

var d3=Date.UTC(2011,10,25,12);
document.write(d3+"<br />");
d.setTime(490594540395);
document.write(d+"<br /><br />");
document.write(d.toDateString()+"<br />");
document.write(d.toTimeString()+"<br />");
document.write(d.toISOString()+"<br />");
document.write(d.toJSON()+"<br />");
document.write(d.toLocaleDateString()+"<br />");
document.write(d.toLocaleTimeString()+"<br />");
document.write(d.toLocaleString()+"<br />");
document.write(d.toUTCString()+"<br />");
</script>
</body>
</html>
```

```
Tue Oct 23 2012 15:10:10 GMT+0800 (Malay
Peninsula Standard Time)
Sat Jan 23 2010 6
15
7
-480
1325692800000
1322222400000
Fri Jul 19 1985 12:15:40 GMT+0800 (Malay
Peninsula Standard Time)

Fri Jul 19 1985
12:15:40 GMT+0800 (Malay Peninsula Standard
Time)
1985-07-19T04:15:40.395Z
1985-07-19T04:15:40.395Z
Friday, July 19, 1985
12:15:40 PM
Friday, July 19, 1985 12:15:40 PM
Fri, 19 Jul 1985 04:15:40 GMT
```

3.2.8 Math

Properties:
E, LN2, LN10, LOG2E, LOG10E, PI, SQRT2, SQRT1_2(square root of 1/2).

Methods:
acos(num), asin(num), atan(num), cos(num), sin(num), tan(num) define trigonometrical functions. **atan2(y,x)** returns the arctangent of (y/x). All degrees are in radians.

abs(num) returns the absolute value. **ceil(num)** returns the ceiling value. **floor(num)** returns the floor value. **round(num)** rounds x to the nearest integer. **max(n1,n2......)** returns the highest value. **min(n1,n2......)** returns the lowest value.

sqrt(num) returns the square root of x. **pow(x,y)** raises x to the power of y. **log(num)** returns the base-e natural logarithm of x. **exp(num)** returns e^x.

random() returns a random number between 0 and 1.

```
<!DOCTYPE html>
<html>
<head></head>
<body>
<script>
document.write(Math.PI+"<br />");
document.write(Math.sin(Math.PI/2)+"<br />");
document.write(Math.random()+"<br />");
</script>
</body>
</html>
```

```
3.141592653589793
1
0.5431340533626983
```

3.2.9 RegExp

A **RegExp()** (regular expression) allows a string to be searched and replaced efficiently by matching patterns. There are two ways to create a regular expression:

var p=new RegExp(*pattern*,*modifiers*);
var p=/*pattern*/*modifiers*;

For example:

var p=new RegExp("hello","gi");
var p=/hello/gi;

properties:
global, **ignoreCase** and **multiline** specify whether the modifier "g","i" or "m" is set respectively (Boolean). **source** stores the pattern as a string. **lastIndex** stores the position at which to start the next match.

methods:
compile(re,m) compiles a regular expression.
exec(s) returns the first match in the string s.
test(s) returns true if a match is found, false otherwise.

modifiers:
i: case-insensitive.
g: global. Find all matches.
m: multiline matching.

patterns:
[fdrw**]** any character within
[^fdrw**]** any character not within
[0-9] any digit from 0 to 9
[A-Z] any uppercase letter
[a-z] any lowercase letter
[A-z] any letter
[\b] backspace
[car**|**bus**|**taxi**]** any options within
. any character except newline or line terminator
\w any letter, digit or _ ([A-Za-z0-9_])
\W any character which is not a letter, digit or _ ([^A-Za-z0-9_])
\d any digit ([0-9])
\D any non-digit ([^0-9])
\s any whitespace character
\S any non-whitespace character
\b a word boundary
\B not a word boundary
\0 NUL character
\n newline character
\f form feed character
\r carriage return character
\t tab character
\v vertical tab character
****xxx character specified by the octal number xxx
\xdd character specified by the hex number dd
\uxxxx character specified by the hex number xxxx
\cX a control character in a string, X is from A-Z
c**+** one or more c's
c+? smallest possible ? match
c***** zero or more c's
c*? smallest possible * match
c**?** zero or one c
c**{**n**}** a sequence of n c's
c**{**n,m**}** a sequence of n to m c's
c**{**n,**}** a sequence of at least n c's
c**$** with c at the end
^c with c at the beginning
(zzz) grouping for back references
(**?=**s) followed by s (excluding s)
(**?!**s) not followed by s (excluding s)

To escape special characters, add a \ in front of:
. \ + * ? [ ] ^ $ ( ) { } = ! < > | : -

```
<!DOCTYPE html>
<html>
<head></head>
<body>
<script>
function print(p){
  document.write(p.exec(s)+"<br />");
}
var s="I say that today is a good day."
p=/DAy/          ; print(p);  //null
p=/DAy/i         ; print(p);  //day
p=/DAy[a-z]/i    ; print(p);  //null
p=/[A-z]DAy/i    ; print(p);  //oday
p=/\Dday/        ; print(p);  //oday
p=/\bday/        ; print(p);  //day
p=/\B\wday/      ; print(p);  //oday
p=/\B.\wday/     ; print(p);  //null
p=/.o{2,5}...../ ; print(p);  //good day
p=/^...../       ; print(p);  //I say
p=/..(?=at)/     ; print(p);  //th
p=/.......day(?!.)/ ; print(p);  //null
document.write(s.replace("day","doyy")+"<br />");
p=/day/i;
document.write(s.replace(p,"doyy")+"<br />");
p=/day/ig;
document.write(s.replace(p,"doyy")+"<br />");
p=/a/gi;
while (p.test(s)){document.write(p.lastIndex+",");}
document.write('<br/>'+s.replace(/(.....)(.....)/,'$2 $1'));
</script>
</body>
</html>
```

```
null
day
null
oday
oday
day
oday
null
good day
I say
th
null
I say that todoyy is a good day.
I say that todoyy is a good day.
I say that todoyy is a good doyy.
4,9,15,21,29,
that I say today is a good day.
```

3.2.10 Error

The error objects include **Error**, **EvalError**, **InternalError**, **RangeError**, **ReferenceError**, **SyntaxError**, **TypeError**, and **URIError**. When throwing any of the error objects, you can specify three parameters: message, filename, and lineNumber.

properties:
name specifies the error name. **message** specifies the error message.

```
<!DOCTYPE html>
<html>
<body>
  <script>
  try {
    throw new Error('Whoops!');
  } catch (e) {
    alert(e.name + ': ' + e.message);
  }
  try {
    foo.bar();
  } catch (e) {
    if (e instanceof EvalError) {
      alert(e.name + ': ' + e.message);
          //...
    } else if (e instanceof RangeError) {
      alert(e.name + ': ' + e.message);
          //...
    } else if (e instanceof ReferenceError){
      alert(e.name + ': ' + e.message);
          //...
    }
  }
  </script>
</body>
</html>
```

3.2.11 Global Properties and Methods

properties:

Infinity refers to mathematical infinity. **NaN** is **n**ot **a** **n**umber. **undefined** is an undefined value. **null** represents a null value. 'NaN', 'undefined' and 'null' evaluate to false in a Boolean context.

```
<!DOCTYPE html>
<html>
<body>
<script>
var a;
if (!a) alert(a);  // undefined
if (!(a+10)) alert(a+10);  // NaN
a=null;
if (!a) alert(a);  // null
alert(a+100);  // 100
</script>
</body>
</html>
```

methods:

encodeURI(s) converts the special characters in s to %-entities and returns the resulting string. **encodeURIComponent(s)** also encodes the characters , / ? : @ & = + $ #. **decodeURI(s)** and **decodeURIComponent(s)** decode an encoded string and return the resulting string.

eval(s) treats the string s as Javascript statements and executes them. If s is an expression, the resulting value will be returned.

isFinite(n) tests if a value is finite. **isNaN(n)** tests if a value is not a number.

number(o) converts o to a number. **string(o)** converts o to a string. **parseFloat(s)** converts o to a float number. **parseInt(s,i)** converts s to an integer of radix i.

```
<!DOCTYPE html>
<html>
<head></head>
<body>
<script>
  var s="Hello, Mike. How do you do?";
  document.write(encodeURIComponent(s)+"<br />"+
                                          "<br />");
  eval ("var a=true, b=false, c='4545fds';");
  document.write(Number(a)+"<br />");
  document.write(Number(b)+"<br />");
  document.write(Number(c)+"<br />");
  document.write(isNaN(c)+"<br />"+"<br />");

  var d=new Date(), e="1.6";
  document.write(Number(d)+"<br />");
  document.write(d.getTime()+"<br />");
  document.write(parseInt(d)+"<br />");
  document.write((e+1)+"<br />");
  document.write(parseInt(e)+"<br />");
  document.write((parseFloat(e)+1)+"<br />"+"<br />");
  var f=undefined;
  document.write(isNaN(s)+"<br />");
  document.write(isFinite(s)+"<br />");
  document.write(isFinite(1/0)+"<br />");
</script>
</body>
</html>
```

```
Hello%2C%20Mike.%20How%20do%20you%20do%3F

1
0
NaN
true

1351038567147
1351038567147
NaN
1.61
1
2.6

true
false
false
```

Without the 'defer' attribute, the script will not run because the body has not been parsed yet.

```
<!DOCTYPE html>
<html>
<head>
  <script src="parseInt.js" defer></script>
</head>
<body>
  <input type="number" value="10"/>+
  <input type="number" value="20"/>
</body>
</html>
```

```
var x = document.getElementsByTagName("input")[0].value;
var y = document.getElementsByTagName("input")[1].value;
alert (y-x);                                // 10
alert (x+y);                                // 1020
alert (parseInt(x,10)+parseInt(y,10));  // 30
alert ((+x)+(+y));                          // 30
```

3.3 Window Objects

(Read-only properties are underlined.)

3.3.1 Window

The 'Window' object is special in the sense that all its properties and methods can be accessed without specifying the 'window.' prefix, as if they are global.

```
Window
Inherits: EventTarget, WindowTimers, WindowBase64,
WindowEventHandlers

Properties:
OfflineResourceList applicationCache
Crypto crypto
nsIArray dialogArguments
HTMLElement frameElement
HTMLCollection(Window) frames
unsigned int length

History history
Navigator navigator
Location location
Performance performance
Screen screen
HTMLDocument document

unsigned int innerHeight
unsigned int innerWidth
unsigned int outerHeight
unsigned int outerWidth
unsigned int screenX
unsigned int screenY

unsigned int pageXOffset
unsigned int pageYOffset
unsigned int scrollX
unsigned int scrollY

bar locationbar
bar menubar
bar personalbar
bar scrollbars
bar statusbar
bar toolbar

Window opener
Window parent
Window self
Window top
Window window

Boolean fullscreen
String name
String status

Methods:
void getAttention()
void dump(String msg)
void alert(String msg)
Boolean confirm(String msg)
String prompt(String msg[, String initialText])

void blur()
void close()
void focus()
void print()
void maximize()
void minimize()
void restore()
void stop()

void moveBy(int xPixels, int yPixels)
void moveTo(int xPixels, int yPixels)
void resizeBy(int xPixels, int yPixels)
void resizeTo(int width, int height)
void scroll(int xPixels, int yPixels)
void scrollByLines(int lines)
void scrollTo(int xCoord, yCoord)
void setCursor(String cursorType)

iID setImmediate(function f [,Object param...])
void clearImmediate(iID immediateID)

Selection getSelection()
find (String text, Boolean caseSensitive, Boolean backwards,
      Boolean wrapAround, Boolean wholeWord,
      Boolean searchInFrames, Boolean showDialog)
void updateCommand(String command)

MediaQueryList matchMedia(String mediaQuery)
CSSStyleDeclaration getComputedStyle(
                              Element e[, String pseudoElt])

Window open(String URL, String name [, String features])
Window openDialog(String URL, String name
                    [, String features [,args......]])
void postMessage(Object data, String targetOrigin
                    [, Transferable[] transfer])
```

Many of the properties and methods are self-explanatory. Some will be described in 3.4. Some others are insignificant or poorly supported, and are hence not further explained.

One particularly useful method is the **print()** function, which brings up a dialog box that will allow the visitor to print the webpage out onto paper with a printer.

This illustrates how to print something different from the current view.

```
<!DOCTYPE html>
<html>
<head><style type="text/css">
@media screen {
  .print { display: none; }
  .noPrint { display: block; }
}
@media print {
  .print { display: block; }
  .noPrint { display: none; }
}
</style></head>
<body>
  <div class="noPrint">
    What you see here will not be printed...<br/>
    <input type="button" onclick="print()" value="print"/>
  </div>
  <div class="print">
    Separate content printed successfully...
  </div>
</body>
</html>
```

You can tell if a '**bar**' is visible with its '**.visible**' property.

alert(...) halts the script execution until the OK button on the popped-up window is clicked. **confirm(...)** halts the script execution until the OK or Cancel button on the popped-up window is clicked. **prompt(...)** halts the script execution, prompts for a string, until the OK or Cancel button on the popped-up window is clicked.

You can open a new window with **open(...)**. **openDialog(...)** is an extension to open(...) in the sense that the former allows extra data to be passed to the new window in the form of 'w.arguments[]'.The *features* include 'left', 'top', 'height', 'width', 'screenX', 'screenY', 'centerscreen', 'outerHeight', 'outerWidth', 'innerHeight', 'innerWidth', 'menubar', 'toolbar', 'location', 'personalbar', 'status', 'dependent', 'dialog', 'minimizable', 'fullscreen', 'resizable', 'scrollbars', 'titlebar', 'alwaysRaised', 'alwaysLowered' and 'close'. If there are only two states for a feature, you can turn it on by specifying '*feature*', '*feature*=yes' or '*feature*=1'.

```
<!DOCTYPE html><html>
<body>
  <script>
  var features = "left=100, top=100,"+
                 "height=200, width=400,"+
                 "resizable=no, location," +
                 "status=1";
  w=open('', 'My New Window', features);
  w.document.body.innerHTML = '<p>Hello World</p>';
  w.alert('Hi! Welcome to '+w.name);
  w.alert(w.statusbar.visible);
  w.close();
  </script>
</body></html>
```

MediaQueryList comes with a Boolean '**.matches**' property. It gives information about the device on which the webpage is displayed.

```
alert(matchMedia('(min-width: 4000px)').matches); // false
```

postMessage(...) allows safe cross-origin communication. (3.6.4)

WindowBase64
Methods: String btoa(String binaryData) String atob(String base64Data)

btoa(...) converts a string of binary data to a string of base-64 data so that it can be transmitted without any problem. **atob(...)** performs the reverse decoding.

```
<!DOCTYPE html><html>
<body>
  <script>
  bData = btoa('(hi)');
  alert(bData); // KGhpKQ==
  alert(atob(bData)); // (hi)
  </script>
</body></html>
```

WindowTimers
Methods: timeoutID setTimeout(function f, Number millisec [,param...]) void clearTimeout(timeoutID tid) intervalID setInterval(function f, Number millisec [,param...]) void clearInterval(intervalID iid)

setTimeout(...) executes a function once after a delay. **setInterval(...)** executes a function repeatedly every 'millisec'. The latter is an important function in the sense that it allows many animation effects to be achieved.

```
<!DOCTYPE html><html>
<body>
  <p>Growing Text</p>
  <script>
  var fs = 10;
  function enlargeFont(step){
    p = document.getElementsByTagName('p')[0];
    fs+=step;
    if (fs>100) clearInterval(sid);
    p.style.fontSize=fs+'px';
  }
  var sid=setInterval(enlargeFont,10,1);
  </script>
</body></html>
```

3.3.2 Navigator

Navigator
Inherits: NavigatorID, NavigatorLanguage, NavigatorOnLine, NavigatorGeolocation, NavigatorPlugins, NavigatorUserMedia, NetworkInformation. (all combined below)
Properties: BatteryManager battery Geolocation geolocation String language String[] languages Boolean onLine String oscpu String userAgent
Methods: void getUserMedia(Object constraints, function(LocalMediaStream) successFunc, function(Error) failureFunc) void registerContentHandler(String mimeType, String uri, String title) void registerProtocolHandler(String protocol, String uri, String title) Boolean vibrate(Number[] pattern)

BatteryManager is currently only supported in Firefox. **geolocation** lets you know the geographical location of the visitor's device, and will be covered in 3.6.2. **getUserMedia()** prompts for the permission to use the camera or the microphone, and will be covered in Chapter 12.

```
<!DOCTYPE html><html>
<body>
  <pre><script>
    document.writeln(navigator.language);
    document.writeln(navigator.onLine);

    // This determines the browser name
    document.writeln(navigator.userAgent);

    // This vibrates a mobile device
    navigator.vibrate([100,30,100,30,100]);
  </script></pre>
</body></html>
```

```
en-US
true
Mozilla/5.0 (Windows NT 6.3) AppleWebKit/537.36
(KHTML, like Gecko) Chrome/38.0.2125.111
Safari/537.36
```

3.3.3 Location

In 1.1.2, we have seen how to redirect to another website using the <meta> tag. You can cause automatic redirection in Javascript using the **location** object too.

Location
Inherits: URLUtils (combined below)
Properties: String href String protocol String host String hostname String port String pathname String search URLSearchParams searchParams String hash String username String password String origin
Methods: void assign(String url) void reload([Boolean fromServer]) void replace(String url) String toString()

The difference between **replace(...)** and **assign(...)** is that replace(...) will not save the current page in **history**, which means that the user won't be able to use the back button to navigate to it. If **fromServer** is false, the **reload(...)** operation may retrieve the webpage from the cache instead of the server.

The three lines are equivalent.
location.assign('http://google.com');
location.href = 'http://google.com';
location = 'http://google.com';

As we will see in (4.21.3) and Chapter 14, there are other ways to initiate a redirection.

3.3.4 History

History
Properties: int length any state
Methods: void back() void forward() void go(int p) void pushState(Object state, String title, String url) void replaceState(Object state, String title, String url)

history allows you to revert back to webpages the visitor has visited in the tab. **back()** is the same as **go(-1). forward()** is the same as **go(1)**.

pushState(...) adds a new history entry. **replaceState(...)** replaces the current history entry.

3.3.5 Screen

Screen
Properties: int top int left int height int width int availTop int availLeft int availHeight int availWidth int colorDepth int pixelDepth String orientation
Methods: Boolean lockOrientation(String[] orientation) Boolean unlockOrientation()

screen returns information about the screen and allows you to change the **orientation**, which can be *{portrait|landscape}[-primary|-secondary]* or *default*.

3.3.6 Performance

Performance
Properties: PerformanceTiming timing PerformanceNavigation navigation
Methods: Number now()

performance contains some handy properties and methods that allow you to measure the performance at various stages of a website access.

PerformanceTiming
Properties: unsigned long long navagationStart unsigned long long unloadEventStart unsigned long long unloadEventEnd unsigned long long redirectStart unsigned long long redirectEnd unsigned long long fetchStart unsigned long long domainLookupStart unsigned long long domainLookupEnd unsigned long long connectStart unsigned long long connectEnd unsigned long long secureConnectionStart unsigned long long requestStart unsigned long long responseStart unsigned long long responseEnd unsigned long long domLoading unsigned long long domInteractive unsigned long long domContentLoadedEventStart unsigned long long domContentLoadedEventEnd unsigned long long domComplete unsigned long long loadEventStart unsigned long long loadEventEnd

PerformanceNavigation

Properties:
int redirectCount
int type
    0 TYPE_NAVIGATENEXT
    1 TYPE_RELOAD
    2 TYPE_BACK_FORWARD
    255 TYPE_UNDEFINED

```
<!DOCTYPE html><html>
<body>
  <pre><script>
    now = new Date().getTime();
    rst = performance.timing.requestStart;
    document.writeln(performance.now());
    document.writeln(now);
    document.writeln(rst);
    document.writeln((now-rst)/1000.0 +" seconds");
  </script></pre>
</body></html>
```

```
12.999999977182597
1415081052368
1415081052354
0.014 seconds
```

3.3.7 Other Media Interfaces

Accessing and manipulating audios, videos, gamepads etc. can get quite complex technically. The subject is beyond the scope of this book. Here we simply list down the relavant web interfaces. The interested reader is directed to:

https://developer.mozilla.org/en-US/docs/Web/API

AnalyserNode, BiquadFilterNode, ChannelMergerNode, ChannelSplitterNode, ConvolverNode, DelayNode, GainNode, Gamepad, GamepadButton, GamepadEvent, MediaElementSourceNode, MediaRecorder, MediaStreamAudioDestinationNode, MediaStreamAudioSourceNode, PannerNode, WaveShaperNode, WebVTT

3.4 DOM Objects

Document Object Model (DOM) treats the entire document as a hierarchy of nodes.

If Object A inherits Object B, then Object A has access to the properties and methods of Object B, in addition to its own members. For instance, if an object is a HTMLAudioElement, then you can access the properties and methods that belong to EventTarget:

```
    EventTarget
         |
        Node
         |
      Element
         |
    HTMLElement
         |
  HTMLMediaElement
         |
  HTMLAudioElement
```

In 3.4.1 and 3.4.2, the read-only properties are underlined.

3.4.1 Core DOM Reference

The Objects in this subsection are shared by HTML (Chapter 1), XML (Chapter 6), and SVG (Chapter 7). In particular, the Document object is inherently available and represents a HTML webpage. It is also obtained by the 'contentDocument' property of an iframe, and the 'responseXML' property of an XMLHttpRequest object.

Attr
Properties: Boolean isId String name String schemaTypeInfo Boolean specified String value

CharacterData
Inherits: Node, ChildNode, NonDocumentTypeChildNode
Properties: String data unsigned long length Element NonDocumentTypeChildNode.nextElementSibling Element NonDocumentTypeChildNode.previousElementSibling
Methods: void appendData(String data) void deleteData(unsigned long offset. unsigned long count) void insertData(unsigned long offset, String data) void replaceData(unsigned long offset, unsigned long count,   String data) String substringData(unsigned long offset, String data)

ChildNode

Comment
Inherits: CharacterData, Node

CustomEvent
Constructor: CustomEvent(String type[, CustomEventInit eventInitDict])
Properties: Any detail
Methods: void initCustomEvent(String type, Boolean canBubble,   Boolean cancelable, Any detail)

Document
Inherits: Node, EventTarget
Properties: DocumentType doctype Element documentElement String documentURI DOMImplementation implementation String lastStyleSheetSet String preferredStyleSheetSet String selectedStyleSheetSet String[] styleSheets String[] styleSheetSets
Methods: Node adoptNode(Node source) Node importNode(Node source, Boolean deep) Element querySelector(String selector) NodeList querySelectorAll(String selector) Element getElementById(String id) HTMLCollection getElementsByClassName(String className) HTMLCollection getElementsByTagName(String tagName) HTMLCollection getElementsByTagNameNS(String namespace, String tagName)

Attr createAttribute(String name)
Attr createAttributeNS(String namespace, String name)
CharacterData createCDATASection(String data)
Comment createComment(String comment)
DocumentFragment createDocumentFragment()
Element createElement(String name)
Element createElementNS(String namespace, String name)
Event createEvent(String interface)
Text createTextNode(String text)
ProcessingInstruction createProcesingInstruction(String target,
String data)

Range createRange()
NodeIterator createNodeIterator(Node root
[,Number whatToShow[, NodeFilter filter]])
TreeWalker createTreeWalker(
Node root[, Number whatToShow[, NodeFilter filter]])

CaretPosition caretPositionFromPoint(Number x, Number y)
Element elementFromPoint(Number x, Number y)
void enableStyleSheetsForSet(String name)
XPathExpression createExpression(
String expression, XPathNSResolver resolver)
XPathNSResolver createNSResolver(Node resolver)
XPathResult evaluate(String expression, Node contextNode,
XPathNSResolver resolver, Number type, Object result)

DocumentFragment

Inherits: Node, ParentNode

Methods:
Element querySelector(String selector)
NodeList querySelectorAll(String selector)

DocumentType

Inherits: Node, ChildNode

Properties:
String name
String publicId
String systemId

DOMError

Properties:
String name

DOMException

Properties:
String name

DOMImplementation

Methods:
XMLDocument createDocument(String namespaceURI,
String qualifiedName[, DocumentType docType])
DocumentType createDocumentType(
String qualifiedName, String publicId, String systemId)
Document createHTMLDocument([String title])
Boolean hasFeature(String feature, String version)

DOMString

(mapped to String in Javascript)

DOMStringList

Properties:
int length

Methods:
DOMString item(int index)
Boolean contains(String str)

DOMTimeStamp

(in milliseconds)

DOMTokenList

Properties:
int length

Methods:
String item(int index)
Boolean contains(String str)
void add(String str)
void remove(String str)
Boolean toggle(String str)

Element

Inherits: Node, EventTarget, ParentNode, ChildNode, NonDocumentTypeChildNode, Animatable

Properties:
NamedNodeMap attributes
int childElementCount
HTMLCollection children
DOMTokenList classList
String className
String id
String tagName
String innerHTML
Element firstElementChild
Element lastElementChild
Element NonDocumentTypeChildNode.nextElementSibling
Element NonDocumentTypeChildNode.previousElementSibling

Methods:
String getAttribute(String name)
String getAttributeNS(String namespace, String name)
Boolean hasAttribute(String name)
Boolean hasAttributeNS(String namespace, String name)
void removeAttribute(String name)
void removeAttributeNS(String namespace, String name)
void setAttribute(String name, String value)
void setAttributeNS(
String namespace, String name, String value)

HTMLCollection getElementsByClassName(
String space-separated-names)
HTMLCollection getElementsByTagName(String name)
HTMLCollection getElementsByTagNameNS(
String namespace, String name)
Element querySelector(String selectors)
NodeList querySelectorAll(String selectors)
void ChildNode.remove()

Event

Properties:
Boolean bubbles
Boolean cancelable
EventTarget currentTarget
Boolean defaultPrevented
unsigned short eventPhase
EventTarget target
DOMTimeStamp timestamp
String type
Boolean isTrusted

Methods:
void initEvent(String type, Boolean canBubble,
Boolean cancelable)
preventDefault()
stopImmediatePropagation()
stopPropagation()

Subclasses: AnimationEvent, AudioProcessingEvent, BeforeInputEvent, BeforeUnloadEvent, BlobEvent, ClipboardEvent, CloseEvent, CompositionEvent, CSSFontFaceLoadEvent, CustomEvent, DeviceLightEvent, DeviceMotionEvent, DeviceOrientationEvent, DeviceProximityEvent, DOMTransactionEvent, DragEvent, EditingBeforeInputEvent, ErrorEvent, FocusEvent, GamepadEvent, HashChangeEvent, IDBVersionChangeEvent, **KeyboardEvent**, MediaStreamEvent, MessageEvent, **MouseEvent**, MutationEvent, OfflineAudioCompletionEvent, PageTransitionEvent, PointerEvent, PopStateEvent, ProgressEvent, RelatedEvent, RTCDataChannelEvent, RTCIdentityErrorEvent, RTCIdentityEvent, RTCPeerConnectionIceEvent, SensorEvent, StorageEvent, SVGEvent, SVGZoomEvent, TimeEvent, TouchEvent, TrackEvent, TransitionEvent, UIEvent, UserProximityEvent, WheelEvent

(Fully documented at: https://developer.mozilla.org/en-US/docs/Web/API/Event)

KeyboardEvent

Properties:
Boolean altKey
Boolean ctrlKey
Boolean metaKey
Boolean shiftKey
String code
Boolean isComposing
String key
String locale
unsigned long location
Boolean repeat

Methods:
Boolean getModifierState(String key)

MouseEvent

Properties:
Boolean altKey
Boolean ctrlKey
Boolean metaKey
Boolean shiftKey
int button = {0:left, 1:wheel, 2:right}
int buttons = {1:left, 2:right, 4:wheel, 8:back, 16:forward}
int which = {0:no, 1:left, 2:wheel, 3:right}
int clientX
int clientY
int movementX
int movementY
int screenX
int screenY
EventTarget relatedTarget

Methods:
Boolean getModifierState(String key)

EventTarget

Methods:
void addEventListener(String type,
function/EventListener listener [,Boolean useCapture])
Boolean dispatchEvent(Event e)
void removeEventListener(String type,
function/EventListener listener [,Boolean useCapture])

HTMLCollection

Properties:
int length

Methods:
Node item(int index) → [index]
Node namedItem(String name) → ['name']

MutationObserver

Constructor:
MutationObserver(function(MutationRecord[]) callback)

Methods:
void observe(Node target, MutationObserverInit options)
void disconnect()
Array takeRecords()

Properties of MutationObserverInit:
Boolean childList
Boolean attributes
Boolean characterData
Boolean subtree
Boolean attributeOldValue
Boolean characterDataOldValue
Array attributeFilter

Properties of MutationRecord:
String type
Node target
NodeList addedNodes
NodeList removedNodes
Node previousSibling
Node nextSibling
String attributeName
String attributeNamespace
String oldValue

Node

Inherits: EventTarget

Properties:
String baseURI
NodeList childNodes
Node parentNode
Node firstChild
Node lastChild
Node nextSibling
Node previousSibling
String nodeName
unsigned short nodeType
1:element 2:attribute 3:text 4:CDATA
5:entity ref 6:entity 7:pro. ins. 8: comment
9:document 10:doc type 11:doc frag. 12: notation
String nodeValue
Document ownerDocument
Element parentElement
String textContent

Methods:
Node appendChild(Node n)
Node cloneNode(Boolean deep)
Node insertBefore(Node new, Node reference)
Node removeChild(Node n)
Node replaceChild(Node new, Node old)
unsigned short compareDocumentPosition(Node n)
DOCUMENT_POSITION_{DISCONNECTED | PRECEDING | FOLLOWING | CONTAINS | CONTAINED_BY | IMPLEMENTATION_SPECIFIC}
Boolean contains(Node n)
Boolean hasChildNodes()
Boolean isDefaultNamespace(String namespace)
Boolean isEqualNode(Node n)
String lookupPrefix(String namespace)
String lookupNamespaceURI(String prefix)
void normalize()

NodeFilter

Methods:
unsigned short acceptNode(Node n)
FILTER_{ACCEPT | REJECT | SKIP}

NodeIterator

Properties:
Node root
unsigned long whatToShow
NodeFilter.SHOW_{ALL | COMMENT | DOCUMENT | DOCUMENT_FRAGMENT | DOCUMENT_TYPE | ELEMENT | PROCESSING_INSTRUCTION | TEXT}
NodeFilter filter

Methods:
Node previousNode()
Node nextNode()

NodeList

Properties:
int length

Methods:
Node item(int index) → [index]

ParentNode

ProcessingInstruction

Inherits: Node

Range

Properties:
Boolean collapsed
Node commonAncestorContainer
Node endContainer
Number endOffset
Node startContainer
Number startOffset

Methods:
void setStart(Node start, int startOffset)
void setEnd(Node end, int endOffset)
void setStartBefore(Node reference)
void setStartAfter(Node reference)
void setEndBefore(Node reference)
void setEndAfter(Node reference)
void selectNode(Node reference)
void selectNodeContents(Node reference)
void collapse([Boolean toStart])
DocumentFragment cloneContents()
void deleteContents()
DocumentFragment extractContents()
void insertNode(Node new)
void surroundContents(Node new)
int compareBoundaryPoints(unsigned short H, Range source)
H: {END | START}_TO_{END | START}
Range cloneRange()
void detach()
toString()

Text
Properties:
String wholeText
Methods:
Node splitText(offset)

TreeWalker
Properties:
Node root
unsinged long whatToShow (see NodeIterator)
NodeFilter filter
Node currentNode
Methods:
Node parentNode()
Node firstChild()
Node lastChild()
Node previousSibling()
Node nextSibling()
Node previousNode()
Node nextNode()

3.4.2 HTML DOM Reference

The objects in this subsection are meant for HTML only.

HTMLElement
Inherits: Element, GlobalEventHandlers, TouchEventHandlers
Properties:
String accessKey
String accessKeyLabel
String contentEditable = {'true'|'false'}
Boolean isContentEditable
HTMLMenuElement contextMenu
DOMStringMap dataset
String dir
Boolean draggable
DOMSettableTokenList dropzone
Boolean hidden
String lang
Boolean spellcheck
CSSStyleDeclaration style
long tabIndex
String title
Methods:
void blur()
void click()
void focus()

URLUtils
Properties:
String href
String protocol
String host
String hostname
String port
String pathname
String search
String hash
String username
String password
String origin
URLSearchParams searchParams
Methods:
String toString()

HTMLAnchorElement for <a>
Inherits: HTMLElement, URLUtils
Properties:
String hreflang
String media
String rel
DOMTokenList relList
long tabIndex
String target
String text
String type

HTMLAreaElement for <area>
Inherits: HTMLElement, URLUtils
Properties:
String alt
String cords
String hreflang
String media
String rel
DOMTokenList relList
String search
String shape
long tabIndex
String target
String type

HTMLAudioElement for <audio>
Inherits: HTMLElement, HTMLMediaElement
Constructor:
Audio([URLString])

HTMLBaseElement for <base>
Inherits: HTMLElement
Properties:
String href
String target

HTMLBodyElement for <body>
Inherits: HTMLElement, WindowEventHandlers

HTMLBRElement for
Inherits: HTMLElement

HTMLButtonElement for <button>
Inherits: HTMLElement
Properties:
Boolean autofocus
Boolean disabled
HTMLFormElement form
String formAction
String formEncType
String formMethod
Boolean formNoValidate
String formTarget
NodeList labels
String name
long tabIndex
String type
String validationMessage
ValidityState validity
String value
Boolean willValidate

Methods:
Boolean checkValidity() void setCustomValidity(String error)

HTMLCanvasElement for <canvas>
Inherits: HTMLElement
Properties: unsinged int height unsinged int width
Methods: RenderingContext getContext(String contextType) String toDataURL(String type, Number quality) void toBlob(function callback(Blob) [,String type [, Number quality]])

HTMLDataElement for <data>
Inherits: HTMLElement
Properties: String value

HTMLDataListElement for <datalist>
Inherits: HTMLElement
HTMLCollection options

HTMLDivElement for <div>
Inherits: HTMLElement

HTMLDListElement for <dl>
Inherits: HTMLElement

HTMLDocument
Inherits: Document
Properties: HTMLElement head HTMLElement body HTMLCollection anchors HTMLCollection embeds HTMLCollection forms HTMLCollection images HTMLCollection links HTMLCollection plugins HTMLCollection scripts Element activeElement String cookie window defaultView String designMode String domain String lastModified String location String readyState String referrer String title String URL
Methods: void close() void execCommand(String command[, Boolean showUI[, String value]]) NodeList getElementsByName(String name) Selection getSelection() Boolean hasFocus() void open() Boolean queryCommandEnabled(String command) Boolean queryCommandIndeterm(String command) Boolean queryCommandState(String command) Boolean queryCommandSupported(String command) Boolean queryCommandValue(String command) void write(String text) void writeln(String text)

HTMLEmbedElement for <embed>
Inherits: HTMLElement
Properties: String height String src String type String width

HTMLFieldSet for <fieldset>
Inherits: HTMLElement
Properties: Boolean disabled HTMLFormControlsCollection elements HTMLFormElement form String name String type String validationMessage ValidityState validity Boolean willValidate
Methods: Boolean checkValidity() void SetCustomValidity(String msg)

HTMLFormControlsCollection
Inherits: HTMLCollection
Methods: RadioNodeList/Element namedItem(String name) → ['name']

HTMLFormElement for <form>
Inherits: HTMLElement
Properties: String acceptCharset String action String autocomplete HTMLFormControlsCollection elements String encoding String enctype long length String method String name Boolean noValidate String target
Methods: Boolean checkValidity() HTMLElement item(int index) → [index] HTMLElement namedItem(String name) → ['name'] void submit() void reset()

HTMLHeadElement for <head>
Inherits: HTMLElement

HTMLHeadingElement for <h1> - <h6>
Inherits: HTMLElement

HTMLHtmlElement for <html>
Inherits: HTMLElement

HTMLHRElement for <hr>
Inherits: HTMLElement

HTMLIFrameElement for <iframe>
Inherits: HTMLElement
Properties: Document contentDocument WindowProxy contentWindow String height String name DOMSettableTokenList sandbox String src String srcDoc String width

HTMLImageElement for <img>

Inherits: HTMLElement

Properties:
String alt
Boolean complete
String crossOrigin
Boolean isMap
String src
String useMap
unsigned long height
unsigned long width
unsigned long naturalHeight
unsigned long naturalWidth

Constructor:
Image([unsigned long width, unsigned long height])

HTMLInputElement for <input>

Inherits: HTMLElement

Properties:
String accept
String alt
String autocomplete
Boolean autofocus
Boolean checked
Boolean defaultChecked
String defaultValue
Boolean disabled
FileList files
HTMLFormElement form
String formAction
String formEncType
String formMethod
Boolean formNoValidate
String formTarget
String height
Boolean indeterminate
NodeList labels
HTMLElement list
String max
long maxLength
String min
Boolean multiple
String name
String pattern
String placeholder
Boolean readOnly
Boolean required
String selectionDirection = {'forward' | 'backward' | 'none'}
unsigned long selectionEnd
unsigned long selectionStart
unsigned long size
String src
String step
long tabIndex
String type
String validationMessage
ValidityState validity
String value
Date valueAsDate
double valueAsNumber
String width
Boolean willValidate

Methods:
Boolean checkValidity()
void select()
void setCustomValidity(String error)
void setSelectionRange(int selectionStart, int selectionEnd,
[,String selectionDirection])
void setRangeText(String replacement,
[int start [, int end [, String selectMode]]])
void stepDown(Number n)
void stepUp(Number n)

HTMLKeygenElement for <keygen>

Inherits: HTMLElement

Properties:
Boolean autofocus
String challenge
Boolean disabled
HTMLFormElement form
String keytype
String name
String type
String validationMessage
ValidityState validity
Boolean willValidate

Methods:
Boolean checkValidity()
void setCustomValidity(String error)

HTMLLabelElement for <label>

Inherits: HTMLElement

Properties:
HTMLElement control
HTMLFormElement form
String htmlFor

HTMLLegendElement for <legend>

Inherits: HTMLElement

Properties:
HTMLFormElement form

HTMLLIElement for <li>

Inherits: HTMLElement

Properties:
long value

HTMLLinkElement for <link>

Inherits: HTMLElement, LinkStyle

Properties:
Boolean disabled
String href
String hreflang
String media
String rel
DOMTokenList relList
DOMSettableTokenList sizes
StyleSheet sheet
String type

HTMLMapElement for <map>

Inherits: HTMLElement

Properties:
String name
HTMLCollection areas
HTMLCollection images

HTMLMediaElement

Inherits: HTMLElement

Properties:
AudioTrackList audioTracks
Boolean autoplay
TimeRanges buffered
MediaController controller
Boolean controls
String crossOrigin
String currentSrc
double currentTime
Boolean defaultMuted
double defaultPlaybackRate
double duration
Boolean ended
MediaError error
Boolean loop
String mediaGroup
Boolean muted
unsigned short networkState
Boolean paused

double playbackRate
TimeRanges played
String preload
unsigned short readyState
TimeRanges seekable
Boolean seeking
String src
TextTrackList textTracks
VideoTrackList videoTracks
double volume

Methods:
String canPlayType(String type)
void fastSeek(double time)
void load()
void pause()
void play()

HTMLMetaElement for <meta>

Inherits: HTMLElement

Properties:
String content
String httpEquiv
String name

HTMLMeterElement for <meter>

Inherits: HTMLElement

Properties:
double high
double low
double max
double min
double optimum
NodeList labels

HTMLModElement for <del> and <ins>

Inherits: HTMLElement

Properties:
String cite
String datetime

HTMLObjectElement for <object>

Inherits: HTMLElement

Properties:
Document contentDocument
WindowProxy contentWindow
String data
HTMLFormElement form
String height
String name
long tabindex
String type
Boolean typeMustMatch
String useMap
String validationMessage
ValidityState validity
String width
Boolean willValidate

Methods:
Boolean checkValidity()
void setCustomValidity(String error)

HTMLOListElement for <ol>

Inherits: HTMLElement

Properties:
Boolean reversed
long start
String type

HTMLOptGroupElement for <optgroup>

Inherits: HTMLElement

Properties:
Boolean disabled
String label

HTMLOptionsCollection

Properties:
unsigned long length

Methods:
HTMLOptionElement item(int index) → [index]
HTMLOptionElement namedItem(String name) → ['name']

HTMLOptionElement for <option>

Inherits: HTMLElement

Properties:
Boolean defaultSelected
Boolean disabled
HTMLFormElement form
long index
String label
Boolean selected
String text
String value

Constructor:
Option([String text [, String value
[, Boolean defaultSelected [, Boolean selected]]]])

HTMLOutputElement for <output>

Inherits: HTMLElement

Properties:
String defaultValue
HTMLFormElement form
DOMSettableTokenList htmlFor
NodeList labels
String name
String type
String validationMessage
ValidityState validity
String value
Boolean willValidate

Methods:
Boolean checkValidity()
void setCustomValidity(String error)

HTMLParagraphElement for <p>

Inherits: HTMLElement

HTMLParamElement for <param>

Inherits: HTMLElement

Properties:
String name
String value

HTMLPreElement for <pre>

Inherits: HTMLElement

HTMLProgressElement for <progress>

Inherits: HTMLElement

Properties:
double max
double position
double value
NodeList labels

HTMLQuoteElement for <q>

Inherits: HTMLElement

Properties:
String cite

HTMLScriptElement for <script>

Inherits: HTMLElement

Properties:
String type
String src
String charset
Boolean async
Boolean defer
String text

HTMLSelectElement for <select>

Inherits: HTMLElement

Properties:
Boolean autofocus
Boolean disabled
HTMLFormElement form
NodeList labels
long length
Boolean multiple
String name
HTMLOptionsCollection options
Boolean required
long selectedIndex
HTMLCollection selectedOptions
long size
String type
String validationMessage
ValidityState validity
String value
Boolean willValidate

Methods:
void add(HTMLOptionElement o, long before)
HTMLOptionElement item(int index) → [index]
HTMLOptionElement namedItem(String name) → ['name']
Boolean checkValidity()
void setCustomValidity(String error)

HTMLSourceElement for <source>

Inherits: HTMLElement

Properties:
String media
String src
String type

HTMLSpanElement for <span>

Inherits: HTMLElement

HTMLStyleElement for <style>

Inherits: HTMLElement, LinkStyle

Properties:
String media
String type
Boolean disabled
StyleSheet sheet
Boolean scoped

HTMLTableElement for <table>

Inherits: HTMLElement

Properties:
HTMLTableCaptionElement caption
HTMLTableSectionElement tHead
HTMLTableSectionElement tFoot
HTMLCollection rows
HTMLCollection tBodies

Methods:
HTMLTableSectionElement createTHead()
void deleteTHead()
HTMLTableSectionElement createTFoot()
void deleteTFoot()
HTMLTableCaptionElement createCaption()
void deleteCaption()
HTMLTableRowElement insertRow([int index])
void deleteRow(int index)

HTMLTableCaptionElement for <caption>

Inherits: HTMLElement

HTMLTableCellElement

Inherits: HTMLElement

Propertie:
unsigned long colSpan
unsigned long rowSpan
DOMSettableTokenList headers
long cellIndex

HTMLTableDataCellElement for <td>

Inherits: HTMLElement, HTMLTableCellElement

HTMLTableHeaderCellElement for <th>

Inherits: HTMLElement, HTMLTableCellElement

Properties:
String abbr
String scope = {'row' | 'col' | 'colgroup' | 'rowgroup'}

HTMLTableColElement for <col>

Inherits: HTMLElement

Properties:
unsigned long span

HTMLTableRowElement for <row>

Inherits: HTMLElement

HTMLCollection cells
long rowIndex
long sectionRowIndex

void deleteCell(int index)
HTMLTableCellElement insertCell(int index)

HTMLTableSectionElement

Inherits: HTMLElement

Propeties:
HTMLCollection rows

Methods:
void deleteRow(int index)
HTMLTableRowElement insertRow(int index)

HTMLTextAreaElement

Inherits: HTMLElement

Propeties:
Boolean autofocus
unsigned long cols
String defaultValue
Boolean disabled
HTMLFormElement form
long maxLength
String name
String placeholder
Boolean readOnly
Boolean required
unsigned long rows
String selectionDirection = {'forward' | 'backward' | 'none'}
unsigned long selectionEnd
unsigned long selectionStart
long tabIndex
long textLength
String type
String validationMessage
ValidityState validity
String value
Boolean willValidate
String wrap

Methods:
void select()
void setSelectionRange(int start, int end [, String direction])
Boolean checkValidity()
void setCustomValidity(String error)

HTMLTimeElement for <time>

Inherits: HTMLElement

Propeties:
String dateTime

HTMLTitleElement for <title>

Inherits: HTMLElement

Propeties:
String text

HTMLTrackElement
Inherits: HTMLElement
Propeties: String kind String src String srclang String label Boolean default unsigned short readyState TextTrack track

HTMLUListElement for <ul>
Inherits: HTMLElement

HTMLUnknownElement
Inherits: HTMLElement

HTMLVideoElement for <video>
Inherits: HTMLElement, HTMLMediaElement
Propeties: String height String poster unsigned long videoHeight unsigned long videoWidth String width

LinkStyle
Properties: StyleSheet sheet

StyleSheet
Properties: Boolean disabled String href MediaList media Node ownerNode StyleSheet parentStyleSheet String title String type

3.4.3 getElementX()

You can obtain an element by tag, class, name or id using the functions getElement**X**(...). When multiple elements are returned, use [index] or ['name/id'] to obtain a particular element.

```
<!DOCTYPE html><html>
<body>
  <p id="p1" class="c1">A</p>
  <p id="p2" class="c1 c2">B</p>
  <p id="p3" class="c2 c3">C<b>E</b></p>
  <p id="p4" class="c2">D</p>
  <input id="i1" type="text" name="it1"/>

  <script>
    document.getElementsByTagName('p')[3].innerHTML =
   document.getElementsByClassName('c2')['p2'].innerHTML;
                                                    // D -> B

    var e1 = document.getElementsByName('it1')[0];
    e1.setAttribute('class','c3');
    alert(e1.hasAttribute('class')); // true
    e1.value = 'Hello World';
    e1.focus();

    var e2 = document.getElementById('p3');
    alert(e2.attributes['class'].value); // c2 c3
    alert(e2.classList.item(1)); // c3
    alert(e2.tagName); // P
    alert(e2.nodeName); // P
    alert(e2.nodeType); // 1
    alert(e2.childNodes[0].nodeValue); // C
    alert(e2.textContent); // CE
    alert(e2.innerHTML); // C<b>E</b>
    alert(e1.compareDocumentPosition(e2)==
          Node.DOCUMENT_POSITION_PRECEDING); // true
    alert(e2.nextSibling.nextSibling.nextSibling.nextSibling
          .isEqualNode(e1)); // true
  </script>
</body></html>
```

A

B

CE

B

Hello World

3.4.4 querySelector()

You can call querySelector() if you wish to obtain the first element that matches a CSS selector.

```
<!DOCTYPE html><html>
<body>
  <form>
    <textarea>Hello</textarea>
    <select name='sl'>
      <option value='m'>Male</option>
      <option value='f' selected>Female</option>
    </select>
    <input type='checkbox' name='cb' class='c1' checked/>
    <input type='radio' name='rd' class='c1' value='r1'/>
    <input type='radio' name='rd' class='c1' value='r2'
           checked/>
  </form>
  <script>
  alert(document.forms[0][0].value); // hello
  alert(document.querySelectorAll('form>.c1')[1].value); // r1
  alert(document.querySelector('body .c1').value); // on
  alert(document.forms[0]['rd'].value); // r2
  </script>
</body></html>
```

Hello Female ▼

3.4.5 NodeIterator and TreeWalker

NoteIterator allows you to iterate through the selected nodes in a tree in a depth-first order.

```
<!DOCTYPE html><html>
<body>
  <p>A</p>
  <span>Z</span>
  <p>B<b>1</b></p>
  <!-- hi -->
  <p>C</p>
  <script>
  ni = document.createNodeIterator(
        document.body,
        NodeFilter.SHOW_ELEMENT|
        NodeFilter.SHOW_COMMENT,
        function(node){
          return node.nodeName=='SPAN'?
                 NodeFilter.FILTER_REJECT:
                 NodeFilter.FILTER_ACCEPT;
        });
  var i=0;
  while (i++, n = ni.nextNode()){
    alert(i+" "+n.textContent);
  }
  /* 1: (<body> text)
     2: A
     3: B1
     4: 1
     5: hi
```

```
    6: C
    7: (<script> text) */
  </script>
</body></html>
```

TreeWalker allows more traversal options than NodeIterator.

```
<!DOCTYPE html><html>
<body>
  <p>A</p>
  <span>Z</span>
  <p>B<b>1</b></p>
  <!-- hi -->
  <p>C</p>
  <script>
  ni = document.createTreeWalker(
         document.body,
         NodeFilter.SHOW_ELEMENT|
         NodeFilter.SHOW_COMMENT,
         function(node){
           return node.nodeName=='SPAN'?
                  NodeFilter.FILTER_REJECT:
                  NodeFilter.FILTER_ACCEPT;
       });
  alert(ni.lastChild().textContent); // (<script> text)
  alert(ni.previousSibling().textContent); // C
  alert(ni.previousNode().textContent); // hi
  alert(ni.parentNode().textContent); // (<body> text)
  </script>
</body></html>
```

3.4.6 Range

```
<!DOCTYPE html><html>
<body>
  <p><span><i>Hello</i> World</span></p>
  <p>A</p>
  <p>B</p>
  <p>C</p>
  <script>
    r = document.createRange();
    p = document.getElementsByTagName('p');
    r.selectNodeContents(p[0]);
                      // excluding <p>, unlike selectNode()
    alert(r.startContainer.innerHTML);
                      // <span><i>Hello</i> World</span>
    r.setStartBefore(p[1]);
    r.setEndAfter(p[2]);
    alert(r); // A   B
  </script>
</body></html>
```

3.4.7 CaretPosition

You can obtain a node if you know its position on the screen. Only Firefox supports this feature at the time of writing.

```
<!DOCTYPE html><html>
<body>
  <h4 onclick="showTag(event)">A</h4>
  <p onclick="showTag(event)">B</p>
  <span onclick="showTag(event)">C</span>
  <script>
    function showTag(e){
   cp = document.caretPositionFromPoint(e.clientX,e.clientY);
     alert(cp.offsetNode.nodeName+" "+cp.offset); // #text 1
    }
  </script>
</body></html>
```

3.4.8 CSS

You can set a css property of an element using '*element*.**style**.*property*'. If the property name is hyphenated, convert it to camel case.

```
<!DOCTYPE html><html>
<head>
  <style type="text/css">
    p {background-color:orange}
  </style>
</head>
<body>
  <p>ABC</p>
  <script>
    p=document.getElementsByTagName('p')[0];
    ps=p.style;
    ps.fontSize='100px';
    ps.color='red';
    alert(ps.fontSize); // 100px
    alert(ps.backgroundColor); // (empty)!
    alert(getComputedStyle(p,null).backgroundColor);
                                          // rgb(255,165,0)
  </script>
</body></html>
```

3.4.9 Node Addition/Removal

Nodes can be added to, replaced in, or removed from the DOM tree.

Note that the last two lines in the script plays an mp3 in the background.

```
<!DOCTYPE html><html>
<body>
  <div></div>
  <script>
   d=document.getElementsByTagName('div')[0];
   p1=document.createElement('p');
   p1.setAttribute('id','p1');
   p1.appendChild(document.createTextNode('Hello '));
   s1=document.createElement('span');
   s1.appendChild(document.createTextNode('World'));
   p1.appendChild(s1);
   p1.appendChild(document.createTextNode('!!!'));
   d.appendChild(p1);

   alert(d.innerHTML);
   // <p id="p1">Hello <span>World</span>!!!</p>

   d.innerHTML='Hello <span>World</span>!!!';
   s=d.getElementsByTagName('span')[0];
   alert(document.contains(s)); // true

   d.insertBefore(document.createTextNode('Earth'),s);
   d.replaceChild(document.createTextNode(''),s);
   //d.removeChild(s);
   alert(d.innerHTML); // Hello Earth!!!

   a = new Audio('http://example.com/song.mp3');
   a.play();
  </script>
</body></html>
```

3.4.10 <table> and <select>

```
<!DOCTYPE html><html>
<head>
  <style type="text/css">
    table,td {border: 1px solid;}
  </style>
<head>
<body>
  <script>
    t = document.createElement('table');
    r0 = t.insertRow(0);
    t0 = r0.insertCell(0);
    t1 = r0.insertCell(1);
    t2 = r0.insertCell(2);
    t0.appendChild(document.createTextNode('A'));
    t1.appendChild(document.createTextNode('B'));
    t2.appendChild(document.createTextNode('C'));
    c = t.createCaption();
```

```
    c.appendChild(document.createTextNode('a table'));
    document.body.appendChild(t);
  </script>
</body></html>
```

a table

A	B	C

```
<!DOCTYPE html><html>
<body>
  <select>
    <option id='o1' value='1'>A</option>
    <option id='o2' value='2'>B</option>
    <option id='o3' value='3'>C</option>
  </select>
  <script>
    s = document.getElementsByTagName('select')[0];
    alert(s.namedItem('o1').text); // A
    alert(s[1].value);  // 2
  </script>
</body></html>
```

3.4.11 Node Copying

adoptNode() moves a node, while importNode() copies a node.

At the time of writing, this example does not work in Chrome locally without a server due to its cross-origin policy.

```
<!DOCTYPE html><html>
<body>
  <iframe src="DOM-copyB.html" onload="copy_nodes()"
       height="80" width="150"></iframe>
  <script>
    function copy_nodes(){
      ed = document.getElementsByTagName('iframe')[0].
                                          contentDocument;
      edp0 = ed.getElementsByTagName('p')[0];
      edp1 = ed.getElementsByTagName('p')[1];
      p0 = document.importNode(edp0,true);
      p1 = document.adoptNode(edp1);
      p2 = p1.cloneNode(true);
      document.body.appendChild(p0);
      document.body.appendChild(p1);
      document.body.appendChild(p2);
    }
  </script>
</body></html>
```

```
<!-- DOM-copyB.html -->
<!DOCTYPE html><html>
<body>
  <p>A<b>B</b>C</p>
  <p>1<b>2</b>3</p>
</body></html>
```

ABC

ABC

123

123

3.4.12 Text Selection

You can automatically select a part of some text in a textbox.

```
<!DOCTYPE html><html>
<body>
  <input type='text' size='100' value='hello world'/>
  <script>
    i = document.getElementsByTagName('input')[0];
    i.setSelectionRange(3,9);
  </script>
</body></html>
```

hello world

execCommand() affects the selected region of a contentEditable element.

```
<!DOCTYPE html><html>
<body>
  <div contenteditable="true" onmouseup="SetToBold();">
    Select a part of this text!</div>
  <script>
    function SetToBold () {
      document.execCommand ('bold', false, null);
      document.execCommand ('fontSize', false, '20px');
    }
  </script>
</body>></html>
```

Select **a part** of this text!

Other commands: backColor, bold, contentReadOnly, copy, createLink, cut, decreaseFontSize, delete, enableInlineTableEditing, enableObjectResizing, fontName, fontSize, foreColor, formatBlock, forwardDelete, heading, hiliteColor, increaseFontSize, indent, insertBrOnReturn, insertHorizontalRule, insertImage, insertOrderedList, insertUnorderedList, insertParagraph, insertText, italic, justifyCenter, justifyFull, justifyLeft, justifyRight, outdent, paste, redo, removeFormat, selectAll, strikethrough, subscript, superscript, underline, undo, unlink, styleWithCSS

You can also obtain the selected region with window.getSelection().

3.4.13 Node Normalization

normalize() removes empty nodes, and merges adjacent text nodes.

Originally <body> has 6 child nodes: 2 <p> nodes, 1 <script> node, and 3 text nodes spacing the elements.

```
<!DOCTYPE html><html>
<body>
  <p>A</p>
  <p>B</p>
  <script>
    bd = document.body;
    alert(bd.childNodes.length); // 6
    pb = document.getElementsByTagName('p')[1];
    bd.insertBefore(document.createTextNode('  '),pb);
    bd.insertBefore(document.createTextNode('  '),pb);
    bd.appendChild(document.createTextNode(''));
    alert(bd.childNodes.length);  // 9
    bd.normalize();
    alert(bd.childNodes.length);  // 6(Chrome),7(IE)
  </script>
</body></html>
```

3.4.14 Validation

You can change the validity message to show when a visitor submits invalid data.

Notice in this example, the input element is obtained by using the form id and the input name directly.

```
<!DOCTYPE html><html>
<body>
  <form id='frm'>
    <input type="number" onkeyup="vMsg()" name='tb' />
    <input type="submit"/>
```

```
  </form>
  <p></p>
  <script>
  function vMsg(){
    inp = document.forms.frm.tb;
    p = document.getElementsByTagName('p')[0];
    p.innerHTML = "<br/>willValidate: "+
                        inp.willValidate + "<br/>";
    p.innerHTML += "checkValidity(): "+
                          inp.checkValidity() + "<br/>";
    for (vp in inp.validity)
       p.innerHTML += vp+": "+inp.validity[vp]+"<br/>" ;

    // The following changes the error message when
    // the Submit button is clicked.
    inp.setCustomValidity("A number please!");
  }
  </script>
</body></html>
```

```
1a    Submit
A number please!
willValidate: true
checkValidity(): false
valid: false
customError: true
badInput: true
stepMismatch: false
rangeOverflow: false
rangeUnderflow: false
tooLong: false
patternMismatch: false
typeMismatch: false
valueMissing: false
```

3.4.15 Events

In 1.5.2, we have seen how to capture some mouse, keyboard and scrolling events. We did this by attaching some Javascript code to the 'onX' event attributes in an element. There are *two other ways* by which an event can be defined.

You can attach a function directly to the 'onX' property of an element.

```
<!DOCTYPE html><html>
<body>
  <button>Click</button>
  <script>
    window.onload = alert(1);
    document.onkeyup =
              function(e){alert(e.keyCode);};
    document.getElementsByTagName('button')[0].onclick =
              function(e){alert(e.button);};
  </script>
</body></html>
```

You can also register 'X' event listeners on objects. (As we shall in chapter 4, XMLHttpRequest can have events defined too.)

```
<!DOCTYPE html><html>
<body>
  <button>Click</button>
  <script>
    window.addEventListener('DOMContentLoaded',alert(1));
    document.addEventListener('keyup',
          function(e){alert(e.keyCode);});
    document.getElementsByTagName('button')[0].
          addEventListener('click',
                                  function(e){alert(e.button);});
  </script>
</body></html>
```

You can stop the default action of a HTML element by using event.preventDefault(). The default action can also be stopped by 'return false;'.

In this example, clicking the link or the checkbox won't change or trigger anything. Only small letters can be entered in the textbox.

```
<!DOCTYPE html><html>
<head>
  <script>
    function clk(e){e.preventDefault();}

    function prs(e){
      var charCode = e.charCode;
      if (charCode < 97 || charCode > 122) {
        e.preventDefault();
        alert(
           "Please use lowercase letters only."
           + "\n" + "charCode: " + charCode + "\n"
        );
      }
    }
  </script>
</head>
<body>
  <a href="http://google.com" onclick="clk(event)">
     Google</a>
  <input type='checkbox' onclick="clk(event)"/>
  <input type='text' onkeypress="prs(event)"/>
</body></html>
```

The GlobalEventHandlers interface is inherited by HTMLElement, Document, Window, and WorkerGlobalScope. Its propeties have been listed in 1.5.2.

3.4.16 MutationObserver

Constrasting events on existing elements, a MutationObersver allows you to invoke a function when a DOM tree is modified.

```
<!DOCTYPE html><html>
<body>
  <p>A</p>
  <p>B</p>
  <p>C</p>
  <script>
    mo = new MutationObserver(function(mutations) {
            mutations.forEach(function(mutation) {
              alert(mutation.type);  // childList
            });
          });
    mo.observe(document.body,
         {childList:true, attributes:true, characterData:true});
    document.body.insertBefore(
         document.createTextNode('haha'),
         document.getElementsByTagName('p')[1]);
    mo.disconnect();
  </script>
</body></html>
```

3.5 Client Storage

A cookie can store only about 4kB of data, whereas web/DOM storage (localStorage and sessionStorage) can store 5MB-25MB of data. To store an unlimited amount of data, consider IndexedDB.

3.5.1 Cookie

A cookie is a piece of data that remains on the visitor's computer after the browser window is closed. Every time a web page is requested from a server, the cookie is added to the HTTP header, so that the server can read the cookie too.
A cookie contains the name-value pair, the expiry date, and the path. Using Javascript, it can be set or returned with **document.cookie**, which must not be regarded as a normal string property. Applying the assignment = operator to it adds a cookie to the end, instead of replacing the whole series of values with a new value. If the name already exists, only the value of the name will be replaced. The following shows an example of how to set a cookie:

document.cookie= '*cname=value*;
expires=*Thu, 2 Aug 2001 20:47:11 UTC*;
domain=google.com;
path=/;
secure';

expires specifies the expiry time of the cookie. If omitted, the cookie is deleted when the visitor quits the browser.

domain and **path** designate which locations have access to the cookie in the future. Sub-directories of the path will have access to the cookie too. Note that setting the domain to 'www.example.com' denies access from 'example.com'. If they are not set, it becomes the domain of the page that sets the cookie.

secure, if present, restricts access to the cookie to be via https only.

When *document.cookie* is used in an expression, only the name=value pairs are returned as a string, separated by semicolons.:
'cname1=value1; cname2=value2......'

For security reasons, this example won't work in Chrome without a server.

```
<!DOCTYPE html>
<html>
<head>
<script>
  function getCookie(name){
    var i,x,y,cookies=
          decodeURIComponent(document.cookie).split(";");
    for (i=0;i<cookies.length;i++){
      x=cookies[i].substr(0,cookies[i].indexOf("="));
      y=cookies[i].substr(cookies[i].indexOf("=")+1);
      x=x.replace(/^\s+|\s+$/g,"");
      if (x==name) {return y;}
    }
    return "";
  }
  function setCookie(name,v,exp_days){
    var exp_date=new Date();
    exp_date.setDate(exp_date.getDate() + exp_days);
    var c_value=encodeURIComponent(v) + ";expires=" +
                                  exp_date.toUTCString();
    document.cookie=name + "=" + c_value;
  }
  function eraseCookie(n){
    setCookie(n,"",-1);
  }
  setCookie("name","Adam",1);
  setCookie("age",25,1);
  setCookie("sex","male",1);
  setCookie("age",30,1);
  setCookie("data","~!@#$%^&*()_+ ",1);
  eraseCookie("sex");
  document.write(document.cookie);
  alert(getCookie("data")); // ~!@#$%^&*()_+
</script>
</head>
<body></body>
</html>
```

```
name=Adam; age=30;
data=~!%40%23%24%25%5E%26*()_%2B%20;
```

3.5.2 Local Storage

Like a cookie, a localStorage variable remains on the visitor's computer after the browser window is closed. Unlike a cookie, it is not sent to the server and does not expire. It can only be accessed by the web page that stores it. Only used when asked for, it can store large amounts of data without affecting the performance.

For information about how to store files and images in localStorage, refer to:

https://hacks.mozilla.org/2012/02/saving-images-and-files-in-localstorage/

3.5.3 Session Storage

A sessionStorage variable is like a localStorage variable, except that it is deleted when the visitor closes the browser window or tab.

Here 'test' is an arbitrarily defined property, and can only be assigned a string value. When the page first loads, localStorage.test and sessionStorage. test are undefined. As the user refreshes the page, the browser alerts the messages.

```
<!DOCTYPE html>
<html>
<body>
<script>
if(Storage){
  alert(localStorage.test);
  localStorage.test="Local Storage Detected";

  alert(sessionStorage.test);
  sessionStorage.test="Session Storage Detected";
} else {
  alert("Sorry, your browser does not support web
storage...");
}
</script>
</body>
</html>
```

3.5.4 JSON

JSON stands for Javascript Object Notation. It is a syntax for serializing objects and arrays. A JSON string can be easily stored or transmitted. Although it uses Javascript syntax for storing information, it is language independent and may be used in various programming languages.

Methods:
JSON.parse(s1[, f(s2,a)]) converts the string s1 to a JSON object. f(s2,a) transforms the returned value, using the key s2 and the value a.

JSON.stringify(o [,f(s1,a) [, s2]]) or **JSON.stringify(o [,arr [, s2]])** converts a JSON object o to a string. f(s1,a) transforms the returned value, using the key s1 and the value a. arr specifies the set of properties included. s2 is a string of space that causes the resulting string to be pretty-printed.

All property names in a JSON string must be double-quoted.

```
<!DOCTYPE html><html><body>
<script>
var JSON_string='\
   {"students":\
     [{"firstName":"Ali", "lastName":"Ahmad"}, \
      {"firstName":"Anna", "lastName":"Chan"}, \
      {"firstName":"Jacinta", "lastName":"May"}],\
    "teachers":\
     [{"firstName":"Jason", "lastName":"Ian"},\
      {"firstName":"Keown", "lastName":"Deary"}]}';
var JObj=JSON.parse(JSON_string);
alert(JObj.students[1].lastName);  // Chan
alert(JObj.teachers[0].firstName);  // Jason
</script>
</body></html>
```

```
<!DOCTYPE html><html><body>
<script>
o1 = {a:10, b:100, c:1000, '@':10000};
s1 = JSON.stringify(o1,['a','b','@'],"  ");

// toJSON() is a special object method
o2 = {foo:'X', toJSON:function(){return 'bar'}};
s2 = JSON.stringify({a:o2}); // {"a":"bar"}
alert(s2);

o3 = ['a',3,4,'b'];
s3 = JSON.stringify(o3);
alert(s3);  // ["a",3,4,"b"]
</script>
</body></html>
```

3.5.5 IndexedDB

An IndexedDB is organized into databases. A database contains object stores (comparable to tables in SQL), which in turn contain objects or other types of data. An object store can be structured in 4 ways:

keyPath	autoIncrement	
(none)	false	The object store can hold any value. You must supply a separate key argument whenever you want to add a new value.
'key'	false	The object store can only hold objects. The object must have a property with the same name as the key path.
(none)	true	The object store can hold any value. The key is generated for you automatically, or you can supply a separate key argument if you want to use a specific key.
'key'	true	The object store can only hold objects. Usually a key is generated and the value of the generated key is stored in the objet in a property with the same name as the key path. If such a property already exists, the value of that property is used as the key rather than generating a new key.

The operations for IndexedDB are mostly asynchronous, which means that before a function returns, other code may continue.

For information about how to store files and images in IndexedDB, refer to:

https://hacks.mozilla.org/2012/02/storing-images-and-files-in-indexeddb/

Note that window.indexedDB implements IDBFactory.

IDBFactory
Methods:
IDBOpenDBRequest open(String dbName, int version)
IDBOpenDBRequest delete(String dbName)
int cmp(Any a, Any b)

IDBOpenDBRequest
Inherits: IDBRequest
Handlers:
function(e) onblocked
function(e) onupgradeneeded

IDBDatabase
Inherits: EventTarget
Properties:
String name
int version version
DOMStringList objectStoreNames
Handlers:
function(e) onabort
function(e) onerror
function(e) onversionchange
Methods:
void close()
IDBObjectStore createObjectStore(String name, Object opt)
void deleteObjectStore(String name)
IDBTransaction transaction(String[] stores[, String mode])
... mode : 'readwrite', 'readonly', 'versionchange'

IDBRequest
Inherits: EventTarget
Properties:
IDBObjectStore result
DOMError error
Object source
IDBTransaction transaction
IDBRequestReadyState readyState
Handlers:
function(e) onerror
function(e) onsuccess

IDBTransaction
Inherits: EventTarget
Properties:
IDBDatabase db
IDBTransactionMode mode
DOMError error
Methods:
void abort()
IDBObjectStore objectStore(String name)
Handlers:
function(e) onabort
function(e) oncomplete
function(e) onerror

IDBObjectStore

Properties:
DOMStringList indexNames
Any keyPath
String name
IDBTransaction transaction
Boolean autoIncrement

Methods:
IDBRequest add(Any item [, Any key])
IDBRequest clear()
IDBRequest delete(Any key)
IDBRequest get(Any key)
IDBIndex createIndex(String index, Any key [, Object options])
void deleteIndex(String index)
IDBIndex IDBRequest index(String index)
IDBRequest put(Any item [,Any key])
IDBRequest openCursor([KeyRange r [, String direction]])

IDBIndex

Inherits: EventTarget

Properties:
String name
IDBObjectStore objectStore
Any keyPath
Boolean multiEntry
Boolean unique

Methods:
IDBRequest count()
IDBRequest get(Any key)
IDBRequest getKey(Any key)
IDBRequest openCursor()
IDBRequest openKeyCursor()

IDBCursor

Properties:
IDBObjectStore/IDBIndex source
String direction
Any key
Any primaryKey

Methods:
void advance(int positions)
void continue([Any key])
IDBRequest delete()
IDBRequest update(Any new)

IDBCursorWithValue

Inherits: IDBCursor

Properties:
Any value

IDBKeyRange

Properties:
Any lower
Any upper
Boolean lowerOpen
Boolean upperOpen

Methods:
IDBKeyRange bound(Any lower, Any upper, Boolean lowerOpen, Boolean upperOpen)
IDBKeyRange only(Any value)
IDBKeyRange lowerBound(Any value[, Boolean open])
IDBKeyRange upperBound(Any value[, Boolean open])

IDBVersionChangeEvent

Properties:
unsigned long long oldVersion
unsigned long long newVersion

```
<!DOCTYPE html>
<html><head>
<script>
var db;
const students = [
  {id:'H423498', name:'Mike', clss:'5D', age:11},
  {id:'A213132', name:'Bill', clss:'4H', age:10},
  {id:'H234324', name:'Paul', clss:'4H', age:7}];

if(indexedDB){
  //indexedDB.deleteDatabase('myDB');
  var request = indexedDB.open('myDB',3);
  request.onerror = function(e){
    alert("Why didn't you allow me to use IndexedDB?");
  };
  request.onsuccess = function(e){
    // This event is fired after the 'upgradeneeded' event
    // if the latter is ever fired.
    db = e.target.result;
  };
  request.onupgradeneeded = function(e){
    // This event is fired when you create a new database
    // or increase the version number. Furthermore, you
    // can only create object stores in this event.
    db = e.target.result;
    var os = db.createObjectStore('students',
                                   {keyPath:'id'});
    os.createIndex('name','name',{unique:true});
    os.createIndex('clss','clss',{unique:false});
    os.transaction.oncomplete = function(e){
      T = db.transaction(['students'],'readwrite');
      var sos = T.objectStore('students');
      for (i in students) {sos.add(students[i]);}
    };
  };
}


function addStudents(){
  var T = db.transaction(['students'],'readwrite');
  var sos = T.objectStore('students');
  sos.add({id:'C577564', name:'Alam', clss:'3A', age:10});
  sos.add({id:'C234464', name:'Alex', clss:'2B', age:8});
}

function removeStudents(){
  var T = db.transaction(['students', 'teachers'],'readwrite');
  var sos = T.objectStore('students');
  sos.delete('C577564');
  sos.delete('C234464');
}

function getStudent(){
  var sos = db.transaction(['students', 'teachers'],'readwrite')
              .objectStore('students');
  var index = sos.index('name');
  index.get('Bill').onsuccess = function(e) {// access by index
  data = event.target.result;
  document.getElementsByTagName('p')[0].innerHTML =
     data.id + " " + data.name + " " +
     data.clss + " " + data.age + "<br/>";
  }
}

function getStudents(){
  document.getElementsByTagName('p')[0].innerHTML = "";
  var sos = db.transaction(['students', 'teachers'],'readwrite')
              .objectStore('students');
  var index = sos.index('clss'); // access by index
  var range = IDBKeyRange.bound('1A','4H',false,false);
                                         // including 1A and 4H
  index.openCursor(range,'prev').onsuccess =
    function(e){
      var cursor = e.target.result;
      if (cursor){
     document.getElementsByTagName('p')[0].innerHTML +=
        cursor.value.id + " " + cursor.key + " " +
        cursor.value.clss + " " + cursor.value.age + "<br/>";
        cursor.continue();
      };
    };
}

function changeStudent(){
  var sos = db.transaction(['students', 'teachers'],'readwrite')
```

```
                .objectStore('students');
  var request = sos.get('C577564');  // access by key
  request.onsuccess = function(e) {
    data = request.result;
    data.age = 9;
    request2 = sos.put(data);
  }
}

function printStudents(){
  document.getElementsByTagName('p')[0].innerHTML="";

  // A transaction will become inactive if you return to
  // the event loop without using it. 'T' here must
  // not be declared globally once only.
  var T = db.transaction(['students'],'readwrite');

  var sos = T.objectStore('students');
  sos.openCursor().onsuccess = function(e){ // access by key
    var cursor = e.target.result;
    if (cursor){
   document.getElementsByTagName('p')[0].innerHTML +=
      cursor.key + " " + cursor.value.name + " " +
      cursor.value.clss + " " + cursor.value.age + "<br/>";
      cursor.continue();
    };
  };
}

</script></head>
<body>
  <p></p>
  <button onclick="addStudents();">
      Add students</button>
  <button onclick="removeStudents();">
      Remove students</button>
  <button onclick="getStudent();">
      Get by name</button>
  <button onclick="getStudents();">
      Get by class</button>
  <button onclick="changeStudent();">
      Change by id</button>
  <button onclick="printStudents();">
      Print students</button>
</body>
</html>
```

H234324 4H 4H 7
A213132 4H 4H 10
C577564 3A 3A 10
C234464 2B 2B 8

Add students | Remove students | Get by name
Get by class | Change by id | Print students

3.6 Advanced Techniques

3.6.1 FileReader

FileReader allows you to read the contents of a local file stored on the client computer.

FileReader
Inherits: EventTarget
Constructor: FileReader()
Properties: DOMError <u>error</u> int <u>readyState</u> = 0:EMPTY 1:LOADING 2:DONE String/ArrayBuffer <u>result</u>
Methods: void abort() void readAsArrayBuffer(Blob/File data) void readAsBinaryString(Blob/File data) void readAsDataURL(Blob/File data) void readAsText(Blob/File data [, String encoding])
Handlers: function(Event e) onabort function(Event e) onerror function(Event e) onload function(Event e) onloadstart function(Event e) onloadend function(Event e) onprogress

File
Inherits: Blob (combined below)
Properties: Date <u>lastModifiedData</u> String <u>name</u> int <u>size</u> String <u>type</u>
Methods: Blob slice([int start [, int end [, String contentType]]])

This shows how to preview an image. It also shows how to check the file size and type.

```
<!DOCTYPE html><html>
<head><script>
  function previewImg(){
    var i = document.querySelector('img');
    var f = document.querySelector('input[type=file]').files[0];
    var r = new FileReader();
    if (!f) return;
    r.onloadend = function () {i.src = r.result;};
    if (f.size>1024*1024) {
      alert('The file size must be smaller than 1MB.');
      return;
    }
    if (f.name.substr(-4)!='.jpg'){
      alert('The file type must be .jpg.');
      return;
    }
    r.readAsDataURL(f);
  }
</script></head>
<body>
  Choose a .jpg file:
  <input type="file" onchange="previewImg()"/><br/>
  <img/>
</body>
</html>
```

This shows how to obtain a file in the browser by dragging it from the outside. As of 12th Nov 2014, this works in Chrome, but other browsers may not support this drag-and-drop feature.

```
<!DOCTYPE html><html>
<body>
 <div style=" border: 10px dashed #ccc; margin: 20px auto;
              width: 300px; height: 300px;"></div>
  <script>
  var d = document.querySelector('div');
  d.ondragover = function () {return false;};
  d.ondrop = function(e) {
    this.className = '';
    var f = e.dataTransfer.files[0],
        r = new FileReader();
    r.onload = function (event) {
      d.style.background = 'url(' + event.target.result + ')';
    };
    r.readAsDataURL(f);
    return false;
  };
  </script>
</body>
</html>
```

3.6.2 Geolocation and Google Maps API

The Geolocation object is part of Navigator. It allows you to track the geographical position of the visitor. Different browsers have different security policies with regard to the use of geolocation.

Geolocation

Methods:
Position getCurrentPosition(
    function(Position p) success
    [,function(PositionError e) error
    [, PositionOptions options]])
 	
int watchPosition(
    function(Position p) success
    [,function(PositionError e) error
    [, PositionOptions options]])
 	
void clearWatch(int id)

watchPosition(...) registers a function that is invoked whenever the location changes. It returns an id that may be passed to clearWarch(...).

```
<!DOCTYPE html><html>
<body><script>
var options = {
  enableHighAccuracy: true,
  timeout: 5000,  // 5000ms
  maximumAge: 0   // 0ms, ie. don't use cache
};
function success(pos) {
  var crd = pos.coords;
  alert('Timestamp: '+ pos.timestamp);
  alert('Latitude : ' + crd.latitude);
  alert('Longitude: ' + crd.longitude);
  alert('Altitude: ' + crd.altitude);
  alert('More or less ' + crd.accuracy + ' meters.');
  alert('More or less ' + crd.altitudeAccuracy +
       ' meters for altitude.');
  alert('Heading: ' + crd.heading);
  alert('Speed: ' + crd.speed);
};
function error(err) {
  alert('ERROR(' + err.code + '): ' + err.message);
};
p = navigator.geolocation
            .getCurrentPosition(success, error, options);
</script></body></html>
```

To obtain the name of the place at a particular latitude and longtitude, you should use Google Maps API.

```
<!DOCTYPE html><html>
<body>
<script
src="http://maps.google.com/maps/api/js?sensor=false">
</script>
<script type="text/javascript">
  var geocoder = new google.maps.Geocoder();
  var latLng = new google.maps.LatLng(5.98,116);
  if (geocoder) {
    geocoder.geocode({ 'latLng': latLng},
                     function (results, status) {
      if (status == google.maps.GeocoderStatus.OK) {
        alert(results[0].formatted_address);
      } else {
        alert("Geocoding failed: " + status);
      }
    });
  }
</script>
</body></html>
```

3.6.3 Device Orientation

Many mobile devices contain an accelerometer which allows the orientation to be determined.

```
var ball   = document.querySelector('.ball');
var garden = document.querySelector('.garden');
var output = document.querySelector('.output');

var maxX = garden.clientWidth  - ball.clientWidth;
var maxY = garden.clientHeight - ball.clientHeight;

function handleOrientation(event) {
  var x = event.beta;  // In degree in the range [-180,180]
  var y = event.gamma; // In degree in the range [-90,90]

  output.innerHTML  = "beta : " + x + "\n";
  output.innerHTML += "gamma: " + y + "\n";

  // Because we don't want to have the device upside down
  // We constrain the x value to the range [-90,90]
  if (x >  90) { x =  90};
  if (x < -90) { x = -90};

  // To make computation easier we shift the range of
  // x and y to [0,180]
  x += 90;
  y += 90;

  // 10 is half the size of the ball
  // It center the positioning point to the center of the ball
  ball.style.top  = (maxX*x/180 - 10) + "px";
  ball.style.left = (maxY*y/180 - 10) + "px";
}
window.addEventListener('deviceorientation',
                        handleOrientation);
```

Partial code (Courtesy of https://developer.mozilla.org/en-US/docs/Web/API/Detecting_device_orientation)

3.6.4 Web Worker

A web worker is an external Javascript that runs in the background independently.

This example won't work in Chrome without a server.

```
<!DOCTYPE html>
<html>
<body>
<p>Prime numbers: <output id="result"></output></p>
<button onclick="startWorker()">Start Worker</button>
<button onclick="stopWorker()">Stop Worker</button>
<br /><br />
<script>
var w;
function startWorker() {
  if(Worker) {
    if(w) return;
    w=new Worker("primes.js");
    w.onmessage = function (e) {
       document.getElementById("result").innerHTML=e.data;
    };
  } else {
    document.getElementById("result").innerHTML=
        "Your browser does not support Web Workers...";
  }
}
function stopWorker(){w.terminate();}
</script>
</body>
</html>
```

```
// primes.js
var n=2;
function timedCount(){
  var prime=true;
  for (i=2; i<Math.sqrt(n)+1; i++){
    if (n%i==0){prime=false; break;}
  }
  if (prime||n==2) postMessage(n);
  setTimeout("timedCount()",500);
  if (n==2) n++; else n+=2;
}
timedCount();
```

Prime numbers: 409

Start Worker | Stop Worker

3.6.5 SMS Gateways

If you wish to send an SMS from a computer, you should first sign up for an account at an SMS gateway such as Clickatell, ViaNett, Nexmo etc. While it is possible to send an SMS through Javascript alone via HTTP GET (or POST), it is possibly a better idea to send it through PHP cURL(Chapter 16) so that your account credentials are hidden from the user at the client end. The official websites of the gateways contain information about how to send an SMS in various ways.

3.6.6 Facebook Like, Share & Comments

The Facebook Like and Share Buttons can be clicked to create a connection between a piece of content and the person clicking the button. A count of all the likes can be displayed.

To integrate the Facebook Like and Share Buttons, first create a Facebook App at:
https://developers.facebook.com/apps

Then go to:
https://developers.facebook.com/docs/plugins/like-button
to configure the buttons and get the JavaScript code.

Similarly, after you have registered an App, you can implement Facebook Comments at:
https://developers.facebook.com/docs/plugins/comments/

A list of possible Facebook plugins can be found at:
https://developers.facebook.com/docs/plugins

3.6.7 Others in this Book

Javascript provides some other web APIs which may be premature to illustrate here.

AJAX (4.25), a very important technique, allows data to be fetched from the server without loading a whole page. Closely related to AJAX is the **FormData** (4.25.5) interface, which allows all data in a form to be submitted at once without loading another page.

Server-Sent Events (12.1.6) allow dynamic communication between the server and the client.

Web Sockets (4.22.6) create a permanent connection between a page and the server.

WebRTC (12.5) allows videoconferencing to be performed in the browser without using a plugin.

Canvas 2D (Chapter 8) and **WebGL** (Chapter 9) allow you to draw on the canvas.

You can switch many elements to **fullscreen mode** (8.5.4).

jQuery (Chapter 15) is a Javascript library that calls for the 'write less; do more' principle.

If you wish to learn Javascript beyond this book, you should study a full-stack platform called **MEAN** (MongoDB, Express.js, Angular.js, Node.js).

4. Hypertext Preprocessor

PHP runs on the server. Particularly, it can process forms, files and databases over the internet.

To use PHP, you must first rent a server from a web host such as iPage, or set up your own server (Chapter 13). There are all-in-one packages that allow PHP to be run on a local computer, such as XAMPP and WampServer. These distributions contain Apache, PHP, MySQL and other applications.

Usage of Server-Side Languages, 15 Nov 2014	
PHP	82.0%
ASP.NET	17.3%
Java	2.7%
ColdFusion	0.7%
Perl	0.6%
Ruby	0.5%
Python	0.2%
JavaScript	0.1%
Erlang	0.1%
Others (<0.1% each): Lasso, Scala, Tcl, Smalltalk, C++, Haskell, Lisp, Ada	
(Courtesy of http://w3techs.com/technologies/overview/programming_language/all)	

A manual for PHP, protected by the Creative Commons Attribution 3.0 License, can be found at the PHP official website: http://php.net/manual/en/.

When a PHP file is requested from the server, the server first executes blocks of PHP code within the file. A 'normal HTML file' is then returned to the client's browser. As such, there is no way for a casual visitor to read the PHP code. These blocks of code are contained by the symbols **<?php** ... **?>**:

The server, after replacing the PHP block with the output, returns a converted document to the browser. (**echo** and **print** output the value of an expression, and they can be used interchangeably.)

```
<!-- intro.php -->
<!DOCTYPE html>
<html>
<head></head>
<body><?php
  echo "Hello ";
  print "<b>World!</b>";
?>
</body>
</html>
```

```
<!-- intro.php -->
<!DOCTYPE html>
<html>
<head></head>
<body>Hello <b>World!</b></body>
</html>
```

Hello **World!**

One can choose to return only certain parts of the document:

```
<!-- intro.php -->
<!DOCTYPE html>
<html>
<head></head>
<body>
  <?php
    $expression=true;
    if ($expression == true): ?>
   This part will be shown.
<?php else: ?>
   This part will not be shown.
<?php endif; ?>
</body>
</html>
```

```
<!-- intro.php -->
<!DOCTYPE html>
<html>
<head></head>
<body>
 This part will be shown.
</body>
</html>
```

This part will be shown.

With PHP, it becomes possible to generate HTML code automatically. This is especially useful if the webpage contains a lot of repetitive HTML code segments.

4.1 Basic Syntax

Statements are separated by '**;**'. Inline comments are denoted by **//** or **#**. Block comments are denoted by **/*** ... ***/**.

At any point, the script may be terminated with **return, die,** or **exit**, which can take on several forms:

```
return;          # returning from a global scope
exit;            # termination
exit();          # termination
exit(0);         // successful termination
exit(200);       // status 200 returned
exit("ERROR");   // prints the string before exiting
die("ERROR");    // die is the same as exit
```

After a script has been terminated in one of these ways, the remaining HTML part of the document after ?> is discarded.

4.1.1 Variables and Constants

All variable names are preceded by the $ symbol. Variables need not be declared before values can be assigned to them:

```
$a = trUE;              // boolean
$b = Null;              // NULL
$c = 033;               // octal integer
$d = -0x1C;             // hexadecimal integer
$e = 0b101;             // binary integer
$f = 1.331;             // float
$g = 1234e-3;           // exponential float
$h = intval("5.7");     # 5, integer conversion
$i = isset($a,$b,$c);   # false, $b is NULL
$j = empty($c);         #false, $c is not false
$k = empty($z);         # true, $z is undefined
```

While the names of variables are case-sensitive, the values true, false and NULL are not. 0, the empty string"", the string "0", an array with zero elements and NULL are considered false.

The size of an integer can be determined using **PHP_INT_SIZE**. The maximum allowed value of an integer can be determined using **PHP_INT_MAX**. If an integer overflows, it will be interpreted as a float instead.

Use **&**$variable for assignment by reference. For example, {$a=4; $b= &$a; $a=5;} will result in $b getting a value of 5 since $a and $b now point to the same value. The bindings of variables may be broken with the **unset()** function, eg.: unset($a,$b). Note that unsetting $a alone will not unset $b after the assignment by reference.

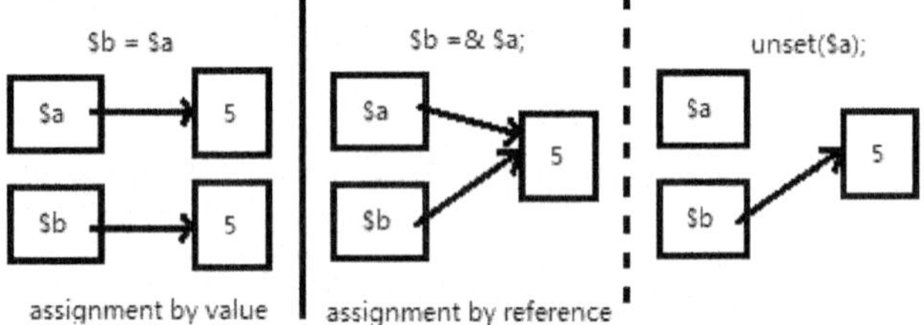

Constants are identifiers with values that do not change. The names of constants do not start with $. Their values can be directly accessed anywhere, even in a function:

```
define ("a",100);// one way to define a constant
const b=3;    // another way to define a constant
echo a*b;     // one way to use a constant
echo constant("b");  //another way to use it
echo defined("a");   // true
```

4.1.2 Operators

The operators, in order of decreasing precedence, are:

clone new	clone, new
[]	array
++ -- ~ @ (bool) (int) (float) (string) (array) (object)	pre-ncrement, pre-decrement, error suppression type casting
instanceof	types
!	logical
* / %	arithmetic
+ - .	arithmetic and string
<< >>	bitwise
< <= > >=	comparison
== != === !== <>	comparison
&	bitwise and references
^	bitwise
|	bitwise
&&	logical
||	logical
?:	ternary
= += -= *= /= .= %= &= |= <<= >>= =>	assignment
and	logical
xor	logical
or	logical
,	many uses
++ --	post-increment, post-decrement

Note the shorthand notations for assignment operators. ($a = $a % 5) is the same as ($a%=5), which is the remainder of $a divided by 5. An assignment evaluates to the value of the assignment, so ($a=$b=5) assign 5 to $a because ($b=5) evaluates to 5.

Placing ++ at the back of a variable increases its value by one after the whole statement has been executed. Placing it in front of a variable increases its value by one before the statement is executed.

The comparison operators are:
- == equals
- === equals in value and type
- !=,<> does not equal
- !== equals in neither value nor type
- \> is strictly greater than
- < is strictly less than
- \>= is greater than or equal to
- <= is less than or equal to

Caution must be taken when comparing floats for equality, for the internal representation of floats may offset the precise value slightly.

The logical operators are: **!**(not), **&&**(and), **||**(or), **and**, **xor** and **or**. Notice that the two variations of the logical operators **and** and **or** operate at different precedences. A **xor** expression evaluates to true only if one of the operands (but not both) evaluates to true. For example,

```
echo ($b=("5"==5) xor $d=("5"===5));
```

The resulting output is 1 because $b=("5"==5) evaluates to true while $d=("5"===5) evaluates to false.

For bitwise operators:
$a&$b: 1 for which both corresponding bits are 1s
$a|$b: 1 for which either corresponding bit is 1
$a^$b: 1 for which either but not both bit is 1
~$a: inverts the bits
$a >> 3: shifts the binary form 3 bits to the right
$a << 2: shifts the binary form 2 bits to the left

To cast a type out of an expression, include the bracketed type in front of the expression:

```
echo ((int)4.7+1);    # 5
echo ((bool)5.7);     # 1
```

The casts available are:
- (int), (integer) -- integer
- (bool), (boolean) -- boolean
- (float), (double), (real) -- float
- (string) -- string
- (array) -- array
- (object) -- object
- (unset) -- null

If 'display_errors' is set to 'on' in php.ini, error and warning messages will be displayed. These messages can be suppressed with the @ operator.

```
<!DOCTYPE html>
<html><body>
<?php
ini_set("display_errors","on");
echo @(10/0);
$my_file = @file ('non_existent_file') or
            die ("Failed opening file");
?>
</body></html>
```

4.1.3 Arrays

In PHP, an array is an ordered map that associates keys to values. A key can be an integer or a string. These two statements do the same assignment:

```
$arr = array("a"=>"Hello", 5 => "World");
$arr = ["a"=>"Hello", 5 => "World"]; // PHP 5.4+
```

If a key is a float, a string containing an integer or a boolean, it will be cast to an integer. If the key is not specified, it will be regarded as the largest integer index plus 1. Eg.:

```
$arr = ["orange",                    // key 0
        "apple",                     // key 1
        5.7=> "pineapple",           // key 5
        "special" => "cucumber",     // key "special"
        "watermelon"];               // key 6
$arr[]="pear";                       // key 7
```

To access $arr, use the square brackets [], eg.: $arr[1], $arr["special"].

Assign an array to a key in an array to create a multidimensional array.

```
$arr = ["ma"=>["foo"=>"bar"]];
$arr[1][2] = "live";
```

To access the value "foo", use $arr["ma"]["foo"].

Applying the + operator to two arrays returns an array which is a union of the two arrays. If the arrays contain the same keys, the key-value pairs of the left operand will be preserved.

```
<!DOCTYPE html>
<html>
<head></head>
<body><?php

$a=[4,5,6];
$b=[1,2,3,7,8];
var_dump ($a + $b);

?></body>
</html>
```

```
array(5) { [0]=> int(4) [1]=> int(5) [2]=> int(6) [3]=> int(7)
[4]=> int(8) }
```

Arrays may be compared with comparison operators.

```
<!DOCTYPE html>
<html>
<head></head>
<body><?php

$a=["hello","hi"];
$b=[1=>"hi",0=>"hello"];
var_dump ($a==$b);   // true; same key-value pairs
var_dump ($a===$b); // false; different order
var_dump ($a!==$b); // true; different order
var_dump ($a<>$b);   // false; same key-value pairs
var_dump ($a!=$b);   // false; same key-value pairs

?></body>
</html>
```

```
bool(true) bool(false) bool(true) bool(false) bool(false)
```

The values of an array can be assigned to a **list**() of variables directly:

```
<!DOCTYPE html>
<html>
<head></head>
<body><?php

$arr = ['apple',2=>'orange','mango'];
list($a0,,,$a3)=$arr;  // index 1 and index 2 skipped
echo ($a0." ".$a3."<br />");

list($a,list($b,$c)) = ['fruits',['vege','meat']];  // nested
echo ($a." ".$b." ".$c);

?></body>
</html>
```

```
apple mango
fruits vege meat
```

4.1.4 Strings

A string may may span multiple lines without using any multiline character. Strings can be joined with the . operator. Applying an arithmetic operator to a string converts the string to a number, while applying ++ and to a string variable shifts its last character to the next character. Eg.:

```
echo (30+"10.5 meters"); //outputs 40.5
$a="bus"; $a++;            // $a is now "but"
```

<,<=,> and>= compare the character codes of the first characters of the strings. If they are the same, the second characters will be compared, and so on. For example: "ACD">"ABD" is true.

In double-quoted strings, the following will escape: $variable, \n(new line),\r(carriage return), \t (horizontal tab),\v(vertical tab),\e(escape),\f(form feed),\\(backslash),\$(dollar sign),\"(double quote),\ddd(octal sequence), and \xdd(hexadecimal sequence).

In single-quoted strings, only \\ (backslash) and \'(single quote) will escape.

```
<!DOCTYPE html>
<html>
<head></head>
<body><?php
  $a=5;
  echo ("Give me $a" . "<br />");
  echo ('Give me $a' . '<br />');
  echo ('This isn\'t
        "bad"' . '<br />');
  echo ("\n");
  echo ('\n');
?></body>
</html>
```

```
Give me 5
Give me $a
```

```
This isn't "bad"
\n
```

A string may be specified with <<<. An identifier immediately follows the operator, then a new line, then the string. The string is closed when the identifier is again encountered in a line with nothing else except possibly the closing ;. The line with the closing identifier must not contain any extra spaces or characters.

If the opening identifier is not quoted or double-quoted, characters expand and escape as in double quoted strings. If the opening identifier is single-quoted, nothing expands nor escapes, not even \\ and \'.

```
<!DOCTYPE html>
<html>
<head></head>
<body><?php
$a=3;

echo <<<MSG1
Testing $a \\  " <br />
MSG1;

echo <<<'MSG2'
Testing $a \\  \'
MSG2;

?></body>
</html>
```

```
Testing 3 \ "
Testing $a \\ \'
```

Arrays and object properties can also be expanded in double-quoted strings. Enclose the identifier with {} so that the parser will not regard any irrelevant characters as part of the identifier. Functions, static class variables, and class constants inside {} will cause the return value to be interpreted as variable names for expansion.

Omitting the curly brackets will cause an error because *$fruits* is undefined.

```
<!DOCTYPE html>
<html>
<head></head>
<body><?php
$drinks=['Cola','7 Up','Sarsi'];
$fruit='apple';
echo ("He drank some $drinks[1]. ");
echo ("He ate some {$fruit}s. ");
echo ("I said ${fruit}s.");
?></body>
</html>
```

```
He drank some 7 Up. He ate some apples. I said apples.
```

A single character in a string may be accessed with **[]** or **{}**:

```
$str="abcd";
$str[2]="e";      // changes the string to "abed"
echo ($str{0});  // outputs "a"
```

A string can be executed as if it is some PHP code with **eval(...)**.Eg.: eval("echo 100; return 100;"); will return 100. eval(...) returns NULL by default, and returns false if there is a parse error within.

A string may be used as the name of a variable. For instance, {$a="hello"; $$a="world";} is equivalent to {$a="hello"; $hello=world;}. In the case of an array, ${$a[1]} treats $a[1] as the variable name while ${$a}[1] treats $$a as the variable name.

4.1.5 Conditionals

A conditional statement can be specified by **if**:

> **if** (*condition1*) {*statements1*;}
> **elseif** (*condition2*) {*statements2*;}
> **elseif......**
> **else** {statements3;}

If *condition1* evaluates to true, *statements1* will be executed. Otherwise *condition2* will be checked, and so on. If all the conditions are false, *statements3* will be executed. The elseif and else clauses are optional, and there may be any number of elseif clauses.

If the expression that is compared needs to be evaluated only once, **switch** may be used instead.

> **switch**(*expression*){
> **case** *value1*: *statements1;* **break**;
> **case** *value2*: *statements2;* **break**;
> **case** *value3*: *statements3;* **break**;
> ......
> **default**: *statements4;*
> }

On the other hand, the ternary operators ?: allow a value to be chosen among multiple values within an expression.

Note: Syntactically PHP allows a second form for **if**, **while**, **for**, **foreach**, and **switch**. '{' is changed to ':' and '}' to **endif;**, **endwhile;**, **endfor;**, **endforeach;**, or **endswitch;**, respectively.

The following three code segments are similar:

```
if ($a+$b==2): $x="two";
elseif ($a+$b==1): $x="one";
else : $x="zero";
endif;
```

```
switch ($a+$b){
  case 2: $x="two"; break;
  case 1: $x="one"; break;
  default: $x="zero";
}
```

```
$x = ($a+$b==2)?"two"
     : ($a+$b==1)?"one"
     :"zero";
```

If *break;* is omitted at the end of a *case* clause in the *switch* statement, PHP will go on running the statements in the next case.

4.1.6 Loops

There are several ways to run a block of statements repeatedly:

while(*cycle condition*){*statements*;}
do {*statements*;} **while**(*cycle condition*);
for (*pre-loop statements*;
cycle condition;
cycle statements;){*statements*;}
foreach (*$array* **as** *$value*){*statements;*}
foreach(*$array* **as** *$key* **=>** *$value*){*statements;*}

Each of these code segments calculates the sum of 0 to 9.

```
$a=0; $sum=0;
while ($a<10) $sum+=$a++;
```

```
$a=0; $sum=0;
do {$sum+=$a++;} while ($a<10);
```

```
for ($a=0,$sum=0;$a<10;$a++) $sum+=$a;
```

foreach is used to loop through the values of an array or class object.

The reference, '&', allows the values in the array to be changed. Note that the variables retain their last values after the loop.

```
<!DOCTYPE html>
<html>
<head></head>
<body><?php

$a=[3,4,"foo"=>5,6,100];

foreach($a as $k => &$v) {
  $v*=2;
  echo $k.$v."<br />";
}
echo $k.$v."<br />";
foreach($a as $v2) {
  echo $v2."<br />";
}


?></body>
</html>
```

```
06
18
foo10
212
3200
3200
6
8
10
12
200
```

break [i]; ends the loop instantly. **continue [i];** ends the current iteration of loop and starts the next iteration by evaluating the *cycle condition*. i is an optional integer that tells how many levels of loops to end. If omitted, it will be regarded as 1, ie. the current level.

```
<!DOCTYPE html>
<html>
<head></head>
<body><?php

for ($a=0; $a<5; $a++){ // level 3 for continue
  for ($b=0; $b<5; $b++){ // level 2 for continue
    for ($c=0; $c<5; $c++){ // level 1 for continue
      echo ($a+$b+$c).",";
      if ($a+$b+$c>5) continue 3;
    }
    echo "<br />";
  }
  if ($a>3) break;
}

?></body>
</html>
```

```
0,1,2,3,4,
1,2,3,4,5,
2,3,4,5,6,1,2,3,4,5,
2,3,4,5,6,2,3,4,5,6,3,4,5,6,4,5,6,
```

goto causes the exectution to jump to a point specified by a label, which is a name followed by a ':'. It can also be used to run the same statements repeatedly, or get out of multi-level loops.

This calculates the sum of 0 to 9.

```
<!DOCTYPE html>
<html>
<head></head>
<body><?php

$i=0; $sum=0;

sectionA:
$sum+=$i++;
if ($i<10) goto sectionA;

echo $sum;

?></body>
</html>
```

```
45
```

4.1.7 Functions

A function is a piece of code which may be called using its name. It can take in arguments and return a value. Unlike variable names, function names are case-insensitive. Structuring a code with functions makes it readable and maintainable.

This function takes an array as an argument and returns an array.

```
<!DOCTYPE html>
<html>
<head></head>
<body><?php

function sum_product($arr){
  $s=0; $p=1;
  foreach ($arr as $v){
    $s+=$v;
    $p*=$v;
  }
  return [$s,$p];
}

$a=[10,20,30,40];
list($sum,$product)=sum_product($a);
echo $sum.",".$product;

?></body>
```

```
</html>
```

```
100,240000
```

Default values, when passed to arguments after **=**, must appear at the end of the arguments list.

```
<!DOCTYPE html>
<html>
<head></head>
<body><?php

function shout($s,$s1="I say: ",$s2="!"){
  echo $s1.$s.$s2."<br />";
}
shout ("Hello World");
shout ("Hello World","He says: ");
shout ("Hello World","She says: ",".");

?></body>
</html>
```

```
I say: Hello World!
He says: Hello World!
She says: Hello World.
```

A string may be used as a function name.

```
<!DOCTYPE html>
<html>
<head></head>
<body><?php
function shout(){
  echo "Hello World";
}
$f = "shout";
$f();
?></body>
</html>
```

```
Hello World
```

A function needs not exist in a place before where it is called. However, if it is defined within an if-block or within a function, it needs to be 'executed' before it becomes visible globally.

```
<!DOCTYPE html>
<html>
<head></head>
<body><?php
shout();
shout_again(); // error without first calling shout();

function shout(){
  echo "Hello World <br />";
  function shout_again(){
    echo "Hello World";
  }
}
?></body>
</html>
```

```
Hello World
Hello World
```

Variables inside a function are not visible outside the function. For global variables outside a function to be visible inside a function, they must first be referenced with **global**.

```
<!DOCTYPE html>
<html>
<head></head>
<body><?php
$a=2; $b=3;
function add(){
  global $a, $b;//binds
  $a=&$GLOBALS["a"];
  $b=&$GLOBALS["b"];
  $a+=$b;
  unset($a); // no effect on global $a, local $a unbound only
  $c=10;
}
add();
echo $a."<br />";
echo isset($c);  // false, NULL
?></body>
</html>
```

```
5
```

The value of a **static** variable in a function is preserved after the function ends. It resumes its value on the next function call.

```
<!DOCTYPE html>
<html>
<head></head>
<body><?php
function f(){
   static $a=0;
   echo $a;
   $a++;
}
f();f();f();
?></body>
</html>
```

```
012
```

To allow a function to change the value of an external variable passed to it, use a reference symbol '&' in the arguments list.

```
<!DOCTYPE html>
<html>
<head></head>
<body><?php
function change_noref($n1,$n2){$n1++; $n2++;}
function change_ref(&$n1,&$n2){$n1++; $n2++;}
$a=5; $b=5;
change_noref($a,$b);echo ($a+$b)."<br />";
change_ref($a,$b);echo ($a+$b);
?></body>
</html>
```

```
10
12
```

To return a reference, include '&' before the function name, and include it again when assigning the function.

```
<!DOCTYPE html>
<html>
<head></head>
<body><?php
$a=5;
function &ref(){
  global $a;
  return $a;
}
$b =& ref();
$a=10;
echo $b;
?></body>
</html>
```

```
10
```

An anonymous function can be assigned to a variable, or passed in as an argument to another function. When you declare an anonymous function, remember to add the semicolon at the end of the statement.

```
<!DOCTYPE html>
<html>
<head></head>
<body><?php
$f = function(){echo "Hello World";};
function f2($func){
  $g=$func;
  $g();
}
f2($f);
?></body>
</html>
```

```
Hello World
```

Sometimes we need to **use** variables in the parent scope in an anonymous function in PHP (unlike a Javascript closure).

```
<html>
<head></head>
<body><?php
function f($s){
  $s2="I say";
  $f2= function () use ($s, $s2){
    echo $s2." ".$s;
  };
  $f2();
}
f("Hello World.");
?></body>
</html>
```

```
I say Hello World.
```

A function can take in any number of additional arguments. These arguments can be retrieved with **func_num_args()**, **func_get_arg(i)**, **func_get_args()**.

```
<!DOCTYPE html>
<html>
<head></head>
<body><?php
function f($v1,$v2){
  for ($i=0; $i<func_num_args(); $i++){
    echo func_get_arg($i);
  }
  echo "<br />";
  echo
   func_get_args()[0].func_get_args()[1].func_get_args()[2];
}
f(1,2,3,4,5,6,7);
?></body>
</html>
```

```
1234567
123
```

A function may enforce its arguments to be of particular types. An enforced type can be an **array**, a **callable**, a class, or an interface.

```
<!DOCTYPE html>
<html>
<head></head>
<body><?php

function f(array $v1, callable $fa, MyClass $ca){
  echo $fa().$ca->v2.$v1[1];
}

$g = function(){echo "Hello World";};
class MyClass{public $v2=100;}
$c = new MyClass;

f([100,200],$g,$c);

?></body>
</html>
```

```
Hello World100200
```

4.1.8 Code Insertion

To use the code from another file, **include** the file. The scope applied is the scope at the point of inclusion. The included file must start with <?php and end with ?>, otherwise it will be treated as HTML code. 1 is returned if the inclusion is successful, otherwise false is returned. An arbitrary value may be returned in the middle of the included file.

```
<?php //test.php
$a=100;
return 5;
?>
```

```
<!DOCTYPE html>
<html>
<head></head>
<body><?php
$b=include "test.php";
echo $a.".$b";
?>
</body>
</html>
```

```
100.5
```

An alternative is to use **require**. The only difference is that upon failure, **include** merely generates a warning, whereas **require** results in an error and halts the script. To make sure files that have been included will not be included again, use **include_once** or **require_once** instead.

Try to **declare** a tick directive for a function to be called automatically after every one or more (tickable) statements.

```
<!DOCTYPE html>
<html>
<head></head>
<body><?php

declare(ticks=1); // calls the tick handler after every
                  // tickable statement for the  rest of the code
function f(){
  echo "Tick Handler f Called.<br />";
}
register_tick_function('f'); // registers the tick handler

echo "testing..."; $a=1;
echo "testing..."; $a=1;
echo "testing..."; $a=1;
echo "testing..."; $a=1;

declare (ticks=2){ // calls the tick handler after every 2
                   // tickable statements for the block
```

```
    echo "testing..."; $a=1;
    echo "testing..."; $a=1;
    echo "testing..."; $a=1;
    echo "testing..."; $a=1;
}
unregister_tick_function('f');
?>
</body>
</html>
```

```
Tick Handler f Called.
testing...Tick Handler f Called.
Tick Handler f Called.
testing...Tick Handler f Called.
Tick Handler f Called.
testing...Tick Handler f Called.
Tick Handler f Called.
testing...Tick Handler f Called.
Tick Handler f Called.
testing...Tick Handler f Called.
testing...Tick Handler f Called.
testing...Tick Handler f Called.
testing...Tick Handler f Called.
Tick Handler f Called.
```

Another directive to **declare** would be the encoding directive.

```
<?php
declare(encoding='ISO-8859-1');
// code here
?>
```

4.1.9 Namespaces

A **namespace** is used to prevent the name collisions of constants, functions, classes and interfaces. Its declaration must precede all other statements in a file, including any HTML code. The only statement that can precede it is the declare() statement used for the encoding directive.

A namespace can take on the brace {} form, or the free statement form. However, the two different forms must not appear within a single file.

```
<?php //bar.php, namespaces in {} form
namespace Bar {
    const a=10; // defined as \Bar\a
}
namespace {
    const a=50; // defined as \a, in the global namespace
}
?>
```

```
<?php //foo.php, namespaces in free statement form
namespace Foo;
include "bar.php";
const a=20;          // defined as \Foo\a;
echo a;              // 20, resolves to \Foo\a
echo \Foo\a;         // 20, resolves to \Foo\a
echo \Bar\a;         // 10, resolves to \Bar\a
echo \a;             // 50, resolves to \a, the global namespace
echo namespace\a; // 20, resolves to \Foo\a
//echo Foo\a;        // error, resolves to \Foo\Foo\a
//echo Bar\a;        // error, resolves to \Foo\Bar\a

namespace Foo\Alpha;
const a=30;          // defined as \Foo\Alpha\a
echo a;              // 30, resolves to \Foo\Alpha\a;

namespace Foo;
echo Alpha\a;      // 30, resolves to \Foo\Alpha\a;
echo strlen("hi") // 2, fall back to \strlen(), the global nspc;

?>
```

```
<!DOCTYPE html>
<html>
<head></head>
<body><?php
include "foo.php";
echo a;          // 50, resolves to \a
echo \Bar\a;  // 10, resolves to \Bar\a
?>
</body>
</html>
```

```
2020105020303025010
```

If a namespaced function or constant does not exist, PHP will automatically fall back to global functions or constants. On the other hand, class names always resolve to the current namespace.

We can **use** an alias for a class name, an interface name or a namespace.

```
<?php //alpha_beta.php
namespace Alpha\Beta;
class MyClass{
    public static $v=100;
}
?>
```

```
<?php //foo.php
namespace Foo;
include "alpha_beta.php";

$o=new \Alpha\Beta\MyClass;
$ns='Alpha\Beta\MyClass'; // no leading \ needed
$o2=new $ns;
echo $o2::$v;

use Alpha\Beta as A;   // aliasing a namespace
echo A\MyClass::$v;

use Alpha\Beta\MyClass as C;  // aliasing a class name
echo C::$v;

use Alpha\Beta\MyClass;  // Alpha\Beta\MyClass as MyClass;
echo MyClass::$v;

use Alpha\Beta\MyClass as D, Alpha\Beta;  // Multiple decl.
echo Beta\MyClass::$v;
?>
```

```
<!DOCTYPE html>
<html>
<head></head>
<body><?php
include "foo.php";
?>
</body>
</html>
```

```
100100100100100
```

4.1.10 Magical Constants

PHP provides some predefined, compile-time constants.

```
<?php  // test.php
namespace test;
class C{
  public $v;
  function print_names(){
    echo __LINE__."<br />";
    echo __FILE__."<br />";
    echo __DIR__."<br />";
    echo __CLASS__."<br />";
    echo __METHOD__."<br />";
    echo __FUNCTION__."<br />";
    echo __NAMESPACE__."<br />"; // NULL
    // echo __TRAIT__;
  }
}
$o= new C;
$o->print_names();
?>
```

```
<html>  // intro.php
<head></head>
<body><?php
include "test.php";
?></body>
</html>
```

```
6
E:\Program Files\xampp\htdocs\intro.php
E:\Program Files\xampp\htdocs
test\C
test\C::print_names
print_names
test
```

4.2 Classes and Objects

Not to be confused with the HTML/CSS 'class' attribute, a **class** in PHP may be regarded as a data type. It can contain properties (variables) and methods (functions). Use **new** to instantiate an object out of a class. Use **->** on an instantiated object to access the object properties and methods. A string may be used as the class name, the method name or the object name.

```
<!DOCTYPE html>
<html>
<head></head>
<body><?php

class MyClass{
  public $v=10; // a property
  function shout(){ // a method
    echo "Hello World! <br />";
  }
  function smile(){ // another method
    echo "Smile World! <br />";
  }
}

$test=new MyClass;
$test->shout();
echo $test->v."<br />";

$s="MyClass";
$test2=new $s;
$test2->smile();

$s="shout";
$test->$s();

$s="test";
$$s->smile();
?></body>
</html>
```

```
Hello World!
10
Smile World!
Hello World!
Smile World!
```

4.2.1 Scope

A class often **extends** another class and inherits its members. The child may override a property or method from the parent class (using the same arguments and visibility signature). Methods declared **final** must not be overridden, whereas **final** classes must not be inherited.

Properties and method declared **public** are accessible everywhere. If they are declared as **private**, they are accessible only within the class and are not inheritable. If they are declared **protected**, they are only accessible within the class, any inheriting classes, and any inherited classes. If undeclared, a method in a class is public by default.

Properties, when being initialized, must take constant values, instead of other variables or expressions.

$this-> is used within a class method to represent the current object.

```
<!DOCTYPE html>
<html>
<head></head>
<body><?php

class P{
  public $v1=1;
  protected $v2=2;
  private $v3=3;
  function smile(){ // accessible everywhere
    echo $this->v1.")Smile, Universe!<br />";
  }
  final protected function laugh(){ // inheritable
    echo $this->v3.")Laugh, Earth!<br />";
  }
  private function shout(){ // accessible within P only
    echo "Hello World! <br />";
  }
}

final class C extends P{ // cannot extend C due to 'final'
  function smile(){ // method overriding
    echo $this->v2.")Smile, World!<br />";
  }
  //protected function laugh(){} // error due to 'final'

}

$p = new P();
$c = new C;   // ()are optional when creating an instance
with new
$p->smile();
$c->smile();
$p->shout(); // error

?></body>
</html>
```

```
1)Smile, Universe!
2)Smile, World!
```

```
Fatal error: Call to private method P::shout() from context ''
in E:\Program Files\xampp\htdocs\intro.php on line 33
```

The properties of an object can be looped through with **foreach**.

```
<!DOCTYPE html>
<html>
<head></head>
<body><?php

class MyClass{
  public $a=1;
  public $b=2;
  private $c=3;
  function f(){
    foreach ($this as $key => $value)
      echo $key.":".$value."<br />";
  }
}

$Obj = new MyClass;
foreach ($Obj as $key => $value){ // $c not printed
  echo $key.":".$value."<br />";

}
$Obj->f(); // $c printed

?></body>
</html>
```

```
a:1
b:2
a:1
b:2
c:3
```

Two objects are equal (==) if they belong to the same class, and their properties have equal values. Two objects are identical (===) only if they refer to the same instance. The **instanceof** operator tests if an object belongs to a class.

If two objects are of the same class, they will have access to each other's private and protected members.

```
<!DOCTYPE html>
<html>
<head></head>
<body><?php
class C{
  private $a=3;
  function f($o){
    echo $o->a; // accessible even if it is private
  }
}
$v1=new C;
$v2=new $v1;
echo ($v1==$v2);          // 1,true
echo ($v1===$v2);         // NULL, false
echo ($v2 instanceof C); // 1, true
$v1->f($v2);              // 3
?></body>
</html>
```

```
113
```

When an object's variable is assigned to another variable, or passed into a function as an argument, the new variable points to the same object instance. Hence any change made to the one variable affects the other. This form of assignment by reference, is different from the assignment by value form used in the assignment of scalar values and arrays. Use **clone** to get another copy of the object.

```
<!DOCTYPE html>
<html>
<head></head>
<body><?php

class MyClass{
  public $v=1;
}
$a= new MyClass;

$b=$a; $a->v=2; echo $b->v;
$c=&$a;$a->v=3; echo $c->v;
function f($o){$o->v=4;}f($a);echo $a->v;
$d=clone $a; $a->v=5; echo $d->v;
$a=NULL; echo $b->v;
echo $c->v; // error

?></body>
</html>
```

```
23445
Notice: Trying to get property of non-object in E:\Program
Files\xampp\htdocs\intro.php on line 16
```

4.2.2 The 'static' Keyword and Constants

A **const**ant, value of which does not change, can be declared for a class. It can be overridden in the child class. A **static** property or method can be accessed without any instantiation of the class. While a class constant can only be public, a static property can be protected or private. A constant or a static member can be accessed with ::.

> Only constants and static members may be accessed without any instantiation. They must be accessed with ::, with the exeception of *$obj->static_func()*. **parent::** and **self::** refer to the parent class and current class respectively. **$this** must not be used in a static method.

```
<!DOCTYPE html>
<html>
<head></head>
<body><?php
class P{
  const c=1;
  static private $v1=2;
  static $v2=3;
  public $v3=4;
  static function f(){
    echo self::$v1;
    //echo $this->v3=1; //error
  }
  function g(){
    echo 5;
  }
}
class C extends P{
  static function f(){ // method overriding
    echo parent::c;
    echo self::c; // also visible
  }
}
echo P::c;        //1
echo P::$v2;      //3
P::f();           //2
C::f();           //11
$s="P";$s::f(); //2
$s="f";P::$s(); //2
$a=new P;
echo $a::c;       //1
echo $a::$v2;  //3
$a::f();          //2
```

```
$a->f();           //2
//P::g();          // 5, warning
//$a::g();         // 5, warning
//echo $a->c;  // error
//echo $a->$v2;// error
//echo $a::$v3; // error
//echo P::$v3;  // error
//P->f();          // error
//P->c1;           // error
?></body>
</html>
```

```
13211221322
```

An object can be created out of a static function.

```
<!DOCTYPE html>
<html>
<head></head>
<body><?php
class C{
  static function getNew(){
    return new static;
  }
}
$a=C::getNew();
var_dump($a instanceof C);
?></body>
</html>
```

```
bool(true)
```

Late static binding can be achieved with **static::**. It allows an overriding member to be chosen, when the member is used from the base class.

```
<!DOCTYPE html>
<html>
<head></head>
<body><?php
class P1 {
  public static function which() {
    echo __CLASS__;
  }
  public static function test() {
     self::which();    //P1
     static::which(); //C1
     P1::which();     //P1
     C1::which();     //C1
  }
}
class C1 extends P1 {
   public static function which() { // overriding method
     echo __CLASS__;
   }
}
C1::test();

class P2 {
  private function which() {
    echo __CLASS__;
  }
  public function test() {
     $this->which(); //P2
     self::which();   //C2
  }
}
class C2 extends P2 {
   public function which() {
     echo __CLASS__;
   }
}
$v2=new C2;
$v2->test();
?></body>
</html>
```

```
P1C1P1C1P2P2
```

4.2.3 Undefined Methods and Traits

An **abstract** method is an undefined method. A class containing an abstract method must be declared **abstract**, and may not be instantiated. If a child class extending an abstract class does not define all its abstract methods, the child class must be declared abstract too.

```
<!DOCTYPE html>
<html>
<head></head>
<body><?php
abstract class P{
  protected $v1=3;
  protected $v2=2;
  abstract function calculate();
}
class product extends P{
  function calculate(){
    echo $this->v1*$this->v2;
  }
}
$a=new product;
$a->calculate();
?></body>
</html>
```

```
6
```

An **interface** contains only constants and undefined public methods. It may not be instantiated on its own. Any class that **implements** an interface must define all its methods. A class cannot implement two interfaces that share function or constant names, and an interface constant cannot be overridden.

```
<!DOCTYPE html>
<html>
<head></head>
<body><?php
interface I1{
  const c=100;
}
interface I2{
  const d=200;
}
interface STAR extends I1,I2{
  public function star();
}
interface CROSS{
  public function cross();
}
class C implements STAR,CROSS{
  public function star(){
    echo C::c * C::d."<br />";
  }
  public function cross(){
    echo C::c + C::d."<br />";
  }
}
$a=new C;
$a->star();  //20000
$a->cross(); //300
echo I1::c;   //100
?></body>
</html>
```

```
20000
300
100
```

A **trait** cannot be instantiated on its own. A class can **use** multiple traits at once. A method defined inside a class overrides the trait method, which in turn overrides the method from the parent class.

```
<!DOCTYPE html>
<html>
<head></head>
<body><?php

trait T{
  public $v=3;
  private function shout(){
    echo "Hello World!<br />";
  }
}
class P{
  function shout(){
    echo "Hello Universe!<br />";
  }
}
class C extends P{
  use T; // overrides shout() from P
  function shout(){  // overrides shout() from T
    echo "Smile World!<br />";
  }
}
$o=new C;
$o->shout();
echo $o->v;
?></body>
</html>
```

```
Smile World!
3
```

A trait can use another trait. If two traits used contain the same function names, they need to be resolved with **insteadof**. An alias name can be assigned to a function with **as**, which may also change the visibility.

```
<!DOCTYPE html>
<html>
<head></head>
<body><?php
trait T1{
  function shout(){
    echo "Hello World!<br />";
  }
}
trait T2{
  use T1 {shout as protected;}
  function smile(){
    echo "Smile World!<br />";
  }
}
trait T3{
  function shout(){
    echo "Hello Universe!<br />";
  }
  function smile(){
    echo "Smile Universe!<br />";
  }
}
class C{
  use T2,T3{
    T2::shout insteadof T3;
    T3::smile insteadof T2;
    T2::smile as private sm;
  }
  function start(){
    $this->shout();
    $this->smile();
    $this->sm();
  }
}
$o=new C;
$o->start();
?></body>
</html>
```

```
Hello World!
Smile Universe!
Smile World!
```

A trait method can be static. It can also be abstract, which forces the class that uses it to define it. Traits can't contain constants.

4.2.4 Magic Functions

Magic functions are functions that are triggered automatically when special events happen. They can be defined in any class.

__construct([$m1,$m2......]) is called when an object is created. A child class can override the parent's 'constructor' with a different arguments signature. $m1, $m2 can be any content type (mixed). **__destruct()** is called when there are no more references to an object. **__clone()** is called when an object is cloned.

The destructor is called before the script ends.

```
<!DOCTYPE html>
<html>
<head></head>
<body><?php

class C{
  function __construct($s){ echo "Constructor".$s;}
  function __destruct(){ echo "Destructor called. ";}
  function __clone(){ echo "__clone() called. ";}
}

$a=new C(" called. ");  // Constructor called.
$b=clone $a;            // __clone() called.
$a=$b;                  // Destructor called.
$c=clone $a;            // __clone called().

?></body>
</html>
```

```
Constructor called. __clone() called. Destructor called.
__clone() called. Destructor called. Destructor called.
```

__set($s,$m) is called when writing data to undeclared properties. **__get($s)** is called when reading data from undeclared properties. It can return any type. **__isset($s)** is triggered by calling isset() or empty() on undeclared properties. It returns a boolean value. **__unset($s)** is triggered when unset() is used on undeclared properties.

__call($s,$arr) is called when invoking undeclared methods in an object context. It can return any type. **__callStatic($s,$arr)** is triggered when invoking undeclared methods in a static context. It can return any type. **__invoke ([$m1,$m2......])** is called when a script tries to call an object as a function. It can return any type.

__toString() is called when the object is treated like a string. It returns a string.

```
<!DOCTYPE html>
<html>
<head></head>
<body><?php

class C{
  function __set($name,$value){
    echo "Trying to set \$$name to $value...<br />";
  }
  function __get($name){
    echo "Trying to get a value from \$$name...<br />";
    return 5;
  }
  function __isset($name){
    echo "Checking if \$$name is set...<br />";
    return true;
  }
  function __unset($name){
    echo "Trying to unset \$$name...<br />";
  }
  function __call($name,$arr){
    echo "Trying to call $name() with $arr[0]...<br />";
  }
  static function __callStatic($name,$arr){
    echo
      "Trying to call $name() statically with $arr[0]...<br />";
  }
  function __invoke($s){
    echo "Trying to invoke a function with $s...<br />";
  }
  function __toString(){
    return "Trying to be treated like a string...<br />";
  }
}
$a=new C; // $a->x is an undeclared property
$a->x=5;
$b=$a->x;
$c=isset($a->x);
unset($a->x);
$a->x("TEST");
$a::x("TEST");
$a("TEST");
echo $a;
?></body>
</html>
```

```
Trying to set $x to 5...
Trying to get a value from $x...
Checking if $x is set...
Trying to unset $x...
Trying to call x() with TEST...
Trying to call x() statically with TEST...
Trying to invoke a function with TEST...
Trying to be treated like a string...
```

4.2.5 Serialization

An object can be serialized to a string (and stored into a file). As **serialize($o)** is called, PHP first runs the magic function **__sleep()**, which returns an array of the variable names to be serialized.

To restore a serialized string to an object, use **unserialize($s)**. **__wakeup()** will be called after an object has been unserialized.

```
<!DOCTYPE html>
<html>
<head></head>
<body><?php
class MyClass{
  public $a;
  public $b;
  public $c;
  public $arr=['hello','world'];
  function __sleep(){
    return ['a','b','arr'];
  }
  function __wakeup(){
    $this->c=50000;
  }
}
$o=new MyClass;
$o->a=100;
$o->b=2000;
$o->c=30000;
$s=serialize($o);
echo $s;

$o2=unserialize($s);
echo "<br />$o2->a";
echo "<br />$o2->b";
echo "<br />$o2->c";
?></body>
</html>
```

```
O:7:"MyClass":3:{s:1:"a";i:100;s:1:"b";i:2000;s:3:"arr";a:2:{i:0;s:5:"hello";i:1;s:5:"world";}}
100
2000
50000
```

__set_state($arr) is called when **var_export($o)** is called on an object. The latter is a function similar to var_dump(), which outputs the content of a variable, except that the output is PHP code.

```
<!DOCTYPE html>
<html>
<head></head>
<body><?php

class A{
   public $v1;
   public $v2;
   public static function __set_state($arr) {
      $obj = new A;
      $obj->v1 = $arr['v1'];
      $obj->v2 = $arr['v2'];
      return $obj;
   }
}
$a = new A;
$a->v1 = 5;
$a->v2 = 'Hello';
var_export($a);
eval('$b = ' . var_export($a, true) . ';');
echo "<br />";
var_export($b);

?></body>
</html>
```

```
A::__set_state(array( 'v1' => 5, 'v2' => 'Hello', ))
A::__set_state(array( 'v1' => 5, 'v2' => 'Hello', ))
```

4.2.6 Exceptions

An **Exception** object is thrown when an error occurs. It can be caught in a **try** block, and handled in a **catch** block. More than one catch blocks may be used to catch various exception classes, and the first matching clause will be used. We can **throw** our own exceptions.

```
<!DOCTYPE html>
<html>
<head></head>
<body><?php
function inverse($x) {
   if (!$x) {
      throw new Exception('Division by zero.');
   }
   else return 1/$x;
```

```
}
try {
   echo inverse(4);
   echo inverse(0);  // exception thrown
   echo "This part is not executed.";
} catch (Exception $e) {
   echo '<br />*** Caught exception ***';
   echo "<br /> Message:". $e->getMessage();
   echo "<br /> Code:". $e->getCode();
   echo "<br /> File:". $e->getFile();
   echo "<br /> Line:". $e->getLine();
   echo "<br /> Previous:". $e->getPrevious();
   echo "<br /> Trace String:". $e->getTraceAsString();
}
echo '<br />This part is printed.';
?> </body>
</html>
```

```
0.25
*** Caught exception ***
Message:Division by zero.
Code:0
File:E:\Program Files\xampp\htdocs\intro.php
Line:7
Previous:
Trace String:#0 E:\Program
Files\xampp\htdocs\intro.php(13): inverse(0) #1 {main}
This part is printed.
```

The thrown object must be an instance of the Exception class or a subclass of Exception. The Exception class has the following members:

```
<?php
class Exception{
protected $message = 'Unknown exception';
private $string;
protected $code = 0;
protected $file;
protected $line;
private $trace;
private $previous; // previous exception if nested exception

public function __construct
   ($message = null, $code = 0, Exception $previous = null);
final private function __clone(); // no cloning of exceptions
final public function getMessage();
final public function getCode();
final public function getFile();
final public function getLine();
final public function getTrace(); // an array of the backtrace()
final public function getPrevious(); // previous exception
final public function getTraceAsString(); // formatted trace
public function __toString(); // formatted string for display
}
?>
```

Exceptions can be nested. An uncaught inner exception will be thrown to the outer try{...} catch(...) {...} block.

```
<!DOCTYPE html>
<html>
<head></head>
<body><?php
class E extends Exception{}
class F extends Exception{}
class G extends Exception{}
try{
  try {
    throw new E;
  } catch (F $exc){
    echo "Caught in the inner try block F.";
  } catch (G $exc){
    echo "Caught in the inner try block G.";
  }
} catch (E $exc){
  echo "Caught in the outer try block E.";
}
?> </body>
</html>
```

```
Caught in the outer try block E.
```

An uncaught exception causes a fatal error. Use **set_exception_handler($f($e))** to handle any uncaught exceptions. set_exception_handler() takes in the exception $e, and returns the name of the previously defined exception handler. NULL is returned on error or if no exception handler was previously defined. If NULL is passed, resetting the handler to its default state, TRUE is returned.

```
<!DOCTYPE html>
<html>
<head></head>
<body><?php
function Exc_Handler($E){
  echo $E->getMessage();
}
set_exception_handler('Exc_Handler');
throw new Exception('Testing the exception handler...');
?> </body>
</html>
```

```
Testing the exception handler...
```

4.3 SuperGlobals

Superglobals are built-in arrays that are available in all scopes. They can be accessed in functions without having to do **global $variable** first. You should study this section (4.3) carefully for it contains many crucial PHP concepts.

4.3.1 Accessing Global Variables

$GLOBALS[s] provides a means to manipulate global variables directly in functions.

```
<!DOCTYPE html>
<html>
<head></head>
<body><?php

function f(){
  $v=1;
  echo $v;                  // 1, local variable
  echo $GLOBALS['v'];       // 2, global variable
  $GLOBALS['w']=3;
  unset($GLOBALS['v']);  // global variables can now be unset
}
$v=2;
f();
echo $w;  // 3, global variable
echo $v;  // Notice, already unset

?> </body>
</html>
```

```
123
Notice: Undefined variable: v in E:\Program
Files\xampp\htdocs\intro.php on line 16
```

4.3.2 Retrieving Form Data

Any form data passed to a PHP script is stored in the $_POST or $_GET array. Dots and spaces in variable names are converted to underscores. (eg. <input name="a.b" /> becomes $_GET["a_b"].

Unlike AJAX data, form data is automatically URL-encoded when the form is submitted. The form data is automatically URL-decoded again at the PHP end, so that you can use $_GET, $_POST, and $_REQUEST directly.

If you wish to prevent spamming, you should consider Akismet and Google's reCAPTCHA.

If the form method "get" is used instead of "post", the data will be stored in the array $_GET. For the "get" method, because the parameters are added to the URL, the page can be bookmarked with all the parameters intact. However, the "get" method is not a secure way of passing sensitive data to the server.

```
<!DOCTYPE html>
<html>
<head></head>
<body>
<form id="test" method="post" action="action.php">
  Username:
        <input type="text" name="username" size="15"/>
        <br /><br />
  Passwod:
        <input type="password" name="password" size="15"/>
        <br /><br />
  Country: <select name="country">
              <option>France</option>
              <option>Italy</option>
              <option>Germany</option>
              <option>United Kingdom</option>
           </select> <br /><br />
  Sex: <input type="radio" name="sex" value="female"/>
         <label for "female">female</label>
       <input type="radio" name="sex" value="male"/>
         <label for "male">male</label><br /><br />
  Conditions read:
 <input type="checkbox" name="cond[read]"/>
 <br /><br />
  Conditions agreed:
 <input type="checkbox" name="cond[agreed]"/>
 <br /><br />
 <input type="image" src="submit.gif"
                                 height="50" width="150"/>
</form>
</body>
</html>
```

```
<!DOCTYPE html> <!-- action.php -->
<html>
<head></head>
<body><?php
echo $_POST['username']."<br />";
echo $_POST['password']."<br />";
echo $_POST['country']."<br />";
echo $_POST['sex']."<br />";
echo $_POST['cond']['read']."<br />";
echo $_POST['cond']['agreed']."<br />";
echo $_POST['x']."<br />"; // where the submit img is clicked
echo $_POST['y']."<br />"; // where the submit img is clicked
?> </body>
</html>
```

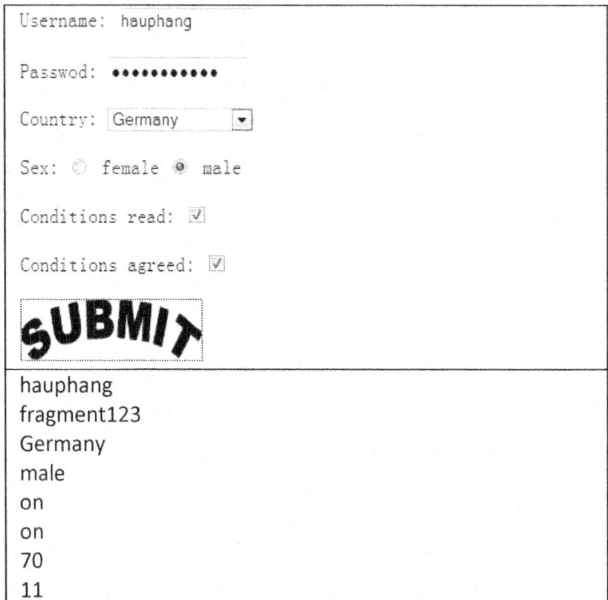

4.3.3 Uploading a File

Here, **$_FILE** is a two-dimensional array that stores information about an uploaded file.

To upload a large file, make sure **memory_limit**, **post_max_size** and **upload_max_filesize** in php.ini have been set appropriately.

After the user has chosen a file and clicked the "Submit" button, the file is copied to the server and stored as a temporary file, which is then again moved to a new location in the server. Any temporary files are automatically deleted as the PHP script exits. You must first create the directory 'upload' for this code to work.

```
<!DOCTYPE html>
<html>
<head></head>
<body>
<form action="upload.php" method="post"
        enctype="multipart/form-data">
    <input type="hidden" name="MAX_FILE_SIZE"
         value="3000000"/>
   <label for="file">Filename:</label>
   <input type="file" name="file" /> <br />
   <input type="submit" value="Submit" />
</form>
</body>
</html>
```

```
<html> <!-- upload.php -->
<body>
<?php
  if ($_FILES["file"]["error"] > 0){
    echo "Return Code: " . $_FILES["file"]["error"] . "<br />";
  } else {
    echo "Upload: " . $_FILES["file"]["name"] . "<br />";
    echo "Type: " . $_FILES["file"]["type"] . "<br />";
    echo "Size: ".($_FILES["file"]["size"] / 1024)." Kb<br />";
    echo "Temp file: ".$_FILES["file"]["tmp_name"]."<br />";
    if (file_exists("upload/" . $_FILES["file"]["name"])) {
      echo $_FILES["file"]["name"] . " already exists. ";
    } else {
      move_uploaded_file($_FILES["file"]["tmp_name"],
                       "upload/" . $_FILES["file"]["name"]);
                                //returns true if successful
      echo "Stored in: upload/" . $_FILES["file"]["name"];
    }
  }
```

```
?>
</body>
</html>
```

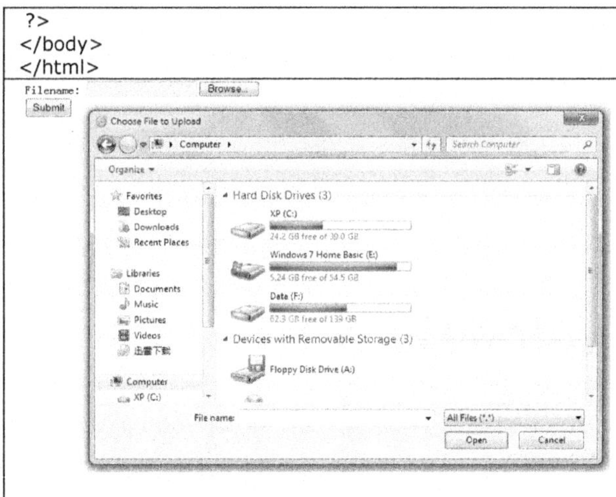

Upload: neptune.jpg
Type: image/pjpeg
Size: 2.759765625 Kb
Temp file: E:\Program Files\xampp\tmp\php67FE.tmp
Stored in: upload/neptune.jpg

4.3.4 Uploading Multiple Files

```
<!DOCTYPE html>
<html>
<head></head>
<body>
<form action="upload2.php" method="post"
    enctype="multipart/form-data">
  <label for="file">Filename:</label>
  <input type="file" name="file[]" multiple /> <br />
  <input type="submit" value="Submit" />
</form>
</body>
</html>
```

```
<html> <!-- upload2.php -->
<body>
<?php
 for ($i=0; $i<count($_FILES["file"]["name"]); $i++){
   move_uploaded_file($_FILES["file"]["tmp_name"][$i],
                      $_FILES["file"]["name"][$i]);
 }
?>
</body>
</html>
```

4.3.5 Cookies

PHP can send a cookie for it to be stored on the user's computer using the function: **setcookie ($s1,$s2 [,$i[,$s3[,$s4[,$b1=false[,$b2=false]]]]]);**
This function must precede any output, including the <html> tag as well as any whitespace.
$s1 is the name of the cookie. **$s2** is the value. **i** is the expiration time in seconds. The default is 0, which means that the cookie expires when the browser closes. **$s3** is the path which will have access to the cookie. **$s4** is the domain which will have access to the cookie. If **$b1** is true, the cookie will be sent only over a secure HTTPS connection, if one exists. If **$b2** is true, the cookie will be accessible only through HTTP, which means that JavaScript won't be able to access it.

As the user refreshes the page, the browser prints "abc123".

```
<?php
$t=time()+60*60; // expires in 1 hour
setcookie("test","abc",$t,"/"); // / for the current domain
setcookie("arr[a]","123",$t,"/"); // storing into an array
?>
<!DOCTYPE html>
<html>
<head></head>
<body><?php
if (isset($_COOKIE["test"])) echo $_COOKIE["test"]; //abc
if (isset($_COOKIE["arr"]["a"])) echo $_COOKIE["arr"]["a"];
//123
?>
</body>
</html>
```

abc123

Every time a page is requested from the server, all associated cookies are sent along from the local computer. All cookies, including those saved by JavaScript, can be accessed using the array **$_COOKIE.** To delete a cookie, set the expiration time to an expired time.

The array **$_REQUEST** stores the combined key-value pairs of $_GET, $_POST and $_COOKIE. These superglobals are already decoded. Using urldecode() on them could have unexpected and dangerous results.

4.3.6 Session Variables

Accessible to all web pages, a session variable can be set or accessed with **$_SESSION**. It lasts until the user has closed the browser.

One must first start up a session before information can be stored in a session. **session_start()** has to be used before the <html> tag.

```
<?php session_start(); ?>
<!DOCTYPE html>
<html>
<body>
<?php
if(isset($_SESSION['views']))
  $_SESSION['views']=$_SESSION['views']+1;
else
   $_SESSION['views']=1;
 echo "Views=". $_SESSION['views'];
?>
</body>
</html>
```

Views=4

session_destroy() closes a session, deleting all session variables.

4.3.7 Server Information

$_SERVER is an array that contains information about the server and execution environment. The keys available include:

PHP_SELF	GATEWAY_INTERFACE
SERVER_ADDR	SERVER_NAME
SERVER_SOFTWARE	SERVER_PROTOCOL
REQUEST_METHOD	REQUEST_TIME
REQUEST_TIME_FLOAT	QUERY_STRING
DOCUMENT_ROOT	HTTP_ACCEPT
HTTP_ACCEPT_CHARSET	HTTP_ACCEPT_ENCODING
HTTP_ACCEPT_LANGUAGE	HTTP_CONNECTION
HTTP_HOST	HTTP_REFERER
HTTP_USER_AGENT	HTTPS
REMOTE_ADDR	REMOTE_HOST
REMOTE_PORT	REMOTE_USER
REDIRECT_REMOTE_USER	SCRIPT_FILENAME
SERVER_ADMIN	SERVER_PORT
SERVER_SIGNATURE	PATH_TRANSLATED
SCRIPT_NAME	REQUEST_URI
PHP_AUTH_DIGEST	PHP_AUTH_USER
PHP_AUTH_PW	AUTH_TYPE
PATH_INFO	ORIG_PATH_INFO

```
<!DOCTYPE html>
<html>
<head></head>
<body>
<?php
echo $_SERVER["PHP_SELF"]."<br />";
echo $_SERVER["GATEWAY_INTERFACE"]."<br />";
echo $_SERVER["SERVER_NAME"]."<br />";
echo $_SERVER["REQUEST_TIME"]."<br />";
echo $_SERVER["REQUEST_METHOD"]."<br />";
echo $_SERVER["DOCUMENT_ROOT"]."<br />";
echo $_SERVER["SERVER_SIGNATURE"]."<br />";
?>
</body>
</html>
```

```
/intro.php
CGI/1.1
localhost
1352882888
GET
E:/Program Files/xampp/htdocs
Apache/2.4.3 (Win32) OpenSSL/1.0.1c PHP/5.4.7 Server at localhost Port 80
```

4.3.8 Client's IP Address & Location

$_SERVER['REMOTE_ADDR'] may not contain the real client's IP address. It will give you a proxy address for a client connected through a proxy, for example.

With the client's IP address, you can determine its location using a service by http://ipinfo.io.

```
<!DOCTYPE html>
<html><body>
<pre>
<?php
$ip = getenv('HTTP_CLIENT_IP')?:
      getenv('HTTP_X_FORWARDED_FOR')?:
      getenv('HTTP_X_FORWARDED')?:
      getenv('HTTP_FORWARDED_FOR')?:
      getenv('HTTP_FORWARDED')?:
      getenv('REMOTE_ADDR');
$details = json_decode(
            file_get_contents("http://ipinfo.io/{$ip}/json"));
print_r($details);
?>
</pre>
</body></html>
```

```
stdClass Object
(
    [ip] => 115.133.78.155
    [hostname] => No Hostname
    [city] => Kota Kinabalu
    [region] => Sabah
    [country] => MY
    [loc] => 5.8626,115.9946
    [org] => AS4788 TM Net, Internet Service Provider
    [postal] => 88000
)
```

(Function Parameters Legend)

To save space, the following sections abbreviate function prototypes by using a short form for the parameters. Some of the data types are listed below:

$b : boolean
$i : integer
$f : float
$s : string
$e : exception
$m : mixed
$r : $resource
$arr : array
$f() : function
$cf() : comparison function
$ts : timestamp in integer

4.4 Variable Functions

4.4.1 Identity Booleans

is_null($m) returns true if $m is NULL. **empty($m)** returns true if $m does not exist or equals false. **isset($m1[,$m2......])** returns true if $m1, $m2 are set and are not NULL. **unset ($m1[,$m2......])** destroys the specified variables.

is_array($m) returns true if $m is an array. **is_bool($m)** returns true if $m is a boolean. **is_float($m), is_double($m)** or **is_real($m)** returns true if $m is a float. **is_int($m), is_integer($m)** or **is_long($m)** returns true if $m is an integer. **is_numeric($m)** returns true if $m is a number or a numeric string. **is_object($m)** returns true if $m is an object. **is_resource($m)** returns true if $m is a resource. **is_scalar($m)** returns true if $m is an integer, float, string or boolean. **is_string($m)** returns true if $m is a string. **is_callable($m[,$b=false[,&$s]])** returns true if $m can be called as a function. $s stores the callable name. If $b is true, the function returns true as long as $m is a valid function name, even if the function does not exist. It then only rejects non-string variables or invalid arrays. The valid arrays have only two entries, the first of which is an object or a string, and the second a string.

```
<!DOCTYPE html>
<html>
<head></head>
<body>
<?php

function func() {}
$fv = 'func';
var_dump(is_callable($fv, false, $callable_name));
echo $callable_name. "<br />";

$fv = function(){};
var_dump(is_callable($fv, false, $callable_name));
echo $callable_name. "<br />";

class C{function method(){}}
$obj = new C;
$mv = array('C', 'method');
var_dump(is_callable($mv, false, $callable_name));
echo $callable_name. "<br />";

$mv = array($obj, 'method');
var_dump(is_callable($mv, false, $callable_name));
echo $callable_name. "<br />";

var_dump(is_callable('funX',true, $callable_name));
$fv=10;
var_dump(is_callable($fv, true, $callable_name));
$mv=['CX','methodX'];
var_dump(is_callable($mv, true, $callable_name));
$mv=[1,2,3];
var_dump(is_callable($mv, true, $callable_name));
?>
</body>
</html>
```

```
bool(true) func
bool(true) Closure::__invoke
bool(true) C::method
bool(true) C::method
bool(true) bool(false) bool(true) bool(false)
```

4.4.2 Typing

strval($m) returns the string value of $m. **floatval($m)** returns the float value of $m. **intval($m[,$i])** returns the integer value of $m, using base $i.

```
<!DOCTYPE html>
<html>
<head></head>
<body>
<?php
echo intval(042)."<br />";
echo intval('042')."<br />";
echo intval(123e2)."<br />";
echo intval('123e2')."<br />";
echo intval('111',2)."<br />";
echo intval([])."<br />";
echo intval([1])."<br />";
?>
</body>
</html>
```

```
34
42
12300
123
7
0
1
```

gettype($m) returns the type of $m as a string, which can be "boolean", "integer", "double", "string", "array", "object", "resource", "NULL", or "unknown type". **settype($m,$s)** sets the type of $m to $s, which can be "boolean", "integer", "float", "string", "array", "object" or "null". **get_resource_type($r)** returns the resource type as a string.

4.4.3 Display

get_defined_vars() returns an array of all defined variables, be them environment, server, or user-defined variables.

```
<!DOCTYPE html>
<html>
<head></head>
<body>
<?php
$v=10;
$va=get_defined_vars();
echo $va['v'];
echo $va['_COOKIE']['test'];
?>
</body>
</html>
```

print_r($m[,$b=false]) displays information about $m. If $b is true, the function will return the information rather than print it. **var_dump ($m1[,$m2......])** displays information about $m1, $m2...... **var_export($m[,$b=false])** displays information about $m. The output is valid PHP code. If $b is true, the function will return the information rather than print it. **debug_zval_dump($m)** displays information about an internal zend value $m.

```
<!DOCTYPE html>
<html>
<head></head>
<body>
<?php
$a=[1,2,['hello','world']];
print_r($a); echo '<br /><br />';
var_dump($a); echo '<br /><br />';
var_export($a); echo '<br /><br />';
debug_zval_dump($a);
?>
</body>
</html>
```

```
Array ( [0] => 1 [1] => 2 [2] => Array ( [0] => hello [1] =>
world ) )

array(3) { [0]=> int(1) [1]=> int(2) [2]=> array(2) { [0]=>
string(5) "hello" [1]=> string(5) "world" } }

array ( 0 => 1, 1 => 2, 2 => array ( 0 => 'hello', 1 => 'world', ), )

array(3) refcount(2){ [0]=> long(1) refcount(1) [1]=> long(2)
refcount(1) [2]=> array(2) refcount(1){ [0]=> string(5) "hello"
refcount(1) [1]=> string(5) "world" refcount(1) } }
```

4.5 Array Functions

4.5.1 Searching and Counting

array_key_exists($m,$arr) returns true if the key $m can be found in $arr. **in_array ($m, $arr[,$b=false])** returns true if the value $m can be found in $arr. If $b is true, the types are also compared. **array_search($m,$arr[,$b=false])** returns the first matching key of the value $m. FALSE is returned if the value does not exist. If $b is true, the types are also compared. **count($arr[,$i])** or **sizeof($arr[,$i])** returns the number of elements in $arr. If $i is set to COUNT_RECURSIVE, the elements in sub arrays will be counted as well. **array_count_values($arr)** returns an array which uses the values of $arr as keys, and their frequencies as values.

```
<!DOCTYPE html><html><head></head>
<body>
<?php
$a=["hello",1,1,"hello",1,2];
print_r(array_count_values($a));
?>
</body></html>
```

```
Array ( [hello] => 2 [1] => 3 [2] => 1 )
```

4.5.2 New Formation

range($m1, $m2[,$num=1]) returns an array with values from $m1 to $m2, with $num as the incrementing step. **array_fill($i1,$i2,$m)** returns an array with $i2 elements, all with value $m, starting from index $i1. **array_fill_keys($arr,$m)** returns an array that uses the values of $arr as keys, and uses $m as the value. **array_pad($arr,$i,$m)** returns a copy of $arr, padded to the size of $i with value $m. If $i >= 1 then the array is padded on the right, if $i <= -1 then on the left. If |$i| <= the length of $arr then no padding takes place.

```
<!DOCTYPE html><html><head></head>
<body>
<?php
print_r(range(-10,10,3)); echo "<br />";
print_r(array_fill(3,4,"HI")); echo "<br />";
$a=['smile','hello','world'];
print_r(array_fill_keys($a,"HI")); echo "<br />";
print_r(array_pad($a,-6,"HI"))
?>
</body></html>
```

```
Array ( [0] => -10 [1] => -7 [2] => -4 [3] => -1 [4] => 2 [5] => 5
[6] => 8 )
Array ( [3] => HI [4] => HI [5] => HI [6] => HI )
Array ( [smile] => HI [hello] => HI [world] => HI )
Array ( [0] => HI [1] => HI [2] => HI [3] => smile [4] => hello
[5] => world )
```

array_values($arr) returns an array with the values of $arr as values, indexed numerically. **array_keys ($arr[,$m[,$b=false]])** returns an array with keys of $arr as values, indexed numerically. If $m is specified, then only the keys for that value are returned. If $b is true, then the types are compared as well. **array_combine($arr1, $arr2)** returns an array with the values of $arr1 as keys, and the values of $arr2 as the corresponding values.

array_merge($arr1[,$arr2......]) returns an array that combines $arr1, $arr2...... If the input arrays have the same string keys, then the later value will overwrite the previous one. Values with numeric keys will be renumbered starting from zero. **array_merge_recursive($arr1[$,arr2......])** is similar to array_merge(), except that when the input arrays have the same string keys, the values will be merged into an array. Any array values will be merged recursively. **array_chunk($arr,$i [,$b=false])** returns a multidimensional array that is formed by splitting $arr into chunks, each containing $i elements. If $b is true, the keys will be preserved.

```
<!DOCTYPE html><html><head></head>
<body>
<?php
$a1=['apple','banana','special'=>'pear'];
$a2=['cat','dog','special'=>'fish'];
print_r(array_values($a1)); echo "<br /><br />";
print_r(array_keys($a1)); echo "<br /><br />";
print_r(array_combine($a1,$a2)); echo "<br /><br />";
print_r(array_merge_recursive($a1,$a2)); echo "<br /><br
/>";
print_r(array_chunk(['a','b','c','d','e'],2));
?>
</body></html>
```

```
Array ( [0] => apple [1] => banana [2] => pear )

Array ( [0] => 0 [1] => 1 [2] => special )

Array ( [apple] => cat [banana] => dog [pear] => fish )

Array ( [0] => apple [1] => banana [special] => Array ( [0] =>
pear [1] => fish ) [2] => cat [3] => dog )

Array ( [0] => Array ( [0] => a [1] => b ) [1] => Array ( [0] => c
[1] => d ) [2] => Array ( [0] => e ) )
```

array_slice($arr,$i1[,$i2[,$b=FALSE]]) returns an array which is a sequence of $i2 elements from $arr, starting from $i1. If $i1 is negative, the sequence will start that far from the end. If $i2 is negative, the sequence will stop that many elements from the end. If $i2 is omitted, the sequence will have everything from $i up until the end. If $b is true, the keys will be preserved. **array_splice (&$arr1, $i1[,$i2=0[,$arr2]])** removes $i2 elements from $arr1, starting from $i1, and then inserts the elements of $arr2 into the position of removal. An array consisting of the extracted elements is returned. If $i1 is negative, the removal starts that far from the end. If $i2 is omitted, everything from $i1 to the end will be removed. If $i2 is negative, the end of the removed portion will be that many elements from the end. **array_replace($arr1,$arr2[,$arr3......])** returns an array formed by replacing the values in $arr1 with values of the same keys from $arr2. If three or more arrays are passed, then the values of the later arrays will be used. **array_replace_ recursive ($arr1,$arr2[,$arr3......])** is similar to array_replace(...), except that the replacement will recurse into deeper arrays, when both values are arrays.

```
<!DOCTYPE html><html><head></head>
<body>
<?php

$a=[1,2,3,4,5,6,7];
print_r(array_slice($a,-3,2)); echo "<br />";
print_r(array_slice($a,1,-2)); echo "<br />";

array_splice($a,2,2,[100,200,300]);
print_r($a); echo "<br />";

$a=[1,2,3,4,5,6,7];
print_r(array_replace($a,[100,200,5=>300,400,500,600]));

?>
</body></html>
```

```
Array ( [0] => 5 [1] => 6 )
Array ( [0] => 2 [1] => 3 [2] => 4 [3] => 5 )
Array ( [0] => 1 [1] => 2 [2] => 100 [3] => 200 [4] => 300 [5] => 5 [6] => 6 [7] => 7 )
Array ( [0] => 100 [1] => 200 [2] => 3 [3] => 4 [4] => 5 [5] => 300 [6] => 400 [7] => 500 [8] => 600 )
```

4.5.3 Elements Conversion

array_change_key_case($arr[, $i= CASE_LOWER]) returns a copy of $arr with the keys uppercased or lowercased. $i can be CASE_LOWER or CASE_UPPER. **array_flip ($arr)** returns an array with the values of $arr as keys, and the keys of $arr as corresponding values. If a value has several occurrences, the latest key will be used as its value. **array_unique ($arr [,$i= SORT_STRING])** returns a copy of $arr without all duplicate values. $i can be SORT_REGULAR, SORT_NUMERIC, SORT_STRING, or SORT_LOCALE_STRING. **array_filter($arr [,$f($m)=""])** returns a copy of $arr with the key-value pairs filtered out by the function $f. $m corresponds a value in $arr. Only if $f($m) returns true on a value, the value will be added to the returned array. Array keys are preserved. If $f is not supplied, all entries of $arr equal to FALSE will be removed. **array_map($f($m1[,$m2......]), $arr1 [,$arr2......])** returns an array that contains the resultant elements after applying $f to each element in $arr1....... The number of parameters that $f accepts should match the number of arrays passed. If $arr1 contains string keys, then the returned array will contain string keys if and only if exactly one array is passed. If $f is NULL, an array of arrays will be returned from the arrays passed.
array_walk(&$arr, $f(&$m1,$m2[,$m3])[,$m4= NULL]) applies $f to each element in $arr, with $m1 and $m2 corresponding to the value and key respectively. $m4 is the optional data supplied to $f as the third parameter $m3. Only the values of $arr may be changed, with the reference symbol & added in front of $m1. This function returns TRUE on success. **array_walk_recursive(&$arr, $f(&$m1, $m2[,$m3])[,$m4= NULL])** is similar to array_walk() except that the function will recurse into deeper arrays.

```
<!DOCTYPE html><html><head></head>
<body>
<?php
function filter($m){
  return ($m>'b');
}
function map($m1,$m2){
  return ($m2.' '.$m1);
}
function walk(&$m1,$m2,$m3){
  $m1="$m3 $m1";
}
$a=['a'=>'apple','b'=>'banana','c'=>'pear','d'=>'banana'];
$b=['sweet','nice','delicious','awesome'];
print_r(array_change_key_case($a,CASE_UPPER));
                                        echo "<br /><br />";
print_r(array_flip($a)); echo "<br /><br />";
print_r(array_unique($a)); echo "<br /><br />";
print_r(array_filter($a,'filter')); echo "<br /><br />";
print_r(array_map('map',$a,$b)); echo "<br /><br />";
print_r(array_map(NULL,$a,$b)); echo "<br /><br />";
array_walk($a,'walk','the');
print_r($a);
?>
</body></html>
```

```
Array ( [A] => apple [B] => banana [C] => pear [D] => banana )

Array ( [apple] => a [banana] => d [pear] => c )

Array ( [a] => apple [b] => banana [c] => pear )

Array ( [b] => banana [c] => pear [d] => banana )

Array ( [0] => sweet apple [1] => nice banana [2] => delicious pear [3] => awesome banana )

Array ( [0] => Array ( [0] => apple [1] => sweet ) [1] => Array ( [0] => banana [1] => nice ) [2] => Array ( [0] => pear [1] => delicious ) [3] => Array ( [0] => banana [1] => awesome ) )

Array ( [a] => the apple [b] => the banana [c] => the pear [d] => the banana )
```

4.5.4 Reduction

array_sum($arr) returns the sum of the values in $arr. **array_product($arr)** returns the product of the values in $arr. **array_reduce($arr, $f(&$m1, $m2)[,$m3=NULL])** returns a single value obtained by applying $f to the elements in $arr iteratively, with $m3 being the initial value.

```
<!DOCTYPE html><html><head></head>
<body>
<?php
function minus($result, $item){
  return ($result-$item);
}
$a=[1,2,3,4,5];
echo array_sum($a); echo "<br />";
echo array_product($a); echo "<br />";
echo array_reduce($a,'minus',100);
?>
</body></html>
```

```
15
120
85
```

4.5.5 Symbols Table

compact($m1[,$m2......]) returns an array containing all variables named in $m1......**extract (&$arr[,$i=EXTR_OVERWRITE[,$s=NULL]])** imports variables from an array into the symbols table. $i can be EXTR_OVERWRITE, EXTR_SKIP, EXTR_PREFIX_SAME, EXTR_PREFIX_ALL, EXTR_PREFIX_INVALID, EXTR_IF_EXISTS, EXTR_PREFIX_IF_EXISTS, EXTR_REFS. $s is the prefix attached to a variable name.

```
<!DOCTYPE html><html><head></head>
<body>
<?php

$v1=1; $v2=2; $v3=3; $v4=4; $v5=5; $v6=6;
print_r(compact('v1',['v2','v3',['v4','v5']],'v6'));
echo "<br />";

$a=["c"=>"lemon","orange","banana"];
extract($a,EXTR_PREFIX_INVALID,'v');
echo "$c $v_0 $v_1 <br />";

$b=["v_0"=>"watermelon","v_1"=>"apple","v_2"=>"pear"];
extract($b,EXTR_SKIP|EXTR_REFS);
                                    // skip if names collide; ref.
echo "$v_0 $v_1 $v_2 <br />";

$v_2="mango";
echo $b["v_2"];

?></body></html>
```

```
Array ( [v1] => 1 [v2] => 2 [v3] => 3 [v4] => 4 [v5] => 5 [v6] =>
6 )
lemon orange banana
orange banana pear
mango
```

4.5.6 Iteration and Selection

array_push(&$arr,$m1[,$m2......]) adds $m1...... onto the the end of $arr. It returns the new number of elements in $arr. **array_pop(&$arr)** removes and returns the last value of $arr. The array pointer will be reset. **array_unshift(&$arr, $m1 [,$m2......])** adds $m1......onto the front of $arr. It returns the new number of elements in $arr. All numerical keys will be modified to start counting from zero. **array_shift(&$arr)** removes and returns the first value of $arr. The array pointer will be reset. All numerical keys will be modified to start counting from zero. **array_rand($arr[,$i=1])** picks $i random keys from $arr. If more than one entries are picked, an array will be returned.

```
<!DOCTYPE html><html><head></head>
<body>
<?php
$a=['a','b','c','d','e','f'];
array_pop($a);
array_push($a,'X','Y');
array_shift($a);
array_unshift($a,'M','N');
print_r($a); echo "<br />";
$r=array_rand($a,3);
echo $a[$r[0]]." ".$a[$r[1]]." ".$a[$r[2]];
?>
</body></html>
```

```
Array ( [0] => M [1] => N [2] => b [3] => c [4] => d [5] => e [6]
=> X [7] => Y )
M c d
```

current(&$arr) or **pos(&$arr)** returns the value of the element in $arr currently pointed to by the internal pointer. **key(&$arr)** returns the key of the element in $arr currently pointed to by the internal pointer. **prev(&$arr)** rewinds the internal array pointer one place backward and returns the value at that position in $arr. FALSE is returned if there are no more elements. **next(&$arr)** advances the internal array pointer one place forward and returns the value at that position in $arr. FALSE is returned if there are no more elements. **each(&$arr)** returns an array containing the current key-value pair and advances the array cursor. **reset(&$arr)** rewinds $arr's internal pointer to the first element and returns its value. **end(&$arr)** advances $arr's internal pointer to the last element and returns its value.

```
<!DOCTYPE html><html><head></head>
<body>
<?php
$a=['a','b','c','test'=>'d','e','f'];
do{
  echo "[".key($a)."=>".pos($a)."]";
} while (next($a));
reset($a); echo "<br />";
print_r(each($a)); echo "<br />";
print_r(each($a)); echo "<br />";
print_r(each($a)); echo "<br />";
echo prev($a).prev($a).prev($a);
?>
</body></html>
```

```
[0=>a][1=>b][2=>c][test=>d][3=>e][4=>f]
Array ( [1] => a [value] => a [0] => 0 [key] => 0 )
Array ( [1] => b [value] => b [0] => 1 [key] => 1 )
Array ( [1] => c [value] => c [0] => 2 [key] => 2 )
cba
```

4.5.7 Difference and Intersection

The difference functions are:

array_diff($arr1,$arr2[,$arr3......])
array_diff_ key($arr1,$arr2[,$arr3......])
array_diff_ukey($arr1, $arr2 [,$arr3......], $cf($m1,$m2))
array_diff_assoc($arr1,$arr2[,$arr3......])
array_diff_uassoc($arr1, $arr2 [,$arr3......], $cf($m1,$m2))
array_udiff($arr1, $arr2 [,$arr3......], $cf($m1,$m2))
array_udiff_assoc($arr1, $arr2 [,$arr3......], $cf($m1,$m2))
array_udiff_uassoc($arr1, $arr2 [,$arr3......], $cf($m1,$m2), $cf2($m3,$m4))

array_diff() returns a copy of $arr1, removing entries with values repeated in the subsequent arrays. array_diff_key() is similar, but compares the keys instead. 'assoc' requires the keys to be repeated too for an entry to be removed. 'u' requires a comparison function to be supplied. The comparison function $cf has to return an integer < 0 if the first argument is less than the second, 0 if the first argument equals the second, > 1 if the first argument is greater than the second.

The intersection functions are:
array_intersect($arr1,$arr2[,$arr3......])
array_intersect_ key($arr1,$arr2[,$arr3......])
array_intersect_ukey($arr1, $arr2 [,$arr3......], $cf($m1,$m2))
array_intersect_assoc($arr1,$arr2[,$arr3......])
array_intersect_uassoc($arr1, $arr2 [,$arr3......], $cf($m1,$m2))
array_uintersect($arr1, $arr2 [,$arr3......], $cf($m1,$m2))
array_uintersect_assoc($arr1, $arr2 [,$arr3......], $cf($m1,$m2))
array_uintersect_uassoc($arr1, $arr2 [,$arr3......], $cf($m1,$m2), $cf2($m3,$m4))
While the difference functions remove repeated elements, these intersection functions return only the repeated elements.

```
<!DOCTYPE html><html><head></head>
<body>
<?php
$a=['a'=>'apple','b'=>'banana','c'=>'carrot','d'=>'pear'];
$b=['a'=>'apple','b'=>'orange','carrot'];
print_r(array_diff($a,$b)); echo "<br />";
print_r(array_diff_key($a,$b)); echo "<br />";
print_r(array_diff_assoc($a,$b)); echo "<br />";
print_r(array_intersect($a,$b)); echo "<br />";
print_r(array_intersect_key($a,$b)); echo "<br />";
print_r(array_intersect_assoc($a,$b)); echo "<br />";
?>
</body></html>
```

```
Array ( [b] => banana [d] => pear )
Array ( [c] => carrot [d] => pear )
Array ( [b] => banana [c] => carrot [d] => pear )
Array ( [a] => apple [c] => carrot )
Array ( [a] => apple [b] => banana )
Array ( [a] => apple )
```

4.5.8 Sorting

The sorting functions are:
sort(&$arr[,$i=SORT_REGULAR])
rsort(&$arr[,$i=SORT_REGULAR])
usort(&$arr,$cf($m1,$m2))

ksort(&$arr[,$i=SORT_REGULAR])
krsort(&$arr[,$i=SORT_REGULAR])
uksort(&$arr,$cf($m1,$m2))

asort(&$arr[,$i=SORT_REGULAR])
arsort(&$arr[,$i=SORT_REGULAR])
uasort(&$arr,$cf($m1,$m2))

natsort(&$arr)
natcasesort(&$arr)

'k' sorts the keys instead of the values. 'a' maintains the associations with keys. 'r' sorts the elements in reverse order. 'nat' sorts the elements in natural order. 'natcase' performs a case-insensitive sort on the elements, in natural order. 'u' requires a comparison function to be supplied. The comparison function $cf has to return an integer < 0 if the first argument is less than the second, 0 if the first argument equals the second, > 1 if the first argument is greater than the second. $i can be SORT_REGULAR, SORT_NUMERIC, SORT_STRING, SORT_FLAG_CASE, SORT_LOCALE_STRING, SORT_NATURAL. These functions return TRUE on success, FALSE on failure.

```
<!DOCTYPE html><html><head></head>
<body>
<?php
function s($m1,$m2){
  return strcmp($m1,$m2);
}
$a = ["c"=>"lemon","a"=>"orange","z"=>"banana",
      "e"=>"apple","g"=>"watermelon"];
$b = $a; sort($b)     ; print_r($b); echo "<br />";
$b = $a; usort($b,'s'); print_r($b); echo "<br />";
$b = $a; ksort($b)    ; print_r($b); echo "<br />";
$b = $a; asort($b)    ; print_r($b); echo "<br /><br />";

$a = ["img.gif","img1.gif","img11.gif","img2.gif"];
$b = $a;    sort($b); print_r($b); echo "<br />";
$b = $a; natsort($b); print_r($b); echo "<br /><br />";

$a = ["c"=>"Lemon","a"=>"orange","z"=>"Banana",
      "e"=>"apple", "g"=>"watermelon"];
$b = $a; sort($b); print_r($b); echo "<br />";
$b = $a; sort($b,SORT_STRING|SORT_FLAG_CASE);
print_r($b); echo "<br />";

?></body></html>
```

```
Array ( [0] => apple [1] => banana [2] => lemon [3] => orange [4] => watermelon )
Array ( [0] => apple [1] => banana [2] => lemon [3] => orange [4] => watermelon )
Array ( [a] => orange [c] => lemon [e] => apple [g] => watermelon [z] => banana )
Array ( [e] => apple [z] => banana [c] => lemon [a] => orange [g] => watermelon )

Array ( [0] => img.gif [1] => img1.gif [2] => img11.gif [3] => img2.gif )
Array ( [0] => img.gif [1] => img1.gif [3] => img2.gif [2] => img11.gif )

Array ( [0] => Banana [1] => Lemon [2] => apple [3] => orange [4] => watermelon )
Array ( [0] => apple [1] => Banana [2] => Lemon [3] => orange [4] => watermelon )
```

shuffle(&$arr) randomizes the order of the elements of $arr. It returns TRUE on success, FALSE on failure. **array_reverse($arr[,$b])** returns an array with a reversed order of the elements. If $b is true, then the numeric keys are preserved. **array_multisort(&$arr [,&$arg1= SORT_ASC[,&$arg2=SORT_REGULAR[,......]]])** can be used to sort several arrays at once. It returns TRUE on success, FALSE on failure. $arg can be another array, or sort options for the previous array argument: SORT_ASC, SORT_DESC, SORT_REGULAR, SORT_NUMERiC, SORT_STRING. Only string keys will be maintained.

For array_multisort(), $b is sorted according to the order by which $a is sorted. When $a contains the same values, $b is sorted according to its own sorting order.

```
<!DOCTYPE html><html><head></head>
<body>
<?php
$a = ["c"=>"lemon","orange","banana",
      "apple","watermelon"];
print_r(array_reverse($a)); echo "<br />";
shuffle($a);  print_r($a); echo "<br /><br />";
```

```
$a = ["10",11,100,100,100,"a"];
$b = [    1, 2, "2",  3,   6,"1"];
array_multisort($a,$b);
print_r($a); echo "<br />";
print_r($b); echo "<br /><br />";

array_multisort($a,SORT_ASC,SORT_STRING,
                $b,SORT_NUMERIC,SORT_DESC);
print_r($a); echo "<br />";
print_r($b); echo "<br /><br />";
?></body></html>
```

```
Array ( [0] => watermelon [1] => apple [2] => banana [3] => orange [c] => lemon )
Array ( [0] => apple [1] => orange [2] => lemon [3] => banana [4] => watermelon )

Array ( [0] => 10 [1] => a [2] => 11 [3] => 100 [4] => 100 [5] => 100 )
Array ( [0] => 1 [1] => 1 [2] => 2 [3] => 2 [4] => 3 [5] => 6 )

Array ( [0] => 10 [1] => 100 [2] => 100 [3] => 100 [4] => 11 [5] => a )
Array ( [0] => 1 [1] => 6 [2] => 3 [3] => 2 [4] => 2 [5] => 1 )
```

4.6 Date Functions

4.6.1 Creation and Setting

Synopsis for the class **DateTime**:

Creation and output
__construct ([string $time = "now" [,DateTimeZone $timezone=NULL]]) **ALIAS** date_create(......)
static DateTime createFromFormat(string $format , string $time [,DateTimeZone $timezone]) **ALIAS** date_create_from_format(......)
string format (string $format) **ALIAS** date_format(......)
static array getLastErrors () **ALIAS** date_get_last_errors(......)
Modification
DateTime modify (string $modify) **ALIAS** date_modify(......)
DateTime setDate (int $y , int $m , int $d) **ALIAS** date_date_set(......)
DateTime setISODate (int $y , int $w [,int $d=1]) **ALIAS** date_isodate_set(......)
DateTime setTime (int $h , int $m [,int $s=0]) **ALIAS** date_time_set(......)
DateTime setTimestamp (int $unixtimestamp) **ALIAS** date_timestamp_set(......)
int getTimestamp () **ALIAS** date_timestamp_get(......)
DateInterval
DateTime add (DateInterval $itv) **ALIAS** date_add(......)
DateTime sub (DateInterval $itv) **ALIAS** date_sub(......)
DateInterval diff (DateTime $datetime2 [, bool $absolute=false]) **ALIAS** date_dif(......)
DateTimeZone
int getOffset (void) **ALIAS** date_offset_get(......)
DateTime setTimezone(DateTimeZone $timezone) **ALIAS** date_timezone_set(......)
DateTimeZone getTimezone(void) **ALIAS** date_timezone_get(......)

Eg. creating and setting a date:

```
<!DOCTYPE html><html><head></head>
<body><?php

// Setting a new time with today's date
$dt = new DateTime('5 am');
$dt = new DateTime('5:30 pm');
$dt = new DateTime('5:30:30 pm');

// Setting a new date with midnight time
$dt = new DateTime('2000/12/25');
$dt = new DateTime('25.12.00');
$dt = new DateTime('25DEC00');
$dt = new DateTime('25-DEC-00');
$dt = new DateTime('25-December 2000');
$dt = new DateTime('25-12-2000');
$dt = new DateTime('2000-12-25');
$dt = new DateTime('12/25/2000');
$dt = new DateTime('2000/12/25');

// Setting a new date and time together
$dt = new DateTime();  // current date and time
$dt = new DateTime('2000-12-25 18:30:30');
$dt = new DateTime('2000:12:25 18:30:30');
$dt = new DateTime('25/Dec/2000:18:30:30 -0700');

// Modification
$dt->modify('2001/01/01');
$dt->setDate(2000,12,25);
$dt->setISODate(2000,15,5);  // 5th day of week 15
$dt->setTime(18,30,30);
$dt->setTimestamp(1234567890);
$dt=new DateTime();
echo $dt->getTimestamp()."<br />";

// Procedural form (ALIAS)
$dt = date_create('2000/12/25');
date_modify($dt,'2001/01/01');
date_date_set($dt,2000,12,25);
date_isodate_set($dt,2000,15,5);  // 5th day of week 15
date_time_set($dt,18,30,30);
date_timestamp_set($dt,1234567890);
echo date_timestamp_get($dt)."<br />";

?></body></html>
```

4.6.2 Formatting

The characters are supported in the $format are:

	Day	
d	01 -- 31	Day of the month
j	1 -- 31	Day of the month
S	st, nd, rd, th	Suffix, works well with j
z	0 – 365	Day of the year
	Week	
W	1 – 52	Week number of the year
l	Sunday -- Saturday	Day of the week
D	Mon -- Sun	Day of the week
N	1(Mon)—7(Sun)	Day of the week
w	0(Sun)—6(Sat)	Day of the week
	Month	
F	January – December	Month of the year
M	Jan – Dec	Month of the year
m	01 -- 12	Month of the year
n	1 – 12	Month of the year
t	28 – 31	No. of days in the month
	Year	
L	0 – 1	1 if leap year, 0 otherwise
o	0000 – 9999	Year, overflowing week
Y	0000 – 9999	Year
y	00 -- 99	Year
	Time	
a	am / pm	Ante or Post Meridiem

A	AM / PM	Ante or Post Meridiem
B	000 - 999	Swatch Internet time
g	1 - 12	Hour
G	0 - 23	Hour
h	01 - 12	Hour
H	00 - 23	Hour
i	00 - 59	Minutes
s	00 - 59	Seconds
u	Eg. 123456	Macroseconds
	Timezone	
e	Eg. UTC, GMT, Atlantis/Azores	Timezone identifier
I	0 - 1	1 if daylight saving, 0 otherwise
O	-1200 -- +1200	Difference to GMT
P	-12:00 -- +12:00	Difference to GMT
T	Eg. EST, MDT	Timezone abbreviation
Z	-43200 -- 50400	Timezone offset in seconds
	Full Date and Time	
c	Eg. 2004-02-12 T15:30:30+00:00	Full Date and Time
r	Eg. Thu, 21 Dec 2000 16:01:07 +0200	Full Date and Time
U	Eg. 12345678	Seconds since 1 Jan 1970

```
<!DOCTYPE html><html><head></head>
<body>
<?php
$dt = DateTime::createFromFormat('j-M-Y', '15-Mar-2014');
$dt = date_create_from_format('j-M-Y', '15-Mar-2014');
echo $dt->format("d/m/y")."<br />";
echo $dt->format("jS F Y")."<br />";
echo $dt->format("r")."<br />";
echo date_format($dt,"e T P I Z")."<br />"; // procedural

try {
   $dt = new DateTime('asdfasdf');
} catch (Exception $e) {
   print_r(DateTime::getLastErrors());
}
?></body></html>
```

```
15/03/14
15th March 2014
Sat, 15 Mar 2014 12:46:03 +0100
Europe/Berlin CET +01:00 0 3600
Array ( [warning_count] => 1 [warnings] => Array ( [6] =>
Double timezone specification ) [error_count] => 1 [errors]
=> Array ( [0] => The timezone could not be found in the
database ) )
```

4.6.3 Interval

Synopsis for the class **DateInterval**:

Properties
int $y
int $m
int $d
int $h
int $i
int $s
int $invert
mixed $days
Methods
__construct(string $interval_spec)
static DateInterval createFromDateString(string $time) **ALIAS** date_interval_create_from_date_string(......)
string format(string $format) **ALIAS** date_interval_format(......)

For DateInterval, the following characters are recognized in $interval_spec:

P	All format strings start with P
Y	Years
M	Months
D	Days
W	Weeks
T	Any time portion is preceded by T
H	Hours
M	Minutes
S	Seconds

Eg. Using DateInterval:

```
<!DOCTYPE html><html><head></head>
<body>
<?php

$dt = new DateTime();
$di = new DateInterval('P3Y3M3DT3H3M3S');

echo $dt->format("r")."<br />";
$dt->add($di);
echo $dt->format("r")."<br />";
date_sub($dt,$di); // alias
echo $dt->format("r")."<br />";

$dt2 = new DateTime('2000-12-25');
$dd=$dt->diff($dt2);
var_dump($dd);
echo "<br />".$dd->invert."<br />";
// invert==1 means $dt2 occurs before $dt
echo $dd->format("%r%y years %m months %d days %h
                  hours %i minutes %s seconds")."<br />";
echo $dd->format("%r%Y years %M months %D days %H
                  hours %I minutes %S seconds")."<br />";
echo date_interval_format($dd,"%r%a days.")."<br />";
                                                  // alias
?></body></html>
```

```
Sun, 18 Nov 2012 04:12:13 +0100
Sun, 21 Feb 2016 07:15:16 +0100
Sun, 18 Nov 2012 04:12:13 +0100
object(DateInterval)#4 (8) { ["y"]=> int(11) ["m"]=> int(10) ["d"]=>
int(24) ["h"]=> int(4) ["i"]=> int(12) ["s"]=> int(13) ["invert"]=> int(1)
["days"]=> int(4346) }
1
-11 years 10 months 24 days 4 hours 12 minutes 13 seconds
-11 years 10 months 24 days 04 hours 12 minutes 13 seconds
-4346 days.
```

Eg. Using DateInterval::createFromDateString:

```
<!DOCTYPE html><html><head></head>
<body>
<?php
$di=date_interval_create_from_date_string('3600 seconds');
$di=DateInterval::createFromDateString('1 day');
$di=DateInterval::createFromDateString('2 weeks');
$di=DateInterval::createFromDateString('3 months');
$di=DateInterval::createFromDateString('4 years');
$di=DateInterval::createFromDateString('1 year + 1 month');
$di=DateInterval::createFromDateString('1 day + 12 hours');
$dt = new DateTime();
$dt->add($di);
echo $dt->format('H:i:sA');
?></body></html>
```

```
16:53:59PM
```

4.6.4 Timezone

Synopsis for the class **DateTimeZone:**

__construct (string $timezone) **ALIAS** timezone_open(......)
array getLocation () **ALIAS** timezone_location_get(......)
string getName () **ALIAS** timezone_name_get(......)
int getOffset (DateTime $dttime) **ALIAS** timezone_offset_get(......)
array getTransitions ([int $timestamp_begin [, int $timestamp_end]]) **ALIAS** timezone_transitions_get(......)
static array listAbbreviations () **ALIAS** timezone_abbreviations_list()
static array listIdentifiers ([int $what=DateTimeZone::ALL [,string $country=NULL]]) **ALIAS** timezone_identifiers_list(......)

date_default_timezone_set($s) sets to $s the default timezone used by all date/time functions. It returns true if $s is a valid timezone, false otherwise . **date_default_timezone_get()** gets the default timezone used by all date/time functions. **timezone_version_get()** returns the current version of the timezone as a string. **timezone_name_from_abbr($s)** returns the timezone name from abbreviation.

Eg. Using DateTimeZone:

```
<!DOCTYPE html><html><head></head>
<body><?php
echo date_default_timezone_get()."<br />";
echo timezone_version_get()."<br />";
echo timezone_name_from_abbr("CET")."<br />";

$dtz = new DateTimeZone('Asia/Kuching');
$dt = new DateTime('now',$dtz);
echo $dt->format('r')."<br />";

// prints the timezone name, Asia/Kuching
echo $dtz->getName()."<br />";

// prints the timezone offset in seconds, 28800
echo $dtz->getOffset($dt)."<br />";

// prints an array of geographical information
print_r($dtz->getLocation()); echo "<br />";

// prints all transitions for the timezone
//print_r($dtz->getTransitions()); echo "<br />";

// prints an associative array containing
// dst, offset and the timezone name
//print_r($dtz->listAbbreviations()); echo "<br />";

// prints a numerically indexed array with all timezone names
//print_r($dtz->listIdentifiers()); echo "<br />";

?></body></html>
```

```
Europe/Berlin
2012.3
Europe/Berlin
Sun, 18 Nov 2012 13:47:26 +0800
Asia/Kuching
28800
Array ( [country_code] => MY [latitude] => 1.55 [longitude]
=> 110.33333 [comments] => Sabah & Sarawak )
```

Timezone names for DateTimeZone				
Africa/Abidjan	Africa/Accra	Africa/Addis_Ababa	Africa/Algiers	Africa/Asmara
Africa/Asmera	Africa/Bamako	Africa/Bangui	Africa/Banjul	Africa/Bissau
Africa/Blantyre	Africa/Brazzaville	Africa/Bujumbura	Africa/Cairo	Africa/Casablanca
Africa/Ceuta	Africa/Conakry	Africa/Dakar	Africa/Dar_es_Salaam	Africa/Djibouti
Africa/Douala	Africa/El_Aaiun	Africa/Freetown	Africa/Gaborone	Africa/Harare
Africa/Johannesburg	Africa/Juba	Africa/Kampala	Africa/Khartoum	Africa/Kigali
Africa/Kinshasa	Africa/Lagos	Africa/Libreville	Africa/Lome	Africa/Luanda
Africa/Lubumbashi	Africa/Lusaka	Africa/Malabo	Africa/Maputo	Africa/Maseru
Africa/Mbabane	Africa/Mogadishu	Africa/Monrovia	Africa/Nairobi	Africa/Ndjamena
Africa/Niamey	Africa/Nouakchott	Africa/Ouagadougou	Africa/Porto-Novo	Africa/Sao_Tome
Africa/Timbuktu	Africa/Tripoli	Africa/Tunis	Africa/Windhoek	
America/Adak	America/Anchorage	America/Anguilla	America/Antigua	America/Araguaina
America/Argentina/ Buenos_Aires	America/Argentina/ Catamarca	America/Argentina/ ComodRivadavia	America/Argentina/ Cordoba	America/Argentina/Jujuy
America/Argentina/ La_Rioja	America/Argentina/ Mendoza	America/Argentina/ Rio_Gallegos	America/Argentina/Salta	America/Argentina/San_Juan
America/Argentina/ San_Luis	America/Argentina/ Tucuman	America/Argentina/ Ushuaia	America/Aruba	America/Asuncion
America/Atikokan	America/Atka	America/Bahia	America/Bahia_Banderas	America/Barbados
America/Belem	America/Belize	America/Blanc-Sablon	America/Boa_Vista	America/Bogota
America/Boise	America/Buenos_Aires	America/Cambridge_Bay	America/Campo_Grande	America/Cancun
America/Caracas	America/Catamarca	America/Cayenne	America/Cayman	America/Chicago
America/Chihuahua	America/Coral_Harbour	America/Cordoba	America/Costa_Rica	America/Creston
America/Cuiaba	America/Curacao	America/Danmarkshavn	America/Dawson	America/Dawson_Creek
America/Denver	America/Detroit	America/Dominica	America/Edmonton	America/Eirunepe
America/El_Salvador	America/Ensenada	America/Fort_Wayne	America/Fortaleza	America/Glace_Bay
America/Godthab	America/Goose_Bay	America/Grand_Turk	America/Grenada	America/Guadeloupe
America/Guatemala	America/Guayaquil	America/Guyana	America/Halifax	America/Havana
America/Hermosillo	America/Indiana/ Indianapolis	America/Indiana/Knox	America/Indiana/Marengo	America/Indiana/Petersburg
America/Indiana/ Tell_City	America/Indiana/Vevay	America/Indiana/ Vincennes	America/Indiana/ Winamac	America/Indianapolis
America/Inuvik	America/Iqaluit	America/Jamaica	America/Jujuy	America/Juneau
America/Kentucky/ Louisville	America/Kentucky/ Monticello	America/Knox_IN	America/Kralendijk	America/La_Paz
America/Lima	America/Los_Angeles	America/Louisville	America/Lower_Princes	America/Maceio
America/Managua	America/Manaus	America/Marigot	America/Martinique	America/Matamoros
America/Mazatlan	America/Mendoza	America/Menominee	America/Merida	America/Metlakatla
America/Mexico_City	America/Miquelon	America/Moncton	America/Monterrey	America/Montevideo
America/Montreal	America/Montserrat	America/Nassau	America/New_York	America/Nipigon
America/Nome	America/Noronha	America/North_Dakota/ Beulah	America/North_Dakota/ Center	America/North_Dakota/ New_Salem
America/Ojinaga	America/Panama	America/Pangnirtung	America/Paramaribo	America/Phoenix
America/ Port-au-Prince	America/Port_of_Spain	America/Porto_Acre	America/Porto_Velho	America/Puerto_Rico
America/ Rainy_River	America/Rankin_Inlet	America/Recife	America/Regina	America/Resolute
America/ Rio_Branco	America/Rosario	America/Santa_Isabel	America/Santarem	America/Santiago
America/ Santo_Domingo	America/Sao_Paulo	America/Scoresbysund	America/Shiprock	America/Sitka
America/ St_Barthelemy	America/St_Johns	America/St_Kitts	America/St_Lucia	America/St_Thomas
America/St_Vincent	America/ Swift_Current	America/Tegucigalpa	America/Thule	America/Thunder_Bay
America/Tijuana	America/Toronto	America/Tortola	America/Vancouver	America/Virgin
America/Whitehorse	America/Winnipeg	America/Yakutat	America/Yellowknife	
Antarctica/Casey	Antarctica/Davis	Antarctica/DumontDUrville	Antarctica/Macquarie	Antarctica/Mawson
Antarctica/McMurdo	Antarctica/Palmer	Antarctica/Rothera	Antarctica/South_Pole	Antarctica/Syowa
Antarctica/Vostok				
Arctic/Longyearbyen				
Asia/Aden	Asia/Almaty	Asia/Amman	Asia/Anadyr	Asia/Aqtau
Asia/Aqtobe	Asia/Ashgabat	Asia/Ashkhabad	Asia/Baghdad	Asia/Bahrain
Asia/Baku	Asia/Bangkok	Asia/Beirut	Asia/Bishkek	Asia/Brunei
Asia/Calcutta	Asia/Choibalsan	Asia/Chongqing	Asia/Chungking	Asia/Colombo
Asia/Dacca	Asia/Damascus	Asia/Dhaka	Asia/Dili	Asia/Dubai
Asia/Dushanbe	Asia/Gaza	Asia/Harbin	Asia/Hebron	Asia/Ho_Chi_Minh
Asia/Hong_Kong	Asia/Hovd	Asia/Irkutsk	Asia/Istanbul	Asia/Jakarta
Asia/Jayapura	Asia/Jerusalem	Asia/Kabul	Asia/Kamchatka	Asia/Karachi
Asia/Kashgar	Asia/Kathmandu	Asia/Katmandu	Asia/Kolkata	Asia/Krasnoyarsk
Asia/Kuala_Lumpur	Asia/Kuching	Asia/Kuwait	Asia/Macao	Asia/Macau
Asia/Magadan	Asia/Makassar	Asia/Manila	Asia/Muscat	Asia/Nicosia

Asia/Novokuznetsk	Asia/Novosibirsk	Asia/Omsk	Asia/Oral	Asia/Phnom_Penh
Asia/Pontianak	Asia/Pyongyang	Asia/Qatar	Asia/Qyzylorda	Asia/Rangoon
Asia/Riyadh	Asia/Saigon	Asia/Sakhalin	Asia/Samarkand	Asia/Seoul
Asia/Shanghai	Asia/Singapore	Asia/Taipei	Asia/Tashkent	Asia/Tbilisi
Asia/Tehran	Asia/Tel_Aviv	Asia/Thimbu	Asia/Thimphu	Asia/Tokyo
Asia/Ujung_Pandang	Asia/Ulaanbaatar	Asia/Ulan_Bator	Asia/Urumqi	Asia/Vientiane
Asia/Vladivostok	Asia/Yakutsk	Asia/Yekaterinburg	Asia/Yerevan	
Atlantic/Azores	Atlantic/Bermuda	Atlantic/Canary	Atlantic/Cape_Verde	Atlantic/Faeroe
Atlantic/Faroe	Atlantic/Jan_Mayen	Atlantic/Madeira	Atlantic/Reykjavik	Atlantic/South_Georgia
Atlantic/St_Helena	Atlantic/Stanley			
Australia/ACT	Australia/Adelaide	Australia/Brisbane	Australia/Broken_Hill	Australia/Canberra
Australia/Currie	Australia/Darwin	Australia/Eucla	Australia/Hobart	Australia/LHI
Australia/Lindeman	Australia/Lord_Howe	Australia/Melbourne	Australia/North	Australia/NSW
Australia/Perth	Australia/Queensland	Australia/South	Australia/Sydney	Australia/Tasmania
Australia/Victoria	Australia/West	Australia/Yancowinna		
Europe/Amsterdam	Europe/Andorra	Europe/Athens	Europe/Belfast	Europe/Belgrade
Europe/Berlin	Europe/Bratislava	Europe/Brussels	Europe/Bucharest	Europe/Budapest
Europe/Chisinau	Europe/Copenhagen	Europe/Dublin	Europe/Gibraltar	Europe/Guernsey
Europe/Helsinki	Europe/Isle_of_Man	Europe/Istanbul	Europe/Jersey	Europe/Kaliningrad
Europe/Kiev	Europe/Lisbon	Europe/Ljubljana	Europe/London	Europe/Luxembourg
Europe/Madrid	Europe/Malta	Europe/Mariehamn	Europe/Minsk	Europe/Monaco
Europe/Moscow	Europe/Nicosia	Europe/Oslo	Europe/Paris	Europe/Podgorica
Europe/Prague	Europe/Riga	Europe/Rome	Europe/Samara	Europe/San_Marino
Europe/Sarajevo	Europe/Simferopol	Europe/Skopje	Europe/Sofia	Europe/Stockholm
Europe/Tallinn	Europe/Tirane	Europe/Tiraspol	Europe/Uzhgorod	Europe/Vaduz
Europe/Vatican	Europe/Vienna	Europe/Vilnius	Europe/Volgograd	Europe/Warsaw
Europe/Zagreb	Europe/Zaporozhye	Europe/Zurich		
Indian/Antananarivo	Indian/Chagos	Indian/Christmas	Indian/Cocos	Indian/Comoro
Indian/Kerguelen	Indian/Mahe	Indian/Maldives	Indian/Mauritius	Indian/Mayotte
Indian/Reunion				
Pacific/Apia	Pacific/Auckland	Pacific/Chatham	Pacific/Chuuk	Pacific/Easter
Pacific/Efate	Pacific/Enderbury	Pacific/Fakaofo	Pacific/Fiji	Pacific/Funafuti
Pacific/Galapagos	Pacific/Gambier	Pacific/Guadalcanal	Pacific/Guam	Pacific/Honolulu
Pacific/Johnston	Pacific/Kiritimati	Pacific/Kosrae	Pacific/Kwajalein	Pacific/Majuro
Pacific/Marquesas	Pacific/Midway	Pacific/Nauru	Pacific/Niue	Pacific/Norfolk
Pacific/Noumea	Pacific/Pago_Pago	Pacific/Palau	Pacific/Pitcairn	Pacific/Pohnpei
Pacific/Ponape	Pacific/Port_Moresby	Pacific/Rarotonga	Pacific/Saipan	Pacific/Samoa
Pacific/Tahiti	Pacific/Tarawa	Pacific/Tongatapu	Pacific/Truk	Pacific/Wake
Pacific/Wallis	Pacific/Yap			
Brazil/Acre	Brazil/DeNoronha	Brazil/East	Brazil/West	Canada/Atlantic
Canada/Central	Canada/ East-Saskatchewan	Canada/Eastern	Canada/Mountain	Canada/Newfoundland
Canada/Pacific	Canada/ Saskatchewan	Canada/Yukon	CET	Chile/Continental
Chile/EasterIsland	CST6CDT	Cuba	EET	Egypt
Eire	EST	EST5EDT	Etc/GMT	Etc/GMT+0
Etc/GMT+1	Etc/GMT+10	Etc/GMT+11	Etc/GMT+12	Etc/GMT+2
Etc/GMT+3	Etc/GMT+4	Etc/GMT+5	Etc/GMT+6	Etc/GMT+7
Etc/GMT+8	Etc/GMT+9	Etc/GMT-0	Etc/GMT-1	Etc/GMT-10
Etc/GMT-11	Etc/GMT-12	Etc/GMT-13	Etc/GMT-14	Etc/GMT-2
Etc/GMT-3	Etc/GMT-4	Etc/GMT-5	Etc/GMT-6	Etc/GMT-7
Etc/GMT-8	Etc/GMT-9	Etc/GMT0	Etc/Greenwich	Etc/UCT
Etc/Universal	Etc/UTC	Etc/Zulu	Factory	GB
GB-Eire	GMT	GMT+0	GMT-0	GMT0
Greenwich	Hongkong	HST	Iceland	Iran
Israel	Jamaica	Japan	Kwajalein	Libya
MET	Mexico/BajaNorte	Mexico/BajaSur	Mexico/General	MST
MST7MDT	Navajo	NZ	NZ-CHAT	Poland
Portugal	PRC	PST8PDT	ROC	ROK
Singapore	Turkey	UCT	Universal	US/Alaska
US/Aleutian	US/Arizona	US/Central	US/East-Indiana	US/Eastern
US/Hawaii	US/Indiana-Starke	US/Michigan	US/Mountain	US/Pacific
US/Pacific-New	US/Samoa	UTC	W-SU	WET
Zulu				

4.6.5 Checking and Parsing

checkdate($i1,$i2,$i3) returns true if a date, given by month=$i1, day=$i2, year=$i3, is a valid date. **date_parse($s)** returns an associative array with information about the date $s. **date_parse_from_format($format, $s)** is similar to date_parse() but uses a specified format instead.

```
<!DOCTYPE html><html><head></head>
<body><?php
var_dump(checkdate(2,29,2001)); echo "<br />";
var_dump(checkdate(12,29,2001)); echo "<br />";
print_r(date_parse('2000-12-25 18:30:30')); echo "<br />";
print_r(date_parse_from_format("j.n.Y H:iP",
                                    "6.1.2009 13:00+01:00" ));
?></body></html>
```

```
bool(false)
bool(true)
Array ( [year] => 2000 [month] => 12 [day] => 25 [hour] => 18 [minute] => 30 [second] => 30 [fraction] => 0 [warning_count] => 0 [warnings] => Array ( ) [error_count] => 0 [errors] => Array ( ) [is_localtime] => )
Array ( [year] => 2009 [month] => 1 [day] => 6 [hour] => 13 [minute] => 0 [second] => 0 [fraction] => [warning_count] => 0 [warnings] => Array ( ) [error_count] => 0 [errors] => Array ( ) [is_localtime] => 1 [zone_type] => 1 [zone] => -60 [is_dst] => )
```

4.6.6 Timestamp

time() returns the current Unix timestamp, which is the number of seconds since 1 Jan 1970 Midnight GMT. **microtime($b)** returns the current Unix timestamp with microseconds. If $b is true, a float instead of a string is returned. **gettimeofday($b)** returns the current Unix timestamp. If $b is true, a float instead of an array is returned. **mktime([$i1[, $i2[, $i3[, $i4[, $i5[, $i6]]]]]])** returns a Unix timestamp for the date and time. The parameters are respectively the hour, minute, second, month, day and year. **gmmktime**(......) is similar to mktime(......) except that the passed parameters represent a GMT date.

```
<!DOCTYPE html><html><head></head>
<body><?php

echo time()."<br />";
echo microtime()."<br />";
echo microtime(true)."<br />";
echo gettimeofday(true)."<br />";
print_r(gettimeofday()); echo "<br /><br />";

echo mktime(23,59,59,12,30,2012)."<br />";
echo gmmktime(23,59,59,12,30,2012)."<br />";

?></body></html>
```

```
1353229775
0.16088300 1353229775
1353229775.1609
1353229775.1609
Array ( [sec] => 1353229775 [usec] => 160895 [minuteswest] => -60 [dsttime] => 0 )

1356908399
1356911999
```

For the following functions in this paragraph, $ts refers to the timestamp integer. If omitted, it means the current timestamp. **date($format[,$ts])** returns a string representing the datetime in the specified format. **gmdate($format[,$ts])** is identical to date() except that the time returned is GMT. **idate($format[,$ts])** returns an integer according to the given format string which is a single character. **getdate([$ts])** returns an associative array containing the datetime information. **localtime([$ts[,$b=false]])** returns an array containing information about the local time. If $b is true, an associative array will be returned. **strtotime($s[,$ts])** returns a timestamp integer from the textual datetime specified by $s. $ts here signifies the relative timestamp.

```
<!DOCTYPE html><html><head></head>
<body><?php

echo date('d-M-Y h:i:sa')."<br />";
echo gmdate('d-M-Y h:i:sa')."<br />";
echo idate('Y')."<br />";
print_r(getdate()); echo "<br />";
print_r(localtime()); echo "<br />";
print_r(localtime(time(),true)); echo "<br />";

echo strtotime('30-12-2012')."<br />";
echo strtotime('now')."<br />";
echo strtotime('yesterday')."<br />";
echo strtotime('+1 day')."<br />";
echo strtotime('+1 week')."<br />";
echo strtotime('+1 week 2 days 4 hours 2 seconds')."<br />";
echo strtotime('next Thursday')."<br />";
echo strtotime('last Monday')."<br />";
echo strtotime('2000-12-25 18:30:30')."<br />";
echo strtotime('2000:12:25 18:30:30')."<br />";

?></body></html>
```

```
18-Nov-2012 11:10:39am
18-Nov-2012 10:10:39am
2012
Array ( [seconds] => 39 [minutes] => 10 [hours] => 11 [mday] => 18 [wday] => 0 [mon] => 11 [year] => 2012 [yday] => 322 [weekday] => Sunday [month] => November [0] => 1353233439 )
Array ( [0] => 39 [1] => 10 [2] => 11 [3] => 18 [4] => 10 [5] => 112 [6] => 0 [7] => 322 [8] => 0 )
Array ( [tm_sec] => 39 [tm_min] => 10 [tm_hour] => 11 [tm_mday] => 18 [tm_mon] => 10 [tm_year] => 112 [tm_wday] => 0 [tm_yday] => 322 [tm_isdst] => 0 )

1356822000
1353233439
1353106800
1353319839
1353838239
1354025441
1353538800
1352674800
977765430
977765430
```

4.6.7 Sun Motion

date_sun_info($ts, $f1, $f2) returns an array with information about sunset/sunrise and twilight beginning/ending. $f1 and $f2 represent the latitude and longitude respectively. $f1 defaults to North; pass in a negative value for South. $f2 defaults to East; pass in a negative value for West. **date_sunrise ($ts[,$i[,$f1[,$f2[,$f3[,$f4=0]]]]])** returns the sunrise time for a given day (specified as a timestamp $ts) and location. $i represents the return format, and it can be SUNFUNCS_RET_ STRING, SUNFUNCS_RET_DOUBLE, SUNFUNCS_ RET_TIMESTAMP. $f1, $f2 and $f3 represent the latitude, longitude and zenith respectively. $f4 is the GMT offset in hours. **date_sunset(......)** is similar to date_sunrise(......) but returns the sunset time instead. The three functions in this paragraph return FALSE on failure.

```
<!DOCTYPE html><html><head></head>
<body><?php
date_default_timezone_set('Asia/Kuching');
$sun_info = date_sun_info(strtotime("2012-11-18"),
                    5.974, 116.069);
foreach ($sun_info as $key => $val) {
   echo "$key: ".date("H:i:s",$val)."<br />";
}
echo date("D M d Y"). ', sunrise time : ' .
    date_sunrise(time(), SUNFUNCS_RET_STRING,
                    5.974, 116.069, 90, 8)."<br />";
echo date("D M d Y"). ', sunset time : ' .
    date_sunset(time(), SUNFUNCS_RET_STRING,
                    5.974, 116.069, 90, 8)."<br />";
?></body></html>
```

```
sunrise: 06:05:44
sunset: 17:56:10
transit: 12:00:57
civil_twilight_begin: 05:43:49
civil_twilight_end: 18:18:04
nautical_twilight_begin: 05:18:21
nautical_twilight_end: 18:43:33
astronomical_twilight_begin: 04:52:54
astronomical_twilight_end: 19:08:59
Sun Nov 18 2012, sunrise time : 06:08
Sun Nov 18 2012, sunset time : 17:53
```

4.7 String Functions

4.7.1 ASCII Code

chr($i) returns a character specified by the ASCII code $i. **ord($s)** returns the ASCII value of the first character of $s.

4.7.2 Reordering

strrev($s) returns a string that is $s reversed. **str_repeat($s,$i)** returns a string that is $s repeated $i times. **str_pad($s1,$i1[,$s2=" ", [$i2=STR_PAD_RIGHT]])** returns a string that is $s1 padded with $s2 to the length $i1. $i2 can be STR_PAD_RIGHT, STR_PAD_LEFT, or STR_PAD_BOTH. **str_shuffle($s)** returns a string that is $s randomly shuffled.

4.7.3 Space Removal and Wrapping

rtrim($s1[,$s2]) or **chop($s1[,$s2])** returns a copy of $s1 with whitespace stripped from the end. $s2 is the list containing the characters to be stripped. **ltrim(......)** is similar but strips whitespace from the beginning. **trim(......)** is similar but strips whitespace from both the beginning and end. **wordwrap($s1[,$i=75[,$s2="\n"[,$b=false]]])** returns a copy of $s1 wrapped to $i characters using $s2 as a string break character. If $b is true, a word at the end is broken so that the string is wrapped with a width of exactly $i characters.

4.7.4 Conversion

strtolower($s) returns a copy of $s with all alphabets converted to lowercase. **strtoupper($s)** returns a copy of $s with all alphabets converted to uppercase. **lcfirst($s)** returns a copy of $s with the first character lowercased, if that character is an alphabet. **ucfirst($s)** returns a copy of $s with the first character capitalized, if that character is an alphabet. **ucwords($s)** returns a copy of $s with the first character of each word capitalized, if that character is an alphabet.

quotemeta($s) returns a copy of $s with backslashes added before . \ + * ? [^] ($). **addslashes($s)** returns a copy of $s with backslashes added before single quotes('), double quotes ("), backslashes (\) and NULs (the NULL byte). **addcslashes($s1,$s2)** returns a copy of $s1 with backslashes added before characters listed in $s2. **stripslashes($s)** returns a copy of $s with backslashes stripped off. **stripcslashes($s)** returns a copy of $s with backslashes stripped off. C-like \n, \r...... octal and hexadecimal representations are recognized.

```
<!DOCTYPE html><html><head></head>
<body><?php

echo ord('A')."<br />";
echo chr(66)."<br />";
echo strrev('abcde')."<br />";
echo str_repeat('abc',3)."<br />";
echo str_pad('abc',10,'+-',STR_PAD_BOTH)."<br />";
echo str_shuffle('abcdef')."<br />";
echo trim('   .-.-.-.-abc.-.-.-.-.   ',".-   ")."<br /><br />";

echo wordwrap('I say it is quite fun to learn PHP. Do you
agree?',13,"<br />")."<br /><br />";;

echo ucwords(strtolower('hElLo WolRd!'))."<br />";
echo quotemeta('(can you hear me?)')."<br />";
echo addcslashes('Hello World','A..Z')."<br />";
echo addcslashes('Hello World','HWc..f')."<br />";
echo stripcslashes('\" \' \101 \x41 \\\ \n \r \t');
;
?></body></html>
```

```
65
B
edcba
abcabcabc
+-+abc+-+-
```

```
fecabd
abc

I say it is
quite fun to
learn PHP. Do
you agree?

Hello Wolrd!
\(can you hear me\?\)
\Hello \World
\H\ello \Worl\d
" ' A A \
```

4.7.5 Counting

strlen($s) returns an integer denoting the length of $s. **str_word_count($s1[,$i=0[,$s2]])** returns the number of words in $s1. If $i is 1, an array containing all the words will be returned. If $i is 2, an associative array will be returned, where the key is the character position and the value is the word itself. $s2 is a list of additional characters which will be considered as 'word'. **substr_count($s1, $s2 [,$i1[,$i2]])** returns the no. of times $s2 is found in $s1. $i1 is the offset of where to start the counting. $i2 is the maximum length after the specified offset to search for the substring. **count_chars($s[,$i=0])** counts the no. of times every byte value (from 0 to 255) is found in $s. If $i is 0, it gives an array with the byte-value as key and the frequency as value. $i=1 is same as $i=0, but it only lists byte-values occurring at least once. $i=2 is the same as $i=0 but it only lists byte-values occurring zero time. $i=3 returns a string of all unique characters. $i=4 returns a string of all not used characters.

4.7.6 Group Searching

strspn($s1,$s2[,$i1[,$i2]]) returns the position of the first character in $s1 that cannot be found in $s2. $i1 is the position to start searching. If $i1 is negative, then the function will start searching at $i -th position from the end. $i2 is the length of the segment to examine. If $i2 is negative, $s1 will be examined from $i1 up to $i2 characters from the end. **strcspn(......)** is similar but returns the position of the first character in $s1 that can be found in $s2.

```
<!DOCTYPE html><html><head></head>
<body><?php

$s = 'I say it is quite fun to learn funny PHP at 3am.';
echo strlen($s)."<br />";
echo str_word_count($s)."<br />";
print_r(str_word_count($s,1)); echo "<br />";
print_r(str_word_count($s,2,'3')); echo "<br />";
echo substr_count($s,'fun')."<br />";
echo count_chars($s,3)."<br />";
print_r(count_chars($s,1)); echo "<br />";
echo strspn($s,'Is ')."<br />";
echo strcspn($s,'qt');

?></body></html>
```

```
48
12
Array ( [0] => I [1] => say [2] => it [3] => is [4] => quite [5] =>
fun [6] => to [7] => learn [8] => funny [9] => PHP [10] => at
[11] => am )
Array ( [0] => I [2] => say [6] => it [9] => is [12] => quite [18]
=> fun [22] => to [25] => learn [31] => funny [37] => PHP [41]
=> at [44] => 3am )
2
.3HIPaefilmnoqrstuy
Array ( [32] => 11 [46] => 1 [51] => 1 [72] => 1 [73] => 1 [80]
=> 2 [97] => 4 [101] => 2 [102] => 2 [105] => 3 [108] => 1
[109] => 1 [110] => 4 [111] => 1 [113] => 1 [114] => 1 [115]
=> 2 [116] => 4 [117] => 3 [121] => 2 )
3
7
```

4.7.7 Splitting and Joining

chunk_split($s1[,$i=76[,$s2="\r\n"]]) returns a copy of $s1 with $s2 inserted every $i characters. **str_split($s[,$i=1])** returns an array of strings formed by splitting $s into segments of $i characters. **str_getcsv($s1[,$s2=','[,$s3='"'[,$s4='\\']]])** returns an array of strings formed by splitting $s1 at $s2. $s3 is the enclosure character. $s4 is the escape character. **explode($s1,$s2[,$i])** returns an array of strings formed by splitting $s2 at $s1. A positive $i will return a maximum of $i elements with the last element containing the rest of the string. If $i is negative, all components except the last -$i are returned. **implode([$s,]$arr)** returns a string formed by joining the elements of $arr with $s. **strtok([$s1,]$s2)** splits $s1 into smaller string tokens, with each token delimited by any character from $s2. $s1 is required on the first call to the function.

```
<!DOCTYPE html><html><head></head>
<body><?php
echo chunk_split("abcdefghi",3,"...")."<br />";
print_r(str_split("abcdefghi",3));
echo "<br />";
print_r(str_getcsv('"Sally,Irene",Osman'));
echo "<br />";
print_r(explode(",","Sally,Irene,Osman,Henry",3));
echo "<br />";
echo implode("---",["Sally","Irene","Osman"]).
     "<br /><br />";

$s = "This is\tan example\nstring";
$t = strtok($s, " \n\t");
while ($t !== false) {
   echo "($t)";
   $t = strtok(" \n\t");
}

?></body></html>
```

```
abc...def...ghi...
Array ( [0] => abc [1] => def [2] => ghi )
Array ( [0] => Sally,Irene [1] => Osman )
Array ( [0] => Sally [1] => Irene [2] => Osman,Henry )
Sally---Irene---Osman

(This)(is)(an)(example)(string)
```

4.7.8 Comparison

The string comparison functions are:

strcmp($s1,$s2)
strcasecmp($s1,$s2)
strncmp($s1,$s2,$i)
strncasecmp($s1,$s2,$i)
strnatcmp($s1,$s2)
strnatcasecmp($s1,$s2)
strcoll($s1,$s2)
substr_compare($s1,$s2,$i1[,$i2[,$b]])

These functions return <0 if $s1 is less than $s2, >0 if $s1 is greater than $s2, and 0 if they are equal. 'case' performs a case-insensitive comparison. 'n' compares the first $i characters from each string. 'nat' performs a 'natural order' comparison. strcoll(......) is similar to strcmp(......) except that the comparison is not binary safe, and is locale based. **substr_compare(......)** compares $s1 from position $i1 with $s2 up to $i2 characters. If $i1 is negative, it starts counting from the end. If $b is true, the comparison is case-insensitive.

```
<!DOCTYPE html><html><head></head>
<body><?php

echo strcmp("abc","abd"); // -1
echo strcasecmp("abc","ABC"); // 0
echo strncmp("abcd","abce",3); // 0
echo strncasecmp("aBcD","AbcE",3); // 0
echo strnatcmp("image2","image11"); // -1
echo strcmp("imAgE11","iMage2"); // 1
echo strcoll("abc","abcd"); // -1
echo substr_compare("abcdef","cDE",2,3,true); // 0

?></body></html>
```

```
-1000-11-10
```

4.7.9 Searching

To find the position of $s2 in $s1, use:

strpos($s1,$s2[,$i=0]);
stripos($s1,$s2[,$i=0]);
strrpos($s1,$s2[,$i=0]);
strripos($s1,$s2[,$i=0]);

FALSE is returned if $s2 cannot be found. 'i' performs a case-insensitive search. 'r' searches for the last instead of the first occurrence. $i denotes the starting position of the search. For strrpos(......) and strripos(......), if $i is negative, the search will start -$i characters from the end, searching backwards.

Notice the use of ===. FALSE and 0 are equivalent in values but not in types.

```
<!DOCTYPE html><html><head></head>
<body><?php
echo strpos("abcabc","abc",1);
echo stripos("abcabc","ABC",1);
echo strrpos("abcabc","abc",-4);
echo strripos("abcabc","ABC",-4);
echo "<br/>";
if (strpos("aaa","bb")===FALSE) echo "string not found";
?></body></html>
```

```
3300
string not found
```

4.7.10 Substring

substr($s1,$i1[,$i2]) returns a substring of $s1 that is $i2 long, starting from position $i1. If $i1 is negative, the returned string will start at the $i-th character from the end. If $i2 is negative, that many characters will be omitted from the end. **strstr($s1,$s2[,$b=false])** or **strchr(......)** returns a substring of $s1, starting from the first occurrence of $s2 to the end. If $b is true, the function returns the part of $s1 before the first occurrence of $s2. FALSE is returned if $s2 cannot be found. **stristr(......)** is similar to strstr(......) but is case-insensitive. **strrchr($s1,$s2)** returns a substring of $s1, starting at the last occurrence of $s2 until the end. If $s2 contains more than one character, only the first is used. **strpbrk($s1,$s2)** returns a substring of $s1, starting from the first occurrence of any character from $s2, to the end.

```
<!DOCTYPE html><html><head></head>
<body><?php
echo substr("abcdefgh",3)."<br />"; // defgh
echo substr("abcdefgh",-3,2)."<br />"; // fg
echo substr("abcdefgh",3,-2)."<br />"; //def
echo strstr("abcdefgh","cde")."<br />"; //cdefgh
echo stristr("abcdefgh","cDE",true)."<br />"; //ab
echo strrchr("abcabcdef","aXX")."<br />"; //abcdef
echo strpbrk("abcdefgh","xyze")."<br />"; //efgh
?></body></html>
```

```
defgh
fg
def
cdefgh
ab
abcdef
efgh
```

4.7.11 Replacement

substr_replace($s1,$s2,$i1,[$i2]) returns a copy of $s1, with the portion of length $i2 starting from $i1 replaced by $s2. If $s1 is an array of strings, the replacement will occur on each srting, in which case $s2, $i1 and $i2 can be scalar values or arrays. If $i1 is negative, the replacement will begin at the $i1-th character from the end. If $i2 is negative, it represents the number of characters from the end of $s1 at which to stop replacing. If $i2 is omitted, it will default to strlen($s1).
str_replace($s1,$s2,$s3[,&$i]) returns a copy of $s3 with all $s1 replaced by $s2. $i stores the number of replacements performed. If $s3 is an array, the search and replace is performed with every entry, and the return value is an array. If $s1 and $s2 are arrays, then a value from each array will be taken to search and replace on $s3. **str_ireplace(......)** is the case-insensitive version of str_replace(......).
strtr($s1,$s2,$s3) gives a copy of $s1 where all occurrences of each character in $s2 have been translated to the corresponding character in $s3.
strtr($s1,$arr) does almost the same thing, but the second argument is an array in the form ('from'=>'to').

```
<!DOCTYPE html><html><head></head>
<body><?php
echo substr_replace("hello world","*",4)."<br />";
echo substr_replace("hello world","*",-5,-2)."<br />";
print_r (substr_replace(["abc","def"],"*",1,1));
echo "<br />";
print_r (substr_replace(["abc","def"],"*",[1,2],1));
echo "<br />";
print_r (substr_replace(["abc","def"],"*",1,[1,2]));
echo "<br />";
print_r (substr_replace(["abc","def"],"*",[0,1],[1,2]));
echo "<br /><br />";

echo str_replace("l","*","hello world",$i)."---$i<br />";
print_r (str_replace("a","*",["cat","car"])); echo "<br />";
echo str_replace(["ll","rl"],"*","hello world")."<br />";
echo str_replace(["ll","rl"],["**","##"],"hello world").
    "<br /><br />";

echo strtr("abcdef","ace","XYZ")."<br />";
echo strtr("abcdef",["ab"=>"X","de"=>"MNO"])."<br />";
?></body></html>
```

```
hell*
hello *ld
Array ( [0] => a*c [1] => d*f )
Array ( [0] => a*c [1] => de* )
Array ( [0] => a*c [1] => d* )
Array ( [0] => *bc [1] => d* )

he**o wor*d---3
Array ( [0] => c*t [1] => c*r )
he*o wo*d
he**o wo##d

XbYdZf
XcMNOf
```

4.7.12 Display and Formatting

To produce or output a string, use:

print ($s) or echo ($s)
printf($format[,$m1......])
sprintf($format[,$m1......])
fprintf($resource,$format[,$m1......])
vprintf($format,$arr)
vsprintf($format,$arr)
vfprintf($resource,$format,$arr)
sscanf($s1,$format[,&$m1......])

printf(), fprint(), vprintf(), vfprintf() returns the length of the string written. The prefix 's' returns a string. The prefix 'f' prints the string on the resource provided. The prefix 'v' uses an array, instead of a variable-length arguments list.

sscanf() parses $s1 according to $format and stores the values in $m1......If we pass only 2 arguments, it will return an array. Otherwise the number of values assigned will be returned.

$format can contain the following conversion specifiers, which are preceded by the % sign.

spc	Treated as	Presented as
b	integer	binary number
c	integer	character of that ASCII value
d	integer	decimal number
e	scientific notation	scientific notaion
u	integer	unsigned decimal number
f	float	float (locale)
F	float	float (non-locale)
o	integer	octal number
s	string	string
x	integer	lowercase hex
X	integer	uppercase hex
E	like %e but uses uppercase E	
g	shorter of %e and %f	
G	shorter of %E and %f	
%	The % literal	

Between the % sign and the specifier symbol, additional specifications may be defined to format the output. See the example below.

number_format($f,$i=0) and **number_format ($f, $i=0, $s1='.', $s2=',')** return a string that is $f formatted with grouped thousands. $i sets the number of decimal points. $s1 is the separator for the decimal point. $s2 is the thousands separator.

```
<!DOCTYPE html><html><head></head>
<body><?php

printf("%d ducks and %d %s<br />",20,3,"alligators");
vprintf("%d ducks and %d %s<br />",[20,3,"alligators"]);
printf("the number is %03d<br />",7);
printf("the value of PI is %.3f<br />",3.14159265359);
printf("the hex of 110 is %X<br />",110);
printf("%+.3e%%<br />",6425.6892);
printf("%c<br />",65);

sscanf("20 ducks and 3 alligators",
        "%d ducks and %d %s",$a,$b,$c);
echo "$a pigs and $b $c<br />";

list($m,$d,$y)=sscanf("February 02 2002", "%s %d %d");
echo "$d $m $y<br />";

echo number_format(1234567890.123456,2,'|',' ');

?></body></html>
```

```
20 ducks and 3 alligators
20 ducks and 3 alligators
the number is 007
the value of PI is 3.142
the hex of 110 is 6E
+6.426e+3%
A
20 pigs and 3 alligators
2 February 2002
1 234 567 890|12
```

4.7.13 HTML

nl2br($s[,$b=true]) returns a copy of $s with '<br />' inserted before all newlines. If $b is false, '<br>' will be inserted instead. **strip_tags($s1 [,$s2])** returns a copy of $s1 with all NUL bytes, HTML and PHP tags stripped off. $s2 specifies the allowed tags. **parse_str($s[,$arr])** parses $s as if it were the query string passed via a URL and sets variables in the current scope.

The PHP code and the converted HTML document:
`<!DOCTYPE html><html><head></head>` `<body><?php` `echo nl2br("Hello\nWorld\n");` `$text = '<p>Test 123.</p>` `        <!-- Comment --><a href="#abc">Some text</a>';` `echo strip_tags($text); echo " \n";` `echo strip_tags($text,"<p><a>"); echo " \n";` `$s = "a=value&arr[]=foo+bar&arr[]=baz";` `parse_str($s);` `echo $a." ".$arr[0]." ".$arr[1]." \n";` `parse_str($s, $output);` `echo $output['a']." ".$output['arr'][0]." ".$output['arr'][1];` `?></body></html>`
`<!DOCTYPE html><html><head></head>` `<body>Hello ` `World ` `Test 123.Some text ` `<p>Test 123.</p><a href="#abc">Some text</a> ` `value foo bar baz ` `value foo bar baz</body></html>`

htmlspecialchars($s[,$flags[,$encoding= 'UTF-8'[,$b=true]]]) returns a copy of $s with the following characters translated to HTML entities: & " ' < >. If $b is false, the function will not convert existing entities. **htmlspecialchars_decode($s, $flags)** converts these HTML entities back to special characters. **htmlentities(......)** is identical to htmlspecialchars(), except that ALL characters which have HTML entity equivalents are translated into these entities. **html_entity_decode($s [,$flags [,$encoding='UTF-8']])** returns a copy of $s with all HTML entities converted to their applicable characters. It is the opposite of htmlentities(). **get_html_translation_table ([$table= HTML_SPECIALCHARS [,$flag[, $encoding='UTF-8']]])** returns an array, which is a translation table used by htmlspecialchars() and htmlentities(). The original characters are returned as keys while the entities are returned as values. $table is either HTML_ENTITIES or HTML_SPECIALCHARS.

$flag	
ENT_COMPAT	Default. Encodes double quotes and without encoding single quotes.
ENT_QUOTES	Encodes double and single quotes.
ENT_NOQUOTES	Does not encode double and single quotes.
ENT_IGNORE	Discards invalid sequences instead of returning an empty string.
ENT_SUBSTITUTE	Replaces invalid sequences with U+FFFD or &#FFFD instead of returning an empty string.
ENT_DISALLOWED	Replaces invalid code points for the given document type with U+FFFD or &#FFFD instead of returning an empty string.
ENT_HTML401	Default. Handles code as HTML 4.01.
ENT_XML1	Handles code XML 1.
ENT_XHTML	Handles code as XHTML
ENT_HTML5	Handles code as HTML 5.

$encoding		
ISO-8859-1	cp866	BIG5
ISO-8859-5	cp1251	GB2312
ISO-8859-15	cp1252	BIG5-HKSCS
UTF-8	KOI8-R	Shift-JIS
"" (empty string)	MacRoman	EUC-JP

The PHP code and the converted HTML document:

`<!DOCTYPE html><html><head></head>`
`<body><?php`
 	
`$e = htmlspecialchars('<p>"Hello World"</p>'`
`                  ,ENT_QUOTES|ENT_HTML5);`
`echo "\n$e\n";`
`$s = htmlspecialchars_decode($e,ENT_QUOTES|ENT_HTML5);`
`echo "$s\n";`
 	
`$e = htmlentities('I asked:"are you alright?"',`
`                  ENT_QUOTES|ENT_HTML5);`
`echo "\n$e\n";`
`$s = html_entity_decode($e,ENT_QUOTES|ENT_HTML5);`
`echo "$s\n\n";`
 	
`print_r(get_html_translation_table());`
`?></body></html>`

`<!DOCTYPE html><html><head></head>`
`<body>`
`<p>"Hello World"</p>`
`<p>"Hello World"</p>`
 	
`I asked:"are you alright?"`
`I asked:"are you alright?"`
 	
`Array`
`(`
`  ["] => "`
`  [&] => &`
`  [<] => <`
`  [>] => >`
`)`
`</body></html>`

4.7.14 Special Calculations

similar_text($s1,$s2[,&$f]) returns the similarity between two strings, ie. the number of matching characters. If $f is passed, it stores the similarity in percent. **levenshtein($s1,$s2[,$i1,$i2,$i3])** returns the Levenshtein distance between two strings, which is the minimal number of characters you have to replace, insert or delete to transform $s1 to $s2. $i1, $i2 and $i3 define the cost of insertion, replacement and deletion respectively. **soundex($s)** returns the soundex key of $s as a string that is 4 characters long. Words pronounced similarly produce the same soundex key. **metaphone($s[,$i])** returns the metaphone key of $s as a string that is $i characters long. Similar to soundex(), metaphone creates the same key for similarly sounding words.

```
<!DOCTYPE html><html><head></head>
<body><?php

echo similar_text("a cat","cars",$f)." $f<br />";
echo levenshtein("a cat","cars")."<br />";
echo soundex("Kathy")."<br />";
echo soundex("kittie")."<br />";
echo metaphone("programming")."<br />";
echo metaphone("programmer")."<br />";
echo metaphone("programmer",3)."<br />";

?></body></html>
```

```
2 44.444444444444
4
K300
K300
PRKRMNK
PRKRMR
PRK
```

4.8 Math Functions

4.8.1 Trigonometry

The trigonometrical functions are:

sin($f)	**sinh($f)**	**asin($f)**	**asinh($f)**
cos($f)	**cosh($f)**	**acos($f)**	**acosh($f)**
tan($f)	**tanh($f)**	**atan($f)**	**atan($f)**
atan2($f1,$f2) returns the arc tangent of $f1/$f2.			
hypot($f1,$f2) returns the length of the hypotenuse of a right-angle triangle with sides of length $f1 and $f2.			

All angles are measured in radians. **deg2rad($f)** converts $f from degrees to radians. **rad2deg($f)** converts $f from radians to degrees. **pi()** returns an approximation of pi.

4.8.2 Radix

base_convert($s,$i1,$i2) returns a string containing a number that is the number in $s converted from base $i1 to base $i2. **bindec($s), octdec($s),** and **hexdec($s)** convert to a decimal number from a binary, octal and hexadecimal number respectively. **decbin($num), decoct($num),** and **dechex($num)** return the binary, octal and hexadecimal representation strings of $num.

```
<!DOCTYPE html><html><head></head>
<body><?php

var_dump(asin(sin(pi()))); echo "<br />"; // approx. 0
var_dump(base_convert('a2d3',16,3)); echo "<br />";
var_dump(octdec('234')); echo "<br />";
var_dump(decbin('243234')); echo "<br />";

?></body></html>
```

```
float(1.2246467991474E-16)
string(10) "2010011211"
int(156)
string(18) "111011011000100010"
```

4.8.3 Rational Numbers

max($arr) or **max($m1,$m2......)** returns the highest of the parameter values. A non-numeric string is evaluated as 0. If arrays are passed, the longest array is returned. **min($arr)** or **min($m1,$m2......)** is similar but returns the lowest of the parameter values.

abs($num) returns the absolute value of $num. **ceil($f)** returns the next higher integer value. **floor($f)** returns the next lower integer value. **round($f[,$i1=0[$,i2]])** rounds $f to the specified precision $i1 (number of digits after the decimal point). $i2 can be **PHP_ROUND_HALF_UP**, PHP_ROUND_HALF_DOWN, PHP_ROUND_HALF_ODD, or PHP_ROUNd_HALF_EVEN.

```
<!DOCTYPE html><html><head></head>
<body><?php
var_dump(max(["car","cats","bus"])); echo "<br />";
var_dump(max(-2,"hello","world",-1)); echo "<br />";
var_dump(max([1,2,3],[4,5],6)); echo "<br />";
var_dump(abs(-3)); echo "<br />";
var_dump(ceil(-3.2)); echo "<br />";
var_dump(floor(3.8)); echo "<br />";
var_dump(round(3.856,1)); echo "<br />";
var_dump(round(3.55,1,PHP_ROUND_HALF_ODD));
echo "<br />";
var_dump(round(3.55,1,PHP_ROUND_HALF_EVEN));
echo "<br />";
var_dump(round(3.551,1,PHP_ROUND_HALF_ODD));
echo "<br />";
?></body></html>
```

```
string(4) "cats"
string(5) "world"
array(3) { [0]=> int(1) [1]=> int(2) [2]=> int(3) }
int(3)
float(-3)
float(3)
float(3.9)
float(3.5)
float(3.6)
float(3.6)
```

fmod($f1,$f2) returns the floating point remainder of $f1 divided by $f2. **sqrt($f)** returns the square root of $f. **pow($num1,$num2)** returns the result of $num1 raised to the power of $num2. **exp($f)** returns the result of e raised to the power of $f. **expm1($f)** returns 'exp($f)-1', computed in a way that is accurate even when $f is near zero. **log10 ($f)** returns the base-10 logarithm of $f. **log($f1 [,$f2=M_E])** returns the natural algorithm of $f1. If $f2 is specified, the function returns log$f2$f1, ie using $f2 as the base of the logarithm. **log1p($f)** returns log(1+$f), computed in a way that is accurate even when $f is near zero.

```
<!DOCTYPE html><html><head></head>
<body><?php

var_dump(fmod(4.2,1.5)); echo "<br />";
echo sqrt(2)."<br />";
echo pow(2,3.5)."<br />";
echo log(8,2)."<br />";
echo expm1(0)."<br />";
echo log1p(0)."<br />";

?></body></html>
```

```
float(1.2)
1.4142135623731
11.313708498985
3
0
0
```

is_finite($f) returns true if $f is finite, false otherwise. **is_infinite($f)** returns true if $f is infinite, false otherwise. **is_nan($f)** returns true if $f is not a number, false otherwise.

4.8.4 Randomization

rand([$i1,$i2]) generates a random integer between 0 and **getrandmax()**, or between $i1 and $i2 if they are supplied. **srand($i)** seeds the random number generator for rand(). **mt_rand ([$i1,$i2])** generates a random integer between 0 and **mt_getrandmax()**, or between $i1 and $i2 if they are supplied. Using the Mersenne Twister, mt_rand() is four times faster than rand(). **mt_srand([$i])** seeds the random number generator for mt_rand(). **lcg_value()** returns a random float between 0 and 1, using the combined linear congruential generator.

```
<!DOCTYPE html><html><head></head>
<body><?php

echo getrandmax()."<br />";
echo mt_getrandmax()."<br />";
echo rand()."<br />";  // already seeded randomly
echo mt_rand(-100,2)."<br />"; // already seeded randomly
echo lcg_value()."<br />";

?></body></html>
```

```
32767
2147483647
18499
-90
0.68047841956385
```

Constant	Description
M_PI	Π
M_E	e
M_LOG2E	$\log_2 e$
M_LOG10E	$\log_{10} e$
M_LN2	$\log_e 2$
M_LN10	$\log_e 10$
M_PI_2	Π/2
M_PI_4	Π/4
M_1_PI	1/Π
M_2_PI	2/Π
M_SQRTPI	sqrt(Π)
M_2_SQRTPI	2/sqrt(Π)
M_SQRT2	sqrt(2)
M_SQRT3	sqrt(3)
M_SQRT1_2	1/sqrt(2)
M_LNPI	$\log_e Π$
M_EULER	Euler constant
NAN	Not A Number (float)
INF	The Infinite (float)

4.9 Function Functions

4.9.1 Invocation

call_user_func($s[,$m......]) calls the function $s and passes the remaining parameters as arguments to the function $s. It returns the return value of the callback, or FALSE on error. **call_user_func_array ($s,$arr)** is similar to call_user_func() except that the arguments are supplied as an array.

```
<!DOCTYPE html><html><head></head>
<body><?php

function shout($a,$b){
  echo $a.$b."!<br />";
}

call_user_func('shout','Hello',' World');
call_user_func_array('shout',['Hello',' World']);

?></body></html>
```

```
Hello World!
Hello World!
```

forward_ static_call($s[,$m......]) calls a user-defined method $s, with the following arguments. This function uses late static bindinig and must be called within a method. $s can be a string with a function name, or an array with a class name and a method name. This function returns the result of calling $s, or FALSE on error. **forward_static_ call_array ($s,$arr)** is similar to forward_static_ call() except that the arguments are supplied as an array.

```
<!DOCTYPE html><html><head></head>
<body><?php
class P{
  const NAME = 'P';
  public static function test() {
    $args = func_get_args();
    echo static::NAME, " ".join(',', $args)." <br />";
  }
}
class C extends P{
   const NAME = 'C';
   public static function test() {
      echo self::NAME, "<br />";
      forward_static_call(array('P','test'),'AB','CD');
      forward_static_call('test','OP', 'QR');
      forward_static_call_array( 'test',['OP', 'QR']);
   }
}
C::test('foo');
function test() {
  $args = func_get_args();
   echo "test ".join(',', $args)." <br />";
}
?></body></html>
```

```
C
C AB,CD
test OP,QR
test OP,QR
```

4.9.2 Registration

create_function($s1,$s2) creates an anonymous function and returns a unique name for it. $s1 is the arguments string while $s2 contains the function code.

```
<!DOCTYPE html><html><head></head>
<body><?php

$f = create_function('$a,$b','echo $a.$b;');
$f('Hello',' World');

?></body></html>
```

```
Hello World
```

register_shutdown_function($s[,$m......]) registers a callback function $s to be executed after the script execution finishes or exit() is called.

```
<!DOCTYPE html><html><head></head>
<body><?php
function shout($s){echo "$s!";}
function laugh($s){echo "$s!";}
register_shutdown_function('shout','Bye World');
register_shutdown_function('laugh',' Haha');
?></body></html>
```

```
Bye World! Haha!
```

4.9.3 Checking

function_exists($s) returns true if the given function $s has been defined. It checks both built-in and user-defined functions. **get_defined_functions()** returns a multidimensional array containing all functions, both built-in and user-defined. The internal functions will be accessible via $arr['internal] and the user defined ones via $arr['user'].

```
<!DOCTYPE html><html><head></head>
<body><?php

function shout(){
  echo "Hello World";
}
var_export(function_exists('shout'));
$arr=get_defined_functions();
print_r($arr);

?></body></html>
```

```
trueArray ( [internal] => Array ( [0] => zend_version [1] =>
func_num_args [2] => func_get_arg ......[1392] =>
xmlrpc_server_register_introspection_callback )
[user] => Array ( [0] => shout ) )
```

4.10 Class Functions

4.10.1 Existence

class_exists($s) returns true if the class $s has been defined. **interface_exists($s)** returns true if the interfacce $s has been defined. **trait_exists ($s)** returns true if the trait $s has been defined. **method_exists($m,$s)** returns true if the method $s has been defined. $m is an object instance or the class name. **property_exists($m,$s)** returns true if the property $s has been defined. $m is an object instance or the class name.

get_declared_classes() returns an array with the names of the defined classes. **get_declared_interfaces()**returns an array with the names of the declared interfaces. **get_declared_traits()** returns an array of all declared traits.

get_class($o) returns the class name of $o as a string. **is_a($o,$s[,$b=FALSE])** returns true if $o belongs to the class $s or has this class as its ancestor. If $b is false, a string class name for $o is not allowed. **is_subclass_of($m,$s[,$b=TRUE])** returns true if a class or object $m has the class $s as its ancestor. If $b is false, a string class name for $o is not allowed. **get_parent_class($m)** returns the parent class name for the object or class $m.

```
<!DOCTYPE html><html><head></head>
<body><?php
class P {public $a=0;}
class C extends P{private $b=0;}

$o = new C;
var_dump(class_exists('C'));
var_dump(property_exists($o,'b'));
var_dump(property_exists('C','a'));
echo "<br />";
echo get_class($o)."<br />";
echo is_a($o,'P')."<br />";
echo is_subclass_of($o,'P')."<br />";
echo get_parent_class($o)."<br />";
echo get_parent_class('C')."<br />";
print_r(get_declared_interfaces());
?></body></html>
```

```
bool(true) bool(true) bool(true)
C
1
1
P
P
Array ( [0] => Traversable [1] => IteratorAggregate [2] =>
Iterator [3] => ArrayAccess [4] => Serializable [5] =>
JsonSerializable [6] => RecursiveIterator [7] => OuterIterator
[8] => Countable [9] => SeekableIterator [10] => SplObserver
[11] => SplSubject [12] => Reflector [13] =>
SessionHandlerInterface )
```

4.10.2 Members

class_alias($s1,$s2) creates an alias $s2 for the class $s1. **get_called_class()** returns the name of the class the method is called in. **get_object_vars($o)** returns an associative array of the non-static properties of the object $o. **get_class_vars($s)** returns an associative array of the declared properties of the class $s. The properties are visible from the current scope. **get_class_ methods($m)** returns an array of the names of the methods in the class $m. $m is the class name or an object instance.

```
<!DOCTYPE html><html><head></head>
<body><?php

class P {
  function shout(){
    echo get_called_class()."<br />";
  }
}
class C extends P{
  const x=10;
  private $a=1;
  public $b=2;
  static public $c=3;
}

class_alias('C','D');
$o = new D;
$o->shout();
$arr = get_object_vars($o); print_r($arr); echo "<br />";
$arr = get_class_vars('D'); print_r($arr); echo "<br />";
$arr = get_class_methods('D'); print_r($arr); echo "<br />";
$arr = get_class_methods($o); print_r($arr); echo "<br />";

?></body></html>
```

```
C
Array ( [b] => 2 )
Array ( [b] => 2 [c] => 3 )
Array ( [0] => shout )
Array ( [0] => shout )
```

4.11 Filter

4.11.1 Synopsis

filter_var($m[,$filter[,$options]]) filters a variable with a specified filter. It returns the filtered data, or FALSE if the filter fails. **filter_var_array ($arr[,$definition])** filters an array of data. It returns an array containing the filtered variables, which have a value of FALSE on failure.

$filter, $options, $definition

Validation filters merely checks if the data meets certain qualification. Sanitization filters, on the other hand, may change the data.

Validation Filters

FILTER_VALIDATE_BOOLEAN
flags:
FILTER_NULL_ON_FAILURE
returns TRUE for "1","true","on" and "yes", FALSE otherwise. If FILTER_NULL_ON_FAILURE is set, FALSE is returned only for "0","false","off","no" and "", and NULL is returned for all non-boolean values.

FILTER_VALIDATE_EMAIL

FILTER_VALIDATE_FLOAT
flags:
FILTER_FLAG_ALLOW_THOUSAND
options:
decimal
FILTER_FLAG_ALLOW_THOUSAND allows a comma as a thousands separator in numbers.

FILTER_VALIDATE_INT
flags:
FILTER_FLAG_ALLOW_OCTAL
FILTER_FLAG_ALLOW_HEX
options:
min_range
max_range

FILTER_VALIDATE_IP
flags:
FILTER_FLAG_IPV4
FILTER_FLAG_IPV6
FILTER_FLAG_NO_PRIV_RANGE
FILTER_FLAG_NO_RES_RANGE
validates the value as an IP address, optionally only IPv4 or IPv6 or not from private (10.0.0.0/8, 172.16.0.0/12, 192.168.0.0/16) or reserved (0.0.0.0/8, 169.254.0.0/16, 192.0.2.0/24, 224.0.0.0/4) ranges.

FILTER_VALIDATE_REGEXP
options:
regexp

FILTER_VALIDATE_URL
flags:
FILTER_FLAG_PATH_REQUIRED
FILTER_FLAG_QUERY_REQUIRED

Sanitization Filters

FILTER_SANITIZE_EMAIL
removes all characters except letters, digits and !#$%&'*+-/=?^_`{|}~@.[].

FILTER_SANITIZE_ENCODED
flags:
FILTER_FLAG_STRIP_LOW
FILTER_FLAG_STRIP_HIGH
FILTER_FLAG_ENCODE_LOW
FILTER_FLAG_ENCODE_HIGH
URL-encodes the string, optionally stripping or encoding special characters.

FILTER_SANITIZE_MAGIC_QUOTES
applies addslashes().

FILTER_SANITIZE_NUMBER_FLOAT
flags:
FILTER_FLAG_ALLOW_FRACTION
FILTER_FLAG_ALLOW_THOUSAND
FILTER_FLAG_ALLOW_SCIENTIFIC
removes all characters except digits, +- and optionally .,eE.

FILTER_SANITIZE_NUMBER_INT
removes all characters except digits, +-.

FILTER_SANITIZE_SPECIAL_CHARS
flags:
FILTER_FLAG_STRIP_LOW
FILTER_FLAG_STRIP_HIGH
FILTER_FLAG_ENCODE_HIGH
HTML-escapes '"<>& and characters with an ASCII value less than 32.

FILTER_SANITIZE_FULL_SPECIAL_CHARS
flags:
FILTER_FLAG_NO_ENCODE_QUOTES
applies htmlspecialchars() with ENT_QUOTES set.

FILTER_SANITIZE_STRING
or
FILTER_SANITIZE_STRIPPED
flags:
FILTER_FLAG_NO_ENCODE_QUOTES
FILTER_FLAG_STRIP_LOW
FILTER_FLAG_STRIP_HIGH
FILTER_FLAG_ENCODE_LOW
FILTER_FLAG_ENCODE_HIGH
FILTER_FLAG_ENCODE_AMP

FILTER_SANITIZE_URL
removes all characters except letters, digits and $-_.+!*'(),{}|\^~[]`<>#%";/?:@&=.

FILTER_UNSAFE_RAW
flags:
FILTER_FLAG_STRIP_LOW
FILTER_FLAG_STRIP_HIGH
FILTER_FLAG_ENCODE_LOW
FILTER_FLAG_ENCODE_HIGH
FILTER_FLAG_ENCODE_AMP
does nothing, optionally stripping or encoding special characters

Callback Filter

FILTER_CALLBACK
options:
callable function or method

For the flags, FILTER_FLAG_STRIP_LOW strips characters that has a numerical value <32. FILTER_FLAG_STRIP_HIGH strips characters that has a numerical value >127. FILTER_FLAG_ENCODE_LOW encodes characters with a numerical value <32. FILTER_FLAG_ENCODE_HIGH encodes characters with a numerical value >127. FILTER_ FLAG_ENCODE_AMP encodes ampersands &.

4.11.2 Examples

An example of using **filter_var()**:

```
<!DOCTYPE html><html><head></head>
<body><?php
var_dump(filter_var('yes',
                FILTER_VALIDATE_BOOLEAN,
                FILTER_NULL_ON_FAILURE));
echo "<br />";
var_dump(filter_var('hi',
                FILTER_VALIDATE_BOOLEAN,
                ['flags' => FILTER_NULL_ON_FAILURE]));
echo "<br />";
var_dump(filter_var('0654',
                FILTER_VALIDATE_INT,
                ['options' => ['default' => 3, // if the filter fails
                               'min_range' => 0],
                 'flags' => FILTER_FLAG_ALLOW_OCTAL]));
echo "<br />";
var_dump(filter_var('http://www.example.com/test/test.php?
username=hello&password=world',
                FILTER_VALIDATE_URL,
                FILTER_FLAG_PATH_REQUIRED|
                   FILTER_FLAG_QUERY_REQUIRED));
echo "<br />";
var_dump(filter_var('(testing@example.com)',
                FILTER_SANITIZE_EMAIL));
echo "<br />";

function foo($value){return "$value (verified)";}
var_dump(filter_var('William, Thomas Lee',
                FILTER_CALLBACK,
                ['options' => 'foo']));
?></body></html>
```

```
bool(true)
NULL
int(428)
string(66) "http://www.example.com/test/test.php?

username=hello&password=world"
string(19) "testing@example.com"
string(30) "William, Thomas Lee (verified)"
```

An example of using **filter_var_array()**:

```
<!DOCTYPE html><html><head></head>
<body><?php
$data = [
   'test_id'     => 'link<meta>',
   'number'      => '6',
   'version'     => '4.3.31',
   'testscalar'  => ['1','12','30','82'],
   'testarray'   => '2'];

$args = [
   'test_id'        => FILTER_SANITIZE_ENCODED,
   'number'         => ['filter'  => FILTER_VALIDATE_INT,
                        'flags'   => FILTER_FORCE_ARRAY,
                        'options' => ['min_range'=>1,
                                      'max_range'=>100]],
   'version'        => FILTER_SANITIZE_ENCODED,
   'doesnotexist'   => FILTER_VALIDATE_INT,
   'testscalar'     => ['filter' => FILTER_VALIDATE_INT,
                        'flags'  => FILTER_REQUIRE_SCALAR],
   'testarray'      => ['filter' => FILTER_VALIDATE_INT,
                        'flags'  => FILTER_FORCE_ARRAY]];

var_dump(filter_var_array($data, $args));

?></body></html>
```

```
array(6) {
   ["test_id"]=> string(14) "link%3Cmeta%3E"
   ["number"]=> array(1) { [0]=> int(6) }
   ["version"]=> string(6) "4.3.31"
   ["doesnotexist"]=> NULL
   ["testscalar"]=> bool(false)
   ["testarray"]=> array(1) { [0]=> int(2) } }
```

4.11.3 Checking Filters

filter_list() returns an array of the names of all supported filters. **filter_id($s)** returns the filter ID belonging to a filter named $s.

```
<!DOCTYPE html><html><head></head>
<body><?php

print_r(filter_list());
echo "<br /><br />";
$f=filter_id("validate_email");
var_dump(filter_var("hello@yahoo.com",$f));

?></body></html>
```

```
Array ( [0] => int [1] => boolean [2] => float [3] =>
validate_regexp [4] => validate_url [5] => validate_email [6]
=> validate_ip [7] => string [8] => stripped [9] => encoded
[10] => special_chars [11] => full_special_chars [12] =>
unsafe_raw [13] => email [14] => url [15] => number_int [16]
=> number_float [17] => magic_quotes [18] => callback )

string(15) "hello@yahoo.com"
```

4.11.4 External Data

To filter external variables passed to the script, use:

filter_input($type, $s[,$filter[,$options]])
filter_input_array($type, $definition)
filter_has_var($type, $s)

$type can be INPUT_GET, INPUT_POST, INPUT_COOKIE, INPUT_SERVER or INPUT_ENV. filter_input() is similar to filter_var() except that the name of the external variable is passed as a string. filter_input_array is similar to filter_var_array() except that the type of the external variables is passed. filter_has_var() checks if the variable of a specified type exists.

4.12 Regular Expression Functions

For an explanation about how to form a regular expression, read (3.2.9).

4.12.1 Basics

preg_quote($s1[,$s2]) returns a copy of $s1 with a backslash \ added in front of every character that is part of the regular expression syntax. The special characters are .\+*?[]^$(){}=!<>|:-. If the delimiter $s2 is specified, it will also be escaped. **preg_grep($s,$arr[,$i])** returns an array with entries that match the pattern $s. If $i is set to PREG_GREP_INVERT, the function returns elements that do not match the pattern. **preg_last_error()** returns the error code of the last regex execution. The return value can be:

PREG_NO_ERROR
PREG_INTERNAL_ERROR
PREG_BACKTRACK_LIMIT_ERROR
PREG_RECURSION_LIMIT_ERROR
PREG_BAD_UTF8_ERROR
PREG_BAD_UTF8_OFFSET_ERROR

```
<!DOCTYPE html><html><head></head>
<body><?php

// filtering an array with preg_grep()
$arr=['abc','aab','acd','ade'];
print_r(preg_grep('/ab/',$arr)); echo "<br />";
print_r(preg_grep('/ab/',$arr,PREG_GREP_INVERT));
echo "<br />";

// using other delimiters and the case-insensitive modifier i
print_r(preg_grep('/ab/i',$arr)); echo "<br />";
print_r(preg_grep('|Ab|i',$arr)); echo "<br />";
print_r(preg_grep('+aB+i',$arr)); echo "<br />";
print_r(preg_grep('?AB?i',$arr)); echo "<br />";
print_r(preg_grep('{ab}i',$arr)); echo "<br />";

// using preg_quote()
$word="*very*";
echo preg_quote($word)."<br />";
print_r(preg_grep('/'.preg_quote($word).'/',
             ['PHP is *very* fun'])); echo "<br />";

// accessing preg_last_error()
switch (preg_last_error()){
  case PREG_NO_ERROR:
    echo "PREG_NO_ERROR";
  break; case PREG_INTERNAL_ERROR:
    echo "PREG_INTERNAL_ERROR";
  break; case PREG_BACKTRACK_LIMIT_ERROR:
    echo "PREG_BACKTRACK_LIMIT_ERROR";
  break; case PREG_RECURSION_LIMIT_ERROR:
    echo "PREG_RECURSION_LIMIT_ERROR";
  break; case PREG_BAD_UTF8_ERROR:
    echo "PREG_BAD_UTF8_ERROR";
  break; case PREG_BAD_UTF8_OFFSET_ERROR:
    echo "PREG_BAD_UTF8_OFFSET_ERROR";
}
?></body></html>
```

```
Array ( [0] => abc [1] => aab )
Array ( [2] => acd [3] => ade )
Array ( [0] => abc [1] => aab )
Array ( [0] => abc [1] => aab )
Array ( [0] => abc [1] => aab )
Array ( [0] => abc [1] => aab )
Array ( [0] => abc [1] => aab )
\*very\*
Array ( [0] => PHP is *very* fun )
PREG_NO_ERROR
```

4.12.2 Splitting

preg_split($s1,$s2[,$i1=-1,[$i2]]) splits $s2 into an array of strings, using the regular expression $s1 as the separator. If $i1 is specified, up to $i1 substrings are returned, with the rest of the string being placed in the last substring. $i1=-1,0 or NULL means no limit. If $i2 is set to PREG_SPLIT_NO_EMPTY, only non-empty pieces will be returned. If $2 is set to PREG_SPLIT_DELIM_CAPTURE, parenthesized expression in the pattern will be captured as well. If $i2 is set to PREG_SPLIT_ OFFSET_CAPTURE, the string offset too will be returned for each element.

```
<!DOCTYPE html><html><head></head>
<body><?php
$s = 'XXabYYacadZZ';
print_r(preg_split('/a./',$s));
echo "<br />";
print_r(preg_split('/a./',$s,2));
echo "<br />";
print_r(preg_split('/a./',$s,0,PREG_SPLIT_NO_EMPTY));
echo "<br />";
print_r(preg_split('/a.(..)/',$s,0,
                PREG_SPLIT_DELIM_CAPTURE));
echo "<br />";
print_r(preg_split('/a./',$s,0,
                PREG_SPLIT_OFFSET_CAPTURE));
echo "<br />";

?> </body></html>
```

```
Array ( [0] => XX [1] => YY [2] => [3] => ZZ )
Array ( [0] => XX [1] => YYacadZZ )
Array ( [0] => XX [1] => YY [2] => ZZ )
Array ( [0] => XX [1] => YY [2] => [3] => ad [4] => ZZ )
Array ( [0] => Array ( [0] => XX [1] => 0 )
        [1] => Array ( [0] => YY [1] => 4 )
        [2] => Array ( [0] => [1] => 8 )
        [3] => Array ( [0] => ZZ [1] => 10 ) )
```

4.12.3 Matching

preg_match($s1,$s2[,&$arr[,$i1[,$i2]]]) returns 1 if the there is a match for the regular expression $s1 in $s2. $arr[0] contains the substring that matches the full pattern, $arr[1] contains the substring that matches the first parenthesized subpattern, and so on. If $i1 is set to PREG_OFFSET_CAPTURE, the string offset too will be returned. $i2 specifies the position from which to start the search. **preg_match_all($s1,$s2[,&$arr [,$i1=PREG_PATTERN_ORDER[,$i2]]])** is similar to preg_match() except that all matches are stored in $arr. It returns the number of full pattern matches. $i1=PREG_SET_ORDER orders the results so that $arr[0] is an array of the first set of matches, $arr[1] is an array of the second set of matches, and so on.

```
<!DOCTYPE html><html><head></head>
<body><?php

$s = '--abcXXYY--abcMMNN--';
preg_match('/abc(..)(..)/',$s,$arr);
print_r($arr); echo "<br />";
preg_match('/abc(..)(..)/',$s,$arr,PREG_OFFSET_CAPTURE);
print_r($arr); echo "<br /><br />";

preg_match_all('/abc(..)(..)/',$s,$arr);
print_r($arr); echo "<br />";
preg_match_all('/abc(..)(..)/',$s,$arr,PREG_SET_ORDER);
print_r($arr); echo "<br />";
preg_match_all('/abc(..)(..)/',$s,$arr,PREG_SET_ORDER|PREG
_OFFSET_CAPTURE);
print_r($arr); echo "<br />";
?> </body></html>
```

```
Array ( [0] => abcXXYY
        [1] => XX
        [2] => YY )
Array ( [0] => Array ( [0] => abcXXYY [1] => 2 )
        [1] => Array ( [0] => XX [1] => 5 )
        [2] => Array ( [0] => YY [1] => 7 ) )

Array ( [0] => Array ( [0] => abcXXYY [1] => abcMMNN )
        [1] => Array ( [0] => XX [1] => MM )
        [2] => Array ( [0] => YY [1] => NN ) )
Array ( [0] => Array ( [0] => abcXXYY [1] => XX [2] => YY )
        [1] => Array ( [0] => abcMMNN [1] => MM [2] =>
NN ) )
Array ( [0] => Array ( [0] => Array ( [0] => abcXXYY [1] => 2 )
                      [1] => Array ( [0] => XX [1] => 5 )
                      [2] => Array ( [0] => YY [1] => 7 ) )
        [1] => Array ( [0] => Array ( [0] => abcMMNN [1] =>
11 )
                      [1] => Array ( [0] => MM [1] => 14 )
                      [2] => Array ( [0] => NN [1] => 16 ) ) )
```

4.12.4 Replacement

preg_replace($s1,$s2,$s3[,$i1=-1[,&$i2]]) searches $s3 for matches to the pattern $s1 and replaces them with $s2. $s1,$s2 and $s3 can be strings or arrays of strings. The replacement $s2 may contain references of the form \N or $N, which replaces the text by the n'th parathesized pattern. \0 or $0 refers to the text matched by the whole pattern. $i1 sets the maximum possible replacements. The default is -1(no limit). If specified, $i2 will be filled with the number of replacements done. **preg_replace_callback(s1,$f($arr),$s2 [,$i1=-1[,&$i2]])** is similar to preg_replace() except that instead of the replacement string, a callback function should be specified. **preg_filter ($s1,$s2,$s3[,$i1=-1[,&$i2]])** is similar to preg_replace() except that it only returns the subjects where there is a match.

```
<!DOCTYPE html><html><head></head>
<body><?php

echo preg_replace('/(\w+) (\d+), (\d+)/i',
                  '($2 $1 ${3})',
                  'January 20, 2000')."<br />";
echo preg_replace(['/is/','/fun/','/learn/','/\s+/'],
                  ['is not','easy','master',' '],
                  'PHP is fun to      learn')."<br />";
echo preg_replace(['/is/','/fun/','/learn/'],
                  '***',
                  'PHP is fun to learn')."<br />";

?> </body></html>
```

```
(20 January 2000)
PHP is not easy to master
PHP *** *** to ***
```

```
<!DOCTYPE html><html><head></head>
<body><?php

function next_year($matches){
  return $matches[1].($matches[2]+1);
}
echo preg_replace_callback(
          "|(\d{2}/\d{2}/)(\d{4})|",
          "next_year",
          "The event will be held on 29/03/2003.");

?> </body></html>
```

```
The event will be held on 29/03/2004.
```

```
<!DOCTYPE html><html><head></head>
<body><?php

$subject = array('1', 'a', '2', 'b', '3', 'A', 'B', '4');
$pattern = array('/\d/', '/[a-z]/', '/[1a]/');
$replace = array('A:$0', 'B:$0', 'C:$0');
print_r(preg_filter($pattern, $replace, $subject));
echo "<br />";
print_r(preg_replace($pattern, $replace, $subject));

?> </body></html>
```

```
Array ( [0] => A:C:1 [1] => B:C:a [2] => A:2 [3] => B:b [4] =>
A:3 [7] => A:4 )
Array ( [0] => A:C:1 [1] => B:C:a [2] => A:2 [3] => B:b [4] =>
A:3 [5] => A [6] => B [7] => A:4 )
```

4.13 Error Functions

4.13.1 Backtrace

debug_backtrace([$i1[,$i2=0]]) returns an associative array containing the backtrace. $i1 can be DEBUG_BACKTRACE_PROVIDE_OBJECT or DEBUG_BACKTRACE_IGNORE_ARGS. $i2 limits the number of stack frames returned. By default ($i2=0) it returns all stack frames. **debug_print_ backtrace ([$i1[,$i2]])** prints the backtrace. $i1 can be DEBUG_BACKTRACE_IGNORE_ARGS. $i2 limits the number of stack frames used. By default ($i2=0) it prints all stack frames.

```
<?php  // test.php

function a() {b();}
function b() {
  print_r(debug_backtrace());
  echo "<br /><br />";
  debug_print_backtrace();
}
a();
?>
```

```
<!DOCTYPE html><html><head></head>
<body><?php
include "test.php";
?> </body></html>
```

```
Array ( [0] => Array ( [file] => E:\Program
Files\xampp\htdocs\test.php
                       [line] => 3
```

```
                    [function] => b
                    [args] => Array ( ) )
        [1] => Array ( [file] => E:\Program Files\
                              xampp\htdocs\test.php
                    [line] => 10
                    [function] => a
                    [args] => Array ( ) )
        [2] => Array ( [file] => E:\Program Files\
                              xampp\htdocs\intro.php
                    [line] => 4
                   [args] => Array ( [0] => E:\Program Files\
                                xampp\htdocs\test.php )
                    [function] => include ) )

#0 b() called at [E:\Program Files\xampp\htdocs\test.php:3]
#1 a() called at [E:\Program
Files\xampp\htdocs\test.php:10]
 #2 include(E:\Program Files\xampp\htdocs\test.php) called
at [E:\Program Files\xampp\htdocs\intro.php:4]
```

error_get_last() returns an associative array containing information about the last error, or NULL if there has not been any error.

```
<!DOCTYPE html><html><head></head>
<body><?php
echo $a;
print_r(error_get_last());
?> </body></html>
```

```
Notice: Undefined variable: a in E:\Program
Files\xampp\htdocs\intro.php on line 4
Array ( [type] => 8
        [message] => Undefined variable: a
        [file] => E:\Program Files\xampp\htdocs\intro.php
        [line] => 4 )
```

4.13.2 Logging and Reporting

error_log($s1[,$i=0[,$s2[,$s3]]]) sends an error message $s1 somewhere. It returns TRUE on success and FALSE on failure. $i can be:

0	sends $s1 to PHP's system logger
1	sends $s1 as an email to the address in $s2, using the extra headers $s3
2	no longer an option
3	appends $s1 to the file $s2
4	sends $s1 to the SAPI logging handler

```
<!DOCTYPE html><html><head></head>
<body><?php
error_log("\nTesting 123. An error has occurred.\n",0);

if (error_log("\nTesting 123. An error has occurred.\n",
            1,"fragment_shader@yahoo.com")){
  echo "Error Logging Successful.";
}

print_r(error_get_last());

error_log("\nTesting 123. An error has
occurred.\n",3,"error.txt");

?> </body></html>
```

```
Error Logging Successful.
```

error_reporting([$i]) sets the error_reporting directive at runtime. It returns the old error_reporting level. $i can be:

constant of error level	value
E_ERROR	1
E_WARNING	2
E_PARSE	4
E_NOTICE	8
E_CORE_ERROR	16
E_CORE_WARNING	32
E_COMPILE_ERROR	64
E_COMPILE_WARNING	128
E_USER_ERROR	256
E_USER_WARNING	512
E_USER_NOTICE	1024
E_STRICT	2048
E_RECOVERABLE_ERROR	4096
E_DEPRECATED	8192
E_USER_DEPRECATED	16384
E_ALL	32767

```
<!DOCTYPE html><html><head></head>
<body><?php
// Turn off all error reporting
error_reporting(0);

// Report simple running errors
error_reporting(E_ERROR | E_WARNING | E_PARSE);

// Reporting E_NOTICE can be good too (to report uninitialized
// variables or catch variable name misspellings ...)
error_reporting(E_ERROR | E_WARNING | E_PARSE |
               E_NOTICE);

// Report all errors except E_NOTICE
// This is the default value set in php.ini
error_reporting(E_ALL ^ E_NOTICE);

// Report all PHP errors (see changelog)
error_reporting(E_ALL);

// Report all PHP errors
error_reporting(-1);

// Same as error_reporting(E_ALL);
ini_set('error_reporting', E_ALL);

?> </body></html>
```

4.13.3 Error Handler

set_error_handler($f($i1,$s1[,$s2[,$i2[,$arr]]]) [,$i3=E_ALL|E_STRICT]) sets a user function $f() to handle errors. $i1 contains the level of the error raised. $s1 contains the error message. $s2 contains the filename. $i2 contains the line number. $arr contains all variables in the scope. If $f() returns FALSE then the normal error handler continues. $i3 dictates what error levels trigger the error handler $f(). **restore_error_handler()** reverts to the previous error handler function, which can be a built-in or a user-defined function.

```
<!DOCTYPE html><html><head></head>
<body><?php
function eh($errno,$errmsg,$file,$line,$var){
   echo "Error level $errno<br />";
   echo "$errmsg<br />";
   echo "$file<br />";
   echo "Line $line<br />";
   print_r($var);
}
function eh2(){
   echo "Error";
}
set_error_handler('eh');
set_error_handler('eh2');
restore_error_handler();
echo $a;

?> </body></html>
```

```
Error level 8
Undefined variable: a
E:\Program Files\xampp\htdocs\intro.php
Line 16
Array ( [_GET] => Array ( ) [_POST] => Array ( ) [_COOKIE] =>
Array ( ) [_FILES] => Array ( ) )
```

Similarly, **restore_exception_handler()** reverts to the previous exception handler, after changing the exception handler using set_exception_handler() (4.2.6).

4.13.4 Error Generation

trigger_error($s[,$i=E_USER_NOTICE]) or **user_error(......)** generates a user-level error/warning/notice. $i can be E_USER_NOTICE, E_USER_WARNING, E_USER_ERROR.

```
<!DOCTYPE html><html><head></head>
<body><?php
user_error("NOTICE!",E_USER_NOTICE);
trigger_error("WARNING!",E_USER_WARNING);
trigger_error("ERROR!",E_USER_ERROR);
?> </body></html>
```

Notice: NOTICE! in **E:\Program Files\xampp\htdocs\intro.php** on line **3**

Warning: WARNING! in **E:\Program Files\xampp\htdocs\intro.php** on line **4**

Fatal error: ERROR! in **E:\Program Files\xampp\htdocs\intro.php** on line **5**

4.14 File System Functions

4.14.1 Directory

is_dir($s) returns true if $s is a directory. **getcwd()** returns the current working directory as a string. **chdir($s)** changes the current directory to $s and returns true on success. **scandir($s[,$i= SCANDIR_SORT_ASCENDING])** returns an array of files and directories from the directory $s, or false on failure. $i can be SCANDIR_SORT_ASCENDING, SCANDIR_SORT_DESCEDING, or SCANDIR_SORT_NONE. **mkdir($s[,$i=0777[,$b=false]])** creates the directory $s with an access code *(see chmod())* of $i, and returns true on success. If $b is set to true, then nested directories can be created.

rename($s1,$s2) renames a file or directory $s1 to $s2, moving it between directories if necessary, and returns true on success. If $s2 exists, it will be overwritten. **rmdir($s)** removes an empty directory $s, and returns true on success.

```
<!DOCTYPE html><html><head></head>
<body><?php

mkdir("testing");
rename ("testing","testing2");
var_dump(is_dir("testing2"));echo "<br />";
print_r(scandir("./testing2/..")); // back to the current dir
chdir("testing2");
echo getcwd();
rename("../a.html","b.html");
rmdir("../testing2");

?></body></html>
```

bool(true)
Array ([0] => . [1] => .. [2] => a.html [3] => action.php [4] => alpha_beta.php [5] => apache_pb.gif [6] => apache_pb.png [7] => apache_pb2.gif [8] => apache_pb2.png [9] => apache_pb2_ani.gif [10] => bar.php [11] => error.txt [12] => favicon.ico [13] => foo.php [14] => forbidden [15] => index.html [16] => intro.php [17] => restricted [18] => submit.gif [19] => test.php [20] => testing2 [21] => upload [22] => upload.php [23] => upload_file.php [24] => xampp)
E:\Program Files\xampp\htdocs\testing2
Warning: rmdir(../testing2): Directory not empty in **E:\Program Files\xampp\htdocs\intro.php** on line **11**

opendir($s) opens a directory handle and returns the resource. False is returned on failure. **dir($s)** returns an instance of the Directory class for the directory $s.

Synopsis for the class Directory:

Properties
string $path
resource $handle
Methods
void close([resource $dir_handle]) **ALIAS** closedir(......) This closes the directory handle.
string read([resource $dir_handle]) **ALIAS** readdir(......) This returns the next entry. False is returned on failure.
void rewind([resource $dir_handle]) **ALIAS** rewinddir(......) This rewinds the stream to the beginning.

```
<!DOCTYPE html><html><head></head>
<body><?php

$r=opendir(".");
while (false !== ($entry = readdir($r)))
    echo "$entry"."<br />";
closedir($r);

$d=dir(".");
echo $d->path."<br />";
echo $d->read()."<br />";
echo $d->read()."<br />";
```

```
echo $d->read()."<br />";
$d->rewind();
echo $d->read()."<br />";
$d->close();

?></body></html>
```

```
.
..
action.php
alpha_beta.php
apache_pb.gif
apache_pb.png
apache_pb2.gif
apache_pb2.png
apache_pb2_ani.gif
bar.php
error.txt
favicon.ico
foo.php
forbidden
index.html
intro.php
restricted
submit.gif
test.php
testing2
upload
upload.php
upload_file.php
xampp
.
.
..
action.php
.
```

basename($s1[,$s2]) returns the trailing name component of the path $s1. Any suffix $s2 will be cut off. **dirname($s)** returns the parent directory of the path $s. **pathinfo($s[,$i= PATHINFO_DIRNAME|PATHINFO_BASENAME|PATHINFO_EXTENSION|PATHINFO_FILENAME])** returns information about a file path $s, as an array or string. **realpath($s)** returns the absolute pathname of $s. **realpath_cache_get()** returns an array of realpath cache entries. **realpath_cache_size()** returns the amount of memory used by the realpath cache. **disk_free_space($s)** or **diskfreespace($s)** returns the available space of a filesystem as specified by the path $s. **disk_total_space($s)** returns the total size of a filesystem as specified by the path $s.

```
<!DOCTYPE html><html><head></head>
<body><?php

echo basename("/abc/def/ghi","i")."<br />";
echo dirname("xampp/external")."<br />";
print_r(pathinfo("xampp/external/cds.php"));echo "<br />";
echo realpath(".")."<br />";
echo realpath_cache_sizE()."<br />";
echo disk_free_space(".")."<br />";
echo disk_total_space(".")."<br />";

?></body></html>
```

```
gh
xampp
Array ( [dirname] => xampp/external [basename] => cds.php
[extension] => php [filename] => cds )
E:\Program Files\xampp\htdocs
748
1088978944
58558771200
```

4.14.2 General Files

file_exists($s) returns true if the file or directory $s exists. **is_file($s)** returns true if $s is a regular file. **is_executable($s)** returns true if $s is an executable file. **is_link($s)** returns true if $s is a symbolic link. **is_readable($s)** returns true if $s is a readable file. **is_writable($s)** or **is_writeable ($s)** returns true if $s is a writable file. **fnmatch($s1,$s2[,$i])** returns true if the passed string $s2 matches the shell wildcard pattern $s1. $i can be any combination of:

FNM_NOESCAPE	Disable backslash escaping.
FNM_PATHNAME	A slash in the string only matches a slash in the given pattern.
FNM_PERIOD	A leading period in the string must be exactly matched by a period in the given pattern.
FNM_CASEFOLD	Caseless match.

glob($s[,$i]) returns an array of pathnames matching the shell wildcard pattern $s. $i can be:

GLOB_MARK	Adds a slash to each directory returned.
GLOB_NOSORT	No sorting.
GLOB_NOCHECK	Returns the search pattern if no matching files were found.
GLOB_NOESCAPE	Backslashes do not quote metacharacters.
GLOB_BRACE	Expands {a,b,c} to match 'a','b' or 'c'.
GLOB_ONLYDIR	Returns only matching directories.
GLOB_ERR	Stops on read errors.

```
<!DOCTYPE html><html><head></head>
<body><?php

var_dump(fnmatch("a?c","abc")); // true
var_dump(fnmatch("*A",".CBA")); // true
var_dump(fnmatch("*A",".CBA",FNM_PERIOD)); //false
var_dump(fnmatch("[abc]","B",FNM_CASEFOLD)); //true

echo "<br /><br />";
print_r(glob("*",GLOB_MARK|GLOB_NOSORT));

?></body></html>
```

```
bool(true) bool(true) bool(false) bool(true)

Array ( [0] => action.php [1] => alpha_beta.php [2] => apache_pb.gif
[3] => apache_pb.png [4] => apache_pb2.gif [5] => apache_pb2.png
[6] => apache_pb2_ani.gif [7] => bar.php [8] => error.txt [9] =>
favicon.ico [10] => foo.php [11] => forbidden\ [12] => index.html
[13] => intro.php [14] => restricted\ [15] => submit.gif [16] =>
```

```
test.php [17] => testing2\ [18] => upload\ [19] => upload.php [20]
=> upload_file.php [21] => xampp\ )
```

fileatime($s) returns the last access time of the file $s in the form of a Unix timestamp. **filemtime ($s)** returns the last modification time of the file $s in the form of a Unix timestamp. **touch($s[,$i1 =time()[,$i2]])** sets the touch time of the file $s to be $i1, and the access time to be $i2. It returns true on success or false on failure. **filectime($s)** returns the inode change time of the file $s in the form of a Unix timestamp. **fileinode($s)** returns the inode number of the file $s.

filesize($s) returns the size of the file $s. **filetype($s)** returns the type of the file $s, which can be "fifo","char","dir","block","link","file","socket" and "unknown".

stat($s) returns an array containing information about a file $s. **fstat($r)** is similar to stat() except that it operates on an open file pointer $r. **lstat($s)** is similar to stat() except that if the file $s is a symbolic link, the status of the symbolic link is returned.

clearstatcache([$b=false[,$s]]) clears the file status cache. When you call a function that returns information about a file, PHP often caches it to provide faster performance. In case the file is changed, the cache needs to be cleared in order to reflect the reality. If $b is true, the realpath cache is cleared. If $s is set, the realpath and stat cache are cleared for the file $s only.

```
<!DOCTYPE html><html><head></head>
<body><?php

print_r(stat("test.php")); echo "<br />";
echo fileatime("test.php")."<br />";
touch("test.php");
echo fileatime("test.php")."<br />";
clearstatcache();
echo fileatime("test.php")."<br />";

?></body></html>
```

```
Array ( [0] => 4 [1] => 0 [2] => 33206 [3] => 1 [4] => 0 [5] => 0
[6] => 4 [7] => 310 [8] => 1365504496 [9] => 1365504496
[10] => 1352526964 [11] => -1 [12] => -1 [dev] => 4 [ino] => 0
[mode] => 33206 [nlink] => 1 [uid] => 0 [gid] => 0 [rdev] => 4
[size] => 310 [atime] => 1365504496 [mtime] =>
1365504496 [ctime] => 1352526964 [blksize] => -1 [blocks]
=> -1 )
1365504496
1365504496
1365504517
```

filegroup($s) returns the group ID of the file $s. **fileowner($s)** returns the user ID of the owner of the file $s. **chgrp($s,$m)** changes the group of the file $s to $m, which is a group name or number. It returns true on success or false on failure. **lchgrp($s,$m)** is similar but changes the group of a symlink instead. **chown($s,$m)** changes the owner of the file $s to $m, which is a user name or number. It returns true on success or false on failure. **lchown($s,$m)** is similar but changes the owner of a symlink instead.
chmod($s,$i) changes the permission mode of the file $s to $i. $i consists of three octal number components for the owner, the user group, and everybody else, in this order. One component can be computed by adding up the needed permissions for that target user base. Number 1 means execution rights, number 2 means writeable rights, number 4 means readable rights. Add up these numbers to specify the needed rights. **fileperms($s)** returns the permissions for the file $s, along with other information. Lower bits are the same as the permissions expected by chmod().

umask([$i]) sets PHP's umask to $i & 0777 and returns the old umask. Without any arguments, it simply returns the current umask.

```
<!DOCTYPE html><html><head></head>
<body><?php

echo sprintf("%o",fileperms("test.php"))."<br />";
chmod("test.php",0764);

?></body></html>
```

```
100666
```

copy($s1,$s2) copies the file $s1 to $s2. It returns true on success. **unlink($s)** deletes the file $s. It returns true on success. **link($s1,$s2)** creates a hard link $s2 for the file $s1. It returns true on success. **symlink($s1,$s2)** creates a symbolic link $s2 for the file $s1. It returns true on success. **linkinfo($s)** is used to verify if a link $s really exists. It returns the st_dev field of the Unix C stat structure returned by the lstat system call, and 0 or false in case of error. **readlink($s)** returns the contents of the symbolic link path $s, or false on error. **tempnam($s1,$s2)** creates a file with a unique filename, with the prefix $s2 and access permission set to 0600, in the specified directory $s1. It returns the new temporary filename, or FALSE on failure. **tmpfile()** creates a temporary file with a unique name in read-write mode and returns the file handle. The file is automatically closed when the script ends. **is_uploaded_file($s)** returns true if the file $s was uploaded via HTTP POST. **move_uploaded_file ($s1,$s2)** moves an uploaded file $s1 to $s2.

parse_ini_file($s[,$b=false[,$i=INI_SCANNER_ NORMAL]]) returns an array consisting of the settings in the ini file $s. If $b is set to true, you get a multidimensional array, with the section names included. If $i is set to INI_SCANNER_RAW, then option values will not be parsed. **parse_ini_ string(......)** is similar but takes in a string $s instead of a file.

```
<!DOCTYPE html><html><head></head>
<body><?php

$tmp = tempnam(".","TEST");
copy($tmp,"TESTING");
unlink($tmp);
unlink("TESTING");

$ini = "
[SECTION 1]
a=123
b=456";

print_r(parse_ini_string($ini));
echo "<br />";
print_r(parse_ini_string($ini,true));

?></body></html>
```

```
Array ( [a] => 123 [b] => 456 )
Array ( [SECTION 1] => Array ( [a] => 123 [b] => 456 ) )
```

4.14.3 Reading/Writing

fopen($s1,$s2[,$b]) opens a file $s1 for reading or writing, using the mode $s2. It returns the file handler resource. If $b is set to true, files in the include_path will be searched too. To read a remote URL (eg. http:// or ftp://), **allow_url_fopen** in php.ini needs to be enabled. $s2 can be:

flag	r	w	pointer	file already exists
r	Y		Start	
r+	Y	Y	Start	
w		Y	Start	Truncate to 0 length
w+	Y	Y	Start	Truncate to 0 length
a		Y	End	
a+	Y	Y	End	
x		Y	Start	Error
x+	Y	Y	Start	Error
c		Y	Start	
c+	Y	Y	Start	
additional flag				
b	binary files.			
t	plain-text files. translates \n to \r\n.			

fclose($r) closes an open file pointer opened by fopen(). It returns true on success.

fwrite($r,$s[,$i]) or **fputs(......)** writes the string $s to the file $r. If $i is specified, writing will stop after that many bytes have been written. This function returns the number of bytes written, or false on error.

file_put_contents($s,$m[,$i]) is identical to calling fopen(), fwrite() and fclose() successively to write data to a file $s. $m can be either a string, an array(implode()), or a stream resource(remaining buffer). This function returns the number of bytes written, or false on error. $i can be any combination of:

FILE_USE_INCLUDE_PATH	Search for the file in the include directory.
FILE_APPEND	Append data to the file instead of overwriting it.
LOCK_EX	Use an exclusive lock.

fputcsv($r,$arr[,$s1=',’[,$s2='"']]) formats the array $arr as CSV and writes it to the file $r. $s1 is the delimiter character, and $s2 is the enclosure character.

fflush($r) forces all buffered output to be written to the file $r. It returns true on success or false on failure.

ftruncate($r,$i) truncates the file $r to length $i. It returns true on success or false on failure.

```
<!DOCTYPE html><html><head></head>
<body><?php

file_put_contents("test.txt","ABCDEF");

$r=fopen("test.txt","ab");
fwrite($r,"1234567890",3);
fwrite($r,"---");
fflush($r);
ftruncate($r,12);
fclose($r);

$r=fopen("test.txt","c");
fwrite($r,"XXX");
fclose($r);

?></body></html>
```

```
XXXDEF123---
```

fread($r,$i) reads $i bytes from the file $r and returns the string. **fscanf($r,$s[,&$m...])** reads one line from the file $r and stores the values into &$m......, according to the format $s (see sscanf() and sprint()). If &$m is omitted, the values parsed will be returned as an array. Otherwise, the function will return the number of assigned values.

fgetc($r) reads and returns one character from the file $r. **fgets ($r[,$i])** reads and returns one line from the file $r. If $i is specified, reading ends when $i-1 bytes, a newline or EOF has been read (whichever comes first). **fgetss($r[,$i[,$s]])** is identical to fgets() except that it strips any NUL bytes, HTML and PHP tags from the text it reads. $s specifies the allowed tags. **fgetcsv ($r[,$i[,$s1=','[,$s2='"'[,$s3='\\']]]])** reads a line from the file $r, and returns an array containing the fields read. $i must be greater than the longest line in characters. $s1 sets the delimiter character. $s2 sets the enclosure character. $s3 sets the escape character. **file_get_contents($s[,$b=false[,$r[,$i1= -1 [,$i2]]]])** reads the entire file $s into a string. If $b is true, *include_path* will be searched. $r denotes the context resource and can be skipped by setting it to NULL. $i1 tells where the reading starts. $i2 tells the number of bytes to read. **file($s[,$i=0])** splits an entire file $s into lines and stores them into an array. $i can be any combination of:

FILE_USE_INCLUDE_PATH: Search the include_path.
FILE_IGNORE_NEW_LINES: Do not add a newline at the end of each array element.

FILE_SKIP_EMPTY_LINES
Skip empty lines.

readfile($s[,$b]) reads a file $s and outputs it. Set $b to true to search the include_path. This function returns the number of bytes read from the file, or false on error. **fpassthru($r)** reads to EOF on the file $r and outputs the results. It returns the number of bytes read from the file, or false on error.

```
<!DOCTYPE html><html><head></head>
<body><?php

file_put_contents("test.txt",
              "1,2,3,4,5
               a,b,c,d,e
               @,#,$,%,&");

readfile("test.txt");
echo "<br /><br />";

$r=fopen("test.txt","rb");
echo fread($r,3)."<br />";
echo fgets($r)."<br />";
print_r(fgetcsv($r));
echo "<br />";
fpassthru($r);
echo "<br /><br />";
fclose($r);

echo file_get_contents ("test.txt",false,NULL,0,10)."<br />";
print_r(file("test.txt"));

?></body></html>
```

```
1,2,3,4,5 a,b,c,d,e @,#,$,%,&

1,2
,3,4,5
Array ( [0] => a [1] => b [2] => c [3] => d [4] => e )
@,#,$,%,&

1,2,3,4,5
Array ( [0] => 1,2,3,4,5 [1] => a,b,c,d,e [2] => @,#,$,%,& )
```

feof($r) returns true if the position indicator in the file $r has reached the end-of-file. **ftell($r)** returns the current position of the position indicator in the file $r. **rewind($r)** sets the position indicator in the file $r to the beginning. **fseek($r,$i1[,$i2])** sets the position indicator in the file $r to be $i1 bytes away. It returns 0 upon success or -1 otherwise. $i2 can be:

SEEK_SET	$i1 bytes from the start
SEEK_CUR	$i1 bytes from the current position
SEEK_END	$i1 bytes from EOF

flock($r,$i) performs a portable advisory locking on the file $r. By default, this function will block until the requested lock is acquired. It returns true on success or false on failure. $i can be:

LOCK_SH	Acquire a shared lock (reader).
LOCK_EX	Acquire an exclusive lock (writer).
LOCK_UN	Release a lock.

```
<!DOCTYPE html><html><head></head>
<body><?php

file_put_contents("test.txt","1234567890");

$r=fopen("test.txt","rb");
fscanf($r,"123%d",$i);
echo $i."<br />";                    // 4567890
echo ftell($r)."<br />";             // 10
var_dump(feof($r));echo "<br />";  // bool(true)
rewind($r);
echo ftell($r)."<br />";             // 0
fseek($r,-3,SEEK_END);
echo ftell($r)."<br />";             // 7
fclose($r);

$r=fopen("test2.txt","wb");
if (flock($r,LOCK_EX)){
  $r2=fopen("test2.txt","wb");
  fwrite($r2,"ABC123");              // nothing written!
  fwrite($r,"DEF");
  fflush($r);
  flock($r,LOCK_UN);
} else {
  echo "Coundn't acquire the lock!";
}
fclose($r); fclose($r2);

?></body></html>
```

```
4567890
10
bool(true)
0
7
DEF
```

4.15 Mail Functions

mail($s1,$s2,$s3[,$s4[,$s5]]) sends an email to $s1, with the subject $s2, and the message $s3. $s5 are additional command line options. This function returns true if the mail was successfully accepted for delivery.

$s4 specifies extra headers separated by "\r\n" (if "\r\n" doesn't work, try "\n"). These headers include "From", "To", "Cc", "Bcc","Reply-To", "MIME-Version", "Content-type", "X-Mailer"......

4.15.1 Simple Mail

It is easy to send a simple mail.

```
<!DOCTYPE html><html><head></head>
<body><?php

mail("ambrose@yahoo.com, John<john1982@yahoo.com>",
       "Test 1",
       "This is a simple mail.",
       "From: admin@webpal-exchange.com \n".
         "To: mary2013@yahoo.com \n".
         "Cc: admin2@webpal-exchange.com \n".
         "Bcc: admin3@webpal-exchange.com \n".
   "Reply-To: Help Desk<support@webpal-exchange.com>\n".
         "X-Mailer: PHP/".phpversion())
or die("MAIL ERROR");

mail("Justine@yahoo.com",
       "Test 1",
       "This is a simple mail with an extra option.",
       null,
       "-fwebmaster@yahoo.com");

?> </body></html>
```

4.15.2 HTML Mail

To send an HTML mail, you need to change the content type in the header.

```
<!DOCTYPE html><html><head></head>
<body><?php

mail("fragment_shader@yahoo.com",
      "Test 2",
      "This is a <b>HTML mail</b>.".
        "<img src=http://www.example.com/image.gif>",
      "MIME-Version: 1.0 \n".
        "Content-type: text/html; charset=iso-8859-1 \n");

?> </body></html>
```

4.15.3 Alternative Part

For receivers that do not support HTML mails, you can send a multi-part mail with an alternative part. Notice the two dashes that precede each boundary and that mark the end of the entire message. Leave an empty line before and after the sub-messages.

```
<!DOCTYPE html><html><head></head>
<body><?php

// This creates a random hash for the boundary string
$boundary=md5(time());

$msg="
If you can see this then your client doesn't accept MIME types!

--$boundary
Content-Type: text/plain; charset=\"iso-8859-1\"
Content-Transfer-Encoding: 7bit

This is the simple, alternative mail.

--$boundary
Content-Type: text/html; charset=\"iso-8859-1\"
Content-Transfer-Encoding: 7bit

<h1>This is the HTML mail.</h1>

--$boundary--";

mail("example@yahoo.com",
  "Test 3",
  $msg,
  "From: admin@example.com\n".
  "Content-type: multipart/alternative;
                  boundary=\"$boundary\"");

?> </body></html>
```

4.15.4 Attachment

To send small attachment files, first capture the file contents into strings.

```
<!DOCTYPE html><html><head></head>
<body><?php

$boundary=md5(time());
$file1 =
chunk_split(base64_encode(file_get_contents('a.zip')));
$file2 =
chunk_split(base64_encode(file_get_contents('b.exe')));

$msg="
--$boundary
Content-Type: text/html; charset=\"iso-8859-1\"
Content-Transfer-Encoding: 7bit

<h1>This is the HTML mail.</h1>

--$boundary
Content-Type: application/octet-stream; name=\"a.zip\"
Content-Transfer-Encoding: base64
Content-Disposition: attachment

$file1

--$boundary
Content-Type: application/octet-stream; name=\"b.exe\"
Content-Transfer-Encoding: base64
Content-Disposition: attachment

$file2

--$boundary--";

mail("example@yahoo.com",
      "Test 4",
       $msg,
      "From: admin@example.com\n".
      "MIME-Version: 1.0\n".
      "Content-type: multipart/mixed;\n".
      "boundary=\"$boundary\"")
or die("MAIL ERROR");

?> </body></html>
```

4.16 JSON Functions

Apart from a text file, SQL and XML, JSON may be used to store, transport and manipulate data. An interesting comparison may be made between JSON-encoding and serialization(4.2.5). While serialization gives control over what to be encoded, a JSON-encoded string is more readable.

4.16.1 Encoding

An object or array can be encoded to become a JSON string: **json_encode($m [,$i1=0 [,$i2=512]])**. $m can be an object, an array, scalar types or NULL. $i1 is a bitmask consisting of JSON_HEX_QUOT, JSON_HEX_TAG, JSON_HEX_AMP, JSON_HEX_APOS, JSON_NUMERIC_CHECK, JSON_PRETTY_PRINT, JSON_UNESCAPED_SLASHES, JSON_FORCE_OBJECT, JSON_UNESCAPED_UNICODE. $i2 is a positive integer representing the maximum depth.

The string representation of a JSON object may be in the form of an object, denoted by {}, or an array, denoted by []. Scalar values are encoded into the same, corresponding types.

```
<?php

$a = array('a' => 1, 'b' => 2, 'c' => 3, 'd' => 4, 'e' => 5);
echo json_encode($a),"<br/>";

$a = array('<cat>',"'dog'",'"cow"','&fish&', "\xc4\xa9");
echo json_encode($a, JSON_HEX_TAG | JSON_HEX_APOS |
                      JSON_HEX_QUOT | JSON_HEX_AMP |
                      JSON_UNESCAPED_UNICODE),"<br/>";

$a = array(array(1,2,3));
echo json_encode($a), "<br/>";
echo json_encode($a, JSON_FORCE_OBJECT), "<br/>";

$a = array("cat", "dog", "cow", "fish");
echo json_encode($a), "<br/>";

unset($a[0]);
echo json_encode($a), "<br/>";

class cl{
  public $v1=1;
  private $v2=2;
}
```

```
$a = new cl;
echo json_encode($a), "<br/>";

echo json_encode("abc"), "<br/>";
echo json_encode(3);
?>
```

```
{"a":1,"b":2,"c":3,"d":4,"e":5}
["\u003Ccat\u003E","\u0027dog\u0027","\u0022cow\u0022",
"\u0026fish\u0026","Ã©"]
[[1,2,3]]
{"0":{"0":1,"1":2,"2":3}}
["cat","dog","cow","fish"]
{"1":"dog","2":"cow","3":"fish"}
{"v1":1}
"abc"
3
```

4.16.2 Decoding

To decode a JSON string $s, use **json_decode($s [,$b=false [,$i1=512 [,$i2=0]]])**. If $b is true, returned objects will be converted into associative arrays. $i1 specifies the recursion depth. $i2 can be JSON_BIGINT_AS_STRING. For the JSON strings, the names and string values must be enclosed in double quotes. Single quotes are not allowed.

```
<?php

$a = '{"a":1,"b":2,"c":3,"special-X":100}';
var_dump(json_decode($a));
var_dump(json_decode($a, true));

$b = json_decode($a);
echo $b->{'special-X'};  // - is not allowed originally

$a = '{"num": 12345678901234567890}';
var_dump(json_decode($a));
var_dump(json_decode($a, false, 512,
                        JSON_BIGINT_AS_STRING));

?>
```

```
object(stdClass)#1 (4) { ["a"]=> int(1) ["b"]=> int(2)
["c"]=> int(3) ["special-X"]=> int(100) }

array(4) { ["a"]=> int(1) ["b"]=> int(2) ["c"]=>
int(3) ["special-X"]=> int(100) }

100

object(stdClass)#2 (1) { ["num"]=>
float(1.2345678901235E+19) }

object(stdClass)#2 (1) { ["num"]=> string(20)
"12345678901234567890" }
```

4.16.3 Error Handling

json_last_error_msg() returns the error string of the last json_encode() or json_decode() call.

json_last_error() returns an integer which can be JSON_ERROR_{NONE|DEPTH|STATE_MISMATCH|CTRL_CHAR|SYNTAX|UTF8|RECURSION|INF_OR_NAN|UNSUPPORTED_TYPE}.

```
<?php
$o = json_decode('{"a":1,"b":2,"c":3,'); // extra comma
echo json_last_error_msg();
if (json_last_error() == JSON_ERROR_SYNTAX) echo 1;
?>
```

```
Syntax error1
```

4.17 Cryptography Functions

4.17.1 Password Hashing

Storing passwords as hashes adds an additional level of security to your system.

password_hash($s, $i [,$arr]) creates a one-way, password hash for the password $s. Password hashes created with crypt() can be used with password_hash(). $i denotes the algorithm, and can be PASSWORD_DEFAULT or PASSWORD_BCRYPT. The latter causes password $s to be truncated to 72 characters, and results in a hash that is always 60 characters. For PASSWORD_BCRYPT, you may specify $arr, an array containing the keys 'salt' and 'cost'. 'cost' denotes the algorithmic cost, and is 10 by default. **password_verify($s1, $s2)** returns true if the password $s1 matches the hash $s2. Note that password_hash() returns the algorithm, cost and salt as part of the returned hash.
password_needs_rehash($s, $i [,$arr]) returns true if the supplied hash $s does not implement the algorithm $i and $options $arr.
password_get_info($s) returns an array containing information about the hash.

```
<?php

$P = 'myPassword';
$O = [
   'cost' => 11,
   'salt' => mcrypt_create_iv(22, MCRYPT_DEV_URANDOM)];
$H = password_hash($P,PASSWORD_BCRYPT,$O);

echo $H;
var_dump(password_verify($P,$H));
var_dump(password_needs_rehash(
          $H,PASSWORD_BCRYPT,$O));
print_r(password_get_info($H));

?>
```

```
$2y$11$i9NVGbfeHnhlosoJr74r8.HtRLqlpcPzT5QBL0uWcuHDHF
zq6JxnO

bool(true)

bool(false)

Array ( [algo] => 1 [algoName] => bcrypt [options] => Array
( [cost] => 11 ) )
```

This determines for BCRYPT the maximum algorithmic cost given a time limit.

```
<?php

$timeTarget = 1.0;

$cost = 9;
do {
   $cost++;
   $start = microtime(true);
   password_hash("test", PASSWORD_BCRYPT,
                        ["cost" => $cost]);
   $end = microtime(true);
} while (($end - $start) < $timeTarget);

echo "Appropriate Cost Found: " . $cost . "\n";

?>
```

```
Appropriate Cost Found: 14
```

4.17.2 General Hashing

crc32($s) returns an integer which is the cyclic-redundancy-checksum polynomial of $s. It is 32 bits long. **crypt($s1[,$s2])** returns a hashed string of $s1, using the standard Unix DES-based algorithm. $s2 is the salt string to base the hashing on. **md5 ($s[,$b=false])** returns the MD5 hash of $s, which is a string storing a 32-character hexadecimal number. If $b is true, the hash is in raw binary format with a length of 16. **md5_file($s [,$b=false])** is similar to md5() except that instead of a string, $s is the name of the file to be hashed. **sha1($s [,$b=false])** returns the sha1 hash of $s, which is a string storing a 40-character hexadecimal number. If $b is true, the hash is in raw binary format with a length of 20. **sha1_file ($s[,b])** is similar to sha1() except that instead of a string, $s is the name of the file to be hashed.

```
<!DOCTYPE html><html><head></head>
<body><?php

$s = "hello world";
echo crc32($s)."<br />";
echo crypt($s)."<br />"; // different each time
echo crypt($s,"ABC")."<br />";
echo md5($s)."<br />";
echo sha1($s)."<br />";

?></body></html>
```

```
222957957
$1$wO/.3N0.$hDclc7tqBHh2mTlmamkxg1
AB5Fm/mCd2lgM
5eb63bbbe01eeed093cb22bb8f5acdc3
2aae6c35c94fcfb415dbe95f408b9ce91ee846ed
```

str_rot13($s) returns a copy of $s with ROT13 performed. ROT13 encoding shifts every letter by 13 places in the alphabet. Passing an encoded string as an argument will return the original version. **bin2hex($s)** returns a string containing the hexadecimal representation of $s. **hex2bin($s)** is the reverse of bin2hex(). **convert_uuencode($s)** returns a string that is $s encoded using the uuencode algorithm. Uuencode translates all strings into printable characters, making them safe for network transmissions. Uuencoded data is about 35% larger than the original. **convert_uudecode($s)** is the reverse of convert_uuencode(). **quoted_printable_encode($s)** returns a quoted printable string created according to RFC2045, Section 6.7, from a 8 bit string. **quoted_printable_decode($s)** is the reverse of quoted_printable_encode().

```
<!DOCTYPE html><html><head></head>
<body><?php

$s = "PHP 5.4.0\n\r";
echo str_rot13($s)."<br />";
echo str_rot13(str_rot13($s))."<br />";
echo bin2hex($s)."<br />";
echo hex2bin(bin2hex($s))."<br />";
echo convert_uuencode($s)."<br />";
echo convert_uudecode(convert_uuencode($s))."<br />";
echo quoted_printable_encode($s)."<br />";
echo quoted_printable_decode(
    quoted_printable_encode($s))."<br />";

?></body></html>
```

```
CUC 5.4.0
PHP 5.4.0
50485020352e342e300a0d
PHP 5.4.0
+4$A0(#4N-"XP"@T``
PHP 5.4.0
PHP 5.4.0=0A=0D
PHP 5.4.0
```

hash_algos() returns an array containing the names of all registered hashing algorithms.

```
<?php
print_r(hash_algos());
?>
```

```
Array ( [0] => md2 [1] => md4 [2] => md5 [3] => sha1 [4] => sha224 [5] => sha256 [6] => sha384 [7] => sha512 [8] => ripemd128 [9] => ripemd160 [10] => ripemd256 [11] => ripemd320 [12] => whirlpool [13] => tiger128,3 [14] => tiger160,3 [15] => tiger192,3 [16] => tiger128,4 [17] => tiger160,4 [18] => tiger192,4 [19] => snefru [20] => snefru256 [21] => gost [22] => adler32 [23] => crc32 [24] => crc32b [25] => fnv132 [26] => fnv164 [27] => joaat [28] => haval128,3 [29] => haval160,3 [30] => haval192,3 [31] => haval224,3 [32] => haval256,3 [33] => haval128,4 [34] => haval160,4 [35] => haval192,4 [36] => haval224,4 [37] => haval256,4 [38] => haval128,5 [39] => haval160,5 [40] => haval192,5 [41] => haval224,5 [42] => haval256,5 )
```

hash_file($s1, $s2 [,$b=false]) returns a hash for string $s2 using algorithm $s1. **hash_file($s1, $s2 [,$b=false])** returns a hash for file $s2 using algorithm $s1. If $b is true, raw binary data is output.

```
<?php
echo hash('sha1','Please code PHP well.')."<br/>";
file_put_contents('eg.txt', 'Please code PHP well.');
echo hash_file('sha1', 'eg.txt');
?>
```

```
8de35e94d666d764056f4750591c7d00aa416a7e
8de35e94d666d764056f4750591c7d00aa416a7e
```

hash_init($s1 [, $i=0 [, $s2=NULL]]) initializes an incremental hashing context, using algorithm $s1. $i can be HASH_HMAC. If $i is HASH_HMAC, $s2 specifies the secret key. **hash_update($r, $s)** pumps string $s into active hashing context $r. **hash_update_file($r, $s)** pumps data from file $s into active hashing context $r. **hash_final($r, $b=false)** finalizes an incremental hash (context $r) and returns the resulting digest. If $b is true, raw binary data is output.

```
<?php
$c = hash_init('md5');
hash_update($c, 'PHP is really fun.');
hash_update($c, 'Do you agree?');
hash_update_file($c,'eg.txt');
echo hash_final($c);
?>
```

```
751644bb4b3f66972833c561a2808faf
```

4.17.3 Encryption

```
<?php
  # --- ENCRYPTION ---

  # The key should be a random binary. Use scrypt, bcrypt or
  # PBKDF2 to convert a string into a key.
  # The key is specified using hexadecimal.
  $key = pack('H*', "bcb04b7e103a0cd8b54763051cef08bc".
                   "55abe029fdebae5e1d417e2ffb2a00a3");

  # This shows the key size. Use either 16-, 24- or 32- byte
  # keys for AES-128, 192 and 256 respectively
  $key_size =  strlen($key);
  echo "Key size: " . $key_size . "\n";

  $plaintext = "This string was AES-256 / CBC / ".
               "ZeroBytePadding encrypted.";

  # create a random IV to use with CBC encoding
  $iv_size = mcrypt_get_iv_size(MCRYPT_RIJNDAEL_128,
                                MCRYPT_MODE_CBC);
  $iv = mcrypt_create_iv($iv_size, MCRYPT_RAND);

  # creates a cipher text compatible with AES (Rijndael
  # block size = 128) to keep the text confidential
  # only suitable for encoded input that never ends with
  # value 00h (because of default zero padding)
  $ciphertext = mcrypt_encrypt(MCRYPT_RIJNDAEL_128,
               $key, $plaintext, MCRYPT_MODE_CBC, $iv);

  # prepend the IV for it to be available for decryption
  $ciphertext = $iv . $ciphertext;

  # encode the resulting cipher text so it can be
  # represented by a string
  $ciphertext_base64 = base64_encode($ciphertext);

  echo  $ciphertext_base64 . "\n";

  # === WARNING ===
  # Resulting cipher text has no integrity or authenticity
  # added and is not protected against padding oracle
  # attacks.

  # --- DECRYPTION ---

  $ciphertext_dec = base64_decode($ciphertext_base64);

  # retrieves the IV, iv_size should be created using
  # mcrypt_get_iv_size()
  $iv_dec = substr($ciphertext_dec, 0, $iv_size);

  # retrieves the cipher text (everything except the
  # $iv_size in the front)
  $ciphertext_dec = substr($ciphertext_dec, $iv_size);

  # may remove 00h valued characters from end of plain text
  $plaintext_dec = mcrypt_decrypt(MCRYPT_RIJNDAEL_128,
        $key, $ciphertext_dec, MCRYPT_MODE_CBC, $iv_dec);

  echo  $plaintext_dec . "\n";
?>
```

(courtesy of http://my1.php.net/manual/en/function.mcrypt-encrypt.php)

Key size: 32
XpcI9sgPpRsX6QZ4kTqSBQ2LzAQhI49720KMVLEQbousnLyKmaQAfM4MkNVYW1Z81uPBdihv0eTRfftFzfCV9lwOB2FGqtSEc5IuoQJG5yE=
This string was AES-256 / CBC / ZeroBytePadding encrypted.

4.18 ZIP Compression Functions

4.18.1 Adding Files

If archive.zip already exists, the files will be added to the archive. The second parameter to $zip->addFile() is optional.

```
<?php

$zip = new ZipArchive();
$filename = "./archive.zip";

if ($zip->open($filename, ZipArchive::CREATE)!==TRUE)
  exit("cannot open <$filename>\n");

$zip->addFile("test.php","new_name.php");

echo "numfiles: " . $zip->numFiles . "<br/>";
echo "status:" . $zip->status . "<br/>";
$zip->close();

?>
```

numfiles: 1
status:0

4.18.2 Retrieving Files

This extracts all entries.

```
<?php
$zip = new ZipArchive;
if ($zip->open('test.zip') === TRUE) {
   $zip->extractTo('.');
   $zip->close();
   echo 'ok';
} else {
   echo 'failed';
}
?>
```

This extracts two entries.

```
<?php
$zip = new ZipArchive;
$res = $zip->open('test_im.zip');
if ($res === TRUE) {
   $zip->extractTo('/myFolder/',array('a.gif', 'b.php'));
   $zip->close();
   echo 'ok';
} else {
   echo 'failed';
}
?>
```

4.18.3 Obtaining Information

This obtains the information about the individual files in the zip archive and prints their contents.

```
<?php
$zip = zip_open("test.zip");
if ($zip) {
   while ($zip_entry = zip_read($zip)) {
      echo "Name: " . zip_entry_name($zip_entry) . "<br/>";
      echo "Actual Filesize: " . zip_entry_filesize($zip_entry) .
           "<br/>";
      echo "Compressed Size:" .
           zip_entry_compressedsize($zip_entry) . "<br/>";
      echo "Compression Method: " .
           zip_entry_compressionmethod($zip_entry) .
           "<br/>";

      if (zip_entry_open($zip, $zip_entry, "r")) {
         echo "File Contents:<br/>";
         $buf = zip_entry_read($zip_entry,
                              zip_entry_filesize($zip_entry));
         echo "$buf<br/>";

         zip_entry_close($zip_entry);
```

```
        }
        echo "<br/>";
    }
    zip_close($zip);
}
?>
```

(Courtesy of http://my1.php.net/manual/en/zip.examples.php)

```
Name: new_name.php
Actual Filesize: 2214
Compressed Size: 948
Compression Method: deflated
File Contents: ...

Name: new_name2.php
Actual Filesize: 151
Compressed Size: 106
Compression Method: deflated
File Contents: ...

Name: new_name3.php
Actual Filesize: 302
Compressed Size: 202
Compression Method: deflated
File Contents: ...
```

4.19 Image Processing Functions

4.19.1 File Conversion

This function converts an image from any format to any format.

```
<?php

function image_convert($file, $targetType){
  // Obtain the file into memory
  $last3 = strtolower(substr($file, -3));
  $last4 = strtolower(substr($file, -4));
  $r = ($last3=='gif')?imagecreatefromgif($file):
       ($last3=='png')?imagecreatefrompng($file):
       ($last3=='jpg'||$last4=='jpeg')?
                        imagecreatefromjpeg($file):
       NULL;
  if (!r) die('Invalid source file');

  // Output the file
  $filebase = ($last4=='jpeg')?substr($file,0,-4):
                                substr($file,0,-3);
  $targetType = strtolower($targetType);
  if ($targetType=='gif') imagegif($r,$filebase."gif");
  else if ($targetType=='png') imagepng($r,$filebase."png");
  else if ($targetType=='jpg') imagejpeg($r,$filebase."jpg");
  else if ($targetType=='jpeg')imagejpeg($r,$filebase."jpeg");

  // Free the file from memory
  imagedestroy($r);
}

image_convert("testing.jpeg","png");

?>
```

4.19.2 Resizing

imagescale($r,$i1[,$i2=-1[,$i3=IMG_ BILINAER_FIXED]]) scales an image $r using the new width $i1 and new height $i2. A new image resource is returned. $i3 can be IMG_NEAREST_NEIGHBOUR, IMG_BILINEAR_FIXED, IMG_BICUBIC, IMG_BICUBIC_FIXED.

```
<?php

$rs=imagecreatefromjpeg("testing.jpg");
$rd=imagescale($rs,100,100);
imagejpeg($rd,"testing5.jpg");

?>
```

4.19.3 Cropping

```
<?php

$rs=imagecreatefromjpeg("testing.jpg");
$rd=imagecrop($rs,
        ['x'=>100,'y'=>100,'width'=>200,'height'=>200]);
imagejpeg($rd,"testing6.jpg");

?>
```

4.19.4 Watermarking

You can place an image on another image. You can make the background transparent by using the Magic Wand in Paint.NET.

```
<?php

$rd=imagecreatefromjpeg('testing.jpg');
$rs=imagecreatefrompng('watermark.png');
imagecopyresized($rd,
                 $rs,
                 0,              // destination X
                 0,              // destination Y
                 0,              // source X
                 0,              // source Y
                 100,            // destination width
                 100,            // destination height
                 imagesx($rs),   // source width
                 imagesy($rs));  // source height
imagejpeg($rd,'testing8.jpg');

?>
```

4.19.5 Translucent Watermarking

```
<?php

$rd=imagecreatefromjpeg('testing.jpg');
$rs=imagecreatefrompng('watermark2.png');
imagecopymerge($rd,
               $rs,
               0,              // destination X
               0,              // destination Y
               0,              // source X
               0,              // source Y
               imagesx($rs),   // source width
               imagesy($rs),   // source height
               30);            // opacity 0-100
imagejpeg($rd,'testing9.jpg');

?>
```

4.19.6 Adding Text

The return value is an array with 8 integers, corresponding in order, the lower-left corner, the lower-right corner, the upper-right corner, and the upper-left corner of the bounding box.

```
<?php

$rd=imagecreatefromjpeg('testing.jpg');
var_dump(
  imagettftext($rd,
               15,  // font size
               20,  // anticlockwise angle
               100, // x
               100, // y
               imagecolorallocate($rd, 255, 0, 0), // color
               'CURLZ___.ttf',   // font file
               'Hello World!!')); // text
imagejpeg($rd,'testing10.jpg');

?>
```

```
array(8) { [0]=> int(101) [1]=> int(104) [2]=> int(201)
[3]=> int(67) [4]=> int(194) [5]=> int(45) [6]=> int(92)
[7]=> int(82) }
```

4.19.7 Grayscaling

```
<?php

$rd=imagecreatefromjpeg('testing.jpg');
$W=imagesx($rd);
$H=imagesy($rd);
for ($x=0; $x<$W; $x++){
  for ($y=0; $y<$H; $y++){
    $rgb = imagecolorat($rd, $x, $y);
    $r = ($rgb >> 16) & 0xFF;
    $g = ($rgb >> 8) & 0xFF;
    $b = $rgb & 0xFF;
    $Ave = ($r+$g+$b)/3;
    imagesetpixel($rd, $x, $y,
                  imagecolorallocate($rd, $Ave, $Ave, $Ave));
  }
}
imagejpeg($rd,'testing11.jpg');

?>
```

4.19.8 Drawing

```
<?php

$I = imagecreatetruecolor(800,800);

$w = imagecolorallocate($I, 255, 255, 255);
$r = imagecolorallocate($I, 255, 0, 0);

imagefill($I,100,100,$w); // flood-fill the background to white

imagesetthickness($I,3);
imageline($I,30,20,770,20,$r);

imagesetstyle($I,[$r,$r,$r,$r,$w,$w,$w,$w]);
imageline($I,30,40,770,40,IMG_COLOR_STYLED);


// *** FIGURES DOWN FROM UPPER LEFT ***

// imagearc(img, center-X, center-Y, width, height,
//             start-angle, end-angle, color)
imagearc($I,100,150,100,100,0,270,$r);
imagefilledarc($I,100,250,100,100,0,270,$r,IMG_ARC_PIE);
imagefilledarc($I,100,350,100,100,0,90,$r,
                      IMG_ARC_CHORD|IMG_ARC_NOFILL);
imagefilledarc($I,100,450,100,100,0,270,$r,
                      IMG_ARC_PIE|IMG_ARC_NOFILL);
imagefilledarc($I,100,550,100,100,0,270,$r,
        IMG_ARC_PIE|IMG_ARC_NOFILL|IMG_ARC_EDGED);

// imagerectangle(img, upper-left-X, upper-left-Y
//                 lower-right-X, lower-right-Y, color)
imagerectangle($I,220,100,350,300,$r);
imagefilledrectangle($I,220,350,350,500,$r);

// imageellipse(img, center-X, center-Y,
//             width, height, color)
imageellipse($I,450,120,80,120,$r);
imagefilledellipse($I,450,300,80,120,$r);

// imagepolygon(img, points, pointsTotal, color)
imagepolygon($I,[600,120,700,120,600,250],3,$r);
imagefilledpolygon($I,[600,320,700,320,600,450],3,$r);

// output to browser
header('Content-Type: image/png');
imagepng($I);

?>
```

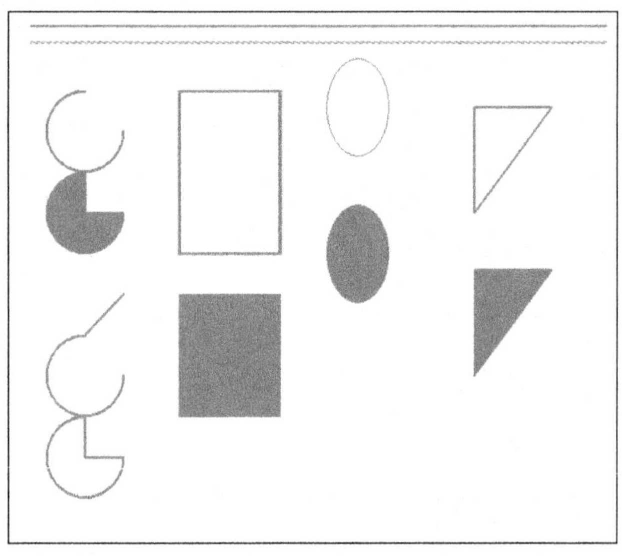

4.20 Program Execution Functions

In (4.1.4) we have seen how to execute PHP command strings with eval(...). You may also issue Unix or Windows commands within PHP.

escapeshellcmd($s) returns a string that escapes any characters in $s that might be used to 'hack' the shell command. In Unix, *# & ; ` | * ? ~ < > ^ ( ) [ ] { } $ \ ,* *\x0A* and *\xFF* are preceded by a backslash. ' and " are escaped only if they are not paired. In Windows, all these characters and % are replaced by a space instead, or preceded by ^.
escapeshellarg($s) returns a string that adds quotes around $s and replaces several special characters with a space, allowing you to pass a string directly, having it be treated as a single safe argument.

4.20.1 With Output Displayed

passthru($s [, &$i]) executes an external command $s and displays the raw output by passing the data back directly without any interference. $i stores the return status of the Unix command. No value is returned. **system($s [, &$i])** is identical to passthru() but tries to flush the web server's output buffer after each line of output. The latter function returns the last line of command output.

```
<?php

passthru('whoami');
echo "\n\n";

$cmd = "dir /w "; // from visitor's input
$arg = "tmp";     // from visitor's input
system(escapeshellcmd($cmd).escapeshellarg($arg));

?>
```

```
nt authority\system


 Volume in drive C has no label.
 Volume Serial Number is 8007-B8AB
```

```
 Directory of C:\Program
Files\Zend\Apache2\htdocs\PHP\tmp

[.]                        [..]
image_conversion.php  image_crop.php
image_drawing.php      image_greyscale.php
image_resize.php       image_resize2.php
image_text.php          image_watermark.php
image_watermark_translucent.php
              9 File(s)         3,521 bytes
              2 Dir(s)  205,990,244,352 bytes free
```

4.20.2 Without Output Displayed

Identical to the backtick operator ``, **shell_exec($s)** executes the external command $s and returns the output as a string. NULL is returned if an error occurred or the command produces no output.
exec($s [, &$arr [, &i]]) executes the external command $s, and stores the output lines and return status in the array $arr and the integer $i respectively. It returns the last line from the result of the command.

popen($s1, $s2) forks the external command $s1, and returns a file pointer that can be used by fgets(), fgetss(), and fwrite(). When $s2 is 'r', the returned file pointer equals STDOUT. When $s2 is 'w', the returned file pointer equals STDIN. **pclose($r)** closes a file pointer opened by popen().

```
<?php

echo `dir`; // not single quotes!
echo shell_exec('dir');
shell_exec('dir',$arr);
$r = popen('dir','r');
echo fgets($r);

?>
```

proc_open($s1, $arr1, $arr2 [, $s2 [, $arr3 [, $arr4]]]) forks the external command $s1 and returns a file pointer. $arr1 is an indexed array where the keys can be 0(stdin), 1(stdout), or 2(stderr), and the value represents how PHP will pass that descriptor to the child process. The valid values are arrays with the first element being 'pipe' (the second element is 'r' or 'w') or 'file' (the second element is a filename). $arr2 will be set to an index array of file pointers that correspond to PHP's end of any pipes created.
$s2 is the absolute working directory of the command.
$arr3 is an array with the environment variables for the command that will be run, or NULL to use the same environment as the current PHP process.
$arr4 currently work for Windows only, and can include the keys 'suppress_error' (TRUE or FALSE) and 'bypass_shell' (TRUE or FALSE).
proc_close($r) closes the resource opened by proc_open().

```
<?php
$descriptorspec = array(
   0 => array("pipe", "r"),  // pipe that the child will read from
   1 => array("pipe", "w"),  // pipe that the child will write to
   2 => array("file", "/tmp/error-output.txt", "a") //file to write
);

$cwd = '/tmp';
$env = array('some_option' => 'aeiou');

$process = proc_open('php',
                     $descriptorspec, $pipes, $cwd, $env);

if (is_resource($process)) {
   // $pipes now looks like this:
   // 0 => writeable handle connected to child stdin
   // 1 => readable handle connected to child stdout
   // Any error output will be appended to
   //  /tmp/error-output.txt

   fwrite($pipes[0], '<?php print_r($_ENV); ?>');
   fclose($pipes[0]);

   echo stream_get_contents($pipes[1]);
   fclose($pipes[1]);

   // It is important that you close any pipes before calling
   // proc_close in order to avoid a deadlock
   $return_value = proc_close($process);

   echo "command returned $return_value\n";
}
?>
```

(courtesy of http://www.php.net/manual/en/function.proc-open.php)

4.21 Network Functions

4.21.1 IP Address

checkdnsrr($s1 [,$s2="MX"]) or **dns_check_record($s1 [,$s2="MX"])** searches DNS for records of type $s2 corresponding to host $s1. $s2 can be A, MX, NS, SOA, PTR, CNAME, AAAA, A6, SRV, NAPTR, TXT or ANY. TRUE is returned if any records are found.

getmxrr($s, &$arr1 [,&$arr2]) or **dns_get_mx($s, &$arr1 [,&$arr2])** searches DNS for MX records corresponding to host $s and stores them in $arr1. $arr2 stores the weight information.

dns_get_record($s [, $i=DNS_ANY [, &$arr1 [, &$arr2 [, &$b=false]]]]) returns an associative array of DNS Resource Records associated with the host $s. $i specifies the type and can be DNS_A, DNS_CNAME, DNS_HINFO, DNS_MX, DNS_NS, DNS_PTR, DNS_SOA, DNS_TXT, DNS_AAAA, DNS_SRV, DNS_NAPTR, DNS_A6, DNS_ALL or DNS_ANY. $arr1 stores the Resource Records for the Authoritative Name Servers. $arr2 stores Additional Records. $b specifies whether to use raw mode, in which only the requested type is queried, instead of looping type by type before going with the additional information.

```
<?php
echo "<pre>";
var_dump(checkdnsrr("www.google.com","A"));
var_dump(getmxrr("binarybehemoth.com",$arr));
print_r($arr);
print_r(dns_get_record("binarybehemoth.com"));
echo "</pre>";
?>
```

```
bool(true)
bool(true)
Array
(
    [0] => mail.binarybehemoth.com
)
Array
(
    [0] => Array
        (
            [host] => binarybehemoth.com
            [class] => IN
            [ttl] => 900
            [type] => MX
            [pri] => 5
            [target] => mail.binarybehemoth.com
        )

    [1] => Array
        (
            [host] => binarybehemoth.com
            [class] => IN
            [ttl] => 899
            [type] => NS
            [target] => ns4.no-ip.com
        )

    [2] => Array
        (
            [host] => binarybehemoth.com
            [class] => IN
            [ttl] => 899
            [type] => NS
            [target] => ns5.no-ip.com
        )

    [3] => Array
        (
            [host] => binarybehemoth.com
            [class] => IN
            [ttl] => 899
            [type] => NS
            [target] => ns2.no-ip.com
        )

    [4] => Array
        (
            [host] => binarybehemoth.com
            [class] => IN
            [ttl] => 899
            [type] => NS
            [target] => ns1.no-ip.com
        )

    [5] => Array
        (
            [host] => binarybehemoth.com
            [class] => IN
            [ttl] => 899
            [type] => NS
            [target] => ns3.no-ip.com
        )

)
```

gethostname() returns the host name for the local machine as a string. **gethostbyname($s)** returns as a string the IPv4 address of the Internet host $s.

gethostbynamel($s) returns as an array a list of IPv4 addresses of the Internet host $s. **gethostbyaddr($s)** returns as a string the host name of the Internet host specified by the IP address $s.

```
<?php
echo "<pre>";
echo gethostname()."\n";
echo gethostbyname('www.google.com')."\n";
print_r(gethostbynamel('www.google.com'));
echo gethostbyaddr('173.194.127.80');
echo "</pre>";
?>
```

```
Phang
173.194.127.83
Array
(
    [0] => 173.194.127.83
    [1] => 173.194.127.84
    [2] => 173.194.127.80
    [3] => 173.194.127.81
    [4] => 173.194.127.82
)
hkg03s11-in-f16.1e100.net
```

getprotobynumber($i) returns as a string the protocol name associated with a protocol number. **getprotobyname($s)** returns as an integer the protocol number associated with a protocol name $s. **getservbyport($i,$s)** returns as a string the Internet service associated with port $i and protocol $s. **getservbyname($s1, $s2)** returns as an integer the port number associated with the Internet service $s1 and protocol $s2.

```
<?php
echo "<pre>";

for ($i=0; $i<70; $i++) echo $i."(".getprotobynumber($i).")";

echo "\n".getprotobyname('tcp')."\n";

$services = array('http', 'ftp', 'ssh', 'telnet', 'imap','smtp',
                  'nicname', 'gopher', 'finger', 'pop3', 'www');
foreach ($services as $service) {
   $port = getservbyname($service, 'tcp');
   echo $service . ": " . $port . "\n";
}

echo getservbyport(80,'tcp');

echo "</pre>";
?>
```

```
0(ip)1(icmp)2()3(ggp)4()5()6(tcp)7()8(egp)9()10()11()12(pu
p)13()14()15()16()17(udp)18()19()20(hmp)21()22(xns-
idp)23()24()25()26()27(rdp)28()29()30()31()32()33()34()35(
)36()37()38()39()40()41(ipv6)42()43(ipv6-route)44(ipv6-
frag)45()46()47()48()49()50(esp)51(ah)52()53()54()55()56()
57()58(ipv6-icmp)59(ipv6-nonxt)60(ipv6-opts)61()62()63()
64()65()66(rvd)67()68()69()

6
http: 80
ftp: 21
ssh: 22
telnet: 23
imap: 143
smtp: 25
nicname: 43
gopher: 70
finger: 79
pop3: 110
```

```
www: 80
http
```

inet_pton($s) converts a human-readable IP address $s to its packed string representation. **inet_ntop($s)** converts a packed string internet address $s to a human-readable representation. **ip2long($s)** converts an IP address into an integer. **long2ip($i)** converts an integral IP address into a string in Internet-standard dotted format.

```
<?php
echo "<pre>";
echo inet_pton('115.135.180.20')."\n";
echo inet_ntop(inet_pton('115.135.180.20'))."\n";
echo ip2long('115.135.180.20')."\n";
echo long2ip(1938273300)."\n";
echo "</pre>";
?>
```

```
s‡´
115.135.180.20
1938273300
115.135.180.20
```

4.21.2 System Logging

syslog($i, $s) generates a log message $s with the priority $i. $i can be LOG_EMERG, LOG_ALERT, LOG_CRIT, LOG_ERR, LOG_WARNING, LOG_NOTICE, LOG_INFO, or LOG_DEBUG. '%m' in $s will be replaced by the error message corresponding to the present value of errno. TRUE is returned on success.

```
<?php
var_dump(syslog(LOG_ERR, "System failed"));
?>
```

```
bool(true)
```

4.21.3 HTTP Header

header($s [,$b=true [, $i]]) sends a raw HTTP header as specified by $s. Its call must precede any output, including HTML tags, spaces, and PHP output. $b specifies whether to replace a previous similar header. If $b is FALSE, a second header of the same type will be added. $i specifies the HTTP response code.

This forces *test.exe* to be downloaded as *download.exe*. Note that this hides the URL of the source.

```
<?php

// The MIME type
header('Content-type: application/octet-stream');

// The target name
header('Content-Disposition: attachment;
filename="download.exe"');

// The source
readfile('test.exe');

?>
```

This also forces *test.exe* to be downloaded, but the URL may be shown in a download manager.

```
<?php
header("Location: test.exe");
?>
```

This redirects the browser to a new page. A status code of 302 (REDIRECT) will also be sent. Here an absolute URL path instead of a relative one is used.

```
<?php
header("Location: http://binarybehemoth.com");
?>
```

This disables caching at the client's side.

```
<?php
header("Cache-Control: no-cache, must-revalidate");
header("Expires: Mon, 26 Jul 2010 08:00:00 GMT"); // past
?>
```

header_remove($s) removes a header previously set using header(). **headers_list()** returns an array of response headers sent (or ready to be sent). **headers_sent([&$s [, &$i]])** returns true if the header block has been sent. No more header lines can be sent using header(), once the headers have been sent. $s stores the PHP source file name while $i stores the line number where output started. **header_register_callback($func)** registers a function that will be called after PHP prepares all headers to be sent, before any other output is sent, and before any headers are sent. **http_presponse_ code([$i])** returns or sets the HTTP response code. If $i is provided, the response code will be set; otherwise you will get the response code.

```
<?php
header("Field1: ABC");
header("Field2: DEF");
header("Field3: GHI");
header_remove("Field2");
header_register_callback(callback);
$headers=headers_list();
var_dump(headers_sent());
print_r($headers);
echo http_response_code();

function callback(){
  header_remove("Field2");
}
?>
```

```
bool(false) Array ( [0] => X-Powered-By: ZendServer 6.3.0
[1] => Field1: ABC [2] => Field3: GHI ) 200
```

4.21.4 URL

urlencode($s) returns an encoded string by replacing in $s all non-alphanumeric characters (except -_.) with a % sign followed by two hex digits, and all spaces by a + sign. This allows data to be passed along with the URL using the GET method. **urldecode($s)** decodes any %## encoding in the string $s. + signs are decoded to a space character.

rawurlencode($s) is similar to urlencode($s) except that ~ signs are not encoded and spaces are encoded as %##. **rawurldecode($s)** is similar to urldecode($s) except that + signs are not decoded.

base64_encode($s) encodes $s with MIME base64 to make binary data survive transport through transport layers that are not 8-bit clean. **base64_ decode($s)** is the reverse of base64_ encode($s).

```
<?php

echo "<pre>";

$test = ' -_.~+!@#$%^&';
echo urlencode($test)."\n";
echo rawurlencode($test)."\n";
echo base64_encode($test);

echo "</pre>";

?>
```

```
+-_.%7E%2B%21%40%23%24%25%5E%26
%20-_.~%2B%21%40%23%24%25%5E%26
IC1fLn4rIUAjJCVeJg==
```

parse_url($s [, $i=-1]) returns an array containing the URL components of $s. If $i is one of PHP_URL_SCHEME, PHP_URL_HOST, PHP_URL_PORT, PHP_URL_USER,PHP_URL_PASS, PHP_URL_PATH, PHP_URL_QUERY or PHP_URL_FRAGMENT, a string is returned instead, and the string contains just the specified component.

```
<?php
echo "<pre>";
print_r(parse_url('http://username:password@hostname/path
?arg=value#anchor'));
echo "</pre>";
?>
```

```
Array
(
    [scheme] => http
    [host] => hostname
    [user] => username
    [pass] => password
    [path] => /path
    [query] => arg=value
    [fragment] => anchor
)
```

get_headers($s [,$i=0]) returns an array with the headers sent by the server in response to the HTTP request $s. If $i is set to non-zero, the response is parsed and the array's keys are set.

```
<?php
echo "<pre>";
print_r(get_headers("http://www.google.com",1));
echo "</pre>";
?>
```

```
Array
(
    [0] => HTTP/1.0 302 Found
    [Location] =>
http://www.google.com.my/?gws_rd=cr&ei=27FPU-S7O-
fniAf4v4GoCQ
    [Cache-Control] => Array
        (
            [0] => private
            [1] => private, max-age=0
        )

    [Content-Type] => Array
        (
            [0] => text/html; charset=UTF-8
            [1] => text/html; charset=ISO-8859-1
        )

    [Set-Cookie] => Array
        (
            [0] =>
PREF=ID=d115201d75f3707f:FF=0:TM=1397731803:LM=139
7731803:S=IiTOX1VG8tEZBzxv; expires=Sat, 16-Apr-2016
10:50:03 GMT; path=/; domain=.google.com
            [1] => NID=67=T_q3Tm11ZZXK6PSDi2QoPpzfQ1r8-
rged9RopxpI5d1ikLo8-
RpjczHHS4QtVhbxL8r_XHkrVb2RZlFduHmcKtkDxyVM4GQa3j1L
cKLLlM9h9-6COnFpHAEZ5Yv7y1Au; expires=Fri, 17-Oct-2014
10:50:03 GMT; path=/; domain=.google.com; HttpOnly
            [2] =>
PREF=ID=92c098fcba592628:FF=0:TM=1397731804:LM=139
7731804:S=MI0uB5GJFK7ZZ0-w; expires=Sat, 16-Apr-2016
10:50:04 GMT; path=/; domain=.google.com.my
            [3] =>
NID=67=PNjAby1rLsDXZwsY0c9DKEKLw1N9aAZblB9KoOFiUp
ZZq0Ktg3yfczdeu4YsoX2p2LwWYYk-
qxKIl6PIuppc8VHzCnrwMzyL1GAVbM7zc5MUMY0xTRiCHTUhLZ
YOJbfW; expires=Fri, 17-Oct-2014 10:50:04 GMT; path=/;
domain=.google.com.my; HttpOnly
        )

    [P3P] => Array
        (
            [0] => CP="This is not a P3P policy! See
http://www.google.com/support/accounts/bin/answer.py?hl=e
n&answer=151657 for more info."
            [1] => CP="This is not a P3P policy! See
http://www.google.com/support/accounts/bin/answer.py?hl=e
n&answer=151657 for more info."
        )

    [Date] => Array
        (
            [0] => Thu, 17 Apr 2014 10:50:03 GMT
            [1] => Thu, 17 Apr 2014 10:50:04 GMT
        )

    [Server] => Array
        (
            [0] => gws
            [1] => gws
        )

    [Content-Length] => 262
    [X-XSS-Protection] => Array
        (
            [0] => 1; mode=block
            [1] => 1; mode=block
        )

    [X-Frame-Options] => Array
        (
            [0] => SAMEORIGIN
            [1] => SAMEORIGIN
        )

    [Alternate-Protocol] => Array
        (
            [0] => 80:quic
            [1] => 80:quic
        )

    [1] => HTTP/1.0 200 OK
    [Expires] => -1
)
```

get_meta_tags($s [,$b=false]) opens the file $s and parses it for <meta> tags in the file, until </head> is met, and returns an associative array. If $b is true, the path specified by the include_path directive will be searched as well.

```
<?php
echo "<pre>";
print_r(get_meta_tags('test.html'));
echo "</pre>";
?>
```

```
<html>
<head>
  <title>Test Page</title>
  <meta name="author" content="Lip Phang"/>
  <meta name="keywords" content="Advanced PHP"/>
  <meta name="DESCRIPTION" content="URL Functions"/>
</head>
<body>
Hello
</body>
</html>
```

```
Array
(
    [author] => Lip Phang
    [keywords] => Advanced PHP
    [description] => URL Functions
)
```

http_build_query($arr [,$s1 [,$s2 [$i=PHP_QUERY_RFC1738]]]) generates a URL-encoded query string from the array provided. $s1 specifies the prefix to be prepended to any numeric indices in the array. $s2 specifies the arguments separator, which is & by default. $i specifies the encoding type, which can be PHP_QUERY_RFC1738 (spaces encoded as +), or PHP_QUERY_RFC3986 (spaces encoded as %20).

```
<?php
$arr = ['a'=>1, 'b'=>2, 3];
echo http_build_query($arr,'num')."<br/>";

class O{
   private $a=1;
   public $b=2;
}
$obj = new O;
echo http_build_query($obj);
?>
```

```
a=1&b=2&num0=3
b=2
```

4.22 Socket Functions

(The material presented in this section can get rather technical. If you find it too complex, you may wish to skip to 4.22.6 to see how sockets really work with PHP. The codes for WebSocket can be downloaded at the official website of this book.)

Before a client can connect to the server over a socket connection, a listening socket needs to be set up first at the server's end.

4.22.1 Initialization

socket_create($i1, $i2, $i3) creates and returns a socket resource. **socket_create_pair($i1, $i2, $i3, &$arr)** creates two connected, indistinguishable sockets and stores them in $arr. The latter function is often used in IPC (Interprocess Communication).

$i1	
AF_INET	IPv4
AF_INET6	IPv6
AF_UNIX	Efficient local communication (for Interprocess Communication)
$i2	
SOCK_STREAM	Sequenced, reliable, full-duplex, connection-based byte streams. (TCP)
SOCK_DGRAM	Connectionless, unreliable datagrams of fixed maximum length. (UDP)
SOCK_SEQPACKET	Sequenced, reliable, two-way connection-based datagrams of fixed maximum length.
SOCK_RAW	Raw protocol access used to construct any type of protocol such as ICMP requests.
SOCK_RDM	Datagram layer that does not guarantee ordering. Probably not implemented on your operating system.
$i3	
SOL_TCP	TCP is reliable, connection-based, stream oriented, and full-duplexed.
SOL_UDP	UDP is connectionless, unreliable, and uses fixed record lengths, requiring a minimum amount of protocol overhead.
(icmp)	ICMP is mainly used to report errors in datagram communication. The 'ping' command is an example of ICMP. The integral parameter should be retrieved with getprotobyname('icmp').

socket_bind($r, $s [, $i=0]) binds the address $s and the port $i to the socket $r. If AF_INET is used, $s is in dotted-quad notation (eg. 127.0.0.1); if AF_UNIX is used, $s is the path of a Unix-domain socket (eg. Tmp/my.sock). TRUE is returned on success and FALSE on failure.

socket_set_option($r, $i1, $i2, $m) sets, for socket $r, at protocol level $i1, the option $i2 to a value of $m. For $i1, SOL_SOCKET is used for the socket level, and the protocol numbers (by getprotobyname()) for other levels. TRUE is returned on success and FALSE on failure:

$i2
SO_DEBUG (int): whether debugging information is being recorded.
SO_BROADCAST (int): whether the transmission of broadcast messages is supported.
SO_REUSEADDR (int): whether local addresses can be reused.
SO_KEEPALIVE (int): whether connections are kept active with periodic transmission of messages. If the connected socket fails to respond to these messages, the connection is broken and the processes writing to that socket are notified with a SIGPIPE signal.
SO_LINGER (array with two keys: *l_onoff* and *l_linger*): whether the socket lingers on socket_close() if data is present. By default, when the socket is closed, it attempts to send all unsent data. In the case of a connection-oriented socket, socket_close() will wait for its peer to acknowledge the data. If *l_onoff* is non-zero and *l_linger* is zero, all the unsent data will be discarded and RST (reset) is sent to the peer in the case of a connection-oriented socket. If *l_onoff* is non-zero and *l_linger* is non-zero, socket_close() will block until all the data is sent or the time specified in *l_linger* elapses. If the socket is non-blocking, socket_close() will fail and return an error.
SO_OOBINLINE (int): whether the socket leaves out-of-band data inline.
SO_SNDBUF (int): the size of the send buffer.
SO_RCVBUF (int): the size of the receive buffer.

SO_ERROR (int): information about error status and clears it, for socket_get_option() only.
SO_TYPE (int): the socket type (eg. SOCK_STREAM), for socket_get_option() only.
SO_DONTROUTE (int): whether outgoing messages bypass the standard routing facilities.
SO_RCVLOWAT (int): the minimum number of bytes to process for socket input operations.
SO_RCVTIMEO (array with two keys: *sec*, for seconds part, and *usec*, for microseconds part): the timeout value for input operations.
SO_SNDTIMEO (as in SO_RECVTIMEO): the timeout value specifying the amount of time that an output function blocks because flow control prevents data from being sent.
SO_SNDLOWAT (int): the minimum number of bytes to process for socket output operations.
TCP_NODELAY (int): whether the Nagle TCP algorithm is disabled.
MCAST_JOIN_GROUP (array with two keys: *group*, for multicast address, and *interface* for interface number or name): joins a multicast group, for socket_set_option() only.
MCAST_LEAVE_GROUP (array as in MCAST_JOIN_GROUP): leaves a multicast group, for socket_set_option() only.
MCAST_BLOCK_SOURCE (array as in MCAST_JOIN_GROUP, plus the key *source*, which maps to a string specifying an IPv4 or IPv6 address of the source to be blocked): blocks packets arriving from a specific source to a specific multicast group, for socket_set_option() only.
MCAST_UNBLOCK_SOURCE (array as in MCAST_BLOCK_ SOURCE): unblocks packets arriving from a specific source address to a specific multicast group, for socket_set_option() only.
MCAST_JOIN_SOURCE_GROUP (array as in MCAST_BLOCK_ SOURCE): receives packets destined to a specific multicast group whose source address matches a specific value, for socket_set_option() only.
MCAST_LEAVE_SOURCE_GROUP (array as in MCAST_BLOCK_ SOURCE): stops receiving packets destined to a specific multicast group whose source address matches a specific value, for socket_set_option() only.
IP_MULTICAST_IF (int, for the interface number, or string with an interface name like eth0): the outgoing interface for IPv4 multicast packets.
IPV6_MULTICAST_IF (as in IP_MULTICAST_IF): the outgoing interface for IPv6 multicast packets.
IP_MULTICAST_LOOP (int): the multicast loopback policy for IPv4 packets, which determines whether multicast packets sent by this socket also reach receivers in the same host that have joined the same multicast group on the outgoing interface used by this socket. This is the case by default.
IPV6_MULTICAST_LOOP (int): analogous to IP_MULTICAST_ LOOP but for IPv6.
IP_MULTICAST_TTL (int between 0 and 255): the time-to-live of outgoing IPv4 multicast packets. This should be a value between 0 (don't leave the interface) and 255. The default value is 1 (only the local network is reached).
IPV6_MULTICAST_HOPS (int between -1 and 255): analogous to IP_MULTICAST_TTL, but for IPv6 packets. -1 is also accepted, meaning the route default should be used.

socket_set_block($r) sets blocking mode on the socket $r. When an operation (receive, send, connect, accpt...) is performed on a blocking socket, the script will pause its execution until it receives a signal or it can perform the operation. **socket_set_nonblock ($r)** is the opposite of the previous function. For these functions, TRUE is returned on success and FALSE on failure.

socket_import_stream($r) imports a stream that encapsulates a socket and returns an extension socket.

socket_close($r) closes the socket $r, which was created with socket_create() or socket_accept().

4.22.2 Connecting

socket_listen($r [,$i=0]) listens for incoming connections on socket $r, applicable only to types SOCK_STREAM and SOCK_SEQPACKET. $i specifies the maximum number of incoming connections that will be queued for processing. (The maximum is given by SOMAXCONN).

socket_create_listen($i1 [,$i2=128]) returns a socket on port $i1 which only listens to accept new connections. $i2 specifies the maximum number of incoming connections that will be queued for processing.

socket_accept($r) accepts incoming connections to the listening socket $r, and returns a new socket. This function will block until a connection becomes present.

socket_connect($r, $s [,$i=0]) connects to the address $s using the socket $r and port $i. **socket_select(&$arr1, &$arr2, &$arr3, $i1 [,$i2])** waits for arrays of sockets to change status. $arr1 will be watched to see if characters become available for reading. $arr2 will be watched to see if write will not block. $arr3 will be watched for exceptions. $i1 is the seconds and $i2 is the microseconds for the timeout parameter, which is an upper bound on the time elapsed before socket_ select() return. If $i1 is NULL, the function can block indefinitely. On exit, this function modifies the arrays to indicate which sockets changed status. It returns the number of sockets contained in the modified arrays.

4.22.3 Reading

socket_read($r, $i1 [,$i2=PHP_BINARY_READ]) reads a maximum of $i1 bytes from the socket $r and returns the string read. If $i2 is PHP_NORMAL_READ, reading stops at \n or \r. FALSE is returned on error.

socket_recv($r, &$s, $i1, $i2) retrieves $i1 bytes of data from the socket $r and stores it into $s. **socket_recvfrom($r, &$s1, $i1, $i2, &$s2 [,$i3])** retrieves $i1 bytes of data from address $s2 on port $i3 through socket $r and stores it in $s1. **socket_ recvmsg($r, $s [,$i2])** reads message $s on socket $r. These functions return the number of bytes received, or FALSE on error. $i2 is a combination of:

MSG_OOB	Processes out-of-band data.
MSG_PEEK	Receives data from the beginning of the queue without removing it from the queue.
MSG_WAITALL	Blocks until at least $i bytes are received. If a signal is caught or the remote host disconnects, the function may return less data.
MSG_DONTWAIT	Returns even if it would normally have blocked.

4.22.4 Writing

socket_write($r, $s [, $i]) writes $i bytes of data from $s on the socket $r. This function returns the number of bytes written, or FALSE on failure.

socket_send($r, $s, $i1, $i2) sends $i2 bytes of data from $s to the socket $r using the flags $i2. **socket_sendto($r, $s1, $i1, $i2, $s2 [, $i3])** sends $i1 bytes of data from $s1 through the socket $r to port $i3 at the address $s2. **socket_sendmsg ($r, $arr [,$i2])** sends the message in $arr through the socket $r using the flags $i2. These functions return the number of bytes sent, or FALSE on error. $i2 is a combination of:

MSG_OOB	Sends out-of-band data.
MSG_EOR	Indicates a record mark. The sent data completes the record.
MSG_EOF	Closes the sender side of the socket and includes an appropriate notification of this at the end of the sent data. The sent data completes the transaction.
MSG_DONTROUTE	Bypasses routing, uses direct interface.

socket_shutdown($r [,$i]) shuts down a socket for receiving, sending, or both. $i can be 0 (stops reading), 1 (stops writing), or 2 (stops reading and writing).

4.22.5 Information

socket_get_option($r, $i1, $i2) gets the value of socket option $i2 on the protocol level $i1 for socket $r. For more information, refer to socket_set_option ().

socket_cmsg_space($i1, $i2) calculates the message buffer size for type $i2 on protocol level $i1.

socket_getpeername($r, &$s [,&$i]) retrieves the address and port of the remote side of the socket $r and stores them in $s and $i respectively. TRUE is returned on success and FALSE on failure. **socket_getsockname($r, &$s [,&$i])** retrieves the address and port of the local side of the socket $r and stores them in $s and $i respectively. TRUE is returned on success and FALSE on failure.

socket_last_error([$r]) returns the last error on the socket $r as an integer. **socket_strerror($i)** returns a string describing an error integer. **socket_clear_error([$r])** clears the error on the socket $r or the last error code.

4.22.6 Chat App with Web Socket

If you are using a domain name, make sure you forward the port at your modem router appropriately.

To maintain a persistent listening socket at the server, you must run the following PHP script in the Windows command line on the computer where PHP is installed. Simply enter 'PHP -q server.php' and leave the window open. To run the command automatically in the background, place the command in a batch file and use a service manager such as NSSM, RunAsService, and AlwaysUp.

```
<?php
// server.php
$host = 'localhost';
$port = '30000';
$null = NULL; // to be passed by reference

$socket = socket_create(AF_INET, SOCK_STREAM, SOL_TCP);
socket_set_option($socket, SOL_SOCKET,
                             SO_REUSEADDR, 1);
socket_bind($socket, 0, $port);
socket_listen($socket);
$clients = array($socket);

while (true) {
  $changed = $clients;
  socket_select($changed, $null, $null, 0, 10);

  // check for any new socket
  if (in_array($socket, $changed)) {
    $socket_new = socket_accept($socket);
    $clients[] = $socket_new;
    $header = socket_read($socket_new, 1024);
    perform_handshaking($header, $socket_new, $host,
                                                  $port);
    socket_getpeername($socket_new, $ip); // the ip address
    $response = json_encode(array('type'=>'system',
                       'message'=>$ip.' connected'));
    send_message($response);
    $found_socket = array_search($socket, $changed);
    unset($changed[$found_socket]);
  }

  foreach ($changed as $changed_socket) {
    while(socket_recv($changed_socket, $buf, 1024, 0)>=1){
      $received_text = unmask($buf);
      $tst_msg = json_decode($received_text);
      $user_name = $tst_msg->name;
      $user_message = $tst_msg->message;
      $user_color = $tst_msg->color;
      $response_text = json_encode(array(
              'type'=>'usermsg', 'name'=>$user_name,
          'message'=>$user_message, 'color'=>$user_color));
      send_message($response_text);
      break 2;
    }

    // check disconnected client
    $buf = @socket_read($changed_socket, 1024,
                        PHP_NORMAL_READ);
    if ($buf === false) {
      $found_socket = array_search($changed_socket,
                                     $clients);
      socket_getpeername($changed_socket, $ip);
      unset($clients[$found_socket]);
      $response = json_encode(array('type'=>'system',
                        'message'=>$ip.' disconnected'));
      send_message($response);
    }
  }
}
socket_close($sock);

// sends a message to all connected clients
```

```
function send_message($msg){
  global $clients;
  $msg = mask($msg);
  foreach($clients as $changed_socket)
    @socket_write($changed_socket,$msg,strlen($msg));
  return true;
}

function unmask($text) {
  $length = ord($text[1]) & 127;
  if($length == 126) {
    $masks = substr($text, 4, 4);
    $data = substr($text, 8);
  } elseif($length == 127) {
    $masks = substr($text, 10, 4);
    $data = substr($text, 14);
  } else {
    $masks = substr($text, 2, 4);
    $data = substr($text, 6);
  }
  $text = "";
  for ($i = 0; $i < strlen($data); ++$i) {
    $text .= $data[$i] ^ $masks[$i%4];
  }
  return $text;
}

//Encode message for transfer to client.
function mask($text){
  $b1 = 0x80 | (0x1 & 0x0f);
  $length = strlen($text);
  if($length <= 125)
    $header = pack('CC', $b1, $length);
  elseif($length > 125 && $length < 65536)
    $header = pack('CCn', $b1, 126, $length);
  elseif($length >= 65536)
    $header = pack('CCNN', $b1, 127, $length);
  return $header.$text;
}

function perform_handshaking($receved_header,$client_conn,
                                                $host, $port){
  $headers = array();
  $lines = preg_split("/\r\n/", $receved_header);
  foreach($lines as $line){
    $line = chop($line);
    if(preg_match('/\A(\S+): (.*)\z/', $line, $matches))
    $headers[$matches[1]] = $matches[2];
  }
  $secKey = $headers['Sec-WebSocket-Key'];
  $secAccept = base64_encode(pack('H*', sha1($secKey .
            '258EAFA5-E914-47DA-95CA-C5AB0DC85B11')));
  $upgrade  = "HTTP/1.1 101 Web Socket Protocol
Handshake\r\n" .
       "Upgrade: websocket\r\n" .
       "Connection: Upgrade\r\n" .
       "WebSocket-Origin: $host\r\n" .
       "WebSocket-Location: ws://$host:$port/index.php\r\n".
       "Sec-WebSocket-Accept:$secAccept\r\n\r\n";
  socket_write($client_conn,$upgrade,strlen($upgrade));
}
```

```
<!DOCTYPE html>
<html>
<head>
<meta charset='UTF-8' />
<script>
  var colors = ['007AFF','FF7000','FF7000','15E25F',
               'CFC700','CFC700','CF1100','CF00BE','F00'];
  var userColor = colors[Math.floor(Math.random()*10)];

  var wsUri = "ws://binarybehemoth.com:30000/server.php";
  websocket = new WebSocket(wsUri);
  websocket.onopen = function(ev) {
                    systemMessage('Connected');};
  websocket.onerror = function(ev){
                    systemMessage('Error:'+ev.data);};
  websocket.onclose = function(ev){
                    systemMessage('Connection closed');};
  websocket.onmessage = function(ev) {
    var msg = JSON.parse(ev.data);
    if(msg.type == 'usermsg')
      userMessage(msg.name,msg.message,msg.color);
    if(msg.type == 'system') systemMessage(msg.message);
    document.getElementById('message').value="";
  };

  function send(){
    var mymessage = document.getElementById('message').
                                                  value;
    var myname = document.getElementById('name').value;
    if(myname == ""){
      alert("Please enter a nickname!");
      return;
    }
    if(mymessage == ""){
      alert("Please enter a message!");
      return;
    }
    var msg = { message: mymessage,
               name: myname,
               color : userColor
             };
    websocket.send(JSON.stringify(msg));
  }

  function systemMessage(msg){
    document.getElementById('message_box').innerHTML +=
          "<span style='font-size:14px; color: #BDBDBD;"+
          "font-style: italic;'>"+msg+"</span><br/>";
  }

  function userMessage(username, msg, color){
    if (String(username)=='null' ||
       String(msg)=='null') return;
    document.getElementById('message_box').innerHTML +=
"<span style='color:#"+color+";'>"+username+":</span>"+
"<span style='color:#88B6E0;'>"+msg+"</span><br/>";
  }
</script>

</head>
<body>

<div style="width: 500px; background: #CCCCCC;
          padding: 10px; border: 1px solid #999999; ">
  <div id="message_box" style="background: #FFFFFF;
     height: 150px; overflow: auto; padding: 10px;
     border: 1px solid #999999;font-size: 14px;"></div>
  <input type="text" id="name" placeholder="Your Name"
       maxlength="10" style="width:20%" />
  <input type="text" id="message" placeholder="Message"
       maxlength="80" style="width:60%" />
  <button onclick="send()">Send</button>
</div>

</body>
</html>
```

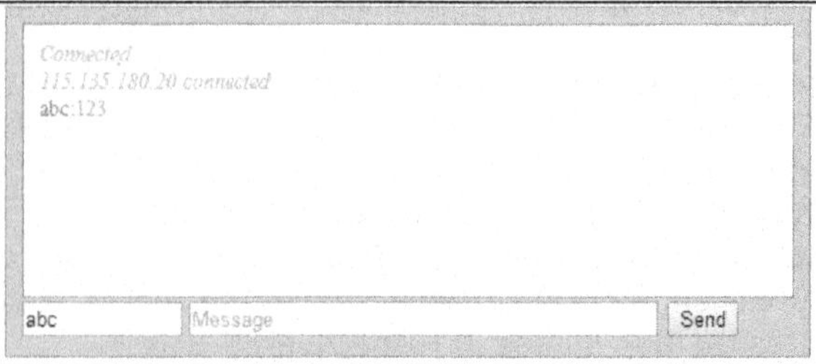

Connected
115.135.180.20 connected
abc:123

abc | Message | Send

4.23 Miscellaneous Functions

4.23.1 PHP Options (php.ini)

phpinfo($i=INFO_ALL) outputs information about the PHP system, including the configuration options and EGPCS (Environment, GET, POST, Cookie, Server) data. $i can be INFO_GENERAL, INFO_ CREDITS, INFO_CONFIGURATION, INFO_MODULES, INFO_ENVIRONMENT, INFO_VARIABLES, INFO_ LICENSE, and INFO_ALL. **ini_get($s)** returns the value of the configuration option $s, or FALSE if the option does not exist. **ini_set($s1,$s2)** sets the value of the configuration option $s1 to be $s2. The configuration option will keep this new value during the script's execution, and will be restored at the script's ending. **ini_restore($s)** restores a given configuration option $s to its original value.

set_time_limit($i) sets the number of seconds a script is allowed to run. The default is 30s or the value of 'max_execution_time' in php.ini.

4.23.2 Connection and Browser

connection_aborted() returns 1 if the client is disconnected (stop button clicked), 0 otherwise. **connection_status()** returns 0 if the connection is normal, 1 if the connection is aborted, 2 if the script is timed out, 3 if the script is both aborted and timed out. **ignore_user_abort([$m])** sets whether a client disconnection should abort the script. It sets the ignore_user_abort ini setting to $m and returns the previous setting as an integer. $m should be set to *true* to prevent the script from dying the next time it tries to write anything. **get_browser([$s[,$b=false]])** returns information about the capabilities of the browser (user agent $s). If $b is set to true, an array instead of an object is returned.

```
<!DOCTYPE html><html><head></head>
<body><?php
echo $_SERVER['HTTP_USER_AGENT'] . "<br />";
print_r(get_browser(null, true));
?></body></html>
```

```
Mozilla/5.0 (compatible; MSIE 9.0; Windows NT 6.1;
Trident/5.0; yie9)
Array (
[browser_name_regex] => ▯.*$�
[browser_name_pattern] => *
[browser] => Default Browser
[version] => 0
[majorver] => 0
[minorver] => 0
[platform] => unknown
[alpha] =>
[beta] =>
[win16] =>
[win32] =>
[win64] =>
[frames] => 1
[iframes] =>
[tables] => 1
[cookies] =>
[backgroundsounds] =>
[cdf] =>
[vbscript] =>
[javaapplets] =>
[javascript] =>
[activexcontrols] =>
[isbanned] =>
[ismobiledevice] =>
[issyndicationreader] =>
[crawler] =>
[cssversion] => 0
[supportscss] =>
[aol] =>
[aolversion] => 0 )
```

4.23.3 Formatting

highlight_string($s[,$b=false]) returns a highlighted version of $s, using the colors defined in the built-in syntax highlighter for PHP. If $b is true, the highlighted code is returned, and no ouput is printed out. **highlight_file($s[,$b=false])**or **show_source(......)** is similar except that the content in the file $s is used. It nicely colours different parts of the piece of PHP code according to their meanings.

```
<!DOCTYPE html><html><head></head>
<body><?php
highlight_string("<ABC>");
?></body></html>
```

```
<!DOCTYPE html><html><head></head>
<body><code><span style="color: #000000">
&lt;ABC&gt;</span>
</code></body></html>
```

```
<ABC>
```

php_strip_whitespace($s) returns a string which is the source code in the file $s with comments and whitespace removed.

```
<!DOCTYPE html><html><head></head>
<body><?php
// Displaying the size of this piece of code...
echo strlen(php_strip_whitespace(__FILE__));



?></body></html>
```

```
112
```

4.23.4 Sleep and Halt

sleep($i) delays the execution for $i seconds. **usleep($i)** delays the execution for $i microseconds. **time_nanosleep($i1,$i2)** delays the execution for $i1 seconds and $i2 nanoseconds. It returns TRUE on success or FALSE on failure. If the delay was interrupted by a signal, an associative array will be returned with the components: *seconds* (the number of seconds remaining) and *nanoseconds*(the number of nanoseconds remaining). **time_sleep_until($f)** delays the execution until the timestamp $f.

```
<!DOCTYPE html><html><head></head>
<body><?php
$nano = time_nanosleep(3, 200000);
if ($nano === true) {
   echo "Slept for 3 seconds, 200 microseconds.\n";
} elseif ($nano === false) {
   echo "Sleeping failed.\n";
} elseif (is_array($nano)) {
   $seconds = $nano['seconds'];
   $nanoseconds = $nano['nanoseconds'];
   echo "Interrupted by a signal.\n";
   echo "Time remaining: $seconds seconds, $nanoseconds
nanoseconds.";
}

// sleeps for another second
time_sleep_until(microtime(true)+1);
?></body></html>
```

```
Slept for 3 seconds, 200 microseconds.
```

__halt_compiler() halts the compiler execution of the current file. The byte position of the data start can be determined by the __COMPILER_HALT_OFFSET__ constant.

```
<!DOCTYPE html><html><head></head>
<body><?php
echo "A<br />";
require "test.php";
echo "<br />B";
?></body></html>
```

```
<?php  // test.php
// open this file
$fp = fopen(__FILE__, 'r');

// seek file pointer to data
fseek($fp, __COMPILER_HALT_OFFSET__);

// and output it
var_dump(stream_get_contents($fp));

// the end of the script execution
__halt_compiler();
 the installation data (eg. tar, gz, PHP, etc.) <br />
```

```
A
string(56) " the installation data (eg. tar, gz, PHP, etc.)
"
B
```

4.23.5 More String

uniqid([$s=""[,$b=false]]) returns a unique string with prefix $s. It is based on the current time (milliseconds). If $b is true, the unique string is 23 instead of 13 characters long.

```
<!DOCTYPE html><html><head></head>
<body><?php
echo uniqid("",true);
?></body></html>
```

```
50d44533d57d82.97508534
```

pack($format, $m1,$m2......) returns a binary string which is made up of $m1, $m2...... packed in the specified format. The format string consists of format codes followed by an optional repeater argument, which can be either an integer or * for repeating to the end of the input data. **unpack ($format,$s)** returns an array of unpacked data by unpacking the binary string $s using the specified format. $format consists of format codes separated by a slash /. A key name for the array follows each format code.

Format codes	
a	NUL-padded string
A	SPACE-padded string
h	Hex string, low nibble first
H	Hex string, high nibble first
c	signed char
C	unsigned char
s	signed short(always 16 bit, machine byte order)
S	unsigned short(always 16 bit, machine byte order)
n	unsigned short(always 16 bit, big endian byte order)
v	unsigned short(always 16 bit, little endian byte order
i	signed int (machine dependent size and byte order)
I	unsigned int (machine dependent size and byte order)
l	signed long (always 32 bit, machine byte order)
L	unsigned long (always 32 bit, machine byte order)
N	unsigned long (always 32 bit, big endian byte order)
V	unsigned long (always 32 bit, little endian byte order)
f	float (machine dependent size and representation)
d	double (machine dependent size and representation)
x	NUL byte
X	Back up one byte
@	NUL-fill to absolution position

```
<!DOCTYPE html><html><head></head>
<body><?php

//stores the byte seq. 0x12, 0x34, 0x78, 0x56, 0x41, 0x42
$binarydata = pack("nvc*", 0x1234, 0x5678, 65, 66);

print_r(unpack("c2chars1/nint/c2chars2",$binarydata));

?></body></html>
```

```
Array ( [chars11] => 18 [chars12] => 52 [int] => 30806
        [chars21] => 65 [chars22] => 66 )
```

4.24 (Excluded Information)

For various reasons, some PHP libraries have been excluded in this book. This is intended to help the reader to focus on functions that are truly useful and widely supported. Should the need arise, the reader is encouraged to read the documentation at php.net.

4.24.1 Rar Compression

Rar is a very efficient archiver. You can read Rar archives without installing any external library. However, you can't write Rar archives in PHP because that is prohibited by the license.

4.24.2 PDF

The Portable Document Format is a widely used file format that presents documents in a way independent of software, hardware, and operating systems. This PECL extension is not bundled with PHP. The full version of PDFlib can be downloaded but you need a license for commercial use. The PDFlib Lite supports a limited subset of functionality, and can be used freely under certain conditions.

4.24.3 Streams

Built-in within PHP, streams are a way to generalize file, network, data compression, and other operations which share a common set of functions and uses. A stream can be read from and written to linearly, and may be able to fseek() to an arbitrary location.

4.24.4 FTP and HTTP

There are many FTP and HTTP functions which allow you to read a file at a remote site, and perform downloading and uploading. In favour of using the cURL library(Chapter 16), this book has not covered these FTP and HTTP functions.

4.24.5 BC Math

The Binary Calculator allows you to perform mathematical operations on numbers of arbitrary precision. Numbers of any size are represented as strings.

4.24.6 Tokenizer

"The tokenizer functions provide an interface to the PHP tokenizer embedded in the Zend Engine. Using these functions you may write your own PHP source analyzing or modification tools without having to deal with the language specification at the lexical level."

4.24.7 Predefined Interfaces and Classes

ArrayAccess allows a class to be accessed using [...].

Traversable, *Iterator* and *IteratorAggregate* allow a class to be traversable using 'foreach'.

Serializable allows custom serialization.

Closure allows control of anonymous functions.

Generator allows the creation of generator objects.

4.25 AJAX

Asynchronous Javascript And XML is the art of exchanging data with a server and updating parts of a webpage, without reloading the whole page. To achieve this, the client must create, set and then send a Javascript XMLHttpRequest object, and wait for the response from the server.

The same-origin policy applies to XMLHttpRequests unless the server provides an Access-Control-Allow-Origin (CORS) header. If you wish to access the session variables in an AJAX call, remember to start the PHP script with: <?php session_start(); ?>

4.25.1 Synopsis

Synopsis for an XMLHttpRequest object:

Properties
onreadystatechange is used to set the callback function called when the response from the server is ready.
readyState returns the status of the request. It changes from 0 to 4: 0: request not initialized 1: server connection established 2: request received 3: processing request 4: request finished and the response is ready
status returns the status of the request: 200: OK 404: Page not found
responseText contains the response data in the form of a string.
responseXML contains the response data in the form of XML data (6.6.1).
Methods
open($s1,$s2,$b) sets the connection type to $s1 and requests the server to return the output of $s2. $s1 can be "GET" or "POST". If "GET" is used, the query string is to be attached to the url in $s2, and the result may be cached. "POST" is more robust and secure, with no size limitations. If "POST" is used, the query string must be specified in send(), and setRequestHeader() must be called. $s2 can be a ".php",".asp" or any data file. $b specifies whether the execution is asynchronous. If it is set to true, Javascript will execute other scripts while waiting for the server response. The callback function must also be set with *onreadystatechange*. If it is set to false, the execution flow will block until the server response is ready.
setRequestHeader($s1,$s2) needs to be called if the "POST" method is used. $s1 specifies the header name. $s2 specifies the header value.
send([$s]) sends the request after it has been set. $s contains the query string when the "POST" method is used.

A very detailed synopsis of XMLHttpRequest can be found at:

https://developer.mozilla.org/en-US/docs/Web/API/XMLHttpRequest

4.25.2 Retrieving a Static File

When the button is clicked, the content of the file "test.txt" in the server is displayed.

```
<!DOCTYPE html><html><head>
<script>

function loadText(){
  var xhr;
  xhr=new XMLHttpRequest();
  xhr.onreadystatechange=function(){
    if (xhr.readyState==4 && xhr.status==200)
    document.getElementById("div").innerHTML=
                                          xhr.responseText;
  };
  xhr.open("GET","test.txt",true);
  xhr.send();
}
</script></head>

<body>
  <div id="div"></div>
  <button type="button" onclick="loadText()">
    Retrieve Text</button>

</body></html>
```

Retrieve Text

testing 123
Retrieve Text

4.25.3 Synchronous Transfer (POST)

Unlike form data, AJAX data is not automatically URL-encoded (unless you use FormData). However, the AJAX data is automatically URL-decoded at the PHP end, so that you can use $_GET, $_POST, and $_REQUEST directly.

This example demonstrates the use of the "POST" method in carrying out an online poll. Because the asynchronous parameter in *xhr.open()* is set to false, there is no need to define the callback function using *xhr.onreadystatechange*.

```
<!DOCTYPE html><html><head>
<script>

function vote(v){
  var xhr;
  xhr=new XMLHttpRequest();
  xhr.open("POST","poll.php",false);
  xhr.setRequestHeader("Content-type",
                  "application/x-www-form-urlencoded");
  xhr.send("vote="+v);
  document.getElementById("poll").innerHTML=
                                          xhr.responseText;
}
</script></head>

<body>
  <div id="poll">
    <h3>Do you think AJAX is fun?</h3>
    Yes: <input type="radio" name="vote" value="0"
                onclick="vote(this.value)"/>
    No: <input type="radio" name="vote" value="1"
                onclick="vote(this.value)"/>
  </div>
</body></html>
```

```
<?php
$v = $_POST['vote'];
$content=file("poll.txt");
list($yes,$no)=explode("|",$content[0]);
if ($v==0) $yes++;
if ($v==1) $no++;
file_put_contents("poll.txt","$yes|$no");
?>
<h3>Yes: <?php echo $yes; ?> </h3><br />
<h3>No: <?php echo $no; ?> </h3>
```

Do you think AJAX is fun?

Yes: ○ No: ○

Yes: 11

No: 5

4.25.4 Asynchronous Transfer (GET)

Syntactically, an asynchronous transfer may look more complex to the coder. However, it allows the webpage to be responsive. For example, with it, you can display an animated gif while some data is being retrieved.

This PHP script searches as you type. Because the "GET" method is used, the results may be cached. A random parameter is passed using Math.random() to ensure that the latest version of "gethint.php" is used.

```
<!DOCTYPE html><html><head>
<script>
function showHint(s){
  var xhr;
  if (s.length==0){
    document.getElementById("hints").innerHTML="";
    return;
  }
  xhr=new XMLHttpRequest();
  xhr.onreadystatechange=function() {
    if (xhr.readyState==4 && xhr.status==200)
      document.getElementById("hints").innerHTML=
        xhr.responseText;
  }
  xhr.open("GET","gethint.php?q="+s+"&r="+
                  Math.random(),true);
  xhr.send();
}
</script>
</head><body>
  <h3>Start typing a name:</h3>
  Name:
  <input type="text" onkeyup="showHint(this.value)" />
  <p>Suggestions: <span id="hints"></span></p>
</body></html>
```

```
<?php
$a = ["Paul","Crowe","Betrand","Mary","Irene","Fiona",
     "Gundesen","Hegel","Singa","Johan","Katherine","Jacky",
     "Lina","Opheus","Petronas","Ananda","Racheal","Cindy",
     "Doris","Eva","Livita","Sunny","Trovalta","Inu",
     "Purple","Liza","Alexander","Ellen","Wendy","Vincent"];
$q=$_GET["q"];
if (strlen($q) > 0){
  $hint="";
  for($i=0; $i<count($a); $i++){
    if (stripos($a[$i],$q)) {
      $hint=($hint=="")?$a[$i]:$hint." , ".$a[$i];
    }
  }
}

echo ($hint=="")?"no suggestion":$hint;
?>
```

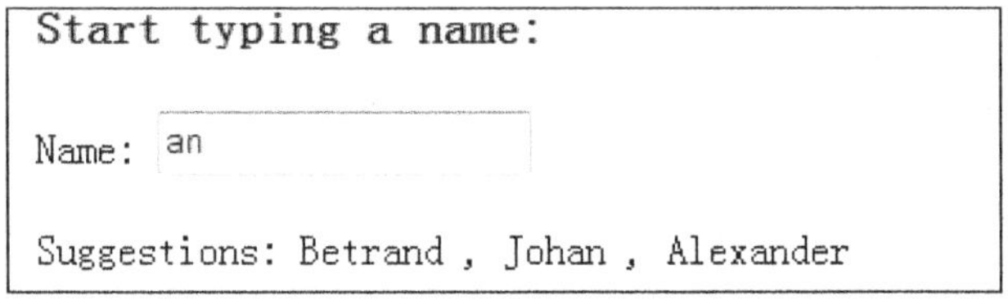

```
Start typing a name:

Name: an

Suggestions: Betrand , Johan , Alexander
```

4.25.5 Upload Progress and FormData

This script displays the upload progress. A form is submitted without reloading the whole page. Note that when using FormData(), the strings in the form are already %-encoded. Note also that the execution must be asynchronous, ie. the third parameter to xhr.open() must be true.

```
<!DOCTYPE html><html>
<head>
<script>

var start_time;

function start_upload() {
  d=new Date();
  start_time=d.getTime();

  f = document.getElementById("file_uploader").files[0];
  if (f.size > 10*1024*1024){
    document.getElementById("msg").innerHTML=
                                        "file too large";
    return;
  }
  if (f.name.substr(-4,4)!=".exe"){
    document.getElementById("msg").innerHTML=
                                        "invalid type";
    return;
  }

  fd = new
       FormData(document.getElementById('upload_form'));
  fd.append("input_text2","===&&&===");
  var xhr = new XMLHttpRequest();
  xhr.upload.addEventListener('progress',
                          upload_progress, false);
  xhr.addEventListener('load', upload_finish, false);
  xhr.addEventListener('error', upload_error, false);
  xhr.open('POST', 'upload.php');
  xhr.send(fd);
}

function upload_progress(e) {
  if (!e.lengthComputable) return;
  p = e.loaded * 100 / e.total;
  p = p.toFixed(3);
  d = new Date();
  r = e.loaded/((d.getTime()-start_time)/1000)/1024;
  r = r.toFixed(3);
  document.getElementById("msg").innerHTML=
           p+"% completed.<br/>rate: "+r+"KB/s.<br/>";
}

function upload_finish(e) {
  document.getElementById("msg").innerHTML+=
                                   e.target.responseText;
}

function upload_error(e){
  document.getElementById("msg").innerHTML=
                                        "Upload error.";
}
</script>
</head>
<body>
  <form id="upload_form">
    <input type="hidden" name="secret"
           value="~!@#$%^&*()_+ "/>
    <input type="text" name="input_text1"/><br/>
    <input type="file" name="upload_file"
           id="file_uploader"/>
  </form>
  <button onclick="start_upload();">Upload</button>
  <p id="msg"></p>
</body>
</html>
```

```
<?php
// upload.php
move_uploaded_file($_FILES["upload_file"]["tmp_name"],
                   $_FILES["upload_file"]["name"]);
echo "input_text1: ".$_REQUEST["input_text1"]."<br/>";
echo "input_text2: ".$_REQUEST["input_text2"]."<br/>";
//echo "secret: ".$_REQUEST["secret"];
?>
```

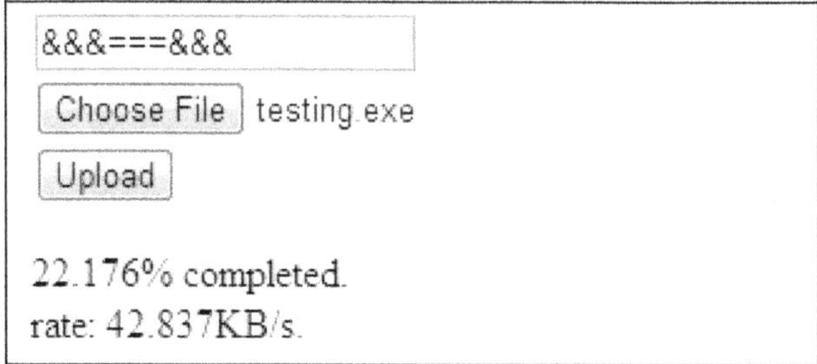

```
&&&===&&&
Choose File  testing.exe
Upload

22.176% completed.
rate: 42.837KB/s.
```

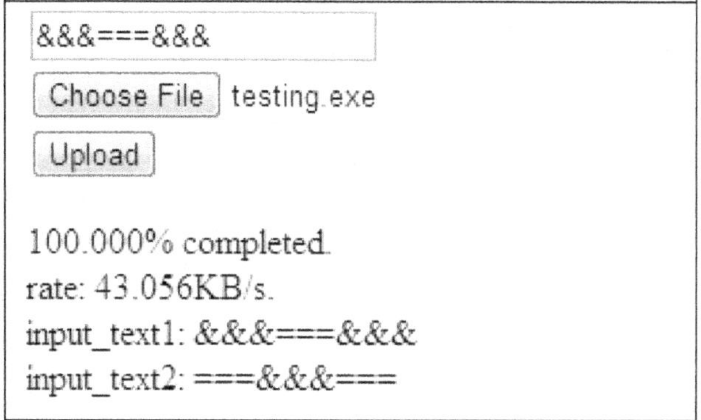

```
&&&===&&&
Choose File  testing.exe
Upload

100.000% completed.
rate: 43.056KB/s.
input_text1: &&&===&&&
input_text2: ===&&&===
```

To upload large files, make sure **memory_limit**, **post_max_size** and **upload_max_filesize** in php.ini have been set appropriately.

4.26 PHP 5.6 New Features

As of 15 Nov 2014, PHP 5.6 has been released but few web hosts support it. Here are some interesting new features:

(courtesy of http://php.net/manual/en/ migration56.new-features.php)

4.26.1 Constant Scalar Expressions

```
<?php
const ONE = 1;
const TWO = ONE * 2;

class C {
   const THREE = TWO + 1;
   const ONE_THIRD = ONE / self::THREE;
   const SENTENCE = 'The value of THREE is '.self::THREE;

   public function f($a = ONE + self::THREE) {
      return $a;
   }
}

echo (new C)->f()."\n";
echo C::SENTENCE;
?>
```

```
4
The value of THREE is 3
```

4.26.2 Variadic Functions via ...

```
<?php
function f($req, $opt = null, ...$params) {
   // $params is an array containing the remaining arguments.
   printf('$req: %d; $opt: %d; number of params: %d'."\n",
         $req, $opt, count($params));
}

f(1);
f(1, 2);
f(1, 2, 3);
f(1, 2, 3, 4);
f(1, 2, 3, 4, 5);
?>
```

```
$req: 1; $opt: 0; number of params: 0
$req: 1; $opt: 2; number of params: 0
$req: 1; $opt: 2; number of params: 1
$req: 1; $opt: 2; number of params: 2
$req: 1; $opt: 2; number of params: 3
```

4.26.3 Argument Unpacking via ...

```
<?php
function add($a, $b, $c) {
   return $a + $b + $c;
}

$operators = [2, 3];
echo add(1, ...$operators);
?>
```

```
6
```

4.26.4 Exponentiation via **

```
<?php
printf("2 ** 3 ==      %d\n", 2 ** 3);
printf("2 ** 3 ** 2 == %d\n", 2 ** 3 ** 2);

$a = 2;
$a **= 3;
printf("a ==          %d\n", $a);
?>
```

```
2 ** 3 ==      8
2 ** 3 ** 2 == 512
a ==           8
```

4.26.5 'use function' and 'use const'

The *use* operator has been extended to support importing functions and constants in addition to classes.

```
<?php
namespace Name\Space {
   const FOO = 42;
   function f() { echo __FUNCTION__."\n"; }
}

namespace {
   use const Name\Space\FOO;
   use function Name\Space\f;

   echo FOO."\n";
   f();
}
?>
```

```
42
Name\Space\f
```

4.26.6 hash_equals()

This compares two strings in constant time.

```
<?php
$expected  = crypt('12345',
                   '$2a$07$usesomesillystringforsalt$');
$correct   = crypt('12345',
                   '$2a$07$usesomesillystringforsalt$');
$incorrect = crypt('1234',
                   '$2a$07$usesomesillystringforsalt$');

var_dump(hash_equals($expected, $correct));
var_dump(hash_equals($expected, $incorrect));
?>
```

```
bool(true)
bool(false)
```

4.26.7 __debuginfo()

This changes the values that are shown when an object is output using var_dump().

```
<?php
class C {
   private $prop;

   public function __construct($val) {
      $this->prop = $val;
   }

   public function __debugInfo() {
      return [
         'propSquared' => $this->prop ** 2,
      ];
   }
}
var_dump(new C(42));
?>
```

```
object(C)#1 (1) {
  ["propSquared"]=>
  int(1764)
}
```

5. Structured Query Language

SQL handles a relational database management system (RDMBS) in which a lot of data can be stored, modified and retrieved in an efficient and orderly manner. SQL is widely regarded as a fourth-generation language, which means that the commands are English-like and can be understood intuitively. We shall focus on MySQL, a popular open-sourced implementation of SQL acquired by Oracle.

MySQL commands can be issued to a MySQL server either through a direct front end such as PhpMyAdmin and MySQL Workbench, or through an external script such as a PHP script.

An SQL DBMS is typically organized into a collection of databases (also known as schemas). Each database contains a number of tables, views, stored procedures and functions. Each table or view, in turn, is made up of a number of relations (records). In this regard, the tables and views, where data is stored, are two-dimensional. Each row corresponds to a record or relation, and each column corresponds to a field.

We start by assuming that you already have access to a database and an account. We shall cover the more important concepts first. Advanced details will be discussed later.

The official documentation, which includes the various system variables and command-line options not covered here, can be found at:
http://dev.mysql.com/doc/refman/5.7/en/index.html
(This chapter reorganizes the official documentation and presents extra topics. Howerver, for the purpose of education, a few sections follow the official documentation closely. With due respect to the original writers, it is pointless to make changes to good writing.)

In this chapter, no meaningful example will be given until 5.5. As you read 5.1 – 5.4, you may wish to refer to 5.5.1 and 5.5.2 for two working examples. Study these two examples very carefully for they illustrate all the central concepts of SQL.

5.1 Data Types

When a table is being created, the data type for each column is declared.

5.1.1 Numeric

Integer Type	Bytes	Range
TINYINT	1	-128 **to** 127
SMALLINT	2	-32 768 **to** 32 767
MEDIUMINT	3	-8 388 608 **to** 8 388 607
INT	4	-2 147 483 648 **to** 2 147 483 647
BIGINT	8	-9 223 372 036 854 775 808 **to** 9 223 372 036 854 775 807
You can append an **UNSIGNED** attribute to an integer type, so that only non-negative integers can be stored. This increases the upper limit of the type. For instance, 'TINYINT UNSIGNED' stores integers from 0 to 255.		
You can append a **bracketed integer** to an integer type, to set the display width. For example, for the type 'TINYINT (5)', a value of 10 will be left-padded with three spaces when displayed.		
You can append a **ZEROFILL** attribute to an integer type with a display width, so that the integers are left-padded with zeros when displayed. For example, for the type 'TINYINT(5) ZEROFILL', a value of 10 will be displayed as 00010. When ZEROFILL is specified, the UNSIGNED attribute is automatically added.		

Point Type
DECIMAL(8,3), for instance, can be used to store exact values from -99999.999 to 99999.999, where the precision is 8 digits and the scale is 3. The number of bytes used varies. DECIMAL(10) is the same as DECIMAL(10,0). DECIMAL is the same as DECIMAL(10) in MySQL. DECIMAL(8,3) is the same as NUMERIC(8,3).
FLOAT, **REAL**, **DOUBLE** and **DOUBLE PRECISION** store approximate numeric values. REAL, DOUBLE, and DOUBLE PRECISION are the same. In MySQL, single-precision values use 4 bytes, while double-precision values use 8 bytes. You can specify the precision p using the syntax FLOAT(p). If necessary, that will use double precision for the storage. MySQL allows the nonstandard syntax: FLOAT(M,D) or REAL(M,D), DOUBLE(M,D) or DOUBLE PRECISION(M,D), where M is the total number of digits, and D is the number of digits after the decimal point.
You can also append UNSIGNED to these types, to prevent negative values from being stored. However, the upper limits of the ranges are not increased.

Bit Type
BIT(10), for instance, can be used to store values of 10 bits. A binary representation is specified using a notation like b'1001010101'.

5.1.2 String

Character Type
CHAR(10), for example, can hold up to 10 characters. 10 bytes are used regardless of how long the string is. **VARCHAR(10)**, for example, can hold up to 10 characters. The number of bytes used equals the length of the string plus one or two bytes.
BINARY(10) and **VARBINARY(10)** are similar to CHAR(10) and VARCHAR(10), except that the former types contain *byte strings* rather than *character strings*. Without using any character sets, BINARY(n) and VARBINARY(n) perform sorting and comparison based on the numeric values of the bytes.
CHAR(10) BINARY and **VARCHAR(10) BINARY** use the binary collations for the column character sets.

Text Type	Storage Required
TINYBLOB, TINYTEXT	L+1 bytes, L <2^{8}
BLOB, TEXT	L+2 bytes, L <2^{16}
MEDIUMBLOB, MEDIUMTEXT	L+3 bytes, L <2^{24}
LONGBLOB, LONG TEXT	L+4 bytes, L <2^{32}
Where L is the number of bytes of the string. BLOB values are regarded as byte strings. TEXT values are regarded as character strings.	
Custom Type	
ENUM('cat', 'dog'), for instance, can contain the values NULL, '', 'cat', and 'dog'. Each predefined value equals an	

integer, starting with 1. 0 is reserved for the empty string. Using ENUM() saves storage space.
SET('cat','dog'), for instance, can contain the values NULL, '', 'cat', 'dog' and 'cat,dog'. Multiple members are separated by commas. A maximum of 64 members are allowed. In this case, 'cat' has a binary value of 01 while 'dog' has a binary value of 10.

5.1.3 Date and Time

Date and Time Type
DATE supports the values from '1000-01-01' to '9999-12-31'.
TIME supports the values from '-838:59:59.000000' to '838:59:59.999999'. '11:30' means '11:30:00'. '1130' means '00:11:30'.
YEAR(4) stores a year value using 1 byte. The display width is 4 characters. You may specify its value as an integer or a string, in the range 1901-2155.
DATETIME supports the values from '1000-01-01 00:00:00.000000' to '9999-12-31 23:59:59.999999'.
TIMESTAMP supports the values from '1000-01-01 00:00:00.000000' UTC to '9999-12-31 23:59:59.999999' UTC. Values are converted from the current time zone to UTC for storage, and from UTC to the current time zone for retrieval.
If two-digit year values are used, 00-69 are converted to 2000-2069, while 70-99 are converted to 1970-1999.
For DATETIME and TIMESTAMP, to set an initial default value use DEFAULT. For example, if you specify dt DATETIME **DEFAULT CURRENT_TIMESTAMP** the column dt is automatically initialized to the current timestamp if no value is specified for the column during an insertion.
For DATETIME and TIMESTAMP, to automatically update to the current date and time, use ON UPDATE. For instance, when defining a table, if you specify dt TIMESTAMP **ON UPDATE CURRENT_TIMESTAMP** the column dt is automatically set to the current timestamp when one of the other columns changes its value.

5.2 Table Definitions

5.2.1 CREATE TABLE

```
CREATE [TEMPORARY] TABLE [IF NOT EXISTS] tbl_name
    (create_definition,...)
    [table_options]
    [partition_options]
```

```
CREATE [TEMPORARY] TABLE [IF NOT EXISTS] tbl_name
    [(create_definition,...)]
    [table_options]
    [partition_options]
    select_statement
```

```
CREATE [TEMPORARY] TABLE [IF NOT EXISTS] tbl_name
    { LIKE old_tbl_name | (LIKE old_tbl_name) }
```

create_definition:

```
    col_name column_definition
  | [CONSTRAINT [symbol]] PRIMARY KEY [index_type]
      (index_col_name,...) [index_option] ...
  | {INDEX|KEY} [index_name] [index_type]
      (index_col_name,...) [index_option] ...
  | [CONSTRAINT [symbol]] UNIQUE [INDEX|KEY]
     [index_name] [index_type] (index_col_name,...)
     [index_option] ...
  | {FULLTEXT|SPATIAL} [INDEX|KEY] [index_name]
     (index_col_name,...) [index_option] ...
  | [CONSTRAINT [symbol]] FOREIGN KEY
     [index_name] (index_col_name,...) reference_definition
  | CHECK (expr)
```

column_definition:

```
    data_type [NOT NULL | NULL] [DEFAULT default_value]
      [AUTO_INCREMENT] [UNIQUE [KEY] | [PRIMARY] KEY]
      [COMMENT 'string']
      [COLUMN_FORMAT {FIXED|DYNAMIC|DEFAULT}]
      [reference_definition]
```

data_type:

```
    BIT[(length)]
  | TINYINT[(length)] [UNSIGNED] [ZEROFILL]
  | SMALLINT[(length)] [UNSIGNED] [ZEROFILL]
  | MEDIUMINT[(length)] [UNSIGNED] [ZEROFILL]
  | INT[(length)] [UNSIGNED] [ZEROFILL]
  | INTEGER[(length)] [UNSIGNED] [ZEROFILL]
  | BIGINT[(length)] [UNSIGNED] [ZEROFILL]
  | REAL[(length,decimals)] [UNSIGNED] [ZEROFILL]
  | DOUBLE[(length,decimals)] [UNSIGNED] [ZEROFILL]
  | FLOAT[(length,decimals)] [UNSIGNED] [ZEROFILL]
  | DECIMAL[(length[,decimals])] [UNSIGNED] [ZEROFILL]
  | NUMERIC[(length[,decimals])] [UNSIGNED] [ZEROFILL]
  | DATE
  | TIME
  | TIMESTAMP
  | DATETIME
  | YEAR
  | CHAR[(length)]
      [CHARACTER SET charset_name]
      [COLLATE collation_name]
  | VARCHAR(length)
      [CHARACTER SET charset_name]
      [COLLATE collation_name]
  | BINARY[(length)]
  | VARBINARY(length)
  | TINYBLOB
  | BLOB
  | MEDIUMBLOB
  | LONGBLOB
  | TINYTEXT [BINARY]
      [CHARACTER SET charset_name]
      [COLLATE collation_name]
  | TEXT [BINARY]
      [CHARACTER SET charset_name]
      [COLLATE collation_name]
  | MEDIUMTEXT [BINARY]
      [CHARACTER SET charset_name]
      [COLLATE collation_name]
  | LONGTEXT [BINARY]
      [CHARACTER SET charset_name]
      [COLLATE collation_name]
  | ENUM(value1,value2,value3,...)
      [CHARACTER SET charset_name]
      [COLLATE collation_name]
  | SET(value1,value2,value3,...)
      [CHARACTER SET charset_name]
      [COLLATE collation_name]
  | spatial_type
```

index_col_name:

```
    col_name [(length)] [ASC | DESC]
```

index_type:

```
    USING {BTREE | HASH}
```

index_option:

```
    KEY_BLOCK_SIZE [=] value
  | index_type
  | WITH PARSER parser_name
  | COMMENT 'string'
```

reference_definition:

```
    REFERENCES tbl_name (index_col_name,...)
      [MATCH FULL | MATCH PARTIAL | MATCH SIMPLE]
      [ON DELETE reference_option]
      [ON UPDATE reference_option]
```

reference_option:

```
    RESTRICT | CASCADE | SET NULL | NO ACTION
```

To create a table in a particular database, use db_name.tbl_name.

A **TEMPORARY** table is valid only during the current connection. Two connections can use the same temporary table name without conflicting with each other.

IF NOT EXISTS prevents an error when the table already exists. If a table of the same name already exists, the new definition is not adopted.

Integer and floating-point types can have the **AUTO_INCREMENT** attribute. If you insert NULL or 0 into such a type, the column is set to the largest value for the column plus 1. A table can only contain one AUTO_INCREMENT column. It must be indexed. It must not have a DEFAULT value. Inserting a negative number is assumed to be inserting a large positive number.

BLOB or TEXT types should not have the **DEFAULT** attribute.

NOT NULL requires the column to be filled during an insertion. The default is **NULL**.

The **DEFAULT** value must be a constant, not a function or expression. CURRENT_TIMESTAMP is the exception.

The **COMMENT** value can be up to 1024 characters long.

KEY and **PRIMARY KEY** are the same. A table can only have one PRIMARY KEY, which is a NOT NULL unique index. A PRIMARY KEY is stored first, followed by the UNIQUE indexes, and then the other indexes. To specify a PRIMARY KEY that spans multiple columns, use a separate PRIMARY KEY(index_col_name,...) clause. The name of a PRIMARY KEY is PRIMARY. If you do not assign a name for other indexes, they will be assigned the same name as the first indexed column, with an optional suffix (_2,_3...).

An error will be encountered when you try to insert, for a **UNIQUE** column, a value that already exists.

Some storage engines allow you to be **USING** an index type when creating an index. The **WITH PARSER** option, usable only with **FULLTEXT** indexes, associates a parser plugin with the index if full-text indexing and searching operations need special handling. For CHAR, VARCHAR, BINARY, and VARBINARY, use the col_name(length) syntax to specify an index prefix length. Specifying a prefix length is mandatory for indexes of BLOB and TEXT types.

The **CHECK** clause is ignored.

INDEX, **CONSTRAINT** and **FOREIGN KEY** will be discussed in 5.11.

table_options:

```
  table_option [[,] table_option] ...
```

table_option:

```
   ENGINE [=] engine_name
 | AUTO_INCREMENT [=] value
 | AVG_ROW_LENGTH [=] value
 | [DEFAULT] CHARACTER SET [=] charset_name
 | CHECKSUM [=] {0 | 1}
 | [DEFAULT] COLLATE [=] collation_name
 | COMMENT [=] 'string'
 | CONNECTION [=] 'connect_string'
 | DATA DIRECTORY [=] 'absolute path to directory'
 | DELAY_KEY_WRITE [=] {0 | 1}
 | INDEX DIRECTORY [=] 'absolute path to directory'
 | INSERT_METHOD [=] { NO | FIRST | LAST }
 | KEY_BLOCK_SIZE [=] value
 | MAX_ROWS [=] value
 | MIN_ROWS [=] value
 | PACK_KEYS [=] {0 | 1 | DEFAULT}
 | PASSWORD [=] 'string'
 | ROW_FORMAT [=] {DEFAULT|DYNAMIC|FIXED|
                   COMPRESSED|REDUNDANT|COMPACT}
 | STATS_AUTO_RECALC [=] {DEFAULT|0|1}
 | STATS_PERSISTENT [=] {DEFAULT|0|1}
 | STATS_SAMPLE_PAGES [=] value
 | UNION [=] (tbl_name[,tbl_name]...)
```

AUTO_INCREMENT sets the initial AUTO_INCREMENT value for the table.

AVG_ROW_LENGTH specifies the approximated average row length for the table. For MyISAM, MySQL uses the product of MAX_ROWS and AVG_ROW_LENGTH to decide how big the table is.

Values for **CHARACTER SET** and **COLLATE** are listed in 5.2.2.

Setting 1 to **CHECKSUM** causes MySQL to maintain a live checksum for all rows. This makes it easier to find corrupted tables.

Setting 1 to **DELAY_KEY_WRITE** delays key updates until the table is closed. (MyISAM only)

If you want to use a MERGE table, specify for **INSERT_METHOD** FIRST or LAST, to have insertions go to the first or last table respectively. NO prevents insertions.

For compressed InnoDB tables, you can specify the **KEY_BLOCK_SIZE** in kilobytes to use for pages. 0 causes the default compressed page size to be used.

MAX_ROWS and **MIN_ROWS** are hints to the storage engine about the maximum and minimum numbers of rows in the table.

Setting 1 to **PACK_KEYS** in MyISAM tables causes smaller indexes to be used. This makes updates slower and reads faster. The default is to pack strings, but not numbers. Significant benefit is obtained from the prefix compression only if many numbers are the same.

PASSWORD is unused. You need to contact the sales department of Oracle, if you wish to scramble the .frm files.

UNION is used when you want to access a collection of identical MyISAM tables as one. It works only with MERGE tables.

partition_options:

```
  PARTITION BY
     { [LINEAR] HASH(expr)
     | [LINEAR] KEY [ALGORITHM={1|2}] (column_list)
     | RANGE{(expr) | COLUMNS(column_list)}
     | LIST{(expr) | COLUMNS(column_list)} }
  [PARTITIONS num]
  [SUBPARTITION BY
     { [LINEAR] HASH(expr)
     | [LINEAR] KEY [ALGORITHM={1|2}] (column_list) }
    [SUBPARTITIONS num]
  ]
  [(partition_definition [, partition_definition] ...)]
```

partition_definition:

```
  PARTITION partition_name
     [VALUES
        {LESS THAN {(expr | value_list) | MAXVALUE}
        |
        IN (value_list)}]
     [[STORAGE] ENGINE [=] engine_name]
     [COMMENT [=] 'comment_text' ]
     [DATA DIRECTORY [=] 'data_dir']
     [INDEX DIRECTORY [=] 'index_dir']
     [MAX_ROWS [=] max_number_of_rows]
     [MIN_ROWS [=] min_number_of_rows]
     [(subpartition_definition [, subpartition_definition] ...)]
```

subpartition_definition:

```
  SUBPARTITION logical_name
     [[STORAGE] ENGINE [=] engine_name]
     [COMMENT [=] 'comment_text' ]
     [DATA DIRECTORY [=] 'data_dir']
     [INDEX DIRECTORY [=] 'index_dir']
     [MAX_ROWS [=] max_number_of_rows]
     [MIN_ROWS [=] min_number_of_rows]
```

select_statement:

```
  [IGNORE | REPLACE] [AS] SELECT ...
                     (Some valid select statement)
```

Partitioning will be described in 5.16.

5.2.2 Character Sets and Collations

> SHOW CHARACTER SET;

Charset	Desctiption	Default collation	Max Len
big5	Big5 Traditional Chinese	big5_chinese_ci	2
dec8	DEC West European	dec8_swedish_ci	1
cp850	DOS West European	cp850_general_ci	1
hp8	HP West European	hp8_english_ci	1
koi8r	KOI8-R Relcom Russian	koi8r_general_ci	1
latin1	cp1252 West European	latin1_swedish_ci	1
latin2	ISO 8859-2 Central European	latin2_general_ci	1
swe7	7bit Swedish	swe7_swedish_ci	1
ascii	US ASCII	ascii_general_ci	1
ujis	EUC-JP Japanese	ujis_japanese_ci	3
sjis	Shift-JIS Japanese	sjis_japanese_ci	2
hebrew	ISO 8859-8 Hebrew	hebrew_general_ci	1
tis620	TIS620 Thai	tis620_thai_ci	1
euckr	EUC-KR Korean	euckr_korean_ci	2
koi8u	KOI8-U Ukrainian	koi8u_general_ci	1
gb2312	GB2312 Simplified Chinese	gb2312_chinese_ci	2
greek	ISO 8859-7 Greek	greek_general_ci	1
cp1250	Windows Central European	cp1250_general_ci	1
gbk	GBK Simplified Chinese	gbk_chinese_ci	2
latin5	ISO 8859-9 Turkish	latin5_turkish_ci	1
armscii8	ARMSCII-8 Armenian	armscii8_general_ci	1
utf8	UTF-8 Unicode	utf8_general_ci	3
ucs2	UCS-2 Unicode	ucs2_general_ci	2
cp866	DOS Russian	cp866_general_ci	1
keybcs2	DOS Kamenicky Czech-Slovak	keybcs2_general_ci	1
macce	Mac Central European	macce_general_ci	1
macroman	Mac West European	macroman_general_ci	1
cp852	DOS Central European	cp852_general_ci	1
latin7	ISO 8859-13 Baltic	latin7_general_ci	1
utf8mb4	UTF-8 Unicode	utf8mb4_general_ci	4
cp1251	Windows Cyrillic	cp1251_general_ci	1
utf16	UTF-16 Unicode	utf16_general_ci	4
utf16le	UTF-16LE Unicode	utf16le_general_ci	4
cp1256	Windows Arabic	cp1256_general_ci	1
cp1257	Windows Baltic	cp1257_general_ci	1
utf32	UTF-32 Unicode	utf32_general_ci	4
binary	Binary pseudo charset	binary	1
geostd8	GEOSTD8 Georgian	geostd8_general_ci	1
cp932	SJIS for Windows Japanese	cp932_japanese_ci	2
eucjpms	UJIS for Windows Japanese	eucjpms_japanese_ci	3
big5	Big5 Traditional Chinese	big5_chinese_ci	2
dec8	DEC West European	dec8_swedish_ci	1
cp850	DOS West European	cp850_general_ci	1
hp8	HP West European	hp8_english_ci	1
koi8r	KOI8-R Relcom Russian	koi8r_general_ci	1
latin1	cp1252 West European	latin1_swedish_ci	1
latin2	ISO 8859-2 Central European	latin2_general_ci	1
swe7	7bit Swedish	swe7_swedish_ci	1
ascii	US ASCII	ascii_general_ci	1
ujis	EUC-JP Japanese	ujis_japanese_ci	3
sjis	Shift-JIS Japanese	sjis_japanese_ci	2
hebrew	ISO 8859-8 Hebrew	hebrew_general_ci	1
tis620	TIS620 Thai	tis620_thai_ci	1
euckr	EUC-KR Korean	euckr_korean_ci	2
koi8u	KOI8-U Ukrainian	koi8u_general_ci	1
gb2312	GB2312 Simplified Chinese	gb2312_chinese_ci	2
greek	ISO 8859-7 Greek	greek_general_ci	1
cp1250	Windows Central European	cp1250_general_ci	1
gbk	GBK Simplified Chinese	gbk_chinese_ci	2
latin5	ISO 8859-9 Turkish	latin5_turkish_ci	1
armscii8	ARMSCII-8 Armenian	armscii8_general_ci	1
utf8	UTF-8 Unicode	utf8_general_ci	3
ucs2	UCS-2 Unicode	ucs2_general_ci	2
cp866	DOS Russian	cp866_general_ci	1
keybcs2	DOS Kamenicky Czech-Slovak	keybcs2_general_ci	1
macce	Mac Central European	macce_general_ci	1
macroman	Mac West European	macroman_general_ci	1
cp852	DOS Central European	cp852_general_ci	1
latin7	ISO 8859-13 Baltic	latin7_general_ci	1

> SHOW COLLATION LIKE 'latin1%';

Collation	Char set	Id	De-fault	Com-piled	Sort-len
latin1_german1_ci	latin1	5		Yes	1
latin1_swedish_ci	latin1	8	Yes	Yes	1
latin1_danish_ci	latin1	15		Yes	1
latin1_german2_ci	latin1	31		Yes	2
latin1_bin	latin1	47		Yes	1
latin1_general_ci	latin1	48		Yes	1
latin1_general_cs	latin1	49		Yes	1
latin1_spanish_ci	latin1	94		Yes	1

5.2.3 ALTER TABLE

```
ALTER [IGNORE] TABLE tbl_name
    [alter_specification [, alter_specification] ...]
    [partition_options]
```

algorithm_option:
```
    ALGORITHM [=] {DEFAULT|INPLACE|COPY}
```

lock_option:
```
    LOCK [=] {DEFAULT|NONE|SHARED|EXCLUSIVE}
```

alter_specification:
```
    table_options
  | ADD [COLUMN] col_name column_definition
        [FIRST | AFTER col_name ]
  | ADD [COLUMN] (col_name column_definition,...)
  | ADD {INDEX|KEY} [index_name]
        [index_type] (index_col_name,...) [index_option] ...
  | ADD [CONSTRAINT [symbol]] PRIMARY KEY
        [index_type] (index_col_name,...) [index_option] ...
  | ADD [CONSTRAINT [symbol]]
        UNIQUE [INDEX|KEY] [index_name]
        [index_type] (index_col_name,...) [index_option] ...
  | ADD FULLTEXT [INDEX|KEY] [index_name]
        (index_col_name,...) [index_option] ...
  | ADD SPATIAL [INDEX|KEY] [index_name]
        (index_col_name,...) [index_option] ...
  | ADD [CONSTRAINT [symbol]]
        FOREIGN KEY [index_name] (index_col_name,...)
        reference_definition
  | ALGORITHM [=] {DEFAULT|INPLACE|COPY}
  | ALTER [COLUMN] col_name
                   {SET DEFAULT literal | DROP DEFAULT}
  | CHANGE [COLUMN] old_col_name new_col_name
                   column_definition [FIRST|AFTER col_name]
  | LOCK [=] {DEFAULT|NONE|SHARED|EXCLUSIVE}
  | MODIFY [COLUMN] col_name column_definition
                   [FIRST | AFTER col_name]
  | DROP [COLUMN] col_name
  | DROP PRIMARY KEY
  | DROP {INDEX|KEY} index_name
  | DROP FOREIGN KEY fk_symbol
  | DISABLE KEYS
  | ENABLE KEYS
  | RENAME [TO|AS] new_tbl_name
  | RENAME {INDEX|KEY} old_index_name TO
                   new_index_name
  | ORDER BY col_name [, col_name] ...
  | CONVERT TO CHARACTER SET charset_name
                   [COLLATE collation_name]
```

```
  | [DEFAULT] CHARACTER SET [=] charset_name
                              [COLLATE [=] collation_name]
  | DISCARD TABLESPACE
  | IMPORT TABLESPACE
  | FORCE
  | ADD PARTITION (partition_definition)
  | DROP PARTITION partition_names
  | DISCARD PARTITION {partition_names | ALL} TABLESPACE
  | IMPORT PARTITION {partition_names | ALL} TABLESPACE
  | TRUNCATE PARTITION {partition_names | ALL}
  | COALESCE PARTITION number
  | REORGANIZE PARTITION partition_names INTO
                        (partition_definitions)
  | EXCHANGE PARTITION partition_name WITH TABLE
                        tbl_name
  | ANALYZE PARTITION {partition_names | ALL}
  | CHECK PARTITION {partition_names | ALL}
  | OPTIMIZE PARTITION {partition_names | ALL}
  | REBUILD PARTITION {partition_names | ALL}
  | REPAIR PARTITION {partition_names | ALL}
  | REMOVE PARTITIONING
```

index_col_name:

```
  col_name [(length)] [ASC | DESC]
```

index_type:

```
  USING {BTREE | HASH}
```

index_option:

```
  KEY_BLOCK_SIZE [=] value
  | index_type
  | WITH PARSER parser_name
  | COMMENT 'string'
```

table_options:

```
  table_option [[,] table_option] ...
  (see CREATE TABLE options)
```

partition_options:

```
  (see CREATE TABLE options)
```

Setting **ALGORITHM** to COPY causes a temporary copy of the original table to be made during the alteration. MySQL waits for modifications on the table, alters the copy, deletes the original table and renames the new one. Updates and writes after the ALTER TABLE operation are stalled until the new table is ready.

Setting ALGORITHM to INPLACE uses the in-place technique for clauses and storage engines that support it, and fails otherwise.

Setting ALGORITHM to DEFAULT is the same as specifying no ALGORITHM at all.

Setting **LOCK** to DEFAULT results in maximum concurrency. Setting it to NONE permits concurrent reads and writes if supported, and returns an error message otherwise. Setting it to SHARED permits concurrent reads but block writes, and returns an error message if concurrent reads are not supported. Setting it to EXCLUSIVE blocks reads and writes.

If **IGNORE** is specified, when duplicates are found for unique keys, only one row is used on a unique key, the other conflicting rows are removed, and incorrect values are truncated to the closest matching acceptable value. If IGNORE is not specified, the copy is aborted and rolled back.

ALTER TABLE cannot be used to change the storage engine of a table to MERGE or BLACKHOLE, to prevent loss of data.

ORDER BY allows you to create the new table with the rows in a particular order after the ALTER TABLE operation.

5.2.4 RENAME TABLE

```
RENAME TABLE tbl_name TO new_tbl_name
           [, tbl_name2 TO new_tbl_name2] ...
```

The RENAME operation is performed atomically. No other session can access the table while it is being renamed.

Renaming operations occur from left to right. To swap two table names, you can use:

```
  RENAME TABLE old_table TO tmp_table,
               new_table TO old_table,
               tmp_table TO new_table;
```

You can RENAME TABLE to move a table from one database to another:

```
  RENAME TABLE this_db.tbl_name TO that_db.tbl_name;
```

You cannot RENAME a TEMPORARY table.

5.2.5 TRUNCATE TABLE

```
TRUNCATE [TABLE] tbl_name
```

This empties a table completely.

5.2.6 DROP TABLE

```
DROP [TEMPORARY] TABLE [IF EXISTS]
  tbl_name [, tbl_name] ...
  [RESTRICT | CASCADE]
```

This removes one or more tables.

IF EXISTS prevents an error for non-existent tables.

RESTRICT and **CASCADE** are not supported in MySQL 5.7.

TEMPORARY drops only TEMPORARY tables, does not end an ongoing transaction, and does not check access rights.

5.3 Basic Data Management

5.3.1 INSERT

```
INSERT [LOW_PRIORITY | HIGH_PRIORITY]
  [IGNORE]
  [INTO] tbl_name
  [PARTITION (partition_name,...)]
  [(col_name,...)]
  {VALUES | VALUE} ({expr | DEFAULT},...),(...),...
  [ ON DUPLICATE KEY UPDATE
   col_name=expr
     [, col_name=expr] ... ]
```

```
INSERT [LOW_PRIORITY | HIGH_PRIORITY]
  [IGNORE]
  [INTO] tbl_name
  [PARTITION (partition_name,...)]
  SET col_name={expr | DEFAULT}, ...
  [ ON DUPLICATE KEY UPDATE
   col_name=expr
     [, col_name=expr] ... ]
```

```
INSERT [LOW_PRIORITY | HIGH_PRIORITY] [IGNORE]
  [INTO] tbl_name
  [PARTITION (partition_name,...)]
  [(col_name,...)]
  SELECT ...
  [ ON DUPLICATE KEY UPDATE
   col_name=expr
     [, col_name=expr] ... ]
```

INSERT...VALUES inserts one or more new rows by specifying the values for the specified columns. If no column name is specified, the value for every column must be provided in order. **INSERT...SET** inserts a new row by specifying the values for *specific* columns. **INSERT...SELECT** inserts one or more new rows by obtaining the rows from another table or tables.

If multiple value lists are inserted, MySQL returns a string in the format: '*Records: 100 Duplicates:0 Warnings: 0*' , where *records* refer to the number of processed rows, *duplicates* the number of rows that could not be inserted because of duplicates for unique indexes, *warnings* the number of problematic attempts.

If the types of the inserted values do not match the defined types for the table, the inserted values may be clipped, truncated, or converted.

LOW_PRIORITY delays the insertion until the table is not being read. **HIGH_PRIORITY** prevents concurrent insertions. These two attributes affect only storage engines that use only table-level locking (such as MyISAM, MEMORY, and MERGE).

IGNORE causes errors to be ignored.

If **ON DUPLICATE KEY UPDATE** is specified, and a duplicate is found in a UNIQUE index or PRIMARY KEY, an UPDATE of the old row is performed.

To insert special characters such as the apostrophe, precede the character with a slash, eg. \'.

5.3.2 REPLACE

```
REPLACE [LOW_PRIORITY]
    [INTO] tbl_name
    [PARTITION (partition_name,...)]
    [(col_name,...)]
    {VALUES | VALUE} ({expr | DEFAULT},...),(...),...
```

```
REPLACE [LOW_PRIORITY]
    [INTO] tbl_name
    [PARTITION (partition_name,...)]
    SET col_name={expr | DEFAULT}, ...
```

```
REPLACE [LOW_PRIORITY]
    [INTO] tbl_name
    [PARTITION (partition_name,...)]
    [(col_name,...)]
    SELECT ...
```

REPLACE is the same as INSERT, except that when there is a duplicate value for a PRIMARY KEY or a UNIQUE index, the old row is deleted before the insertion.

A REPLACE statement returns the sum of the rows deleted and inserted.

5.3.3 UPDATE

```
UPDATE [LOW_PRIORITY] [IGNORE] table_reference
    SET col_name1={expr1|DEFAULT}
        [, col_name2={expr2|DEFAULT}] ...
    [WHERE where_condition]
    [ORDER BY ...]
    [LIMIT row_count]
```

```
UPDATE [LOW_PRIORITY] [IGNORE] table_references
    SET col_name1={expr1|DEFAULT}
      [, col_name2={expr2|DEFAULT}] ...
    [WHERE where_condition]
```

With the **ORDER BY** clause, the rows are updated in the order that is specified.

LIMIT limits the number of rows that can be updated.

LOW_PRIORITY delays the execution until the table is not being read. This affects storage engines that use only table-level locking (such as MyISAM, MEMORY, and MERGE).

IGNORE suppresses errors.

An UPDATE operation returns the number of rows that were changed.

5.3.4 DELETE

```
DELETE [LOW_PRIORITY] [QUICK] [IGNORE] FROM tbl_name
    [PARTITION (partition_name,...)]
    [WHERE where_condition]
    [ORDER BY ...]
    [LIMIT row_count]
```

```
DELETE [LOW_PRIORITY] [QUICK] [IGNORE]
    tbl_name[.*] [, tbl_name[.*]] ...
    FROM table_references
    [WHERE where_condition]
```

```
DELETE [LOW_PRIORITY] [QUICK] [IGNORE]
    FROM tbl_name[.*] [, tbl_name[.*]] ...
    USING table_references
    [WHERE where_condition]
```

A DELETE statement returns the number of deleted rows.

LOW_PRIORITY, IGNORE, ORDER BY and **LIMIT** are the same as for UPDATE.

QUICK tells the storage engine not to merge the index leaves, which may speed up the deletion.

5.4 Basic Data Retrieval

Data retrieval in SQL generally fetches a number of rows, which may be regarded as a two-dimensional table.

5.4.1 SELECT

```
SELECT
    [ALL | DISTINCT | DISTINCTROW ]
      [HIGH_PRIORITY]
      [MAX_STATEMENT_TIME]
      [STRAIGHT_JOIN]
      [SQL_SMALL_RESULT]
      [SQL_BIG_RESULT]
      [SQL_BUFFER_RESULT]
      [SQL_CACHE | SQL_NO_CACHE]
      [SQL_CALC_FOUND_ROWS]
    select_expr [, select_expr ...]
    [FROM table_references
      [PARTITION partition_list]
    [WHERE where_condition]
    [GROUP BY {col_name | expr | position}
      [ASC | DESC], ... [WITH ROLLUP]]
    [HAVING where_condition]
    [ORDER BY {col_name | expr | position}
      [ASC | DESC], ...]
    [LIMIT {[offset,] row_count | row_count OFFSET offset}]
    [PROCEDURE procedure_name(argument_list)]
    [INTO OUTFILE 'file_name'
        [CHARACTER SET charset_name] export_options
      | INTO DUMPFILE 'file_name'
      | INTO var_name [, var_name]]
    [FOR UPDATE | LOCK IN SHARE MODE]]
```

select_expr can be a single * to retrieve all columns.

You may specify an alias for select_expr, as in the following:
SELECT CONCAT(a,'-',b) **AS** c FROM myTable ORDER BY c;
or
SELECT CONCAT(a,'-',b) c FROM myTable ORDER BY c;

You may specify an alias for each table using the syntax:
tbl_name [[AS] new_name] [index_int]

ORDER BY and **GROUP BY** can use column names, column aliases, or column positions. Column positions are integers beginning with 1.

The **HAVING** clause can use aggregate functions and merge rows with the same values for the specified columns, but the **WHERE** clause cannot:

```
SELECT a, MAX(b) FROM users
    GROUP BY a HAVING MAX(b) > 10;
```

LIMIT constrains the number of rows fetched:

```
SELECT * FROM tbl LIMIT 3,10;  # Fetch rows 4-13
SELECT * FROM tbl LIMIT 35,9999999; # Fetch rows 36-last
```

PROCEDURE processes data in the result set.

If **FOR UPDATE** is used with a storage engine that uses page or row locks, before the end of the transaction, examined rows cannot be written, cannot be doing SELECT...LOCK IN SHARE MODE, and cannot be read in certain transaction isolation levels.

LOCK IN SHARE MODE prevents affected rows from being modified until your transaction commits. Other sessions can still read the rows.

ALL returns all rows including duplicates. **DISTINCT** removes duplicate rows. **DISTINCTROW** is the same as DISTINCT.

For storage engines that use only table-level locking (such as MyISAM, MEMORY, and MERGE), **HIGH_PRIORITY** runs the query even if the table is locked for reading.

MAX_STATEMENT_TIME sets the execution timeout in milliseconds.

STRAIGHT_JOIN joins the tables in the order in which they appear in the FROM clause.

SQL_BIG_RESULT tells the optimizer that the result set has many rows. **SQL_SMALL_RESULT** tells the optimizer that the result set has few rows.

SQL_BUFFER_RESULT puts the result into a temporary table, thus freeing the table locks early. This helps when it takes a long time to send the result set to the client.

SQL_CALC_FOUND_ROWS calculates the number of rows in the result set without regard to any LIMIT clause. The total can then be retrieved with SELECT_FOUND_ROWS().

SQL_CACHE stores the result in the query cache if it is cacheable. With **SQL_NO_CACHE**, the server neither checks the query cache to see if the result is already cached, nor does it cache the query result.

The **INTO** clause will be discussed in 5.9.2.

5.4.2 JOIN

```
table_references:
   escaped_table_reference [, escaped_table_reference] ...

escaped_table_reference:
   table_reference
 | { OJ table_reference }

table_reference:
   table_factor
 | join_table

table_factor:
   tbl_name [PARTITION (partition_names)]
      [[AS] alias] [index_hint_list]
 | table_subquery [AS] alias
 | ( table_references )

join_table:
   table_reference [INNER | CROSS] JOIN table_factor
                   [join_condition]
 | table_reference STRAIGHT_JOIN table_factor
 | table_reference STRAIGHT_JOIN table_factor ON
                   conditional_expr
 | table_reference {LEFT|RIGHT} [OUTER] JOIN
                   table_reference join_condition
 | table_reference NATURAL [{LEFT|RIGHT} [OUTER]] JOIN
                   table_factor

join_condition:
   ON conditional_expr
 | USING (column_list)

index_hint_list:
   index_hint [, index_hint] ...

index_hint:
   USE {INDEX|KEY}
     [FOR {JOIN|ORDER BY|GROUP BY}] ([index_list])
 | IGNORE {INDEX|KEY}
     [FOR {JOIN|ORDER BY|GROUP BY}] (index_list)
 | FORCE {INDEX|KEY}
     [FOR {JOIN|ORDER BY|GROUP BY}] (index_list)

index_list:
   index_name [, index_name] ...
```

JOIN, **CROSS JOIN**, and **INNER JOIN** are the same in MySQL. They yield a Cartesian product between the specified tables. Each row in the first table is joined to each row in the second table. For instance:

SELECT * FROM t1 JOIN (t2, t3) ON(t2.a=t1.a AND t3.a=t2.a) results in a new table formed by joining t1, t2, and t3 where t1.a, t2.a, and t3.a are the same.

For a **LEFT JOIN,** if there is no matching row for the right table in the ON or USING part, a row with all columns set to NULL will be used for the right table. **RIGHT JOIN** is identical, but works in the other way round.

USING compares columns of the same name in both tables, and joins the rows when the values are the same.

A **NATURAL** [LEFT] JOIN is the same as an INNER JOIN or LEFT JOIN with a USING clause that names all columns that exist in both tables.

The **{OJ...}** syntax is meant for compatibility with ODBC. The curly brace should be specified literally.

STRAIGHT_JOIN is similar to JOIN, except that the left table is always read before the right table.

5.4.3 UNION

```
SELECT ...
UNION [ALL | DISTINCT] SELECT ...
[UNION [ALL | DISTINCT] SELECT ...]
```

A **UNION** statement combines the results from multiple SELECT statements.

To use an ORDER BY or LIMIT clause for the entire UNION result, parenthesize the individual SELECT statements and place the ORDER BY or LIMIT clause at the end:

```
(SELECT a FROM t1 WHERE a=100 AND b=5)
UNION
(SELECT a FROM t2 WHERE a=101 AND b=3)
ORDER BY a LIMIT 15;
```

5.4.4 Index Hint

```
tbl_name [[AS] alias] [index_hint_list]

index_hint_list:
   index_hint [, index_hint] ...

index_hint:
   USE {INDEX|KEY}
     [FOR {JOIN|ORDER BY|GROUP BY}] ([index_list])
 | IGNORE {INDEX|KEY}
     [FOR {JOIN|ORDER BY|GROUP BY}] (index_list)
 | FORCE {INDEX|KEY}
     [FOR {JOIN|ORDER BY|GROUP BY}] (index_list)

index_list:
   index_name [, index_name] ...
```

You can tell the optimizer how to choose indexes when performing a query. For example,

SELECT * FROM t1 USE INDEX (c1,c2) WHERE c1=1;

Specifying an empty index_list for USE INDEX means 'use no indexes'.

5.4.5 HANDLER

```
HANDLER tbl_name OPEN [ [AS] alias]

HANDLER tbl_name READ index_name
   { = | <= | >= | < | > } (value1,value2,...)
   [ WHERE where_condition ] [LIMIT ... ]
HANDLER tbl_name READ index_name
   { FIRST | NEXT | PREV | LAST }
   [ WHERE where_condition ] [LIMIT ... ]
HANDLER tbl_name READ
   { FIRST | NEXT }
   [ WHERE where_condition ] [LIMIT ... ]

HANDLER tbl_name CLOSE
```

HANDLER is faster than SELECT, and is sometimes a more natural way to treat data.

HANDLER...OPEN makes a table accessible with subsequent **HANDLER...READ**, until **HANDLER...CLOSE** is called or the session terminates.

HANDLER...READ fetches a row where the index specified satisfies the given values and the WHERE condition is met. If an index spans multiples columns, you can specify values for

only the leftmost columns. For example: HANDLER tb READ idx = (1,2,3) HANDLER tb READ idx = (1,2) HANDLER tb READ idx = (1)
Use the quoted **'PRIMARY'** to use a table's PRIMARY KEY: HANDLER tb READ 'PRIMARY' pk...
LIMIT fetches specific number of (instead of one) rows. The syntax is specified in 5.4.1.

5.5 PHP Integration

5.5.1 Example: Procedural Style

Note that the equivalence comparison operator in SQL is = and not ==.

```
<!DOCTYPE html><html><head>
<style type="text/css">
  table, td {border: 1px solid;}
</style></head><body>
<?php

// ****** 1. Database Connection
$link=mysqli_connect("localhost","root","password","testDB");
if (mysqli_connect_errno()) {
  echo "Connection failed: ".mysqli_connect_error();
  exit();
}


// ****** 2. Table Definition
mysqli_query($link, "DROP TABLE IF EXISTS tbl1, tbl2");

mysqli_query($link, "
CREATE TABLE IF NOT EXISTS tbl1 (
  a TINYINT (5) ZEROFILL,
  b INT UNSIGNED AUTO_INCREMENT UNIQUE,
  c DECIMAL(5,2) PRIMARY KEY,
  d DATETIME DEFAULT CURRENT_TIMESTAMP
                ON UPDATE CURRENT_TIMESTAMP,
  e BINARY(3) NOT NULL,
  z TEXT)
  AUTO_INCREMENT 5,
  CHARACTER SET 'latin1'
");
echo mysqli_error($link); // reports any error

mysqli_query($link,"
ALTER TABLE tbl1
  ADD f VARCHAR(5) AFTER e,
  CHANGE z g TEXT
");

mysqli_query($link, "
CREATE TABLE IF NOT EXISTS tbl2 (
  a TINYINT (5) ZEROFILL,
  x BLOB)
");
echo mysqli_error($link); // reports any error


// ****** 3. Data Management
mysqli_query($link, "
INSERT INTO tbl1 VALUES
(1,10,1.23,'2015-06-25 19:30:00','abc','aaaaa','Hello World'),
(2,99,1.1,'2016-04-23 13:30:00','def','bbb','Testing 123')
");

mysqli_query($link, "
REPLACE tbl1 SET
a=3,c=9.9,e='mno',g='Good day'
");

mysqli_query($link, "
UPDATE tbl1 SET
c=8.8 WHERE a=3
");

mysqli_query($link, "
INSERT INTO tbl2 VALUES
(4,'PHP'),
(5,'SQL')
");


// ****** 4. Data Retrieval
$result = mysqli_query($link, "
SELECT * FROM tbl1 ORDER BY a ASC,b DESC");
tabulate($result);

$result = mysqli_query($link, "
SELECT * FROM tbl2");
tabulate($result);

$result = mysqli_query($link, "
(SELECT a AS c1,g c2 FROM tbl1) UNION
(SELECT * FROM tbl2) ORDER BY c1 DESC");
tabulate($result);

$result = mysqli_query($link, "
SELECT * FROM tbl1 JOIN tbl2 ON tbl1.a <= 3");
tabulate($result);

$result = mysqli_query($link, "
SELECT * FROM tbl1 JOIN tbl2 GROUP BY tbl1.a, tbl1.b
HAVING SUM(tbl1.a)>3");
tabulate($result);

$result = mysqli_query($link, "
SELECT * FROM tbl1 T1 RIGHT JOIN tbl2 T2 ON T2.a <= 4");
tabulate($result);

mysqli_query($link, "UPDATE tbl2 SET a=3 WHERE a=4");
$result = mysqli_query($link, "
SELECT * FROM tbl1 JOIN tbl2 USING (a)");
tabulate($result);


// ****** A useful, general-purpose result printer
function tabulate($result){
  $fInfo = mysqli_fetch_fields($result);
  echo "<table><tr>";
  foreach($fInfo as $col){
    echo "<td>".$col->name."</td>";
  }
  while ($row = mysqli_fetch_row($result)){
    echo "</tr><tr>";
    foreach ($row as $val){
      echo "<td>".$val."</td>";
    }
  }
  echo "</tr></table><br/>";
}

?>
</body>
</html>
```

a	b	c	d	e	f	g
00001	10	1.23	2015-06-25 19:30:00	abc	aaaaa	Hello World
00002	99	1.10	2016-04-23 13:30:00	def	bbb	Testing 123
00003	100	8.80	2014-04-27 09:29:05	mno		Good day

a	x
00004	PHP
00005	SQL

c1	c2
5	SQL
4	PHP
3	Good day
2	Testing 123
1	Hello World

a	b	c	d	e	f	g	a	x
00002	99	1.10	2016-04-23 13:30:00	def	bbb	Testing 123	00004	PHP
00002	99	1.10	2016-04-23 13:30:00	def	bbb	Testing 123	00005	SQL
00001	10	1.23	2015-06-25 19:30:00	abc	aaaaa	Hello World	00004	PHP
00001	10	1.23	2015-06-25 19:30:00	abc	aaaaa	Hello World	00005	SQL
00003	100	8.80	2014-04-27 09:29:05	mno		Good day	00004	PHP
00003	100	8.80	2014-04-27 09:29:05	mno		Good day	00005	SQL

a	b	c	d	e	f	g	a	x
00002	99	1.10	2016-04-23 13:30:00	def	bbb	Testing 123	00004	PHP
00003	100	8.80	2014-04-27 09:29:05	mno		Good day	00004	PHP

a	b	c	d	e	f	g	a	x
00002	99	1.10	2016-04-23 13:30:00	def	bbb	Testing 123	00004	PHP
00001	10	1.23	2015-06-25 19:30:00	abc	aaaaa	Hello World	00004	PHP
00003	100	8.80	2014-04-27 09:29:05	mno		Good day	00004	PHP
							00005	SQL

a	b	c	d	e	f	g	x
00003	100	8.80	2014-04-27 09:29:05	mno		Good day	PHP

5.5.2 Example: Object-Oriented Style

```
<!DOCTYPE html><html><head>
<style type="text/css">
  table, td {border: 1px solid;}
</style></head><body>
<?php
// ****** 1. Database Connection
$S=new mysqli("localhost","root","password","testDB");
if ($S->connect_errno) {
  echo "Connect failed: ".$S->connect_error;
  exit();
}


// ****** 2. Table Definition & Data Management
$S->query("
DROP TABLE IF EXISTS tbl, tmp");

$S->query("
CREATE TABLE tbl (
  a INT,
  b VARCHAR(20))");

$S->query("
CREATE TABLE tmp LIKE tbl");

$S->query("
INSERT INTO tbl VALUES
  (1,'Hello World'),
  (2,'Testing 123'),
  (3,'Good Day!'),
  (4,'How Are You?'),
  (5,'Good Luck!')");

$S->query("
INSERT INTO tmp
SELECT * FROM tbl");

echo $S->error."<br/>";


// ****** 3. Data Retrieval by HANDLER
$S->query("HANDLER tbl OPEN");
tabulate($S->query(
        "HANDLER tbl READ FIRST WHERE a>=2 LIMIT 2"));
tabulate($S->query(
        "HANDLER tbl READ NEXT WHERE a>=2 LIMIT 2"));
$S->query("HANDLER tbl CLOSE");


// ****** 4. Data Retrieval by multi_query()
$S->multi_query("
SELECT * FROM tbl WHERE a>1 AND a<5;
SELECT * FROM tbl WHERE a>2 AND a<4;");
do{
  tabulate($S->store_result());
} while ($S->next_result());


// ****** A useful, general-purpose result printer
function tabulate($result){
  $fInfo = $result->fetch_fields();
  echo "<table><tr>";
  foreach($fInfo as $col){
    echo "<td>".$col->name."</td>";
  }
  while ($row = $result->fetch_row()){
    echo "</tr><tr>";
    foreach ($row as $val){
             echo "<td>".$val."</td>";
           }
  }
  echo "</tr></table><br/>";
}?>
</body>
</html>
```

a	b
2	Testing 123
3	Good Day!

a	b
4	How Are You?
5	Good Luck!

a	b
2	Testing 123
3	Good Day!
4	How Are You?

a	b
3	Good Day!

5.5.3 Conventions of Functions

If the following sections, each function appears in the object-oriented form for the class *mysqli*. With some exceptions, the procedural form of each function can be obtained by prepending it with *mysqli_* and adding the link as the first parameter. For example:

The procedural form of
query($s [,$i=MYSQLI_STORE_RESULT])
is
mysqli_query($l,$s [,$i=MYSQLI_STORE_RESULT])

The procedural form of
$error
is
mysqli_error($l)

Unless otherwise specified, each function returns TRUE on success and FALSE on failure.

5.5.4 Connection Functions

__construct(
[$s1=ini_get("mysqli.default_host")
[,$s2=ini_get("mysqli.default_user")
[,$s3=ini_get("mysqli.default_pw")
[,$s4=""
[,$i=ini_get("mysqli.default_port")
[,$s5=ini_get("mysqli.default_socket")]]]]]])
connects to the MySQL server, using the database $s4. Nothing is returned. The procedural form mysqli_connect(......) returns the link. **$connect_errno** gives the error number for the last connection attempt. Zero means no error. **$connect_error** gives the error message in the form of a string for the last connection attempt. NULL means no error. **get_connection_stats()** gives an array of connection statistics. **stat()** obtains the status.

init() returns a resource to be used with real_connect(). **real_connect([$s1 [,$s2 [,$s3 [, $s4 [, $i [, $s5 [, $i2]]]]]]])** is similar to __construct(......) except that real_connect(......) needs an object created by init(), there is a flags parameter $i2, and various options can be set with options(). The flags $i2 can be

MYSQLI_CLIENT_COMPRESS uses a protocol for compression.
MYSQLI_CLIENT_FOUND_ROWS returns the no. of matched rows, instead of the no. of affected rows.
MYSQLI_CLIENT_IGNORE_SPACE allows spaces beyond function names, and reserves all function names as keywords.
MYSQLI_CLIENT_INTERACTIVE allows interactive_timeout (rather than wait_timeout) seconds of inactivity before timeout.
MYSQLI_CLIENT_SSL uses SSL encryption.

options($i, $m) is used to set extra connection options. Where $i can be:

MYSQLI_OPT_CONNECT_TIMEOUT sets the no. of seconds for connection timeout.
MYSQLI_OPT_LOCAL_INFILE enables/disables the use of LOAD LOCAL INFILE.
MYSQLI_INIT_COMMAND is executed during the establishment of a connection to the server.
MYSQLI_READ_DEFAULT_FILE reads settings from the specified file rather than my.cnf.
MYSQLI_READ_DEFAULT_GROUP reads settings from the specified group from my.cnf or the file given by MYSQL_READ_DEFAULT_FILE.
MYSQLI_SERVER_PUBLIC_KEY sets the RSA public key file used with the SHA-256 based authentication.

ssl_set($s1, $s2, $s3, $s4, $s5) establishes secure connections using SSL. $s1 specifies the path to the key. $s2 specifies the path to the certificate. $s3 specifies the path to the certificate authority. $s4 specifies the path to a directory containing trusted SSL CA certificates in PEM format. $s5 specifies a list of allowable ciphers to use for SSL encryption.

ping() pings a server. It attempts to reconnect if the server connection has been lost.

change_user($s1, $s2, $s3) changes the user using username $s1, password $s2, and database $s3. **select_db($s)** selects $s as the current database. **close()** closes the connection.

```
<?php
$mysqli = mysqli_init();
if (!$mysqli) die('mysqli_init failed');
$mysqli->options(MYSQLI_INIT_COMMAND,
                 'SET AUTOCOMMIT = 0');
$mysqli->options(MYSQLI_OPT_CONNECT_TIMEOUT, 5);
if (!$mysqli->real_connect('localhost', 'root', 'pw', 'testDB')) {
   die('Connect Error (' . mysqli_connect_errno() . ') '
        . mysqli_connect_error());
}
echo $mysqli->stat()."\n";
print_r($mysqli->get_connection_stats());
$mysqli->close();
?>
```

```
Uptime: 435665  Threads: 3  Questions: 2624  Slow queries:
0  Opens: 527  Flush tables: 1  Open tables: 104  Queries per
second avg: 0.006
Array
(
   [bytes_sent] => 142
   [bytes_received] => 104
   [packets_sent] => 4
   [packets_received] => 3
   [protocol_overhead_in] => 12
   [protocol_overhead_out] => 16
   [bytes_received_ok_packet] => 0
   [bytes_received_eof_packet] => 0
   [bytes_received_rset_header_packet] => 0
   [bytes_received_rset_field_meta_packet] => 0
   [bytes_received_rset_row_packet] => 11
   [bytes_received_prepare_response_packet] => 0
   [bytes_received_change_user_packet] => 0
   [packets_sent_command] => 1
   [packets_received_ok] => 0
   [packets_received_eof] => 0
   [packets_received_rset_header] => 0
......
```

5.5.5 Query Functions

query($s [, $i=MYSQLI_STORE_RESULT]) performs a query $s. If $i=MYSQLI_USE_RESULT, all ensuing invocations will return the error 'Commands out of sync' unless free_result() is called, This function gives mysqli_result on success, or FALSE on failure. For non-DML queries (not INSERT, UPDATE or DELETE), it is similar to invoking **real_query($s)** followed by store_result() or use_result().

escape_string($s) encodes NUL, \n, \r, \, ', ", and Control-Z for use in an SQL statement.

refresh($i) updates caches or tables, or resets the replication server information. $i can be MYSQLI_ REFRESH_ {LOG | TABLES | HOSTS | STATUS | THREADS | SLAVE | MASTER}.

$affected_rows gives the no. of affected rows in a previous INSERT, UPDATE, REPLACE or DELETE operation. **$field_count** gives the no. of columns for the last query. **$insert_id** gives the AUTO_INCREMENT value changed by the previous query, or 0 if there was no previous query or if the query did not update an AUTO_INCREMENT value.

$info returns a string providing information about the last query.

Query type	Example result string
INSERT INTO	Records:50 Duplicate:0 Warnings:0
LOAD DATA INFILE	Records:10 Duplicate:0 Warnings:0
ALER TABLE	Records:1 Deleted:0 Skipped:0 Warnings:0
UPDATE	Rows matched:30 Changed:30 Warnings:0

multi_query($s) runs multiple queries $s joined by ';'. To obtain the resultset from the first query you can use **use_result()** or **store_result()**. The queries after that can be processed using **more_results()** and **next_result().**

$errno gives the error code for the last function invocation. Zero means no error occurred. **$error** gives a string describing the last error. An empty string is returned if there was no error. **$error_list** gives a list of errors from the last executed command. **$sqlstate** returns the SQLSTATE error string from the last operation. '00000' means no error. **get_warnings()** gets the result of SHOW WARNINGS. **$warning_count** gives the no. of warnings from the most recent query.

5.5.6 Information Functions

get_charset() returns the default character set as an object. **character_set_name()** gives the default character set as a string. **set_charset($s)** changes the default character set.

```
<?php
$link=mysqli_connect("localhost","root","pwd","testDB");
echo mysqli_character_set_name($link)."\n";
print_r(mysqli_get_charset($link));
mysqli_set_charset($link,'utf8');
?>
```

```
utf8
stdClass Object
(
    [charset] => utf8
    [collation] => utf8_general_ci
    [dir] =>
    [min_length] => 1
    [max_length] => 3
    [number] => 33
    [state] => 1
    [comment] => UTF-8 Unicode
)
```

set_local_infile_handler($func) sets the callback for LOAD DATA LOCAL INFILE.

set_local_infile_default() unsets user defined handler previously set with set_local_infile_handler().

```
<?php
$db = mysqli_init();
$db->real_connect("localhost","root","pwd","test");

function loadMe($stream, &$buffer, $buflen, &$errmsg){
  $buffer = fgets($stream);
  echo $buffer;
  $buffer = strtoupper(str_replace(",", "\t", $buffer));
  return strlen($buffer);
}

$db->set_local_infile_handler("loadMe");
$db->query(
      "LOAD DATA LOCAL INFILE 'input.txt' INTO TABLE t1");
$db->set_local_infile_default();
?>
```

$client_info gives a string of client information. **$client_version** gives an integer of client version. **$server_info** gives a string describing the server. **$server_version** gives an integer describing the server version. **$host_info** gives a string representing the type of connection used. **$protocol_version** gives the version of MySQL protocol used. For the procedural forms for these six variables, you need to prepend mysqli_get_ instead of mysqli_. The procedural form of $protocol_version is mysqli_get_proto_info($l).

```
<?php
$S=new mysqli("localhost","root","password","testDB");
echo $S->client_info."\n";
echo $S->client_version."\n";
echo $S->server_info."\n";
echo $S->server_version."\n";
echo $S->host_info."\n";
echo $S->protocol_version."\n";
?>
```

```
mysqlnd 5.0.11-dev - 20120503 - $Id:
40933630edef551dfaca71298a83fad8d03d62d4 $
50011
5.6.16-log
50616
localhost via TCP/IP
10
```

5.5.7 The mysqli_result class

This section documents the functions for the *mysqli_result* object, which is returned by queries. With some exceptions, the procedural form of each function can be obtained by prepending each function name with mysqli_ and passing the *mysqli_result* object as the first parameter. For example, the procedural form of fetch_row() is mysqli_fetch_row($result).

fetch_row() gets the next row as an numeric array. **fetch_assoc()** gets the next row as an associative array. **fetch_array([$i = MYSQLI_BOTH])** gets the next row as an associative array, a numeric array, or both. $i can be MYSQLI_BOTH, MYSQLI_NUM, or MYSQLI_ASSOC. **fetch_object([$s1 [, $s2]])** gets the current row as an object. $s1 is the name of the class to instantiate. $s2 is an optional array which passes arguments to the constructor $s1.

fetch_all([$i =MYSQLI_NUM]) fetches all rows and gives an array of numeric or associative arrays. $i can be MYSQLI_BOTH, MYSQLI_NUM, or MYSQLI_ASSOC. **data_seek($i)** sets the pointer to a row specified by the offset $i.

fetch_field() returns the next field as an object. **fetch_fields()** gives an array of all field objects. **$current_field** gets the current field offset as an integer. The procedural form is mysqli_field_tell ($result). **field_seek($i)** brings the field cursor to the offset $i.

$num_rows gives the no. of resultant rows. **$field_count** gives the no. of resultant fields. The procedural form is mysqli_num_fields($result). **$lengths** returns an array with the lengths of all columns for the current row. The procedural form is mysqli_fetch_lengths($result).

free(), **close()**, or **free_result()** clears the memory used for a result. The procedural form is mysqli_free_result($result).

```
<!DOCTYPE html><html><head></head><body><pre>

<?php
// S for SQL
$S=new mysqli("localhost","root","password","testDB");

$S->query("
DROP TABLE IF EXISTS tbl");

$S->query("
CREATE TABLE tbl (
  a INT,
  b VARCHAR(20))");

$S->query("
INSERT INTO tbl VALUES
  (0,'Hello World'),
  (1,'Testing 123'),
  (2,'Good Day!'),
  (3,'How Are You?'),
  (4,'Good Luck!')");


// R for result
$R = $S->query("SELECT * FROM tbl");

$row = $R->fetch_row();
echo $row[0]."|".$row[1]."<br/>";

$row = $R->fetch_assoc();
echo $row['a']."|".$row['b']."<br/>";

$row = $R->fetch_array();
echo $row[0]."|".$row['b']."<br/>";

class C{
  public $c=5;
}
$row = $R->fetch_object("C");
echo $row->a."|".$row->b."|".$row->c."<br/>";

$R->data_seek(3);
$row = $R->fetch_all();
print_r($row);

while ($field = $R->fetch_field()){
  echo "\n".$R->current_field."|";
  print_r($field);
}
free($R);

?>
</pre></body></html>
```

```
0|Hello World
1|Testing 123
2|Good Day!
3|How Are You?|5
Array
(
    [0] => Array
        (
            [0] => 3
            [1] => How Are You?
        )

    [1] => Array
        (
            [0] => 4
            [1] => Good Luck!
        )

)

1|stdClass Object
(
    [name] => a
    [orgname] => a
    [table] => tbl
    [orgtable] => tbl
    [def] =>
    [db] => test
    [catalog] => def
    [max_length] => 12
    [length] => 11
    [charsetnr] => 63
    [flags] => 32768
    [type] => 3
    [decimals] => 0
)

2|stdClass Object
(
    [name] => b
    [orgname] => b
    [table] => tbl
    [orgtable] => tbl
    [def] =>
    [db] => test
    [catalog] => def
    [max_length] => 0
    [length] => 60
    [charsetnr] => 33
    [flags] => 0
    [type] => 253
    [decimals] => 0
)
```

5.6 Functions and Operators

To illustrate the use of various MySQL functions and operators, many examples in this section use the SELECT clause. You may use the functions and operators in some other clauses such as the WHERE clause and the HAVING clause.

5.6.1 Operators

The operators, in the order of precedence, are:

BINARY (binary string casting), COLLATE
!
-(unary minus), ~(unary bit inversion)
^ (bitwise XOR)
*, /, DIV (integer division), %, MOD (same as %)

-, +
<< (bit left shift), >> (bit right shift)
& (bitwise AND)
|
= (comparison), <=> (NULL-safe equal), >=, >, <=, <, <>, !=, IS, LIKE, REGEXP, IN
BETWEEN...AND CASE...WHEN...THEN...ELSE...END
NOT
&&, AND
XOR
!!, OR
= (assignment), :=

SELECT 11 DIV 2;	5
SELECT 1 = 1, NULL = NULL, 1 = NULL;	1 NULL NULL
SELECT 1 <=> 1, NULL <=> NULL, 1 <=> NULL;	1 1 0
SELECT 1 IS TRUE, 0 IS FALSE, NULL IS UNKNOWN, NULL IS NOT UNKNOWN;	1 1 1 0
SELECT 0 IS NULL, 0 IS NOT NULL, FALSE IS NULL, NULL IS FALSE;	0 1 0 0
SELECT 'ab' LIKE 'a%b', 'axxb' LIKE 'a%b', 'abx' LIKE 'a%b';	1 1 0
SELECT 'ab' LIKE 'a_b', 'axb' LIKE 'a_b', 'axxb' LIKE 'a_b';	0 1 0
SELECT 'a_b%' LIKE 'a_b\%';	1
SELECT 'a_b%' NOT LIKE 'a_b\%';	0
SELECT 'abc' REGEXP '^[a-d]*';	1
SELECT 'x\n' REGEXP 'X\n', 'x\n' REGEXP BINARY 'X\n';	1 0
SELECT 'a' NOT REGEXP 'A';	0
SELECT 'a' IN ('ab','0','c');	0
SELECT 10 NOT IN (10,20,30);	0
SELECT 4 BETWEEN '4' AND 5;	1
SELECT 'y' BETWEEN 'x' AND 'Z';	1
SELECT 2 NOT BETWEEN 3 AND 1;	1
SELECT @a:=5,@b=5;	5 NULL

*** RLIKE is a synonym for REGEXP.

5.6.2 Type Conversion

The *type* for a **CONVERT(expr, type)** and **CAST(expr AS type)** can be BINARY [(N)], CHAR[(N)], DATE. DATETIME, DECIMAL [(M [,D])], TIME, UNSIGNED [INTEGER].

SELECT 2 + '2';	4
SELECT CONCAT(2, '2');	22
SELECT CONVERT(2, CHAR) + CAST(2 AS UNSIGNED INT);	4
SELECT 1 > NULL;	NULL
SELECT 1 = 0x01, '1' = 0x01;	1 0
SELECT 2 > '5x', 0 = 'x5';	0 1
SELECT 'a' = 'A', BINARY 'a' = 'A';	1 0
SELECT CONVERT('xyz' USING 'utf8');	xyz

5.6.3 Comparison

SELECT COALESCE(NULL, NULL, 3, 4, 5, NULL); -- first non-NULL argument	3
SELECT COALESCE(NULL, NULL, NULL);	NULL
SELECT GREATEST(1, 3.2, 2);	3.2
SELECT LEAST('x','y','z');	x
SELECT INTERVAL(5,1,3,7,8,9); -- 2 smaller integers between 5 and 7	2
SELECT INTERVAL(5,5,1,3);	3

5.6.4 Flow Control

SELECT CASE 2 WHEN 1 THEN 'one' WHEN 2 THEN 'two' ELSE 'three' END;	two
SELECT CASE WHEN 1 = 2 THEN 'first' WHEN 2 = 2 THEN 'SECOND' ELSE 'THIRD' END; -- first TRUE result	SECOND
SELECT IF(5<8, 'smaller', 'greater');	smaller
SELECT IFNULL(5,'abc'), IFNULL(NULL, 'abc');	5 abc
SELECT NULLIF(10,10), NULLIF(9,10);	NULL 9

5.6.5 Numeric

The trigonometrical functions are **SIN(x)**, **COS(x)**, **TAN(x)** and **COT(x)**, where x is specified in radians. The inverse functions are **ASIN(x)**, **ACOS(x)**, **ATAN(x)**, **ATAN(Y,X)** and **ATAN2(Y,X)**.

PI() returns the value of PI. **RADIANS(x)** converts x from degrees to radians. **DEGREES(x)** converts x from radians to degrees.

POW(x,y) or **POWER(x,y)** returns the value of x raised to the power of y. **SQRT(x)** returns the square root of a non-negative x. **EXP(x)** returns the value of e raised to the power of x. **LOG(x)** or **LN(x)** returns ln(x). **LOG(B,x)** returns the logarithm of x to be base B. **LOG2(x)** returns the base-2 logarithm of x. **LOG10(x)** returns the base-10 logarithm of x.

MOD(N,M) is the same as N % M and N MOD M. **SIGN(x)** returns the sign as -1, 0, or 1. **ABS(x)** returns the absolute value of x. **CEIL(x)** and **CEILING(x)** returns the smallest integer not less than x. **FLOOR(x)** returns the largest integer not greater than x. **ROUND(x)** rounds x to the nearest integer. **ROUND(x, D)** rounds x to D decimal places, where D can be negative. **TRUNCATE(x,D)** truncates x to D decimal places, where D can be negative.

CONV(N,B1,B2) converts N from base B1 to base B2. **CRC32(expr)** computes a cyclic redundancy check value and returns a 32-bit unsigned value. **RAND()** returns a random float in the range 0 to 1.0. **RAND(s)** uses s as the seed to produce the random number.

5.6.6 String

Numeric Conversion	
SELECT ASCII('abc'); -- code for 'a'	97
SELECT ORD('好'); -- multibyte code	15050173
SELECT CHAR(77,121,83,81,'76');	MySQL
SELECT BIN(13);	1101
SELECT OCT(51);	51
SELECT HEX(47);	2F
SELECT UNHEX('4D7953514C'), 0x4D7953514C;	MySQL MySQL
SELECT FORMAT(123456.123456, 4);	1,234.1235

Length	
SELECT LENGTH('abc 永');	6
SELECT BIT_LENGTH('abc 永');	48
SELECT OCTET_LENGTH('abc 永');	6
SELECT CHAR_LENGTH('abc 永');	4
SELECT CHARACTER_LENGTH('abc 永');	4
SELECT HEX(WEIGHT_STRING('永')); -- comparison value	6C38

Comparison	
SELECT STRCMP('abc','def'),STRCMP('def','abc');	-1 1
SELECT STRCMP('abc','abc');	0
SELECT STRCMP('abc','abcd'); -- abc precedes abcd	-1

Case	
SELECT UCASE('aBcd'), UPPER('EFgh'); -- synonyms	ABCD EFGH
SELECT LCASE('aBcd'), LOWER('EFgh'); -- synonyms	abcd efgh

Spacing and Padding	
SELECT SPACE(5);	' '
SELECT TRIM(' abc ');	'abc'
SELECT LTRIM(' abc ');	'abc '
SELECT RTRIM(' abc ');	' abc'
SELECT LPAD('abcd',7,'--');	---abcd
SELECT RPAD('abcd',3,'--');	abc

Concatenation	
SELECT CONCAT('ab',12,'cd');	ab12cd
SELECT CONCAT('ab',12,NULL);	NULL
SELECT CONCAT_WS(',','ab',12,'cd');	ab,12,cd
SELECT CONCAT_WS(',','ab',12,NULL);	ab,12
SELECT REPEAT('abc',3);	abcabcabc

Arguments Set	
SELECT ELT(2,'ab','cd','ef');	cd
SELECT EXPORT_SET(6,'1','0','|',8); -- 6 is 0110	0|1|1|0|0|0|0|0
SELECT MAKE_SET(5,'ab','cd','ef'); -- 5 is 101	ab,ef
SELECT FIELD('cd','ab','cd','ef','gh'); -- cd is the second one	2
SELECT FIND_IN_SET('cd','ab,cd,ef,gh'); -- cd is the second one	2

Substring	
SELECT LOCATE('cd','abcdef'); -- synonym: POSITION()	3
SELECT LOCATE('cd','abcdefcd',4);	7
SELECT LOCATE('zz','abcdefcd',4);	0
SELECT INSTR('abcdef','cd');	3
SELECT LEFT('abcdef',3);	abc
SELECT RIGHT('abcdef',3);	def
SELECT SUBSTR('abcdef',3); -- synonym: SUBSTRING()	cdef
SELECT SUBSTR('abcdef' FROM 3);	cdef
SELECT SUBSTR('abcdef', 3,2);	cd
SELECT SUBSTR('abcdef' FROM 3 FOR 2);	cd
SELECT SUBSTR('abcdef',-2);	ef
SELECT INSERT('abcdef',3,2,'XXXX');	abXXXXef
SELECT REPLACE('abcdabef','ab','XX');	XXcdXXef
SELECT REVERSE('abcd');	dbca
SELECT SUBSTRING_INDEX('www.google.com','.',2);	www.google
SELECT SUBSTRING_INDEX('www.google.com','.',-2);	google.com

Miscellaneous	
SELECT '\\\'',QUOTE('\\\'');	\' '\\\''
SELECT SOUNDEX('hello'),SOUNDEX('helo');	H400 H400
SELECT 'hello' SOUNDS LIKE 'helo';	1
SELECT TO_BASE64('xyz'), FROM_BASE64(TO_BASE64('xyz'));	eHI6 xyz
SELECT LOAD_FILE('file.txt');	<file content>

5.6.7 Date and Time

Current Date and Time	
SELECT CURRENT_DATE, CURRENT_DATE(), CURDATE(); -- synonyms	2014-04-27 2014-04-27 2014-04-27
SELECT CURRENT_TIME, CURRENT_TIME(), CURTIME(); -- synonyms	13:16:54 13:16:54 13:16:54
SELECT NOW(), CURRENT_TIMESTAMP, CURRENT_TIMESTAMP(), LOCALTIME, LOCALTIME(), LOCALTIMESTAMP, LOCALTIMESTAMP(); -- synonyms	2014-04-27 13:16:54 ......
SELECT NOW(2), SLEEP(1), NOW(2);	2014-04-27 13:16:54.28 0 2014-04-27 13:16:54.28
SELECT SYSDATE(), SLEEP(1), SYSDATE();	2014-04-27 13:16:54 0 2014-04-27 13:16:55
SELECT SYSDATE(2);	2014-04-27 13:16:55.72
SELECT UNIX_TIMESTAMP(); -- seconds since 1970-01-01 00:00:00	1398576430
SELECT UNIX_TIMESTAMP('2014-04-27 13:28:00'); -- seconds since 1970-01-01 00:00:00	1398576480
SELECT UTC_DATE, UTC_DATE()+0; -- synonyms	2014-04-27 20140427
SELECT UTC_TIME, UTC_TIME()+0; -- synonyms	05:30:42 53042
SELECT UTC_TIMESTAMP, UTC_TIMESTAMP()+0; -- synonyms	2014-04-27 05:32:57 20140427053257

Additions and Subtractions	
SELECT DATE_ADD('2014-04-27', INTERVAL 15 DAY), ADDDATE('2014-04-27', INTERVAL 15 DAY); -- synonyms	2014-05-12 2014-05-12
SELECT ADDDATE('2014-04-27', 15); -- second argument treated as days	2014-05-12
SELECT DATE_SUB('2014-04-27', INTERVAL 15 DAY), SUBDATE('2014-04-27', INTERVAL 15 DAY); -- synonyms	2014-04-12 2014-04-12
SELECT SUBDATE('2014-04-27', 15); -- second argument treated as days	2014-04-12
SELECT ADDTIME('2014-04-27 13:30:00', '1 05:30:30.123456');	2014-04-28 19:00:30.123456
SELECT ADDTIME('13:30:00', '1 05:30:30.123456');	43:00:30.123456

SELECT SUBTIME('13:30:00', '05:30:30.123456');	07:59:29.876544
SELECT DATEDIFF('2014-04-27 14:00:00','2015-04-27'); -- time not used	-365
SELECT TIMEDIFF('2014-04-27 14:00:00', '2014-03-27 06:30:30');	751:29:30
SELECT TIMESTAMPDIFF(DAY, '2014-04-27 14:00:00','2013-03-27');	-396
SELECT TIMESTAMPADD(WEEK,15, '2014-04-27 13:30:30.1');	2014-08-10 13:30:30.100000
SELECT PERIOD_DIFF(201311,201404); -- 5 months	-5
SELECT PERIOD_ADD(201404,12); -- 12 months	201504
SELECT TIMESTAMP('2007-02-10 14:30:00','05:10:10');	2007-02-10 19:40:10
SELECT EXTRACT(YEAR FROM '2014-04-27');	2014
INTERVAL units: MICROSECOND: 123456 SECOND: 30 MINUTES: 30 HOUR: 12 DAY: 4 WEEK: 25 MONTH: 6 QUARTER: 2 YEAR: 2000 SECOND_MICROSECOND: '30.123456' MINUTE_MICROSECOND: '30:30.123456' MINUTE_SECOND: '30:30' HOUR_MICROSECOND: '06:30:30.123456' HOUR_SECOND: '06:30:30' HOUR_MINUTE: '06:30' DAY_MICROSECOND: '15 06:30:30.123456' DAY_SECOND: '15 06:30:30' DAY_MINUTE: '15 06:30' DAY_HOUR: '15 06' YEAR_MONTH: '15-06'	

Formatting	
SET @d = '2014-04-27 14:30:00.123456'; SELECT YEAR(@d),MONTH(@d),DAY(@d), HOUR(@d),MINUTE(@d),SECOND(@d), MICROSECOND(@d); -- DAYOFMONTH() is a synonym for DAY()	2014 4 27 14 30 0 123456
SELECT DATE('2007-05-10 14:30:30.123456');	2007-05-10
SELECT TIME('2007-05-10 14:30:30.123456');	14:30:30. 123456
SELECT DAYOFWEEK('2007-02-10'); -- 1 to 7, SUNDAY to SATURDAY	7
SELECT WEEKDAY('2007-02-10'); -- 0 to 6, MONDAY TO SUNDAY	5
SELECT DAYNAME('2007-02-10');	Saturday
SELECT DAYOFYEAR('2007-05-10'); -- 1 to 366	130
SELECT MAKEDATE(2014,100); -- 100 is day of the year	2014-04-10
SELECT MAKETIME(12,30,30);	12:30:30
SELECT WEEK('2014-12-31');	52
SELECT WEEK('2014-12-25'), WEEKOFYEAR('2014-12-25');	51 52
SELECT YEARWEEK('2014-12-25');	201451
SELECT MONTHNAME('2007-02-10');	February
SELECT QUARTER('2007-02-10'); -- 1 to 4	1
SELECT LAST_DAY('2007-02-10');	2007-02-28
SELECT FROM_DAYS(1000);	0002-09-27
SELECT FROM_UNIXTIME(10);	1970-01-01 08:00:10
SELECT FROM_UNIXTIME(10)+0;	19700101 080010

SELECT SEC_TO_TIME(12345);	03:25:45
SELECT TIME_TO_SEC('03:25:45');	12345
SELECT TO_DAYS('0000-02-01');	32
SELECT TO_SECONDS('0000-02-01');	2764800
SELECT DATE_FORMAT('2014-04-27 12:00:00' , '%Y,%M');	2014,April
SELECT TIME_FORMAT('100:30:30.123456','%f');	123456
SELECT STR_TO_DATE('2014,January','%Y,%M');	2014-01-00
SELECT FROM_UNIXTIME(10,"%Y %D %M");	1970 1st January
SELECT GET_FORMAT(DATE,'USA');	%m.%d.%Y
SELECT GET_FORMAT(DATE,'JIS');	%Y-%m-%d
SELECT GET_FORMAT(DATE,'ISO');	%Y-%m-%d
SELECT GET_FORMAT(TIME,'EUR');	%H.%i.%s
SELECT GET_FORMAT(DATETIME,'INTERNAL');	%Y%m%d %H%i%s
SELECT CONVERT_TZ('2014-04-27 14:00:00','+00:00','+08:00');	2014-04-27 22:00:00

Format Specifier	Description	Example
%a	Abbreviated weekday name	Sun
%b	Abbreviated month name	Jan
%c	Month, numeric	2
%D	Day of the month, with suffix	2nd
%d	Day of the month, numeric	02
%e	Day of the month, numeric	2
%f	Microseconds	123456
%H	Hour (00...23)	18
%h	Hour (01...12)	12
%I	Hour (01...12)	12
%i	Minutes, numeric	09
%j	Day of year (001...366)	002
%k	Hour (0...23)	18
%l	Hour(1...12)	12
%M	Month name	January
%m	Month, numeric	02
%p	AM or PM	AM
%r	Time	12:30:30 AM
%S	Seconds	05
%s	Seconds	05
%T	Time	18:30:30
%U	Week(0...53), Sunday first	05
%u	Week(0...53), Monday first	05
%V	Week(1...53), Sunday first	05
%v	Week(1...53), Monday first	05
%W	Weekday name	Sunday
%w	Day of the week (0=Sunday)	0
%X	Year for the week, Sunday first	2000
%x	Year for the week, Monday first	2000
%Y	Year, numeric	2000
%y	Year, numeric	99
%%	Literal % character	%

5.6.8 Encryption and Compression

ENCRYPT(str[,salt]) encrypts str using the Unix crypt() system call. If salt is not provided, a random value is used.

AES_ENCRYPT(str, key [, init_vector]) encrypts str with key using the AES algorithm. **AES_DECRYPT (str, key [, init_vector])** decrypts str with key using the AES algorithm.

DES_ENCRYPT(str, key [, init_vector]) encrypts str with key using the Triple-DES algorithm. **DES_DECRYPT(str, key [, init_vector])** decrypts str with key using the Triple-DES algorithm.

SHA1(str) and **SHA(str)** calculates an SHA-1 160-bit checksum for str and returns a string of 40 hex digits. **SHA2(str, hash_length)** calculates the SHA-2 family of hash functions (SHA-224, SHA-256, SHA-384, SHA-512). The second argument must have a value of 224, 256, 384, 512, or 0(256). **MD5(str)** calculates an MD5 128-bit checksum for str, and returns a string of 32 hex digits.

PASSWORD(str) returns a hashed password string calculated from str, and returns a nonbinary string in the connection character set. **VALIDATE_ PASSWORD_STRENGTH(str)** returns an integer in the range 0(weak) to 100(strong) indicating the strength of the password str.

COMPRESS(str) returns a compressed version of str as a binary string. **UNCOMPRES(str)** returns an uncompressed version of a string str compressed by COMPRESS(str). **UNCOMPRESSERD_LENGTH(str)** returns the length of str before compression.

RANOM_BYTES(len) returns a binary string of len random bytes.

5.6.9 Database Information

VERSION() returns the MySQL server version. **DATABASE()** or **SCHEMA()** returns the current database name. **CONNECTION_ID()** returns the ID for the connection.

USER(), **SESSION_USER()**, or **SYSTEM_USER()** returns the current username and hostname. **CURRENT_USER**, or **CURRENT_USER()** returns the username and hostname combination used to authenticate the current client.

LAST_INSERT_ID() returns the first generated value for an AUTO_INCREMENT column during the last INSERT operation. **ROW_COUNT()** returns the number of affected rows during the last operation. **FOUND_ROWS()** returns the number of rows returned without the LIMIT clause. To use this function, include the SQL_CALC_FOUND_ROWS option in the SELECT statement:

```
> SELECT SQL_CALC_FOUND_ROWS *
  FROM tbl LIMIT 10;
> SELECT FOUND_ROWS();
```

CHARSET(str) returns the character set of str. **COLLATION(str)** returns the collation of str. **COERCIBILITY(str)** returns the collation coercibility of str.

BENCHMARK(count, expr) executes expr count times. The returned value is always zero, but the query execution times may be reported elsewhere.

5.6.10 GROUP BY Aggregate

COUNT([DISTINCT] expr) returns the number of values retrieved. **MAX([DISTINCT] expr)** returns the maximum value retrieved. **MIN([DISTINCT] expr)** returns the minimum value retrieved. **SUM ([DISTINCT] expr)** returns the sum of the values retrieved. **AVG([DISTINCT] expr)** returns the average of the values retrieved. **GROUP_CONCAT ([DISTINCT] expr)** returns a string that is the concatenation of the retrieved values.

```
SELECT COUNT(*) FROM tbl;
SELECT a FROM tbl GROUP BY a HAVING MAX(b)>9
SELECT GROUP_CONCAT(DISTINCT score SEPARATOR ' ')
FROM class GROUP BY student
```

BIT_AND(expr), **BIT_OR(expr)**, and **BIT_XOR (expr)** perform bitwise operations on the values retrieved.

STD(expr), STDDEV(expr), or **STDDEV_POP (expr)** returns the population standard deviation. **STDDEV_SAMP(expr)** returns the sample standard deviation. **VARIANCE(expr)** or **VAR_POP(expr)** returns the population standard variance. **VAR_SAMP (expr)** returns the sample variance.

5.6.11 Miscellaneous

DEFAULT(column) returns the default value for a table column. **NAME_CONST(name,value)** names the column as *name* and returns *value*. **BIT_ COUNT(arg)** returns the number of set bits in *arg*. **SLEEP(sec)** pauses for *sec* seconds.

GET_LOCK(str, timeout) tries to obtain a lock named str. **RELEASE_LOCK(str)** releases the lock acquired by GET_LOCK(). **IS_USED_LOCK(str)** returns the client's connection identifier if str is a used lock, NULL otherwise. **IS_FREE_LOCK(str)** returns 1 if no one is using str as a lock, 0 if the lock is in use, NULL if an error occurs. **MASTER_POS_WAIT (log_name, log_pos [,timeout])** blocks until the slave has read and applied all updates up to the specified position in the master log. It returns the number of log events the slave had to wait for to advance to the specified position.

INET_ATON(ip_address) returns an integer representing the IPv4 ip_address. **INET_NTOA(int)** returns the dotted-quad ip address represented by int. **INET6_ATON(ip_address)** returns a binary string representing the IPv6 ip_address. **INET6_NTOA(str)** returns the IPv6 address represented by str. **IS_IPV4(str)** returns 1 if str is a valid IPv4 IP address, 0 otherwise. **IS_IPV6(str)** returns 1 if str is a valid IPv6 IP address, 0 otherwise. **IS_IPV4_COMPAT(str)** returns 1 if str is a valid IPv4-compatible IPv6 address, 0 otherwise. str is a binary string as returned by INET6_ATON(). **IS_IPV4_MAPPED(str)** returns 1 if str is a valid

IPv4-mapped IPv6 address, 0 otherwise. str is a binary string as returned by INET6_ATON().

UUID() returns a Universal Unique Identifier according to DCE 1.1: Remote Procedure Call, CAE Specifications published by The Open Group in October 1997. A UUID is globally unique in space and time. It has a format like: '6ccd780c-baba-1026-9564-0040f4311e29'. **UUID_SHORT()** returns a short version of UUID as a 64-bit unsigned integer. It has a format like: 92395783831158784.

ExtractValue(xml_frag, xpath_expr) returns the text (CDATA) of the first text node which is a child of the elements of elements matched by the Xpath expression. **UpdateXML(xml_target, xpath_expr, new_xml)** replaces a single portion of xml_target matched by xpath_expr with new_xml.

5.7 Information and Variables

5.7.1 Information

Comments within an SQL statement are denoted from '#' to the end of line, from '-- ' (ending with a whitespace character) to the end of line, and from '/*' to '*/'. The last form of comment syntax can span multiple lines.

```
CREATE TABLE tbl(
   a INT,  # this is a comment
   b INT,  -- this is another comment
   c INT   /* this is a multiline
              comment */
);
```

To obtain information from MySQL Reference Manual, use: **HELP** 'search_string', where 'search_string' can contain the wildcard characters % and _ as with the LIKE operator.

```
<!DOCTYPE html><html><head></head><body><pre>
<?php

$S=new mysqli("localhost","root","password","testDB");
tabulate($S->query("HELP 'contents'"));  // the contents page
tabulate($S->query("HELP 'Data Types'"));  // a topic
tabulate($S->query("HELP 'REPLACE'"));  // a command

// ****** A useful, general-purpose result printer
function tabulate($result){
   $fInfo = $result->fetch_fields();
   echo "<table border='1'><tr>";
   foreach($fInfo as $col){
      echo "<td>".$col->name."</td>";
   }
   while ($row = $result->fetch_row()){
      echo "</tr><tr>";
      foreach ($row as $val){
         echo "<td>".$val."</td>";
      }
   }
   echo "</tr></table><br/>";
}
?>
</pre></body></html>
```

source_category_name	name	is_it_category
Contents	Account Management	Y
Contents	Administration	Y
Contents	Compound Statements	Y
Contents	Data Definition	Y
Contents	Data Manipulation	Y
Contents	Data Types	Y
Contents	Functions	Y
Contents	Functions and Modifiers for Use with GROUP BY	Y
Contents	Geographic Features	Y
Contents	Help Metadata	Y
Contents	Language Structure	Y
Contents	Plugins	Y
Contents	Procedures	Y
Contents	Storage Engines	Y
Contents	Table Maintenance	Y
Contents	Transactions	Y
Contents	User-Defined Functions	Y
Contents	Utility	Y

source_category_name	name	is_it_category
Data Types	AUTO_INCREMENT	N
Data Types	BIGINT	N
Data Types	BINARY	N
Data Types	BIT	N
Data Types	BLOB	N
Data Types	BLOB DATA TYPE	N
Data Types	BOOLEAN	N
Data Types	CHAR	N
Data Types	CHAR BYTE	N
Data Types	DATE	N
Data Types	DATETIME	N
Data Types	DEC	N
Data Types	DECIMAL	N
Data Types	DOUBLE	N
Data Types	DOUBLE PRECISION	N
Data Types	ENUM	N
Data Types	FLOAT	N
Data Types	INT	N
Data Types	INTEGER	N
Data Types	LONGBLOB	N
Data Types	LONGTEXT	N
Data Types	MEDIUMBLOB	N
Data Types	MEDIUMINT	N
Data Types	MEDIUMTEXT	N
Data Types	SET DATA TYPE	N
Data Types	SMALLINT	N
Data Types	TEXT	N
Data Types	TIME	N
Data Types	TIMESTAMP	N
Data Types	TINYBLOB	N
Data Types	TINYINT	N
Data Types	TINYTEXT	N
Data Types	VARBINARY	N
Data Types	VARCHAR	N
Data Types	YEAR DATA TYPE	N

name	description	example

REPLACE	Syntax:
	REPLACE [LOW_PRIORITY | DELAYED]
	    [INTO] tbl_name
	    [PARTITION (partition_name,...)]
	    [(col_name,...)]
	    {VALUES | VALUE} ({expr | DEFAULT},...),(...),...
	
	Or:
	
	REPLACE [LOW_PRIORITY | DELAYED]
	    [INTO] tbl_name
	    [PARTITION (partition_name,...)]
	    SET col_name={expr | DEFAULT}, ...
	
	Or:
	
	REPLACE [LOW_PRIORITY | DELAYED]
	    [INTO] tbl_name
	    [PARTITION (partition_name,...)]
	    [(col_name,...)]
	    SELECT ...
	
	REPLACE works exactly like INSERT, except that if an old row in the table has the same value as a new row for a PRIMARY KEY or a UNIQUE index, the old row is deleted before the new row is inserted. See [HELP INSERT].
	
	REPLACE is a MySQL extension to the SQL standard. It either inserts, or deletes and inserts. For another MySQL extension to standard SQL---that either inserts or updates---see http://dev.mysql.com/doc/refman/5.6/en/insert-on-duplicate.html.
	
	Note that unless the table has a PRIMARY KEY or UNIQUE index, using a REPLACE statement makes no sense. It becomes equivalent to INSERT, because there is no index to be used to determine whether a new row duplicates another.
	
	Values for all columns are taken from the values specified in the REPLACE statement. Any missing columns are set to their default values, just as happens for INSERT. You cannot refer to values from the current row and use them in the new row. If you use an assignment such as SET col_name = col_name + 1, the reference to the column name on the right hand side is treated as DEFAULT(col_name), so the assignment is equivalent to SET col_name = DEFAULT(col_name) + 1.
	
	To use REPLACE, you must have both the INSERT and DELETE privileges for the table.
	
	Beginning with MySQL 5.6.2, REPLACE supports explicit partition selection using the PARTITION option with a comma-separated list of names of partitions, subpartitions, or both. As with INSERT, if it is not possible to insert the new row into any of these partitions or subpartitions, the REPLACE statement fails with the error Found a row not matching the given partition set. See http://dev.mysql.com/doc/refman/5.6/en/partitioning-selection.html, for more information.
	
	URL: http://dev.mysql.com/doc/refman/5.6/en/replace.html	

EXPLAIN, **DESCRIBE**, or **DESC** can be used to obtain information about a specific table or statement.

```
{EXPLAIN | DESCRIBE | DESC}
   tbl_name [col_name | wild]

{EXPLAIN | DESCRIBE | DESC}
   [explain_type]
   {explainable_stmt | FOR CONNECTION connection_id}

explain_type: {
   EXTENDED
 | PARTITIONS
 | FORMAT = format_name
}

format_name: {
   TRADITIONAL
 | JSON
}

explainable_stmt: {
   SELECT statement
 | DELETE statement
 | INSERT statement
 | REPLACE statement
 | UPDATE statement
}
```

```
<!DOCTYPE html><html><head></head><body><pre>
<?php

$S=new mysqli("localhost","root","password","testDB");
$S->query("DROP TABLE IF EXISTS tbl;");
$S->query("
CREATE TABLE tbl(
  a INT PRIMARY KEY,
  b INT DEFAULT 5,
  c INT AUTO_INCREMENT UNIQUE
)");

tabulate($S->query("EXPLAIN tbl"));
tabulate($S->query("EXPLAIN SELECT * FROM tbl"));

// ****** A useful, general-purpose result printer
function tabulate($result){
  $fInfo = $result->fetch_fields();
  echo "<table border='1'><tr>";
  foreach($fInfo as $col){
    echo "<td>".$col->name."</td>";
  }
  while ($row = $result->fetch_row()){
    echo "</tr><tr>";
    foreach ($row as $val){
      echo "<td>".$val."</td>";
    }
  }
  echo "</tr></table><br/>";
}

?>
</pre></body></html>
```

Field	Type	Null	Key	Default	Extra
a	int(11)	NO	PRI		
b	int(11)	YES		5	
c	int(11)	NO	UNI		auto_increment

id	select_type	table	type	possible_keys	key	key_len	ref	rows	Extra
1	SIMPLE	tbl	ALL					1	

5.7.2 SHOW

SHOW BINARY LOGS SHOW MASTER LOGS
These list the log files on the server and the sizes.

SHOW BINLOG EVENTS [IN 'log_name'] [FROM pos] [LIMIT [offset,] row_count]
This shows the events in the binary log. If 'log_name' is not specified, the first binary log is used.

SHOW CHARACTER SET [LIKE 'pattern' | WHERE expr]
This shows all available character sets.

SHOW COLLATION [LIKE 'pattern' | WHERE expr]
This lists collations supported by the server.

SHOW [FULL] COLUMNS {FROM | IN} tbl [{FROM|IN} db] [LIKE 'pattern' | WHERE expr]
This displays information about the columns in a table.

SHOW CREATE {DATABASE|SCHEMA} [IF NOT EXISTS] db
This shows the statement that creates the database.

SHOW CREATE EVENT event
This displays the statement that creates an event.

SHOW CREATE FUNCTION function
This displays the statement that defines a function.

SHOW CREATE PROCEDURE procedure
This displays the statement that creates a stored procedure.

SHOW CREATE TABLE tbl
This displays the statement that creates a table.

SHOW CREATE TRIGGER trigger
This displays the statement that creates a trigger.

SHOW CREATE VIEW view
This displays the statement that creates a view.

SHOW {DATABASES | SCHEMAS} [LIKE 'pattern' | WHERE expr]
This lists the databases on the server.

SHOW ENGINE engine {STATUS | MUTEX}
This displays the operational information about a storage engine.

SHOW [STORAGE] ENGINES
This displays information about the server's storage engines.

SHOW ERRORS [LIMIT [offset,] row_count] SHOW COUNT(*) ERRORS
These display information about errors resulting from executing a statement in the current session.

SHOW EVENTS [{FROM | IN} schema] [LIKE 'pattern' | WHERE expr]
This displays information about Event Manager events.

SHOW FUNCTION CODE function
This displays a representation of the internal implementation of the function.

SHOW FUNCTION STATUS [LIKE 'pattern' | WHERE expr]
This shows the characteristics of a function.

SHOW GRANTS [FOR user]
This lists the statement that can be used to duplicate the privileges granted to an account.

SHOW {INDEX | INDEXES | KEYS} {FROM|IN} tbl [{FROM|IN} db] [WHERE expr]
This displays information about the indexes in a table.

SHOW MASTER STATUS
This displays status information about the binary log files of the master.

SHOW OPEN TABLES [{FROM|IN} db] [LIKE 'pattern'| WHERE expr]
This lists the non-temporary tables that are currently open in the table cache.

SHOW PLUGINS
This displays information about server plugins.

SHOW PRIVILEGES
This lists the supported system privileges.

SHOW PROCEDURE CODE procedure
This displays a representation of the internal implementation of the stored procedure.

SHOW PROCEDURE STATUS [LIKE 'pattern' | WHERE expr]
This displays the chraracteristics about a stored procedure.

SHOW PROCESSLIST
This displays which threads are running.

SHOW RELAYLOG EVENTS [IN 'log_name'] [FROM pos] [LIMIT [offset,] row_count]
This shows the events in the relay log of a replication slave.

SHOW SLAVE HOSTS
This displays a list of replication slaves currently registered with the master.

SHOW SLAVE STATUS [NONBLOCKING]
This provides status information on essential parameters of the slave threads.

SHOW [GLOBAL|SESSION] STATUS [LIKE 'pattern' | WHERE expr]
This provides server status information.

SHOW TABLE STATUS [{FROM|IN} db] [LIKE 'pattern' | WHERE expr]
This works like 'SHOW TABLES', but provides a lot of information about each non-TEMPORARY table.

SHOW TRIGGERS [{FROM|IN} db] [LIKE 'pattern' | WHERE expr]
This lists the triggers currently defined for the tables in a database.

SHOW [GLOBAL|SESSION] VARIABLES [LIKE 'pattern' | WHERE expr]
This shows the values of the system variables.

SHOW WARNINGS [LIMIT [offset,] row_count] SHOW COUNT(*) WARNINGS
This displays information about the errors, warnings and notes resulting from a statement in the current session.

5.7.3 INFORMATION_SCHEMA

INFORMATION_SCHEMA is a predefined database which stores meta-information about all the other databases. It contains several read-only views. They are not tables, so there are no files associated with them, and you cannot set triggers on them. However, you can select INFORMATION_SCHEMA as the default database with a USE statement.

Much information in INFORMATION_SCHEMA can be retrieved with the SHOW statement. For instance, the two statements below are equivalent:

```
SELECT table_name FROM INFORMATION_SCHEMA.TABLES
  WHERE table_schema = 'db_name'
  [AND table_name LIKE 'wild']
```

```
SHOW TABLES
  FROM db_name
  [LIKE 'wild']
```

INFORMATION_SCHEMA contains the following tables:

CHARACTER_SETS
COLLATIONS
COLLATION_CHARACTER_SET_APPLICABILITY
COLUMNS
COLUMN_PRIVILEGES
ENGINES
EVENTS
FILES
GLOBAL_STATUS and SESSION_STATUS
GLOBAL_VARIABLES and SESSION_VARIABLES
KEY_COLUMN_USAGE
OPTIMIZER_TRACE
PARAMETERS
PARTITIONS
PLUGINS
PROCESSLIST
PROFILING
REFERENTIAL_CONSTRAINTS
ROUTINES
SCHEMATA
SCHEMA_PRIVILEGES
STATISTICS
TABLES
TABLESPACES
TABLE_CONSTRAINTS
TABLE_PRIVILEGES
TRIGGERS Table
USER_PRIVILEGES
VIEWS

5.7.4 SET

```
SET variable_assignment [, variable_assignment] ...

variable_assignment:
    user_var = expr
  | [GLOBAL | SESSION] system_var = expr
  | [@@global. | @@session. | @@]system_var = expr
```

A user-defined variable begins with the symbol @.

Any change to a **SESSION** system variable lasts until a session closes. Any change to a **GLOBAL** system variable lasts until the server restarts.

Some system variables exist as both SESSION and GLOBAL variables.

To view the values for the various system variables, tabulate the result retrieved by the query:

```
SHOW [GLOBAL|SESSION] VARIABLES
[LIKE 'pattern' | WHERE expr]
```

```
SET @a = 900 + 99;
SELECT @a,
       @@system_time_zone,
       @@global.autocommit;
```

999	Malay Peninsula Standard Time	1

5.8 Injection Attacks

By submitting carefully devised input to a poorly designed system, an attacker can trick a server script into executing SQL commands that are not allowed for a client. An open-sourced software package may be especially vulnerable to SQL injection, because the database architecture is publicly open. Never trust any form of input, even if it originates from a select box, a hidden input field, or a cookie.

To prevent injection attacks, a web developer should properly validate all input from the client. Prepared statements with paramerized queries are very effective in this regard, because they compile all runnable parts of a query beforehand, and accept the input as simple data that cannot be executed. Prepared statements also increase the computational efficiency of repeated SQL commands, as they need not be parsed multiple times.

Additionally, privileges can be limited for casual visitors.

5.8.1 Hacking Techniques

Example 1

Server Code:
```
SELECT * FROM users WHERE userid = $input
```
Injection for $input:
```
99 OR TRUE
```
Executed Command:
```
SELECT * FROM users WHERE userid = 99 OR TRUE
```
This may permit the hacker to obtain all usernames and passwords, as the WHERE clause always evaluates to TRUE.

Example 2

Server Code:
```
SELECT * FROM users WHERE username = '$input'
```
Injection for $input:
```
' OR TRUE --
```
Executed Command:
```
SELECT * FROM users WHERE username = '' OR TRUE -- '
```
This may permit the hacker to obtain all usernames and passwords, as the WHERE clause always evaluates to TRUE. Ending a string immediately with the single quote and commenting out the rest of the query are common forms of SQL injection.

Example 3

Server Code:
```
SELECT id, name, dt, size FROM products WHERE size='$size'
```
Injection for $size:
```
'
UNION
SELECT '1', CONCAT(uname,'-',passwd) AS NAME,
'2000-01-01', '0' FROM users --
```
Executed Command:
```
SELECT id, name, dt, size FROM products WHERE size=''
UNION
SELECT '1', CONCAT(uname,'-','passwd) AS NAME,
'2000-01-01', '0' FROM users --'
```
This obtains the usernames and passwords even when the table containing them is not being accessed directly.

Example 4

Server Code:
```
UPDATE usertable SET password='$pwd'
WHERE username='$uid'
```
Injection for $pwd:
```
xxx
```
Injection for $uid:
```
' OR uid LIKE '%admin%
```
Executed Command:
```
UPDATE usertable SET password='xxx'
WHERE username='' OR uid LIKE '%admin%'
```
This changes the admin's password.

Example 5
Server Code: UPDATE usertable SET password='$pwd' WHERE username='$uid'
Injection for $pwd: xxx', trusted=100, admin='yes
Executed Command: UPDATE usertable SET passwordwd='xxx', trusted=100, admin='yes' WHERE username='...'
This grants more priveleges to an account illegally.

Example 6
Server Code: SELECT * FROM products WHERE id LIKE '%$prod%'
Injection for $prod: *a%'* *exec master..xp_cmdshell 'net user test testpass /ADD' --*
Executed Command: SELECT * FROM products WHERE id LIKE '%*a%'* *exec master..xp_cmdshell 'net user test testpass /ADD'* -- %'
This gives the attacker access to a machine running MSSQL Server.

Example 7
Server Code: SELECT * FROM users WHERE userid = $input
Injection for $input: 99; DROP TABLE suppliers
Executed Command: SELECT * FROM users WHERE userid = 99; DROP TABLE suppliers
This deletes a table from the table illegally. Note that this hacking technique works only in systems that support multiple batched SQL statements within a query. Some PHP systems support only one SQL statement per query.

Example 8
Server Code: SELECT id, name FROM products ORDER BY name LIMIT 30 OFFSET $offset
Injection for $offset: 0; insert into pg_shadow(usename,usesysid,usesuper,usecatupd,passwd) select 'crack', usesysid, 't','t','crack' from pg_shadow where usename='postgres'; --
Executed Command: SELECT id, name FROM products ORDER BY name LIMIT 30 OFFSET 0; insert into pg_shadow(usename,usesysid,usesuper,usecatupd,passwd) select 'crack', usesysid, 't','t','crack' from pg_shadow where usename='postgres'; --
This grants the hacker superuser access. Note that this hacking technique works only in systems that support multiple batched SQL statements within a query. Some PHP systems support only one SQL statement per query.

5.8.2 Validating Input

Simple preventive measures against SQL injection involve converting the input to numbers when numbers are expected, and escaping the single quotes when strings are expected. Three functions are useful here:

1.
settype(&$m, $s) sets the type of variable $m to type $s. $s can be 'bool', 'boolean', 'int', 'integer', 'float', 'double', 'string', 'array', 'object', 'null'.

2.
mysqli_real_escape_string($l, $s) encodes NUL, \n, \r, \, ', ", and Control-Z to be used in an SQL statement.

3.
str_replace($s1, $s2, $s3 [,$i]) returns a copy of $s3 with all $s1 replaced by $s2. This can be used to convert the single quotes forth and back.

```
<!DOCTYPE html><html><head></head><body><pre>
<?php

// Example 1
$input = "99 OR TRUE";
settype($input,"int");
echo $input."\n\n";

// Example 2
$input = "' OR TRUE --";
$link=mysqli_connect("localhost","root","passwd","testDB");
echo mysqli_real_escape_string($link,$input)."\n\n";

// Example 3
$size = "'
UNION
SELECT '1', CONCAT(uname,'-',passwd) AS NAME,
'2000-01-01', '0' FROM users -- ";
$size = str_replace("'","--SQ--",$size);
echo $size."\n\n";
$size = str_replace("--SQ--","'",$size);
echo $size;

?>
</pre></body></html>
```

```
99

\' OR TRUE --

--SQ--
UNION
SELECT --SQ--1--SQ--, CONCAT(uname,--SQ-----SQ--,passwd) AS NAME,
--SQ--2000-01-01--SQ--, --SQ--0--SQ-- FROM users --

'
UNION
SELECT '1', CONCAT(uname,'-',passwd) AS NAME,
'2000-01-01', '0' FROM users --
```

5.8.3 MySQL Prepared Statements

PREPARE ps_name FROM preparable_stmt
EXECUTE ps_name [USING @var1 [,@var2]...]
{DEALLOCATE | DROP} PREPARE ps_name
A prepared statement is deallocated automatically at the end of a session. A prepared statement is not shared by other sessions.
Prepared statements cannot be nested or contain multi-statements.
If a prepared statement is constructed in a stored routine, it won't be cleared when the stored routine exits. As such, a prepared statement cannot refer to stored routines' parameters or local variables.
? is used as parameter markers in preparable_stmt.

Preparable statements
ALTER TABLE ALTER USER ANALYZE TABLE CACHE INDEX CALL CHANGE MASTER CHECKSUM {TABLE | TABLES} COMMIT {CREATE | DROP} INDEX {CREATE | RENAME | DROP} DATABASE {CREATE | DROP} TABLE {CREATE | RENAME | DROP} USER {CREATE | DROP} VIEW DELETE DO FLUSH {TABLE | TABLES | TABLES WITH READ LOCK | HOSTS | PRIVILEGES | LOGS | STATUS | MASTER | SLAVE | DES_KEY_FILE | USER_RESOURCES} GRANT INSERT INSTALL PLUGIN KILL LOAD INDEX INTO CACHE OPTIMIZE TABLE RENAME TABLE REPAIR TABLE REPLACE RESET {MASTER | SLAVE | QUERY CACHE} REVOKE SELECT SET SHOW {WARNINGS | ERRORS} SHOW BINLOG EVENTS SHOW CREATE {PROCEDURE | FUNCTION | EVENT | TABLE | VIEW} SHOW {MASTER | BINARY} LOGS SHOW {MASTER | SLAVE} STATUS SLAVE {START | STOP} TRUNCATE TABLE UNINSTALL PLUGIN UPDATE

PREPARE ps FROM 'SELECT ? + ?;'; SET @a=1, @b=2; EXECUTE ps USING @a, @b; DEALLOCATE PREPARE ps;	3

5.8.4 PHP Prepared Statements

mysqli::prepare($s) or **mysqli_prepare($l, $s)** prepares a single query $s and returns a mysqli_stmt prepared statement object. **mysqli::stmt_init()** or **mysqli_stmt_init($l)** initializes a prepared statement appropriate for mysqli_stmt_prepare().

The following functions in this sub-section (5.8.4) belong to the mysqli_stmt class, which represents a prepared object. Only the object-oriented forms are desribed. The procedural form of each function for a prepared statement object can be obtained by prepending the function name with mysqli_stmt_, and using the mysqli_stmt object as the first parameter. For example, the procedural form for PS->prepare($s) is mysqli_stmt_prepare ($stmt,$s). Unless otherwise specified, these functions return true on SUCCESS or FALSE on failure.

```
<!DOCTYPE html><html><head></head><body><pre>
<?php

// ****** 1. Database Connection
$S=mysqli_connect("localhost","root","password","testDB");


// ****** 2. Table Definition
$S->query("DROP TABLE IF EXISTS tbl");
$S->query("
CREATE TABLE tbl(
  a INT,
  b DOUBLE,
  c VARCHAR(10),
  d BLOB
)");


// ****** 3. Data Management
$PS = $S->prepare("INSERT INTO tbl VALUES (?,?,?,?)");
$PS->bind_param("idsb",$i,$d,$s,$b);// i for integer
                                    // d for double
                                    // s for string
                                    // b for blob
$i = 100;
$d = 3.14;
$s = "Hello";
$b = "Some long long long long text";
$PS->execute(); // inserts the first row
$PS->execute(); // inserts the second row
$PS->execute(); // inserts the third row


// ****** 4. Data Retrieval
$PS->prepare("SELECT a,b FROM tbl");

$PS->execute();
$PS->bind_result($i,$d);
while ($PS->fetch()){
  echo "$i,$d\n";
}

$PS->execute();
tabulate($PS->get_result());

$PS->execute();
$PS->store_result(); // needed by data_seek()
$PS->data_seek(1);
while ($PS->fetch()){
  echo "$i,$d\n";
}

echo "\n";
echo "num_rows:".$PS->num_rows."\n";
echo "affected_rows:".$PS->affected_rows."\n";
echo "field_count:".$PS->field_count."\n";
echo "param_count:".$PS->param_count."\n";
echo "insert_id:".$PS->insert_id."\n";
echo "sqlstate:".$PS->sqlstate."\n";
echo "errno:".$PS->errno."\n";
echo "error:".$PS->error."\n";
echo "error_list:"; print_r($PS->error_list); echo "\n";
echo "get_warnings():"; print_r($PS->get_warnings()); echo
"\n";

$PS->free_result();
//$PS->reset(); // resets the statement
$PS->close();   // frees the memory


// ****** A useful, general-purpose result printer
function tabulate($result){
  $fInfo = $result->fetch_fields();
  echo "<table border='1'><tr>";
  foreach($fInfo as $col){
    echo "<td>".$col->name."</td>";
  }
  while ($row = $result->fetch_row()){
    echo "</tr><tr>";
```

```
    foreach ($row as $val){
             echo "<td>".$val."</td>";
           }
  }
  echo "</tr></table><br/>";
}

?>
</pre></body></html>
```

```
100,3.14
100,3.14
100,3.14
```

a	b
100	3.14
100	3.14
100	3.14

```
100,3.14
100,3.14

num_rows:3
affected_rows:3
field_count:2
param_count:0
insert_id:0
sqlstate:00000
errno:0
error:
error_list:Array
(
)

get_warnings():
```

5.8.5 PDO

PHP Data Objects defines a lightweight, consistent interface for accessing databases in PHP.

```
<!DOCTYPE html><html><head></head><body><pre>
<?php

$P = new PDO ("mysql:dbname=test;host=localhost",
                  "root",
                  "password");
$P->exec("DROP TABLE IF EXISTS tbl;");
$P->exec("
CREATE TABLE tbl (
  a INT,
  b VARCHAR(5))");
echo "****************************************\n";

// *** Style 1
$P->exec("INSERT INTO tbl VALUES (1,'abc')");
$P->exec("INSERT INTO tbl VALUES (2,'def')");
$P->exec("INSERT INTO tbl VALUES (3,'ghi')");
$PS = $P->query("SELECT a,b FROM tbl");
foreach ($PS as $row){
  echo $row['a'],",",$row['b'],"\n";
}
echo "****************************************\n";

// *** Style 2
$PS = $P->prepare("INSERT INTO tbl VALUES (:a,:b)");
$PS->execute([":a"=>4, ":b"=>"jkl"]);
$PS->execute([":a"=>5, ":b"=>"mno"]);
$PS = $P->query("SELECT a,b FROM tbl");
echo "rows:".$PS->rowCount()."
columns:".$PS->columnCount()."\n";
while ($row = $PS->fetch(PDO::FETCH_BOTH)){
  echo $row['a'],",",$row['b'],"\n";
}
echo "****************************************\n";

// *** Style 3
$PS = $P->prepare("INSERT INTO tbl VALUES (:a,:b)");
echo "PDO errorCode():".$P->errorCode()."\n";
echo "PDO errorInfo():"; print_r($P->errorInfo()); echo "\n";
$PS->bindValue(":a",6,PDO::PARAM_INT); // by value
$PS->bindParam(":b",$b,PDO::PARAM_STR,3);// by reference
echo "PS errorCode():".$PS->errorCode()."\n";
echo "PS errorInfo():"; print_r($PS->errorInfo()); echo "\n";
$b = "pqr";
$PS->execute();
$PS = $P->query("SELECT a,b FROM tbl");
while ($row = $PS->fetchObject()){
  echo $row->a,",",$row->b,"\n";
}
echo "****************************************\n";

// *** Style 4
$P->beginTransaction(); // disables auto-commit
  $P->exec("INSERT INTO tbl VALUES(7,'stu')"); //rolled back
  $P->exec("INSERT INTO tbl VALUES(8,'vwx')");//rolled back
$P->rollBack();            // re-enables auto-commit
$P->beginTransaction(); // disables auto-commit
  $P->exec("INSERT INTO tbl VALUES(9,'yz')");
$P->commit();              // re-enables auto-commit
$PS = $P->prepare(
              "SELECT a,b FROM tbl WHERE a > ? AND a<?");
$PS->execute([0,10]);
$PS->bindColumn(1,$a);   // by column number
$PS->bindColumn('b',$b); // by column name
while ($PS->fetch(PDO::FETCH_BOUND)){
  echo "$a,$b\n";
}
?>
</pre></body></html>
```

```
****************************************
1,abc
2,def
3,ghi
****************************************
rows:5  columns:2
1,abc
2,def
3,ghi
4,jkl
5,mno
****************************************
PDO errorCode():00000
PDO errorInfo():Array
(
    [0] => 00000
    [1] =>
    [2] =>
)

PS errorCode():
PS errorInfo():Array
(
    [0] =>
    [1] =>
    [2] =>
)

1,abc
2,def
3,ghi
4,jkl
5,mno
6,pqr
****************************************
1,abc
2,def
3,ghi
4,jkl
5,mno
6,pqr
9,yz
```

Possible values for the first parameter for $PS->fetch(......)
PDO::FETCH_ASSOC gets an array indexed by the column name.
PDO::FETCH_BOTH gets an array indexed by the column name and the column number.
PDO::FETCH_BOUND assigns the values of the columns in the result set to the PHP variables bound with bindColumn().
PDO::FETCH_CLASS gets an object of the requested class,
PDO::FETCH_INTO updates an existing object of the requested class.
PDO::FETCH_NAMED is similar to PDO:FETCH_ASSOC. If there are columns with the same name, the value referred by that key will be an array of all the values.
PDO::FETCH_NUM gets an array indexed by the column number, starting at column 0.
PDO::FETCH_OBJ gets an object with property names corresponding to the column names returned.

Possible values for the third parameter for $PS->bindParam(...) and $PS->bindValue(...)
PDO::PARAM_BOOL
PDO::PARAM_NULL
PDO::PARAM_INT
PDO::PARAM_STR
PDO::PARAM_LOB

5.9 Backup and Recovery

Physical backups consist of raw copies of database directories and files. *Logical backups* save a database by storing the structures and data in custom logical formats. While physical backups are fast and compact, logical backups are highly portable and can be performed with the SQL server running.

5.9.1 Physical Backups

Different storage engines store a database in different file formats. Storing data from the MEMORY storage engine is not that straightforward because the contents are not stored on disk. MySQL Enterprise Backup allows you to retrieve data from MEMORY tables during a backup.

In Windows, for instance, a database using the InnoDB storage engine may be stored in:
  C:\ProgramData\MySQL\MySQL Server 5.6\data
. Each database is represented by a directory. Each table is stored as tbl.frm and tbl.ibd in the directory.

If the server is running during a physical backup, appropriate locking needs to be done so that the database contents do not change during the backup. When you try to restore a physical backup by copying the files back, you may need to stop MySQL Server first.

5.9.2 Internal Commands

SELECT ... INTO @var1, @var2...
This stores the column values of a single row into variables.
SELECT * FROM tbl LIMIT 1 INTO @a , @b;

SELECT ... INTO OUTFILE filename ...
This stores multiple rows to a file using a specified format.

SELECT * FROM tbl INTO OUTFILE 'a.txt'
  FIELDS TERMINATED BY ','
    OPTIONALLY ENCLOSED BY '"'
    ESCAPED BY '^'
  LINES TERMINATED BY '\r\n';

1,"abc" 2,"def" 3,"ghi" 4,"jkl" 5,"mno" 6,"pqr" 9,"yz" 10,"^""
Special characters should be escaped so that the file can be read back in reliably.

SELECT ... INTO DUMPFILE filename
This stores a single row to a file without any formatting.
SELECT * FROM tbl LIMIT 1 INTO DUMPFILE 'aa.txt';
1abc

LOAD DATA [LOW_PRIORITY | CONCURRENT] [LOCAL]
  INFILE 'file_name'
  [REPLACE | IGNORE]
  INTO TABLE tbl_name
  [CHARACTER SET charset_name]
  [{FIELDS | COLUMNS}
    [TERMINATED BY 'string']
    [[OPTIONALLY] ENCLOSED BY 'char']
    [ESCAPED BY 'char']
  ]
  [LINES
    [STARTING BY 'string']
    [TERMINATED BY 'string']
  ]
  [IGNORE number LINES]
  [(col_name_or_user_var,...)]
  [SET col_name = expr,...]

This reads rows from a text file into a table at a very high speed.
LOW_PRIORITY causes the loading to be delayed until no other clients are reading the table. **CONCURRENT** allows data to be read from the table during the loading.
If **LOCAL** is specified, the file is read on the client host and sent to the server.
REPLACE replaces existing rows with the same value for a primary key or unique index. **IGNORE** ignores the additions of such rows. Without both REPLACE and IGNORE, the rest of the text file is ignored if LOCAL is not specified.
IGNORE number LINE ignores *number* lines at the start of the file.

If the field starts with the **ENCLOSED BY** character, instances of that character are recognized as terminating a field value only if followed by the field or line TERMINATED BY sequence. If the ENCLOSED BY character is ",
  "Hello ""WORLD"" !"
is interpreted as
  Hello "WORLD"!

LOAD DATA INFILE 'data.txt' INTO TABLE tbl;
LOAD DATA INFILE 'data.txt'   INTO TABLE tbl(column1, @var) SET column2 = @var*100;

```
LOAD XML [LOW_PRIORITY | CONCURRENT]
    [LOCAL] INFILE 'file_name'
    [REPLACE | IGNORE]
    INTO TABLE [db_name.]tbl_name
    [PARTITION (partition_name,...)]
    [CHARACTER SET charset_name]
    [ROWS IDENTIFIED BY '<tagname>']
    [IGNORE number {LINES | ROWS}]
    [(column_or_user_var,...)]
    [SET col_name = expr,...]
```
This reads data from an XML file into a table.

5.9.3 External Commands

In Windows, first, get access to various MySQL external commands by setting a path to the binary directory. For instance, enter in the command prompt (run as Administrator):

> path=%path%;"c:\progra~1\MySQL\MySQL Server 5.6\bin"

>mysqldump –uroot –pPASSWORD testDB > backup.sql	
This saves the database named testDB into the file backup.sql. Here the username is 'root' while the password is 'PASSWORD'. As the host (-h) is not specified, localhost is assumed. To specify a port, use –P.	
>mysqldump –uroot –pPASSWORD testDB t1 t2> backup.sql	
This saves the tables named 't1' and 't2' from the database 'testDB' into 'backup.sq'.	
>mysqldump -uroot -pPASSWORD -- databases db1 db2 db3 t1 t2> backup.sql	
This saves the databases named 'db1', 'db2', and 'db3'. '-- databases' causes the CREATE DATABASE and USE statements to be included as well.	
>mysqldump -uroot -pPASSWORD --all-databases > x.sql	
This dumps all databases.	
Other options	
--events	Dumps event schedulers.
--routines	Dumps stored procedures and functions.
--triggers	Dumps triggers.
--no-data	Dumps definitions only.
--no-create-info	Dumps data only.
--tab=*dir_name*	Dumps all output to the directory 'dir_name", using two files for each table. The .sql file contains the table definitions, while the .txt file contains the table data.
--fields-terminated-by=*str*	Specifies the fields separator for the .txt file.
--fields-enclosed-by=*str*	Specifies the fields enclosing character for the .txt file.
--fields-optionally-enclosed-by=*str*	Specifies the fields optional enclosing character for the .txt file.
--fields-escaped-by=*str*	Specifies the escape character for the .txt file.
--lines-terminated-by=*str*	Specifies the lines separator for the .txt file.

If you try to read the .sql files saved above using a text editor, you will notice that they are runnable SQL commands that can be issued to recreate the databases. The following describes how to restore the databases using the .sql files.

>mysql < backup.sql
This restores the databases, assuming backup.sql contains the CREATE DATABASE and USE statements.
>mysqladmin create db2 >mysql db2 < backup.sql
This restores the database in backup.sql to db2, even if it does not contain the CREATE DATABASE and USE statements.
>mysql db < backup.sql >mysqlimport db backup.txt
This restores the table by using the two files generated by: mysqldump --tab To restore the data, you may also issue within MySQL the command LOAD DATA INFILE...
SOURCE backup.sql
This restores the database from within MySQL.

5.9.4 Binary Logging

All transactions within MySQL are recorded in the binary logs automatically. Incremental changes are normally made using the binary logs to bring a restored database up-to-date. You need to locate the binary log files before you can use them.

>mysqlbinlog binlog.000001 | more
This views the events from the log.
>mysqlbinlog binlog.000001 binlog.000002 | mysql –uroot –pPASSWORD
This execute events from the binary logs.
>mysqlbinlog --start-datetime="2014-04-01 10:00:00" --stop-datetime="2014-05-01 19:00:00" binlog.000001| mysql –uroot -pPASSWORD
This executes the events in the specified time.
>mysqlbinlog --start-position=123456 --stop-position=123499 binlog.000001 | mysql –uroot –pPASSWORD
This executes the events in the specified transaction positions.

5.10 Views

A view is a virtual table created by referencing an existing table or another view.

The view definition is frozen at creation time, so that changes to the underlying tables afterward do not affect the view definition. For example, if a view is defined by referencing another table, new columns added to the table later do not become part of the view.

However, new rows added to the underlying tables will become part of the view.

5.10.1 Basic Syntax

```
CREATE
    [OR REPLACE]
    [ALGORITHM = {UNDEFINED | MERGE | TEMPTABLE}]
    [DEFINER = { user | CURRENT_USER }]
    [SQL SECURITY { DEFINER | INVOKER }]
    VIEW view_name [(column_list)]
    AS select_statement
    [WITH [CASCADED | LOCAL] CHECK OPTION]
```

OR REPLACE replaces an existing view of the same name.

ALGORITHM will be discussed in the next subsection, ie. 5.10.2.

select_statement cannot
- contain a subquery in the FROM clause
- refer to system or user variables
- refer to program parameters or local variables within a stored program
- refer to prepared statement parameters
- refer to a temporary table
- be associated with a trigger

DEFINER and **SQL SECURITY** determine which account to use when checking for access privileges. **DEFINER** indicates that the required privileges must be held by the user who defined the view. **INVOKER** indicates that the required privileges must be held by the user who invoked the view.

For an updatable view, **WITH CHECK OPTION** prevents inserts and updates to rows except those for which the WHERE clause in the select_statement is true. **CASCADED** (default) causes the checks for other underlying views to be evaluated as well. **LOCAL** restricts CHECK OPTION to the view being defined only.

```
ALTER
    [ALGORITHM = {UNDEFINED | MERGE | TEMPTABLE}]
    [DEFINER = { user | CURRENT_USER }]
    [SQL SECURITY { DEFINER | INVOKER }]
    VIEW view_name [(column_list)]
    AS select_statement
    [WITH [CASCADED | LOCAL] CHECK OPTION]
```

This alters an existing view. The syntax is similar to that of view creation.

```
DROP VIEW [IF EXISTS]
    view_name [, view_name] ...
    [RESTRICT | CASCADE]
```

This removes one or more views. **RESTRICT** and **CASCADE** are ignored.

```
DROP TABLE IF EXISTS tbl;
DROP VIEW IF EXISTS vw;
CREATE TABLE tbl (a INT, b INT);
INSERT INTO tbl VALUES (1,2),(3,4),(5,6);
CREATE VIEW vw AS SELECT a,b,a+b FROM tbl WHERE a>1;
INSERT INTO tbl VALUES (7,8);
SELECT * FROM vw;
```

a	b	a+b
3	4	7
5	6	11
7	8	15

```
DROP TABLE IF EXISTS tbl;
CREATE TABLE tbl (a INT, b INT);
INSERT INTO tbl VALUES (1,2),(3,4),(5,6);
CREATE OR REPLACE
   DEFINER = 'root'@'localhost'
   SQL SECURITY DEFINER
   VIEW vw(x,y)
   AS SELECT a,b FROM tbl WHERE a>1
   WITH LOCAL CHECK OPTION;
INSERT INTO vw VALUES (2,9);  // updatable view
SELECT * FROM tbl;             // table updated as well
```

a	b
1	2
3	4
5	6
2	9

5.10.2 Algorithms

For **MERGE,** the text of a statement that refers to the view and the view definition are merged such that parts of the view definition replace corresponding parts of the statement. MERGE is usually more efficient than TEMPTABLE. For example:

```
CREATE
  ALGORIGHM=MERGE
  VIEW vw(vc1,vc2) AS
  SELECT c1,c2 FROM tbl WHERE c3>10;
```

If the query is:

```
SELECT c1,c2 FROM vw WHERE vc1<50;
```

The resulting statement to be executed is:

```
SELECT c1,c2 FROM tbl WHERE (c3>10) and (c1<50);
```

For **TEMPTABLE**, the results from the view are retrieved into a temporary table, which then is used to execute the statement. This allows locks to be released on underlying tables after the temporary table has been created and before it is used to finish processing the statement. The view cannot be updated.

For **UNDEFINED**(default), MySQL chooses which algorithm to use, preferring MERGE over TEMPTABLE.

5.10.3 Updatable Views

For a view to be updatable, there must be a one-to-one relationship between the rows in the view and the rows in the underlying table. A view is not updatable if it contains any of the following:

- Aggregate functions
- DISTINCT
- GROUP BY
- HAVING
- UNION
- Subquery in the select list
- Certain joins
- Nonupdatable view in the FROM clause
- A subquery in the WHERE clause that refers to a table in the FROM clause
- Refers only to literal values
- ALGORITHM = TEMPTABLE
- Multiple references to any column of a base table

A view is insertable if it also satisfies the following:

- There must be no duplicate view column names.
- The view must contain all columns in the base table that do not have a default value.
- The view columns must be simple column references and not derived columns.

5.11 Indexes

5.11.1 INDEX

Indexes allow rows to be retrieved quickly. They also speed up other operations such as joins, sorting, grouping, MIN(), MAX(), rows eliminations etc.

Without an index, MySQL reads through the entire table to find the requested rows. If a table has 1 000 000 rows, using an index to find a row allows the searching time to be reduced by at least 50 000 times.

Most indexes (PRIMARY KEY, UNIQUE, INDEX, and FULLTEXT) are stored in B-trees. Indexes of spatial data types use R-trees, and that MEMORY tables also support hash indexes.

However, when a query accesses most of the rows, reading sequentially is faster than working through an index.

Unlike PRIMARY KEY and UNIQUE columns, an INDEX column allows duplicate values to be stored.

```
CREATE TABLE tbl(
  a INT,
  b INT,
  INDEX USING BTREE (a,b));
INSERT INTO tbl VALUES (1,2),(1,2);
```

Most indexes are created during table definitions. However, it can be added at a later stage with an ALTER TABLE statement. It can also be added using CREATE INDEX, which is mapped to an ALTER TABLE statement.

```
CREATE [UNIQUE|FULLTEXT|SPATIAL] INDEX index_name
   [index_type]
   ON tbl_name (index_col_name,...)
   [index_option]
   [algorithm_option | lock_option] ...

index_col_name:
   col_name [(length)] [ASC | DESC]

index_type:
   USING {BTREE | HASH}

index_option:
   KEY_BLOCK_SIZE [=] value
  | index_type
  | WITH PARSER parser_name
  | COMMENT 'string'

algorithm_option:
   ALGORITHM [=] {DEFAULT|INPLACE|COPY}

lock_option:
   LOCK [=] {DEFAULT|NONE|SHARED|EXCLUSIVE}
```

```
DROP INDEX index_name ON tbl_name
   [algorithm_option | lock_option] ...

algorithm_option:
   ALGORITHM [=] {DEFAULT|INPLACE|COPY}

lock_option:
   LOCK [=] {DEFAULT|NONE|SHARED|EXCLUSIVE}
```

Prefixes can be specified for CHAR, VARCHAR, BINARY, and VARBINARY. A prefix length must be specified for BLOB and TEXT. Prefix values cannot be given for spatial columns.
FULLTEXT indexes are supported only for InnoDB and MyISAM tables and can include only CHAR, VARCHAR and TEXT columns. Indexing always happens over the entire column.
KEY_BLOCK_SIZE is a hint for the size in bytes to use for pages.
InnoDB and MySAIM support only the **BTREE** index type. MEMORY/HEAP/NDB support both **BTREE** and **HASH**.
Information about **ALGORITHM** and **LOCK** can be found in 5.2.3.

```
CREATE TABLE tbl(
  name VARCHAR(64)
) ENGINE=MEMORY;
CREATE INDEX nameInd USING HASH ON tbl(name(10));
DROP INDEX nameInd ON tbl;
```

5.11.2 FOREIGN KEY

Foreign keys can be defined for a table to cross-reference related data across tables. A foreign key value can only be created in the child table, if there is a matching candidate key value in the parent table.

The FOREIGN KEY clause is specified in the child table. The parent and child tables must use the same storage engine. They must not be TEMPORARY tables. Corresponding columns must have similar data types. The size and sign of integer types must be the same. The length of string types need not be the same. The character set and collation must be the same.

If the **CONSTRAINT symbol** clause is given, the symbol value must be unique in a database.

ON UPDATE and ON DELETE
CASCADE: Delete or update the rows from the parent table and child table automatically.
SET NULL: Delete or update the rows from the parent table, and set the foreign key columns in the child table to NULL.
RESTRICT (default)**:** Rejects the deletion or update operation for the parent table
NO ACTION: Same as RESTRICT in MySQL.
SET DEFAULT: Recognized by the MySQL parser, but rejected by InnoDB.

```
DROP TABLE IF EXISTS parent1,parent2,child;
CREATE TABLE parent1(
  a INT,
  b INT,
  PRIMARY KEY (a,b)
);
CREATE TABLE parent2(
  c VARCHAR(10) PRIMARY KEY
);
CREATE TABLE child(
  x INT,
  y INT,
  z VARCHAR(10),
  FOREIGN KEY (x,y) REFERENCES parent1(a,b)
    ON DELETE CASCADE
```

```
    ON UPDATE RESTRICT,
  CONSTRAINT zc
    FOREIGN KEY (z) REFERENCES parent2(c)
    ON DELETE CASCADE
);
INSERT INTO parent1 VALUES (1,2);
INSERT INTO parent2 VALUES ('hello');
INSERT INTO child VALUES (1,2,'hello');
#INSERT INTO child VALUES (1,2,'world');  # this fails!
ALTER TABLE child DROP FOREIGN KEY zc;
INSERT INTO child VALUES (1,2,'world');  # this works!
```

5.12 Subquery

A subquery is a bracketed SELECT statement within another outer statement. The outer statement can be any one of SELECT, INSERT, UPDATE, DELETE, SET or DO.

A subquery sometimes becomes useful when it is impossible to formulate a query using JOIN otherwise. Sometimes it is also faster to use a subquery.

5.12.1 Scalar Subquery

A scalar subquery is one that returns a single row containing a single column.

```
SELECT (SELECT 500);
```
```
500
```

```
DROP TABLE IF EXISTS t1,t2;
CREATE TABLE t1 (a INT);
INSERT INTO t1 VALUES (200);
CREATE TABLE t2 (b INT);
INSERT INTO t2 VALUES (200),(300),(400);
SELECT * FROM t2 WHERE b>(SELECT * FROM t1);
```
```
300
400
```

```
SELECT * FROM t1
  WHERE column1 = (SELECT MAX(column2) FROM t2);
```

```
SELECT * FROM t1 AS t
  WHERE 2 = (SELECT COUNT(*) FROM t1 WHERE t1.id = t.id);
```

5.12.2 Column Subquery

A column subquery returns a single column over multiple rows.

SOME() and ANY() are the same.

```
DROP TABLE IF EXISTS t1,t2;
CREATE TABLE t1 (a INT);
INSERT INTO t1 VALUES (100),(200),(300),(400);
CREATE TABLE t2 (b INT);
INSERT INTO t2 VALUES (10),(20),(300),(400),(500);
SELECT b FROM t2 WHERE b > ANY(SELECT a FROM t1);
```
```
300
400
500
```

```
DROP TABLE IF EXISTS t1,t2;
CREATE TABLE t1 (a INT);
INSERT INTO t1 VALUES (100),(200),(300),(400);
CREATE TABLE t2 (b INT);
INSERT INTO t2 VALUES (10),(20),(300),(400),(500);
SELECT b FROM t2 WHERE b IN (SELECT a FROM t1);
```
```
300
400
```

```
DROP TABLE IF EXISTS t1,t2;
CREATE TABLE t1 (a INT);
INSERT INTO t1 VALUES (100),(200),(300),(400);
CREATE TABLE t2 (b INT);
INSERT INTO t2 VALUES (10),(20),(300),(400),(500);
SELECT b FROM t2 WHERE b > ALL(SELECT a FROM t1);
```
```
500
```

EXISTS(SELECT...) returns TRUE if one or more rows are returned. The opposite is NOT EXISTS(SELECT...).

```
DROP TABLE IF EXISTS t1,t2;
CREATE TABLE t1 (a INT);
INSERT INTO t1 VALUES (100),(200),(300),(400);
CREATE TABLE t2 (b INT);
INSERT INTO t2 VALUES (10),(20),(300),(400),(500);
SELECT EXISTS (SELECT a FROM t1);
```
```
1
```

5.12.3 Table Subquery

```
DROP TABLE IF EXISTS t1,t2;
CREATE TABLE t1 (a INT, b INT);
INSERT INTO t1 VALUES (1,100),(2,200),(3,300),(4,400);
CREATE TABLE t2 (c INT, d INT);
INSERT INTO t2 VALUES
(1,10),(2,20),(3,300),(4,400),(5,500);
SELECT * FROM t2 WHERE (c,d) IN (SELECT a,b FROM t1);
```
```
3   300
4   400
```

```
DROP TABLE IF EXISTS t1,t2;
CREATE TABLE t1 (a INT, b INT);
INSERT INTO t1 VALUES (1,100),(2,200),(3,300),(4,400);
CREATE TABLE t2 (c INT, d INT);
INSERT INTO t2 VALUES
(1,10),(2,20),(3,300),(4,400),(5,500);
SELECT col1,col2 FROM
  (SELECT a AS col1,b AS col2 FROM t1) AS t WHERE t.col1>2;
```
```
3   300
4   400
```

```
SELECT * FROM t1
  WHERE col1 = ANY (SELECT col1 FROM t2
                    WHERE t2.col2 = t1.col2);
```

5.13 Automation

Statements can be set to run automatically in future, either periodically (EVENT) or when a specific operation occurs (TRIGGER).

5.13.1 EVENT

The event scheduler thread must be first turned on, for events to work.

Setting @@global.event_scheduler to DISABLED prevents the state from changing during runtime.

```
SET @@global.event_scheduler=ON;
SHOW PROCESSLIST;
```

```
......
35, event_scheduler, localhost, , Daemon, 39,
Waiting on empty queue,
```

```
CREATE
   [DEFINER = { user | CURRENT_USER }]
   EVENT
   [IF NOT EXISTS]
   event_name
   ON SCHEDULE schedule
   [ON COMPLETION [NOT] PRESERVE]
   [ENABLE | DISABLE | DISABLE ON SLAVE]
   [COMMENT 'comment']
   DO event_body;

schedule:
   AT timestamp [+ INTERVAL interval] ...
  | EVERY interval
   [STARTS timestamp [+ INTERVAL interval] ...]
   [ENDS timestamp [+ INTERVAL interval] ...]

interval:
   quantity {YEAR | QUARTER | MONTH | DAY | HOUR |
MINUTE | WEEK | SECOND | YEAR_MONTH | DAY_HOUR |
DAY_MINUTE | DAY_SECOND | HOUR_MINUTE |
HOUR_SECOND | MINUTE_SECOND}
```

DEFINER records the user who defines the event.

ON COMPLETION PRESERVE prevents the event from being dropped once it expires. **ON COMPLETION NOT PRESERVE** is the default.

DISABLE prevents the event from running. **ENABLE** is the default. **DISABLE ON SLAVE** prevents the event from running on the replicated slave.

```
ALTER
   [DEFINER = { user | CURRENT_USER }]
   EVENT event_name
   [ON SCHEDULE schedule]
   [ON COMPLETION [NOT] PRESERVE]
   [RENAME TO new_event_name]
   [ENABLE | DISABLE | DISABLE ON SLAVE]
   [COMMENT 'comment']
   [DO event_body]
```

```
DROP EVENT [IF EXISTS] event_name
```

This runs the INSERT statement exactly once, one and a half hour from now.

```
CREATE TABLE tbl (a INT);
CREATE
   DEFINER = 'root'@'localhost'
   EVENT myEvent
   ON SCHEDULE AT CURRENT_TIMESTAMP
                    + INTERVAL 1 HOUR
                    + INTERVAL 30 MINUTE
   DO
     INSERT INTO tbl VALUES (1);
```

This runs the INSERT statement once every hour, in the period specified.

```
DROP TABLE IF EXISTS tbl;
DROP EVENT IF EXISTS myEvent;
CREATE TABLE tbl (a INT);
CREATE EVENT myEvent
   ON SCHEDULE EVERY 1 HOUR
         STARTS '2014-05-02 11:00:00'
         ENDS '2014-05-02 19:00:00'
   DO
     INSERT INTO tbl VALUES (1);
```

5.13.2 TRIGGER

```
CREATE
   [DEFINER = { user | CURRENT_USER }]
   TRIGGER trigger_name
   { BEFORE | AFTER } { INSERT | UPDATE | DELETE }
   ON tbl_name FOR EACH ROW
   [{ FOLLOWS | PRECEDES } other_trigger_name]
   trigger_body
```

INSERT activates the trigger through INSERT, LOAD DATA and REPLACE statements. **UPDATE** activates the trigger through UPDATE statements. **DELETE** activates the trigger through DELETE and REPLACE statements.

Cascaded foreign key actions do not activate triggers.

There must not be triggers for a given table that have the same trigger name and action time. For instance, you cannot have two BEFORE INSERT triggers for a table.

```
DROP TRIGGER [IF EXISTS] [schema_name.]trigger_name
```

The column values can be accessed within a trigger with OLD.colName or NEW.colName.

```
SET @sum=0;
DROP TABLE IF EXISTS account;
DROP TRIGGER IF EXISTS sumT;
CREATE TABLE account (amount DECIMAL(10,2));
CREATE TRIGGER sumT
      BEFORE INSERT ON account
      FOR EACH ROW SET @sum = @sum + NEW.amount;
INSERT INTO account VALUES (300),(200);
SELECT @sum;
```

```
500.00
```

5.14 Compound Statements

A compound statement such as BEGIN...END is a block of SQL commands. It is useful for EVENT, TRIGGER, PROCEDURE and FUNCTION.

5.14.1 PROCEDURE and FUNCTION

```
CREATE
   [DEFINER = { user | CURRENT_USER }]
   PROCEDURE routine ([proc_parameter[,...]])
   [characteristic ...] routine_body

CREATE
   [DEFINER = { user | CURRENT_USER }]
   FUNCTION routine ([func_parameter[,...]])
   RETURNS type
   [characteristic ...] routine_body

proc_parameter:
   [ IN | OUT | INOUT ] param_name type

func_parameter:
   param_name type

type:
   Any valid MySQL data type

characteristic:
   COMMENT 'string'
  | LANGUAGE SQL
  | [NOT] DETERMINISTIC
  | { CONTAINS SQL | NO SQL | READS SQL DATA |
     MODIFIES SQL DATA }
  | SQL SECURITY { DEFINER | INVOKER }
```

An **IN** parameter passes a value into a procedure. Any modification to it within the procedure is not visible outside the procedure. An **OUT** parameter passes a value from the procedure out to the caller's variable. An **INOUT** parameter passes a value into a procedure, and any modification to it is visible outside the procedure.

For a **FUNCTION**, parameters are always regarded as **IN** parameters.

A stored **FUNCTION** cannot return a result set.

LANGUAGE SQL is ignored currently as only SQL routines are supported.

A routine is **DETERMINISTIC** if it always produces the same result for the same input parameters. The optimizer executes statements faster with this choice. The default is **NOT DETERMINISTIC**. A routine containing NOW() or RAND() is nondeterministic.

CONTAINS SQL, the default, indicates the routine does not contain statements that read or write data. **NO SQL** indicates that the routine contains no SQL statements. **READS SQL DATA** indicates that the routine contains statements that read data (SELECT), but not statements that write data. **MODIFIES SQL DATA** indicates that the routine contains statements that writes data (INSERT, DELETE).

SQL SECURITY specifies whether the routine uses the privileges of the account in the DEFINER clause, or the user who invokes it.

The following statements are not permitted in stored routines:

- LOCK TABLES and UNLOCK TABLES
- ALTER VIEW
- LOAD DATA and LOAD TABLE
- Statements not permitted in SQL prepared statements (except SIGNAL, RESIGNAL, and GET DIAGNOSTICS)

To begin a transaction within a stored program, use START TRANSACTION.

The following statements are not permitted in stored functions:

- Commit or rollback statements
- Statements returning a result set
- FLUSH statements
- Recursive functions
- Statements that modify a table that is already being used by the statement that invoked the function

```
ALTER {PROCEDURE|FUNCTION routine [characteristic ...]

characteristic:
   COMMENT 'string'
  | LANGUAGE SQL
  | { CONTAINS SQL | NO SQL | READS SQL DATA |
     MODIFIES SQL DATA }
  | SQL SECURITY { DEFINER | INVOKER }
```

```
DROP {PROCEDURE | FUNCTION} [IF EXISTS] routine
```

Invoked with the **CALL** keyword, the procedure generates a table of 0-8 random integers in the specified range. The function returns the average of the integers in the table.

Notice the use of DELIMITER to temporarily change the delimiter character for the outer statements.

```
DROP PROCEDURE IF EXISTS initialize_tbl;
DROP FUNCTION IF EXISTS tAverage;

DELIMITER //
CREATE PROCEDURE initialize_tbl
      (IN min INT, IN max INT, OUT cnt INT)
      NOT DETERMINISTIC
      MODIFIES SQL DATA
  BEGIN
    DROP TABLE IF EXISTS tbl;
    CREATE TABLE tbl(num INT, INDEX (num));
    INSERT INTO tbl VALUES
                (rand()*100),(rand()*100),(rand()*100),
                (rand()*100),(rand()*100),(rand()*100),
                (rand()*100),(rand()*100);
    DELETE FROM tbl WHERE num<min OR num>max;
    SET cnt = (SELECT count(num) FROM tbl);
  END //
CREATE FUNCTION tAverage()
      RETURNS INT
      DETERMINISTIC
      READS SQL DATA
  BEGIN
    RETURN (SELECT AVG(num) FROM tbl);
  END //
DELIMITER ;

CALL initialize_tbl(30,70,@C);
SELECT @C,tAverage(),num FROM tbl;
```

@C	tAverage()	num
3	47	30
3	47	53
3	47	59

5.14.2 Flow Control

Labels allow a set of statements to be executed multiple times.

```
[begin_label:] BEGIN
    [statement_list]
END [end_label]
```

```
[begin_label:] LOOP
    statement_list
END LOOP [end_label]
```

```
[begin_label:] REPEAT
    statement_list
UNTIL search_condition
END REPEAT [end_label]
```

```
[begin_label:] WHILE search_condition DO
    statement_list
END WHILE [end_label]
```

begin_label can be given without end_label. If end_label is present, it must be the same as begin_label. end_label cannot be given without begin_label.

Use **ITERATE** or **LEAVE** to refer to a label within a labeled construct. ITERATE jumps the execution to the beginning of the construct. LEAVE gets out of the statements block.

```
DROP PROCEDURE IF EXISTS sum100;
DELIMITER //
CREATE PROCEDURE sum100(INOUT p INT)
BEGIN
 lbl: LOOP
   SET p = p + 1;
   IF p < 100 THEN ITERATE lbl; END IF;
   LEAVE lbl;
 END LOOP lbl;
END //
DELIMITER ;
SET @s=0;
CALL sum100(@s);
SELECT @s;
```

```
100
```

You may use **RETURN** to terminate a stored function and return the value.

Unlike a CASE expression, a **CASE** statement here cannot have an ELSE NULL clause. It is terminated with **END CASE** instead of END.

```
DROP FUNCTION IF EXISTS func;
DELIMITER //
CREATE FUNCTION func()
RETURNS INT
DETERMINISTIC
BEGIN
  DECLARE v INT DEFAULT 1;
  CASE v
    WHEN 2 THEN RETURN v*v;
    WHEN 3 THEN RETURN v*v*v;
    ELSE
      BEGIN
        RETURN v;
      END;
  END CASE;
END; //
DELIMITER ;
SELECT func();
```

```
1
```

5.14.3 Local Variables

DECLARE must be used inside and at the beginning of BEGIN...END. Variable and condition declarations must appear before cursor or handler declarations.

```
DECLARE var_name [, var_name] ...
            type
            [DEFAULT value]
```

```
DROP PROCEDURE IF EXISTS proc ;
DELIMITER //
CREATE PROCEDURE proc()
BEGIN
  DECLARE a,b,c INT DEFAULT 2;
  SELECT a,b,c;
END //
DELIMITER ;
CALL proc();
```

```
2    2    2
```

5.14.4 Cursors

A cursor is a result set within a stored routine. It cannot be updated and it can only be traversed in one direction without skipping rows. Cursor declarations must appear before handler declarations and after variable and condition declarations.

```
CREATE PROCEDURE curDemo()
BEGIN
  DECLARE done INT DEFAULT FALSE;
  DECLARE a CHAR(20);
  DECLARE x, y INT;
  DECLARE cur1 CURSOR FOR SELECT id,data FROM test.t1;
  DECLARE cur2 CURSOR FOR SELECT i FROM test.t2;
  DECLARE CONTINUE HANDLER FOR NOT FOUND
      SET done = TRUE;

  OPEN cur1;
  OPEN cur2;

  read_loop: LOOP
    FETCH cur1 INTO x, y;
    FETCH cur2 INTO c;
    IF done THEN
      LEAVE read_loop;
    END IF;
    IF x < y THEN
      INSERT INTO test.t3 VALUES (a,x);
    ELSE
      INSERT INTO test.t3 VALUES (a,y);
    END IF;
  END LOOP;

  CLOSE cur1;
  CLOSE cur2;
END;
```

5.14.5 Conditions

A HANDLER specifies what to do when a CONDITON occurs.

```
DECLARE condition_name CONDITION FOR condition_value

condition_value:
    mysql_error_code
  | SQLSTATE [VALUE] sqlstate_value
```

```
DECLARE handler_action HANDLER
    FOR condition_value [, condition_value] ...
    statement

handler_action:
    CONTINUE
  | EXIT
  | UNDO

condition_value:
    mysql_error_code
  | SQLSTATE [VALUE] sqlstate_value
  | condition_name
  | SQLWARNING
  | NOT FOUND
  | SQLEXCEPTION
```

CONTINUE causes the execution to continue. **EXIT** terminates the BEGIN...END compound statement. **UNDO** is not supported so far.

NOT FOUND is used to control what happens when a cursor reaches the end of a data set.

Use **SHOW WARNINGS** or **SHOW ERRORS** to see conditions or errors.

```
DECLARE no_such_table CONDITION FOR 1051;
DECLARE CONTINUE HANDLER FOR no_such_table
  BEGIN
    -- body of handler
  END;
```

SQL statements produce diagnostic information. GET DIAGNOSTICS allows you to obtain either statement or condition information.

```
GET [CURRENT | STACKED] DIAGNOSTICS
{
    statement_information_item
    [, statement_information_item] ...
  | CONDITION condition_number
    condition_information_item
    [, condition_information_item] ...
}

statement_information_item:
    target = statement_information_item_name

condition_information_item:
    target = condition_information_item_name

statement_information_item_name:
    NUMBER
  | ROW_COUNT
```

```
condition_information_item_name:
   CLASS_ORIGIN
 | SUBCLASS_ORIGIN
 | RETURNED_SQLSTATE
 | MESSAGE_TEXT
 | MYSQL_ERRNO
 | CONSTRAINT_CATALOG
 | CONSTRAINT_SCHEMA
 | CONSTRAINT_NAME
 | CATALOG_NAME
 | SCHEMA_NAME
 | TABLE_NAME
 | COLUMN_NAME
 | CURSOR_NAME
```

CURRENT, the default, retrieves information from the current diagnostic area. **STACKED** retrieves information from the second diagnostic area, which is available only if the current context is a condition handler.

```
GET CURRENT DIAGNOSTICS
  @a=NUMBER, @b=ROW_COUNT;
GET CURRENT DIAGNOSTICS
  CONDITION 1
  @c=RETURNED_SQLSTATE, @d=MESSAGE_TEXT;
SELECT @a,@b,@c,@d;
```

```
1  0  42000  FUNCTION test.func does not exist
```

RESIGNAL passes on the error condition information that is available during the execution of a condition handler within a compound statement, making it possible to both handle an error and return the error information. Without it, by executing an SQL statement within the handler, information causing the handler's activation is destroyed. RESIGNAL may change the information before passing it.

```
RESIGNAL [condition_value]
    [SET signal_information_item
    [, signal_information_item] ...]

condition_value:
   SQLSTATE [VALUE] sqlstate_value
 | condition_name

signal_information_item:
   condition_information_item_name =
     simple_value_specification

condition_information_item_name:
   CLASS_ORIGIN
 | SUBCLASS_ORIGIN
 | MESSAGE_TEXT
 | MYSQL_ERRNO
 | CONSTRAINT_CATALOG
 | CONSTRAINT_SCHEMA
 | CONSTRAINT_NAME
 | CATALOG_NAME
 | SCHEMA_NAME
 | TABLE_NAME
 | COLUMN_NAME
 | CURSOR_NAME
```

A simple **RESIGNAL** alone means 'pass on the error with no change'. It 'pops' the diagnostics area stack.

RESIGNAL with a condition value means 'push a condition into the current diagnostics area'.

```
DROP TABLE IF EXISTS xx;
delimiter //
CREATE PROCEDURE p ()
BEGIN
  DECLARE EXIT HANDLER FOR SQLEXCEPTION
  BEGIN
    SET @error_count = @error_count + 1;
    IF @a = 0 THEN RESIGNAL SQLSTATE '45000' SET
MYSQL_ERRNO=5; END IF;
  END;
  DROP TABLE xx;
END//
delimiter ;
SET @error_count = 0;
SET @a = 0;
SET @@max_error_count = 2;
CALL p();
SHOW ERRORS;
```

Level	Code	Message
Error	1051	Unknown table 'xx'
Error	5	Unknown table 'xx'

SIGNAL returns an error, providing information to a handler, to an outer portion of the application, or to the client.

```
SIGNAL condition_value
    [SET signal_information_item
    [, signal_information_item] ...]

condition_value:
   SQLSTATE [VALUE] sqlstate_value
 | condition_name

signal_information_item:
   condition_information_item_name =
     simple_value_specification

condition_information_item_name:
   CLASS_ORIGIN
 | SUBCLASS_ORIGIN
 | MESSAGE_TEXT
 | MYSQL_ERRNO
 | CONSTRAINT_CATALOG
 | CONSTRAINT_SCHEMA
 | CONSTRAINT_NAME
 | CATALOG_NAME
 | SCHEMA_NAME
 | TABLE_NAME
 | COLUMN_NAME
 | CURSOR_NAME
```

```
CREATE PROCEDURE p (pval INT)
BEGIN
  DECLARE specialty CONDITION FOR SQLSTATE '45000';
  IF pval = 0 THEN
    SIGNAL SQLSTATE '01000';
  ELSEIF pval = 1 THEN
    SIGNAL SQLSTATE '45000'
      SET MESSAGE_TEXT = 'An error occurred';
  ELSEIF pval = 2 THEN
    SIGNAL specialty
      SET MESSAGE_TEXT = 'An error occurred';
  ELSE
    SIGNAL SQLSTATE '01000'
      SET MESSAGE_TEXT = 'A warning occurred',
MYSQL_ERRNO = 1000;
    SIGNAL SQLSTATE '45000'
      SET MESSAGE_TEXT = 'An error occurred',
          MYSQL_ERRNO = 1001;
  END IF;
END;
```

5.15 Transactions and Locks

5.15.1 Transactions

By default, MySQL autocommits, which means that statements are executed immediately as they are issued. By starting a transaction with START TRANSACTION, you turn off autocommit. Changes made by statements are not permanent until you COMMIT them explicitly. You also have the choice to ROLLBACK statements that have not been committed, so that the changes are cancelled. A transaction ends with COMMIT or ROLLBACK unless the AND CHAIN clause is used.

```
START TRANSACTION
   [transaction_characteristic [, transaction_characteristic] ...]

transaction_characteristic:
   WITH CONSISTENT SNAPSHOT
  | READ WRITE
  | READ ONLY

BEGIN [WORK]

COMMIT [WORK] [AND [NO] CHAIN] [[NO] RELEASE]

ROLLBACK [WORK] [AND [NO] CHAIN] [[NO] RELEASE]

SET autocommit = {0 | 1}

SAVEPOINT identifier

ROLLBACK [WORK] TO [SAVEPOINT] identifier

RELEASE SAVEPOINT identifier
```

WITH CONSISTENT SNAPSHOT starts a consistent read for InnoDB. The only isolation level that permits a consistent read is REPEATABLE READ. **READ ONLY** allows optimizations to be made for InnoDB. **READ WRITE** is the default.
After **autocommit** has been **SET** to zero, you must use COMMIT to make the changes permanent or ROLLBACK to ignore the changes.
BEGIN is the same as **START TRANSACTION,** but the latter permits modifiers.
WORK is ignored.
AND CHAIN starts a new transaction as soon as the current one ends. **RELEASE** disconnects the current client session after terminating the current transaction.
ROLLBACK TO rolls back to the named savepoint without terminating the transaction. **RELEASE SAVEPOINT** removes the named savepoint without performing any COMMIT or ROLLBACK. Savepoints are deleted with COMMIT or ROLLBACK.
Beginning a transaction causes any pending transaction to be committed. Thus, transactions cannot be nested.
Transactions should be performed using only tables managed by a single transaction-safe storage engine, for best results.
Transactions that are rolled back are not logged.

```
SET [GLOBAL | SESSION] TRANSACTION
   transaction_characteristic [, transaction_characteristic] ...

transaction_characteristic:
   ISOLATION LEVEL level
  | READ WRITE
  | READ ONLY

level:
    REPEATABLE READ
  | READ COMMITTED
  | READ UNCOMMITTED
  | SERIALIZABLE
```

This sets the transaction properties. Without **SESSION** or **GLOBAL**, this statement applies to the next transaction within the current session.
For **REPEATABLE READ**, the default isolation level for InnoDB, all consistent reads within the same transaction read the snapshot established by the first read.
For **READ COMMITTED**, each consistent read, even within the same transaction, sets and reads its own fresh snapshot.
For **READ UNCOMMITTED**, SELECT statements are performed in a nonblocking fashion, but a possible earlier version of a row might be used. Reads are not consistent.
SERIALIZABLE is like REPEATEABLE READ, but InnoDB implicitly converts all plain SELECT statements to SELECT...LOCK IN SHARE MODE if autocommit is disabled.

```
DROP TABLE IF EXISTS tbl;
CREATE TABLE tbl (a INT);

START TRANSACTION;
  INSERT INTO tbl VALUES (100);
  SAVEPOINT sp;
  INSERT INTO tbl VALUES (200);
  ROLLBACK TO sp;
COMMIT;

SELECT * FROM tbl;
```

```
100
```

Some statements cannot be rolled back. These include data definition language (DDL) statements, such as those that create or drop databases, and those that create, drop, or alter tables or stored routines. A transaction cannot be fully rolled back if it contains such a statement.

Some statements cause an implicit commit:

- Data Definition Language (DDL) statements that define or modify database objects, such as {ALTER| CREATE| DROP} {DATABASE| EVENT| PROCEDURE| SERVER|, TABLE| VIEW| INDEX| FUNCTION} etc.
- Statements that implicitly use or modify tables in the mysql database, such as {CREATE| DROP| RENAME} USER, GRANT, REVOKE, SET PASSWORD.
- Transaction-control and locking statements, such as BEGIN, LOCK TABLES, SET autocommit=1, START TRANSACTION, UNLOCK TABLES.
- Data loading statements such as LOAD DATA INFILE using the NDB storage engine.
- Administrative statements such as ANALYZE TABLE, CACHE INDEX, CHECK TABLE, LOAD INDEX INTO CACHE, OPTIMIZE TABLE, and REPAIR TABLE.
- Replication control statements such as START SLAVE, STOP SLAVE, RESET SLAVE, and CHANGE MASTER TO.

5.15.2 PHP Transactions

Transactions can also be executed at the PHP level.

```
<!DOCTYPE html><html><head></head><body>

<?php
$S=new mysqli("localhost","root","password","testDB");
$S->query("DROP TABLE IF EXISTS tbl");
$S->query("CREATE TABLE tbl (a INT)");
$S->begin_transaction();
  $S->query("INSERT INTO tbl VALUES(100)");
$S->rollback();

$S->autocommit(FALSE);
  $S->query("INSERT INTO tbl VALUES(200)");
//$S->commit();
$S->autocommit(TRUE); // also commits transaction

tabulate($S->query("SELECT * FROM tbl"));

// ****** A useful, general-purpose result printer
function tabulate($result){
  $fInfo = $result->fetch_fields();
  echo "<table border='1'><tr>";
  foreach($fInfo as $col){
    echo "<td>".$col->name."</td>";
  }
  while ($row = $result->fetch_row()){
    echo "</tr><tr>";
    foreach ($row as $val){
              echo "<td>".$val."</td>";
            }
  }
  echo "</tr></table><br/>";
}
?>
</body>
</html>
```

a
200

5.15.3 Locks

A lock can be used to prevent other sessions from accessing or modifying tables or views. Locking a view locks all underlying tables automatically. Any tables used in triggers are also locked automatically. While locks are held, the session can access only the locked tables. Use aliases if you need to refer to a locked table multiple times in a single query.

Sometimes it is much faster to lock MyISAM tables, because MySQL does not flush the key cache while a lock is in effect. At other times, you must LOCK TABLES if you want to ensure that no other session modifies the tables between a SELECT and an UPDATE. However, sometimes this can be avoided by using relative updates
(eg.: UPDATE tbl SET v=v+10).

```
LOCK TABLES
   tbl_name [[AS] alias] lock_type
   [, tbl_name [[AS] alias] lock_type] ...

lock_type:
   READ [LOCAL]
 | [LOW_PRIORITY] WRITE

UNLOCK TABLES
```

Lock Type	Holding Session	Other Sessions
READ	Can read Can't write	Can read Can't write
WRITE	Can read Can write	Can't read Can't write

For a **READ** lock, no session can update the table. The session holding the lock can read the table but not write it. Other sessions can read the table without explicitly acquiring a READ lock. Multiple sessions can acquire a READ lock for the table at the same time. **LOCAL** enables non-conflicting INSERT statements by other sessions. If InnoDB is used, READ LOCAL is the same as READ.

For a **WRITE** lock, the session that holds the lock can read and write the table. No other session can access it. Lock requests for the table by other sessions block. **LOW_PRIORITY** is ignored.

All locks are released automatically when the session terminates.

LOCK TABLES and **UNLOCK TABLES** cannot be used within stored programs. The following statements cannot be run while a table is being locked: CREATE TABLE, CREATE VIEW, DROP VIEW, DDL statements on stored functions and procedures and events.

Beginning a transaction releases existing table locks. ROLLBACK does not release table locks.

FLUSH TABLES WITH READ LOCK acquires a global read lock. START TRANSACTION does not release it.

This illustrates the correct way to use LOCK TABLES with transactional tables.

```
SET autocommit=0;
LOCK TABLES t1 WRITE, t2 READ, ...;
... do something with tables t1 and t2 here ...
COMMIT;
UNLOCK TABLES;
```

5.16 Partitioning

A table may be divided into multiple partitions which may be stored in different directories. Partitioning allows data stored in a table to span multiple disks, and related data to be moved easily. Some queries can be optimized with partition pruning (built-in), which excludes non-matching partitions when retrieving rows that satisfy a given WHERE clause. Moreover, you may specify the specific partitions to search, for a SELECT statement.

MySQL supports only horizontal partitioning, in which different rows may be assigned to different partitions. The MERGE, CSV, or FEDERATED storage engines do not support partitioning.

To specify the storage locations, use **DATA DIRECTORY** and **INDEX DIRECTORY**. However, these two options have no effect for the InnoDB storage engine, and Windows.

5.16.1 Creation

A unique index must include all columns in the partitioning function.

RANGE

```
CREATE TABLE tbl(
  a INT
) PARTITION BY RANGE (a) (  -- expression or any data type
  PARTITION p0 VALUES LESS THAN (10),
  PARTITION p1 VALUES LESS THAN (20),
  PARTITION p2 VALUES LESS THAN (30),
  PARTITION p3 VALUES LESS THAN MAXVALUE
);
```

```
CREATE TABLE tbl (
   ts TIMESTAMP
) PARTITION BY RANGE (UNIX_TIMESTAMP(ts) ) (
   PARTITION p0 VALUES LESS THAN
                  (UNIX_TIMESTAMP('2013-01-01 00:00:00') ),
   PARTITION p1 VALUES LESS THAN
                  (UNIX_TIMESTAMP('2014-01-01 00:00:00') ),
   PARTITION p2 VALUES LESS THAN
                  (UNIX_TIMESTAMP('2015-01-01 00:00:00') ),
   PARTITION p3 VALUES LESS THAN (MAXVALUE)
);
```

RANGE COLUMN

```
CREATE TABLE tbl (
   d DATE,
   s VARCHAR(10)
) PARTITION BY RANGE COLUMNS (s,d) ( -- no expression
   PARTITION p0 VALUES LESS THAN ('d','2015-01-01'),
   PARTITION p1 VALUES LESS THAN ('f','2015-01-01'),
   PARTITION p2 VALUES LESS THAN ('n','2015-01-01'),
   PARTITION p3 VALUES LESS THAN (MAXVALUE,
                                  MAXVALUE)
);
```

```
SELECT PARTITION_NAME, TABLE ROWS
  FROM INFORMATION_SCHEMA.PARTITIONS
  WHERE TABLE_NAME = 'tb';
```

```
SELECT (0,25,50)< (20,20,0),  -- 1
         (100,0,0)< (0,10,20);  -- 0
```

LIST

```
CREATE TABLE tbl(
  a INT
) PARTITION BY LIST (a) (  -- only integer columns allowed
  PARTITION odd VALUES IN(1,3,5,7,9),
  PARTITION even VALUES IN(0,2,4,6,8)
);
```

LIST COLUMN

```
CREATE TABLE tbl(
  a VARCHAR(3),
  b VARCHAR(3)
) PARTITION BY LIST COLUMNS (a,b) (
  PARTITION pt1 VALUES IN(('a','x'),('c','x')),
  PARTITION pt2 VALUES IN(('b','y'))
);
```

HASH

```
CREATE TABLE tbl(
  d1 DATE,
  d2 DATE,
  UNIQUE(c,d)
) PARTITION BY LINEAR HASH (YEAR(d1)+YEAR(d2)) #integer
  PARTITIONS 4;
```

HASH uses a simple modulo function to map the rows to the partitions.

LINEAR HASH

```
CREATE TABLE tbl(
  d DATE
) PARTITION BY LINEAR HASH (YEAR(d)) # integer
  PARTITIONS 6;
```

To determine the partition which stores a row

1. Find the next power of 2 greater than the partitions total:
   v = POWER(2, CEILING(LOG(2, pTotal)))
2. Set N = F(columns) & (v-1)
3. While N>= pTotal
   Set v=CEILING(v/2)
   Set N=N & (v -1)

For instance, if '1998-01-01' is inserted into tbl, the partition number is given by:

```
  v = POWER(2,CESILING(LOG(2,6))) = 8
  N = Year('1998-01-01') & (8-1)
     = 1998 & 7
     = 6        (>=pTotal)
  N'= 6 & (CEILING(8/2)-1)
     = 6 & 3
     = 2
```

Linear hashing allows adding, dropping, merging, and splitting of partitions to be much faster. The disadvantage is that data is less likely to be evenly distributed compared to regular hashing.

KEY

```
CREATE TABLE tbl(
  a DATE,
  b VARCHAR(10),
  PRIMARY KEY (a,b)
) PARTITION BY KEY(a,b)  -- non-integers allowed
  PARTITIONS 6;
```

```
CREATE TABLE tbl(
  a DATE PRIMARY KEY,
  b VARCHAR(10)
) PARTITION BY KEY() -- a used
  PARTITIONS 6;
```

This causes MySQL to use its own hashing function, one which is the same for PASSWORD().

LINEAR KEY

```
CREATE TABLE tbl(
  a DATE,
  b VARCHAR(10),
  PRIMARY KEY (a,b)
) PARTITION BY LINEAR KEY(a,b)  -- non-integers allowed
  PARTITIONS 6;
```

subpartitioning

CREATE TABLE tbl (a INT, b DATE)
  PARTITION BY RANGE(YEAR(b)) -- RANGE or LIST
  SUBPARTITION BY HASH(TO_DAYS(b)) -- HASH or KEY
  SUBPARTITIONS 2 (-- 2 subpartitions per partition
    PARTITION p0 VALUES LESS THAN (2016),
    PARTITION p1 VALUES LESS THAN (2018),
    PARTITION p2 VALUES LESS THAN MAXVALUE
  );

CREATE TABLE tbl(a INT, b DATE)
  PARTITION BY RANGE(YEAR(b))
  SUBPARTITION BY HASH(TO_DAYS(b)) (
    PARTITION p0 VALUES LESS THAN (2016) (-- explicit
      SUBPARTITION s0
        DATA DIRECTORY = '/disk0/data'
        INDEX DIRECTORY = '/disk0/idx',
      SUBPARTITION s1
        DATA DIRECTORY = '/disk1/data'
        INDEX DIRECTORY = '/disk1/idx'
    ),
    PARTITION p1 VALUES LESS THAN (2018) (
      SUBPARTITION s2
        DATA DIRECTORY = '/disk2/data'
        INDEX DIRECTORY = '/disk2/idx',
      SUBPARTITION s3
        DATA DIRECTORY = '/disk3/data'
        INDEX DIRECTORY = '/disk3/idx'
    ),
    PARTITION p2 VALUES LESS THAN MAXVALUE (
      SUBPARTITION s4
        DATA DIRECTORY = '/disk4/data'
        INDEX DIRECTORY = '/disk4/idx',
      SUBPARTITION s5
        DATA DIRECTORY = '/disk5/data'
        INDEX DIRECTORY = '/disk5/idx'
)
  );

5.16.2 Management

Altering RANGE or LIST partitions
ALTER TABLE tbl TRUNCATE PARTITION p3;
ALTER TABLE tbl DROP PARTITION p4;

ALTER TABLE tbl
  ADD PARTITION (
  PARTITION p5 VALUES LESS THAN (2010)); -- the end only

ALTER TABLE members
  REORGANIZE PARTITION p0 INTO (
    PARTITION n0 VALUES LESS THAN (1960),
    PARTITION n1 VALUES LESS THAN (1970)
); -- splitting

ALTER TABLE members REORGANIZE PARTITION s2,p3 INTO (PARTITION p0 VALUES LESS THAN (1980)); -- merging

ALTER TABLE members REORGANIZE PARTITION p0,p1,p2,p3
INTO (
  PARTITION m0 VALUES LESS THAN (1980),
  PARTITION m1 VALUES LESS THAN (2000)
); -- merging and splitting

ALTER TABLE tbl
  PARTITION BY HASH(YEAR(dob))
  PARTITIONS 8; -- changing partitioning type

Altering HASH or KEY partitions
ALTER TABLE tbl COALESCE PARTITION 4; -- reduce by 4
ALTER TABLE tbl ADD PARTITION PARTITIONS 6; -- add 6

Others

ALTER TABLE pt -- partitioned tabled
  EXCHANGE PARTITION p
  WITH TABLE tbl; -- non-partitioned table
   # exchanges all the rows in pt with the rows in tbl

ALTER TABLE e2 REMOVE PARTITIONING;   # removes partitioning
ALTER TABLE tbl REBUILD PARTITION p0, p1;   # removes and reinserts all rows

ALTER TABLE tbl OPTIMIZE PARTITION p0, p1;
  # same as running CHECK PARTITION,
  # ANALYZE PARTITION, REPAIR PARTITION

ALTER TABLE tbl ANALYZE PARTITION p3;   # reads and stores key distributions
ALTER TABLE t1 REPAIR PARTITION p0,p1;   # repairs corrupted partitions
ALTER TABLE trb3 CHECK PARTITION p1;   # like CHECK TABLE
ALTER TABLE tbl TRUNCATE PARTITION ALL;   # empties all partitions
SHOW CREATE TABLE
SHOW CREATE STATUS
EXPLAIN PARTITIONS SELECT * FROM tbl

5.16.3 Selection

You can select which partitions to use for SELECT, DELETE, INSERT, REPLACE, UPDATE, LOAD DATA, LOAD XML operations. The partition clause usually follows the table name.

```
SELECT a, b FROM tbl PARTITION (p1,p2);
DELETE FROM tbl PARTITION (p0, p1) WHERE a=10;
UPDATE tbl PARTITION (p0) SET a=2 WHERE b=3;
```

5.17 Replication

Replication is the process by which selected data from one database server (the master) is replicated to one or more database servers (the slaves). It is asynchronous by default, which means that the slaves need not be connected permanently to receive updates.

Normally, all writes and updates must occur at the root master. Reads, however, can take place on the slaves.

Replication spreads the load among multiple slaves to improve performance. It can be used to run backup services. It can also distribute data over long distances, thus reducing transmission overhead.

During the replication process, the slaves read the binary log from the master, and execute selected events in the binary log on the local database.

A slave can be the master of another slave. Thus a replication setup may use various arbitrary topologies, including the tree, linear, and circular topologies.

5.17.1 Setting Up

Step 1: Configure the Master

Enable binary logging, and assign a unique server ID to the master. These can be done by editing my.cnf or my.ini(in C:\ProgramData\MySQL\MySQL Server 5.6 for Windows).

```
[mysqld]
log-bin=mysql-bin
server-id=1
```

Restart the server after making the changes.

Step 2: Configure the Slaves

Assign a unique server ID to each slave, as in Step 1.

```
[mysqld]
server-id=2
```

Restart the server after making the changes.

Step 3: Create a User for Replication

There must be a user account on the master that the slave can use to connect.

```
CREATE USER 'repl'@'%.mydomain.com'
    IDENTIFIED BY 'slavepass';
GRANT REPLICATION SLAVE ON *.*
    TO 'repl'@'%.mydomain.com';
```

Step 4: Determine the Master Binary Log Coordinates

You must know the master's current coordinates within its binary log, so that the slaves can start processing events from the binary log at the correct point. You may need to temporarily stop processing statements on the master first.

Start a session on the master, flush all tables, and block write statements:

```
FLUSH TABLES WITH READ LOCK;
```

In a different session on the master, obtain information about the current binary log file name and position:

```
SHOW MASTER STATUS;
```

File	Position	......
mysql--bin.000033	14665	

If binary logging has not been previously enabled, you need to use the empty string '' and 4 for the slave's log file and position respectively.

Step 5: Copy a Data Snapshot

To copy all existing databases on the master to the slaves, run in the command line:

```
mysqldump --all-databases --master-data > dbdump.db
```

You may also choose to dump specific databases only. Once the dump is created, copy the dump file to each slave. If the database is large, you may choose to copy the raw data files instead.

On each slave, import the dump file in the command line:

```
mysql < dbdump.db
```

Step 6: Start the Replication

On the master, release the read lock:

```
UNLOCK TABLES;
```

On each slave, set the master replication server configuration.

```
CHANGE MASTER TO
    MASTER_HOST='master_host_name',
    MASTER_USER='replication_user_name',
    MASTER_PASSWORD='replication_password',
    MASTER_LOG_FILE='recorded_log_file_name',
    MASTER_LOG_POS=recorded_log_position;
START SLAVE;
```

5.17.2 Using SSL

To use an encrypted SSL connection, specify the paths to the certificate and keys in the [mysqld] section of the master's my.cnf or my.ini file:

```
[mysqld]
ssl-ca=cacert.pem
ssl-cert=server-cert.pem
ssl-key=server-key.pem
```

where ssl-ca identifies the Certificate Authority certificate, ssl-cert identifies the server public key, and ssl-key identifies the server private key.

On the slave you can specify in the [client] section of the my.cnf or my.ini file the following options. Restart the server with the --skip-slave-start option to prevent the slave from connecting to the master. Then run the subsequent statements below.

```
[client]
ssl-ca=cacert.pem
ssl-cert=client-cert.pem
ssl-key=client-key.pem
```

```
CHANGE MASTER TO
    MASTER_HOST='master_hostname',
    MASTER_USER='replicate',
    MASTER_PASSWORD='password',
    MASTER_SSL=1;
START SLAVE;
```

Alternatively, you can specify the certificate and the keys in the CHANGE MASTER statement:

```
CHANGE MASTER TO
    MASTER_HOST='master_hostname',
    MASTER_USER='replicate',
    MASTER_PASSWORD='password',
    MASTER_SSL=1,
    MASTER_SSL_CA = 'ca_file_name',
    MASTER_SSL_CAPATH = 'ca_directory_name',
    MASTER_SSL_CERT = 'cert_file_name',
    MASTER_SSL_KEY = 'key_file_name';
START SLAVE;
```

5.17.3 Replication with GTIDs

Transaction-based replication using ***global transaction identifiers (GTIDs)*** allows for seamless failover, in which one of the slaves is promoted to a master when the master crashes.

A GTID is represented as:
  GTID = source_id:transaction_id
which uniquely identifies a transaction across the entire replication setup. *source_id*, which is usually the server's server_uuid, refers to the originating server. *transaction_id* is an integer that increases by one every time a transaction executes within the master. For example, a GTID looks like:
  3E11FA47-71CA-11E1-9E33-C80AA9429562:23

In the binary log, each transaction is associated with a GTID. During a replication process when the slave reads a GTID from the master, it retains the same GTID after committing the corresponding transaction. The slave does not generate a new GTID. In other words, a GTID remains the same throughout the replication setup after the transaction was first committed on the master.

The following steps describe how to set up transaction-based replication:

Step 1: Make the master and slave read-only.

```
SET @@global.read_only = ON;
```

Then, allow the slave to catch up with the master.

Step 2: Stop both servers. In the command line:

```
mysqladmin –uusername –p shutdown
```

Step 3: Restart both servers with GTIDs enabled. For the master, enter in the command line:

```
mysqld_safe --gtid_mode=ON --log-bin
--log-slave-updates --enforce-gtid-consistency &
```

For the slave, add the option --skip-slave-start:

```
mysqld_safe --gtid_mode=ON --log-bin
--log-slave-updates --enforce-gtid-consistency
--skip-slave-start &
```

Step 4: Connect the slave to the master.

```
CHANGE MASTER TO
    MASTER_HOST = host,
    MASTER_PORT = port,
    MASTER_USER = user,
    MASTER_PASSWORD = password,
    MASTER_AUTO_POSITION =1;
START SLAVE;
```

Step 5: Disable read-only mode for the master.

```
SET @@global.read_only = OFF;
```

To see the GTIDs in the binary log, enter SHOW MASTER STATUS, SHOW SLAVE STATUS, or SHOW BINLOG EVENTS. You can read the system variable gtid_exceuted. Moreover, the log file can be read using mysqlbinlog --base-64-output=DECODE-ROWS in the command line. You should notice that consecutive GTIDs may be collapsed into the range form:
  3E11FA47-71CA-11E1-9E33-C80AA9429562:20-23
  3E11FA47-71CA-11E1-9E33-C80AA5698468:40-99

During a failover, the slave sends to the master the range of GTIDs that have been committed. The master then sends all other transactions that have not been committed on the salve, along with the corresponding GTIDs.

When a slave has just been set up, executing the entire transaction history from the master can be time consuming. To speed things up, you can manually copy the data and transactions to the slave:

- To copy the data, you can use ***mysql --gtid-mode=ON*** (slave) to import a dump file created with ***mysqldump --master_data --set-gtid-purged*** (master), or copy the contents of the master's data directory to the slave data's directory.
- To copy the transactions, import the binary log using ***mysqlbinlog***, with the options ***--read-from-remote-server*** and ***--read-from-remote-master***.
    - You can also copy the master's binary log files to the slave directly. To read the logs on the slave, update the slave's binlog.index file to point to the copied logs, then execute a **CHANGE MASTER TO** statement to point to the first log file, and **START SLAVE** to read them. To read the logs on the slave, you can also use ***mysqlbinlog > file*** to export the binary log files to SQL files that can be processed by the ***mysql*** client.

However, sometimes it is not feasible to copy the entire binary log files because of their sheer sizes. To solve this problem, you can commit an empty transaction on the slave for each transaction identifier contained in the master's gtid_executed system variable, like this:

```
SET GTID_NEXT='aaa-bbb-ccc-ddd:N';
BEGIN;
COMMIT;
SET GTID_NEXT='AUTOMATIC';
```

After all transaction identifiers have been reinstated like this, run the following commands:

```
FLUSH LOGS;
PURGE BINARY LOGS TO 'master-bin.00000N';
```

FLUSH LOGS creates a new binary log. PURGE BINARY LOGS purges the empty transactions, which allows the slave to catch up with the master in time.

Instead of committing empty transactions and using the PURGE BINARY LOGS statement, you can also set the system variable gtid_purged on the slave directly, based on the value of gtid_executed on the master. gtid_purged contains the set of all transactions that have been purged from the master's binary log.

Note that the following are not supported by GTID-based replication:

- Non-transactional storage engines such as MyISAM.
- CREATE TABLE ... SELECT statements.
- Temporary tables.
- sql_slave_skip_counter. Use the master's gtid_executed variable instead.
- Importing a dump made using mysqldump into a server running with GTID mode enabled, when there are GTIDs in the target server's binary log.

5.17.4 Statement-based vs Row-based

Events are recorded within the binary log in statements-based format or row-based format. Statement-based logging, the default, logs statements that made any changes, whereas row-based logging logs changes in individual table rows. A third type of logging, mixed-format logging, changes the logging format in real time according to the type of event.

To change the format for binary logging, SET the system variable binlog_format. Restart the server if the variable is set globally.

```
SET binlog_format = 'ROW';
SET @@binlog_format = 'STATEMENT';
SET SESSION binlog_format = 'MIXED';
SET GLOBAL binlog_format = 'ROW';
SET @@session.binlog_format = 'STATEMENT';
SET @@global.binlog_format = 'MIXED';
```

Statement-based logging requires much less storage space, so statement-based replication (SBR) can be completed more quickly.

However, SBR has its limitations when compared to row-based replication (RBR). SBR:

- is unsafe as not all statements which modify data can be replicated using it.
- requires more row-level locks for INSERT, UPDATE or DELETE statements.
- must re-evaluate and re-execute complex statements.
- requires deterministic user-defined functions (UDFs) to be applied on the slaves.

The following statements are unsafe for SBR. They generate a warning if statement-based logging is used. If the MIXED binary logging format is used, these unsafe statements are logged using row-based format, while the other statements are logged using statement-based format.

- Statements containing system functions that may return a different value on slave: FOUND_ROWS(), GET_LOCK(), IS_FREE_LOCK(), IS_USED_LOCK(), LOAD_FILE(), MASTER_POS_WAIT(), PASSWORD(), RAND(), RELEASE_LOCK(), ROW_COUNT(), SESSION_USER(), SLEEP(), SYSDATE(), SYSTEM_USER(), USER(), UUID(), and UUID_SHORT().
- References to system variables
- User-defined functions (UDFs)
- Fulltext plugin
- Trigger or stored program updates a table having an AUTO_INCREMENT column
- INSERT...ON DUPLICATE KEY UPDATE statements on tables with multiple primary or unique keys.
- Updates using LIMIT
- Accesses or references log tables
- Non-transactional operations after transactional operations.
- LOAD DATA INFILE statements.

However, the following non-deterministic functions are safe: CONNECTION_ID(), CURDATE(), CURRENT_DATE(), CURRENT_TIME(), CURRENT_TIMESTAMP(), CURTIME(), LAST_INSERT_ID(), LOCALTIME(), LOCALTIMESTAMP(), NOW(), UNIX_TIMESTAMP(), UTC_DATE(), UTC_TIME(), and UTC_TIMESTAMP().

5.17.5 Administration

To check the replication status on the slave, run **SHOW SLAVE STATUS**. To check the status of connected slaves on the master, run **SHOW PROCESSLIST**. If the slaves were started with the --report-host option, you can obtain basic information about the slave on the master with **SHOW SLAVE HOSTS**.

To pause or resume replication on a slave, consider:

```
[STOP|START] SLAVE  [IO_THREAD|SQL_THREAD]
```

The **IO_THREAD** reads events from the master while the **SQL_THREAD** executes the received events. You can stop one while allowing the other to run.

To replicate different databases on different slaves, use, on each slave, in the command line, the configuration option --replicate-wild-do-table:

```
--replicate-wild-do-table=databaseX.%
```

To delay replication such that the slave lags behind the master by at least N seconds:

```
CHANGE MASTER TO MASTER_DELAY = N;
```

You can get more control over the replication and binary logging by manipulating the system variables or command-line options. You can also perform semisynchronous replication. These and some other issues are not covered in this book, but you can always refer to the official online documentation to get an in-depth knowledge of replication.

5.18 Administration

5.18.1 Accounts

The predefined ***mysql*** database store account information.

```
CREATE USER user_specification [, user_specification] ...

user_specification:
   user
   [
     | IDENTIFIED WITH auth_plugin [AS 'auth_string']
     IDENTIFIED BY [PASSWORD] 'password'
   ]
```

'%' is used, if **user** does not contain the host name.

If **IDENTIFIED WITH** is used, the server does not assign a password. If **IDENTIFIED BY** is used instead, the server uses the implicit, default authentication plugin.

auth_plugin can be *mysql_native_password* or *sha256_password*. If *sha256_password* is used, the *old_passwords* system variable must be set to 2.

The system variable *default_authentication_plugin* defines the implicit, default plugin. Permitted values are *mysql_native_password* (default) and *sha256_password*. If the implicitly assigned plugin is *mysql_native_password*, the *old_passwords* system variable must be set to 0.

'auth_string' is a quoted string to pass to the plugin.

Specify **PASSWORD**, if you want to avoid specifying the password in plain text and you know its hash value (the value that PASSWORD() would return).

```
CREATE USER 'janet'@'localhost'
         IDENTIFIED WITH sha256_password;
SET old_passwords =2;
SET PASSWORD FOR 'janet'@'localhost' =
      PASSWORD('password');
```

```
SET old_passwords = 0;
CREATE USER 'ahmad'@'localhost' IDENTIFIED BY 'password'.
```

```
CREATE USER 'ali'@'localhost' IDENTIFIED BY PASSWORD
  '*90E462C37378CED12064BB3388827D2BA3A9B689'
```

```
SET PASSWORD [FOR user] =
   {
     PASSWORD('cleartext password')
    | OLD_PASSWORD('cleartext password')
    | 'encrypted password'
   }
```

If the **FOR user** clause is omitted, the current user's password is set.

```
ALTER USER user_specification [, user_specification] ...

user_specification:
   user alter_option

alter_option: {
   PASSWORD EXPIRE
  | PASSWORD EXPIRE DEFAULT
  | PASSWORD EXPIRE NEVER
  | PASSWORD EXPIRE INTERVAL N DAY
}
```

Operations will be denied when a password expires.

The first option, **PASSWORD EXPIRE**, expires an account password instantly.

The second option, **PASSWORD EXPIRE DEFAULT**, expires the account after the number of days specified by the *default_password_lifetime* system variable. If that system variable (default:360) is set to 0, the password never expires.

The third option, **PASSWORD EXPIRE NEVER**, disables automatic password expiration.

The fourth option, **PASSWORD EXPIRE INTERVAL N DAY**, causes the password to expire after N days.

```
RENAME USER old_user TO new_user
   [, old_user TO new_user] ...
```

This changes the user name.

```
RENAME USRE 'jane'@'localhost' TO 'jean'@'localhost';
```

```
DROP USER user [, user] ...
```

This removes a user.

5.18.2 Privileges

```
GRANT
   priv_type [(column_list)]
     [, priv_type [(column_list)]] ...
   ON [object_type] priv_level
   TO user_specification [, user_specification] ...
   [REQUIRE {NONE | ssl_option [[AND] ssl_option] ...}]
   [WITH with_option ...]

GRANT PROXY ON user_specification
   TO user_specification [, user_specification] ...
   [WITH GRANT OPTION]

object_type:
   TABLE
  | FUNCTION
  | PROCEDURE

priv_level:
   *
  | *.*
  | db_name.*
  | db_name.tbl_name
  | tbl_name
  | db_name.routine_name

user_specification:
   user
   [
     | IDENTIFIED WITH auth_plugin [AS 'auth_string']
     IDENTIFIED BY [PASSWORD] 'password'
   ]
```

```
ssl_option:
    SSL
  | X509
  | CIPHER 'cipher'
  | ISSUER 'issuer'
  | SUBJECT 'subject'

with_option:
    GRANT OPTION
  | MAX_QUERIES_PER_HOUR count
  | MAX_UPDATES_PER_HOUR count
  | MAX_CONNECTIONS_PER_HOUR count
  | MAX_USER_CONNECTIONS count
```

This grants prvileges to one or more user accounts.

```
GRANT SELECT (col1), INSERT (col1,col2) ON mydb.mytbl
  TO 'someuser'@'somehost';
```

```
GRANT EXECUTE ON PROCEDURE mydb.myproc
  TO 'someuser'@'somehost';
```

```
GRANT ALL PRIVILEGES ON test.* TO 'root'@'localhost'
  IDENTIFIED BY 'goodsecret'
  REQUIRE
    SUBJECT '/C=EE/ST=Some-State/L=Tallinn/
          O=MySQL demo client certificate/
          CN=Tonu Samuel/emailAddress=tonu@example.com'
    AND ISSUER '/C=FI/ST=Some-State/L=Helsinki/
               O=MySQL Finland AB/CN=Tonu
               Samuel/emailAddress=tonu@example.com'
    AND CIPHER 'EDH-RSA-DES-CBC3-SHA';
```

Privileges
ALL [PRIVILEGES] grants all privileges except GRANT OPTION.
ALTER (global, database, table) enables the use of ALTER TABLE.
ALTER ROUTINE (global, database, table) enables stored routines to be altered or dropped.
CREATE (global, database, table) enables database and table creation.
CREATE ROUTINE (global, database, table) enables stored routine creation.
CREATE TABLESPACE (global) enables tablespaces and log file groups to be created, altered or dropped.
CREATE TEMPORARY TABLES (global, database) enables the use of CREATE TEMPORARY TABLE.
CREATE USER (global) enables thes use of CREATE USER, DROP USER, RENAME USER, and REVOKE ALL PRIVILEGES.
CREATE VIEW (global, database, table) enables views to be created and altered.
DELETE (global, database, table) enables the use of DELETE.
DROP (global, database, table) enables databases, tables, and views to be dropped.
EVENT (global, database) enables the use of events for the Event Scheduler.
EXECUTE (global, database, table) enables the user to execute stored routines.
FILE (global) enables the user to cause the server to read or write files.
GRANT_OPTION (global, database, table, procedure, proxy) enables privileges to be granted to or removed from other accounts.
INDEX (global, database, table) enables indexes to be created or dropped.
INSERT (global, database, table, column) enables the use of INSERT.
LOCK TABLES (global, database) enables the use of LOCK TABLES on tables for which you have the SELECT privilege.
PROCESS (global) enables the user to see all processes with SHOW PROCESSLIST.
PROXY (from user to user) enables user proxying.
REFERENCES (implemented)
RELOAD (global) enables the use of FLUSH operations.
REPLICATION CLIENT (global) enables the user to ask where the the master or slave servers are.
REPLICATION SLAVE (global) enables replication slaves to read binary log events from the master.
SELECT (global, database, table, column) enables the use of SELECT.
SHOW DATABASES (global) enables the use of SHOW DATABASES to show all databases.
SHOW VIEW (global, database, table) enables the use of SHOW CREATE VIEW.
SHUTDOWN (global) enables the use of *mysqladmin shutdown*.
SUPER (global) enables the use of other administrative operations such as CHANGE MASTER TO, KILL, PURGE BINARY LOGS, SET GLOBAL, and *mysqladmin debug* command.
TRIGGER (global, database, table) enables trigger operations.
UPDATE (global, database, table, column) enables the use of UPDATE.
USAGE (no privileges)

```
REVOKE
   priv_type [(column_list)]
     [, priv_type [(column_list)]] ...
   ON [object_type] priv_level
   FROM user [, user] ...

REVOKE ALL PRIVILEGES, GRANT OPTION
   FROM user [, user] ...

REVOKE PROXY ON user
   FROM user [, user] ...
```

5.18.3 Connections

```
CREATE {DATABASE | SCHEMA} [IF NOT EXISTS] db_name
   [create_specification] ...

create_specification:
   [DEFAULT] CHARACTER SET [=] charset_name
 | [DEFAULT] COLLATE [=] collation_name
```

```
ALTER {DATABASE | SCHEMA} [db_name]
   alter_specification ...
ALTER {DATABASE | SCHEMA} db_name
   UPGRADE DATA DIRECTORY NAME

alter_specification:
   [DEFAULT] CHARACTER SET [=] charset_name
 | [DEFAULT] COLLATE [=] collation_name
```

```
DROP {DATABASE | SCHEMA} [IF EXISTS] db_name
```

```
USE db_name
```

```
CREATE SERVER server_name
   FOREIGN DATA WRAPPER wrapper_name
   OPTIONS (option [, option] ...)

option:
  { HOST character-literal
  | DATABASE character-literal
  | USER character-literal
  | PASSWORD character-literal
  | SOCKET character-literal
  | OWNER character-literal
  | PORT numeric-literal }
```

```
ALTER SERVER  server_name
   OPTIONS (option [, option] ...)
```

```
DROP SERVER [ IF EXISTS ] server_name
```

This defines a server for use with the FEDERATED storage engine.
Currently 'mysql' is the only supported **wrapper_name**.

CREATE SERVER s
FOREIGN DATA WRAPPER mysql
OPTIONS (
  USER 'Remote',
  HOST '192.168.1.106',
  DATABASE 'test');

CREATE TABLE t (s1 INT)
  ENGINE=FEDERATED
  CONNECTION='s';

INSTALL PLUGIN plugin_name SONAME 'shared_library_name'
UNINSTALL PLUGIN plugin_name
The shared library must be located in the plugin directory, as indicated by the *plugin_dir* system variable.
Refer to the online official documentation for more information about using plugins.

5.18.4 Table Maintenance

ANALYZE [NO_WRITE_TO_BINLOG | LOCAL] TABLE   tbl_name [, tbl_name] ...
This analyses and stores, for a table, the key distribution. A key distribution is used to decide which indexes to use and the order in which tables should be joined.
This works with InnoDB, NDB and MyISAM tables. For InnoDB and MyISAM, the table is read-locked during the analysis.
NO_WRITE_TO_BINLOG and **LOCAL** are the same.
The SHOW INDEX statement checks a stored key distribution.

CHECK TABLE tbl_name [, tbl_name] ... [option] ... option = {FOR UPGRADE | QUICK | FAST | MEDIUM | EXTENDED | CHANGED}
This checks tables for errors.
This works for InnoDB, MyISAM, ARCHIVE and CSV tables. For MyISAM tables, the key statistics are also updated.
FOR UPGRADE checks whether the tables are compatible with the current version of MySQL. If the full check succeeds, the server marks the table's .frm file with the current MySQL version number. Incompatibilities might occur because the storage format for a data type has changed or because its sort order has changed.
QUICK does not scan the rows for incorrent links. This applies to InnoDB and MyISAM tables and views.
FAST checks only tables that have not been closed properly. This applies only to MyISAM tables and views.
CHANGED checks only tables that have been changed since the last check or that have not been closed properly. This applies only to MyISAM tables and views, and is ignored for InnoDB.
MEDIUM scans rows to verify that deleted links are valid. This also calculates a key checksum for the rows and verifies this with a calculated checksum for the keys. This applies only to MyISAM tables and views, and is ignored for InnoDB.
EXTENDED does a full key lookup for all keys for each row. This ensures that the table is 100% consistent, but takes a long time. This applies only to MyISAM tables and views, and is ignored for InnoDB.
CHECK TABLE might change the table. This happens if the table is marked as 'corrupted' or 'not closed properly' but CHECK TABLE does not find any problems in the table. In this case, CHECK TABLE marks the table as okay

CHECKSUM TABLE tbl_name [, tbl_name] ...   [QUICK | EXTENDED]
This reports a checksum for the contents of a table. The checksum can be used to make sure the contents are the same before and after a backup, rollback, or other operation.
EXTENDED, the default, performs the calculation row-by-row.
For MyISAM tables created with the CHECKSUM=1 clause, the 'live' table checksum can be returned very fast. If the table does not meet all these conditions, the **QUICK** method returns NULL.

OPTIMIZE [NO_WRITE_TO_BINLOG | LOCAL] TABLE   tbl_name [, tbl_name] ...
This reorganizes the physical storage of table data and associated data, to reduce storage space and improve I/O efficiency when accessing the table.

REPAIR [NO_WRITE_TO_BINLOG | LOCAL] TABLE
  tbl_name [, tbl_name] ...
  [QUICK] [EXTENDED] [USE_FRM]

This repairs a possibly corrupted table. The statement only applies to MyISAM, ARCHIVE and CSV tables.
QUICK tries to repair only the index file, and not the data file.
EXTENDED creates the index row by row instead of creating one index at a time with sorting.
The **USE_FRM** option is available for use if the .MYI index file is missing or if its header is corrupted. This option tells MySQL not to trust the information in the .MYI file header and to re-create it using information from the .frm file. Use the USE_FRM option only if you cannot use regular REPAIR modes! Telling the server to ignore the .MYI file makes important table metadata stored in the .MYI unavailable to the repair process, which can have deleterious consequences.
If USE_FRM is not used, REPAIR TABLE checks the table to see whether an upgrade is required. If so, it performs the upgrade.
By default, the server writes REPAIR TABLE statements to the binary log so that they replicate to replication slaves. To suppress logging, specify the optional **NO_WRITE_TO_ BINLOG** keyword or its alias **LOCAL**. In the event that a table on the master becomes corrupted and you run REPAIR TABLE on it, any resulting changes to the original table are not propagated to slaves.

5.18.5 Others

BINLOG 'str'
BINLOG is an internal-use statement generated by the mysqlbinlog program as the printable representation of certain events in binary log files.
'str' value is a base 64-encoded string that the server decodes to determine the data change indicated by the corresponding event.

CACHE INDEX
  tbl_index_list [, tbl_index_list] ...
  [PARTITION (partition_list | ALL)]
  IN key_cache_name
 	
tbl_index_list:
  tbl_name [[INDEX|KEY] (index_name[, index_name] ...)]
 	
partition_list:
  partition_name[, partition_name][, ...]

This assigns table indexes to a specific key cache. It is used only for MyISAM tables. After the indexes have been assigned, they can be preloaded into the cache if desired with LOAD INDEX INTO CACHE.
A key cache must exist before you can assign indexes to it. The key cache referred to in a CACHE INDEX statement can be created by setting its size with a parameter setting statement or in the server parameter settings: SET GLOBAL keycache1.key_buffer_size=128*1024;
Index assignment affects the server globally.

CREATE TABLE pt (c1 INT, c2 VARCHAR(50), INDEX i(c1))
  PARTITION BY HASH(c1)
  PARTITIONS 4;
 	
SET GLOBAL kc_fast.key_buffer_size = 128 * 1024;

```
SET GLOBAL kc_slow.key_buffer_size = 128 * 1024;

CACHE INDEX pt PARTITION (p0) IN kc_fast;
CACHE INDEX pt PARTITION (p1, p3) IN kc_slow;
```

```
FLUSH [NO_WRITE_TO_BINLOG | LOCAL]
    flush_option [, flush_option] ...

flush_option:
  DES_KEY_FILE
| HOSTS
| [log_type] LOGS
| PRIVILEGES
| QUERY CACHE
| STATUS
| TABLES [tbl_name......] [WITH READ LOCK | FOR EXPORT]
| USER_RESOURCES

log_type:
  BINARY
| ENGINE
| ERROR
| GENERAL
| RELAY
| SLOW
```

DES_KEY_FILE reloads the DES keys from the file that was specified with the --des-key-file option at server startup time.
HOSTS empties the host cache. You should flush the host cache if some of your hosts change IP address or if the error message *Host 'host_name' is blocked* occurs.
FLUSH LOGS closes and reopens all log files. **BINARY** closes and reopens the binary log files. **ENGINE** closes and reopens any flushable logs for installed storage engines. Currently, this causes InnoDB to flush its logs to disk. **ERROR** closes and reopens the error log file. **GENERAL** closes and reopens the general query log file. **RELAY** closes and reopens the relay log files. **SLOW** closes and reopens the slow query log file.
PRIVILEGES reloads the privileges from the grant tables in the mysql database.
QUERY CACHE defragments the query cache to better utilize its memory.
STATUS adds the current thread's session status variable values to the global values and resets the session values to zero.
USER_RESOURCES resets all per-hour user resources to zero.
FLUSH TABLES or **FLUSH TABLE** closes all open tables, forces all tables in use to be closed, and flushes the query cache. This also removes all query results from the query cache.
FLUSH TABLES WITH READ LOCK acquires a global read lock and not table locks, so it is not subject to the same behavior as LOCK TABLES and UNLOCK TABLES with respect to table locking and implicit commits. Use UNLOCK TABLES to release the lock.
FOR EXPORT ensures that changes to the tables have been flushed to disk.

```
KILL [CONNECTION | QUERY] thread_id
```

CONNECTION, the default, terminates the associated connection. **QUERY** terminates the statement that the connection is currently executing, but leaves the connection itself intact.
Enter SHOW PROCESSLIST to see which threads are running.
Killing a REPAIR TABLE or OPTIMIZE TABLE operation on a MyISAM table results in a table that is corrupted and unusable.

```
LOAD INDEX INTO CACHE
  tbl_index_list [, tbl_index_list] ...

tbl_index_list:
  tbl_name
    [PARTITION (partition_list | ALL)]
    [[INDEX|KEY] (index_name[, index_name] ...)]
    [IGNORE LEAVES]

partition_list:
    partition_name[, partition_name][, ...]
```

This preloads a table index into the key cache to which it has been assigned by an explicit CACHE INDEX statement, or into the default key cache otherwise.
The **IGNORE LEAVES** modifier causes only blocks for the nonleaf nodes of the index to be preloaded.
IGNORE LEAVES fails unless all indexes in a table have the same block size. You can determine index block sizes for a table by using *myisamchk -dv* and checking the Blocksize column.

```
RESET {reset_option [,...]}

reset_option: MASTER | QUERY CACHE | SLAVE
```

MASTER deletes all binary logs listed in the index file, resets the binary log index file to be empty, and creates a new binary log file.
QUERY CACHE removes all query results from the query cache.
SLAVE makes the slave forget its replication position in the master binary logs. It also resets the relay log by deleting any existing relay log files and beginning a new one.

5.19 Storage Engines

You can use the SHOW ENGINES statement to see the supported engines.

5.19.1 InnoDB

Balancing high reliability and performance, InnoDB is the default storage engine.

The advantages of using InnoDB are:

- The DML (Data Manipulative Language) operations follow the ACID (atomicity, consistency, isolation and durability) model, featuring commit, rollback, and crash-recovery capabilities.
- Row-level locking and Oracle-style consistent reads increase performance and multi-user concurrency.
- The tables arrange your data on disk to optimize queries based on primary keys.
- FOREIGN KEY constraints are supported.
- You can freely mingle InnoDB tables with tables from other storage engines, even within the same statement. For example, you can use a join operation to combine data from InnoDB and MEMORY tables in a single query.
- InnoDB has been designed for maximum performance when processing large data volumes.
- InnoDB maintains its own buffer pool for caching data and indexes in main memory.

- The tables can handle a lot of data, even on operating systems where the file size is limited to 2GB.

Storage Limits	64TB
Transactions	Yes
Locking granularity	Row
MVCC	Yes
Geospatial data type support	Yes
Geospatial indexing support	No
B-tree indexes	Yes
T-tree indexes	No
Hash indexes	No
Full-text search indexes	Yes
Clustered indexes	Yes
Data caches	Yes
Index caches	Yes
Compressed data	Yes
Encrypted data	Yes
Cluster database support	No
Replication support	Yes
Foreign key support	Yes
Backup/ Point-in-time recovery	Yes
Query cache support	Yes
Update statistics for data dictionary	Yes

5.19.2 MyISAM

MyISAM is based on the older (and no longer available) ISAM storage engine but has many useful extensions.

Storage Limits	256TB
Transactions	No
Locking granularity	Table
MVCC	No
Geospatial data type support	Yes
Geospatial indexing support	Yes
B-tree indexes	Yes
T-tree indexes	No
Hash indexes	No
Full-text search indexes	Yes
Clustered indexes	No
Data caches	No
Index caches	Yes
Compressed data	Yes
Encrypted data	Yes
Cluster database support	No
Replication support	Yes
Foreign key support	No
Backup/ Point-in-time recovery	Yes
Query cache support	Yes
Update statistics for data dictionary	Yes

5.19.3 MEMORY

The MEMORY storage engine (formerly known as HEAP) creates contents that are stored in memory. Because the data is vulnerable to crashes, hardware issues, or power outages, only use these tables as temporary work areas or read-only caches for data pulled from other tables.

MEMORY performance is limited by contention due to single-thread execution and table lock overhead when processing updates. This limits scalability when load increases, especially for statement mixes that include writes.

Despite the in-memory processing for MEMORY tables, they are not necessarily faster than InnoDB tables on a busy server, for general-purpose queries, or under a read/write workload. Particularly, the table locking involved with performing updates can slow down concurrent usage of MEMORY tables from multiple sessions.

The maximum size of MEMORY tables is limited by the max_heap_table_size system variable, which has a default value of 16MB.

Storage Limits	RAM
Transactions	No
Locking granularity	Table
MVCC	No
Geospatial data type support	No
Geospatial indexing support	No
B-tree indexes	Yes
T-tree indexes	No
Hash indexes	Yes
Full-text search indexes	No
Clustered indexes	No
Data caches	N/A
Index caches	N/A
Compressed data	No
Encrypted data	Yes
Cluster database support	No
Replication support	Yes
Foreign key support	No
Backup/ Point-in-time recovery	Yes
Query cache support	Yes
Update statistics for data dictionary	Yes

5.19.4 CSV

The CSV storage engine stores data in text files using comma-separated values format.

5.19.5 ARCHIVE

The ARCHIVE storage engine produces special-purpose tables that store large amounts of unindexed data in a very small footprint. Rows are compressed as they are inserted. On retrieval, rows are uncompressed on-the-fly.

It supports INSERT and SELECT, but not DELETE, REPLACE, or UPDATE. It does support ORDER BY operations, BLOB columns, and basically all but spatial data types. It uses row-level locking. It supports the AUTO_INCREMENT column attribute.

Storage Limits	None
Transactions	No
Locking granularity	Table
MVCC	No
Geospatial data type support	Yes
Geospatial indexing support	No
B-tree indexes	No
T-tree indexes	No
Hash indexes	No
Full-text search indexes	No
Clustered indexes	No
Data caches	No
Index caches	No
Compressed data	Yes
Encrypted data	Yes
Cluster database support	No
Replication support	Yes

Foreign key support	No
Backup/ Point-in-time recovery	Yes
Query cache support	Yes
Update statistics for data dictionary	Yes

5.19.6 BLACKHOLE

The BLACKHOLE storage engine accepts data but throws it away. No data is stored. Retrievals always return an empty result.

5.19.7 MERGE

The MERGE storage engine, also known as the MRG_MyISAM engine, is a collection of identical MyISAM tables that can be used as one. "Identical" means that all tables have identical column and index information.

```
CREATE TABLE t1 (
  a INT NOT NULL AUTO_INCREMENT PRIMARY KEY,
  message CHAR(20)) ENGINE=MyISAM;
CREATE TABLE t2 (
  a INT NOT NULL AUTO_INCREMENT PRIMARY KEY,
  message CHAR(20)) ENGINE=MyISAM;
INSERT INTO t1 (message) VALUES ('Testing'),('table'),('t1');
INSERT INTO t2 (message) VALUES ('Testing'),('table'),('t2');
CREATE TABLE total (
  a INT NOT NULL AUTO_INCREMENT,
  message CHAR(20), INDEX(a))
  ENGINE=MERGE UNION=(t1,t2) INSERT_METHOD=LAST;
```

5.19.8 FEDERATED

The FEDERATED storage engine allows you to access data from a remote MySQL database without using replication or cluster technology. No data is stored on the local tables. Querying a local FEDERATED table automatically pulls the data from the remote (federated) tables.

To enable FEDERATED, you must start the MySQL server binary using the --federated option.

5.19.9 EXAMPLE

A stub engine that does nothing, the EXAMPLE storage engine is meant to serve as an example in the MySQL source code that illustrates how to begin writing new storage engines.

When you create an EXAMPLE table, the server creates a table format file in the database directory. The file begins with the table name and has an .frm extension. No other files are created. No data can be stored into the table. Retrievals return an empty result.

6. Extensible Markup Language

So far we have seen how to store data in Javascript (Chapter 3), text files (Chapter 4), and structured tables (Chapter 5). XML represents yet another way to store data. Although somewhat verbose, an XML document is both human-readable and machine-readable. It may be regarded as something intermediate between a text file and a structured table.

Whereas an SQL table is two-dimensional, an XML document is hierarchical. While SQL operates at the server, XML is a client technology as much as a server technology. In general, SQL should be used for very dynamic data because of its storage efficiency, while XML should be used for static content. Where it gives significant advantages in retrieval efficiency, storage space and security, SQL is more appropriate. However, to the human coder, with XML, data can be easily prepared, transformed and transported.

The following is an example of an XML document. Containing different tags and attributes, an XML document resembles a HTML document, except that the names for the XML tags and attributes are defined by the coder.

```
<bookslist>
  <book id="123321">
    <title>Harry Potter</title>
    <author>J. K. Rowling</author>
    <ISBN>9780545010221</ISBN>
    <price>22.90</price>
    <bestseller/>
  </book>
  <book id="456654">
    <title>Fantasy in Death</title>
    <author>J. D. Robb</author>
    <ISBN>9781101185360</ISBN>
    <price>7.81</price>
  </book>
</bookslist>
```

A *well-formed* XML document must:

- have a root element. In the example above, <booklist> is the root element.
- close all elements. This means that for each opening tag <tag>, there must be a closing tag </tag>. Empty tags can be abbreviated by <tag/>.
- quote all attributes values. In the example above, 'id' is an attribute for the element <book>, and its value (123321) must be quoted.
- be case-sensitive in tags.
- escape some special characters like < and & when they are not markup. In XML, there are only five built-in character entities: <(<), >(>), &(&), '('), "("). Additional entities may be defined in a DTD as we shall see later.
- use hexadecimal references for any Unicode character, such as &.

Note that white space is preserved in XML and not truncated as in HTML.

You can use the browsers to view an XML document. We recommend using Altova XMLSpy or OxygenXML to process XML documents in various ways as described later in this chapter. A free plugin for Notepad++ called XML Tools, available at http://sourceforge.net/projects/npp-plugins/files/XML%20Tools/, can be used to format XML documents, perform XSD validation, apply XSLT etc.

6.1 Markup Components

Text in an XML document consists of intermingled *character data* and *markup*. Markup specifies the structure of the document and some other special semantics. Text that is not markup constitutes the character data.

So far you have seen elements, attributes, and entities. We shall use this example throughout this section to illustrate various other markup components permitted in an XML document. One other markup component, document type declarations (DTDs), will be described later.

```
<?xml version="1.0" encoding="UTF-8" standalone="yes" ?>
<bookslist xml:base="http://GoldenBookstore.com">
           xmlns:gb="http://GoldenBookstore.com"
           xmlns:xlink="http://www.w3.org/1999/xlink"
           xmlns:xi="http://www.w3.org/2003/XInclude">
  <!-- These are the books in Golden Bookstore. -->
  <?xml-stylesheet type="text/xsl" href="style.xsl"?>
  <gb:book xml:id="b123321" xml:base="/branch1">
    <title xml:lang="en" xml:space="preserve">
      Harry Potter</title>
    <author gb:gender="f"
            xlink:type="simple"
            xlink:href="/images/jkrowling.gif"
            xlink:show="new">
      J. K. Rowling</author>
    <ISBN>9780545010221</ISBN>
    <price>22.90</price>
    <description>
      <![CDATA[<old_price>30.00</old_price>]]>
    </description>
    <bestseller/>
  </gb:book>
  <gb:book xml:id="b456654" xml:space="preserve">
    <title xml:lang="en">Fantasy in Death</title>
    <author gb:gender="f"
            xlink:type="simple"
            xlink:href="/images/jdrobb.gif"
            xlink:show="new">
      J. D. Robb</author>
    <ISBN>9781101185360</ISBN>
    <price>7.81</price>
  </gb:book>
  <xi:include href="books.xml" parse="xml" />
</bookslist>
```

6.1.1 Document Declaration

An XML document should begin with an XML declaration denoted by <?xml ...... ?>. The three possible attributes are:

- **version**: There are currently version 1.0 and version 1.1. Version 1.1 has not been widely implemented. The main changes are to enable the use of line-ending characters used on EBCDIC platforms, and the use of scripts and characters absent from Unicode 3.2. XML 1.1 came out of a desire to support all the world's languages, and is generally not used.
- **encoding**: This specifies the encoding of the document.
- **standalone:** The valid values are 'yes' and 'no'. A standalone XML document is one that tells the XML processor to ignore any DTDs. 'yes' indicates that there are no external markup declarations which affect the information passed from the XML processor to the application.

6.1.2 Comment

<!--......--> denotes a comment, and can appear anywhere outside other markup. Not part of any character data, it may or may not allow the XML processor to retrieve the comment text. The characters <, & etc may appear in it. Entity references will not be recognized. Avoid double-hyphens -- within comments for compatibility reasons.

6.1.3 CDATA

<![CDATA[......]]> denotes a section of character data. This is used to escape blocks of text containing characters which would otherwise be recognized as markup. In the previous example, <old_price> is recognized as character data, not markup. CDATA sections can contain the < and & literals. They cannot be nested.

6.1.4 Processing Instruction

<? ......?> denotes a processing instruction that is meant to inform the XML processor to process the data in a certain way. A processing instruction begins with a target name used to identify the application to which the instruction is directed. In the previous example, we request the XML document to be rendered using a stylesheet using the 'xml-stylesheet' target. Target names such as 'XML' and 'xml' are reserved.

6.1.5 Namespace

A namespace is used to prevent name clashes of the elements and attributes. This can be important when different people are working together, each creating his or her own XML documents. By convention, a HTTP-style URL is used as a namespace, although no connection to the URL is needed to process the XML document.

A namespace is declared in an opening tag like this:
xmlns:prefixName='namespaceName'

A namespace can only be used after it has been declared in an ancestor or current element. To use a namespace, preprend an element name or attribute name with 'prefixName:'.

If the part ':prefixName' is omitted, a *default namespace* is assumed. The scope of the namespace is the content of the tag itself. To use the default namespace, the descendant element names and attribute names need not be prefixed with any prefix name.

Reserved Prefix Names
The prefix name '**xml**' is reserved and bound to 'http://www.w3.org/XML/1998/namespace'. It may be declared, but must not be bound to any other namespace name. Other prefix names must not be bound to this namespace name, and it must not be declared as the default namespace.
The prefix name '**xmlns**' is reserved and bound to 'http://www.w3.org/2000/xmlns/'. It must not be declared. Other prefix names must not be bound to this namespace name. It must not be declared as the default namespace. Element names must not have the prefix xmlns.
Prefix names beginning with 'xml' are reserved.

No tag may contain two attributes which have the same names, or the same local names prefixed by prefix names bound to the same namespace name.

6.1.6 xml:lang

This special attribute declares the formal language for the content of the tag. It can be overridden.

6.1.7 xml:space

This special attribute can be assigned a value of 'preserve' or 'default'. 'preserve' indicates that white space is to be preserved. 'default' tells the XML processor to use its own scheme to handle white space.

6.1.8 xml:id

This special attribute is used to assign a single, unique name to an element. This helps XML processors to make sub-resource linking robust.

6.1.9 xml:base

This specifies the base URL for any relative URLs. When nested, the declaration in the descendent element can be appended to that in the ancestor element. xml:base is also recognized in XLink, XPointer and XInclude.

6.1.10 XLink

XLink allows an element to behave like a hyperlink. It exists as a special namespace that should be declared in an ancestor element.

xlink:actuate specifies when the linked resource is read and shown. The valid values are 'onLoad', 'onRequest', 'other', and 'none'.
xlink:href specifies the URL of the resource.
xlink:show specifies where to open the link. The valid values are 'embed', 'new', 'replace', 'other' and 'none'.
xlink:type specifies the type of the link. The valid values are 'simple', 'extended', 'locator', 'arc', 'resource', 'title', and 'none'.
xlink:role, **xlink:arcrole**, and **xlink:title** describe the meaning of the resources within the context of the link.
xlink:label, **xlink:from**, and **xlink:to** are used for traversal.

XLink is not supported by browsers currently but other XML processors may use it.

6.1.11 XPointer

XPointer allows the links to points to specific parts of an XML document instead of the whole XML document. For instance:
xlink:href="http://example.com/cars.xml#xpointer(id('BMW'))"
Because the above example references the 'id' attribute, it can be rewritten as:
xlink:href=http://example.com/cars.xml#BMW
XPointer recognizes XPath, which will be explained later.

```
<foobar id="foo">
  <bar/>
  <baz>
    <bom a="1"/>
  </baz>
  <bom a="2"/>
</foobar>
```

```
xpointer(id("foo")) => foobar
 xpointer(/foobar/1) => bar
 xpointer(//bom) => bom (a=1), bom (a=2)
 element(/1/2/1) => bom (a=1)
                         (/1 descend into first element (foobar),
                          /2 descend into second child element (baz),
                          /1 select first child element (bom))
```

(Courtesy of http://en.wikipedia.org/wiki/XPointer)

XLink is not supported by browsers currently but other XML processors may use it.

6.1.12 XInclude

XInclude is a generic mechanism for merging XML documents. The valid values for the attribute 'parse' are 'text' and 'xml'. Like XLink, its special namespace should be declared becfore it is used. For a working PHP example, refer to 6.7.2.

The following demonstrates range inclusion. The second row below shows how XInclude may be invoked. The third row shows 'source.xml'. The fourth row shows the XML obtained.

```
<?xml version='1.0'?>
<document>
  <p>The relevant excerpt is:</p>
  <quotation>
    <include xmlns="http://www.w3.org/2001/XInclude"
   href="source.xml"
   xpointer="xpointer(string-range(chapter/p[1],'Sentence 2')/
            range-to(string-range(/chapter/p[2]/i,'3.',1,2)))"/>
  </quotation>
</document>
```

```
<chapter>
  <p>Sentence 1.  Sentence 2.</p>
  <p><i>Sentence 3.  Sentence 4.</i>  Sentence 5.</p>
</chapter>
```

```
<?xml version='1.0'?>
<document>
  <p>The relevant excerpt is:</p>
  <quotation>
    <p xml:base="http://www.example.com/source.xml">
      Sentence 2.</p>
    <p xml:base="http://www.example.com/source.xml">
      <i>Sentence 3.</i></p>
  </quotation>
</document>
```

(Courtesy of http://www.w3.org/TR/xinclude/#examples)

The following demonstrates fallback. If neither example.txt nor fallback-example.txt is available, the XML obtained is shown in the third row.

```
<?xml version='1.0'?>
<div>
  <xi:include href="example.txt" parse="text"
    xmlns:xi="http://www.w3.org/2001/XInclude">
     <xi:fallback>
        <xi:include href="fallback-example.txt" parse="text">
           <xi:fallback>
              <a href="mailto:bob@example.org">
               Report error</a>
           </xi:fallback>
        </xi:include>
     </xi:fallback>
  </xi:include>
</div>
```

```
<?xml version='1.0'?>
<div>
  <a href="mailto:bob@example.org">Report error</a>
</div>
```

(Courtesy of http://www.w3.org/TR/xinclude/#examples)

Currently browsers do not support XLink and XPointer in general. However, they support simple XLinks in SVG.

6.2 XPath

XPath is a language for selecting nodes from an XML document. It can also be used to compute values in the context of an XML document.

XPath is used in XPointer, XInclude, XSD, Schematron, XQuery, XSLT and XForms. XPath can be evaluated in GUI tools such as XML ValidatorBuddy and online tools such as http://videlibri.sourceforge.net/cgi-bin/xidelcgi.

6.2.1 Data Types

The following tree shows all available data types in XPath, with the subtypes indented to the right.

```
item()
  function(*)
  node()
    attribute()
    comment()
    document()
    element()
    namespace()
    processing-instruction()
    text()
  xs:anyAtomicType
    xs:untypedAtomic
    xs:boolean
    xs:base64Binary (eg. ' AAAA FFFF ', groups of 4-digit HEX)
    xs:hexBinary (eg. ' AF12 ', 4-digit HEX)
    xs:anyURI
    xs:QName (eg. ' ab12 ', no symbol, no intermediate space)
    xs:NOTATION
    xs:float
    xs:double
    xs:decimal
      xs:integer
        xs:nonPositiveInteger
          xs:negativeInteger
        xs:long
          xs:int
            xs:short
              xs:byte
        xs:nonNegativeInteger
          xs:positiveInteger
          xs:unsignedLong
            xs:unsignedLong
              xs:unsignedInt
                xs:unsignedShort
                  xs:unsignedByte
    xs:string
      xs:normalizedString
        xs:token (eg. '  a  b c 1 2 $%^&*&*&3  ')
          xs:language (eg. 'abc', no space, no symbol, no digit)
          xs:NMTOKEN (eg. 'abc123', no space, no symbol)
          xs:Name (eg. ' abc',one leading space only, no symbol)
            xs:NCName
              xs:ID
              xs:IDREF
              xs:ENTITY
    xs:gYearMonth (eg. '2014-05')
    xs:gYear (eg. '2014')
    xs:gMonthDay (eg. '--05-31')
    xs:gDay (eg. '---30')
    xs:gMonth (eg. '--06')
    xs:date (eg. '2015-08-31')
    xs:time (eg. '18:30:30')
    xs:dateTime (eg. '2015-03-04T12:00:00')
      xs:dateTimeStamp (eg. '2015-03-04T12:00:00Z')
    xs:duration (eg. 'P1Y2M3D')
      xs:yearMonthDuration (eg. 'P1Y2M')
      xs:dayTimeDuration (eg. 'P10DT6H30M30S')

xs:anyType
  user-defined complex types
  xs:untyped
  xs:anySimpleType
    xs:IDREFS
    xs:NMTOKENS
    xs:ENTITIES
    xs:anyAtomicType
```

(A normalizedString is a string that does not contain line feeds, carriage returns, or tabs.)

(A token is a string that does not contain line feeds, carriage returns, tabs, leading or trailing spaces, or multiple spaces.)

(Some other string types are also described in 6.3.1.)

Date and Time examples
date: 2015-03-04 2015-03-04Z (UTC time) 2015-03-04+08:00
time: 13:30:10 13:30:10.6 12:00:00Z (UTC time) 12:00:00+08:00
datetime: 2015-03-04T12:00:00 2015-03-04T12:00:00Z (UTC time) 2015-03-04T12:00:00+08:00
duration: P5Y3M9DT15H30M30S P3M (3 months) PT3M (3 minutes) -P3D

6.2.2 Path Expressions

Basic Syntax	
A	All <A> nodes within the current context, ie. relative to the current path.
/A	The <A> root node, ie. an absolute path.
//A	All <A> nodes in the document, regardless of how deeply nested they are.
.	The current context, ie. the current node.
..	The parent context, ie. the parent node.
A/B	All <B> nodes that are the direct children of <A> nodes within the current context.
A//B	All <B> nodes that are the descendants of <A> nodes within the current context.

A/*	All nodes that are the direct children of <A> nodes within the current context.
@A	The 'A' attribute of the current context/node. (An attribute may be treated as the child of its node.)
@*	All attributes of the current context/node.
N:A	All <A> child nodes from the N namespace within the current context.
N:*	All nodes from the N namespace within the current context.
*:A	All <A> nodes from all namespaces within the current context.
A[B]	All <A> nodes *containing* a <B> child node.
A[@B]	All <A> nodes containing the attribute B.
A/@B	All B attributes in <A> within the current context.
A[3]	The third <A> node within the current context.
A[B][3]	The third <A> node containing a <B> child within the current context.
(A/B)[3]	The third <B> node that is a child of an <A> node within the current context.
A/text()[2]	The second text node in each <A> node within the current context.
A|B	All <A> and <B> child nodes within the current context.

The square brackets [] at the right can assume a Boolean value, an integer, or a node. A complex Boolean expression joined by and/or can be formed out of the three types of values.

Axes

child::*	* matches only element nodes. If node() is used instead, text, comment and processing instruction nodes are matched as well.
descendant::*	
descendant-or-self::*	
self::*	
following::*	Multiple nodes may be returned. For example, preceding-sibling::node()[2] returns the previous node that is two siblings away.
following-sibling::*	
ancestor::*	
ancestor-or-self::*	
parent::*	
preceding::*	Any derived types of node() can be used in place of node(), eg. child::comment().
preceding-sibling::*	
namespace::*	
attribute::*	

Complex Filters

A[position()<3]	The first two <A> nodes.
A[last()]	The last <A> child node.
A[B][C]	All <A> nodes containing a <B> node and a <C> node.
A[(B or C) and D]	All <A> nodes containing a <D> node, and a <B> node or a <C> node.
A[not(B)]	All <A> nodes which do not contain a <B> node.
A[B="C"]	All <A> nodes containing the <B> nodes with the value C.
A[.!="B"]	All <A> nodes with a value that is not "B".
(B|C) [@at eq A/@at]	All <B> nodes and <C> nodes with the attribute @at equals that of <A>.

Examples

```
<?xml version="1.0"?>
<menu restaurant="Golden Outlet">
  <dish id="1">Satay <i>Cooked</i></dish>
  <drink id="2">Cola</drink>
  <dish id="3">Curry Chicken</dish>
  <dish id="4" xmlns="http://example.com">
    Sweet and Sour Pork
  </dish>
</menu>
```

(1) .
(2) /.
(3) self::node()
(4) /self::node()
(5) let $p := /. return $p
(6) menu/..
(7) menu!..
(8) root()
(9) root(menu/drink)
(10) doc('menu.xml')

GIVE

```
<?xml version="1.0"?>
<menu restaurant="Golden Outlet">
  <dish id="1">Satay <i>Cooked</i></dish>
  <drink id="2">Cola</drink>
  <dish id="3">Curry Chicken</dish>
  <dish id="4" xmlns="http://example.com">
    Sweet and Sour Pork
  </dish>
</menu>
```

(1) menu
(2) /menu
(3) menu[1]
(4) menu[@restaurant]
(5) menu[@restaurant="Golden Outlet"]
(6) menu[drink]
(7) menu[drink="Cola"]
(8) menu[drink][dish]
(9) child::node()
(10) node()
(11) menu[last()]|menu[position()=1]|menu[1]
(12) if (//dish) then menu else //dish

GIVE

```
<menu restaurant="Golden Outlet">
  <dish id="1">Satay <i>Cooked</i></dish>
  <drink id="2">Cola</drink>
  <dish id="3">Curry Chicken</dish>
  <dish id="4" xmlns="http://example.com">
    Sweet and Sour Pork
  </dish>
</menu>
```

(1) /menu/@restaurant
(2) menu//@restaurant
(3) //@restaurant

```
(4) (//@*)[1]
(5) (//attribute::node())[1]
(6) //attribute(restaurant)
```

GIVE

```
restaurant="Golden Outlet"
```

```
(1) //dish
(2) menu/dish
(3) //dish[1] | //dish[2]
(4) //dish[1] union //dish[2]
(5) //dish[position()=(1,2)] intersect //dish
(6) /menu/child::node()[@id] except
    /menu/child::node()[@id=2 or @id=4]
(7) /menu/dish[@id]
(8) /menu/dish[@id<10]
(9) /menu/dish[@id=1 or @id=3]
(10)/menu/dish[@id=1]|//dish[@id=3]
(11)menu/child::node()[@id!=2 and not(@id=4)]
(12)menu/dish[i]|menu/dish[.="Curry Chicken"]
(13)/menu/element(dish)
```

GIVE

```
(1) <dish id="1">Satay <i>Cooked</i></dish>
(2) <dish id="3">Curry Chicken</dish>
```

```
(1) //i/text()
(2) (//text()[1])[3]
(3) /menu/dish/*/text()
(4) /menu[1]/dish[1]/i[1]/text()
```

GIVE

```
Cooked
```

```
(1) /menu/dish[2]/following::node()
```

GIVES

```
(1) (space)
(2) <dish id="4" xmlns="http://example.com">
(3) Sweet and Sour Pork
(4) (space)
```

```
(1) //dish[1] is //dish[@id=1]
(2) //dish[2] >> //dish[@id=1]
(3) //dish[@id=1] << //dish[2]
(4) some $x in //dish satisfies $x[@id>0]
(5) every $x in //dish satisfies $x[@id>0]
(6) count(/menu/child::node()) > count(/menu/child::*)
(7) not(. instance of element())
(8) menu instance of element()
(9) menu instance of element(menu)
```

GIVE

```
true
```

```
(1) menu/dish/string-length()
(2) ('abcdefghijkl',
     'xmnopqrstuvwx')!string-length()
```

GIVE

```
(1) 12
(2) 13
```

6.2.3 Sequence, Flow Control and Typing

Examples

```
(1) (3 idiv 2,(2,(3)),(),4 to 6)
(2) reverse(reverse(1 to 6))
(3) (1 to 6)[. mod 1 eq 0]
(4) (1 to 6)[. < 10]
(5) (0 to 5)!(. + 1)
(6) (1 to 3)!(.*2-1 , .*2)
(7) let $a := (1 to 3), $b := (4 to 6)
    return ($a,$b)
(8) for $i in (0,3), $j in (1,2,3) return ($i + $j)
(9) if (5 le 5) then (1 to 6) else (0)
(10)(1 to 6) treat as xs:decimal+
```

GIVE

```
(1) 1
(2) 2
(3) 3
(4) 4
(5) 5
(6) 6
```

```
(1) 2 = (1,2,3)
(2) 3 > (2,4)
(3) (1,2) = (2,3)
(4) (1,2) != (2,3)
(5) some $x in (1 to 3), $y in (2 to 4)
    satisfies $x + $y < 4
(6) every $x in (1 to 3), $y in (2 to 4)
    satisfies $x + $y > 0
(7) 15 instance of xs:integer
(8) 15 instance of item()
(9) (1,2) instance of xs:integer+
(10)  xs:unsignedByte(1) instance of xs:integer
(11)  xs:dateTime('2015-03-04T12:00:00')
      instance of xs:anyType
(12)  xs:dayTimeDuration('P9DT15H30M30S')
      instance of xs:duration
(13)  1.3 castable as xs:integer
(14)  1.3 cast as xs:Boolean
(15)  xs:date('2015-08-31') >
      xs:date('2015-07-31')
```

GIVE

```
True
```

```
(1) xs:dayTimeDuration("P30D")
(2) "P30D" cast as xs:dayTimeDuration?
(3) xs:dayTimeDuration('P20D') +
    xs:dayTimeDuration('P10D')
(4) xs:date('2015-03-04') - xs:date('2015-02-02')
```

GIVE

```
P30D
```

(1,2) = (2,3) is equivalent to: 1=2 or 1=3 or 2=2 or 2=3

6.2.4 Node Functions

```
<?xml version="1.0"?>
<menu restaurant="Golden Outlet"
      xmlns:ns="http://example.com"
      xml:lang="en">
  <dish xml:id="1">Satay <i>Cooked</i></dish>
  <drink id="2">Cola</drink>
  <dish id="3">Curry Chicken</dish>
  <dish id="4" xmlns="http://example.com">
     Sweet and Sour Pork
  </dish>
</menu>
```

Expression	Result
(1) name(menu/ns:dish) (2) menu/dish[1]/name() (3) node-name(menu/ns:dish) (4) local-name(menu/ns:dish) (5) id("1")/name() (6) element-with-id("1")/ name() (7) idref("1")/name()	dish
namespace-uri(menu/ns:dish)	http://example.com
(1) base-uri(menu/ns:dish) (2) base-uri() (3) static-base-uri()	/home/project-web/videlibri/cgi-bin/
(1) document-uri() (2) document-uri(menu)	(empty)
(1) string() (2) string(menu)	Satay Cooked Cola Curry Chicken Sweet and Sour Pork

(3) data(menu)	
(1) path() (2) path(.)	/
innermost(menu) **GIVES** (1) <i>Cooked</i> (2) <drink id="2">Cola</drink> (3) <dish id="3">Curry Chicken</dish> (4) <dish id="4" xmlns="http://example.com">Sweet and Sour Pork</dish>	
outermost(menu/dish/i) **GIVES** <?xml version="1.0"?> <menu restaurant="Golden Outlet" xmlns:ns="http://example.com"> <dish id="1">Satay <i>Cooked</i></dish> <drink id="2">Cola</drink> <dish id="3">Curry Chicken</dish> <dish id="4" xmlns="http://example.com"> Sweet and Sour Pork </dish> </menu>	
nilled(menu)	false
(1) has-children() (2) has-children(menu)	true
(1) lang("en") (2) lang("en",menu/dish)	true
generate-id()	

6.2.5 Numeric Functions

abs(-3)	3
ceiling(1.1)	2
floor(1.9)	1
round(1.5)	2
round(1.125,2)	1.13
round(8452,-2)	-8500
round-half-to-even(2.5)	2
round-half-to-even(35612.25, -2)	35600
number("15")	15
format-integer(123,'0000')	0123
format-integer(123,'w')	one hundred and twenty-three
format-integer(21,'1;o','en')	21st
format-integer(14,'Ww;o(-e)','de')	Vierzehnte
format-integer(7,'a')	g
format-integer(57,'I')	LVII
format-integer(1234,'#;##O;')	1;234
format-number(12345.6, '#,###.00')	12,345.60
format-integer(12345678.9, '9,999.99')	12,345,678.90
format-integer(123.9,'9999')	0124
format-integer(0.14,'01%')	14%
format-integer(-6,'000')	-006
format-integer(12.34,'0.000e00')	1.234e01
format-integer(12.34,'#.000e0')	0.123e2
format-integer(1234.5678, '#;##0*00', 'ch')	1;234*57
(Courtesy of http://www.w3.org/TR/2014/ REC-xpath-functions-30-20140408/#func-number)	

6.2.6 Math Functions

The namespace for the prefix 'math' is http://www.w3.org/2005/xpath-functions/math.

2*math:pi()	6.283185307179586e0
math:exp(1)	2.7182818284590455e0
math:exp10(1)	1.0e1
math:log(math:exp(1))	1.0e0
math:log10(1.0e3)	3.0e0
math:pow(2,3)	8.0e0
math:sqrt(1.0e6)	1.0e3
math:sin(math:pi())	0.0e0
math:cos(math:pi())	-1.0e0
math:tan(math:pi())	0.0e0
math:asin(1.0e0)	1.5707963267948966e0
math:acos(1.0e0)	0.0e0
math:atan(1.0e0)	0.7853981633974483e0
math:atan2(-0.0e0,+1)	-0.0e0

6.2.7 String Functions

codepoints-to-string((66, 65, 67, 72))	BACH
string-to-codepoints("BACH")	(66, 65, 67, 72)
compare("ABC","AAB")	1
codepoint-equal("ABC","ABC ")	false
concat("AB","CD")	ABCD
"AB"||"CD"	ABCD
string-join(('A','B','C'),'-')	A-B-C
substring("ABCDE",2,3)	BCD
string-length("ABCDE")	5
normalize-space('A B C')	A B C
normalize-unicode('ABC')	ABC
upper-case('Abc')	ABC
lower-case('Abc')	abc
translate("bar","abc","ABC")	BAr
contains("ABCDE","CD")	true
starts-with("ABCDE","ABC")	true
ends-with("ABCDE","cde")	true
substring-before("ABCDE","CDE")	AB
substring-after("ABCDE","B")	CDE
matches("ABCDE","^A.C.E$")	true
replace("abracadabra", "bra", "*")	a*cada*
tokenize("AB,CD,E",",")	('AB','CD','E')
analyze-string("The cat sat on the mat.", "\w+") **GIVES** <analyze-string-result xmlns="http://www.w3.org/2005/xpath-functions"> <match>The</match> <non-match> </non-match> <match>cat</match> <non-match> </non-match> <match>sat</match> <non-match> </non-match> <match>on</match> <non-match> </non-match> <match>the</match> <non-match> </non-match> <match>mat</match> <non-match>.</non-match> </analyze-string-result>	

6.2.8 URI Functions

resolve-uri("AB/C","http://D")	http://D/AB/C
encode-for-uri("http://A B")	http%3A%2F%2F A%20B
iri-to-uri("http://www. example.com/~bébé"	http://www.exam ple.com/~b%C3 %A9b%C3%A9
resolve-QName("ns",menu)	ns
QName("http://example.com", "hello")	hello
prefix-from-QName(QName("http://example.com", "hello"))	()
local-name-from-QName(QName("http://example.com", "hello"))	hello
namespace-uri-from-QName(QName("http://example.com", "hello"))	http://example.com
namespace-uri-for-prefix("ns",menu)	http://example.com
in-scope-prefixes(menu)	(1) xml (2) ns

6.2.9 Datetime Functions

years-from-duration(xs:yearMonthDuration("P20Y15M"))	21
months-from-duration(xs:yearMonthDuration("-P20Y18M"))	-6
days-from-duration(xs:dayTimeDuration("P3DT55H"))	5
hours-from-duration(xs:dayTimeDuration("P3DT12H32M12S"))	12
minutes-from-duration(xs:dayTimeDuration("P3DT10H"))	0
seconds-from-duration(xs:dayTimeDuration("-PT256S"))	-16
dateTime(xs:date("1999-12-31"), xs:time("12:00:00"))	xs:dateTime('1999-12-31 T12:00:00')
year-from-dateTime(xs:dateTime("1999-05-31 T13:20:00-05:00"))	1999
month-from-dateTime(xs:dateTime("1999-05-31 T13:20:00-05:00"))	5
day-from-dateTime(xs:dateTime("1999-05-31 T13:20:00-05:00"))	31
hours-from-dateTime(xs:dateTime("1999-05-31 T08:20:00-05:00"))	8
minutes-from-dateTime(xs:dateTime("1999-05-31 T13:20:00-05:00"))	20
seconds-from-dateTime(xs:dateTime("1999-05-31 T13:20:00-05:00"))	0
timezone-from-dateTime(xs:dateTime("1999-05-31 T13:20:00-05:00"))	xs:dayTimeDur ation("-PT5H")
year-from-date(xs:date("1999-05-31"))	1999
month-from-date(xs:date("1999-05-31-05:00"))	5
day-from-date(xs:date("1999-05-31-05:00"))	31
timezone-from-date(xs:date("1999-05-31-05:00"))	xs:dayTimeDur ation("-PT5H")
hours-from-time(xs:time("11:23:00"))	11
minutes-from-time(xs:time("13:00:00Z"))	0
seconds-from-time(xs:time("13:20:10.5"))	10.5
timezone-from-time(xs:time("13:20:00Z"))	xs:dayTimeDur ation('PT0S')
adjust-dateTime-to-timezone(xs:dateTime('2002-03-07 T00:00:00+01:00'), xs:dayTimeDuration("-PT8H"))	xs:dateTime('2 002-03- 06T15:00:00- 08:00')
adjust-date-to-timezone(xs:date("2002-03-07-07:00"), xs:dayTimeDuration("-PT10H"))	xs:date("2002 -03-06- 10:00")
adjust-time-to-timezone(xs:time("10:00:00-07:00"), xs:dayTimeDuration("-PT10H"))	xs:time("07:0 0:00-10:00")
format-date(xs:date('2002-12-31'), "[MNn] [D], [Y]", "en", (), ())	December 31, 2002
format-time(xs:time('15:58:45'), "[h]:[m01]:[s01] [Pn]","en",(),())	3:58:45 pm
format-dateTime($xs:dateTime("2002-12-31T15:58:45"), "[M01]/[D01]/[Y0001] at [H01]:[m01]:[s01]")	12/31/2002 at 15:58:45
current-dateTime()	xs:dateTimeSt amp('2014-09- 06T07:30:58.7 67')
current-date()	xs:date('2014- 09-06')
current-time()	xs:time('07:31 :54.574')
implicit-timezone()	xs:dayTimeDur ation('PT8H')
default-collation()	http://www.be nibela.de/2012 /pxp/case- insensitive- clever

6.2.10 Sequence Functions

empty((1,2))	false
exists((1,2))	true
head((1,2,3))	1
tail((1,2,3))	(2,3)
insert-before((1,2,3),2,(4,5))	(1,4,5,2,3)
remove((1,2,3),2)	(1,3)
reverse((1,2,3))	(3,2,1)
subsequence((1,2,3,4,5),2,2)	(2,3)
unordered((1,2,3,4,5))	(1,2,3,4,5)
distinct-values((1,2,3,2,1))	(1,2,3)
index-of((10,20,30,30,40,50),30)	(3,4)
deep-equal((1,2,3),(1,(2),3))	true
zero-or-one((10))	10
zero-or-one(())	()
one-or-more((1,2,3))	(1,2,3)
exactly-one((10))	10
count((1,2,3))	3
avg((3,4,7))	4.6666666667
max((1,2,3))	3
min((1,2,3))	1
sum((1,2,3))	6

6.2.11 File Functions

For the functions in this table, any filename can be started with 'http://' or 'file://'. A query string starting with ? can be appended to a URL too.
doc("data.xml") returns the document node for the file data.xml. Further node paths can be added to it. For example, doc("data.xml")//a returns all 'a' nodes in the document.
doc-available("data.xml") returns true if data.xml exists and can be returned as a document node.
collection("s*.xml") returns a sequence of document nodes for files with names starting with s.
uri-collection("s*.xml") returns a sequence of URI strings for files with names starting with s, ie. their file names.
unparsed-text("data.dat") returns a string representation of the content of the file data.dat.
unparsed-text-lines("data.dat") returns a sequence of strings that are lines of content within the file data.dat.
unparsed-text-available("data.dat") returns true if the file data.dat is available to be called within unparsed-text().
environment-variable("APPDATA") returns the value of a system environment variable "APPDATA".
available-environment-variables() returns a sequence of names of the system environment variables.

6.2.12 String Parsing Functions

parse-xml("<a>Hello <b>World</b></a>") creates an XML document from an XML string and returns the root node.
parse-xml-fragment("I say<a>Hello <b>World</b></a>") creates an XML fragment from an XML string and returns the root node. Note that the example does not return an error even though the XML is not well-formed itself (no root), unlike the case for parse-xml().
serialize(1 to 3) returns a serialized representation of the sequence as a string.

6.2.13 Higher-order Functions

function-lookup(xs:QName("fn:substring"),2)("abcd",2) returns bcd.
function-name(fn:substring#2) returns fn:substring
function-arity(fn:substring#3) returns 3
for-each(1 to 5, function($a) { $a * $a }) returns (1,4,9,16,25)
filter(1 to 10, function($a) {$a mod 2 = 0}) returns (2,4,6,8,10)
fold-left(1 to 5, 10000, function($a, $b) { $a + $b }) returns 10015
fold-right(1 to 5, "***", fn:concat(?, ".", ?)) returns 1.2.3.4.5.***
for-each-pair(("a", "b", "c"), ("x", "y", "z"), concat#2) returns ("ax","by","cz")

6.2.14 Error Functions

error(fn:QName('http://www.example.com/HR', 'myerr:toohighsal')) raises an error which may be caught in a try-catch construct in XQuery or XSLT.
trace($v, 'the value of $v is:') reports the value of $v.

6.2.15 Custom Functions

XPath 3.0 has advanced support for custom functions.

```
(1)
  let $f := function ($v) {$v * 2} return $f(3)

(2)
  let
  $process :=function($v as xs:double,
                       $f as function(xs:double) as xs:double)
                      as xs:double
                      {$f($v)},
  $mult2 := function ($n as xs:double) as xs:double
            {$n*2}
  return $process(3,$mult2)

(3)
  let
  $compose:=function($f as function(xs:double) as xs:double,
                     $g as function(xs:double) as xs:double)
                     as function(xs:double) as xs:double
                     {function ($x as xs:double)
                             {$g($f($x))}},
  $mult2 := function($x as xs:double) {$x *2},
  $mult3 := function($x as xs:double) {$x *3}
  return $compose($mult2,$mult3)(1)

(4)
  let $plus := function($x as xs:integer,
                        $y as xs:integer)
                        as xs:integer
                        {$x+$y}
  return $plus(?,?)(2,4)

(5)
  let $plus := function ($m as xs:integer)
                         as (function(xs:integer) as xs:integer)
                         {function ($n as xs:integer)
                                {$m + $n}}
  return $plus(2)(4)

(6)
  let $s := function ($n as xs:integer,
                      $f as function(xs:integer,
                         function()) as xs:integer) as xs:integer
                      {if ($n<1) then 0 else $n+$f($n - 1,$f)},
  $sum := function($n as xs:integer)
                      {$s($n,$s)}
  return $sum(3)
```

GIVE

6

(1) a simple function
(2) passing a function to a function
(3) functions composition
(4) partial function application
(5) function closure
(6) recursive function (not supported by all)

6.3 Schema Languages

A grammar-based schema language such as DTD or Relax NG declares the grammar for an XML document. It defines the permissible structures, contents, and orders of the elements, attributes, and entities.

A rule-based schema language such as Schematron specifies the relationships that must hold for the values of the elements and attributes.

Very expressive, XSD is both grammar-based and rule-based.

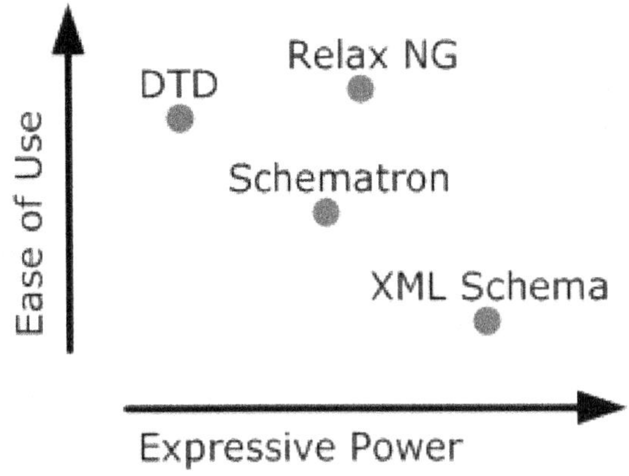

An XML document that conforms to the schema defined in a schema language is said to be *valid*.

You can validate your XML document online at:
http://validator.w3.org/check
http://www.validome.org/grammar/
http://www.xmlvalidation.com/
http://www.freeformatter.com/xml-validator-xsd.html

You can also use any other offline tools such as:
1. XML Check (DTD and XSD)
(http://download.cnet.com/XML-Validator/3000-7241_4-75765753.html)
2. Jing (Relax NG and Relax NG Compact)
(http://www.thaiopensource.com/relaxng/jing.html)
3. XML Validator Buddy (Schematron)
(http://www.xml-buddy.com/download.htm)

6.3.1 DTD

Document Type Definition is declared internally or externally using <!DOCTYPE ...>. It is the only schema language that allows entities to be defined.

The name of an external DTD file ends with ".dtd".

This shows an internal DTD.

```
<?xml version="1.0" ?>
<!DOCTYPE class [
  <!ELEMENT class (student*) >
  <!ELEMENT student (name,DOB,(top|last)?,description)>
  <!ELEMENT name (#PCDATA)>
  <!ELEMENT DOB (#PCDATA)>
  <!ELEMENT top EMPTY>
  <!ELEMENT last EMPTY>
  <!ELEMENT description ANY>
  <!ATTLIST student
            id CDATA #IMPLIED
            sex (M|F) #REQUIRED>
  <!ENTITY school "Hwa Chung Junior College">
]>
<class>
  <student id="H901234" sex="M">
    <name>Alex Lee</name>
    <DOB>23-03-1990</DOB>
    <top/>
    <description>studying at &school;.</description>
  </student>
  <student id="H904321" sex="F">
    <name>Mary Chan</name>
    <DOB>25-06-1990</DOB>
    <description>studying at &school;.</description>
```

```
  </student>
</class>
```

A DTD declares all elements, attributes, and entities used.

',' denotes a sequence. When separated by the comma, the child elements must appear in the specified order. '**|**' denotes a choice.

+ means one or more.
***** means zero or more.
? means zero or one.

The valid attribute types are:

- **CDATA:** character data
- **(en1|en2...):** one of the enumerated values
- **ID:** unique id
- **IDREF:** the id of another element
- **IDREFS:** a list of other ids
- **NMTOKEN:** a valid XML name
- **NMTOKENS:** a list of valid XML names
- **ENTITY:** an entity
- **ENTITIES:** a list of entities
- **NOTATION:** a notation

The valid attribute defaults are:

- **value:** the default value
- **#REQUIRED:** required
- **#IMPLIED:** optional
- **#FIXED value:** must be a fixed value

This demonstrates the use of an external DTD and parameter entities. Parameter entities, to be prefixed by %, are meant to cause substitutions within a DTD and must be declared in an external DTD.

```
<?xml version="1.0" encoding="UTF-8" ?>
<!DOCTYPE p SYSTEM "p.dtd">
<p>
  'ANY' allows you to mix <b>tags</b>
  with <b>parsed character data</b>.
</p>
```

```
<!ENTITY % x.y "p">
<!ENTITY % x.z "ANY">
<!ELEMENT %x.y; %x.z;>
<!ELEMENT b (#PCDATA)>
```

A public DTD is one what is commonly used and widely shared. The XML processor may replace the public ID with a built-in URI. The second string after PUBLIC is a system identifier(URI), and may be used if the public ID is not recognized.

```
<?xml version="1.0" encoding="utf-8"?>
<!DOCTYPE html PUBLIC
     "-//W3C//DTD XHTML 1.0 Transitional//EN"
     "http://www.w3.org/TR/xhtml1/DTD/xhtml1-transitional.dtd">
<html xmlns="http://www.w3.org/1999/xhtml">
</html>
```

(Courtesy of http://en.wikipedia.org/wiki/Document_type_definition#Examples) (modified)

Generally, NMTOKEN, a valid XML name, is one made up of alphanumeric characters, -, _ etc.

```
<?xml version="1.0" encoding="UTF-8" ?>
<!DOCTYPE p [
  <!ELEMENT p ANY>
  <!ELEMENT b (#PCDATA)>
  <!ATTLIST b
              att NMTOKEN #FIXED "1">
]>
<p>
  <b att="1">!1, @1, #1, $1...</b> are valid CDATA
  but not valid NMTOKEN.
</p>
```

This illustrates how to use attributes declared as ID, IDREF, and IDREFS.

```
<?xml version="1.0" encoding="UTF-8" ?>
<!DOCTYPE p [
  <!ELEMENT p ANY>
  <!ELEMENT b (#PCDATA)>
  <!ATTLIST p
              ir IDREFS #IMPLIED>
  <!ATTLIST b
              id ID #IMPLIED>
]>
<p ir="b1 b2">
  The value of an attribute declared as
  <b id="b1">ID</b> must be <b id="b2">unique</b>.
</p>
```

Here are some examples of external entity declarations. The first two are *parsed external entities*, which means that the parsers retrieve the contents of the files and parse them as if they are internal entities. The third is an *unparsed external entity*, which means how it is processed is left to the application according to the notation assigned. Here gif is a notation declared elsewhere.

```
<!ENTITY open-hatch SYSTEM
      "http://www.textuality.com/boilerplate/OpenHatch.xml">
<!ENTITY open-hatch PUBLIC
      "-//Textuality//TEXT Standard open-hatch boilerplate//EN"
      "http://www.textuality.com/boilerplate/OpenHatch.xml">
<!ENTITY hatch-pic SYSTEM
      "../grafix/OpenHatch.gif"
      NDATA gif >
```

(Courtesy of http://www.w3.org/TR/2008/REC-xml-20081126/#sec-external-ent)

The value of an attribute declared as ENTITY must be an unparsed external entity.

```
<?xml version="1.0" standalone="no" ?>
<!DOCTYPE img [
  <!ELEMENT img EMPTY>
  <!ATTLIST img
              src ENTITY #REQUIRED>
  <!ENTITY logo SYSTEM
              "http://www.xmlwriter.net/logo.gif" NDATA gif>
  <!NOTATION gif PUBLIC "gif viewer">
]>
<img src="logo"/>
```

(Courtesy of http://xmlwriter.net/xml_guide/entity_declaration.shtml)

6.3.2 XSD

XML Schema Definition, or W3C XML Schema (WXS), is XML-based. All its elements can have the 'id' attribute as well as other attributes. The name of a XSD file ends with ".xsd".

Instead of coding an XSD file from scratch, you can use the XSD inference tool in XMLSpy or OxygenXML to generate an XSD file from an XML file. Such a tool can also be found in Microsoft's XML Schema Definition Tool (XSD.exe), Apache's XMLBeans, Trang, xmlgrid.net etc.

This illustrates the basic features of XSD.

```
<?xml version="1.0"?>
<zoo xmlns="http://www.example.com"
  xmlns:xsi="http://www.w3.org/2001/XMLSchema-instance"
  xsi:schemaLocation="http://www.example.com zoo.xsd">
  <animal id="l123444">
    <name>Mighty</name>
    <type>lion</type>
    <kg>135</kg>
    <imported/>
  </animal>
  <animal id="b355345">
    <name>Lucky</name>
     <type>bear</type>
     <kg>205</kg>
  </animal>
</zoo>
```

```
<?xml version="1.0"?>

<xs:schema
          xmlns:xs="http://www.w3.org/2001/XMLSchema"
          targetNamespace="http://www.example.com"
          xmlns="http://www.example.com"
          elementFormDefault="qualified">

<xs:element name="zoo"><xs:complexType><xs:sequence>
  <xs:element name="animal" maxOccurs="unbounded">
    <xs:complexType>
      <xs:sequence>
        <xs:element name="name" type="xs:string"/>
        <xs:element name="type"><xs:simpleType>
          <xs:restriction base="xs:string">
            <xs:enumeration value="lion"/>
            <xs:enumeration value="bear"/>
            <xs:enumeration value="tiger"/>
          </xs:restriction>
        </xs:simpleType></xs:element>
        <xs:element name="kg"><xs:simpleType>
          <xs:restriction base="xs:integer">
            <xs:minInclusive value="10"/>
            <xs:maxInclusive value="5000"/>
          </xs:restriction>
        </xs:simpleType></xs:element>
        <xs:element name="imported" minOccurs="0">
          <xs:complexType/>
        </xs:element>
      </xs:sequence>
      <xs:attribute name="id" type="xs:string"/>
    </xs:complexType>
  </xs:element>
</xs:sequence></xs:complexType></xs:element>

</xs:schema>
```

schama can have the following attributes:

- *attributeFormDefault*: 'qualified' or 'unqualified'
- *elementFormDefault*: 'qualified' or 'unqualified'
- *defaultAttributes*: the name of a defined attribute group which will be included to each complex type, unless overridden by the 'defaultAttributesApply' in complexType.
- *blockDefault*: '#all' or a list of 'extension', 'resctriction', or 'substitution'.
- *finalDefault:* '#all' or a list of of 'extension', 'resctriction', or 'substitution', additionally 'list' and 'union'
- *xpathDefaultNamespace*: '##local', '##defaultNamespace', '##targetNamespace' or any URI.
- *version:* a version of the schema

element and attribute can have the following attributes:

- *default* : the default value
- *fixed* : a fixed value
- *form* : 'unqualified' indicates that this element is not required to be qualified with the namespace prefix. 'qualified' indicates that this element must be qualified with the namespace prefix. The default is given by the value of the elementFormDefault or attributeFormDefault attribute of the schema element.

attribute can have the following attribute:

- *use* : 'optional', 'prohibited', or 'required'
- *inheritable*: 'true' or 'false'

complexType can have the following attributes:

- *abstract*: 'true' or 'false'
- *block*: '#all' or a list of 'extension' or 'restriction'. This prevents the element from being a subtype. Unlike 'final', a subtype can still be declared.
- *final*: '#all' or a list of 'extension' or 'restriction'. This prevents type derivation by extension, restriction, or both.
- *mixed*: 'true' or 'false'
- *name*: NCName
- *defaultAttributesApply*: 'true' or 'false'

If an attribute or element does not have the 'type' attribute, its type must be declared as its child element.

You can specify multiple XSD files in the XML file like this:

```
<ns1:root
  xmlns:ns1="http://example.com/1"
  xmlns:ns2="http://example.com/2"
  xmlns:xsi="http://www.w3.org/2001/XMLSchema-instance"
  xsi:schemaLocation="http://example.com/1 ns1.xsd
                      http://example.com/2 ns2.xsd">
   <ns2:a/>
</ns1:root>
```

Elements Hierarchy (simplified)

schema
    group, attributeGroup
    redefine
    notation
    import
    include
    element
        alternative
        simpleType
            union
            list
            restriction
                (assert)
                enumeration
                fractionDigits
                length
                {max|min}Exclusive
                {max|min}Inclusive
                {max|min}Length
                pattern
                totalDigits
                whitespace
        complexType
            openContent
            sequence, choice, all
                (element)
                (group)
                any
            attribute, anyAttribute
            (group), (attributeGroup)
            simpleContent, complexContent
                (restriction)
                  (assert)
                extension
                  (assert)
            assert
        unique,key,keyref
            selector
            field
 	
annotation
    appinfo
    documentation

(schema is always the document root.) *(annotation can be the child of any element.)* *(simpleType can be a child of attribute, element, list, restriction, schema, and union.)* *(complexType can be a child of element, redefine, and schema.)* *(attribute can be a child of attributeGroup, schema, complexType, restriction (both simpleContent and complexContent), and extension (both simpleContent and complexContent).)* *(anyAttribute can be a child of complexType, restriction (both simpleContent and complexContent), and extension (both simpleContent and complexContent), attributeGroup.)*

(group can be a child of schema, choice, sequence, all, complexType, restriction (both simpleContent and complexContent), and extension (both simpleContent and complexContent).) *(attributeGroup can be a child of attributeGroup, complexType, schema, restriction (both simpleContent and complexContent), and extension (both simpleContent and complexContent).)* *(sequence and choice can be a child of group, choice, sequence, complexType, restriction (both simpleContent and complexContent), extension (both simpleContent and complexContent).)* *(all can be a child of group, complexType, restriction (both simpleContent and complexContent), and extension (both simpleContent and complexContent).)* *(restriction can be a child of simpleType, simpleContent, and complextContent.)*
sequence means that the child elements must appear in the specified order, each occurring one time. choice means that only one of the child elements can appear. all means that the child elements can appear in any order, each occurring one time.
For element, sequence, choice, all, any, or group, you can specify the 'minOccurs' and 'maxOccurs' attributes, which dictate the minimum and maximum numbers of times an element (or group of elements) can appear.

This uses assertions to deny certain attribute and element values, as well as to validate the order of the attribute values.

```
<?xml version="1.0" encoding="UTF-8"?>
<Transactions
  xmlns:xsi="http://www.w3.org/2001/XMLSchema-instance"
  xsi:noNamespaceSchemaLocation="transactions.xsd">
  <Transaction OrderID="50">-1000</Transaction>
  <Transaction OrderID="60">1000</Transaction>
  <Transaction OrderID="70">3000</Transaction>
  <Transaction OrderID="300">2000</Transaction>
</Transactions>
```

```
<?xml version="1.0" encoding="UTF-8"?>
<xs:schema
  xmlns:xs="http://www.w3.org/2001/XMLSchema">
  <xs:element name="Transactions">
    <xs:complexType>
      <xs:sequence>
        <xs:element name="Transaction"
                    maxOccurs="unbounded">
          <xs:complexType>
            <xs:simpleContent>
              <xs:extension base="xs:integer">
                <xs:attribute name="OrderID"
                              type="xs:integer"/>
                <xs:assert test=
                    "empty(index-of((8,9,10),@OrderID))"/>
```

```
                <xs:assert test=
                    "$value = (-3000 to 3000)"/>
              </xs:extension>
            </xs:simpleContent>
          </xs:complexType>
        </xs:element>
      </xs:sequence>
      <xs:assert test="every $x in Transaction satisfies
          (empty($x/preceding-sibling::*) or
          ($x/@OrderID gt
                $x/preceding-sibling::*[1]/@OrderID))"/>
    </xs:complexType>
  </xs:element>
</xs:schema>
```

The value for the 'test' attribute in assert is an XPath.

This illustrates how to use annotations, groups, references, and restrictions.

```
<?xml version="1.0"?>
<dictionary
  xmlns="http://www.example.com"
  xmlns:xsi="http://www.w3.org/2001/XMLSchema-instance"
  xsi:schemaLocation="http://www.example.com
                      dictionary.xsd">
  <word id="w5445353" initial="b">
    <spelling>beautiful</spelling>
    <type>adjective</type>
  </word>
  <word id="w1222234" initial="t">
    <spelling>table</spelling>
    <type form="singular">noun</type>
  </word>
</dictionary>
```

```
<?xml version="1.0"?>
<!-- dictionary.xsd -->

<xs:schema
        xmlns:xs="http://www.w3.org/2001/XMLSchema"
        targetNamespace="http://www.example.com"
        xmlns="http://www.example.com"
        elementFormDefault="qualified">

<xs:include schemaLocation="dictDef.xsd"/>
<xs:element name="dictionary" type="dType"/>

</xs:schema>
```

```
<?xml version="1.0"?>
<!-- dictDef.xsd -->

<xs:schema
        xmlns:xs="http://www.w3.org/2001/XMLSchema"
        targetNamespace="http://www.example.com"
        xmlns="http://www.example.com"
        elementFormDefault="qualified">

<xs:annotation>
  <xs:appinfo source="http://example.com/info/">
    Example Note
  </xs:appinfo>
  <xs:documentation source="http://example.com/info/">
    A group, attribute group, or custom
    type may be reused multiple times.
  </xs:documentation>
</xs:annotation>

<xs:simpleType name="wType">
  <xs:restriction base="xs:string">
    <xs:enumeration value="noun"/>
    <xs:enumeration value="verb"/>
    <xs:enumeration value="adjective"/>
  </xs:restriction>
</xs:simpleType>

<xs:group name="wSequence">
  <xs:sequence>
    <xs:element name="spelling"><xs:simpleType>
      <xs:restriction base="xs:string">
        <xs:pattern value="[a-zA-Z ]+"/>
        <xs:maxLength  value="50"/>
        <xs:whiteSpace  value="collapse"/>
      </xs:restriction>
    </xs:simpleType></xs:element>
    <xs:element name="type">
      <xs:complexType><xs:simpleContent>
        <xs:extension base="wType">
          <xs:attribute name="form">
            <xs:simpleType>
              <xs:restriction base="xs:string">
                <xs:enumeration value="singular"/>
                <xs:enumeration value="plural"/>
                <xs:enumeration value="present"/>
                <xs:enumeration value="past"/>
              </xs:restriction>
            </xs:simpleType>
          </xs:attribute>
        </xs:extension>
      </xs:simpleContent></xs:complexType>
    </xs:element>
  </xs:sequence>
</xs:group>

<xs:attributeGroup name="wAttributes">
  <xs:attribute name="id" type="xs:ID" />
  <xs:attribute name="initial" type="xs:NMTOKEN" />
  <xs:anyAttribute/>
</xs:attributeGroup>

<xs:complexType name="dType"><xs:sequence>
  <xs:element name="word" maxOccurs="999999">
    <xs:complexType>
      <xs:group ref="wSequence"/>
      <xs:attributeGroup ref="wAttributes"/>
    </xs:complexType>
  </xs:element>
</xs:sequence></xs:complexType>

</xs:schema>
```

Here we custom-define a simple data type, a complex data type, a group of elements, and a group of attributes to be used later.

element and attribute can have the attribute 'rel'.

include adds an external XSD schema with the same target namespace. To add a schema with a different target namespace, use import:

```
<xs:import namespace="http://example.com/schema"/>
<xs:import schemaLocation="http://example.com/schema"/>
```

For restriction and extension, you must specify the base attribute, which can be either a built-in primitive data type or a custom data type.

You can't include both a restriction and an extension within complexType. If you wish to restrict and declare an attribute for an element at the same time, you must first declare a restricted simpleType, and use that type as the base for the extension of the element.

anyAttribute allows the element to include attributes not declared by the schema.

complexContent contains an extension or a restriction for a complexType.

simpleContent contains an extension or a restriction for a simpleType, or for a complexType containing text only.

This demonstrates conditional type assignment, in which the type of an element depends on one of its attributes. This also shows how to specify XSD versions for the validator.

```
<?xml version="1.0" encoding="UTF-8"?>
<integer xmlns:xsi=
          "http://www.w3.org/2001/XMLSchema-instance"
        xsi:noNamespaceSchemaLocation=
          "file:///C:/Zend/Apache2/htdocs/xml/integer.xsd"
        kind="b">127</integer>
```

```
<?xml version="1.0" encoding="UTF-8"?>
<xs:schema xmlns:xs=
          "http://www.w3.org/2001/XMLSchema"
          xmlns:vc=
          "http://www.w3.org/2007/XMLSchema-versioning"
          elementFormDefault="qualified"
          attributeFormDefault="unqualified"
          vc:minVersion="1.1">
  <xs:complexType name="bInt">
    <xs:simpleContent>
      <xs:extension base="xs:byte">
        <xs:attribute name="kind" type="xs:string"/>
      </xs:extension>
    </xs:simpleContent>
  </xs:complexType>
  <xs:complexType name="sInt">
    <xs:simpleContent>
      <xs:extension base="xs:short">
        <xs:attribute name="kind" type="xs:string"/>
      </xs:extension>
    </xs:simpleContent>
  </xs:complexType>
  <xs:complexType name="iInt">
    <xs:simpleContent>
      <xs:extension base="xs:int">
        <xs:attribute name="kind" type="xs:string"/>
      </xs:extension>
    </xs:simpleContent>
  </xs:complexType>
  <xs:complexType name="lInt">
    <xs:simpleContent>
      <xs:extension base="xs:long">
        <xs:attribute name="kind" type="xs:string"/>
      </xs:extension>
    </xs:simpleContent>
  </xs:complexType>
  <xs:complexType name="gInt">
    <xs:simpleContent>
      <xs:extension base="xs:integer">
        <xs:attribute name="kind" type="xs:string"/>
      </xs:extension>
    </xs:simpleContent>
  </xs:complexType>
  <xs:element name="integer"
            vc:minVersion="1.1" vc:maxVersion="3.0">
    <xs:alternative test="@kind='b'" type="bInt"/>
    <xs:alternative test="@kind='s'" type="sInt"/>
    <xs:alternative test="@kind='i'" type="iInt"/>
    <xs:alternative test="@kind='l'" type="lInt"/>
    <xs:alternative                  type="gInt"/>
  </xs:element>
</xs:schema>
```

This illustrates notation, list, union, dateTime, and numeric restrictions.

```
<?xml version="1.0"?>
<dtList
  xmlns="http://www.example.com"
  xmlns:xsi="http://www.w3.org/2001/XMLSchema-instance"
  xsi:schemaLocation="http://www.example.com date.xsd">
  2013-03-02Z
  12:00:00+08:00
  2013-03-02T12:00:00+08:00
  123
  321.444
</dtList>
```

```
<?xml version="1.0"?>

<xs:schema
       xmlns:xs="http://www.w3.org/2001/XMLSchema"
       targetNamespace="http://www.example.com"
       xmlns="http://www.example.com"
       elementFormDefault="qualified">

<xs:notation name="jpeg"
          public="image/jpeg" system="viewer.exe" />

<xs:simpleType name="numbers">
  <xs:restriction base="xs:decimal">
    <xs:totalDigits value="10"/>
    <xs:fractionDigits value="3"/>
  </xs:restriction>
</xs:simpleType>

<xs:simpleType name="dUnion">
  <xs:union memberTypes="xs:date
                         xs:time
                         xs:dateTime
                         numbers"/>
</xs:simpleType>

<xs:element name="dtList">
  <xs:simpleType>
    <xs:list itemType="dUnion"/>
  </xs:simpleType>
</xs:element>

</xs:schema>
```

totalDigits specifies the maximum number of digits allowed. fractionDigits specifies the maximum number of digits allowed after the decimal point.

This shows how to declare any element, notation, and 'mixed' content.

Here, <nameslist> must start with one single arbitrary element. An element named <description> must appear after another element named <name>, with any number of arbitrarily named elements in between.

```
<?xml version="1.0" encoding="UTF-8"?>

<nameslist
 xmlns="http://www.example.com"
 xmlns:xsi="http://www.w3.org/2001/XMLSchema-instance"
 xsi:schemaLocation="http://www.example.com
                     nameslist.xsd">

<group>Famous People</group>

<person>
  <name>Bruce</name>
  <age>30</age>
  <description>He is a real <b>fighter</b>.</description>
</person>

<person>
```

```
  <name>Stephen</name>
  <sex>male</sex>
  <status>married</status>
  <description>He is a real <b>writer</b>.</description>
</person>

</nameslist>
```

```
<?xml version="1.0"?>
<xs:schema
    xmlns:xs="http://www.w3.org/2001/XMLSchema"
    xmlns="http://www.example.com"
    targetNamespace="http://www.example.com"
    elementFormDefault="qualified">
  <xs:notation name="jpeg"
               public="image/jpeg" system="viewer.exe" />
  <xs:element name="nameslist">
    <xs:complexType>
      <xs:sequence>
        <xs:any namespace="##any" processContents="lax"
                notQName="name description person"/>
        <xs:element name="person" maxOccurs="10">
          <xs:complexType>
            <xs:openContent>
              <xs:any namespace="##any"
                       processContents="lax"/>
            </xs:openContent>
            <xs:sequence>
              <xs:element name="name" type="xs:string"/>
              <xs:element name="description">
                <xs:complexType mixed="true">
                  <xs:sequence>
                   <xs:element name="b" type="xs:string"/>
                  </xs:sequence>
                </xs:complexType>
              </xs:element>
            </xs:sequence>
          </xs:complexType>
        </xs:element>
      </xs:sequence>
    </xs:complexType>
  </xs:element>
</xs:schema>
```

Group references are allowed in <u>all</u> model groups.

A notation describes the format of non-XML data.

A <u>complexType</u> or <u>complexContent</u> with the mixed attribute declared as 'true' can have text around its child elements, ie. a mixture of elements and text.

<u>openContent</u> can have the 'mode' attribute, which can have a value of 'none', 'interleave', or 'suffix'. The default is 'interleave'.

<u>any</u> and <u>anyAttribute</u> can have the following attributes:

- namespace:
  - ##any – from any namespace(default)
  - ##other – any namespace that is not the namespace of the parent element
  - ##local – no namespace
  - ##targetNamesapce – the namespace of the parent element
  - List of {namespace URIs, ##targetNamespace, ##local} – a space-delimited list
- notNamespace:
  - ##targetNamespace
  - ##local
  - List of the anyURI and the previous two
- notQName:
  - List of QName, ##defined, or ##definedSibling
- processContents:
  - strict – the processor must obtain the schema for the required namespaces and validate the elements (default)
  - lax – same as strict; if the schema cannot be obtained, no errors will occur.
  - skip – the processor does not attempt to validate any elements from the specified namespaces

<u>redefine</u> allows you to redefine simple and complex types, groups and attribute groups from an external schema. This construct is ***deprecated*** in XSD 1.1.

```
<?xml version="1.0"?>
<item
  xmlns="http://www.example.com"
  xmlns:xsi="http://www.w3.org/2001/XMLSchema-instance"
  xsi:schemaLocation="http://www.example.com item.xsd">
  <name>ruler</name>
  <price>1.00</price>
</item>
```

```
<?xml version="1.0"?>
<!-- item.xsd -->

<xs:schema
        xmlns:xs="http://www.w3.org/2001/XMLSchema"
        targetNamespace="http://www.example.com"
        xmlns="http://www.example.com"
        elementFormDefault="qualified">

<xs:redefine schemaLocation="item2.xsd">
  <xs:complexType name="iDetails">
    <xs:complexContent>
      <xs:extension base="iDetails">
        <xs:sequence>
          <xs:element name="price"/>
        </xs:sequence>
      </xs:extension>
    </xs:complexContent>
  </xs:complexType>
</xs:redefine>

<xs:element name="item" type="iDetails"/>

</xs:schema>
```

```
<?xml version="1.0"?>
<!-- item2.xsd -->

<xs:schema
        xmlns:xs="http://www.w3.org/2001/XMLSchema"
        targetNamespace="http://www.example.com"
        xmlns="http://www.example.com"
        elementFormDefault="qualified">
<xs:complexType name="iDetails">
  <xs:sequence>
    <xs:element name="name"/>
  </xs:sequence>
</xs:complexType>
</xs:schema>
```

Rather similar to redefine is override.

```
<?xml version="1.0"?>
<item
  xmlns="http://www.example.com"
  xmlns:xsi="http://www.w3.org/2001/XMLSchema-instance"
  xsi:schemaLocation="http://www.example.com item.xsd">
  <price>1.00</price>
</item>
```

```
<?xml version="1.0"?>
<!-- item.xsd -->
<xs:schema
   xmlns:xs="http://www.w3.org/2001/XMLSchema"
   xmlns="http://www.example.com"
   targetNamespace="http://www.example.com"
   elementFormDefault="qualified">
  <xs:override schemaLocation="item2.xsd">
    <xs:complexType name="iDetails">
      <xs:sequence>
        <xs:element name="price"/>
      </xs:sequence>
    </xs:complexType>
  </xs:override>
  <xs:element name="item" type="iDetails"/>
</xs:schema>
```

```
<?xml version="1.0"?>
<!-- item2.xsd -->
<xs:schema
      xmlns:xs="http://www.w3.org/2001/XMLSchema"
      xmlns="http://www.example.com"
      targetNamespace="http://www.example.com"
      elementFormDefault="qualified">
  <xs:complexType name="iDetails">
    <xs:sequence>
      <xs:element name="name"/>
    </xs:sequence>
  </xs:complexType>
</xs:schema>
```

This demonstrates substitution. All three XML documents are valid against the schema.

```
<?xml version="1.0" ?>
<section
  xmlns:xsi="http://www.w3.org/2001/XMLSchema-instance"
  xsi:noNamespaceSchemaLocation="body.xsd">
  <p>Hello World!</p>
</section>
```

```
<?xml version="1.0" ?>
<body
  xmlns:xsi="http://www.w3.org/2001/XMLSchema-instance"
  xsi:noNamespaceSchemaLocation="body.xsd">
  <div>Hello World!</div>
</body>
```

```
<?xml version="1.0" ?>
<section
  xmlns:xsi="http://www.w3.org/2001/XMLSchema-instance"
  xsi:noNamespaceSchemaLocation="body.xsd">
  <div>Hello World!</div>
</section>
```

```
<xs:schema
     xmlns:xs="http://www.w3.org/2001/XMLSchema"
     elementFormDefault="qualified">
  <xs:complexType name="sContent">
    <xs:sequence>
      <xs:element ref="p"/>
    </xs:sequence>
  </xs:complexType>
  <xs:element name="section" type="sContent"/>
  <xs:element name="body" substitutionGroup="section"/>

  <xs:element name="p" type="xs:string"/>
  <xs:element name="span" type="xs:string"/>
  <xs:element name="div" substitutionGroup="p span"/>
</xs:schema>
```

element and complexType can have the following attributes:

- *abstract* : true or false
- *block* : #all or a list that is a subset of substitution, extension or restriction.
- *final* : #all or a list that is a subset of extension or restriction.

This example illustrates identity constraints. Each child of <items> must have a 'number' attribute whose value matches one of these unique product numbers. Each <product> element must have a <number> child whose value is unique.

```
<?xml version="1.0" ?>
<shipment
  xmlns:xsi="http://www.w3.org/2001/XMLSchema-instance"
  xsi:noNamespaceSchemaLocation="shipment.xsd">
  <number>987QWERTY</number>
  <items>
    <thermometer number="876">
      <quantity>1</quantity>
      <color value="blue"/>
    </thermometer>
    <thermometer number="876">
      <quantity>1</quantity>
      <color value="sage"/>
    </thermometer>
    <pump number="432">
      <quantity>1</quantity>
    </pump>
  </items>
  <products>
    <product>
      <number>876</number>
      <name>TM-902C K Type Digital Thermometer</name>
      <price currency="USD">14.99</price>
    </product>
    <product>
      <number>432</number>
      <name>3CFM 1/4HP Rotary Vane Vacuum Pump</name>
      <price currency="USD">59.99</price>
    </product>
  </products>
</shipment>
```

```
<xs:schema
        xmlns:xs="http://www.w3.org/2001/XMLSchema"
        elementFormDefault="qualified">
  <xs:element name="shipment" type="OrderType">
    <xs:keyref name="prodNumKeyRef" refer="prodNumKey">
      <xs:selector xpath="items/*"/>
      <xs:field xpath="@number"/>
    </xs:keyref>
    <xs:key name="prodNumKey">
      <xs:selector xpath=".//product"/>
      <xs:field xpath="number"/>
    </xs:key>
  </xs:element>
  <xs:complexType name="OrderType">
    <xs:sequence>
      <xs:element name="number" type="xs:string"/>
      <xs:element name="items" type="ItemsType"/>
      <xs:element name="products" type="ProductsType"/>
    </xs:sequence>
  </xs:complexType>
  <xs:complexType name="ItemsType">
    <xs:choice maxOccurs="unbounded">
      <xs:element name="thermometer"
                  type="ProductOrderType"/>
      <xs:element name="pump" type="ProductOrderType"/>
    </xs:choice>
  </xs:complexType>
  <xs:complexType name="ProductOrderType">
    <xs:sequence>
      <xs:element name="quantity" type="xs:integer"/>
      <xs:element name="color" type="ColorType"
                                  minOccurs="0"/>
    </xs:sequence>
```

```
    <xs:attribute name="number" type="xs:integer"/>
  </xs:complexType>
  <xs:complexType name="ProductsType">
    <xs:sequence>
      <xs:element name="product" type="ProductType"
                                     maxOccurs="unbounded"/>
    </xs:sequence>
  </xs:complexType>
  <xs:complexType name="ProductType">
    <xs:sequence>
      <xs:element name="number" type="xs:integer"/>
      <xs:element name="name" type="xs:string"/>
      <xs:element name="price" type="PriceType"/>
    </xs:sequence>
  </xs:complexType>
  <xs:complexType name="ColorType">
    <xs:attribute name="value" type="xs:string"/>
  </xs:complexType>
  <xs:complexType name="PriceType">
    <xs:simpleContent>
      <xs:extension base="xs:decimal">
        <xs:attribute name="currency" type="xs:token"/>
      </xs:extension>
    </xs:simpleContent>
  </xs:complexType>
</xs:schema>
```

6.3.3 Relax NG

Relax NG (REgular LAnguage for XML Next Generation) is XML based. It is somewhat simpler to learn than XSD.

The name of a Relax NG file ends with ".rng".

This illustrates the basic features of RelaxNG.

```
<?xml version="1.0"?>
<zoo>
  <animal id="l123444" id2="L234423">
    <name>Mighty</name>
    <type>lion</type>
    <kg>135</kg>
    <imported/>
  </animal>
  <animal id="b355345">
    <name>Lucky</name>
    <type>bear</type>
    <kg>205</kg>
  </animal>
</zoo>
```

```
<?xml version="1.0"?>
<element name="zoo"
         xmlns="http://relaxng.org/ns/structure/1.0">
  <zeroOrMore>
    <element name="animal">
      <attribute name="id"/>
      <element name="name"><text/></element>
      <element name="type"><text/></element>
      <element name="kg"><text/></element>
      <optional>
        <element name="imported"><empty/></element>
        <attribute name="id2"/>
      </optional>
    </element>
  </zeroOrMore>
</element>
```

oneOrMore can be used in place zeroOrMore, if at least one child element must be present.

RelaxNG does not allow element to be empty. So the following is invalid: <element name="x"/>

The order of elements is significant, but the order of the attributes is not.

This illustrates the use of choice, group, and data.

```
<?xml version="1.0"?>
<personalDetails>
  <person>
    <name>Ali</name>
    <sex>m</sex>
  </person>
  <person sex="f">
    <firstName>Sharon</firstName>
    <lastName>Ann</lastName>
  </person>
</personalDetails>
```

```
<?xml version="1.0"?>
<element name="personalDetails"
         xmlns="http://relaxng.org/ns/structure/1.0">
  <zeroOrMore>
    <element name="person">
      <choice>
        <element name="name"><text/></element>
        <group>
          <element name="firstName"><text/></element>
          <element name="lastName"><text/></element>
        </group>
      </choice>
      <choice>
        <element name="sex">
          <data type="string" datatypeLibrary=
          "http://www.w3.org/2001/XMLSchema-datatypes">
            <param name="maxLength">1</param>
          </data>
        </element>
        <attribute name="sex">
          <choice>
            <value>m</value>
            <value>f</value>
          </choice>
        </attribute>
      </choice>
    </element>
  </zeroOrMore>
</element>
```

The attribute datatypeLibrary can appear in any ancestor element instead.

This illustrates the use of list, interleave, and mixed.

```
<?xml version="1.0"?>
<data>
  <myList1>SN 4432 1234 3287 ZZ</myList1>
  <myList2><b/><c/><a/></myList2>
  <myList3>as324<a/>23423<b/>4sd</myList3>
</data>
```

```
<?xml version="1.0"?>
<element
  name="data"
  xmlns="http://relaxng.org/ns/structure/1.0"
  datatypeLibrary=
          "http://www.w3.org/2001/XMLSchema-datatypes">
  <element name="myList1">
    <list>
      <data type="string"/>
      <oneOrMore>
        <data type="int"/>
      </oneOrMore>
      <optional>
        <data type="string"/>
      </optional>
    </list>
  </element>
  <element name="myList2">
    <interleave>
      <element name="a"><empty/></element>
      <element name="b"><empty/></element>
      <optional>
        <element name="c"><empty/></element>
      </optional>
```

```
    </interleave>
  </element>
  <element name="myList3">
    <mixed>
      <element name="a"><empty/></element>
      <element name="b"><empty/></element>
    </mixed>
  </element>
</element>
```

Combining attributes with interleave has the same effect as combining them with group.

This is a rather complex example that demonstrates the various ways to use references.

```
<?xml version="1.0"?>
<!-- badminton.xml -->

<badminton id="3432">
  <players.min>2</players.min>
  <players.max>4</players.max>
</badminton>
```

```
<?xml version="1.0"?>
<!-- badminton1.rng -->

<element
  name="badminton"
  xmlns="http://relaxng.org/ns/structure/1.0">

  <externalRef href="badminton2.rng"/>
</element>
```

```
<?xml version="1.0"?>
<!-- badminton2.rng -->

<grammar xmlns="http://relaxng.org/ns/structure/1.0">
  <include href="badminton3.rng">
    <define name="idd">
      <attribute name="id"/>
    </define>
  </include>
  <define name="pNum" combine="interleave">
    <element name="players.min">
      <text/>
    </element>
    <ref name="idd"/>
  </define>
  <start>
    <ref name="pNum"/>
  </start>
</grammar>
```

```
<?xml version="1.0"?>
<!-- badminton3.rng -->

<grammar xmlns="http://relaxng.org/ns/structure/1.0">
  <define name="pNum">
    <element name="players.max">
      <text/>
    </element>
  </define>
  <define name="idd">
    <element name="id">
      <text/>
    </element>
  </define>
</grammar>
```

Theoretically, the three schema files could be merged into one. They appear as separate files to illustrate externalRef and include here. The include element, if not empty, contains definitions that override the included definitions.

The 'combine' attribute can take other values such as choice.

In a grammar definition, there can be recursive references within an element.

If a nested grammar is used, parentRef can be used in place of ref to escape out of the current grammar and reference a definition from the parent.

<notAllowed/> never matches anything. It can be used with combine="choice" to allow the including pattern to specify additional choices.

You can declare a namespace for an element or an attribute with the attribute 'ns'.

```
<?xml version="1.0"?>
<xn1:section id="199"
             xmlns:xn1="http://example1.com"
             xmlns:xn2="http://example2.com">
  <xn1:subsection1/>
  <xn2:subsection2/>
</xn1:section>
```

```
<?xml version="1.0"?>
<element name="section"
         xmlns="http://relaxng.org/ns/structure/1.0"
         xmlns:myNS="http://example2.com"
         ns="http://example1.com">
 <element name="subsection1"><empty/></element>
 <element name="myNS:subsection2"><empty/></element>
 <attribute name="id"/>
</element>
```

Note that element inherits the value of the 'ns' attribute of the nearest ancestor, but attribute does not. The XML document will be invalid if xn1:id="199" is used instead, because the id attribute is declared to have the empty (or absent) namespace.

Here

```
  <element name="myNS:subsection2">
```

is equivalent to:

```
  <element name="subsection2" ns="http://example2.com">
```

This allows an element to have any attribute with a qualified name, but if there was an 'xml:space' attribute, it had the value 'default' or 'preserve'.

```
<?xml version="1.0"?>
<element
  name="example"
  xmlns="http://relaxng.org/ns/structure/1.0">
  <zeroOrMore>
    <attribute>
      <anyName>
        <except>
          <name>xml:space</name>
        </except>
      </anyName>
    </attribute>
  </zeroOrMore>
  <optional>
    <attribute name="xml:space">
      <choice>
        <value>default</value>
        <value>preserve</value>
      </choice>
    </attribute>
  </optional>
</element>
```

Instead of name, you can use nsName to contain any name with the namespace URI specified by the 'ns' attribute. Eg.:

```
<element>
  <anyName>
    <except>
      <nsName/>
```

```
      <nsName ns=""/>
    </except>
  </anyName>
</element>
```

will contain any namespace-qualified element provided it is qualified with namespace other than that of parent element.

(Courtesy of http://relaxng.org/tutorial-20011203.html#IDAFLZR)

You can attach annotations anywhere. div allows an annotation to be applied to a group of definitions in a grammar.

```
<?xml version="1.0"?>
<grammar xmlns:m="http://www.example.com/module">
  <m:documentation>Here are the animals.
  </m:documentation>
  <div m:name="These are reptiles.">
    <define name="crocodile">
      <attribute name="crocodile"/></define>
    <define name="snake">
      <attribute name="snake"/></define>
    <define name="alligator">
      <attribute name="alligator"/></define>
  </div>
  <div m:name="These are mammals.">
    <define name="dog">
      <attribute name="dog"/></define>
    <define name="cat">
      <attribute name="cat"/></define>
    <define name="tiger">
      <attribute name="tiger"/></define>
  </div>
</grammar>
```

6.3.4 Relax NG Compact

The name of a Relax NG Compact document ends with ".rnc".

This illustrates the basic semantics of Relax NG Compact.

```
<?xml version="1.0" ?>
<emailsList>
  <person id="232133">
    <firstName>Adam</firstName>
    <lastName>Khoo</lastName>
    <email>adamkhoo@yahoo.com</email>
    <sex>M</sex>
    <scores>88 97</scores>
    <description>
      This is a <b>smart guy</b>.
    </description>
    <VIP/>
  </person>
  <person>
    <id>234023</id>
    <name>Serena</name>
    <email>serena@yahoo.com</email>
    <sex> F </sex>
    <scores>50 78.5</scores>
  </person>
</emailsList>
```

```
datatypes xs=
           "http://www.w3.org/2001/XMLSchema-datatypes"

element emailsList {
  element person {
    (element id {xs:integer} |   # a comment
     attribute id {xs:integer}),
    (element name {text} |
     (element firstName {text} &
      element lastName {text})),
    element email {
      xsd:string {
        minLength="5"
        maxLength="125"}
      },
    element sex {string "M" | "F"},
    element scores {
      list {xsd:float, xsd:float}
    },
    element description{
      mixed {element b{text}}
    }?,
    element VIP {empty}?
  }*
}
```

* denotes zero or more.
\+ denotes one or more.
? denotes zero or one.
() denotes grouping.
, denotes a sequence.
| denotes a choice.
& denotes interleaving (out-of-order sequence).
# denotes a comment

'xsd' is a built-in datatypes library. Its URI is "http://www.w3.org/2001/XMLSchema-datatypes".

The 'string' before "M" means that there must not be spaces before and after "M".

The order of elements in a sequence (denoted by ,) is significant. The order of attributes in a sequence is not.

This is a rather complex example that demonstrates the various ways to use references.

```
<?xml version="1.0"?>
<!-- badminton.xml -->

<badminton id="3432">
  <players.min>2</players.min>
  <players.max>4</players.max>
</badminton>
```

```
#badminton1.rnc
element badminton {
  external "badminton2.rnc"
}
```

```
#badminton2.rnc
grammar {
  include "badminton3.rnc" {
    idd = attribute id{text}
  }
  pNum &= element players.min {text}
  pNum &= idd
  start = pNum
}
```

```
#badminton3.rnc
grammar {
  pNum=element players.max {text}
  idd=element id {text}
}
```

'external' references another .rnc document as if the content of that document is at the current place.

'include' allows grammars to be merged. The optional {...} clause next to 'include' overrides the included definitions. The content designator, 'start', can be replaced likewise.

&= combines the definitions, interleaving them.
|= combines the definitions, joining them with |.

In a grammar definition, there can be recursive references within an element. Eg.:

```
inline = element span {inline | text}
```

To use keywords such as 'element', 'attribute', 'text', 'empty', 'grammar' as the name of a definition, it must be prefixed with \, Eg.:

```
start = \element
\element = element element {text}
```

In a nested grammar, to use the definition from the parent, prefix the name with 'parent '.

'notAllowed' is typically used to allow an including pattern to specify additional choices with |=. Eg.:

```
grammar {
  inline =notAllowed        # inline.rnc
}
------------------------------------------------
grammar {
  include "inline.rnc"
  inline |= element code {inline} | element em {inline}
}
```

This illustrates various ways to use namespaces.

```
<?xml version="1.0"?>
<book xmlns="http://example2.com">
  <title xmlns="http://example1.com">
    Web Coding Bible
  </title>
  <genre xmlns="http://example1.com">
    Manual
  </genre>
</book>
```

```
#book.rnc
namespace a = "http://example1.com"
default namespace = "http://example2.com"

element book {
  element a:title {text},
  external "book2.rnc" inherit = a
}
```

```
#book2.rnc
namespace c = inherit
element c:genre {text}
```

Unless 'inherit'ed explicitly, a namespace declaration applies only to the file in which it appears. A file referenced using 'include' or 'external' cannot take advantage of the namespace declarations of the referencing file.

A default namespace does not apply to attributes. The attribute name in an attribute declaration must be prefixed with the namespace prefix if so desired.

```
default namespace eg = "http://example.com"
```

is equivalent to

```
default namespace = "http://example.com"
namespace eg = "http://example.com"
```

In the example above, 'inherit = a' can be omitted if the default namespace is to be inherited instead.

* can be used to denote any element or any attribute.

```
<?xml version="1.0"?>
<house id="100">
  <type>bungalow</type>
  <cost xmlns="http://example.com">500000</cost>
  <area>10000</area>
</house>
```

```
namespace a = "http://example.com"
element house {
  attribute * {text}+,      #any attribute
  element * {text},         #any element
  element (a:*|*) {text}, #union of namespaces
  element * - a:* {text}  #difference
}
```

This shows how to use annotations.

```
namespace an = "http://example.com"
grammar {
  [an:dummy = "elements"]
  div {
    a = element a {text}
    an:entity [name="picture"]
    b = element b {text}
  }
  [an:dummy = "attributes"]
  div {
    c = attribute c {text}
    d = attribute d {text}
  }
  start = a
}
```

```
## This is the documentation syntax.
element a {text}
```

is equivalent to

```
namespace d=
      "http://relaxng.org/ns/compatibility/annotations/1.0"
[d:documentation [ This is documentation syntax."]]
element a {text}
```

```
"Line 1\x{A}" ~ "Line 2"
```

is equivalent to

```
'''Line 1
Line 2'''
```

and

```
"""Line 1
Line 2"""
```

Here, \x{A} denotes an escaped newline, and ~ concatenation. String literals can be delimited by triple quotes.

6.3.5 Schematron

Like XSD and Relax NG, a Schematron schema is an XML document which has the suffix ".sch".

An XML document can be validated against a Schematron schema using GUI-based tools such as XML ValidatorBuddy or Oxygen XML. There is also an XSLT stylesheet which implements Schematron validation, thus allowing the XML document to be dynamically validated by invoking any XSLT processor (eg. SAXON or XALAN).

XPath is heavily used in Schematron.

This demonstrates *co-constraints* with <pattern>-<rule>-<assert>, *progressive validation* with <phase>, and <diagnostics>.

```
<?xml version="1.0"?>
<superior rank="colonel" id="c123">
   <subordinate rank="major" id="m456">
       A subordinate must be ranked lower than the superior.
   </subordinate>
</superior>
```

```
<?xml version="1.0"?>
<schema
  xmlns="http://purl.oclc.org/dsdl/schematron"
  queryBinding='xslt2'
  schemaVersion='ISO19757-3'
  defaultPhase="#ALL">

  <phase><active pattern="CR"/></phase>
  <phase><active pattern="CS"/></phase>

  <pattern name="Check Subordinate" id="CS">
    <rule context="superior">
      <assert test="subordinate">
        A superior must have a subordinate.
      </assert>
```

```
    </rule>
  </pattern>
  <pattern name="Check Rank" id="CR">
    <rule context="subordinate[@rank='general']">
      <assert test="/superior/@rank='general'">
        A general's superior must be a general.
      </assert>
    </rule>
    <rule context="subordinate[@rank='colonel']">
      <assert test="(/superior/@rank='general') or
                    (/superior/@rank='colonel')"
              diagnostics="iColonel">
        A colonel's superior must be a colonel or a general.
      </assert>
    </rule>
    <rule context="subordinate[@rank='major']">
      <assert test="(/superior/@rank='general') or
                    (/superior/@rank='colonel') or
                    (/superior/@rank='major')"
              diagnostics="iMajor">
        A major's superior must be a major, a colonel,
        or a general.
      </assert>
    </rule>
  </pattern>

  <diagnostics>
    <diagnostic id="iColonel">
      Invalid <value-of select="@id"/>.
    </diagnostic>
    <diagnostic id="iMajor">
      Invalid <value-of select="@id"/>.
    </diagnostic>
  </diagnostics>
</schema>
```

A <rule> context specifies the XML fragments which should be checked against. The content for <assert> is the error message that will appear when the assertion fails.

The optional <phase> elements specify the order of validation. Here, the pattern "CS" will not be checked if the pattern "CR" failed. If no <phase> element is specified, all patterns will be checked against. <phase> elements should appear before any <pattern> element.

The optional <diagnostics> element contains error messages that are user-friendly to domain experts. It should appear after any <pattern> element. A <diagnostic> is invoked when an assertion fails.

This demonstrates *cardinality* and the use of a namespace.

```
<?xml version="1.0"?>
<sentence xmlns="http://example.com/myNamespace">
  Be polite!
</sentence>
```

```
<?xml version="1.0"?>
<schema
  xmlns="http://purl.oclc.org/dsdl/schematron"
  queryBinding='xslt2'
  schemaVersion='ISO19757-3'>
  <ns prefix="n" uri="http://example.com/myNamespace"/>
  <pattern name="Language Filter">
    <rule context="n:sentence">
     <assert test="count(/n:sentence[contains(.,'fuck')])=0">
         The sentence must not contain the word fuck.
     </assert>
     <assert test="count(/n:sentence[contains(.,'shit')])=0">
         The sentence must not contain the word shit.
     </assert>
    </rule>
  </pattern>
</schema>
```

This attaches some messages and demonstrates the third kind of validation – *algorithmic validation*.

```
<?xml version="1.0"?>
<demography country="Malaysia">
    <group race="Malay">60</group>
    <group race="Chinese">23</group>
    <group race="Indian">7</group>
    <group race="Others">10</group>
</demography>
```

```
<?xml version="1.0"?>
<schema
  xmlns="http://purl.oclc.org/dsdl/schematron"
  queryBinding='xslt2'
  schemaVersion='ISO19757-3'>
  <title>Checking if the ethnic groups add up to 100%.
  </title>
  <pattern name="Demographic Make-up Check">
    <title>Main check.</title>
    <p>The groups must add up to 100%.</p>
    <rule context="demography">
      <assert test="sum(group) = 100">
        The sum of the group proportions must be 100%.
      </assert>
      <report test="group">
         Ethnic groups found.
      </report>
    </rule>
  </pattern>
</schema>
```

<report> is the opposite of <assert>. It prints its content when the test passes during the validation process.

<title> is valid in <schema> and <pattern>. It provides a title.

<p> is valid in <schema>, <pattern> and <phase>. It provides additional information.

<emph> is valid in <active>, <assert>, <diagnostic>, <p> and <report>. It provides some emphasis.

<span> is an inline element which can apply a stylesheet with the 'class' attribute.

Other elements which can enhance the appearance of the output are: <icon>, <fpi>, <flag>, <role>, and <subject>.

This illustrates the use of references.

```
<?xml version="1.0"?>
<menu restaurant="Golden Outlet">
  <dish>Satay</dish>
  <dish>Curry Chicken</dish>
</menu>
```

```
<?xml version="1.0"?>
<schema
  xmlns="http://purl.oclc.org/dsdl/schematron"
  queryBinding='xslt2'
  schemaVersion='ISO19757-3'>

  <include href="menu.incl"/>

  <pattern name="Extends and uses an abstract rule.">
    <let name="v" value="//menu/@restaurant"/>
    <rule context="menu">
      <extends rule="eod"/>
      <assert test="$v='Golden Outlet'">
        The restaurant must be Golden Outlet.
      </assert>
    </rule>
  </pattern>
</schema>
```

```
<!-- menu.incl -->
  <pattern name="Contains an abstract rule.">
  <rule abstract="true" id="eod" role="ExOfDish">
    <assert test="dish">
      There must be at least a dish.
    </assert>
  </rule>
</pattern>
```

<include> treats the tag as if the content of the referenced file is at its place.

<let> can appear at the top of <schema>, <pattern> or <rule>. It is applicable only within that parent element

A <rule> declared as 'abstract' must be extended to be effective.

6.4 XQuery

Although XQuery was initially conceived as a query language for large collections of XML documents, it is also capable of transforming individual documents. Syntactically, XQuery shares some similarities with SQL.

XQuery is essentially a functional language. The name of an XQuery file ends with ".xq", ".xql", or ".xquery".

Escape Characters	
(new line)
(space)	
(tab)	
{	{
}	}
&	&
`	"

6.4.1 FLWOR

At the heart of XQuery are FLWOR expressions (for-let-where-order by-return).

```
<?xml version="1.0" encoding="UTF-8"?>
<richestMen>
  <billionaire id="1">
    <name>Carlos Slim Helu</name>
    <age>74</age>
    <country>Mexico</country>
    <net_worth>86.1</net_worth>
  </billionaire>
  <billionaire id="2">
    <name>Bill Gates</name>
    <age>58</age>
    <country>USA</country>
    <net_worth>81.2</net_worth>
  </billionaire>
  <billionaire id="3">
    <name>Warren Buffett</name>
    <age>84</age>
    <country>USA</country>
    <net_worth>67.6</net_worth>
  </billionaire>
  <billionaire id="4">
    <name>Amancio Ortega</name>
    <age>78</age>
    <country>Spain</country>
    <net_worth>64.2</net_worth>
  </billionaire>
  <billionaire id="5">
    <name>Larry Ellison</name>
    <age>70</age>
    <country>USA</country>
    <net_worth>51.1</net_worth>
  </billionaire>
</richestMen>
```

```
for $man in richestMen/billionaire
where $man/net_worth > 70
let $id :=$man/@id
order by $man/name/text()
return '&#10;Rank&#32;'||$id||')&#32;'||($man/name)
```

GIVES

```
Rank 2) Bill Gates
Rank 1) Carlos Slim Helu
```

```
for $man in doc('richestMen.xml')/richestMen/billionaire
let $c := $man/country/text()
group by $c
return document {element {$c} {count($man)}}
```

GIVES

```
<Mexico>1</Mexico><Spain>1</Spain><USA>3</USA>
```

```
for $age in richestMen/billionaire/age
count $num
stable order by $age descending, $num ascending empty least
return <man num='{$num}'>{$age}</man>
```

GIVES

```
<man num="3"><age>84</age></man>
<man num="4"><age>78</age></man>
<man num="1"><age>74</age></man>
<man num="5"><age>70</age></man>
<man num="2"><age>58</age></man>
```

```
<table>
  {for $man at $i in richestMen/billionaire
  return (<tr><td>{$i}.{$man/name/text()}</td>
              <td>{$man/net_worth/text()}</td></tr>,
          '&#10;') }
</table>
```

GIVES

```
<table>
<tr><td>1.Carlos Slim Helu</td><td>86.1</td></tr>
<tr><td>2.Bill Gates</td><td>81.2</td></tr>
<tr><td>3.Warren Buffett</td><td>67.6</td></tr>
<tr><td>4.Amancio Ortega</td><td>64.2</td></tr>
<tr><td>5.Larry Ellison</td><td>51.1</td></tr>
</table>
```

6.4.2 Other Expressions

This subsection demonstrates how to use other kinds of other XQuery expressions.

```
comment{'This shows the use of various contructors'},
'&#10;',
element student {
   namespace school {'http://tchs.example.com'},
   attribute id {'U027218N'},
   text {'&#10;1. '},
   element firstName {'Chong'},
   element lastName {'Lip Phang'}}
```

GIVES

```
<!--This shows the use of various contructors-->
<student xmlns:school="http://tchs.example.com"
id="U027218N">
```

```
1. <firstName>Chong</firstName><lastName>Lip
Phang</lastName></student>
```

```
let $f := substring(?,1,3)
return (
  $f('cat123'),
  $f('dog456')
)
```

GIVES

```
cat dog
```

```
for $n allowing empty at $i in (300,200,100,())
return ($n,$i,'&#10;')
```

GIVES

```
300 1
 200 2
 100 3
```

```
for tumbling window $w in (20,40,60,80,100,120,140)
start at $s when true()
only end at $e when $e - $s = 2
return <window>{$w}</window>
```

GIVES

```
<window>20 40 60</window>
<window>80 100 120</window>
```

```
for sliding window $w in (20,40,60,80,100,120,140)
start at $s when true()
only end at $e when $e - $s = 2
return <window>{$w}</window>
```

GIVES

```
<window>20 40 60</window>
<window>40 60 80</window>
<window>60 80 100</window>
<window>80 100 120</window>
<window>100 120 140</window>
```

```
declare namespace
        err = "http://www.w3.org/2005/xqt-errors";
try {
  3 div 0
} catch err:XPTY0004{
  'typing error'
} catch * {
  $err:code || '&#10;' ||
  $err:description || '&#10;' ||
  $err:value || '&#10;' ||
  $err:module || '&#10;' ||
  $err:line-number || '&#10;' ||
  $err:additional
}
```

GIVES

```
err:FOAR0001
division_by_zero
0
file:///C:/Zend/Apache2/htdocs/xml/richestMen.xq
3
```

```
switch (5)
  case 3
  case 5 return "three or five"
  case 7 return "seven"
  default return "unknown"
```

GIVES

```
three or five
```

```
declare variable $pi external :=
      Q{http://www.w3.org/2005/xpath-functions/math}pi();
$pi
```

GIVES

```
3.14159265358979
```

```
declare namespace
output = "http://www.w3.org/2010/xslt-xquery-serialization";

declare option output:omit-xml-declaration "no";
declare option output:method "xml";
declare option output:encoding "iso-8859-1";
declare option output:indent "yes";
declare option output:item-separator "&#10;";
<html/>
```

GIVES

```
<?xml version="1.0" encoding="iso-8859-1"?><html/>
```

```
declare context item := document {
  <person>
    <firstName>Lin</firstName>
    <lastName>Dan</lastName>
  </person>
};
//text()
```

GIVES

```
LinDan
```

```
(: A private variable/function is hidden from module import. :)
declare %private variable $v := 10;
declare %private function local:mult2($x) {$x * 2};
local:mult2($v)
```

GIVES

```
20
```

```
import schema namespace
  geometry = "http://example.org/geo-schema-declarations";
import module namespace
  geo = "http://example.org/geo-functions";
declare variable
  $t as geometry:triangle := geo:make-triangle();
$t
```

```
declare decimal-format local:de
     decimal-separator = ","
     grouping-separator = ".";
declare decimal-format local:en
     decimal-separator = "."
     grouping-separator = ",";
let $numbers := (1234.567, 789, 1234567.765)
for $i in $numbers
return (
  format-number($i, "#.###,##", "local:de"),
  format-number($i, "#,###.##", "local:en")
)
```

GIVES

```
1.234,57 1,234.57 789 789 1.234.567,76 1,234,567.76
```

```
(: more prolog declarations :)
(: http://www.w3.org/TR/2014/
REC-xquery-30-20140408/#id-query-prolog :)

xquery version "3.0" encoding "utf-8";
module namespace gis = "http://example.org/gis-functions";
declare boundary-space preserve;
declare default collation
      "http://example.org/languages/Icelandic";
declare base-uri "http://example.org";
declare construction strip;
declare ordering unordered;
declare default order empty least;
declare copy-namespaces preserve, no-inherit;
declare default element namespace
      "http://example.org/names";
declare default function namespace
      "http://www.w3.org/2005/xpath-functions/math";
```

6.4.3 Version 3.1

At the time of writing, XQuery 3.1 is a working draft in W3C. It is under development as of 09-09-2014.

```
let $m1 := map {'abc':123, 1:'hello'},
    $m2 := map:remove($m1,'abc'),
    $m3 := map:merge (for $i in 1 to 5
                         return map {$i: 'value'||$i})
return (map:keys($m1),
        $m1('abc'),
        deep-equal($m1,$m2))
                         GIVES

1 abc 123 false
```

```
let $a := [(1,2),3],                 (: two members :)
    $b := array {1 to 2,3},          (: three members :)
    $c := array:size($a),            (: 2 :)
    $d := $b(1),                     (: 1 :)
    $e := [1,2,3]=2,                 (: true :)
    $f := function ($x as xs:integer*){count($x)}
return $f([1 to 5])                  (: 5 :)
```

```
let $m := map {'R':'red', 'G':'green', 'B':'blue'}
return ($m?*,                       (: red green blue :)
        map:keys($m) ! $m(.)        (: red green blue :)
        $m?R,                       (: red :)
        $m?2,                       (: green :)
        $m?('G',3))                 (: green blue :)
```

```
'w e l c o m e'
=> upper-case() => tokenize() => string-join('-')
                         GIVES

W-E-L-C-O-M-E
```

Map Functions:
map:merge, map:size, map:keys, map:contains, map:get, map:entry, map:put, map:remove, map:for-each-entry

Array Functions:
array:size, array:append, array:subarray, array:remove, array:insert-before, array:head, array:tail, array:reverse, array:join, array:for-each-member, array:filter, array:fold-left, array:fold-right, array:for-each-pair

More:
contains-token, parse-ietf-date, format-number, tokenize, xs:hexBinary, xs:hex64Binary, json-doc, parse-json, collation-key, load-module, transform

6.4.4 XQFT

XQuery Full Text is an extension to XQuery. It is used to query strings for words and phrases. BaseX (http://basex.org/) is a program that supports XQFT.

"abc" contains text "a"	false
"a bc" contains text "Bc"	true
"ab...bc!" contains text "ab,bc"	true
"ab...bc..de!" contains text "ab,de"	false
"aa aa bb cc" contains text "aa" occurs exactly 2 times	true
"aa aa bb cc" contains text "aa" occurs at least 2 times	true
"aa aa bb cc" contains text "aa" occurs at most 2 times	true
"aa aa bb cc" contains text "aa" occurs from 2 to 3 times	true
"aa bb cc" contains text {"aa","ac"} any	true
"aa bb cc" contains text {"aa","ac"} all	false
"aa bb cc" contains text {"aa ab","ac"} any word	true
"aa bb cc" contains text {"bb aa","cc"} all words	true
"aa bb cc" contains text {"aa bb","cc"} phrase	true
"aa bb cc" contains text {"aa","cc"} phrase	false
"aa bb cc" contains text {"aa bb","cc"} ftor {"ab"}	true
"aa bb cc" contains text {"aa bb","cc"}ftand {"ab"}	false
"aa bb cc" contains text ftnot {"aa","cc"}	false
"aa bb cc" contains text "aa" not in "aa bb"	false
"a b c d e" contains text {"a","c","e"} all ordered distance at most 1 words	true
"a b c d e" contains text {"a","c","e"} all distance at most 1 paragraphs	false
"a b c d e" contains text {"a","e"} all window 4 words	false
"a b c d e" contains text {"a","e"} all window 5 words	true
"a b c d e" contains text {"a","e"} all window 1 sentences	true
"a b c! d e." contains text {"a","e"} all words same sentence	false
"a b c! d e." contains text {"a","e"} all words same paragraph	true
"a b c! d e." contains text {"b","a"} at start	true
"a b c! d e." contains text {"b","a"} at end	false
"a b c! d e." contains text {"a b c! d e."} entire content	true
"a b c! d e." contains text {"a","b","c","d","e"} entire content	false
"Hello World" contains text "world" using case sensitive	false
"cry" contains text "crying" using stemming	true
"a b c d e" contains text "a x c y e" using stop words("b","d","x","y")	true
"regular expression" contains text "r.?.+.*.{1,10}" using wildcards	true
for $x score $i in ("a","a b","a b c") [. contains text "a"] return $x || $i || '
'	a1 a b0.6 a b c0.4
let score $s := "a b c d" contains text "a b" return $s	0.62011
'angry' contains text 'furious' using thesaurus default	(true)
'a <b>x y z</b> c' contains text 'a c' without content b	(true)
//p[.//text() contains text 'a c']	(eg.)

6.4.5 XQUF

XQuery Update Facility is an extension to XQuery. It is used to update an XML document. BaseX (http://basex.org/) is a program that supports XQUF.

```
<?xml version="1.0" encoding="UTF-8" ?>
<a>
  <b>Hello</b>
  <b>World</b>
</a>
```

```
insert node (attribute {'id'}{5},'Yes!',<c/>) into /a
```

GIVES

```
<a id="5">
  <b>Hello</b>
  <b>World</b>Yes!<c/>
</a>
```

```
insert node <c/> as first into /a
(: 'as last into' can be used too :)
```

GIVES

```
<a>
  <c/>
  <b>Hello</b>
  <b>World</b>
</a>
```

```
insert node <c/> before /a/b[2]
(: ' after' can be used too :)
```

GIVES

```
<a>
  <b>Hello</b>
  <c/>
  <b>World</b>
</a>
```

```
delete node (a/b[1],a/b[2])
```

GIVES

```
<a/>
```

```
replace node a/b[2] with <c>Kitty</c>
```

GIVES

```
<a>
  <b>Hello</b>
  <c>Kitty</c>
</a>
```

```
replace value of node a/b[2] with <c>Kitty</c>
```

GIVES

```
<a>
  <b>Hello</b>
  <b>Kitty</b>
</a>
```

```
rename node a/b[1] as 'x'
```

GIVES

```
<a>
  <x>Hello</x>
  <b>World</b>
</a>
```

```
copy $v := /a
modify (
  rename node $v/b[1] as 'c',
  insert node ('Kitty') into $v/b[2]
) return $v
```

GIVES

```
<a>
  <c>Hello</c>
  <b>WorldKitty</b>
</a>
```

```
for $v in a/b
return $v update delete node text()
```

GIVES

```
<b/>
<b/>
```

```
declare %updating function {...}
```

6.5 XSLT

Extensible Stylesheet Language Transformations is a language for transforming XML documents. The functionalities of XSLT overlap with those of XQuery. XSLT is an XML-based stylesheet language while XQuery is a functional language. XSLT is stronger in its handling of narrative documents with more flexible structure, while XQuery is stronger in its data handling, for example when performing relational joins.

To let the browsers XSLT-transform an XML document, include the following line in the XML document:
<?xml-stylesheet type="text/xsl" href="x.xslt"?>
where x.xslt contains the stylesheet.

An XSLT 3.0 processor is available online at http://exselt.net/demo.

Throughout this section, instruction tags that are underlined at the top of the tables are intended to be part of XSLT 3.0, which is under development at the time of writing.

To give more focus to the important concepts, a full coverage of the meaning of every attribute is beyond the scope of this book. The interested reader is encouraged to read the W3C documentation at: http://www.w3.org/TR/2014/WD-xslt-30-20141002/.

6.5.1 Basic Flow Control

<xsl:stylesheet> <xsl:output> <xsl:template> <xsl:variable> <xsl:for-each> <xsl:value-of> <xsl:copy-of> <xsl:copy>

```
<?xml version="1.0" encoding="UTF-8"?>
<?xml-stylesheet type="text/xsl" href="a.xslt"?>
<a>
  <b>1<c>Cat</c></b>
  <b>2<c>Cow</c></b>
  <b>3<c>Dog</c></b>
  <b>4<c>Fish</c></b>
</a>
```

```
<?xml version="1.0" encoding="UTF-8"?>
<!--a.xslt -->
<xsl:stylesheet version="1.0"
      xmlns:xsl="http://www.w3.org/1999/XSL/Transform"
      xmlns:xs="http://www.w3.org/2001/XMLSchema"
      xmlns:fn="http://www.w3.org/2005/xpath-functions">
  <xsl:output method="xml" version="1.0"
             encoding="UTF-8" indent="yes"/>
  <xsl:template match="a">
    <xsl:variable name="v" as="xs:integer" select="2"/>
    <xsl:variable name="header" as="node()*">
      <head>
        <title>A B C</title>
      </head>
    </xsl:variable>
    <html>
      <xsl:copy-of select="$header"/>
      <body>
        <table><xsl:for-each select="b[position() > $v]">
          <tr><td><xsl:value-of select="text()"/></td>
              <td><xsl:value-of select="c"/></td>
          </tr>
        </xsl:for-each></table>
```

```
    </body>
   </html>
  </xsl:template>
</xsl:stylesheet>
```

GIVES

```
<?xml version="1.0" encoding="UTF-8"?>
<html xmlns:xs="http://www.w3.org/2001/XMLSchema"
      xmlns:fn="http://www.w3.org/2005/xpath-functions">
  <head>
    <title>A B C</title>
  </head>
  <body>
    <table>
      <tr>
        <td>3</td>
        <td>Dog</td>
      </tr>
      <tr>
        <td>4</td>
        <td>Fish</td>
      </tr>
    </table>
  </body>
</html>
```

<xsl:stylesheet> defines a stylesheet module. It can have the following attributes:

- id = id
- version = decimal
- default-mode = eqname | "#unnamed"
  This attribute defines the default value for the mode attribute of all <xsl:template> and <xsl:apply-templates> elements within its scope.
- default-validation = "preserve" | "strip" *(6.5.3)*

  'The value strip indicates that the new node and each of the contained nodes will have the type annotation xs:untyped if it is an element, or xs:untypedAtomic if it is an attribute. Any previous type annotation present on a contained element or attribute node is also replaced by xs:untyped or xs:untypedAtomic as appropriate. The typed value of the node is changed to be the same as its string value, as an instance of xs:untypedAtomic. In the case of elements the nilled property is set to false.'

  'The value preserve indicates that nodes that are copied will retain their type annotations, but nodes whose content is newly constructed will be annotated as xs:anyType in the case of elements, or xs:untypedAtomic in the case of attributes.'
- input-type-annotations = "preserve" | "strip" | "unspecified" *(6.5.3)*
  'When type annotations are stripped: 1) the type annotation of every element node is changed to xs:untyped 2) the type annotation of every attribute node is changed to xs:untypedAtomic 3) the typed value of every element and attribute is set to be the same as its string value, as an instance of xs:untypedAtomic 4) the is-nilled property of every element node is set to false.'
- default-collation = URIs
- extension-element-prefixes = prefixes
- exclude-result-prefixes = prefixes
- expand-text = "yes" | "no"
- use-when = expression
- xpath-default-namespace = URI

<xsl:transform> is a synonym of <xsl:stylesheet>.

<xsl:template>, <xsl:variable>, <xsl:param>, <xsl:function> etc. can have the 'visibility' attribute:

- 'public' : A using package may use <xsl:apply-templates> to invoke templates in this mode; it may also declare additional template rules in this mode, which are selected in preference to template rules in the used package. These may appear only as children of the <xsl:override>element within the <xsl:use-package> element.
- 'private': A using package may neither reference the mode nor provide additional templates in this mode; the name of the mode is not even visible in the using package, so no such attempt is possible. The using package can use the same name for its own modes without risk of conflict.
- 'final': A using package may use <xsl:apply-templates> to invoke templates in this mode, but it must not provide additional template rules in this mode.
- 'abstract': The sequence constructor defining the template body must be empty: that is, the only permitted children are <xsl:context-item> and <xsl:param>, and. There must be no 'match' attribute.

<xsl:output> can have the following attributes:

- name = *eqname*
- method = "xml" | "html" | "xhtml" | "text" | *eqname*
- byte-order-mark = "yes" | "no"
- cdata-section-elements = *eqnames*
- doctype-public = *string*
- doctype-system = *string*
- encoding = *string*
- escape-uri-attributes = "yes" | "no"
- html-version = *decimal*
- include-content-type = "yes" | "no"
- indent = "yes" | "no"
- item-separator = *string*
- media-type = *string*
- normalization-form = "NFC" | "NFD" | "NFKC" | "NFKD" | "fully-normalized" | "none" | *nmtoken*
- omit-xml-declaration = "yes" | "no"
- parameter-document = *uri*
- standalone = "yes" | "no" | "omit"
- suppress-indentation = *eqnames*
- undeclare-prefixes = "yes" | "no"
- use-character-maps = *eqnames*
- version = *nmtoken*

If you are trying to print XML or HTML data and wish the output to be properly indented, remember to use:

```
<xsl:output method="xml" indent="yes"/>
```

<xsl:template> can have the 'mode' and 'priority' attributes. When a selected item matches more than one template rule with a given mode, only one template rule is evaluated for the item. A template rule with a higher priority will be preferred

<xsl:value-of> can have the 'separator' attribute. It defines the separating string to use between adjacent items when the value is a sequence.

While <xsl:copy-of> performs a deep copy, <xsl:copy> performs a shallow copy.

<xsl:copy-of> can have the following attributes:

- copy-namespaces = "yes" | "no"
- type = *eqname (6.5.3)*
- validation = "strict" | "lax" | "preserve" | "strip" *(6.5.3)*

<xsl:copy> can have the following attributes:

- copy-namespaces = "yes" | "no"
- inherit-namespaces = "yes" | "no"
- use-attribute-sets = *eqnames*
- type = *eqname (6.5.3)*
- validation = "strict" | "lax" | "preserve" | "strip" *(6.5.3)*
- on-empty = *expression*

You can use the function deep-copy($nodes) to perform a deep copy of nodes too.

<xsl:variable> and <xsl:param> can have the 'static' attribute. When declared as true, the attribute causes the variable or parameter to become global. It can then also be used in <xsl:use-when> expressions.

Whenever the 'select' attribute is not present, the value should be declared as the child element.

<xsl:for-each-group>

```
<?xml version="1.0" encoding="UTF-8"?>
<testScores>
  <test>
    <subject>Math</subject>
    <score>78</score>
  </test>
  <test>
    <subject>English</subject>
    <score>90</score>
  </test>
  <test>
    <subject>Malay</subject>
    <score>59</score>
  </test>
  <test>
    <subject>Math</subject>
    <score>95</score>
  </test>
  <test>
    <subject>English</subject>
    <score>85</score>
  </test>
</testScores>
```

```
<?xml version="1.0" encoding="UTF-8"?>
<xsl:stylesheet version="3.0"
      xmlns:xsl="http://www.w3.org/1999/XSL/Transform"
      xmlns:xs="http://www.w3.org/2001/XMLSchema"
      xmlns:fn="http://www.w3.org/2005/xpath-functions">
  <xsl:template match="testScores">
    <xsl:for-each-group
          select="test"
          group-by="subject">
      <xsl:value-of select="current-grouping-key()"/>
      <xsl:value-of select="avg(current-group()/score)"/>
    </xsl:for-each-group>
  </xsl:template>
</xsl:stylesheet>
```

GIVES

```
<?xml version="1.0" encoding="UTF-8"?>
Math86.5English87.5Malay59
```

<xsl:for-each-group> can have the following attributes:

- group-adjacent = *expression*
- group-starting-with = *pattern*
- group-ending-with = *pattern*
- bind-group = *eqname*
- bind-grouping-key = *eqname*
- composite = "yes" | "no"
- collation = { *uri* }

<xsl:iterate> <xsl:next-iteration> <xsl:break> <xsl:on-complettion> <xsl:param> <xsl:choose> <xsl:when> <xsl:otherwise>

```
<?xml version="1.0" encoding="UTF-8"?>
<primes>
  <i>2</i>
  <i>3</i>
  <i>5</i>
  <i>7</i>
  <i>11</i>
  <i>13</i>
</primes>
```

```
<?xml version="1.0" encoding="UTF-8"?>
<xsl:stylesheet version="3.0"
      xmlns:xsl="http://www.w3.org/1999/XSL/Transform"
      xmlns:xs="http://www.w3.org/2001/XMLSchema"
      xmlns:fn="http://www.w3.org/2005/xpath-functions">
  <xsl:output method="xml" version="1.0"
              encoding="UTF-8" indent="yes"/>
  <xsl:template match="/primes">
    <xsl:iterate select="i">
      <xsl:param name="cnt" select="1"/>
      <xsl:choose>
        <xsl:when test="position()=1">
         &#10; Prime: 2
        </xsl:when>
        <xsl:when test="position() le 5">
         &#10; Prime <xsl:value-of select="."/> Leap:
          <xsl:value-of select=". - /*//i[$cnt - 1]"/>
        </xsl:when>
        <xsl:otherwise>
          <xsl:break/>
        </xsl:otherwise>
      </xsl:choose>
      <xsl:next-iteration>
        <xsl:with-param name="cnt" select="$cnt+1"
                        as="xs:integer"/>
      </xsl:next-iteration>
      <!-- <xsl:on-completion>
        Primes are fun.
      </xsl:on-completion> -->
    </xsl:iterate>
  </xsl:template>
</xsl:stylesheet>
```

GIVES

```
<?xml version="1.0" encoding="UTF-8"?>

Prime: 2


Prime 3 Leap: 1

Prime 5 Leap: 2

Prime 7 Leap: 2

Prime 11 Leap: 4
```

By contrast with <xsl:for-each>, with <xsl:iterate>, the processing is explicitly sequential.

<xsl:param> can have the following attributes:

- as = *sequence-type*
- required = "yes" | "no"
- tunnel = "yes" | "no": Tunnel parameters have the property that they are automatically passed on by the called template to any further templates that it calls, and so on recursively. Tunnel parameters thus allow values to be set that are accessible during an entire phase of stylesheet processing, without the need for each template that is used during that phase to be aware of the parameter.
  <xsl:with-param> can have this attribute too.
- static = "yes" | "no"
- visibility = "public" | "private" | "final" | "abstract"

<xsl:if> <xsl:try> <xsl:catch> <xsl:function> <xsl:message>

```
<?xml version="1.0" encoding="UTF-8"?>
<division>
  <num1>9999</num1>
  <num2>9</num2>
</division>
```

```
<?xml version="1.0" encoding="UTF-8"?>
<xsl:transform version="3.0"
     xmlns:xsl="http://www.w3.org/1999/XSL/Transform"
     xmlns:xs="http://www.w3.org/2001/XMLSchema"
     xmlns:fn="http://www.w3.org/2005/xpath-functions"
     xmlns:err="http://www.w3.org/2005/xqt-errors"
     xmlns:ns ="http://example.com">

  <xsl:function name="ns:divide" as="xs:decimal">
    <xsl:param name="x" as="xs:double"/>
    <xsl:param name="y" as="xs:double"/>
    <xsl:value-of select="$x div $y"/>
  </xsl:function>

  <xsl:template match="division">hi
    <xsl:if test="num1 > 999 or num2 > 999">
      One or two of the integers are greater than 999.
    </xsl:if>
    <xsl:try select="ns:divide(num1,num2)">
      <xsl:catch errors="err:FAOR0001">
```

```
        <xsl:message>Division by zero.
         Code: <xsl:value-of select="$err:code"/>
         Description: <xsl:value-of
                             select="$err:description"/>
         Value: <xsl:value-of select="$err:value"/>
         Module: <xsl:value-of select="$err:module"/>
         Line-number: <xsl:value-of
                             select="$err:line-number"/>
         Column-number: <xsl:value-of
                             select="$err:column-number"/>
        </xsl:message>
      </xsl:catch>
    </xsl:try>
  </xsl:template>

</xsl:transform>
```

GIVES

```
<?xml version="1.0" encoding="UTF-8"?>hi

      One or two of the integers are greater than 999.
   1111
```

<xsl:try> or <xsl:catch> can have the 'select' attribute. If that attribute is omitted, the value must be defined in the content as its children.

A custom function must use a namespace.

<xsl:message> can have the 'terminate' (yes|no) and error-code attributes.

<xsl:function> can have the following attributes:

- visibility = "public" | "private" | "final" | "abstract"
- override-extension-function = "yes" | "no"
- identity-sensitive = "yes" | "no"
- cache = "full" | "partial" | "no"

6.5.2 Constructing Nodes

<xsl:document> <xsl:result-docunent> <xsl:element> <xsl:attribute> <xsl:namespace> <xsl:comment> <xsl:processing-instruction> <xsl:text> <xsl:sequence> <xsl:number>

```
<?xml version="1.0" encoding="UTF-8"?>
<xsl:transform version="3.0"
    xmlns:xsl="http://www.w3.org/1999/XSL/Transform"
    xmlns:xs="http://www.w3.org/2001/XMLSchema"
    xmlns:fn="http://www.w3.org/2005/xpath-functions">

  <xsl:template match="/">
    <xsl:text>&#10;</xsl:text>
    <xsl:document>
      <xsl:element name="a">
        <xsl:namespace name="ns"
                       select="'http://example.com'"/>
        <xsl:attribute name="x" select="division/num2"/>
        <xsl:attribute name="y">10</xsl:attribute>
        <xsl:text>&#10;</xsl:text>
        <xsl:comment>COMMENT</xsl:comment>
        <xsl:processing-instruction name="pi"
                              select="'INSTRUCTION'"/>
        <xsl:text>&#10;</xsl:text>
        <xsl:sequence select="(1 to 5)"/>
        <xsl:text>&#10;</xsl:text>
        <xsl:number value="100000000"
              grouping-separator="," grouping-size="3"/>
        <xsl:text>&#10;</xsl:text>
      </xsl:element>
    </xsl:document>
  </xsl:template>
</xsl:transform>
```

GIVES

```
<?xml version="1.0" encoding="UTF-8"?>
<a xmlns:ns="http://example.com" x="9" y="10">
<!--COMMENT--><?pi INSTRUCTION?>
1 2 3 4 5
100,000,000
</a>
```

<xsl:attribute>, <xsl:namespace>, <xsl:comment>, <xsl:processing-instruction>, <xsl:sequence> or <xsl:number>can have the 'select' attribute. If this attribute is not defined, the value should be defined within its content as its child element(s).

<xsl:attribute> can have the following attributes:

- namespace = { *uri* }
- separator = { *string* }
- type = *eqname (6.5.3)*
- validation = "strict" | "lax" | "preserve" | "strip" *(6.5.3)*
- on-empty = *expression*

<xsl:element> can have the following attributes:

- namespace = { uri }
- inherit-namespaces = "yes" | "no"
- use-attribute-sets = *eqnames*
- type = *eqname (6.5.3)*
- validation = "strict" | "lax" | "preserve" | "strip" *(6.5.3)*
- on-empty = *expression*

<xsl:number> can have the following attributes:

- select = *expression*
- level = "single" | "multiple" | "any"
- count = *pattern*
- from = *pattern*
- format = { *string* }
- lang = { *language* }
- letter-value = { "alphabetic" | "traditional" }
- ordinal = { *string* }
- start-at = { *integer* }

<xsl:result-document> can have the following attributes:

- validation = "strict" | "lax" | "preserve" | "strip"
- type = *eqname*

To construct a document that is to form a final result rather than an intermediate result, use the <xsl:result-document> instruction. <xsl:result-document> can have the following attributes:

- format = { *eqname* }
- href = { *uri* }
- validation = "strict" | "lax" | "preserve" | "strip"
- type = *eqname (6.5.3)*
- method = { "xml" | "html" | "xhtml" | "text" | *eqname* }
- byte-order-mark = { "yes" | "no" }
- cdata-section-elements = { *eqnames* }
- doctype-public = { *string* }
- doctype-system = { *string* }
- encoding = { *string* }
- escape-uri-attributes = { "yes" | "no" }
- html-version = { *decimal* }
- include-content-type = { "yes" | "no" }
- indent = { "yes" | "no" }
- item-separator = { *string* }
- media-type = { *string* }
- normalization-form = { "NFC" | "NFD" | "NFKC" | "NFKD" | "fully-normalized" | "none" | *nmtoken* }
- omit-xml-declaration = { "yes" | "no" }
- parameter-document = { *uri* }
- standalone = { "yes" | "no" | "omit" }
- suppress-indentation = { *eqnames* }
- undeclare-prefixes = { "yes" | "no" }
- use-character-maps = *eqnames*
- output-version = { *nmtoken* }

6.5.3 Validation

Notice in the previous sections that <xsl:element>, <xsl:attribute>, <xsl:copy>, <xsl:copy-of>, <xsl:document> and <xsl:result-document> can have the 'type' and 'validate' attributes. It is possible to perform an XSD validation on the generated XML file, during an XSLT transformation.

<xsl:import-schema>

```
<?xml version="1.0" encoding="UTF-8"?>
<!-- transactions_transformed.xsd -->
<xs:schema
  xmlns:xs="http://www.w3.org/2001/XMLSchema">
  <xs:complexType name="rootType">
    <xs:sequence>
      <xs:element name="elem"/>
      <xs:element name="elem"/>
      <xs:element name="elem"/>
      <xs:element name="elem"/>
      <xs:element name="elem"/>
    </xs:sequence>
  </xs:complexType>
  <xs:element name="elem">
    <xs:complexType>
      <xs:simpleContent>
        <xs:extension base="xs:int">
          <xs:attribute name="id"
                        type="xs:NMTOKEN" use="required"/>
        </xs:extension>
      </xs:simpleContent>
    </xs:complexType>
  </xs:element>
</xs:schema>
```

```
<?xml version="1.0" encoding="UTF-8"?>
<xsl:stylesheet version="3.0"
      xmlns:xsl="http://www.w3.org/1999/XSL/Transform"
      xmlns:xs="http://www.w3.org/2001/XMLSchema">
  <xsl:output method="xml" indent="yes"/>
  <xsl:import-schema
          schema-location="transactions_transformed.xsd"/>
  <xsl:template match="/">
    <xsl:element name="root" type="rootType">
      <xsl:element name="elem" type="xs:byte">
        <xsl:value-of select="50"/>
      </xsl:element>
      <xsl:element name="elem" validation="strip">
        <xsl:value-of select=" 'Hello' "/>
      </xsl:element>
      <xsl:element name="elem" validation="preserve">
        <xsl:value-of select=" 'Hello' "/>
      </xsl:element>
      <xsl:element name="elem" validation="strict">
        <xsl:attribute name="id">E1</xsl:attribute>
        <xsl:value-of select="100"/>
      </xsl:element>
      <xsl:element name="elem" validation="lax">
        <xsl:attribute name="id">E2</xsl:attribute>
        <xsl:value-of select="200"/>
      </xsl:element>
    </xsl:element>
  </xsl:template>
</xsl:stylesheet>
```

GIVES

```
<?xml version="1.0" encoding="UTF-8"?>
<root xmlns:xs="http://www.w3.org/2001/XMLSchema">
  <elem>50</elem>
  <elem>Hello</elem>
  <elem>Hello</elem>
  <elem id="E1">100</elem>
  <elem id="E2">200</elem>
</root>
```

The attribute 'type' and the attribute 'validation' must not appear together at the same time. 'type' validates against a built-in type such as xs:integer or a type defined in the schema. 'validation' performs a global validation against the schema declared.

The attribute 'validation' can be assigned one of the four following values:

- strip : The new node and the contained nodes will be typed as xs:untyped if it is an element, or xs:untypefdAtomic if it is an attribute. XSD validation is not invoked.
- preserve: The nodes that are copied or contained will preserve their types. Nodes with newly constructed content will be annotated as xs:anyType in the case of elements, or xs:untypedAtomic in the case of attributes. XSD validation is not invoked.
- strict: XSD validation is invoked. Validation fails if there is no matching top-level element declaration or if the outcome is 'invalid' or 'notKnown'.
- lax: XSD validation is invoked. Validation fails only if the outcome is 'invalid'.

<xsl:import-schema> can omit the 'schema-location' attribute, in which case the XSD is defined as the child content of the tag.

6.5.4 Sorting and Merging

For simplicity, the examples in this subsection use sequences of integers. You can use xpaths and nodes instead of integers. For instance, you can use:

```
<xsl:merge-source
      for-each="doc(a.xml), doc(b.xml)"
      select="a/b/@c">...
```

<xsl:perform-sort> <xsl:sort>

```
<?xml version="1.0" encoding="UTF-8"?>
<xsl:transform version="3.0"
    xmlns:xsl="http://www.w3.org/1999/XSL/Transform"
    xmlns:xs="http://www.w3.org/2001/XMLSchema"
    xmlns:fn="http://www.w3.org/2005/xpath-functions">
  <xsl:template match="/">
    <xsl:perform-sort select="('1a','3b','8b','4b','2','1c','1b')">
      <xsl:sort select="substring(.,1,1)"/>
      <xsl:sort select="substring(.,2,1)"
                order="descending"/>
    </xsl:perform-sort>
  </xsl:template>
</xsl:transform>
```

GIVES

```
<?xml version="1.0" encoding="UTF-8"?>1c 1b 1a 2 3b 4b 8b
```

<xsl:sort> can have the following attributes:

- select = *expression*
- lang = { *language* }
- order = { "ascending" | "descending" }
- collation = { *uri* }
- stable = { "yes" | "no" }
- case-order = { "upper-first" | "lower-first" }
- data-type = { "text" | "number" | *eqname* }

<xsl:merge> <xsl:merge-source> <xsl:merge-key> <xsl:merge-action>

```
<?xml version="1.0" encoding="UTF-8"?>
<xsl:transform version="3.0"
    xmlns:xsl="http://www.w3.org/1999/XSL/Transform"
    xmlns:xs="http://www.w3.org/2001/XMLSchema"
    xmlns:fn="http://www.w3.org/2005/xpath-functions">
  <xsl:template match="/">
    <xsl:merge bind-group="g" bind-key="k">
      <xsl:merge-source for-each="(1,100)"
                        select="(.*5,.*3,.*1,.*7,.*9)">
        <xsl:merge-key select="."/>
      </xsl:merge-source>
      <xsl:merge-source select="(4,10,2,8,6)">
        <xsl:merge-key select=". * 10" order="descending"/>
      </xsl:merge-source>
      <xsl:merge-source select="(5)">
        <xsl:merge-key select=". * 10"/>
      </xsl:merge-source>
      <xsl:merge-action>
        <xsl:value-of select="$g"/>
        <xsl:text>&#32;</xsl:text>
        <xsl:value-of select="$k"/>
        <xsl:text>&#10;</xsl:text>
      </xsl:merge-action>
    </xsl:merge>
  </xsl:template>
</xsl:transform>
```

GIVES

```
<?xml version="1.0" encoding="UTF-8"?>
    1 1
3 3
5 5
7 7
9 9
2 20
4 40
5 50
6 60
8 80
10 100
100 100
300 300
500 500
700 700
900 900
```

<xsl:merge-source> can have the following attributes:

- bind-source = *eqname*
- streamable = "yes" | "no"
- sort-before-merge = "yes" | "no"

<xsl:merge-key> can have the following attributes:

- lang = { *language* }
- order = { "ascending" | "descending" }
- collation = { *uri* }
- case-order = { "upper-first" | "lower-first" }
- data-type = { "text" | "number" | *eqname* }

6.5.5 Multiple Templates

<xsl:apply-templates>

```
<?xml version="1.0" encoding="UTF-8"?>
<Root>
  <Employee>
    <Name>Dash</Name>
    <Age>23</Age>
  </Employee>
  <Employee>
    <Name>Gwen</Name>
    <Age>22</Age>
  </Employee>
</Root>
```

```
<xsl:stylesheet version="1.0"
      xmlns:xsl="http://www.w3.org/1999/XSL/Transform">
  <xsl:output method="xml" indent="yes"/>
  <xsl:template match="/Root">
    <Root>
      <Employee>
        <Name>
          <xsl:apply-templates select="Employee/Name"/>
        </Name>
        <Age>
          <xsl:apply-templates select="Employee/Age"/>
        </Age>
      </Employee>
    </Root>
  </xsl:template>
  <xsl:template match="Name|Age">
    <xsl:value-of select="."/>
    <xsl:if test="position()!=last()">
      <xsl:text>,</xsl:text>
    </xsl:if>
  </xsl:template>
</xsl:stylesheet>
```

GIVES

```
<?xml version="1.0" encoding="UTF-8"?>
<Root>
  <Employee>
    <Name>Dash,Gwen</Name>
    <Age>23,22</Age>
  </Employee>
</Root>
```

The same result can be obtained in a simpler way by using <xsl:value-of separator="," select=...>.

<xsl:apply-templates> is similar to <xsl:value-of> in that it replaces itself with some data. Unlike <xsl:value-of> which copies data from an xpath in the context, <xsl:apply-templates> copies data from a matching template in the context.

The 'select' attribute of <xsl:apply-templates> is optional, in which case the context data is returned.

<xsl:apply-templates> can contain <xsl:sort> and <xsl:with-param> as its child elements. It can have the following attribute:

- mode = *token*

```
<?xml version="1.0" encoding="UTF-8"?>
<treeview>
  <treenode>
    <caption>Directory Z</caption>
    <nodes>
      <treenode><caption>File B</caption></treenode>
      <treenode><caption>File Z</caption></treenode>
      <treenode><caption>File A</caption></treenode>
    </nodes>
  </treenode>
  <treenode>
    <caption>Directory G</caption>
    <nodes>
      <treenode><caption>File F</caption></treenode>
      <treenode><caption>File O</caption></treenode>
      <treenode><caption>File B</caption></treenode>
    </nodes>
  </treenode>
</treeview>
```

```
<?xml version="1.0" encoding="UTF-8"?>
<xsl:stylesheet version="1.0"
      xmlns:xsl="http://www.w3.org/1999/XSL/Transform">
  <xsl:output method="xml" indent="yes" />
  <xsl:template match="/">
    <treeview>
      <xsl:apply-templates select="treeview/treenode">
        <xsl:sort select="caption" data-type="text"/>
      </xsl:apply-templates>
    </treeview>
  </xsl:template>
  <xsl:template match="treenode">
    <treenode>
      <xsl:copy-of select="caption"/>
      <nodes>
        <xsl:apply-templates select="nodes/treenode">
          <xsl:sort select="caption" data-type="text"/>
        </xsl:apply-templates>
      </nodes>
    </treenode>
  </xsl:template>
  <xsl:template match=
                    "/treeview/treenode/nodes/treenode">
    <xsl:copy-of select="."/>
  </xsl:template>
</xsl:stylesheet>
```

GIVES

```
<?xml version="1.0" encoding="UTF-8"?>
<treeview>
  <treenode>
    <caption>Directory G</caption>
    <nodes>
      <treenode>
        <caption>File B</caption>
      </treenode>
      <treenode>
        <caption>File F</caption>
      </treenode>
      <treenode>
        <caption>File O</caption>
      </treenode>
    </nodes>
  </treenode>
  <treenode>
    <caption>Directory Z</caption>
    <nodes>
```

```
      <treenode>
        <caption>File A</caption>
      </treenode>
      <treenode>
        <caption>File B</caption>
      </treenode>
      <treenode>
        <caption>File Z</caption>
      </treenode>
    </nodes>
  </treenode>
</treeview>
```

<xsl:next-match>

```
<?xml version="1.0" encoding="UTF-8"?>
<element bold="true"
         subscript="false"
         italic="true"
         text="stuff"/>
```

```
<?xml version="1.0" encoding="UTF-8"?>
<xsl:stylesheet version="3.0"
xmlns:xsl="http://www.w3.org/1999/XSL/Transform">
  <xsl:output method="xml" indent="yes"/>
  <xsl:template match="element" priority="1">
    <xsl:value-of select="@text" />
  </xsl:template>
  <xsl:template match="element[@italic = 'true']"
                priority="2">
    <sup><xsl:next-match/></sup>
  </xsl:template>
  <xsl:template match="element[@subscript = 'true']"
                priority="3">
    <sub><xsl:next-match/></sub>
  </xsl:template>
  <xsl:template match="element[@bold = 'true']"
                priority="4">
    <strong><xsl:next-match/></strong>
  </xsl:template>
</xsl:stylesheet>
```

GIVES

```
<?xml version="1.0" encoding="UTF-8"?>
<strong>
  <sup>stuff</sup>
</strong>
```

<xsl:next-match/> is similar to <xsl:apply-templates> in that it matches another template. However, unlike <xsl:apply-templates> which builds on the current context, <xsl:next-match/> resets the context and excludes itself from the next match. Note that it is always possible to create a recursive template.

<xsl:call-template>
<xsl:context-item>

```
<?xml version="1.0" encoding="UTF-8"?>
<a>
  <b>1<c/>a</b>
  <b>2<c/>b</b>
  <b>3<c/>c</b>
  <b>4<c/>d</b>
</a>
```

```
<?xml version="1.0" encoding="UTF-8"?>
<xsl:stylesheet version="3.0"
     xmlns:xsl="http://www.w3.org/1999/XSL/Transform"
     xmlns:xs="http://www.w3.org/2001/XMLSchema"
     xmlns:fn="http://www.w3.org/2005/xpath-functions">
  <xsl:template name="T">
    <xsl:context-item as="node()"/>
    <xsl:param name="P"/>
    <xsl:apply-templates select="b[position() lt 3]"/>
    <xsl:value-of select="$P"/>
  </xsl:template>
  <xsl:template match="a">
    <xsl:call-template name="T">
      <xsl:with-param name="P" select="'X'"/>
    </xsl:call-template>
  </xsl:template>
</xsl:stylesheet>
```

GIVES

```
<?xml version="1.0" encoding="UTF-8"?>1a2bX
```

<xsl:context-item> declares the required type of the context item when the containing template is called. It can exist as a child element to <xsl:mode> too. It can have the following attribute:

- use = "required" | "optional" | "prohibited"

6.5.6 Module Assembly

<xsl:package> <xsl:use-package>
<xsl:global-context-item> <xsl:expose>
<xsl:accept> <xsl:override>
<xsl:include> <xsl:import>
<xsl:apply-imports>

```
<?xml version="1.0"?>
<xsl:package name="P" version="9.0">
  <xsl:global-context-item as="item()" use="optional"
                           streamable="true" />
  <xsl:expose component="template" names="T1 T2"
              visibility="public"/>
  <xsl:use-package name="P2" version="10.0">
    <xsl:accept component="template" names="T1 T2"
                visibility="public"/>
    <xsl:override>
      <xsl:template match="object">
        <dummy/>
      </xsl:template>
    </xsl:override>
  </xsl:use-package>

  <xsl:stylesheet version="3.0"
       xmlns:xsl="http://www.w3.org/1999/XSL/Transform">
    <xsl:import href="a.xsl"/>
    <xsl:include href="b.xsl"
      use-when="system-property('xsl:vendor')='vendorX'"/>
    <xsl:template match="person">
      <override>
        <xsl:apply-imports/>
      </override>
    </xsl:template>
    <xsl:template match="animal">
      <override>
        <xsl:next-match/>
      </override>
    </xsl:template>
  </xsl:stylesheet>
</xsl:package>
```

A package is made up of one or more stylesheet modules.

'XSLT provides two mechanisms to construct a stylesheet from multiple stylesheet modules:

- an inclusion mechanism that allows stylesheet modules to be combined without changing the semantics of the modules being combined, and
- an import mechanism that allows stylesheet modules to override each other.' Template rules and declarations in the importing module take precedence over those in the imported module.

'A template rule that is being used to override another template rule can use the <xsl:apply-imports> or <xsl:next-match> instruction to invoke the overridden template rule. The <xsl:apply-imports> instruction only considers template rules in imported stylesheet modules; the <xsl:next-match> instruction considers all other template rules of lower import precedence and/or priority, and also declarations of the same precedence and priority that appear earlier in declaration order.'

<xsl:apply-imports> can have <xsl:with-param> as its child element. <xsl:next-match> can have <xsl:with-param> and <xsl:fallback> as its child elements.

<xsl:package> can have the following attributes:

- name = *uri*
- package-version = *string*
- version = *decimal*

- input-type-annotations = "preserve" | "strip" | "unspecified"
- default-mode = *eqname* | "#unnamed"
- default-validation = "preserve" | "strip"
- default-collation = *uris*
- extension-element-prefixes = *prefixes*
- exclude-result-prefixes = *prefixes*
- expand-text = "yes" | "no"
- use-when = *expression*
- xpath-default-namespace = *uri*

The 'component' attribute can have these values: "template", "function", "accumulator", "attribute-set", "variable", "mode".

The 'visibility' attribute can have these values: "public", "private", "final", "abstract", "hidden", "absent".

<xsl:override> can contain the following child elements: <xsl:template>, <xsl:function>, <xsl:accumulator>, <xsl:variable>, <xsl:param>, <xsl:attribute-set>.

6.5.7 Declarations

This subsection describes the declarations that may appear at the start of a stylesheet.

<xsl:preserves-space> <xsl:strip-space>

```
<?xml version="1.0" encoding="UTF-8"?>
<root>
  <a>   <e/>   </a>
  <b>   <e/>   </b>
  <c>   <e/>   </c>
</root>
```

```
<?xml version="1.0"?>
<xsl:stylesheet version="3.0"
       xmlns:xsl="http://www.w3.org/1999/XSL/Transform">
  <xsl:preserve-space elements="a c"/>
  <xsl:strip-space elements="b"/>
  <xsl:template match="root">
    <xsl:text>&#10;</xsl:text>
    <xsl:copy-of select="a,b,c"/>
    <xsl:text>&#10;</xsl:text>
    <d xml:space="preserve">   <e/>   </d>
    <f>   <g/>   </f>
  </xsl:template>
</xsl:stylesheet>
```

GIVES

```
<?xml version="1.0" encoding="UTF-8"?>
<a>   <e/>   </a><b><e/></b><c>   <e/>   </c>
<d xml:space="preserve">   <e/>   </d><f><g/></f>
```

<xsl:decimal-format>

```
<?xml version="1.0"?>
<?xml-stylesheet type="text/xsl" href="decimalformat.xsl"?>
<xsl:stylesheet version="1.0"
      xmlns:xsl="http://www.w3.org/1999/XSL/Transform" >
  <xsl:decimal-format name="df"
                     decimal-separator="."
                     grouping-separator=","
                     infinity="INFINITY"
                     NaN="Not a Number"
                     minus-sign="-"
                     percent="%"
                     per-mille="m"
                     zero-digit="0"
                     digit="#"
                     pattern-separator=";" />
  <xsl:template match="/">
    <xsl:value-of
      select="format-number(1 div 0, '###,###.00', 'df')"/>
  </xsl:template>
</xsl:stylesheet>
```

GIVES

```
<?xml version="1.0" encoding="UTF-8"?>INFINITY
```

<xsl:namespace-alias> <xsl:mode> <xsl:attribute-set> <xsl:key> <xsl:character-map> <xsl:output-character>

```
<?xml version="1.0" encoding="UTF-8"?>
<r att="hello">
  <a att="one_hundred">100</a>
  <a att="two_hundred">200</a>
  <b att="three_hundred">300</b>
</r>
```

```
<xsl:stylesheet version="3.0"
    xmlns:xsl="http://www.w3.org/1999/XSL/Transform"
    xmlns:fo="http://www.w3.org/1999/XSL/Format"
    xmlns:x="http://www.w3.org/1999/XSL/Transform">
  <xsl:namespace-alias
                 stylesheet-prefix="x" result-prefix="xsl"/>
  <xsl:mode on-multiple-match="use-last"/>
  <xsl:attribute-set name="aGrp">
    <xsl:attribute name="a1" select="1"/>
    <xsl:attribute name="a2" select="2"/>
    <xsl:attribute name="a3" select="3"/>
  </xsl:attribute-set>
  <xsl:character-map name="cm">
    <xsl:output-character character="«" string="[[["/>
    <xsl:output-character character="»" string="]]]"/>
    <xsl:output-character character="§" string='"'/>
  </xsl:character-map>
  <xsl:output use-character-maps="cm" />
  <xsl:key name="k" match="a" use="@att"/>
  <xsl:key name="k" match="b" use="@att"/>

  <xsl:template match="r">
    This will not be printed because of the mode set.
  </xsl:template>
  <xsl:template match="r">
    <xsl:text>&#10;1</xsl:text>
    <fo:block xsl:use-attribute-sets="aGrp"/>
    <x:text>&#10;2</x:text>
    <xsl:copy-of select="key('k',a/@att)"/>
    <x:text>&#10;3</x:text>
    <xsl:copy-of select="key('k',b/@att)"/>
    <x:text>&#10;4</x:text>
    <xsl:copy-of select="key('k',a)"/>
    <x:text>&#10;5</x:text>
    «<dummy att='§'/>»
  </xsl:template>
</xsl:stylesheet>
```

GIVES

```
<?xml version="1.0" encoding="UTF-8"?>
1<fo:block xmlns:fo="http://www.w3.org/1999/XSL/Format"
a1="1" a2="2" a3="3"/>
2<a att="one_hundred">100</a><a
att="two_hundred">200</a>
3<b att="three_hundred">300</b>
4
5
[[[<dummy xmlns:fo="http://www.w3.org/1999/XSL/Format"
att='"'/>]]]
```

<xsl:mode> can have the following attributes:

- name = *eqname*
- streamable = "yes" | "no"
- on-no-match = "deep-copy" | "shallow-copy" | "deep- skip" | "shallow-skip" | "text-only-copy" | "fail"
- on-multiple-match = "use-last" | "fail"
- warning-on-no-match = "yes" | "no"
- warning-on-multiple-match = "yes" | "no"
- typed = "yes" | "no" | "strict" | "lax" | "unspecified"
- visibility = "public" | "private" | "final"

<xsl:character-map> can have the following attribute:

- use-character-maps = *eqnames*

<xsl:key> can have the following attributes:

- composite = "yes" | "no"
- collation = *uri*

6.5.8 Analysis

<xsl:analyze-string> <xsl:matching-substring> <xsl:non-matching-substring> <xsl:fallback>

```
<xsl:stylesheet version="3.0"
    xmlns:xsl="http://www.w3.org/1999/XSL/Transform">
  <xsl:template match="/">
    <xsl:analyze-string select="'abcdef'" regex="^(a.)(..)"
                                          flags="msix">
      <xsl:matching-substring>
        <xsl:value-of select="regex-group(2)"/>
      </xsl:matching-substring>
      <xsl:non-matching-substring>
        (<xsl:value-of select="."/>)
      </xsl:non-matching-substring>
      <xsl:fallback>
        Your processor does not support this feature.
      </xsl:fallback>
    </xsl:analyze-string>
  </xsl:template>
</xsl:stylesheet>
```

GIVES

```
<?xml version="1.0" encoding="UTF-8"?>cd
        (ef)
```

<xsl:assert> <xsl:evaluate>

```
<xsl:stylesheet version="3.0"
    xmlns:xsl="http://www.w3.org/1999/XSL/Transform">
  <xsl:template match="/">
    <xsl:assert test="101 ge 100">
      Is smaller than 100.
    </xsl:assert>
    <xsl:message select="10 ge 10">
      Is greater than or equals 10
    </xsl:message>
    <xsl:evaluate xpath="(1 to 3)!(.*.)"/>
  </xsl:template>
</xsl:stylesheet>
```

GIVES

(The processor reports 'Is greater than or equals 10'.)

<xsl:assert> can have the following attributes:

- select = *expression*
- error-code = { *eqname* }

<xsl:message> can have the following attributes:

- terminate = { "yes" | "no" }
- error-code = { *eqname* }

<xsl:evaluate> can have the following attributes:

- as = *sequence-type*
- base-uri = { *uri* }
- with-params = *expression*
- context-item = *expression*
- namespace-context = *expression*
- schema-aware = { "yes" | "no" }

6.5.9 Streaming, Accumulators and Maps

Streaming refers to the process by which an XML document is read on-the-fly, without loading the whole document in memory. The process can be 'forked' so that more than one computations happen during the same pass, effectively in parallel.

An accumulator allows you to define processing that occurs effectively as a side-effect of reading the document. It allows a value to be computed progressively during streamed processing of a document, and accessed as a function of a node in the document, without compromise to the functional nature of the XSLT language.

<xsl:stream> <xsl:fork>

```
<?xml version="1.0"?>
<xsl:stylesheet version="3.0"
      xmlns:xsl="http://www.w3.org/1999/XSL/Transform">
  <xsl:template match="/">
    <xsl:stream href="in.xml">
      <xsl:fork>
        <xsl:sequence>
          <min><xsl:value-of
                  select="min(//employee/@salary)"/>
          </min>
        </xsl:sequence>
        <xsl:sequence>
          <max><xsl:value-of
                  select="max(//employee/@salary)"/>
          </max>
        </xsl:sequence>
      </xsl:fork>
    </xsl:stream>
  </xsl:template>
</xsl:stylesheet>
```

<xsl:stream> can have the following attributes:

- validation = "strict" | "lax" | "preserve" | "strip"
- type = *eqname*

<xsl:accumulator> <xsl:accumulator-rule>

```
<?xml version="1.0" encoding="UTF-8"?>
<book>
  <chapter>
    <figure/>
    <figure/>
    <figure/>
  </chapter>
  <chapter>
    <figure/>
    <figure/>
    <figure/>
  </chapter>
  <chapter>
    <figure/>
    <figure/>
    <figure/>
  </chapter>
</book>
```

```
<?xml version="1.0" encoding="UTF-8"?>
<xsl:stylesheet version="3.0"
      xmlns:xsl="http://www.w3.org/1999/XSL/Transform">
  <xsl:accumulator name="figNum" as="xs:integer"
                initial-value="0" streamable="yes">
    <xsl:accumulator-rule match="chapter" select="0"/>
    <xsl:accumulator-rule match="figure"
                            select="$value+1"/>
  </xsl:accumulator>
  <xsl:mode streamable="yes"/>

  <xsl:template match="book">
   <xsl:apply-templates/>
   <p>Figure
      <xsl:value-of select="accumulator-before('figNum')"/ >
   </p>
  </xsl:template>
</xsl:stylesheet>
```

```
<?xml version="1.0" encoding="UTF-8"?>

    <p>Figure 1</p>
    <p>Figure 2</p>
    <p>Figure 3</p>

    <p>Figure 1</p>
    <p>Figure 2</p>
    <p>Figure 3</p>

    <p>Figure 1</p>
    <p>Figure 2</p>
    <p>Figure 3</p>
```

Note the special variable $value within the accumulator context.

<xsl:accumulator> can have the following attributes:

- as = *sequence-type*
- visibility = "public" | "private" | "final" | "abstract"
- streamable = "yes" | "no"

<xsl:accumulator-rule> can have the following attribute:

- phase = "start" | "end"

To retrieve the value of the accumulator, use accumulator-before() or accumulator-after(), which respectively gets the value before or after visiting the descendent nodes.

Streaming use cases motivate the introduction of maps into XSLT, because its flexible structure allows data to be stored temporarily. Note that at the time of writing, it has been proposed that the map construct, along with the related functions, be incorporated into XPath instead.

<xsl:map> <xsl:map-entry>

```
<xsl:stylesheet version="3.0"
    xmlns:xsl="http://www.w3.org/1999/XSL/Transform"
    xmlns:xs="http://www.w3.org/2001/XMLSchema"
    xmlns:map=
            "http://www.w3.org/2005/xpath-functions/map">
  <xsl:variable name="m1" as="map(*)"
                      select="map{0:'hello',1:'world'}"/>
  <xsl:variable name="m2" as="map(xs:string, xs:string)">
    <xsl:map>
      <xsl:map-entry key="'Mo'" select="'Monday'"/>
      <xsl:map-entry key="'Tu'" select="'Tuesday'"/>
      <xsl:map-entry key="'We'" select="'Wednesday'"/>
      <xsl:map-entry key="'Th'" select="'Thursday'"/>
      <xsl:map-entry key="'Fr'" select="'Friday'"/>
      <xsl:map-entry key="'Sa'" select="'Saturday'"/>
      <xsl:map-entry key="'Su'" select="'Sunday'"/>
    </xsl:map>
  </xsl:variable>
  <xsl:variable name="m3" select="map:merge($m2)" />
  <xsl:variable name="m4" select="map:merge(
                              (map:entry($m2,'Mo'),
                               map:entry($m2,'Mo')))" />
  <xsl:variable name="m5" select=
                              "map:remove($m2,'Su')"/>
  <xsl:variable name="m6" select="map:merge(
            map:for-each($m1,
            function($k,$v){map:entry($k, $v+1)}))"/>

  <xsl:template match="/">
    <xsl:value-of select="$m1(0)"/>
    <xsl:value-of select="$m2('Mo')"/>
    <xsl:value-of select="map:keys($m2)"/>
    <xsl:value-of select="map:contains($m2,'Mo')"/>
    <xsl:value-of select="map:get($m2,'Mo')"/>
    <xsl:value-of select="deep-equal($m2,$m3)"/>
    <xsl:value-of select="deep-equal(/. , /)"/>
    <xsl:value-of select="
       let $C:='http://www.w3.org/2005/xpath-functions/
            collations/UCA?strength=primary'
       return map:merge((map{collation-key('A', $C):1},
                       map{collation-key('a', $C):2}))
                       (collation-key('A', $C)) "/>
  </xsl:template>
</xsl:stylesheet>
```

```
<?xml version="1.0" encoding="UTF-8"?>
helloMondayFr Mo Sa Su Th Tu WetrueMondaytruetrue2
```

The values in a map can be nodes and functions. You can also, for instance, use <xsl:for-each> to list the <xsl:map-entry> elements within <xsl:map>.

6.5.10 Other Built-in Functions

document() json-to-xml() xml-to-json()

```
<xsl:value-of select="document('zoo.xml')"/>
```

IS THE SAME AS

```
<xsl:value-of select="doc('zoo.xml')"/>
```

```
json-to-xml('{"x": 1, "y": [3,4,5]}')
```

GIVES

```
<map xmlns="http://www.w3.org/2013/XSL/json">
  <number key="x">1</number>
  <array key="y">
    <number>3</number>
    <number>4</number>
    <number>5</number>
  </array>
</map>
```

```
xml-to-json($input as node()) as xs:string

xml-to-json($input    as node(),
            $options as map(*)) as xs:string
```

element-available()
function-available()
type-available()

```
<?xml version="1.0" encoding="UTF-8"?>
<xsl:stylesheet version="3.0"
        xmlns:xsl="http://www.w3.org/1999/XSL/Transform"
        xmlns:xs="http://www.w3.org/2001/XMLSchema" >
  <xsl:template match="/">
    <xsl:value-of select="element-available('xsl:for-each')"/>
    <xsl:value-of select="function-available('substring')"/>
    <xsl:value-of select="type-available('xs:string')"/>
  </xsl:template>
</xsl:stylesheet>
```

```
<?xml version="1.0" encoding="UTF-8"?>truetruetrue
```

current() system-property()
unparsed-entity-public-id() unparsed-entity-uri()

```
<xsl:apply-templates
        select="//glossary/entry[@name=current()/@ref]"/>
```

IS DIFFERENT FROM

```
<xsl:apply-templates
        select="//glossary/entry[@name=./@ref]"/>
```

In the upper case, current() refers to the current context item. In the lower case, the dot operator './' is optional, and the @ref attribute belongs to the 'entry' elements.

system-property($property) returns the value of a system property. $property can be:

- 'xsl:version'
- 'xsl:vendor'
- 'xsl:vendor-url'
- 'xsl:product-name'
- 'xsl:product-version'
- 'xsl:is-schema-aware'
- 'xsl:supports-serialization'
- 'xsl:supports-backwards-compatibility'
- 'xsl:supports-namespace-axis'
- 'xsl:supports-streaming'
- 'xsl:supports-dynamic-evaluation'

unparsed-entity-public-id($entity) returns the public identifier of an unparsed entity identified by the string $entity.

unparsed-entity-uri($entity) returns the URI (system identifier) of an unparsed entity identified by the string $entity.
snapshot($nodes) returns a copy of a node together with its ancestors and descendants and their attributes and namespaces.

6.6 JavaScript Integration

JavaScript treats an XML document as a DOM tree. For a reference on how to manipulate the XML nodes, refer to Chapter 3.

6.6.1 Document Loading with AJAX

For security reasons, both the HTML file and the XML file must be located in the same server. Note that the use of 'innerHTML' is permitted in some browsers, even though it is really XML. If it doesn't work, use .childNodes[i].nodeValue or XMLSerializer.

```
<?xml version="1.0" encoding="UTF-8" ?>
<a>
  <b>Hello <c/> <d>World</d></b>
  <b>!</b>
</a>
```

```
<!DOCTYPE html>
<html>
<head>
  <script>
    function loadXMLDoc(file){
      xhr=new XMLHttpRequest();
      xhr.open("GET",file,false);
      xhr.send();
      return xhr.responseXML;
    }
    XML = loadXMLDoc("a.xml");
    b = XML.getElementsByTagName("b")[0];
    document.write(b.innerHTML+"<br/>");
    bc= b.childNodes;
    for (i=0; i<bc.length; i++){
      if (bc.item(i).nodeType==1)
        document.write(bc.item(i).nodeName);
    }
    b.setAttribute("id","10");
    document.write("<br/>"+
                        b.getAttributeNode("id").textContent);
  </script>
</head>
<body></body>
</html>
```

Hello World
cd
10

6.6.2 String Loading with DOMParser

Using the <xml> tag implicitly displays the XML data in the browser.

```
<!DOCTYPE html>
<html>
<head>
  <script id="x1" type="text/xmldata">
    <a><b>Hello <c/> <d>World</d></b>
      <b>!</b></a>
  </script>
  <xml id="x2">
    <a><b>Hello <c/> <d>World</d></b>
      <b>!</b></a>
  </xml>
  <script>
    Xstring = document.getElementById("x1").innerHTML;
    parser=new DOMParser();
    XML=parser.parseFromString(Xstring,"text/xml");

    b2=XML.createElement("b");
    b2.textContent="Hello Earth!";
    root=XML.getElementsByTagName("a")[0];
    root.appendChild(b2);

    serializer=new XMLSerializer();
    alert(serializer.serializeToString(root));
  </script>
</head>
<body></body>
</html>
```

Hello World !

The page at binarybehemoth.com says:

<a><b>Hello <c/> <d>World</d></b>
<b>!</b><b>Hello Earth!</b></a>

OK

6.6.3 XQuery with XQIB

XQuery In the Browser is a JavaScript library which can be found at http://www.xqib.org/. At the time of writing, XQIB supports XQUF fully and XQFT partially.

The prefix b: is special in XQIB.

```
<!DOCTYPE html>
<html xmlns="http://www.w3.org/1999/xhtml">
  <head>
    <title>XQIB: Sample page</title>
    <meta charset="UTF-8"/>
    <script type="text/javascript"
          src="mxqueryjs/mxqueryjs.nocache.js"></script>
    <script type="application/xquery">
     declare updating function local:onclick($loc, $evtObj) {
       insert node <hr color="red"/>
         as last into b:dom()//body
     };
     b:addEventListener
       (b:dom()//input, "onclick", local:onclick#2)
    </script>
  </head>
  <body>
    <h1>Insert example</h1>
    <input type="button" value="Click to add a line!"/>
  </body>
</html>
```

(Courtesy of http://www.xqib.org/js/Update.html)

6.6.4 XSLT

At the time of writing, the browsers support XSLT 1.0. If you wish to use a higher version of XSLT, consider Saxon CE, which is available at:

http://www.saxonica.com/ce/index.xml

```
<?xml version="1.0" encoding="UTF-8" ?>
<!-- people.xml -->
<people>
  <person>
    <name>Eric Lee</name>
    <gender>m</gender>
    <age>35</age>
  </person>
  <person>
    <name>Serena</name>
    <gender>f</gender>
    <age>25</age>
  </person>
</people>
```

```
<?xml version="1.0" encoding="UTF-8"?>
<!-- people.xslt -->
<xsl:stylesheet version="3.0"
      xmlns:xsl="http://www.w3.org/1999/XSL/Transform">
  <xsl:output method="html" version="5.0"
            encoding="UTF-8" indent="yes"/>
  <xsl:template match="people">
    <table border="1">
    <xsl:for-each select="person">
      <tr>
        <td><xsl:value-of select="name"/></td>
        <td><xsl:value-of select="gender"/></td>
        <td><xsl:value-of select="age"/></td>
      </tr>
    </xsl:for-each>
    </table>
  </xsl:template>
</xsl:stylesheet>
```

```
<!DOCTYPE html>
<html>
<head></head>
<body></body>
  <script>
    function loadXMLDoc(file){
      xhr=new XMLHttpRequest();
      xhr.open("GET",file,false);
      xhr.responseType ='msxml-document';
      xhr.send();
      return xhr.responseXML;
    }
    XML  = loadXMLDoc("people.xml");
    XSLT = loadXMLDoc("people.xslt");

    // code for IE
    if (window.ActiveXObject || "ActiveXObject" in window ){
      newXML = XML.transformNode(XSLT);
      document.getElementsByTagName("body")[0].
                                    innerHTML = newXML;
    } // code for Chrome, Firefox, Opera, etc.
    else if (document.implementation &&
           document.implementation.createDocument){
      xsltProcessor = new XSLTProcessor();
      xsltProcessor.importStylesheet(XSLT);
      newXML =
        xsltProcessor.transformToFragment(XML, document);
      document.getElementsByTagName("body")[0].
                                    appendChild(newXML);
    }
  </script>
</html>
```

Eric Lee	m	35
Serena	f	25

6.6.5 jQuery

Most of the traversing and manipulation methods provided by jQuery will work with XML documents.

```
<!doctype html>
<html lang="en">
<head>
  <meta charset="utf-8">
  <title>jQuery.parseXML demo</title>
  <script src= "//code.jquery.com/jquery-2.1.1.min.js">
   </script>
</head>
<body>

<p id="someElement"></p>
<p id="anotherElement"></p>

<script>
var xml = "<rss version='2.0'><channel><title>RSS
Title</title></channel></rss>",
  xmlDoc = $.parseXML( xml ),
  $xml = $( xmlDoc ),
  $title = $xml.find( "title" );

// Append "RSS Title" to #someElement
$( "#someElement" ).append( $title.text() );

// Change the title to "XML Title"
$title.text( "XML Title" );

// Append "XML Title" to #anotherElement
$( "#anotherElement" ).append( $title.text() );
</script>

</body>
</html>
```

RSS Title
XML Title

(Courtesy of http://api.jquery.com/jQuery.parseXML/)

6.7 PHP Integration

Here we focus on DOM. There are several other PHP libraries that implement XML such as SimpleXML and XMLReader. If you wish to use XQuery in PHP, consider Zorba.

6.7.1 DOM Reference

DOMNode

```
readonly string $nodeName ;
string $nodeValue ;
readonly int $nodeType ;
readonly DOMNode $parentNode ;
readonly DOMNodeList $childNodes ;
readonly DOMNode $firstChild ;
readonly DOMNode $lastChild ;
readonly DOMNode $previousSibling ;
readonly DOMNode $nextSibling ;
readonly DOMNamedNodeMap $attributes ;
readonly DOMDocument $ownerDocument ;
readonly string $namespaceURI ;
string $prefix ;
readonly string $localName ;
readonly string $baseURI ;
readonly string $textContent ;
```

```
DOMNode appendChild ( DOMNode $newnode )
string C14N ([ bool $exclusive [, bool $with_comments
                [, array $xpath [, array$ns_prefixes ]]]] )
int C14NFile ( string $uri [, bool $exclusive
                [, bool $with_comments [, array $xpath
                [, array $ns_prefixes ]]]] )
```

```
DOMNode cloneNode ([ bool $deep ] )
int getLineNo ( void )
string getNodePath ( void )
bool hasAttributes ( void )
bool hasChildNodes ( void )
DOMNode insertBefore ( DOMNode $newnode
                       [, DOMNode $refnode ] )
bool isDefaultNamespace ( string $namespaceURI )
bool isSameNode ( DOMNode $node )
bool isSupported ( string $feature , string $version )
string lookupNamespaceURI ( string $prefix )
string lookupPrefix ( string $namespaceURI )
void normalize ( void )
DOMNode removeChild ( DOMNode $oldnode )
DOMNode replaceChild ( DOMNode $newnode ,
                       DOMNode $oldnode )
```

DOMDocument extends DOMNode

```
readonly string $actualEncoding ;
readonly DOMConfiguration $config ;
readonly DOMDocumentType $doctype ;
readonly DOMElement $documentElement ;
string $documentURI ;
string $encoding ;
bool $formatOutput ;
readonly DOMImplementation $implementation ;
bool $preserveWhiteSpace = true ;
bool $recover ;
bool $resolveExternals ;
bool $standalone ;
bool $strictErrorChecking = true ;
bool $substituteEntities ;
bool $validateOnParse = false ;
string $version ;
readonly string $xmlEncoding ;
bool $xmlStandalone ;
string $xmlVersion ;
```

```
__construct ([ string $version [, string $encoding ]] )
DOMAttr createAttribute ( string $name )
DOMAttr createAttributeNS ( string $namespaceURI ,
                            string $qualifiedName )
DOMCDATASection createCDATASection ( string $data )
DOMComment createComment ( string $data )
DOMDocumentFragment createDocumentFragment ( void )
DOMElement createElement ( string $name [, string $value ] )
DOMElement createElementNS ( string $namespaceURI ,
                 string $qualifiedName [, string$value ] )
DOMEntityReference createEntityReference ( string $name )
DOMProcessingInstruction createProcessingInstruction (
                          string $target [, string $data] )
DOMText createTextNode ( string $content )
DOMElement getElementById ( string $elementId )
DOMNodeList getElementsByTagName ( string $name )
DOMNodeList getElementsByTagNameNS (
              string $namespaceURI , string $localName )
DOMNode importNode ( DOMNode $importedNode
                     [, bool $deep ] )
mixed load ( string $filename [, int $options = 0 ] )
bool loadHTML ( string $source [, int $options = 0 ] )
bool loadHTMLFile ( string $filename [, int $options = 0 ] )
mixed loadXML ( string $source [, int $options = 0 ] )
void normalizeDocument ( void )
bool registerNodeClass ( string $baseclass ,
                         string $extendedclass )
bool relaxNGValidate ( string $filename )
bool relaxNGValidateSource ( string $source )
int save ( string $filename [, int $options ] )
string saveHTML ([ DOMNode $node = NULL ] )
int saveHTMLFile ( string $filename )
string saveXML ([ DOMNode $node [, int $options ]] )
bool schemaValidate ( string $filename [, int $flags ] )
bool schemaValidateSource ( string $source [, int $flags ] )
bool validate ( void )
int xinclude ([ int $options ] )
```

For the saving functions, only LIBXML_NOEMPTYTAG is supported for $options. For the loading functions and xinclude(), $options is any combination of

LIBXML_COMPACT	LIBXML_NOXMLDECL
LIBXML_DTDATTR	LIBXML_NSCLEAN
LIBXML_DTDLOAD	LIBXML_PARSEHUGE
LIBXML_DTDVALID	LIBXML_PEDANTIC
LIBXML_HTML_NOIMPLIED	LIBXML_XINCLUDE
LIBXML_HTML_NODEFDTD	LIBXML_ERR_ERROR
LIBXML_NOBLANKS	LIBXML_ERR_FATAL
LIBXML_NOCDATA	LIBXML_ERR_NONE
LIBXML_NOEMPTYTAG	LIBXML_ERR_WARNING
LIBXML_NOENT	LIBXML_VERSION
LIBXML_NOERROR	LIBXML_DOTTED_VERSION
LIBXML_NONET	LIBXML_SCHEMA_CREATE
LIBXML_NOWARNING	

(http://php.net/manual/en/libxml.constants.php)

loadXML(), loadHTML(), saveXML(), saveHTML(), relaxNGValidateSource(), schemaValidateSource() deal with a string.

DOMElement extends DOMNode

```
readonly bool $schemaTypeInfo ;
readonly string $tagName ;
```

```
__construct ( string $name
              [, string $value [, string $namespaceURI ]] )
string getAttribute ( string $name )
DOMAttr getAttributeNode ( string $name )
DOMAttr getAttributeNodeNS ( string $namespaceURI ,
                             string $localName )
string getAttributeNS ( string $namespaceURI ,
                        string $localName )
DOMNodeList getElementsByTagName ( string $name )
DOMNodeList getElementsByTagNameNS (
              string $namespaceURI , string $localName )
bool hasAttribute ( string $name )
bool hasAttributeNS ( string $namespaceURI ,
                      string $localName )
bool removeAttribute ( string $name )
bool removeAttributeNode ( DOMAttr $oldnode )
bool removeAttributeNS ( string $namespaceURI ,
                         string $localName )
DOMAttr setAttribute ( string $name , string $value )
DOMAttr setAttributeNode ( DOMAttr $attr )
DOMAttr setAttributeNodeNS ( DOMAttr $attr )
void setAttributeNS ( string $namespaceURI ,
                      string $qualifiedName , string $value )
void setIdAttribute ( string $name , bool $isId )
void setIdAttributeNode ( DOMAttr $attr , bool $isId )
void setIdAttributeNS ( string $namespaceURI ,
                        string $localName , bool $isId )
```

DOMAttr extends DOMNode

```
readonly string $name ;
readonly DOMElement $ownerElement ;
readonly bool $schemaTypeInfo ;
readonly bool $specified ;
string $value ;
```

```
__construct ( string $name [, string $value ] )
bool isId ( void )
```

DOMDocumentFragment extends DOMNode

```
bool appendXML ( string $data )
```

DOMDocumentType extends DOMNode
readonly string *$Id* ;
readonly string *$systemId* ;
readonly string *$name* ;
readonly DOMNamedNodeMap *$entities* ;
readonly DOMNamedNodeMap *$notations* ;
readonly string *$internalSubset* ;

DOMNotation extends DOMNode
readonly string *$Id* ;
readonly string *$systemId* ;

DOMEntity extends DOMNode
readonly string *$Id* ;
readonly string *$systemId* ;
readonly string *$notationName* ;
string *$actualEncoding* ;
readonly string *$encoding* ;
readonly string *$version* ;

DOMEntityReference extends DOMNode
__construct (string $name)

DOMProcessingInstruction extends DOMNode
readonly string *$target* ;
string *$data* ;
__construct (string $name [, string $value])

DOMCharacterData extends DOMNode
string *$data* ;
readonly int *$length* ;
void appendData (string $data)
void deleteData (int $offset , int $count)
void insertData (int $offset , string $data)
void replaceData (int $offset , int $count , string $data)
string substringData (int $offset , int $count)

DOMComment extends DOMCharacterData
__construct ([string $value])

DOMText extends DOMCharacterData
readonly string *$wholeText* ;
__construct ([string $value])
bool isWhitespaceInElementContent (void)
DOMText splitText (int $offset)

DOMCdataSection extends DOMText
__construct (string $value)

DOMNamedNodeMap implements Traversable
readonly int *$length* ;
DOMNode getNamedItem (string $name)
DOMNode getNamedItemNS (string $namespaceURI , string $localName)
DOMNode item (int $index)

DOMNodeList implements Traversable
readonly int *$length* ;
DOMNode DOMNodelist::item (int $index)

DOMException extends Exception
readonly int *$code* ;

```
DOMImplementation
__construct ( void )
DOMDocument createDocument (
                    [ string $namespaceURI = NULL
                    [, string $qualifiedName =NULL
                    [, DOMDocumentType $doctype = NULL ]]] )
DOMDocumentType createDocumentType (
                    [ string $qualifiedName = NULL
                    [, string$Id = NULL
                    [, string $systemId = NULL ]]] )
bool hasFeature ( string $feature , string $version )
```

6.7.2 Reading

```
<?xml version="1.0" encoding="UTF-8" ?>
<!-- people.xml -->
<people xmlns:xi="http://www.w3.org/2003/XInclude">
  <xi:include href="people2.xml" parse="xml">
    <xi:fallback>
    <error>xinclude: people2.xml not found</error>
    </xi:fallback>
  </xi:include>

  <person id="p3">
    <name>Eric Lee</name>
    <gender>m</gender>
    <age>35</age>
  </person>
  <person id="p4">
    <name>Serena</name>
    <gender>f</gender>
    <age>25</age>
  </person>
</people>
```

```
<?xml version="1.0" encoding="UTF-8" ?>
<!-- people2.xml -->
<people>
  <person id="p1">
    <name>Alexander Mike</name>
    <gender>m</gender>
    <age>40</age>
  </person>
  <person id="p2">
    <name>Celeste</name>
    <gender>f</gender>
    <age>15</age>
  </person>
</people>
```

```
<!DOCTYPE html>
```

```
<html><head></head><body><?php
$doc = new DOMDocument();
$doc->load('people.xml');
$doc->xinclude();
$persons = $doc->getElementsByTagName('person');
foreach ($persons as $person){
  $v = $person->getElementsByTagName('*');
  for ($i=0; $i<$v->length; $i++){
    echo $v->item($i)->nodeValue.",";
  }
  echo $person->attributes->getNamedItem('id')->value;
  echo "<br/>";
}
?><body></html>
```

```
Alexander Mike,m,40,p1
Celeste,f,15,p2
Eric Lee,m,35,p3
Serena,f,25,p4
```

6.7.3 Writing

```
<!DOCTYPE html>
<html><head></head><body><?php

$doc = new DOMDocument("1.0","UTF-8");
$comment=$doc->createComment("This is 'book.xml'.");
$doc->appendChild($comment);
$book=$doc->createElement("book");
$doc->appendChild($book);

$part1 = new DOMElement("part");
$book->appendChild($part1);
$part1->setAttribute("title","Core");
$part1->setIdAttribute("title",true);

$chapters = ["HTML","CSS","JavaScript","PHP","SQL","XML"];
foreach ($chapters as $chapter){
  $c = new DOMElement("chapter",$chapter);
  $part1->appendChild($c);
}
$doc->save("book.xml");

?><body></html>
```

```
<!-- This is 'book.xml'. -->
▼<book>
  ▼<part title="Core">
      <chapter>HTML</chapter>
      <chapter>CSS</chapter>
      <chapter>JavaScript</chapter>
      <chapter>PHP</chapter>
      <chapter>SQL</chapter>
      <chapter>XML</chapter>
    </part>
  </book>
```

6.7.4 Validation

relaxNG and XSD are the supported schema languages. relaxNG Compact is not supported.

```
<!DOCTYPE html>
<html><head></head><body><?php
$doc = new DOMDocument();
$doc->load('zoo.xml');
$doc->relaxNGValidate('zoo.rng');
$doc->schemaValidate('zoo.xsd');
?><body></html>
```

Warning: DOMDocument::relaxNGValidate(): Expecting no namespace for element zoo in **C:\Program Files\Zend\Apache2\htdocs\xml\zoo.php** on line **5**

Warning: DOMDocument::schemaValidate(): Element '{http://www.w3.org/2001/XMLSchema}complexType': The content is not valid. Expected is (annotation?, (simpleContent | complexContent | ((group | all | choice | sequence)?, ((attribute | attributeGroup)*, anyAttribute?)))). in **C:\Program Files\Zend\Apache2\htdocs\xml\zoo.php** on line **6**

Warning: DOMDocument::schemaValidate(): Invalid Schema in **C:\Program Files\Zend\Apache2\htdocs\xml\zoo.php** on line **6**

6.7.5 XPath

DOMXPath
DOMDocument *$document* ;
__construct (DOMDocument $doc) mixed evaluate (string $expression [, DOMNode $contextnode [, bool $registerNodeNS = true]]) DOMNodeList query (string $expression [, DOMNode $contextnode [, bool$registerNodeNS = true]]) bool registerNamespace (string $prefix , string $namespaceURI) void registerPhpFunctions ([mixed $restrict])

```
<?xml version="1.0" encoding="UTF-8" ?>
<!-- people.xml -->
<people>
  <person id="p3">
    <name>Eric Lee</name>
    <gender>m</gender>
    <age>35</age>
  </person>
  <person id="p4">
    <name>Serena</name>
    <gender>f</gender>
    <age>25</age>
  </person>
</people>
```

```
<!DOCTYPE html>
<html><head></head><body><?php
$doc = new DOMDocument();
$doc->load('people.xml');
$xpath = new DOMXPath($doc);
$query = 'count(/people/person/name)';
echo $xpath->evaluate($query); //2
echo $xpath->query($query); // error
?><body></html>
```

2
Catchable fatal error: Object of class DOMNodeList could not be converted to string in **C:\Program Files\Zend\Apache2\htdocs\xml\people2.php** on line **9**

6.7.6 XSLT

XSLTProcessor
string getParameter (string $namespaceURI , string $localName) int XsltProcessor::getSecurityPrefs (void) bool hasExsltSupport (void) void importStylesheet (object $stylesheet) void registerPHPFunctions ([mixed $restrict]) bool removeParameter (string $namespaceURI , string $localName) bool setParameter (string $namespace , string $name , string $value) bool setProfiling (string $filename) int XsltProcessor::setSecurityPrefs (int $securityPrefs) DOMDocument transformToDoc (DOMNode $doc) int transformToURI (DOMDocument $doc , string $uri) string transformToXML (DOMDocument $doc)

For the source XML and XSLT files, refer to 6.5.1.

```
<?php
$xml = new DOMDocument;
$xml->load('ab.xml');
$xslt = new DOMDocument;
$xslt->load('ab.xslt');
$proc = new XSLTProcessor;
$proc->importStyleSheet($xslt);
echo $proc->transformToXML($xml); // string printed
echo $proc->transformToDoc($xml); // error
?>
```

```
<?xml version="1.0" encoding="UTF-8"?>
<html xmlns:xs="http://www.w3.org/2001/XMLSchema"
    xmlns:fn="http://www.w3.org/2005/xpath-functions">
  <head>
    <title>A B C</title>
  </head>
  <body>
    <table>
      <tr>
        <td>3</td>
        <td>Dog</td>
      </tr>
      <tr>
        <td>4</td>
        <td>Fish</td>
      </tr>
    </table>
  </body>
</html>
<br />
<b>Catchable fatal error</b>: Object of class
DOMDocument could not be converted to string in
<b>C:\Program Files\Zend\Apache2\htdocs\xml\
ab.php</b> on line <b>9</b><br />
```

6.8 Parsers and Programs

6.8.1 DOM

Cross-platform and language-independent, Document Object Model is a convention for interacting with objects in HTML and XML documents. A DOM program reads from the parser and builds a tree representation of the entire document, called the DOM tree, in the memory. This can take considerable space and time. Once loaded, random access is possible in any order, which is important for document rearrangement, validation, XPath, XSLT, etc.

6.8.2 SAX

Where DOM operates on the document as a whole, SAX (Simple API for XML) parsers use streaming, operating on each piece of an XML document sequentially in one shot. The result from the parser is fed to the application directly. Unlike DOM, SAX is state-independent. The memory required by a SAX parser is minimal. Because SAX is event-driven, document processing is ***generally*** faster than DOM.

6.8.3 StAX

Streaming API for XML is intermediate between DOM and SAX. The entry point is a cursor that represents a point within the document. The application moves the cursor forward, 'pulling' data from the parser when necessary. This is different from SAX, which 'pushes' data to the application, requiring the application to maintain state between events as necessary to keep track of the location within the document.

6.8.4 VTD-XML

Virtual Token Descriptor for XML is a group of cross-platform non-extractive processing methods. Traditionally in extractive parsing, a lexical analyzer represents tokens as discrete string objects. By contrast, 'document-centric', VTD-XML keeps the source intact, and uses offsets and lengths to describe those tokens. With a persistent internal representation, object-oriented modeling is skipped, thus eliminating creation cost. However, the document size is increased by about 30% to 50%. Moreover, it is incompatible with DOM, SAX, external DTD entities, and certain validation techniques.

6.8.5 Expat

Expat is a parser library written in C. It is stream-oriented, open-source, and used in the Apache HTTP Server, Mozilla, Perl, Python, and PHP, among many other languages.

6.8.6 Pull Parsing

Pull parsing regards the document as a series of objects which are read sequentially using the Iterator design pattern. This makes it compatible with recursive-descent parsers which mirror the XML structure. StAX in Java and XMLReader in PHP are examples of pull parsers. Pull-parsing code is generally easier to undertand than SAX parsing code.

6.8.7 Xerces

Xerces is a set of Apache libraries for parsing, validating, serializing and manipulating XML. It implements DOM and SAX.

6.8.8 MSXML

Microsoft XML Core Services is a collection of services that allow JScript appplications, VBScript applications and Microsoft development tools to create XML applications in Windows. DOM, SAX, XSLT, XSD etc. are supported.

6.8.9 libxml2

libxml2 is an XML parser library. Written in C, it provides bindings to C++, PHP5, Python, Pascals, Common Lisp etc.

6.9 Web Services

A **web service** is a way of communication between two machines over a network. Different software systems often need to exchange data with each other, and a web service allows just that over the internet. How to use a web service will be briefly explained in this section.

6.9.1 WSDL

The **Web Services Description Language** defines the functionalities offered by a web service. It is often used together with SOAP and XSD.

The WSDL file can be read by a client program to find out what operations are available on the server. Any special datatypes used are embedded in the form of XSD. SOAP can then be used to call one of the operations over HTTP.

```
<definitions name="HelloService"
  targetNamespace=
            "http://www.examples.com/wsdl/HelloService.wsdl"
  xmlns="http://schemas.xmlsoap.org/wsdl/"
  xmlns:soap="http://schemas.xmlsoap.org/wsdl/soap/"
  xmlns:tns="http://www.examples.com/wsdl/HelloService.wsdl"
  xmlns:xsd="http://www.w3.org/2001/XMLSchema">

  <message name="SayHelloRequest">
    <part name="firstName" type="xsd:string"/>
  </message>
  <message name="SayHelloResponse">
    <part name="greeting" type="xsd:string"/>
  </message>

  <portType name="Hello_PortType">
    <operation name="sayHello">
      <input message="tns:SayHelloRequest"/>
      <output message="tns:SayHelloResponse"/>
    </operation>
  </portType>

  <binding name="Hello_Binding" type="tns:Hello_PortType">
  <soap:binding style="rpc"
    transport="http://schemas.xmlsoap.org/soap/http"/>
  <operation name="sayHello">
    <soap:operation soapAction="sayHello"/>
    <input>
      <soap:body encodingStyle=
                "http://schemas.xmlsoap.org/soap/encoding/"
        namespace="urn:examples:helloservice"
        use="encoded"/>
    </input>
    <output>
      <soap:body encodingStyle=
                "http://schemas.xmlsoap.org/soap/encoding/"
        namespace="urn:examples:helloservice"
        use="encoded"/>
    </output>
  </operation>
  </binding>

  <service name="Hello_Service">
    <documentation>WSDL File for HelloService</documentation>
    <port binding="tns:Hello_Binding" name="Hello_Port">
      <soap:address
        location="http://www.examples.com/SayHello/">
    </port>
  </service>
</definitions>
```

(Courtesy of *http://www.tutorialspoint.com/wsdl/wsdl_example.htm*)

6.9.2 SOAP

Simple Object Access Protocol, is used to exchange structured information in web services.

```
<?xml version="1.0"?>
<soap:Envelope
      xmlns:soap="http://www.w3.org/2003/05/soap-envelope">
  <soap:Header>
  </soap:Header>
  <soap:Body>
    <m:GetPrice xmlns:m="http://www.example.org/stock">
      <m:StockName>Google</m:StockName>
    </m:GetPrice>
  </soap:Body>
</soap:Envelope>
```

6.9.3 REST

Representational State Transfer is an abstraction of the World Wide Web.

A web service is 'RESTful' if it conforms to the following constraints:

- Client-server
- Stateless
- Cacheable
- Layered system
- Code on demand
- Uniform interface

Whereas SOAP is a protocol, REST is an architectural style. As such, there is no 'official' standard for RESTful web APIs. Nevertheless, a RESTful implementation such as the Web can use standards like HTTP, URI, XML, etc.

6.9.4 XML-RPC

XML Remote Procedure Call uses XML to encode calls and HTTP for transport. 'XML-RPC' also refers, in general, to the use of XML for remote procedure call, independently of the specific protocol.

XML-RPC works by sending a HTTP request to a server. Multiple input parameters can be supplied, and one value is returned. These input and output parameters can contain larger structures like lists and maps.

REST transports resources such as documents, while XML-RPC deals with method calls. XML-RPC is simpler than SOAP because XML-RPC:

- uses one method of method serialization, whereas SOAP defines multiple varying encodings.
- has simpler security operations.
- does not use WSDL, although XRDL provides a subset of WSDL.

A typical request.

```
<?xml version="1.0"?>
<methodCall>
  <methodName>examples.getStateName</methodName>
  <params>
    <param>
      <value><i4>100</i4></value>
    </param>
  </params>
</methodCall>
```

A typical response.

```
<?xml version="1.0"?>
<methodResponse>
  <params>
    <param>
      <value><string>Chong Lip Phang</string></value>
    </param>
  </params>
</methodResponse>
```

A typical fault.

```
<?xml version="1.0"?>
<methodResponse>
  <fault>
    <value>
      <struct>
        <member>
          <name>faultCode</name>
          <value><int>4</int></value>
        </member>
        <member>
          <name>faultString</name>
          <value><string>Too many parameters.
          </string></value>
        </member>
      </struct>
    </value>
  </fault>
</methodResponse>
```

6.10 Applications

XML has been used widely in numerous applications. Here we briefly describe several important XML applications.

6.10.1 RSS and ATOM

Web feeds allow publishers to syndicate information automatically, publishing frequently updated blog entries, news headlines, audio, video etc.

Subscribers to a website RSS no longer need to manually check the website for new content. Instead, their software program or browser constantly monitors the site, informs the user of any updates, and download any data if necessary.

A software program called "aggregator" or "feed reader", which can be web-based, desktop-based, or mobile-device-based, presents feed data to subscribers. They can receive timely updates from multiple favourite websites from their program.

RSS (Rich Site Summary), often dubbed Really Simple Syndication, has become popular due to early feed reader support.

```
<?xml version="1.0" encoding="UTF-8" ?>
<rss version="2.0">
<channel>
  <title>RSS Title</title>
  <description>This is an example of an RSS feed
  </description>
  <link>http://www.example.com/main.html</link>
  <lastBuildDate>Mon, 06 Sep 2010 00:01:00 +0000
  </lastBuildDate>
  <pubDate>Sun, 06 Sep 2009 16:20:00 +0000</pubDate>
  <ttl>1800</ttl>

  <item>
    <title>Example entry</title>
    <description>Here is some text containing an interesting
                description. </description>
    <link>http://www.example.com/blog/post/1</link>
    <guid>7bd204c6-1655-4c27-aeee-53f933c5395f</guid>
    <pubDate>Sun, 06 Sep 2009 16:20:00 +0000</pubDate>
  </item>
</channel>
</rss>
```

Atom is technically more advanced. It has less restrictive licensing, IANA registered MIME type, XML namespace, URI support, Relax NG support.

```
<?xml version="1.0" encoding="utf-8"?>
  <feed xmlns="http://www.w3.org/2005/Atom">
  <title>Example Feed</title>
  <subtitle>A subtitle.</subtitle>
  <link href="http://example.org/feed/" rel="self" />
  <link href="http://example.org/" />
  <id>urn:uuid:60a76c80-d399-11d9-b91C-0003939e0af6</id>
  <updated>2003-12-13T18:30:02Z</updated>

  <entry>
    <title>Atom-Powered Robots Run Amok</title>
    <link href="http://example.org/2003/12/13/atom03" />
    <link rel="alternate" type="text/html"
      href="http://example.org/2003/12/13/atom03.html"/>
    <link rel="edit"
      href="http://example.org/2003/12/13/atom03/edit"/>
    <id>urn:uuid:1225c695-cfb8-4ebb-aaaa-80da344efa6a</id>
    <updated>2003-12-13T18:30:02Z</updated>
    <summary>Some text.</summary>
    <content type="xhtml">
      <div xmlns="http://www.w3.org/1999/xhtml">
        <p>This is the entry content.</p>
      </div>
    </content>
    <author>
      <name>John Doe</name>
      <email>johndoe@example.com</email>
    </author>
  </entry>
</feed>
```

RSS 2.0	Atom 1.0
author	author*
category	category
channel	feed
copyright	rights
description	subtitle
description*	summary, content
generator	generator
guid	id*
image	logo
item	entry
lastBuildDate	updated*
link*	link*
managingEditor	author or contributor
pubDate	published
title*	title*
ttl	--
* indicates that an element must be provided except for Atom elements "author" and "link" which are only required under certain conditions.	

6.10.2 DocBook

DocBook documents technical information. As a semantic language that captures the structure of a document, DocBook is neutral in presentation. The content can be published in a variety of formats like HTML, XHTML, EPUB, PDF, man pages, Web help and HTML Help.

```
<?xml version="1.0" encoding="UTF-8"?>
<book xml:id="simple_book"
      xmlns="http://docbook.org/ns/docbook" version="5.0">
  <title>Very simple book</title>
  <chapter xml:id="chapter_1">
    <title>Chapter 1</title>
    <para>HTML</para>
    <para>HTML deals with many
        <emphasis>tags</emphasis>!</para>
  </chapter>
  <chapter xml:id="chapter_2">
    <title>Chapter 2</title>
    <para>CSS</para>
  </chapter>
</book>
```

6.10.3 DITA

Darwin Information Typing Architecture is used for authoring and, with the DITA Open Toolkit, publishing. Adopting the principles of specialization and inheritance, it is comparable to the Charles Darwin's concept of evolutionary adaptation.

Each DITA 'topic', an XML file, can be reused across multiple publications. The generic Topic type contains a title element, a prolog element for metadata, and a body element. The body element contains paragraph, table, and list elements, as in HTML. There are three specializaed topic types: Task, Concept, and Reference.

Extensive metadata elements and attributes, both at topic level and within elements, can be included. Conditional text allows filtering or styling content based on attributes for audience, platform, product, and other properties. A .ditaval file identifies which values are to be used for conditional processing.

A DITA map is a container for topics. Giving the topics sequence and structure, it is used to transform a collection of content into a publication. A map can include relationship tables which define hyperlinks between topics, be nested, reference topics or other maps, and contain a variety of content types and metadata.

New elements and attributes can be added for specific industries and companies, through specialization of base DITA elements and attributes.

Ditamap file (table of Contents)

```
<?xml version="1.0" encoding="utf-8" standalone="no"?>
<!DOCTYPE map PUBLIC "-//OASIS//DTD DITA Map//EN"
"map.dtd">
<map id="map" xml:lang="en">
  <topicref format="dita" href="sample.dita"
            navtitle="Sample" type="topic"/>
</map>
```

Hello world (topic DTD)

```
<?xml version="1.0" encoding="utf-8" standalone="no"?>
<!DOCTYPE topic PUBLIC "-//OASIS//DTD DITA Topic//EN"
"topic.dtd">
<topic xml:lang="en" id="sample">
  <title>Sample</title>
  <body>
    <p audience="foo">Hello world</p>
  </body>
</topic>
```

.ditaval file (for conditionalizing text)

```
<?xml version="1.0" encoding="UTF-8"?>
<val>
  <prop att="audience" val="foo" action="include"/>
  <prop att="audience" val="bar" action="exclude"/>
</val>
```

6.10.4 MathML

Mathematical Markup Language describes mathematical notations. It aims at integrating mathematical formulae into World Wide Web and other documents. Not all browsers support MathML.

This shows a representation of ax^2+bx+c.

```
<?xml version="1.0" encoding="UTF-8"?>
 <!DOCTYPE math PUBLIC "-//W3C//DTD MathML 2.0//EN"
      "http://www.w3.org/Math/DTD/mathml2/mathml2.dtd">
 <math xmlns="http://www.w3.org/1998/Math/MathML">
   <mrow>
     <mi>a</mi>
     <mo>&InvisibleTimes;</mo>
     <msup>
       <mi>x</mi>
       <mn>2</mn>
     </msup>
     <mo>+</mo>
     <mi>b</mi>
     <mo>&InvisibleTimes; </mo>
     <mi>x</mi>
     <mo>+</mo>
     <mi>c</mi>
   </mrow>
 </math>
```

6.11 Peripheral XMLs

In this section, we show a few more XML-related techonologies. A full documentation of these standards is beyond the scope of this book, either because their use is limited or because their nature is not directly related to the web.

6.11.1 XHTML

Extesible HyperText Markup Language is a stricter version of HTML in the sense that the document must be well-formed in the XML sense, as described in the beginning of this chapter. Its development was motivated by interoperability with other formats, as an XHTML document can be processed by an XML processor. Moreoever, the XML namespaces allow the document to be extended by other XML-based languages such as SVG and MathML.

There are currently two stable versions of XHTML - 1.0 and 1.1. XHTML 1.1 adds modularization, along with ruby annotation elements (ruby, rbc, rtc, rb, rt, and rp). XHTML is supported by major browsers.

Besides the need to be well-formed in the XML sense, an XHTML document differs from a HTML document in several other important aspects:

- An XHTML document begins with an XML declaration.
- The DOCTYPE declares the document to be XHTML-compliant, as described in Chapter 1.
- The root element, <html>, contains an 'xmlns' attribute to relate it with the XHTML namespace.
- All tag names and attribute names must be in a lower case in XHTML.
- Attribute minimization is not allowed in XHTML. For instance, <textarea readonly> is incorrect. Use <textarea readonly="readonly"> instead.

```
<?xml version="1.0" encoding="UTF-8"?>
<!DOCTYPE html PUBLIC "-//W3C//DTD XHTML 1.0 Strict//EN"
      "http://www.w3.org/TR/xhtml1/DTD/xhtml1-strict.dtd">
<html xmlns="http://www.w3.org/1999/xhtml"
       xml:lang="en">
 <head>
 <title>XHTML 1.0 Strict Example</title>
 <script type="application/javascript">
 <![CDATA[
 function start() {
   alert("Hello World");
 }
 ]]>
 </script>
 </head>
 <body onload="start()">
   <p>The name of an XHTML file ends with .xhtml. </p>
 </body>
</html>
```

6.11.2 XSL-FO (a.k.a. XSL)

Extensible Stylesheet Language - Formatting Objects is a markup language for formatting XML data for output to screen, paper or other media.

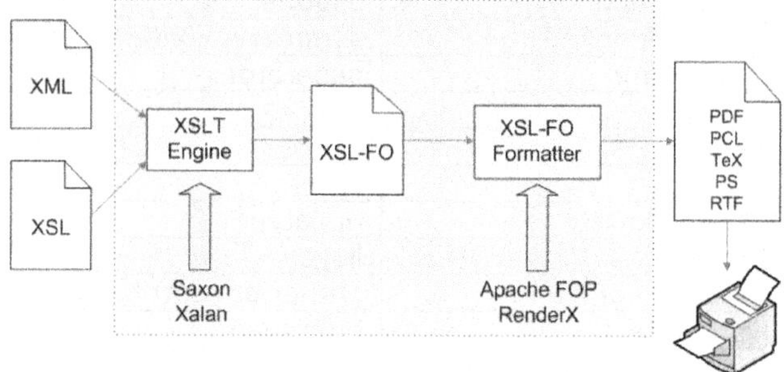

(Courtesy of http://cscie153.dce.harvard.edu/lecture_notes/2009/20091013/handout.html)

```
<?xml version="1.0" encoding="utf-8"?>
<fo:root xmlns:fo="http://www.w3.org/1999/XSL/Format">
  <fo:layout-master-set>
    <fo:simple-page-master master-name="simple"
           page-height="11in" page-width="8.5in"
           margin-top="1.0in" margin-bottom="1.0in"
           margin- left="1.25in" margin-right="1.25in">
      <fo:region-body margin-top="0.25in" />
    </fo:simple-page-master>
  </fo:layout-master-set>
  <fo:page-sequence master-reference="simple">
    <fo:flow flow-name="xsl-region-body">
      <fo:block font-size="18pt" font-family="sans-serif"
           line-height="24pt" space-after.optimum="15pt"
           background-color="blue" color="white"
           text-align="center" padding-top="3pt">
          Title
      </fo:block>
      <fo:block font-size="12pt" font-family="sans-serif"
                line-height="15pt" space-after.optimum="3pt"
                text-align="justify">
          Some Text
      </fo:block>
    </fo:flow>
  </fo:page-sequence>
</fo:root>
```

6.11.3 XBRL

Extensible Business Reporting Language is an XML-based standard for reporting business information.

```
<?xml version="1.0" encoding="UTF-8"?>

<xbrli:xbrl
xmlns:ifrs-gp="http://xbrl.iasb.org/int/fr/ifrs/gp/2005-05-15"
xmlns:iso4217="http://www.xbrl.org/2003/iso4217"
xmlns:xbrli="http://www.xbrl.org/2003/instance"
xmlns:xbrll="http://www.xbrl.org/2003/linkbase"
xmlns:xlink="http://www.w3.org/1999/xlink">

  <xbrll:schemaRef
        xbrll:href="http://www.org.com/xbrl/taxonomy"
        xlink:type="simple"/>
   <ifrs-gp:OtherOperatingIncomeTotalFinancialInstitutions
        contextRef="J2004" decimals="0" unitRef="EUR">
        38679000000
   </ifrs-gp:OtherOperatingIncomeTotalFinancialInstitutions>
   <ifrs-gp:OtherAdministrativeExpenses
        contextRef="J2004" decimals="0" unitRef="EUR">
        35996000000
   </ifrs-gp:OtherAdministrativeExpenses>
   <ifrs-gp:OtherOperatingExpenses
        contextRef="J2004" decimals="0" unitRef="EUR">
        870000000
   </ifrs-gp:OtherOperatingExpenses>
  ...
   <ifrs-gp:OtherOperatingIncomeTotalByNature
        contextRef="J2004" decimals="0" unitRef="EUR">
        10430000000
   </ifrs-gp:OtherOperatingIncomeTotalByNature>
   <xbrli:context id="BJ2004">
     <xbrli:entity>
        <xbrli:identifier scheme="www.iqinfo.com/xbrl">
          ACME
        </xbrli:identifier>
     </xbrli:entity>
     <xbrli:period>
        <xbrli:instant>2004-01-01</xbrli:instant>
     </xbrli:period>
   </xbrli:context>
   <xbrli:context id="EJ2004">
     <xbrli:entity>
        <xbrli:identifier scheme="www.iqinfo.com/xbrl">
          ACME
        </xbrli:identifier>
     </xbrli:entity>
     <xbrli:period>
        <xbrli:instant>2004-12-31</xbrli:instant>
     </xbrli:period>
   </xbrli:context>
   <xbrli:context id="J2004">
     <xbrli:entity>
        <xbrli:identifier scheme="www.iqinfo.com/xbrl">
          ACME
        </xbrli:identifier>
     </xbrli:entity>
     <xbrli:period>
        <xbrli:startDate>2004-01-01</xbrli:startDate>
        <xbrli:endDate>2004-12-31</xbrli:endDate>
     </xbrli:period>
   </xbrli:context>
   <xbrli:unit id="EUR">
     <xbrli:measure>iso4217:EUR</xbrli:measure>
   </xbrli:unit>
</xbrli:xbrl>
```

(Courtesy of http://en.wikipedia.org/wiki/XBRL)

6.11.4 XProc

XML Processing is a language that describes a pipeline of operations to be performed on XML documents. Possible operations include file inclusions, validations, and XSLT transformations. Implementations include Calabash, Calumet, QuiXProc and Tubular.

```
<pipeline xmlns="http://www.w3.org/ns/xproc">
  <xinclude name="included">
    <input port="source">
      <pipe step="pipeline" port="source"/>
    </input>
  </xinclude>
  <validate-with-xml-schema>
    <input port="schema">
      <document
        href="http://example.com/schema.xsd"/>
    </input>
  </validate-with-xml-schema>
  <xslt>
    <input port="stylesheet">
      <document
        href="http://example.com/stylesheet.xsl"/>
    </input>
  </xslt>
</pipeline>
```

6.11.5 XForms

XForms is the next-generation HTML web forms. It is generic enough to be a standalone. At the time of writing, no major browser supports XForms. Based on the model-view-controller (MVC) approach, it has many advanced features. For example, new data can be used to update the form while it is running, without scripting.

```
<xforms:model>
  <xforms:instance>
    <ecommerce xmlns="">
      <method/>
      <number/>
      <expiry/>
    </ecommerce>
  </xforms:instance>
  <xforms:submission action="http://example.com/submit"
   method="post" id="submit" includenamespaceprefixes=""/>
</xforms:model>
```

(Courtesy of http://www.w3.org/TR/2009/REC-xforms-20091020/)

6.11.6 XKMS

XML Key Management Specification uses public key infrastructure (PKI) to secure communication among applications. Web services can receive updated key information from an XKMS compliant server for encryption and authentication.

XKMS is made up of:

- X-KISS: XML Key Information Service Specification outlines the syntax that delegates tasks required to process the key information element of an XML signature to a trust service.
- X-KRSS: XML Key Registration Service Specification outlines the registration of public key information.

This demonstrates encryption.

```
<?xml version="1.0"?>

<PaymentInfo xmlns="http://example.org/paymentv2">
  <Name>John Smith</Name>
  <CreditCard Limit="5,000" Currency="USD">
   <Number>
    <EncryptedData
       xmlns="http://www.w3.org/2001/04/xmlenc#"
       Type="http://www.w3.org/2001/04/xmlenc#Content">
     <CipherData>
      <CipherValue>A23B45C56</CipherValue>
     </CipherData>
    </EncryptedData>
   </Number>
   <Issuer>Example Bank</Issuer>
   <Expiration>04/02</Expiration>
  </CreditCard>
</PaymentInfo>
```

(Courtesy of http://www.w3.org/TR/2013/REC-xmlenc-core1-20130411/)

This shows a signature.

```
<Signature Id="MyFirstSignature"
           xmlns="http://www.w3.org/2000/09/xmldsig#">
  <SignedInfo>
    <CanonicalizationMethod
     Algorithm="http://www.w3.org/2006/12/xml-c14n11"/>
    <SignatureMethod
     Algorithm=
  "http://www.w3.org/2001/04/xmldsig-more#rsa-sha256"/>
    <Reference
     URI=
      "http://www.w3.org/TR/2000/REC-xhtml1-20000126/">
      <Transforms>
        <Transform
     Algorithm="http://www.w3.org/2006/12/xml-c14n11"/>
      </Transforms>
      <DigestMethod
       Algorithm=
           "http://www.w3.org/2001/04/xmlenc#sha256"/>

      <DigestValue>
              dGhpcyBpcyBub3QgYSBzaWduYXR1cmUK...
      </DigestValue>
    </Reference>
  </SignedInfo>

  <SignatureValue>...</SignatureValue>

  <KeyInfo>
    <KeyValue>
      <DSAKeyValue>
        <P>...</P><Q>...</Q><G>...</G><Y>...</Y>
      </DSAKeyValue>
    </KeyValue>
  </KeyInfo>
</Signature>
```

(Courtesy of http://www.w3.org/TR/2013/REC-xmldsig-core1-20130411/)

6.11.7 appML

Application Modeling Language (appML) is an HTML extension specifically designed for web-based apps. It is a framework made up XML, Javascript and PHP.

7. Scalable Vector Graphics

Using SVG, images can be zoomed in (CTRL +) without degradation. Based on XML, SVG images can be searched, indexed, scripted, compressed and animated. It is easier to use a drawing program such as Inkscape to draw SVG images, and to convert other image files to the SVG format.

An SVG image can be used in a variety of ways.

A. Using the browser directly.

```
<?xml version="1.0" standalone="no"?>
<!DOCTYPE svg PUBLIC "-//W3C//DTD SVG 1.1//EN"
"http://www.w3.org/Graphics/SVG/1.1/DTD/svg11.dtd">

<svg xmlns="http://www.w3.org/2000/svg" version="1.1">
  <circle cx="120" cy="120" r="50" stroke="black"
   stroke-width="2" fill="red" />
</svg>
```

B. Using <img>.

```
<!DOCTYPE html>
<html>
  <head></head>
  <body>
    <img src="circle.svg"/>
  </body>
</html>
```

C. Using <object>.

```
<!DOCTYPE html>
<html>
  <head></head>
  <body>
    <object data="circle.svg" type="image/svg+xml">
     Your browser does not support SVG.
    </object>
</body>
</html>
```

D. Using <embed>.

```
<!DOCTYPE html>
<html>
  <head></head>
  <body>
    <embed src="circle.svg" type="image/svg+xml" />
  </body>
</html>
```

E. Using <iframe>.

```
<!DOCTYPE html>
<html>
  <head></head>
  <body>
    <iframe src="circle.svg"></iframe>
  </body>
</html>
```

F. Using <a>.

```
<!DOCTYPE html>
<html>
  <head></head>
  <body>
    <a href="circle.svg">SVG image</a>
  </body>
</html>
```

G. Using inline SVG.

```
<!DOCTYPE html>
<html>
  <head></head>
  <body>
    <svg xmlns="http://www.w3.org/2000/svg"
         version="1.1">
      <circle cx="120" cy="120" r="50" stroke="black"
        stroke-width="2" fill="red"/>
    </svg>
  </body>
</html>
```

SVG libraries include Snap.svg, svg.js, Raphael, Fabric.js, D3.js and many more.

(Manipulation of the SVG DOM is beyond the scope of this book. The interested reader is referred to:
https://developer.mozilla.org/en-US/docs/Web/API/Document_Object_Model)

7.1 Values and Attributes

Colors and lengths in SVG can be specified in the same ways as CSS (2.1).

The value of an <angle> has the form:
<number> [deg|gard|rad]

In this chapter, underlined tags are not closed with a separate closing tag. To facilitate future references, the SVG attributes are grouped and abbreviated here:

A: animation event attributes (7.8.2)
onbegin, onend, onload, onrepeat
O: conditional processing attributes (7.4.3)
requiredExtensions, requiredFeatures, systemLanguage
C: core attributes (7.2.1)
id, xml:base, xml:lang, xml:space
D: document event attributes (7.8.2)
onabort, onerror, onresize, onscroll, onunload, onzoom
F: filter primitive attributes (7.6.2)
height, result, width, x, y
G: graphical event attributes (7.9)
onactivate, onclick, onfocusin, onfocusout, onload, onmousedown, onmousemove, onmouseout, onmouseover, onmouseup
P: presentation attributes
markers (7.3.2):marker-end, marker-mid, maker-start **stroking** (7.3.3): stroke-dasharray, stroke-dashoffset, stroke-linecap, stroke-linejoin, stroke-miterlimit, stroke-opacity, stroke-width, stroke **filling** (7.5): opacity, fill-opacity, fill-rule, fill, visibility, stop-color, stop-opacity, clip-path, clip-rule, clip, mask **filters** (7.6.2): filter, flood-color, flood-opacity **text** (7.7.1): text-anchor, text decoration, text-rendering, direction, unicode-bidi, letter-spacing, word-spacing, writing-mode **fonts** (7.7.2): font-family, font-size-adjust, font-size, font-stretch, font-style, font-variant, font-weight **glyphs** (7.7.3): glyph-orientation-horizontal, glyph-orientation-vertical, kerning

rendering: color-rendering, image-rendering, shape-rendering, text-rendering

color: color-interpolation-filters, color-interpolation, color-profile, color, lighting-color(7.6.5)

others: cursor, display, enable-background, overflow, pointer-events

S: style attributes (7.2)

class, style, externalResourcesRequired

X: XLink attributes (7.4.1)

xlink:href, xlink:type, xlink:role, xlink:arcrole, xlink:title, xlink:actuate, xlink:show

7.2 <svg>

7.2.1 Essential Attributes

<svg> specifies an SVG image......OCDGPS

......id="<name>": a unique name of the element
......style="<style>": the style information
......class="<list>": as a style sheet selector, other processing
......version="<number>": the SVG language version
......xml:base="<iri>": the base IRI
......xml:lang="<language>": the language
......xml:space="{<u>default</u>|preserve}": is space preserved?
......baseProfile="<profile-name>": the minimum lang. profile
......contentScriptType="<MIME type>": the scripting language. The default is "<u>application/ecmascript</u>".
......externalResourcesRequired="{true|false}": whether external resources are needed to render the content. The resources include style sheets, color profiles, and fonts.
......width="<length>": the width
......height="<length>": the height
......zoomAndPan="{disable|<u>magnify</u>}": allows magnification?
......viewBox(7.2.2)
......preserveAspectRatio(7.2.2)

```
<!DOCTYPE html>
<html>
<head>
  <title>C</title>
</head>
<body>
  <p>A SVG circle</p>
  <svg xmlns="http://www.w3.org/2000/svg"
        id="test_circle"
        style="border:solid 1px; left:50px; position:relative"
        version="1.1"
        xml:base="http://www.example.com/circle.html"
        xml:lang="en"
        xml:space="preserve"
        width="200px" height="200px"
        zoomAndPan="magnify">
    <circle cx="100" cy="100" r="50" stroke="black"
     stroke-width="2" fill="red"/>
  </svg>
</body>
</html>
```

A SVG circle

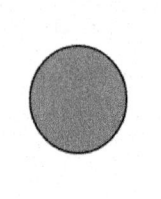

7.2.2 Viewing

(Note: At the time of writing, apparently some browsers have not fully supported the SVG viewing capabilities. Any discrepancies are to be regretted.)

......viewBox="<x> <y> <width> <height>": specifies a rectangular region for the viewport.
......preserveAspectRatio="none" or "[defer] x{Min|Mid|Max} Y{Min|Mid|Max} [meet|slice]": specifies how to preserve the aspect ratio, applicable only if a viewBox is specified. The middle mandatory term specifies where to place the content in the viewport. 'defer', when specified for an image element, causes the 'preserveAspectRatio' attribute on the referenced content to be used. 'meet' causes the viewport to (just) contain the content. 'slice' causes the content to (just) contain the viewport.

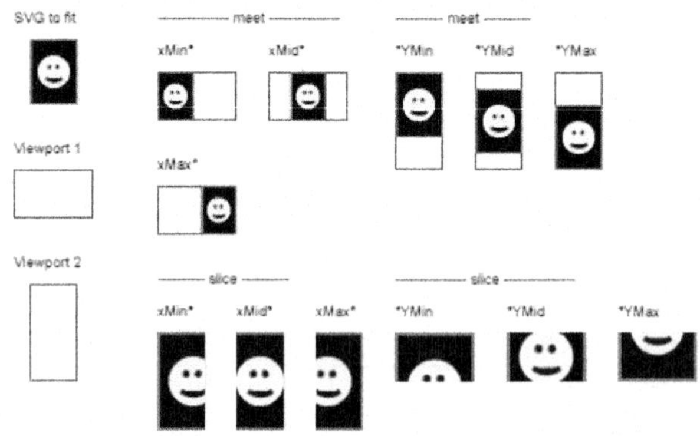

(courtesy of http://www.w3.org/TR/SVG11/coords.html)

<view> defines a custom viewBox......C

......externalResourcesRequired(7.2.1)
......viewBox(7.2.2)
......preserveAspectRatio(7.2.2)
......zoomAndPan(7.2.1)
......viewTarget="<XML name>": the target object associated with the view.

```
<!DOCTYPE html>
<html>
<head>
  <title>C</title>
</head>
<body>
  <svg width="400px" height="400px"
        viewBox="0 0 100 100">
    <view id="normalView" viewBox="0 0 100 100"/>
    <view id="halfView"   viewBox="0 0 200 200"/>
    <view id="doubleView" viewBox="0 0  50  50"/>

    <circle fill="none" stroke="black" stroke-width="1"
            cx="50" cy="50" r="40"/>

    <a xlink:href="#doubleView">
       <text x="2" y="6" font-size="5">
        [double size]</text></a>
    <a xlink:href="#normalView">
      <text x="39" y="6" font-size="5">
        [normal size]</text></a>
    <a xlink:href="#halfView">
       <text x="77" y="6" font-size="5">
        [half size]</text></a>
</svg>
</body>
</html>
```

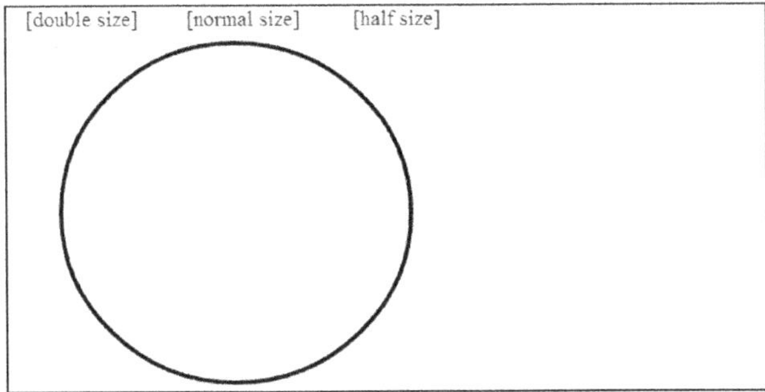

7.3 Outlining

7.3.1 Shapes

<rect> draws a rectangle......OCGPS
......transform (7.3.4)
......x="<coord.>": the x coord. of the upper-left corner
......y="<coord.>": the y coord. of the upper-left corner
......width="<length>": the width
......height="<length>": the height
......rx="<length>": the x radius of the corner roundness
......ry="<length>": the y radius of the corner roundness

<circle> draws a circle......OCGPS
......transform (7.3.4)
......cx="<coord.>": the x coord. of the center
......cy="<coord.>": the y coord. of the center
......r="<length>": the radius

<ellipse> draws an ellipse......OCGPS
......transform (7.3.4)
......cx="<coord.>": the x coord. of the center
......cy="<coord.>": the y coord. of the center
......rx="<length>": the x radius
......ry="<length>": the y radius

<polygon> draws a polygon......OCGPS
......transform (7.3.4)
......points="<x1,y1 x2,y2......>": the corner points

```
<!DOCTYPE html>
<html>
<head></head>
<body>
  <svg>
    <rect x="20" y="20" width="80" height="50"
          rx="10" ry="20"/>
    <circle cx="200" cy="50" r="50"/>
    <ellipse cx="120" cy="150" rx="100" ry="50"/>
    <polygon points="20,220 260,250 50,340" />
  </svg>
</body>
</html>
```

7.3.2 Lines

<line> draws a straight line......OCGPS
......transform (7.3.4)
......x1="<coord.>": the x coord. of the start of the line
......y1="<coord.>": the y coord. of the start of the line
......x2="<coord.>": the x coord. of the end of the line
......y2="<coord.>": the y coord. of the end of the line

<polyline> draws joined straight lines......OCGPS
......transform (7.3.4)
......points="<x1,y1 x2,y2......>": the points of the joined straight lines

```
<!DOCTYPE html>
<html>
<head></head>
<body>
  <svg>
    <line x1="20" y1="20" x2="200" y2="20"
          stroke="black"/>
    <polyline points="20,40 200,40 20,80 200,80"
              fill="none" stroke="black"/>
  </svg>
</body>
</html>
```

<path> draws straight lines or curves......OCGPS
......transform (7.3.4)
......pathLength
......d="<path data>": the paths of the lines

<path data>: a capitalized command (eg. M) means the use of absolute values. A small command (eg. m) means the use of relative values.
M <x1>,<y1> <x2>,<y2>...... lifts the 'drawing pen' and moves to a new location. Subsequent pairs of coordinates are treated as implicit L commands.
L <x1>,<y1> <x2>,<y2>......draws a straight line to the specified location. Subsequent pairs of coordinates may be specified to use the L command repeatedly.
H <x>: draws a horizontal line to the x location.
V <y>: draws a vertical line to the y location.
Z: closes the path by drawing a straight line from the current point to the initial point.
A <rx>,<ry> <x-axis-rotation> <large-arc-flag>, <sweep-flag> <x>, <y>: draws an elliptical arc to (x,y). (rx, ry) define the two radii. x-axis-rotation determines the orientation. large-arc-flag and sweep-flag determine how the arc is drawn.
Q <x1>,<y1> <x>,<y>......: draws a quadratic Bezier curve to (x,y), using (x1,y1) as the control point.
T <x>,<y>......: draws a quadratic Bezier curve to (x,y). The control point is assumed to be the reflection of the control point on the previous command. If there is no previous Q/T command, the control point is assumed to be coincident with the current point.
C <x1>,<y1> <x2>,<y2> <x>,<y>......: draws a cubic Bezier curve to (x,y), using (x1,y1) as the control point at the beginning and (x1,y2) as the control point at the end.
S <x1>,<y1> <x>,<y>......: draws a cubic Bezier curve to (x,y). The first control point is assumed to be the reflection of the second control point on the previous command relative to the current point. If there is no previous C/S command, assume the first control point to be coincident with the current point.

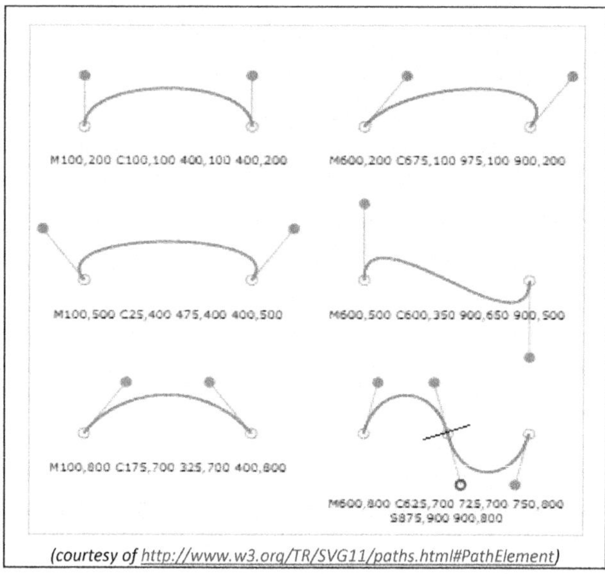

(courtesy of http://www.w3.org/TR/SVG11/paths.html#PathElement)

```
<!DOCTYPE html>
<html>
<head></head>
<body>
  <svg>
    <path d="M50,0 50,100 q-50,30 0,100 l0,100 50,50
                M300,200 h-150 a150,150 0 1,0 150,-150 z
                M275,175 v-150 a150,150 0 0,0 -150,150 z"
          fill="none" stroke="black"/>
  </svg>
</body>
</html>
```

<marker> defines an arrowhead for lines......CPS. To use a marker, specify the marker name in the referencing element using '......marker-start', '......marker-mid', and '......marker-end'.

......viewBox="<x> <y> <width> <height>": the view box
......preserveAspectRatio(7.2.2)
......refX="<x coord.>": the x coord. of the reference point
......refY="<y coord.>": the y coord. of the reference point
......markerUnits="{strokeWidth|userSpaceOnUse}": the units for 'markerWidth', 'markerHeight' and the contents. If strokeWidth is used, one unit equals the stroke width of the graphical object referencing the marker. If userSpaceOnUse is used, the coordinate system of the graphical object referencing the marker is used.
......markerWidth="<length>": the width of the marker
......markerHeight="<length>": the height of the marker
......orient="auto|<angle>": how the marker is rotated

```
<!DOCTYPE html>
<html>
<head></head>
<body>
  <svg>
    <marker id="Triangle"
          viewBox="0 0 10 10" refX="0" refY="5"
          markerUnits="strokeWidth"
          markerWidth="4" markerHeight="3"
          orient="auto">
      <path d="M0,0 L10,5 L0,10 z" />
    </marker>
    <path d="M100,75 L200,75 L250,125"
        fill="none" stroke="black" stroke-width="10"
        marker-end="url(#Triangle)" />
  </svg>
</body>
</html>
```

7.3.3 Stroking

......stroke="<paint>": the color of the outline, which can be a solid color or a gradient. The possible values are the same as for ......fill.

......stroke-width="<length>": the width of the stroke.

......stroke-opacity="<0.0 to 1.0>": the opacity of the stroke. 0.0 means fully transparent. 1.0 means fully opaque.

......stroke-dasharray="<length>, <length>......": the lengths of the alternating dashes and gaps.

......stroke-dashoffset="<length>": the distance into the dash pattern to start the dash.

......stroke-linecap="{butt|round|square}": the shape at the ends of a line.

'butt' cap 'round' cap 'square' cap

(courtesy of http://www.w3.org/TR/SVG11/painting.html#StrokeProperty)

......stroke-linejoin="{miter|round|bevel}": the shape at the corners

'miter' join 'round' join 'bevel' join

(courtesy of http://www.w3.org/TR/SVG11/painting.html#StrokeProperty)

......stroke-miterlimit="<greater than or equal to 1>": the limit of the miter length, for stroke-linejoin="miter". If the limit is exceeded, a 'bevel' join will be used.

```
<!DOCTYPE html>
<html>
<head></head>
<body>
  <svg>
    <path d="M20,20 200,20 200,100"
          fill="none"
          stroke="black"
          stroke-width="10"
          stroke-opacity="0.3"
          stroke-dasharray="20,3,5,8"
          stroke-dashoffset="10"
          stroke-linejoin="miter"
          stroke-miterlimit="1.414"/>
  </svg>
</body>
</html>
```

7.3.4 Transformation

......transform="<transform-list>": the transformation to be performed. <transform-list> is a space-separated list of transformation definitions.

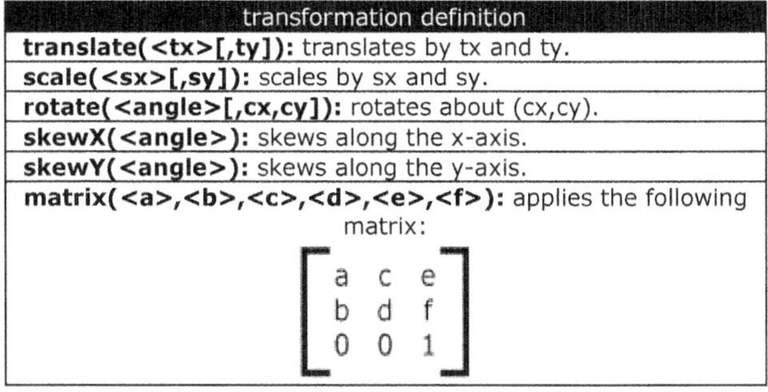

transformation definition
translate(<tx>[,ty]): translates by tx and ty.
scale(<sx>[,sy]): scales by sx and sy.
rotate(<angle>[,cx,cy]): rotates about (cx,cy).
skewX(<angle>): skews along the x-axis.
skewY(<angle>): skews along the y-axis.
matrix(<a>,<b>,<c>,<d>,<e>,<f>): applies the following matrix: $\begin{bmatrix} a & c & e \\ b & d & f \\ 0 & 0 & 1 \end{bmatrix}$

```
<!DOCTYPE html>
<html>
<head></head>
<body>
  <svg>
    <circle cx="100" cy="300" r="60"
            transform="rotate(30,100,100)
                       translate(50,-50)
                       scale(1.5,0.5)
                       skewX(30)"/>
  </svg>
</body>
</html>
```

7.4 Structuring

7.4.1 Grouping

<defs> contains definitions for referenced elements...... OCGPS. Elements contained by <defs> are not rendered directly but are rendered only when referenced later. To improve readability, accessibility and execution efficiency, coders are encouraged to place all template definitions within this element.
......transform (7.3.4)

<g> groups a set of directly rendered graphical elements ......OCGPS. For a well-defined set of elements, the use of this element promotes accessibility, allows attributes to be shared, facilitates transformation, enables animation, and makes it possible for an object to be reused.
......transform (7.3.4)

<symbol> groups a set of graphical elements that are rendered only when referenced somewhere else with <use>......CGPS
......viewBox (7.2.2)
......preserveAspectRatio (7.2.2)

<u><use></u> instantiates an object copy......OCGPSX. Any <svg>, <symbol>, <g>, graphical element, or other <use> is potentially a template object that can be re-used via this element.
......transform (7.3.4)
......x="<coord.>": the x coord. of the upper-left corner
......y="<coord.>": the y coord. of the upper-left corner
......width="<length>": the width
......height="<length>": the height
......xlink:href="<iri>": the id of the fragment.
......xlink:type="simple": the type of XLink used.
......xlink:role="<iri>": the resource that describes it.
......xlink:arcrole="<iri>": the resource that describes it.
......xlink:title="<anything>": a human-readable description.
......xlink:actuate="{onLoad|onRequest}" : for XLink-aware processors.
......xlink:show="{new|replace|embed|other|none}": for XLink-aware processors.

```
<!DOCTYPE html>
<html>
<head>
  <title></title>
</head>
<body>
  <svg>
    <defs>
      <linearGradient id="Gradient01">
        <stop offset="20%" stop-color="#39F" />
        <stop offset="90%" stop-color="#F3F" />
      </linearGradient>
      <rect id="square" width="50" height="50"
        fill="url(#Gradient01)"/>
    </defs>
    <symbol id="circle">
      <circle cx="50" cy="50" r="40" stroke="black"
        stroke-width="2" fill="yellow"/>
      <circle cx="50" cy="50" r="25" stroke="black"
        stroke-width="2" fill="yellow"/>
    </symbol>

    <!-- actual drawing starts here -->
    <use x="0" y="0"  xlink:href="#square"/>
    <use x="60" y="0" xlink:href="#circle"/>
    <g transform="rotate(45,50,100)">
      <rect x="40" y="90" width="70" height="70"
        fill="none" stroke="black" stroke-width="2"/>
      <use x="50" y="100"  xlink:href="#square"/>
    </g>
  </svg>
</body>
</html>
```

7.4.2 Describing

<!-- --> denotes a comment.

<desc> denotes a description......CS.

<title> denotes a human-readable title......CS. It is often displayed as a tooltip as the pointing device moves over the element. It should be the first child element of its parent.

```
<!DOCTYPE html>
<html>
<head></head>
<body>
  <svg>
    <g>
      <title>circle</title>
      <desc>
        displays a tooltip as the pointer moves over the shape.
      </desc>
      <circle cx="60" cy="60" r="50"/>
    </g>
  </svg>
</body>
</html>
```

circle

<metadata> specifies metadata......C. It should contain elements from other XML namespaces.

(courtesy of http://www.w3.org/TR/SVG11/metadata.html#MetadataElement)

```
<?xml version="1.0" standalone="yes"?>
<svg width="4in" height="3in" version="1.1"
   xmlns = 'http://www.w3.org/2000/svg'>
   <desc xmlns:myfoo="http://example.org/myfoo">
     <myfoo:title>This is a financial report</myfoo:title>
     <myfoo:descr>The global description uses markup from
        the <myfoo:emph>myfoo</myfoo:emph> namespace.
     </myfoo:descr>
     <myfoo:scene>
        <myfoo:what>widget $growth</myfoo:what>
        <myfoo:contains>$three $graph-bar</myfoo:contains>
        <myfoo:when>1998 $through 2000</myfoo:when>
     </myfoo:scene>
   </desc>
   <metadata>
     <rdf:RDF
xmlns:rdf = "http://www.w3.org/1999/02/22-rdf-syntax-ns#"
     xmlns:rdfs = "http://www.w3.org/2000/01/rdf-schema#"
        xmlns:dc = "http://purl.org/dc/elements/1.1/" >
       <rdf:Description about="http://example.org/myfoo"
          dc:title="MyFoo Financial Report"
          dc:description="$three $bar $thousands $dollars "
          dc:publisher="Example Organization"
          dc:date="2000-04-11"
          dc:format="image/svg+xml"
          dc:language="en" >
        <dc:creator>
          <rdf:Bag>
            <rdf:li>Irving Bird</rdf:li>
            <rdf:li>Mary Lambert</rdf:li>
          </rdf:Bag>
        </dc:creator>
       </rdf:Description>
     </rdf:RDF>
   </metadata>
</svg>
```

7.4.3 Linking

<a> specifies a hyperlink......OCGPSX.
......transform (7.3.4)
......xlink:href="<iri>": the referenced resource.
......target="{_replace|_self|_parent|_top|_blank|<XML name>"}: the target display. '_replace' displays in the same rectangular area in the same frame. '_self' displays in the same frame. '_parent' displays in the immediate frameset parent. '_top' displays in the full window or tab. '_blank' displays in a new un-named window or tab. <XML name> displays in the named frame/pane. If it does not exist, it is created with the name.

Clicking the circle displays 'markers.html' in the current window.

```
<!DOCTYPE html>
<html>
<head></head>
<body>
  <svg>
    <a xlink:href="markers.html">
      <circle cx="50" cy="50" r="50"/>
    </a>
  </svg>
</body>
</html>
```

<style> embeds a style sheet......C.
......type="<MIME type>": the type. The default is "text/css".
......media=<media descriptors>": (1.1.5)
......title="<text>": an advisory title.

Notice that a style may be defined with the 'style' attribute as well.

```
<!DOCTYPE html>
<html>
<head></head>
<body>
  <svg>
    <defs>
      <style type="text/css"><![CDATA[
        #rect {fill: red;
              stroke: blue;
              stroke-width: 3}
      ]]></style>
    </defs>
    <rect id="rect" x="20" y="20" width="60" height="30"/>
    <rect x="20" y="60" width="60" height="30"
          style="fill:none; stroke:black; stroke-width:3;"/>
  </svg>
</body>
</html>
```

<foreignObject> includes a foreign object......OCGPS.
......transform (7.3.4)
......x="<coord.>": the x coord. of the upper-left corner
......y="<coord.>": the y coord. of the upper-left corner
......width="<length>": the width
......height="<length>": the height

<switch> processes one of the direct child elements......OCGPS. It evaluates the 'requiredFeatures', 'requiredExtensions' and 'systemLanguage' attributes on its direct child elements in order, and then processes the first child for which these attributes evaluates to true. All other direct child elements will be bypassed.

......transform (7.3.4)

......requiredFeatures="<space-separated Feature Strings>": evaluates to true if all features are supported. It evaluates to false otherwise, thus skipping the element. For a complete list of Feature Strings, refer to: http://www.w3.org/TR/SVG11/feature.html

......requiredExtensions="<space-separated IRIs>": evaluates to true if all extensions are supported. It evaluates to false otherwise, thus skipping the element.

......systemLanguage="<comma-separated language names>": evaluates to true if one of the languages specified is supported. It evaluates to false otherwise, thus skipping the element. Eg.: <text systemLanguage="ch, en"><!-- content goes here --></text>

(courtesy of http://www.w3.org/TR/SVG11/extend.html)

```
<?xml version="1.0" standalone="yes"?>
<svg width="4in" height="3in" version="1.1"
  xmlns = 'http://www.w3.org/2000/svg'>
   <desc>This example uses the 'switch' element to provide a
          fallback graphical representation of an paragraph, if
          XMHTML is not supported.</desc>
   <!-- The 'switch' element will process the first child element
      whose testing attributes evaluate to true.-->
   <switch>
      <!-- Process the embedded XHTML if the
requiredExtensions attribute evaluates to true (i.e., the user
agent supports XHTML embedded within SVG). -->
      <foreignObject width="100" height="50"
        requiredExtensions=
       "http://example.com/SVGExtensions/EmbeddedXHTML">
         <!-- XHTML content goes here -->
         <body xmlns="http://www.w3.org/1999/xhtml">
            <p>Here is a paragraph that requires word wrap</p>
          </body>
       </foreignObject>
       <!-- Else, process the following alternative SVG.
            Note that there are no testing attributes on the 'text'
         element. If no testing attributes are provided, it is as if
    there were testing attributes and they evaluated to true.-->
      <text font-size="10" font-family="Verdana">
         <tspan x="10" y="10">
            Here is a paragraph that</tspan>
         <tspan x="10" y="20">requires word wrap.</tspan>
       </text>
   </switch>
</svg>
```

7.5 Painting

7.5.1 Filling

......fill="{none|<color>|<func. iri>}": paints the interior of the given graphical element with the specified colour/method. If a path is open and this attribute is not 'none', the path is closed by joining the end with the start.

......fill-rule="{nonzero|evenodd}": specifies which parts are considered 'inside' and to be painted. To determine if a part is considered 'inside', draw a ray from that point to infinity in any direction. For nonzero, starting with zero, add one each time a path segment crosses the ray from left to right and subtract one each time a path segment crosses the ray from right to left. The point is inside if the result is non-zero. For evenodd, count the number of path segments that the ray crosses. The point is inside if the number is odd.

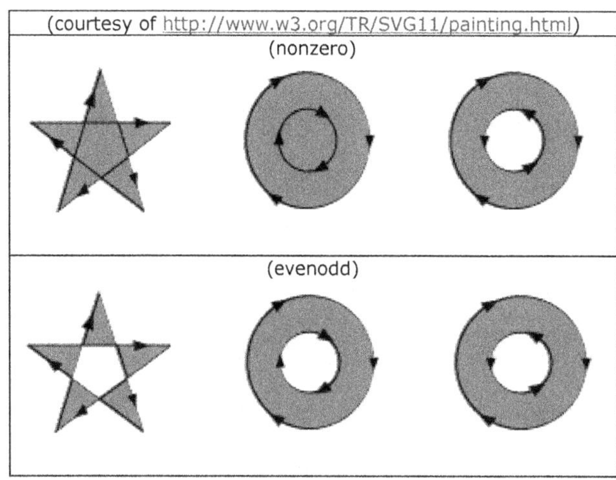

(courtesy of http://www.w3.org/TR/SVG11/painting.html)

......fill-opacity="{0.0 to 1.0}": specifies the opacity of the paint for the interior. 0.0 means fully transparent. 1.0 means fully opaque.

......opacity="{0.0 to 1.0}": combines stroke-opacity, fill-opacity etc.

......visibility="{visible|hidden|collapse}": specifies whether the element is visible.

```
<!DOCTYPE html>
<html>
<head></head>
<body>
  <svg>
    <circle cx="300" cy="100" r="50"
            stroke="black" stroke-width="5" />
    <path d="M20,20 200,200 200,100 20,100
                 100,20 200,20  100,200 300,100"
             stroke="black" stroke-width="5"
             fill="orange" fill-rule="evenodd" fill-opacity="0.7"
/>
  </svg>
</body>
</html>
```

7.5.2 Gradient

<linearGradient> defines a linearGradient for 'fill'......CPSX

......x1="<coord.>": x coord. of the starting point. % may be used.

......y1="<coord.>": y coord. of the starting point. % may be used.

......x2="<coord.>": x coord. of the ending point. % may be used.

......y2="<coord.>": y coord. of the ending point. % may be used.

......gradientUnits="{userSpaceOnUse|objectBoundingBox}: the coord. system for 'x1', 'y1', 'x2', and 'y2'.

......gradientTransform="<transform-list as described in 7.3.4>": the transformation from the gradient coordinate system onto the target coordinate system.

......spreadMethod="{pad|reflect|repeat}": what happens if the gradient starts or ends inside the bounds of the target rectangle. 'pad' fills the remainder of the region with terminal colors. 'reflect' fills the region start-to-end, end-to-start, start-to-end etc. 'repeat' fills the region start-to-end, start-to-end, start-to-end etc.

......xlink:href="<iri>": reference to a different 'linearGradient' or 'radialGradient' element. The attributes and gradient stops of the referenced element are inherited.

<radialGradient> defines a radial gradient for 'fill'......CPSX

......cx="<coord.>": x coord. of the center of the outermost circle.
......cy="<coord.>": y coord. of the center of the outermost circle.
......r="<length>": the radius of the outermost circle.
......fx="<coord.>": the x coord. of the focal point (ie. 0% stop)
......fy="<coord.>": the y coord. of the focal point (ie. 0% stop)
......gradientUnits (see <linearGradient>)
......gradientTransform (see <linearGradient>)
......spreadMethod (see <linearGradient>)
......xlink:href (see <linearGradient>)

<stop> defines the ramp of colors to use within <linearGradient> and <radialGradient>......CPS

......offset="<0.0 to 1.0| 0% to 100%>": where the stop is placed.
......stop-color="<color>": the color for the stop.
......stop-opacity="<0.0 to 1.0>": the opacity of the stop.

```
<!DOCTYPE html>
<html>
<head></head>
<body>
  <svg>
    <defs>
      <linearGradient id="lg" x1="20%" x2="80%"
                spreadmethod="reflect">
        <stop offset="0%" stop-color="black"/>
        <stop offset="100%" stop-color="white"/>
      </linearGradient>
      <radialGradient id="rg" cx="50%" cy="50%" r="25%"
                spreadmethod="repeat">
        <stop offset="0%" stop-color="black"/>
        <stop offset="50%" stop-color="orange"/>
        <stop offset="100%" stop-color="white"/>
      </radialGradient>
    </defs>
    <rect x="20" y="20" width="200" height="50"
        fill="url(#lg)"/>
    <rect x="20" y="90" width="200" height="50"
        fill="url(#rg)"/>
  </svg>
</body>
</html>
```

7.5.3 Advanced Techniques

<image> displays an image file such as a PNG, JPG, or SVG file......OCGPSX

......preserveAspectRatio (7.2.2)
......transform (7.3.4)
......x="<coord.>": the x coord. of the upper-left corner.
......y="<coord.>": the y coord. of the upper-left corner.
......width="<length>": the width.
......height="<length>": the height.
......xlink:href="<iri>": the source of the image.

```
<!DOCTYPE html>
<html>
<head></head>
<body>
  <svg>
    <image width="100" height="200"
            xlink:href="flower.jpg">
      <title>a flower</title>
    </image>
  </svg>
</body>
</html>
```

<pattern> defines a graphical object to be tiled repeatedly using 'fill' and 'stroke'......OCPSX

......viewBox (7.2.2)
......preserveAspectRatio (7.2.2)
......x="<coord.>": how the pattern tiles are placed.
......y="<coord.>": how the pattern tiles are placed.
......width="<length>": the width of each displayed tile.
......height="<length>": the height of each displayed tile.
......patternUnits="{userSpaceOnUse|objectBoundingBox}": the coordinate system for 'x', 'y', 'width' and 'height'.
......patternContentUnits="{userSpaceOnUse|objectBoundingBox}" : the coordinate system for the contents of the pattern. This attribute has no effect if 'viewBox' is specified.
......patternTransform="<transform-list as described in 7.3.4>": transformation for the pattern.
......xlink:href="<iri>": another pattern which provides the attributes and child elements for inheritance.

```
<!DOCTYPE html>
<html>
<head></head>
<body>
  <svg>
    <defs>
      <pattern id="flowers" patternUnits="userSpaceOnUse"
              x="0" y="0" width="40" height="80"
              viewBox="0 5 10 20">
        <image width="10" height="20"
              xlink:href="flower.jpg">
        </image>
      </pattern>
      <pattern id="circles" patternUnits="userSpaceOnUse"
              x="0" y="0" width="10" height="10"
              viewBox="0 0 35 35">
        <circle cx="20" cy="20" r="15"/>
      </pattern>
    </defs>
    <circle cx="200" cy="200" r="150" stroke-width="30"
          fill="url(#flowers)" stroke="url(#circles)"/>
  </svg>
</body>
</html>
```

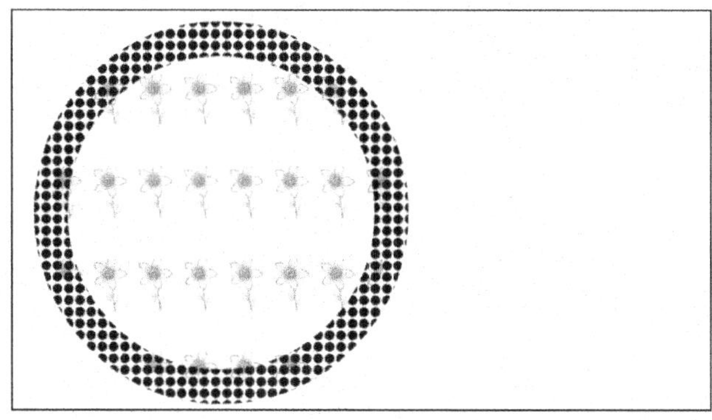

<clipPath> defines a shape where overlapping contents can be viewed using the 'clip-path' attribute......OCPS

......transform (7.3.4)
......clip-rule (see 7.5.1 fill-rule)
......clipPathUnits="{userSpaceOnUse|objectBoundingBox}": the coordinate system for the contents of the 'clipPath'.

```
<!DOCTYPE html>
<html>
<head></head>
<body>
  <svg>
    <defs>
      <clipPath id="circle">
        <circle cx="100" cy="100" r="100">
      </clipPath>
    </defs>
  <g clip-path="url(#circle)">
  <rect x="0" y="0" width="1000" height="25" fill="black"/>
  <rect x="0"y="25"width="1000" height="25" fill="orange"/>
  <rect x="0" y="50" width="1000" height="25" fill="white"/>
  <rect x="0" y="75" width="1000" height="25" fill="black"/>
  <rect x="0"y="100"width="1000"height="25"fill="orange"/>
  <rect x="0"y="125"width="1000" height="25" fill="white"/>
  <rect x="0"y="150"width="1000" height="25" fill="black"/>
  </g>
  </svg>
</body>
</html>
```

<mask> specifies a semi-transparent mask for compositing foreground objects into the current background......OCPS. For each pixel, a mask value is calculated from the RGB and alpha channels of the mask. The effect of a mask is identical to multiplying the alpha channel(transparency) of the given object with the mask's mask value. The brighter/whiter a pixel on the mask, the more opaque is the object.

......x="<coord.>": the x coord. of the upper-left corner.
......y="<coord.>": the y coord. of the upper-left corner.
......width="<length>": the width.
......height="<length>": the height.
......maskUnits="{userSpaceOnUse|<u>objectBoundingBox</u>}": the coordinate system for 'x', 'y', 'width', and 'height'.
......maskContentUnits="{<u>userSpaceOnUse</u>|objectBoundingBox}": the coordinate system for the contents of the 'mask'.

```
<!DOCTYPE html>
<html>
<head></head>
<body>
  <svg>
    <defs>
      <mask id="flower">
        <image width="100" height="200"
            xlink:href="flower.jpg">
        </image>
      </mask>
    </defs>
    <rect width="100" height="200" mask="url(#flower)"/>
  </svg>
</body>
</html>
```

7.6 Filter

A filter is used to perform complex pixel operations that enhance the look of a piece of graphical content. With a filter, a lot of common artwork can be achieved. The filter effects include shadowing, blurring, protrusion, lighting etc.

7.6.1 An Example

<filter> defines a filter......CPSX. A filter element is referenced via the 'filter' attribute.

......x="<coord.>": the region to which the filter applies.
......y="<coord.>": the region to which the filter applies.
......width="<length>": the region to which the filter applies.
......height="<length>": the region to which the filter applies.
......filterRes="<width> [height]": the dimensions of the intermediate images in pixels.
......filterUnits="{userSpaceOnUse|<u>objectBoundingBox</u>}": the coordinate system for 'x', 'y', 'width', and 'height'.
......primitiveUnits="{<u>userSpaceOnUse</u>|objectBoundingBox}": the coordinate system for the various length values within the filter primitives and for the attributes that define the filter primitive subregion.
......xlink:href="<iri>": another filter which provides the attributes and child elements for inheritance.

(courtesy of http://www.w3.org/TR/SVG11/filters.html)

```
<?xml version="1.0"?>
<!DOCTYPE svg PUBLIC "-//W3C//DTD SVG 1.1//EN"
    "http://www.w3.org/Graphics/SVG/1.1/DTD/svg11.dtd">
<svg width="7.5cm" height="5cm" viewBox="0 0 200 120"
   xmlns="http://www.w3.org/2000/svg" version="1.1">
  <title>Example filters01.svg - introducing filter
      effects</title>
  <desc>An example which combines multiple filter primitives
     to produce a 3D lighting effect on a graphic consisting
     of the string "SVG" sitting on top of an oval filled in red
     and surrounded by an oval outlined in red.</desc>
  <defs>
    <filter id="MyFilter" filterUnits="userSpaceOnUse"
          x="0" y="0" width="200" height="120">
      <feGaussianBlur in="SourceAlpha" stdDeviation="4"
                     result="blur"/>
```

```
      <feOffset in="blur" dx="4" dy="4" result="offsetBlur"/>
      <feSpecularLighting in="blur" surfaceScale="5"
          specularConstant=".75" specularExponent="20"
          lighting-color="#bbbbbb" result="specOut">
        <fePointLight x="-5000" y="-10000" z="20000"/>
      </feSpecularLighting>
      <feComposite in="specOut" in2="SourceAlpha"
                   operator="in" result="specOut"/>
      <feComposite in="SourceGraphic" in2="specOut"
        operator="arithmetic" k1="0" k2="1" k3="1" k4="0"
          result="litPaint"/>
      <feMerge>
        <feMergeNode in="offsetBlur"/>
        <feMergeNode in="litPaint"/>
      </feMerge>
    </filter>
  </defs>
  <rect x="1" y="1" width="198" height="118"
        fill="#888888" stroke="blue" />
  <g filter="url(#MyFilter)" >
    <path fill="none" stroke="#D90000" stroke-width="10"
          d="M50,90 C0,90 0,30 50,30 L150,30
             C200,30 200,90 150,90 z" />
    <path fill="#D90000"
          d="M60,80 C30,80 30,40 60,40 L140,40
             C170,40 170,80 140,80 z" />
    <g fill="#FFFFFF" stroke="black" font-size="45"
       font-family="Verdana" >
      <text x="52" y="76">SVG</text>
    </g>
  </g>
</svg>
```

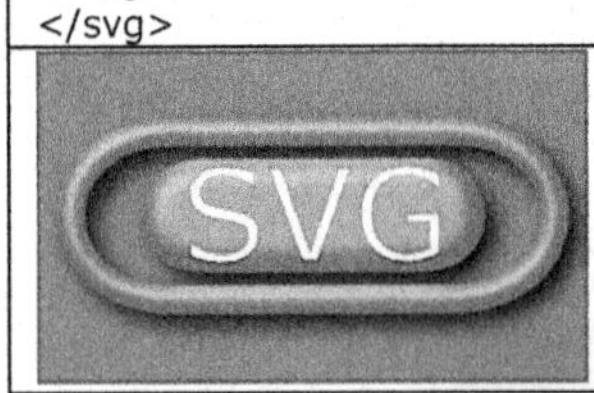

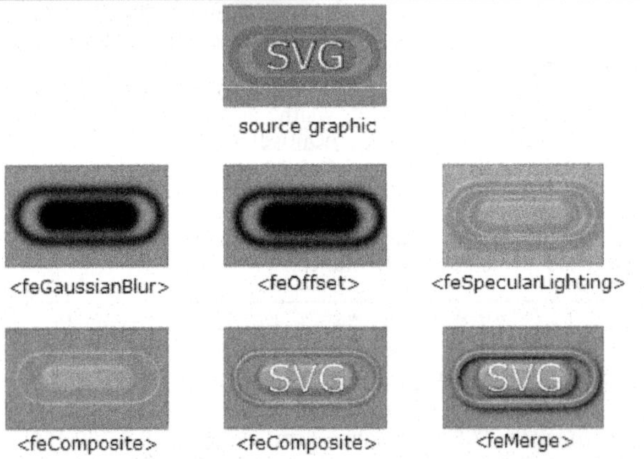

source graphic

<feGaussianBlur> <feOffset> <feSpecularLighting>

<feComposite> <feComposite> <feMerge>

7.6.2 Simple Operations

<feFlood> creates a rectangle filled with the color and opacity values from the properties 'flood-color' and 'flood-opacity'......CPFS.

......x="<coord.>": the x coord. of the upper-left corner.
......y="<coord.>": the y coord. of the upper-left corner.
......width="<length>": the width of the rectangle.
......height="<length>": the height of the rectangle.
......result="<filter primitive name>": the reference name to be used via 'in' in another filter primitive.
......flood-color="<color>": the filling color.
......flood-opacity="{0.0 to 1.0}": the filling opacity.

<feImage> loads an external image......CPFSX

......preserveAspectRatio (7.2.2)
......xlink:href="<iri>": the image source.

<feTile> fills a target rectangle with a repeated, tiled pattern of an input image......CPFS

......in="{SourceGraphic | SourceAlpha | BackgroundImage | BackgroundAlpha | FillPaint | StrokePaint | <filter primitive name>}": SourceGraphic represents the original input into the <filter> element. SourceAlpha represents the alpha channel of the original input into the <filter> element. BackgroundImage represents the background under the filter region. BackgroundAlpha represents the alpha channel of the background under the filter region. FillPaint represents the value of the 'fill' property on the target element for the filter effect. StrokePaint represents the value of the 'stroke' property on the target element for the filter effect.

```
<!DOCTYPE html>
<html>
<head></head>
<body>
  <svg>
    <defs>
      <filter id="rectangle">
        <feFlood width="100" height="200"
                 flood-color="green" flood-opacity="0.5"/>
      </filter>
      <filter id="flowers">
        <feImage xlink:href="flower.jpg" width="40"
                 height="80" result="one"/>
        <feTile in="one"/>
      </filter>
    </defs>
    <rect width="400" height="200" filter="url(#flowers)"/>
    <rect width="400" height="200"
                       filter="url(#rectangle)"/>
  </svg>
</body>
</html>
```

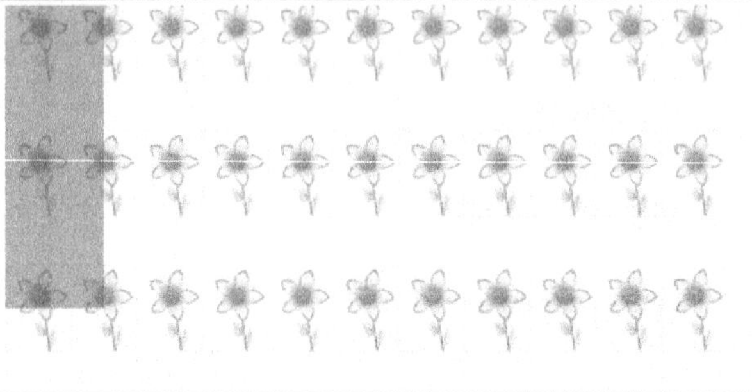

7.6.3 Blurring

<feGaussianBlur> performs a Gaussian blur on the input image......CPFS

......in (7.6.2)
...... stdDeviation="<number> [number]": the blurness. If two numbers are provided, they represent the standard deviation along the x-axis and y-axis respectively. If one number is provided, then that value is used for both X and Y.

<feTurbulence> creates an image using the Perlin turbulence function......CPFS. It allows the synthesis of artificial textures like clouds and marble.

......baseFrequency="<number> [number]": a parameter for the noise function. If two numbers are provided, they represent values in the X and Y directions respectively. If one number is provided, then that value is used for both X and Y. The higher the frequency, the smaller the individual 'noise patches' look.

......numOctaves="<integer>": a parameter for the noise function.
......seed="<number>": the starting number for the pseudo random number generator.
......stitchTiles="{stitch|noStitch}": whether to attempt smoothness at the border of tiles.
......type="{fractalNoise|turbulence}": whether to perform a noise or turbulence function. Compared to a 'turbulence', a 'noise' looks softer with less obvious boundaries.

For <feTurbulence>, the resulting images are noises made up of various colours.

```
<!DOCTYPE html>
<html>
<head></head>
<body>
  <svg>
    <defs>
      <filter id="g5">
        <feGaussianBlur in="SourceGraphic"
                        stdDeviation="5">
      </filter>
      <filter id="g20">
        <feGaussianBlur in="SourceGraphic"
                        stdDeviation="20">
      </filter>
      <filter id="n05-8">
        <feTurbulence type="fractalNoise"
                  baseFrequency="0.05" numOctaves="8">
      </filter>
      <filter id="t05-8">
        <feTurbulence type="turbulence"
                  baseFrequency="0.05" numOctaves="8">
      </filter>
      <filter id="n1-8">
        <feTurbulence type="fractalNoise"
                  baseFrequency="0.1" numOctaves="8">
      </filter>
      <filter id="t1-8">
        <feTurbulence type="turbulence"
                  baseFrequency="0.1" numOctaves="8">
      </filter>
      <filter id="n05-4">
        <feTurbulence type="fractalNoise"
                  baseFrequency="0.05" numOctaves="4">
      </filter>
      <filter id="t05-4">
        <feTurbulence type="turbulence"
                  baseFrequency="0.05" numOctaves="4">
      </filter>
      <symbol id="SVG">
        <rect width="200" height="100"/>
        <g fill="orange" stroke="black" font-size="45"
                                  font-family="Verdana">
          <text x="52" y="66">SVG</text>
        </g>
      </symbol>
    </defs>

    <use xlink:href="#SVG" x="5" y="20"
          filter="url(#g5)"/>
    <use xlink:href="#SVG" x="250" y="20"
          filter="url(#g20)"/>

    <use xlink:href="#SVG" x="5" y="160"
          filter="url(#n05-8)"/>
    <use xlink:href="#SVG" x="250" y="160"
          filter="url(#t05-8)"/>

    <use xlink:href="#SVG" x="5" y="300"
          filter="url(#n1-8)"/>
    <use xlink:href="#SVG" x="250" y="300"
          filter="url(#t1-8)"/>
    <use xlink:href="#SVG" x="5" y="440"
          filter="url(#n05-4)"/>
    <use xlink:href="#SVG" x="250" y="440"
          filter="url(#t05-4)"/>
  </svg>
</body>
</html>
```

7.6.4 Offsetting

<feOffset> offsets the input image relative to its current position in the image space by the specified vector......CPFS. This is important for effects like drop shadows.
......in (7.6.2)
......dx="<number>": the amount to offset along the x-axis.
......dy="<number>": the amount to offset along the y-axis.

<feDisplacementMap> uses the pixel values from 'in2' to spatially displace the image pixels from 'in'......CPFS
......in (7.6.2)
......in2 (7.6.2)
......scale="<number>": the displacement scale factor.
......xChannelSelector="{R|G|B|A}": the channel from 'in2' used to displace the pixels in 'in' along the x-axis.
......yChannelSelector="{R|G|B|A}": the channel from 'in2' used to displace the pixels in 'in' along the y-axis

<feMorphology> fattens or thins the artwork......CPFS
......in (7.6.2)
......operator="{erode|dilate}": whether to thin(erode) or fatten(dilate) the source graphic.
......radius="<number> [number]": the radius(radii) for the operation. If two numbers are provided, the first represents the x-radius and the second represents the y-radius.

```
<!DOCTYPE html>
<html>
<head></head>
<body>
  <svg>
    <defs>
      <filter id="e2">
        <feMorphology in="SourceGraphic" operator="erode"
                                          radius="2"/>
      </filter>
      <filter id="e4">
```

```
      <feMorphology in="SourceGraphic" operator="erode"
                                        radius="4"/>
    </filter>
    <filter id="d2">
      <feMorphology in="SourceGraphic" operator="dilate"
                                        radius="2"/>
    </filter>
    <filter id="d4">
      <feMorphology in="SourceGraphic" operator="dilate"
                                        radius="4"/>
    </filter>
    <symbol id="flower">
      <image width="100" height="200"
             xlink:href="flower.jpg">
      </image>
    </symbol>
  </defs>
  <use xlink:href="#flower" x="0"/>
  <use xlink:href="#flower" x="110" filter="url(#e2)"/>
  <use xlink:href="#flower" x="220" filter="url(#e4)"/>
  <use xlink:href="#flower" x="330" filter="url(#d2)"/>
  <use xlink:href="#flower" x="440" filter="url(#d4)"/>
</svg>
</body>
</html>
```

7.6.5 Lighting

The lighting calculation follows the standard Phong lighting model. The alpha channel of the image is used as the bump map. There are two types of lighting - specular lighting and diffuse lighting. Specular lighting is observed at smooth surfaces, while diffuse lighting is observed at rough surfaces. For a lighting primitive, exactly one light source must be specified as its child element. A light source can be a 'point light', a 'spot light' or a 'distant light'.

<feSpecularLighting> defines specular lighting......CPFS

......in (7.6.2)
......lighting-color="<color>": the color of the light source.
......surfaceScale="<number>": the height of the surface when the input alpha channel equals 1.
......specularConstant="<number>": k_s in Phong lighting model.
......specularExponent="<number>": the 'brightness'/'shininess'.
......kernelUnitLength="<number> [number]": the intended distance in current filter units for dx and dy respectively, in the surface normal calculation formulas.

<feDiffuseLighting> defines diffuse lighting......CPFS

......in (7.6.2)
......lighting-color="<color>": the color of the light source.
......surfaceScale="<number>": the height of the surface when the input alpha channel equals 1.
......diffuseConstant="<number>": k_d in Phong lighting model.
......kernelUnitLength="<number> [number]": the intended distance in current filter units for dx and dy respectively, in the surface normal calculation formulas.

<fePointLight> defines a light source made up of a 'point light'......C

......x="<number>": the x location for the light source.
......y="<number>": the y location for the light source.
......z="<number>": the z location for the light source.

<feSpotLight> defines a light source made up of a 'spot light'......C

......x="<number>": the x location for the light source.
......y="<number>": the y location for the light source.
......z="<number>": the z location for the light source.
......pointsAtX="<number>": the x location of the pointed place.
......pointsAtY="<number>": the y location of the pointed place.
......pointsAtZ="<number>": the z location of the pointed place.
......specularExponent="<number>": the focus for the light source.
......limitingConeAngle="<number>": the angle in degrees between the spot light axis and the spot light cone.

<feDistantLight> defines a light source made up of a 'distant light'......C

......azimuth="<number>": angle in degrees for the light source on the XY plane from the x-axis.
......elevation="<number>": angle in degrees for the light source from the XY plane towards the z-axis.

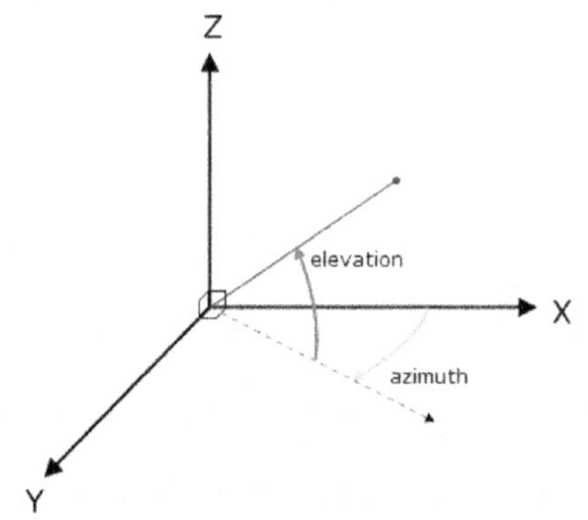


```
<!DOCTYPE html>
<html>
<head></head>
<body>
  <svg>
    <defs>
      <filter id="point-50">
        <feSpecularLighting surfaceScale="5" lighting-color="red"
             specularConstant="0.75" specularExponent="50">
          <fePointLight x="50" y="80" z="100"/>
        </feSpecularLighting>
      </filter>
      <filter id="spot-20">
        <feSpecularLighting surfaceScale="5" lighting-color="red"
             specularConstant="0.75" specularExponent="50">
          <feSpotLight x="50" y="80" z="100" limitingConeAngle="20"
               pointsAtX="50" pointsAtY="50" pointsAtZ="0"/>
        </feSpecularLighting>
      </filter>
      <filter id="distant-50">
        <feSpecularLighting surfaceScale="5" lighting-color="red"
             specularConstant="0.75" specularExponent="50">
          <feDistantLight azimuth="40" elevation="60" />
        </feSpecularLighting>
      </filter>
      <filter id="point-150">
        <feSpecularLighting surfaceScale="5" lighting-color="red"
             specularConstant="0.75" specularExponent="150">
          <fePointLight x="50" y="80" z="100"/>
        </feSpecularLighting>
      </filter>
      <filter id="spot-40">
        <feSpecularLighting surfaceScale="5" lighting-color="red"
             specularConstant="0.75" specularExponent="50">
          <feSpotLight x="50" y="80" z="100" limitingConeAngle="40"
               pointsAtX="50" pointsAtY="50" pointsAtZ="0"
        </feSpecularLighting>
      </filter>
      <filter id="diffuse">
        <feDiffuseLighting surfaceScale="5" lighting-color="red"
             diffuseConstant="0.75">
          <fePointLight x="50" y="80" z="10"/>
        </feSpecularLighting>
      </filter>
      <symbol id="circle">
        <circle cx="50" cy="50" r="40" fill="green"/>
```

```
      </symbol>
    </defs>
    <use xlink:href="#circle" x="0" filter="url(#point-50)"/>
    <use xlink:href="#circle" x="110" filter="url(#spot-20)"/>
    <use xlink:href="#circle" x="220" filter="url(#distant-50)"/>
    <use xlink:href="#circle" x="0" y="120" filter="url(#point-150)"/>
    <use xlink:href="#circle" x="110" y="120" filter="url(#spot-40)"/>
    <use xlink:href="#circle" x="220" y="120" filter="url(#diffuse)"/>
  </svg>
</body>
</html>
```

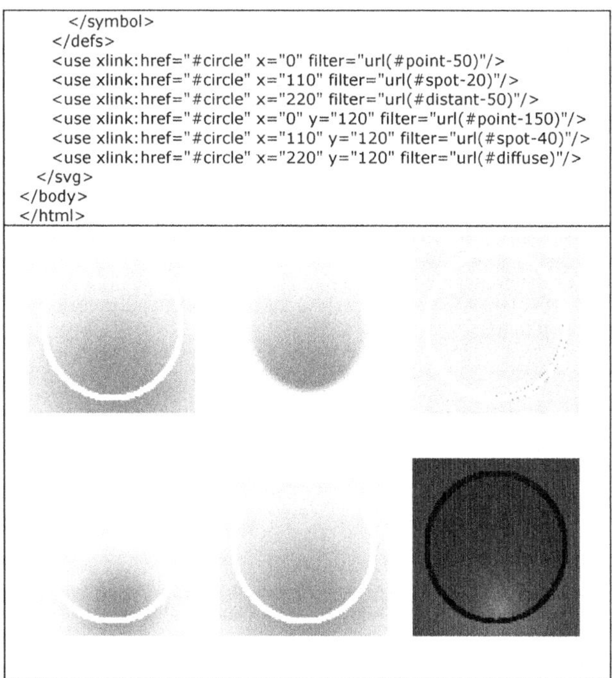

7.6.6 Merging

<feBlend> composites two objects together using commonly used imaging software blending modes......CPFS. It performs a pixel-wise combination of two input images.

......in (7.6.2)
......in2 (7.6.2)
......mode="{normal | multiply | screen | darken | lighten}": how the two images are blended.

mode	resultant color
normal	$(1-O_a)*C_b + C_a$
multiply	$(1-O_a)*C_b + (1-O_b)*C_a + C_a*C_b$
screen	$C_b + C_a - C_a*C_b$
darken	$Min((1-O_a)*C_b + C_a, (1-O_b)*C_a + C_b)$
lighen	$Max((1-O_a)*C_b + C_a, (1-O_b)*C_a + C_b)$

```
<!DOCTYPE html>
<html>
<head></head>
<body>
  <svg>
    <defs>
      <filter id="normal" >
        <feFlood width="100" height="200"
                 flood-color="yellow" flood-opacity="0.5"
                 result="b"/>
        <feBlend mode="normal" in="b"
                 in2="SourceGraphic"/>
      </filter>
      <filter id="multiply" >
        <feFlood width="100" height="200"
                 flood-color="yellow" flood-opacity="0.5"
                 result="b"/>
        <feBlend mode="multiply" in="b"
                 in2="SourceGraphic"/>
      </filter>
      <filter id="screen" >
        <feFlood width="100" height="200"
                 flood-color="yellow" flood-opacity="0.5"
                 result="b"/>
        <feBlend mode="screen" in="b"
                 in2="SourceGraphic"/>
      </filter>
      <filter id="darken" >
        <feFlood width="100" height="200"
                 flood-color="yellow" flood-opacity="0.5"
                 result="b"/>
        <feBlend mode="darken" in="b"
                 in2="SourceGraphic"/>
      </filter>
      <filter id="lighten" >
        <feFlood width="100" height="200"
                 flood-color="yellow" flood-opacity="0.5"
                 result="b"/>
        <feBlend mode="lighten" in="b"
                 in2="SourceGraphic"/>
      </filter>
      <symbol id="flower">
        <image width="90" height="200"
               xlink:href="flower.jpg"></image>
      </symbol>
    </defs>
    <use xlink:href="#flower" x="0" filter="url(#normal)"/>
    <use xlink:href="#flower" x="100"
        filter="url(#multiply)"/>
    <use xlink:href="#flower" x="200" filter="url(#screen)"/>
    <use xlink:href="#flower" x="300" filter="url(#darken)"/>
    <use xlink:href="#flower" x="400" filter="url(#lighten)"/>
  </svg>
</body>
</html>
```

<feComposite> performs a combination of two input images pixel-wise using one of the Porter-Duff compositing operations......CPFS. The 'arithmetic' operation is useful for combining the output from a lighting filter with texture data. It is also useful for implementing dissolve.

......in (7.6.2)
......in2 (7.6.2)
......operator="{over|in|out|atop|xor|arithmetic}": the operation to perform. For 'arithmetic', result = k1*i1*i2 + k2*i1 + k3*i2 + k4.
......k1="<number>": an attribute for the 'arithmetic' operation.
......k2="<number>": an attribute for the 'arithmetic' operation.
......k3="<number>": an attribute for the 'arithmetic' operation.
......k4="<number>": an attribute for the 'arithmetic' operation.

opacity 1.0 (with feFlood)
opacity 0.5 (with feFlood)
over in out atop xor arithmetic

opacity 1.0 (without feFlood)
opacity 0.5 (without feFlood)
over in out atop xor arithmetic

<feMerge> stacks two or more images on top of each other......CPFS. Although the same effect can be achieved by applying the 'over' operator of the <feComposite> filter repeatedly, it is more convenient to have this common form. The last specified <feMergeNode> child element appears at the top.

<feMergeNode> specifies a graphic to be stacked using <feMerge>......C
......in (7.6.2)

7.6.7 Low-level Operations

<feConvolveMatrix> combines pixels in the input image with neighboring pixels to produce a resulting image......CPFS. The effects that can be achieved through convolutions include blurring, edge detection, sharpening, embossing and beveling.
......in (7.6.2)
......order="<integer> [integer]": the number of cells in each dimension for 'kernelMatrix'.
......kernelMatrix="<number> [number]......": the values in the kernel matrix for the convolution.
......divisor="<number>": the divisor. The default value is the sum of all values in kernelMatrix.
......bias="<number>": the bias term.
......targetX="<integer>": the positioning in X of the convolution matrix relative to a given target pixel in the input image. By default, it equals floor(orderX/2).
......targetY="<integer>": the positioning in Y of the convolution matrix relative to a given target pixel in the input image. By default, it equals floor(orderY/2).
......edgeMode="{duplicate|wrap|none}": how to extend the input image with color values so that the matrix operations can be applied at the edge. "duplicate" extends by duplicating the color values at the given edge. "wrap" extends by taking the color values from the opposite edge. "none" extends with pixel value of zero for R,G,B, and A.
......kernelUnitLength="<number> [number]": the intended distance between successive columns and rows, respectively, in the 'kernelMatrix'.
......preserveAlpha="{false|true}": whether to apply the convolution to the color channels only. A value of 'false' will apply to all channels including the alpha channel.

$$\mathbf{COLOR}_{x,y}=\Big(\sum_{i=0 \text{ to } orderY-1}\sum_{j=0 \text{ to } orderX-1} \mathbf{SOURCE}_{x-targetX+J,\ y-targetY+I} * \mathbf{kernelMatrix}_{orderX-J-1,\ orderY-I-1}\Big) / \text{divisor} + \text{bias} * \text{ALPHA}_{x,y}$$

When 'preserveAlpha=false',

$$\mathbf{ALPHA}_{x,y}=\Big(\sum_{i=0 \text{ to } orderY-1}\sum_{j=0 \text{ to } orderX-1} \mathbf{SOURCE}_{x-targetX+J,\ y-targetY+I} * \mathbf{kernelMatrix}_{orderX-J-1,\ orderY-I-1}\Big) / \text{divisor} + \text{bias}$$

When 'preserveAlpha=true',

$$\mathbf{ALPHA}_{x,y}=\mathbf{SOURCE}_{x,y}$$

<feColorMatrix> applies a matrix transformation by multiplying the matrix with the RGBA values of the pixel......CPFS
......in (7.6.2)
......type="{matrix | saturate | hueRotate | luminanceToAlpha}": the type of matrix operation.
......values="<number> [number]......": the content of the operation. For type='matrix', it is a list of 20 matrix values (a00 a01 a02 a03 a04 a10 a11 ...... a34). For type='saturate', it is a single real number value from 0.0 to 1.0. For type='hueRotate', it is a single real number value representing the degrees. For type='luminanceToAlpha', it is not applicable.

$$\begin{bmatrix} R' \\ G' \\ B' \\ A' \\ 1 \end{bmatrix} = \begin{bmatrix} a00 & a01 & a02 & a03 & a04 \\ a10 & a11 & a12 & a13 & a14 \\ a20 & a21 & a22 & a23 & a24 \\ a30 & a31 & a32 & a33 & a34 \\ 0 & 0 & 0 & 0 & 0 \end{bmatrix} * \begin{bmatrix} R \\ G \\ B \\ A \\ 1 \end{bmatrix}$$

<feComponentTransfer> performs component-wise remapping of data for every pixel......CPFS. It should contain the next 4 listed tags.
......in (7.6.2)

<feFuncR>, <feFuncG>, <feFuncB>, and **<feFuncA>** specify the transfer functions for the four channels......C
......type="{identity | table | discrete | linear | gamma}": the type of component transfer function.
......tableValues="<number> [number]......": the values for the lookup table.
......slope="<number>": the slope of the linear function when type='linear'.
......intercept="<number>": the intercept of the linear function when type='linear'.
......amplitude="<number>": the amplitude of the gamma function when type='gamma'.
......exponent="<number>": the exponent of the gamma function when type='gamma'.
......offset="<number>": the offset of the gamma function when type='gamma'.

type	remapped component (interval [0,1]).
identity	C
table	Given n+1 values(v_0 to v_n)find k such that: k/n <=C < (k+1)/n. The remapped component is given by: $v_k + (C-k/n)*n*(v_{k+1}-v_k)$ OR v_n when C=1.
discrete	Given n values(v_0 to v_{n-1}) find k such that: k/n <=C < (k+1)/n. The remapped component is given by: v_k OR v_{n-1} when C=1.
linear	slope*C + intercept
gamma	amplitude*$C^{exponent}$ + offset

```
<!DOCTYPE html>
<html>
<head></head>
<body>
  <svg>
    <defs>
      <linearGradient id="lg">
        <stop offset="0" stop-color="white" />
        <stop offset="0.33" stop-color="orange" />
        <stop offset="0.67" stop-color="black" />
        <stop offset="1" stop-color="red" />
      </linearGradient>
      <filter id="ct">
        <feComponentTransfer>
          <feFuncR type="table" tableValues="0 1 0.5 0.8"/>
          <feFuncG type="discrete"
                   tableValues="1 0 0.5 0.8"/>
          <feFuncB type="linear" slope="0.5"
                   intercept="0.25"/>
          <feFuncA type="gamma" amplitude="2"
                  exponent="3" offset="0.1"/>
        </feComponentTransfer>
      </filter>
    </defs>
    <rect width="500" height="100" fill="url(#lg)"
        filter="url(#ct)"/>
  </svg>
```

```
</body>
</html>
```

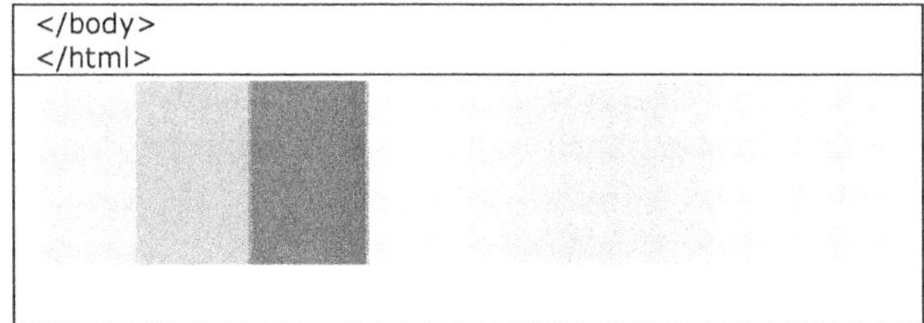

7.7 Text

A glyph, where mentioned here, refers to a unit of rendered content within a font. Often, there is a one-to-one correspondence between characters to be drawn and corresponding glyphs, but other times multiple glyphs are used to render a single character (eg. accents) or a single glyph can be used to render multiple characters (eg. ligatures).

7.7.1 Displaying

<text> creates text......OCGPS

......transform(7.3.4)

......x="<coord.> [coord.]......": the x positions of the glyphs. If there are more glyphs than the coordinates, then the text continues at the end of the last glpyph.

......y="<coord.> [coord.]......": the y positions of the glyphs. If there are more glyphs than the coordinates, then the text continues at the end of the last glpyph.

......dx="<length> [length]......": the x offsets of the glyphs. If there are more glyphs than the lengths, the extra glyphs use the last offset.

......dy="<length> [length]......": the y offsets of the glyphs. If there are more glyphs than the lengths, the extra glyphs use the last offset.

......rotate="<number> [number]......": the degrees to rotate for the glyphs. If there are more glyphs than the numbers, the extra glyphs use the last number.

......textLength="<length>": the total length of the whole text. The text is stretched or compressed to fit this length.

......lengthAdjust="{spacing|spacingAndGlyphs}": how to stretch or compress the text to fit the 'textLength'. 'spacing' adjusts only the spacing. 'spacingAndGlyphs' adjusts the lengths of the individual glyphs as well.

......text decoration="{none|underline|overline|line-through|blink}": how to decorate the text.

......direction="{ltr|rtl}": the writing direction of the text.

......unicode-bidi="{normal|embed|bidi-override}": how to treat unicode.

......letter-spacing="{normal|<length>}": the spacing between characters.

......word-spacing="{normal|<length>}": the spacing between words.

......text-anchor="{start|middle|end}": the text alignment.

......writing-mode="{lr|rl|tb}": the initial inline progression direction. 'lr' means left-to-right. 'rl' means right-to-left. 'tb' means top-to-bottom.

```
<!DOCTYPE html>
<html>
<head></head>
<body>
  <svg>
    <text x="100 200" y="40" dy="30 -30" rotate="-30 30"
          textLength="400" lengthAdjust="spacing"
          font-size="40">
      Hello World!
    </text>
    <text y="140" x="100" text-decoration="underline"
          letter-spacing="10" word-spacing="50"
          text-anchor="end"
      font-size="40">
      Helllo World!
    </text>
  </svg>
</body>
</html>
```

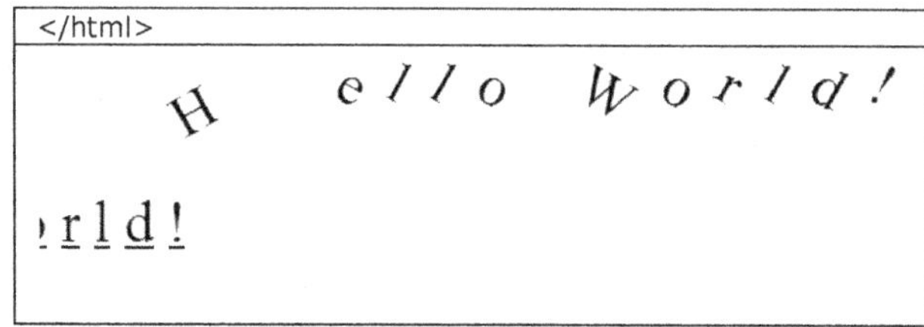

<tspan> adjust text properties within a <text> element......OCGPS

......x (see 7.7.1 <text>)
......y (see 7.7.1 <text>)
......dx (see 7.7.1 <text>)
......dy (see 7.7.1 <text>)
......rotate (see 7.7.1 <text>)
......textLength (see 7.7.1 <text>)
......lengthAdjust (see 7.7.1 <text>)

<tref> references the text data of a <text> element......OCGPSX

......xlink:href="<iri>": the <text> element whose character data shall be used.

<textPath> draws the text along the shape of a <path> element......OCGPSX

......xlink:href="<iri>"

......startOffset="<length>": the offset from the start of the <path> for the initial current text position.

......method="{align|stretch}": the method by which text is rendered.

......spacing="{auto|exact}": the spacing between glyphs.

```
<!DOCTYPE html>
<html>
<head></head>
<body>
  <svg>
    <defs>
      <path id="p" d="m 300 100
                      c 200 100 300   0 400 100
                      c 500 200 600 300 700 200
                      c 800 100 900 100 900 100" />
      <text id="when">Today </text>
    </defs>
    <text x="50" y="50" font-size="40">
      <tref xlink:href="#when"/>
      is a
      <tspan fill="orange">good day</tspan>
      to
      <textPath xlink:href="#p">
        learn SVG! Don't you agree?
      </textPath>
    </text>
  </svg>
</body>
</html>
```

Today is a good day to

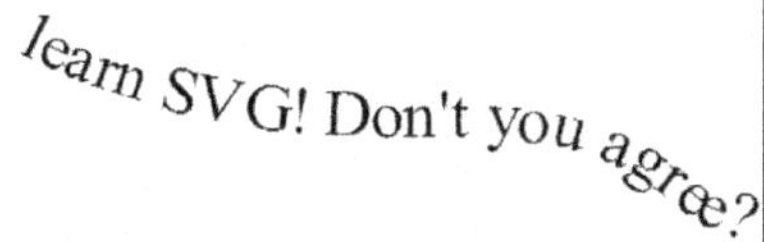

7.7.2 Fonts

(Note: At the time of writing this, apparently some browsers have not fully supported the SVG font elements. Any discrepancies are to be regretted.)

<font> defines a font......OPS. Each 'font' element must have a <font-face> child element which describes the various characteristics of the font.
......horiz-origin-x="<number>": the X coord. of the origin of a glyph to be used when drawing horizontally oriented text.
......horiz-origin-y="<number>": the Y coord of the origin of a glyph to be used when drawing horizontally oriented text.
......horiz-adv-x="<number>": the horizontal advance after rendering a glyph in horizontal orientation.
......vert-origin-x="<number>": the X coord. of the origin of a glyph to be used when drawing vertically oriented text.
......vert-origin-y="<number>": the Y coord. of the origin of a glyph to be used when drawing vertically oriented text.
......vert-adv-y="<number>": the vertical advance after rendering a glyph in vertical orientation.

<font-face> describes the characteristics of a font......C
......font-family="<string>": the name of the font to use. The font name can be a family name or a generic name(2.4.5).
......font-style="all|{normal|italic|oblique}......": the style.
......font-variant="{normal|small-caps}......": whether to display in a small, capitalized font.
......font-weight="all|{normal|bold|<number>}......": the weight.
......font-stretch="all|{normal | ultra-condensed | extra-condensed | condensed | semi-condensed | semi-expanded | expanded | extra-expanded | ultra-expanded}......:
......font-size="<number>": the font size.
......unicode-range="<urange>": the unicode range. The default value is 'U+0-10FFFF'.
......units-per-em="<number>": the size of the design grid on which the glyphs are laid out. It is necessary for 'stemv', 'stemh', 'cap-height', 'x-height', 'accent', 'descent' etc. The default is '1000'.
......stemv="<number>": the vertical stem width.
......stemh="<number>": the horizontal stem width.
......slope="<number>": the vertical stroke angle.
......cap-height="<number>": the height of uppercase glyphs.
......x-height="<number>": the height of lowercase glyphs.
......accent-height="<number>": the distance from the origin to the top of accent characters.
......ascent="<number>": the maximum unaccented height.
......descent="<number>": the maximum unaccented depth.
......underline-position="<number>": the position of an underline.
......underline-thickness="<number>": the thickness of an underline.
......strikethrough-position="<number>": the position of a strikethrough.
......strikethrough-thickness="<number>": the thickness of a strikethrough.
......overline-position="<number>": the position of an overline.
......overline-thickness="<number>": the thickness of an overline.

<font-face-src> references another font......C. It contains <font-face-name> and <font-face-uri>, which are used for referencing local and external fonts respectively.

<font-face-name> references a local font......C.
......name="<string>": the name of the local font.

<font-face-uri> references an external <font> element CX
......xlink:href="<iri>": the location of the referenced font.

<font-face-format> specifies the supported formats of the font referenced by the <font-face-uri> element......C
......string="{ truedoc-pfr | embedded-opentype | type-1 | truetype | opentype | truetype-gx | speedo | intellifont }+": the supported formats.

```
<!DOCTYPE html>
<html>
<head></head>
<body>
  <svg>
  <defs>
    <font id="Font1">
      <font-face font-family="My Font" font-weight="bold">
        <font-face-src> <!-- try the fonts one by one -->
          <font-face-name name="Jokerman"/>
          <font-face-uri xlink:href="jokerman.ttf">
            <font-face-format string="truetype, opentype"/>
          </font-face-uri>
          <font-face-name name="Arial"/>
          <font-face-name name="Verdana"/>
        </font-face-src>
      </font-face>
    </font>
  </defs>
  <text x="50" y="50" font-weight="bold"
      font-family="dummy, 'My Font', Helvetica, Fantasy">
    Testing 123
  </text>
</svg>
</body>
</html>
```

Testing 123

7.7.3 Glyphs

<glyph> defines the graphics for a glyph......CPS
......d="<path data>": The definition of the outline of the glyph, using the same syntax as for the 'd' attribute on a <path> element. (7.3.2)
......horiz-adv-x="<number>": the horizontal advance after rendering the glyph in horizontal orientation.
......vert-origin-x="<number>": the x coord. of the origin of the glyph to be used when drawing vertically oriented text.
......vert-origin-y="<number>": the y coord. of the origin of the glyph to be used when drawing vertically oriented text.
......vert-adv-y="<number>": the vertical advance after rendering the glyph in vertical orientation.
......unicode="<string>": the sequence of Unicode characters corresponding to the glyph.
......glyph-name="<name>......": the glyph name to be referenced in <hkern> and <vkern>.
......orientation="{h|v}": the particular progression direction.
......arabic-form="{initial | medial | terminal | isolated": the form for Arabic glyphs.
......lang="<language code>......": a comma-separated list of language names.

<missing-glyph> defines the graphics to use if the given glyph has not been defined......CPS
......d="<path data>": The definition of the outline of the glyph, using the same syntax as for the 'd' attribute on a <path> element. (7.3.2)
......horiz-adv-x="<number>": the horizontal advance after rendering the glyph in horizontal orientation.
......vert-origin-x="<number>": the x coord. of the origin of the glyph to be used when drawing vertically oriented text.
......vert-origin-y="<number>": the y coord. of the origin of the glyph to be used when drawing vertically oriented text.
......vert-adv-y="<number>": the vertical advance after rendering the glyph in vertical orientation.

<altGlyph> uses a glyph in <text> for the content data......OCGPSX

......x (7.7.1)
......y (7.7.1)
......dx (7.7.1)
......dy (7.7.1)
......format (7.7.2 <font-face-format>)
......rotate (7.7.1)
......xlink:href="<iri>": the <glyph> or <altGlyphDef> element.

<altGlyphDef> defines a set of possible glyph substitutions......C. It contains the <glyphRef> elements.

<glyphRef> defines a possible glyph to use in <altGlyphyDef>......CPSX
......x (7.7.1)
......y (7.7.1)
......dx (7.7.1)
......dy (7.7.1)
......format (7.7.2 <font-face-format>)
......xlink:href="<iri>": the <glyph> or <altGlyphDef> element.

<hkern> and **<vkern>** define the amount of spacing to decrease when two specific characters appear together, in the horizontal and vertical orientations respectively......C
......u1="<character>+": a set of comma-separated, possible first glyphs in the kerning pair.
......u2="<character>+": a set of comma-separated, possible second glyphs in the kerning pair.
......g1="<glyph name>+": a set of glyphs for the first glyph.
......g2="<glyph name>+": a set of glyphs for the second glyph.
......k="<number>": the amount of spacing to decrease.

```
<!DOCTYPE html>
<html>
<head></head>
<body>
<svg>
  <defs>
    <font id="Font1">
      <font-face font-family="My Font" font-weight="bold">
        <font-face-src>
          <font-face-name name="Arial"/>
        </font-face-src>
      </font-face>
      <missing-glyph horiz-adv-x="2400"
          d="M0,0 L3000,2000 0,2000 2000,0"/>
      <glyph id="hourglass" unicode="^^"
            horiz-adv-x="2400"
          d="M0,0 L2000,2000 0,2000 2000,0"/>
      <glyph id="wave" unicode="@@" horiz-adv-x="2400"
     d="M0,0 Q2000,2000 2000,1000 Q1000,1000 2000,0"/>
      <altGlyphDef id="hourglass2">
        <glyphRef xlink:href="#hourglass"/>
      </altGlyphDef>
      <hkern u1="a" u2="b,c,d" k="300">
    </font>
  </defs>
  <text x="50" y="50" font-weight="bold"
      font-family="dummy, 'My Font', Helvetica, Fantasy">
    ^^
    @@
    <altGlyph xlink:href="#hourglass2">XXXX</altGlyph>
    acae
  </text>
</svg>
</body>
</html>
```

7.8 Animation

7.8.1 Using Elements

<animate> animates an attribute over time......AOCPX.
......attributeName="<attribute>": the attribute to animate.
......attributeType="{CSS|XML|auto}": the namespace for the attribute.
......begin="<clock value>": the initial delay.
......dur="<clock value>": the duration to interpolate for each iteration.
......end="<clock value>": the time that constrains the active duration for all iterations.
......min="<clock value>": the minimum value of the active duration for all iterations.
......max="<clock value>": the maximum value of the active duration for all iterations..
......restart="{always|whenNotActive|never}": whether the animation can be restarted.
......repeatCount="<number>|indefinite": the number of iterations. 'number' can be a partial fraction.
......repeatDur="<clock value>|indefinite": the total duration for all iterations. After this duration ends, the animation jumps to the point specified by 'end'.
......fill="{freeze|remove}": what happens when the active duration is over. 'freeze' uses the last value. 'remove' uses the original value.
......calcMode="{discrete|linear|paced|spline}": the interpolation mode. 'discrete' jumps from one value to the next without any interpolation. 'linear' uses simple interpolation between values. 'paced' produces an even pace of change. 'spline' interpolates according to a cubic Bezier spline.
......values="<number>+": a semicolon-separated list of one or more values.
......keyTimes="{0.0 to 1.0}+": a semicolon-separated list of time values used to control the pacing. This attribute must have exactly as many values as there are in the 'values' attribute. Each successive time value must be greater than the preceding time value.
......keySplines="<0.0 to 1.0 control point descriptions>+": a list of semicolon-separated list of Bezier control point descriptions associated with 'keyTimes'. Each control point description is a set of four values: x1 y1 x2 y2, where x corresponds to the time interval, and y corresponds to the attribute value.
......from="<value>": the starting value of the animation.
......to="<value>": the ending value of the animation.
......by="<value>": a relative offset for the animation.
......additive="{replace|sum}": whether the animation will add to the underlying value of the attribute.
......accumulate="{none|sum}": whether each repeat iteration builds upon the last value of the previous iteration.

<clock value>	actual time meaning
50:00:10.25	50 hours, 10 seconds and 250 milliseconds
00:10.5	10 seconds and 500 milliseconds
3.2h	3 hours and 12 minutes
45min	45 minutes
30s	30 seconds
5ms	5 milliseconds
12.467	12 seconds and 467 milliseconds

(courtesy of http://www.w3.org/TR/SVG11/animate.html)

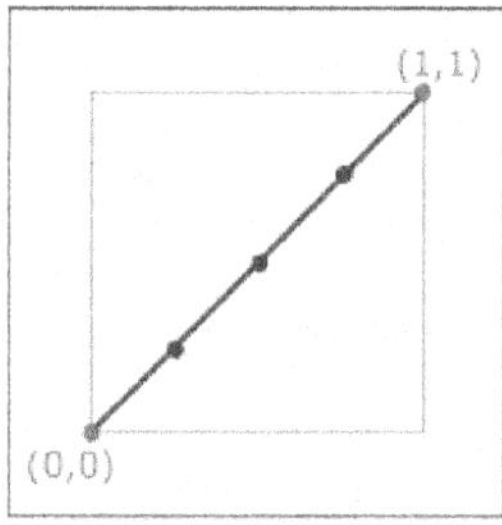

keySplines="0 0 1 1" (the default)

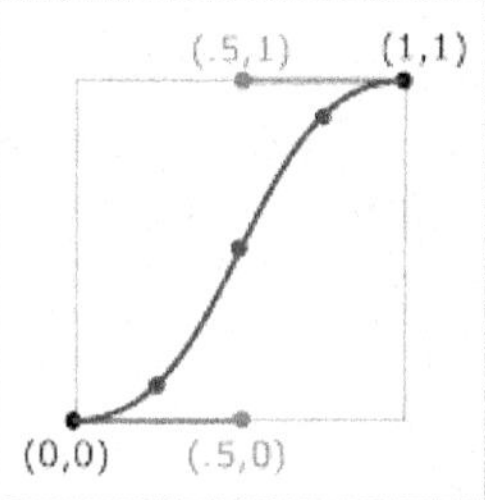

keySplines=".5 0 .5 1"

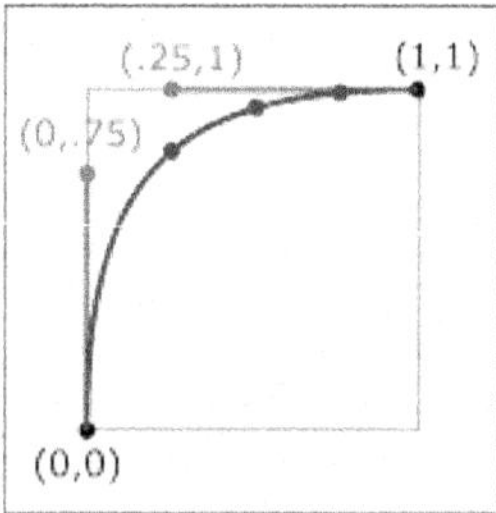

keySplines="0 .75 .25 1"

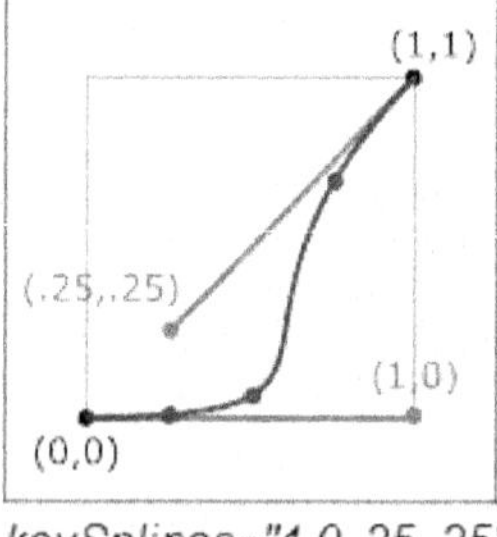

keySplines="1 0 .25 .25"

Examples of keySplines

A rectangle that moves left-to-right and keeps changing its color.

```
<!DOCTYPE html>
<html>
<head></head>
<body>
<svg>
  <rect y="100" width="100" height="50">
    <animate attributeName="x"
                  from="0" to="1000"
                  begin="0" dur="10" end="15" min="36"
                  repeatCount="5" repeatDur="15"
                  fill="freeze"/>
    <animate attributeName="fill"
                  begin="2" dur="5" repeatCount="indefinite"
                  keyTimes="0;0.25;0.5;1"
                  values="black;red;green;white"/>
  </rect>
</svg>
</body>
</html>
```

<set> sets the value of an attribute for a specified duration...... AOCX
......to="<value>": the ending value of the animation.
......attributeName (see <animate>)
......attributeType (see <animate>)
......begin (see <animate>)
......dur (see <animate>)
......end (see <animate>)
......min (see <animate>)
......max (see <animate>)
......restart (see <animate>)
......repeatCount (see <animate>)
......repeatDur (see <animate>)
......fill (see <animate>)

After an initial delay of 5 seconds, the rectangle jumps to the right for 3 seconds, and then returns to its original position instantly.

```
<!DOCTYPE html>
<html>
<head></head>
<body>
<svg>
  <rect y="100" width="100" height="50">
    <set attributeName="x"
           to="1000" begin="5" dur="3"/>
  </rect>
</svg>
</body>
</html>
```

<animateMotion> moves an element along a path...... AOCX
......begin (see <animate>)
......dur (see <animate>)
......end (see <animate>)
......min (see <animate>)
......max (see <animate>)
......restart (see <animate>)
......repeatCount (see <animate>)
......repeatDur (see <animate>)
......fill (see <animate>)
......calcMode (see <animate>)
......values (see <animate>)
......keyTimes (see <animate>)
......keySplines (see <animate>)
......from (see <animate>)
......to (see <animate>)
......by (see <animate>)
......additive (see <animate>)
......accumulate (see <animate>)
......path="<path data>": the path to move along. (see 7.3.2)
......keyPoints="{0.0 to 1.0}+": a semicolon-separated list indicating how far the object has moved at various 'keyTimes'.
......rotate="{<number>|auto|auto-reverse}": the rotation over time. 'number' is the number of degrees of the constant rotation. 'auto' rotates the object by the angle of the direction of the motion path. 'auto-reverse' is like 'auto' plus 180 degrees.

<mpath> specified within <animateMotion> to reference the <path> element that defines the motion path......CX
......xlink:href="<iri>": the <path> element.

```
<!DOCTYPE html>
<html>
<head></head>
<body>
<svg>
  <defs>
    <path id="p" d="M0,0 q0,100 100,0
                              q200,0 100,100
                              q150,150 300,300"/>
  </defs>
  <rect width="100" height="50">
    <animateMotion begin="0" dur="10" rotate="auto"
               path="M0,0 q100,100 0,100
                          q300,500 200,400
                          q500,-500 1000,300"
               keyTimes="0; 0.3; 0.8; 1"
               keyPoints="0; 0.7; 0.8; 1"/>
  </rect>
  <circle r="50">
    <animateMotion begin="0" dur="10">
      <mpath xlink:href="#p"/>
    </animateMotion>
  </circle>
```

```
</svg>
</body>
</html>
```

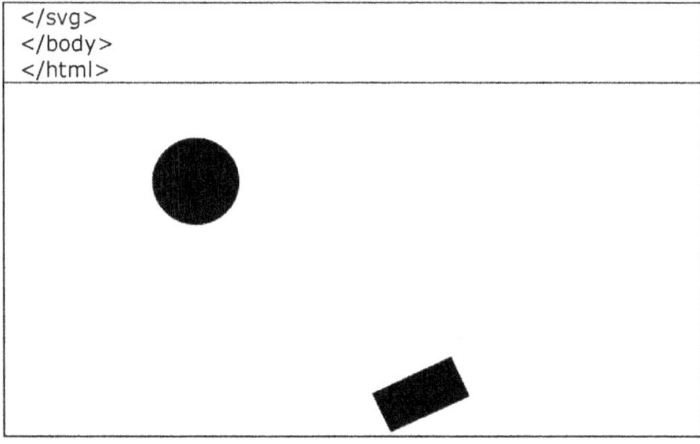

<u><animateTransform></u> animates a transformation attribute on a target element......AOCX

......type="{<u>translate</u>|scale|rotate|skewX||skewY}": the type of transformation.
......attributeName (see <animate>)
......attributeType (see <animate>)
......begin (see <animate>)
......dur (see <animate>)
......end (see <animate>)
......min (see <animate>)
......max (see <animate>)
......restart (see <animate>)
......repeatCount (see <animate>)
......repeatDur (see <animate>)
......fill (see <animate>)
......calcMode (see <animate>)
......values (see <animate>)
......keyTimes (see <animate>)
......keySplines (see <animate>)
......form (see <animate>)
......to (see <animate>)
......by (see <animate>)
......additive (see <animate>)
......accumulate (see <animate>)

type	syntax of values for 'from', 'by', 'to'
translate	<tx> [,<ty>]
scale	<sx> [,<sy>]
rotate	<rotate-angle> [<cx> <cy>]
skewX	<skew-angle>
skewY	<skew-angle>

```
<!DOCTYPE html>
<html>
<head></head>
<body>
<svg>
  <rect y="100" width="100" height="50">
    <animateTransform
          attributeName="transform" type="rotate"
          from="0 100 100" to="720 200 200" dur="10"
          fill="freeze"/>
  </rect>
</svg>
</body>
</html>
```

7.8.2 Using DOM

Animation in SVG can also be achieved by manipulating the DOM.

As time passes, the text grows in size, and becomes increasingly clear.

```
<!DOCTYPE html>
<html>
<head></head>
<body>

<svg width="20cm" height="2cm" viewBox="0 0 400 200"
      onload="StartAnimation(evt)">
  <script type="application/ecmascript"><![CDATA[
    var timevalue = 0;
    var timer_increment = 50;
    var max_time = 5000;
    var text_element;
    function StartAnimation(evt) {
      text_element =

evt.target.ownerDocument.getElementById("TextElement");
        ShowAndGrowElement();
    }
    function ShowAndGrowElement() {
      timevalue = timevalue + timer_increment;
      if (timevalue > max_time) return;
      scalefactor = (timevalue * 20.) / max_time;
      text_element.setAttribute("transform",
                        "scale(" + scalefactor + ")");
      opacityfactor = timevalue / max_time;
      text_element.setAttribute("opacity", opacityfactor);
      setTimeout("ShowAndGrowElement()", timer_increment)
    }
    window.ShowAndGrowElement = ShowAndGrowElement
  ]]></script>
  <g transform="translate(50,150)" fill="red" font-size="7">
    <text id="TextElement">Let's animate SVG.</text>
  </g>
</svg>

</body>
</html>
```

Let's animate SVG.

7.9 Interaction

An interactive SVG image can be created by using the <script> tag (JavaScript) and specifying functions for various events.

Moving the pointer over the red circle changes its color to blue. Clicking it enlarges it. Leaving it changes its color back to red.

```
<!DOCTYPE html>
<html>
<head></head>
<body>

<svg width="6cm" height="6cm">
  <script type="application/ecmascript"> <![CDATA[
   function enlarge(evt) {
     var circle = evt.target;
     var currentRadius = circle.getAttribute("r");
     circle.setAttribute("r", parseInt(currentRadius) + 5);
   }
   function blue(evt) {
     var circle = evt.target;
     circle.setAttribute("fill", "blue");
   }
   function red(evt) {
     var circle = evt.target;
     circle.setAttribute("fill", "red");
   }
  ]]> </script>

  <circle cx="100" cy="100" r="10" fill="red"
          onclick="enlarge(evt)"
          onmouseover="blue(evt)"
          onmouseout="red(evt)"/>
</svg>
</body>
</html>
```

8. 2D Canvas

In an HTML document, we can draw 2D graphics using the <canvas> element and JavaScript. Games have been developed with 2D Canvas. Compared to SVG, a canvas graphic is computationally faster to draw. While a canvas lacks many SVG features like the filters and event-driven interactivity, a canvas provides per-pixel control of the graphic. Perhaps more importantly, a canvas allows you to display the webcam, thereby letting you take and save a photo with it.

The upper-left corner of the canvas has the co-ordinates (0,0). All lengths are expressed in pixels. Colors can be specified in the same ways as CSS.

```
<!DOCTYPE html>
<html>
<head></head>
<body>
  <canvas id="myCanvas" width="600" height="200"
          style="border:solid 2px"></canvas>
  <script>
    var canvas = document.getElementById('myCanvas');
    var context = canvas.getContext('2d');
    context.beginPath();
      context.moveTo(100, 150);
      context.lineTo(450, 50);
      context.lineWidth=10;
      context.strokeStyle="#F00";
    context.stroke();
  </script>
</body>
</html>
```

Libraries for 2D Canvas include Kinetic.js and Three.js.

8.1 Outlining

8.1.1 Beginning/Ending

Beginning/Ending Methods
beginPath() declares that a path is about to be drawn. This method should be called before other drawing methods have been called.
stroke() declares that a path has been drawn completely and that the path should be made visible. This method should be called after other drawing methods have been called.

8.1.2 Line Drawing

Line Drawing Methods
moveTo(x,y) 'lifts up the pen' and moves to (x,y), without drawing anything.
lineTo(x,y) draws a straight line to (x,y).
arcTo(x1,y1,x2,y2,r) draws a circular arc with radius r, just touching the tangents formed by joining (x0,y0)-(x1,y1) and (x1,y1)-(x2,y2), where (x0,y0) represents the current point. 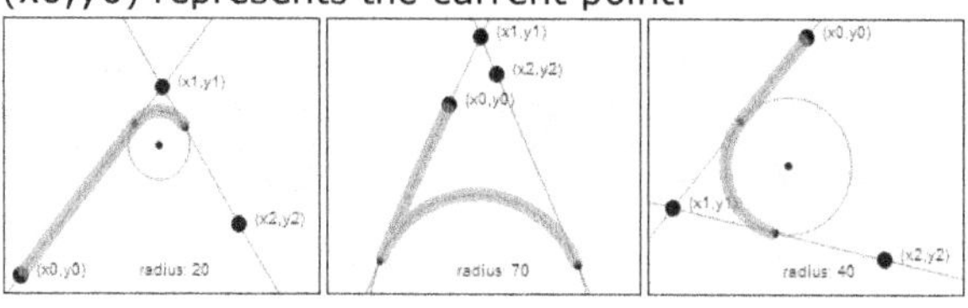 *(courtesy of http://www.dbp-consulting.com/tutorials/canvas/CanvasArcTo.html)*
quadraticCurveTo(cpx,cpy,x,y) draws a quadratic Bezier curve to (x,y), using (cpx,cpy) as the control point.
bezierCurveTo(cp1x,cp1y,cp2x,cp2y,x,y) draws a Bezier curve to (x,y), using (cp1x,cp1y) and (cp2x,cp2y) as the control points.
closePath() draws a straight line back to the starting point.

8.1.3 Shape Drawing

Shape Drawing Methods
rect(x,y,width,height) draws a rectangle with the upper-left corner at (x,y), and the dimensions 'width' and 'height'.
strokeRect(x,y, width,height) draws a rectangle with the upper-left corner at (x,y), and the dimensions 'width' and 'height'. stroke() needs not be called for the rectangle to be drawn.
fillRect(x,y, width,height) draws a rectangle with the upper-left corner at (x,y), and the dimensions 'width' and 'height'. The rectangle is filled with the filling color. stroke() needs not be called for the rectangle to be drawn.
clearRect(x,y, width,height) clears a rectangular area with the upper-left corner at (x,y), and the dimensions 'width' and 'height'. The color displayed at the area is the background color of the canvas. stroke() needs not be called for the rectangle to be drawn.
arc(x,y,r,sRad,eRad[,cc]) draws a circular arc with radius r, centered at (x,y). The starting angle is defined by 'sRad', while the ending angle is defined by 'eRad'. 'cc' is a boolean value indicating whether to draw the arc in a counter clockwise manner.

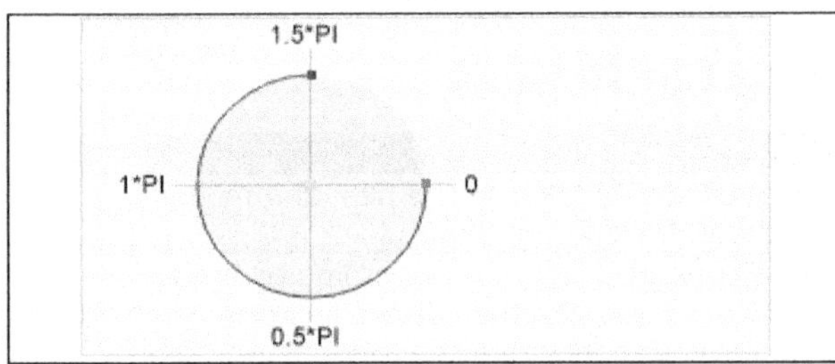

8.1.4 Outlining

Outlining Properties
strokeStyle stores the color of the line. The default stroke color is black.
lineWidth stores the width of the line.
lineCap stores the shape at the ends of the line. The value can be 'butt', 'round', or 'square'. (see 7.3.3)
lineJoin sets the shape at the corners of the line. The value can be 'miter', 'round', or 'bevel'. (see 7.3.3)
miterLimit stores the maximum miter length (when lineJoin='miter'). If it is exceeded, the corner will be displayed as lineJoin type 'bevel'. The miter length is the distance between the inner corner and the outer corner. 

```
<!DOCTYPE html>
<html>
<head></head>
<body>
  <canvas id="myCanvas"
          width="600" height="600"></canvas>
  <script>
    var canvas = document.getElementById('myCanvas');
    var c = canvas.getContext('2d');

    c.beginPath();
      c.moveTo(50,50);
      c.lineTo(150, 150);
      c.arcTo(200, 100,250,300,60);
      c.bezierCurveTo(100,100,300,300,200,50)
      c.closePath();
      c.lineWidth=4;
      c.strokeStyle="#F00";
    c.stroke();

    c.fillRect(250,50,250,150);
  </script>
</body>
</html>
```

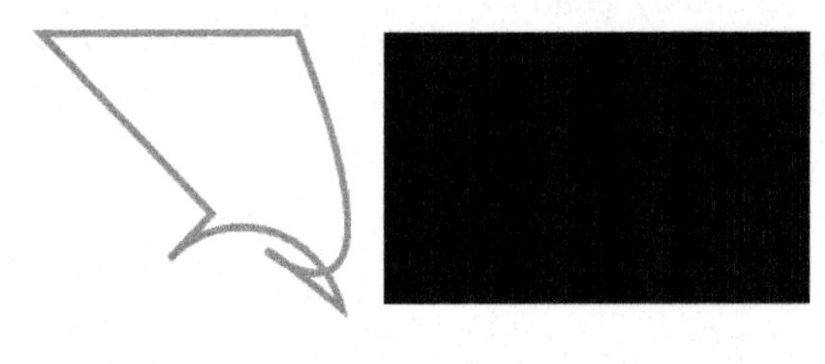

8.2 Painting

8.2.1 Filling

fillStyle stores the internal filling style, which can be a solid color, a gradient, or a pattern.
fill() initiates the actual filling according to 'fillStyle'.
createLinearGradient(x1,y1,x2,y2) creates a linear gradient object to be used by 'fillStyle', starting from (x1,y1) and ending at (x2,y2).
createRadialGradient(x1,y1,r1,x2,y2,r2) creates a circular gradient object to be used by 'fillStyle', starting from the circle defined by (x1,y1,r1), ending at the circle defined by (x2,y2,r2).
gradient.addColorStop(stop,color) specifies the color at a position in the gradient object. 'stop' must be between 0.0 and 1.0.
createPattern(image, rep) loads an image and tile it in the interior, to be used by 'fillStyle'. 'rep' can be 'repeat', 'repeat-x', 'repeat-y', or 'no-repeat'.

```
<!DOCTYPE html>
<html>
<head></head>
<body>
  <canvas id="myCanvas" width="1200"
                        height="600"></canvas>
  <script>
    var canvas = document.getElementById('myCanvas');
    var c = canvas.getContext('2d');

    c.beginPath();
    c.rect(50,50,200,200);
    c.fillStyle='brown';
    c.fill();

    c.beginPath();
    c.rect(260,50,200,200);
    g=c.createLinearGradient(260,150,460,150);
    g.addColorStop(0,'white');
    g.addColorStop(0.5,'brown');
    g.addColorStop(1,'black');
    c.fillStyle=g;
    c.fill();

    c.beginPath();
    c.rect(470,50,200,200);
    g=c.createRadialGradient(570,150,20,620,200,100);
    g.addColorStop(0,'white');
    g.addColorStop(0.5,'brown');
    g.addColorStop(1,'black');
    c.fillStyle=g;
    c.fill();

    var imageObj = new Image();
    imageObj.onload = function(){
      c.beginPath();
      var p=c.createPattern(imageObj,'repeat');
      c.rect(680,50,200,200);
      c.fillStyle=p;
      c.fill();
    }
    imageObj.src = "brick.jpg";
  </script>
</body>
</html>
```

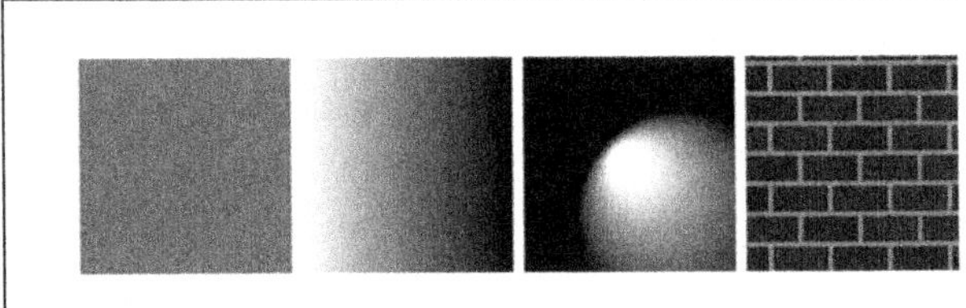

8.2.2 Shadow

shadowColor stores the color to use for shadows.

shadowBlur stores the blur level for shadows.

shadowOffsetX stores the horizontal distance of the shadow from the shape.

shadowOffsetY stores the vertical distance of the shadow from the shape.

```
<!DOCTYPE html>
<html>
<head></head>
<body>
  <canvas id="myCanvas"
          width="1200" height="600"></canvas>
  <script>
    var canvas = document.getElementById('myCanvas');
    var c = canvas.getContext('2d');

    c.rect(50,50,200,200);
    c.shadowColor='purple';
    c.shadowBlur='20';
    c.shadowOffsetX='30';
    c.shadowOffsetY='15';
    c.fillStyle='brown';
    c.fill();
  </script>
</body>
</html>
```

8.2.3 Transparency

globalAlpha stores the opacity value of the figure. The value ranges from 0.0 (fully transparent) to 1.0 (fully opaque).

```
<!DOCTYPE html>
<html>
<head></head>
<body>
  <canvas id="myCanvas"
          width="1200" height="600"></canvas>
  <script>
    var canvas = document.getElementById('myCanvas');
    var c = canvas.getContext('2d');

    c.beginPath();
    c.arc(100,100,75,0,2*Math.PI,false);
    c.fillStyle='red';
    c.fill();

    c.beginPath();
    c.arc(200,100,75,0,2*Math.PI,false);
    c.fillStyle='blue';
    c.globalAlpha=0.5;
    c.fill();
  </script>
</body>
</html>
```

8.2.4 Clipping

clip() indicates that all subsequent drawing is to occur within the clipping region (defined by the current shape).

save() saves the current context, to be restored at a later point of time.

restore() restores the canvas context to the last saved context.

```
<!DOCTYPE html>
<html>
<head></head>
<body>
  <canvas id="myCanvas"
          width="600" height="600"></canvas>
  <script>
    var canvas = document.getElementById('myCanvas');
    var c = canvas.getContext('2d');

    c.save();

    c.beginPath();
    c.arc(100,100,75,0,2*Math.PI,false);
    c.fillStyle='red';
    c.fill();
    c.clip();

    c.beginPath();
    c.rect(100,100,200,50);
    c.rect(0,0,100,100);
    c.fillStyle='orange';
    c.fill();

    c.restore();
  </script>
</body>
</html>
```

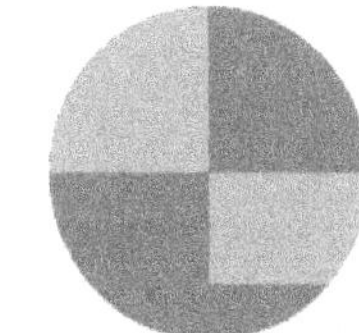

8.2.5 Composite Operation

globalCompositeOperation stores and describes how any subsequent drawing overlaps with the existing drawing.

```
<!DOCTYPE html>
<html>
<head></head>
<body>
  <canvas id="myCanvas"
          width="600" height="600"></canvas>
  <script>
    var canvas = document.getElementById('myCanvas');
    var c = canvas.getContext('2d');

    c.fillStyle = 'blue';
    c.fillRect(0,0,100,100);

    c.globalCompositeOperation='source-atop';

    c.arc(100,100,80,0,2*Math.PI,false);
    c.fillStyle = 'red';
    c.fill();
  </script>
</body>
</html>
```

source-atop source-in source-out source-over

destination-atop destination-in destination-out destination-over

lighter darker xor copy

(coustesy of http://www.html5canvastutorials.com/advanced/html5-canvas-global-composite-operations-tutorial/)

8.3 Text

8.3.1 Basics

fillText(text,x,y[,maxWidth]) draws filled text.

strokeText(text,x,y[,maxWidth]) draws text without any interior filling (outline only).

measureText(text).width returns the width of the specified text, in pixels.

textAlign stores the alignment for text content. The value can be 'start', 'end', 'center', 'left' or 'right'. For instance, setting a value of 'end' or 'right' will cause the text to end at the specified location.

textBaseline stores the text baseline. The value can be 'alphabetic', 'top', 'hanging', 'middle', 'ideographic', or 'bottom'.

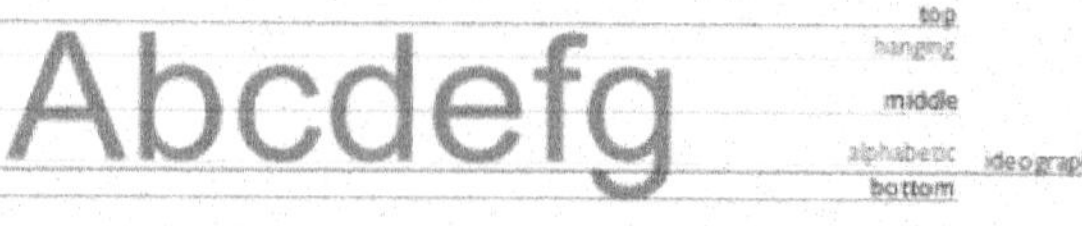

(courtesy of http://www.w3schools.com/tags/canvas_textbaseline.asp)

font stores a list of space separated font properties.

Property	Description
<font-style>	Possible values: normal, italic, oblique
<font-variant>	Possible values: normal, smapp-caps
<font-weight>	Possible values: normal, bold, bolder, lighter, 100, 200, 300, 400, 500, 600, 700, 800, 900
<font-size>	<font size, eg. 12em>
<font-family>	<font family name, eg. Arial>
caption	Use the font in captioned controls
icon	Use the font in icons
menu	Use the font in menus
message-box	Use the font in dialog boxes
small-caption	Use the font in small controls
status-bar	Use the font in the status bar

```
<!DOCTYPE html>
<html>
<head></head>
<body>
  <canvas id="myCanvas"
          width="600" height="600"></canvas>
  <script>
    var canvas = document.getElementById('myCanvas');
    var c = canvas.getContext('2d');

    c.beginPath();
      c.moveTo(0,200);
      c.lineTo(400,200);
      c.moveTo(200,0);
      c.lineTo(200,400);
    c.stroke();

    c.font='800 6em Arial';
    c.strokeStyle='red';
    c.textAlign='center';
    c.textBaseline='middle';
    c.strokeText("Text",200,200);

    w=c.measureText('Text').width;
    c.font='italic 18px caption';
    c.fillStyle='blue';
    c.fillText(w+" pixels wide",200,270);
  </script>
</body>
</html>
```

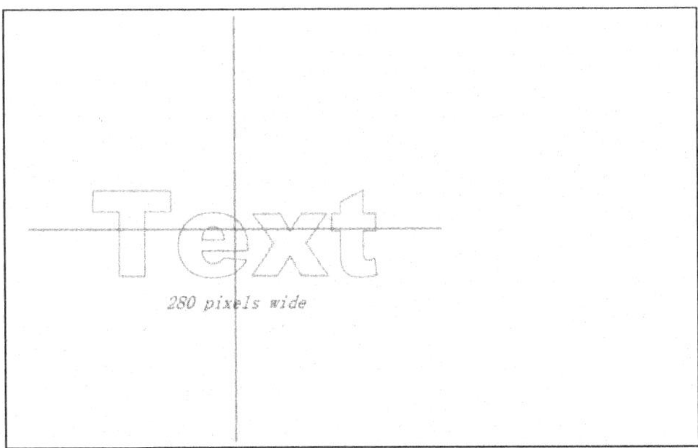

8.3.2 Word Wrapping

This example demonstrates word wrapping.
(courtesy of http://www.html5canvastutorials.com/tutorials/html5-canvas-wrap-text-tutorial/)

```
<!DOCTYPE HTML>
<html>
  <head></head>
  <body>
    <canvas id="myCanvas" width="578"
                          height="200"></canvas>
    <script>
     function wrapText(context, text, x, y,
                       maxWidth, lineHeight) {
       var words = text.split(' ');
       var line = '';

       for(var n = 0; n < words.length; n++) {
         var testLine = line + words[n] + ' ';
         var metrics = context.measureText(testLine);
         var testWidth = metrics.width;
         if (testWidth > maxWidth && n > 0) {
           context.fillText(line, x, y);
           line = words[n] + ' ';
           y += lineHeight;
         } else {
           line = testLine;
         }
       }
       context.fillText(line, x, y);
     }

     var canvas = document.getElementById('myCanvas');
     var context = canvas.getContext('2d');
     var maxWidth = 400;
     var lineHeight = 25;
     var x = (canvas.width - maxWidth) / 2;
     var y = 60;

     var text = 'All the world \'s a stage, and all the men and \
women merely players. They have their exits and their \
entrances; And one man in his time plays many parts.';

     context.font = '16pt Calibri';
     context.fillStyle = '#333';
     wrapText(context, text, x, y, maxWidth, lineHeight);

    </script>
  </body>
</html>
```

All the world 's a stage, and all the men and
women merely players. They have their exits
and their entrances; And one man in his time
plays many parts.

8.4 Images

8.4.1 Displaying

drawImage(img,x,y) or **drawImage(img,x,y,width,height)** or **drawImage(img,sx,sy,swidth,sheighty,x,y,width,height)** loads and displays an image. 'sx', 'sy', 'swidth', and 'sheight' define the clipping region on the source image file.

```
<!DOCTYPE html>
<html>
<head></head>
<body>
  <canvas id="myCanvas"
          width="600" height="600"></canvas>
  <script>
    var canvas = document.getElementById('myCanvas');
    var c = canvas.getContext('2d');

    var I = new Image();
    I.onload = function(){
      c.drawImage(I,10,10);
      c.drawImage(I,100,50,300,340,10,400,300,300);
    }
    I.src='puppy.jpg';
  </script>
</body>
</html>
```

8.4.2 Pixel Operations

getImageData(x,y,width,height).data returns the array of pixel values of the specified rectangular region on the canvas. The array contains pixel values of the R-G-B-A components, left-to-right, then top-to-bottom. Each value is an integer in the range [0,255].

putImageData(imageData,x,y) displays the imageData on the canvas.

While not a very efficient implementation, this example shows how each component of the individual pixels can be accessed.

```
<!DOCTYPE html>
<html>
<head></head>
<body>
  <img id="image" src='puppy.jpg'
          width="300" height="300"/><br/>
  <canvas id="sourceCanvas" width="300" height="300"
          style="border:1px solid"></canvas>
  <canvas id="targetCanvas" width="300" height="300"
          style="border:1px solid"></canvas><br/>
  <button onclick="displayImage()">Display Image</button>
  <button onclick="grayscaleConvert()">
          Convert to Grayscale</button>

  <script>
    var scanvas = document.getElementById('sourceCanvas');
    var sc = scanvas.getContext('2d');
    var tcanvas = document.getElementById('targetCanvas');
    var tc = tcanvas.getContext('2d');

    function displayImage(){
      var I = document.getElementById("image");
      sc.drawImage(I,0,0,300,300);
    }

    function getPixelComponentValue(idp,x,y,c){
      return idp[((y*300)+x)*4+c];
    }

    function grayscaleConvert(){
      var I = document.getElementById("image");
      var ImgData = sc.getImageData(0,0,300,300);
      var ImgDataPixels = ImgData.data;
      for (y=0; y<I.height; y++){
        for (x=0; x<I.width; x++){
          brightness =
          (getPixelComponentValue(ImgDataPixels,x,y,0) +
           getPixelComponentValue(ImgDataPixels,x,y,1) +
           getPixelComponentValue(ImgDataPixels,x,y,2))
/3;
          ImgDataPixels[((y*I.width)+x)*4]   = brightness;
          ImgDataPixels[((y*I.width)+x)*4+1] = brightness;
          ImgDataPixels[((y*I.width)+x)*4+2] = brightness;
        }
      }
      tc.putImageData(ImgData,0,0);
    }
  </script>
</body>
</html>
```

Display Image | Convert to Grayscale

8.4.3 Client-side Saving

canvas.toDataURL([MIME_type][, quality]) converts the canvas to an image file. The default image type is PNG. When 'image/jpeg' is passed as the first argument, the second argument (0.0 to 1.0) specifies the image quality.

Passing 0 as the second argument to toDataURL() results in the poorest quality but smallest file size. Note that right-clicking on the image will bring up a dialog box that allows you to save the image as a file.

```
<!DOCTYPE HTML>
<html>
  <head></head>
  <body>
    <canvas id="myCanvas"
            width="300" height="300"></canvas>
    <br/>
    <script>
      var canvas = document.getElementById('myCanvas');
      var c = canvas.getContext('2d');

      var I = new Image();
      I.onload = function(){
        c.drawImage(I,0,0,300,300);
        var img = canvas.toDataURL("image/jpeg",0);
        document.write('<img src="'+img+'"/>');
      }
      I.src='puppy.jpg';
    </script>
  </body>
</html>
```

8.4.4 Server-side Saving

toDataURL() inherently base64-encodes the image data, so it can be transmitted directly over an AJAX call. To save the image data in the server, remove the header and base64-decode it first.

This method is crucial in capturing a snapshot from the webcam and saving it into the server, as we shall see in Chapter 12.

```
<!DOCTYPE HTML>
<html>
  <head></head>
  <body>
    <canvas id="myCanvas"
            width="300" height="300"></canvas>
    <br/>
    <script>
      var canvas = document.getElementById('myCanvas');
      var c = canvas.getContext('2d');

      c.beginPath();
        c.moveTo(100, 150);
        c.lineTo(450, 50);
        c.lineWidth=10;
        c.strokeStyle="#F00";
      c.stroke();

      var canvasData = canvas.toDataURL("image/png");
      xhr = new XMLHttpRequest();
      xhr.open('POST', 'saveImage.php', false);
      xhr.setRequestHeader('Content-Type',
                           'application/x-www-form-urlencoded');
      xhr.send("imgData="+canvasData);
    </script>
  </body>
</html>
```

```
<?php
// saveImage.php
$I = $_POST['imgData'];
$I = str_replace('data:image/png;base64,', '', $I);
$I = str_replace(' ', '+', $I);
file_put_contents("test.png",base64_decode($I));
?>
```

8.5 Advanced Techniques

8.5.1 Transformation

translate(x,y) further translates the canvas drawing.
rotate(rad) further rotates about the top-left corner.
scale(scalewidth,scaleheight) further scales the drawing. The values are in the range [0.0,1.0].
transform(a,b,c,d,e,f) multiplies the current transformation matrix with a custom matrix. $$\begin{bmatrix} x' \\ y' \\ 1 \end{bmatrix} = \begin{bmatrix} a & c & e \\ b & d & f \\ 0 & 0 & 1 \end{bmatrix} \begin{bmatrix} x \\ y \\ 1 \end{bmatrix}$$
setTransform(a,b,c,d,e,f) resets the current transformation matrix to the identity matrix, and then runs transform() with the same arguments.

```
<!DOCTYPE HTML>
<html>
  <head></head>
  <body>
    <canvas id="myCanvas"
            width="1200"  height="1200"></canvas>
    <script>
      var canvas = document.getElementById('myCanvas');
      var c = canvas.getContext('2d');

      c.save();
      c.fillRect(0,0,100,100);
      c.translate(200,0);

      c.save();
      c.fillRect(0,0,100,100);
      c.translate(200,0);

      c.save();
      c.fillRect(0,0,100,100);
      c.translate(200,0);

      c.restore();
      c.fillRect(0,200,100,100);

      c.restore();
      c.fillRect(0,200,100,100);

      c.restore();
      c.fillRect(0,200,100,100);
    </script>
  </body>
</html>
```

8.5.2 Animation

To animate an object, we can use setTimeout() to impose a small delay between frames. We can also use the requestAnimFrame shim which enables the browser to determine the optimal FPS.

A square moving left-to-right.

```
<!DOCTYPE HTML>
<html>
  <head></head>
  <body>
    <canvas id="myCanvas" width="600" height="200">
    </canvas>

    <script>
      window.requestAnimFrame = (function() {
        return window.requestAnimationFrame ||
            window.webkitRequestAnimationFrame ||
            window.mozRequestAnimationFrame ||
            window.oRequestAnimationFrame ||
            window.msRequestAnimationFrame ||
            function(callback) {
              window.setTimeout(callback, 1000 / 60);
            };
      })();

      var x=0;
      var canvas = document.getElementById('myCanvas');
      var c = canvas.getContext('2d');

      function animate(){
        c.clearRect(0,0,canvas.width,canvas.height);
        c.fillRect(x,100,100,100);
        x++;
        requestAnimFrame(animate);
      }
      animate();
    </script>
  </body>
</html>
```

8.5.3 Mouse Tracking

```
<!DOCTYPE HTML>
<html>
  <head></head>
  <body>
    <canvas id="myCanvas" width="600" height="200"
          onmousemove="displayPosition(event)"
          style="border:1px solid"></canvas>
    <script>
      var canvas = document.getElementById('myCanvas');
      var c = canvas.getContext('2d');

      function displayPosition(evt){
        c.clearRect(0,0,canvas.width,canvas.height);
        r=canvas.getBoundingClientRect();
        x=evt.clientX - r.left;
        y=evt.clientY - r.top;
        c.font='20px Verdana';
        c.fillText("x:"+x+"  y:"+y,10,30);
      }
    </script>
  </body>
</html>
```

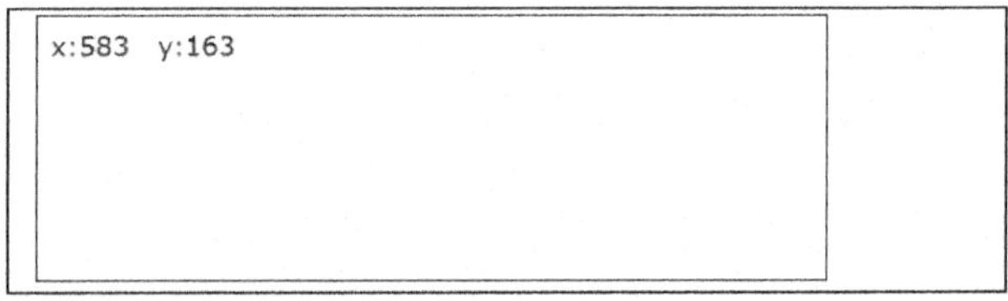

8.5.4 Fullscreen Mode

Many elements, such as <video>, <canvas>, <div> and <body>, can be switched to fullscreen mode. This is done by obtaining the element and then calling requestFullscreen() on it. As of 23 Nov 2014, this is an experimental technology, so you should include the browser-specific prefixes when calling the method.

Here we call requestFullscreen() on *document.documentElement*. In practice, you can call the method on other types of elements obtained by calling, for example, getElementById(...). *document.fullscreenElement* points to the element currently in fullscreen mode, and is NULL if no element is in fullscreen mode.

```
<!DOCTYPE HTML>
<html>
  <head>
    <script>
    function toggleFullScreen() {
      if (!document.fullscreenElement &&
          !document.mozFullScreenElement &&
          !document.webkitFullscreenElement &&
          !document.msFullscreenElement ) {
        if (document.documentElement.
            requestFullscreen) {
          document.documentElement.
          requestFullscreen();
        } else if (document.documentElement.
                msRequestFullscreen) {
          document.documentElement.
          msRequestFullscreen();
        } else if (document.documentElement.
                mozRequestFullScreen) {
          document.documentElement.
          mozRequestFullScreen();
        } else if (document.documentElement.
                webkitRequestFullscreen) {
          document.documentElement.
          webkitRequestFullscreen(
                        Element.ALLOW_KEYBOARD_INPUT);
        }
      } else {
        if (document.exitFullscreen) {
          document.exitFullscreen();
        } else if (document.msExitFullscreen) {
          document.msExitFullscreen();
        } else if (document.mozCancelFullScreen) {
          document.mozCancelFullScreen();
        } else if (document.webkitExitFullscreen) {
          document.webkitExitFullscreen();
        }
      }
    }
    document.addEventListener("keydown", function(e) {
      if (e.keyCode == 13) {
        toggleFullScreen();
      }
    }, false);
        </script>
  </head>
  <body>
    <canvas id="myCanvas" width="600"
            height="200"></canvas>
```

```
    <script>
    var canvas = document.getElementById('myCanvas');
    var c = canvas.getContext('2d');
    c.beginPath();
      c.moveTo(50,50);
      c.lineTo(150, 150);
      c.arcTo(200, 100,250,300,60);
      c.closePath();
    c.stroke();
    </script>
  </body>
</html>
```

Note that you can't switch an element to fullscreen mode as the document is loading. The switch must be triggered by a user-invoked event such as a mouse click or a pressed key.

9. WebGL Canvas

WebGL is a technology that allows sophisticated 3D graphics to be drawn using HTML5 Canvas and JavaScript. At the core of the WebGL pipeline are the vertex and fragment shaders. A vertex shader processes the defining vertices of the graphical primitives, while a fragment shader interpolates these vertices (and the varying variables) to obtain the pixel (fragment) values in the framebuffer.

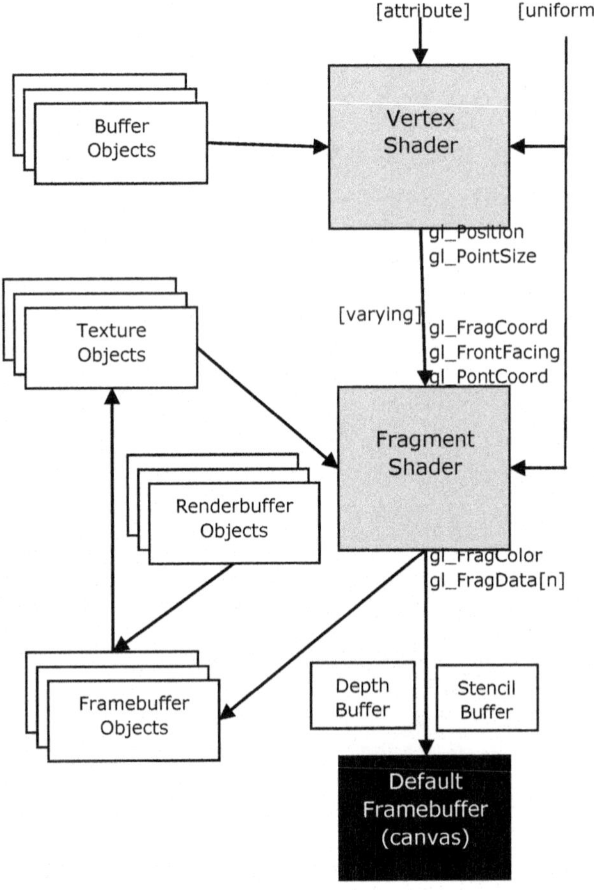

WebGL is a low-level language. In this chapter, we shall develop, step-by-step, a library that contains many useful functions. The library will be named 'webgl-library.js' (available for download at the official website of this book).

The official specification of WebGL can be found at:
https://www.khronos.org/registry/webgl/specs/1.0/

9.1 The Shading Language

Defined as JavaScript strings, the programs for the vertex and fragment shaders are written in the Shading Language.

9.1.1 Data Types

Basic Types	
void	no function return value or empty parameter list
bool	Boolean
int	signed integer
float	floating scalar
vec2, vec3, vec4	float vector
bvec2, bvec3, bvec4	boolean vector
ivec2, ivec3, ivec4	signed integer vector
mat2, mat3, mat4	float matrix
sampler2D	2D texture access
samplerCube	cube-mapped texture access
Examples	
bool b1=true;	
int i1=3;	
float f1=5; //error	
float f2=5.0;	
float f3=float(5);	
float f4=float(i1);	
bool b2=bool(5.0);	
int i2=int(true)+3,i3,i4=5;	
vec3 va=5.0; //error	
vec3 vb=vec3(1.0,2.0,3.0);	
vec2 vc=vec2(vb); //sets to (1.0,2.0);	
vec4 vd=vec4(5.0); //sets to (5.0,5.0,5.0,5.0);	
vec4 ve=vec4(vc,vd); //sets to (1.0,2.0,5.0,5.0);	
mat3 ma=mat3(1.0,2.0,3.0,4.0,5.0,6.0,7.0,8.0,9.0); $$ma = \begin{bmatrix} 1.0 & 4.0 & 7.0 \\ 2.0 & 5.0 & 8.0 \\ 3.0 & 6.0 & 9.0 \end{bmatrix}$$	
mat2 mb=mat2(ve);	
mat3 mc=mat3(vb,vb,vb);	
mat2 md=mat2(1.0,2.0,vc);	
mat4 me=mat4(1.0); // identity matrix	

float f5=vb.x; // the first to fourth components of a
// vector can be accessed via
// (x,y,z,w), (r,g,b,a), or (s,t,p,q),
// where v.x, v.r, and v.s are the
// same, and so on.	

vec2 vf=vb.zx; // sets to (3.0,1.0)	
vec3 vg=vb.rgr; // sets to (1.0,2.0,1.0)	
vg.sp=vec2(5.0,6.0); // vg becomes (5.0,2.0,6.0)	
vg=vb.xrs; // error: components not of the same set	
vec3 vh=ma[1]; //sets to (4.0,5.0,6.0)	
float f6=ma[2][0]; //sets to 7.0	
float f7=ma[1].y; //sets to 5.0	

const int ind=0;
vec3 vi=ma[ind+1];
// in the [] operator, there can only be an integral
// literal, a const variable, a loop index, or an
// expression composed from any of the preceding.	

Arrays
Only 1-dimensional arrays are supported. Arrays cannot be initialized during declaration. Arrays cannot also be qualified as const. The index of an array must be an integral literal, a const variable, or an expression composed from any of the preceding.
Examples
float floatArray[3];
vec4 vec4Array[5];

Structures
Unlike C, the 'typedef' keyword is not necessary when defining a new aggregate structure type.
Examples

struct light {
  vec4 color;
  vec3 position;
};
light l1,l2;
l1=light(vec4(0.0,1.0,0.0,1.0),
        vec3(8.0,3.0,8.0));

struct light {
  vec4 color[3];
  vec3 position;
}l3[5]; // an array of structures
vec3 p=l3[2].position;

9.1.2 Qualifiers

Storage Qualifiers	
(none)	local read/write; input parameter
const	compile-time constant; read-only function parameter; must be initialized during declaration
attribute	used to pass per-vertex data to the vertex shader; must be global; can only be used with float, vec2, vec3, vec4, mat2, mat3, and mat4
uniform	used to pass data to the vertex and fragment shaders; read-only; value does not change across the primitive being drawn
varying	used to pass data from the vertex shader to the fragment shader; must be global; can only be used with float, vec2, vec3, vec4, mat2, mat3, and mat4. The value passed to a fragment shader is interpolated across the vertices according to the shape drawn.
Precision Qualifiers	

(none)	Vertex Shader (default):
	    int: highp
	    float: highp
	    sampler2D: lowp
	    samplerCube: lowp
	Fragment Shader (default):
	    int: mediump
	    float: **None**
	    sampler2D: lowp
	    samplerCube: lowp

highp	float range: (-262,262) float precision: 2-16 int range: (-216,216)
mediump	float range: (-214,214) float precision: 2-10 int range: (-210,210)
lowp	float range: (-2,2) float precision: 2-8 int range: (-28 ,28)
Function Parameter Qualifiers	
(none)	same as 'in'
in	passes values in as function parameters; values not passed out during return time
out	passes values out of functions during return time; values not initialized when the variables are passed in
inout	passes values both in and out of functions
Examples ([storage][parameter][precision]<type><var>)	
varying lowp vec2 v;	

precision mediump float; //all floats are mediump
precision highp int; // all ints are highp
        // ivec4 now has 4 highp int components	

void luma(const in vec3 color, out float brightness){
  brightness=0.2*color.r +0.7*color.g+0.7*color.b;
}	

9.1.3 Operators

The operators, in order of precedence, are:

<table>
<tr><th>No.</th><th>Operator</th><th>Description</th><th>Associativity</th></tr>
<tr><td>1</td><td>()</td><td>bracket grouping</td><td>NA</td></tr>
<tr><td>2</td><td>[]
()
.
++, --</td><td>array subscript
function call
selector
increment,decrement</td><td>L-R</td></tr>
<tr><td>3</td><td>+- !</td><td>unary</td><td>R-L</td></tr>
<tr><td>4</td><td>* /</td><td>multiplicative</td><td>L-R</td></tr>
<tr><td>5</td><td>+ -</td><td>additive</td><td>L-R</td></tr>
<tr><td>6</td><td><><= >=</td><td>relational</td><td>L-R</td></tr>
<tr><td>7</td><td>== !=</td><td>equality</td><td>L-R</td></tr>
<tr><td>8</td><td>&&</td><td>Logical and</td><td>L-R</td></tr>
<tr><td>9</td><td>^^</td><td>Logical exclusive or</td><td>L-R</td></tr>
<tr><td>10</td><td>||</td><td>Logical inclusive or</td><td>L-R</td></tr>
<tr><td>11</td><td>?:</td><td>Ternary selection</td><td>L-R</td></tr>
<tr><td>12</td><td>= += -=
*= /=</td><td>Assignment</td><td>L-R</td></tr>
<tr><td>13</td><td>,</td><td>Sequence</td><td>L-R</td></tr>
<tr><td colspan="4">Examples</td></tr>
<tr><td colspan="4">m=f*m; // component-wise</td></tr>
<tr><td colspan="4">v=f*v; // component-wise</td></tr>
<tr><td colspan="4">v=v*v; // component-wise</td></tr>
<tr><td colspan="4">m=m*m; // linear algebraic</td></tr>
</table>

v=v*m; // linear algebraic
v=m*v; // linear algebraic
f=dot(v,v); // vector dot product
v=cross(v,v); // vector cross product
m=matrixCompMult(m,m); // component-wise

9.1.4 Statements

The syntaxes for the various statements in WebGL Shading Language share some similarities with the C syntaxes.

Function Call	returnType functionName([type0 arg0][, type1 arg1]......){...}

Iteration	for(...;...;...){...};
	while (...){...};
	do {...}while(...);

Selection	if (...){...} if (...){...}else{...}

Jump	break, continue, return,
	discard // used in the fragment
	// shader to skip the current
	// fragment operation

Entry	void main(...){...}

9.1.5 Built-in Constants

There are built-in constants that store the number of variables that can be defined for each data type.

Built-in Constant	Minimum
gl_MaxVertexAttribs	8
gl_MaxVertexUniformVectors	128
gl_MaxVaryingVectors	8
gl_MaxVertexTextureImageUnits	0
gl_MaxCombinedTextureImageUnits	8
gl_MaxTextureImageUnits	8
gl_MaxFragmentUniformVectors	16
gl_MaxDrawBuffers	1

9.1.6 Built-in Functions

Where specified, T denotes a float, vec2, vec3, or vec4. U denotes vec2, vec3, vec4, ivec2, ivec3, or ivec4. M denotes any matrix type. B denotes bvec2, bvec3, or bvec4.

Trigonometrical Functions (returning T): radians(T degrees), degrees(T radians), sin(T radians), cos(T radians), tan(T radians), asin(T x), acos(T x), atan(T x), atan(T y, T x).
Exponential Functions (returning T): pow(T x, T y), exp(T x), log(T x), exp2(T x), log2(T x), sqrt(T x), inversesqrt(T x)
Common Functions (returning T): abs(T x), floor(T x), ceil(T x) , mod(T x, T y), min(T x,T y), max(T x,T y) sign(T x): returns -1.0, 0.0, or 1.0 fract(T x): x-floor(x) clamp(T x, T m1, T m2): min(max(x,m1),m2) mix(T x, T y, T a): linear blend of x and y step(T edge, T x): 0.0 if x<edge, else 1.0 smoothstep(T edge0, T edge1, T x): clip, smooth
Geometric Functions returning float: length(T x), distance(T p0, T p1), dot(T x, T y) returning vec3: cross(vec3 x, vec3 y) returning M: matrixCompMult(M x, M y): multiplies x by y component-wise returning T: normalize(T x) faceforward(T N,T I, T N_{ref}): returns N if dot(N_{ref},I)<0, else -N reflect(T I, T N): reflection direction I-2*dot(N,I)*N refract(T I, T N, float eta): refraction vector
Vector Relational Functions: returning B: lessThan(U x,U y) lessThanEqual(U x, U y) greaterThan(U x, U y) greaterThanEqual(U x, U y) equal(U x, U y) equal(B x, B y) notEqual(U x, U y) notEqual(B x, B y) not(B x) returning bool: any(B x): true if any component is true all(B x): true if all components are true
Texture Lookup Functions (returning vec4): only in vertex shaders: texture2DLod(sampler2D s, vec2 coord, float lod) texture2DProjLod(sampler2D s, vec3 coord, float lod) texture2DProjLod(sampler2D s, vec4 coord, float lod) textureCudeLod(samplerCube s, vec3 coord,float lod) only in fragment shaders: texture2D(sampler2D s, vec2 coord, float bias) texture2DProj(sampler2D s, vec3 coord, float bias) texture2DProj(sampler2D s,vec4 coord, float bias) textureCube(samplerCube s, vec3 coord, float bias) in both shaders: texture2D(sampler2D s, vec2 coord) texture2DProj(sampler2D s, vec3 coord) texture2DProj(sampler2D s,vec4 coord) textureCube(samplerCube s, vec3 coord)

9.1.7 Preprocessors and Macros

As in C, there exist pre-processors which are executed before compilation. Macros can also be defined to use meaningful names in place of value literals. However, unlike C, macros in GLSL cannot have parameters.

Preprocessors (examples)
#if constant-expression   // statements to run if the expression is true #endif

#if constant-expression1
  // statements to run if the expression is true
#elif constant-expression2
  //...
#else
  //...
#endif

#ifdef macro-name   // statements to run if 'macro-name' is defined #endif
#ifndef macro-name   // statements to run if 'macro-name' is undefined #endif
#define macro-name value
#undefine macro-name
#version 101 // must be at the top of the program
#error...
#pragma...
#extension...
#line...
Built-in Macros
__LINE__ yields the line number in the shader program.
__VERSION__ yields the version of GLSL used. 100 means version 1.00.
GL_ES is defined and set to 1 if the program is running on an OpenGL-ES Shading Language.
GL_FRAGMENT_SHADER_PRECISION_HIGH is defined and set to 1 if highp is supported in the fragment language.

9.2 2D Drawing

Unlike 2D Canvas, WebGL does not allow one to draw in a straightforward manner. Before any drawing can be done, one first needs to know how to use shaders, and how to pass data to the shaders. In 9.2.1, we shall write a general-purpose shaders-initializing function that will be used throughout the rest of the chapter. In 9.2.2, we discuss how to pass data from the JavaScript program to the shaders. In 9.2.3, we explore how to pass large quantities of data efficiently using typed arrays and buffer objects.

By default, the eye is looking at the origin (0.0,0.0,0.0), viewing along the negative direction of the z-axis (into the screen). The x and y coordinates range from -1.0 to 1.0, which correspond to the edges of the canvas. (0.0,0.0) is the center of the canvas. In this section, z is always zero for all vertices, allowing 2D graphics to be studied exclusively.

9.2.1 Initializing Shaders

10 steps are involved in the use of the vertex and fragment shaders.

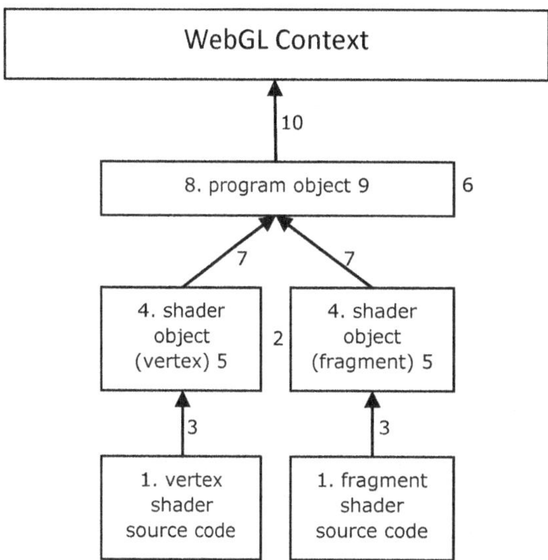

Step 1: Code both shaders using the Shading Language. The code for a shader can be exist as string literals inside a JavaScript, or as text content inside the <script> tags outside a JavaScript. We shall see how to do both.

Step 2: Create a shader object for both shaders. This is done by calling the constructor **createShader(type)** where 'type' can be VERTEX_SHADER or FRAGMENT_SHADER.

Step 3: Specify the source code for the shader objects. This is done by calling **shaderSource(shader, source)**. Note that if the sources exist as text inside the <script> tags, they need to be parsed into strings first.

Step 4: Compile the shaders objects. This is done by calling **compileShader(shader)**.

Step 5: Check the status of the shader compilation. This is done by calling **getShaderParameter (shader,pname)**. pname can be SHADER_TYPE, DELETE_STATUS, COMPILE_STATUS.

Step 6: Create a program object. This is done by calling **createProgram()**.

Step 7: Attach both shader objects to the program object. This is done by calling **attachShader (program, shader)**.

Step 8: Link the program object. This is done by calling **linkProgram(program)**.

Step 9: Check the status of the linking of the program object. This is done by calling **getProgramParameter(program,pname)** where pname can be DELETE_STATUS, LINK_STATUS, VALIDATE_STATUS, ATTACHED_SHADERS, ACTIVE_ATTRIBUTES, ACTIVE_UNIFORMS. The first three return true or false; the last three return an integer.

Step 10: Tell WebGL to use the program. This is done by calling **useProgram(program)**.

The function initShaders() can automatically tell whether the parameters are strings of shader programs, or the tag ids of the shader programs. If the strings passed in contain "main" and "(", the strings are shader programs.

```
// webgl-library.js
function initShaders(gl,vs,fs){
  vsScript = (vs.indexOf("main")>0 && vs.indexOf("(")>0)?
    vs:document.getElementById(vs).innerHTML;
  fsScript = (fs.indexOf("main")>0 && fs.indexOf("(")>0)?
    fs:document.getElementById(fs).innerHTML;
  vsObj = gl.createShader(gl.VERTEX_SHADER);
  fsObj = gl.createShader(gl.FRAGMENT_SHADER);
  gl.shaderSource(vsObj,vsScript);
  gl.shaderSource(fsObj,fsScript);
  gl.compileShader(vsObj);
  gl.compileShader(fsObj);
  if (!gl.getShaderParameter(vsObj,gl.COMPILE_STATUS)){
    alert("Can't compile the vertex shader.");
  }
  if (!gl.getShaderParameter(fsObj,gl.COMPILE_STATUS)){
    alert("Can't compile the fragment shader.");
    return;
  }
  var p = gl.createProgram();
  gl.attachShader(p,vsObj);
  gl.attachShader(p,fsObj);
  gl.linkProgram(p);
  if (!gl.getProgramParameter(p, gl.LINK_STATUS)){
    alert("Can't link the shaders-attached program.");
    return;
  }
  gl.useProgram(p);
  shaderProgram=p;
  return p;
}
```

```
<!DOCTYPE html>
<html>
<head>
<script src="webgl-library.js"></script>
<script id="vs" type="x-shader/x-vertex">
  void main(){
    gl_Position = vec4(0.0,0.5,0.0,1.0);
    gl_PointSize=30.0;
  }
</script>
<script id="fs" type="x-shader/x-fragment">
  precision mediump float;
  void main(){
    gl_FragColor=vec4(1.0,1.0,1.0,1.0);
  }
</script>

<script>
function draw_point(){
  var canvas = document.getElementById("myCanvas");
  var gl = canvas.getContext("webgl");
  initShaders(gl,"vs","fs");

  gl.clearColor(0.0,0.0,0.0,1.0);
  gl.clear(gl.COLOR_BUFFER_BIT);
  gl.drawArrays(gl.POINTS,0,1);
}
</script>
</head>

<body onload="draw_point()">
  <canvas id="myCanvas" width="500" height="500">
    Please use a browser that supports 'canvas'.
  </canvas>
</body>
</html>
```

Here are some other related functions:

isShader(shader) returns true if 'shader' is a shader object. **isProgram(program)** returns true if 'program' is a program object.

getShaderInfoLog(shader) returns the information about a shader object as a string. **getProgramInfoLog(program)** return the information about a program object as a string. **validateProgram(program)** checks to see if the program is executable given the current states. The information is stored in the program's information log.

deleteShader(shader) deletes a shader object. **deleteProgram(program)** deletes a program object.

detachShader(program,shader) detaches a shader object from a program object. **getShaderSource(shader)** returns the source code of the shader object as a string. **getAttachedShaders(program)** returns an array of shader objects that are attached to 'program'.

bindAttribLocation(program,index, attribute-name) associates a user-defined attribute variable in 'program' with a generic vertex attribute index. If attribute-name refers to a matrix attribute variable, index refers to the first column, (index+1) refers to the second column and so on.

9.2.2 Passing Data to the Shaders

Step 1: To pass data to the shaders, first we have to determine the locations of the variables using:
getAttribLocation(program,name)
getUniformLocation(program,name)
Each of these functions returns the location of the variable as an integer which is greater than or equal to 0. -1 is returned if the variable does not exist or if it starts with 'gl_' or 'webgl_'.

Step 2: Using the locations we have obtained, we then specify the values:
vertexAttrib{1234}{fi}[v](location,...)
uniform{1234}{fi}[v](location,...)
{fi} specifies whether a float or an integer is passed. {1234} indicates how many values are to be passed. If the variable in the shader has more components than the parameters, the second and third components will be set to zero while the fourth component will be set to one. If 'v' is specified, there will be only one parameter other than 'location', and it will be an array containing the few components.

```
<!DOCTYPE html>
<html>
<head>
<script src="webgl-library.js"></script>
<script>
var VS_SOURCE="\
  attribute vec4 p;\
  void main(){\
    gl_Position = p; \
    gl_PointSize=30.0;\
  }\
";

var FS_SOURCE="\
  precision mediump float;\
  uniform vec4 c;\
  void main(){\
    gl_FragColor=c;\
  }\
";

function draw_point(){
  var canvas = document.getElementById("myCanvas");
  var gl = canvas.getContext("webgl");
  initShaders(gl,VS_SOURCE,FS_SOURCE);

  var pL=gl.getAttribLocation(gl.program, 'p');
  if (pL<0) alert("Failed to get the location of p");
  gl.vertexAttrib2f(pL,0.5,0.0);

  var cA=[1.0,0.3,0.6,1.0];
  var cL=gl.getUniformLocation(gl.program,'c');
  if (cL<0) alert("Failed to get the location of c");
  gl.uniform4fv(cL,cA);

  gl.clearColor(0.0,0.0,0.0,1.0);
  gl.clear(gl.COLOR_BUFFER_BIT);
  gl.drawArrays(gl.POINTS,0,1);
}
</script>
</head>

<body onload="draw_point()">
  <canvas id="myCanvas" width="500"
                        height="500"></canvas>
</body>
</html>
```

Here are some other related functions:

uniformMatrix{234}fv(location, transpose, Array) passes in the values for a matrix uniform.

getVertexAttribOffset(location, pname) returns the address of the specified generic 'location'. 'pname' must be VERTEX_ATTRIB_ARRAY_POINTER.

getActiveAttrib(program,location) and **getActiveUniform(program,location)** return a WebGLActiveInfo object with three members: 'name', 'size', and 'type'.

9.2.3 Typed Arrays and Buffer Objects

JavaScript is a loosely typed language. To process large quantities of data of the same type efficiently, the data types have to be specified for arrays. This is where typed arrays come in. The only way to create a typed array is by using the 'new' operator.

View	Bytes	Description
Int8Array	1	Signed integer
Uint8Array	1	Unsigned integer
Int16Array	2	Signed integer
Uint16Array	2	Unsigned integer
Int32Array	4	Signed integer
Uint32Array	4	Unsigned integer
Float32Array	4	Signed float
Float64Array	8	Signed float

Methods, Properties	Description
get(index)	Gets the index-th element.
set(index,value)	Sets value to the index-th element.
set(array,offset)	Sets the elements of array from offset-th element.
subset(begin,end)	Returns a subset of the array.
length	The number of elements.
BYTES_PER_ELEMENT	The number of bytes per element.
At the time of writing, some methods are not supported by the browsers.	

Example:

```
var v1=new Float64Array(4); //4 elements
var v2=new Float32Array(
            [0.3,0.3, -0.3,0.3, -0.3,-0.3]);
var v3=new Float32Array(v2); // copies v2
alert(v3.length); // yields 6
```

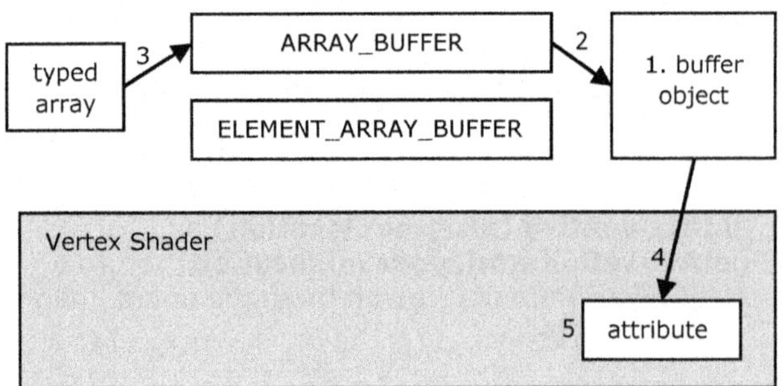

A buffer object is a memory area allocated by WebGL to hold the vertices. By using a buffer object, multiple vertices can, at once, be passed to a vertex shader through one of its attribute variables, as WebGL draws the primitive. There are five steps involved in using a buffer object.

Step 1: Create a buffer object. This is done by calling **createBuffer()**.

Step 2: Bind the buffer object to a target. This is done by calling **bindBuffer(target,buffer)**, where target can be ARRAY_BUFFER(vertex data) or ELEMENT_ARRAY_BUFFER(index values to vertex data, see the example at 9.4.3).

Step 3: Write data into the buffer object. This is done by calling **bufferData(target,data,usage)**. 'target' can be ARRAY_BUFFER or ELEMENT_ARRAY_BUFFER. 'data' is the typed array to be passed in. 'usage' can be STATIC_DRAW (specified once, used many times), STREAM_DRAW (specified once, used a few times), or DYNAMIC_DRAW (specified repeatedly, used many times).

Step 4: Assign the buffer object to an attribute variable. This is done by calling **vertexAttribPointer(location, size, type, normalized, stride, offset).** 'size' can be 1 to 4 and specifies the number of components per vertex. 'type' can be UNSIGNED_BYTE (Uint8Array), SHORT (Int16Array), UNSIGNED_SHORT (Uint16Array), INT (Int32Array), UNSIGNED_INT(Uint32Array), FLOAT(Float32Array). 'normalized' can be true or false, and indicates whether nonfloating data should be normalized to [0,1] or [-1,1]. 'stride' specifies the number of bytes between different vertex data elements, or zero for default stride. 'offset' specifies in bytes the starting location of the vertex data in the buffer object.

Step 5: Enable assignment. This is done by calling **enableVertexAttribArray(location)**.

A red point appears whenever and wherever the mouse is clicked on the canvas.

```
<!DOCTYPE html>
<html>
<head>
<script src="webgl-library.js"></script>
<script>
var VS_SOURCE="\
  attribute vec4 p;\
  void main(){\
    gl_Position = p; \
    gl_PointSize=30.0;\
  }\
";

var FS_SOURCE="\
  precision mediump float;\
  uniform vec4 c;\
  void main(){\
    gl_FragColor=c;\
  }\
";

var n=0;
var points=new Array();

function initialize_webgl(){
  var canvas = document.getElementById("myCanvas");
  var gl = canvas.getContext("webgl");
  initShaders(gl,VS_SOURCE,FS_SOURCE);
  gl.clearColor(0.0,0.0,0.0,1.0);
  gl.clear(gl.COLOR_BUFFER_BIT);
  canvas.onclick=function(ev){draw_point(ev,canvas,gl);};
}

function draw_point(ev,canvas,gl){
  // Stores the locations of the mouse click in points[]
  var x=ev.clientX;
  var y=ev.clientY;
  var rect=ev.target.getBoundingClientRect();
  x=((x-rect.left)-canvas.height/2)/(canvas.height/2);
  y=(canvas.width/2-(y-rect.top))/(canvas.width/2);
  points.push(x);
  points.push(y);
  n++;

  // Use a buffer object to pass points[] to the attribute p
  var pL=gl.getAttribLocation(gl.program, 'p');
  if (pL<0) alert("Failed to get the location of p");
  var b=gl.createBuffer();
  gl.bindBuffer(gl.ARRAY_BUFFER,b);
  gl.bufferData(gl.ARRAY_BUFFER,
               new Float32Array(points),gl.STATIC_DRAW);
  gl.vertexAttribPointer(pL,2,gl.FLOAT,false,0,0);
  gl.enableVertexAttribArray(pL);

  // Specifies the pixel/fragment color
  var cA=[1.0,0.0,0.0,1.0];
  var cL=gl.getUniformLocation(gl.program,'c');
  if (cL<0) alert("Failed to get the location of c");
  gl.uniform4fv(cL,cA);

  gl.clearColor(0.0,0.0,0.0,1.0);
  gl.clear(gl.COLOR_BUFFER_BIT);
  gl.drawArrays(gl.POINTS,0,n); // draws n points
  gl.deleteBuffer(b); // frees the memory
}
</script>
</head>

<body onload="initialize_webgl()">
  <canvas id="myCanvas" width="500"
                        height="500"></canvas>
</body>
</html>
```

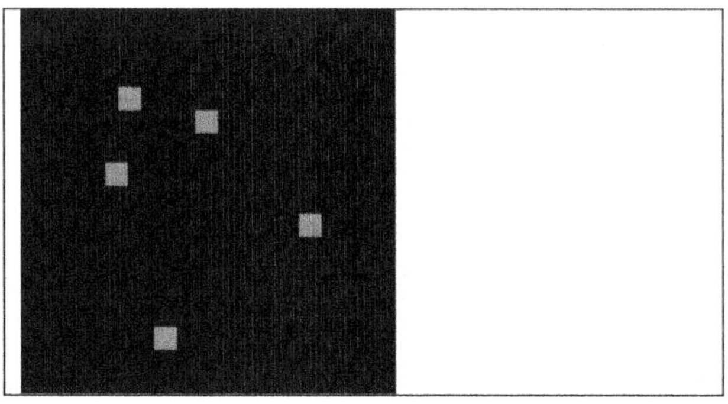

Here are some other related functions:

isBuffer(buffer) returns true if 'buffer' is a defined buffer object. **deleteBuffer(buffer)** deletes the specified buffer object. **bufferSubData(target, offset, data)** updates a portion of the buffer object, starting at 'offset', with 'data'. **disableVertexAttrib Array(location)** disables attribute assignment.

getVertexAttrib(location,pname) and **getUniform(program,location)** return the values passed to the attribute or uniform attributes, or information about the variables. 'pname' can be: CURRENT_VERTEX_ATTRIB, VERTEX_ATTRIB_ARRAY_BUFFER_BINDING, VERTEX_ATTRIB_ARRAY_ENABLED, VERTEX_ATTRIB_ARRAY_SIZE, VERTEX_ATTRIB_ARRAY_STRIDE, VERTEX_ATTRIB_ARRAY_TYPE, or VERTEX_ATTRIB_ARRAY_NORMALIZED.

9.2.4 Drawing Modes

There are two functions that allow drawing to be initiated:

drawArrays(mode, first, count) uses the buffer object bound to ARRAY_BUFFER.

drawElements(mode,count,type,offset) uses the buffer object bound to ELEMENT_ARRAY_BUFFER, where the indices to the vertices are specified. (see the example at 9.4.3)

'mode' can be POINTS, LINE_STRIP, LINE_LOOP, LINES, TRIANGLE_STRIP, TRIANGLE_FAN, TRIANGLES.

'first' specifies the first vertex to draw from.

'count' specifies the number of vertices to be used for drawing.

'type' can be UNSIGNED_BYTE, or UNSIGNED_SHORT.

'offset' specifies a pointer to the location where the vertices are stored.

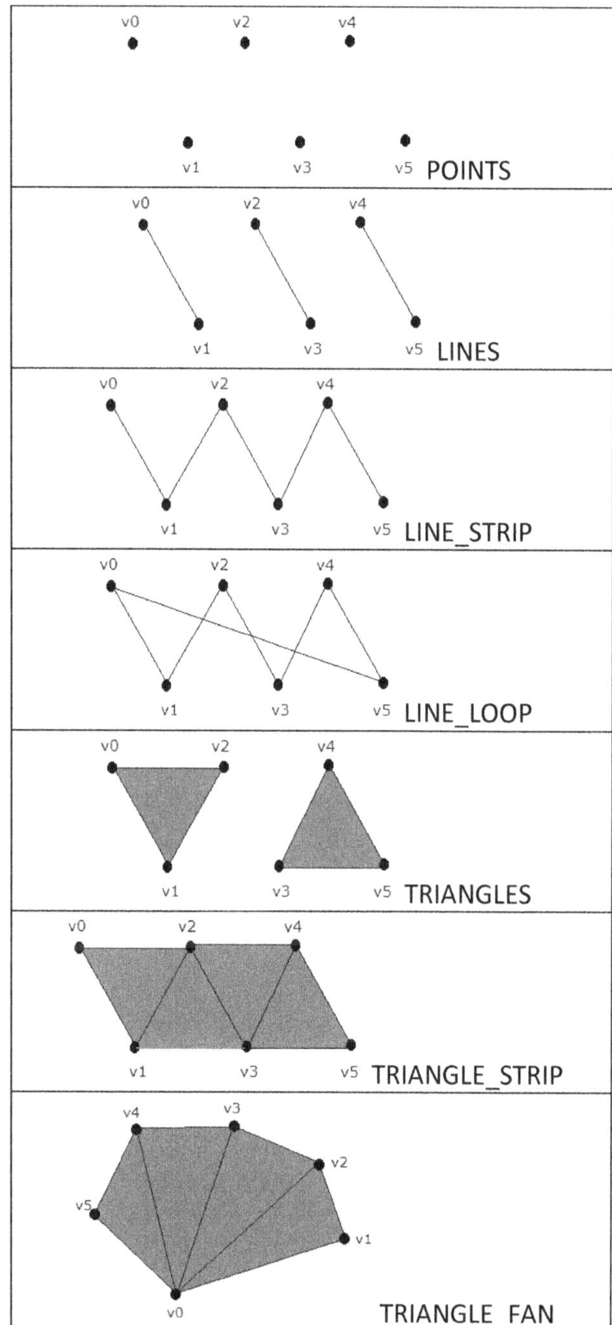

During the rasterization process, the fragment_shader interpolates the varying variable c2, drawing a colorful triangle. As the value of a uniform variable is the same throughout the entire primitive, to pass a changing variable to the fragment shader, one has to pass the values to an attribute variable first.

```
<!DOCTYPE html>
<html>
<head>
<script src="webgl-library.js"></script>
<script>
var VS_SOURCE="\
  attribute vec4 p;\
  attribute vec4 c;\
  varying vec4 c2;\
  void main(){\
    c2=c;\
    gl_Position = p; \
  }\
";

var FS_SOURCE="\
  precision mediump float;\
  varying vec4 c2;\
  void main(){\
    gl_FragColor=c2;\
  }\
";

var points=new Array();
var vc= new Float32Array([ 0.0,-0.5,  1.0, 0.0, 0.0,
                          -0.5, 0.5,  0.0, 1.0, 0.0,
                           0.5, 0.5,  0.0, 0.0, 1.0]);

function colored_triangle(){
  var canvas = document.getElementById("myCanvas");
  var gl = canvas.getContext("webgl");
  initShaders(gl,VS_SOURCE,FS_SOURCE);

  var ESIZE=vc.BYTES_PER_ELEMENT;
  var b=gl.createBuffer();
  gl.bindBuffer(gl.ARRAY_BUFFER,b);
  gl.bufferData(gl.ARRAY_BUFFER,vc,gl.STATIC_DRAW);

  pL=gl.getAttribLocation(gl.program,'p');
  gl.vertexAttribPointer(pL,2,gl.FLOAT,false,ESIZE*5,0);
  gl.enableVertexAttribArray(pL);

  cL=gl.getAttribLocation(gl.program,'c');
  gl.vertexAttribPointer(cL,3,gl.FLOAT,false,ESIZE*5,
                         ESIZE*2);
  gl.enableVertexAttribArray(cL);
  gl.clearColor(0.0,0.0,0.0,1.0);
  gl.clear(gl.COLOR_BUFFER_BIT);
  gl.drawArrays(gl.TRIANGLES,0,3);
}
</script>
</head>

<body onload="colored_triangle()">
  <canvas id="myCanvas" width="500"
height="500"></canvas>
</body>
</html>
```

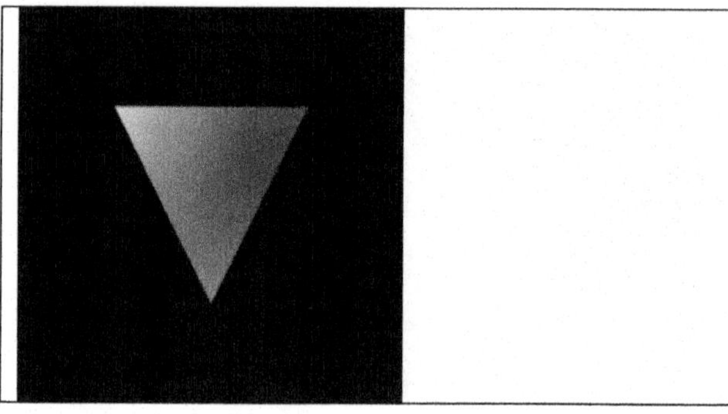

The color buffer in the default framebuffer stores the pixels of the resultant image on the canvas. In the framebuffer, there also exist the depth and stencil buffers.

clearColor(red,green,blue,alpha) specifies the clear color for a drawing area. The parameters range from 0.0 to 1.0.

clear(mask) clears the specific buffers in the framebuffer. 'mask' is a bitwise OR of COLOR_BUFFER_BIT, DEPTH_BUFFER_BIT, and STENCIL_BUFFER_BIT.

clearDepth(depth) specifies the clear value for the depth buffer. 'depth' is a float.

clearStencil(s) specifies the clear value for the stencil buffer. 's' is an integer.

9.2.5 Fragment Coordinates

The fragment shader provides two built-in variables: **gl_FragCoord** stores the window coordinates of the fragment. **gl_PointCoord** is a 2-dimensional vector which stores the position of the fragment in the drawn point (0.0,1.0).

Note that gl_PointSize and gl_PointCoord are applicable only for point rasterization only, ie. when the drawing 'mode' is POINTS.

This draws a round, colorful circle at the center.

```
<!DOCTYPE html>
<html>
<head>
<script src="webgl-library.js"></script>
<script id="vs" type="x-shader/x-vertex">
  void main(){
    gl_Position = vec4(0.0,0.0,0.0,1.0);
    gl_PointSize=100.0;
  }
</script>
<script id="fs" type="x-shader/x-fragment">
  precision mediump float;
  void main(){
    float dist=distance(gl_PointCoord,vec2(0.5,0.5));
    if (dist<0.5){
      gl_FragColor=vec4(gl_PointCoord,0.0,1.0);
    } else {
      discard;
    }
  }
</script>
```

```
<script>
function draw_point(){
  var canvas = document.getElementById("myCanvas");
  var gl = canvas.getContext("webgl");
  initShaders(gl,"vs","fs");

  gl.clearColor(0.0,0.0,0.0,1.0);
  gl.clear(gl.COLOR_BUFFER_BIT);
  gl.drawArrays(gl.POINTS,0,1);
}
</script>
</head>

<body onload="draw_point()">
  <canvas id="myCanvas" width="500"
height="500"></canvas>
</body>
</html>
```

9.2.6 Display Regions

viewport(x, y, width, height) scales the entire resultant image onto the specified region of the canvas, transforming the image from device coordinates to window coordinates. **scissor (x,y,width,height)** cuts away the region that falls outside the specified region on the canvas, leaving the cutaway region in background color.

(x,y) is a pair of integers that denotes the lower-left corner of the region. By default, 'width' and 'height' are the width and height of the canvas in integers. scissor() is performed after all the viewport() operations.

```
<!DOCTYPE html>
<html>
<head>
<script src="webgl-library.js"></script>
<script>
var VS_SOURCE="\
  attribute vec4 p;\
  attribute vec4 c;\
  varying vec4 c2;\
  void main(){\
    c2=c;\
    gl_Position = p; \
  }\
";

var FS_SOURCE="\
  precision mediump float;\
  varying vec4 c2;\
  void main(){\
    gl_FragColor=c2;\
  }\
";

var gl,m,mL;
function start(){
  var canvas = document.getElementById("myCanvas");
  gl = canvas.getContext("webgl");
  initShaders(gl,VS_SOURCE,FS_SOURCE);

  var points=new Array();
  var vc= new Float32Array([ 0.0,-0.5,  1.0, 0.0, 0.0,
                            -0.5, 0.5,  0.0, 1.0, 0.0,
                             0.5, 0.5,  0.0, 0.0, 1.0]);
  var ESIZE=vc.BYTES_PER_ELEMENT;
  var b=gl.createBuffer();
  gl.bindBuffer(gl.ARRAY_BUFFER,b);
  gl.bufferData(gl.ARRAY_BUFFER,vc,gl.STATIC_DRAW);

  pL=gl.getAttribLocation(gl.program,'p');
  gl.vertexAttribPointer(pL,2,gl.FLOAT,false,ESIZE*5,0);
  gl.enableVertexAttribArray(pL);


  cL=gl.getAttribLocation(gl.program,'c');
  gl.vertexAttribPointer(cL,3,gl.FLOAT,false,ESIZE*5,
                         ESIZE*2);
  gl.enableVertexAttribArray(cL);

  gl.clearColor(0.0,0.0,0.0,1.0);
  gl.clear(gl.COLOR_BUFFER_BIT);

  gl.enable(gl.SCISSOR_TEST);
  gl.scissor(0,0,500,250);
  gl.viewport(0,0,250,500)  // scales to left half of the canvas
  gl.drawArrays(gl.TRIANGLES,0,3);
  gl.viewport(250,0,250,500)
                            // scales to right half of the canvas
  gl.drawArrays(gl.TRIANGLES,0,3);

}
</script>
</head>

<body onload="start()">
  <canvas id="myCanvas" width="500"
height="500"></canvas>
</body>
</html>
```

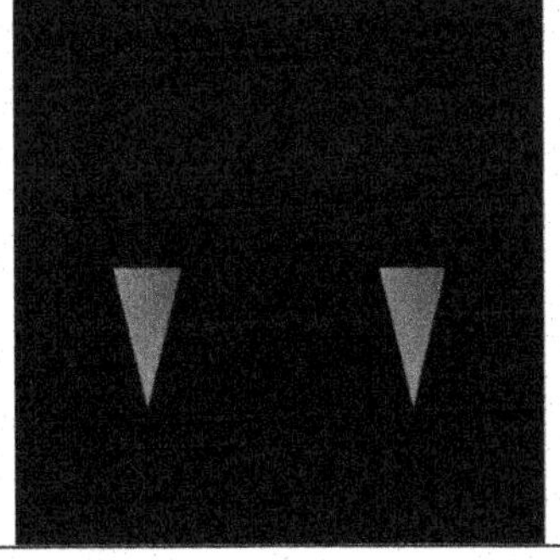

enable(capability) enables a capability.
disable(capability) disables a capability.
isEnabled(capability) returns true if a capability is enabled.

'capability' can be:
BLEND,
CULL_FACE,
DEPTH_TEST,
DITHER,
POLYGON_OFFSET_FILL,
SAMPLE_ALPHA_TO_COVERAGE,
SAMPLE_COVERAGE,

SCISSOR_TEST,
STENCIL_TEST

By default, all capabilities are disabled to speed up drawing.

9.3 Positional Matrices

A transformation can be achieved by multiplying the positional vectors of the vertices with a 4*4 matrix in the vertex shader. In this section, we will develop a JavaScript object called Matrix4 that contains many useful methods for transformations, viewing and projection. The matrix object defined is passed to the vertex shader as a uniform variable.

Here three functions are added to webgl-library.js, allowing the coder to construct a Matrix4, set it to I, and multiply a matrix to it. This example does not perform any transformation but it teaches how to use Matrix4 at the basic level. It will serve as a template for other examples in this section.

```
//webgl-library.js
function Matrix4(s){
  var i;
  this.entries = new Array();
  if (s && (typeof s)==='object' && s.length &&
     s.length==16){
    for (i=0; i<16; i++) this.entries.push(s[i]);
  } else {
    this.entries=[1,0,0,0, 0,1,0,0, 0,0,1,0, 0,0,0,1];
  }
}

Matrix4.prototype.setIdentity = function(){
  var e = this.entries;
  e[0] = 1; e[4] = 0; e[8]  = 0; e[12] = 0;
  e[1] = 0; e[5] = 1; e[9]  = 0; e[13] = 0;
  e[2] = 0; e[6] = 0; e[10] = 1; e[14] = 0;
  e[3] = 0; e[7] = 0; e[11] = 0; e[15] = 1;
  return this;
}

Matrix4.prototype.multiply_matrix = function(other){
 var i, e, a, b, ai0, ai1, ai2, ai3;
 e = this.entries;
 a = this.entries;
 b = other;
 for (i = 0; i < 4; i++) {
  ai0=a[i]; ai1=a[i+4]; ai2=a[i+8]; ai3=a[i+12];
  e[i]    = ai0*b[0]  + ai1*b[1]  + ai2*b[2]  + ai3*b[3];
  e[i+4]  = ai0*b[4]  + ai1*b[5]  + ai2*b[6]  + ai3*b[7];
  e[i+8]  = ai0*b[8]  + ai1*b[9]  + ai2*b[10] + ai3*b[11];
  e[i+12] = ai0*b[12] + ai1*b[13] + ai2*b[14] + ai3*b[15];
 }
 return this;
}
```

```
<!DOCTYPE html>
<html>
<head>
<script src="webgl-library.js"></script>
<script>
function draw_colored_triangle(){
  var points=new Array();
  var vc= new Float32Array([ 0.0,-0.5,  1.0, 0.0, 0.0,
                            -0.5, 0.5,  0.0, 1.0, 0.0,
                             0.5, 0.5,  0.0, 0.0, 1.0]);
  var ESIZE=vc.BYTES_PER_ELEMENT;
  var b=gl.createBuffer();
  gl.bindBuffer(gl.ARRAY_BUFFER,b);
  gl.bufferData(gl.ARRAY_BUFFER,vc,gl.STATIC_DRAW);

  pL=gl.getAttribLocation(gl.program,'p');
  gl.vertexAttribPointer(pL,2,gl.FLOAT,false,ESIZE*5,0);
  gl.enableVertexAttribArray(pL);

  cL=gl.getAttribLocation(gl.program,'c');
  gl.vertexAttribPointer(cL,3,gl.FLOAT,false,ESIZE*5,|
                                ESIZE*2);
  gl.enableVertexAttribArray(cL);

  gl.clearColor(0.0,0.0,0.0,1.0);
  gl.clear(gl.COLOR_BUFFER_BIT);
  gl.drawArrays(gl.TRIANGLES,0,3);
}

var VS_SOURCE="\
  uniform mat4 I;\
  attribute vec4 p;\
  attribute vec4 c;\
  varying vec4 c2;\
  void main(){\
    c2=c;\
    gl_Position = I*p; \
  }\
";

var FS_SOURCE="\
  precision mediump float;\
  varying vec4 c2;\
  void main(){\
    gl_FragColor=c2;\
  }\
";

var gl,m,mL;
function start(){
  var canvas = document.getElementById("myCanvas");
  gl = canvas.getContext("webgl");
  initShaders(gl,VS_SOURCE,FS_SOURCE);

  m = new Matrix4();
  mL = gl.getUniformLocation(gl.program, 'I');
  gl.uniformMatrix4fv(mL,false,m.entries);
  draw_colored_triangle();
}
</script>
</head>

<body onload="start()">
  <canvas id="myCanvas"
          width="500" height="500"></canvas>
</body>
</html>
```

9.3.1 Model Matrix

To peform a translation by (Tx,Ty,Tz), we multiply the modelview matrix by:

$$\begin{bmatrix} 1 & 0 & 0 & Tx \\ 0 & 1 & 0 & Ty \\ 0 & 0 & 1 & Tz \\ 0 & 0 & 0 & 1 \end{bmatrix}$$

To peform a scaling by (Sx,Sy,Sz), we multiply the modelview matrix by:

$$\begin{bmatrix} Sx & 0 & 0 & 0 \\ 0 & Sy & 0 & 0 \\ 0 & 0 & Sz & 0 \\ 0 & 0 & 0 & 1 \end{bmatrix}$$

To perform a rotation by Θ about an axis in the direction of the unit vector (u_x,u_y,u_z), we multiply the modelview matrix by:

$$\begin{bmatrix} \cos\theta + u_x^2(1-\cos\theta) & u_x u_y(1-\cos\theta) - u_z\sin\theta & u_x u_z(1-\cos\theta) + u_y\sin\theta & 0 \\ u_y u_x(1-\cos\theta) + u_z\sin\theta & \cos\theta + u_y^2(1-\cos\theta) & u_y u_z(1-\cos\theta) - u_x\sin\theta & 0 \\ u_z u_x(1-\cos\theta) - u_y\sin\theta & u_z u_y(1-\cos\theta) + u_x\sin\theta & \cos\theta + u_z^2(1-\cos\theta) & 0 \\ 0 & 0 & 0 & 1 \end{bmatrix}$$

This displays a rotating rectangle at the right of the canvas. Note that the transformations are applied in the reversed order, because of the way they are multiplied.

```
// webgl-library.js
Matrix4.prototype.translate = function(x,y,z){
  this.multiply_matrix([1,0,0,0, 0,1,0,0, 0,0,1,0, x,y,z,1]);
}

Matrix4.prototype.scale = function(x,y,z){
  this.multiply_matrix([x,0,0,0, 0,y,0,0, 0,0,z,0, 0,0,0,1]);
}

Matrix4.prototype.rotate = function(degrees,x,y,z){
  var e = new Array(16);
  var r = Math.PI * degrees / 180;
  var s = Math.sin(r);
  var c = Math.cos(r);
  var nc = 1-c;

  // Normalize (x,y,z) to a unit vector
  var l = Math.sqrt(x*x + y*y + z*z);
  x/=l;
  y/=l;
  z/=l;

  e[ 0] = x*x*nc + c;
  e[ 1] = x*y*nc + z*s;
  e[ 2] = z*x*nc - y*s;
  e[ 3] = 0;
  e[ 4] = x*y*nc - z*s;
  e[ 5] = y*y*nc + c;
  e[ 6] = y*z*nc + x*s;
  e[ 7] = 0;
  e[ 8] = z*x*nc + y*s;
  e[ 9] = y*z*nc - x*s;
  e[10] = z*z*nc + c;
  e[11] = 0;
  e[12] = 0;
  e[13] = 0;
  e[14] = 0;
  e[15] = 1;

  this.multiply_matrix(e);
}
```

```
...
var VS_SOURCE="\
  uniform mat4 modelMatrix;\
  attribute vec4 p;\
  attribute vec4 c;\
  varying vec4 c2;\
  void main(){\
    c2=c;\
    gl_Position = modelMatrix * p; \
  }\
";

var FS_SOURCE="\
  precision mediump float;\
  varying vec4 c2;\
  void main(){\
    gl_FragColor=c2;\
  }\
";

var gl,mm,mmL;
function start(){
  var canvas = document.getElementById("myCanvas");
  gl = canvas.getContext("webgl");
  initShaders(gl,VS_SOURCE,FS_SOURCE);

  mm = new Matrix4();
  mmL = gl.getUniformLocation(gl.program, 'modelMatrix');
  mm.translate(0.5,0,0);
  mm.scale(0.5,0.5,0.5);
  var tick = function(){
    mm.rotate(1,0,0,1); // rotates one degree every frame
    gl.uniformMatrix4fv(mmL,false,
                        new Float32Array(mm.entries));
    draw_colored_triangle();
    requestAnimationFrame(tick);
  };
  tick();
}
...
```

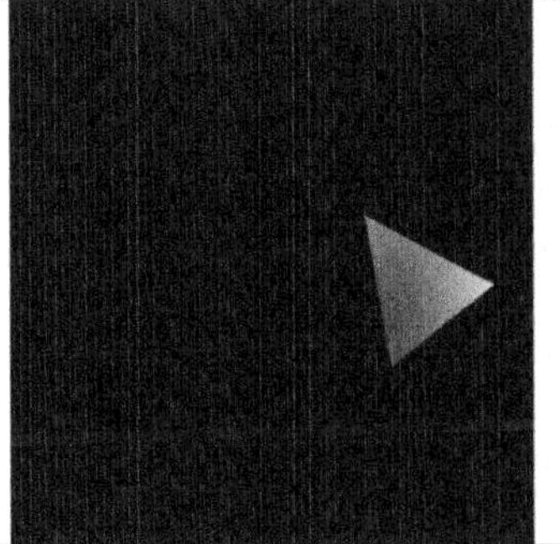

9.3.2 View Matrix

So far we have been looking at the origin in the negative-y direction. It is possible to move the imaginary camera around so that the object can be viewed from a different perspective. Precisely, the viewing can be defined by 3 vectors:

V_{eye} specifies the location of the camera.

V_{target} specifies the target of the camera.

V_{up} specifies the rotation of the camera.

The view matrix can be obtained by the following pseudo-code:

```
mat4 lookAt(vec3 eye, vec3 target, vec3 up){
  vec3 vz=normalize(eye - target);
  vec3 vx=normalize(crossProduct(up,vz));
  vec3 vy=crossProduct(vz,vx);
  inverse=mat4(vec4(vx,0),
               vec4(vy,0),
               vec4(vz,0),
               vec4(eye,1));
```

```
    return inverse.getInverse();
}
```

Pressing the arrow keys move the camera around. The triangle becomes thin as the camera moves horizontally to the edge.

```
//webgl-library.js

Matrix4.prototype.lookAt = function(eyeX, eyeY, eyeZ,
                    targetX, targetY, targetZ, upX, upY, upZ) {
  var e, fx, fy, fz, l, sx, sy, sz, ux, uy, uz;

  fx = targetX - eyeX;
  fy = targetY - eyeY;
  fz = targetZ - eyeZ;

  // Normalize f.
  l = Math.sqrt(fx*fx + fy*fy + fz*fz);
  fx /= l;
  fy /= l;
  fz /= l;

  // Calculate cross product of f and up.
  sx = fy * upZ - fz * upY;
  sy = fz * upX - fx * upZ;
  sz = fx * upY - fy * upX;

  // Normalize s.
  l = Math.sqrt(sx*sx + sy*sy + sz*sz);
  sx /= l;
  sy /= l;
  sz /= l;

  // Calculate cross product of s and f.
  ux = sy * fz - sz * fy;
  uy = sz * fx - sx * fz;
  uz = sx * fy - sy * fx;

  // A pre-calculated shortcut.
  this.entries[0] = sx;
  this.entries[1] = ux;
  this.entries[2] = -fx;
  this.entries[3] = 0;
  this.entries[4] = sy;
  this.entries[5] = uy;
  this.entries[6] = -fy;
  this.entries[7] = 0;
  this.entries[8] = sz;
  this.entries[9] = uz;
  this.entries[10] = -fz;
  this.entries[11] = 0;
  this.entries[12] = 0;
  this.entries[13] = 0;
  this.entries[14] = 0;
  this.entries[15] = 1;

  this.translate(-eyeX, -eyeY, -eyeZ);
}
```

```
...
var VS_SOURCE="\
  uniform mat4 modelMatrix;\
  uniform mat4 viewMatrix;\
  attribute vec4 p;\
  attribute vec4 c;\
  varying vec4 c2;\
  void main(){\
    c2=c;\
    gl_Position = viewMatrix * modelMatrix * p; \
  }\
";

var FS_SOURCE="\
  precision mediump float;\
  varying vec4 c2;\
  void main(){\
    gl_FragColor=c2;\
  }\
";

var eyeX=0,eyeY=0,eyeZ=0.5;
var gl,mm,mmL,vm,vmL;

function keydown(ev){
  switch (ev.keyCode){
          case 37: eyeX-=0.01; // left arrow key
    break; case 38: eyeY+=0.01; // up arrow key
    break; case 39: eyeX+=0.01; // right arrow key
    break; case 40: eyeY-=0.01; // down arrow key
  }
  vm.lookAt(eyeX,eyeY,eyeZ, 0,0,0, 0,1,0);
  gl.uniformMatrix4fv(vmL,false, new
                              Float32Array(vm.entries));
}

function start(){
  var canvas = document.getElementById("myCanvas");
  gl = canvas.getContext("webgl");
  initShaders(gl,VS_SOURCE,FS_SOURCE);
  document.onkeydown = function(ev){keydown(ev);};

  mm = new Matrix4();
  mm.translate(0.5,0,0);
  mm.scale(0.5,0.5,0.5);
  mmL = gl.getUniformLocation(gl.program, 'modelMatrix');
  gl.uniformMatrix4fv(mmL,false, new
                              Float32Array(mm.entries));

  vm = new Matrix4();
  vm.lookAt(eyeX,eyeY,eyeZ, 0,0,0, 0,1,0);
  vmL = gl.getUniformLocation(gl.program, 'viewMatrix');
  gl.uniformMatrix4fv(vmL,false, new
                              Float32Array(vm.entries));

  var tick = function(){
    mm.rotate(1,0,0,1);  // rotates one degree every frame
    gl.uniformMatrix4fv(mmL,false,
                     new Float32Array(mm.entries));
    draw_colored_triangle();
    requestAnimationFrame(tick);
  };
  tick();
}
...
```

9.3.3 Projection Matrix

There are two ways by which 3D objects in the visible viewing volume (the frustum) are projected onto the 2D screen. By orthographic projection (the default), the light rays travel in a parallel fashion, covering a viewing area as large as the screen. By perspective projection, the light rays converge and meet at the eye point. Orthographic projection is used for many technical drawings, whereas perspective projection simulates the human vision and is thus used for characters in games.

To use orthographic projection, six parameters need to be supplied to 'orthographic()': 'left', 'right', 'bottom', 'top', 'near', and 'far'.

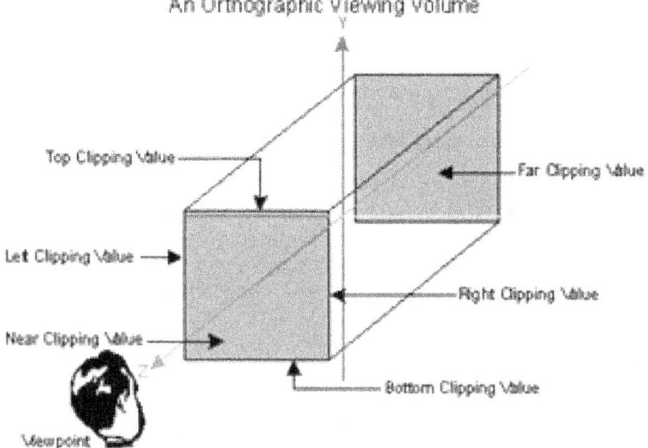

(courtesy of http://www.microsoft.com/msj/archive/S2085.aspx)

There are two ways to use perspective projection. The first form, called 'frustum()' here, takes in the same six parameters as the orthographic projection. The second form, called 'perspective()' here, takes in four parameters: 'fovy', 'aspect', 'near', and 'far'.

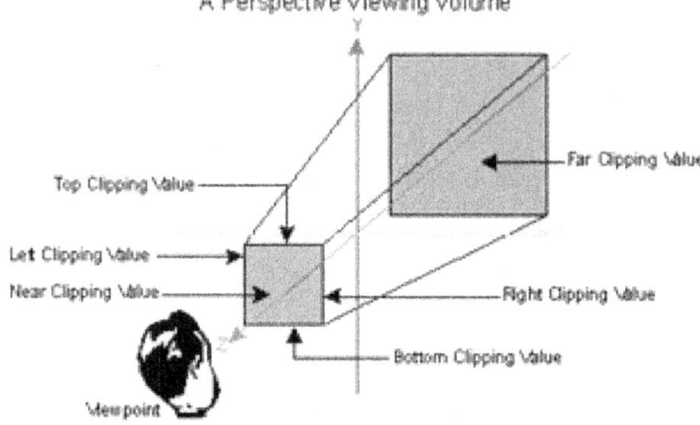

(courtesy of http://www.microsoft.com/msj/archive/S2085.aspx)

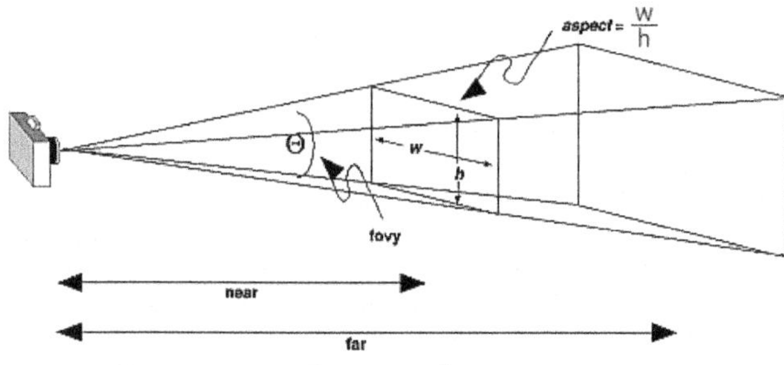

(courtesy of http://www.felixgers.de/teaching/jogl/perspectiveProjection.html)

For orthographic projection, adjusting the 'near' value has no effect on the display, as long as the object is contained by the frustum.

```
//webgl-library.js
Matrix4.prototype.orthographic = function(
                              left, right, bottom, top, near, far) {
  var e, rw, rh, rd;

  if (left === right || bottom === top || near === far)
    throw 'null frustum';

  rw = 1 / (right - left);
  rh = 1 / (top - bottom);
  rd = 1 / (far - near);

  e = this.entries;
  e[0]  = 2 * rw;
  e[1]  = 0;
  e[2]  = 0;
  e[3]  = 0;
  e[4]  = 0;
  e[5]  = 2 * rh;
  e[6]  = 0;
  e[7]  = 0;
  e[8]  = 0;
  e[9]  = 0;
  e[10] = -2 * rd;
  e[11] = 0;
  e[12] = -(right + left) * rw;
  e[13] = -(top + bottom) * rh;
  e[14] = -(far + near) * rd;
  e[15] = 1;

  return this;
};

Matrix4.prototype.frustum = function(
                              left, right, bottom, top, near, far) {
  var e, rw, rh, rd;

  if (left === right || top === bottom || near === far)
     throw 'null frustum';
  if (near <= 0) throw 'near <= 0';
  if (far <= 0) throw 'far <= 0';

  rw = 1 / (right - left);
  rh = 1 / (top - bottom);
  rd = 1 / (far - near);

  e = this.entries;
  e[ 0] = 2 * near * rw;
  e[ 1] = 0;
  e[ 2] = 0;
  e[ 3] = 0;
  e[ 4] = 0;
  e[ 5] = 2 * near * rh;
  e[ 6] = 0;
  e[ 7] = 0;
  e[ 8] = (right + left) * rw;
  e[ 9] = (top + bottom) * rh;
  e[10] = -(far + near) * rd;
  e[11] = -1;
  e[12] = 0;
  e[13] = 0;
  e[14] = -2 * near * far * rd;
  e[15] = 0;

  return this;
};


Matrix4.prototype.perspective =
                              function(fovy, aspect, near, far){
  var e, rd, s, ct;

  if (near === far || aspect === 0) throw 'null frustum';
  if (near <= 0) throw 'near <= 0';
  if (far <= 0) throw 'far <= 0';

  fovy = Math.PI * fovy / 180 / 2;
  s = Math.sin(fovy);
  if (s === 0) throw 'null frustum';
```

```
    rd = 1 / (far - near);
    ct = Math.cos(fovy) / s;

    e = this.entries;
    e[0]  = ct / aspect;
    e[1]  = 0;
    e[2]  = 0;
    e[3]  = 0;
    e[4]  = 0;
    e[5]  = ct;
    e[6]  = 0;
    e[7]  = 0;
    e[8]  = 0;
    e[9]  = 0;
    e[10] = -(far + near) * rd;
    e[11] = -1;
    e[12] = 0;
    e[13] = 0;
    e[14] = -2 * near * far * rd;
    e[15] = 0;

    return this;
};
```

```
...
var VS_SOURCE="\
  uniform mat4 modelMatrix;\
  uniform mat4 viewMatrix;\
  uniform mat4 projectionMatrix;\
  attribute vec4 p;\
  attribute vec4 c;\
  varying vec4 c2;\
  void main(){\
    c2=c;\
    gl_Position=projectionMatrix*viewMatrix*modelMatrix*p; \
  }\
";

var FS_SOURCE="\
  precision mediump float;\
  varying vec4 c2;\
  void main(){\
    gl_FragColor=c2;\
  }\
";

var eyeX=0,eyeY=0,eyeZ=0.5,near=0.25,far=10,ortho=true;
var gl,mm,mmL,vm,vmL,pm,pmL;

function keydown(ev){
  switch (ev.keyCode){
        case 37: eyeX-=0.01;  // left arrow key
    break; case 38: eyeY+=0.01;  // up arrow key
    break; case 39: eyeX+=0.01;  // right arrow key
    break; case 40: eyeY-=0.01;  // down arrow key
    break; case 49: ortho=true;  // '1' key
    break; case 50: ortho=false; // '2' key
    break; case 81: near+=0.01;  // 'Q' key
    break; case 65: near-=0.01;  // 'A' key
  }
  vm.lookAt(eyeX,eyeY,eyeZ, 0,0,0, 0,1,0);
  gl.uniformMatrix4fv(vmL,false,vm.entries);
  if (ortho) pm.orthographic(-0.25,0.25,-0.25,0.25,near,far);
  else pm.frustum(-0.25,0.25,-0.25,0.25,near,far);
  gl.uniformMatrix4fv(pmL,false,new
                                    Float32Array(pm.entries));
}

function start(){
  var canvas = document.getElementById("myCanvas");
  gl = canvas.getContext("webgl");
  initShaders(gl,VS_SOURCE,FS_SOURCE);
  document.onkeydown = function(ev){keydown(ev);};

  mm = new Matrix4();
  mm.scale(0.5,0.5,0.5);
  mmL = gl.getUniformLocation(gl.program, 'modelMatrix');
  gl.uniformMatrix4fv(mmL,false,new
                                    Float32Array(mm.entries));

  vm = new Matrix4();
  vm.lookAt(eyeX,eyeY,eyeZ, 0,0,0, 0,1,0);
  vmL = gl.getUniformLocation(gl.program, 'viewMatrix');
  gl.uniformMatrix4fv(vmL,false,new
                                    Float32Array(vm.entries));

  pm = new Matrix4();
  pm.orthographic(-0.25,0.25,-0.25,0.25,near,far);
  pmL = gl.getUniformLocation(gl.program,
                                  'projectionMatrix');
  gl.uniformMatrix4fv(pmL,false,new
                                    Float32Array(pm.entries));

  var tick = function(){
    mm.rotate(1,0,0,1);  // rotates one degree every frame
    gl.uniformMatrix4fv(mmL,false,
                        new Float32Array(mm.entries));
    draw_colored_triangle();
    requestAnimationFrame(tick);
  };
  tick();
}
...
```

9.4 Light Rays

Lighting gives the scene a sense of depth, which is important in creating a realistic 3D scene. For an object to be visible, the light rays reflected from the object must reach the eyes or camera.

9.4.1 Depth Test

By default, WebGL draws objects in the order in which they are specified inside the buffer objects. This means that the objects behind that are supposed to be blocked by the objects in front may appear in the front instead. To correctly display the foreground and background objects, the DEPTH_TEST capability has to be enabled.

However, even with the capability enabled, hidden surface removal may fail when the objects are extremely close to one another. The phenomenon, known as Z fighting, causes the object to appear unnatural. Z fighting occurs because of the limited precision of the depth buffer. To resolve the problem, WebGL provides a feature known as 'polygon offset'.

WebGL hidden surface removal uses a left-handed clip coordinate system. This means that objects with smaller z values appear in front of objects with bigger z values.

If 'polygon_offset' is not enabled, the red triangle will cover the smaller green triangle entirely, even though the smaller green triangle is located just in front of the red triangle.

```
<!DOCTYPE html>
<html>
<head>
<script src="webgl-library.js"></script>
<script>
var VS_SOURCE="\
  attribute vec4 p;\
  attribute vec4 c;\
  varying vec4 c2;\
  void main(){\
    c2=c;\
    gl_Position = p; \
    gl_PointSize=20.0;\
  }\
";

var FS_SOURCE="\
  precision mediump float;\
  varying vec4 c2;\
  void main(){\
    gl_FragColor=c2;\
  }\
";

var gl,m,mL;
function start(){
  var canvas = document.getElementById("myCanvas");
  gl = canvas.getContext("webgl");
  initShaders(gl,VS_SOURCE,FS_SOURCE);

  var points=new Array();
  var vc= new Float32Array([ 0.0,-0.5,0.0,  1.0, 0.0, 0.0,
                            -0.5, 0.5,0.0,  1.0, 0.0, 0.0,
                             0.5, 0.5,0.0,  1.0, 0.0, 0.0,
                    0.0,-0.4,-0.000000001,  0.0, 1.0, 0.0,
                   -0.4, 0.4,-0.000000001,  0.0, 1.0, 0.0,
                    0.4, 0.4,-0.000000001,  0.0, 1.0, 0.0]);
  var ESIZE=vc.BYTES_PER_ELEMENT;
  var b=gl.createBuffer();
  gl.bindBuffer(gl.ARRAY_BUFFER,b);
  gl.bufferData(gl.ARRAY_BUFFER,vc,gl.STATIC_DRAW);

  pL=gl.getAttribLocation(gl.program,'p');
  gl.vertexAttribPointer(pL,3,gl.FLOAT,false,ESIZE*6,0);
  gl.enableVertexAttribArray(pL);


  cL=gl.getAttribLocation(gl.program,'c');
  gl.vertexAttribPointer(cL,3,gl.FLOAT,false,ESIZE*6,
                         ESIZE*3);
  gl.enableVertexAttribArray(cL);

  gl.enable(gl.DEPTH_TEST);
  gl.enable(gl.POLYGON_OFFSET_FILL);

  gl.clearColor(0.0,0.0,0.0,1.0);
  gl.clear(gl.COLOR_BUFFER_BIT | gl.DEPTH_BUFFER_BIT);

  gl.drawArrays(gl.TRIANGLES,0,3);
  gl.polygonOffset(-1.0,-1.0);
  gl.drawArrays(gl.TRIANGLES,3,3);

}
</script>
</head>

<body onload="start()">
  <canvas id="myCanvas" width="500"
height="500"></canvas>
</body>
</html>
```

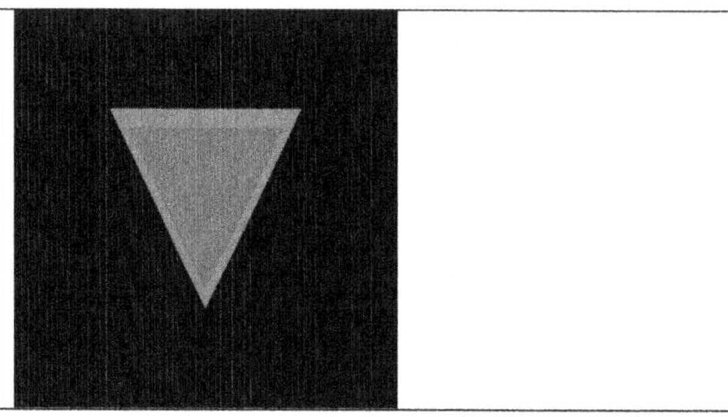

polygonOffset(factor, units) specifies the offset to be added to the depth values, where offset = m * factor + r * units, with m representing the change in depth relative to the screen area of the polygon, and r representing the smallest difference between two depth values the hardware can distinguish. 'polygon offset' is also useful for rendering hidden-line images, for applying decals to surfaces, and for rendering solids with highlighted edges.

depthRange(near,far) specifies the mapping of depth values from normalized device coordinates to window coordinates. Window coordinate depth values in the depth buffer range from 0 to 1, which is also the default range. Values for 'near' and 'far' are clamped to the range [0,1].

9.4.2 Facet Culling

A triangle has two sides – the front side and the back side. It is possible to draw only one side without drawing the other side.

frontFace(mode) specifies which side is considered to be the front side. 'mode' can be 'CCW' (vertices specified in counter-clockwise order) or 'CW' (vertices specified in clockwise order).

cullFace(mode) specifies which side to discard. 'mode' can be 'BACK', 'FRONT', or 'FRONT_AND_BACK'.

Nothing is drawn, as the front side is discarded.

```
<!DOCTYPE html>
<html>
<head>
<script src="webgl-library.js"></script>
<script>
var VS_SOURCE="\
  attribute vec4 p;\
  attribute vec4 c;\
  varying vec4 c2;\
  void main(){\
    c2=c;\
    gl_Position = p; \
    gl_PointSize=20.0;\
  }\
";

var FS_SOURCE="\
  precision mediump float;\
  varying vec4 c2;\
  void main(){\
    gl_FragColor=c2;\
```

```
  }\
";

var gl,m,mL;
function start(){
  var canvas = document.getElementById("myCanvas");
  gl = canvas.getContext("webgl");
  initShaders(gl,VS_SOURCE,FS_SOURCE);

  var points=new Array();
  var vc= new Float32Array([ 0.0,-0.5,0.0,  1.0, 0.0, 0.0,
                            -0.5, 0.5,0.0,  1.0, 0.0, 0.0,
                             0.5, 0.5,0.0,  1.0, 0.0, 0.0]);
  var ESIZE=vc.BYTES_PER_ELEMENT;
  var b=gl.createBuffer();
  gl.bindBuffer(gl.ARRAY_BUFFER,b);
  gl.bufferData(gl.ARRAY_BUFFER,vc,gl.STATIC_DRAW);

  pL=gl.getAttribLocation(gl.program,'p');
  gl.vertexAttribPointer(pL,3,gl.FLOAT,false,ESIZE*6,0);
  gl.enableVertexAttribArray(pL);


  cL=gl.getAttribLocation(gl.program,'c');

gl.vertexAttribPointer(cL,3,gl.FLOAT,false,ESIZE*6,ESIZE*3);
  gl.enableVertexAttribArray(cL);

  gl.enable(gl.CULL_FACE);
  gl.frontFace(gl.CW);
  gl.cullFace(gl.FRONT);

  gl.clearColor(0.0,0.0,0.0,1.0);
  gl.clear(gl.COLOR_BUFFER_BIT | gl.DEPTH_BUFFER_BIT);
  gl.drawArrays(gl.TRIANGLES,0,3);

}
</script>
</head>

<body onload="start()">
  <canvas id="myCanvas" width="500"
                        height="500"></canvas>
</body>
</html>
```

9.4.3 Directional Light (Per Vertex)

If the light source is very far away, the incoming light rays will be almost parallel, giving rise to directional light. An example of such a light source is the sun.

Diffuse reflection is caused by direct light rays hitting a rough surface. The light is scattered equally in all directions from where it hits:
<surface color by diffuse reflection>
*=<light color> * <base color of surface> * cosΘ*
*=<light color> * <base color of surface> **
(<light direction>•<surface normal>)
<surface normal> is a vector representing the direction perpendicular to the surface. The vectors <light direction> and <surface normal> must be normalized unit vectors, which means that their lengths must be 1. Because the normal may be changed by a rotation or a scaling of the object, it needs to be multiplied by the inverse transpose matrix of the model matrix first.

Ambient reflection is caused by indirect light emitted from a combination of light sources and reflected by various surfaces. It may be thought of as the background light. Ambient light models the light that hits an object from all directions with constant intensity:
<surface color by ambient reflection>
*=<light color> * <base color of surface>*

To render a realistic scene, these two types of reflections need to be combined:
<surface color by diffuse and ambient reflection>
=<surface color by diffuse reflection> +
<surface color by ambient reflection>

```
//webgl-library.js
function Vector3(s){
  var i;
  this.entries = new Array();
  if (s && (typeof s)==='object' &&
     s.length && s.length==3){
    for (i=0; i<3; i++) this.entries.push(s[i]);
  } else {
    this.entries=[0,0,0];
  }
}

Vector3.prototype.normalize = function() {
  var v = this.entries;
  var c = v[0], d = v[1], e = v[2],
      g = Math.sqrt(c*c+d*d+e*e);
  v[0] = c/g; v[1] = d/g; v[2] = e/g;
  return this;
};

Matrix4.prototype.inverse = function(){
 var i, s, d, inv, det;
 s = this.entries;
 inv = new Array(16);

inv[0] = s[5]*s[10]*s[15]- s[5]*s[11]*s[14]-s[9] *s[6]*s[15]
      +s[9]*s[7] *s[14]+s[13]*s[6] *s[11]-s[13]*s[7]*s[10];
inv[1]=-s[1]*s[10]*s[15]+s[1] *s[11]*s[14]+
         s[9] *s[2]*s[15]-s[9]*s[3] *s[14]-
         s[13]*s[2] *s[11]+s[13]*s[3]*s[10];
inv[2]=  s[1]*s[6]*s[15]-s[1] *s[7]*s[14]-s[5] *s[2]*s[15]
        +s[5]*s[3]*s[14]+s[13]*s[2]*s[7] -s[13]*s[3]*s[6];
inv[3]=-s[1]*s[6]*s[11]+s[1]*s[7]*s[10]+s[5]*s[2]*s[11]
        -s[5]*s[3]*s[10]-s[9]*s[2]*s[7] +s[9]*s[3]*s[6];
inv[4]=-s[4]*s[10]*s[15]+s[4] *s[11]*s[14]+
         s[8] *s[6]*s[15]-s[8]*s[7] *s[14]-
         s[12]*s[6] *s[11]+s[12]*s[7]*s[10];
inv[5] =   s[0]*s[10]*s[15]-s[0] *s[11]*s[14]-
           s[8] *s[2]*s[15]+s[8]*s[3] *s[14]+
           s[12]*s[2] *s[11]-s[12]*s[3]*s[10];
inv[6]=-s[0]*s[6]*s[15]+s[0] *s[7]*s[14]+s[4] *s[2]*s[15]
        -s[4]*s[3]*s[14]-s[12]*s[2]*s[7] +s[12]*s[3]*s[6];
inv[7]=  s[0]*s[6]*s[11]-s[0]*s[7]*s[10]-s[4]*s[2]*s[11]
        +s[4]*s[3]*s[10]+s[8]*s[2]*s[7] -s[8]*s[3]*s[6];
inv[8]=  s[4]*s[9] *s[15]-s[4] *s[11]*s[13]-
          s[8] *s[5]*s[15]+s[8]*s[7] *s[13]+
          s[12]*s[5] *s[11]-s[12]*s[7]*s[9];
inv[9]=-s[0]*s[9] *s[15]+s[0] *s[11]*s[13]+
         s[8] *s[1]*s[15] -s[8]*s[3] *s[13]-
         s[12]*s[1] *s[11]+s[12]*s[3]*s[9];
inv[10]= s[0]*s[5]*s[15]-s[0] *s[7]*s[13]-s[4] *s[1]*s[15]+
         s[4]*s[3]*s[13]+s[12]*s[1]*s[7] -s[12]*s[3]*s[5];
inv[11]=-s[0]*s[5]*s[11]+s[0]*s[7]*s[9] +s[4]*s[1]*s[11]
        -s[4]*s[3]*s[9] -s[8]*s[1]*s[7] +s[8]*s[3]*s[5];
inv[12]=-s[4]*s[9] *s[14]+s[4] *s[10]*s[13]+
          s[8] *s[5]*s[14] -s[8]*s[6] *s[13]-
          s[12]*s[5] *s[10]+s[12]*s[6]*s[9];
inv[13]=s[0]*s[9]*s[14]-s[0]*s[10]*s[13]-s[8] *s[1]*s[14]+
         s[8]*s[2] *s[13]+s[12]*s[1] *s[10]-s[12]*s[2]*s[9];
inv[14]=-s[0]*s[5]*s[14]+s[0] *s[6]*s[13]+s[4] *s[1]*s[14]
        -s[4]*s[2]*s[13]-s[12]*s[1]*s[6] +s[12]*s[2]*s[5];
inv[15]= s[0]*s[5]*s[10]-s[0]*s[6]*s[9] -s[4]*s[1]*s[10]+
        s[4]*s[2]*s[9] +s[8]*s[1]*s[6] -s[8]*s[2]*s[5];
```

```
  det = s[0]*inv[0] + s[1]*inv[4] + s[2]*inv[8] +
        s[3]*inv[12];
  if (det === 0) return this;
  for (i = 0; i < 16; i++) s[i] = inv[i] / det;
  return this;
}

Matrix4.prototype.transpose = function() {
  var e, t;
  e = this.entries;
  t = e[ 1];  e[ 1] = e[ 4];  e[ 4] = t;
  t = e[ 2];  e[ 2] = e[ 8];  e[ 8] = t;
  t = e[ 3];  e[ 3] = e[12];  e[12] = t;
  t = e[ 6];  e[ 6] = e[ 9];  e[ 9] = t;
  t = e[ 7];  e[ 7] = e[13];  e[13] = t;
  t = e[11];  e[11] = e[14];  e[14] = t;
  return this;
};


function initArrayBuffer(gl, attrib, data, num) {
   var b = gl.createBuffer();
   gl.bindBuffer(gl.ARRAY_BUFFER, b);
   gl.bufferData(gl.ARRAY_BUFFER, data, gl.STATIC_DRAW);
   var attL = gl.getAttribLocation(gl.program, attrib);
   gl.vertexAttribPointer(attL, num, gl.FLOAT, false, 0, 0);
   gl.enableVertexAttribArray(attL);
}
```

```
<!DOCTYPE html>
<html>
<head>
<script src="webgl-library.js"></script>
<script id="vs" type="x-shader/x-vertex">
  attribute vec4 p;  // position
  attribute vec4 c;  // color
  attribute vec4 n;  // normal

  uniform mat4 modelMatrix;
  uniform mat4 viewMatrix;
  uniform mat4 projectionMatrix;
  uniform mat4 normalMatrix;
  uniform vec3 lightColor;
  uniform vec3 lightDirection;
  uniform vec3 ambientLight;
  varying vec4 color;
  void main() {
    gl_Position = projectionMatrix * viewMatrix *
                  modelMatrix * p;
    vec3 normal = normalize(vec3(normalMatrix * n));
    float nDotL = max(dot(lightDirection, normal), 0.0);
    vec3 diffuse = lightColor * c.rgb * nDotL;
    vec3 ambient = ambientLight * c.rgb;
    color = vec4(diffuse + ambient, c.a);
  }
</script>
<script id="fs" type="x-shader/x-fragment">
  #ifdef GL_ES
  precision mediump float;
  #endif
  varying vec4 color;
  void main() {
    gl_FragColor = color;
  }
</script>

<script>
function main() {
  var canvas = document.getElementById('myCanvas');
  var gl = canvas.getContext('webgl');
  initShaders(gl, 'vs', 'fs');
  var n = initVertexBuffers(gl);

  var cvL = gl.getUniformLocation(gl.program, 'lightColor');
  var dvL = gl.getUniformLocation(gl.program,
                                  'lightDirection');
  var avL = gl.getUniformLocation(gl.program,
                                  'ambientLight');
```

```
  gl.uniform3f(cvL, 1.0, 1.0, 1.0);
  var dir = new Vector3([0.0,2.0,5.0]);
  dir.normalize();
  gl.uniform3fv(dvL, dir.entries);
  gl.uniform3f(avL, 0.2, 0.2, 0.2);

  var mmL = gl.getUniformLocation(gl.program,
                                  'modelMatrix');
  var vmL = gl.getUniformLocation(gl.program, 'viewMatrix');
  var pmL = gl.getUniformLocation(gl.program,
                                  'projectionMatrix');
  var mm = new Matrix4();
  var vm = new Matrix4();
  var pm = new Matrix4();
  mm.translate(0, 0.4, 0);
  mm.rotate(90, 0, 0, 1);
  pm.perspective(30, canvas.width/canvas.height, 1, 100);
  vm.lookAt(3, 3, 7, 0, 0, 0, 0, 1, 0);
  gl.uniformMatrix4fv(mmL, false,
                      new Float32Array(mm.entries));
  gl.uniformMatrix4fv(vmL, false, new
                      Float32Array(vm.entries));
  gl.uniformMatrix4fv(pmL, false, new
                      Float32Array(pm.entries));

  var nmL = gl.getUniformLocation(gl.program,
                                  'normalMatrix');
  var nm = new Matrix4(mm.entries);
  nm.inverse();
  nm.transpose();
  gl.uniformMatrix4fv(nmL, false, new
                      Float32Array(nm.entries));

  gl.clearColor(0, 0, 0, 1);
  gl.enable(gl.DEPTH_TEST);
  gl.clear(gl.COLOR_BUFFER_BIT | gl.DEPTH_BUFFER_BIT);
  gl.drawElements(gl.TRIANGLES, n, gl.UNSIGNED_BYTE, 0);
}

function initVertexBuffers(gl) {
  //    v6----- v5
  //   /|      /|
  //  v1------v0|
  //  | |     | |
  //  | |v7---|-|v4
  //  |/      |/
  //  v2------v3
  var vertices = new Float32Array([
 1.0, 1.0, 1.0,  -1.0, 1.0, 1.0,  -1.0,-1.0, 1.0,   1.0,-1.0, 1.0,
 1.0, 1.0, 1.0,   1.0,-1.0, 1.0,   1.0,-1.0,-1.0,   1.0, 1.0,-1.0,
 1.0, 1.0, 1.0,   1.0, 1.0,-1.0,  -1.0, 1.0,-1.0,  -1.0, 1.0, 1.0,
-1.0, 1.0, 1.0,  -1.0, 1.0,-1.0,  -1.0,-1.0,-1.0,  -1.0,-1.0, 1.0,
-1.0,-1.0,-1.0,   1.0,-1.0,-1.0,   1.0,-1.0, 1.0,  -1.0,-1.0, 1.0,
 1.0,-1.0,-1.0,  -1.0,-1.0,-1.0,  -1.0, 1.0,-1.0,   1.0, 1.0,-1.0
  ]);

  var colors = new Float32Array([
    1, 0, 0,   1, 0, 0,   1, 0, 0,  1, 0, 0,    // v0-v1-v2-v3 front
    1, 0, 0,   1, 0, 0,   1, 0, 0,  1, 0, 0,    // v0-v3-v4-v5 right
    1, 0, 0,   1, 0, 0,   1, 0, 0,  1, 0, 0,    // v0-v5-v6-v1 up
    1, 0, 0,   1, 0, 0,   1, 0, 0,  1, 0, 0,    // v1-v6-v7-v2 left
    1, 0, 0,   1, 0, 0,   1, 0, 0,  1, 0, 0,    // v7-v4-v3-v2 down
    1, 0, 0,   1, 0, 0,   1, 0, 0,  1, 0, 0     // v4-v7-v6-v5 back
 ]);

  var normals = new Float32Array([
 0.0, 0.0, 1.0,   0.0, 0.0, 1.0,   0.0, 0.0, 1.0,   0.0, 0.0, 1.0,
 1.0, 0.0, 0.0,   1.0, 0.0, 0.0,   1.0, 0.0, 0.0,   1.0, 0.0, 0.0,
 0.0, 1.0, 0.0,   0.0, 1.0, 0.0,   0.0, 1.0, 0.0,   0.0, 1.0, 0.0,
-1.0, 0.0, 0.0,  -1.0, 0.0, 0.0,  -1.0, 0.0, 0.0,  -1.0, 0.0, 0.0,
 0.0,-1.0, 0.0,   0.0,-1.0, 0.0,   0.0,-1.0, 0.0,   0.0,-1.0, 0.0,
 0.0, 0.0,-1.0,   0.0, 0.0,-1.0,   0.0, 0.0,-1.0,   0.0, 0.0,-1.0
  ]);

  var indices = new Uint8Array([
    0, 1, 2,   0, 2, 3,      // front
    4, 5, 6,   4, 6, 7,      // right
    8, 9,10,   8,10,11,      // up
   12,13,14,  12,14,15,      // left
```

```
    16,17,18,  16,18,19,    // down
    20,21,22,  20,22,23     // back
  ]);

  initArrayBuffer(gl, 'p', vertices, 3);
  initArrayBuffer(gl, 'c', colors, 3);
  initArrayBuffer(gl, 'n', normals, 3);

  gl.bindBuffer(gl.ARRAY_BUFFER, null);
  var b = gl.createBuffer();
  gl.bindBuffer(gl.ELEMENT_ARRAY_BUFFER, b);
  gl.bufferData(gl.ELEMENT_ARRAY_BUFFER, indices,
                                              gl.STATIC_DRAW);

  return indices.length;
}

</script>
</head>

<body onload="main()">
  <canvas id="myCanvas" width="500"
height="500"></canvas>
</body>
</html>
```

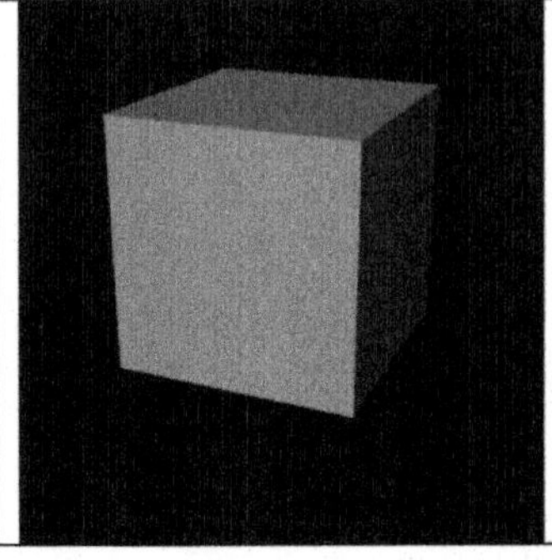

9.4.4 Pointed Light (Per Fragment)

A nearby light source gives rise to pointed light. The direction of the light from a point light source differs at each position. So the light direction needs to be calculated at each position:

<light direction> = <light source position> - <surface position>

While it is possible to implement the shading in the vertex shader, implementing it in the fragment shader yields a more realistic result.

```
<!DOCTYPE html>
<html>
<head>
<script src="webgl-library.js"></script>
<script id="vs" type="x-shader/x-vertex">
  attribute vec4 p;
  attribute vec4 n;
  uniform mat4 modelMatrix;
  uniform mat4 viewMatrix;
  uniform mat4 projectionMatrix;
  uniform mat4 normalMatrix;
  varying vec3 v_Normal;
  varying vec3 v_Position;
  void main() {
    gl_Position =
                projectionMatrix*viewMatrix*modelMatrix*p;
    v_Position = vec3(modelMatrix * p);
    v_Normal = normalize(vec3(normalMatrix * n));
  }
</script>
<script id="fs" type="x-shader/x-fragment">
  #ifdef GL_ES
  precision mediump float;
  #endif
  uniform vec3 lightColor;
  uniform vec3 lightPosition;
  uniform vec3 ambientLight;
  varying vec3 v_Normal;
  varying vec3 v_Position;
  void main() {
    vec4 surfaceColor = vec4(1.0,1.0,1.0,1.0);
    vec3 normal = normalize(v_Normal);
    vec3 lightDirection = normalize(lightPosition - v_Position);
    float nDotL = max(dot(lightDirection, normal), 0.0);
    vec3 diffuse = lightColor * surfaceColor.rgb * nDotL;
    vec3 ambient = ambientLight * surfaceColor.rgb;
    gl_FragColor = vec4(diffuse + ambient, surfaceColor.a);
  }
</script>

<script>

function main() {
  var canvas = document.getElementById('myCanvas');
  var gl = canvas.getContext('webgl');
  initShaders(gl, 'vs', 'fs');
  var n = initVertexBuffers(gl);

  var cvL = gl.getUniformLocation(gl.program, 'lightColor');
  var pvL = gl.getUniformLocation(gl.program, 'lightPosition');
  var avL = gl.getUniformLocation(gl.program,
                                          'ambientLight');
  gl.uniform3f(cvL, 0.8, 0.8, 0.8);
  gl.uniform3f(pvL, 3.0, 6.0, 5.0);
  gl.uniform3f(avL, 0.1, 0.1, 0.1);
  var mmL = gl.getUniformLocation(gl.program,
                                          'modelMatrix');
  var vmL = gl.getUniformLocation(gl.program, 'viewMatrix');
  var pmL = gl.getUniformLocation(gl.program,
                                          'projectionMatrix');
  var mm = new Matrix4();
  var vm = new Matrix4();
  var pm = new Matrix4();
  mm.scale(1, 1.5, 1);
  pm.perspective(30, canvas.width/canvas.height, 1, 10);
  vm.lookAt(3, 1, 5, 0, 0, 0, 0, 1, 0);
  gl.uniformMatrix4fv(mmL, false,
                      new Float32Array(mm.entries));
  gl.uniformMatrix4fv(vmL, false, new
                                  Float32Array(vm.entries));
  gl.uniformMatrix4fv(pmL, false, new
                                  Float32Array(pm.entries));

  var nmL = gl.getUniformLocation(gl.program,
                                          'normalMatrix');
  var nm = new Matrix4(mm.entries);
  nm.inverse();
  nm.transpose();
  gl.uniformMatrix4fv(nmL, false, new
                                  Float32Array(nm.entries));

  gl.clearColor(0, 0, 0, 1);
  gl.enable(gl.DEPTH_TEST);
  gl.clear(gl.COLOR_BUFFER_BIT | gl.DEPTH_BUFFER_BIT);
 gl.drawElements(gl.TRIANGLES, n, gl.UNSIGNED_SHORT, 0);
}

function initVertexBuffers(gl) { // Create a sphere
  var SPHERE_DIV = 50;

  var i, ai, si, ci;
  var j, aj, sj, cj;
  var p1, p2;
  var positions = [];
  var indices = [];

  for (j = 0; j <= SPHERE_DIV; j++) {
    aj = j * Math.PI / SPHERE_DIV;
    sj = Math.sin(aj);
    cj = Math.cos(aj);
    for (i = 0; i <= SPHERE_DIV; i++) {
```

```
      ai = i * 2 * Math.PI / SPHERE_DIV;
      si = Math.sin(ai);
      ci = Math.cos(ai);
      positions.push(si * sj); // X
      positions.push(cj);      // Y
      positions.push(ci * sj); // Z
    }
  }

  for (j = 0; j < SPHERE_DIV; j++) {
    for (i = 0; i < SPHERE_DIV; i++) {
      p1 = j * (SPHERE_DIV+1) + i;
      p2 = p1 + (SPHERE_DIV+1);
      indices.push(p1);
      indices.push(p2);
      indices.push(p1 + 1);
      indices.push(p1 + 1);
      indices.push(p2);
      indices.push(p2 + 1);
    }
  }

  initArrayBuffer(gl, 'p', new Float32Array(positions), 3);
  initArrayBuffer(gl, 'n', new Float32Array(positions), 3);

  gl.bindBuffer(gl.ARRAY_BUFFER, null);
  var indexBuffer = gl.createBuffer();
  gl.bindBuffer(gl.ELEMENT_ARRAY_BUFFER, indexBuffer);
  gl.bufferData(gl.ELEMENT_ARRAY_BUFFER,
                new Uint16Array(indices), gl.STATIC_DRAW);
  return indices.length;
}
</script>
</head>

<body onload="main()">
  <canvas id="myCanvas" width="500"
                        height="500"></canvas>
</body>
</html>
```

9.4.5 Specular Lighting

Specular lighting causes a bright spot of light to appear on a surface, making the surface looks shiny.

In the Phong Reflection Model, the intensity of the specular highlight is given by

$$k_{\text{spec}} = (\hat{R} \cdot \hat{V})^n$$

where R is the mirror reflection of the light vector off the surface, and V is the viewpoint vector. As n increases, the size of the spot decreases.

The middle of the triangle 'lights up', as it reflects the light directly in front of it, making the material looks shiny.

```
<!DOCTYPE html>
<html>
<head>
<script src="webgl-library.js"></script>
<script id="vs" type="x-shader/x-vertex">
  uniform mat4 u_perspectiveMatrix;
  uniform mat4 u_modelMatrix;
  uniform mat4 u_viewMatrix;

  attribute vec4 a_Position;
  attribute vec3 a_Normal;

  varying vec4 v_Position;
  varying vec3 v_Normal;

  void main() {
    mat4 modelViewMatrix = u_viewMatrix * u_modelMatrix;
    v_Position = modelViewMatrix * a_Position;
    gl_Position = u_perspectiveMatrix * v_Position;
    v_Normal = normalize( mat3(modelViewMatrix) *
                          a_Normal);
  }
</script>
<script id="fs" type="x-shader/x-fragment">
  #ifdef GL_ES
  precision mediump float;
  #endif
  uniform mat4 u_fViewMatrix;
  uniform vec3 u_lightPosition;

  varying vec4 v_Position;
  varying vec3 v_Normal;
  void main() {
    vec3 normal = normalize(v_Normal);
    vec3 lightPosition = vec3(u_fViewMatrix*
                         vec4(u_lightPosition, 1) - v_Position);
    vec3 lightDir = normalize(lightPosition);
    float lightDist = length(lightPosition);

    float specular = 0.0;
    float d = max(dot(v_Normal, lightDir), 0.0);
    if (d > 0.0) {
      vec3 viewVec = vec3(0,0,1.0);
      vec3 reflectVec = reflect(-lightDir, normal);
     specular = pow(max(dot(reflectVec, viewVec), 0.0),
                    120.0);
    }
    gl_FragColor.rgb = vec3(0.1,0.1,0.1) +
                       vec3(0.4, 0.4, 0.4) * d + specular;
    gl_FragColor.a = 1.0;
  }
</script>

<script>
var g_perspectiveMatrix = new Matrix4();
var g_modelMatrix = new Matrix4();
var g_viewMatrix = new Matrix4();

function main() {
  var canvas = document.getElementById("myCanvas");
  var gl = canvas.getContext("webgl");
  initShaders(gl, "vs", "fs");

  var perspectiveMatrixShaderLocation =
       gl.getUniformLocation(gl.program,
                             'u_perspectiveMatrix');
  var modelMatrixShaderLocation =
       gl.getUniformLocation(gl.program, 'u_modelMatrix');
  var viewMatrixShaderLocation =
       gl.getUniformLocation(gl.program, 'u_viewMatrix');
  var lightPositionShaderLocation =
       gl.getUniformLocation(gl.program, 'u_lightPosition');
  var f_viewMatrixShaderLocation =
       gl.getUniformLocation(gl.program, 'u_fViewMatrix');
```

```
  gl.enable(gl.DEPTH_TEST);
  gl.clearColor(0, 0, 0, 1);
  drawCommon(gl,
                    canvas,
                    perspectiveMatrixShaderLocation,
                    viewMatrixShaderLocation,
                    lightPositionShaderLocation,
                    f_viewMatrixShaderLocation);
  drawCube(gl,
               canvas,
               perspectiveMatrixShaderLocation,
               modelMatrixShaderLocation,
               lightPositionShaderLocation);
}

function drawCommon(gl, canvas,
                         perspectiveMatrixShaderLocation,
                         viewMatrixShaderLocation,
                         lightPositionShaderLocation,
                         f_viewMatrixShaderLocation) {
  gl.clear(gl.COLOR_BUFFER_BIT | gl.DEPTH_BUFFER_BIT);
  g_perspectiveMatrix.perspective(
                      30, canvas.width/canvas.height, 1, 10000);
  g_viewMatrix.lookAt(0, 3, 10,  0, 0, 0,   0, 1, 0);
  gl.uniformMatrix4fv(perspectiveMatrixShaderLocation, false,
                         g_perspectiveMatrix.entries);
  gl.uniformMatrix4fv(viewMatrixShaderLocation, false,
                         g_viewMatrix.entries);
  gl.uniformMatrix4fv(f_viewMatrixShaderLocation, false,
                         g_viewMatrix.entries);
  var lightPosition = new Float32Array([0, 0, 2]);
  gl.uniform3fv(lightPositionShaderLocation, lightPosition);
}

function drawCube(gl, canvas,
                    perspectiveMatrixShaderLocation,
                    modelMatrixShaderLocation,
                    lightPositionShaderLocation) {
  var vertices = new Float32Array([-1.5,1.5,0.0,
                                        1.5,1.5,0.0,
                                        0.0,-1.5,0.0]);
  var normals = new Float32Array([0.0,0.0,1.0,
                                       0.0,0.0,1.0,
                                       0.0,0.0,1.0]);
  initArrayBuffer(gl,'a_Position',vertices,3);
  initArrayBuffer(gl,'a_Normal',normals,3);
  gl.uniformMatrix4fv(modelMatrixShaderLocation, false,
                         g_modelMatrix.entries);
  gl.drawArrays(gl.TRIANGLES,0,3);
}

</script>
</head>

<body onload="main()">
  <canvas id="myCanvas" width="500"
height="500"></canvas>
</body>
</html>
```

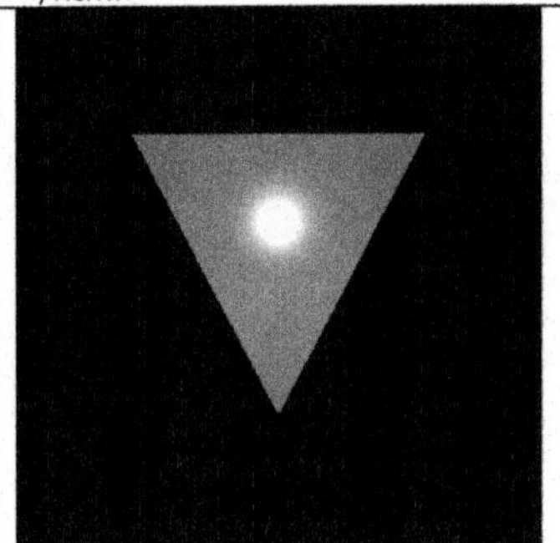

9.4.6 Fogging

Fogging is the phenomenon in which a distant object looks hazy. We will explore linear fog here, although there exist other fog calculations such as the exponential fog.

The *fog factor* describes how clearly we can see the object. When it is 1.0, the object can be seen completely. When it is 0.0, the object cannot be seen at all.

<fog factor>
= (<end point> - <distance from the eye point) /
(<end point> - <starting point>)
where
<starting point>
<= <distance from the eye point>
<= <end point>

The lower tip of the triangle is farther away, and is thus more obscured.

```
<!DOCTYPE html>
<html>
<head>
<script src="webgl-library.js"></script>
<script id="vs" type="x-shader/x-vertex">
  attribute vec4 p;
  attribute vec4 c;
  uniform mat4 modelMatrix;
  uniform mat4 viewMatrix;
  uniform mat4 projectionMatrix;
  uniform vec4 eyePosition;
  varying vec4 color;
  varying float dist;
  void main() {
    gl_Position =
                   projectionMatrix*viewMatrix*modelMatrix*p;
    color = c;
    dist = distance(modelMatrix * p, eyePosition);
  }
</script>
<script id="fs" type="x-shader/x-fragment">
  #ifdef GL_ES
  precision mediump float;
  #endif
  uniform vec3 fogColor;
  uniform vec2 fogDistance;
  varying vec4 color;
  varying float dist;
  void main() {
    float fogFactor = clamp((fogDistance.y-dist)/
                         (fogDistance.y-fogDistance.x),0.0,1.0);
    vec3 finalColor = mix(fogColor, vec3(color), fogFactor);
    gl_FragColor = vec4(finalColor, color.a);
  }
</script>

<script>

function main() {
  var canvas = document.getElementById('myCanvas');
  var gl = canvas.getContext('webgl');
  initShaders(gl, 'vs', 'fs');

  var fogColor = new Float32Array([0.0,0.0,0.0]);
  var fogDistance = new Float32Array([3,8]);
  var eye = new Float32Array([0,0,3,1.0]);
  var epL = gl.getUniformLocation(gl.program, 'eyePosition');
  var fcL = gl.getUniformLocation(gl.program, 'fogColor');
  var fdL = gl.getUniformLocation(gl.program, 'fogDistance');
  gl.uniform3fv(fcL, fogColor);
```

```
  gl.uniform2fv(fdL, fogDistance);
  gl.uniform4fv(epL, eye);

  var mmL = gl.getUniformLocation(gl.program,
                                  'modelMatrix');
  var vmL = gl.getUniformLocation(gl.program, 'viewMatrix');
  var pmL = gl.getUniformLocation(gl.program,
                                  'projectionMatrix');
  var mm = new Matrix4();
  var vm = new Matrix4();
  var pm = new Matrix4();
  mm.scale(1, 1.5, 1);
  pm.perspective(30, canvas.width/canvas.height, 1, 10);
  vm.lookAt(eye[0], eye[1], eye[2], 0, 0, 0, 0, 1, 0);
  gl.uniformMatrix4fv(mmL, false,
                 new Float32Array(mm.entries));
  gl.uniformMatrix4fv(vmL, false, new
                                Float32Array(vm.entries));
  gl.uniformMatrix4fv(pmL, false, new
                                Float32Array(pm.entries));

  gl.clearColor(0, 0, 0, 1);
  gl.clear(gl.COLOR_BUFFER_BIT);
  draw_colored_triangle(gl);
}

function draw_colored_triangle(gl){
  var points=new Array();
  var vc= new Float32Array([ 0.0,-0.5,-5.0,  1.0, 1.0, 1.0,
                            -0.5, 0.5, 0.0,  1.0, 1.0, 1.0,
                             0.5, 0.5, 0.0,  1.0, 1.0, 1.0]);
  var ESIZE=vc.BYTES_PER_ELEMENT;
  var b=gl.createBuffer();
  gl.bindBuffer(gl.ARRAY_BUFFER,b);
  gl.bufferData(gl.ARRAY_BUFFER,vc,gl.STATIC_DRAW);

  pL=gl.getAttribLocation(gl.program,'p');
  gl.vertexAttribPointer(pL,3,gl.FLOAT,false,ESIZE*6,0);
  gl.enableVertexAttribArray(pL);

  cL=gl.getAttribLocation(gl.program,'c');
  gl.vertexAttribPointer(cL,3,gl.FLOAT,false,ESIZE*6,
                     ESIZE*3);
  gl.enableVertexAttribArray(cL);

  gl.clearColor(0.0,0.0,0.0,1.0);
  gl.clear(gl.COLOR_BUFFER_BIT);
  gl.drawArrays(gl.TRIANGLES,0,3);
}
</script>
</head>

<body onload="main()">
  <canvas id="myCanvas" width="500"
height="500"></canvas>
</body>
</html>
```

9.4.7 Alpha Blending

For a surface, WebGL allows you to mix its color(the source color) with the color of the surface behind it(the destination color). Alpha blending means using the alpha values to achieve blending effects such as transparency. To use blending:

<u>Step 1: Enable the blending function:</u>
gl.enable(gl.BLEND);

<u>Step 2: Specify the blending function:</u>
gl.blendFunc(src_factor, dst_factor);

where <color> = <source color> * src_factor + <destination color> * dst_factor

Factor Constant	Factor for R	Factor for G	Factor for B
ZERO	0.0	0.0	0.0
ONE	1.0	1.0	1.0
SRC_COLOR	Rs	Gs	Bs
ONE_MINUS_SRC_COLOR	(1-Rs)	(1-Gs)	(1-Bs)
DST_COLOR	Rd	Gd	Bd
ONE_MINUS_DST_COLOR	(1-Rd)	(1-Gd)	(1-Bd)
SRC_ALPHA	As	As	As
ONE_MINUS_SRC_ALPHA	(1-As)	(1-As)	(1-As)
DST_ALPHA	Ad	Ad	Ad
ONE_MINUS_DST_ALPHA	(1-Ad)	(1-Ad)	(1-Ad)
SRC_ALPHA_SATURATE	min (As,Ad)	min (As,Ad)	min (As,Ad)

This program simulates transparency. As the alpha values approach zero, the triangles become more transparent.

```
<!DOCTYPE html>
<html>
<head>
<script type="text/javascript"
       src="webgl-library.js"></script>

<script id="shader-fs" type="x-shader/x-fragment">
  #ifdef GL_ES
  precision mediump float;
  #endif
  varying vec4 v_Color;
  void main() {
    gl_FragColor = v_Color;
  }
</script>

<script id="shader-vs" type="x-shader/x-vertex">
  attribute vec4 a_Position;
  attribute vec4 a_Color;
  uniform mat4 u_ViewMatrix;
  uniform mat4 u_ProjMatrix;
  varying vec4 v_Color;
  void main() {
    gl_Position = u_ProjMatrix * u_ViewMatrix * a_Position;
    v_Color = a_Color;
  }
</script>

<script type="text/javascript">

function WebGLStart() {
  var canvas = document.getElementById('cv');
  var gl = canvas.getContext("webgl");
  initShaders(gl, "shader-vs", "shader-fs");
  var n = initVertexBuffers(gl);
  gl.clearColor(0, 0, 0, 1);
  gl.enable (gl.BLEND);
```

```
  gl.blendFunc(gl.SRC_ALPHA, gl.ONE_MINUS_SRC_ALPHA);

  var u_ViewMatrix = gl.getUniformLocation(gl.program,
                                            'u_ViewMatrix');
  var u_ProjMatrix = gl.getUniformLocation(gl.program,
                                            'u_ProjMatrix');
  var viewMatrix = new Matrix4();
  window.onkeydown = function(ev){
     keydown(ev, gl, n, u_ViewMatrix, viewMatrix); };
  var projMatrix = new Matrix4();
  projMatrix.orthographic(-1, 1, -1, 1, 0, 2);
  gl.uniformMatrix4fv(u_ProjMatrix, false, projMatrix.entries);
  draw(gl, n, u_ViewMatrix, viewMatrix);
}

function initVertexBuffers(gl) {
   var verticesColors = new Float32Array([
     // Vertex coordinates and color(RGBA)
     0.0, 0.5, -0.4, 0.4, 1.0, 0.4, 0.4, // The green front
    -0.5, -0.5, -0.4, 0.4, 1.0, 0.4, 0.4,
     0.5, -0.5, -0.4, 1.0, 0.4, 0.4, 0.4,

     0.5, 0.4, -0.2, 1.0, 0.4, 0.4, 0.4, // The yellow middle
    -0.5, 0.4, -0.2, 1.0, 1.0, 0.4, 0.4,
     0.0, -0.6, -0.2, 1.0, 1.0, 0.4, 0.4,

     0.0, 0.5, 0.0, 0.4, 0.4, 1.0, 0.4, // The blue back
    -0.5, -0.5, 0.0, 0.4, 0.4, 1.0, 0.4,
     0.5, -0.5, 0.0, 1.0, 0.4, 0.4, 0.4,
   ]);
   var n = 9;
   var vertexColorbuffer = gl.createBuffer();
   if (!vertexColorbuffer) {
     console.log('Failed to create the buffer object');
     return -1;
   }
   gl.bindBuffer(gl.ARRAY_BUFFER, vertexColorbuffer);
   gl.bufferData(gl.ARRAY_BUFFER, verticesColors,
                                      gl.STATIC_DRAW);
   var FSIZE = verticesColors.BYTES_PER_ELEMENT;

   var a_Position = gl.getAttribLocation(gl.program,
                                     'a_Position');
   gl.vertexAttribPointer(a_Position, 3,
                          gl.FLOAT,false,FSIZE*7,0);
   gl.enableVertexAttribArray(a_Position);
   var a_Color = gl.getAttribLocation(gl.program, 'a_Color');
   gl.vertexAttribPointer(a_Color, 4, gl.FLOAT,false,
                          FSIZE*7, FSIZE * 3);
   gl.enableVertexAttribArray(a_Color);
   gl.bindBuffer(gl.ARRAY_BUFFER, null);
   return n;
}

function keydown(ev, gl, n, u_ViewMatrix, viewMatrix) {
   if(ev.keyCode == 39) { // The right arrow key was pressed
     g_EyeX += 0.01;
   } else if (ev.keyCode == 37) {
                              // The left arrow key was pressed
     g_EyeX -= 0.01;
   } else return;
   draw(gl, n, u_ViewMatrix, viewMatrix);
}

var g_EyeX = 0.20, g_EyeY = 0.25, g_EyeZ = 0.25;
function draw(gl, n, u_ViewMatrix, viewMatrix) {
  viewMatrix.lookAt(g_EyeX, g_EyeY, g_EyeZ, 0, 0, 0, 0, 1, 0);
  gl.uniformMatrix4fv(u_ViewMatrix, false, viewMatrix.entries);
  gl.clear(gl.COLOR_BUFFER_BIT | gl.DEPTH_BUFFER_BIT);
  gl.drawArrays(gl.TRIANGLES, 0, n);
}
</script>

</head>

<body onload="WebGLStart();">
   <canvas id="cv" style="border: none;"
                              width="500"
height="500"></canvas>
    <br/>
</body>

</html>
```

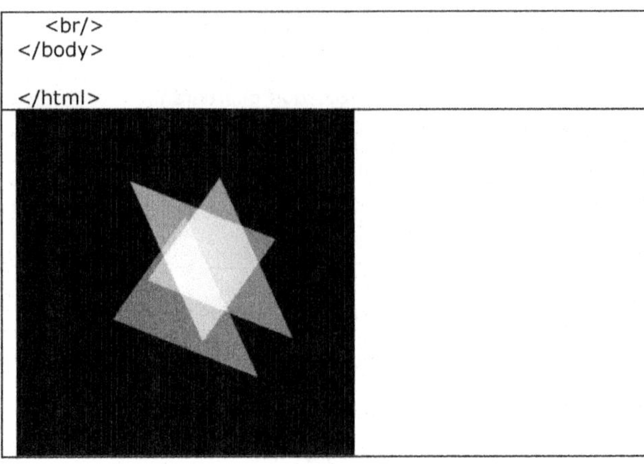

With hidden surface removal enabled, objects at the back may not be drawn. This may cause alpha blending to behave in an unexpected manner. To counter this problem, follow these steps:

Step 1: Enable hidden surface removal
gl.enable(gl.DEPTH_TEST);

Step 2: Draw all opaque objects (alpha values=1.0)

Step 3: Make the depth buffer read-only
gl.depthMask(false);

Step 4: Draw all the transparent objects back to front.

Step 5: Make the depth buffer readable and writable
gl.depthMask(true);

9.4.8 Stencil Shadow Volume

Drawing a shadowed scene with this technique involves drawing the scene four times. This shadowing technique is accurate to the pixel, but can be computationally intensive.

The **first pass** prepares the depth buffer. Writing to the color buffer is disabled.

colorMask(red, green, blue, alpha) enables or disables the writing of frame buffer color components. **depthMask(flag)** enables or disables writing into the depth buffer. The parameters for these two functions can be false or true. **stencilMask(mask)** specifies a bit mask to enable and disable writing of individual bits in the stencil planes. 'mask' is an unsigned int. **stencilMaskSeparate(face, mask)** is similar but specifies for a 'face', which can be FRONT, BACK, FRONT_AND_BACK.

The **second pass** prepares the stencil buffer, using the depth buffer just prepared. Writing to the color buffer and depth buffer is disabled. Face culling is also disabled.

The second pass is where things become interesting.

To render a shadow volume we extend the silhouette of an occluder. (A silhouette edge on a 3D body projected onto a 2D plane is the collection of points whose outwards surface normal is perpendicular to the view vector.)

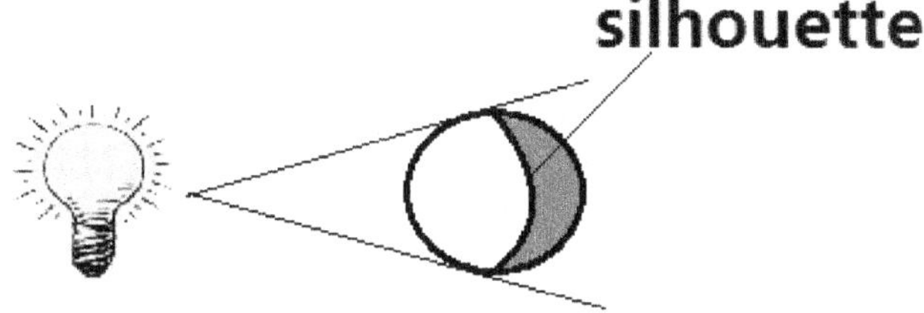

This is done by emitting a quad for each silhouette edge.

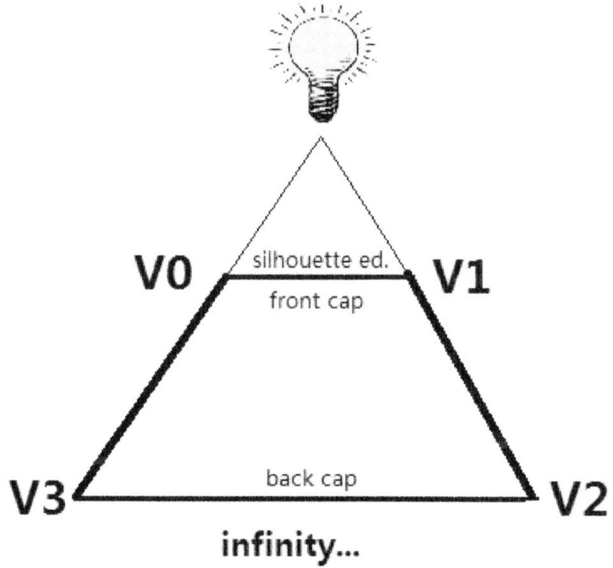

After all edges have been extended, we seal off the volume by adding the front and back caps. Each triangle which faces the light becomes part of the front cap. For the back cap, we need to extend the vertices of light facing triangle to infinity (along the vector from the light to each vertex) and reverse their order. While a point is extended to infinity along the light vector we can still project it to the near plane.

If the depth test fails when rendering the back facing polygons of the shadow volume we increment the value in the stencil buffer. If the depth test fails when rendering the front facing polygons of the shadow volume we decrement the value in the stencil buffer. We do nothing if depth test passes, stencil stencil test fails. A point is rendered only if its stencil value is zero.

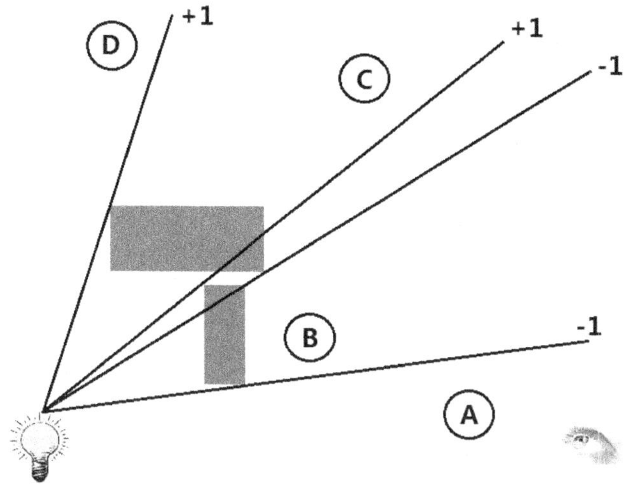

	Stencil Operations	Final Stencil Value	Drawn?
A	+1 +1 -1 -1	0	Yes
B	+1 +1 -1	+1	No
C	+1	+1	No
D		0	Yes

stencilOp(fail, zfail, zpass) sets the front and back stencil test actions. 'fail' specifies the action to take when the stencil test fails. 'zfail' specifies the action to take when the stencil test passes, but the depth test fails. 'zpass' specifies the action to take when both the stencil test and the depth test pass, or when the stencil test passes and either there is no depth buffer or depth testing is not enabled. 'fail', 'zfail', and 'zpass' can be KEEP, ZERO, REPLACE, INCR, DECR, INVERT, INCR_WRAP, or DECR_WRAP. **stencilOpSeparate(face, fail, zfail, zpass)** is a similar function but specifies for a 'face' only, which can be FRONT, BACK, or FRONT_AND_BACK.

stencilFunc(func, ref, mask) set the front and back function and reference value for stencil testing. 'func' can be NEVER, ALWAYS, LESS, EQUAL, LEQUAL, GREATER, GEQUAL, NOTEQUAL. 'ref' specifies the reference value for the stencil test. 'mask' specifies a mask that is ANDed with both the reference value and the stored stencil value when the test is done. **stencilFuncSeparate(face, func, ref, mask)** is a similar function but specifies for a 'face' only, which can be FRONT, BACK, or FRONT_AND_BACK.

The **third pass** draws on the color buffer, using the stencil buffer just prepared.

depthFunc(func) specifies the function used to compare each incoming pixel depth value with the depth value present in the depth buffer. 'func' can be NEVER, ALWAYS, LESS, EQUAL, LEQUAL, GREATER, GEQUAL, or NOTEQUAL.

The **fourth pass** draws on the color buffer again. The use of alpha blending gives rise to the addition of ambient lighting.

Because a stencil buffer is not present by default, you need to request for it when getting the context with .getContext() at the beginning.

```
// webgl-library.js
// We are using the w = 0.0 trick to send vertices to infinity,
// but we have to use an infinite projection matrix for this to
// work
Matrix4.prototype.frustumInfinite =
  function(left, right, bottom, top, near) {
    var e, rw, rh;
    if (left === right || top === bottom) throw 'null frustum';
    if (near <= 0) throw 'near <= 0';

    rw = 1 / (right - left);
    rh = 1 / (top - bottom);

    e = this.entries;
    e[ 0] = 2 * near * rw;
    e[ 1] = 0;
    e[ 2] = 0;
    e[ 3] = 0;
    e[ 4] = 0;
    e[ 5] = 2 * near * rh;
    e[ 6] = 0;
    e[ 7] = 0;
    e[ 8] = (right + left) * rw;
    e[ 9] = (top + bottom) * rh;
    e[10] = -1;
    e[11] = -1;
    e[12] = 0;
    e[13] = 0;
    e[14] = -2 * near;
    e[15] = 0;
    return this;
};
```

```
<!DOCTYPE html>
<html>
<head>
<script type="text/javascript" src="webgl-
library.js"></script>
<script id="vs" type="x-shader/x-vertex">
  attribute vec4 a_Position;
  attribute vec4 a_Normal;
  attribute vec4 a_Color;
  uniform mat4 u_MvpMatrix;
  uniform vec4 u_LightPos;
  uniform float u_Diffuse;
  uniform float u_Ambient;
  varying vec4 v_Color;
  void main() {
    gl_Position = u_MvpMatrix * a_Position;
    v_Color =
             vec4(a_Color.rgb*(u_Diffuse*dot(a_Normal.xyz,
             normalize(u_LightPos.xyz)) + u_Ambient), 1.0);
  }
</script>

<script id="vs_shadow" type="x-shader/x-vertex">
  attribute vec4 a_Position;
  attribute vec4 a_Normal;
  uniform mat4 u_MvpMatrix;
  uniform vec4 u_LightPos;
  varying vec4 v_Color;
  void main() {
    gl_Position = u_MvpMatrix * (a_Position.w == 0.0 ||
                  dot(a_Normal.xyz, u_LightPos.xyz) < 0.0 ?
                  vec4(a_Position.xyz * u_LightPos.w -
                  u_LightPos.xyz, 0.0) : a_Position);
    v_Color = vec4(0.0, 1.0, 1.0, 1.0);
  }
</script>

<script id="fs" type="x-shader/x-fragment">
  #ifdef GL_ES
  precision mediump float;
  #endif
  varying vec4 v_Color;
  void main() {
    gl_FragColor = v_Color;
  }
</script>

<script type="text/javascript">
  var sceneRotation = 40.0;
  var Light = { x : -16.0, y : 24.0, z : -4.0, w : 1.0 };
      // w = 1.0 for Point light and w = 0.0 for Directional light

  function WebGLStart() {
    var canvas = document.getElementById('cv');
    var gl = canvas.getContext('experimental-webgl',
                                          { stencil : true });
    var program = initShaders(gl, "vs", "fs");
    program.a_Position = gl.getAttribLocation(program,
                                              'a_Position');
    program.a_Normal=gl.getAttribLocation(program,
                                              'a_Normal');
    program.a_Color = gl.getAttribLocation(program,
                                              'a_Color');
    program.u_MvpMatrix = gl.getUniformLocation(program,
                                              'u_MvpMatrix');
    program.u_Diffuse = gl.getUniformLocation(program,
                                              'u_Diffuse');
    program.u_Ambient = gl.getUniformLocation(program,
                                              'u_Ambient');
    program.u_LightPos = gl.getUniformLocation(program,
                                              'u_LightPos');

    var programShadow = initShaders(gl, "vs_shadow", "fs");
    programShadow.a_Position =
        gl.getAttribLocation(programShadow, 'a_Position');
    programShadow.a_Normal =
        gl.getAttribLocation(programShadow, 'a_Normal');
    programShadow.u_MvpMatrix =
      gl.getUniformLocation(programShadow, 'u_MvpMatrix');
    programShadow.u_LightPos =
        gl.getUniformLocation(programShadow, 'u_LightPos');

    var plane = initVertexBuffersForPlane(gl);
    var cubeMesh = initVertexBuffersForCubeMesh(gl);

    var tmp = new Matrix4();
    var viewProjMatrix = new Matrix4();
    viewProjMatrix.frustumInfinite(-1.0, 1.0, -1.0, 1.0, 2);
    tmp.lookAt(0.0, 7.0, 9.0, 0.0, 0.0, 0.0, 0.0, 1.0, 0.0);
    viewProjMatrix.multiply_matrix(tmp.entries);
    viewProjMatrix.rotate(sceneRotation, 0, 1, 0);

    // Initialize
    gl.clearColor(0, 0, 0, 1);
    gl.clearStencil(0);
    gl.enable(gl.DEPTH_TEST);
    gl.depthFunc(gl.LESS);
    gl.clear(gl.COLOR_BUFFER_BIT | gl.DEPTH_BUFFER_BIT |
             gl.STENCIL_BUFFER_BIT);

    // First pass: depth buffer
    gl.useProgram(program);
    gl.colorMask(false, false, false, false);
    gl.uniform4f(program.u_LightPos,
                 Light.x, Light.y, Light.z, Light.w);
    draw(gl, program, plane, viewProjMatrix);
    drawMesh(gl, program, cubeMesh, viewProjMatrix);

    // Second pass: stencil buffer
    gl.useProgram(programShadow);
    gl.enable(gl.STENCIL_TEST);
    gl.disable(gl.CULL_FACE);
    gl.depthMask(false);
    gl.stencilOpSeparate(gl.FRONT, gl.KEEP, gl.INCR_WRAP,
                                                  gl.KEEP);
    gl.stencilOpSeparate(gl.BACK, gl.KEEP, gl.DECR_WRAP,
                                                  gl.KEEP);
    gl.stencilFunc(gl.ALWAYS, 0, 0xFF);
    gl.uniform4f(programShadow.u_LightPos,
                 Light.x, Light.y, Light.z, Light.w);
    drawMeshShadowVolume(gl, programShadow, cubeMesh,
                                          viewProjMatrix);
```

```
  // Third pass: color buffer
  gl.useProgram(program);
  gl.colorMask(true, true, true, true);
  gl.enable(gl.CULL_FACE);
  gl.depthMask(true);
  gl.stencilOpSeparate(gl.FRONT, gl.KEEP, gl.KEEP,
                       gl.KEEP);
  gl.stencilOpSeparate(gl.BACK, gl.KEEP, gl.KEEP, gl.KEEP);
  gl.depthFunc(gl.LEQUAL);
  gl.uniform1f(program.u_Diffuse, 0.5);
  gl.uniform1f(program.u_Ambient, 0.0);
  gl.stencilFunc(gl.EQUAL, 0, 0xFF);
  draw(gl, program, plane, viewProjMatrix);
  drawMesh(gl, program, cubeMesh, viewProjMatrix);

  // Fourth pass: alpha blending for ambient lighting
  gl.enable(gl.BLEND);
  gl.disable(gl.STENCIL_TEST);
  gl.blendEquation(gl.FUNC_ADD);
  gl.blendFunc(gl.ONE, gl.ONE);
  gl.uniform1f(program.u_Diffuse, 0.0);
  gl.uniform1f(program.u_Ambient, 0.5);
  draw(gl, program, plane, viewProjMatrix);
  drawMesh(gl, program, cubeMesh, viewProjMatrix);

  gl.disable(gl.BLEND);
  gl.disable(gl.DEPTH_TEST);
}

var g_modelMatrix = new Matrix4();
var g_mvpMatrix = new Matrix4();

function draw(gl, program, o, viewProjMatrix) {
  initAttributeVariable(gl, program.a_Position,
                        o.vertexBuffer);
  initAttributeVariable(gl, program.a_Normal,
                        o.normalBuffer);
  initAttributeVariable(gl, program.a_Color, o.colorBuffer);
  gl.bindBuffer(gl.ELEMENT_ARRAY_BUFFER,
               o.indexBuffer);
  g_mvpMatrix.set(viewProjMatrix);
  g_mvpMatrix.multiply_matrix(g_modelMatrix.entries);
  gl.uniformMatrix4fv(program.u_MvpMatrix, false,
                      g_mvpMatrix.entries);
  gl.drawElements(gl.TRIANGLES, o.numIndices,
                  gl.UNSIGNED_BYTE, 0);
  gl.disableVertexAttribArray(program.a_Position);
  gl.disableVertexAttribArray(program.a_Normal);
  gl.disableVertexAttribArray(program.a_Color);
}

function initAttributeVariable(gl, a_attribute, buffer) {
  gl.bindBuffer(gl.ARRAY_BUFFER, buffer);
  gl.vertexAttribPointer(a_attribute, buffer.num,
                         buffer.type,false, 0, 0);
  gl.enableVertexAttribArray(a_attribute);
}

function initVertexBuffersForPlane(gl) {
  // Vertex coordinates
  var vertices = new Float32Array([  // v0-v1-v2-v3
       3.0, -1.0, 2.5,    -3.0, -1.0, 2.5,
      -3.0, -1.0, -2.5,    3.0, -1.0, -2.5,
  ]);

  // Normals
  var normals = new Float32Array([
    0.0, 1.0, 0.0, 0.0, 1.0, 0.0, 0.0, 1.0, 0.0, 0.0, 1.0, 0.0,
  ]);

  // Colors
  var colors = new Float32Array([
    1.0, 1.0, 1.0, 1.0, 1.0, 1.0, 1.0, 1.0, 1.0, 1.0, 1.0, 1.0,
  ]);

  // Indices of the vertices
  var indices = new Uint8Array([0, 2, 1, 0, 3, 2]);
```

```
// Utilize Object object to return multiple buffer objects
// together
  var o = {};
  o.vertexBuffer = initArrayBufferForLaterUse(gl, vertices,
                                              3, gl.FLOAT);
  o.normalBuffer = initArrayBufferForLaterUse(gl, normals,
                                              3, gl.FLOAT);
  o.colorBuffer = initArrayBufferForLaterUse(gl, colors,
                                             3, gl.FLOAT);
  o.indexBuffer= initElementArrayBufferForLaterUse(gl,
                                  indices, gl.UNSIGNED_BYTE);
  if (!o.vertexBuffer || !o.normalBuffer || !o.colorBuffer
                         || !o.indexBuffer) return null;
  o.numIndices = indices.length;

  gl.bindBuffer(gl.ARRAY_BUFFER, null);
  gl.bindBuffer(gl.ELEMENT_ARRAY_BUFFER, null);

  return o;
}

function drawMesh(gl, program, o, viewProjMatrix) {
  initAttributeVariable(gl, program.a_Position,
                        o.vertexBuffer);
  initAttributeVariable(gl, program.a_Normal,
                        o.normalBuffer);
  initAttributeVariable(gl, program.a_Color, o.colorBuffer);
  g_mvpMatrix.set(viewProjMatrix);
  g_mvpMatrix.multiply_matrix(g_modelMatrix.entries);
  gl.uniformMatrix4fv(program.u_MvpMatrix, false,
                      g_mvpMatrix.entries);
  gl.drawArrays(gl.TRIANGLES, 0, o.count);
  gl.disableVertexAttribArray(program.a_Position);
  gl.disableVertexAttribArray(program.a_Normal);
  gl.disableVertexAttribArray(program.a_Color);
}

function dotL(normal) {
  return ((Light.x * normal[0] +
          Light.y * normal[1] + Light.z * normal[2]));
}

function drawMeshShadowVolume(
                        gl,program,o,viewProjMatrix){
  initAttributeVariable(gl, program.a_Position,
                        o.vertexBuffer);
  initAttributeVariable(gl, program.a_Normal,
                        o.normalBuffer);
  g_mvpMatrix.set(viewProjMatrix);
  g_mvpMatrix.multiply_matrix(g_modelMatrix.entries);
  gl.uniformMatrix4fv(program.u_MvpMatrix, false,
                      g_mvpMatrix.entries);
  gl.drawArrays(gl.TRIANGLES, 0, o.count);
  gl.disableVertexAttribArray(program.a_Position);
  gl.disableVertexAttribArray(program.a_Normal);

  // Silhouette detection
  var shadowVolumeEdges = [];
  for(var i = o.edges.length; i--;) {
    var dL0 = dotL(o.edges[i].n[0]);
    var dL1 = dotL(o.edges[i].n[1]);
    o.edges[i].c = dL0 < 0.0;
    if(dL0 * dL1 <= 0.0)
      shadowVolumeEdges.push(o.edges[i]);
  }

  // Silhouette extrusion
  var shadowVolumeVertices = new
        Float32Array(shadowVolumeEdges.length * 6 * 4);
  for(var i = shadowVolumeEdges.length; i--;) {
    var t;
    shadowVolumeVertices[i * 24 + 19] = 0.0;
    shadowVolumeVertices[i * 24 + 3] = 1.0;
    shadowVolumeVertices[i * 24 + 7] =
      shadowVolumeVertices[i * 24 + 15] =
      shadowVolumeEdges[i].c ? 0.0 : 1.0;
    shadowVolumeVertices[i * 24 + 11] =
      shadowVolumeVertices[i * 24 + 23] =
      shadowVolumeEdges[i].c ? 1.0 : 0.0;
```

```
        for(t = 3; t--;) shadowVolumeVertices[i * 24 + 0 + t] =
                            shadowVolumeEdges[i].v[0][t];
        for(t = 3; t--;) shadowVolumeVertices[i * 24 + 4 + t] =
                            shadowVolumeEdges[i].v[1][t];
        for(t = 3; t--;) shadowVolumeVertices[i * 24 + 8 + t] =
                            shadowVolumeEdges[i].v[1][t];
        for(t = 3; t--;) shadowVolumeVertices[i * 24+12+t] =
                            shadowVolumeEdges[i].v[0][t];
        for(t = 3; t--;) shadowVolumeVertices[i * 24 + 16+t]=
                            shadowVolumeEdges[i].v[1][t];
        for(t = 3; t--;) shadowVolumeVertices[i * 24 + 20+t] =
                            shadowVolumeEdges[i].v[0][t];
    }
    o.shadowBuffer = initArrayBufferForLaterUse(gl,
                        shadowVolumeVertices, 4, gl.FLOAT);
    initAttributeVariable(gl,
                        program.a_Position,o.shadowBuffer);
    g_mvpMatrix.set(viewProjMatrix);
    g_mvpMatrix.multiply_matrix(g_modelMatrix.entries);
    gl.uniformMatrix4fv(program.u_MvpMatrix,false,
                        g_mvpMatrix.entries);
    gl.drawArrays(gl.TRIANGLES,0,
                    shadowVolumeEdges.length*6);
    gl.disableVertexAttribArray(program.a_Position);
}

function initVertexBuffersForCubeMesh(gl) {
    var arrVertices = [ [1.0, 1.0, 1.0],   [-1.0, 1.0, 1.0],
                        [-1.0, -1.0, 1.0],[1.0, -1.0, 1.0],
                        [1.0, -1.0, -1.0],[1.0, 1.0, -1.0],
                        [-1.0, 1.0, -1.0],[-1.0, -1.0, -1.0]];

    var arrTriangles = [ {v: [0, 1, 2], n: [0.0, 0.0, 1.0]},
                        {v: [0, 2, 3], n: [0.0, 0.0, 1.0]},
                        {v: [0, 3, 4], n: [1.0, 0.0, 0.0]},
                        {v: [0, 4, 5], n: [1.0, 0.0, 0.0]},
                        {v: [0, 5, 6], n: [0.0, 1.0, 0.0]},
                        {v: [0, 6, 1], n: [0.0, 1.0, 0.0]},
                        {v: [1, 6, 7], n: [-1.0, 0.0, 0.0]},
                        {v: [1, 7, 2], n: [-1.0, 0.0, 0.0]},
                        {v: [7, 4, 3], n: [0.0, -1.0, 0.0]},
                        {v: [7, 3, 2], n: [0.0, -1.0, 0.0]},
                        {v: [4, 7, 6], n: [0.0, 0.0, -1.0]},
                        {v: [4, 6, 5], n: [0.0, 0.0, -1.0]}];

    var color = [1.0, 0.0, 1.0];

// This could be a function but we have to make sure that we
// use the same vertices/triangles structures
    var edges = [];
    for(var i = arrTriangles.length; --i;) {
      for(var r = i; r--;) {
        var numShared = 0;
        var last_vi = -1;
        var flip_n = false;
        var edge = {v: [], n: []};
        for(var vi = 3; vi--;) {
          for(var vr = 3; vr--;) {
            if(arrTriangles[i].v[vi] == arrTriangles[r].v[vr]) {
           edge.v.push(arrVertices[arrTriangles[r].v[vr]]);
           edge.n.push(arrTriangles[numShared++ ? r : i].n);
              if(numShared == 2) {
                if(vi + 1 != last_vi) edge.n.reverse();
                edges.push(edge);
              }
              last_vi = vi;
              break;
            }
          }
        }
      }
    }

    var size = arrTriangles.length * 3 * 3;
    var vertices = new Float32Array(size);
    var normals = new Float32Array(size);
    var colors = new Float32Array(size);
    for(var i = arrTriangles.length; i--;){
        for(var v = 3; v--;) {
          for(var r = 3; r--;) {
            vertices[i * 9 + v * 3 + r] =
                        arrVertices[arrTriangles[i].v[v]][r];
            normals[i * 9 + v * 3 + r] = arrTriangles[i].n[r];
            colors[i * 9 + v * 3 + r] = color[r];
          }
        }
    }

 // Utilize Object object to return multiple buffer objects
 // together
    var o = {};
    o.edges = edges;
    o.count = arrTriangles.length * 3;
    o.vertexBuffer = initArrayBufferForLaterUse(gl, vertices,
                                                    3, gl.FLOAT);
    o.normalBuffer = initArrayBufferForLaterUse(gl, normals,
                                                    3, gl.FLOAT);
    o.colorBuffer = initArrayBufferForLaterUse(gl, colors,
                                                    3, gl.FLOAT);
    if (!o.vertexBuffer || !o.colorBuffer) return null;
    gl.bindBuffer(gl.ARRAY_BUFFER, null);
    return o;
  }

  function initArrayBufferForLaterUse(gl, data, num, type) {
    var buffer = gl.createBuffer();
    gl.bindBuffer(gl.ARRAY_BUFFER, buffer);
    gl.bufferData(gl.ARRAY_BUFFER, data, gl.STATIC_DRAW);
    buffer.num = num;
    buffer.type = type;
    return buffer;
  }

  function initElementArrayBufferForLaterUse(gl, data, type) {
    var buffer = gl.createBuffer();
    gl.bindBuffer(gl.ELEMENT_ARRAY_BUFFER, buffer);
    gl.bufferData(gl.ELEMENT_ARRAY_BUFFER, data,
                gl.STATIC_DRAW);
    buffer.type = type;
    return buffer;
  }
</script>
</head>
<body onload="WebGLStart();">
  <canvas id="cv" style="border: none;"
          width="500" height="500"></canvas>
</body>
</html>
```

9.5 Texturing

A texture is an image file applied onto a primitive surface. WebGL has limited support for non-power-of-two (NPOT) image sizes. Unless the 'TEXTURE_WRAP_S' and 'TEXTURE_WRAP_T' parameters are set to 'CLAMP_TO_EDGE', valid texture images must have sizes such as 128*128 and 256*512.

When dealing with textures, the horizontal axis is referred to the s-axis while the vertical axis is denoted by the t-axis.

By default, some browsers block access to files on your local disk. You need to enable the option before proceeding, should you decide to run on your local disk. Remember to block the access after completion because enabling local file access opens a security loophole.

9.5.1 Image Texture

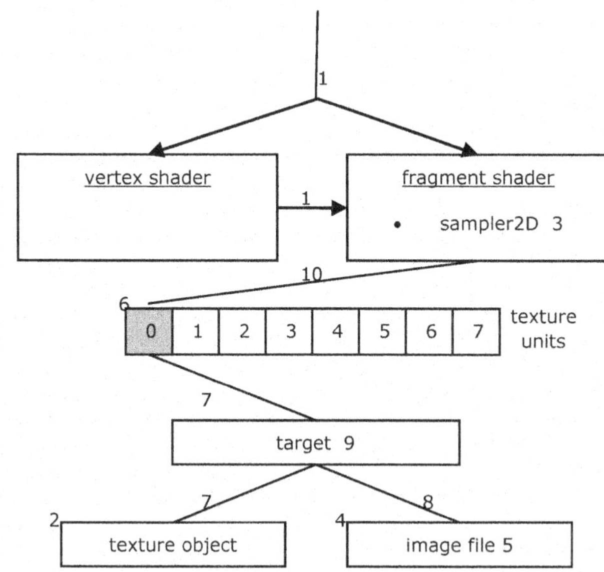

Step 1: Pass the texture coordinates to the shaders. Include the texture coordinates in the buffer object. In the vertex shader, pass the texture coordinates to the fragment shader as varying variables. In the fragment shader, retrieve the texels (texture elements) by calling texture2D(). The texture coordinates range from (0.0,0.0) to (1.0,1.0), corresponding to the lower-left and upper-right corners.

Step 2: Create a texture object. This is done by calling **createTexture()**. A texture object can be deleted by calling **deleteTexture(texture)**. **isTexture(texture)** returns true if 'texture' is a texture object.

Step 3: Get the location of the texture sampler in the fragment shader. This is done by calling **getUniformLocation(program,sampler)**.

Step 4: Load the image file. Create a new Image object with 'new Image()' and specify the source with 'img.src'. Because images are loaded asynchronously, subsequent operations should be called after the image has been loaded completely. Use 'img.onload' to achieve this. The final drawing should be called only after all texture images have been loaded.

Step 5: Flip the y-axis. Because the image coordinate system is such that greater y values lie below, you need to flip the y-axis. This is done by calling **pixelStorei(pname, param)** where 'pname' can be 'UNPACK_FLIP_Y_WEBGL' or 'UNPACK_PREMULTIPLY_ALPHA_WEBGL', and 'param' can be non-zero(true) or zero(false;default).

Step 6: Activate a texture unit. This is done by calling **activeTexture(texUnit)**, where 'texUnit' can be TEXTURE1, TEXTURE2...By default at least eight texture units are supported.

Step 7: Bind the texture object to the active texture unit. This is done by calling **bindTexture(target, texture_obj)** where 'target' can be 'TEXTURE_2D' or 'TEXTURE_CUBE_MAP'.

Step 8: Assign an image in the client memory. This is done by calling **texImage2D(target, level, internalformat, format, type, image)**, where 'target' can be 'TEXTURE_2D' or 'TEXTURE_CUBE_MAP', level is the mipmapping level. 'internalformat' and 'format' must be the same.

After the assignment, you may choose to replace a rectangular portion of the existing texture by calling **texSubImage2D(target, level, xOffset, yOffset, format, type, image)**. The offset subimage 'image' must not extend beyond the existing texture.

Alternatively, you may choose to assign a portion of the current framebuffer(canvas output) as the texture by calling **copyTexImage2D(target, level, internalformat, x, y, width, height, 0)**. Similar to texSubImage2D(), **copyTexSubImage2D(target, level, xoffset, yoffset, x, y, width, height)** replaces a portion of the existing texture with a portion of the existing framebuffer.

internalformat/ format	Components in a texel
RGB	red, green, blue
RGBA	red, green, blue, alpha
ALPHA	0.0, 0.0 , 0.0 , alpha
LUMINANCE	L,L,L,1 L:luminance
LUMINANCE_ALPHA	L,L,L, alpha

type	description
UNSIGNED_BYTE	Each component has 1 byte.
UNSIGNED_SHORT_5_6_5	RGB: each component has 5,6,5 bits respectively.
UNSIGNED_SHORT_4_4_4_4	RGBA: each component has 4,4,4,4 bits respectively.
UNSIGNED_SHORT_5_5_5_1	RGBA: each RGB component has 5 bits, and A has 1 bit.

Step 9 : Set the texture parameters. This is done by calling **texParameteri(target,pname, param)**, where 'target' can be 'TEXTURE_2D' or 'TEXTURE_CUBE_MAP'.

pname	param
TEXTURE_MAG_FILTER: magnification TEXTURE_MIN_FILTER: minification (NEAREST_MIPMAP_LINEAR)	• NEAREST: uses the texel nearest the center of the textured pixel. • LINEAR: uses the weighted average of the four texels nearest the center of the textured pixel.
TEXTURE_WRAP_S: wrapping in s-axis TEXTURE_WRAP_T: wrapping in t-axis	• REPEAT: repeats the image • MIRRORED_REPEAT: repeats the image in a mirrored manner • CLAMP_TO_EDGE: uses the edge color and allows non-power-of-two image sizes

In order for 'TEXTURE_WRAP_S' and 'TEXTURE_WRAP_T' to show their effects, the mapping texture coordinates in the fragment shader should extend beyond 1.0.

Step 10: Pass the texture unit to the shader. This is done by calling **uniform1i(samplerLocation, textureUnit)**.

Instead of simply attaching one texture, this example illustrates how to merge two textures, resulting in a circular view.

```
//webgl-library.js
function loadTexture(gl, n, texture, u_Sampler, image,
aTexture,

texUnit) {
  gl.pixelStorei(gl.UNPACK_FLIP_Y_WEBGL, 1);
                                        // Flip the y-axis
  gl.activeTexture(aTexture);
  gl.bindTexture(gl.TEXTURE_2D, texture);
  gl.texImage2D(gl.TEXTURE_2D, 0, gl.RGBA, gl.RGBA,
               gl.UNSIGNED_BYTE, image);
  gl.texParameteri(gl.TEXTURE_2D, gl.TEXTURE_MIN_FILTER,
                                  gl.LINEAR);
  gl.uniform1i(u_Sampler, texUnit);
  gl.clear(gl.COLOR_BUFFER_BIT);
}
```

```
<!DOCTYPE html>
<html>
<head>

<script type="text/javascript" src="webgl-
library.js"></script>

<script id="shader-vs" type="x-shader/x-vertex">
  attribute vec4 a_Position;
  attribute vec2 a_TexCoord;
  varying vec2 v_TexCoord;
  void main() {
    gl_Position = a_Position;
    v_TexCoord = a_TexCoord;
  }
</script>

<script id="shader-fs" type="x-shader/x-fragment">
  #ifdef GL_ES
  precision mediump float;
  #endif
  uniform sampler2D u_Sampler0;
  uniform sampler2D u_Sampler1;
  varying vec2 v_TexCoord;
  void main() {
    vec4 c0 = texture2D(u_Sampler0, v_TexCoord);
    vec4 c1 = texture2D(u_Sampler1, v_TexCoord);
    gl_FragColor = c0 * c1;
  }
</script>

<script type="text/javascript">

function WebGLStart() {
  var canvas = document.getElementById('cv');
  var gl = canvas.getContext('webgl');
  initShaders(gl, "shader-vs", "shader-fs");
  var n=initVertexBuffers(gl);
  gl.clearColor(0.0, 0.0, 0.0, 1.0);
  initTextures(gl, n);
}

function initVertexBuffers(gl) {
  var verticesTexCoords = new Float32Array([
   // Vertex coordinate --> Texture coordinate
   -0.9, 0.9,  0.0, 1.0,
   -0.9, -0.9,  0.0, 0.0,
    0.9, 0.9,  1.0, 1.0,
    0.9, -0.9,  1.0, 0.0,
  ]);
  var n = 4; // The number of vertices

  var vertexTexCoordBuffer = gl.createBuffer();
  gl.bindBuffer(gl.ARRAY_BUFFER, vertexTexCoordBuffer);
  gl.bufferData(gl.ARRAY_BUFFER, verticesTexCoords,
                                   gl.STATIC_DRAW);

  var FSIZE = verticesTexCoords.BYTES_PER_ELEMENT;

  var a_Position = gl.getAttribLocation(gl.program,
                                        'a_Position');
  gl.vertexAttribPointer(a_Position,2,gl.FLOAT,false,
                         FSIZE*4, 0);
  gl.enableVertexAttribArray(a_Position);

  var a_TexCoord=gl.getAttribLocation(gl.program,
                                       'a_TexCoord');
  gl.vertexAttribPointer(a_TexCoord, 2, gl.FLOAT,false,
                         FSIZE*4, FSIZE*2);
  gl.enableVertexAttribArray(a_TexCoord);

  return n;
}

function initTextures(gl, n) {
  var texture0 = gl.createTexture();
  var texture1 = gl.createTexture();
  var u_Sampler0 = gl.getUniformLocation(gl.program,
                                          'u_Sampler0');
  var u_Sampler1 = gl.getUniformLocation(gl.program,
                                          'u_Sampler1');
  var img0 = new Image();
  var img1 = new Image();
  img0.onload = function(){
    loadTexture(gl, n, texture0, u_Sampler0, img0,
                gl.TEXTURE0,0);
  };
  img1.onload = function(){
    loadTexture(gl, n, texture1, u_Sampler1, img1,
                gl.TEXTURE1,1);
    gl.drawArrays(gl.TRIANGLE_STRIP, 0, n);
  };
  img0.src = 'dog.jpg';
  img1.src = 'circle.gif';
}
</script>

</head>
<body onload="WebGLStart();">
```

```
   <canvas id="cv" style="border: none;"
           width="500" height="500">
</canvas>
</body>

</html>
```

	dog.jpg
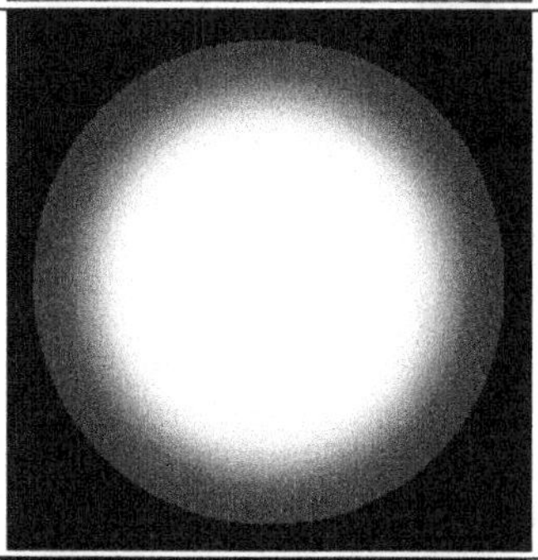	circle.gif
	(final output)

9.5.2 Mipmapping

Mipmapping is a technique that improves performance and reduces aliasing artifacts by using images of different sizes for a texture. These images normally show the same graphic, but their sizes are different. When a texture displayed is small or faraway, a small image is used. When a texture displayed is large or near, a large image is used.

To perform mipmapping:

Step 1: Generate all the mipmaps. After the level-0 base image has been specified with texImage2D(), you can automatically generate all mipmaps by calling **generateMipmap()**. This generates all mipmaps (with the same graphic as the base image), down to size 1*1. Note that the base image must have power-of-two dimensions.

```
gl.texImage2D(gl.TEXTURE_2D, 0, gl.RGBA, gl.RGBA,
              gl.UNSIGNED_BYTE, image256);
gl.generateMipmap(gl.TEXTURE_2D);
```

Alternatively, you can manually generate the mipmaps by calling **texImage2D()** repeatedly. In each successive call, 'level' should be increased by one, and 'image' should have the dimensions halved. All reduction mipmaps must be generated, which means the mipmap with the highest level should have a dimension of 1*1.

```
gl.texImage2D(gl.TEXTURE_2D, 0, gl.RGBA, gl.RGBA,
              gl.UNSIGNED_BYTE, image256);
gl.texImage2D(gl.TEXTURE_2D, 1, gl.RGBA, gl.RGBA,
              gl.UNSIGNED_BYTE, image128);
gl.texImage2D(gl.TEXTURE_2D, 2, gl.RGBA, gl.RGBA,
              gl.UNSIGNED_BYTE, image64);
gl.texImage2D(gl.TEXTURE_2D, 3, gl.RGBA, gl.RGBA,
              gl.UNSIGNED_BYTE, image32);
gl.texImage2D(gl.TEXTURE_2D, 4, gl.RGBA, gl.RGBA,
              gl.UNSIGNED_BYTE, image16);
gl.texImage2D(gl.TEXTURE_2D, 5, gl.RGBA, gl.RGBA,
              gl.UNSIGNED_BYTE, image8);
gl.texImage2D(gl.TEXTURE_2D,6, gl.RGBA, gl.RGBA,
              gl.UNSIGNED_BYTE, image4);
gl.texImage2D(gl.TEXTURE_2D, 7, gl.RGBA, gl.RGBA,
              gl.UNSIGNED_BYTE, image2);
gl.texImage2D(gl.TEXTURE_2D, 8, gl.RGBA, gl.RGBA,
              gl.UNSIGNED_BYTE, image1);
```

Step 2: Specify the mipmapping parameter. This is done by calling **texParameteri(gl.TEXTURE_2D, gl.TEXTURE_MIN_FILTER, param)**, where 'param' can be 'NEAREST_MIPMAP_NEAREST', 'NEAREST_MIPMAP_LINEAR', 'LINEAR_MIPMAP_NEAREST', and 'LINEAR_MIPMAP_LINEAR'. The word 'NEAREST' after 'MIPMAP' means that the mipmap with a size nearest the display size will be used. If 'LINEAR' is specified after 'MIPMAP', a weighted average from the two closest mipmaps will be used. You may omit this step if the default 'NEAREST_MIPMAP_LINEAR' is used.

hint(gl.GENERATE_MIPMAP_HINT, mode) specifies implementation-specific hints. 'mode' can be FASTEST, NICEST, DON'T_CARE.

9.5.3 Video Texture

You may use video files in place of image files. texImage2D() then fetches the current video frame for the texture image. For the video to play in the texture, texImage2D() must be called repeatedly.

flush() forces the execution of GL commands in finite time.

This example uses requestAnimationFrame() to call texImage2D() repeatedly.

```
<!DOCTYPE html>
<html>
<head>

<script type="text/javascript"
        src="webgl-library.js"></script>

<script id="shader-vs" type="x-shader/x-vertex">
  attribute vec4 a_Position;
  attribute vec2 a_TexCoord;
  varying vec2 v_TexCoord;
```

```
  void main() {
    gl_Position = a_Position;
    v_TexCoord = a_TexCoord;
  }
</script>

<script id="shader-fs" type="x-shader/x-fragment">
  #ifdef GL_ES
  precision mediump float;
  #endif
  uniform sampler2D u_Sampler;
  varying vec2 v_TexCoord;
  void main() {
    gl_FragColor = texture2D(u_Sampler, v_TexCoord);
  }
</script>

<script>

function WebGLStart() {
  var canvas = document.getElementById('cv');
  var gl = canvas.getContext('webgl');
  initShaders(gl, "shader-vs", "shader-fs");
  var n=initVertexBuffers(gl);
  gl.clearColor(0.0, 0.0, 0.0, 1.0);

  var bunny_video = document.createElement('video');
  bunny_video.src = 'bunny.ogv';
  bunny_video.autoplay=true;

  var texture = gl.createTexture();
  gl.pixelStorei(gl.UNPACK_FLIP_Y_WEBGL, true);
  gl.bindTexture(gl.TEXTURE_2D,texture);
  gl.texParameteri(gl.TEXTURE_2D, gl.TEXTURE_MIN_FILTER,
                   gl.LINEAR);
  gl.texParameteri(gl.TEXTURE_2D, gl.TEXTURE_WRAP_S,
                   gl.CLAMP_TO_EDGE );
  gl.texParameteri(gl.TEXTURE_2D, gl.TEXTURE_WRAP_T,
                   gl.CLAMP_TO_EDGE );

  var refresh_texture = function (){
    gl.bindTexture(gl.TEXTURE_2D, texture);
    gl.texImage2D(gl.TEXTURE_2D, 0, gl.RGBA, gl.RGBA,
                  gl.UNSIGNED_BYTE, bunny_video);
  }

  var animate = function (time){
    gl.clear(gl.COLOR_BUFFER_BIT);
    if (bunny_video.currentTime>0) {
      gl.activeTexture(gl.TEXTURE0);
      refresh_texture();
    }
    gl.drawArrays(gl.TRIANGLE_STRIP, 0, 4);
    gl.flush();
    window.requestAnimationFrame(animate);
  }

  animate(0);
}

function initVertexBuffers(gl) {
  var verticesTexCoords = new Float32Array([
   // Vertex coordinate --> Texture coordinate
   -0.9, 0.9,  0.0, 1.0,
   -0.9, -0.9,  0.0, 0.0,
    0.9, 0.9,  1.0, 1.0,
    0.9, -0.9,  1.0, 0.0,
  ]);
  var n = 4;

  var vertexTexCoordBuffer = gl.createBuffer();
  gl.bindBuffer(gl.ARRAY_BUFFER, vertexTexCoordBuffer);
  gl.bufferData(gl.ARRAY_BUFFER, verticesTexCoords,
                gl.STATIC_DRAW);

  var FSIZE = verticesTexCoords.BYTES_PER_ELEMENT;

  var a_Position = gl.getAttribLocation(gl.program,
                                        'a_Position');
  gl.vertexAttribPointer(a_Position,2,gl.FLOAT,false,
                         FSIZE*4, 0);
  gl.enableVertexAttribArray(a_Position);

 var a_TexCoord=gl.getAttribLocation(gl.program,
                                      'a_TexCoord');
  gl.vertexAttribPointer(a_TexCoord, 2, gl.FLOAT, false,
                         FSIZE * 4, FSIZE * 2);
  gl.enableVertexAttribArray(a_TexCoord);

  return n;
}
</script>
</head>

<body onload="WebGLStart();">
  <canvas id="cv" style="border: none;"
    width="500" height="500"></canvas>
</body>
</html>
```

9.5.4 Canvas Texture

Besides an Image object and a video object, you may also pass a canvas object to texImage2D(). Like them, the canvas object must have power-of-two sizes, unless the 'TEXTURE_WRAP_S' and 'TEXTURE_WRAP_T' parameters are set to 'CLAMP_TO_EDGE'.

One may choose to show the additional Image object, video object or canvas object by coding their tags directly in the HTML file, or choose to hide them by creating them dynamically in the JavaScript.

Here we draw a red square on another canvas, and then use that canvas as the texture.

```
<!DOCTYPE html>
<html>
<head>

<script type="text/javascript" src="webgl-
library.js"></script>

<script id="shader-vs" type="x-shader/x-vertex">
  attribute vec4 a_Position;
  attribute vec2 a_TexCoord;
  varying vec2 v_TexCoord;
  void main() {
    gl_Position = a_Position;
    v_TexCoord = a_TexCoord;
  }
</script>

<script id="shader-fs" type="x-shader/x-fragment">
  #ifdef GL_ES
  precision mediump float;
  #endif
  uniform sampler2D u_Sampler0;
  varying vec2 v_TexCoord;
```

```
  void main() {
    gl_FragColor = texture2D(u_Sampler0, v_TexCoord);
  }
</script>

<script type="text/javascript">

function WebGLStart() {
  var canvas = document.getElementById('cv');
  var gl = canvas.getContext('webgl');
  initShaders(gl, "shader-vs", "shader-fs");
  var n=initVertexBuffers(gl);
  gl.clearColor(0.0, 0.0, 0.0, 1.0);

  var canvas2=document.createElement('canvas');
  canvas2.width=512;
  canvas2.height=512;
  g = canvas2.getContext('2d');
  g.fillStyle="rgb(255,0,0)";
  g.fillRect(100,100,300,300);

  var texture0 = gl.createTexture();
  var u_Sampler0 = gl.getUniformLocation(gl.program,
                                          'u_Sampler0');

  loadTexture(gl, n, texture0, u_Sampler0, canvas2,
             gl.TEXTURE0,0);
  gl.drawArrays(gl.TRIANGLE_STRIP, 0, n);
}

function initVertexBuffers(gl) {
  var verticesTexCoords = new Float32Array([
   // Vertex coordinate --> Texture coordinate
   -0.3, 0.3,   0.0, 1.0,
   -0.3, -0.3,  0.0, 0.0,
    0.3, 0.3,   1.0, 1.0,
    0.3, -0.3,  1.0, 0.0,
  ]);
  var n = 4; // The number of vertices

  var vertexTexCoordBuffer = gl.createBuffer();

  gl.bindBuffer(gl.ARRAY_BUFFER, vertexTexCoordBuffer);
  gl.bufferData(gl.ARRAY_BUFFER, verticesTexCoords,
               gl.STATIC_DRAW);
  var FSIZE = verticesTexCoords.BYTES_PER_ELEMENT;

  var a_Position = gl.getAttribLocation(gl.program,
                                        'a_Position');
  gl.vertexAttribPointer(a_Position,2,gl.FLOAT,false,
                        FSIZE*4, 0);
  gl.enableVertexAttribArray(a_Position);

 var a_TexCoord=gl.getAttribLocation(gl.program,
                                        'a_TexCoord');
  gl.vertexAttribPointer(a_TexCoord, 2, gl.FLOAT, false,
                        FSIZE * 4, FSIZE * 2);
  gl.enableVertexAttribArray(a_TexCoord);

  return n;
}

</script>

</head>
<body onload="WebGLStart();">
  <canvas id="cv" style="border: none;"
   width="500" height="500"></canvas>
</body>

</html>
```

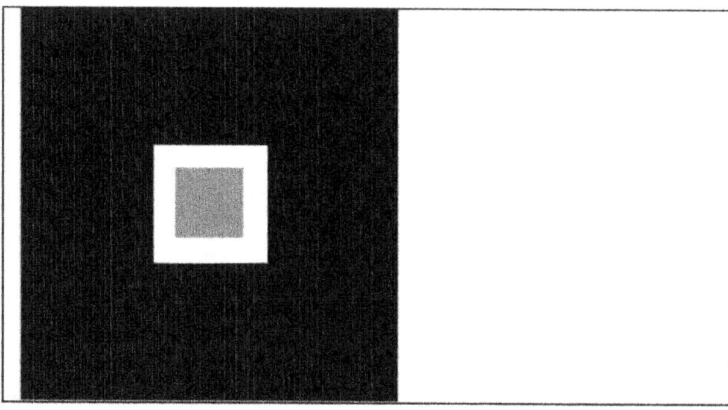

9.5.5 Rendered Texture

By default, WebGL draws on the default color framebuffer, causing the canvas to display the drawing. You may draw on a manually created framebuffer in the memory, without showing the drawing on the canvas. The drawing may then be used as a texture.

To initialize a framebuffer object:

Step 1: Create a framebuffer object. This is done by calling **createFramebuffer()**. The framebuffer object may be deleted by calling **deleteFramebuffer(framebuffer)**.

Step 2: Prepare a texture object.

Step 3: Prepare a renderbuffer object for the depth buffer. A renderbuffer object may be created by **createRenderbuffer()**. (It can be deleted by **deleteRenderbuffer()**.) Then, bind it by calling **bindRenderbuffer(gl.RENDERBUFFER, renderbuffer)**. When the binding is complete, specify the storage parameters by calling **renderbufferStorage(gl.RENDERBUFFER, internalformat, width, height)**.

internalformat	
DEPTH_COMPONENT16	This uses the renderbuffer as a depth buffer.
STENCIL_INDEX8	This uses the renderbuffer as a stencil buffer.
RGBA4	This uses the renderbuffer as a color buffer. Each component has 4 bits.
RGB5_A1	This uses the renderbuffer as a color buffer. Each RGB component has 5 bits, and A has 1 bit.
RGB565	This uses the renderbuffer as a color buffer. Each RGB component has 5, 6, 5 bits respectively.

Step 4: Attach the texture object to the framebuffer obect. First, bind the framebuffer by calling **bindFramebuffer(gl.FRAMEBUFFER, framebuffer)**. Then, set the texture object by calling **framebufferTexture2D(gl.FRAMEBUFFER, attachment, textarget, texture, level)**, where 'attachment' can be 'COLOR_ATTACHMENT0' for a color buffer, or 'DEPTH_ATTACHMENT' for a depth buffer.

Step 5: Attach the renderbuffer object to the framebuffer object. This is done by calling **framebufferRenderbuffer(gl.FRAMEBUFFER, attachment, gl.RENDERBUFFER, renderbuffer)**, where 'attachment' can be 'COLOR_ATTACHMENT0', 'DEPTH_ATTACHMENT' or 'STENCIL_ATTACHMENT'.

Step 6: Check the configuration of the framebuffer object. This is done by calling **checkFramebufferStatus(gl.FRAMEBUFFER)**.

Return value for checkFramebufferStatus()
FRAMEBUFFER_COMPLETE: Correct configuration.
FRAMEBUFFER_INCOMPLETE_ATTACHMENT: An incomplete framebuffer attachment point.
FRAMEBUFFER_INCOMPLETE_DEMENSIONS: The width or height of the attachment is different.
FRAMEBUFFER_INCOMPLETE_MISSING_ATTACHMENT: No valid attachment found.

To draw in the framebuffer object, call:

```
gl.bindFramebuffer(gl.FRAMEBUFFER, fbo);
```

To draw in the default color framebuffer, call:

```
gl.bindFramebuffer(gl.FRAMEBUFFER, null);
```

This example renders a textured image in the framebuffer, and then uses the framebuffer as a texture for a square. Although this is not particularly interesting, it clearly illustrates the technique by which rich effects can be accomplished. For example, with this, you can animate a square containing a rotating cube with a texture image on each side.

```
//webgl-library.js

function initFramebufferObject(gl,width,height) {
  var framebuffer, texture, depthBuffer;

  framebuffer = gl.createFramebuffer();

  texture = gl.createTexture();
  gl.bindTexture(gl.TEXTURE_2D, texture);      |
  gl.texImage2D(gl.TEXTURE_2D, 0, gl.RGBA,width,height, 0,
                    gl.RGBA, gl.UNSIGNED_BYTE, null);
  gl.texParameteri(gl.TEXTURE_2D, gl.TEXTURE_MIN_FILTER,
                    gl.LINEAR);
  framebuffer.texture = texture;
  depthBuffer = gl.createRenderbuffer();
  gl.bindRenderbuffer(gl.RENDERBUFFER, depthBuffer);
  gl.renderbufferStorage(gl.RENDERBUFFER,
                    gl.DEPTH_COMPONENT16, width,height);
  gl.bindFramebuffer(gl.FRAMEBUFFER, framebuffer);
  gl.framebufferTexture2D(gl.FRAMEBUFFER,
      gl.COLOR_ATTACHMENT0, gl.TEXTURE_2D, texture, 0);
  gl.framebufferRenderbuffer(gl.FRAMEBUFFER,
    gl.DEPTH_ATTACHMENT, gl.RENDERBUFFER, depthBuffer);

  var e = gl.checkFramebufferStatus(gl.FRAMEBUFFER);
  if (gl.FRAMEBUFFER_COMPLETE !== e) {
    alert('Frame buffer object is incomplete: ' + e.toString());
    return error();
  }

  // Unbind the buffer object
  gl.bindFramebuffer(gl.FRAMEBUFFER, null);
  gl.bindTexture(gl.TEXTURE_2D, null);
  gl.bindRenderbuffer(gl.RENDERBUFFER, null);

  return framebuffer;
}
```

```
<!DOCTYPE html>
<html>
<head>

<script type="text/javascript"
        src="webgl-library.js"></script>

<script id="shader-vs" type="x-shader/x-vertex">
  attribute vec4 a_Position;
  attribute vec2 a_TexCoord;
  varying vec2 v_TexCoord;
  void main() {
    gl_Position = a_Position;
    v_TexCoord = a_TexCoord;
  }
</script>

<script id="shader-fs" type="x-shader/x-fragment">
  #ifdef GL_ES
  precision mediump float;
  #endif
  uniform sampler2D u_Sampler;
  varying vec2 v_TexCoord;
  void main() {
    gl_FragColor = texture2D(u_Sampler, v_TexCoord);
  }
</script>

<script type="text/javascript">

function WebGLStart() {
  var canvas = document.getElementById('cv');
  var gl = canvas.getContext('webgl');
  initShaders(gl, "shader-vs", "shader-fs");

  img = new Image();
  img.onload = function(){
    var fbo = draw_in_framebufferObject(gl,img);
    draw_in_defaultFramebuffer(gl,fbo.texture);
  }
  img.src = 'dog.jpg';
}

function draw_in_framebufferObject(gl,img){
  var n=initVertexBuffers(gl);
  var texture = gl.createTexture();
  var u_Sampler = gl.getUniformLocation(gl.program,
                                          'u_Sampler');

  var fbo = initFramebufferObject(gl,512,512);
  gl.bindFramebuffer(gl.FRAMEBUFFER, fbo);
  gl.viewport(0, 0, 512, 512);
  gl.clearColor(0.7, 0.7, 0.0, 1.0);
  gl.clear(gl.COLOR_BUFFER_BIT | gl.DEPTH_BUFFER_BIT);

  loadTexture(gl, n, texture, u_Sampler, img,
                  gl.TEXTURE0,0);
  gl.drawArrays(gl.TRIANGLE_STRIP, 0, n);
  return fbo;
}

function draw_in_defaultFramebuffer(gl,texture){
  var n=initVertexBuffers(gl);

  gl.bindFramebuffer(gl.FRAMEBUFFER, null);
  gl.viewport(0, 0, 500, 500);
  gl.clearColor(0.0, 0.0, 0.0, 1.0);
  gl.clear(gl.COLOR_BUFFER_BIT | gl.DEPTH_BUFFER_BIT);

  gl.activeTexture(gl.TEXTURE0);
  gl.bindTexture(gl.TEXTURE_2D, texture);
  gl.drawArrays(gl.TRIANGLE_STRIP, 0, n);
}

function initVertexBuffers(gl) {
  var verticesTexCoords = new Float32Array([
    // Vertex coordinate --> Texture coordinate
    -0.8, 0.8,  0.0, 1.0,
    -0.8, -0.8,  0.0, 0.0,
     0.8, 0.8,  1.0, 1.0,
```

```
    0.8, -0.8,   1.0, 0.0,
  ]);
  var n = 4; // The number of vertices

  var vertexTexCoordBuffer = gl.createBuffer();

  gl.bindBuffer(gl.ARRAY_BUFFER, vertexTexCoordBuffer);
  gl.bufferData(gl.ARRAY_BUFFER, verticesTexCoords,
                gl.STATIC_DRAW);

  var FSIZE = verticesTexCoords.BYTES_PER_ELEMENT;

  var a_Position = gl.getAttribLocation(gl.program,
                                        'a_Position');
  gl.vertexAttribPointer(a_Position,2,gl.FLOAT,false,
                         FSIZE*4, 0);
  gl.enableVertexAttribArray(a_Position);

  var a_TexCoord=gl.getAttribLocation(gl.program,
                                        'a_TexCoord');
  gl.vertexAttribPointer(a_TexCoord, 2, gl.FLOAT, false,
                         FSIZE * 4, FSIZE * 2);
  gl.enableVertexAttribArray(a_TexCoord);

  return n;
}

</script>

</head>
<body onload="WebGLStart();">
  <canvas id="cv" style="border: none;"
          width="500" height="500"></canvas>
</body>

</html>
```

isFramebuffer(fb) returns true if 'fb' is a framebuffer object.

framebufferTexture2D(gl.FRAMEBUFFER, attachment, textarget, texture, level) attaches a texture image to a framebuffer object. 'attachment' can be 'COLOR_ATTACHMENT0', 'DEPTH_ATTACHMENT' or 'STENCIL_ATTACHMENT'. 'textarget' can be 'TEXTURE_2D', 'TEXTURE_CUBE_MAP_POSITIVE{X,Y,Z}' or 'TEXTURE_CUBE_MAP_NEGATIVE{X,Y,Z}'.

getFramebufferAttachmentParameter(gl.FRAMEBUFFER, attachment, pname) returns attachment parameters for a framebuffer object. 'attachment' can be 'COLOR_ATTACHMENT0', 'DEPTH_ATTACHMENT' or 'STENCIL_ATTACHMENT'. 'pname' can be FRAMEBUFFER_ATTACHMENT_OBJECT_{TYPE,NAME}, FRAMEBUFFER_ATTACHMENT_TEXTURE_LEVEL, or FRAMEBUFFER_ATTACHMENT_TEXTURE_CUBE_MAP_FACE.

isRenderbuffer(rbf) returns true if 'rbf' is is a renderbuffer object.

getRenderbufferParameter(gl.RENDERBUFFER, pname) returns the paratemeters for a renderbuffer. 'pname' can be RENDERBUFFER_{WIDTH, HEIGHT, INTERNAL_FORMAT}, RENDERBUFFER_{RED, GREEN, BLUE, ALPHA, DEPTH, STENCIL}_SIZE.

9.5.6 Shadow Mapping

We can implement shadows by drawing the scene twice, using two pairs of shaders. Compared to stencil shadow volume, shadow mapping is often faster, but may use more memory.

In the first pass, the drawing occurs in a framebuffer object. The camera is assumed to be at the location of the light source. Its distances to each fragment are recorded in a texture image known as the image map. We shall use gl_FragCoord, a built-in vec4, in the fragment shader. gl_FragCoord.x and gl_FragCoord.y represent the position of the fragment on the screen, and gl_FragCoord.z represents the depth distance in the range [0,1] which correspond to the near clipping plane and far clipping plane.

In the second pass, we draw on the default framebuffer. If the distance from the light source to the fragment in this step is greater than the distance recorded in the shadow map, the fragment is in the shadow.

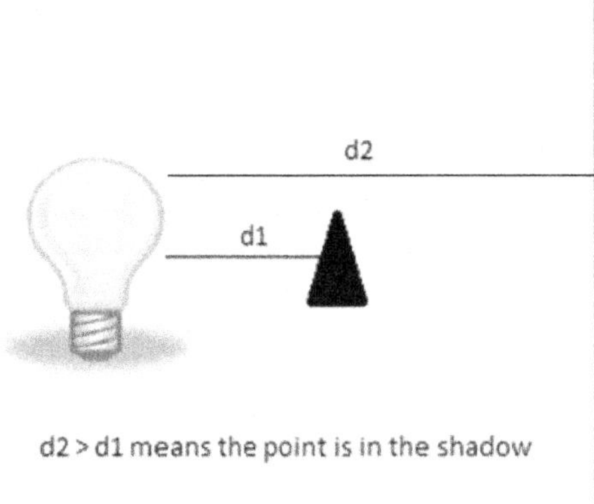

d2 > d1 means the point is in the shadow

Because gl_FragCoord.z has only an 8-bit precision, it is not stored in gl_FragColor directly.Rather, all the R, G, B, and A components are used to store it.

```
// webgl-library.js
Matrix4.prototype.set = function(src) {
  var i, s, d;
  s = src.entries;
  d = this.entries;
  if (s === d) return;
  for (i = 0; i < 16; ++i) d[i] = s[i];
  return this;
};
```

```
<!DOCTYPE html>
<html>
<head>

<script type="text/javascript"
        src="webgl-library.js"></script>

<script id="shadow-vs" type="x-shader/x-vertex">
  attribute vec4 a_Position;
  uniform mat4 u_MvpMatrix;
  void main() {
    gl_Position = u_MvpMatrix * a_Position;
  }
</script>

<script id="shadow-fs" type="x-shader/x-fragment">
  #ifdef GL_ES
  precision mediump float;
  #endif
  void main() {
    const vec4 bitShift = vec4(1.0, 256.0, 256.0 * 256.0,
                                 256.0 * 256.0 * 256.0);
    const vec4 bitMask = vec4(1.0/256.0, 1.0/256.0,
                                 1.0/256.0, 0.0);
    vec4 rgbaDepth = fract(gl_FragCoord.z * bitShift);
    rgbaDepth -= rgbaDepth.gbaa * bitMask;
    gl_FragColor = rgbaDepth;
  }
</script>

<script id="vs" type="x-shader/x-vertex">
  attribute vec4 a_Position;
  attribute vec4 a_Color;
  uniform mat4 u_MvpMatrix;
  uniform mat4 u_MvpMatrixFromLight;
  varying vec4 v_PositionFromLight;
  varying vec4 v_Color;
  void main() {
    gl_Position = u_MvpMatrix * a_Position;
    v_PositionFromLight = u_MvpMatrixFromLight *
                            a_Position;
    v_Color = a_Color;
  }
</script>

<script id="fs" type="x-shader/x-fragment">
  #ifdef GL_ES
  precision mediump float;
  #endif
  uniform sampler2D u_ShadowMap;
  varying vec4 v_PositionFromLight;
  varying vec4 v_Color;
  float unpackDepth(const in vec4 rgbaDepth) {
    const vec4 bitShift = vec4(1.0, 1.0/256.0,
           1.0/(256.0*256.0), 1.0/(256.0*256.0*256.0));
    float depth = dot(rgbaDepth, bitShift);
    return depth;
  }
  void main() {
    vec3 shadowCoord = (v_PositionFromLight.xyz/
                        v_PositionFromLight.w)/2.0 + 0.5;
    vec4 rgbaDepth=texture2D(
                        u_ShadowMap,shadowCoord.xy);
    float depth = unpackDepth(rgbaDepth);
    float visibility = (shadowCoord.z>depth+0.0015) ?
                                          0.7 : 1.0;
    gl_FragColor = vec4(v_Color.rgb * visibility, v_Color.a);
  }
</script>

<script type="text/javascript">

var LIGHT_X = 0, LIGHT_Y = 40, LIGHT_Z = 2;

function WebGLStart() {
  var canvas = document.getElementById('cv');
  var gl = canvas.getContext('webgl');
```

```
  var shadowProgram=initShaders(gl,"shadow-vs",
                                    "shadow-fs");
  shadowProgram.a_Position = gl.getAttribLocation(
                              shadowProgram, 'a_Position');
  shadowProgram.u_MvpMatrix = gl.getUniformLocation(
                              shadowProgram, 'u_MvpMatrix');

  var normalProgram = initShaders(gl, "vs", "fs");
  normalProgram.a_Position = gl.getAttribLocation(
                          normalProgram, 'a_Position');
  normalProgram.a_Color = gl.getAttribLocation(
                          normalProgram, 'a_Color');
  normalProgram.u_MvpMatrix = gl.getUniformLocation(
                          normalProgram, 'u_MvpMatrix');
  normalProgram.u_MvpMatrixFromLight=
       gl.getUniformLocation(normalProgram,
                             'u_MvpMatrixFromLight');
  normalProgram.u_ShadowMap = gl.getUniformLocation(
                          normalProgram, 'u_ShadowMap');

  var triangle = initVertexBuffersForTriangle(gl);
  var plane = initVertexBuffersForPlane(gl);

  var fbo = initFramebufferObject(gl,2048,2048);
  gl.activeTexture(gl.TEXTURE0);
  gl.bindTexture(gl.TEXTURE_2D, fbo.texture);

  gl.clearColor(0, 0, 0, 1);
  gl.enable(gl.DEPTH_TEST);

  var tmp = new Matrix4();
  var viewProjMatrixFromLight = new Matrix4();
  viewProjMatrixFromLight.perspective(70.0, 1.0, 1.0, 200.0);
  tmp.lookAt(LIGHT_X, LIGHT_Y, LIGHT_Z,
            0.0, 0.0, 0.0, 0.0, 1.0, 0.0);
  viewProjMatrixFromLight.multiply_matrix(tmp.entries);

  var tmp = new Matrix4();
  var viewProjMatrix = new Matrix4();
  viewProjMatrix.perspective(
                45, canvas.width/canvas.height, 1.0, 100.0);
  tmp.lookAt(0.0, 7.0, 9.0, 0.0, 0.0, 0.0, 0.0, 1.0, 0.0);
  viewProjMatrix.multiply_matrix(tmp.entries);

  var currentAngle = 0.0;
  var mvpMatrixFromLight_t = new Matrix4();
  var mvpMatrixFromLight_p = new Matrix4();

  gl.bindFramebuffer(gl.FRAMEBUFFER, fbo);
  gl.viewport(0, 0,2048, 2048);
  gl.clear(gl.COLOR_BUFFER_BIT | gl.DEPTH_BUFFER_BIT);
  gl.useProgram(shadowProgram);
  draw(gl, shadowProgram, triangle,
       viewProjMatrixFromLight);
  mvpMatrixFromLight_t.set(g_mvpMatrix);
  draw(gl, shadowProgram, plane, viewProjMatrixFromLight);
  mvpMatrixFromLight_p.set(g_mvpMatrix);

  gl.bindFramebuffer(gl.FRAMEBUFFER, null);
  gl.viewport(0, 0, canvas.width, canvas.height);
  gl.clear(gl.COLOR_BUFFER_BIT | gl.DEPTH_BUFFER_BIT);
  gl.useProgram(normalProgram);
  gl.uniform1i(normalProgram.u_ShadowMap, 0);
  gl.uniformMatrix4fv(normalProgram.u_MvpMatrixFromLight,
                      false, mvpMatrixFromLight_t.entries);
  draw(gl, normalProgram, triangle, viewProjMatrix);
  gl.uniformMatrix4fv(normalProgram.u_MvpMatrixFromLight,
                      false, mvpMatrixFromLight_p.entries);
  draw(gl, normalProgram, plane, viewProjMatrix);
}

var g_modelMatrix = new Matrix4();
var g_mvpMatrix = new Matrix4();

function draw(gl, program, o, viewProjMatrix) {
 initAttributeVariable(gl, program.a_Position, o.vertexBuffer);
 if (program.a_Color != undefined)
   initAttributeVariable(gl, program.a_Color, o.colorBuffer);
 gl.bindBuffer(gl.ELEMENT_ARRAY_BUFFER, o.indexBuffer);
```

```
  g_mvpMatrix.set(viewProjMatrix);
  g_mvpMatrix.multiply_matrix(g_modelMatrix.entries);
  gl.uniformMatrix4fv(
        program.u_MvpMatrix, false, g_mvpMatrix.entries);
  gl.drawElements(
         gl.TRIANGLES, o.numIndices, gl.UNSIGNED_BYTE, 0);
}

function initAttributeVariable(gl, a_attribute, buffer) {
  gl.bindBuffer(gl.ARRAY_BUFFER, buffer);
  gl.vertexAttribPointer(a_attribute, buffer.num, buffer.type,
                                                   false, 0, 0);
  gl.enableVertexAttribArray(a_attribute);
}

function initVertexBuffersForPlane(gl) {
   // Create a plane
   //  v1------v0
   //  |          |
   //  |          |
   //  |          |
   //  v2------v3

   var vertices = new Float32Array([
     3.0, -1.7, 2.5,  -3.0, -1.7, 2.5,
    -3.0, -1.7, -2.5,   3.0, -1.7, -2.5    // v0-v1-v2-v3
   ]);
   var colors = new Float32Array([
     1.0, 1.0, 1.0,    1.0, 1.0, 1.0,  1.0, 1.0, 1.0,   1.0, 1.0, 1.0
   ]);
   var indices = new Uint8Array([0, 1, 2,   0, 2, 3]);

   var o = new Object();
   o.vertexBuffer = initArrayBufferForLaterUse(
                                  gl, vertices, 3, gl.FLOAT);
   o.colorBuffer = initArrayBufferForLaterUse(
                                  gl, colors, 3, gl.FLOAT);
   o.indexBuffer = initElementArrayBufferForLaterUse(
                              gl, indices, gl.UNSIGNED_BYTE);
   if (!o.vertexBuffer||!o.colorBuffer||!o.indexBuffer)
     return null;
   o.numIndices = indices.length;
   gl.bindBuffer(gl.ARRAY_BUFFER, null);
   gl.bindBuffer(gl.ELEMENT_ARRAY_BUFFER, null);
   return o;
}

function initVertexBuffersForTriangle(gl) {
   // Create a triangle
   //       v2
   //      / |
   //     /  |
   //    /   |
   //  v0----v1

   var vertices = new Float32Array(
                  [-0.8, 3.5, 0.0,  0.8, 3.5, 0.0,  0.0, 3.5, 1.8]);
   var colors = new Float32Array(
                  [1.0, 0.5, 0.0,  1.0, 0.5, 0.0,  1.0, 0.0, 0.0]);
   var indices = new Uint8Array([0, 1, 2]);

   var o = new Object();
   o.vertexBuffer = initArrayBufferForLaterUse(
                                  gl, vertices, 3, gl.FLOAT);
   o.colorBuffer = initArrayBufferForLaterUse(
                                  gl, colors, 3, gl.FLOAT);
   o.indexBuffer = initElementArrayBufferForLaterUse(
                              gl, indices, gl.UNSIGNED_BYTE);
   if (!o.vertexBuffer||!o.colorBuffer||!o.indexBuffer)
     return null;
   o.numIndices = indices.length;
   gl.bindBuffer(gl.ARRAY_BUFFER, null);
   gl.bindBuffer(gl.ELEMENT_ARRAY_BUFFER, null);
   return o;
}

function initArrayBufferForLaterUse(gl, data, num, type) {
   var buffer = gl.createBuffer();
   gl.bindBuffer(gl.ARRAY_BUFFER, buffer);
   gl.bufferData(gl.ARRAY_BUFFER, data, gl.STATIC_DRAW);
   buffer.num = num;
   buffer.type = type;
   return buffer;
}

function initElementArrayBufferForLaterUse(gl, data, type) {
   var buffer = gl.createBuffer();
   gl.bindBuffer(gl.ELEMENT_ARRAY_BUFFER, buffer);
   gl.bufferData(gl.ELEMENT_ARRAY_BUFFER, data,
                 gl.STATIC_DRAW);
   buffer.type = type;
   return buffer;
}

</script>

</head>
<body onload="WebGLStart();">
   <canvas id="cv" style="border: none;"
           width="500" height="500"></canvas>
   <p id="msg"></p>
</body>

</html>
```

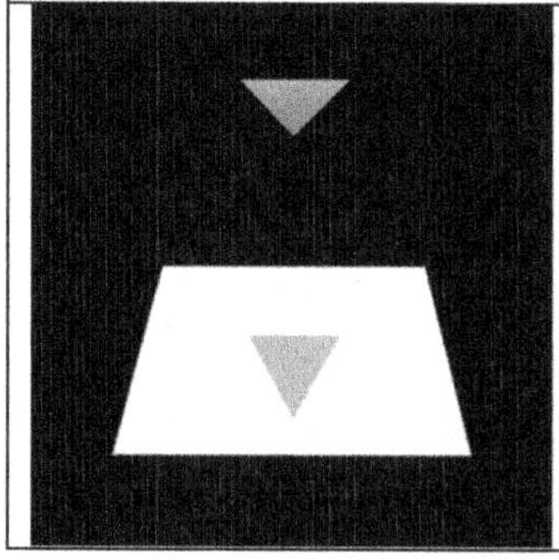

9.6 Mouse Interaction

9.6.1 Rotation

We can rotate an object by dragging the mouse, recording the coordinates and calculating the distances covered.

```
<!DOCTYPE html>
<html>
<head>
<script src="webgl-library.js"></script>

<script id="vs" type="x-shader/x-vertex">
  attribute vec4 p;
  uniform mat4 u_modelMatrix;
  void main(){
    gl_Position = u_modelMatrix * p;
  }
</script>

<script id="fs" type="x-shader/x-fragment">
  precision mediump float;
  void main(){
    gl_FragColor=vec4(1.0,1.0,1.0,1.0);
  }
</script>

<script>

function initEventHandlers(canvas, currentAngle) {
  var dragging = false;
  var lastX = -1, lastY = -1;

  canvas.onmousedown = function(ev) {
    var x = ev.clientX, y = ev.clientY;
```

```
    var rect = ev.target.getBoundingClientRect();
    if (rect.left <= x && x < rect.right &&
        rect.top <= y && y < rect.bottom) {
      lastX = x; lastY = y;
      dragging = true;
    }
  };

  canvas.onmouseup = function(ev) { dragging = false; };

  canvas.onmousemove = function(ev) {
    var x = ev.clientX, y = ev.clientY;
    if (dragging) {
      var factor = 100/canvas.height;
      var dx = factor * (x - lastX);
      var dy = factor * (y - lastY);
      currentAngle[0] = Math.max(Math.min(
                         currentAngle[0] + dy, 90.0), -90.0);
      currentAngle[1] = currentAngle[1] + dx;
    }
    lastX = x, lastY = y;
  };
}

function WebGLStart(){
   var canvas = document.getElementById("myCanvas");
   var gl = canvas.getContext("webgl");
   initShaders(gl,"vs","fs");
   var vertices = new Float32Array([
                  0.0,-0.5,0.0,  -0.5,0.5,0.0,  0.5,0.5,0.0]);
   initArrayBuffer(gl, 'p', vertices, 3);
   gl.clearColor(0.0, 0.0, 0.0, 1.0);
   var u_modelMatrix = gl.getUniformLocation(gl.program,
                                            'u_modelMatrix');
   var modelMatrix = new Matrix4();
   var currentAngle = [0.0, 0.0]; // ([x-axis, y-axis] degrees)
   initEventHandlers(canvas, currentAngle);

   var tick = function() {
   modelMatrix.setIdentity();
   modelMatrix.rotate(currentAngle[0], 1.0, 0.0, 0.0); // x-axis
   modelMatrix.rotate(currentAngle[1], 0.0, 1.0, 0.0); // y-axis
      gl.uniformMatrix4fv(u_modelMatrix,false,
                         modelMatrix.entries);
      gl.clear(gl.COLOR_BUFFER_BIT);
      gl.drawArrays(gl.TRIANGLES,0,3);
      requestAnimationFrame(tick, canvas);
   };
   tick();
}
</script>
</head>

<body onload="WebGLStart()">
  <canvas id="myCanvas" width="500"
height="500"></canvas>
</body>
</html>
```

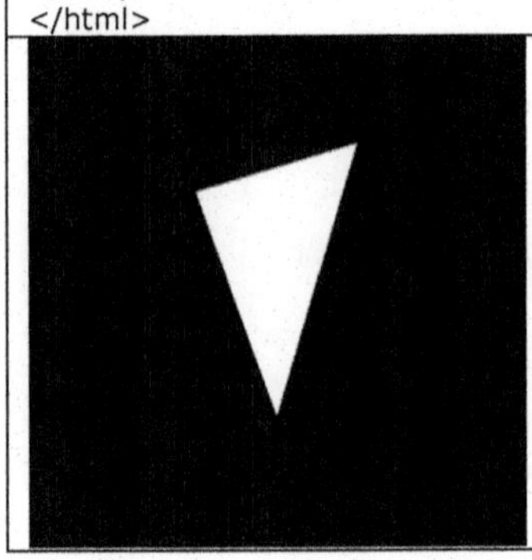

9.6.2 Object Selection

To know if an object has been clicked, we draw the object two times. In the first time, we color the whole object with a specific color. We then check if the pixel clicked is of that specific color. We then quickly draw the object the second time, using the original colors.

To check the color of a pixel, use **readPixels(x,y,width,height,gl.RGBA, gl.UNSIGNED_BYTE,typed_array)**. 'typed_array' must be of the type Uint8Array.

A message pops up when the triangle is clicked. In more complex examples, the camera and the object may be moving, but this has no effect on this technique.

```
<!DOCTYPE html>
<html>
<head>
<script src="webgl-library.js"></script>

<script id="vs" type="x-shader/x-vertex">
  varying vec4 vc;
  uniform bool clicked;
  attribute vec4 p;
  void main(){
    if (clicked){
      vc = vec4(1.0,0.0,0.0,1.0);
    } else {
      vc = vec4(0.0,0.5,0.5,1.0);
    }
    gl_Position = p;
  }
</script>

<script id="fs" type="x-shader/x-fragment">
  precision mediump float;
  varying vec4 vc;
  void main(){
    gl_FragColor=vc;
  }
</script>

<script>

function WebGLStart(){
  var canvas = document.getElementById("myCanvas");
  var gl = canvas.getContext("webgl");
  initShaders(gl,"vs","fs");
  var vertices = new Float32Array([
                 0.0,-0.5,0.0,  -0.5,0.5,0.0,  0.5,0.5,0.0]);
  initArrayBuffer(gl, 'p', vertices, 3);
  gl.clearColor(0.0, 0.0, 0.0, 1.0);
  var u_Clicked = gl.getUniformLocation(gl.program,
                                        'clicked');
  gl.uniform1i(u_Clicked, 0);

  canvas.onmousedown = function(ev) {
    var x = ev.clientX, y = ev.clientY;
    var rect = ev.target.getBoundingClientRect();
    if (rect.left <= x && x < rect.right &&
        rect.top <= y && y < rect.bottom) {
      var x_in_canvas = x - rect.left,
          y_in_canvas = rect.bottom - y;
      var picked =
              check(gl,x_in_canvas,y_in_canvas,u_Clicked);
      if (picked) alert('The triangle was selected! ');
    }
  };

  var tick = function() {
    draw(gl);
    requestAnimationFrame(tick, canvas);
  };
  tick();
```

```
}

function draw(gl) {
  gl.clear(gl.COLOR_BUFFER_BIT);
  gl.drawArrays(gl.TRIANGLES,0,3);
}

function check(gl, x, y, u_Clicked) {
 var picked = false;
 gl.uniform1i(u_Clicked, 1);
 draw(gl);
 var pixels = new Uint8Array(4);
 gl.readPixels(x, y, 1, 1, gl.RGBA,
              gl.UNSIGNED_BYTE, pixels);
 if (pixels[0] == 255) picked = true;
 gl.uniform1i(u_Clicked, 0);
 draw(gl);
 return picked;
}

</script>
</head>

<body onload="WebGLStart()">
  <canvas id="myCanvas" width="500"
                          height="500"></canvas>
</body>
</html>
```

9.6.3 Part Selection

This technique goes one step further by allowing you to select different parts of an object. Each part is numbered, and this information is passed to the vertex shader. Again, the object is drawn twice. In the first pass, the part number is stored in the alpha component of the color variable, allowing you to retrieve it using readPixels() later.

Originally the two triangles were blue. When one of them is clicked, its color changes to white. The white triangle may be switched by clicking the other triangle.

```
<!DOCTYPE html>
<html>
<head>
<script src="webgl-library.js"></script>

<script id="vs" type="x-shader/x-vertex">
  attribute vec4 p;
  attribute float part;
  uniform int pickedPart;
  varying vec4 vc;
  void main(){
    gl_Position = p;
    int pa = int(part);
    vec3 color =
            (pa==pickedPart)?vec3(1.0):vec3(0.0,0.0,1.0);
    if (pickedPart == 0){
      vc = vec4(color, part/255.0);
    } else {
      vc = vec4(color, 1.0);
    }
  }
</script>

<script id="fs" type="x-shader/x-fragment">
  precision mediump float;
  varying vec4 vc;
  void main(){
    gl_FragColor=vc;
  }
</script>

<script>

function WebGLStart(){
  var canvas = document.getElementById("myCanvas");
  var gl = canvas.getContext("webgl");
  initShaders(gl,"vs","fs");

  var vertices = new Float32Array([
          0.0,0.0,0.0,  -0.5, 0.5,0.0,  0.5, 0.5,0.0,
          0.0,0.0,0.0,  -0.5,-0.5,0.0,  0.5,-0.5,0.0 ]);
  initArrayBuffer(gl, 'p', vertices, 3);
  var parts = new Float32Array([
    1.0,1.0,1.0, 2.0,2.0,2.0]);
  initArrayBuffer(gl, 'part', parts, 1);

  gl.clearColor(0.0, 0.0, 0.0, 1.0);
  var pickedPart=
          gl.getUniformLocation(gl.program,'pickedPart');
  gl.uniform1i(pickedPart, -1);

  canvas.onmousedown = function(ev) {
    var x = ev.clientX, y = ev.clientY;
    var rect = ev.target.getBoundingClientRect();
    if (rect.left <= x && x < rect.right &&
       rect.top <= y && y < rect.bottom) {
      var x_in_canvas = x - rect.left,
          y_in_canvas = rect.bottom - y;
      var part = checkPart(
                    gl, x_in_canvas, y_in_canvas, pickedPart);
      gl.uniform1i(pickedPart, part);
      draw(gl);
    }
  }

  var tick = function() {
    draw(gl);
    requestAnimationFrame(tick, canvas);
  };
  tick();
}

function draw(gl) {
  gl.clear(gl.COLOR_BUFFER_BIT);
  gl.drawArrays(gl.TRIANGLES,0,6);
}

function checkPart(gl, x, y, pickedPart) {
 var pixels = new Uint8Array(4);
 gl.uniform1i(pickedPart, 0);
 draw(gl);
 gl.readPixels(x, y, 1, 1, gl.RGBA,
              gl.UNSIGNED_BYTE, pixels);
 return pixels[3];
}

</script>
</head>

<body onload="WebGLStart()">
  <canvas id="myCanvas" width="500"
                          height="500"></canvas>
</body>
</html>
```

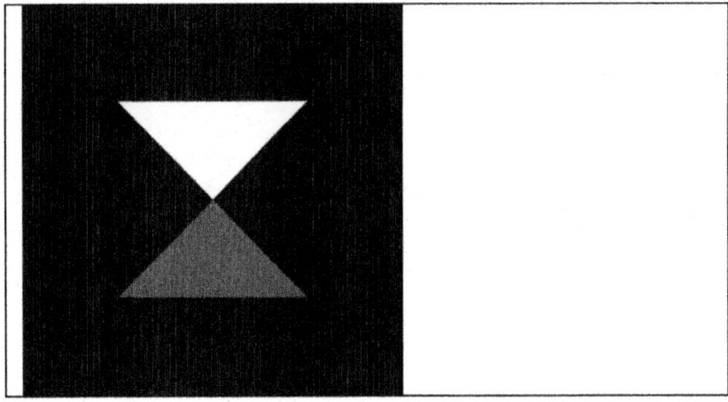

9.7 General Structuring

9.7.1 Head-Up Display (HUD)

To write text, place a 2D canvas on top. The 2D canvas background is transparent by default. You can also make the background of the WebGL canvas transparent by setting the alpha value of the clear color to 0.0.

```
<!DOCTYPE html>
<html>
<head>
<script src="webgl-library.js"></script>

<script id="vs" type="x-shader/x-vertex">
  attribute vec4 p;
  void main(){
    gl_Position = p;
  }
</script>

<script id="fs" type="x-shader/x-fragment">
  precision mediump float;
  void main(){
    gl_FragColor=vec4(1.0,0.0,0.0,1.0);
  }
</script>

<script>

function WebGLStart(){
  var webglCanvas =
                  document.getElementById("webglCanvas");
  var gl = webglCanvas.getContext("webgl");
  var canvas2D = document.getElementById("2DCanvas");
  var hud = canvas2D.getContext("2d");

  initShaders(gl,"vs","fs");
  var vertices = new Float32Array([
    0.0,-0.5,0.0,  -0.5,0.5,0.0,  0.5,0.5,0.0]);
  initArrayBuffer(gl, 'p', vertices, 3);
  gl.clearColor(0.0, 0.0, 0.0, 0.0);
  gl.clear(gl.COLOR_BUFFER_BIT);
  gl.drawArrays(gl.TRIANGLES,0,3);

  hud.font = '40px "Arial"';
  hud.fillStyle = 'rgba(0,255,0,1)';
  hud.fillText('This is a triangle.',100,250);
}
</script>
</head>

<body onload="WebGLStart()">
  <p style="position:relative; top:200px">
  WebGL Canvas and 2D Canvas can work side by side.
  The backgrounds are transparent here.
  </p>
  <canvas id="webglCanvas" width="500" height="500"
    style="position:absolute; left:0px; z-index:0"></canvas>
  <canvas id="2DCanvas" width="500" height="500"
    style="position:absolute; left:0px; z-index:1"></canvas>
</body>
</html>
```

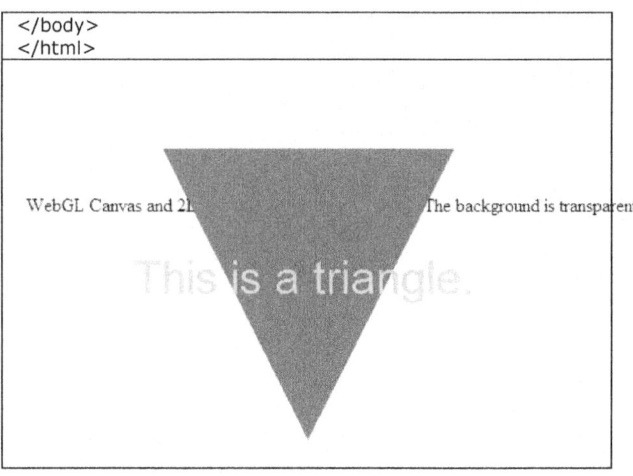

9.7.2 Reading an OBJ File

Complex 3D figures are usually drawn using 3D modeler software such as Blender. Here we shall briefly explain how to export 3D figure data to WebGL.

Let's draw a cube with one side colored in blue. Launch Blender. You will see a cube. Press 'Tab' to change to 'Edit Mode'. Choose 'Face select' at the 3D View bar at the bottom of the screen.

Select the top face of the cube by right-clicking it. Now, at the right panel of the screen, search for the Material icon which is displayed as a circle. Click on it. Then click on the plus sign to add a new material. Next, click on 'New'. Click on the bar below 'Diffuse' and change its color to blue. Click 'Assign'.

After everything is done, go to File -> Export -> Wavefront (.obj), select a file name, and click 'Export OBJ'. You will obtain two files, called 'cube.obj' and 'cube.mtl' here. The documentation for these two file formats can be found at

'http://www.fileformat.info/format/wavefrontobj/egff.htm'
and
'http://www.fileformat.info/format/material/'.

cube.obj	
# Blender v2.69 (sub 0) OBJ File: ''	comment
# www.blender.org	comment
mtllib cube.mtl	use this as the material f.
o Cube	the object name
v 1.00000 -1.00000 -1.00000	vertex 1 of Cube
v 1.00000 -1.00000 1.000000	vertex 2 of Cube
v -1.00000 -1.00000 1.00000	vertex 3 of Cube
v -1.00000 -1.00000 -1.00000	vertex 4 of Cube
v 1.00000 1.00000 -0.99999	vertex 5 of Cube
v 0.99999 1.00000 1.00001	vertex 6 of Cube
v -1.00000 1.00000 1.00000	vertex 7 of Cube
v -1.00000 1.00000 -1.00000	vertex 8 of Cube
usemtl Material	use Material for faces
s off	smoothing group off
f 1 2 3 4	face 1 of Cube
f 1 5 6 2	face 2 of Cube
f 2 6 7 3	face 3 of Cube
f 3 7 8 4	face 4 of Cube
f 5 1 4 8	

usemtl Material.002 f 5 8 7 6	face 5 of Cube use Material.002 for face face 6 of Cube

cube.mtl	
# Blender MTL File: 'None' # Material Count: 2	Comment comment
newmtl Material Ns 96.078431 Ka 0.000000 0.000000 0.000000 Kd 0.640000 0.640000 0.640000 Ks 0.500000 0.500000 0.500000 Ni 1.000000 d 1.000000 illum 2	defines 'Material' weight of specular color ambient color diffuse color specular color optical density transparency illumination model
newmtl Material.002 Ns 96.078431 Ka 0.000000 0.000000 0.000000 Kd 0.000000 0.149642 0.640000 Ks 0.500000 0.500000 0.500000 Ni 1.000000 d 1.000000 illum 2	defines 'Material.002' weight of specular color ambient color diffuse color specular color optical density transparency illumination model

To retrieve these files over the internet, pass these filenames to AJAX calls. Generic functions should be created to translate the data so that they can be passed into buffer objects. Use the JavaScript **split('\n')** function to separate the lines. Among the useful generic parsing functions are:

StringParser.init(str)
StringParser.getWord()
StringParser.skipToNextWord()
StringParser.getInt()
StringParser.getFloat()

9.7.3 Model Matrix Stack

Imagine a more complex scene in which many objects are moving, each according to its own rules. Some of these objects may move together as a group, which in turn may be a member of another group, thus forming a hierarchical tree of objects. For example, a walking man's arms and hands swing as groups. The hands, arms, and the rest of the body, in turn form another major group. We don't want the hands to be detached from the arms and we don't want the arms to be detached from the body.

As another example, satellites rotate around planets, which in turn revolve around the sun. In this case, a planet and its satellites form a group. It is always easier to determine the location of the moon if we can somehow remember the position of the Earth and then use the relative information, instead of re-calculating everything from scratch.

The key to properly drawing a hierarchy of objects lies in implementing a stack of model matrices. Everytime before we progress to a deeper level of hierarchy, we push the current model matrix to a stack. To backtrack, we pop and recall the model matrix. The last pushed matrix is always retrieved first.

Conveniently, JavaScript arrays can be manipulated as a stack using push() and pop().

If we are to animate the solar system, the code should resemble the following.

```
......
var matrixStack = [];
function pushMatrix(m) {
  var m2 = new Matrix4(m);
  matrixStack.push(m2);
}

function popMatrix() {
  return matrixStack.pop();
}

var modelMatrix = new Matrix4();
function drawSolarSystem(){
   draw(sun......);
   pushMairix(modelMatrix);
      modelMatrix.rotate(......);
      modelMatrix.translate(......);
      draw(planet1......);
      pushMatrix(modelMatrix);
         modelMatrix.rotate(......);
         modelMatrix.translate(......);
         draw(satellite1......);
      modelMatrix = popMatrix();
      pushMatrix(modelMatrix);
         modelMatrix.rotate(......);
         modelMatrix.translate(......);
         draw(satellite2......);
      modelMatrix = popMatrix();
   modelMatrix = popMatrix();
   pushMairix(modelMatrix);
      modelMatrix.rotate(......);
      modelMatrix.translate(......);
      draw(planet2......);
      pushMatrix(modelMatrix);
         modelMatrix.rotate(......);
         modelMatrix.translate(......);
         draw(satellite3......);
      modelMatrix = popMatrix();
      pushMatrix(modelMatrix);
         modelMatrix.rotate(......);
         modelMatrix.translate(......);
         draw(satellite4......);
      modelMatrix = popMatrix();
   modelMatrix = popMatrix();
   ......
}
......
```

If the manipulation of a model matrix seems confusing, you may mentally visualize the three axes in a 3D space instead. A translation moves the origin of the three axes. A rotation rotates the three axes. A scaling shrinks or elongates an axis. Using these transformed axes, draw an object, or make a further axes transformation. Popping a model matrix stack will cause the last stored axes to be used.

9.7.4 Lost Context

Information in the shared graphics hardware can be lost when another program takes over the hardware or when the machine hibernates, resulting in a lost display. To circumvent the problem, use **addEventListener(type, handler, useCapture)**. 'type' can be 'webglcontextlost' or 'webglcontextrestored'. 'handler' is the function to call when the event occurs. 'useCapture' specifies whether the event needs to be captured.

```
<!DOCTYPE html>
<html>
<head>
<script src="webgl-library.js"></script>
<script id="vs" type="x-shader/x-vertex">
  attribute vec4 a_Position;
  uniform mat4 u_ModelMatrix;
  void main() {
    gl_Position = u_ModelMatrix * a_Position;
  }
</script>
<script id="fs" type="x-shader/x-fragment">
  void main() {
    gl_FragColor = vec4(1.0, 0.0, 0.0, 1.0);
  }
</script>
<script>

function main() {
  var canvas = document.getElementById("myCanvas");
  canvas.addEventListener('webglcontextlost',
                          contextLost,false);
  canvas.addEventListener('webglcontextrestored',
                     function(ev) { start(canvas); }, false);
  start(canvas);
}

var ANGLE_STEP = 45.0;
var g_currentAngle = 0.0;
var g_requestID;

function start(canvas) {
  var gl = canvas.getContext("webgl");
  initShaders(gl, "vs", "fs");
  var n = initVertexBuffers(gl);
  gl.clearColor(0.0, 0.0, 0.0, 1.0);

  var u_ModelMatrix = gl.getUniformLocation(gl.program,
                                          'u_ModelMatrix');
  var modelMatrix = new Matrix4();
  var tick = function() {
    g_currentAngle = animate(g_currentAngle);
    draw(gl, n, g_currentAngle, modelMatrix, u_ModelMatrix);
    g_requestID = requestAnimationFrame(tick, canvas);
  };
  tick();
}

function contextLost(ev) {
  cancelAnimationFrame(g_requestID);
  ev.preventDefault();
}

function initVertexBuffers(gl) {
  var vertices = new Float32Array ([
    0.0, 0.5,   -0.5, -0.5,   0.5, -0.5
  ]);
  initArrayBuffer(gl,'a_Position',vertices,2);
  return 3;
}

function draw(gl, n, currentAngle, modelMatrix,
                u_ModelMatrix) {
  modelMatrix = new Matrix4();
  modelMatrix.rotate(currentAngle, 0, 0, 1);
  gl.uniformMatrix4fv(u_ModelMatrix, false,
                          modelMatrix.entries);
  gl.clear(gl.COLOR_BUFFER_BIT);
  gl.drawArrays(gl.TRIANGLES, 0, n);
}

var g_last = Date.now();
function animate(angle) {
  var now = Date.now();
  var elapsed = now - g_last;
  g_last = now;
  var newAngle = angle + (ANGLE_STEP * elapsed) / 1000.0;
  return newAngle %= 360;
}

</script>
</head>

<body onload="main()">
  <canvas id="myCanvas" width="500"
                          height="500"></canvas>
</body>
</html>
```

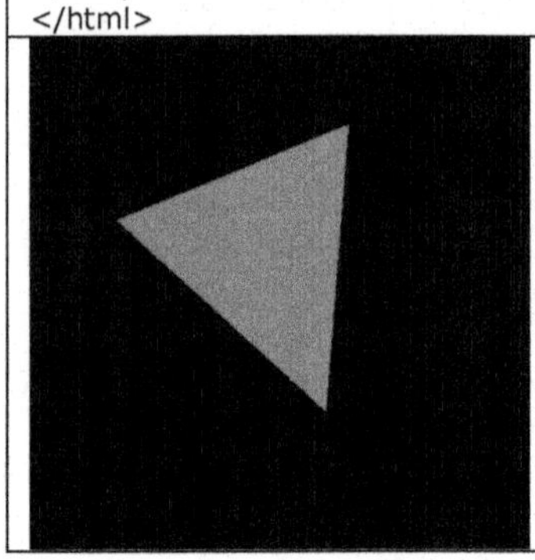

isContextLost() returns true if the context is lost.

9.7.5 Miscellaneous Information

getSupportedExtensions() returns a string containing the supported extensions.

getExtension(name) returns an extension object. 'name' is a string.

getParameter(pname) gets the value of a parameter. 'pname' can be

{ALPHA, RED, GREEN, BLUE, SUBPIXELS}_BITS,
ACTIVE_TEXTURE,
ALIASED_{LINE_WIDTH, POINT_SIZE}_RANGE,
ARRAY_BUFFER_BINDING,
BLEND_DST_{ALPHA, RGB},
BLEND_EQUATION_{ALPHA, RGB},
BLEND_SRC_{ALPHA, RGB},
BLEND[_COLOR],
COLOR_{CLEAR_VALUE, WRITEMASK},
[NUM_]COMPRESSED_TEXTURE_FORMATS,
CULL_FACE[_MODE],
CURRENT_PROGRAM,
DEPTH_{BITS, CLEAR_VALUE, FUNC, RANGE, TEST,
WRITEMASK},
ELEMENT_ARRAY_BUFFER_BINDING,
DITHER,
FRAMEBUFFER_BINDING,
FRONT_FACE,
GENERATE_MIPMAP_HINT,
LINE_WIDTH,
MAX_[COMBINED_]TEXTURE_IMAGE_UNITS
MAX_{CUBE_MAP_TEXTURE, RENDERBUFFER, TEXTURE}_SIZE
MAX_VARYING_VECTORS,
MAX_VERTEX_{ATTRIBS, TEXTURE_IMAGE_UNTIS,
UNIFORM_VECTORS},
MAX_VIEWPORT_DIMS,
PACK_ALIGNMENT,
POLYGON_OFFSET_{FACTOR, FILL, UNITS},
RENDERBUFFER_BINDING,
RENDERER,
SAMPLE_BUFFERS,
SAMPLE_COVERAGE_{INVERT, VALUE},
SAMPLES,
SCISSOR_{BOX, TEST},
SHADING_LANGUAGE_VERSION,
STENCIL_{BITS, CLEAR_VALUE, TEST},
STENCIL_[BACK_]{FAIL, FUNC, REF, VALUE_MASK, WRITEMASK}
STENCIL_[BACK_]PASS_DEPTH_{FAIL,PASS}
TEXTURE_BINDING_{2D, CUBE_MAP},
UNPACK_ALIGNMENT,
UNPACK_{COLORSPACE_CONVERSION_WEBGL, FLIP_Y_WEBGL,
PREMULTIPLY_ALPHA_WEBGL},
VENDOR,
VERSION,
VIEWPORT

9.7.6 Context Attributes

We saw in 9.4.8 that we can pass a second parameter to .getContext(). Here we show the other attributes available.

alpha (true): If true, requests a drawing buffer with an alpha channel.
depth (true): If true, requests a drawing buffer with a depth buffer of at least 16 bits.
stencil (false): If true, requests a stencil buffer of at least 8 bits.
antialias (true): If true, requests a drawing buffer with antialiasing.
premultipliedAlpha (true): If true, requests a drawing buffer which contains colors with premultiplied alpha.
preserveDrawingBuffer (true): If true, requests that contents of the drawing buffer remain in between frames, at potential performance cost.

9.7.7 WebGL 2

WebGL 2 is based on OpenGL ES 3.0. As of 23 Nov 2014, it is not widely supported by browsers, but this may change in the future. Changes include:

- Non-power-of-two texture access
- ETC2 and EAC compressed texture formats
- Pixel buffer objects
- Primitive restart
- Rasterizer discard
- GLSL token size of 1024 characters
- Non-zero vertex attribute divisor

10. Java Applet

An applet is a small application designed to run within another application. While the term "applet" is sometimes used to describe a small program included in a computer's operating system, it usually refers to a small program written in the Java programming language.
While applets can serve as basic desktop applications, they have limited access to system resources and therefore are not ideal as complex programs. However, their small size and cross-platform nature make them suitable as web-based applications. Examples of applets designed to run in web browsers include calculators, drawing programs, animations, and video games. Web-based applets can run in any browser on any operating system as long as the Java plug-in is installed.

The main difference between a stand-alone Java application and a Java applet is that a Java applet is typically executed in an Applet Viewer or a Java-compatible web browser.

JBuilder provides an environment for developing Java programs. The full documentation for the Java API can be found at:

http://docs.oracle.com/javase/7/docs/api/

.

10.1 The Applet Environment

10.1.1 The Applet Class

Every applet is an extension of the java.applet.Applet class. The base Applet class provides methods that may be called to do the following:

- Getting the applet parameters
- Getting the network location of the HTML file
- Printing a status message
- Fetching an image
- Fetching an audio clip
- Playing an audio clip
- Resizing the applet

10.1.2 Advantages and Disadvantages

Some advantages of using applets are:

- Applets are cross-platform and can run on Windows, Mac OS and Linux platforms.
- Applets can work in all versions of Java plug-in.
- Applets run in a sandbox, so the user can trust the code (without any security approval).
- Applets are supported by most web browsers.
- Applets are cached (until the browser closes) in most web browsers, so they will be quick to load when returning to the same web page. Because of this, you may need to restart the browser when you update and upload an applet.
- The user can also have full access to the machine if the user allows it.

Here are a few disadvantages.

- A Java plug-in is required to run an applet.
- A Java applet requires JVM, so for the first time it takes significant time to startup.
- If an applet is not already cached in the machine, it will be downloaded from the internet and that will take time.
- It is difficult to design and build a good user interface in applets compared to HTML technology.

10.1.3 Creating "Hello World.java"

A simple applet that will print "Hello World" when invoked from a browser.

```
import java.applet.*;
import java.awt.*;

public class HelloWorld extends Applet {
  public void init () {
    //this method will be called when the applet is started
  }

  public void stop (){
    //this method will be called when the applet is terminated
  }

  public void paint(Graphics g){
    // String first, then the x and y coordinates.
    g.drawString("Hello world",20,20);
  }
}
```

The import statements at the start of our program bring the classes into the scope of our applet class.

The overridden paint() method appears as

```
public void paint(Graphics g) {
   g.drawString("Hello World",20,20);
}
```

The paint() method receives a reference to an object of the type 'Graphics'. This reference is known locally by the name 'g'.

The Graphics class provides a method named drawString() that is used to "draw" a text string onto the Graphics object at the specified location. The string will be drawn at a location of 20 pixels to the right and 20 pixels down from the top-left corner of the screen space occupied by the applet.

Save the code in a notepad and name it HelloWorld.java (same name as the public class). Now, you have to compile the source code to generate a bytecode file called HelloWorld.class.

If you're using the Java Development Kit, you can compile it by typing 'javac HelloWorld.java' at a command prompt (on Microsoft Windows, this is done within an MS-DOS shell). Check that the .class file was indeed generated.

10.1.4 Life Cycle of an Applet

You create an applet by implementing four methods in the Applet class:

- **init()**: This is called at the very beginning.
- **start()**: This is called after init(), and whenever the user returns from other pages.
- **stop()**: This is called when the user moves off the page.
- **destroy()**: This is called when the browser exits.

10.1.5 Invoking an Applet in HTML

Below is an example that invokes the "Hello World" applet. Create a .html file containing the following code:

HTML code, invoking a Java applet

```
<html>
  <head></head>
  <body>
    <div >
      <object type="application/x-java-applet"
              height="70" width="300" >
        <param name="code" value="HelloWorld"/>
        <param name="codebase" value="."/>
        Your browser does not support the 'object' tag.
      </object>
    </div>
  </body>
</html>
```

Hello world

To refer to a .class file in an html file you will use the <object> tag.

- **type:** The type of the application. Here we indicate that we are going to embed a Java applet.
- **width**: The width of the window pane within which the applet will be displayed.
- **height**: The height of the window pane within which the applet will be displayed.
- **<param name="code">** : The name of the Java bytecode (.class) file to execute.
- **<param name="codeabse">**: The URL (absolute or relative) of the directory containing the code file. If the bytecode file resides on a machine different from that of the HTML file invoking it, the codebase must be the absolute URL of the directory containing this file. Eg.:

  codedebase="http://www.vivids.com/java/assorted/Coalesce/"

  If the bytecode file and the HTML file invoking it reside in different directories on the same machine, the value of the codebase attribute is usually a relative URL. Eg.:

Location of test.class	Location of test.html	Value of the 'codebase' attribute within test.html
/applets/programs/examples	/applets	programs/example
/	/applets	..
/applets	/applets	.

- **<param>:** Additional nested *<param>* elements are optional and can be used to feed data to the applet from the HTML document. An example would be
  <param name="var_color" value="blue">
  The applet would use
  varColor=getParameter("var_color");
  to access the value.

10.1.6 JDK

Java Development Kit contains the software and tools that you need to compile, debug, and run applets and applications that you've written using the Java programming language. JDK has as its primary components a collection of programming tools, including javac, and the archiver, which packages related class libraries into a single JAR file.
Follow the steps below:

1. Download the latest version of JDK from Sun Microsystems.
2. Double-click the installation file and it should open an installer.
3. Click next, then read and accept the license.
4. The next page you encounter should install (and in some cases download) the Java Development Kit.
5. Go to the command prompt and add the Java binary path. For example, on a windows platform, this can be done by:
   path "e:\program files\java\ jdk1.7.0_25\bin";%path%
6. Try typing 'javac'.
   The command prompt should start showing the javac source file information.

10.1.7 Applet Viewer

We generally use web browsers to run applets. It's not mandatory to open a Web browser to run an applet. We can use a Java Applet viewer as well.
An Applet viewer is a command line program that runs Java applets. It is included in the SDK. It helps you to test an applet before you run it in a browser. The Applet viewer runs on the HTML document, and uses embedded <object> tags.

appletviewer <option> <html file>

We can use only one option: -debug that starts the applet viewer in the Java debugger. Using this option we can debug an applet.

Build the java file, and then view your applet by running the following commands
C:\javac>javac Myapplet.java
C:\javac>appletviewer Myapplet.html

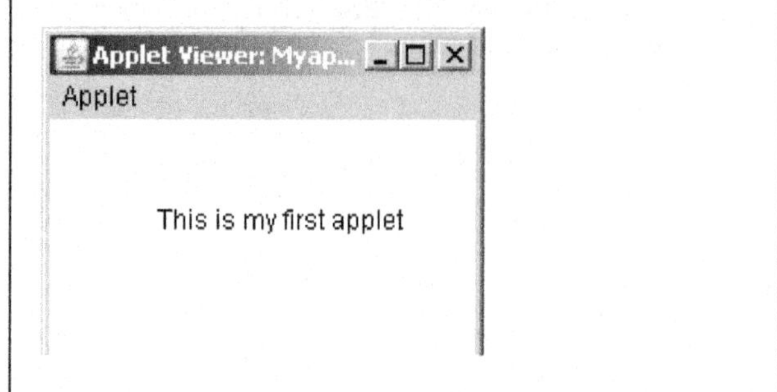

10.1.8 Making a JAR File

The JAR file format is a compressed format used primarily to distribute Java applications and libraries. It is built on the ZIP file format, and functions in a similar way; many files are compressed and packaged together in a single file, making it easy to distribute the files over a network. If you need to package a Java application or library, you can create a JAR file using the Java Development Kit (JDK) at your computer's command prompt.

Prepare your files. Place all the files you want to include in the JAR file inside a single folder. They will need to be referenced through a single command line, so specifying separate paths is not feasible.

Open the command prompt. This can be done by clicking on **Start** and then **Run.** Type "cmd" into the text box and click the "OK" button.

Navigate to the folder where you stored your files.

- To navigate deeper into the hard drive, use the "change directory" command by typing "cd."
- For example, if your files are stored at "C:\myfiles," then you should type "cd \myfiles."

Set the path to the directory of the JDK bin. You will need to run the jar.exe utility to create a JAR file, and that file is located in the bin directory.

- Use the "path" command to specify the JDK bin directory. For example, if you installed JDK to the default location, you would type: path "e:\program files\java\ jdk1.7.0_25\bin";%path%
- If you aren't sure of the exact directory, navigate to it in Windows Explorer and take note of the directory's full path.

Create the JAR file. The format of the command line for creating the JAR file looks like this:
"jar cf <jar-file> <input-file(s)>"

- The "jar" portion refers to the jar.exe program, which compiles the JAR file.
- The "c" option specifies that you want to create a JAR file.
- The "f" option means that you want to specify the filename.
- The "jar-file" portion is where you should type the name that you want the file to have.

- "input-file(s)" is a space-separated list of all the files to be included in the JAR file.

- For example, you might type "jar cf myjar.jar manifest.txt myclass.class". This would create a JAR file with the filename "myjar.jar" which would include the files "manifest.txt" and "myclass.class."

- If you add directories to the JAR file, the jar.exe utility will automatically add their contents.

10.1.9 Using a JAR File

If the applet is bundled as a JAR file, the only thing you need to do differently is to use the archive parameter to specify the relative path of a jar file.

If the HelloWorld.class is packaged in a JAR file named HelloWorld.jar, you can modify the HTML file with the addition of an archive parameter:

```
<object type="application/x-java-applet"
        height="70" width="300">
  <param name="code" value="HelloWorld.class"/>
  <param name="archive" value="HelloWorld.jar"/>
  <param name="codebase" value="."/>
</object>
```

'archive' specifies the relative path to the JAR file that contains HelloWorld.class.

10.1.10 Passing Parameters

A Java applet can retrieve the parameter values passed from the HTML page.

The <param> tag is used in the HTML file to pass parameters to the applet.

<param name="var" value="Hello">

The value of a parameter passed to an applet can be retrieved using the getParameter() function. E.g.:

String strParameter = this.getParameter("varname");

```
import java.applet.*;
import java.awt.*;

public class appletParameter extends Applet {
  private String strDefault = "Applet Programming";
  public void paint(Graphics g) {
    String strParameter = this.getParameter("message");
    if (strParameter == null) strParameter = strDefault;
    g.drawString(strParameter, 50, 25);
  }
}
```

```
<html>
  <head></head>
  <body>
    <div >
      <object type="application/x-java-applet"
        height="300" width="300">
        <param name="code"
                value="appletParameter.class"/>
        <param name="codebase" value="."/>
        <param name="message" value="Welcome"/>
      </object>
    </div>
  </body>
</html>
```

Welcome

It is often useful to be able to pass parameters from a HTML page to an applet. This allows us to modify the action of an applet without actually having to re-code or re-compile the applet.

10.2 Basic Syntax

10.2.1 Variables and Primitive Types

A variable is a container that holds a value. To be able to use a variable it needs to be declared first. Declaring a variable is normally the first thing that happens in any program.

a) Declcaration. To declare a variable in Java, all that is needed is the data type followed by the variable name. Eg.:

String myName;

In the above example, a variable called "myName" has been declared with a data type of String.

b) Initialization. Before a variable can be used it must be given an initial value. This is called initializing the variable. Eg.:

myName = "Java Applet";

```
byte b1 = 127,             // 1-byte integer
     b2 = 0b10,            //  binary integer
     b3 = 07,              //  octal integer
     b4 = 0x1a;            //  hexadecimal integer
short s = 32767;           // 2-byte integer
int i = 2147483647;        // 4-byte integer
long l = 9223372036854775807L;   // 8-byte integer
float f = 3.141f;          // 4-byte floating point
double d = 3.14159;        // 8-byte floating point
boolean bl = true;         // true or false; the default is false.
char c = 'x';              // 2-byte Unicode
String s = "Hello"         // a String
```

Special characters	
\n	Newline
\r	Carriage return
\f	Formfeed
\b	Backspace
\s	Space
\t	Tab
\"	Double quote
\'	Single quote
\\	Backslash
\ddd	Octal character
\uxxxx	Hexadecimal Unicode character

c) Location and Scope. There are two kinds of variables in Java applets:

- **Instance variables** are declared in a class, outside any block. They are visible within the class.
- **Local variables** are declared inside the methods in a class. They are destroyed once the method exits.

```
import java.awt.Font;
import javax.swing.*;
import java.awt.*;
public class InstanceVariables extends JApplet {
  String fruit; //instance variable declared outside all methods
  String season;
  public void paint( Graphics g ){
    fruit = "Favorite fruit";
    season = "Favorite season";
    g.setColor( Color.RED );
    g.drawString( fruit, 30, 45 );
    g.setColor( new Color( 12,34,52) );
    g.drawString( season, 30, 80 );
  }
}
```

```
import java.awt.Font;
import javax.swing.*;
import java.awt.*;
public class LocalVariables extends JApplet {
  public void paint( Graphics g ){
    String fruit; //local variable declared inside a method.
    String season;
    fruit = "Favorite fruit";
    season = "Favorite season";
    g.setColor( Color.RED );
    g.drawString( fruit, 30, 45 );
    g.setColor( new Color( 12,34,52) );
    g.drawString( season, 30, 80 );
  }
}
```

10.2.2 Methods

A Java method is a collection of statements that are grouped together for an operation to be performed. It is used to make code easier to read. It also makes sure that no code is duplicated.

In general, a method definition has the following syntax:

```
modifiers returnType methodName(list of parameters) {
   // Method body;
}
```

```
import java.awt.Font;
import java.awt.Graphics;
import java.awt.*;
import javax.swing.*;

public class Calculate extends JApplet {
  public void paint (Graphics g ) {
    int addition = add(2, 7);
    String added = "2 + 7 = " + addition;
    g.drawString ( added, 0, 12 );
    String subtracted = "2 - 7 = " + subtract(2, 7 );
    g.drawString ( subtracted, 0, 24 );
  }
  public int add( int num1, int num2 ) {
    return num1 + num2;
  }
  public int subtract( int n1, int n2 ) {
    return n1 - n2;
  }
}
```

10.2.3 Operators

a) Comparison Operators:

Operators	Meaning
<	Strictly less than
<=	Less than or equal to
>	Strictly greater than
>=	Greater than or equal to
==	Equal to
!=	Not equal to

b) Arithmetic Operators

Operator	Meaning	Example
+	Addition	a + b
-	Subtraction	a - b
*	Multiplication	a * b
/	Division	a / b
%	Modulo	a % b
+	Unary Plus	+4
-	Unary Minus	-4

```
import java.applet.Applet;
import java.awt.Button;
import java.awt.Graphics;
import java.awt.TextField;
import java.awt.event.ActionEvent;
import java.awt.event.ActionListener;

public class SumTwoNum extends Applet implements

ActionListener{
  TextField Num1, Num2, Num3;
  Button Sum;
  String total = "";
  public void init(){
    Num1 = new TextField(10); add(Num1);
    Num2 = new TextField(10); add(Num2);

    Sum = new Button("SUM"); add(Sum);
    Num3 = new TextField(10); add(Num3);
    Num3.setText("Result");
    Sum.addActionListener(this);
  }
  public void actionPerformed(ActionEvent e) {
    int tot;
    tot=Integer.parseInt(Num1.getText()) +
         Integer.parseInt(Num2.getText());
    total = " "+ tot;
    Num3.setText(total);
    repaint();
  }
}
```

Applet Viewer: SumTwoNum

Applet

111 222 SUM

333

Precedence of Arithmetic Operators

Highest to Lowest	Operator
1	*, /, %
2	+, -

c) Increment and Decrement Operators

Operator	Meaning and Example
x++	Post-increment adds 1 to the value. The value is returned before the increment is made. Example: a = 1; b = a++; After the execution of the statements above, the value of a is 2 and the value of b is 1.
x--	Post-decrement subtracts 1 from the value. The value is returned before the decrement is made. Example: a = 1; b = a--; After the execution of the statements above, the value of a is 0 and the value of b is 1.
++x	Pre-increment adds 1 to the value. The value is returned after the increment is made. Example: a = 1; b = ++a; After the execution of the statements above, the value of a is 2 and the value of b is 2.
--x	Pre-decrement subtracts 1 from the value. The value is returned after the decrement is made. Example: a = 1; b = --a; After the execution of the statements above, the value of a is 0 and the value of b is 0.

d) Assignment Operators

Operator	Meaning and Example
=	Assignment operation. Example: a = b b is evaluated and a set to this value.
+=, -=, *=, /=, %=	Arithmetic operation and then assignment. Example: a -= b is equivalent to a = a - b
&=, |=, ^=	Bitwise operation and then assignment. Example: a &= b is equivalent to a = a & b
<<=, >>=, >>>=	Shift operation and then assignment. Example: a <<= b is equivalent to a = a << b

e) Boolean Operators

Boolean Operators	Meaning
a && b	Conditional AND. If both a and b are true, the result is true. If either is false, the result is false. If a is false then b is not evaluated.
a || b	Conditional OR. If either is true, the result is true. If a is true, b is not evaluated.
! a	Boolean NOT. If a is true, the result is false. If a is false, the result is true.

f) Bitwise Operators

Bitwise Operators	Meaning
~varName	Compliment - Change all zeros to ones and ones to zeros.
var1 & var2	And - And each bit of var1 with the corresponding bit in var2.
var1 | var2	OR - Or each bit of var1 with the corresponding bit in var2.
var1 ^ var2	XOR - XOR each bit of var1 with the corresponding bit in var2.
x << y	Shift left - Shift x to the left by y bits. High-order bits are lost. Zero bits fill in the right bits. 0b111100 << 2 gives 0b11110000.
x >> y	Shift right - Shift x to the right by y bits. Low-order bits are lost. Zero bits fill in the left bits. 0b111100 >> 2 gives 0b1111.

g) Class and Object Operators

Below are the classes and object operators available in java.

Class & Object Operators	Meaning
a instanceOf b	Class test operator - If a is an instance of class/subclass/interface/sub-interface b, then true is returned.
new a(args)	Class instantiation - Creates an instance of the class a using the constructor a(args). .
class.member	Class member access - Accesses a method or field of a class or object : Eg. o.f - field access for object o. o.m() - method access for object o.
( )	Method invocation - Parentheses after a method name invokes (i.e. calls) the code for the method, E.g. o.m(), o.m(x,y) .
(className)	Object cast - Treats an object as the type of class or interface a. Eg. a a1=(a)a2; Treat a2 as an instance of class or interface a.
+	String concatenation – This joins two strings. E.g. String a = "123"; String b = "456"; String c = a + b; results in c holding "123456". If either a or b in (a + b) is a string, concatenation to a string will occur. Primitives will be converted to strings and the toString() methods of objects will be called. (This is the only case of operator overloading in Java.) The equivalence operator "+=" will also perform string concatenation.

h) Conditional Operator

This operator has the form 'condition?value1:value2'. If *condition* evaluates to true, value1 will be returned. If *condition* evaluates to false, value2 will be returned.

10.2.4 Conversion of Data

Two kinds of data conversions are common:

- **String-to-Number:** To convert a string to an integer we use **parseInt(String)**. To convert a string to a double we use **parseDouble(String)**. Eg.:

  to=Integer.parseInt(Num1.getText());
- **Number-to-String:** We can convert a number to a String with **valueOf(number)**. Eg.:

```
to=String.valueOf(100);
```

10.2.5 Conditional Execution

a) If Statements:

The **if** statement has the following form. Syntax:

if (*boolean-expression*) {
  then-clause
}

Here,

- 'boolean-expression' is an expression that can be true or false.
- 'then-clause' is a sequence of statements. If there is only one statement in the sequence then the surrounding braces may be omitted. The then-clause statements are executed only if the boolean-expression is true.

```
void applyBrakes() {
  // the "if" clause: bicycle must be moving
  if (isFast){
   // the "then" clause: decrease current speed
      currentSpeed--;
   }
}
```

b) If-else Statements:

The **if-then-else** statement provides an alternative path of execution when an "if" clause evaluates to false.

Syntax:
if(*boolean-expression*){
//Executes when the boolean expression is true
}**else**{
//Executes when the boolean expression is false
}

```
void applyBrakes() {
   if (isFast){
      currentSpeed--;
   } else {
      currentSpeed++;
   }
}
```

c) Extended If-else Statements:

An if statement can be followed by an optional **else if...else** statement, which is very useful to test many conditions witin a single statement.

The extended if-else form has the syntax:

```
if(Boolean_expression 1){
  //Executes when the Boolean expression 1 is true
}else if(Boolean_expression 2){
  //Executes when the Boolean expression 2 is true
}else if(Boolean_expression 3){
  //Executes when the Boolean expression 3 is true
}else {
  //Executes when none of the above is true.
}
```

```
import java.awt.*;
import java.applet.Applet;
import java.awt.event.*;

public class AgeSpecificGreetingApplet extends Applet
                                        implements ActionListener {

  // The string variable for the greeting.
  String greeting;

  // The text fields in which the user enter strings.
  TextField nameField;
  TextField ageField;

  public void init (){
    // GUI stuff
    setLayout (new BorderLayout());
    Panel bottomPanel = new Panel ();

    Label nameLabel = new Label ("Name: ");
    bottomPanel.add (nameLabel);
    nameField = new TextField (15);
    bottomPanel.add (nameField);
    Label ageLabel = new Label (" Age: ");
    bottomPanel.add (ageLabel);
    ageField = new TextField (2);
    bottomPanel.add (ageField);
    Button doneButton = new Button ("Press when done");
    bottomPanel.add (doneButton);
    doneButton.addActionListener (this);
    add (bottomPanel, BorderLayout.SOUTH);
    greeting = "";
  }


 // This method is called when the button is clicked.

  public void actionPerformed (ActionEvent click){
    // Retrieve the strings from the two text fields:
    String name = nameField.getText ();
    int age = new Integer
                  (ageField.getText().trim()).intValue();

    if (age < 2) {
      greeting = "Coo coo, little baby " + name;
    } else if (age < 10) {
      greeting = "Yo, kid, what's up?";
    } else if (age < 17) {
      greeting = "Hi " + name +  ", how's school these days?";
    }  else {
      greeting = "Good day " + name + "!";
    }

    // Redraw the applet:
    repaint ();
  }

 public void paint (Graphics g) {
    // The Face, as before:
    g.drawOval (40,40, 120,150);         // Head
    g.drawOval (57,75, 30,20);           // Left eye
    g.drawOval (110,75, 30,20);          // Right eye
    g.fillOval (68,81, 10,10);           // pupil (left)
    g.fillOval (121,81, 10,10);          // pupil (right)
    g.drawOval (85,100, 30,30);          // Nose
    g.fillArc (60,125,80,40, 180,180);   // Mouth
    g.drawOval (25,92, 15,30);           // Left ear
    g.drawOval (160,92, 15,30);          // Right ear

    // Draw the greeting:
    g.drawString (greeting, 190,150);
  }
}
```

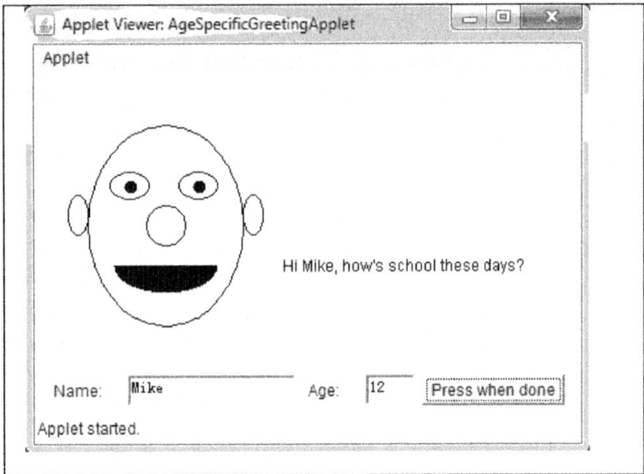

d) Switch

A switch statement allows a variable to be tested for equality against a list of values. Syntax:

switch(*expression*){
    case *value* :
        //Statements
        break; //optional
    case *value* :
        //Statements
        break; //optional
    //You can have any number of cases
    default : //Optional
        //Statements
}

```
switch(x){
   case 1:
      y = 1;
   break; case 2:
      y = 2;
   break; case 3:
      y = 3;
   break; default:
      y = 0;
}
```

10.2.6 Repetition

For a loop, the number of iterations is controlled by a boolean expression. The boolean expression is evaluated before each iteration (pre-test) in while loops and for loops, and after each iteration (post-test) in do-while loops. When the boolean expression becomes false the loop is terminated.

a)For Loops

The for loop is a pre-test loop statement. It has the following form.

for (*initialization*; *boolean-expression*; *increment*) {
        nested-statements
}

Here,

- *initialization* is an expression (usually an assignment expression).
- *boolean-expression* is an expression that can be true or false.
- *increment* is a statement that is executed at the end of each iteration.
- *nested-statements* is a sequence of statements. If there is only one statement then the braces may be omitted.

```
import java.awt.*;
import java.applet.Applet;
import java.awt.event.*;

public class ForLoop extends Applet {
  public void paint (Graphics g) {
     for (int x=0; x<=90; x+=30) {
        g.drawLine (x,0, x,90);
     }
    for (int y=0; y<=90; y+=30) {
       g.drawLine (0,y, 90,y);
   }
  }
}
```

b)While Loops

The while loop is a pre-test loop statement. It has the following form.

while (*boolean-expression*) {
        nested-statements
}

Here,

- *boolean-expression* is an expression that can be true or false.
- *nested-statements* is a sequence of statements. If there is only one statement then the braces can be omitted.

```
import java.awt.*;
import java.applet.Applet;
import java.awt.event.*;

public class WhileLoop extends Applet {
  public void paint (Graphics g) {
     int x = 0;
     while (x <= 240) {
       g.drawLine (x,0, x,240);
       x = x + 30;
     }
     int y = 0;
     while (y <= 240) {
       g.drawLine (0,y, 240,y);
       y = y + 30;
     }
  }
}
```

c)Do-While Loops
The do-while loop is a post-test loop statement. It has the following form.

do {
nested-statements
} **while** (*boolean-expression*);

Here,

- *nested-statements* is a sequence of statements. If there is only one statement then the braces may be omitted.
- *boolean-expression* is an expression that can be true or false.

10.2.7 Arrays

An array is a sequence of variables of the same data type (homogenous). The data type can be any of Java's primitive types or a class (user-defined type). Each variable in the array is an element. We use an index to specify the position of each element in the array. Array indexes always begin with zero.

In Java Arrays are objects, so they need to be declared and instantiated. Elements get default values inside the array, just as they do during normal instantiation.

Examples:

```
int[] array = {1,2,3,4,5};
Auto[] array = {new Auto()};
double [] dailyTemps;
String [] cdTracks;
boolean [] answers;
int [] cs101, bio201; // two integer arrays
dailyTemps = new double[365]; // 365 elements
cdTracks = new String[15]; // 15 elements
int numberOfQuestions = 30;
answers = new boolean[numberOfQuestions];
cars = new Auto[3]; // 3 elements
cs101 = new int[5]; // 5 elements
bio201 = new int[4]; // 4 elements
```

```
import java.awt.*;
import java.applet.*;

public class Array extends Applet{
   int Boxes[];      // Declare an array of integers

   public void init () {
      resize (320, 50);
      Boxes = new int[5];
      for ( int i=0; i<5; i++ ){
          Boxes[i] = 0;
      }
      Boxes[2] = 1;
      Boxes[4] = 1;
   }

   public void paint( Graphics g ){
      for ( int i = 0; i<5; i++ ){
         if (Boxes[i] == 1 ) {
            g.drawString ( "X", i*60 , 25 );
         } else {
            g.drawString ( "O", i*60 , 25 );
         }
      }
   }
}
```

O O X O X

10.2.8 Exceptions

Exceptions are the customary way in Java to indicate to a calling method that an abnormal condition has occurred.

An exception can occur for many different reasons, including the following:

- A user has entered invalid data.
- A file that needs to be opened cannot be found.
- A network connection has been lost in the middle of communication
- The JVM has run out of memory.

Syntax:

```
try {
  //Run some code here
} catch(err) {
  //Handle errors here
}
```

```
import java.awt.*;
import java.applet.Applet;
import java.util.*;
import java.awt.event.*;

public class ExceptionDemo extends Applet  implements
                                                    ActionListener {
  private TextField stringField, resultField;
  private Label resultLabel, stringLabel;
  public void init()  {
    stringLabel = new Label("Type an integer: ");
    resultLabel = new Label("Answer: ");
    stringField = new TextField(20);
    resultField = new TextField(20);
    resultField.setEditable(false);

     add(stringLabel); add(stringField);
     stringField.addActionListener(this);
     add(resultLabel); add(resultField);
  }

  public void actionPerformed(ActionEvent event) {
    if (event.getSource() == stringField) {
      try{
        int number = Integer.parseInt(stringField.getText());
        resultField.setText("Doubled value is "+(2*number));
      } catch (NumberFormatException e) {
        resultField.setText("Error in number: retype ");
      }
    }
  }
}
```

Applet Viewer: ExceptionDemo....
Applet
Type an integer: a
Answer: Error in number: retype
Applet started.

10.2.9 Objects

An object is a software bundle of related states (variable fields) and behaviors (function methods). Software objects are often used to model the real-world objects that you find in everyday life.

In the next topic we will see how to create classes. In OOP an instance of a class is known as an object.

10.2.10 Classes

Till now, we have been using the built-in classes like Color, Text, Buttons etc. Now we will create our own class and use it in the main applet class.

Classes can be very useful when you create large applets because you can organize a lot of the application's complexity in the inner class files.

The benefits of breaking your code into smaller pieces are that the code will be more maintainable, testable, resusable etc.

```
import java.awt.*;
import java.awt.Color;
import java.awt.Graphics;
import javax.swing.*;

public class MyShape extends JPanel {
  public void paintComponent(Graphics g) {
    int x[] = { 70, 150, 190, 80, 100 };
    int y[] = { 80, 110, 160, 190, 100 };
    g.drawPolygon (x, y, 5);
    int x1[] = { 210, 280, 330, 210, 230 };
    int y1[] = { 70, 110, 160, 190, 100 };
    g.setColor(Color.red);
    g.fillPolygon (x1, y1, 5);
  }
}
```

```
import java.awt.*;
import javax.swing.*;

public class DrawShape  extends JApplet {
  MyShape s;
  JButton button;
  public void init( ) {
    rect1 = new rect( );
    rect1.setPreferredSize( new Dimension( 400,400 ) );
    button = new JButton( " My Shape!" );
    setLayout( new FlowLayout( ) );
    add(button);
    add(s);
  }
}
```

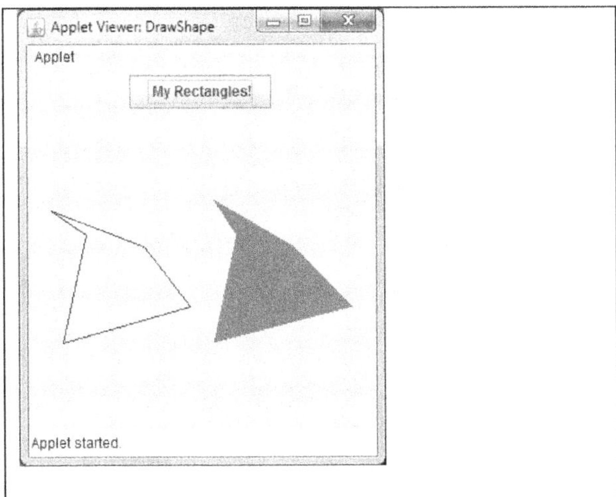

10.2.11 Inheritance

The extension of a class is called inheritance.

The new class inherits all the variables, constants, and methods from the parent class. The class header specifies that it extends another class.

```
import java.awt.*;
import java.applet.Applet;

public class ShapesApplet extends Applet{
   private Shape s;
   private Circle c;
   private Rectangle r;

   public void init () {
      s = new Shape (Color.blue, 50, 100);
      c = new Circle (Color.red,100, 100, 30);
      r = new Rectangle (Color.green, 200, 100, 60, 40);
   }
   public void paint (Graphics g) {
      s.drawShape (g);
      s = c;
      s.drawShape (g);
      s = r;
      s.drawShape (g);
   }
}
```

```
import java.awt.Color;
import java.awt.Graphics;

public class Shape {
   protected Color color;
   protected int x, y;

   Shape (Color c, int xPosition, int yPosition)  {
      color = c;
      x = xPosition;
      y = yPosition;
   } // constructor
   public void drawShape (Graphics g)  {
      g.setColor (color);
      g.drawString ("Shape", x, y);
   }
}
```

```
import java.awt.Color;
import java.awt.Graphics;

public class Circle extends Shape {
   private int radius;
   Circle (Color c, int x, int y, int r)    {
      super (c, x, y);
      radius = r;
   } // constructor
   public void drawShape (Graphics g)  {
      g.setColor (color);
      g.fillOval (x, y, 2*radius, 2*radius);
   }
}
```

```
import java.awt.Color;
import java.awt.Graphics;

class Rectangle extends Shape {
   private int width, height;
   Rectangle (Color c, int x, int y, int w, int h)  {
      super (c, x, y);
      width = w;
      height = h;
   } // constructor
   public void drawShape (Graphics g)  {
      g.setColor (color);
      g.fillRect (x, y, width, height);
   }
}
```

Applet

10.2.12 Modifiers

Access Control Modifiers

Java provides a number of access modifiers to set the access levels for classes, variables, methods and constructors:

- No modifier . Visible to the package.
- **Private**: Visible to the class only.
- **Public**: Visible to the world.
- **Protected**: Visible to the package and all subclasses.

Non Access Modifiers

Java provides a number of non-access modifiers to achieve other functionalities.

- The **static** modifier indicates that the member exists independently. Only a single copy of a static variable exists regardless of the number of instantiations. Local variables cannot be static. A static method does not take in non-static instance variables. Static members can be referenced as in the following:
  ClassName.fieldName or
  ClassName.methodName()
- The **final** modifier indicates that something cannot be changed. A final variable cannot be reassigned another value after the initial initialization. A final method cannot be overridden in a subclass. A final class cannot be inherited.
- The **abstract** modifier indicates that something is to be inherited. An abstract method does not have any implementation within the class. The implementation is given by a subclass. An abstract method must exist within an abstract class. A subclass that extends an abstract class must implement all the abstract methods unless the subclass is abstract too.
- The **synchronized** modifier indicates that a method can only be accessed by one thread at a time.
- The **transient** modifier indicates that a variable will not be included when the object is serialized.
- The **volatile** modifier indicates that a thread accessing the variable must always merge the private copy with the master copy.

```
import java.applet.*;
import java.awt.*;

public class Modifiers extends Applet {
  private Car c;
  public void paint(Graphics g){
    c = new Car("BDN1768");
    g.drawString(c.getVehicleDescription(),20,20);
  }
}
```

```
abstract class Vehicle {
  String Number;
  protected abstract String getVehicleDescription();
}
```

```
class Car extends Vehicle{
  private final static String Type="Car";
  Car(String cn){
    Number=cn;
  }
  public String getVehicleDescription(){
    return Type+": "+Number;
  }
}
```

Applet Viewer: Modifiers
Applet
Car: BDN1768

10.2.13 Interface

An interface is purely a collection of abstract methods. It does not contain any constructor and cannot be instantiated. The fields in an interface must be static and final. A class sometimes 'implements' multiple interfaces. An interface sometimes 'extends' multiple interfaces.

```
// InterfaceDemo.java
import java.applet.*;
import java.awt.*;

public class InterfaceDemo extends Applet {
  private Individual x;
  public void paint(Graphics g){
    x = new
        Individual("English","White","USA","Male","Mike",30);
    g.drawString(x.getName()+", "+x.getAge(),20,20);
  }
}
```

```
// Individual.java
public class Individual implements Person{
  private String language,skinColor,location,sex,name;
  private int age;
  Individual(String g, String k, String l, String s, String n,
                                                        int a){
    language=g;
    skinColor=k;
    location=l;
    sex=s;
    name=n;
    age=a;
  }
  public String getLanguage(){return language;}
  public String getSkinColor(){return skinColor;}
  public String getLocation(){return location;}
  public String getSex(){return sex;}
  public String getName(){return name;}
  public int getAge(){return age;}
}
```

```
// Person.java
public interface Person extends Race, Nationality{
  abstract String getSex();
  abstract String getName();
  abstract int getAge();
}
```

```
// Race.java
public interface Race{
  abstract String getLanguage();
```

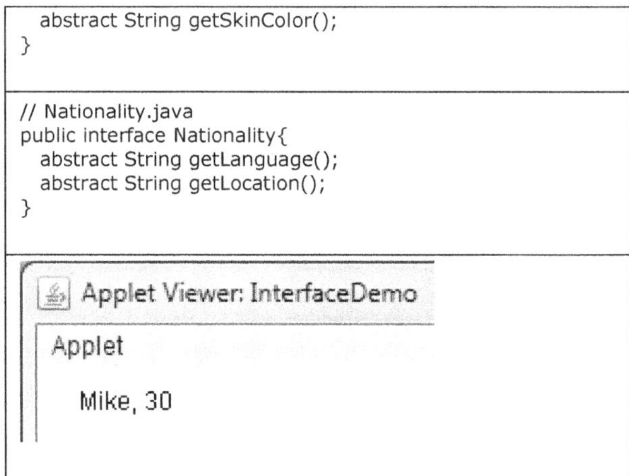

```
  abstract String getSkinColor();
}
```

```
// Nationality.java
public interface Nationality{
  abstract String getLanguage();
  abstract String getLocation();
}
```


10.2.14 Package

You may create and 'import' your own package by placing all the relevant classes and interfaces within a directory, and adding the the 'package' line at the beginning of each of them.

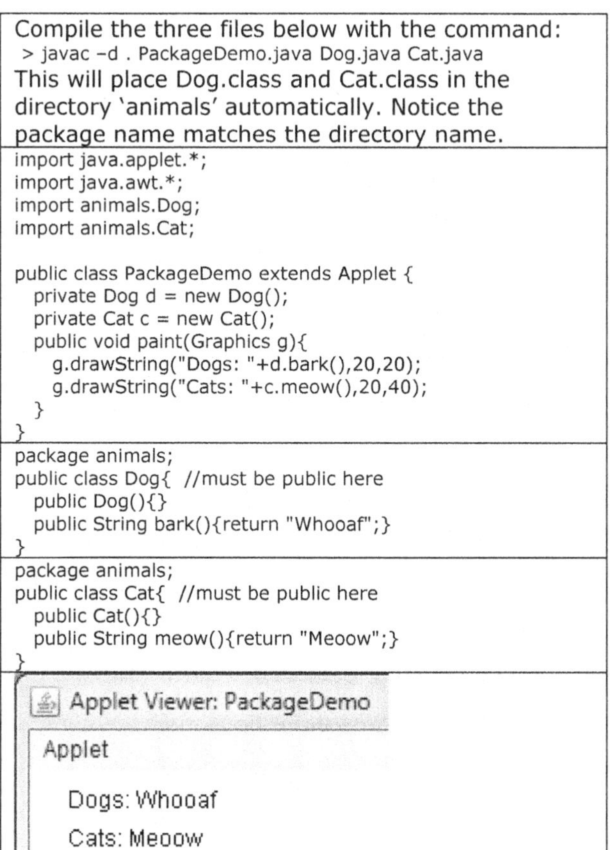

Compile the three files below with the command:
> javac -d . PackageDemo.java Dog.java Cat.java
This will place Dog.class and Cat.class in the directory 'animals' automatically. Notice the package name matches the directory name.

```
import java.applet.*;
import java.awt.*;
import animals.Dog;
import animals.Cat;

public class PackageDemo extends Applet {
  private Dog d = new Dog();
  private Cat c = new Cat();
  public void paint(Graphics g){
    g.drawString("Dogs: "+d.bark(),20,20);
    g.drawString("Cats: "+c.meow(),20,40);
  }
}
```

```
package animals;
public class Dog{  //must be public here
  public Dog(){}
  public String bark(){return "Whooaf";}
}
```

```
package animals;
public class Cat{  //must be public here
  public Cat(){}
  public String meow(){return "Meoow";}
}
```


10.3 Media

The origin (0,0) is at the upper-left corner. All pixel values are integers.

10.3.1 Fonts

To draw text of a particular font on the screen, first you need to create an instance of the Font class. To create an individual Font object, pass three arguments to the Font constructor.

```
import java.awt.Font;
import java.awt.Graphics;

public class Fonts extends java.applet.Applet {
  public void init(){}
  public void stop(){}
  public void paint(Graphics g) {
    Font f1 = new Font("TimesRoman", Font.PLAIN, 18);
    Font f2 = new Font("TimesRoman", Font.BOLD, 18);
    Font f3 = new Font("TimesRoman", Font.ITALIC, 18);
    Font f4 = new Font("TimesRoman", Font.BOLD+
                                     Font.ITALIC, 18);
    g.setFont(f1);
    g.drawString("This is a plain font", 10, 25);
    g.setFont(f2);
    g.drawString("This is a bold font", 10, 50);
    g.setFont(f3);
    g.drawString("This is an italic font", 10, 75);
    g.setFont(f4);
    g.drawString("This is a bold italic font", 10, 100);
  }
}
```

This is a plain font
This is a bold font
This is an italic font
This is a bold italic font

You can find out some basic information about fonts and font objects by using the simple methods of the Font class. The methods of the Font object include:

getName() returns the name of the font as a string.

getSize() returns the current font size (an integer).

getStyle() returns the current style of the font as an integer (0 is plain. 1 is bold. 2 is italic. 3 is bold italic.)

isPlain() returns true if the font's style is plain.

isBold() returns true if the font's style is bold.

isItalic() returns true if the font's style is italic.

10.3.2 Colors

Java uses a 24-bit color system, wherein a color is represented as a combination of red, green, and blue values. Each component of the color can have a number between 0 and 255. 0,0,0 is black; 255,255,255 is white etc.

To draw an object in a particular color, you must create an instance of the Color class to represent that color. To set the current color use the setColor() method.

```
g.setColor(Color.green)
```

Java defines thirteen predefined colors. They are: BLACK, BLUE, CYAN, DARK_GRAY, GRAY, GREEN, LIGHT_GRAY, MAGENTA, ORANGE, PINK, RED, WHITE, YELLOW.

In addition to the predefined colors you can also create your own colors by mixing the three basic video colors of red, green, and blue.

```
Color c = new Color(140,140,140);
```

In addition to **setColor()**, there are other methods like **setForeground()**, and **setBackground()** that set the colors of the foreground and background respectively.

```
import java.applet.*;
import java.awt.*;

public class MyColor extends Applet{
  public void paint(Graphics g){
    setBackground(Color.blue);
    g.setColor(Color.green);
    g.drawString("Colors in Java Applet",100,100);
  }
}
```

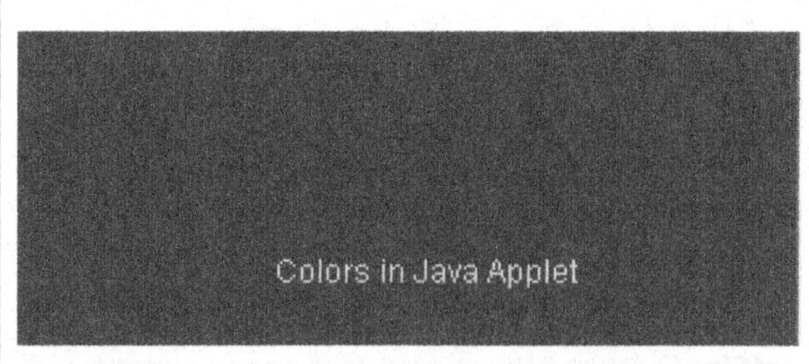

10.3.3 Images

To display an image, the MediaTracker class of the java.awt package can be used. MediaTracker is a utility class that tracks the status of a number of media objects. This type of object can include images and audio clips.

The method **getImage()** is used to obtain an image. It takes two arguments. The first is getCodeBase() while the other is the image name. getCodeBase() returns the url of the directory from where the image was loaded.

Then the **addImage()** method of MediaTracker is used.

```
import java.applet.*;
import java.awt.*;

public class appletImage extends Applet{
  Image img;
  MediaTracker tr;
  public void paint(Graphics g) {
    tr = new MediaTracker(this);
    img = getImage(getCodeBase(), "sunset.gif");
    tr.addImage(img,0);
    g.drawImage(img, 0, 0, this);
  }
}
```

10.3.4 Audio Files

Java provides the ability to play an audio file in applications and applets.

An applet can play an audio file, as represented by **AudioClip** in the java.applet package.

```
AudioClip MyClip;
```

After instantiating an AudioClip object, we have to load the actual audio file to be played. This is achieved with the **getAudioClip()** method- a method of the Applet class.

```
MyClip = getAudioClip(getcodeBase(),
                      "sound.wav");
```

In the above example, an audio file named sound.wav is loaded as the audio file to be played.

AudioClip has three methods:

- **public void play():** Plays the audio clip one time, from the beginning.
- **public void loop():** Causes the audio clip to replay in loops.
- **public void stop():** Stops playing the audio clip.

```
import java.applet.Applet;
import java.applet.AudioClip;
import java.awt.Button;
import java.awt.event.ActionEvent;
import java.awt.event.ActionListener;

public class LoadSoundApplet extends Applet
                              implements ActionListener {
  Button play, stop;
  AudioClip audioClip;

  private static final String PLAY = "PLAY";
  private static final String STOP = "STOP";

  public void init(){
    play = new Button();
    play.setLabel(PLAY);
    play.setActionCommand(PLAY);
    play.addActionListener(this);
    add(play);

    stop = new Button();
    stop.setLabel(STOP);
    stop.setActionCommand(STOP);
    stop.addActionListener(this);
    add(stop);

    audioClip = getAudioClip(getCodeBase(), "ding.wav");
  }

  public void actionPerformed(ActionEvent e) {
    if(e.getActionCommand().equals(PLAY)){
      audioClip.play();
    } else if (e.getActionCommand().equals(STOP)){
      audioClip.stop();
    } else {
      audioClip.stop();
    }
  }
}
```

10.3.5 Displaying a Webpage

A Java applet can load a webpage in a browser window using the **showDocument()** method in the **java.applet.AppletContext** class.
Here are the two forms of showDocument:

```
public void showDocument(java.net.URL url)
public void showDocument(java.net.URL url,
                         String targetWindow)
```

The second argument can have one of the folllowing values:

- "**_blank**" – Displays the document in a new, nameless window.
- "***windowName***" – Displays the document in a window named *windowName*. This window is created if necessary.
- "**_self**" – Displays the document in the window and frame that contain the applet.
- "**_parent**" – Displays the document in the parent frame of the applet's frame. If the applet frame has no parent frame, this acts as "_self".
- "**_top**" – Displays the document in the top-level frame. If the applet's frame is the top-level frame, this acts as "_self".

The following applet redirects the visitor to Google. Notice that a query string is passed. By passing a query string to a PHP script, it is possible to send emails or write to files on the server.

```
import javax.swing.*;
import java.net.URL;
import java.applet.AppletContext;
import java.net.MalformedURLException;

public class ShowDocument extends JApplet{
  public void init() {
    URL url=null;
    try {
      url = new URL("http://www.google.com?a=2");
    } catch (MalformedURLException e){
      System.err.println("Malformed URL");
    }
    getAppletContext().showDocument(url);
  }
}
```

10.4 Drawing Shapes

One of the most important features of a Java applet is its ability to draw graphics. We can write Java applets that draws lines, shapes, images, and text.

Most of the graphical operations in Java are methods defined in the Graphics class. The Graphics class is part of the java.awt package, so if your applet does any painting, make sure you import that class at the beginning of your Java file.

10.4.1 Drawing Methods

The Graphics class provides a set of simple, built-in graphical primitives for drawing lines, rectangles, polygons, ovals, and arcs:

- Lines:
  drawLine(int x1, int y1, int x2, int y2)

- Rectangles:

  drawRect(int x, int y, int width, int height)
  fillRect(int x, int y, int width, int height)
  clearRect(int x, int y, int width, int height)

  fillRect() fills a rectangle with the Graphics object's current color, and **clearRect()** fills a rectangle with the Component's background color

- Raised or lowered rectangles:
  draw3DRect(int x, int y, int width,int height, boolean raised)
  fill3DRect(int x, int y, int width, int height, boolean raised)

  The last parameter **Boolean raised** is a Boolean parameter that results in a raised rectangle effect when set to true. If it's set to false, the face of the rectangle shows a sunken effect.

- Round-edged rectangles:
  drawRoundRect(int x, int y, int width, int height, int arcWidth, int arcHeight)
  fllRoundRect(int x, int y, int width, int height, int arcWidth, int arcHeight)

- Ovals:
  drawOval(int x, int y, int width, int height);
  fillOval(int x, int y, int width, int height);

- Polygons:
  drawPolygon(int xPoints[], int yPoints[], int nPoints);

  fillPolygon(int xPoints[], int yPoints[], int nPoints);

```
import java.applet.*;
import java.awt.*;

public class Shapes extends Applet{
  int x[]={200,290,220},
     y[]={100,300,350};
  public void init(){}
  public void stop(){}

  public void paint(Graphics g){
    setBackground(Color.green);
    g.setColor(Color.blue);

    g.drawLine(3,300,200,10);
    g.fillOval(250,100,100,100);
    g.fillRect(400,50,200,100);
    g.fillRoundRect(400,200,200,100,60,90);
    g.fillPolygon(x,y,3);
  }
}
```

10.4.2 Copying

The copyArea() method copies a rectangular area of the screen to another area of the screen. copyArea() takes six arguments: the x and y coordinates of the top-left corner of the rectangle to copy, the width and the height of that rectangle, and the distances in the x and y directions to which to copy it. For example, this line copies a square (100 pixels on a side) 100 pixels directly to its right:

```
g.copyArea(0,0,100,100,100,0);
```

10.4.3 Finding the Applet Dimensions

The dimensions of the applet can be found by the following method:

```
import java.applet.*;
import java.awt.*;
public class AppletSize extends Applet {
  public void paint(Graphics g) {
    Dimension appletSize = this.getSize();
    int appletHeight = appletSize.height;
    int appletWidth = appletSize.width;

    g.drawString("This applet is " +
                 appletHeight + " pixels high by " +
                 appletWidth + " pixels wide.",
                 15, appletHeight/2);
  }
}
```

This applet is 300 pixels high by 300 pixels wide.

10.5 Graphical User Interface

Java's Abstract Windowing Toolkit, or awt, was designed to support the graphical user interface in Java applications and Java applets.

10.5.1 An AWT Overview

A GUI application extends from java.awt.Frame (AWT) or javax.swing.JFrame (Swing). An applet's top-level container is java.applet Applet (AWT) or javax.swing.JApplet (Swing).

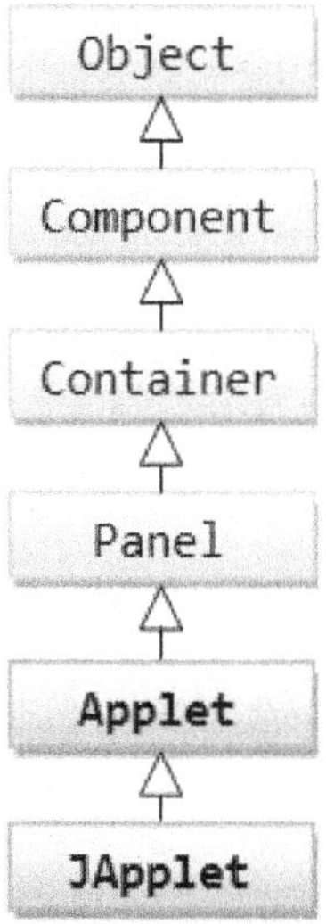

One of the ancestors is java.awt. It is used for producing user interfaces. It gives the ability to draw and handle events. java.awt.Container is designed to hold components such as buttons, list boxes, scrollbars and other user interface objects. It has a layout manager which controls the size and position of each component.

The AWT components include:

- **Containers.** A container can contain components, including other containers.
- **Canvases**. You have been drawing on panels all along. Alternatively, you can use a canvas. A canvas is a drawing surface for painting images or performing graphical operations..
- **UI components.** UI Components include buttons, lists, simple pop-up menus, check boxes, text fields etc.
- **Window construction components**. These include windows, frames, menu bars, and dialog boxes. In an applet, the browser provides the window and menu bar, so there is no need to use these. Nevertheless, your applet may create a new window.

10.5.2 Basic User Interface Components

Because the Applet class inherits from the AWT Container class, it's easy to add (UI) Components to Applets. Each Applet has a layout manager that determines how the Components are placed within the display area. Here are some of the methods the Container class supplies, which you can use to include and position Components in your applet:

add(): Adds the specified Component to this Container. The sytax is

public Component add(Component comp)

remove(): Removes the specified Component from this Container. The syntax is

public void remove(Component comp)

getComponents(): Gets all the Components in this Container. The syntax is

public Component[] getComponents()

locate(): Locates the Component at the specified x,y position. The sytnax is

public Component locate(int x,int y)

preferredSize(): Returns the preferred size of this Container. The syntax is

public Dimension getPreferredSize()

a) Label

A label is a non-editable text string. You can create a label by using one of the following constructors:

- **Label()** creates an empty label, with its text aligned to the left.
- **Label(String)** creates a label with the given text string, also aligned to the left.
- **Label(String, int)** creates a label with the given text string and the given alignment. The second argument can be Label.RIGHT, Label.LEFT, or Label.CENTER.

```
add(new Label("aligned right", Label.RIGHT));
```

b) Button

A button is a simple UI component that triggers some action in your interface when pressed. For example, a calculator applet might have buttons for each digit and operator, or a dialog box might have buttons for OK and Cancel.

You can a button by using one of the following constructors:

- **Button()** creates an empty button with no label.
- **Button(String)** creates a button with the given string as a label.

```
add(new Button("Play"));
```

You can get the button's label by using getLabel() and set the label using setLabel(String).

```
import java.applet.*;
import java.awt.*;

public class ButtonSize extends Applet {
  private boolean laidOut = false;
  private Button  myButton;

  public void init() {
    this.setLayout(null);
    this.myButton = new Button("OK");
    this.add(this.myButton);
  }

  public void paint(Graphics g) {
    if (!this.laidOut) {
      this.myButton.setLocation(25, 50);
      this.myButton.setSize(30, 40);
      this.myButton.setLabel("OK!!");
      this.laidOut = true;
    }
  }
}
```

c) Checkbox

A checkbox has two states -- on and off. To find out the state of a checkbox object we can use getState() that returns a true or false value. We can also get the label of the checkbox using getLabel() that returns a String object.

To create a check box, use one of the following constructors:

- Checkbox() creates an empty check box, unselected.
- Checkbox(String) creates a check box with the given string as a label.
- Checkbox(String, CheckboxGroup, boolean) creates a check box that is either selected or deselected based on whether the boolean argument is true or false, respectively.

```
add(new Checkbox("Apple", null, true));
```

d) Text Fields

Text fields are areas where the user can enter text. They are useful for displaying and receiving text messages.

We can make a text field read-only or editable. We can use setEditable(false) to set a textfield to be read-only. There are numerous ways that we can use to construct a TextField object.

```
TextField text1 = new TextField();

// a text field with a predefined string
TextField text2 = new TextField("Some text");

// a text field with a predefined size
TextField text3 = new TextField(40);
TextField text4 = new TextField("Some text", 50);
```

The value of a text field can be retrieved using the getText() method.

String temp = textField1.getText();

e) Choice Menu

To create a choice menu, instantiate a Choice object and then use addItem() to add items to it. Finally, add the entire choice menu to the panel.

```
import java.applet.Applet;
import java.awt.*;

public class ChoiceMenu extends java.applet.Applet {
  Choice c;
  public void init() {
    c = new Choice();
    c.addItem("Apples");
    c.addItem("Oranges");
    c.addItem("Strawberries");
    c.addItem("Blueberries");
    c.addItem("Bananas");
    add(c);
  }
  public void paint(Graphics g) {
    g.clearRect(0,0,200,200);
    g.drawString(c.getSelectedIndex()+"",50,50);
    g.drawString(c.getSelectedItem(),50,100);
    repaint();
  }
}
```

Bananas

4

Bananas

```
import java.applet.Applet;
import java.awt.*;

public class ComponentApplet extends Applet{
  public void init(){
    Button b = new Button("Test Button");
    this.add(b);

    Checkbox cb = new Checkbox("Test Checkbox");
    this.add(cb);

    CheckboxGroup cbg = new CheckboxGroup();
    this.add(new Checkbox("CB Item 1", cbg, false));
    this.add(new Checkbox("CB Item 2", cbg, false));
    this.add(new Checkbox("CB Item 3", cbg, true));

    Choice choice = new Choice();
    choice.addItem("Choice Item 1");
    choice.addItem("Choice Item 2");
    choice.addItem("Choice Item 3");
    this.add(choice);

    Label l = new Label("Test Label");
    this.add(l);

    TextField t = new TextField("Test TextField",30);
    this.add(t);
  }
}
```

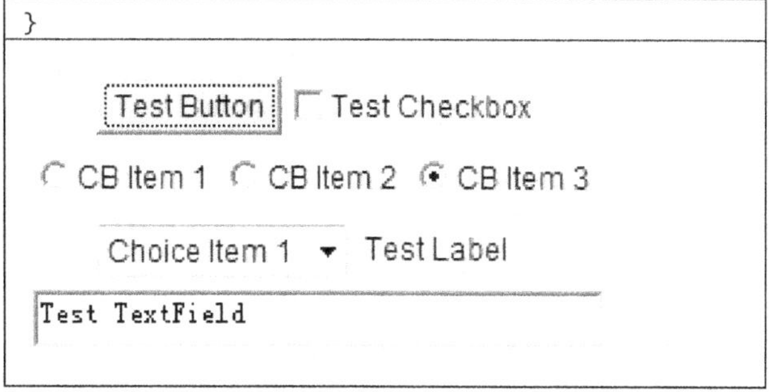

10.5.3 Layout Managers

Each panel has its own layout manager. By nesting panels within panels and using different layout managers, you can arrange your UI components.

The most common layouts are:

- FlowLayout
- GridLayout
- BorderLayout
- CardLayouts
- Grid Bag Layouts

a) FlowLayout

FlowLayout arranges components left-to-right. When a component doesn't fit onto a row, it's wrapped onto the next row. By default, each row is centered.

FlowLayout is the default pane layout. The following line is optional if you plan to use FlowLayout:

setLayout(new FlowLayout());

```
import java.applet.Applet;
import java.awt.*;

  public class FlowLO extends Applet   {
    Button button1, button2, button3, button4, button5;
    public void init()  {
      button1 = new Button("Button 1");
      button2 = new Button("Button 2");
      button3 = new Button("Button 3");
      button4 = new Button("Button 4");
      button5 = new Button("Button 5");
      add(button1);
      add(button2);
      add(button3);
      add(button4);
      add(button5);
    }
  }
```

Button 1 Button 2 Button 3

Button 4 Button 5

To use a specific alignment:

```
setLayout(new FlowLayout(FlowLayout.LEFT));
```

By default, the horizontal and vertical gap values are three pixels. To specify the gap values:

```
setLayout(new FlowLayout(
                    FlowLayout.LEFT, 30, 10));
```

b) Grid Layout

GridLayout lays out the components in a rectangular grid. The container that you apply the layout to divides the area into equally sized squares. Each component that you add is sized to fit that square.

You must specify the number of rows and columns in the grid. So to construct a 3x2 grid we use

```
new GridLayout(3,2)
```

. If you pass a 0 for either the row or the column value to the constructor then you will have unlimited rows or columns. For example,

```
new GridLayout(0,2)
```

will construct a GridLayout object with 2 columns, but an unlimited number of rows.

The order that you use the add() method is still important as it adds the components to the grid from the left to the right, then from the top to the bottom.

```
import java.awt.*;
import java.applet.Applet;

public class GridLO extends Applet  {
  Button button1, button2, button3, button4, button5;
  public void init() {
    this.setLayout(new GridLayout(3,2));
    button1 = new Button("Button 1");
    button2 = new Button("Button 2");
    button3 = new Button("Button 3");
    button4 = new Button("Button 4");
    button5 = new Button("Button 5");
    add(button1);
    add(button2);
    add(button3);
    add(button4);
    add(button5);
  }
}
```

To create gaps:

```
setLayout(new GridLayout(4, 4, 25, 45));
```

c) Border Layout

With Border Layout, the position of a component is indicated as north, south, east, west, or center. Each component occupies as much left-over space as possible and the component in the center, if any, gets any remaining space.

```
import java.awt.*;
import java.applet.Applet;

public class BorderLO extends Applet  {
  Button button1, button2, button3, button4, button5;
  public void init() {
    this.setLayout(new BorderLayout());
    button1 = new Button("Button 1");
    button2 = new Button("Button 2");
    button3 = new Button("Button 3");
    button4 = new Button("Button 4");
    button5 = new Button("Button 5");
    add("North",button1);
    add("South",button2);
    add("East",button3);
    add("West",button4);
    add("Center",button5);
  }
}
```

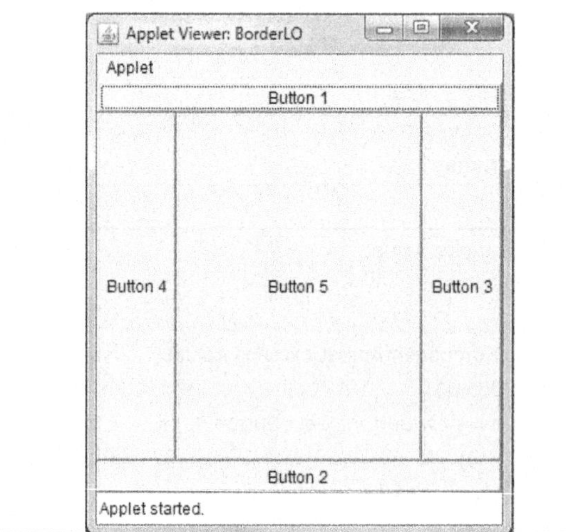

To add gaps:

```
setLayout(new BorderLayout(10, 10));
```

d) Card Layout

A Card layout is used to produce a slides show for components, by displaying them one at a time.

With Card Layout, components share the same display space where a component resembles a stack of playing cards. Only the top card is visible at any time. You can choose the displayed card by:

- specifying the first or last card.
- flipping through the deck backwards or forwards.
- specifying a card with a specific name.

```
import java.awt.*;
import java.awt.event.*;
import java.applet.*;

public class CardLayoutExample extends Applet{
   public void init() {
      new CardLO().MyCardPanel();
   }
}

class CardLO extends Frame {
   private Tab1 p;
   private Tab2 p1;
   private Tab3 p2;
   private Panel cardPanel;
   private CardLayout card;
   private Color activeColor = new Color(200,200,200);
   private Color inactiveColor = new Color(150,150,150);

   public void MyCardPanel() {
      p = new Tab1();
      p1 = new Tab2();
      p2 = new Tab3();

      setBackground(activeColor);
      setBounds(200,200,300,350);
      addWindowListener(new Terminator());

      Panel controls = new Panel(new GridLayout(1,3));
      controls.add(p);
      controls.add(p1);
      controls.add(p2);

      card = new CardLayout();
      cardPanel = new Panel(card);
      cardPanel.add("Card1", new FirstCard());
      cardPanel.add("Card2", new SecondCard());
      cardPanel.add("Card3", new ThirdCard());

      Panel border = new Panel(new BorderLayout());
      border.add(controls, "North");
      border.add(cardPanel, "Center");
      add(border);

      setVisible(true);
   }

   public class Terminator extends WindowAdapter {
      public void windowClosing(WindowEvent e) {
         dispose();
      }
   }

   public class FirstCard extends Panel {
      public FirstCard() {
         add(new Label("First Card"));
         setBackground(activeColor);
      }
   }

   public class SecondCard extends Panel {
      public SecondCard(){
         add(new Label("Second Card"));
         setBackground(activeColor);
      }
   }

   public class ThirdCard extends Panel  {
      public ThirdCard(){
         add(new Label("Third Card"));
         setBackground(activeColor);
      }
   }

   public class Tab1 extends Panel {
      public Tab1() {
         addMouseListener(new MouseAdapter(){
            public void mousePressed(MouseEvent e) {
               card.show(cardPanel, "Card1");
               setBackground(activeColor);
               p1.setBackground(inactiveColor);
               p2.setBackground(inactiveColor);
            }
         });
      }

      public void paint(Graphics g)  {
         g.drawString("Tab 1",25,20);
      }

      public Dimension getPreferredSize(){
        // only need this for one of the tabs
        return new Dimension(100,35);
      }
   }

   public class Tab2 extends Panel {
      public Tab2() {
        setBackground(inactiveColor);
         addMouseListener(new MouseAdapter(){
            public void mousePressed(MouseEvent e) {
               card.show(cardPanel, "Card2");
               setBackground(activeColor);
               p.setBackground(inactiveColor);
               p2.setBackground(inactiveColor);
            }
         });
      }

      public void paint(Graphics g)  {
         g.drawString("Tab 2",25,20);
      }
   }

   public class Tab3 extends Panel {
      public Tab3() {
         setBackground(inactiveColor);
         addMouseListener(new MouseAdapter(){
            public void mousePressed(MouseEvent e) {
               card.show(cardPanel, "Card3");
               setBackground(activeColor);
               p.setBackground(inactiveColor);
               p1.setBackground(inactiveColor);
            }
         });
      }

      public void paint(Graphics g)  {
         g.drawString("Tab 3",25,20);
      }
   }
}
```

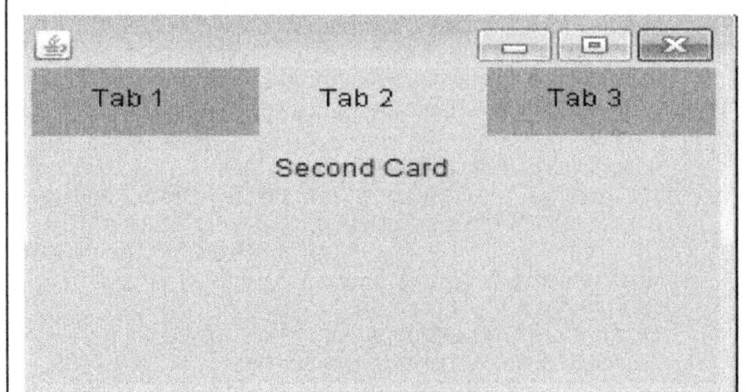

e) GridBag Layout

With GridBag Layout, components are positioned in a grid of rows and columns. Each component can span multiple rows or columns. To utilize GridBad Layout, you use GridBagLayout and GridBagConstraints.

```
// set up layout
GridBagLayout gridbag = new GridBagLayout();
GridBagConstraints constraints = new GridBagConstraints();
setLayout(gridbag);

// define constraints for the button
Button b = new Button("Save");
constraints.gridx = 0;
constraints.gridy = 0;
constraints.gridwidth = 1;
constraints.gridheight = 1;
constraints.weightx = 30;
constraints.weighty = 30;
constraints.fill = GridBagConstraints.NONE;
constraints.anchor = GridBagConstraints.CENTER;

// attach constraints to layout, add button
gridbag.setConstraints(b, constraints);
add(b);
```

```
import java.awt.*;
import java.util.*;
import java.applet.Applet;

public class GridBagLO extends Applet {
  protected void makebutton
(String name, GridBagLayout gridbag, GridBagConstraints c) {
    Button button = new Button(name);
    gridbag.setConstraints(button, c);
    add(button);
  }

  public void init() {
    GridBagLayout gridbag = new GridBagLayout();
    GridBagConstraints c = new GridBagConstraints();

    setFont(new Font("Helvetica", Font.PLAIN, 14));
    setLayout(gridbag);

    c.fill = GridBagConstraints.BOTH;
    c.weightx = 1.0;
    makebutton("Button1", gridbag, c);
    makebutton("Button2", gridbag, c);
    makebutton("Button3", gridbag, c);
    c.gridwidth = GridBagConstraints.REMAINDER;
    makebutton("Button4", gridbag, c);
    c.weightx = 0.0;                    //reset to the default
    makebutton("Button5", gridbag, c); //another row
    c.gridwidth = GridBagConstraints.RELATIVE;
                                        //next-to-last  row
    makebutton("Button6", gridbag, c);
    c.gridwidth = GridBagConstraints.REMAINDER; //end row
    makebutton("Button7", gridbag, c);
    c.gridwidth = 1;                    //reset to the default
    c.gridheight = 2;
    c.weighty = 1.0;
    makebutton("Button8", gridbag, c);
    c.weighty = 0.0; //reset to the default
    c.gridwidth = GridBagConstraints.REMAINDER; //end row
    c.gridheight = 1;                   //reset to the default
    makebutton("Button9", gridbag, c);
    makebutton("Button10", gridbag, c);
    resize(300, 100);
  }

  public static void main(String args[]) {
    Frame f = new Frame("GridBag Layout Example");
    GridBagLO ex1 = new GridBagLO();
    ex1.init();
    f.add("Center", ex1);
    f.pack();
    f.resize(f.preferredSize());
    f.show();
  }
}
```

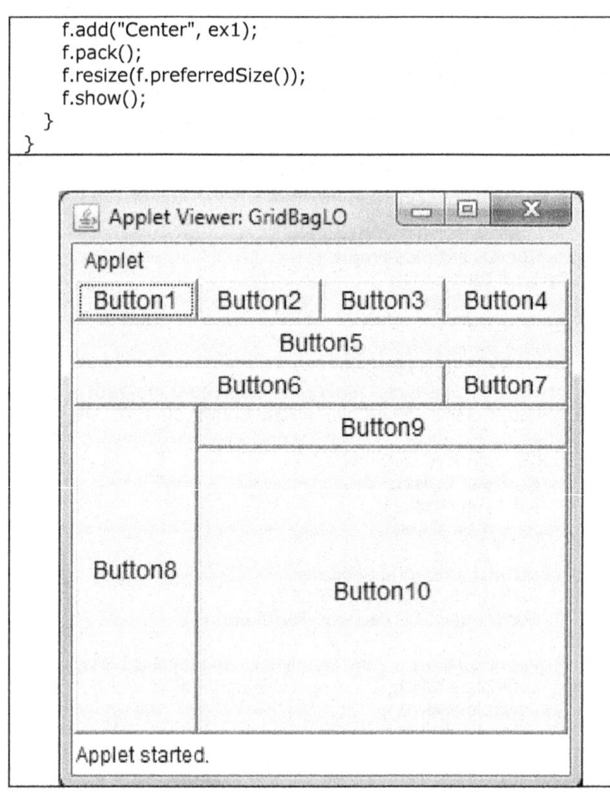

10.5.4 Events and Triggers

A GUI contains components to form the user interface. These components may generate events based on user interactions such as the pressing of the Enter key, a mouse click and so on. When an applet is designed, these events are trapped. Suitable actions to be performed in response to each of those events are provided.

When an event occurs, an Event object is created (an instance of the java.awt.Event class).

To handle events, event handlers must be suitably manipulated. The procedure to be followed when an event is generated is:

1. Determine the type of event that took place.

2. Determine the component which generated the event.

3. Handle the event.

Important Events and Triggers:

- An ActionEvent is generated when a button is clicked.
- An AdjustmentEvent is generated when a scrollbar or any other adjustment element is used.
- A TextEvent is generated when the text of a component is modified.
- An ItemEvent is generated when an item from a list, a choice menu or a checkbox is selected.
- A ContainerEvent is generated when a component is added or removed from the container.
- A ComponentEvent is generated when a component is resized, moved etc.
- A FocusEvent is generated when a component receives focus for input.
- A KeyEvent is generated when a key on the keyboard is pressed, released etc.
- A WindowEvent is generated when a window activity, like maximizing or closing occurs.
- A MouseEvent is generated when a mouse is used.
- A PaintEvent is generated when a component is painted.

Event Listeners

The task of handling an event is assigned to an event listener. When an event occurs, an event object of the appropriate type (as illustrated below) is created. This object is passed to a listener. A listener must implement the interface that has the method for event handling. A component can have multiple listeners, and a listener can be removed using the removeActionListener() method.

The java.awt.event package contains definitions of all event classes and listener interfaces. The listener interfaces defined by AWT for the above events are: ActionListener, AjdustmentListener, ItemListener, TextListener, ComponentListener, ContainerListener, FocusListener, KeyListener, MouseListener, MouseMotionListener, WindowListener.

Three Steps of Event Handling

1) **Prepare to accept events**
Implement the appropriate interface. The applet manifests its desire to accept events by promising to implement certain methods. Example:
"implements ActionListener" for Button events
"implements AdjustmentListener" for Scrollbar events

2) **Start listening for events**
To make the applet "listen" to a particular event, include the appropriate "addxxxListener".

Example:
"addActionListener(this)"

'this' shows that the applet is interested in listening to events generated by the pushing of a certain button.

3) **Respond to events**
Implement the appropriate abstract method.
Example:
"actionPerformed(ActionEvent e)"
is automatically called whenever the user clicks the button.

Thus, implement actionPerformed() to respond to the button event.

10.5.5 ActionEvents

In this example, "Thread.sleep(1000);" stops the execution for 1000 milliseconds. This command must be put in a "try/catch" statement because it will generate an exception.

```
import java.awt.*;
import java.awt.event.*;
import java.applet.*;

import javax.swing.JApplet;
import javax.swing.JButton;

import java.awt.Toolkit;
import java.awt.BorderLayout;
import java.awt.event.ActionListener;
import java.awt.event.ActionEvent;

public class Beeper extends JApplet
                    implements ActionListener {
  JButton b1,b2;
  public void init() {
    setLayout(new FlowLayout());
    b1 = new JButton("Beep Once");
    b2 = new JButton("Beep Twice");
    add(b1);
    add(b2);
    b1.addActionListener(this);
    b2.addActionListener(this);
  }
  public void actionPerformed(ActionEvent e) {
    Object obj = e.getSource();
    if (obj==b1) {
      Toolkit.getDefaultToolkit().beep();
    } else if (obj==b2) {
      Toolkit.getDefaultToolkit().beep();
      try {
        Thread.sleep(1000);
      } catch (InterruptedException exc){}
      Toolkit.getDefaultToolkit().beep();
    }
  }
}
```

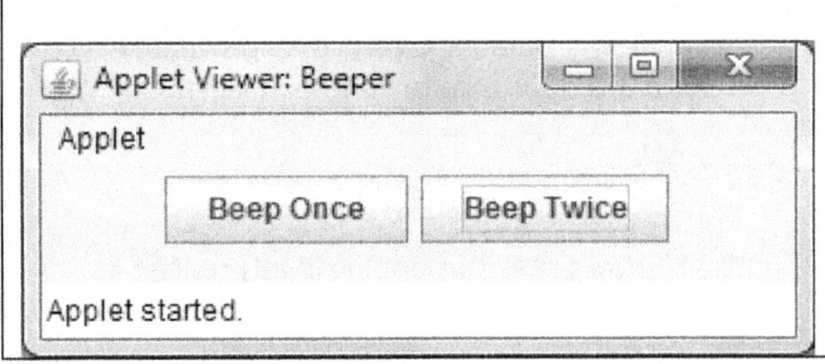

10.5.6 MouseEvents

When the user clicks on the mouse, a MouseEvent is trapped by the applet and processed. The screen coordinates of the position where the mouse click occurred is retrieved and retained in two variables x1 and y1. Similarly when the mouse is released, the corresponding values of the position are stored in x2 and y2. Using these four coordinate values, a rectangle is drawn using the drawRect() method of the Graphics class. When the mouse is dragged by keeping the mouse button pressed, a rectangle is drawn.

```
import java.awt.*;
import java.awt.event.*;
import java.applet.*;

public class MouseRect extends Applet implements
MouseListener{
  int x1, y1, x2, y2;
  public void init() {
    setBounds(100, 100, 300, 300);
    addMouseListener(this);
    this.setVisible(true);
  }

  public void mouseClicked(MouseEvent e) {}

  public void mousePressed(MouseEvent e) {
      x1 = e.getX();
      y1 = e.getY();
  }

   public void mouseMoved(MouseEvent e) {}

   public void mouseReleased(MouseEvent e) {
      x2 = e.getX();
      y2 = e.getY();
      repaint();
   }

   public void mouseEntered(MouseEvent e) { }

   public void mouseDragged(MouseEvent e){ }

   public void mouseExited(MouseEvent e) { }

   public void paint(Graphics g)  {
      g.drawRect(x1, y1, x2-x1, y2-y1);
      x2 = 0;
      y2 = 0;
   }
}
```

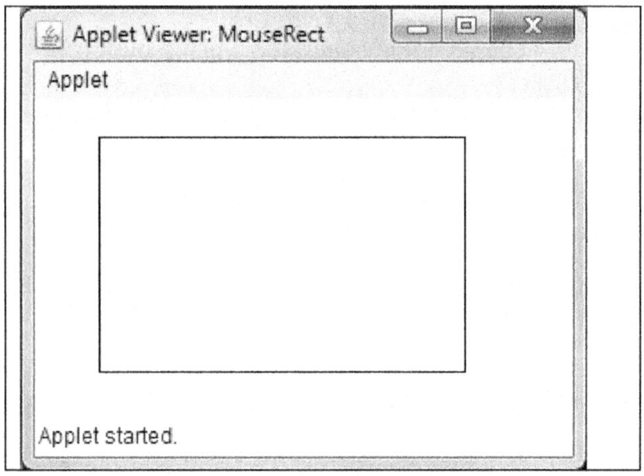

10.5.7 KeyEvents & KeyListener

Keyboard events can also be handled in the same way as mouse events. The only difference is that the KeyListener interface has to be implemented. When a key is pressed, a KEY_PRESSED event is generated and this will in turn call the keyPressed() event handler. When the key is released it will invoke the keyReleased() event handler. If the character is generated by a keystroke, the KEY_TYPED event is generated and the keyTyped() event handler is called. When writing a program to handle keyboard events, input focus is requested by calling the method requestFocus() defined by the Component class. If this method is not invoked in the init() method then the program will not receive any keyboard events.

```
import java.awt.*;
import java.awt.event.*;
import java.applet.*;
import java.awt.*;
import java.awt.event.*;
import java.applet.*;

public class KeyTest extends Applet implements KeyListener{
   String msg = " ";
   public void init(){
      addKeyListener(this);
      requestFocus();
   }
   public void keyPressed(KeyEvent k){
      showStatus("Key Down");
   }
   public void keyReleased(KeyEvent k){
      showStatus("Key is Up");
   }
   public void keyTyped(KeyEvent k){
      msg += k.getKeyChar();
      repaint();
   }
   public void paint(Graphics g){
      g.drawString(msg, 10, 10);
   }
}
```

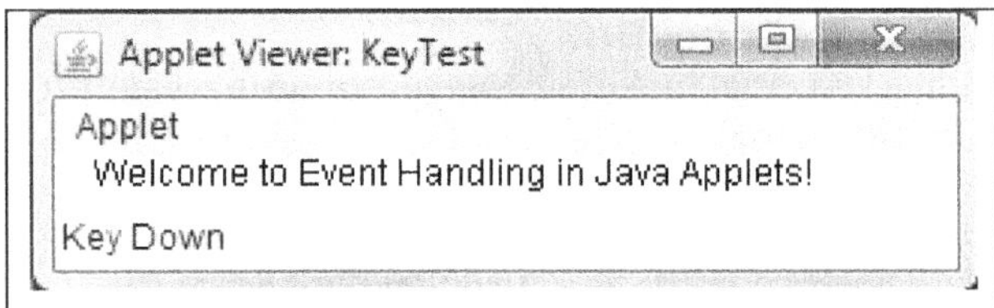

10.6 Swing Components

Allowing more flexibility and functionality, Swing is a graphics library that is more enhanced than AWT. Most components in the Swing package begin with 'J'. To use the Swing package, import it at the top:

    import javax.swing.*;

10.6.1 JLabel

JLabel is a component which simply shows text and/or images. There are at least three constructors for JLabel:

    JLabel(String)
    JLabel(ImageIcon)
    JLabel(String, ImageIcon, horizontalAlignment)

where horizontalAlignment can be JLabel.LEFT, JLabel.RIGHT, or JLabel.CENTER.

If the third constructor is used, we can set the text position with respect to the image using:

    .setHorizontalTextPosition(textPosition)
    .setVerticalTextPosition(textPosition)

where textPosition can be JLabel.LEFT, JLabel.CENTER, or JLabel.RIGHT horizontally; it can be JLabel.TOP, JLabel.CENTER, or JLabel.BOTTOM vertically.

```
import java.awt.*;
import javax.swing.*;

public class JLabelEg extends JApplet {
  JLabel l;
  ImageIcon ic;
  Image img;
  public void init(){
    img = getImage(getCodeBase(),"sunset.gif");
    ic  = new ImageIcon(img);
    l   = new JLabel("Sunset",ic,JLabel.CENTER);
    l.setHorizontalTextPosition(JLabel.CENTER);
    l.setVerticalTextPosition(JLabel.BOTTOM);
    l.setText("Sunset and Bridge");
    add(l);
  }
}
```

Applet Viewer: JLabelEg
Applet
Sunset and Bridge
Applet started.

10.6.2 JButton

JButton can be created with:

    JButton(String)
    JButton(ImageIcon)
    JButton(String, ImageIcon)

As with JLabel, we can set the text position with respect to the image using .setHorizontalTexPosition() and .setVerticalTextPosition().

```
import java.awt.*;
import java.awt.event.*;
import javax.swing.*;

public class JButtonEg extends JApplet implements
                                        ActionListener{
  JLabel l;
  JButton b;
  ImageIcon ic,ic2;
  Image img,img2;
  public void init(){
    setLayout(new FlowLayout());
    img = getImage(getCodeBase(),"location.png");
    img2= getImage(getCodeBase(),"location 2.png");
    ic  = new ImageIcon(img);
    ic2 = new ImageIcon(img2);
    b   = new JButton("Show button info",ic);
    b.setHorizontalTextPosition(JButton.CENTER);
    b.setVerticalTextPosition(JButton.BOTTOM);
    b.setPreferredSize(new Dimension(200,100)); // the size
    b.setBorderPainted(false);        // no border
    b.setContentAreaFilled(false); // button area not filled
    b.setRolloverIcon(ic2);           // image on mouseover
    b.addActionListener(this);
    add(b);
    l   = new JLabel("");
    add(l);
  }
  public void actionPerformed(ActionEvent e){
    b.setEnabled(false);
    l.setText("The button is located at ("+
           b.getX() + "," + b.getY() +
           ") and its dimensions are "
           +b.getWidth() + "*" + b.getHeight()+".");
  }
}
```

Applet Viewer: JButton_Sizes
Applet
Show button info
The button is located at (87,5) and its dimensions are 200*100.
Applet started.

10.6.3 JTextField, JPasswordField and JTextArea

JTextField allows one to enter a single line of text. It can be created by:

JTextField()
JTextField(String)
JTextField(String, columns)

JPasswordField allows one to enter a single line of text that is not shown on the screen. It can be created like JTextField.

JTextArea allows one to enter multiple lines of text. It can be created by:

JTextArea()
JTextArea(String)
JTextArea(rows, columns)
JTextArea(String, rows, columns)

For JTextArea to display the text correctly, it needs to be added through JScrollPane.

```
import java.awt.*;
import javax.swing.*;

public class JTextEg extends JApplet{
  JTextField tf;
  JPasswordField pf;
  JTextArea ta;
  JScrollPane pane;
  public void init(){
    setLayout(new FlowLayout());
    tf = new JTextField("Enter your username",20);
    pf = new JPasswordField(20);
    ta = new JTextArea("Comments",5,20);
    ta.setLineWrap(true);  // enabling line wrapping
    ta.setBackground(Color.GRAY);
    add(tf);
    add(pf);
    pane = new JScrollPane(ta);
    add(pane);
  }
}
```

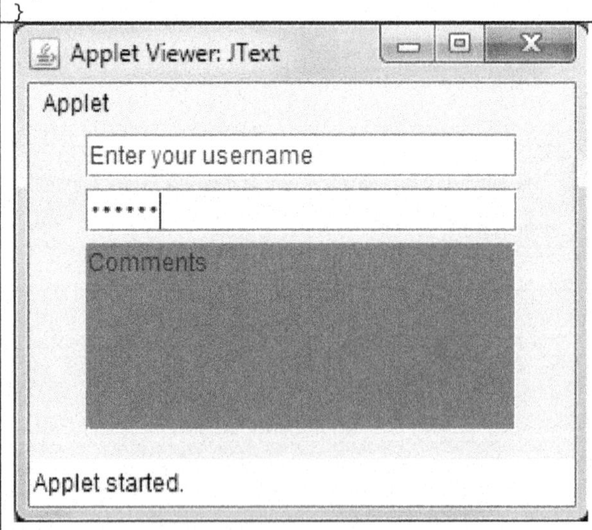

10.6.4 JCheckBox

JCheckBox can be either checked or unchecked. It can be created by:

JCheckBox(String)
JCheckBox(ImageIcon)
JCheckBox(String, ImageIcon)

```
import java.awt.*;
import javax.swing.*;

public class JCheckBoxEg extends JApplet{
  JLabel l;
  JCheckBox cb1,cb2,cb3;
  Image img,img2;
  ImageIcon icon,icon2;
  public void init(){
    setLayout(new FlowLayout());
    img = getImage(getCodeBase(), "location.png");
    icon = new ImageIcon(img);
    img2 = getImage(getCodeBase(), "location 2.png");
    icon2 = new ImageIcon(img2);
    cb1 = new JCheckBox("Red");
    cb2 = new JCheckBox("Green");
    cb3 = new JCheckBox("Blue",icon);
    cb1.setFocusPainted(false);  // no border when selected
    cb2.setFocusPainted(false);  // no border when selected
    cb3.setFocusPainted(false);  // no border when selected
    cb3.setSelectedIcon(icon2);  // display this when selected
    add(cb1);
    add(cb2);
    add(cb3);
    cb1.setSelected(true);
    if (cb1.isSelected()){
      l = new JLabel(cb1.getText());
      add(l);
    }
  }
}
```

10.6.5 JRadioButton

JRadioButton allows the users to select one option among a group of options. It can be created by:

JRadioButton(String)
JRadioButton(ImageIcon)
JRadioButton(String,ImageIcon)

```
import java.awt.*;
import javax.swing.*;

public class JRadioButtonEg extends JApplet{
  JLabel l;
  ButtonGroup g;
  JRadioButton rb1,rb2,rb3;
  public void init(){
    setLayout(new FlowLayout());
    rb1 = new JRadioButton("Orange");
    rb2 = new JRadioButton("Apple");
    rb3 = new JRadioButton("Mango");
    g = new ButtonGroup();
    addButtonsIcon(rb1); g.add(rb1); add(rb1);
    addButtonsIcon(rb2); g.add(rb2); add(rb2);
    addButtonsIcon(rb3); g.add(rb3); add(rb3);
```

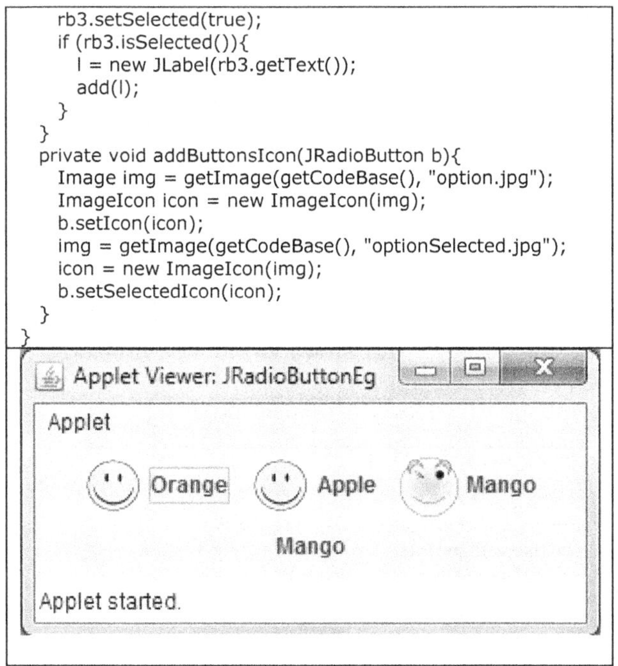

```
    rb3.setSelected(true);
    if (rb3.isSelected()){
      l = new JLabel(rb3.getText());
      add(l);
    }
  }
  private void addButtonsIcon(JRadioButton b){
    Image img = getImage(getCodeBase(), "option.jpg");
    ImageIcon icon = new ImageIcon(img);
    b.setIcon(icon);
    img = getImage(getCodeBase(), "optionSelected.jpg");
    icon = new ImageIcon(img);
    b.setSelectedIcon(icon);
  }
}
```


10.6.6 JComboBox

JComboxBox allows the users to select one option from a drop-down list of items. It can be created by:

JComboBox()

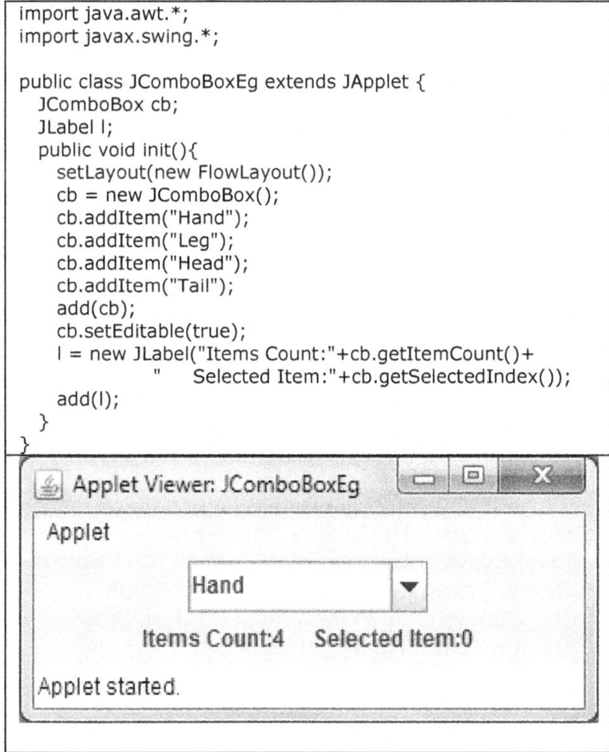

```
import java.awt.*;
import javax.swing.*;

public class JComboBoxEg extends JApplet {
  JComboBox cb;
  JLabel l;
  public void init(){
    setLayout(new FlowLayout());
    cb = new JComboBox();
    cb.addItem("Hand");
    cb.addItem("Leg");
    cb.addItem("Head");
    cb.addItem("Tail");
    add(cb);
    cb.setEditable(true);
    l = new JLabel("Items Count:"+cb.getItemCount()+
              "    Selected Item:"+cb.getSelectedIndex());
    add(l);
  }
}
```


10.6.7 JList and JScrollPane

A JList displays many items from which the user can select one or more. We can add a scrollbar to it using JScrollPane:

JList(DefaultListModel)

JScrollPane(JList)

```
import java.awt.*;
import javax.swing.*;

public class JListEg extends JApplet {
  DefaultListModel model;
  JList list;
  JLabel l;
  public void init(){
    setLayout(new FlowLayout());
    model = new DefaultListModel();
    list = new JList(model);
    model.addElement("What");
    model.addElement(getIcon("option.jpg"));
    model.add(2,"Why");
    model.add(3,getIcon("optionSelected.jpg"));
    model.addElement("When");
    list.setVisibleRowCount(4);
    list.setSelectionMode(
        ListSelectionModel.MULTIPLE_INTERVAL_SELECTION);
    JScrollPane pane = new JScrollPane(list);
    add(pane);
    l = new JLabel(""+list.getSelectedIndex());
    add(l);
  }
  private ImageIcon getIcon(String filename){
    Image img = getImage(getCodeBase(), filename);
    ImageIcon icon = new ImageIcon(img);
    return icon;
  }
}
```

10.6.8 JTabbedPane

JTabbedPane allows us to have tabs that can be clicked to display different page contents. There are different ways to add components/tabs:

JTabbedPane tp = new JTabbedPane();
tp.addTab(tabText, component);
tp.addTab(tabText, ImageIcon, component);
tp.addTab(tabText, ImageIcon, component, toolTip);

To add more than one components to a tab, add the components to a JPanel, then add the JPanel to the JTabbedPane as a component.

```
import java.awt.*;
import javax.swing.*;

public class JTabbedPaneEg extends JApplet {
  public void init(){
    JTabbedPane tp = new JTabbedPane();

    // Tab 1: a JLabel
    tp.addTab("One",new JLabel("This is tab 1"));

    // Tab 2: a JButton
    tp.addTab("Two",new
                JButton("Option",getIcon("option.jpg")));

    // Tab 3: a JPanel containing two buttons
    JPanel panel = new JPanel();
    panel.add(new
            JButton("Location",getIcon("location.png")));
    panel.add(new JButton("option",getIcon("option.jpg")));
    tp.addTab("Three",panel);

    add(tp, BorderLayout.CENTER);
  }
  private ImageIcon getIcon(String filename){
    Image img = getImage(getCodeBase(), filename);
    ImageIcon icon = new ImageIcon(img);
    return icon;
  }
}
```

10.6.9 JFrame

JFrame allows us to open a new window. Components can be added to the new window.

```
import java.awt.*;
import javax.swing.*;

public class JFrameEg extends JApplet {
  public void init(){
    JFrame f = new JFrame("Title");
    f.setSize(250,150);
    f.setVisible(true);
    f.setLocation(30,40);
    f.setLayout(new FlowLayout());
    f.add(new JLabel("A JLabel"));
    f.add(new JButton("A JButton"));

    // resize the frame to the minimum size
    // needed to contain the components
    f.pack();
  }
}
```

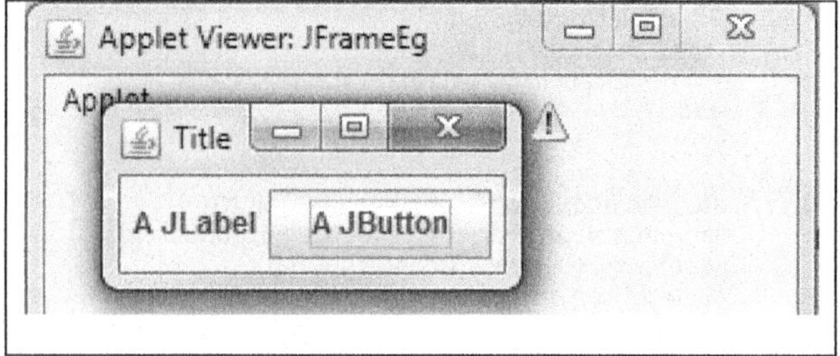

10.6.10 ToolTips

We can display a text string as the mouse pointer moves over a component. Simply call, on the component: .setToolTipText(String).

```
import java.awt.*;
import javax.swing.*;

public class ToolTipEg extends JApplet {
  public void init(){
    setLayout(new FlowLayout());

    JLabel l = new JLabel("JLabel");
    l.setToolTipText("This is a JLabel");
    add(l);

    JButton b = new JButton("JButton");
    b.setToolTipText("This is a JButton");
    add(b);
  }
}
```

10.6.11 DialogBoxes

We can popup a dialog box displaying a title, a message, an icon, and the selected buttons.

```
JOptionPane.showMessageDialog(
   null, String msg, String title, int style)
JOptionPane.showConfirmDialog(
   nuill, String msg, String title, int style)
```

'style' for showMesssgeDialog()
JOptionPane.QUESTION_MESSAGE This displays a question mark and an "OK" button.
JOptionPane.INFORMATION_MESSAGE This displays an 'i' mark and an "OK" button.
JOptionPane.ERROR_MESSAGE This displays an 'x' mark and an "OK" button.
JOptionPane.WARNING_MESSAGE This displays an exclamation mark and an "OK" button.
JOptionPane.PLAIN_MESSAGE This does not display an icon but an "OK" button.
'style' for showConfirmDialog()
JOptionPane.YES_NO_OPTION This displays a question mark, the "YES" button, and the "NO" button.

JOptionPane.YES_NO_CANCEL_OPTION This displays a question mark, the "YES" button, the "NO" button, and the "CANCEL" button.
JOptionPane.OK_CANCEL_OPTION This displays a question mark, the "OK" button, and the "Cancel" button.

```
import java.awt.*;
import javax.swing.*;

public class DialogBoxEg extends JApplet {
  public void init(){
    JLabel l = new JLabel(); add(l);
    int userPick = JOptionPane.showConfirmDialog(
                    null,
                    "Would you like to continue?\n"+
                    "Please answer.",
                    "Continue?",
                    JOptionPane.YES_NO_CANCEL_OPTION);
    switch (userPick){
      case JOptionPane.YES_OPTION:
        l.setText("yes!");
      break; case JOptionPane.NO_OPTION:
        l.setText("no!");
      //break; case JOptionPane.OK_OPTION:
      break; case JOptionPane.CANCEL_OPTION:
        l.setText("cancel!");
    }
  }
}
```

10.6.12 JTable

JTable displays text in a 2D table. To add it, put it into a JScrollPane first. Note that a JTable cannot store an int or any other primitive data type.

```
import java.awt.*;
import javax.swing.*;

public class JTableEg extends JApplet{
  String[] headings = {"Name","Age","Sex","Country"};
  Object content[][]={ {"Mike","23","Male","Malaysia"},
                {"Susan","21","Female","Singapore"},
                {"Katherine","25","Female","Australia"} };
  public void init(){
    JTable table = new JTable(content, headings);

    table.getTableHeader().setBackground(Color.WHITE);
    table.getTableHeader().setForeground(Color.BLACK);
    table.setBackground(Color.YELLOW);
    table.setForeground(Color.RED);
    table.setSelectionBackground(Color.CYAN);
    table.setSelectionForeground(Color.BLUE);
    table.setShowHorizontalLines(true);
    table.setShowVerticalLines(true);
```

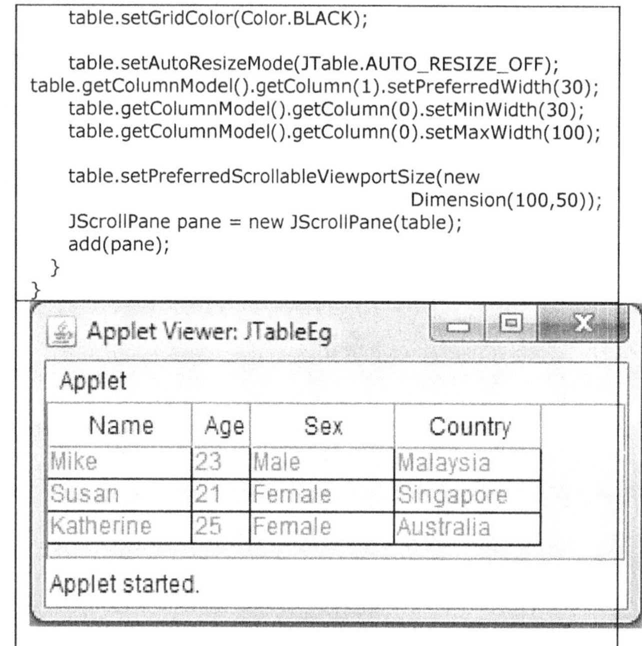

```
    table.setGridColor(Color.BLACK);

    table.setAutoResizeMode(JTable.AUTO_RESIZE_OFF);
table.getColumnModel().getColumn(1).setPreferredWidth(30);
    table.getColumnModel().getColumn(0).setMinWidth(30);
    table.getColumnModel().getColumn(0).setMaxWidth(100);

    table.setPreferredScrollableViewportSize(new
                                        Dimension(100,50));
    JScrollPane pane = new JScrollPane(table);
    add(pane);
  }
}
```


10.7 Timing

10.7.1 Threads

Java allows more than one sequence of execution running in parallel during runtime. Such a sequence is called a thread. You should use a thread to perform a time-consuming task, instead of holding up the machine.

The Java library provides a class called Thread which contains methods for starting, running, stopping, and checking a thread.

a) A single thread

Follow these four steps to get a Thread to work:
1. Implement the **Runnable** interface in the class.
2. Create a **Thread**.
3. Start the Thread inside the **start()** method.
4. Create a method named **run()**.

Runnable is an interface in java.lang that contains only one method which is the **run()** method.

repaint() causes the applet to use the paint() method. When this Java Applet is run, you will see an image growing from nothing to a gigantic image. The growth of the image will not stop until the Java Applet stops running.

```
import java.awt.*;
import java.applet.*;


public class Threading extends Applet implements Runnable{
  private Image theImage = null;
  private Thread theThread = null;
  private int imageWidth = 0;
  private int imageHeight = 0;
  private boolean keepGoing = true;

  public void init() {
    theImage = this.getImage(this.getCodeBase() , "9.jpg");
  }
  public void paint(Graphics g) {
    g.drawImage(theImage, 0, 0,
                    imageWidth, imageHeight, this );
  }
  public void start() {
    theThread = new Thread(this);
    theThread.start();
  }
  public void stop() {
    if( theThread != null )  theThread = null;
    keepGoing = false;
  }
  public void run() {
    do {
      try  {Thread.sleep(50); }
      catch(InterruptedException ie){}
      imageWidth += 5;
      imageHeight += 5;
      repaint();
    } while(keepGoing);
  }
}
```

b) Two threads

An applet which blends the Digtial Clock and Swirling Colors examples. The applet uses two threads. The first changes the color and the second changes the date and time. The color changing thread sleeps for 50 milliseconds, while the date changing thread sleeps for an entire second.

```
import java.awt.*;
import java.util.*;
public class SwirlyClock extends java.applet.Applet {
  Font theFont = new Font("TimesRoman", Font.BOLD, 24);
  Date theDate;
  Color txColor;
  Color bgColor;
  Image buffImg;
  Graphics buffG;
  float hue;
  ColorThread myColorThread;
  DateThread myDateThread;
  public void start() {
    if (myColorThread == null) {
      myColorThread = new ColorThread(this);
      myColorThread.start();
    }
    if (myDateThread == null) {
      myDateThread = new DateThread(this);
      myDateThread.start();
    }
  }
  public void stop() {
    if (myColorThread != null) {
      myColorThread.stop();
      myColorThread = null;
    }
    if (myDateThread != null) {
      myDateThread.stop();
      myDateThread = null;
    }
  }
  public void paint(Graphics g) {
    float thue;
    bgColor = Color.getHSBColor(hue, 1.0f, 0.5f);
    buffG.setColor(bgColor);
    buffG.fillRect(0,0,this.size().width,this.size().height);
    if ( hue > 0.5f ) thue = hue - 0.5f;
    else thue = hue + 0.5f;
    txColor = Color.getHSBColor(thue, 1.0f, 1.0f);
    buffG.setColor(txColor);
    buffG.drawString(theDate.toString(),10,50);
    g.drawImage(buffImg,0,0,this);
  }
  public void update(Graphics g) {
    paint(g);
  }
  public void init() {
    buffImg=createImage(this.size().width,
                            this.size().height);
    buffG=buffImg.getGraphics();
    buffG.setFont(theFont);
    hue = 0.0f;
    theDate = new Date();
  }
}
```

```
import java.util.Date;
public class DateThread extends Thread {
  SwirlyClock myClock;
  DateThread( SwirlyClock c ) {
    super();
    myClock = c;
  }
  public void run() {      //Updates the date and time
    while (true) {
      myClock.theDate = new Date();
      myClock.repaint();
      try { Thread.sleep(1000); }
      catch (InterruptedException e) { }
    }
  }
}
```

```
public class ColorThread extends Thread {
  SwirlyClock myClock;
  private float hue;
  ColorThread( SwirlyClock c ) {
    super();
    myClock = c;
  }
  public void run() {    // Generates a new random color
    while (true) {
      hue = (float)Math.random();
      myClock.hue = (myClock.hue + 0.02f) % 1.0f;
      myClock.repaint();
      try { Thread.sleep(50); }
      catch (InterruptedException e) { }
    }
  }
}
```

Fri Oct 04 20:20:52 PKT 2013

10.7.2 Animation

Animation in an applet involves updating the applet multiple times per second. The animation can be carried out in a loop which repaints the applet, with small delays between the invocations of the paint() method.

This applet creates a thread to perform a background task. The thread increments the variable i once every 1000 milliseconds, and cause the applet to redraw itself.

```
import java.awt.*;
import java.applet.*;
import java.applet.*;
import java.awt.*;

public class ChangingLine extends Applet implements
Runnable {
  int width, height;
  int i = 0;
  Thread t = null;
  boolean threadSuspended;

  public void init() {
    System.out.println("init(): begin");
    width = getSize().width;
    height = getSize().height;
    setBackground( Color.black );
    System.out.println("init(): end");
  }

  public void destroy() {
    System.out.println("destroy()");
  }

  public void start() {
    System.out.println("start(): begin");
    if ( t == null ) {
      System.out.println("start(): creating thread");
      t = new Thread( this );
      System.out.println("start(): starting thread");
      threadSuspended = false;
      t.start();
    }
    else {
      if ( threadSuspended ) {
        threadSuspended = false;
        System.out.println("start(): notifying thread");
        synchronized( this ) {
          notify();
        }
      }
    }
    System.out.println("start(): end");
  }

  public void stop() {
    System.out.println("stop(): begin");
    threadSuspended = true;
  }

  public void run() {
    System.out.println("run(): begin");
    try {
      while (true) {
        System.out.println("run(): awake");

        // Here's where the thread does some work
        ++i;
        if ( i == 10 ) {
          i = 0;
        }
        showStatus( "i is " + i );

        // Now the thread checks to see if it should suspend itself
        if ( threadSuspended ) {
          synchronized( this ) {
            while ( threadSuspended ) {
              System.out.println("run(): waiting");
              wait();
            }
          }
        }
        System.out.println("run(): requesting repaint");
        repaint();
        System.out.println("run(): sleeping");
        t.sleep( 1000 ); // interval given in milliseconds
      }
    }
    catch (InterruptedException e) { }
    System.out.println("run(): end");
  }

  public void paint( Graphics g ) {
    System.out.println("paint()");
    g.setColor( Color.green );
    g.drawLine( width, height, i * width / 10, 0 );
  }
}
```

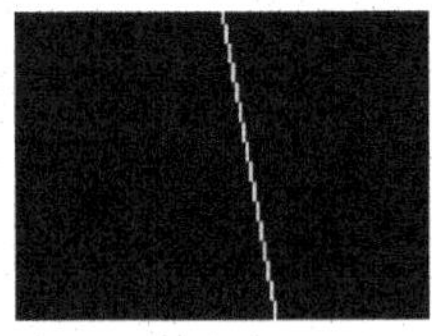
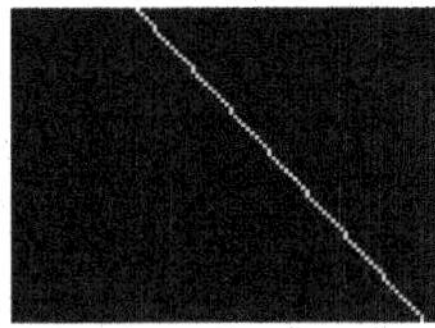

10.7.3 Timers

A timer is useful for repeating a task at particular intervals. Some examples where a timer is used are progress bars, custom clocks, timed animation, tooltips and the blinking cursor. To get a Timer to work:

1. Import the package to handle ActionEvent events.
2. Specify that we're listening for events.
3. Create a Timer object
4. Start the timer.
5. Add an actionToPerform method.
6. Stop the Timer (stop the Timer inside the applet's stop method - and optionally inside the actionPerformed method if you do not want it to continue).

```
import java.awt.BorderLayout;
import java.awt.Color;
import java.awt.Dimension;
import java.awt.Font;
import java.awt.event.ActionEvent;
import java.awt.event.ActionListener;

import javax.swing.JApplet;
import javax.swing.JLabel;
import javax.swing.JPanel;
import javax.swing.Timer;

public class ChangingColor extends JApplet {
  JPanel panel = null;
  JLabel label = null;
  Timer timer = null;

  public void init() {
    try {
      javax.swing.SwingUtilities.invokeAndWait(new
                                                Runnable() {
        public void run() {
          createGUI();
          timer = new Timer(3000, actionToPerform());
        }
      });
    } catch (Exception e) {
      System.err.println(
                    "createGUI didn't successfully complete");
    }
  }

  public void start() {timer.start();}

  public void stop() {timer.stop();}

  public void destroy() {label = null; panel = null;
                                      timer = null;}

  private void createGUI() {
    panel = new JPanel();

    label = new JLabel("Applet Test Program!");
    label.setFont(new Font("Calibri", Font.BOLD, 25));
    label.setHorizontalAlignment(JLabel.CENTER);
    label.setForeground(Color.BLUE);

    setSize(new Dimension(300, 100));
    getContentPane().setBackground(Color.BLACK);
    getContentPane().add(label, BorderLayout.CENTER);
  }

  private ActionListener actionToPerform() {
    return(new ActionListener() {
      public void actionPerformed(ActionEvent e) {
        if (label.getForeground() == Color.RED )
          label.setForeground(Color.GREEN);
        else if (label.getForeground() == Color.GREEN)
          label.setForeground(Color.BLUE);
        else if (label.getForeground() == Color.BLUE)
          label.setForeground(Color.RED);
      }
    });
  }
}
```

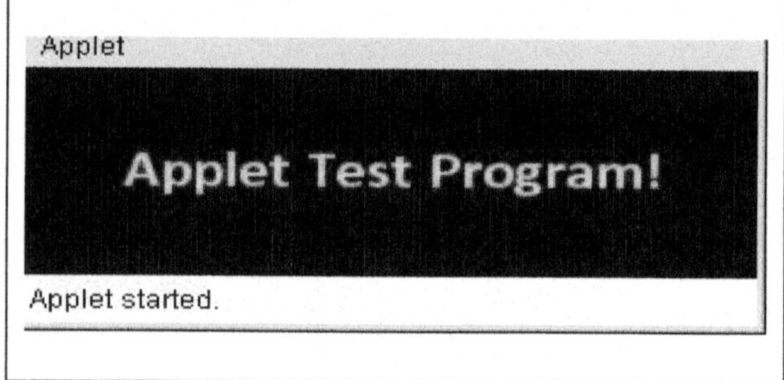

10.8 The Game

It is important to understand how to animate objects, if you wish to write a game. We will first see how to cause a ball to move from the left to the right.

10.8.1 Animation

```
import java.applet.*;
import java.awt.*;
public class MovingBall extends Applet implements Runnable{
  int x_pos  = 10; // x - position of the ball
  int y_pos  = 100; // y - position of the ball
  int radius = 20; // radius of the ball
  public void init (){
    setBackground (Color.blue);
  }
  public void start (){
    Thread th = new Thread (this);
    th.start();
  }
  public void stop(){}
  public void destroy(){}
  public void run (){
    Thread.currentThread ().
                          setPriority(Thread.MIN_PRIORITY);
    while (true){
      x_pos ++;
      repaint ();
      try{
        Thread.sleep (20);
      }catch (InterruptedException ex){ }
      Thread.currentThread().
                          setPriority(Thread.MAX_PRIORITY);
    }
  }
  public void paint (Graphics g){
    g.setColor (Color.red);
    g.fillOval (x_pos - radius, y_pos - radius,
              2 * radius, 2 * radius);
  }
}
```

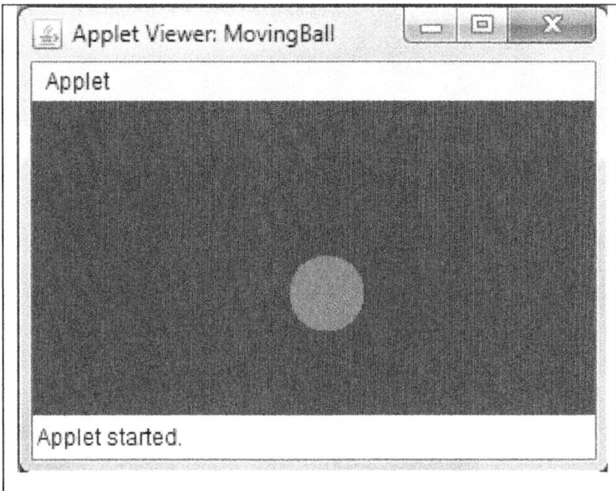

10.8.2 Double Buffering

You should have seen in the previous example that the cirlce is flickering. This is because everytime the paint() method is called the applet screen is cleared completely and becomes completely blank for one millisecond. To suppress this phenomenon, we will use double buffering.

Double buffering

Double buffering involves painting everything in the paint() to an offscreen image. After everything has been painted in the offscreen image, this image is then copied to the applet screen instantly.

The ball bounces in the opposite direction as it touches the wall.

```
import java.applet.*;
import java.awt.*;

public class BouncingBall extends Applet implements Runnable
{
  int x_pos = 30;
  int y_pos = 100;
  int x_speed = 1;
  int radius = 20;
  int appletsize_x = 300;
  int appletsize_y = 300;
  private Image dbImage;
  private Graphics dbg;
  public void init(){
    setBackground (Color.blue);
  }
  public void start (){
    Thread th = new Thread (this);
    th.start ();
  }
  public void stop(){}
  public void destroy(){}
  public void run (){
    Thread.currentThread().
                        setPriority(Thread.MIN_PRIORITY);
    while (true){
      if (x_pos > appletsize_x - radius) {x_speed = -1;}
      else if (x_pos < radius) {x_speed = +1; }
      x_pos += x_speed;
      repaint();
      try {Thread.sleep (20); }
      catch (InterruptedException ex){}
      Thread.currentThread().
                        setPriority(Thread.MAX_PRIORITY);
    }
  }
  public void update (Graphics g){
    if (dbImage == null){
      dbImage = createImage (this.getSize().width,
                             this.getSize().height);
      dbg = dbImage.getGraphics ();
    }
    dbg.setColor (getBackground ());
    dbg.fillRect (0, 0, this.getSize().width,
                  this.getSize().height);
    dbg.setColor (getForeground());
    paint (dbg);
    g.drawImage (dbImage, 0, 0, this);
  }
  public void paint (Graphics g){
    g.setColor  (Color.red);
    g.fillOval (x_pos-radius, y_pos-radius, 2*radius,
                                            2*radius);
  }
}
```

10.8.3 Our Complete Game

The game idea

In our game, the player has to shoot at two balls (a red one and a blue one) which are flying around in our applet. The direction and speed will be chosen randomly. The user can hit a ball by clicking on it with the mouse pointer. If a ball reaches a border of the applet, without being hit, the player looses one life. If the player loses all of his lives, the game is over.

```
public class Player{
  private int score;
  private int lives;
  public Player(){
    lives = 10;
    score = 0;
  }
  public int getScore (){
    return score;
  }
  public int getLives (){
    return lives;
  }
  public void addScore (int plus){
    score += plus;
  }
```

```
    public void looseLife (){
        lives --;
    }
}
```

```
import java.applet.AudioClip;
import java.awt.*;
import java.util.*;
import java.net.*;

public class Ball{
    private int pos_x;
    private int pos_y;
    private int x_speed;
    private int y_speed;
    private int radius;
    private int first_x;
    private int first_y;
    private int maxspeed;
    private final int x_leftout = 10;
    private final int x_rightout = 370;
    private final int y_upout = 45;
    private final int y_downout = 370;
    Color color;
    AudioClip out;
    Player player;
    Random rnd = new Random ();

    public Ball (int radius, int x, int y, int vx, int vy, int ms,
                        Color color, AudioClip out, Player player){
        this.radius = radius;
        pos_x = x;
        pos_y = y;
        first_x = x;
        first_y = y;
        x_speed = vx;
        y_speed = vy;
        maxspeed = ms;
        this.color = color;
        this.out = out;
        this.player = player;
    }

    public void move (){
        pos_x += x_speed;
        pos_y += y_speed;
        isOut();
    }

    public void ballWasHit (){
        pos_x = first_x;
        pos_y = first_y;
        x_speed = (rnd.nextInt ()) % maxspeed;
    }

    public boolean userHit (int maus_x, int maus_y){
        double x = maus_x - pos_x;
        double y = maus_y - pos_y;
        double distance = Math.sqrt ((x*x) + (y*y));
        if (distance < 15){
            player.addScore (10*Math.abs(x_speed) + 10);
            return true;
        } else return false;
    }

    private boolean isOut (){
        if (pos_x < x_leftout){
            pos_x = first_x;
            pos_y = first_y;
            out.play();
            x_speed = (rnd.nextInt ()) % maxspeed;
            player.looseLife();
            return true;
        } else if (pos_x > x_rightout){
            pos_x = first_x;
            pos_y = first_y;
            out.play();
            x_speed = (rnd.nextInt ()) % maxspeed;
            player.looseLife();
            return true;
        } else if (pos_y < y_upout){
            pos_x = first_x;
            pos_y = first_y;
            out.play();
            x_speed = (rnd.nextInt ()) % maxspeed;
            player.looseLife();
            return true;
        } else if (pos_y > y_downout){
            pos_x = first_x;
            pos_y = first_y;
            out.play();
            x_speed = (rnd.nextInt ()) % maxspeed;
            player.looseLife();
            return true;
        } else return false;
    }

    public void DrawBall (Graphics g){
        g.setColor (color);
        g.fillOval (pos_x-radius, pos_y-radius, 2*radius,
                                                    2* radius);
    }
}
```

```
import java.awt.*;
import java.util.*;
import java.applet.*;
import java.net.*;

public class MainGame extends Applet implements Runnable{
    private int speed;
    boolean isStoped = true;
    private Player player;
    private Ball redball;
    private Ball blueball;
    Thread th;
    AudioClip shotnoise;
    AudioClip hitnoise;
    AudioClip outnoise;
    Font f = new Font ("Serif", Font.BOLD, 20);
    Cursor c;
    private Image dbImage;
    private Graphics dbg;

    public void init (){
        c = new Cursor (Cursor.CROSSHAIR_CURSOR);
        this.setCursor (c);
        Color superblue = new Color (0, 0, 255);
        setBackground (Color.black);
        setFont (f);
        if (getParameter ("speed") != null){
            speed = Integer.parseInt(getParameter("speed"));
        } else speed = 15;
        hitnoise = getAudioClip (getCodeBase() , "gun.au");
        hitnoise.play();
        hitnoise.stop();
        shotnoise = getAudioClip (getCodeBase() , "miss.au");
        shotnoise.play();
        shotnoise.stop();
        outnoise = getAudioClip (getCodeBase() , "error.au");
        outnoise.play();
        outnoise.stop();
        player = new Player ();
        redball = new
         Ball (10, 190, 250, 1, -1, 4, Color.red, outnoise,  player);
        blueball = new
         Ball (10, 190, 150, 1, 1, 3, Color.blue, outnoise, player);
    }

    public void start (){
        th = new Thread (this);
        th.start ();
    }

    public void stop (){
        th.stop();
    }

    public boolean mouseDown (Event e, int x, int y){
        if (!isStoped){
```

```
        if (redball.userHit (x, y)) {
          hitnoise.play();
          redball.ballWasHit ();
        }
        if (blueball.userHit (x, y)) {
          hitnoise.play();
          blueball.ballWasHit ();
        } else{
          shotnoise.play();
        }
      } else if (isStoped && e.clickCount == 2)        {
        isStoped = false;
        init ();
      }
      return true;
    }

    public void run (){

Thread.currentThread().setPriority(Thread.MIN_PRIORITY);
      while (true){
        if (player.getLives() >= 0 && !isStoped){
          redball.move();
          blueball.move();
        }
        repaint();
        try{
          Thread.sleep (speed);
         } catch (InterruptedException ex){}
        Thread.currentThread().
                         setPriority(Thread.MAX_PRIORITY);
      }
    }

    public void paint (Graphics g){
      if (player.getLives() >= 0){
        g.setColor (Color.yellow);
        g.drawString ("Score: " + player.getScore(), 10, 40);
        g.drawString ("Lives: " + player.getLives(), 300, 40);
        redball.DrawBall(g);
        blueball.DrawBall(g);
        if (isStoped){
          g.setColor (Color.yellow);
          g.drawString ("Doubleclick on Applet to start Game!",
                                                    40, 200);
        }
      } else if (player.getLives() < 0){
        g.setColor (Color.yellow);
        g.drawString ("Game over!", 130, 100);
        g.drawString ("You scored " + player.getScore() +
                                         " Points!", 90, 140);
        if (player.getScore() < 300)
            g.drawString ("Well, it could be better!", 100, 190);
       else if (player.getScore()<600 &&
              player.getScore() >= 300)
            g.drawString ("That was not so bad", 100, 190);
       else if (player.getScore()<900 &&
              player.getScore()>=600)
            g.drawString ("That was really good", 100, 190);
       else if (player.getScore()<1200 &&
              player.getScore()>=900)
          g.drawString ("You seem to be very good!", 90,190);
       else if (player.getScore() <1500 &&
              player.getScore()>=1200)
          g.drawString ("That was nearly perfect!", 90, 190);
      else if (player.getScore() >= 1500)
      g.drawString ("You are the Champion!",100, 190);
      g.drawString ("Doubleclick on the Applet, to play again!",
                                                    20, 220);
      isStoped = true;
      }
    }

    public void update (Graphics g){
      if (dbImage == null) {
        dbImage = createImage
                (this.getSize().width,this.getSize().height);
        dbg = dbImage.getGraphics ();
      }
        dbg.setColor (getBackground ());
        dbg.fillRect (0, 0, this.getSize().width,
                         this.getSize().height);
        dbg.setColor (getForeground());
        paint (dbg);
        g.drawImage (dbImage, 0, 0, this);
      }
}
```

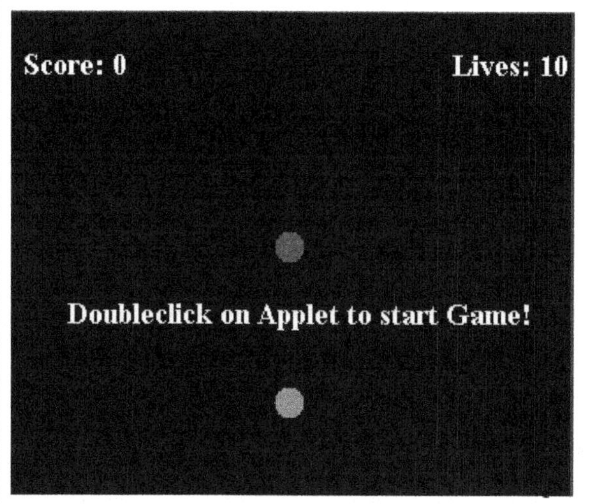

Hit the red ball and the blue ball before they reach the border of the game field by clicking on them with the mouse pointer. If you have lost all your lives, the game is over!

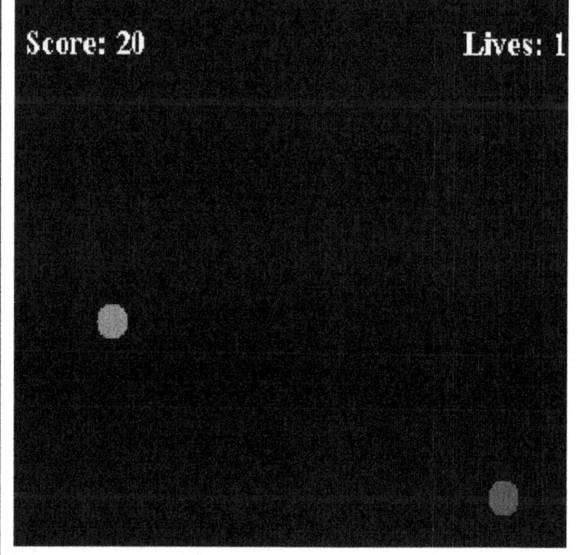

11. Flash ActionScript

ActionScript allows one to add interactivity to graphics, video and other items in Flash Professional. With features like vectors, tweening and inverse kinematics, the graphics can be easily drawn and animated. One of the major strengths of Flash ActionScript is its support for audio and video streaming.

As a start, lets tween a cicle in Flash Professional.
Step 1: Go to 'File -> New -> ActionScript 3.0'.

Step 2: On the side, click 'Rectangular Tool'. Select 'Oval Tool'. Then draw a cicle on the stage.

Step 3: On the Timeline at the bottom, right-click Frame 30 for Layer 1. Choose 'Insert Frame'. Then right-click anywhere between Frame 1 to Frame 30. Choose 'Create Motion Tween'.

Step 4: Click Frame 30. Drag the circle to a new location.

Step 5: Click the symbol at the bottom left to add a new layer. Right-click Frame 1 for Layer 2, and choose 'Actions'. In the editor, enter the line: trace("Hello World");

Step 6: To run it, go to 'Control -> Test Movie -> Test'. Alternatively, press CTRL + ENTER.

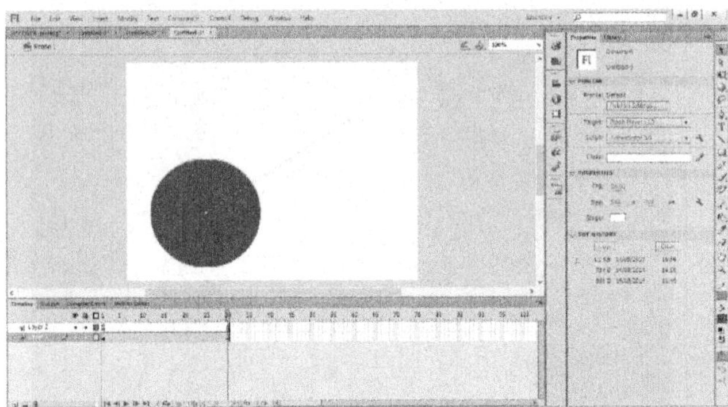

Note that the working space in Flash Professional is saved as a .fla document. Classes and other scipts are saved as .as files. Flash videos are saved as .flv. A .swf file represents the final product. To publish a .swf file in a webpage, press F12, view the page source, and copy the the embedding content. You may modify some of the parameters passed in.

A reference for the ActionScript API can be found at: **http://help.adobe.com/en_US/FlashPlatform/reference/actionscript/3/**

11.1 Basic Syntax

Statements are separated by ';'. Inline comments are denoted by // while block comments are denoted by /* ... */.

11.1.1 Variables and Constants

A variable must be declared before it can be used. A variable declaration has the forms:

```
var name:type;
var name:type = new type;
var name:type = new type(initialValue);
var name:type = initialValue;
```

where 'type' can be Boolean, String, Number, Array, int, uint, Object or any class or interface. For example,

```
var s1:String;
var b1:Boolean = new Boolean;
var n1:Number = new Number(5);
var b2:Boolean = true;
var s2:String = "Hello";
var n2:int = 0x111;   // hexadecimal

var a1:Array = new Array(1,2,3);
var a2:Array = [15,"hello"];
var ma:Array = new Array();
ma[0] = ["abc","def"];
ma[1] = [123,456];
trace (ma[0][1]);

var o1:Object = {p1:5, "p2":"Ali"};
trace(o1.p1); trace(o1["p1"]);
```

A constant is similar to a variable except that its value cannot be changed. A constant declaration has the forms:

```
const name:type = new type;
const name:type = new type(initialValue);
const name:type = initialValue;
```

To escape a special character in a string, lead the character with a '\': \b (backspace), \f (formfeed), \n (line feed), \r (carriage return), \t (tab), \" (double quote), \' (single quote), \\ (backslash), \ddd (octal sequence), \xdd (hexadecimal sequence), \udddd (Unicode sequence).

11.1.2 Operators

The operators, in order of decreasing precedence, are:

[] {x:y} () f(x) new x.y x[y] <> </> @ :: ..
++ -- +(unary) -(unary) ~ ! delete typeof void
* / %
+ -
<< >> >>>
< > <= >= as in instanceof is
== != === !==
&
^

&&
?:
= *= /= %= += -= <<= >>= >>>= $= ^= |=
,

The operators are similar to those in JavaScript. See 3.1.2 for a detailed explanation.

11.1.3 Conditionals

The conditional statements are similar to those in JavaScript (3.1.3):

if (*condition*) *statement1*; [**else** *statement2;*]

if (*condition*) {*statements1;*} [**else** {*statements2;*}]

switch (*expression*){
  case value1: statements1; **break**;
  case value2: statements2; **break**;
  case value3: statements3; **break**;
  ......
  default: statements4;
}

(*expression*)**?***value1***:***value2*

11.1.4 Loops

Similarly, looping statements include:

while (*cycle condition*) {*statements;*}

do {*statements;*} **while** (*cycle condition*);

for (*pre-loop statements;*
    cycle condition;
    cycle statements;) {*statements;*}

for (**var** *element:type* **in** *collection*) {*statements;*}

for each (**var** *element* **in** *collection*) {*statements;*}

```
var myObj:Object = {a:15, b:25};
for (var i:String in myObj) trace(i + ": " + myObj[i]);
```
```
b: 25
a: 15
```

```
var myArray:Array = ["abc", "opq", "xyz"];
for (var i:String in myArray) trace(i + ": " + myArray[i]);
```
```
0: abc
1: opq
2: xyz
```

```
var myObj:Object = {a:15, b:25};
for each(var i in myObj) trace(i);
```
```
25
15
```

```
var myArray:Array = ["abc", "opq", "xyz"];
for each(var i in myArray) trace(i);
```
```
abc
opq
xyz
```

```
var myXML:XML =
<students>
  <fname>Ali</fname>
  <fname>Chan</fname>
  <fname>Bruce</fname>
</students>;

for each (var item in myXML.fname) trace(item);
```
```
Ali
Chan
Bruce
```

A loop can be terminated within by 'break;'. To jump to the next iteration, use 'continue;'.

```
var i:int;
for (i=0; i<100; i++){
  if (i<5) continue;
  trace(i);
  if (i>8) break;
}
```
```
5
6
7
8
9
```

11.1.5 Functions

A function can be defined as a function statement:
function funcName([param:type[=defaultValue]...])
                [:returnType]{...}

or a function expression:
var funcName**:Function** = function
 ([param:type[=defaultValue]...])[:returnType] {...}

In contrast with a function statement, a function expression can be 'delete'd in memory, can only be used on subsequent statements, and can be assigned to elements of arrays or objects.

This demonstrates the use of a function expression.

```
var traceArray:Array = new Array();
traceArray[0] = function
            (aParam:String,bParam:String="world"):void{
  trace(aParam+bParam);
};
traceArray[0]("hello ");
```
```
hello world
```

A function nested within another function is only accessible within the parent function, and has higher precedence over a function of the same name declared outside the parent function.

```
function f1(){
  function f2(){
    trace("inside");
  }
  f2();
}

function f2(){
  trace("outside");
}

f1();
```

```
Inside
```

Function parameters of the primitive types (Boolean, Number, int, uint, String) are passed by value. Function parameters of the other types are passed by reference.

```
function passPrimitive(xParam:int):void {
   xParam++;
}

var xValue:int = 3;
trace(xValue);
passPrimitive(xValue);
trace(xValue);
```

```
3
3
```

```
function passObj(objParam:Object):void{
   objParam.x++;
}
var objVar:Object = {x:10};
trace(objVar.x);
passObj(objVar);
trace(objVar.x);
```

```
10
11
```

You can use the 'arguments' object within a function to access the parameters. The parameters number and the calling function can also be accessed.

```
function argArray(x:int,y:int,z:int):void {
  trace(arguments.callee);
  for (var i:uint = 0; i < arguments.length; i++)
    trace(arguments[i]);

}
argArray(1, 2, 3);
```

```
function Function() {}
1
2
3
```

You can use the ... operator to allow a function to accept an arbitrary number of parameters. With its presence, the 'arguments' becomes no longer available.

```
function argArray(x: int, ... args) {
  for (var i:uint = 0; i < args.length; i++)
    trace(args[i]);
}
argArray(1, 2, 3);
```

```
2
3
```

A function can have properties and methods. The property 'length' is pre-defined and it stores the number of parameters.

```
var f:Function = function ():void {
  trace(f.length);
}
f();
```

```
0
```

11.1.6 Error Handling

Runtime errors may be caught in the '**try**' block, and handled in the '**catch**' block. The '**finally**' block is always executed. You may '**throw**' your own errors. Errors that are not caught are rethrown to the outer block.

```
try {
  trace ("BEGINNING");
  throw "ERROR";
} catch (E){
  trace(E);
} finally {
  trace("FINALLY");
}
```

```
BEGINNING
ERROR
FINALLY
```

You may extend the ActionScript core Error class and throw it during runtime.

11.1.7 Future Reserved Words

Besides the keywords in ActionScript, some words are reserved for the future: **abstract, boolean, byte, cast, char, debugger, double, enum, export, float, goto, intrinsic, long, prototype, short, synchronized, throws, to, transient, type, virtual,** and **volatile.**

11.2 Object Oriented Programming

11.2.1 Classes and Packages

A class is defined like this:

attributes **class** className{...}

where *attributes* can be:

dynamic	Properties may be added to instances at run time.
final	Must not be extended by another class.
internal	(Default). Visible inside the current package only.
public	Visible everywhere.

A class definition may contain variables(or constants), methods, namespaces, and statements. Statements that exist within a class definition outside any methods are executed only once, when the first object

is created out of it.
Classes must not be nested. Because the timeline frames are inherently inside a class, you cannot define a class by right-clicking a frame and choosing Actions. Instead, you must save the public class definition in a separate .as file that has the same name as the class. The package name must also reflect the directory location of the file. The package name should be left as blank if the class file exists within the current working directory. Class files that exist in the current working directory need not be imported.

```
// saved as ./test/testing.as
package test{
  public final class testing {
    trace("hello");
    var message:String = "instance variable";
    public namespace sampleNamespace;
    sampleNamespace function doSomething():void;
  }
}
```

```
import test.testing;
var t:testing = new testing();
var t2:testing = new testing();
```

```
hello
```

11.2.2 Member Attributes

The attributes for a class property or method include:

internal	(Default) Visible inside the same package only.
private	Visible inside the same class only.
protected	Visible in the same class and derived classes only.
public	Visible everywhere.
static	Exists as a single copy that belongs to the class, instead of instances of the class. Static members can be accessed without any instantiation of the class.
final	The method cannot be overriden.
<namespace>	Custom namespace defined.

When referencing the members of an object, the object name may be omitted using **with**.

```
package {
  public class testing {
    private   var num1:int = 1;
    protected var num2:int = 2;
    internal  var num3:int = 3;
    public    var num4:int = 4;
    public function getProduct(){
      trace(num1*num2*num3*num4);
    };

    private   static var snum1:int = 10;
    protected static var snum2:int = 20;
    internal  static var snum3:int = 30;
    public    static var snum4:int = 40;
    public static function getSum(){
      trace(snum1+snum2+snum3+snum4);
    }
  }
}
```

```
import Testing;
var t:Testing = new Testing();
t.getProduct();    // 24
Testing.getSum();  // 100

with (t){
  //trace(num1);     // error
  //trace(num2);     // error
  //trace(num3);     // error
  trace(num4);       // 4
}

with (Testing){
  trace(snum4);      // 40
}
```

```
24
100
4
40
```

11.2.3 Methods

A constructor is a public method within a class that has the same name as the class. It is called automatically whenever an object is instantiated out of the class. A constructor can call the constructor of its parent class by using super(). If super() is not called explicitly, the compiler inserts the call before the first statement in the body. The superclass can also be be referenced with the 'super' prefix. super() should be called before using the 'super' class.

```
class ExampleEx extends Example {
    public function ExampleEx()    {
       super();
       trace(super.status);
    }
}
```

Get and set accessor functions can be defined for a class. A getter function and its associated setter function share the same name, and can be used as if they are variables.

```
package {
  public class GetSet {
    private var privateProperty:String;
    public function get publicAccess():String {
      return privateProperty;
    }
    public function set publicAccess(setValue:String):void {
      privateProperty = setValue;
    }
  }
}
```

```
import GetSet;
var myGetSet:GetSet = new GetSet();
myGetSet.publicAccess = "hello";
trace(myGetSet.publicAccess);
```

```
hello
```

11.2.4 Inheritance

A sub/derived/child class may inherit the properties and methods of a super/base/parent class using the keyword 'extends', as long as the members are not declared as private.

Properties cannot be overriden, but methods can be overriden by using the 'override' keyword at the front of the function declaration. The overriding method must have the same level of access, number of parameters, parameters data types, and return type as the base method.

```
package {
  public class Shape {
    public function area():Number {
      return NaN;
    }
  }
}
```

```
package {
  import Shape;
  public class Circle extends Shape {
    private var radius:Number;
    public function Circle(r:Number){
      radius=r;
    }
    override public function area():Number {
      return (Math.PI * (radius * radius));
    }
  }
}
```

```
package{
  import Shape;
  public class Square extends Shape {
    private var side:Number = 1;
    public function Square(s:Number){
      side=s;
    }
    override public function area():Number {
      return (side * side);
    }
  }
}
```

```
var c:Shape = new Circle(1);
var s:Square = new Square(3);
trace(c.area(),s.area());
```

```
3.141592653589793 9
```

If an instance property is defined and it uses the same name as a static property in the same class or a superclass, the instance property has higher precedence in the scope chain.

11.2.5 Interfaces

An interface is similar to a class. However, it contains a collection of methods that have not been implemented. These methods are meant to be implemented by a class that 'implements' the interface. An interface cannot contain instance variables or constants. A class may implement more than one interfaces. An interface sometimes 'extends' another interface. Interface members cannot be declared as public, private, protected or internal.

```
package {
  public interface A{
    function methodA():void;
  }
}
```

```
package {
  public interface B extends A{
    function methodB():void;
  }
}
```

```
package {
  public interface C{
    function methodC():void;
  }
}
```

```
package {
  public class myClass implements B,C{
    public function methodA():void{
      trace("A");
    }
    public function methodB():void{
      trace("B");
    }
    public function methodC():void{
      trace("C");
    }
  }
}
```

```
var c:myClass = new myClass;
c.methodA();
c.methodB();
c.methodC();
```

```
A
B
C
```

11.2.6 Namespaces

A '**namespace**' can be used to prevent names clash. To reference a namespace, use the **::** operator or simply '**use**' the namespace beforehand.

```
package{
  public namespace mynamespace;
}
```

```
package {
   use namespace mynamespace;
   public class T {
      mynamespace function hello():void{
         trace("Hello World");
      };
   }
}
```

```
var test:T = new T;
test.mynamespace::hello();
```

```
use namespace mynamespace;
var test:T = new T;
test.hello();
```

```
Hello World
```

11.3 Core Classes

11.3.1 Numeric

For Number, int, and uint, you can use:

toExponential(fractionDigits:uint):String
toFixed(fractionDigits:uint):String
toPrecision(precision:uint):String
toString(radix:Number=10):String
valueOf():Number
MAX_VALUE:<varies>
MIN_VALUE:<varies>
NaN:Number
NEGATIVE_INFINITY:Number
POSITIVE_INFINITY:Number

```
var n:Number=1000000;
trace(n.toExponential(3));
trace(n.toFixed(3));
trace(n.toPrecision(3));
trace(n.toString());
trace(n.valueOf());
trace(int.MIN_VALUE);
trace(int.MAX_VALUE);
trace(Number.NaN);
trace(Number.NEGATIVE_INFINITY);
trace(Number.POSITIVE_INFINITY);
```

```
1.000e+6
1000000.000
1.00e+6
1000000
1000000
-2147483648
2147483647
```

```
NaN
-Infinity
Infinity
```

11.3.2 Math

The mathematical functions include:

cos(angleRad:Number):Number
sin(angleRad:Number):Number
tan(angleRad:Number):Number
acos(val:Number):Number
asin(val:Number):Number
atan(val:Number):Number
atan2(y:Number, xNumber):Number
abs(val:Number):Number
ceil(val:Number):Number
floor(val:Number):Number
round(val:Number):Number
max(val1:Number ...rest):Number
min(val1:Number ...rest):Number

exp(val:Number):Number
log(val:Number):Number
pow(base:Number, pow:Number):Number
sqrt(val:Number):Number

random():Number

Mathematical constants (of Number type) include: **E**, **LN10**, **LN2**, **LOG10E**, **LOG2E**, **PI**, **SQRT1_2**, **SQRT2**.

```
trace(Math.atan2(1,2));
trace(Math.random()); //0 to 1
trace(Math.SQRT1_2);
```

```
0.4636476090008061
0.034791987389326096
0.7071067811865476
```

11.3.3 String

The String functions include:

charAt(index:Number=0):String
charCodeAt(index:Number=0):Number
concat(...args):String
fromCharCode(...charCodes):String
indexOf(val:String, startIndex:Number=0):int
lastIndexOf(val:String, startIndex:Number=0x7fffffff):int
localeCompare(other:String,...values):int
match(pattern:*):Array
replace(pattern:*, repl:Object):String
search(pattern:*):int
slice(start:Number=0, end:Number=0x7fffffff):String
split(delimiter:*, limit:Number=0x7fffffff):Array
substr(start:Number=0, len:Number=0x7fffffff):String
toLocaleLowerCase():String
toLocaleUpperCase():String
toLowerCase():String
toUpperCase():String
valueOf():String

length:uint

```
trace("abc".charAt(1));                  // b
trace("abc".charCodeAt(1));              // 98
trace("abc".concat("def","ghi"));        // abcdefghi
trace(String.fromCharCode(97,98,99));    // abc
trace("abc".indexOf("b"));               // 1
trace("abcabc".lastIndexOf("b"));        // 4
trace("a".localeCompare("d"));           // -3
trace("abcdef".match("a..."));           // abcd
trace("abcdef".replace("abcd","X"));     // Xef
trace("abcdef".search("c.."));           // 2
trace("abcdef".slice(1,3));              // bc
trace("a_b_c_d".split("_"));             // a,b,c,d
trace("abcdef".substr(1,3));             // bcd
trace("abcDEF".toLocaleLowerCase());     // abcdef
trace("abcDEF".toLocaleUpperCase());     // ABCDEF
trace("abcDEF".toLowerCase());           // abcdef
trace("abcDEF".toUpperCase());           // ABCDEF
trace("abcDEF".toString());              // abcDEF
trace("abcDEF".length);                  // 6
```

11.3.4 Array

The array functions include:

indexOf(searchElement:*, fromIndex:int=0):int
lastIndexOf(searchElement:*,fromIndex:int=0x7fffffff):int
join(sep:*):String
toLocaleString():String
toString():String

```
var a:Array = [1,2,3,2,1];
trace(a.indexOf(2));
trace(a.lastIndexOf(2));
trace(a.join("_"));
trace(a.toLocaleString());
trace(a.toString());
```

```
1
3
1_2_3_2_1
1,2,3,2,1
1,2,3,2,1
```

pop():*
push(...args):uint
shift():*
unshift(...args):uint
concat(...args):Array
slice(startIndex:int=0, endIndex:int=16777215):Array
splice(startIndex:int, deleteCount:uint, ...values):Array

```
var a:Array = [100,200,300,400,500];
trace(a.pop()); // removes 500
trace(a.pop()); // removes 400
trace(a.push(800,900)); // adds 800,900 to the end
trace(a);

trace(a.shift()); // removes 100
trace(a.shift()); // removes 200
trace(a.unshift(10,20)); // adds 10,20 to the front
trace(a);

// returns a new array with 1000,2000 added to the end
trace(a.concat(1000,2000));

// returns a new array containing elements 2-3
trace(a.slice(2,4));

// removes elements 0-1 and
// adds 8888,9999 to the front
trace(a.splice(0,2,8888,9999));
trace(a);
```

```
500
400
5
100,200,300,800,900
100
200
5
10,20,300,800,900
10,20,300,800,900,1000,2000
```

```
300,800
10,20
8888,9999,300,800,900
```

reverse():Array
sort(...args):Array
sortOn(fieldName:Object, options:Object=null):Array

The parameters used for sorting include:
CASEINSENSITIVE:uint
DESCENDING:uint
UNIQUESORT:uint
RETURNINDEXEDARRAY:uint
NUMERIC:uint

```
var a:Array = [3,20,10,500,400];

a.reverse();trace(a);

a.sort(); trace(a);

function sortInt(a:int,b:int):int{
  if (a>b) return 1;
  if (a<b) return -1;
  return 0;
}
a.sort(sortInt,Array.UNIQUESORT|Array.NUMERIC);trace(a);

var o1:Object = {num1:30, num2:99};
var o2:Object = {num1:10, num2:99};
var o3:Object = {num1:20, num2:99};
var b:Array = new Array(o1,o2,o3);
trace(b[0].num1,b[1].num1,b[2].num1);
b.sortOn("num1",Array.UNIQUESORT|Array.NUMERIC);
trace(b[0].num1,b[1].num1,b[2].num1);
```

```
400,500,10,20,3
10,20,3,400,500
3,10,20,400,500
30 10 20
10 20 30
```

every(callback:Function, thisObject:*=null):Boolean
some(callback:Function, thisObject:*=null):Boolean
filter(callback:Function, thisObject:*=null):Array
forEach(callback:Function, thisObject:*=null):void
map(callback:Function, thisObject:*=null):Array

```
var a:Array = [1,"a","b",7,9];
trace(a.every(isNumeric)); // all elements?
trace(a.some(isNumeric)); // some elements?
trace(a.filter(isNumeric)); // new array constructed
a.forEach(traceIt);
trace(a.map(incr));

function isNumeric(element:*, index:int, arr:Array ):Boolean{
  return (element is Number);
}

function traceIt(element:*, index:int, arr:Array ):void{
  trace(element);
}

function incr(element:*, index:int, arr:Array ):int{
  return(element+1);
}
```

```
false
true
1,7,9
1
a
b
7
9
2,0,0,8,10
```

11.3.5 Date

The properties and methods in the Date class include:

fullYear[UTC]:Number
month[UTC]:Number
date[UTC]:Number
day[UTC]:Number
hours[UTC]:Number
minutes[UTC]:Number
seconds[UTC]:Number
milliseconds[UTC]:Number
time:Number
timezoneOffset:Number

get[UTC]FullYear():Number
get[UTC]Month():Number
get[UTC]Date():Number
get[UTC]Day():Number
get[UTC]Hours():Number
get[UTC]Minutes():Number
get[UTC]Seconds():Number
get[UTC]Milliseconds():Number
getTime():Number
getTimezoneOffset():Number

parse(date:String):Number

set[UTC]FullYear(y:Number, m:Number, d:Number):Number
set[UTC]Month(m:Number, d:Number):Number
set[UTC]Date(d:Number):Number
set[UTC]Hours (h:Number,m:Number,s:Number,ms:Number):Number
set[UTC]Minutes(m:Number,s:Number,ms:Number):Number
set[UTC]Seconds(s:Number,ms:Number):Number
set[UTC]Milliseconds(ms:Number):Number
setTime(ms:Number):Number

to[Locale][Date|Time]String():String
toJSON(k:String):*
toUTCString():String
UTC(y:Number, mo:Number, d:Number=1, h:Number=0, m:Number=0, s:Number=0, ms:Number=0):Number
valueOf():Number

```
var d:Date = new Date;
trace(d.date);  // 1-31
trace(d.getDay()); // 0-6
trace(d.time); // milliseconds since midnight January 1, 1970
trace(d.timezoneOffset); // difference in minutes with UTC
universal time
trace(d.setUTCMinutes(45)); // returns d.time
trace(d.valueOf()); // returns d.time
trace(d.toString());
trace(d.toTimeString());

// Setting an arbitrary date and time
var d2:Date = new Date(2014,3,14,11,29,30,500);
var d3:Date = new Date(d.time);
var d4:Date = new Date("Mon May 1 2006 11:30:00 AM");

// These obtain the number of milliseconds since
// midnight January 1, 1970
var ms1:Number = Date.parse
                ('Wed Apr 12 15:30:17 GMT-0700 2006');
var ms2:Number = Date.parse
                ('Wed 12 Apr 15:30:17 GMT-0700 2006');
var ms3:Number = Date.parse
                ('04/12/2006 15:30:17 GMT-0700');
var ms4:Number = Date.parse
                ('15:30:17 GMT-0700 Wed 04/12/2006');
var ms5:Number = Date.parse
                ('Apr 12 2006 15:30:17 GMT-0700');
```

```
var ms6:Number = Date.parse
                    ('Apr/12/2006 15:30:17 GMT-0700');
var ms7:Number = Date.parse
                    ('2006/04/12 15:30:17 GMT-0700');

// Difference in milliseconds with midnight January 1, 1970
trace(Date.UTC(2010,05));
```

```
14
5
1394767103730
-480
1394768723730
1394768723730
Fri Mar 14 11:45:23 GMT+0800 2014
11:45:23 GMT+0800
1275350400000
```

11.3.6 Regular Expression

The RegExp class includes:

dotall: Boolean (read-only:s)
extended: Boolean (read-only:x)
global: Boolean (read-only:g)
ignoreCase: Boolean (read-only:i)
multiline: Boolean (read-only:m)

source: String
lastIndex: Number

exec(str:String): Object
test(str:String): Boolean

A detailed explanation on the usage of regular expressions can be found at (3.2.9).

```
var r1:RegExp = new RegExp("a..","");
trace("00abc00".search(r1)); // 2
trace("a\n\n axy abc".replace(r1,"X"));

// g performs all replacements
// s matches new-line characters for .
var r2:RegExp = new RegExp("a..","gs");
trace("a\n\n axy abc".match(r2));
trace("a\n\n axy abc".replace(r2,"X"));

// g must be specified to use lastIndex
var r3:RegExp = /a\d\d/g;
trace(r3.test("XYZa12XYZa23")); // true
trace(r3.lastIndex); // 6
trace(r3.exec("XYZa12XYZa23")); // a23
trace(r3.lastIndex); // 12
```

```
2
a

 X abc
a

,axy,abc
X X X
true
6
a23
12
```

11.3.7 XML

The XML class includes:

ignoreComments: Boolean
ignoreProcessingInstructions: Boolean
ignoreWhitespace: Boolean
prettyIndent: int
prettyPrinting: Boolean

appendChild(child:Object):XML
prependChild(child:Object):XML
insertChildAfter(child1:Object, child2:Object):*
insertChildBefore(child1:Object, child2:Object):*

```
var p1:XML = <p>Paragraph 1</p>;
var p2:XML = <p>Paragraph 2</p>;
var B:XML = <body></body> ;
B = B.appendChild(p1);
B = B.appendChild(p2);
B = B.prependChild(<p>Paragraph 0</p>);

var o:Object = {name:"Paragraph 1b"};
var p1b:XML = <p>{o["name"]}</p>;
B = B.insertChildAfter(B.p[1],p1b);

B.span = "Span 1";
B.@id = "testing";

trace(B);
```

```
<body id="testing">
  <p>Paragraph 0</p>
  <p>Paragraph 1</p>
  <p>Paragraph 1b</p>
  <p>Paragraph 2</p>
  <span>Span 1</span>
</body>
```

attribute(attributeName:*):XMLList
attributes():XMLList
childIndex():int
child(propertyName:Object):XMLList
children():XMLList
descendants(name:Object=*):XMLList
parent():*
elements(name:Object=*):XMLList
hasOwnProperty(p:String):Boolean

```
var myXML:XML =
  <school>
    <student NRIC="N2340983123" ID="123456">
      <classRoom>3J</classRoom>
      <fullName>
        <lastName>Julius</lastName>
        <firstName>Patrick</firstName>
      </fullName>
      <sex>male</sex>
    </student>
    <student NRIC="N8907887456" ID="654321">
      <classRoom>4A</classRoom>
      <fullName>
        <lastName>Muiyen</lastName>
        <firstName>Nguyen</firstName>
      </fullName>
      <sex>female</sex>
    </student>
  </school>;
```

```
trace(myXML.student);
```

```
<student NRIC="N2340983123" ID="123456">
  <classRoom>3J</classRoom>
  <fullName>
    <lastName>Julius</lastName>
    <firstName>Patrick</firstName>
  </fullName>
  <sex>male</sex>
</student>
<student NRIC="N8907887456" ID="654321">
  <classRoom>4A</classRoom>
  <fullName>
    <lastName>Muiyen</lastName>
    <firstName>Nguyen</firstName>
  </fullName>
  <sex>female</sex>
</student>
```

```
trace(myXML..fullName);
```

```
<fullName>
  <lastName>Julius</lastName>
  <firstName>Patrick</firstName>
</fullName>
<fullName>
  <lastName>Muiyen</lastName>
  <firstName>Nguyen</firstName>
</fullName>
```

```
trace(myXML.student[0].classRoom.parent().child("sex"));
```

```
male
```

```
trace(myXML.student[0].@NRIC);
trace(myXML.student[0]["@NRIC"]);
trace(myXML.student[0].@["NRIC"]);
trace(myXML.student[0].attribute("NRIC"));
```

```
N2340983123
N2340983123
N2340983123
N2340983123
```

```
trace(myXML.student[0].@*);
```

```
N2340983123123456
```

```
trace(myXML.student.(sex=="male"));
```

```
<student NRIC="N2340983123" ID="123456">
  <classRoom>3J</classRoom>
  <fullName>
    <lastName>Julius</lastName>
    <firstName>Patrick</firstName>
  </fullName>
  <sex>male</sex>
</student>
```

```
trace(myXML.student.(@ID > 600000));
```

```
<student NRIC="N8907887456" ID="654321">
  <classRoom>4A</classRoom>
  <fullName>
    <lastName>Muiyen</lastName>
    <firstName>Nguyen</firstName>
  </fullName>
  <sex>female</sex>
</student>
```

```
trace(myXML.student.(elements("sex")=="male"));
```

```
<student NRIC="N2340983123" ID="123456">
  <classRoom>3J</classRoom>
  <fullName>
    <lastName>Julius</lastName>
    <firstName>Patrick</firstName>
  </fullName>
  <sex>male</sex>
</student>
```

```
for each(var s:String in myXML.student) trace(s);
```

```
<student NRIC="N2340983123" ID="123456">
  <classRoom>3J</classRoom>
  <fullName>
    <lastName>Julius</lastName>
    <firstName>Patrick</firstName>
  </fullName>
  <sex>male</sex>
</student>
<student NRIC="N8907887456" ID="654321">
  <classRoom>4A</classRoom>
  <fullName>
    <lastName>Muiyen</lastName>
    <firstName>Nguyen</firstName>
  </fullName>
  <sex>female</sex>
</student>
```

```
addNamespace(ns:Object):XML
namespace(prefix:String=null):*
namespaceDeclarations():Array
removeNamespace(ns:Namespace):XML
setNamespace(ns:Namespace):void
inScopeNamespaces():Array

comments():XMLList
contains(value:XML):Boolean
copy():XML
defaultSettings():Object
hasComplexContent():Boolean
hasSimpleContent():Boolean
length():int
localName():Object
name():Object
nodeKind():String
normalize():XML
processingInstructions(name:String="*"):XMLList
propertyIsEnumerable(p:String):Boolean
replace(propertyName:Object, value:XML):XML
setChildren(value:Object):XML
setLocalName(name:String):void
setName(name:String):void
setSettings(...rest):void
settings():Object

text():XMLList
toJSON(k:String):*
toString():String
toXMLString():String
valueOf():XML
```

The XMLList class includes:

attribute(attributeName:*):XMLList
attributes():XMLList
child(propertyName:Object):XMLList
children():XMLList
comments():XMLList
contains(value:XML):Boolean
copy():XMLList
descendants(name:Object=*):XMLList
elements(name:Object=*):XMLList
hasComplexContent():Boolean
hasOwnProperty(p:String):Boolean
hasSimpleContent():Boolean
length():int
normalize():XMLList
parent():Object
processingInstructions(name:String="*"):XMLList
propertyIsEnumerable(p:String):Boolean
text():XMLList
toString():String
toXMLString():String
valueOf():XMLList

This reads an external XML file.

```
import flash.events.Event;
import flash.net.URLLoader;

var myXML:XML = new XML();
var XML_URL:String =
                      "http://www.example.com/Sample.xml";
var myXMLURL:URLRequest = new URLRequest(XML_URL);
var myLoader:URLLoader = new URLLoader(myXMLURL);
myLoader.addEventListener(Event.COMPLETE, xmlLoaded);

function xmlLoaded(event:Event):void {
   myXML = XML(myLoader.data);
   trace("Data loaded.");
}
```

11.4 Drawing

11.4.1 DisplayObject

The following shows the hierarchy of subclasses of the DisplayObject class:

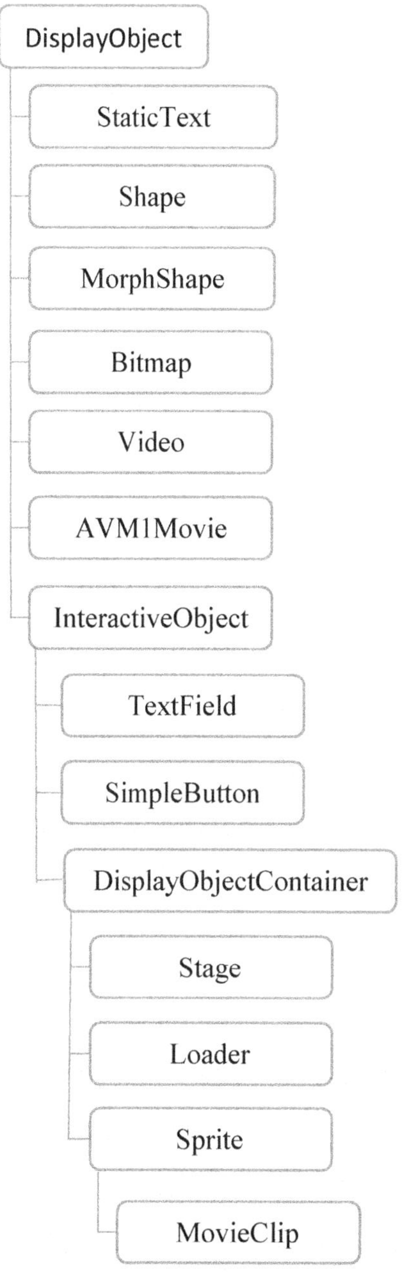

Some common members of DisplayObject are:

alpha: Number
width: Number
height: Number
x: Number
y: Number
scaleX: Number (factor)
scaleY: Number (factor)
rotation: Number (degrees, clockwise)
visible: Boolean
cacheAsBitmap: Boolean
mask: DisplayObject
filters: Array
blendMode: String
blendShader: Shader
transform: Transform
hitTestObject(o:DisplayObject):Boolean
hitTestPoint(x:Number, y:Number, s:Boolean=false):Boolean

11.4.2 Graphics

The Shape, Sprite and MovieClip objects include the Graphics property which can be used to draw vector graphics. The coordinates (0,0) are located at the upper left corner.

The Graphics class includes the following methods:

moveTo(x:Number, y:Number):void

lineTo(x:Number, y:Number):void

curveTo(controlX:Number, controlY:Number, X:Number, Y:Number):void

drawPath(commands:Vector.<int>, data:Vector.<Number>, winding:String ="evenOdd"):void

------

drawRect(x:Number, y:Number, width:Number, height:Number):void

drawRoundRect(x:Number, y:Number, width:Number, height:Number, ellipseWidth:Number, ellipseHeight:Number=NaN):void

drawCircle(x:Number, y:Number, radius:Number):void

drawEllipse(x:Number, y:Number, width:Number, height:Number):void

drawTriangles(vertices:Vector.<Number>, indices:Vector.<int>=null, uvtData:Vector.<Number>=null, culling:String="none"):void

------

lineBitmapStyle(bitmap:BitmapData, matrix:Matrix=null, repeat:Boolean=true, smooth:Boolean=false):void

lineGradientStyle(type:String, colors:Array, alphas:Array, ratios:Array, matrix:Matrix=null, spread:String="pad", interpolation:String="rgb", focalPointRatio:Number=0):void

lineShaderStyle(shader:Shader, matrix:Matrix=null):void

lineStyle(thickness:Number=NaN, color:uint=0, alpha:Number=1.0, pixelHinting:Boolean=false, scaleMode:String="normal", caps:String=null, joints:String=null, miterLimit:Number=3):void

------

beginBitmapFill(bitmap:BitmapData, matrix:Matrix=null, repeat:Boolean=true, smooth:Boolean=false):void

beginFill(color:uint, alpha:Number=1.0):void

beginGradientFill(type:String, colors:Array, alphas:Array, ratios:Array, matrix:Matrix=null, spread:String="pad", interpolation:String="rgb", focalPointRatio:Number=0):void

beginShaderFill(shader:Shader, matrix:Matrix=null):void

endFill():void

------

drawGraphicsData(graphicsData:Vector.<IGraphicsData>):void

copyFrom(sourceGraphics:Graphics):void

clear():void

(**commands** can be GraphicsPathCommand.MOVE_TO, GraphicsPathCommand.LINE_TO, GraphicsPathCommand.CURVE_TO etc.)

(**culling** can be TriangleCulling.POSITIVE or TriangleCulling.NEGATIVE.)

(**winding** can be GraphicsPathWinding.EVEN_ODD, Graphics.PathWinding.NON_ZERO);

(**type** can be GradientType.LINEAR or GradientType.RADIAL.)

(**spread** can be SpreadMethod.PAD, SpreadMethod.REFLECT, or SpreadMethod.REPEAT.)

(**interpolation** can be InterpolationMethod.RGB or InterpolationMethod.LINEAR_RGB.)

```
import flash.display.Shape;
import flash.geom.Matrix;

var s:Shape = new Shape();

s.graphics.lineStyle(5,0x000000);
s.graphics.beginFill(0xFFFF00);
s.graphics.moveTo(50,50);
s.graphics.lineTo(50,150);
s.graphics.lineTo(150,150);
s.graphics.curveTo(150,0,50,50);

var M:Matrix = new Matrix();
// M.createGradientBox(width,height,rotatio,tx,ty);
M.createGradientBox(150,150,0,0,0);
s.graphics.beginGradientFill(GradientType.RADIAL,
                             [0xFF0000, 0x00FF00, 0x0000FF],
                             [1,1,1],
                             [0,127,255],
                             M,
                             SpreadMethod.REFLECT);
s.graphics.drawCircle(300,150,100);

addChild(s);
```

```
var s:Sprite = new Sprite();

var commands:Vector.<int> = new Vector.<int>(5, true);
commands[0] = GraphicsPathCommand.MOVE_TO;
commands[1] = GraphicsPathCommand.LINE_TO;
commands[2] = GraphicsPathCommand.LINE_TO;
commands[3] = GraphicsPathCommand.LINE_TO;
commands[4] = GraphicsPathCommand.LINE_TO;

var coord:Vector.<Number> = new Vector.<Number>(
                                                10, true);
coord[0] = 66; //x1
coord[1] = 10; //y1
coord[2] = 23;
coord[3] = 127;
coord[4] = 122;
coord[5] = 50;
coord[6] = 10;
coord[7] = 49;
coord[8] = 109;
coord[9] = 127;

s.graphics.beginFill(0x663300);
s.graphics.drawPath(commands, coord);
addChild(s);
```

Before running this script, import the pattern file to the library. Then, right click the file in the library, choose Properties, export it for ActionScript, and name the class 'Pattern'.

```
var mc:MovieClip = new MovieClip();

var vertices:Vector.<Number>=new Vector.<Number>(
                                                6, true);
vertices[0] = 150;
vertices[1] = 10;
vertices[2] = 0;
vertices[3] = 200;
vertices[4] = 300;
vertices[5] = 200;

var indices:Vector.<int> = new Vector.<int>(3, true);
indices[0] = 0;
indices[1] = 1;
indices[2] = 2;

var matrix:Matrix = new Matrix();
matrix.rotate(Math.PI/4);

mc.graphics.beginBitmapFill(
                    new Pattern(), matrix, true, false);
mc.graphics.drawTriangles(vertices,indices);
mc.graphics.endFill();

addChild(mc);
```

11.4.3 Geometry

The 'flash.geom' package contains the Point, Rectangle and Matrix classes that ease geometric calculations. A Matrix object has 6 parameters:

$$\begin{bmatrix} a & c & t_x \\ b & d & t_y \\ 0 & 0 & 1 \end{bmatrix}$$

```
import flash.geom.Point;
import flash.geom.Rectangle;
import flash.geom.Matrix;

var p1:Point = new Point(100,200);
var p2:Point = new Point(10,20);
p1.y=150;
trace (p1.length);     // 180.2: (0, 0) to (100,150)
trace(p1.add(p2));     // (x=110, y=170)
trace(p1.equals(p2)); // false
trace(Point.distance(p1,p2));        // 158.1
trace(Point.interpolate(p1,p2,0.1)); //(x=19, y=33)

var r1:Rectangle = new Rectangle(10,10,100,100);
var r2:Rectangle = new Rectangle(20,20,50,150);
trace(r1.contains(50,50));  //true
trace(r1.containsPoint(p1)); // false
trace(r1.containsRect(r2)); // false
trace(r1.equals(r2));         // false
trace(r1.intersects(r2));     // true
trace(r1.intersection(r2)); // (x=20, y=20, w=50, h=90)
trace(r1.union(r2));          // (x=10, y=10, w=100, h=160)
trace(r1.topLeft);            // (x=10, y=10)
r1.inflate(10,20);
r1.offset(10,20);
r1.setTo(10,20,100,100);

// Matrix (a,b,c,d,tx,ty);
var m1:Matrix = new Matrix(1,2,3,4,5,6);
var m2:Matrix = new Matrix(6,5,4,3,2,1);
m1.concat(m2);
m1.identity();
m1.invert();
m1.translate(10,20);
m1.rotate(Math.PI);
m1.scale(5,2);
m1.setTo(1,2,3,4,5,6);
```

11.4.4 Tweening

You may incorporate a motion tween into a script by selecting Edit -> Timeline -> Copy Motion as ActionScript 3.0. Then copy the code into a script by pressing CTRL + V.

This piece of code is generated by Flash Professional automatically. You may edit it to customize the tween.

```
import fl.motion.AnimatorFactory;
import fl.motion.MotionBase;
import fl.motion.Motion;
import flash.filters.*;
import flash.geom.Point;
var __motion_Symbol1_2:MotionBase;
if(__motion_Symbol1_2 == null) {
   __motion_Symbol1_2 = new Motion();
   __motion_Symbol1_2.duration = 30;

   // Call overrideTargetTransform to prevent the scale, skew,
   // or rotation values from being made relative to the target
   // object's original transform.
   // __motion_Symbol1_2.overrideTargetTransform();

  // The following calls to addPropertyArray assign data values
  // for each tweened property. There is one value in the Array
```

```
    // for every frame in the tween, or fewer if the last value
    // remains the same for the rest of the frames.
    __motion_Symbol1_2.addPropertyArray("x",
[0,12.5155,25.031,37.534,50.0621,62.5776,75.0806,87.6086
,100.124,112.64,125.155,137.658,150.174,162.702,175.217,
187.733,200.248,212.764,225.279,237.795,250.31,262.826,2
75.329,287.857,300.36,312.875,325.403,337.919,350.434,36
2.95]);
    __motion_Symbol1_2.addPropertyArray("y", [0,-6.55172,-
13.1034,-19.6486,-26.2069,-32.7586,-39.3038,-45.8621,-
52.4138,-58.9655,-65.5172,-72.0624,-78.6141,-85.1724,-
91.7241,-98.2759,-104.828,-111.379,-117.931,-124.483,-
131.034,-137.586,-144.131,-150.69,-157.235,-163.787,-
170.345,-176.897,-183.448,-190]);

  __motion_Symbol1_2.addPropertyArray("scaleX",[1.000000])
;

  __motion_Symbol1_2.addPropertyArray("scaleY",[1.000000]);
  __motion_Symbol1_2.addPropertyArray("skewX", [0]);
  __motion_Symbol1_2.addPropertyArray("skewY", [0]);
  __motion_Symbol1_2.addPropertyArray("rotationConcat",[0])
;__motion_Symbol1_2.addPropertyArray("blendMode",
                                     ["normal"]);
  __motion_Symbol1_2.addPropertyArray("cacheAsBitmap",
                                     [false]);
  __motion_Symbol1_2.addPropertyArray("opaqueBackground",
                                     [null]);
  __motion_Symbol1_2.addPropertyArray("visible", [true]);

    // Create an AnimatorFactory instance, which will manage
    // targets for its corresponding Motion.
    var __animFactory_Symbol1_2:AnimatorFactory =
                new AnimatorFactory(__motion_Symbol1_2);
    __animFactory_Symbol1_2.transformationPoint =
                new Point(0.500000, 0.500000);

// Call the addTarget function on the AnimatorFactory
// instance to target a DisplayObject with this Motion.
// The second parameter is the number of times the animation
// will play - the default value of 0 means it will loop.
// __animFactory_Symbol1_2.addTarget(<instance name goes
// here>, 0);
}
```

Use the addPropertyArray() method to define the tween properties: **x, y, z, scaleX, scaleY, skewX, skewY, rotationX, rotationY, rotationZ, rotationConcat, useRotationConcat, blendMode, matrix3D.** For the second array parameter, include either one value or a number of values that equals the number of frames.

11.4.5 Coloring

Each DisplayObject contains the transform.colorTransform property, which is an instance of the ColorTransform class. The ColorTransform class includes the following properties:

color: uint
{red|green|blue|alpha}Multiplier:Number
{red|green|blue|alpha}Offset:Number

The multipliers are decimal values to be multiplied with the channel values. The offsets range from -255 to 255, and are added after the multipliers have been applied.

This draws a completely red circle. Notice the change affects both the stroke color and the fill color.

```
import flash.display.Sprite;
import flash.geom.ColorTransform;

var s:Sprite = new Sprite();
s.graphics.lineStyle(5,0x000000);
s.graphics.beginFill(0x00FF00);
s.graphics.drawCircle(100,100,50);

var ct:ColorTransform = new ColorTransform();
ct.color = 0xFF0000;
s.transform.colorTransform = ct;

addChild(s);
```

11.4.6 Masking

You may create a mask for a DisplayObject, so that only the part overlapped by the mask is displayed.

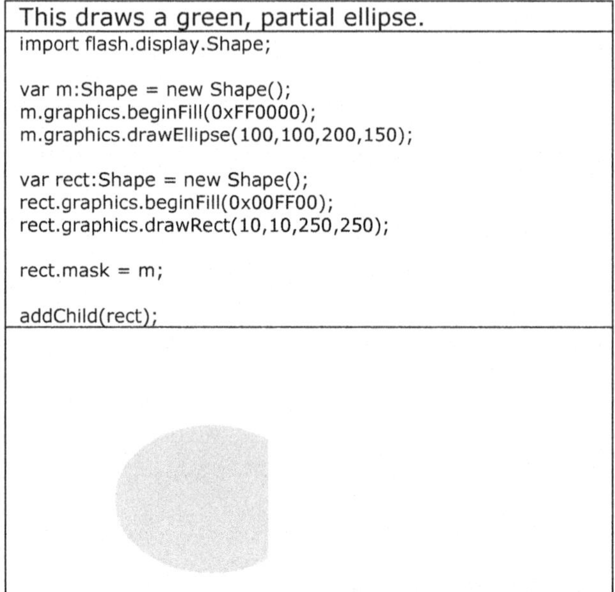

This draws a green, partial ellipse.

```
import flash.display.Shape;

var m:Shape = new Shape();
m.graphics.beginFill(0xFF0000);
m.graphics.drawEllipse(100,100,200,150);

var rect:Shape = new Shape();
rect.graphics.beginFill(0x00FF00);
rect.graphics.drawRect(10,10,250,250);

rect.mask = m;

addChild(rect);
```

11.4.7 Blending

You can set the BlendMode of a DisplayObject, so that the color merges with the background in a specific way. BlendMode includes the following constants: **ADD, ALPHA, DARKEN, DIFFERENCE, ERASE, HARDLIGHT, INVERT, LAYER, LIGHTEN, MULTIPLY, NORMAL, OVERLAY, SCREEN, SHADER, SUBTRACT**.

```
import flash.display.Shape;

var ellipse:Shape = new Shape();
ellipse.graphics.beginFill(0xFF0000);
ellipse.graphics.drawEllipse(100,100,200,150);
addChild(ellipse);

var rect:Shape = new Shape();
rect.graphics.beginFill(0x00FF00);
rect.graphics.drawRect(10,10,250,250);
rect.blendMode = BlendMode.MULTIPLY;
addChild(rect);
```

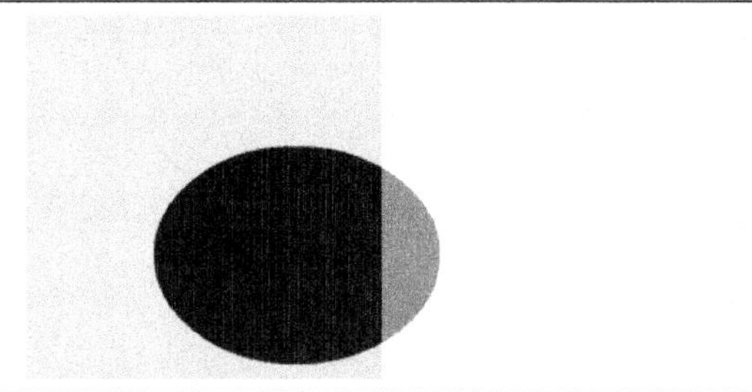

11.4.8 Caching

To optimize performance for an animation, you may cache a DisplayObject as a bitmap. Then, the DisplayObject becomes a surface, which is essentially a bitmap version of the instance's vector data. Updating the vector data recreates the surface. Thus the vector data needs not remain the same.

To cache a DisplayObject, simply set the 'cacheAsBitmap' property to true:

```
mySprite.cacheAsBitmap = true;
```

A surface is not created if the bitmap is greater than 2880 pixels in height or width. The 'opaqueBackground' and 'scrollRect' properties work best when an object is cached as a bitmap.

11.4.9 Filtering

You may apply filters to a display object, to achieve special effects that enhance its appearance. In our examples here, we apply one filter at a time to illustrate its effect. You may, however, apply more than one filters by including more elements in the 'filters' Array property.

BevelFilter
BevelFilter(distance:Number=4.0, angle:Number=45, highlightColor:uint=0xFFFFFF, highlightAlpha:Number=1.0, shadowColor:uint=0x000000, shadowAlpha:Number=1.0, blurX:Number=4.0, blurY:Number=4.0, strength:Number=1, quality:int=1, type:String="inner", knockout:Boolean=false)
angle:Number, blurX:Number, blurY:Number, distance:Number, highlightAlpha:Number, highlightColor:uint, knockout:Boolean, quality:int, shadowAlpha:Number, shadowColor:uint, strength:Number, type:String
'type' can be BitmapFilterType.INNER, BitmapFilterType.OUTER, BitmapFilterType.FULL.

```
import flash.display.Shape;
import flash.geom.Rectangle;
import flash.filters.BevelFilter;

var s:Shape = new Shape();
s.graphics.beginFill(0xFF0000);
s.graphics.drawEllipse(10,10,200,150);
s.filters = [new BevelFilter(10) ]

addChild(s);
```

BlurFilter
BlurFilter(blurX:Number=4.0, blurY:Number=4.0, quality:int=1)
blurX:Number, blurY:Number, quality:int

```
import flash.display.Shape;
import flash.geom.Rectangle;

var s:Shape = new Shape();
s.graphics.beginFill(0xFF0000);
s.graphics.drawEllipse(80,80,200,150);
s.filters = [new BlurFilter(20,70,3) ]
addChild(s);
```

DropShadowFilter
DropShadowFilter(distance:Number = 4.0, angle:Number = 45, color:uint = 0, alpha:Number = 1.0, blurX:Number = 4.0, blurY:Number = 4.0, strength:Number = 1.0, quality:int = 1, inner:Boolean = false, knockout:Boolean = false, hideObject:Boolean = false)
alpha:Number, angle:Number, blurX:Number, blurY:Number, color:uint, distance:Number, hideObject:Boolean, inner:Boolean, knockout:Boolean, quality:int, strength:Number

```
import flash.display.Shape;
import flash.geom.Rectangle;

var s:Shape = new Shape();
s.graphics.beginFill(0xFF0000);
s.graphics.drawEllipse(10,10,200,150);
s.filters = [new DropShadowFilter(20)];
addChild(s);
```

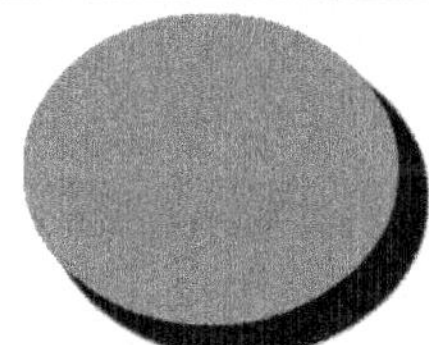

GlowFilter

GlowFilter(color:uint = 0xFF0000, alpha:Number = 1.0, blurX:Number = 6.0, blurY:Number = 6.0, strength:Number = 2, quality:int = 1, inner:Boolean = false, knockout:Boolean = false)

alpha:Number, blurX:Number, blurY:Number, color:uint, inner:Boolean, knockout:Boolean, quality:int, strength:Number

```
import flash.display.Shape;
import flash.geom.Rectangle;

var s:Shape = new Shape();
s.graphics.beginFill(0xFFFF00);
s.graphics.drawEllipse(10,10,200,150);
s.filters = [new GlowFilter(0x0000FF,1.0,10,10)];
addChild(s);
```

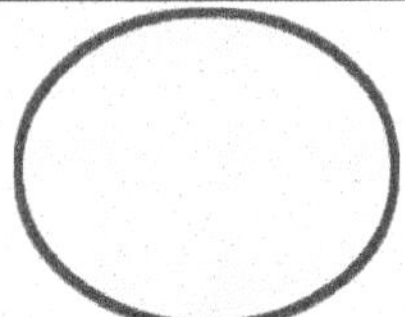

GradientBevelFilter

GradientBevelFilter(distance:Number=4.0, angle:Number=45, colors:Array=null, alphas:Array=null, ratios:Array=null, blurX:Number=4.0, blurY:Number=4.0, strength:Number=1, quality:int=1, type:String="inner", knockout:Boolean=false)

alphas:Array, angle:Number, blurX:Number, blurY:Number, colors:Array, distance:Number, knockout:Boolean, quality:int, ratios:Array, strength:Number, type:String

'type' can be BitmapFilterType.INNER, BitmapFilterType.OUTER, BitmapFilterType.FULL.

```
import flash.display.Shape;
import flash.geom.Rectangle;

var s:Shape = new Shape();
s.graphics.beginFill(0xFFFF00);
s.graphics.drawEllipse(10,10,200,150);
s.filters = [new GradientBevelFilter(10,
                                     45,
                                     [0xFF0000,0x00FF00,0x0000FF],
                                     [1,1,1],
                                     [1,1,1])
            ];
addChild(s);
```

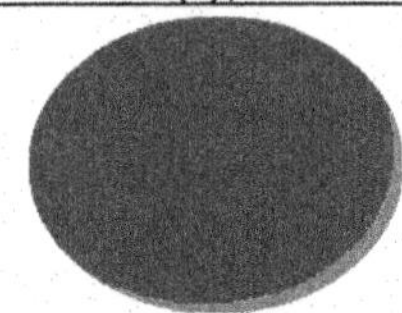

GradientGlowFilter

GradientGlowFilter(distance:Number=4.0, angle:Number=45, colors:Array=null, alphas:Array=null, ratios:Array=null, blurX:Number=4.0, blurY:Number=4.0, strength:Number=1, quality:int=1, type:String="inner", knockout:Boolean=false)

alphas:Array, angle:Number, blurX:Number, blurY:Number, colors:Array, distance:Number, knockout:Boolean, quality:int, ratios:Array, strength:Number, type:String

'type' can be BitmapFilterType.INNER, BitmapFilterType.OUTER, BitmapFilterType.FULL.

```
import flash.display.Shape;
import flash.geom.Rectangle;

var s:Shape = new Shape();
s.graphics.beginFill(0xFFFF00);
s.graphics.drawEllipse(100,100,200,150);
s.filters = [new GradientGlowFilter(0,
                                    0,
                                    [0xFF0000,0x00FF00,0x0000FF],
                                    [1,1,1],
                                    [0,32,64],
                                    150,
                                    150,
                                    1,
                                    2,
                                    "full",
                                    false)
            ];
addChild(s);
```

ColorMatrixFilter

ColorMatrixFilter(matrix:Array=null)

matrix:Array

'matrix' is an array of 20 items for 4 * 5 color transform on the RGBA values of every pixel.

ConvolutionFilter

ConvolutionFilter(matrixX:Number=0, matrixY:Number=0, matrix:Array=null, divisor:Number=1.0, bias:Number=0.0, preserveAlpha:Boolean=true, clamp:Boolean=true, color:uint=0, alpha:Number=0.0)

alpha:Number, bias:Number, clamp:Boolean, color:uint, divisor:Number, matrix:Array, matrixX:Number, matrix:Number, preserveAlpha:Boolean

Convolution can be used to achieve many effects such as blurring, edge detection, sharpening, embossing, and beveling. The convolution filter goes through each pixel and determines the final color of that pixel using the value of the pixel and its surrounding pixels. A matrix, specified as an array of numeric values, indicates to what degree the value of each particular neighboring pixel affects the final resulting value.

```
import flash.display.Shape;
import flash.geom.Rectangle;

var s:Shape = new Shape();
s.graphics.beginFill(0xFFFF00);
s.graphics.drawEllipse(10,10,200,150);
s.filters = [new ConvolutionFilter(3,3,[0,0,0,
                                        0,0,1,
                                        0,0,0])
            ];
addChild(s);
```

DisplacementMapFilter
DisplacementMapFilter(mapBitmap:BitmapData=null, mapPoint:Point=null, componentX:uint=0, componentY:uint=0, scaleX:Number=0.0, scaleY:Number=0.0, mode:String="wrap", color:uint=0, alpha:Number=0.0)
alpha:Number, color:uint, componentX:uint, componentY:uint, mapBitmap:BitmapData, mapPoint:Point, mode:String, scaleX:Number, scaleY:Number
The DisplacementMapFilter class uses the pixel values from the specified BitmapData object to perform a displacement of an object. 'mode' can be DisplacementMapFilterMode.WRAP, DisplacementMapFilterMode.CLAMP, DisplacementMapFilterMode.IGNORE, DisplacementMapFilterMode.COLOR

ShaderFilter
ShaderFilter(shader:Shader = null)
shader:Shader, bottomExtension:int, leftExtension:int, rightExtension:int, topExtension:int
The filtered object is used as an input to the shader, and the shader output becomes the filter result.

11.4.10 Pixel Bender Shaders

Adobe Pixel Bender is a programming language used to manipulate image content. The shader created defines a function that executes on each pixel of an image. Input images and other parameters may be specified. Effects that make can use a shader include the drawing fill, the blend mode and the filter.

An instance of the Shader class must be created to access the shader created using the Adobe Pixel Bender Toolkit, which is a .pbj file. A Shader object has a .data property that stores input images (ShaderInput), input parameters (ShaderParameter), or output metadata.

```
var loader:URLLoader = new URLLoader();
loader.dataFormat = URLLoaderDataFormat.BINARY;
loader.addEventListener(Event.COMPLETE, onLoadComplete);
loader.load(new URLRequest("myShader.pbj"));

var myShader:Shader;
var inputs:Vector.<ShaderInput>=new
Vector.<ShaderInput>();
var parameters:Vector.<ShaderParameter> =
                              new
Vector.<ShaderParameter>();
var metadata:Vector.<String> = new Vector.<String>();

function onLoadComplete(event:Event):void {
  myShader = new Shader(loader.data);
  var shaderData:ShaderData = myShader.data;
  for (var prop:String in shaderData) {
    if (shaderData[prop] is ShaderInput) {
      inputs[inputs.length] = shaderData[prop];
    } else if (shaderData[prop] is ShaderParameter) {
      parameters[parameters.length] = shaderData[prop];
    } else {
      metadata[metadata.length] = shaderData[prop];
    }
  }
}
```

11.4.11 Collision Detection

A value of 'true' is returned even when the shapes have not really touched each other, because their bounding boxes have touched.

```
import flash.display.Shape;

var c1:Shape = new Shape();
c1.graphics.beginFill(0xFF0000);
c1.graphics.drawCircle(100,100,50);

var c2:Shape = new Shape();
c2.graphics.beginFill(0xFFF000);
c2.graphics.drawCircle(180,180,50);

addChild(c1);
addChild(c2);
trace(c1.hitTestObject(c2));
trace(c2.hitTestPoint(220,220));
```

```
true
true
```

11.4.12 Inverse Kinematics

Inverse Kinematics allow you to link parts so they move in relation to one another in a realistic manner. Bones and joins are involved in the motion.

As a demonstration, first create a long, thin, horizontal rectangle. Then create a series of bones in it using the bone tool:

Make sure the bones are joined end-to-end.

Then in the timeline, insert a new frame for the armature. Click the selection tool. Click the last frame, and re-shape the rectangle by dragging the different joins.

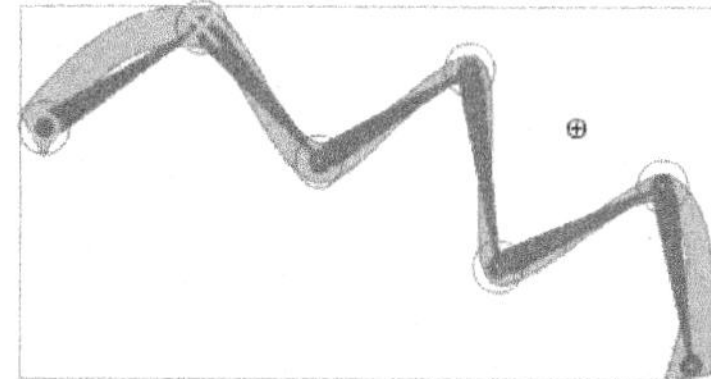

That's it. You have just created a tween that allows you to rotate different parts of a rectangle.

As another example, you may link the limbs of a

moving person to the body.

11.4.13 3D Manipulation

This example illustrates some techniques by which one can manipulate graphics in a 3-dimensional space.

```
import flash.display.Shape;
import flash.geom.Point;

var s:Shape = new Shape();
s.graphics.beginFill(0xFF0000);
s.graphics.drawRect(30,50,200,100);

s.z = 100;
s.rotationY += 50;
root.transform.perspectiveProjection.fieldOfView=40;
root.transform.perspectiveProjection.focalLength=500;
root.transform.perspectiveProjection.projectionCenter =
                                        new Point(100,100);

var matrix:Matrix3D = s.transform.matrix3D;
matrix.appendRotation(25, Vector3D.X_AXIS);
matrix.appendScale(1.5, 1.1, 0.9);
matrix.appendTranslation(50, 50, 0);
matrix.appendRotation(-10, Vector3D.Z_AXIS);
s.transform.matrix3D = matrix;

addChild(s);
```

11.5 Events

To demonstrate various events, let's create a class for a Circle on the stage, so that it can be used in our ActionScripts. First, draw a circle on the stage. Right-click the circle. Choose 'Convert to Symbol'. Name it 'Circle'. (Notice that it is a MovieClip.) Under 'Advanced', check 'Export for ActionScript'. Click OK.

Click the circle on the stage. Press the 'Delete' key to delete it.

At the bottom left, add a new layer. Right-click on Frame 1 of the new layer, and choose 'Actions'. In the editor, type and run the following scripts:

11.5.1 MouseEvent

Using the Circle class in 11.5, try the following code:

Clicking the circle causes it to shrink in size.

```
import flash.events.MouseEvent;

var c:Circle = new Circle;
addChild(c);

c.addEventListener(MouseEvent.CLICK,circleClick);
function circleClick(e:MouseEvent):void{
   c.width--;
   c.height--;
}
```

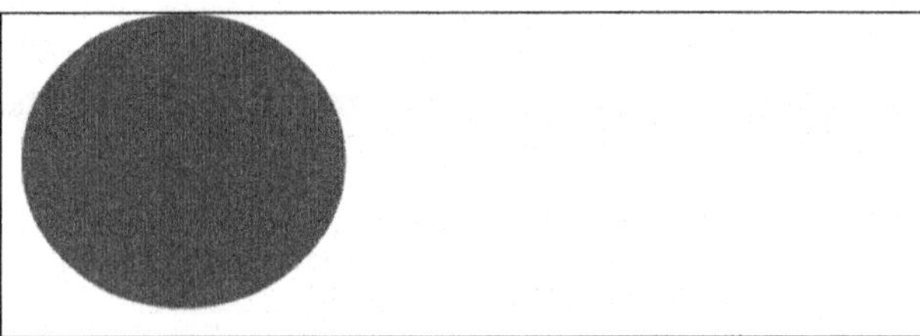

The MouseEvent class has the following constants: **CLICK, CONTEXT_MENU, DOUBLE_CLICK, MIDDLE_CLICK, MIDDLE_MOUSE_DOWN, MIDDLE_MOUSE_UP, MOUSE_DOWN, MOUSE_MOVE, MOUSE_OUT, MOUSE_OVER, MOUSE_UP, MOUSE_WHEEL, RIGHT_CLICK, RIGHT_MOUSE_DOWN, RIGHT_MOUSE_UP, ROLL_OUT, ROLL_OVER**

Additionally, the MouseEvent class has the following properties:

altKey: Boolean
buttonDown: Boolean
commandKey: Boolean
controlKey: Boolean
ctrlKey: Boolean
shiftKey: Boolean

clickCount: int
delta: int
isRelatedObjectInaccessible: Boolean
relatedObject: InteractiveObject

localX: Number
localY: Number
stageX: Number
stageY: Number

11.5.2 KeyboardEvent

Now using the same Circle class in 11.5, try the following code:

Pressing the up key enlarges the circle. Pressing the down key shrinks the circle.

```
var c:Circle = new Circle;
addChild(c);

stage.addEventListener(KeyboardEvent.KEY_DOWN,
                       keyPressed);
function keyPressed(e:KeyboardEvent):void{
  if (e.keyCode == 38){ // up key
     c.width++;
     c.height++;
  } else if (e.keyCode == 40){  // down key
     c.width--;
     c.height--;
  }
}
```

The KeyboardEvent has the following constants: **KEY_DOWN, KEY_UP**

Additionally, the KeyboardEvent has the following properties:

altKey: Boolean
commandKey: Boolean
controlKey: Boolean
ctrlKey: Boolean
shiftKey: Boolean

charCode: uint
keyCode: uint
keyLocation: uint

11.5.3 Screen Panning

Sometimes an object or a scene is too large to fit within the screen. It can be scrolled and panned with the **.scrollRect** property.

Pressing the UP key scrolls the screen upward. Pressing the DOWN key scrolls the screen downward.

```
import flash.events.MouseEvent;
import flash.geom.Rectangle;
import flash.display.Shape;

var s:Shape = new Shape();
s.graphics.beginFill(0xFF0000);
s.graphics.drawCircle(500,500,500);

s.scrollRect = new Rectangle(0, 0, s.width, 350);
s.cacheAsBitmap = true;
addChild(s);

function pan(e:KeyboardEvent):void {
    var rect:Rectangle = s.scrollRect;
    if (e.keyCode == 38) rect.y -= 20;
    else if (e.keyCode == 40) rect.y += 20;
    s.scrollRect = rect;
}

stage.addEventListener(KeyboardEvent.KEY_DOWN, pan);
```

11.5.4 TimerEvent

Using the same Circle class in 11.5, try the following code:

The circle expands every 1 second (1000 ms) , for 10 times.

```
import flash.utils.Timer;
import flash.events.TimerEvent;

var c:Circle = new Circle;
addChild(c);

var timer:Timer = new Timer(1000,10);
timer.start();
timer.addEventListener(TimerEvent.TIMER,enlarge);
timer.addEventListener(TimerEvent.TIMER_COMPLETE,
                            finished);

function enlarge(e:TimerEvent):void{
   c.width += 10;
   c.height += 10;
   // timer.stop();
}

function finished(e:TimerEvent):void{
   trace("FINISHED");
}
```

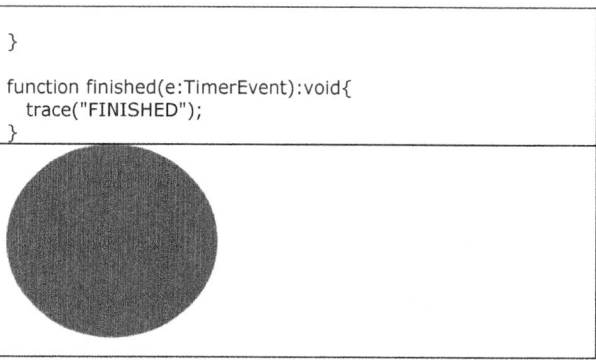

11.5.5 Event.ENTER_FRAME

Using the same Circle class in 11.5, try the following code:

As the stage progresses to a new frame repeatedly, the circle expands.

```
var c:Circle = new Circle;
addChild(c);
//removeChild(c);


c.addEventListener(Event.ENTER_FRAME, expand);

function expand(e:Event):void{
   c.width += 10;
   c.height += 10;
}
```

11.6 External Media

11.6.1 Loader

You may load image files and SWF files using a Loader.

Note that for this to work, the .swf and .fla files need to be saved in the same directory as 'apple.png'. Here we add the loaded image to a Sprite.

```
import flash.display.*;
import flash.net.URLRequest;
import flash.events.Event;

var pictLdr:Loader = new Loader();
pictLdr.load(new URLRequest("apple.png"));
//pictLdr.scaleX =0.1;
//pictLdr.scaleY =0.1;
//addChild(pictLdr);

pictLdr.contentLoaderInfo.addEventListener(
                                Event.COMPLETE, imgLoaded);
function imgLoaded(event:Event):void {
   var container:Sprite = new Sprite();
   container.scaleX=0.1;
   container.scaleY=0.1;
   addChild(container);
   container.addChild(pictLdr.content);
}
```

11.6.2 Bitmap

You may convert display objects to bitmaps so that the individual pixels can be manipulated.

BitmapData(width:Number, height:Number, transparent:Boolean, fillColor:uinit)

Bitmap(bitmapData:BitmapData = null, pixelSnapping:String = "auto", smoothing:Boolean = false)

(pixelSnapping can be PixelSnapping.NEVER, PixelSnapping.ALWAYS, PixelSnapping.AUTO)

This example shows how to draw on a Bitmap and how to manipulate the individual pixels.

```
import flash.geom.Rectangle;
import flash.utils.ByteArray;
import flash.geom.Point;

var s:Sprite = new Sprite();
s.graphics.clear();
s.graphics.beginFill(0xFF0000);
s.graphics.drawCircle(100,100,80);

var b:BitmapData = new BitmapData(200, 200, true, 0x0);
b.draw(s);
b.setPixel(100,100,0x000FFF);
trace(b.getPixel(100,100)); //4095

var ba:ByteArray = b.getPixels(new
                              Rectangle(100,100,80,80));
ba.position = 0;
b.setPixels(new Rectangle(120,120,80,80),ba);
b.copyPixels(b,new Rectangle(20,20,80,80),new Point(0,0));
b.copyChannel(b,
              new Rectangle(50,50,50,50),
              new Point(50,50),
              BitmapDataChannel.RED,
              BitmapDataChannel.GREEN);
b.fillRect(new Rectangle(100,100,50,50),0xFFFF00);
trace(b.hitTest(new Point(50,50), 0xFF, new Point(100,100)));
//true

//b.floodFill(100,50,0x0000FF);
//b.noise(500, 0, 255, BitmapDataChannel.RED,false);
//b.perlinNoise(......);
//b.pixelDissolve(......);

var bitmap:Bitmap = new Bitmap(b);
addChild(bitmap);
```

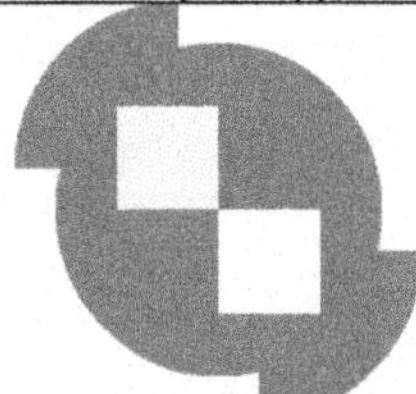

11.6.3 MovieClip

A MovieClip has the following properties and methods:

currentFrame: int
currentFrameLabel: String
currentLabel: String
currentLabels: Array
currentScene: Scene
enabled: Boolean
framesLoaded: int
scenes: Array
totalFrames: int
trackAsMenu: Boolean

gotoAndPlay(frame: Object, scene:String=null):void
gotoAndStop(frame: Object, scene:String=null):void
nextFrame():void
nextScene():void
play():void
prevFrame():void
prevScene():void
stop():void

11.6.4 Text

There are three types of text: Static Text, Dynamic Text, and Input Text.

The TextField class includes the following members:

alwaysShowSelection: Boolean
antiAliasType: String
autoSize: String
background: Boolean
backgroundColor: uint
border: Boolean
borderColor: uint
bottomScrollV: int
caretIndex: int
consdenseWhite: Boolean
defaultTextFormat: flash.text:TextFormat
displayAsPassword: Boolean
embedFonts: Boolean
gridFitType: String
htmlText: String
length: int
maxChars: int
maxScrollH: int
maxScrollV: int
mouseWheelEnabled: Boolean
multiline: Boolean
numLines: int
restrict: String
scrollH: int
scrollV: int
selectable: Boolean
selectionBeginIndex: int
selectionEndIndex: int
sharpness: Number
styleSheet: StyleSheet
text:String
textColor: uint
textHeight: Number
textInteractionMode: String
textWidth: Number
thickness: Number
type: String
useRichTextClipboard: Boolean
wordWrap: Boolean

appendText(newText:String):void
getCharBoundaries(charIndex:int):Rectangle

getCharIndexAtPoint(x:Number, y:Number):int
getFirstCharInParagraph(charIndex:int):int
getImageReference(id:String):DisplayObject
getLineIndexAtPoint(x:Number, y:Number):int
getLineIndexOfChar(charIndex:int):int
getLineLength(lineIndex:int):int
getLineMetrics(lineIndex:int):flash.text:TextLineMetrics
getLineOffset(lineIndex:int):int
getLineText(lineIndex:int):String
getParagraphLength(charIndex:int):int
getTextFormat(begin:int=-1, end:int=-1):flash.text:TextFormat
isFontCompatible(fontName:String, fontStyle:String):Boolean
replaceSelectedText(value:String):void
replaceText(begin:int, end:int, newText:String):void
setSelection(begin:int, end:int):void
setTextFormat(format:flash.text:TextFormat, begin:int=-1, end:int=-1):void

(**antiAliasType** can be flash.text.AntiAliasType.NORMAL, or flash.text.AntiAliasType.ADVANCED)

(**autoSize** can be TextFieldAutoSize.NONE, TextFieldAutoSize.LEFT, TextFieldAutoSize.RIGHT, TextFieldAutoSize.CENTER)

(**gridFitType** can be flash.text.GridFitType.NONE, flash.text.GridFitType.PIXEL, flash.text.GridFitType.SUBPIXEL)

(**type** can be TextFieldType.INPUT or TextFieldType.DYNAMIC)

```
import flash.text.TextField;
import flash.events.MouseEvent;

var t:TextField = new TextField();
t.width=400;
t.height=100;
t.wordWrap=true;
t.multiline=true;
t.border=true;
t.addEventListener(MouseEvent.MOUSE_WHEEL,vscroll);

var format:TextFormat = new TextFormat();
format.font = "Verdana";
format.color = 0xFF0000;
format.size = 20;
t.defaultTextFormat = format;

t.text="Hello world 1! Hello world 2! Hello world 3! Hello \
world 4! Hello world 5! Hello world 6! Hello world 7! Hello \
world 8! Hello world 9! Hello world 10! Hello world 11! Hello \
world 12!";

addChild(t);

function vscroll(e:MouseEvent):void{
  t.scrollV++;
}
```

Hello world 1! Hello world 2! Hello world 3! Hello world 4! Hello world 5! Hello world 6! Hello world 7! Hello

```
import flash.text.TextField;

var t:TextField = new TextField();
t.width=400;
t.height=400;
t.htmlText="<b>Apple</b>\
        <img src='apple.png' width='100' height='100'>";
addChild(t);
```

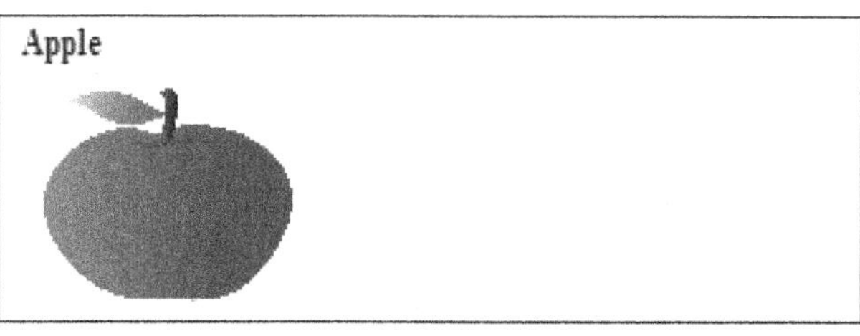


```
var myTextBox:TextField = new TextField();
var myOutputBox:TextField = new TextField();
var myText:String = "Type your text here.";

myTextBox.type = TextFieldType.INPUT;
myTextBox.background = true;
addChild(myTextBox);
myTextBox.text = myText;
myTextBox.addEventListener(TextEvent.TEXT_INPUT,
                        textInput);

function textInput(event:TextEvent):void {
  var str:String = myTextBox.text;
  createOutputBox(str);
}

function createOutputBox(str:String):void {
  myOutputBox.background = true;
  myOutputBox.x = 200;
  addChild(myOutputBox);
  myOutputBox.text = str;
}
```

Hello World! Hello World!

11.6.5 Audio

This plays an external audio file after it has been loaded completely.

```
import flash.events.Event;
import flash.events.ProgressEvent;
import flash.media.Sound;
import flash.net.URLRequest;

var s:Sound = new Sound();
s.addEventListener(ProgressEvent.PROGRESS,
onLoadProgress);
s.addEventListener(Event.COMPLETE, onLoadComplete);
s.addEventListener(IOErrorEvent.IO_ERROR, onIOError);

s.load(new URLRequest("song.mp3"));

function onLoadProgress(event:ProgressEvent):void {
  var loadedPct:uint = Math.round(100 *
                   (event.bytesLoaded / event.bytesTotal));
  trace("The sound is " + loadedPct + "% loaded.");
}

function onLoadComplete(event:Event):void {
  var localSound:Sound = event.target as Sound;
  localSound.play();
}
function onIOError(event:IOErrorEvent) {
  trace("The sound could not be loaded: " + event.text);
}
```

You can embed a sound file into the SWF file by importing it to the Library. Remember to export it for ActionScript in its Properties and give it a proper class name.

```
var ds:DingSound = new DingSound();
var channel:SoundChannel = ds.play();
```

You can play a file while it is being loaded. This is called streaming. The value 3000 here means that the file will be played once a length of 3 seconds has been loaded.

```
import flash.media.Sound;
import flash.media.SoundLoaderContext;
import flash.net.URLRequest;

var s:Sound = new Sound();
var context:SoundLoaderContext = new
SoundLoaderContext(3000, true);
s.load(new
URLRequest("http://www.domain.com/sample.mp3"),
            context);
s.play();
// s.close();  // this stops the sound streaming
```

You can modify a sound file and play it.

```
var mySound:Sound = new Sound();
var sourceSnd:Sound = new Sound();
sourceSnd.load(new URLRequest("song.mp3"));
sourceSnd.addEventListener(Event.COMPLETE, loaded);

function loaded(event:Event):void {
   mySound.addEventListener(
               SampleDataEvent.SAMPLE_DATA,
               processSound);
   mySound.play();
}

function processSound(event:SampleDataEvent):void {
      var bytes:ByteArray = new ByteArray();
      sourceSnd.extract(bytes, 8192);
      event.data.writeBytes(upOctave(bytes));
}

function upOctave(bytes:ByteArray):ByteArray {
   var returnBytes:ByteArray = new ByteArray();
   bytes.position = 0;
   while(bytes.bytesAvailable > 0) {
      returnBytes.writeFloat(bytes.readFloat());
      returnBytes.writeFloat(bytes.readFloat());
      if (bytes.bytesAvailable > 0)
                        bytes.position += 8;
   }
   return returnBytes;
}
```

This routes the microphone's input to the local speakers.

```
import flash.media.Microphone;

var mic:Microphone = Microphone.getMicrophone();

mic.addEventListener(StatusEvent.STATUS, this.onMicStatus);
function onMicStatus(event:StatusEvent):void {
  if (event.code == "Microphone.Unmuted")
     trace("Microphone access was allowed.");
  else if (event.code == "Microphone.Muted")
     trace("Microphone access was denied.");
}

mic.setUseEchoSuppression(true);
mic.setLoopBack(true);
```

You can obtain more information about the microphone.

```
import flash.events.ActivityEvent;
import flash.events.StatusEvent;
import flash.media.Microphone;

var deviceArray:Array = Microphone.names;
trace("Available sound input devices:");
for (var i:int = 0; i < deviceArray.length; i++) {
   trace(" " + deviceArray[i]);
}

var mic:Microphone = Microphone.getMicrophone();
mic.gain = 60;
mic.rate = 11;
mic.setUseEchoSuppression(true);
mic.setLoopBack(true);
mic.setSilenceLevel(5, 1000);

mic.addEventListener(ActivityEvent.ACTIVITY,
                     this.onMicActivity);
mic.addEventListener(StatusEvent.STATUS, this.onMicStatus);

var micDetails:String = "Sound input device name: " +
                     mic.name + '\n';
micDetails += "Gain: " + mic.gain + '\n';
micDetails += "Rate: " + mic.rate + " kHz" + '\n';
micDetails += "Muted: " + mic.muted + '\n';
micDetails += "Silence level: " + mic.silenceLevel + '\n';
micDetails += "Silence timeout: " +
              mic.silenceTimeout + '\n';
micDetails += "Echo suppression: " +
              mic.useEchoSuppression + '\n';
trace(micDetails);

function onMicActivity(event:ActivityEvent):void {
   trace("activating=" + event.activating + ", activityLevel="
        + mic.activityLevel);
}

function onMicStatus(event:StatusEvent):void {
   trace("status: level=" + event.level +
              ", code=" + event.code);
}
```

This demonstrates pausing, volume setting and panning.

The first parameter to SoundTransform() adjusts the volume, and ranges from 0 to 1. The second parameter to SoundTransform() adjusts panning, with -1 being total left panning and 1 being total right panning.

The first parameter to play() sets the initial position in milliseconds. The second parameter to play() sets the number of times to play.

```
import flash.events.Event;
import flash.events.ProgressEvent;
import flash.media.Sound;
import flash.net.URLRequest;
import flash.media.SoundChannel;

var s:Sound = new Sound();
var c:SoundChannel = new SoundChannel();
s.addEventListener(Event.COMPLETE, onLoadComplete);
addEventListener(Event.ENTER_FRAME, onEnterFrame);
s.load(new URLRequest("song.mp3"));

function onLoadComplete(event:Event):void {
  var localSound:Sound = event.target as Sound;
  var trans:SoundTransform = new SoundTransform(0.1, 0);
  c = localSound.play(0,1,trans);
}

function onEnterFrame(event:Event):void {
  if (c.position>10000) c.stop();  // pause after 10 seconds
}
```

11.6.6 Video

This loads an external video and plays it.

```
var nc:NetConnection = new NetConnection();
nc.connect(null); // connection to a media server
var ns:NetStream = new NetStream(nc);
ns.addEventListener(AsyncErrorEvent.ASYNC_ERROR,
asyncErrorHandler);

ns.play("movie.mp4");
//ns.pause();
//ns.seek(5); // 10s from the beginning
//ns.resume();
//ns.togglePause();

function asyncErrorHandler(event:AsyncErrorEvent):void {}

var v:Video = new Video(500,300);
v.attachNetStream(ns);
v.x = 10;
v.y = 10;
addChild(v);
```

11.6.7 Clipboard

This obtains data from the clipboard.

```
import flash.desktop.Clipboard;
import flash.desktop.ClipboardFormats;

if(Clipboard.generalClipboard.hasFormat(
  ClipboardFormats.TEXT_FORMAT)){
    var text:String = Clipboard.generalClipboard.getData(
                        ClipboardFormats.TEXT_FORMAT);
}
```

This writes data to the clipboard.

```
import flash.desktop.Clipboard;
import flash.desktop.ClipboardFormats;

var textToCopy:String = "Copy to clipboard.";
Clipboard.generalClipboard.clear();
Clipboard.generalClipboard.setData(
        ClipboardFormats.TEXT_FORMAT, textToCopy, false);
```

11.6.8 Printer

This demonstrates how to print a display object.

```
var p:PrintJob = new PrintJob();
var s:Sprite = new Sprite();
s.graphics.beginFill(0xFF0000);
s.graphics.drawRect(10,10,200,100);
p.start();
p.addPage(s);
p.send();
```

11.6.9 Webcam

This displays the local webcam input as a video.

```
var cam:Camera = Camera.getCamera();

// The start of optional code
if (cam == null)
  trace("User has no cameras installed.");
else
  trace("User has at least 1 camera installed.");
cam.addEventListener(StatusEvent.STATUS, statusHandler);
function statusHandler(event:StatusEvent):void {
  switch (event.code) {
    case "Camera.Muted":
      trace("User clicked Deny.");
      break;
    case "Camera.Unmuted":
      trace("User clicked Accept.");
      break;
  }
}
// The end of optional code

cam.setMode(640, 480, 25); // width, height, fps
cam.setQuality(0,100);
            // bandwidth(0 for any bytes), quality(0 to 100)

var v:Video = new Video();
v.attachCamera(cam);
addChild(v);
```

11.6.10 Retrieving HTML Parameters

To pass parameters to the root level of a SWF file, include within all <object> tags a <param> tag named 'FlashVars', and specify its value as name-value variable pairs. For example:

```
<param name="FlashVars" value="varA=100&varB=200"/>
<param name="FlashVars" value="varC=300"/>
```

To retrieve the values in the SWF file, follow the code below:

```
var p:String = LoaderInfo(this.root.loaderInfo).
                      parameters.varA.toString();
```

12. Translated Text & Video Chat

In this chapter, we will explore how to code a chat site. At the site, text messages from chatters at different places can be translated to different languages, and the chatters can see and hear one another. Instead of showing the code for such a site all at once, we shall break it into a few sections and explain them one by one.

12.1 Transmitting Text Messages

Push, or **server push**, refers to communication where the request is initiated by the server. It is contrasted with **pull**, where the request for the transmission of information is initiated by the client. **Comet** is a collective term that includes many ways that allow a web server to push data to a browser over a long-held HTTP request. Comet is also known as AJAX Push, Reverse AJAX, Two-way-web, HTTP Streaming, and HTTP server push.

Here we describe a few methods that simulate a server push. We omit the controversial techniques of hidden <iframe> and interactive AJAX as they are poorly supported by browsers.

12.1.1 Long Polling

A common approach to implementing online chat is to use **long polling**, in which an AJAX request is kept open until the server has new data, and upon receiving the server response the browser fires a new AJAX request. Such a method is simple and well-supported by browsers.

Here each message is numbered to keep track of the displayed messages. Two set of AJAX requests are used. The first five bytes of xhr.responseText are used to store the number of the last received message.

```
<!DOCTYPE html><html><head>

<script>

I = 0;  // message number
getMsg();
function getMsg(){
  xhr = new XMLHttpRequest();
  xhr.onreadystatechange = function(){
    if (xhr.readyState==4 && xhr.status==200){
      R = xhr.responseText;
      I = parseInt(R.substr(0,5));
      M = R.substr(5,R.length-5);
      D = document.getElementById("chatZone");
      D.innerHTML+=M;
      D.scrollTop = D.scrollHeight;
      getMsg();
    }
  };
  xhr.open("GET","getMessages.php?num="+I,true);
  xhr.send();
}

document.onkeydown = function (e){
  if (e.keyCode!=13) return;  // ENTER
  name = encodeURIComponent(
                document.getElementById("name").value);
  msg = encodeURIComponent(
                document.getElementById("msg").value);
  xhr2 = new XMLHttpRequest();
  xhr2.open("GET","sendMessage.php?name="+
                name+"&msg="+msg,true);
  xhr2.send();
  document.getElementById("msg").value = "";
}

</script></head>

<body onkeydown="checkEnter()">
  <div id="chatZone" style="width:400px; height:250px;
      background:yellow; overflow-y:scroll;
      border:1px solid black;"></div><br/>
  <input id="name" type="text" size="12"/>:
  <input id="msg"  type="text" size="40" />
</body></html>
```

```
<?php
// sendMessage.php

$N = $_GET['name'];
$M = $_GET['msg'];
$f = fopen("chatlog.txt","a");
fwrite($f,"<b>$N</b>: $M<br/>\r\n");
fclose($f);
?>
```

```
<?php
// getMeesages.php

set_time_limit(90);
$I = $_GET['num'];
for ($j=0; $j<60; $j++){
  $messages = file("chatlog.txt");
  $L = sizeof($messages);
  if ($I<$L) break;
  sleep(1);
}
echo sprintf("%05d",$L);
for ($j=$I; $j<$L; $j++){
  echo $messages[$j];
}
?>
```

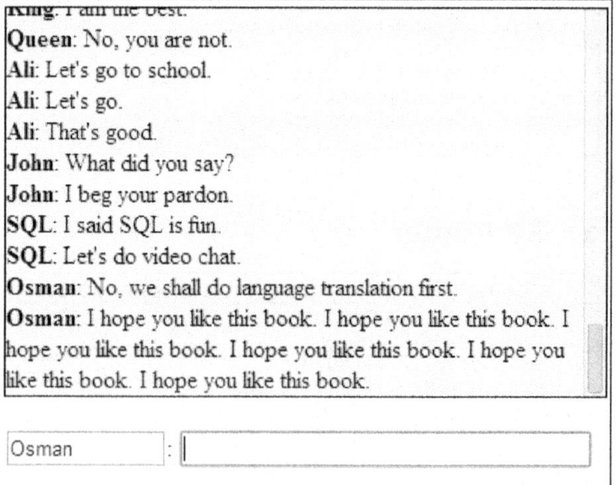

Queen: No, you are not.
Ali: Let's go to school.
Ali: Let's go.
Ali: That's good.
John: What did you say?
John: I beg your pardon.
SQL: I said SQL is fun.
SQL: Let's do video chat.
Osman: No, we shall do language translation first.
Osman: I hope you like this book. I hope you like this book. I hope you like this book. I hope you like this book. I hope you like this book. I hope you like this book.

Osman :

12.1.2 Sockets

In the past, non-polling communication is often achieved by TCP sockets in Java applets and Flash. With the advent of HTML5, it has now been possible to use JavaScript only, with WebSocket. This technique has been discussed in 4.22.6. The advantage of using sockets is that sockets are extremely fast and responsive. The downside is that it requires a listening socket to be first opened at the server, something which is often not allowed on rented shared hosts. WebSockets are not subject to the same-origin policy.

12.1.3 Flash SharedObject

SharedObject in Flash ActionScript can be local or remote. Local SharedObject allows data to be stored on the client's computer. Remote SharedObject allows data to be stored on the server, and synchronized with all subscribers. If you have access to a media server such as Red5, you may use SharedObject.

12.1.4 Server-sent Events

Although it is possible to code a chat site using server-sent events, SSE is currently not supported by Internet Explorer. SSE requires a server to run.

Note the format of the string. As the PHP script gets timed out (30s), it is restarted and the count begins from 0 again.

```
<!DOCTYPE html>
<html>
<body>
  <p></p>
  <script>
  var sse = new EventSource("sse.php");
  sse.onmessage = function(e) {
    document.querySelector('p').innerHTML=e.data;
  }
  sse.onopen = new function(e){};
  sse.onerror = new function(e){};
  var rs = sse.readyState;
  var url = sse.url;
  </script>
</body>
</html>
```

```
<?php
// SSE.php
header("Content-Type: text/event-stream\n\n");
$T = time();
while (1) {
  echo 'data: ' . (time()-$T). "\n\n";
  ob_flush(); flush();
  sleep(1);
}
?>
```

29

12.1.5 Firebase

Firebase provides a service that allows you to synchronize data instantly over multiple clients. When one client updates a piece of data, the other clients can immediately detect and know the update. To use it, first register an account at

https://www.firebase.com/

, the download and include its Javascript library.

As you can see, creating a chat site is pretty straightforward with Firebase.

```
<!DOCTYPE html>
<html>
<head>
  <script
   src="https://cdn.firebase.com/js/client/2.0.5/firebase.js">
  </script>
  <script>
  var fb = new Firebase(
                   'https://popping-torch-7966.firebaseio.com/');
  var fbMsg = fb.child('msg');
  fbMsg.set(null);
  fbMsg.on('value', function(snapshot){
    document.querySelector('div').innerHTML+=
           snapshot.val().n+":"+snapshot.val().m+"<br/>";
  });
  function send(){
    name =
         document.getElementsByTagName('input')[0].value;
    msg  =
         document.getElementsByTagName('input')[1].value;
    fbMsg.set({n:name, m:msg});
  }
  </script>
</head>
<body>
  <div style="background:yellow;
       width:500px; height:300px;"></div>
  <input type='text' placeholder="name"
         style="width:100px"/>:
  <input type='text' style="width:350px"/>
  <button onclick="send()">Send</button>
</body>
</html>
```

Mike:The Firebase manual can be found at their official website.
Alexander:Events include "child_removed", "child_added", "child_changed", "child_moved" and "value".
Rebecca:Security and authentication are extensively supported in Firebase.

Mike : The Firebase manual can be found at their official website Send

12.2 Language Translation

We shall use the free Microsoft Translation API, and develop step-by-step a PHP library called 'ms_translator.php'.

12.2.1 Registering an Application

STEP 1: If you don't already have one, sign up for a Microsoft account at

https://signup.live.com/signup.aspx

. Then login into the account.

STEP 2: Go to Windows Azure Marketplace at https://azure.microsoft.com/en-us/marketplace/ and search for Microsoft Translator. Sign up for the free translation service which allows you to translate 2000000 characters per month.

STEP 3: At the bottom of the page, search for DEVELOP -> Register Your Application, and click on it.

STEP 4: Fill in the form. You may specify https://www.microsoft.com for Redirect URI. Click CREATE.

At any point of time, you may check the number of remaining characters that can be translated for the month at:
https://datamarket.azure.com/account/datasets

12.2.2 Obtaining the Access Token

Every time you want to use the translation service, first you need to obtain an access token, which will be valid for 10 minutes. To protect your credentials, the remote site should be accessed in PHP instead of JavaScript. The 'curl' library (Chapter 16) can be used for this purpose.

The assignments to $clientID and $clientSecret should be replaced with the credentials you received in the previous section. $authUrl, $scopeUrl, and $grantType should be fixed. Here we split some of the strings due to space constraint, but you should leave them connected.

```
<?php
// ms_translator.php

class AccessTokenAuthentication {
  function getTokens($grantType, $scopeUrl, $clientID,
                                         $clientSecret, $authUrl){
    try {
      $ch = curl_init();
      $paramArr = array (
        'grant_type'   => $grantType,
        'scope'        => $scopeUrl,
        'client_id'    => $clientID,
        'client_secret' => $clientSecret
      );
      $paramArr = http_build_query($paramArr);
      curl_setopt($ch, CURLOPT_URL, $authUrl);
      curl_setopt($ch, CURLOPT_POST, TRUE);
      curl_setopt($ch, CURLOPT_POSTFIELDS, $paramArr);
      curl_setopt ($ch, CURLOPT_RETURNTRANSFER, TRUE);
      curl_setopt($ch, CURLOPT_SSL_VERIFYPEER, false);
      $strResponse = curl_exec($ch);
      $curlErrno = curl_errno($ch);
      if($curlErrno){
        $curlError = curl_error($ch);
        throw new Exception($curlError);
      }
      curl_close($ch);
      $objResponse = json_decode($strResponse);
      if ($objResponse->error){
        throw new
            Exception($objResponse->error_description);
      }
      return $objResponse->access_token;
    } catch (Exception $e) {
      echo "Exception-".$e->getMessage();
    }
  }
}

Class HTTPTranslator {
  function curlRequest($url, $authHeader, $postData=''){
    $ch = curl_init();
    curl_setopt ($ch, CURLOPT_URL, $url);
    curl_setopt ($ch, CURLOPT_HTTPHEADER,
              array($authHeader,"Content-Type: text/xml"));
    curl_setopt ($ch, CURLOPT_RETURNTRANSFER, TRUE);
    curl_setopt ($ch, CURLOPT_SSL_VERIFYPEER, False);
    if($postData) {
      curl_setopt($ch, CURLOPT_POST, TRUE);
      curl_setopt($ch, CURLOPT_POSTFIELDS, $postData);
    }
    $curlResponse = curl_exec($ch);
    $curlErrno = curl_errno($ch);
    if ($curlErrno) {
      $curlError = curl_error($ch);
      throw new Exception($curlError);
    }
    curl_close($ch);
    return $curlResponse;
  }

  function createReqXML($languageCode) {
    $requestXml = '<ArrayOfstring
xmlns="http://schemas.microsoft.com/2003/10/Serialization/
Arrays" xmlns:i="http://www.w3.org/2001/XMLSchema-
instance">';
    if($languageCode) {
      $requestXml .= "<string>$languageCode</string>";
    } else {
      throw new Exception('Language Code is empty.');
    }
    $requestXml .= '</ArrayOfstring>';
    return $requestXml;
  }
}

function getAccessTokenHeader(){
  $clientID = "13579753122446688";
  $clientSecret = "nuxNLumB5t14kPQ1VnmAzc".
                  "4hseXJCbKgzySNbWEaIWs=";
  $authUrl = "https://datamarket.accesscontrol.windows.net/"
             ."v2/OAuth2-13/";
  $scopeUrl    = "http://api.microsofttranslator.com";
  $grantType   = "client_credentials";

  $authObj = new AccessTokenAuthentication();
  $accessToken  = $authObj->getTokens("client_credentials",
                $scopeUrl, $clientID, $clientSecret,
$authUrl);
  return "Authorization: Bearer ". $accessToken;
}

?>
```

(courtesy of http://msdn.microsoft.com/en-us/library/hh454950.aspx)

12.2.3 Determining the Language

Except for Chinese Simplified (zh-CHS) and Chinese Traditional (zh-CHT), the language codes are as what are specified in Chapter 1.

getLanguageCode() returns the language code, which is needed for the translation. getLanguage() returns the full name for the language code.

```
<?php
// ms_translator.php

function getLanguageCode($authHeader, $inputStr){
  $translatorObj = new HTTPTranslator();
  $detectMethodUrl = "http://api.microsofttranslator.com/".
           "V2/Http.svc/Detect?text=".urlencode($inputStr);
  $strResponse = $translatorObj->curlRequest(
                              $detectMethodUrl, $authHeader);
  $xmlObj = simplexml_load_string($strResponse);
  foreach((array)$xmlObj[0] as $val){
    $languageCode = $val;
  }
  return $languageCode;
}

function getLanguage($authHeader, $languageCode){
```

```
    $translatorObj = new HTTPTranslator();
    $locale = 'en';
    $getLanguageNamesurl =
                        "http://api.microsofttranslator.com/".
            "V2/Http.svc/GetLanguageNames?locale=$locale";
    $requestXml = $translatorObj->createReqXML(
                                        $languageCode);
    $curlResponse = $translatorObj->curlRequest(
          $getLanguageNamesurl, $authHeader, $requestXml);
    $xmlObj = simplexml_load_string($curlResponse);
    foreach($xmlObj->string as $language){
      return $language;
    }
}

?>
```

12.2.4 Translating to a Language

Here we show a generalized translation function, direct_translate(). To cut down translation time, your application should obtain an access token every ten minutes, and determine the original language beforehand.

```
<?php
// ms_translator.php

function translate($authHeader, $inputStr,
                    $fromLanguageCode, $toLanguageCode){
    $translatorObj = new HTTPTranslator();
    $params = "text=".urlencode($inputStr)."&to=".
            $toLanguageCode."&from=".$fromLanguageCode;
    $translateUrl = "http://api.microsofttranslator.com/".
                    "v2/Http.svc/Translate?$params";
    $curlResponse = $translatorObj->curlRequest(
                            $translateUrl, $authHeader);
    $xmlObj = simplexml_load_string($curlResponse);
    foreach((array)$xmlObj[0] as $val){
      $translatedStr = $val;
    }
    return $translatedStr;
}

function direct_translate($inputStr, $toLanguageCode){
    $authHeader = getAccessTokenHeader();
    $languageCode = getLanguageCode($authHeader,
                                        $inputStr);
    //$language = getLanguage($authHeader, $languageCode);
    return translate($authHeader, $inputStr,
                    $languageCode, $toLanguageCode);
}

?>
```

12.3 Taking a Snapshot

You may let visitors see themselves at your site through their webcams, using solely JavaScript. After you have converted the contents of the <video> tag to the <canvas> tag, you may choose to save the canvas image at the server (8.4.4). For an explanation on how to switch the canvas to fullscreen, refer to (8.5.4).

```
<!DOCTYPE html>
<html>
<body>
  <video style="display:none"></video>
  <canvas width="640" height="480"></canvas>
  <script>
  video = document.querySelector('video');
  canvas = document.querySelector('canvas');
  context = canvas.getContext("2d");

  navigator.getUserMedia = navigator.getUserMedia ||
                          navigator.webkitGetUserMedia ||
                          navigator.mozGetUserMedia ||
                          navigator.msGetUserMedia;

  navigator.getUserMedia({video: true}, onSuccess, onError);

  function onSuccess(stream) {
    video.src = URL.createObjectURL(stream);
    video.play();
    requestAnimationFrame(drawCapture);
  }
  function onError(error){
  function drawCapture() {
    context.drawImage(video, 0, 0, 640, 480);
    requestAnimationFrame(drawCapture);
  }
  </script>
</body>
</html>
```

12.4 Streaming with Red5

Your browsers should have the Adobe Flash Player plugin installed to perform live video streaming.

12.4.1 Setting Up

Red5 is a popular media server implemented in Java. Before installing Red5, you should first install the latest version of Java Standard Edition (SE).

The 'official website' http://www.red5.org/ does not supply the latest versions of Red5. To download the latest version of Red5 (1.0.3 as of 5 Aug 2014), go to

https://github.com/Red5/red5-server

It is important to use this version of Red5 as the earlier versions do not support video recording very well.

Next, set a special environment variable. Right-click Computer, navigate along *Properties -> Advanced system settings -> Advanced -> Environment Variables... -> System variables -> New...* For '*Variable name*', enter ***'JAVA_HOME'***. For 'Variable value', enter the address of Java Development Kit, which looks like ***C:\Program Files\Java\jdk1.8.0***.

Then, go to *Control Panel -> Windows Firewall -> Advanced settings*. Add a new inbound rule and a new outbound rule. For both rules, select the 'Port' type, and enter for *Special ports* **'843,1935,5080,5443'**. Forward these ports in your modem router too.

Go to the Red5 folder, and run the batch file called **Red5.bat**. You should see many text messages. Do not close the window. If you wish to run this batch file automatically in the background every time you switch on the computer, consider using NSSM, RunAsService, or AlwaysUp.

12.4.2 Testing

In the browser address bar, enter **'http://localhost:5080'**, to bring up the Red5 test page. If you see a short video, that means Red5 is running smoothly.

Enter the **'demo'** page where you can run many different demos.

Demo 1: View Publisher, which is a demo about live video streaming. First, select and start a video device under *Video -> Device*. Then, select and start an audio device under *Audio -> Device*. Under *Server -> Location*, enter **'rtmp://localhost:1935/live'** and connect it. Under Publish, click Publish. Then under View, click Play.

Demo 2: View Shared Ball, which is a demo about shared objects. (You must install the app named Shared Object Sample first.) In the browser, open two tabs with the same address as the Shared Ball page. On both tabs, change the RTMP address to : rtmp://localhost:1935/live, and click the connect logo. The yellow lights will turn green. As you move the image in one box, the image in the other box will move accordingly.

Demo 3: View Simple Recorder, which is a demo about recording a movie using the webcam at a website. Enter the address **'rtmp://localhost:1935 /live'**. Start recording, and stop recording after some time. The movie file will be saved at [Red5] \webapps\live\streams as an FLV file.

You can try out other demos yourself. The source codes (.fla files) for these demos are freely available, as indicated on the test page. Just remember that some of the linked files are located in the class/ directory. If you wish to download the entire site, you can use HTTrack. In addition, the various Red5 settings can be set in *[Red5]/conf/red5.properties*.

12.4.3 Live Streaming

Flash ActionScript is called into action for this part.

This script streams a live video to the Red5 server, and streams it back to the client. Before publishing the SWF file, you should go to File -> Publlish Settings, and change 'Local playback security' to 'Access network only'.

Note that you may choose to place and run displayPlaybackVideo() on a separate SWF file. Simply connect to the same address using nc.connect(), and use the same name for nsPlayer.play().

To adjust the video quality, refer to Chapter 11.

```
var nc:NetConnection;
var ns:NetStream;
var nsPlayer:NetStream;
var vid:Video;
var vidPlayer:Video;
var cam:Camera;
var mic:Microphone;

nc = new NetConnection();
nc.addEventListener(NetStatusEvent.NET_STATUS,
                    onNetStatus);
nc.client = { onBWDone: function():void{ } };
nc.connect("rtmp://binarybehemoth.com:1935/live");

function onNetStatus(event:NetStatusEvent):void{
   trace(event.info.code);
   if(event.info.code == "NetConnection.Connect.Success"){
      publishCamera();
      displayPublishingVideo();
      displayPlaybackVideo();
   }
}

function publishCamera() {
   cam = Camera.getCamera();
   mic = Microphone.getMicrophone();
   ns = new NetStream(nc);
   ns.attachCamera(cam);
   ns.attachAudio(mic);
   ns.publish("myCamera", "live");
}

function displayPublishingVideo():void {
   vid = new Video();
   vid.x = 10;
   vid.y = 10;
   vid.attachCamera(cam);
   addChild(vid);
}

function displayPlaybackVideo():void{
   nsPlayer = new NetStream(nc);
   nsPlayer.play("myCamera");
   vidPlayer = new Video();
   vidPlayer.x = cam.width + 20;
   vidPlayer.y = 100;
   vidPlayer.attachNetStream(nsPlayer);
   addChild(vidPlayer);
}
```

12.4.4 Two-way Streaming

This displays two live videos, streamed from the first two connected cameras. Note the use of the event handler onNSPublish, which checks if the first camera has already been connected. For this example to display properly, you should set 1000*500 for the dimensions of the Flash stage. The speakers should not be turned on with the microphone on, as it will result in indefinite echoes.

```
var nc:NetConnection;
var ns:NetStream;
var vid:Video;
var cam:Camera;
var mic:Microphone;
var nsPlayer1:NetStream;
var vidPlayer1:Video;
var nsPlayer2:NetStream;
var vidPlayer2:Video;

nc = new NetConnection();
nc.addEventListener(NetStatusEvent.NET_STATUS,
                    onNetStatus);
nc.client = { onBWDone: function():void{ } };
nc.connect("rtmp://binarybehemoth.com:1935/live");

function onNetStatus(event:NetStatusEvent):void{
   if(event.info.code == "NetConnection.Connect.Success"){
      publishCamera();
      displayPlaybackVideo();
   }
}
```

```
function publishCamera() {
   cam = Camera.getCamera();
   if (!cam) return;
   cam.setMode(640,480,14);
   cam.setQuality(0,100);
   mic = Microphone.getMicrophone();
   ns = new NetStream(nc);
   ns.attachCamera(cam);
   ns.attachAudio(mic);
   ns.addEventListener(NetStatusEvent.NET_STATUS,
                       onNSPublish);
   ns.publish("myCam1", "live");
}

function onNSPublish(event:NetStatusEvent):void{
  if(event.info.code == "NetStream.Publish.BadName"){
    ns.removeEventListener(NetStatusEvent.NET_STATUS,
                           onNSPublish);
    ns.publish("myCam2", "live");
  }
}

function displayPlaybackVideo():void{
   nsPlayer1 = new NetStream(nc);
   nsPlayer1.play("myCam1");
   vidPlayer1 = new Video();
   vidPlayer1.x = 10;
   vidPlayer1.y = 10;
   vidPlayer1.width = 480;
   vidPlayer1.height = 360;
   vidPlayer1.attachNetStream(nsPlayer1);
   addChild(vidPlayer1);

   nsPlayer2 = new NetStream(nc);
   nsPlayer2.play("myCam2");
   vidPlayer2 = new Video();
   vidPlayer2.x = 500;
   vidPlayer2.y = 10;
   vidPlayer2.width = 480;
   vidPlayer2.height = 360;
   vidPlayer2.attachNetStream(nsPlayer2);
   addChild(vidPlayer2);
}
```

12.4.5 Recording

After you have learned how to broadcast a media stream, recording onto a movie file on the server will be pretty easy. The only change that will be required will be the second argument to ns.publish(...). To record a new video, specify 'record'. To add on to an existing video file, specify 'append'. The first argument will become the first part of the resulting movie filename.

Note that the recorded movie files are to be found in the media server instead of the web server. In our example, they will be found at:

[red5]\webapps\live\streams

Also make sure you use Red5 1.0.2 or Red5 1.0.3 for the previous versions contain some bugs when it comes to video recording.

```
var nc:NetConnection;
var ns:NetStream;
var vid:Video;
var cam:Camera;
var mic:Microphone;
var nsPlayer:NetStream;
var vidPlayer:Video;
var vName:String;
```

```
vName = "myWebcam_"+((int)Math.random()*10000);

nc = new NetConnection();
nc.addEventListener(NetStatusEvent.NET_STATUS,
onNetStatus);
nc.client = { onBWDone: function():void{ } };
nc.connect("rtmp://binarybehemoth.com:1935/live");

function onNetStatus(event:NetStatusEvent):void{
   if(event.info.code == "NetConnection.Connect.Success"){
      publishCamera();
      displayPlaybackVideo();
   }
}

function publishCamera() {
   cam = Camera.getCamera();
         if (!cam) return;
         cam.setMode(640,480,14);
         cam.setQuality(0,100);
   mic = Microphone.getMicrophone();
   ns = new NetStream(nc);
   ns.attachCamera(cam);
   ns.attachAudio(mic);
   ns.publish(vName, "record");
}

function displayPlaybackVideo():void{
   nsPlayer = new NetStream(nc);
   nsPlayer.play(vName);
   vidPlayer = new Video();
   vidPlayer.x = 10;
   vidPlayer.y = 10;
         vidPlayer.width = 480;
         vidPlayer.height = 360;
   vidPlayer.attachNetStream(nsPlayer);
   addChild(vidPlayer);
}
```

12.4.6 Alternatives

While Red5 Media Server is free to use, you can choose to use Adobe Media Server(AMS) or Wowza Media Server instead. A license for AMS or Wowza costs a few hundred USD to a few thousand USD to purchase. AMS and Wowza are easy to install, and are known to have the capability to support more concurrent connections than Red5.

You may also choose to lease a media server if you don't want to run one yourself. A leased media server costs around USD10 to USD1000 per month to rent, depending on what type of server and package you choose. A Red5 media server, for example, can be rented at *http://www.red5server.com/*.

If you don't want to run a media server yourself, and wish to use a free media server provided by others, consider ScriptCam. ScriptCam is a popular JQuery plugin to manipulate webcams. Accessible at www.scriptcam.com, it is free for non-commercial use. Among other things, ScriptCam allows you to read bar codes. The main problem with ScriptCam is that the media servers are often non-functional, probably because they are overloaded.

Developers can also choose to build their apps by utilizing pre-built libraries. Two notable examples are *JW Player* and *Red5Chat*. *123 Flash Chat*, the leading chat solution, powering more than 400,000 websites, support 5000 connections per server. It also supports videoconferencing, and logging in with Facebook, Twitter, Yahoo or Google.

12.5 P2P WebRTC

So far all our techniques require the use of a server. Web Real-Time Communication allows text and media data to be transferred peer-to-peer. Like WebSocket and SSE, WebRTC does not require an external plugin. Unlike them, WebRTC does not use a server for the main communication.

12.5.1 Pros and Cons

As the main communication is peer-to-peer without going through a server, many participants can take part in the communication without overloading the server with heavy media data. The load of the server can be greatly lightened.

As the data transfer is direct, there is less communication overhead in term of time delay.

However, as of 28 Nov 2014, WebRTC is natively supported only in Google Chrome, Mozilla Firefox, and Opera. Internet Explorer has not supported it. This means that many visitors may not be able to use it directly. There are, however, WebRTC plugins for Internet Explorer and Safari.

12.5.2 How it Works

To establish contact, two peer computers first need to exchange some information (in the form of JSON strings), over a server. This can be done through your web server using AJAX calls, or through a third-party server using Firebase.

A STUN/TURN ice server is used to traverse Network Address Translation (NAT), allowing you to bypass the routers' restrictions and firewalls. You can use the Google's STUN server for free. To create an account for free access to a TURN server, go to http://numb.viagenie.ca/.

An SDP offer is made by one peer. When an SDP answer is generated by the other contacted peer, a connection is established. If STUN is used, the media will travel directly. If TURN is used, the media will be proxied. TURN is effectively a packet mirror.

Data that can be exchanged over WebRTC includes strings (DataChannel), media (Stream) and files.

12.5.3 Example

Here we use ordinary AJAX polling to listen for an incoming connection during the initial phase. This is a comparatively more complex process. In practice, you can use Firebase, WebSocket etc. to establish contact.

At the time of writing, this example does not work with Google Chrome due to its poor support for conn.createOffer(...). You should use Mozilla Firefox to run it.

```
<!DOCTYPE>
<html>
<head>
  <script>
    var room, ID, video1, video2, stream, conn, channel;
    var PeerConnection = window.RTCPeerConnection ||
                         window.mozRTCPeerConnection ||
                         window.webkitRTCPeerConnection;
    var SessionDescription =
                        window.RTCSessionDescription ||
                        window.mozRTCSessionDescription ||
                        window.webkitRTCSessionDescription;
    var IceCandidate = window.RTCIceCandidate ||
                       window.mozRTCIceCandidate ||
                       window.webkitRTCSessionDescription;
    navigator.getUserMedia = navigator.getUserMedia ||
                             navigator.mozGetUserMedia ||
                             navigator.webkitGetUserMedia;
    function start(){
      video1 = document.getElementById('v1');
      video2 = document.getElementById('v2');
      navigator.getUserMedia({video: true, audio: false},
                             onSuccess, onError);
      function onSuccess(s) {
        stream = s;
        video1.src = URL.createObjectURL(s);
        video1.play();
        obtain_id();
        connect_to_visitor();
      }
    }
    function obtain_id(){
      room = document.querySelector('input').value.trim();
      if (!room) return;
      ID = AJAX('getID.php', room);
      document.querySelector('span').innerHTML = ID;
    }
    function connect_to_visitor(){
      var server = {iceServers: [
        {url: "stun:stun.l.google.com:19302"},
        {url: "turn:www.example.com",
         credential: "wcb2015pass", username: "wcb2015"}]};
      var options =
              {optional: [{DtlsSrtpKeyAgreement: true}]};
      var conn = new PeerConnection(server, options);
      conn.onicecandidate = function(e){
        conn.onicecandidate = null;
      };
      conn.addStream(stream);
      conn.onaddstream = function(e){
        video2.src = URL.createObjectURL(e.stream);
        video2.play();
      };
      var constraints = {mandatory: {
        OfferToReceiveAudio: true,
        OfferToReceiveVideo: true
      }};
      if (ID==1){
        channel = conn.createDataChannel("myChannel",{});
        channel.onmessage = function(e){
          document.querySelector('p').innerHTML = e.data;
        };
        conn.createOffer(function (offer) {
          conn.setLocalDescription(offer);
          AJAX('register_new.php',
               room,
               ID+"|||"+JSON.stringify(offer));
        }, onError, constraints);
        var inv = setInterval(function(){
          var desc =
          AJAX('check_new_connection.php',room,ID);
          if (!desc) return;
          conn.setRemoteDescription(
              new SessionDescription(JSON.parse(desc)));
```

```
          clearInterval(inv);
        },1000);
      }else {
        conn.ondatachannel = function(e){
          channel = e.channel;
          channel.onmessage = function(e){
            document.querySelector('p').innerHTML = e.data;
          };
        };
        var inv = setInterval(function(){
          var desc =
                AJAX('check_new_connection.php',room,ID);
          if (!desc) return;
          conn.setRemoteDescription(
                new SessionDescription(JSON.parse(desc)));
          conn.createAnswer(function (answer) {
            conn.setLocalDescription(answer);
            AJAX('register_new.php',
                room,
                ID+"|||"+JSON.stringify(answer));
          }, onError, constraints);
          clearInterval(inv);
        },1000);
      }
    }
    function send(){
      channel.send(document.getElementById('msg').value);
    }
    function AJAX(action, r, data){
      var xhr;
      xhr = new XMLHttpRequest();
      xhr.open("POST",action,false);
      xhr.setRequestHeader("Content-type",
                "application/x-www-form-urlencoded");
      xhr.send("r="+encodeURIComponent(r)+"&d="+data);
                return xhr.responseText;
    }
    function onError(error){}
  </script>
</head>
<body>
  Room: <input type="text"/> <span></span>
  <button onclick="start()">Connect</button>
  Message: <input type="text" id="msg"/>
  <button onclick="send()">Send</button>
  <p></p>
  <br/><br/>
  <video id="v1" style="width:480px"></video>
  <video id="v2" style="width:480px"></video>
</body>
</html>
```

```
<?php
// getID.php
$R = $_POST['r'].'.total';
if ($data = file($R)){
  $last = $data[0]+1;
  file_put_contents($R,$last);
  echo $last;
} else {
  file_put_contents($R,'1');
  echo '1';
}
?>
```

```
<?php
// register_new.php
$R = $_POST['r'];
$D = $_POST['d'];
list($id, $desc) = explode('|||',$D,2);
file_put_contents($R.$id.".new",$desc);
?>
```

```
<?php
// cneck_new_connection.php
$R = $_POST['r'];
$D = $_POST['d'];
$D = ($D==1)?2:1;
$dat = file($R.$D.".new");
echo $dat[0];
unlink($R.$D.".new");
if ($D==1) unlink($R.".total");
```

```
?>
```

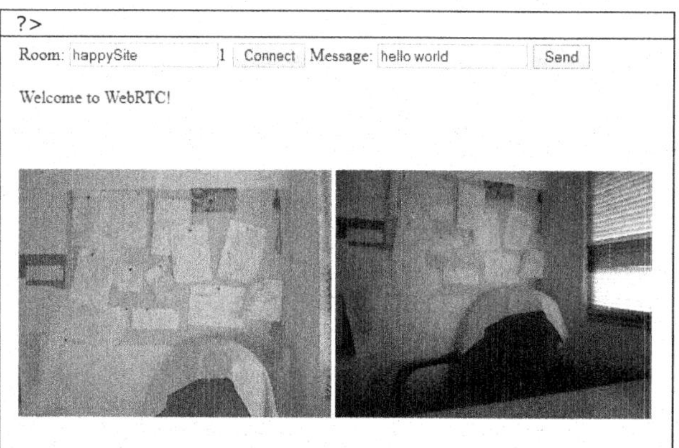

12.5.4 Muaz Khan's Experiments

If you wish to study WebRTC in-depth, you should perhaps visit Muaz Khan's website at:

https://www.webrtc-experiment.com/

Muaz Khan is a WebRTC developer who has created many interesting WebRTC libraries that you can freely use. Among these libraries are utilities that will allow you to perform video recording, screen capture and file sharing.

13. Servers

A server is a physical computer or a piece of specialized software used to serve Internet users. There are different types of software servers that can run on an operating system like Windows and Unix. These servers include the web server, the database server, the mail server, the FTP server, the media server (Chapter 12), the DNS server, and the game server. Different servers may run concurrently together on the same computer.

Usage of operating systems for websites, 16 Dec 2014	
Unix	67.2%
Windows	32.8%
OS X	< 0.1%

(courtesy of http://w3techs.com/technologies/overview/operating_system/all)

Usage of operating systems for personal use, Oct 2014	
Windows	89.85%
OS X	7.05%
Linux	1.41%

(according to Net Applications)

13.1 Networking Essentials

13.1.1 Terminology

A **dedicated server** is a type of Internet hosting in which the client has complete control over the server without sharing it with anyone else. In contrast, a **shared server** is shared by multiple users.

Domain Name System or **DNS** is a hierarchical distributed naming system for computers connected to the Internet. A DNS server is tasked with returning the IP address given a domain name.

A **Demilitarized Zone** or **DMZ** is a subnetwork that contains an organization's external-facing services that are exposed to the Internet. A DMZ adds an additional layer of security to an organization's network. An external attacker has direct access to only the equipment in the DMZ rather than any other part of the network.

A **home server** is a server located in a private residence providing services to others through a home network or the Internet.

A **proxy server** is a server that acts as an intermediary for requests from clients seeking resources from other servers.

On the Internet, a **virtual server** is a server (computer and various server programs) at someone else's location that is shared by multiple website owners. A **virtual private server (VPS)**, also called a **virtual dedicated server (VDS)**, is a virtual server that appears to the user as a dedicated server but is actually installed on a computer serving multiple Websites.

A **virtual private network (VPN)** is a network that uses a public telecommunication infrastructure, such as the Internet, to provide remote users secure access to resources in a way as if they are using a private network. A VPN uses encryption and tunnelling protocols such as the Layer Two Tunnelling Protocol (L2TP).

Cloud computing is the practice of using a network of remote servers hosted on the Internet to store, manage, and process data, rather than a local server or a personal computer.

Network address translation (NAT) is a methodology of modifying network address information in Internet Protocol (IP) datagram packet headers while they are in transit across a traffic routing device for the purpose of remapping one IP address space into another.

Loopback refers to the routing of signals back to the source. Often being 127.0.0.1, it is primarily used to test the transmission infrastructure.

Broadcast refers to the method of transferring a message to all recipients simultaneously. **Multicast** is the delivery of a message to a group of computers simultaneously in a single transmission from the source. **Unicast** is the transmission of messages to a single network destination identified by a unique address.

A **Request for Comments (RFC)** is an official document of Internet specifications, communications protocols, procedures, and events. It is published by the Internet Engineering Task Force (IETF) and the Internet Society. For instance, RFC 793 describes TCP v4.

13.1.2 Protocol Stack

There are numerous protocols in the Internet Protocol Suite. Here we list some of the most important ones.

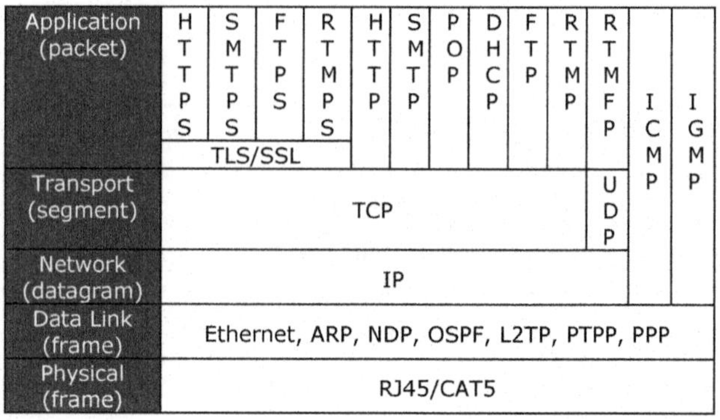

<table>
<tr><td rowspan="2">Application (packet)</td><td>HTTPS</td><td>SMTPS</td><td>FTPS</td><td>RTMPS</td><td rowspan="2">HTTP</td><td rowspan="2">SMTP</td><td rowspan="2">POP</td><td rowspan="2">DHCP</td><td rowspan="2">FTP</td><td rowspan="2">RTMP</td><td rowspan="2">RTMFP</td><td rowspan="4">ICMP</td><td rowspan="4">IGMP</td></tr>
<tr><td colspan="4">TLS/SSL</td></tr>
<tr><td>Transport (segment)</td><td colspan="10">TCP</td><td>UDP</td></tr>
<tr><td>Network (datagram)</td><td colspan="11">IP</td></tr>
<tr><td>Data Link (frame)</td><td colspan="13">Ethernet, ARP, NDP, OSPF, L2TP, PTPP, PPP</td></tr>
<tr><td>Physical (frame)</td><td colspan="13">RJ45/CAT5</td></tr>
</table>

The **data link layer** is the protocol layer that transfers data between network nodes. It might provide the means to detect and possibly correct errors that may occur in the **physical layer**.

Address Resolution Protocol (ARP) is a protocol used for the resolution of network layer addresses into link layer addresses.

The **Internet Protocol (IP)** is the principal communications protocol for relaying datagrams across network boundaries, from the source host to the destination host solely based on the IP addresses in the packet headers.

The **Transmission Control Protocol (TCP)** is a core protocol that provides reliable, ordered, and error-checked delivery of a stream of octets between programs running on computers connected to a network.

The **User Datagram Protocol (UDP)** is a core protocol with minimum mechanism. It has no handshaking prior to communications to set up special transmission channels. There is no guarantee of delivery, ordering, or duplicate protection.

The **Internet Control Message Protocol (ICMP)** is used by network devices like routers to send error messages. It is not typically used to exchange data between systems. Some diagnostic tools like 'ping' and 'traceroute' may use it.

The **Internet Group Management Protocol (IGMP)** is used by hosts and adjacent routers to establish multicast group memberships. It is an integral part of IP multicast.

The **Hypertext Transfer Protocol (HTTP)** (port 80) is a protocol for distributed, collaborative, hypermedia information systems. It is the foundation of World Wide Web.

The **Simple Mail Transfer Protocol (SMTP)** (port 25) is the Internet standard for outgoing email transmission. The **Post Office Protocol (POP)** (port 110) and the **Internet Message Access Protocol (IMAP)** (port 143) are protocols for incoming email retrieval and storage. POP downloads emails from the mail server while IMAP stores emails on the mail server.

The **Dynamic Host Configuration Protocol (DHCP)** (port 67/68) is a networking service that allocates IP addresses to computers. DHCP generally automates the configuration of the IP address, subnet mask, default gateway and DNS server.

The **File Transfer Protocol (FTP)** (port 21) is used to transfer files from one host to another over a TCP network such as the Internet.

The **Real Time Messaging Protocol (RTMP)** (port 1935) is used to stream audio, video and data over the Internet, between a Flash player and a server. (Chapter 12)

The **Secure Real Time Media Flow Protocol (RTMFP)** is used for encrypted, efficient multimedia delivery through both client-server and peer-to-peer models over the Internet.

The **Transport Layer Security (TLS)** and its predecessor, **Secure Sockets Layer (SSL)** are cryptographic protocols designed to provide communication security over the Internet.

13.1.3 IP Address

An **Internet Protocol address (IP address)** is a numerical label assigned to a device in a computer network using the Internet Protocol.

A **subnetwork**, or **subnet**, is a logical division of an IP network. All computers belonging to a subnet are addressed with a common, identical, most-significant bit-group in their IP address.

<table>
<tr><td rowspan="2">Network Prefix</td><td colspan="2">Host Number</td></tr>
<tr><td>Subnet Number</td><td>Host Number</td></tr>
</table>

Apply an 'AND' operation to the IP address and the subnet mask to obtain the network prefix. For instance, given an IP address of 192.168.5.130 and a subnet mask of 255.255.255.192, the host no. will be 0.0.0.2, as shown in the binary analysis below:

IP address	11000000.10101000.00000101.10000010
Subnet mask	11111111.11111111.11111111.11000000
Subnet no.	11000000.10101000.00000101.10000000
Host no.	00000000.00000000.00000000.00000010

There are different classes of IP addresses.

Class A: 0.0.0.0 – 127.255.255.255 (Default subnet mask: 255.0.0.0) 128 networks, 16777216 addresses per network
Class B: 128.0.0.0 – 191.255.255.255 (Default subnet mask: 255.255.0.0) 16384 networks, 65536 addresses per network
Class C: 192.0.0.0 – 223.255.255.255 (Default subnet mask: 255.255.255.0) 2097152 networks, 256 addresses per network
Class D: 224.0.0.0 – 239.255.255.255 (Reserved for Multicasting)
Class E: 240.0.0.0 – 255.255.255.255 (Reserved for Experimental Research)

Reserved IPv4 Addresses
0.0.0.0 – 0.255.255.255 (0.0.0.0/8) 16777216 add. Broadcast messages to the current network
10.0.0.0 – 10.255.255.255 (10.0.0.0/8) 16777216 add. Local communications within a private network **(Class A)**
100.64.0.0 – 100.127.255.255 (100.64.0.0/10) 4194304 add. Communications when using a Carrier-grade NAT
127.0.0.0 – 127.255.255.255 (127.0.0.0/8) 16777216 add. Loopback addresses to the local host
169.254.0.0 – 169.254.255.255 (169.254.0.0/16) 65536 add. Autoconfiguration bewtween two hosts on a single link
172.16.0.0 – 172.31.255.255 (172.16.0.0/12) 1048576 add. Local communications within a private network **(Class B)**
192.0.0.0 – 192.0.0.7 (192.0.0.0/29) 8 add. DS-Lite transition mechanism
192.0.2.0 – 192.0.2.255 (192.0.2.0/24) 256 add. Documentation and example source code
192.88.99.0 – 192.88.99.255 (192.88.99.0/24) 256 add. 6to4 anycast relays
192.168.0.0 – 192.168.255.255 (192.168.0.0/16) 65536 add. Local communications within a private network **(Class C)**
192.18.0.0 – 198.19.255.255 (198.18.0.0/15) 131072 add. Testing inter-network communications between two subnets
198.51.100.0 – 198.51.100.255 (198.51.100.0/24) 256 add. Documentation and example source code
203.0.113.0 – 203.0.113.255 (203.0.113.0/24) 256 add. Documentation and example source code
224.0.0.0 – 239.255.255.255 (224.0.0.0/4) 268435456 add. Multicast assignments
240.0.0.0 – 255.255.255.254 (240.0.0.0/4) 268435455 add. Future use
255.255.255.255 (255.255.255.255/32) 1 add. Limited broadcast destination

Reserved IPv6 Addresses
:: (::/128) 1 add. : Unspecified address
::1 (::1/128) 1 add. : Loopback address to the local host
::ffff:0.0.0.0 - ::ffff:255.255.255.255 (::ffff:0:0/96) 2^{32} add. : IPv4 mapped addresses
100:: - 100::ffff:ffff:ffff:ffff (100::/64) 2^{64} add. : Discard Prefix
64:ff9b::0.0.0.0 – 64:ff9b::255.255.255.255 (64:ff9b::/96) 2^{32} add. : IPv4/IPv6 translation
2001:: - 2001::ffff:ffff:ffff:ffff:ffff:ffff (2001::/32) 2^{96} add. : Teredo tunnelling
2001:10:: - 2001:1f:ffff:ffff:ffff:ffff:ffff:ffff (2001:10::/28) 2^{100} add. : Overlay Routable Cryptographic Hash Identifiers
2001:db8:: - 2001:db8:ffff:ffff:ffff:ffff:ffff:ffff (2001:db8::/32) 2^{96} add. : Addresses used in documentation
2002:: - 2002:ffff:ffff:ffff:ffff:ffff:ffff:ffff (2002::/16) 2^{112} add. : 6to4
fc00:: - fdff:ffff:ffff:ffff:ffff:ffff:ffff:ffff (fc00::/7) 2^{121} add. : Unique local addresses
fe80:: - febf:ffff:ffff:ffff:ffff:ffff:ffff:ffff (fe80::/10) 2^{117} add. : Link-local addresses
ff00:: - :ffff:ffff:ffff:ffff:ffff:ffff:ffff:ffff (ff00::/8) 2^{120} add. : Multicast

13.1.4 Bundled Packages

Although many people prefer to install individual server programs manually to have more control, there are many **AMP** (Apache, MySQL, PHP/Perl/Python) packages that allow you to run a server easily. There are LAMPs (Linux), WAMPs (Windows), MAMPs (Macintosh), SAMPs (Solaris), FAMPs (FreeBSD).

Linux: LAMP, Bitnami LAMPStack, AMPPS

Windows: AppServ, AMPPS, EasyPHP, Apache2Triad, Uniform Server, WampServer, WT-NMP, WPN-XM, Neard, UwAmp.

Mac: AMPPS, MAMP, DAMP, Bitnami MAMPStack

Cross-platform: XAMPP, AMPPS, Zend Server, Bitnami

XAMPP is a popular free and open source cross-platform solution stack that also include FileZilla, Mercury Mail, and other interpreters for scripts. It is however suitable for development use only as it is configured to be as open as possible. Missing security in XAMPP include:

- The MySQL administrator (root) has no password.
- The MySQL daemon is accessible via network.
- ProFTPD uses the password 'lampp' for user 'nobody'.
- PhpMyAdmin is accessible via network.
- Examples are accessible via network.
- MySQL and Apache running under the same user (nobody).

In this chapter, we shall use, on a Windows 8 platform, **Zend Server**, which is suitable for both development and production. Its basic features are free to use, but you may pay a few thousand dollars to use the full functionalities.

Usage of web servers for websites, 16 Dec 2014	
Apache	58.9 %
Nginx	22.7 %
Microsoft-IIS	13.3 %
LiteSpeed	2.1 %
Google Servers	1.3 %
Tomcat	0.4 %
Lighttpd	0.2 %
Apache Traffic Server	0.2 %
Other web servers: IBM Servers, Tengine, Oracle Servers, Zeus, Node.js, Jetty, Zope, Resin, Gunicorn, WEBrick, Kangle, BaseHTTPServer, Cherokee, Mongrel, Tornado, Roxen, AOLserver, WebSTAR, CherryPy, Paste WSGI HTTP Server, Twisted, Abyss, WebToB, IceWarp, WebHare, Orion, Hiawatha, KomHttpServer, PrimeHTTPD, RaidenHTTPD, NaviServer, Caudium, Hunchentoot, Mongrel2, Yaws, AllegroServe, G-WAN, Mahopd, Trifork, Misultin, Swazoo, Tcl-Webserver, Comanche, Inets, Tntnet, TUX, WebSiphon, Wildcat, Blazix	
(courtesy of http://w3techs.com/technologies/overview/web_server/all)	

13.2 Setting Up a Web Server

13.2.1 Installing Zend Server

You may download Zend Server from the official website and install it on your operating system such as Windows 8.

At the time of writing this, I can't get the MySQL program included in the package to work on my Windows 8 platform. When installing the Zend Server package, perhaps you should choose not to install

MySQL together. Download and install MySQL separately instead.

If you are using Windows and a foreign language, when you try to launch Zend Server, you may get a message from the browser saying 'Internal Server Error'. 'Zend Server/Apache2/logs/error.log' would say 'Zend Enabler cannot load because of a problem in its configuration file: XML parse error on line 1 column 1 - invalid byte '?' at position 3 of a 3-byte sequence'. To solve the problem, open 'Zend Server/Zend Server/etc/ZendEnablerConf.xml', delete the messed-up characters in the first line and make sure it is properly tagged. Restart the Apache Zend Server at your system tray.

You should update your Zend server every month. Otherwise it will get expired and you will have to reinstall it to access the control panel, even though the Apache server will still be running.

13.2.2 LAN Access

The Zend Server configuration page may be accessed by clicking the icon or entering 'http://localhost: 10082/ZendServer/' in the browser.

To host a website, place your files at: '\Zend\Apache2\htdocs'.

If you are trying to access the website on the server, simply type 'localhost' in the address bar of a browser.

If you wish to access the website over a Local Area Network (LAN), use the reserved IP address. For a Class C network, it should look like 192.168.0.x, where x is an integer between 0 and 255. This address is the IP address assigned to the server. It can be set by going to Network Connections -> [your network] -> Properties -> Internet Protocol Version 4 (TCP/IPv4).

Anytime, you may choose to view the access and error log files at '\Zend\Apache2\logs'.

13.2.3 Using a Domain Name

An Internet Service Provider usually assigns to the clients **dynamic IP addresses**, which change from time to time. To use a domain name, first you need to obtain a **static IP address** for your server from the Internet Service Provider. If you wish to use a domain name without applying for a static IP address, consider using a Managed DNS Service like *noip.com*. It installs on your computer Dynamic Update Client (DUC) which automatically updates the DNS servers across the globe periodically.

To rent a domain name *for a static IP address instead*, use the service of a domain registrar such as *goDaddy.com*, which is very popular. *goDaddy.com* not only provides a DNS service, it also lets you purchase a TSL/SSL certificate so that your website can be hosted via HTTPS instead of merely HTTP. With it, you can also create subdomains for your domain. Any DNS changes you make can take up to 48 hours to reflect on the Internet. There exist Root DNS servers in the world that obtain information from domain registrars worldwide periodically. Every time a domain name record cannot be found in the DNS server you use (from your ISP), the DNS server queries the Root DNS servers, and caches the record for a limited amount of time if a record can be found. (You may use the DNS server at 8.8.8.8, which is hosted by Google.)

After you have obtained a domain name, launch the admin panel of your modem router. This usually involves entering an address in the browser. The address varies from one modem router to another, but for a Class C network, it can sometimes be accessed via 192.168.0.1. At the admin panel, go to Virtual Servers under Forwarding. Enter the IP address (private IP address) of your server, and forward the port from 80 to 80, which is the default port number for HTTP.

13.2.4 Virtual Host

A virtual host allows a server to host a domain name that is non-existent outside the local network environment. It is often used for development purposes, before the site is transferred to the real Internet site.

A server can host more than one domain names. To set up a virtual host, you need to edit three files:

```
C:\Program Files\Zend\Apache2\conf\extra\httpd-vhosts.conf
......
<VirtualHost *:80>
  DocumentRoot "C:\test"
  ServerName mywebsite.com
  ServerAlias www.mywebsite.com
  ErrorLog "logs/mywebsite.com-error.log"
  CustomLog "logs/mywebsite.com-access.log" common
  <Directory "C:\test">
    Allow from all
    #Require all granted   # new way
  </Directory>
</VirtualHost>
```

```
C:\Program Files\Zend\Apache2\conf\httpd.conf
......
# Virtual hosts
Include conf/extra/httpd-vhosts.conf
......
```

```
C:\Windows\System32\Drivers\etc\hosts
......
# localhost name resolution is handled within DNS itself.
  127.0.0.1       localhost
  ::1             localhost

  127.0.0.1       mywebsite.com
```

After you have changed the three files, you must restart the Apache server. Only then you can access the local files (C:\test\index.html) by pointing to the specific URL (http://mywebsite.com/index.html) in the browser.

13.3 Settings

13.3.1 php.ini

If you use Zend Server, any changes to php.ini should be done through its admin panel, which can be launched by double-clicking its icon on the desktop. It can be accessed through Configurations -> PHP. Click on a category name to view and change the settings. Alternatively, php.ini can be edited at C:\Program Files\Zend\ZendServer\etc.

13.3.2 httpd.conf

The Apache configuration file httpd.conf can be found at '\Zend\Apache2\conf'. Among other things, it specifies what modules to load, the administrator's email address, the directory containing the webpages, the default directory webpage (index.php, index.html), logging and the access to various sites. To change the directory that will be regarded as the server Root Directory, change the directories next to 'DocumentRoot' and within the <Directory> directive.

Note that whatever you learn in Chapter 14 .htaccess can be applied here. 'httpd.conf', however, requires a server restart for the changes to take effect.

13.3.3 Windows Networking Commands

Various commands can be issued at the Command Line Interpreter to obtain information about the network. To get to the command prompt, simply run the command 'cmd' in Windows. Note that each command comes with many options. To see all the additional options available for a command, attach /? to the end of the command and enter it.

(If you are using Windows 8, you may also enter 'VPN' in the search box to set up a Virtual Private Network.)

ipconfig is used to display the network settings currently assigned to all network adapters in the machine. This command can be utilised to verify a network connection.

```
C:\Users\lipphang>ipconfig

Windows IP Configuration


Wireless LAN adapter Local Area Connection* 12:

   Media State . . . . . . . . . . . : Media disconnected
   Connection-specific DNS Suffix  . :

Wireless LAN adapter WiFi 3:

   Media State . . . . . . . . . . . : Media disconnected
   Connection-specific DNS Suffix  . :

Wireless LAN adapter WiFi 2:

   Connection-specific DNS Suffix  . :
   Link-local IPv6 Address . . . . . : fe80::5cd8:6237:97f:d257%15
   IPv4 Address. . . . . . . . . . . : 192.168.1.5
   Subnet Mask . . . . . . . . . . . : 255.255.0.0
   Default Gateway . . . . . . . . . : fe80::1%15
                                       192.168.1.1

Ethernet adapter Ethernet:

   Media State . . . . . . . . . . . : Media disconnected
   Connection-specific DNS Suffix  . :

Tunnel adapter Teredo Tunneling Pseudo-Interface:

   Connection-specific DNS Suffix  . :
   IPv6 Address. . . . . . . . . . . : 2001:0:9d38:6abd:185d:15d3:83ad:81c9
   Link-local IPv6 Address . . . . . : fe80::185d:15d3:83ad:81c9%17
   Default Gateway . . . . . . . . . : ::

Tunnel adapter isatap.{238EA96D-9271-43F2-9207-D14966598804}:

   Media State . . . . . . . . . . . : Media disconnected
   Connection-specific DNS Suffix  . :
```

netstat is used to display active TCP connections.

```
TCP    127.0.0.1:1050         Phang:1051             ESTABLISHED
TCP    127.0.0.1:1051         Phang:1050             ESTABLISHED
TCP    127.0.0.1:1052         Phang:1047             ESTABLISHED
TCP    127.0.0.1:1053         Phang:1048             ESTABLISHED
TCP    127.0.0.1:1054         Phang:9598             ESTABLISHED
TCP    127.0.0.1:1055         Phang:activesync       ESTABLISHED
TCP    127.0.0.1:1056         Phang:9600             ESTABLISHED
TCP    127.0.0.1:1057         Phang:9597             ESTABLISHED
TCP    127.0.0.1:1058         Phang:9601             ESTABLISHED
TCP    127.0.0.1:1059         Phang:9595             ESTABLISHED
TCP    127.0.0.1:1060         Phang:9602             ESTABLISHED
TCP    127.0.0.1:1061         Phang:9596             ESTABLISHED
TCP    127.0.0.1:1062         Phang:9599             ESTABLISHED
TCP    127.0.0.1:1063         Phang:9596             ESTABLISHED
TCP    127.0.0.1:1064         Phang:9595             ESTABLISHED
TCP    127.0.0.1:1065         Phang:9595             ESTABLISHED
TCP    127.0.0.1:1066         Phang:9595             ESTABLISHED
TCP    127.0.0.1:1067         Phang:9595             ESTABLISHED
TCP    127.0.0.1:9595         Phang:1043             ESTABLISHED
TCP    127.0.0.1:9595         Phang:1059             ESTABLISHED
TCP    127.0.0.1:9595         Phang:1064             ESTABLISHED
TCP    127.0.0.1:9595         Phang:1065             ESTABLISHED
TCP    127.0.0.1:9595         Phang:1066             ESTABLISHED
TCP    127.0.0.1:9595         Phang:1067             ESTABLISHED
TCP    127.0.0.1:9596         Phang:1061             ESTABLISHED
TCP    127.0.0.1:9596         Phang:1063             ESTABLISHED
TCP    127.0.0.1:9597         Phang:1057             ESTABLISHED
TCP    127.0.0.1:9598         Phang:1054             ESTABLISHED
TCP    127.0.0.1:9599         Phang:1062             ESTABLISHED
TCP    127.0.0.1:9600         Phang:1056             ESTABLISHED
TCP    127.0.0.1:9601         Phang:1058             ESTABLISHED
TCP    127.0.0.1:9602         Phang:1060             ESTABLISHED
TCP    192.168.1.5:1090       sinwns1011417:https    ESTABLISHED
TCP    192.168.1.5:4369       74.201.176.25:https    ESTABLISHED
TCP    192.168.1.5:6726       5.11.81.104:https      ESTABLISHED
TCP    192.168.1.5:6727       5.11.81.104:https      ESTABLISHED
TCP    192.168.1.5:7723       a118-215:http          CLOSE_WAIT
TCP    192.168.1.5:8502       ni-in-f125:5222        ESTABLISHED
TCP    192.168.1.5:10864      219.93.37.98:http      CLOSE_WAIT
TCP    192.168.1.5:10879      219.93.37.80:http      CLOSE_WAIT
TCP    192.168.1.5:10880      219.93.37.80:http      CLOSE_WAIT
TCP    192.168.1.5:10919      r2:https               ESTABLISHED
TCP    192.168.1.5:10920      119.190.4.52:http      TIME_WAIT
TCP    192.168.1.5:10921      183.60.16.208:8000     TIME_WAIT
TCP    192.168.1.5:10922      112.95.234.84:8000     TIME_WAIT
```

tracert is used to visually see a network packet being sent and received and the number of hops required for that packet to get to its destination.

```
C:\Users\lipphang>tracert www.google.com

Tracing route to www.google.com [173.194.127.83]
over a maximum of 30 hops:

  1     1 ms    <1 ms    <1 ms  ADSL [192.168.1.1]
  2     9 ms     9 ms     9 ms  60.52.73.14
  3     *        *        *     Request timed out.
  4     *        *        *     Request timed out.
  5     *        *        *     Request timed out.
  6     *        *        *     Request timed out.
  7     *        *        *     Request timed out.
  8     *        *        *     Request timed out.
  9     *        *        *     Request timed out.
 10     *        *        *     Request timed out.
 11     *        *        *     Request timed out.
 12     *        *        *     Request timed out.
 13     *        *        *     Request timed out.
 14     *        *        *     Request timed out.
 15     *        *        *     Request timed out.
 16     *        *        *     Request timed out.
 17     *        *        *     Request timed out.
 18     *        *        *     Request timed out.
 19     *        *        *     Request timed out.
 20     *        *        *     Request timed out.
 21     *        *        *     Request timed out.
 22     *        *        *     Request timed out.
 23     *        *        *     Request timed out.
 24     *        *        *     Request timed out.
 25     *        *        *     Request timed out.
 26     *        *        *     Request timed out.
 27     *        *        *     Request timed out.
 28     *        *        *     Request timed out.
 29     *        *        *     Request timed out.
 30     *        *        *     Request timed out.

Trace complete.
```

ping helps in determining TCP/IP Network IP address, as well as issues with the network and assists in resolving them.

```
C:\Users\lipphang>ping www.google.com

Pinging www.google.com [173.194.127.81] with 32 bytes of data:
Reply from 173.194.127.81: bytes=32 time=107ms TTL=56
Reply from 173.194.127.81: bytes=32 time=93ms TTL=56
Reply from 173.194.127.81: bytes=32 time=92ms TTL=56
Reply from 173.194.127.81: bytes=32 time=92ms TTL=56

Ping statistics for 173.194.127.81:
    Packets: Sent = 4, Received = 4, Lost = 0 (0% loss),
Approximate round trip times in milli-seconds:
    Minimum = 92ms, Maximum = 107ms, Average = 96ms
```

pathping provides information about network latency and network loss at intermediate hops between a source and a destination. It sends multiple Echo Request messages to each router over a period of time and then computes results based on the packets returned from each router.

```
C:\Users\lipphang>pathping www.google.com

Tracing route to www.google.com [173.194.127.81]
over a maximum of 30 hops:
  0  Phang [192.168.1.5]
  1  ADSL [192.168.1.1]
  2  175.137.110.38
  3     *        *        *
Computing statistics for 50 seconds...
            Source to Here   This Node/Link
Hop  RTT    Lost/Sent = Pct  Lost/Sent = Pct  Address
  0                                           Phang [192.168.1.5]
                                0/ 100 =  0%   |
  1    0ms     0/ 100 =  0%     0/ 100 =  0%  ADSL [192.168.1.1]
                               16/ 100 = 16%   |
  2   24ms    16/ 100 = 16%     0/ 100 =  0%  175.137.110.38

Trace complete.
```

telnet is a program that allows users to remotely access another computer such as a server, network device, or another computer.

```
Welcome to Microsoft Telnet Client

Escape Character is 'CTRL+]'

Microsoft Telnet> ?

Commands may be abbreviated. Supported commands are:

c    - close                    close current connection
d    - display                  display operating parameters
o    - open hostname [port]     connect to hostname (default port 23).
q    - quit                     exit telnet
set  - set                      set options (type 'set ?' for a list)
sen  - send                     send strings to server
st   - status                   print status information
u    - unset                    unset options (type 'unset ?' for a list)
?/h  - help                     print help information
Microsoft Telnet> _
```

ftp is used to transfer files. At the FTP prompt, you may enter ? to display a list of all the available commands.

```
C:\Users\lipphang>ftp
ftp> open ftp.ipage.com
Connected to ftp.ipage.com.
220-
220 Ipage FTP Server ready
User (ftp.ipage.com:(none)): gamesuriacom
331 Password required for gamesuriacom
Password:
230 User gamesuriacom logged in
ftp> get channel.html
200 PORT command successful
150 Opening ASCII mode data connection for channel.html (60 bytes)
226 Transfer complete
ftp: 60 bytes received in 0.00Seconds 60000.00Kbytes/sec.
ftp> send test.txt
200 PORT command successful
150 Opening ASCII mode data connection for test.txt
226 Transfer complete
ftp: 12 bytes sent in 0.31Seconds 0.04Kbytes/sec.
ftp> ?
Commands may be abbreviated.  Commands are:

!               delete          literal         prompt          send
?               debug           ls              put             status
append          dir             mdelete         pwd             trace
ascii           disconnect      mdir            quit            type
bell            get             mget            quote           user
binary          glob            mkdir           recv            verbose
bye             hash            mls             remotehelp
cd              help            mput            rename
close           lcd             open            rmdir
ftp> !
Microsoft Windows [Version 6.2.9200]
(c) 2012 Microsoft Corporation. All rights reserved.
```

arp displays, adds, or removes arp information from network devices.

```
C:\Users\lipphang>arp

Displays and modifies the IP-to-Physical address translation tables used by
address resolution protocol (ARP).

ARP -s inet_addr eth_addr [if_addr]
ARP -d inet_addr [if_addr]
ARP -a [inet_addr] [-N if_addr] [-v]

  -a            Displays current ARP entries by interrogating the current
                protocol data.  If inet_addr is specified, the IP and Physical
                addresses for only the specified computer are displayed.  If
                more than one network interface uses ARP, entries for each ARP
                table are displayed.
  -g            Same as -a.
  -v            Displays current ARP entries in verbose mode.  All invalid
                entries and entries on the loop-back interface will be shown.
  inet_addr     Specifies an internet address.
  -N if_addr    Displays the ARP entries for the network interface specified
                by if_addr.
  -d            Deletes the host specified by inet_addr. inet_addr may be
                wildcarded with * to delete all hosts.
  -s            Adds the host and associates the Internet address inet_addr
                with the Physical address eth_addr.  The Physical address is
                given as 6 hexadecimal bytes separated by hyphens. The entry
                is permanent.
  eth_addr      Specifies a physical address.
  if_addr       If present, this specifies the Internet address of the
                interface whose address translation table should be modified.
                If not present, the first applicable interface will be used.
Example:
  > arp -s 157.55.85.212   00-aa-00-62-c6-09  .... Adds a static entry.
  > arp -a                                    .... Displays the arp table.
```

route is used to manually configure the routes in the routing table.

```
C:\Users\lipphang>route

Manipulates network routing tables.

ROUTE [-f] [-p] [-4|-6] command [destination]
                  [MASK netmask]  [gateway] [METRIC metric]  [IF interface]

  -f           Clears the routing tables of all gateway entries.  If this is
               used in conjunction with one of the commands, the tables are
               cleared prior to running the command.

  -p           When used with the ADD command, makes a route persistent across
               boots of the system. By default, routes are not preserved
               when the system is restarted. Ignored for all other commands,
               which always affect the appropriate persistent routes.

  -4           Force using IPv4.

  -6           Force using IPv6.

  command      One of these:
                 PRINT     Prints  a route
                 ADD       Adds    a route
                 DELETE    Deletes a route
                 CHANGE    Modifies an existing route
  destination  Specifies the host.
  MASK         Specifies that the next parameter is the 'netmask' value.
  netmask      Specifies a subnet mask value for this route entry.
               If not specified, it defaults to 255.255.255.255.
  gateway      Specifies gateway.
  interface    the interface number for the specified route.
  METRIC       specifies the metric, ie. cost for the destination.

All symbolic names used for destination are looked up in the network database
file NETWORKS. The symbolic names for gateway are looked up in the host name
database file HOSTS.

If the command is PRINT or DELETE. Destination or gateway can be a wildcard,
(wildcard is specified as a star '*'), or the gateway argument may be omitted.

If Dest contains a * or ?, it is treated as a shell pattern, and only
matching destination routes are printed. The '*' matches any string,
and '?' matches any one char. Examples: 157.*.1, 157.*, 127.*, *224*.

Pattern match is only allowed in PRINT command.
Diagnostic Notes:
    Invalid MASK generates an error, that is when (DEST & MASK) != DEST.
    Example> route ADD 157.0.0.0 MASK 155.0.0.0 157.55.80.1 IF 1
             The route addition failed: The specified mask parameter is invalid.
 (Destination & Mask) != Destination.

Examples:

    > route PRINT
    > route PRINT -4
    > route PRINT -6
    > route PRINT 157*          .... Only prints those matching 157*

    > route ADD 157.0.0.0 MASK 255.0.0.0  157.55.80.1 METRIC 3 IF 2
             destination^      ^mask      ^gateway     metric^    ^
                                                         Interface^
      If IF is not given, it tries to find the best interface for a given
      gateway.
    > route ADD 3ffe::/32 3ffe::1

    > route CHANGE 157.0.0.0 MASK 255.0.0.0 157.55.80.5 METRIC 2 IF 2

      CHANGE is used to modify gateway and/or metric only.

    > route DELETE 157.0.0.0
    > route DELETE 3ffe::/32
```

getmac is used to show both the local and remote MAC addresses.

```
C:\Users\lipphang>getmac

Physical Address    Transport Name
=================== ==========================================================
00-1A-4D-4C-53-9A   Media disconnected
D8-FE-E3-64-20-42   \Device\Tcpip_{238EA96D-9271-43F2-9207-D14966598804}
00-11-95-64-30-2C   Media disconnected
```

nslookup displays information that can be used to diagnose DNS infrastructure.

```
C:\Users\lipphang>nslookup
Default Server:  UnKnown
Address:  192.168.1.1

> www.google.com
Server:  UnKnown
Address:  192.168.1.1

Non-authoritative answer:
Name:    www.google.com
Addresses:  2404:6800:4005:802::1011
          173.194.127.84
          173.194.127.80
          173.194.127.81
          173.194.127.82
          173.194.127.83

> ?
Commands:   (identifiers are shown in uppercase, [] means optional)
NAME            - print info about the host/domain NAME using default server
NAME1 NAME2     - as above, but use NAME2 as server
help or ?       - print info on common commands
set OPTION      - set an option
    all                 - print options, current server and host
    [no]debug           - print debugging information
    [no]d2              - print exhaustive debugging information
    [no]defname         - append domain name to each query
    [no]recurse         - ask for recursive answer to query
    [no]search          - use domain search list
    [no]vc              - always use a virtual circuit
    domain=NAME         - set default domain name to NAME
    srchlist=N1[/N2/.../N6] - set domain to N1 and search list to N1,N2, etc.
    root=NAME           - set root server to NAME
    retry=X             - set number of retries to X
    timeout=X           - set initial time-out interval to X seconds
    type=X              - set query type (ex. A,AAAA,A+AAAA,ANY,CNAME,MX,NS,PTR,
SOA,SRV)
    querytype=X         - same as type
    class=X             - set query class (ex. IN (Internet), ANY)
    [no]msxfr           - use MS fast zone transfer
    ixfrver=X           - current version to use in IXFR transfer request
server NAME     - set default server to NAME, using current default server
lserver NAME    - set default server to NAME, using initial server
root            - set current default server to the root
ls [opt] DOMAIN [> FILE] - list addresses in DOMAIN (optional: output to FILE)
    -a          -  list canonical names and aliases
    -d          -  list all records
    -t TYPE     -  list records of the given RFC record type (ex. A,CNAME,MX,NS,
PTR etc.)
view FILE           - sort an 'ls' output file and view it with pg
exit            - exit the program
```

nbtstat is used to display protocol statistics and current TCP/IP connections using NBT.

```
C:\Users\lipphang>nbtstat -A 192.168.1.5

WiFi 3:
Node IpAddress: [0.0.0.0] Scope Id: []

    Host not found.

Ethernet:
Node IpAddress: [0.0.0.0] Scope Id: []

    Host not found.

WiFi 2:
Node IpAddress: [192.168.1.5] Scope Id: []

           NetBIOS Remote Machine Name Table

       Name               Type         Status
    ---------------------------------------------
    PHANG          <00>  UNIQUE      Registered
    WORKGROUP      <00>  GROUP       Registered
    PHANG          <20>  UNIQUE      Registered
    WORKGROUP      <1E>  GROUP       Registered
    WORKGROUP      <1D>  UNIQUE      Registered
    ☺☻__MSBROWSE__☻<01>  GROUP       Registered

    MAC Address = D8-FE-E3-64-20-42


Local Area Connection* 12:
Node IpAddress: [0.0.0.0] Scope Id: []

    Host not found.

C:\Users\lipphang>nbtstat

Displays protocol statistics and current TCP/IP connections using NBT
(NetBIOS over TCP/IP).

NBTSTAT [ [-a RemoteName] [-A IP address] [-c] [-n]
        [-r] [-R] [-RR] [-s] [-S] [interval] ]

  -a   (adapter status) Lists the remote machine's name table given its name
  -A   (Adapter status) Lists the remote machine's name table given its
                        IP address.
  -c   (cache)          Lists NBT's cache of remote [machine] names and their IP
 addresses
  -n   (names)          Lists local NetBIOS names.
  -r   (resolved)       Lists names resolved by broadcast and via WINS
  -R   (Reload)         Purges and reloads the remote cache name table
  -S   (Sessions)       Lists sessions table with the destination IP addresses
  -s   (sessions)       Lists sessions table converting destination IP
                        addresses to computer NETBIOS names.
  -RR  (ReleaseRefresh) Sends Name Release packets to WINS and then, starts Refr
esh

  RemoteName   Remote host machine name.
  IP address   Dotted decimal representation of the IP address.
  interval     Redisplays selected statistics, pausing interval seconds
               between each display. Press Ctrl+C to stop redisplaying
               statistics.
```

netsh is used to, either locally or remotely, display or modify the network configuration of a computer that is currently running.

```
C:\Users\lipphang>netsh
netsh>?

The following commands are available:

Commands in this context:
..             - Goes up one context level.
?              - Displays a list of commands.
abort          - Discards changes made while in offline mode.
add            - Adds a configuration entry to a list of entries.
advfirewall    - Changes to the `netsh advfirewall' context.
alias          - Adds an alias.
branchcache    - Changes to the `netsh branchcache' context.
bridge         - Changes to the `netsh bridge' context.
bye            - Exits the program.
commit         - Commits changes made while in offline mode.
delete         - Deletes a configuration entry from a list of entries.
dhcpclient     - Changes to the `netsh dhcpclient' context.
dnsclient      - Changes to the `netsh dnsclient' context.
dump           - Displays a configuration script.
exec           - Runs a script file.
exit           - Exits the program.
firewall       - Changes to the `netsh firewall' context.
help           - Displays a list of commands.
http           - Changes to the `netsh http' context.
interface      - Changes to the `netsh interface' context.
ipsec          - Changes to the `netsh ipsec' context.
lan            - Changes to the `netsh lan' context.
mbn            - Changes to the `netsh mbn' context.
namespace      - Changes to the `netsh namespace' context.
nap            - Changes to the `netsh nap' context.
netio          - Changes to the `netsh netio' context.
offline        - Sets the current mode to offline.
online         - Sets the current mode to online.
p2p            - Changes to the `netsh p2p' context.
popd           - Pops a context from the stack.
pushd          - Pushes current context on stack.
quit           - Exits the program.
ras            - Changes to the `netsh ras' context.
rpc            - Changes to the `netsh rpc' context.
set            - Updates configuration settings.
show           - Displays information.
trace          - Changes to the `netsh trace' context.
unalias        - Deletes an alias.
wcn            - Changes to the `netsh wcn' context.
wfp            - Changes to the `netsh wfp' context.
winhttp        - Changes to the `netsh winhttp' context.
winsock        - Changes to the `netsh winsock' context.
wlan           - Changes to the `netsh wlan' context.

The following sub-contexts are available:
 advfirewall branchcache bridge dhcpclient dnsclient firewall http interface ips
ec lan mbn namespace nap netio p2p ras rpc trace wcn wfp winhttp winsock wlan

To view help for a command, type the command, followed by a space, and then
 type ?.
```

13.4 Other Servers

13.4.1 MySQL Database Server

You may download and install MySQL Community Edition for free from the official website. Once you have installed it, run MySQL Workbench, and set up a new connection. If the MySQL server is running on the same local computer as the web server, you may specify 'localhost' as the hostname. Here is the PHP code that connects to the database:

```
$link=mysqli_connect("localhost","root","password","testing");
```

where 'root' is the username, and 'testing' is the schema name. By default, MySQL uses the port 3306.

13.4.2 hMailServer

'hMailServer is a free e-mail server for Microsoft Windows. It's used by Internet service providers, companies, governments, schools and enthusiasts in all parts of the world. It supports the common e-mail protocols (IMAP, SMTP and POP3) and can easily be integrated with many existing web mail systems. It has flexible score-based spam protection and can attach to your virus scanner to scan all incoming and outgoing email.' --- *www.hmailserver.com*

Download and install hMailServer. After the installation, launch hMailServer Administrator, add a domain name which should look like *mydomain.com*. Under Domains->*[mydomain.com]*->Accounts, add an email address and click Save. Then go to Settings->Protocols->SMTP-> Delivery of e-mail, for the local host name, enter the domain name again and click Save.

Additionally, under Settings->Logging, enable all the logging options and click Save. Under Domains -> *[mydomain.com]* -> Advanced, enter a catch-all address which is used to receive all emails sent to the domain that do not match any email account.

Next, edit php.ini. If you are using hMailServer on the same computer as the web server, *SMTP* should be set to localhost. *smtp_host* should be set to 25. For Win32 users, also set *sendmail_from* to an email address.

The next step involves adding a mail exchanger record (MX record) for the mail server to the DNS. You need to work with the company that provides your domain for this. The MX mechanism provides the ability to run multiple mail servers for a single domain, and allows administrators to specify an order in which they should be tried.

Most ISPs block any external use of port 25 to reduce spamming. As such, you may need to relay the emails to the mail server of your ISP. Another alternative would be to purchase from *noip.com* Mail Reflector for incoming mails, and Alternate-Port SMTP for outgoing mails.

You also need configure your router to forward all traffic on port 25 to the computer where hMailServer is running. Furthermore, your firewall needs to allow hMailServer to receive and send emails.

hMailServer should be running as a background Windows service. In hMailServer Administrator, go to Utilities -> Diagnostics to test it out.

13.4.3 XAMPP and Gmail

If you are using XAMPP, you can configure it to send emails via Gmail.

In C:\xampp\php\php.ini:

```
[mail function]
SMTP=smtp.gmail.com
smtp_port=587
sendmail_from = myGmail@gmail.com
sendmail_path = "C:\xampp\sendmail\sendmail.exe -t"

extension=php_openssl.dll
```

In C:\xampp\sendmail\sendmail.ini:

```
[sendmail]
smtp_server=smtp.gmail.com
smtp_port=587
smtp_ssl=auto
error_logfile=error.log
debug_logfile=debug.log
auth_username=myGmail@gmail.com
auth_password=myPassword
force_sender=myGmail@gmail.com
```

Then restart Apache in your XAMPP interface.

13.4.4 Filezilla Server

You may install Filezilla Server so that clients can transfer files to or from the server by using an FTP client.

For the server address, enter 127.0.0.1 if you are not trying administer a remote FTP server. Click the 'Users' button, add a user, and specify the shared folders.

Next, configure your modem router to forward all traffic on port 21 to the computer where the FTP server is running(192.168.1.x).

If you are using Windows, you also need to allow Filezilla server to pass through Windows Firewall. In Windows 8, go to 'Windows Firewall' -> 'Allow an app or feature through Windows Firewall'. Click 'Change Settings'. Click 'Allow another app...'. At this point, ***do not*** choose FileZilla Server Interface. Instead, browse for '[FileZilla Server folder]/FileZilla Server.exe'. Click 'Add' and then 'OK'.

Now you can transfer files to or from the server using an FTP client such as FileZilla Client. You may also test your FTP connection at 'http://ftptest.net/'.

14. .htaccess

.htaccess is an Apache configuration file placed in the web server. It is a text file with no name, but with the extension ‘.htaccess’. When placed in a directory, the directives in that file will modify the behavior of access to that directory, and all subdirectories thereof.

On shared hosts, Apache cannot be configured through httpd.conf. As such, .htaccess remains the avenue to configure the server settings (without a server restart). Note that some shared hosts block access to .htaccess or some functionalities of it. Some of the necessary modules may not have been installed.

Because of space constraint, in some of the examples in this chapter, some directives span more than one line. In real life, however, each directive should be specified in exactly one line.

<table>
<tr><td>The following directives in httpd.conf causes .htaccess to be completely ignored.</td></tr>
<tr><td><Directory />
  AllowOverride None
  AllowOverrideList None
</Directory></td></tr>
<tr><td>If ‘All’ instead of ‘None’ is specified, then all directives in an .htaccess file (as specified by AccessFileName) can override earlier configuration directives. Other options beside ‘None’ and ‘All’ include ‘AuthConfig’, ‘FileInfo’, ‘Indexes’, ‘Limit’, ‘Nonfatal=[Override |Unknown|All]’, ‘Options[=Option]’.</td></tr>
</table>

.htaccess directives are fully documented at:
http://httpd.apache.org/docs/

14.1 URL Mapping – Syntaxes

.htaccess allows the request for a URL, whether entered directly in the address bar or linked indirectly in a html file, to be redirected to another URL.

14.1.1 Regular Expressions

Regular expressions may be used to specify which URLs are to be redirected.

<table>
<tr><th colspan="2">Metacharacters</th></tr>
<tr><td>\</td><td>Escapes a special character such as ‘!’, ‘@’, ‘#’, ‘$’, ‘,’, ‘.’ etc.
‘\.’ matches any string containing the dot ‘.’.
‘\s’ matches any string containing a white space.</td></tr>
<tr><td>^</td><td>Marks the starting.
‘^x’ matches any string starting with ‘x’.</td></tr>
<tr><td>$</td><td>Marks the ending.
<i>‘x$’ matches any string ending with ‘x’.</td></tr>
<tr><td>.</td><td>Denotes any character.
‘a.b’ matches strings containing strings suc as ‘abb’, ‘a5b’ etc.</td></tr>
<tr><td>!</td><td>Denotes exception. $N cannot be used at the same time.
‘!xyz’ matches any string except ‘xyz’.</td></tr>
<tr><td>[]</td><td>Denotes a class that defines a character out of a group.
‘[abc]’ matches any string containing ‘a’, ‘b’, or ‘c’.</td></tr>
<tr><td>|</td><td>Denotes logical OR.
‘abc|xyz’ matches any string containing ‘abc’ or ‘xyz’.</td></tr>
<tr><td>()</td><td>Denotes a group and a back reference point for substitution.
‘(ab)+’ means that ‘abab’ can be substituted later with $1.</td></tr>
<tr><td>?</td><td>Denotes a quantifier matching 0 or 1 time.
‘a?b’ matches strings containing ‘b’ or ‘ab’</td></tr>
<tr><td>+</td><td>Denotes a quantifier matching 1 or more times.
‘a+b’ matches strings containing ‘ab’, ‘aab’, ‘aaab’ etc.</td></tr>
<tr><td>*</td><td>Denotes a quantifier matching 0 or more times.
‘a*b’ matches strings containing ‘b’, ‘ab’, ‘aab’ etc.</td></tr>
<tr><td>{}</td><td>Denotes a quantifier matching an arbitrary number of times.
‘a{2,4}b’ matches strings containing ‘aab’, ‘aaab’ or ‘aaaab’.</td></tr>
<tr><th colspan="2">Class Metacharacters within []</th></tr>
<tr><td>\</td><td>Escapes a special character.
‘[ab\+]’ matches any string containing ‘a’, ‘b’ , or ‘+’.</td></tr>
<tr><td>-</td><td>Denotes a range.
‘[0-9]+’ matches any string containing a number.</td></tr>
<tr><td>^</td><td>Denotes negation.
‘^[^/a-z]+’ matches any string that does not begin with ‘/’ and does not contain any small letter.</td></tr>
</table>

For example,

    ^([^/])+/([-a-zA-Z]+)/?

would match

    foo/bar
    foo/B-ar
    foo/bar/
    foo/bar/index.html

where $1 denotes ‘foo’ and $2 denotes ‘bar’ or ‘B-ar’ later.

When matching a URL, the protocol scheme at the front and the query string at the end are not matched. For example, if you type ‘http://example.com/a.php?x=3’ in the address bar, ‘http://’ and ‘?x=3’ will not be considered for matching. On the other hand, even if ‘a.php’ does not exist, it will be matched and the request may be redirected.

14.1.2 ‘Redirect’

This directive has the form:

    Redirect [status] <old URL> <new URL>

It redirects any request for the old URL to the new URL. For both URLs, relative paths are not allowed. <old URL> is a URL path beginning with a ‘/’. <new URL> may include the protocol scheme and host name; otherwise it begins with a ‘/’. Note that the URLs must be valid full paths. ‘/foo’ will not match ‘/foo.html’.

Any GET query string attached to <old URL> will be attached to <new URL>. POST data will be discarded.

The optional [status] is a string or number that informs the client what causes the redirection.

[status]	
permanent (301)	The resource has moved permanently.
temp (302) (default)	The resource has moved temporarily.
seeother (303)	The resource has been replaced.
gone (410)	The resource has been removed permanently.
300-399	<new URL> must be specified.
other numeric status codes	<new URL> must be omitted.

For example, in the domain example.com:

Redirect permanent /foo /bar

would cause 'http://example.com/foo' to be redirected to 'http://example.com/bar'. 'http://example.com/foo/a.html' will not be redirected.

For 'permanent' and 'temp', there exist other notations for Redirect:

RedirectPermanent <old URL> <new URL>
RedirectTemp <old URL> <new URL>

14.1.3 'RedirectMatch'

This directive is the same as 'Redirect', except that now <old URL> is a regular expression that matches the absolute path excluding the protocol scheme and domain name. The absolute path begins with '/'. Any parenthesized matches will cause substitution to be performed on <new URL>.

For example:

RedirectMatch (.*)\.gif$ http://example.com$1.jpg

would cause all '.gif' files to be redirected to like-named '.jpg' files on another server.

14.1.4 'RewriteRule'

This is an even more generic mapping directive. It has the form:

RewriteRule <pattern> <substitution> [flags]

where <pattern> is a regular expression. Subsequent directives of RewriteRule match the output of the last match, unless the L flag is used. The order in which these directives are defined is the order in which they will be applied.

For <pattern>, unlike RedirectMatch, the per-directory prefix (the part of the URL before the directory with the .htaccess file) is not matched. In other words, <pattern> always refers to the relative URLs. The per-directory prefix includes the ending slash /. As such, ^/ never matches here.

<substitution> is an absolute URL (including the protocol scheme and domain name, or starting with a slash /), a relative URL (a path beginning at the .htaccess directory; without a leading slash /), or a dash –(no substitution).

In <substitution>, there can be substitution strings which can be back-references to the RewriteRule pattern ($N), back-references to the last matched RewriteCond pattern (%N), or server variables as in rule condition test-strings (%{VARNAME}) (14.1.5).

To enable the rewrite engine, one needs to set 'RewriteEngine On' and 'Options FollowSymLinks' must be enabled. Unlike 'Redirect' and 'RedirectMatch', 'RewriteRule' is a server-side operation. Using 'RewriteRule' without the R flag, you will not notice a change in the address shown by the browser.

Flags	
B	This escapes non-alphanumeric characters before applying the transformation. Eg.: RewriteRule ^search/(.*)$ /search.php?term$1 'search/x & y/z' will be mapped to 'search.php?term=x & y/z' without the flag, but to '/search.php?term=x%20%26%20y%2Fz' with the flag.
chain|C	If the rule does not match, then the next rule, and any other chained rules, are skipped.
cookie|CO=NAME:VAL:DOMAIN:lifetime:path:secure:httponly	This sets a cookie when a match is found. The last four fields are optional: 'lifetime' is specified in minutes. The default is 0, which means the cookie will persist only for the current session. 'path' is '/' by default, which refers to the entire website. 'secure' can be 'secure', 'true' or '1', which means that the cookie is allowed to be translated via https only. 'httponly' can be 'HttpOnly', 'true', or '1', which means that the cookie is inaccessible to JavaScript. Eg.: RewriteEngine On RewriteRule ^/index\.html - [CO=frontdoor:yes:.example.com:1440:/]
discardpath|DPI	This causes the PATH_INFO portion of the rewritten URI to be discarded. By default, before each rule is mapped, PATH_INFO is appended to the current URI.
env|E=[!]VAR[:VAL]	This sets an environment variable. [E=VAR] sets an empty value. [E=!VAR] unsets a set variable. Eg.: RewriteRule \.(png|gif|jpg)$ - [E=image:1] CustomLog logs/access_log combined env=!image
END	This prevents subsequent rewrite processing from occurring in per-directory context. This is stronger than [L], but does not apply to new, external redirects.

forbidden|F	This causes the server to return a 403 Forbiddden status code to the client. An [L] is implied as the response is returned immediately. For example, to forbid the downloading of all .exe files, use: RewriteRule \.exe – [F]
gone|G	This causes the server to return a 410 Gone status code to the client. An [L] is implied as the response is returned immediately.
Handler|H= Content-handler	This forces the resulting request to be handled with the specified handler. Eg., to force all files without an extension to be parsed by the php handler: RewriteRule !\. - [H=application/x-httpd-php] Eg. to allow .php files to be displayed by mod_php: RewriteRule ^(/source/.+\.php)s$ $1 [H=application/x-httpd-php-source]
last|L	This causes no further rules to be processed if the rule matches. It is important to use this flag to avoid unintended looping.
next|N[=integer]	This causes the ruleset to start over again from the top. An optional integer may be included to specify the maximum number of iterations.
nocase|NC	This causes the match to be performed in a case-insensitive manner. Eg.: to proxy any request for an image file to a dedicated image server: RewriteRule (.*\.(jpg|gif|png))$ http://images.example.com$1 [P,NC]
noescape|NE	This prevents special characters such as & and ? from being converted to their hexcode. Eg. to correctly map to an anchor: RewriteRule ^/anchor/(.+) /bigpage.html#$1 [NE,R]
nosubreq|NS	This prevents the rule from being used on subrequests. For example, you may want to use this flag as the server tries to find out information about possible directory default files such as index.html.
proxy|P	This causes the request to be handled by mod_proxy via a proxy request.
passthrough|PT	This causes the substitution string to be treated as a URI instead of a file path.
qsappend|QSA	This causes the substitution string to combine its query string with the original query string. Eg. for RewriteRule /pages/(.+) /page.php?page=$1 [QSA] '/pages/123?one=two' will be mapped to 'page=123&one=two'
qsdiscard|QSD	This discards the query string from the requested URI. By default, if the requested URI contains a query string and the target URI does not, the query string is copied to the target URI.
redirect|R[=code]	This issues a HTTP redirect to the browser. 'temp'(default), 'permanent' and 'seeother' may be used as the code. If the code is outside the range (300-399), then the substitution string is dropped entirely, and rewriting is stopped as if [L] were used.
skip|S[=integer]	This skips a number of rules following the rule.
type|T=MIMIT-type	This sets the MIME type with which the resulting response will be sent. Eg. to recognize files with 'IMG' in the name to be jpg images: RewriteRule IMG - [T=image/jpg]

When the 'R' flag is used, 'RewriteBase' should be used to specify the prefix-directory for any relative paths in <substitution>. Otherwise, a file-system path will be assumed.

For example, in www.example.com/myapp/,

```
RewriteEngine On
RewriteBase /myapp/
RewriteRule ^index\.html$  welcome.html [R]
```

will map 'www.example.com/myapp/index.html' to 'www.example.com/myapp/welcome.html'.

14.1.5 'RewriteCond'

RewriteCond defines a rule condition. One or more RewriteCond can precede a RewriteRule directive. The following rule is used only if these conditions are met. A RewriteCond only applies to the RewriteRule immediately following it.

This directive takes the form:

RewriteCond *TestString* [*op, CondPattern*] [*flags*]

TestString can contain RewriteRule($0-$9) or RewriteCond(%0-%9) backreferences, where $0 and %0 provides access to the whole string matched by the pattern. TestString can also contain server variables %{variable}.

server variables
API_VERSION 20020903:12
AUTH_TYPE Digest
CACHE_CONTROL max-age=0
CONNECTION keep-alive
CONTENT_TYPE (null)
DOCUMENT_ROOT /web/webroot/askapache.com
HOST www.askapache.com
HTTP
HTTP_ACCEPT text/html,application/xhtml+xml,application/xml;q=0.9,*/*;q=0.8
HTTP_COOKIE __qca=1176541205adf28-5553185; ASKAPACHEID=fdadfa4f33e62a878468; __utmc=1df3893
HTTP_HOST www.askapache.com

HTTP_REFERER
/pro/mod_rewrite/catch.php?k=i

HTTP_USER_AGENT
Mozilla/5.0 (Windows; U; Windows NT 5.1; en-US; rv:1.9) Firefox/3.0.1

IS_SUBREQ
false

KEEP_ALIVE
300

PATH
/bin:/usr/bin:/sbin:/usr/sbin

QUERY_STRING
k=i

REMOTE_ADDR
22.162.134.211

REMOTE_HOST
22.162.134.211

REMOTE_PORT
4220

REMOTE_USER
askapache

REQUEST_FILENAME
/web/webroot/askapache.com/pro/mod_rewrite/index.php

REQUEST_METHOD
GET

REQUEST_PROTOCOL
HTTP/1.1

REQUEST_URI
/pro/mod_rewrite/index.php

SCRIPT_FILENAME
/web/webroot/askapache.com/pro/mod_rewrite/index.php

SCRIPT_GROUP
daemong

SCRIPT_URI
/pro/mod_rewrite/index.php

SCRIPT_URL
/pro/mod_rewrite/index.php

SCRIPT_USER
askapache

SERVER_ADDR
208.113.134.190

SERVER_ADMIN
webmaster@askapache.com

SERVER_NAME
www.askapache.com

SERVER_PORT
80

SERVER_PROTOCOL
HTTP/1.1

SERVER_SOFTWARE
Apache/2.0.61 (Unix) PHP/5.5 OpenSSL/0.9.7e

THE_REQUEST
GET /pro/mod_rewrite/index.php?k=i HTTP/1.1

TIME
20080915152142

TIME_DAY
15

TIME_HOUR
15

TIME_MIN
21

TIME_MON
09

TIME_SEC
42

TIME_WDAY
1

TIME_YEAR
2008

UNIQUE_ID
qOr5tEBvcm8AAE-VoiUAAAAQ

HTTPS
off

SSL_CIPHER
DHE-RSA-AES256-SHA

SSL_CIPHER_ALGKEYSIZE
256

SSL_CIPHER_EXPORT
false

SSL_CIPHER_USEKEYSIZE
256

SSL_CLIENT_VERIFY
NONE

SSL_PROTOCOL
TLSv1

SSL_SERVER_A_KEY
rsaEncryption

SSL_SERVER_A_SIG
sha1WithRSAEncryption

SSL_SERVER_CERT
-----BEGIN CERTIFICATE----- ... MIIFkTC ... -----END CERTIFICATE-----

SSL_SERVER_I_DN
/C=US/ST=Arizona/L=Scottsdale/O=Starfield Technologies, Inc./OU=http://certificates.starfieldtech.com/repository/CN=Starfield Secure Certification Authority/serialNumber=10688435

SSL_SERVER_I_DN_C
US

SSL_SERVER_I_DN_CN
Starfield Secure Certification Authority

SSL_SERVER_I_DN_L
Scottsdale

SSL_SERVER_I_DN_O
Starfield Technologies, Inc.

SSL_SERVER_I_DN_OU
http://certificates.starfieldtech.com/repository

SSL_SERVER_I_DN_ST
Arizona

SSL_SERVER_M_SERIAL
042840B88A2352

SSL_SERVER_M_VERSION
3

SSL_SERVER_S_DN
/O=www.askapache.com/OU=Domain Control Validated/CN=www.askapache.com

SSL_SERVER_S_DN_CN
www.askapache.com

SSL_SERVER_S_DN_O
www.askapache.com

SSL_SERVER_S_DN_OU
Domain Control Validated

SSL_SERVER_V_END
Jul 14 16:53:43 2012 GMT

SSL_SERVER_V_START
Jul 14 20:25:17 2010 GMT

SSL_SESSION_ID
4184083DD1C74547553018174950D88987BD7ED03CE54EBB6638539C34814376

SSL_VERSION_INTERFACE
mod_ssl/2.2.16

SSL_VERSION_LIBRARY
OpenSSL/0.9.8e-fips-rhel5

SCRIPT_FILENAME and REQUEST_FILENAME contain the same value. The values will be updated if a substitution occurred and the rewriting continues.

%{ENV:variable} can be used to access environment variables.

%{SSL:variable} can be used to access SSL environment variables. Eg.: %{SSL:SSK_CIPHER_USERKEYSIZE} may expand to 128.

%{HTTP:header} can be used to obtain the value of a header sent in the HTTP request. %{HTTP:Proxy-Connection} is the value of the HTTP header 'Proxy-Connection:'

%{LA-U:variable} can be used for look-aheads which perform an internal sub-request to determine the future value of 'variable'. This can be used to access the variable for rewriting which is not available currently, but will be set later.

%{LA-F:variable} can be used to perform an internal sub-request to determine the final value of 'variable'. Most of the time, this is the same as LA-U above.

operator	
!	negation; non-matching pattern.
<	lexicographically precedes
>	lexicographically follows
=	lexicographically equal
<=	lexicographically less than or equal to
>=	lexicographically greater than or equal to
-eq	numerically equal to
-ge	numerically greater than or equal to
-gt	numerically greater than
-le	numerically less than or equal to
-lt	numerically less than
-d	is a directory
-f	is a regular file
-F	is an existing file; via subrequest
-H	is a symbolic link; bash convention
-l	is a symbolic link
-L	is a symbolic link; bash convention
-s	is a regular file, with a size greater than zero
-U	is an existing URL; via subrequest
-x	has executable permissions

flags	
nocase|NC	Case-insensitive test.
ornext|OR	Combine with the next RewriteCond using a logical OR.
novary|NV	If a HTTP header is used in the condition, this flag prevents the header from being added to the Vary header of the response.

14.1.6 Status Codes

100	Continue
101	Switching Protocols
102	Processing
200	OK
201	Created
202	Accepted
203	Non-Authoritative Information
204	No Content
205	Reset Content
206	Partial Content
207	Multi-Status
300	Multiple Choices
301	Moved Permanently
302	Found
303	See Other
304	Not Modified
305	Use Proxy
306	<unused>
307	Temporary Redirect
400	Bad Request
401	Authorization Required
402	Payment Required
403	Forbidden
404	Not Found
405	Method Not Allowed
406	Not Acceptable
407	Proxy Authorization Required
408	Request Time-out
409	Conflict
410	Gone
411	Length Required
412	Precondition Failed
413	Request Entity Too Large
414	Request-URI Too Large
415	Unsupported Media Type
416	Requested Range Not Satisfiable
417	Expectation Failed
418	I'm a teapot
419	<unused>
420	<unused>
421	<unused>
422	Unprocessable Entity
423	Locked
424	Failed Dependency
425	No Code
426	Upgrade Required
500	Internal Server Error
501	Method Not Implemented
502	Bad Gateway
503	Service Temporarily Unavailable
504	Gateway Time-out
505	HTTP Version Not Supported
506	Variant Also Negotiates
507	Insufficient Storage
508	<unused>
509	<unused>
510	Not Extended

14.2 URL Mapping – Applications

14.2.1 Rewriting to www

Sometimes an URL is used without the 'www.' prefix. This example forces 'www.' to be appended to the front. The second directive tells Apache not to redirect specific 'system files'.

```
RewriteEngine on
RewriteCond %{REQUEST_URI}
            !^/(robots\.txt|favicon\.ico|sitemap\.xml)$
RewriteCond %{HTTP_HOST}
            !^www\.example\.com$ [NC]
RewriteRule .* http://www.example.com/$0 [L,R=301]
```

14.2.2 Forcing https Connections

For those websites with an SSL cerficate, this piece of code comes in handy. It forces all connections to be made via secure https connections.

```
RewriteEngine on
RewriteCond %{HTTPS} off
RewriteRule .* https://%{HTTP_HOST}%{REQUEST_URI}
```

14.2.3 Changing File Types

Manually changing all the file types in your website can be daunting. .htaccess can help.

```
RewriteEngine on
RedirectMatch 301 (.*)\.html$ $1.php
RedirectMatch 301 (.*)\.(gif|png)$ $1.jpg
```

14.2.4 Redirecting Entire Directory

This allows you to move all your resources to a subfolder.

```
RewriteEngine on
RewriteBase /
RewriteRule .* subfolder/$0 [L,R=301]
```

14.2.5 Maintenance Redirection

This redirects everyone except you (with IP address 111.111.11.11) to /testing/maintenance.html.

```
RewriteEngine on
RewriteBase /testing/
RewriteCond %{REMOTE_HOST} !^111\.111\.11\.11
RewriteCond %{REQUEST_URI} !^/testing/maintenance\.html$
RewriteRule .* maintenance.html [L,R=301]
```

14.2.6. Rewriting a Dynamic URL

As opposed to a dynamic URL with a query string, a static URL is more SEO friendly. Here a RewriteCond back reference is used to change the query string to a specific page.

```
RewriteEngine on
RewriteCond %{QUERY_STRING} page=([^/]+)
RewriteRule  ^old\.php$  %1.php  [L]
```

14.2.7 Modifying a Value in the Query String

```
RewriteCond  %{QUERY_STRING}  ^(.*)val(.*)$
RewriteRule  /path  /path?%1other_val%2
```

14.2.8 Preventing Hotlinking

Hotlinking is the practice of using a resource at another website by linking to it directly, instead of saving a copy of it in your website. Extensive hotlinking to the resources at your website can consume your bandwidth significantly.

To stop hotlinking, the following piece of code displays a warning whenever graphical hotlinking is detected.

```
RewriteEngine on
RewriteCond %{HTTP_REFERRER} !^$
RewriteCond %{HTTP_REFERRER}
            !^http://(www\.)?yourdomain\.com/.*$ [NC]
RewriteRule \.(gif|jpg|swf|flv|png)$
            http://yourdomain.com/warning.gif [R=302,L]
```

14.2.9 Redirecting Non-Existent URLs

```
RewriteEngine On
RewriteCond %{DOCUMENT_ROOT}%{REQUEST_URI} !-d
RewriteCond %{DOCUMENT_ROOT}%{REQUEST_URI} !-f
RewriteRule .* /page-no-found.php
```

14.2.10 Preventing Trackback Spam

Trackback is a method for webmasters to receive a notification when someone links to a document in the website.

This denies obvious trackback spam.

```
RewriteCond %{REQUEST_METHOD} =POST
RewriteCond %{HTTP_USER_AGENT}
            ^.*(opera|mozilla|firefox|msie|safari).*$ [NC]
RewriteCond %{THE_REQUEST}
            ^[A-Z]{3,9}\ /.+/trackback/?\ HTTP/ [NC]
RewriteRule .* - [F,NS,L]
```

14.2.11 Preventing Hacks

Sometimes a website can be hacked by sending malicious query strings.

This blocks malicious query strings.

```
RewriteEngine On
RewriteCond %{QUERY_STRING}
            proc/self/environ [OR]
RewriteCond %{QUERY_STRING}
            mosConfig_[a-zA-Z_]{1,21}(=|\%3D) [OR]
RewriteCond %{QUERY_STRING}
            base64_encode.*(.*) [OR]
RewriteCond %{QUERY_STRING}
            (<|%3C).*script.*(>|%3E) [NC,OR]
RewriteCond %{QUERY_STRING}
            GLOBALS(=|[|\%[0-9A-Z]{0,2}) [OR]
RewriteCond %{QUERY_STRING}
            _REQUEST(=|[|\%[0-9A-Z]{0,2})
RewriteRule ^(.*)$ index.php [F,L]
```

14.2.12 Denying Suspicious Access

This denies access to requests without specific header fields or with an invalid content type.

```
RewriteEngine on
RewriteCond %{HTTP:Content-Length} ^$ [OR]
RewriteCond %{HTTP_HOST} ^$ [OR]
RewriteCond %{HTTP_USER_AGENT} ^-?$ [OR]
RewriteCond %{HTTP_REFERRER} ^-?$ [OR]
RewriteCond %{HTTP:Content-Type}
            !^(application/x-www-form-urlencoded|
               multipart/form-data.*(boundary.*)?)$ [NC]
RewriteRule .* – [F,NS,L]
```

14.2.13 Forbidding POSTing via Proxies

This denies any POST request through a Proxy Server. The site can still be accessed.

```
RewriteCond %{REQUEST_METHOD} =POST
RewriteCond %{HTTP:VIA}
            %{HTTP:FORWARDED}
            %{HTTP:USERAGENT_VIA}
            %{HTTP:X_FORWARDED_FOR}
            %{HTTP:PROXY_CONNECTION}
            !^$ [OR]
RewriteCond %{HTTP:XPROXY_CONNECTION}
            %{HTTP:HTTP_PC_REMOTE_ADDR}
            %{HTTP:HTTP_CLIENT_IP}
            !^$
RewriteCond %{REQUEST_URI}
 !^/(wp-login.php|wp-admin/|wp-content/plugins/|wp-
includes/).* [NC]
RewriteRule .* - [F,NS,L]
```

14.2.14 Denying Request Methods

```
RewriteCond %{REQUEST_METHOD}
            !^(GET|HEAD|OPTIONS|POST|PUT)
RewriteRule .* - [F]
```

14.2.15 Cookies

This sends a cookie called 'lang' to the client.

```
RewriteEngine On
RewriteBase /
RewriteRule ^(.*)(de|es|fr|it|ja|ru|en)/$ -
            [co=lang:$2:.askapache.com:7200:/]
```

This obtains the value of the cookie 'lang'.

```
RewriteEngine On
RewriteBase /
RewriteCond %{HTTP_COOKIE} lang=([^;]+) [NC]
RewriteRule ^(.*)$ /$1?cookie-value=%1 [R,QSA,L]
```

This redirects the page if a cookie is not set.

```
RewriteEngine On
RewriteBase /
RewriteCond %{HTTP_COOKIE} !^.*cookie-name.*$ [NC]
RewriteRule .* /error.php [NC,L]
```

This sets the environment variable 'lang' to the Accept-Language header.

```
RewriteEngine On
RewriteBase /
RewriteCond %{HTTP:Accept-Language}
            ^.*(de|es|fr|it|ja|ru|en).*$ [NC]
RewriteRule ^(.*)$ - [env=lang:%1]
```

This sends the cookie 'language', assuming %{lang} is an existing environment variable.

```
Header set Set-Cookie "language=%{lang}e; path=/;"
env=lang
```

14.3 Error Handling

14.3.1 'ErrorDocument'

You may set your custom error pages by using:

ErrrorDocument <error-code> <handler>

where <handler> can be a file, a message string, or 'default'. If <handler> points to a remote URL, Apache will initiate a redirection, causing the client to miss the original status code. As such, 'ErrorDocument 401' must point to a local document.

```
ErrorDocument 500 http://foo.example.com/cgi-bin/tester
ErrorDocument 404 /cgi-bin/bad_urls.pl
ErrorDocument 401 subscription_info.html
ErrorDocument 403 "Sorry can't allow you access today"
ErrorDocument 403 Forbidden!
```

Microsoft Internet Explorer will by default ignore server-generated error messages when they are "too small" and substitute its own "friendly" error messages.

14.3.2 Administrator Email

You may set the administrator Email for ErrorDocument.

```
SetEnv SERVER_ADMIN
webmaster@example.com
```

14.3.3 ServerSignature

The ServerSignature allows a trailing footer to be generated under server-generated documents such as error messages. The default is off:

ServerSignature <On|Off|Email>

'ServerSignature Email' displays a "mailto:" reference.

14.3.4 Check Spelling

With CheckSpelling on, a visitor that has entered a wrong, non-existent URL will be suggested or redirected to an existing, similar URL.

For example a user types in this to their browser:

http://www.mysite.com/caje/red.html

What was meant was

http://www.mysite.com/cake/red.html

CheckSpelling would pick up this slight mistake and fix it (unless of course there really *was* a page called caje/red.html). The great thing is that it also works for the CaSe sensitive Linux URLs i.e.

http://www.mysite.com/cake/RED.html

is actually a different page to

http://www.mysite.com/cake/red.html

With CheckSpelling enabled it will redirect.

```
CheckSpelling on
```

14.3.5 Error Logging

This suppresses the display of error messages but enables error logging.

```
php_flag display_startup_errors off
php_flag display_errors off
php_flag html_errors off
php_flag log_errors on
php_value error_log /public/errors.log
```

14.4 Blocking

To block certain IP addresses, use the following

Order <Allow,Deny | Deny,Allow>
Allow from <all | address...>
Deny from <all | address ...>

For example, if 'Order Allow,Deny' is used, then all 'Allow' directives are evaluated first, followed by all 'Deny' directives. The default is 'Order Deny,Allow'. Unlike a typical firewall where only the first match is used, the last match is effective. A directive that is evaluated later will override one that is evaluated earlier.

'address' can be:
a) A (partial) domain-name, eg.
  Allow from example.net
  Allow from .com example.org
b) A full IP address:
  Allow from 10.1.2.3
  Allow from 192.168.1.104 192.168.1.205
c) A partial IP address:
  Allow from 10.1
  Allow from 10 172.20 192.168.2
d) A network/netmask pair:
  Allow from 10.1.0.0/255.255.0.0
e) A network/nnn CIDR specification
  Allow from 10.1.0.0/16
 Now the netmask consists of 16 high-order 1 bits.
f) IPv6 address and IPv6 subnets
  Allow from 2001:db8::a00:20ff:fea7:ccea
  Allow from 2001:db8::a00:20ff:fea7:ccea/10
g) An environment variable:
  Allow from env=var
  Allow from env=!var2
The first example allows access if 'var' exists. The second example allows access if 'var2' doesn't exist.

14.4.1 Blocking Specific IPs

```
order allow,deny
deny from 127.0.0.1
deny from 127.0.0.2
deny from 127.0.0.3
allow from all
```

14.4.2 Redirecting Everyone except Specific IPs

```
ErrorDocument 403 http://www.mysite.com
Order deny,allow
Deny from all
Allow from 111.111.111.111
```

14.4.3 Blocking Access to Specific Files

<Files filename>...</Files> are used to enclose directives that apply to the specified file(s) only. Wildcards may be used, where ? matches any single character and * matches any sequence of characters.

```
<Files php.ini>
  order allow,deny
  deny from all
</Files>
<Files .htpasswd>
  order allow,deny
  deny from all
</Files>
```

<FilesMatch regex>...</FilesMatch> are similar to <Files filename>...</Files> but match regular expressions instead.

14.4.4 Disallowing Script Execution

The first line disallows the execution of CGI scripts. The second line treats those files as CGI scripts and let the handler 'cgi-script' handles them. In effect, this stops all those scripts from running.

```
Options -ExecCGI
AddHandler cgi-script
           .php .pl .py .jsp .asp .htm .shtml .sh .cgi
```

14.4.5 Preventing Directory Listing

This prevents all files from being listed.

```
IndexIgnore *
```

This prevents directory index listings and defaulting.

```
Options -Indexes
DirectoryIndex index.html index.php /index.php
```

14.4.6 Blocking Specific User Agents

SetEnvIf <attribute> <regex> [!]env-var[=value]...
Sets an environment variable if <attribute> matches <regex>.

<attribute> can be:
1) An HTTP request header field such as Host and User-Agent, Referrer, and Accept-Language.
2) Remote_Host, Remote_Addr, Server_Addr, Request_Method, Request_Protocol and Request_URI.
3) The name of an environment variable in the list of those associated with the request.

```
SetEnvIfNoCase ^User-Agent$
                 .*(craftbot|download|extract|
                    stripper|sucker|ninja|clshttp|
                    webspider|leacher|collector|
                    grabber|webpictures)
                 HTTP_SAFE_BADBOT
SetEnvIfNoCase ^User-Agent$
                 .*(libwww-perl|aesop_com_spiderman)
                 HTTP_SAFE_BADBOT
Deny from env=HTTP_SAFE_BADBOT
```

14.5 Password Protection

You can prompt a visitor for a username and a password. The file containing the usernames and encrypted passwords are named .htpasswd. To encrypt a password, visit the site http://www.htpasswdgenerator.net/. Additional restrictions should be imposed on this file to prevent it from being downloaded. Its content has the following format:

```
username1:encrypted_password1
username2:encrypted_password2
username3:encrypted_password3
```

AuthName <promptString>

This displays <promptString> in the dialog box asking for the username and password.

AuthType <None|Basic|Digest|Form>

This selects the type of user authentication.

AuthUserFile <.htpasswd path>

This specifies the path containing .htpasswd, which is a file containing the usernames and passwords. Absolute or relative, this should be the file-system path instead of the URL path. You can obtain the file-system path in PHP using dirname(__FILE__).

Require [not] entity-name...

This tests whether an authenticated user is authorized:

Require all granted	Access is allowed unconditionally.
Require all denied	Access is denied unconditionally.
Require env <env-var>...	Access is allowed only if one of the environment variables is set.
Require method <http-method>...	Access is allowed only for the HTTP methods.
Require expr <expression>	Access is allowed if <expression> evaluates to true.
Require user <userid>	Access is allowed only for the named users.
Require group <group-name>	Access is allowed only for the named groups.
Require valid-user	All valid users can access the resource.
Require ip <ip1> <ip2>	Access is only allowed for clients in the IP address range.

14.5.1 Protecting the Entire Directory

```
AuthName "Top Secret"
AuthUserFile /home/mysite/.htpasswd
AuthType basic
Require valid-user
```

14.5.2 Protecting Specific Files

This password-protects all files with names starting with 'admin-'.

```
<FilesMatch "^admin-">
  AuthName "Top Secret"
  AuthUserFile /home/mysite/.htpasswd
  AuthType basic
  Require valid-user
</Files>
```

14.5.3 Allowing Special IP Addresses

'Satisfy Any' tells Apache to allow access if either a valid username and a valid password are entered, or if the client passes the host restriction.

```
AuthUserFile /home/mysite/.htpasswd
AuthName "Top Secret"
AuthType Basic
Require valid-user

Order deny,allow
Deny from all
Allow from 1.2.3.4
Allow from 4.5.6.7
Allow from localhost
Satisfy Any
```

14.5.4 Allowing AJAX Calls

You can allow an AJAX call to bypass a protected page by specifying the URL in the following form:

http://username:password@myserver.com/mypage.php

In jQuery, it will be:

```
$.ajax({
  username: username,
  password: password,
  // ... other params.
});
```

There are obvious security shortcomings with these techniques. To hide the username and password from the visitors, use cURL instead.

14.6 Speed Tweaking

14.6.1 GZIP Compression

This compresses four types of files before they are fetched to the client. 'SetOutputFilter' applies a filter to the output file.

```
<Files *.html> SetOutputFilter DEFLATE
</Files>
<Files *.css> SetOutputFilter DEFLATE
</Files>
<Files *.js> SetOutputFilter DEFLATE
</Files>
<Files *.php> SetOutputFilter DEFLATE
</Files>
```

14.6.2 Caching

This caches the image files for one month in the clients' computers, preventing them from being downloaded every time a visitor returns to the site.

```
<FilesMatch "\.(gif|jpg|jpeg|png|ico|swf|flv)$">
  Header set Cache-Control "max-age=2592000"
</FilesMatch>
```

14.7 Miscellaneous

14.7.1 Setting the Timezone

This sets the server timezone. A list of the timezones can be found in 4.4.3.

```
SetEnv TZ Asia/Kuala_Lumpur
```

14.7.2 Setting the Charset and Language

```
AddDefaultCharset UTF-8
DefaultLanguage en-US
```

14.7.3 Custom Headers

```
Header set P3P
        "policyref="http://www.askapache.com/w3c/p3p.xml"
Header set X-Pingback
"http://www.askapache.com/xmlrpc.php"
Header set Content-Language "en-US"
Header set Vary "Accept-Encoding"
```

14.7.4 Forcing 'Save As' Prompt

This causes files with those extensions to be treated as the media type 'application/octet-stream'.

```
AddType application/octet-
stream .avi .mpg .mov .pdf .xls .mp4
```

14.7.5 IP Logging

This turns off logging.

```
SecFilterSelective REMOTE_ADDR
                    "208\.113\.183\.103"
                    "nolog,noauditlog,pass"
```

This turns on logging.

```
SecFilterSelective REMOTE_ADDR "!^208\.113\.183\.103"
                               "nolog,noauditlog,pass"
SecFilterSelective REMOTE_ADDR "208\.113\.183\.103"
                               "log,auditlog,pass"
```

14.7.6 PHP Settings

To verify that the settings take effect, run the PHP code phpinfo().

```
php_value max_execution_time 50
php_value upload_max_filesize 20M
php_value post_max_size 21M
php_value memory_limit 200M
```

15. jQuery

jQuery is a Javascript library that simplifies many coding tasks. Among many things, jQuery allows multiple elements to be selected for manipulation at once, and some animation effects to take place. Many extensions to Javascript require the use of jQuery.

To use it, first download the file from:
http://jquery.com/download/
Then include the library script as in the following:

```
<!DOCTYPE html>
<html>
<head>
<script src="jquery-2.1.1.min.js"></script>
                                <!-- compressed version -->
<script>
  $(document).ready(function(){
     $("button").click(function(){
         $("p").fadeOut(5000);});});
</script>
</head>
<body>
  <p>Paragraph 1</p>
  <p>Paragraph 2</p>
  <p>Paragraph 3</p>
  <button>remove all paragraphs</button>
</body>
</html>
```

Paragraph 1

Paragraph 2

Paragraph 3

remove all paragraphs

Alternatively, we can use hosted jQuery from Google:

```
......
<head>
<script src=
"//ajax.googleapis.com/ajax/libs/jquery/2.1.1/jquery.min.js"
>< /script>
......
```

or Micosoft:

```
......
<head>
<script src=
"http://ajax.aspnetcdn.com/ajax/jQuery/jquery-2.1.1.min.js"
>< /script>
......
```

Most jQuery functions return the *jQuery object,* thus allowing the functions to be chained.

15.1 Elements Selection

The jQuery object returned from a jQuery function can be treated like an array of Element(s). The selection functions described in this subsection are meant to be appended by other jQuery functions.

15.1.1 Additional Selectors

jQuery shares most of the selectors used in CSS (2.2). Here are some additional jQuery-specific selectors:

$("p:first") the first <p> element
$("p:last") the last <p> element
$("tr:even") all even <tr> elements
$("tr:odd") all odd <tr> elements
$("ul li:eq(2)") the third <li> element in <ul>
$("ul li:gt(2)") all <li> elements after the third
$("ul li:lt(2)") all <li> elements before the third

$("[href!='image1.gif']") all elements with the attribute href not equal to 'image1.gif'
$(" [name!='value']) all elements that don't have the name attribute, or that have the name attribute with a different value.
$(" [name=value][name2!='value2']...) all elements that match all the attribute filters.

$(":header") all <h1>-<h6> elements
$(":input") all <input>, <textarea>, <select> and <button> elements.
$(":button") all<button>&'button'<input>elements.
$(":checkbox") all 'checkbox' <input> elements.
$(":file") all 'file' <input> elements.
$(":image") all 'image' <input> elements.
$(":radio") all 'radio' <input> elements.
$(":reset") all 'reset' <input> elements.
$(":password") all 'password' <input> elements.
$(":submit") all 'submit' <input> elements.
$(":text") all 'text' <input> elements.

$(":root") the document root.
$(":parent") all elements with at least one child.
$(":animated") all animated elements
$(":empty") all elements with no child nodes
$("p:hidden") all hidden <p> elements
$("table:visible") all visible <table>
$("input:not(:empty)")all non-empty <input>
$(":enabled") all enabled input elements
$(":disabled") all disabled input elements
$(":selected") all selected input elements
$(":checked") all checked input elements
$(":focus") the selected element
$(":has(.c)") all elements containing element(s) with a 'c' class.
$(":contains('textbook')") all elements with the text 'textbook' between the opening and closing tags

15.1.2 Expansion

.add(String/Element/jQuery selector)
.add(String selector, Element context)
Create a new jQuery object with elements added.

.addBack([String selector])
Add the previous set of elements on the stack to the current set.

.children([String selector])
The children of each matched element.

.closest(String [, Element context])
.closest(Element/jQuery selector)
The first element of each matched elements that matches the selector up the DOM tree.

.contents()
The children of each matched element, including text and comment nodes.

.find(String/Element/jQuery selector)
The descendants of each matched element.

.next([String selector])
The immediately following sibling of each matched element.

.nextAll([String selector])
All following siblings of each matched element.

.nextUntil([String/Element/jQuery selector [, String filterSelector]])
All following siblings of each matched element up till the specified element.

.offsetParent()
The closest ancestor element that is positioned.

.parent([String selector])
The parent of each matched element.

.parents([String selector])
The ancestors of each matched element.

.parentsUntil([String/Element/jQuery selector [, String filterSelector]])
The ancestors of each matched element up till the specified element.

.prev([String selector])
The immediately preceding sibling of each matched element.

.prevAll([String selector])
All preceding siblings of each matched element.

.prevUntil([String/Element/jQuery selector [, String filterSelector]])
All preceding siblings of each matched element up till the specified element.

.pushStack(String/Elements[] e)
Add a collection of DOM elements onto the jQuery stack.

.siblings([String selector])
All siblings of each matched element.

15.1.3 Reduction

.eq(int index)
Reduce the matched elements to the one at the index.

.filter(String/Element/jQuery selector)
.filter(function (int index, Element e) f)
Reduce the matched elements to those that further match.

.first()
Reduce the matched elements to the first.

.has(String/Element selector)
Reduce the matched elements to those that have a matching descendant.

.last()
Reduce the set of matched elements to the final one.

.not(String/Element/Array/jQuery selector)
.not(function (int index, Element e) f)
Remove elements from the set of matched elements.

.slice(int start [, int end])
Reduce the matched elements to a subset.

```
<!DOCTYPE html><html>
<head>
  <script src="jquery-2.1.1.min.js"></script>
</head>
<body>
  <div>
    <span>1</span>
    <span>2</span>
  </div>
  <p>A</p>
  <p>B</p>
  <p>C</p>
  <script>
 alert($('p').length); // 3
 alert($('p:last').index()); // 3
 alert($('p').index(
            document.getElementsByTagName('p')[0])); // 0
 alert($('p').add('span').length); // 5
 alert($('span:first').next().length); // 1
 alert($('span:first').next().addBack().length); // 2
 alert($('span:first, p:first').nextAll().length); // 4
 alert($('body').children('p')[1].innerHTML); // B
 alert($('p,span').not('p')[1].innerHTML); // 2
 alert($('body').find('p,span').slice(1,3)[1].innerHTML); // A
 alert($('p').next().next().first()[0].innerHTML); // C
 alert($('*').has('span').filter('div')[0].innerHTML);
                                               // contents of <div>
 alert($('span').pushStack(
         document.getElementsByTagName('p')).length); // 3
  </script>
</body>
</html>
```

15.2 DOM Manipulation

15.2.1 Insertion

.after(String/Element/Array/jQuery c [,String/Element/Array/jQuery c])
.after(function(int index) f)
Insert content after each matched element.

.append(String/Element/Array/jQuery c [,String/Element/Array/jQuery c])
.append(function(int index) f)
Insert content to the end of each matched element.

.appendTo(String/Element/Array/jQuery/Selector c)
Insert each matched element to the end of the target.

.before(String/Element/Array/jQuery c [,String/Element/Array/jQuery c])
.before(function(int index) f)
Insert content before each matched element.

.insertAfter(String/Element/Array/jQuery/Selector t)
Insert every matched element after the target.

.clone([Boolean withDataAndEvents

[, Boolean deepWithDataAndEvents]])
Create a deep copy of the matched elements.

.insertBefore(String/Element/Array/jQuery/Selector t)
Insert every matched element abefore the target.

.prepend(String/Element/Array/jQuery c
[,String/Element/Array/jQuery c])
.prepend(function(int index) f)
Insert content to the end of each matched element.

.prependTo(String/Element/Array/jQuery/Selector c)
Insert each matched element to the beginning of the target.

.wrap(String tagsPair)
.wrap(function(int index) f)
Wrap an HTML structure around each matched element.

.wrapAll(String tagsPair)
.wrapAll(function(int index) f)
Wrap an HTML structure around all matched elements together.

.wrapInner(String tagsPair)
.wrapInner (function(int index) f)
Wrap an HTML structure around the content of each matched element.

Consider the following example:

```
<p>A</p>
<p>B</p>
<p>C</p>
```

```
$('p').after('!');
```
GIVES
```
<p>A</p>!
<p>B</p>!
<p>C</p>!
```

```
$('p').append('!');
```
GIVES
```
<p>A!</p>
<p>B!</p>
<p>C!</p>
```

```
$('p:first').appendTo('p:last');
```
GIVES
```
<p>B</p>
<p>C<p>A</p></p>
```

```
$('p:first').clone().appendTo('p:last');
```
GIVES
```
<p>A</p>
<p>B</p>
<p>C<p>A</p></p>
```

```
$('p:first').insertAfter('p:last');
```
GIVES
```
<p>B</p>
<p>C</p><p>A</p>
```

```
$('p').prepend(function (i) {return i;});
```
GIVES
```
<p>0A</p>
<p>1B</p>
<p>2C</p>
```

```
$('p:first').prependTo($('p:last'));
```
GIVES
```
<p>B</p>
<p><p>A</p>C</p>
```

```
$('p').wrap('<span id="s">!</span>');
```
GIVES
```
<span id="s">!<p>A</p></span>
<span id="s">!<p>B</p></span>
<span id="s">!<p>C</p></span>
```

```
$('p').wrapAll('<span id="s">!</span>');
```
GIVES
```
<span id="s">!<p>A</p>
              <p>B</p>
              <p>C</p></span>
```

```
$('p').wrapInner('<span id="s">!</span>');
```
GIVES
```
<p><span id="s">!A</span></p>
<p><span id="s">!B</span></p>
<p><span id="s">!C</span></p>
```

15.2.2 Deletion

.detach([String selector])
Remove the matched elements from the DOM and returns the jQuery object associated with the removed elements.

.empty()
Remove all child nodes of the matched elements from the DOM. The matched elements themselves are not removed.

.remove([String selector])
Remove the matched elements from the DOM.

.replaceAll(String/Element/Array/jQuery selector)
Replace each target element with the set of matched elements.

.replaceWith(String/Element/Array/jQuery newCont)
.replaceWith(function f)
Replace each matched element with the provided new content and return the set of elements that was removed.

.unwrap()
Remove the parent of each matched element from the DOM.

Consider the following example:

```
<p>A</p>
<p>B</p>
<p>C</p>
```

```
var p = $('p:first').detach();
$('p').after(p);
```
GIVES
```
<p>B</p><p>A</p>
<p>C</p><p>A</p>
```

```
$('p').empty();
```
GIVES
```
<p></p>
<p></p>
<p></p>
```

```
$('p:first').remove();
```
GIVES
```
<p>B</p>
<p>C</p>
```

```
$('p:first').replaceAll('p');
```
GIVES
```
<p>A</p>
<p>A</p>
<p>A</p>
```

```
$('p:first').replaceWith('p');
```
GIVES
```
p
<p>B</p>
<p>C</p>
```

```
$('p').contents().unwrap();
```
GIVES
```
A
B
C
```

15.2.3 Values

.data(String key, Any value)
.data(Object o)
Associate data with the matched elements.

.each(function(int index, Element e) f)
Execute a function for each matched element.

.is(String/Element/jQuery selector)
.is(function(int index, Element e) f)
Return true if at least one of the matched elements matches the arguments.

.end()
End the most recent filtering operation in the current chain and return the set of matched elements to its previous state.

.get()

.toArray()
Return an array of matched elements.

.get(int index) → [index]
Retrieves one element.

.index([String/Element/jQuery selector])
Return an integer indicating the position of the first matching element.

.length
Return the number of matched elements.

.map(function(int index, Element e) f)
Pass each matched element through a function, producing a new jQuery object containing the return values.

.removeData(String/Array name)
Remove a previously-stored piece of data.

.text()
.text(String/Number/Boolean data)
.text(function(int index, String text))
Get/set the combined text contents of each matched element.

Consider the following example:

```
<p id="1">A</p>
<p id="2">B</p>
<p id="3">C</p>
```

```
$('p').data('v1',100);
$('p').data({v2:200});
alert($('p:last').data('v1')+$('p:first').data('v2'));
$('p').removeData('v1 v2');
```

GIVES

alerts 300

```
$('p').each(function(i){
    alert($(this)[0].innerHTML + i);
});
```

GIVES

alerts A0 ... alerts B1 ... alerts C2

```
alert($('p').is('p:first'));
```

GIVES

alerts true

```
$('body').find('p:first').css('color','red').end()
         .find('p:last').css('color','green');
```

```
alert($( "p" ).map(function() {
  return this.id;
}).get().join());
```

GIVES

1,2,3

```
alert($('body').text());
```

GIVES

A
B
C
alert($('body').text());

```
alert($('p').toArray()[0].innerHTML);
```

GIVES

A

15.3 Attributes and Properties

15.3.1 General

.attr(String att)
Get the value of an attribute for the first matched element.

.attr(String att, String/Number value)
.attr(Object att)
.attr(String att, function(int index, String att) f)
Set the attributes for the matched elements.

.prop(String prop)
Get the value of a property for the first matched element.

.prop(String prop, Any value)
.prop(Object prop)
.prop(String prop, function(int index, Any oldValue) f)
Set the properties for the matched elements.

.removeAttr(String att)
Remove an attribute from each matched element.

.removeProp(String prop)
Remove a property from each matched element.

.removeClass([String classes])
.removeClass(function (int index, String oldClassVal) f)
Remove classes from each matched element.

.addClass(String classes)
.addClass(function (int index, String currentClass) f)
Add classes to each matched element.

.hasClass(String class)
Return true if any matched element is assigned the class.

.toggleClass([String class][, Boolean switch])
.toggleClass(
  function(int index, String class, Boolean switch) f,
  Boolean switch)
Add or remove classes from each matched element.

.val()
Get the current '.value' of the first matched element.

.val(String/Array value)
.val(function (int index, String value) f)
Set the value of each matched element.

.html()
Get the HTML contents of the first matched element.

.html(String html)
.html(function (int index, String oldHtml) f)
Set the HTML contents of each matched element. This corresponds to the DOM '.innerHTML'.

.css(String/Array prop)
Get the CSS property for the first matched element.

.css(String prop, String/Number value)
.css(String prop, function(int index, String value) f)
.css(Object prop)
Set the CSS properties for each matched element.

$.cssHooks
Hook into jQuery to override how some CSS porperties are retrieved or set, normalize CSS property naming, or create custom properties.

```
<!DOCTYPE html><html>
<head>
  <script src="jquery-2.1.1.min.js"></script>
</head>
<body>
  <input type="text" class="c1"/><br/>
  <input type="text" class="c1"/><br/>
  <input type="text" class="c1"/>
  <script>
  I = $('input');
  alert(I.prop('tagName')); // INPUT
  I.prop('id',function(i){return 'inp'+i;});
  alert(I.prop('id')); // inp0
  I.addClass('c3 c4').toggleClass('c1 c2');
  alert(I.hasClass('c1')); // false
  alert(I.hasClass('c2')); // true
  I.css({'background-color':'yellow', 'color':'red'});
  I.val(100);
  $('body').html('<p>Hello</p>');
  </script>
</body>
</html>
```

If a new property is not well supported by browsers, you can use this technique to set all prefixed variations of the property at once.

```
<!DOCTYPE html><html>
<head>
  <script src="jquery-2.1.1.min.js"></script>
</head>
<body>
  <p>Hello World</p>
  <script>
  $.cssHooks.fSize = {
    get: function(elem, computed, extra){
             return $.css(elem,'font-size');},
    set: function(elem, value){
             elem.style.fontSize = value;}};
  $('p').css('fSize','100px');
  alert($('p').css('fSize')); // 100px
  </script>
</body>
</html>
```

15.3.2 Dimension and Position

.height()
.width()
.innerHeight()
.innerWidth()
Get the height/width of the first matched element.

.height(String/Number value)
.height(function(int index, int height) f)
.width(String/Number value)
.width(function(int index, int height) f)
.innerHeight(String/Number value)
.innerHeight(function(int index, int height) f)
.innerWidth(String/Number value)
.innerWidth(function(int index, int height) f)
Set the height/width for each matched element.

.outerHeight([Boolean includeMargin])
.outerWidth([Boolean includeMargin])
Get the outer height/width of the first matched element.

.offset()
Get the coordinates of the first matched element, relative to the document.

.offset(Object coords)
.offset(function (int index, Object coords) f)
Set the coordinates for each matched element, relative to the document.

.position()
Get the coordinates of the first matched element, relative to the offset parent. The returned object has two properties – 'top' and 'left'.

.scrollLeft()
.scrollTop()
Get the horizontal/vertical position of the scroll bar for the first matched element.

.scrollLeft(Number value)
.scrollLeft(Numbe value)
Set the horizontal/vertical position of the scroll bars for the matched elements.

```
<!DOCTYPE html><html>
<head>
  <script src="jquery-2.1.1.min.js"></script>
</head>
<body>
  <div style="background:orange;
             width:300px; height:100px;
             margin:15px; padding:15px"></div>
  <script>
  var d = $('div');
  alert(d.height()); // 100
  alert(d.innerHeight()); // 130
  alert(d.outerHeight(true)); // 160
  d.offset({top:50, left:200});
  </script>
</body>
</html>
```

15.4 Animation Effects

15.4.1 Hiding and Showing

.hide/show/fadeOut/fadeIn/
slideUp/slideDown/slideToggle(
[Number/String duration] [, function() complete])

.hide/show/fadeOut/fadeIn/fadeToggle/
slideUp/slideDown/slideToggle(Object options)

.hide/show/fadeOut/fadeIn/fadeToggle/
slideUp/slideDown/slideToggle(
[Number/String duration] [, String easing]
[, function() complete])

.fadeTo(String/Number duration, Number opacity
[String easing][, function() complete])

Hide/show the matched elements.

The object 'options' has the following properties:

- Number/String duration = number | 'fast' | 'slow'
- String easing = 'swing' | 'linear'
- Boolean/String queue = (place in queue or instant?)
- Object specialEasing = (CSS properties and functions)
- function(Number now, Tween tween) step
- function(Promise animation, Number progress, Number remainingMs) progress
- function() complete
- function(Promise animation) start
- function(Promise animation, Boolean jumpedToEnd) done
- function(Promise animation, Boolean jumpedToEnd) fail
- function(Promise animation, Boolean jumpedToEnd) always

```
<!DOCTYPE html><html>
<head><script src="jquery-2.1.1.min.js"></script></head>
<body>
  <p>A</p>
  <p>B</p>
  <p>C</p>
  <button>Hide / Show </button>
  <script>
  $('button').click(function(){
    $('p').fadeToggle({duration:1000, easing: 'swing'});
  });
  </script>
</body>
</html>
```

15.4.2 Generic Animation

.animate(Object CSSProperties
[, Number/String duration]
[, String easing]
[, function() complete])
.animate(Object CSSProperties, Object options)
Continually change the CSS properties to the specified targets.

```
<!DOCTYPE html><html>
<head><script src="jquery-2.1.1.min.js"></script></head>
<body>
  <div style='background:green;display:inline-block;'>X
  </div>
  <script>
  $('div').click(function(){
    $(this).animate({height: '200px', width: '200px'},
                    5000,
                    function(){alert('completed!');});
  });
  </script>
</body>
</html>
```

15.4.3 Queue and Others

.queue([String q])
.queue([String q], Array newQueue)
.queue([String q], function(function dqNext()) f)
Show or manipulate the queue of functions.

.dequeue([String q])
Execute the next function on the queue.

.delay(int msDuration [, String q])
Delay execution for subsequent items in the queue.

.stop([String q][, Boolean clearQ][, Boolean toEnd])
Stop the current animation.

.finish([String q])
Stop the current animation, remove all queued animations, and complete all animations.

.clearQueue([String q])
Remove from the queue all items that have not been run.

$.fx.interval
This stores the rate(milliseconds) at which animations fire.

$.fx.off
Setting this to true disables all animation.

```
<!DOCTYPE html>
<html>
<head>
<script src="jquery-2.1.1.min.js"></script>
<style type="text/css">
  div {background:cyan;
       height:100px;width:100px;
       border:2px solid;}
  div:first-child {background:cyan;}
  div:last-child {background:yellow;}
</style>
<script>
$(document).ready(function(){
  alert($.fx.interval); // 13
  var d = $("div");
  setInterval( // fx is the default queue name
    function(){$('p').text(d.queue('fx').length)},
    100);
  $.fx.interval = 1; // smoothing
  $("button").click(function(){
    d.delay(3000)
     .animate({height:300,width:300,marginLeft:300},3000);
    d.delay(3000)
     .animate({width:100},3000); // this is dequeued
    d.dequeue().dequeue();
    d.delay(3000).animate({height:50},3000)
     .delay(3000)
     .animate({height:100,width:100,marginLeft:0},3000)
     .slideUp(3000).fadeIn(3000);
  });
});
</script>
</head>
<body>
  <p>Two moving boxes keep changing their shapes:</p>
  <button>Start</button>
  <div></div>
  <div></div>
</body>
</html>
```

15.5 Event Handlers

15.5.1 Specific Event Binders

.blur([Any data][, function(Event e) handler])
.change([Any data][, function(Event e) handler])
.click([Any data][, function(Event e) handler])
.dblclick([Any data][, function(Event e) handler])
.focus([Any data][, function(Event e) handler])
.focusin([Any data][, function(Event e) handler])
.focusout([Any data][, function(Event e) handler])
.keydown([Any data][, function(Event e) handler])
.keypress([Any data][, function(Event e) handler])
.keyup([Any data][, function(Event e) handler])
.mousedown([Any data][, function(Event e) handler])
.mouseenter([Any data][, function(Event e) handler])
.mouseleave([Any data][, function(Event e) handler])
.mousemove([Any data][, function(Event e) handler])
.mouseout([Any data][, function(Event e) handler])
.mouseover([Any data][, function(Event e) handler])
.mouseup([Any data][, function(Event e) handler])
.resize([Any data][, function(Event e) handler])
.scroll([Any data][, function(Event e) handler])
.select([Any data][, function(Event e) handler])
.submit([Any data][, function(Event e) handler])
Bind an event handler to the specific events.

.hover(function(Event e) handlerIn,
function(Event e) handlerOut)
Bind two handlers, to be executed when the mouse pointer enters or leaves the elements.

.ready(function() handler)
Specify a function to execute when the DOM is fully loaded. The following are the same:

- $(document).ready(handler)
- $().ready(handler)
- $(handler)

15.5.2 The Event Object

event.currentTarget
The current DOM element within the event bubbling phase.

event.delegateTarget
The element where the currently-called jQuery handler was attached.

event.relatedTarget
The other DOM element involved in the event, if any. It indicates the element being entered for 'mouseout', and the element being exited for 'mouseover'.

event.target
The DOM element that initiated the event within the event bubbling phase.

event.data
An optional data object passed to an event method when the current handler is bound.

event.metaKey
Return true if the Meta key was pressed.

event.namespace
The namespace specified when the event was triggered.

event.pageX
event.pageY
The mouse position.

event.result
The last value returned by an event handler that was triggered by this event.

event.timeStamp
The difference in milliseconds between the event time and January 1, 1970.

event.type
A string describing the nature of the event.

event.which
Which keyboard key (charCode) or mouse button (1: left, 2: middle, 3: right) was pressed.

event.preventDefault()
event.stopImmediatePropagation()
event.stopPropagation()
Prevent the default action (3.4.15) or stop the event propagation if the event triggers the handlers of other elements.

event.isDefaultPrevented()
event.isImmediatePropagationStopped()
event.isPropagationStopped()
Return true if the default action is prevented or if the event propagation is stopped.

```
<!DOCTYPE html>
<html>
<head>
<script src="jquery-2.1.1.min.js"></script>
<script>
$().ready(function(){
  $('button').click(function(){return 20;});
  $('button').click({a:10},function(e){
    alert (e.data.a + e.result); // 30
  });
});
</script>
</head>
<body>
  <button>Click</button>
</body>
</html>
```

15.5.3 Generic Event Manipulator

.bind(...) .unbind(...) .delegate(...) .undelegate(...)
(Superceded by .on() and .off().)

.on(String eventTypes [,String selector][, Any data], function(Event e) handler)
.on(Object events [,String selector][, Any data])
Attach a handler to some events for the elements after the descendants have been filtered by 'selector'. The Object 'events' has the form {eventType: function(e), ...}.

.one(String eventTypes [,String selector][, Any data], function(Event e) handler)
.one(Object events [,String selector][, Any data])
Identical to .on(...) except that the event handler is unbound after its first invocation, executing at most once.

.off() → remove all handlers
.off(String eventTypes [,String selector] [, function(Event e) handler])
.off(Object events [,String selector])
Remove an event handler for the elements.

.trigger(String/Event eventType[,Object/Array param])
Execute all handlers for the given event type.

.triggerHandler(String eventType[, Array param])
Identical to .trigger(...) except here: 1) the default behaviour of an event does not occur. 2) only the first matched element is affected. 3) the event does not bubble up. 4) the return value of the last handler is returned instead of the jQuery object.

*** The eventType "click.myPlugin.simple" defines both the myPlugin and simple namespaces for this particular click event.

```
<!DOCTYPE html>
<html>
<head>
  <script src="jquery-2.1.1.min.js"></script>
</head>
<body>
  <p></p>
  <button>Click</button>
  <script>
    // 1.
    $(window).on('load',function(){alert('Hi');});

    // 2.
    $('button').on('focus keydown',function(e){
             $('p').text('Key '+(e.which)+
                         ' has been pressed.');
           }).on('mouseenter', function(){
             $('p').text("Here we go!");
           }).on('mouseout', function(){
             $('p').text("Don't leave me!");
           }).on({mousedown: function(e,x,y){
                   $('p').text('Button down! '+x);},
                 mouseup: function(){
                   $('p').text('Button up!');}});
    $('button').off('mouseup')
               .trigger('mousedown',[10,20]);

    // 3.
    var e = $.Event('myEvent');
    e.v1 = 1000;
    e.v2 = 2000;
    $('button').on('myEvent', function(e,x,y){
                      alert(1000+2000);})
               .trigger(e);
  </script>
</body>
</html>
```

15.6 Functions Container

15.6.1 Callbacks List

You can push functions to a callbacks list, so that whenever the callbacks list is fired in the future, all added functions will be invoked, in the order the functions are added.

$.Callbacks([String flags]) Return a callbacks list. 'flags' can include: • '**once**': the callbacks list can be fire once only. • '**memory**': fires the new function with the previous value when the function has been just added. • '**unique**': a function can only be added once. • '**stopOnFalse**': do not invoke the subsequenct functions when a function returns false.
callbacks.add(function(...)/Array f) Add a function or array of functions. **callbacks.disable()** Disable a callback list from doing anything more. Prevent both adding and firing. **callbacks.empty()** Remove all functions. **callbacks.fire(Any arguments)** Invoke all functions with the specified arguments. **callbacks.fireWith([Object context][, Any arguments])** Invoke all function with the specified arguments within the specified context. **callbacks.lock()** Lock the current state. Prevent firing but allow adding. In a 'memory' callbacks list, a new function may still be invoked. **callbacks.remove(function()/Array f)** Remove a function or array of functions.
callbacks.disabled() **callbacks.fired()** **callbacks.has([function() f])** **callbacks.locked()** Check the various states of the callbacks list.

```
<!DOCTYPE html><html>
<head><script src="jquery-2.1.1.min.js"></script></head>
<body>
  <p></p>
  <script>
  function f1(msg){alert('f1');}
  function f2(msg){alert('f2');}
  function f3(msg){alert('f3');}
  cl = $.Callbacks();
  cl.add(f1)
    .add([f2,f3])
    .remove(f2)
    .fire()  // f1 f3
    .disable()
    .fire();  // (nothing)
  </script>
</body></html>
```

```
<!DOCTYPE html><html>
<head><script src="jquery-2.1.1.min.js"></script></head>
<body>
  <p></p>
  <script>
  function f1(msg){alert('f1: '+msg);}
  function f2(msg){alert('f2: '+msg);}
  cl = $.Callbacks('memory');
  cl.add(f1);
  cl.fire('A');  // f1: A
  cl.add(f2);  // f2: A
  cl.fire('B');  // f1: B
                // f2: B
  </script>
</body></html>
```

15.6.2 Deferred Object

A deferred object is similar to a callbacks list except that once a deferred object is *resolved* or *rejected*, all functions in it can't be invoked again. If the deferred object merely *notifies*, the functions may still be invoked.

Deferred Object
$.Deferred([function(DObject do) f]) Return a deferred object. The function f() is called just before the constructor returns. **deferred.state()** Return a string which can be 'pending', 'resolved', or 'rejected'.
deferred.done(function()[]/function(...) f1 [,function()[]/function(...) f2]) Add handlers to be called when the deferred object is resolved. **deferred.fail(function()[]/function(...) f1 [,function()[]/function(...) f2])** Add handlers to be called when the deferred object is rejected. **deferred.always(function()[]/function(...) f1 [,function()[]/function(...) f2])** Add handlers to be called when the deferred object is resolved or rejected. **deferred.progress(function()[]/function(...) f)** Add handlers to be called when the deferred object generates progress notifications. **deferred.then(function(...) done [,function(...) fail] [,function(...) progress])** Add handlers to be called when the deferred object is resolved, rejected, or stil in progress.
deferred.resolve([Any args]) **deferred.resolveWith(Object context [,Array args])** Resolve by calling functions registered with .done(...), .always(...), and .then(...). **deferred.reject([Any args])** **deferred.rejectWith(Object context [,Array args])** Reject by calling functions registered with .fail(...), .always(...), and .then(...). **deferred.notify([Any args])** **deferred.notifyWith(Object context [,Array args])** Notify by calling functions registered with .progress(...) and .then(...).
A Promise object is a deferred object without the six functions that can change the state of the deferred object, as outlined in the previous row in this table. Note that the jqXHR object returned by $.ajax(...) is a Promise object. **deferred.promise([Object target])** Return a Promise object. If 'target' is provided, methods will be attached onto it, and this object (instead of a new object) will be returned. **$.when(Deffered/Object deferreds)** Return a Promise object. If 'deferreds' is not a Deferred or a Promise, it will be treated as a resolved Deferred and any .done() callbacks attached will be executed immediately, with 'deferreds' as the argument.

```
<!DOCTYPE html><html>
<head><script src="jquery-2.1.1.min.js"></script></head>
<body>
```

```
  <p></p>
  <script>
  function f1(){alert(1);}
  function f2(){alert(2);}
  function f3(){alert(3);}
  function f4(){alert(4);}
  dO = $.Deferred(function(d){
                      this.f5 = function(){alert(5);};
                      d.f6 = function(){alert(6);}});
  dO.f5(); // 5
  dO.f6(); // 6
  dO.done([f1,f2]);
  dO.then(f1,f3,f4);
  dO.notify();  // 4
  dO.notify();  // 4
  alert(dO.state());  // pending
  dO.resolve();  // 1  2  1
  dO.resolve();  // (nothing)
  dO.reject();  // (nothing)
  dO.notify();  // (nothing)
  </script>
</body></html>
```

```
<!DOCTYPE html><html>
<head><script src="jquery-2.1.1.min.js"></script></head>
<body>
  <p></p>
  <script>
  function f1(msg){alert('1'+msg);}
  function f2(msg){alert('2'+msg);}

  dO = $.Deferred();
  dO.done(f1);
  pO1 = dO.promise();
  pO1.done(f1);
  //pO1.resolve('X'); // (error)
  dO.resolve('X'); // 1X  1X

  pO2 = $.when(dO);
  pO1.done(f2);
  dO.resolve('Y'); // 2X

  pO3 = $.when({a:10},{b:20},{c:30});
  dO.reject(f1);  // (nothing)
  dO.done(f2);  // 2X
  </script>
</body></html>
```

15.7 AJAX

15.7.1 Generic $.ajax(...)

A typical, low-level, asynchronous JQuery Ajax request has the form:

$.ajax([String url] [, Object settings])
[.done(function(data, status, xhr) f1)]
[.fail(function(xhr, status, error) f2)]
[.always(function(data|xhr,
status, xhr|error) f3)]
[.then(function(data, status, xhr) f4 ,
function(xhr, status, error) f5)]

'url' is a string that specifies the URL to which the request is sent. 'settings' contains a set, enclosed within {}, of optional key:value pairs.

$.ajax().done() specifies the function to call when the request succeeds. $.ajax().fail() specifies the function to call when the request fails. $ajax().always() specifies the function to call when the request completes, regardless of whether it succeeds or fails. $ajax(). then() combines $ajax().done() and $ajax().fail().

'response' is a string containing the response text. 'status' is a string which can be "success", "notmodified", "error", "timeout", "abort", "parsererror". 'xhr' contains the XMLHttpRequest object. 'error' is a string containing the error message.

Basic Settings
url: string contains the URL to which the request is sent.
type: "GET" / "POST" sets the type of request.
data: plainObject/string contains the data to be sent to the server. The value is a set of key:value pairs, or a query string.
async: true/false specifies whether the request is asynchronous. When set to false, the execution is blocked until a response is received.
cache: true/false specifies whether the request is to be cached.
global: true/false specifies whether to trigger global AJAX event handlers for this request (15.7.3).
timeout: number sets a timeout (in milliseconds) for the request.
statusCode: plainObject sets the function to be called when the response has the corresponding code.

```
<!DOCTYPE html>
<html>
<head>
<script src="jquery-1.8.2.min.js"></script>
<script>

$(document).ready(function(){
  $("button").click(function(){
   num=document.getElementsByTagName("input")[0].value;
    $.ajax("sum.php",
         {type: "POST",
          data: {num:num},
          statusCode:{200:alert_success,
                      404:alert_page_not_found}
         })
     .done(function(msg){
         $("p:first").html(msg);
         })
     .always(function(msg,status,xhr){
       $("p:last").html("Status:"+status+"("+xhr.status+")");
         });
  });
});

function alert_success(){
  alert("SUCCESS!");
}

function alert_page_not_found(){
  alert("PAGE NOT FOUND!");
}
</script></head>

<body>
Enter the number to add:
<input type="text" size="5" value="10"><br/>
<button type="button" id="button">Get the sum</button>
<p></p>
<p></p>
</body></html>
```

```
<?php
```

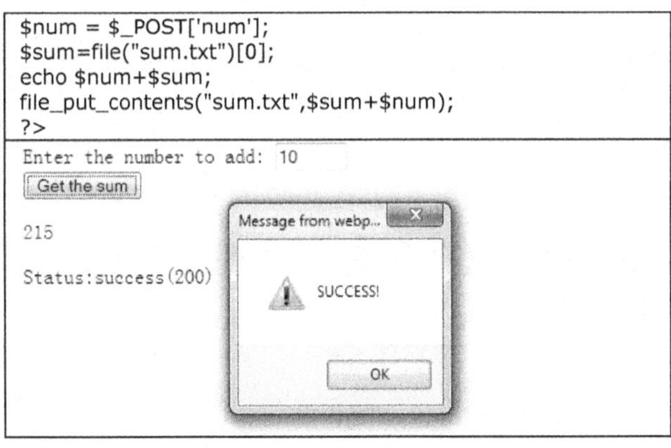

```
$num = $_POST['num'];
$sum=file("sum.txt")[0];
echo $num+$sum;
file_put_contents("sum.txt",$sum+$num);
?>
```


Advanced Settings
accepts: plainObject
beforeSend: function(xhr,settings)
contents: plainObject
contentType: string
context: plainObject
converters: plainObject
crossDomain: true/false
dataFilter: function(data,type)
dataType: "xml", "html", "script", "json", "jsonp", "text"
headers: plainObject
ifModified: true/false
isLocal: true/false
jsonp: string
jsonpCallback: string/function()
mimeType: string
password: string
processData: true/false
scriptCharset: string
traditional: true/false
username: string
xhr: function()
xhrFields: plainObject

$.ajaxPrefilter([String dataTypes,] function(Object opt, Object originalOpt, jqXHR xhr) handler) handle custom Ajax options or modify existing options before each request is sent and before they are processed by $.ajax().

$.ajaxTransport(String dataType, function(Object opt, Object originalOpt, jqXHR xhr) handler) create an object that handles the actual transmission of Ajax data.

15.7.2 Shorthand Methods

```
$.get(String url
      [,Object/String data]
      [,function(Object data, String status,
                 jqXHR xhr) success]
      [,String dataType])
```

is equivalent to

```
$.ajax({url: url,
        data: data,
        dataType: dataType,
        success: success});
```

```
$.post(String url
       [,Object/String data]
       [,function(Object data, String status,
                  jqXHR xhr) success]
       [,String dataType])
```

is equivalent to

```
$.ajax({url: url,
        type: "POST",
        data: data,
        dataType: dataType,
        success: success});
```

```
$.getScript(String url
            [,function(String script, String status,
                       jqXHR xhr) success])
```

is equivalent to

```
$.ajax({url: url,
        dataType: "script",
        success: success});
```

This loads a JavaScript from the server using "GET", then executes it.

```
$.getJSON(String url
          [,Object data]
          [,function (Object data, String status,
                      jqXHR xhr) success])
```

is equivalent to

```
$.ajax({url: url,
        data: data,
        dataType: "json",
        success: success});
```

```
$(selector).load(String url
                 [,Object/String data]
                 [,function (String resText, String status,
                             jqXHR xhr) complete])
```

This method loads data from the server and places the response into the matched element.

15.7.3 Global Event Handlers

jQuery presents a number of event handlers that can be attached to $(document). A callback function is triggered upon a jQuery AJAX event.

.ajaxComplete(function (Event e, jqXHR xhr, Object opt) handler) registers a handler to be called when AJAX requests complete.

.ajaxError(function (Event e, jqXHR xhr, Object settings, String err) handler) registers a handler to be called when AJAX requests complete with an error.

.ajaxSend(function (Event e, jqXHR xhr, Object opt) handler) registers a handler to be called before an AJAX is sent.

.ajaxStart(function() handler) registers a handler to be called when the first AJAX request begins.

.ajaxStop(function() handler) registers a handler to be called when all AJAX requests have completed.

.ajaxSuccess(function (Event e, jqXHR xhr, Object opt, Object data) handler) registers a handler to be called whenever an AJAX request completes successfully.

15.7.4 jQuery Helper Functions

$.param(object[,traditional]) creates a serialized representation of an array or object, suitable for use in a URL query string or Ajax request. If *traditional* is set to true, a shallow serialization is performed.

```
<!DOCTYPE html><html>
<head>
  <script src="jquery-2.0.3.min.js"></script>
  <script>
    var myObject = {
      a: {one: 1,
          two: 2,
          three: 3
         },
      b: [1,2,3]
    };
    var recursiveEncoded = $.param(myObject);
    var recursiveDecoded =
                 decodeURIComponent($.param(myObject));
    alert(recursiveEncoded);
  //a%5Bone%5D=1&a%5Btwo%5D=2&a%5Bthree%5D=3&
  //b%5B%5D=1&b%5B%5D=2&b%5B%5D=3

    alert(recursiveDecoded);
    //a[one]=1&a[two]=2&a[three]=3&b[]=1&b[]=2&b[]=3
  </script>
</head>
<body></body>
</html>
```

```
<!DOCTYPE html><html>
<head>
  <script src="jquery-2.0.3.min.js"></script>
  <script>
    var myObject = {
      a: {one: 1,
          two: 2,
          three: 3
         },
      b: [1,2,3]
    };
    var shallowEncoded = $.param(myObject, true);
    var shallowDecoded =
                 decodeURIComponent(shallowEncoded);
    alert(shallowEncoded);
   // a=%5Bobject+Object%5D&b=1&b=2&b=3

    alert(shallowDecoded);
    //a=[object+Object]&b=1&b=2&b=3
  </script>
</head>
<body></body>
</html>
```

$(this).serialize() encodes a set of form elements as a string for submission.

```
<!doctype html>
<html>
<head>
<script src="jquery-2.0.3.min.js"></script>

</head>
<body>
  <form>
   <select name="single">
     <option>Single</option>
     <option>Single2</option>
   </select><br />

   <select name="multiple" multiple>
     <option selected>Multiple</option>
     <option>Multiple2</option>
     <option selected>Multiple3</option>
   </select><br/>

   <input type="checkbox" name="check"
          value="check1" id="ch1"/>
   <label for="ch1">check1</label>

   <input type="checkbox" name="check"
          value="check2" checked id="ch2"/>
   <label for="ch2">check2</label><br />

   <input type="radio" name="radio"
          value="radio1" checked id="r1"/>
   <label for="r1">radio1</label>

   <input type="radio" name="radio"
          value="radio2" id="r2"/>
   <label for="r2">radio2</label>
  </form>
<p><tt id="results"></tt></p>

<script>
  function showValues() {
    var str = $("form").serialize();
    $("#results").text( str );
  }
  $("input[type='checkbox'], input[type='radio']").
                          on( "click", showValues );
  $("select").on( "change", showValues );
  showValues();
</script>
</body>
</html>
```

Single
Multiple
Multiple2
Multiple3
check1 check2
radio1 radio2

`single=Single&multiple=Multiple&multiple=Multiple3&check=check2&radio=radio1`

$(this).serializeArray() encodes a set of form elements as an array of names and values.

```
<!doctype html>
<html>
<head>
  <script src="jquery-2.0.3.min.js"></script>
</head>
<body>
  <p><b>Results:</b> <span id="results"></span></p>
  <form>
    <select name="single">
      <option>Single</option>
      <option>Single2</option>
    </select>

    <select name="multiple" multiple>
      <option selected>Multiple</option>
      <option>Multiple2</option>
      <option selected>Multiple3</option>
    </select><br/>

    <input type="checkbox" name="check"
           value="check1" id="ch1"/>
    <label for="ch1">check1</label>

    <input type="checkbox" name="check"
           value="check2" checked id="ch2"/>
    <label for="ch2">check2</label>

    <input type="radio" name="radio"
           value="radio1" checked id="r1"/>
    <label for="r1">radio1</label>

    <input type="radio" name="radio"
            value="radio2" id="r2"/>
    <label for="r2">radio2</label>
  </form>
  <script>
    function showValues() {
      var fields = $(":input").serializeArray();
      $("#results").empty();
      jQuery.each(fields, function(i, field){
        $("#results").append(field.value + " ");
      });
    }
    $(":checkbox, :radio").click(showValues);
    $("select").change(showValues);
    showValues();
</script>

</body>
</html>
```

Results: Single Multiple Multiple3 check2 radio1

Multiple
Multiple2
Multiple3
Single

check1 check2 radio1 radio2

15.8 Global $.(...) Functions

We have seen how AJAX functions can be invoked with $.(...). There exist other jQuery functions that do not act on the jQuery object returned by matching elements.

15.8.1 $ Basics

jQuery(String selector [,Element/jQuery context])
jQuery(Element/Element[]/Object/jQuery elements)
jQuery(String html [, Document doc])
jQuery(String html [, Object attributes])
jQuery(function(...) f)
Note that the prefix jQuery is synonymous with the famous $ jQuery symbol. So all forms of selection here are also applicable to $.(...), which has been used throughout the previous sections in this book. For the last form, the function f is execute when the DOM is ready.

.jquery
Return a string containing the jQuery version number.

$.holdReady(Boolean hold)
Hold or release the execution of the jQuery's ready event.

$.noConflict([Boolean removeAll])
Relinquish jQuery's control of the $ variable. The variable assigned to the returned value will become a new jQuery variable.

```
<!DOCTYPE html><html>
<head><script src="jquery-2.1.1.min.js"></script></head>
<script>
  $.holdReady(true);
  $(function(){
    jQuery('p').append('Hello');
    alert($({a:10}).prop('a')); // 10
    j = $.noConflict();
    j('<p>Test</p>').insertAfter('p');
    alert(jQuery('p').jquery); // 2.1.1
    j = $.noConflict(true);
    alert(jQuery('p').jquery); // error
  });
</script>
<body>
  <p></p>
  <script>
    if (confirm('Ready?'))$.holdReady(false);
  </script>
</body></html>
```

15.8.2 Boolean Values

$.contains(Element container, Element contained)
Check to see if an element is a descendant of another element.

$.inArray(Any value, Array arr[, int fromIndex])
Return the index of a value within an array, or -1 if it cannot be found.

$.isArray(Object o)
$.isEmptyObject(Object o)
$.isFunction(Object o)
$.isNumeric(Object o)
$.isPlainObject(Object o)
$.isWindow(Object o)
$.isXMLDoc(Object o)
Determine if an object is a specific type.

```
<!DOCTYPE html><html>
<head><script src="jquery-2.1.1.min.js"></script></head>
<body>
  <p></p>
  <script>
  alert($.contains(document,$('p')[0])); // true
  alert($.contains(5, [1,5,10,3], 2)); //false
  alert($.isArray({a:10})); // false
  alert($.isEmptyObject({f:function(){}})); // false
  alert($.isFunction(alert)); // true
  alert($.isPlainObject({a:10})); // true
  alert($.isPlainObject(window)); // false
  alert($.isWindow(window)); // true
  alert($.isXMLDoc(window)); // false
  </script>
</body></html>
```

15.8.3 Arrays and Objects

$.merge(Array first, Array second)
Merge the contents of two arrays into 'first'.

$.extend([Boolean deep,] Object target [, Object o]...)
Extend the contents of 'target' with the contents of subsequent Object arguments.

$.fn.extend(Object o)
Extend the jQuery prototype.

**$.each(Array/Object ao,
function(Object e, int/String index/key)))**
Execute a function on each item in an array or object.

**$.map(Array/Object ao,
function(Object e, int/String index/key))**
Translate all items in an array or object to a new array and return the new array.

$.unique(Element[] arr)
Sort and return an array of DOM elements with the duplicates removed.

**$.grep(Array arr, function(Object e, int index)
[, Boolean invert])**
Find the elements of an array which pass a function and return a new array.

$.makeArray(Object o)
Convert an object into an array.

```
<!DOCTYPE html><html>
<head><script src="jquery-2.1.1.min.js"></script></head>
<body>
  <p class='c2'></p>
  <p class='c3'></p>
  <p class='c3'></p>
  <p class='c1'></p>
  <script>
  arr = $('p').get();
  arr = arr.concat(arr);
  alert(arr.length); // 8
  $.unique(arr);
  alert(arr.length); // 4

  $.fn.extend({hello:
          function(){alert('hello');}});
  $('p').hello(); // hello
  </script>
</body></html>
```

15.8.4 Element Association

$.data(Element e, String key, Any value)
Associate arbitrary data with an element.

$.data(Element e[, String key])
Return the value associated with an element.

$.hasData(Element e)
Determine if an element has any associated data.

$.removeData(Element e [, String key])
Remove a piece of data previously associated with an element.

The default queueName is 'fx'.

$.queue(Element e[, String queueName])
Return an array of functions to be executed on an element.

**$.queue(Element e, String queueName,
function()[] replacements)**
Replace the queue of functions with an array of functions.

$.queue(Element, String queueName, function() new)
Add a new function to the queue.

$.dequeue(Element [,String queueName])
Execute the next function on the queue.

```
<!DOCTYPE html><html>
<head><script src="jquery-2.1.1.min.js"></script></head>
<body>
  <div></div>
  <script>
  d = $('div')[0];
  $.data(d, 'a', 100);
  $.data(d, 'b', 200);
  alert($.data(d,'a')); // 100
  alert($.data(d).b); // 200
  $.removeData(d);
  alert($.data(d).b); // undefined
  </script>
</body></html>
```

```
<!DOCTYPE html><html>
<head><script src="jquery-2.1.1.min.js"></script></head>
<body>
  <p>Hello World</p>
  <script>
  $('p').fadeOut(5000)
        .fadeIn(5000)
        .slideUp(5000)
        .slideDown(5000);
  $.queue($('p')[0],'fx',function(){
    alert('animation completed!');});
  </script>
</body></html>
```

15.8.5 Parsing

**$.parseHTML(String data [,Element context]
[Boolean keepScripts])**
Parse 'data' and return an array of DOM nodes. 'keepScripts' indicates whether to include scripts passed in 'data'.

$.parseJSON(String data)
Parse 'data' as JSON and return a String, a Number, an Object, an Array, or a Boolean.

$.parseXML(String data)
Parse 'data' and return an XMLDocument.

```
<!DOCTYPE html><html>
<head><script src="jquery-2.1.1.min.js"></script></head>
<body>
  <script>
  // HTML: returns 2
  h = $.parseHTML('<i><b>H</b>ello</i> World')
  alert(h.length);
  $('p').append(h);

  // JSON: returns [object Object]
  alert($.parseJSON('{"a":10,"b":20}'));

  // XML: returns [object XMLDocument]
  alert($.parseXML('<foo>hello</foo>'));
  </script>
</body></html>
```

15.8.6 Others

$.error(String msg)
Throws an exception.

$.globalEval(String code)
Similar to eval() in Javascript except that $.globalEval(...) executes the code within the global context.

$.noop()
A dummy function that does nothing. It is used to be passed as a callback when nothing needs to be done.

$.now()
Return a number representing the current time. It is a shorthand for (new Date).getTime().

$.proxy(function() f, Object context [,Any extraArgs])
$.proxy(Object context, String funcName [,Any extraArgs])
Take a function and return a new one that will always have a particular context.

$.trim(String s)
Return a new string with whitespace removed the beginning and end of 's'.

$.type(Any o)
Return a string describing the type of o. The string can be 'undefined', 'null', 'boolean', 'number', 'string' , 'function', 'array', 'date', 'error' , 'regexp', and 'object'.

```
<!doctype html><html>
<head><script src="jquery-2.1.1.min.js"></script></head>
<body>
 <p><button type="button" id="test">Test</button></p>
<div id="log"></div>
 <script>
var me = {
  type: "zombie",
  test: function( event ) {
    // Without proxy, `this` would refer to the event target
    // use event.target to reference that element.
    var element = event.target;
    $( element ).css( "background-color", "red" );

    // With proxy, `this` refers to the me object encapsulating
    // this function.
    $( "#log" ).append( "Hello " + this.type + "<br>" );
    $( "#test" ).off( "click", this.test );
  }
};

var you = {
  type: "person",
  test: function( event ) {
    $( "#log" ).append( this.type + " " );
  }
};

// Execute you.test() in the context of the `you` object
// no matter where it is called
// i.e. the `this` keyword will refer to `you`
var youClick = $.proxy( you.test, you );

// attach click handlers to #test
$( "#test" )
  // this === "zombie"; handler unbound after first click
  .on( "click", $.proxy( me.test, me ) )

  // this === "person"
  .on( "click", youClick )

  // this === "zombie"
  .on( "click", $.proxy( you.test, me ) )

  // this === "<button> element"
  .on( "click", you.test );
 </script>
 </body></html>
```

(Courtesy of http://api.jquery.com/jQuery.proxy/)

16. cURL

cURL is a multiprotocol file transfer library that allows you to download/upload a webpage or other types of data over the Internet, to the server or the client computer.

"libcurl is free, thread-safe, IPv6 compatible, feature rich, well supported, fast, thoroughly documented and is already used by many known, big and successful companies and numerous applications."

-- http://curl.haxx.se/libcurl/

Supported Protocols
DICT, FILE, FTP, FTPS, Gopher, HTTP, HTTPS, IMAP, IMAPS, LDAP, LDAPS, POP3, POP3S, RTMP, RTSP, SCP, SFTP, SMTP, SMTPS, Telnet and TFTP.

Supported Platforms
Solaris, NetBSD, FreeBSD, OpenBSD, Darwin, HPUX, IRIX, AIX, Tru64, Linux, UnixWare, HURD, Windows, Amiga, OS/2, BeOs, Mac OS X, Ultrix, QNX, OpenVMS, RISC OS, Novell NetWare and DOS.

Language Bindings
Ada95, Basic, C, C++, Ch, Cocoa, D, Dylan, Eiffel, Euphoria, Falcon, Ferite, Gambas, glib/GTK+, Guile, Haskell, ILE/RPG, Java, Lisp, Lua, Mono, .NET, Object-Pascal, OCaml, Pascal, Perl, PHP, Postgres, Python, R, Rexx, Ruby, Scheme, S-Lang, Smalltalk, SP-Forth, SPL, Tcl, Visual Basic, Visual FoxPro, Q, wxWidgets and XBLite.

16.1 Compilation in Microsoft Visual C++ 2010 Express

Step 1: Download the latest curl package from the Source Archives of

http://curl.haxx.se/download.html

. Unzip the package. Here we shall use curl-7.39.0.zip.

Step 2: Download and install Microsoft Visual C++ 2010 Express, if you have not already done so.

Step 3: Launch Visual Studio Command Prompt (2010). It can usually be found in:

Start Menu -> All Programs
-> Microsoft Visual Studio 2010 Express

Step 4: In the command prompt, navigate to the following directory:

[curl directory]\winbuild

Step 5: Build the libcURL library with the following command:

nmake –f Makefile.vc mode=static

. For more compilation options, check out the text file BUILD.WINDOWS.txt. The compilation should produce files and directories in

[curl directory]\builds

Step 6: Run Microsoft Visual C++ 2010 Express. Open a new project. Choose Win32 Console Application. Under Application Settings, choose 'Console application' and check 'Empty project'. Change the mode from 'Debug' to 'Release'.

Step 7: Test out 'simple.c'. From the Explorer, copy the file [curl directory]\docs\examples\simple.c to [project directory]\project\ . Then drag [project directory]\project\simple.c to the 'Source Files' folder under the project.

Step 8: Setup the dependencies. Right click on the project title and choose 'Properties'. For 'Configuration', choose 'Release'.

Go to 'Configuration Properties -> C/C++ -> General'. For 'Additional Include Directories', add '[curl directory]\builds\libcurl-vc-x86-release-static-ipv6-sspi-spnego-winssl\include'.

Go to 'Configuration Properties -> C/C++ -> Preprocessor'. For 'Preprocessor Definitions', add 'CURL_STATICLIB'.

Go to 'Configuration Properties -> Linker -> General'. For 'Additional Library Directories', add '[curl directory]\builds\libcurl-vc-x86-release-static-ipv6-sspi-spnego-winssl\lib'.

Go to 'Configuration Properties -> Linker -> Input'. For 'Additional Dependencies', add 'libcurl_a.lib'.

Step 9: Click the green triangle to build and test-run the program.

16.2 Essential C Functions

libcURL functions in C bear some similarities with PHP curl functions, although they are not entirely the same.

16.2.1 Global Operations

curl_global_init(long flags) sets up the environment for libcURL. curl_global_init (CURL_GLOBAL_ALL) should be called before any other libcURL function. If something went wrong, a non-zero code is returned.

curl_global_cleanup() releases the resources acquired by curl_global_init(). It should be called after all libcURL operations.

16.2.2 The CURL Handle

curl_easy_init() returns an easy handle that can be used as input to other easy functions. It automatically calls curl_global_init() if curl_global_init() has not already been called. This function should be called in the beginning of a libcURL program.

curl_easy_cleanup(CURL *handle) closes the connection opened by curl_easy_init(). It should be called at the end of a libcURL program.

16.2.3 The Heart

curl_easy_perform(CURL *handle) performs the actual file transfer. It represents the heart of every libcURL program. If everything is fine, zero will be returned.

16.2.4 Preparation

curl_easy_setopt(CURL *handle, CURLoption option, parameter) sets the options for the file transfer. It is called between curl_easy_init() and curl_easy_perform(). CURLoption are represented by names starting with 'CURLOPT_'. A non-zero is returned when an error occurs.

16.2.5 Form POST

curl_formadd(struct curl_httppost ** firstitem, struct curl_httppost ** lastitem, ...) adds a section to a multipart/formdata HTTP POST. The first two parameters should be NULL in the first call to this function. Pass firstitem as a parameter to CURLOPT_HTTPPOST. If everything is fine, zero will be returned.

16.2.6 Linked Lists

curl_slist_append(struct curl_slist * list, const char * string**)** adds a string to a linked list of strings. The existing list should be passed as the first argument while the new list is returned from this function.

curl_slists_free_all(struct curl_slist * list) frees a previously built linked list.

16.2.7 Information

A lot of the transfer information can be obtained by setting the option CURLOPT_VERBOSE to 1. Information such as the time spent at various stages, the transfer speed, the transfer size, the response codes, the cookies, the addresses, the ports etc. can be obtained after the transfer by calling **curl_easy_getinfo(CURL *handle, CURLINFO info,...)**. Information about an error can be obtained with **curl_easy_strerror(CURLcode errno)**.

16.3 C Examples

16.3.1 Retrieving a Webpage over HTTP

By default, libcURL outputs the retrieved file to the screen. If the webpage is redirected, the final webpage will be retrieved.

```
#include <stdio.h>
#include <curl/curl.h>

void print_transfer_info(CURL *curl){
  char *lip,*pip,*ct;
  double t;
  long rc;
  curl_easy_getinfo(curl, CURLINFO_LOCAL_IP, &lip);
  printf("\nThe local IP is %s.",lip);
  curl_easy_getinfo(curl, CURLINFO_PRIMARY_IP, &pip);
  printf("\nThe primary IP is %s.",pip);
  curl_easy_getinfo(curl, CURLINFO_CONTENT_TYPE, &ct);
  printf("\nThe content type is %s.",ct);
  curl_easy_getinfo(curl, CURLINFO_TOTAL_TIME, &t);
  printf("\nThe transfer took %.3lf seconds.",t);
  curl_easy_getinfo(curl, CURLINFO_REDIRECT_COUNT, &rc);
  printf("\nRedirection occurred %ld times.",rc);
  return;
}

int main(void){
  char c;
  CURL *curl;
  CURLcode res;
  curl = curl_easy_init();
  if(curl) {
    curl_easy_setopt(curl, CURLOPT_URL,
                     "http://www.example.com/test.php");

    // follows redirection(optional)
    curl_easy_setopt(curl, CURLOPT_FOLLOWLOCATION, 1L);

    // prints the HTTP header(optional)
    curl_easy_setopt(curl, CURLOPT_HEADER, 1L);

    res = curl_easy_perform(curl);

    // prints the transfer details(optional)
    if(res != CURLE_OK){
      fprintf(stderr, "curl_easy_perform() failed: %s\n",
              curl_easy_strerror(res));
    } else print_transfer_info(curl);

    curl_easy_cleanup(curl);
  }
  scanf("%c",&c);
  return 0;
}
```

```
<?php
// http://www.example.com/test.php
echo $_GET['msg'];
?>
```

16.3.2 Retrieving a Webpage over HTTPS

By default, libcURL verifies the SSL certificates, so the program at 16.3.1 can be used to retrieve a webpage over https as well. This program skips the verification process, making the process less secure. Other than the screen, the output can also be produced in a file.

```
#include <stdio.h>
#include <curl/curl.h>

size_t write_data(void *ptr, size_t size, size_t nmemb,
                                    FILE *stream) {
   size_t written;
   written = fwrite(ptr, size, nmemb, stream);
   return written;
}

int main(void){
  char c;
  FILE *f;
  CURL *curl;
  CURLcode res;
  curl = curl_easy_init();
  if(curl) {
    curl_easy_setopt(curl, CURLOPT_URL,
             "https://www.example.com/testing.html");

    // Add the two lines below for a less secure connection
    curl_easy_setopt(curl, CURLOPT_SSL_VERIFYPEER, 0L);
    curl_easy_setopt(curl, CURLOPT_SSL_VERIFYHOST, 0L);

   // Add the three lines below to write to a file
    f = fopen("test.html", "wb");
    curl_easy_setopt(curl,CURLOPT_WRITEFUNCTION,
                                    &write_data);
    curl_easy_setopt(curl, CURLOPT_WRITEDATA, f);

    res = curl_easy_perform(curl);
    fclose(f);
    if(res != CURLE_OK)
      fprintf(stderr, "curl_easy_perform() failed: %s\n",
           curl_easy_strerror(res));
    else printf("File written successfully.");
    curl_easy_cleanup(curl);
  }
  scanf("%c",&c);
  return 0;
}
```

16.3.3 Getting a File into a Variable Only

This example outlines the third way to store the retrieved file -- into a variable in the memory.

```
#include <stdio.h>
#include <curl/curl.h>

struct MemoryStruct {
  char *memory;
  size_t size;
};

static size_t write_data(void *contents, size_t size,
                          size_t nmemb, void *userp){
  size_t realsize = size * nmemb;
  struct MemoryStruct *mem = (struct MemoryStruct *)userp;

  mem->memory = realloc(mem->memory,
                        mem->size + realsize + 1);
  if(mem->memory == NULL) {
    /* out of memory! */
    printf("not enough memory (realloc returned NULL)\n");
    return 0;
  }

  memcpy(&(mem->memory[mem->size]), contents,
              realsize);
  mem->size += realsize;
  mem->memory[mem->size] = 0;
  return realsize;
}

int main(void){
  char c;
  CURL *curl;
  CURLcode res;
  struct MemoryStruct chunk;
  chunk.memory = malloc(1);  // grows as needed by realloc
  chunk.size = 0;

  curl = curl_easy_init();
  if(curl) {
    curl_easy_setopt(curl, CURLOPT_URL,
               "http://www.example.com/testing.html");
    curl_easy_setopt(curl,CURLOPT_WRITEFUNCTION,
                  &write_data);
    curl_easy_setopt(curl, CURLOPT_WRITEDATA,
                 (void *)&chunk);
    res = curl_easy_perform(curl);
    if(res != CURLE_OK)
      fprintf(stderr, "curl_easy_perform() failed: %s\n",
          curl_easy_strerror(res));
    else {
      printf("File written successfully.\n");
      printf("It is %lu bytes long. Content:\n",
           (long)chunk.size);
      printf("%s",chunk.memory);
    }
    curl_easy_cleanup(curl);
  }
  scanf("%c",&c);
  return 0;
}
```

16.3.4 POSTing Form Data over HTTP

This program passes two strings and a file to testing.php.

```
#include <stdio.h>
#include <curl/curl.h>

int main(void){
  char c;
  CURL *curl;
  CURLcode res;
  struct curl_httppost *formpost=NULL;
  struct curl_httppost *lastptr=NULL;
  struct curl_slist *headerlist=NULL;

  curl = curl_easy_init();
  if(curl) {
    curl_formadd(&formpost,&lastptr,
              CURLFORM_COPYNAME, "Name" ,
              CURLFORM_COPYCONTENTS,"Mike",
              CURLFORM_END);
    curl_formadd(&formpost,&lastptr,
              CURLFORM_COPYNAME, "Age" ,
              CURLFORM_COPYCONTENTS, "15" ,
              CURLFORM_END);
    curl_formadd(&formpost,&lastptr,
              CURLFORM_COPYNAME, "my_file" ,
              CURLFORM_FILE, "allexamples.zip",
              CURLFORM_END);
    curl_easy_setopt(curl, CURLOPT_HTTPHEADER,
                  headerlist);
    curl_easy_setopt(curl, CURLOPT_HTTPPOST, formpost);
        curl_easy_setopt(curl, CURLOPT_URL,
               "http://www.example.com/testing.php");
        res = curl_easy_perform(curl);
        curl_formfree(formpost);
        curl_slist_free_all(headerlist);
    curl_easy_cleanup(curl);
  }
  scanf("%c",&c);
```

```
  return 0;
}
```

```
<!-- http://www.example.com/testing.php -->
<!DOCTYPE html>
<html>
<head></head>
<body>
<?php
echo "My name is ".$_POST['Name'].
     ". I am ".$_POST['Age']." years old.";
move_uploaded_file($_FILES['my_file']['tmp_name'],
                   $_FILES['my_file']['name']);
?>
</body>
</html>
```

16.3.5 Retrieving a File over FTP

This downloads a file over FTP. Enabling the CURLOPT_VERBOSE option prints the details about all operations during the file transfer. You can enable the option in other libcurl programs too, whenever you want to trace the transferring process.

```
#include <stdio.h>
#include <curl/curl.h>

struct FtpFile {
  const char *filename;
  FILE *stream;
};

static size_t my_fwrite
       (void *buffer, size_t size, size_t nmemb, void *stream){
  struct FtpFile *out=(struct FtpFile *)stream;
  if(out && !out->stream) {
    out->stream=fopen(out->filename, "wb");
    if(!out->stream) return -1;
  }
  return fwrite(buffer, size, nmemb, out->stream);
}

int main(void){
   char c;
   CURL *curl;
   CURLcode res;
   struct FtpFile ftpfile={
     "test.zip", // filename on the destination
     NULL
   };

   curl_global_init(CURL_GLOBAL_DEFAULT);
   curl = curl_easy_init();
   if(curl) {
     curl_easy_setopt(curl, CURLOPT_URL,
                  "ftp://ftp.example.com/examples.zip");
     curl_easy_setopt(curl, CURLOPT_WRITEFUNCTION,
                                              my_fwrite);
     curl_easy_setopt(curl, CURLOPT_WRITEDATA, &ftpfile);
     curl_easy_setopt(curl, CURLOPT_USERPWD,
                                   "username:password");
     curl_easy_setopt(curl, CURLOPT_VERBOSE, 1L);
     res = curl_easy_perform(curl);
     curl_easy_cleanup(curl);
     if(CURLE_OK != res) fprintf(stderr,
                              "curl told us %d\n", res);
   }

   if(ftpfile.stream) fclose(ftpfile.stream);
   curl_global_cleanup();
   scanf("%c",&c);
   return 0;
}
```

16.3.6 Uploading a File over FTP

This uploads a local file to the server over FTP. If CURLOPT_INFILESIZE_LARGE is used, the next paramenter in curl_easy_setopt() must be cast to curl_off_t, If CURLOPT_INFILESIZE is used, the next parameter must be cast to long.

```
#include <stdio.h>
#include <string.h>
#include <curl/curl.h>
#include <sys/types.h>
#include <sys/stat.h>
#include <fcntl.h>
#include <errno.h>
#ifdef WIN32
  #include <io.h>
#else
  #include <unistd.h>
#endif

#define LOCAL_FILE "test.zip"
#define UPLOAD_FILE_AS "test2.zip"
#define REMOTE_URL "ftp://ftp.example.com/"
#define RENAME_FILE_TO "test3.zip"

static size_t read_callback
        (void *ptr, size_t size, size_t nmemb, void *stream){
  curl_off_t nread;
  size_t retcode = fread(ptr, size, nmemb, stream);
  nread = (curl_off_t)retcode;
  fprintf(stderr, "*** We read %
    " CURL_FORMAT_CURL_OFF_T " bytes from file\n", nread);
  return retcode;
}

int main(void){
  char c;
  CURL *curl;
  CURLcode res;
  FILE *hd_src;
  struct stat file_info;
  curl_off_t fsize;

  struct curl_slist *headerlist=NULL;
  static const char buf_1 [] = "RNFR " UPLOAD_FILE_AS;
  static const char buf_2 [] = "RNTO " RENAME_FILE_TO;

  if(stat(LOCAL_FILE, &file_info)) {
    printf("Couldnt open '%s': %s\n", LOCAL_FILE,
                                     strerror(errno));
    return 1;
  }
  fsize = (curl_off_t)file_info.st_size;

  printf("Local file size: %" CURL_FORMAT_CURL_OFF_T
        " bytes.\n", fsize);

  hd_src = fopen(LOCAL_FILE, "rb");
  curl_global_init(CURL_GLOBAL_ALL);
  curl = curl_easy_init();
  if(curl) {
    headerlist = curl_slist_append(headerlist, buf_1);
    headerlist = curl_slist_append(headerlist, buf_2);
    curl_easy_setopt(curl, CURLOPT_READFUNCTION,
                     read_callback);
    curl_easy_setopt(curl, CURLOPT_UPLOAD, 1L);
    curl_easy_setopt(curl, CURLOPT_URL, REMOTE_URL);
    curl_easy_setopt(curl, CURLOPT_POSTQUOTE,
                     headerlist);
    curl_easy_setopt(curl, CURLOPT_READDATA, hd_src);
    curl_easy_setopt(curl, CURLOPT_VERBOSE, 1L);
    curl_easy_setopt(curl, CURLOPT_USERPWD,
                     "username:password");
    curl_easy_setopt(curl, CURLOPT_INFILESIZE_LARGE,
                                   (curl_off_t)fsize);
    res = curl_easy_perform(curl);
    if(res != CURLE_OK)
```

```
        fprintf(stderr, "curl_easy_perform() failed: %s\n",
                curl_easy_strerror(res));
    curl_slist_free_all (headerlist);
    curl_easy_cleanup(curl);
  }
  fclose(hd_src);
  curl_global_cleanup();
  scanf("%c",&c);
  return 0;
}
```

16.4 PHP Examples

Please note that some web hosts do not allow you to perform curl operations locally, ie. over the same local domain.

16.4.1 Retrieving a Webpage over HTTP(s)

The scripts for retrieving a Webpage over HTTP and HTTPS are the same. Unlike in C, the webpage retrieved is saved directly in a variable, by setting the option CURLOPT_RETURNTRANSFER to TRUE. The following script attempts to recreate the page at 'www.example.com', but will fail to display properly if the page requests other images or pages.

```
<?php
function get_url($url) {
  $ch = curl_init();
  if($ch === false) die('Failed to create curl object');
  curl_setopt($ch, CURLOPT_URL, $url);
  curl_setopt($ch, CURLOPT_RETURNTRANSFER, TRUE);
  //curl_setopt($ch, CURLOPT_FOLLOWLOCATION, TRUE);
  //curl_setopt($ch, CURLOPT_HEADER, TRUE);
  curl_setopt($ch, CURLOPT_CONNECTTIMEOUT, 25);
  $data = curl_exec($ch);
  curl_close($ch);
  return $data;
}
echo get_url('http://www.example.com/');
?>
```

16.4.2 Getting a Remote File over HTTP

This saves the remote file in the server permanently, instead of saving it in a variable.

```
<?php
$source  = 'http://example.com/xyz.zip';
$target = '/var/www/zyx.zip';
$ch = curl_init($source);
if($ch === false) die('Failed to create curl handle');
$fp = fopen($target, 'w');
curl_setopt($ch, CURLOPT_FILE, $fp);
$data = curl_exec($ch);
curl_close($ch);
fclose($fp);
?>
```

16.4.3 POSTing Form Data over HTTP

The '@' symbol at the front of a filename is used to indicate that you are posting a file.

```
<?php
$url = "http://example.com/testing.php";
$post_data = array('Name' => 'Mike',
                   'Age' => '15',
                   'my_file' => '@example/hello3.zip');
$ch = curl_init();
curl_setopt($ch, CURLOPT_URL, $url);
curl_setopt($ch, CURLOPT_RETURNTRANSFER, TRUE);
curl_setopt($ch, CURLOPT_POST, TRUE);
curl_setopt($ch, CURLOPT_POSTFIELDS, $post_data);
$output = curl_exec($ch);
curl_close($ch);
echo $output;
?>
```

```
<!-- http://example.com/testing.php -->
<!DOCTYPE html>
<html>
<head></head>
<body>
<?php
echo "My name is ".$_POST['Name'].
     ". I am ".$_POST['Age']." years old.";
move_uploaded_file($_FILES['my_file']['tmp_name'],
                   $_FILES['my_file']['name']);
?>
</body>
</html>
```

16.4.4 Getting a Remote File over FTP

This gets a remote file over FTP. The syntax is pretty standard except that you have to specify the file pointer for the option CURLOPT_FILE.

```
<?
$curl = curl_init();
$file = fopen("eg.zip", 'w');
curl_setopt($curl, CURLOPT_URL,
                  "ftp://ftp.example.com/examples.zip");
curl_setopt($curl, CURLOPT_RETURNTRANSFER, 1);
curl_setopt($curl, CURLOPT_FILE, $file);
curl_setopt($curl, CURLOPT_USERPWD,
"username:password");
curl_exec($curl);
curl_close($curl);
fclose($file);
?>
```

16.4.5 Uploading a File over FTP

This uploads a file to another server over FTP. Here we obtain any error with curl_errno() and curl_error().

```
<?php
$localfile = 'examples.zip';
$ch = curl_init();
$fp = fopen($localfile, 'r');
curl_setopt($ch, CURLOPT_URL,

'ftp://ftp.example.com/testing/eg.zip');
curl_setopt($ch, CURLOPT_USERPWD, "username:password");
curl_setopt($ch, CURLOPT_UPLOAD, 1);
curl_setopt($ch, CURLOPT_INFILE, $fp);
curl_setopt($ch, CURLOPT_INFILESIZE, filesize($localfile));
curl_exec ($ch);
$error_no = curl_errno($ch);
curl_close ($ch);
if ($error_no == 0) {
  $error = 'File uploaded succesfully.';
} else {
  $error = 'File upload error:'. curl_error($ch);
}
```

```
echo $error;
?>
```

16.5 PayPal Integration

PayPal provides a means to easily integrate credit-card payments into your website. Each online merchant is assigned a token and each successful payment causes the transaction ID to be appended to the return address as a query string.

16.5.1 Obtaining the Identity Token

To obtain a merchant's identity token:
Step 1: Log in into your PayPal account.
Step 2: Under 'My Account', click 'Profile'.
Step 3: Go to 'My selling tools' -> 'Website preferences'.
Step 4: Fill in the form. Turn on 'Auto Return' and 'Payment Data Transfer'. Click 'Save'.

16.5.2 Adding a 'Buy Now' Button

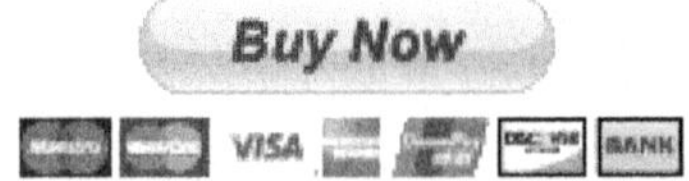

To add a PayPal Buy button:
Step 1: Log in into your PayPal account.
Step 2: Click 'Merchant Services'.
Step 3: Click 'Website Payments Standard'.
Step 4: Under 'Payments Button'->'Sell single items', click 'Create one now'.
Step 5: Fill in the form. Choose 'Use my secure merchant account ID'. Fill in the return URL when the customers finish checkout. Click 'Create Button'.
Step 6: Select and copy the generated code. Paste the code into your file in a place where you want the 'Buy Now' button to appear.

16.5.3 Verifying a Payment

After a customer pays though PayPal and is redirected back to your website, you may want to update some of your records accordingly. The payment can be confirmed by contacting 'https://www.paypal.com/cgi-bin/webscr' and POSTing three pieces of information:

cmd	'_notify-synch' This command string is fixed to be as such.
tx	<transaction id> This string is found in the query string attached to the URL when a customer is returned to your website after checkout.
at	<authorization token> This is the identity token you obtained in 16.5.1.

This will fetch back a lot of information about the payment:

```
SUCCESS
mc_gross=1.00
protection_eligibility=Eligible
address_status=unconfirmed
payer_id=ADHZJ9GRK8GJ6
tax=0.00
address_street=H712+SriMalacca+Condominium%0D%0AJ
alan+Api+Road
payment_date=21%3A15%3A26+Jan+12%2C+2014+PST
payment_status=Completed
charset=windows-1252
address_zip=88100
first_name=Chong
mc_fee=0.34
address_country_code=MY
address_name=GameSuria
custom=
payer_status=verified
business=admin%40hold-em-analyzer.com
address_country=Malaysia
address_city=Kota+Kinabalu
quantity=1
payer_email=topup%40gamesuria.com
txn_id=6D869163D9680983A
payment_type=instant
payer_business_name=GameSuria
btn_id=76791927
last_name=Lip+Phang
address_state=Sabah
receiver_email=admin%40hold-em-analyzer.com
payment_fee=0.34
shipping_discount=0.00
insurance_amount=0.00
receiver_id=BQ75H9QYGTYEG
txn_type=web_accept
item_name=testing+2
discount=0.00
mc_currency=USD
item_number=
residence_country=MY
shipping_method=Default
handling_amount=0.00
transaction_subject=
payment_gross=1.00
shipping=0.00
```

To prevent your website from making repeated sales under the same PayPal transaction (eg. when the customer refreshes the webpage with the transaction ID intact), you should store 'txn_id' in a database and check for its uniqueness.

You should check that 'payment_status' is 'Completed'. You should also check that 'mc_gross', 'mc_currency' and 'receiver_email' are correct.

The <body> content of the second piece of code below is generated by PayPal.

```
<!DOCTYPE html>
<html>
<head>
  <title> PayPal Buy Now </title>
</head>
<body>

<?
$tid = $_GET['tx'];
$auth_token = "nkdHrK7MTSOkCfF1bB3tzgFw-
W4ErH_iM48VdT3p27iR9ewZdJxr4TpZOlK";
$post_vars = "cmd=_notify-synch&tx=" . $tid . "&at=" .
$auth_token;

$ch = curl_init();
curl_setopt($ch, CURLOPT_URL,
"https://www.paypal.com/cgi-bin/webscr");
curl_setopt($ch, CURLOPT_POST, true);
curl_setopt($ch, CURLOPT_POSTFIELDS, $post_vars);
curl_setopt($ch, CURLOPT_FOLLOWLOCATION, true);
curl_setopt($ch, CURLOPT_RETURNTRANSFER, true);
$fetched = curl_exec($ch);

$lines = explode("\n", $fetched);
$keyarray = array();
if (strcmp ($lines[0], "SUCCESS") == 0) {
  for ($i=1; $i<count($lines);$i++){
    list($key,$val) = explode("=", $lines[$i]);
    $keyarray[$key] = urldecode($val);
  }
  // check that txn_id has not been previously processed
  // ......
  // ......
  if ($keyarray['payment_status']!='Completed' ||
      $keyarray['mc_gross']!='1.00' ||
      $keyarray['mc_currency']!='USD' ||
      $keyarray['receiver_email']!=
                                'admin@hold-em-
analyzer.com' ){
    echo "Invalid PayPal transaction.";
  } else echo ("<h2>Thank you for your purchase!</h2>");
} else if (strcmp ($lines[0], "FAIL") == 0) {
  echo ("<h2>Sorry, the PayPal transaction failed.</h2>");
  // log for manual investigation
}
?>

</body>
</html>
```

```
<!DOCTYPE html>
<html>

<body>

<form action="https://www.paypal.com/cgi-bin/webscr"
method="post" target="_top">
<input type="hidden" name="cmd" value="_s-xclick">
<input type="hidden" name="hosted_button_id"
value="F8VPTGBGZMYP4">
<input type="image"
src="https://www.paypalobjects.com/en_US/i/btn/btn_buyno
wCC_LG.gif" border="0" name="submit" alt="PayPal - The
safer, easier way to pay online!">
<img alt="" border="0"
src="https://www.paypalobjects.com/en_US/i/scr/pixel.gif"
width="1" height="1">
</form>

</body>
</html>
```

16.6 Direct Logins

Instead of forcing every visitor to go through the account signing-up process, you can connect to an established website and use the visitor's profile there.

If the visitor is not logged in into the established website, the visitor will be prompted to do so automatically. If it is the first time the visitor tries to log-in into your website, the visitor will be prompted to give permission to your website to access the profile.

16.6.1 Facebook

First, 'Add a New App' at
https://developers.facebook.com/apps

Follow the instructions there to set up Facebook login. Even though you can use Javascript to implement Facebook login, here we shall use PHP cURL.

After you have created an app, go back to click the app. In Settings, add your contact email address. Then in Status and Review, make the app live.

To use the following code, you should replace the values of the variables '$client_id', '$client_secret', and '$redirect_uri'. Here, $redirect_uri should be the URL of the script itself. Note that cURL is used twice here. For the first time, an access token is obtained. The second time retrieves the profile information.

```
<?php
$client_id='775375085836452';
$client_secret='e63348b03e3cbce07720955268cfda6e';
$redirect_uri='http://mydomain.com/logins/facebook/index.p
hp';

if($_GET['code']){
  $code=htmlentities($_GET['code'], ENT_QUOTES, 'UTF-8');
  $url="https://graph.facebook.com/oauth/access_token?".
       "client_id=$client_id&redirect_uri=$redirect_uri&".
       "client_secret=$client_secret&code=$code";
  $ch = curl_init();
  curl_setopt_array($ch, array(CURLOPT_URL => $url,
                        CURLOPT_RETURNTRANSFER => true,
                        CURLOPT_SSL_VERIFYPEER => false,
                        CURLOPT_VERBOSE => true));
  $result1 = curl_exec($ch);
  parse_str($result1,$result1);
  $token=$result1[access_token];

  $url = "https://graph.facebook.com/me?".
         "fields=id,name,picture.type(large),email".
         "&access_token=$token";

  $ch = curl_init();
  curl_setopt_array($ch, array(CURLOPT_URL => $url,
                        CURLOPT_RETURNTRANSFER => true,
                        CURLOPT_SSL_VERIFYPEER => false,
                        CURLOPT_VERBOSE => true));
  $result = curl_exec($ch);
  $result = json_decode($result, true);
  echo '<pre>';
  print_r($result);
  echo '</pre>';
} else {
  header("Location: "
        "https://graph.facebook.com/oauth/authorize?".
        "client_id=$client_id&redirect_uri=$redirect_uri".
        "&scope=email");
```

```
}
?>
```

```
Array
(
    [id] => 100004943772979
    [name] => Chong Lip Phang
    [picture] => Array
        (
            [data] => Array
                (
                    [height] => 0
                    [is_silhouette] =>
                    [url] => https://fbcdn-profile-
                         a.akamaihd.net/hprofile-ak-ash1/t5.0-

1/275962_100004943772979_1930370242_n.jpg
                    [width] => 0
                )

        )

    [email] => webbible2014@gmail.com
)
```

16.6.2 Google

Create a project at:

https://console.developers.google.com/project

Navigate along 'APIs & auth' -> 'Credentials' -> 'CREATE NEW CLIENT ID'. Select 'Web application' as the Application type. For Authorized JavaScript origins, enter your domain name. For Authorized Redirect URI, enter the URL of the script. Click 'Create Client ID'.

This is similar to the case for Facebook. You need to replace the values of '$client_id', '$client_key', and '$redirect_uri'.

```
<?php
$client_id='504638019608-
24ul6lfhf5s7qmvj0otpjm357lq6le58.apps.googleusercontent.co
m';
$client_key='zrK2RcODVLf_PxxM_sBxPMWU';
$redirect_uri='http://mydomain.com/logins/google/index.php'
;

function code2token($code) {
    global $client_id,$client_key,$redirect_uri;
    $oauth2token_url =
                "https://accounts.google.com/o/oauth2/token";
    $clienttoken_post = array(
    "code" => $code,
    "client_id" =>$client_id,
    "client_secret" =>$client_key,
    "redirect_uri" =>$redirect_uri,
    "grant_type" => "authorization_code"
    );

    $curl = curl_init($oauth2token_url);

    curl_setopt($curl, CURLOPT_POST, true);
    curl_setopt($curl, CURLOPT_POSTFIELDS,
                $clienttoken_post);
    curl_setopt($curl, CURLOPT_HTTPAUTH, CURLAUTH_ANY);
    curl_setopt($curl, CURLOPT_SSL_VERIFYPEER, false);
    curl_setopt($curl, CURLOPT_RETURNTRANSFER, 1);

    $json_response = curl_exec($curl);
    curl_close($curl);

    $authObj = json_decode($json_response);

    if (isset($authObj->refresh_token)){
        global $refreshToken;
        $refreshToken = $authObj->refresh_token;
    }

    $accessToken = $authObj->access_token;
    return $accessToken;
}

function call_api($accessToken,$url){
  $curl = curl_init($url);

  curl_setopt($curl, CURLOPT_HTTPAUTH, CURLAUTH_ANY);
  curl_setopt($curl, CURLOPT_SSL_VERIFYPEER,false);
                                                //old: true
  curl_setopt($curl, CURLOPT_RETURNTRANSFER, 1);
  $curlheader[0] = "Authorization: Bearer " . $accessToken;
  curl_setopt($curl, CURLOPT_HTTPHEADER, $curlheader);

  $json_response = curl_exec($curl);
  curl_close($curl);
  $responseObj = json_decode($json_response,1);

  return $responseObj;
}

if(isset($_REQUEST['code'])){
   $data = call_api(code2token($_REQUEST['code']),
             "https://www.googleapis.com/oauth2/v1/userinfo");
   echo '<pre>';
   print_r($data);//array of user profile details name,email,etc
   echo '</pre>';
} else {
   header("Location:
https://accounts.google.com/o/oauth2/auth?response_type=c
ode&client_id=$client_id&redirect_uri=$redirect_uri&scope=ht
tps://www.googleapis.com/auth/userinfo.email+https://www.
googleapis.com/auth/userinfo.profile");
}
?>
```

```
Array
(
    [id] => 107703378425685064164
    [email] => webbible2014@gmail.com
    [verified_email] => 1
    [name] => Chong Lip Phang
    [given_name] => Chong
    [family_name] => Lip Phang
    [link] =>
https://plus.google.com/107703378425685064164
    [picture] => https://lh4.googleusercontent.com/-
WrO4WYcS74A/AAAAAAAAAAI/AAAAAAAAABQ/4dkAc_WQmE4
/photo.jpg
    [gender] => male
    [locale] => en
)
```

16.6.3 Yahoo

Create a project at:

https://developer.apps.yahoo.com/projects

Enter the application name. Select 'Web-based' for 'Application Type'. Write a description. Specify the URL of the script for 'Home Page URL'. For 'Access Scopes', select 'This app requires access to private user data'. Specify the domain. Select the following APIs for private user data access: Contacts -> Read, Social Directory (Profiles) -> Read Public. Tick the checkbox for Terms of Use. Click 'Create Project'. At the next page, follow the instructions to 'Verify Domain'.

Next, head to:

https://developer.yahoo.com/social/sdk/php/

to download a PHP library. Click 'Download'. Then click 'lib'. You should see: JSON.php, OAuth.php, Yahoo.inc, and YahooSessionStore.inc. Click each of them, and copy and paste the contents to files in your server. Place the files in the same directory as the calling script.

The library provided, Yahoo.inc, uses cURL. It is currently somewhat outdated. In line 1166 of Yahoo.inc, you should change 'http' to 'https'.

Remember to change the values for the three constants at the beginning of the script.

```
<?php
require 'Yahoo.inc';
session_start();

define('CONSUMER_KEY',
'dj0yJmk9TWdnaUFrdFRDOE04JmQ9WVdrOWRqQnZTWFptTjJr
bWNHbzlNQS0tJnM9Y29uc3VtZXJzZWNyZXQmeD05Mg--');
define('CONSUMER_SECRET',
'352b25d56e78b3eaac53832b1bc563c6cdb21136');
define('APP_ID', 'vOoIvf7i');

$session = YahooSession::requireSession(CONSUMER_KEY,
                                        CONSUMER_SECRET, APP_ID);
if (is_object($session)){
  $user = $session->getSessionedUser();
  $profile = $user->getProfile();
  echo '<pre>';
  print_r($profile);
  echo '</pre>';
}
?>
```

```
Array
(
   [uri] =>
http://social.yahooapis.com/v1/user/HX4NWUR6M372D7MJNN
NHNG7FTY/profile
   [guid] => HX4NWUR6M372D7MJNNNHNG7FTY
   [birthdate] => 5/25
   [created] => 2009-01-27T12:25:15Z
   [emails] => Array
      (
         [0] => Array
            (
               [handle] => texturing@hotmail.com
               [id] => 3
               [type] => HOME
            )

         [1] => Array
            (
               [handle] => fragment_shader@yahoo.com
               [id] => 5
               [primary] => 1
               [type] => HOME
            )

      )

   [familyName] => Lip Phang
   [gender] => M
   [givenName] => Chong
   [image] => Array
      (
         [height] => 192
         [imageUrl] =>
http://socialprofiles.zenfs.com/images/e7b1b85128144a72921
69ab41f2f7ef9_192.png
         [size] => 192x192
         [width] => 192
      )

   [lang] => en-US
   [location] => NA
   [memberSince] => 2006-08-20T15:10:00Z
   [nickname] => clip
   [phones] => Array
      (
         [0] => Array
            (
               [id] => 6
               [number] => 60-168815123
               [type] => MOBILE
            )

      )

   [profileUrl] =>
http://profile.yahoo.com/HX4NWUR6M372D7MJNNNHNG7FTY
   [searchable] =>
   [timeZone] => America/Los_Angeles
   [updated] => 2013-09-04T11:30:32Z
   [isConnected] =>
)
```

WARNING: Version 7.31.0 of cURL (included in Zend Server 6.3.0) comes with a bug that prevents the script from running successfully. To determine the version of cURL, use: print_r(curl_version());

17. WordPress

A content management system (CMS) is a software interface that simplifies the creation and maintenance of a website. Automating tasks such as publishing and editing, it allows non-programmers to build a website without having to worry about any coding.

There are many CMSs currently available, but in this book, we shall focus on WordPress, the most popular CMS. Open source and originally a blogging system, WordPress has grown to become a full-fledged CMS, powering more than 60 million websites, as of 15 May 2014.

	All Websites	CMSs
[None]	63.1%	---
WordPress	22.1%	59.9%
Joomla	3.1%	8.3%
Drupal	1.9%	5.2%
Blogger	1.1%	3.0%
Magento	1.0%	2.6%
Others: TYPO3, vBulletin, PrestaShop, DataLife Engine, Bitrix, OpenCart, phpBB, Discuz!, ExpressionEngine, DotNetNuke, osCommerce, Shopify, Zen Cart, uCoz, SharePoint, Squarespace, Simple Machines Forum, Bigcommerce, PHP Link Directory, Weebly, Tumblr, IP.Board, xt:Commerce, CMS Made Simple, Wix, Telerik Sitefinity, Pligg, SPIP, Contao, Yahoo! Small Business, Concrete5, GitHub Pages, Movable Type, XenForo, CS-Cart, eZ Publish, Umbraco, Liferay, XOOPS, Media Wiki, Kentico, MyBB, Ning, Webs, Ektron, Plone, 3dcart, SilverStripe, Open Text, eSyndicat, InstantCMS, Shopware, NetCat, UMI.CMS, HostCMS, Google Sites, XpressEngine, TypePad, Homestead, PHP-Nuke, EpiServer CMS, WebsiteBaker CMS		
(courtesy of http://w3techs.com/technologies/overview/content_management/all)		

The online manual for WordPress, WordPress Codex, can be found at *codex.wordpress.org*.

17.1 Files Structure

17.1.1 Installation

Many web hosts support WordPress directly. A notable WordPress hosting provider is *wordpress.com* (free or paid), which is said to host half of all WordPress websites.

To install WordPress manually into your server, first download its latest package from *wordpress.org*. Unzip it to a folder in your server. If your entire site is meant to be run on WordPress, you should unzip the files to the root folder.

WordPress needs PHP and MySQL to run, so make sure you have a running web server and a MySQL instance. Using MySQL, create a database/schema for WordPress.

Notice the file *index.php*. From your browser, launch the site by pointing to the location containing that file. As this is the first time you use WordPress, the configuration file *wp-config.php* has not been set up. WordPress will guide you through the steps to set it up in your browser. Follow the steps and fill in the details about the database you are going to use.

Next, fill in the Site Title, the Username, the Password, and your E-mail. Note that this username and password are different from the username and password which you used for the database just now.

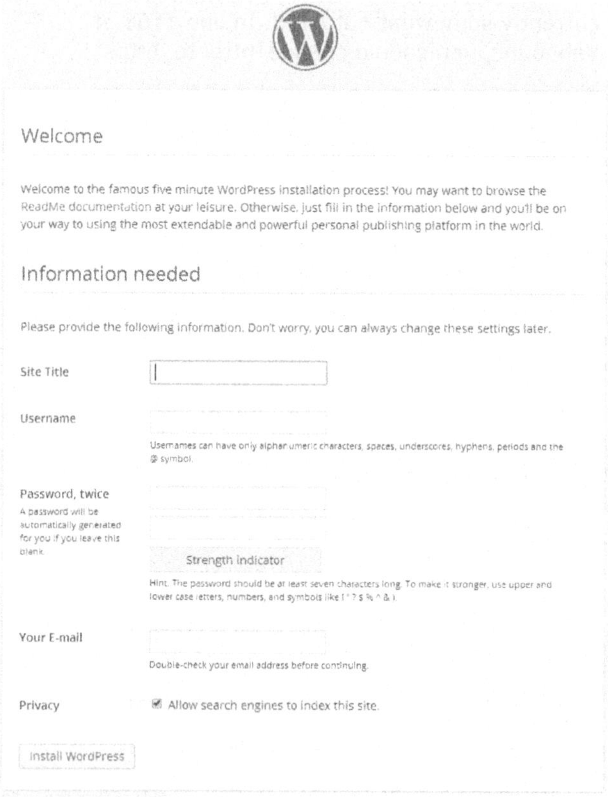

After you have installed WordPress, login to the administrator's panel at *[wordpress]/wp-admin/* via *[wordpress]/wp-login.php*. You can try posting a new post by clicking Posts->Add New. Before you publish the post, try to associate it with some tags and categories.

To view the site, simply enter in the address bar the WordPress root location.

17.1.2 Directories

After you have unzipped the WordPress package, you will notice three directories in the root directory.

wp-admin, *wp-includes*, and the root directories contain the core files. With some exceptions like *wp-config.php*, these core files should generally not be modified because an update of WordPress in future may overwrite these files and conflict with the changes you made. As the core is scrutinized by many experts, hacking it yourself may lead to security vulnerabilities. Hacking the core may also make the website unstable as the functions are inter-related.

wp-content holds all your custom files, including themes, plugins, and media. It controls content manipulation and presentation.

Contents such as pages and posts, along with metadata such as tag and category structures, are stored in the MySQL database.

17.1.3 wp-config.php

As an alternative to the installation method described in 17.1.1, you can actually edit *wp-config-sample.php* and save it as *wp-config.php*, provided you know how to define the various fields in it. You should also edit this file if you wish to change the database settings.

Beside the database settings, this file also contains settings for the authentication unique keys and salts, the localized language and the debugging mode. The debugging mode is set to false by default:

```
define('WP_DEBUG', false);
```

Enabling WP_DEBUG displays errors on the screen, rather than supppressing them with a white screen. You should always disable this option after you have done debugging because error messages might allow hackers to find vulnerabilities.

You can define additional options in *wp-config.php*:

This temporarily changes the WordPress site URL. You can use this during site maintenance. The first line should point to another WordPress site. The second line specifies the link for clicking the site title.

```
define('WP_SITEURL', 'http://mysite.com/temp');
define('WP_HOME', 'http://mysite.com/temp');
```

This redefines the location of the *wp-content* directory.

```
define('WP_CONTENT_DIR',
        $_SERVER['DOCUMENT_ROOT'].
        '/wordpress/new/wp-content');
define('WP_CONTENT_URL',
        'http://domain.com/wordpress/new/wp-content');
```

This redefines the location of the plugins directory. You should define these constants if you move the *wp-content* directory.

```
define('WP_CONTENT_DIR',
        $_SERVER['DOCUMENT_ROOT'].
        '/wordpress/new/wp-content/plugins');
define('WP_CONTENT_URL',
        'http://domain.com/wordpress/new/wp-content/plugins');
```

WordPress saves post revisions for each post and page. Edits are saved by clicking the Save or Publish button, and also by the built-in auto-save feature. The first line below disables post revisions. The second line specifies the maximum number of revisions to keep for each post or page.

```
define('WP_POST_REVISIONS', false);
define('WP_POST_REVISIONS', 5);
```

You can also set the auto-save interval, which is 60 seconds by default.

```
define('AUTOSAVE_INTERVAL',300);
```

You can save all database queries into a global array.

```
define('SAVEQUERIES', true);
```

To view the queries:

```
if (current_user_can('manage_options')){
   global $wpdb;
   print_r($wpdb->queries);
}
```

To enable logging, first create a *php_error.log* file in the root WordPress directory. Then, turn on logging and point to the file.

```
@ini_set('log_errors','On');
@ini_set('display_errors','Off');
@ini_set('error_log',
        '/public_html/wordpress/php_error.log');
```

This increases the memory limit allowed for WordPress.

```
define('WP_MEMORY_LIMIT', '32M');
```

Use the following to translate the display language. The first line will reference your .mo and .po files. The second line defines the directory containing the .mo files, which is defaulted to *wp-content/languages*.

```
define('WPLANG','en-GB');
define('LANGDIR','/wp-content/new/languages');
```

This allows you to share user accounts across multiple WordPress sites. You should set this prior to installing WordPress. The second line should be omitted if you wish the users to have different roles on each WordPress install.

```
define('CUSTOM_USER_TABLE', 'joined_users');
define('CUSTOM_USER_META_TABLE', 'joined_usermeta');
```

This sets the primary domain where cookies can be created and validated on all subdomains.

```
define('COOKIE_DOMAIN', '.domain.com');
define('COOKIEPATH','/');
define('SITECOOKIEPATH','/');
```

You may be asked for your FTP information, every time you try to install a plugin or theme, or update WordPress. You can save your FTP information directly:

```
define('FTP_USER','username');
define('FTP_PASS','password');
define('FTP_HOST','ftp.example.com:21');
```

You can also set various FTP/SSH options:

```
Define('FS_METHOD','ftpext');
define('FTP_BASE','/wordpress/');
define('FTP_CONTENT_DIR','/wordpress/wp-content');
define('FTP_PLUGIN_DIR','/wordpress/wp-content/plugins/');
define('FTP_PUBKEY','/home/username/.ssh/id_rsa.pub');
define('FTP_PRIVKEY','/home/username/.ssh/id_rsa');
define('FTP_SSL',false);
```

This overrides default file permissions in WordPress:

```
define('FS_CHMOD_FILE',0644);
define('FS_CHMOD_DIR',0755);
```

This enables caching, which is required by some plugins to work.

```
define('WP_CACHE',true);
```

This requires users to log in via HTTPS instead of HTTP.

```
define('FORCE_SSL_LOGIN',true);
```

This forces access to all admin pages to be encrypted with SSL.

```
define('FORCE_SSL_ADMIN',true);
```

The trash bin contains any deleted posts, pages, attachments and comments, allowing you to recover them after their deletion. The trash bin is emptied every 30 days by default. To disable the trash bin, set the following value to zero.

```
define('empty_trash_days',14);
```

This disables WordPress cron, which is used to execute scheduled tasks such as posting a scheduled post and checking for new versions of WordPress, themes, and plugins.

```
define('DISABLE_WP_CRON',true);
```

There are many constants that WordPress uses. To list them, run:

print_r(@get_defined_constants());

A great place to learn about these wp-config options can be found at:

http://codex.wordpress.org/Editing_wp-config.php

17.1.4 .htaccess

By default, WordPress refers to your pages and posts using ugly URLs that contain query strings. For instance, a default link to a post may look like:

http://example.com/wordpress/?p=1

You can direct WordPress to, instead, use 'meaningful' permalinks such as :

http://example.com/wordpress/2014/05/hello-world/

Using permalinks gives a boost to your site's SEO. It also enhances the forward compatibility, usability and sharing experience of your site.

To use the permalinks, simply log on to WordPress Dashboard, go to Settings -> Permalinks, choose a URL format, and click 'Save Changes'.

When you do this, WordPress creates a .htaccess file in your root WordPress directory. As you open the file, you will see something like the following:

Basically these lines check to see if the URL refers to any valid, existing file or directory. If it does, no rewriting is done and WordPress tries to load the file. If it does not, it means that it is a permalink, and WordPress runs index.php, where the URL string is converted to a MySQL query.

```
# BEGIN WordPress
<IfModule mod_rewrite.c>
RewriteEngine On
RewriteBase /wordpress/
RewriteRule ^index\.php$ - [L]
RewriteCond %{REQUEST_FILENAME} !-f
RewriteCond %{REQUEST_FILENAME} !-d
RewriteRule . /wordpress/index.php [L]
</IfModule>

# END WordPress
```

You can change the .htaccess file as you like. For instance, you may wish to create a separate .htaccess file in your wp-admin directory, and allow only specific IP addresses to access the directory. Refer to Chapter 14 for more information about .htaccess.

17.1.5 .maintenance

Before the WordPress automatic update process, a .maintenance file is created in the root directory. This displays to all visitors a message 'Briefly unavailable for scheduled maintenance. Check back in a minute.'

You can test this feature by creating the .maintenance file with the following line of code:

```
<?php $upgrading = time(); ?>
```

You can set a custom maintenance page by creating a *maintenance.php* file and placing it in your *wp-content* directory.

17.1.6 Dummy index.php

In your wp-content directory and some other directories, you will find a dummy index.php file with the following content:

```
<?php
// Silence is golden.
```

The existence of this file is actually essential as it prevents anyone from viewing the directory listing by typing the directory name in the address bar. Hackers may find vulnerabilities in a plugin at your site, for example, after seeing all your files and directories.

17.1.7 /uploads

When you upload your first image, WordPress auto-creates the *wp-content/uploads* directory. Before you can upload any files, you need to set the */wp-content* directory to be writable, and you should make it non-writable again after the uploading. If you cannot set the writable option, you can use plugins such as NextGen Gallery for this task.

17.1.8 /upgrade

WordPress auto-creates the *wp-content/upgrade* directory when you run the automatic update process. The new version of WordPress is downloaded from WordPress.org and stored in this folder. It is extracted here prior to the update.

17.1.9 /wp-includes/deprecated.php

When a new version of WordPress is released, certain core API functions may become deprecated. Generally, WordPress is known to have superior backwards compatibility, which allows deprecated functions to be used. However, a deprecated function may be removed in a future release, and should never be used.

All deprecated functions can be found in this file: */wp-includes/deprecated.php*.

17.1.10 APIs

WordPress contains many different APIs in /wp-includes/ which you can use to add custom code. All WordPress APIs are fully documented at:

http://codex.wordpress.org/Category:API

Plugin API
This is used for custom plugin development, utilizing Hooks, Actions, and Filters.

Widgets API
This is used to create and maintain widgets in your plugin. The widget will appear under Appearance -> Widgets SubPanel and can be used on any defined sidebar on your theme.

Shortcode API
A shortcode is a macro code added to a post. It allows a plugin to execute commands and display output in your post.

HTTP API
This is used to grab the content from an external URL. The methods to be tested in order are cURL, Streams, and FSockopen.

Settings API
This is used for developing custom options for your plugins and themes. This API enforces security internally, thereby saving you from worries about nonces, data validation and cross-site scripting attacks.

Options API
This provides an easy way to create, update, retrieve and delete option values.

Dashboard Widgets API
This is used for creating admin dashboard widgets.

Rewrite API
This is used for creating custom rewrite rules.

17.1.11 Site Migration

At times you may need to move your WordPress site from one site to another. For example, you may wish to move it from a local development site to a public live site. While the source codes are easy to move, moving the content (pages and posts) and configuration is not that direct.

WordPress uses fully qualified links instead of relative links in all the content and configuration. To change these links, use the wp-DBManager plugin by Lester Chan. Make a database backup of your site. Next, in the SQL page of the plugin, run the following:

```
UPDATE 'wp_posts' SET post_content =
   replace(post_content, 'href="http://oldsite.com/','href="/');
UPDATE 'wp_posts' SET post_content =
   replace(post_content, 'src="http://oldsite.com/','src="/');
UPDATE 'wp_posts' SET guid =
   replace(guid, 'http://oldsite.com/','http://newsite.com/');
```

Then, in the WordPress dashboard at your old site, go to Tools->Export to download the content file. Lastly, import this file at your new site by going to Tools->Import.

17.2 The Loop

If you open the template file:
[wordpress]\wp-content\themes\twentyfourteen\index.php
you will see something similar to the following:

```
<?php
/**
 * The main template file
 *
 * This is the most generic template file in a WordPress
 * theme and one of the two required files for a theme
 * (the other being style.css). It is used to display
 * a page when nothing more specific matches a query,
 * e.g., it puts together the home page when no home.php
 * file exists.
 *
 * @link http://codex.wordpress.org/Template_Hierarchy
 *
 * @package WordPress
 * @subpackage Twenty_Fourteen
 * @since Twenty Fourteen 1.0
 */

get_header(); ?>
```

```
<div id="main-content" class="main-content">

<?php
  if (is_front_page() &&
      twentyfourteen_has_featured_posts()){
        // Include the featured content template.
        get_template_part( 'featured-content' );
  }
?>

<div id="primary" class="content-area">
  <div id="content" class="site-content" role="main">
    <?php
      if ( have_posts() ) :
        // Start the Loop.
        while ( have_posts() ) : the_post();
          /*
           * Include the post format-specific
           * template for the content. If you want to
           * use this in a child theme, then include
           * a file called called content-___.php
           * (where ___ is the post format) and that
           * will be used instead.
           */
          get_template_part( 'content', get_post_format() );
        endwhile;
          // Previous/next post navigation.
          twentyfourteen_paging_nav();
      else :
        // If no content, include the "No posts found" template.
          get_template_part( 'content', 'none' );
      endif;
    ?>
  </div><!-- #content -->
</div><!-- #primary -->
<?php get_sidebar( 'content' ); ?>
</div><!-- #main-content -->

<?php
get_sidebar();
get_footer();
```

The while loop, affectionately called the Loop, displays all the relevant posts in your main page. It represents the heart of a theme. You can modify this loop to customize the presentation of your posts.

17.2.1 Template Tags

To begin with, you can use various template tags, as documented in *codex.wordpress.org/Template_Tags/*. Some commonly used template tags are:

- the_permalink()
- the_title()
- the_ID()
- the_content()
- the_excerpt()
- the_time()
- the_author()
- the_tags()
- the_category()
- edit_post_link()
- comments_popup_link()

If you replace the Loop with the following, your site will only display the titles of your posts. Clicking a title links to the post.

```
while ( have_posts() ) : the_post();
  echo "<a href='";
  the_permalink();
  echo "'>";
  the_title();
  echo "</a><br/>";
endwhile;
```

If you use the <!--more--> tag in your post, or insert the Read More tag in the editor, the_content() will only display the teaser in the main page.

```
while ( have_posts() ) : the_post();
  the_title('<h1>','</h1>');
  the_content("Read more");
endwhile;
```

17.2.2 Global Variables

Intead of template tags, you can also use some built-in global variables to access various information about a post. You should always avoid modifying the values of these global variables.

Global Variable	Description
$post	Information about the post.
$authordata	Information about the author of the post.
$userdata	Information about the logged-in user.
$is_lynx	Is the browser Lynx?
$is_gecko	Is the browser Firefox?
$is_IE	Is the browser Internet Explorer?
$is_opera	Is the browser Opera?
$is_NS4	Is the browser Netscape?
$is_safari	Is the browser Safari?
$is_chrome	Is the browser Chrome?
$is_iphone	Is the browser iPhone?
$is_mobile	Is the device a smartphone or a tablet?
$is_apache	Is the server Apache?
$is_IIS	Is the server IIS?

Try the following:

```
global $post;
echo "<pre>";
while ( have_posts() ) : the_post();
  the_title('<h1>','</h1>');
  print_r($post);
endwhile;
```

$post

```
WP_Post Object
(
    [ID] => 1
    [post_author] => 1
    [post_date] => 2014-05-15 09:26:54
    [post_date_gmt] => 2014-05-15 09:26:54
    [post_content] => Welcome to WordPress. This is your first
post. Edit or delete it, then start blogging!
    [post_title] => Hello world!
    [post_excerpt] =>
    [post_status] => publish
    [comment_status] => open
    [ping_status] => open
    [post_password] =>
    [post_name] => hello-world
    [to_ping] =>
    [pinged] =>
    [post_modified] => 2014-05-15 09:26:54
    [post_modified_gmt] => 2014-05-15 09:26:54
    [post_content_filtered] =>
    [post_parent] => 0
    [guid] => http://binarybehemoth.com/wordpress/?p=1
    [menu_order] => 0
```

```
    [post_type] => post
    [post_mime_type] =>
    [comment_count] => 2
    [filter] => raw
)
```

$authordata or $userdata

```
WP_User Object
(
    [data] => stdClass Object
        (
            [ID] => 1
            [user_login] => moonvalley
            [user_pass] =>
$P$BeqgoG3agGSExbwTO4U928Ns.2yoUz.
            [user_nicename] => moonvalley
            [user_email] => fragment_shader@yahoo.com
            [user_url] =>
            [user_registered] => 2014-05-15 09:26:54
            [user_activation_key] =>
            [user_status] => 0
            [display_name] => moonvalley
        )

    [ID] => 1
    [caps] => Array
        (
            [administrator] => 1
        )

    [cap_key] => wp_capabilities
    [roles] => Array
        (
            [0] => administrator
        )

    [allcaps] => Array
        (
            [switch_themes] => 1
            [edit_themes] => 1
            [activate_plugins] => 1
            [edit_plugins] => 1
            [edit_users] => 1
            [edit_files] => 1
            [manage_options] => 1
            [moderate_comments] => 1
            [manage_categories] => 1
            [manage_links] => 1
            [upload_files] => 1
            [import] => 1
            [unfiltered_html] => 1
            [edit_posts] => 1
            [edit_others_posts] => 1
            [edit_published_posts] => 1
            [publish_posts] => 1
            [edit_pages] => 1
            [read] => 1
            [level_10] => 1
            [level_9] => 1
            [level_8] => 1
            [level_7] => 1
            [level_6] => 1
            [level_5] => 1
            [level_4] => 1
            [level_3] => 1
            [level_2] => 1
            [level_1] => 1
            [level_0] => 1
            [edit_others_pages] => 1
            [edit_published_pages] => 1
            [publish_pages] => 1
            [delete_pages] => 1
            [delete_others_pages] => 1
            [delete_published_pages] => 1
            [delete_posts] => 1
            [delete_others_posts] => 1
            [delete_published_posts] => 1
            [delete_private_posts] => 1
            [edit_private_posts] => 1
            [read_private_posts] => 1
            [delete_private_pages] => 1
            [edit_private_pages] => 1
            [read_private_pages] => 1
            [delete_users] => 1
            [create_users] => 1
            [unfiltered_upload] => 1
            [edit_dashboard] => 1
            [update_plugins] => 1
            [delete_plugins] => 1
            [install_plugins] => 1
            [update_themes] => 1
            [install_themes] => 1
            [update_core] => 1
            [list_users] => 1
            [remove_users] => 1
            [add_users] => 1
            [promote_users] => 1
            [edit_theme_options] => 1
            [delete_themes] => 1
            [export] => 1
            [administrator] => 1
        )

    [filter] =>
)
```

17.2.3 Generic Functions

You can access generic information outside the loop using various functions. The functions for WordPress are fully documented at: *http://codex.wordpress.org/Function_Reference/.*

wp_list_pages() displays a list of pages as links. **wp_list_categories()** displays a list of categories as links. **wp_list_pages()** displays the links saved in the Links SubPanel. **wp_tag_cloud()** displays a tag cloud from all tags. **get_permalink()** returns the permalink of a post. **next_posts_link()** links to previous posts. **previous_posts_link()** links to next posts.

These two codes are identical, in that they list the page titles as links.

```
echo "<ul>";
wp_list_pages('title_li=');
echo "</ul>";
```

```
wp_page_menu('show_home=1&menu_class=my-menu
&sort_column=menu_order');
```

```
<ul>
  <li class="page_item page-item-2">
    <a href="http://binarybehemoth.com/wordpress/sample-
page/">Sample Page</a></li>
  <li class="page_item page-item-7">
    <a href="http://binarybehemoth.com/wordpress/test-
page/">Test Page</a></li>
</ul>
```

get_post($i) obtains a post object (like the global variable $post in the previous section) with the post ID $i. After calling this function, you can setup your global post data and template tags with **setup_postdata($p)**

```
$myPost = get_post(1);
echo 'Post Title:'.$myPost->post_title.'<br/>';
echo 'Post Content:'.$myPost->post_content.'<br/>';
setup_postdata($myPost);
the_author();
```

get_author_meta($s,$i) obtains information $s about an author with ID $i. **get_post_meta($i)** retrieves metadata about a post with ID $i. **get_the_title($i)** obtains the title for the post with ID $i.

```
the_author_meta('user_email',1);
echo "<br/>";
print_r(get_post_meta(11));
echo "<br/>";
echo get_the_title(1);
```

17.2.4 WP_Query

You can create a custom loop by instantiating a WP-Query object.

This is similar to the default Loop, except that it only shows three posts per page.

```
$myPosts = new WP_Query('posts_per_page=3');
while ($myPosts->have_posts()){
  $myPosts->the_post();
  get_template_part( 'content', get_post_format() );
}
```

When you call the query function, $myPosts->query() converts the parameters into an SQL statement via the function $myPosts->get_posts(), which then executes the query against the MySQL database and extracts the content you have requested. Conditional tags such as is_home() and is_single() are set up. The returned posts array is cached to lighten load on the database server in future.

When formulating the query, you can pass various parameters to WP_Query(). These parameters are documented at: codex.wordpress.org/Class_Reference/WP_Query#Parameters

You may wish to try the following:

```
$myPosts =  new WP_Query(
                      array( 'post_type' => 'post',
                             'post__in' => array( 1, 5, 11) ) );
$myPosts =  new WP_Query(
                      'monthnum=5&day=18&year=2014');
$myPosts = new WP_Query( 'author=1,2,38' );
$myPosts = new WP_Query( 'author_name=ali' );
$myPosts = new WP_Query( 'cat=1,2,3&offset=1' );
$myPosts = new WP_Query( 'p=1' );
$myPosts = new WP_Query( 'tag=songs,books' ); // or
$myPosts = new WP_Query( 'tag=songs+books' ); // and
$myPosts = new WP_Query( 'orderby=title&order=ASC' );
```

Note that the argument can be an array of parameters or a string of parameters concatenated by &.

To implement paging, you need to trick WordPress into using a modified global variable $wp_query, an instance of WP_Query and the default data store for several operations.

```
$tmp = $wp_query;
$paged =(get_query_var('paged'))?get_query_var('paged'):1;
$wp_query = new WP_Query('
                        posts_per_page=10&paged='.$paged);
while ($wp_query->have_posts()): $wp_query->the_post();
  echo "<h2><a href='";
  the_permalink();
  echo "'>";
  the_title();
  echo "</a></h2>";
  the_excerpt();
endwhile;
echo"<div class='navigation'><div class='alignleft'>";
previous_posts_link('&laquo; Previous');
echo "</div><div class='alignright'>";
next_posts_link('Next &raquo;');
echo "</div></div>";
$wp_query=$tmp;
```

17.2.5 Query Functions

Instead of WP_Query, you can also use some other functions to obtain posts for a loop. **query_posts()** modifies the global variable $wp_posts. **get_posts()** returns an array of posts. query_posts() executes another database query, invalidating all cached results from the first, default query.

wp_reset_query() restores $post to the current post in the query. This function actually calls **wp_reset_postdata()**, and destroys the previous query before resetting it. In general, wp_reset_query() should always be called after a query_posts() Loop and wp_reset_postdata() should be used after a WP_Query or get_posts() custom Loop. Otherwise, conditional tags such as is_home() or is_page() may not be subsequently valid.

These two codes are somewhat identical.

```
global $query_string;
query_posts($query_string."&orderby=title&order=ASC");
while ( have_posts() ) : the_post();
  the_ID();
  get_template_part( 'content', get_post_format() );
endwhile;
wp_reset_query();
```

```
$myPosts = get_posts(["orderby"=>"title","order"=>"ASC"]);
foreach ($myPosts as $post){
  setup_postdata($post);
  echo "<h1><a href='";
  the_permalink();
  echo "'>";
  the_title();
  echo "</a></h1>";
  the_content();
}
wp_reset_postdata();
```

rewind_posts() is used to reset the post query and loop counter.

```
while ( have_posts() ) : the_post();
  the_title();
  echo "<br/>";
endwhile;
rewind_posts();
while ( have_posts() ) : the_post();
  the_title();
  echo "<br/>";
  the_content();
  echo "<br/>";
endwhile;
```

Advanced queries can be formulated with the **meta_compare** and **meta_query** parameters. Refer to Codex for more information.

17.3 Database

WordPress stores its content in the MySQL database that you specified at the beginning of the installation. You can query the database directly using traditional means, or using the $wpdb global variable.

17.3.1 Built-in Tables

Although plugins and themes can create custom tables, WordPress uses 11 default tables. The structures of these tables are documented at: *http://codex.wordpress.org/Database_Description*

wp_posts		
ID	bigint(20) unsigned	PRIMARY, IND Pt4, auto_increment
post_author	bigint(20) unsigned	INDEX
post_date	datetime	INDEX Pt3
post_date_gmt	datetime	
post_content	longtext	
post_title	text	
post_excerpt	text	
post_status	varchar(20)	INDEX Pt2
comment_status	varchar(20)	
ping_status	varchar(20)	
post_password	varchar(20)	
post_name	varchar(200)	INDEX
to_ping	text	
pinged	text	
post_modified	datetime	
post_modified_gmt	datetime	
post_content_filtered	longtext	
post_parent	bigint(20) unsigned	INDEX
guid	varchar(255)	
menu_order	int(11)	
post_type	varchar(20)	INDEX Pt1
post_mime_type	varchar(100)	
comment_count	bigint(20)	
Values for post_status: publish, inherit, pending, private, future, draft, trash		
Values for post_type: post, page		
wp_postmeta		
meta_id	bigint(20) unsigned	PRIMARY, auto_increment
post_id	bigint(20) unsigned	INDEX
meta_key	varchar(255)	INDEX
meta_value	longtext	

wp_users		
ID	bigint(20) unsigned	PRIMARY, auto_increment
user_login	varchar(60)	INDEX
user_pass	varchar(64)	
user_nicename	varchar(50)	INDEX
user_email	varchar(100)	
user_url	varchar(100)	
user_registered	datetime	
user_activation_key	varchar(60)	
user_status	int(11)	
display_name	varchar(250)	
wp_usermeta		
umeta_id	bigint(20) unsigned	PRIMARY, auto_increment
user_id	bigint(20) unsigned	INDEX
meta_key	varchar(255)	INDEX
meta_value	longtext	

wp_comments		
comment_ID	bigint(20) unsigned	PRIMARY, auto_increment
comment_post_ID	bigint(20) unsigned	INDEX
comment_author	tinytext	
comment_author_email	varchar(100)	
comment_author_url	varchar(200)	
comment_author_IP	varchar(100)	
comment_date	datetime	
comment_date_gmt	datetime	INDEX, INDEX Pt2
comment_content	text	
comment_karma	int(11)	
comment_approved	varchar(20)	INDEX, INDEX Pt1
comment_agent	varchar(255)	
comment_type	varchar(20)	
comment_parent	bigint(20) unsigned	IND
user_id	bigint(20) unsigned	
wp_commentmeta		
meta_id	bigint(20) unsigned	PRIMARY, auto_increment
comment_id	bigint(20) unsigned	INDEX
meta_key	varchar(255)	INDEX
meta_value	longtext	

wp_terms		
term_id	bigint(20) unsigned	PRIMARY, auto_increment
name	varchar(200)	INDEX
slug	varchar(200)	UNIQUE
term_group	bigint(10)	
wp_term_taxonomy		
term_taxonomy_id	bigint(20) unsigned	PRIMARY, auto_increment
term_id	bigint(20) unsigned	UNIQUE Pt1
taxonomy	varchar(32)	INDEX UNQIUE Pt2
description	longtext	
parent	bigint(20) unsigned	
count	bigint(20)	
wp_term_relationships		
object_id	bigint(20) unsigned	PRIMARY Pt1
term_taxonomy_id	bigint(20) unsigned	PRIMARY Pt2, INDEX
term_order	int(11)	

wp_links		
link_id	bigint(20) unsigned	PRIMARY, auto_increment
link_url	varchar(255)	
link_name	varchar(255)	
link_image	varchar(255)	
link_target	varchar(25)	
link_description	varchar(255)	
link_visible	varchar(20)	INDEX
link_owner	bigint(20) unsigned	
link_rating	int(11)	
link_updated	datetime	
link_rel	varchar(255)	
link_notes	mediumtext	
link_rss	varchar(255)	

wp_options		
option_id	bigint(20) unsigned	PRIMARY, auto_increment
option_name	varchar(64)	UNQIUE
option_value	longtext	
autoload	varchar(20)	

17.3.2 $wpdb

To use the WordPress database global variable $wpdb, simply start with:

    global $wpdb;

Try to learn from these examples:

```
$wpdb->query($wpdb->prepare(
"INSERT INTO $wpdb->myTable(a,b,c) VALUES (%d,%s,%s)",
1,"Hello","World"));
```
```
$cnt = $wpdb->get_var($wpdb->prepare(
            "SELECT COUNT(*) FROM $wpdb->comments;"));
```
```
$p = $wpdb->get_row($wpdb->prepare(
            "SELECT * FROM $wpdb->posts WHERE ID=10"));
echo $p->post_title;
```
```
$p = $wpdb->get_row($wpdb->prepare(
  "SELECT * FROM $wpdb->posts WHERE ID=10"),ARRAY_A);
print_r($p);
```
```
$myPosts = $wpdb->get_results($wpdb->prepare(
"SELECT ID, post_title FROM $wpdb->posts WHERE
post_status='publish'"));

foreach ($myPosts as $p){
   echo $p->post_title."<br/>";
}
```
```
$wpdb->insert($wpdb->myTable,
              ['field1' => 'value1', 'field2' => 'value2']);
```
```
$wpdb->update($wpdb->posts,
               ['post_title'=>'test', 'post_content'=>'ABC'],
               ['ID' => 100]);   // where ID=100
```
```
$wpdb->show_errors();
$wpdb->insert($wpdb->myTable,
              ['field1' => 'value1', 'field2' => 'value2']);
$wpdb->print_error();
$wpdb->hide_errors();
```
```
var_dump($wpdb->num_queries); // total number of queries
var_dump($wpdb->num_rows);  // no. of rows for last query
var_dump($wpdb->last_result); // most recent query results
var_dump($wpdb->last_query); // most recent query
var_dump($wpdb->col_info);// column info. for the last query
```
```
var_dump($wpdb->queries); // all queries executed
  // define('SAVEQUERIES', true);   // in wp-config.php
```

Notice that we reference a table in a query using a syntax like *$wpdb->myTable*. This translates to *wp_myTable* if *wp_* is the table prefix.

17.4 Custom Additions

17.4.1 Post Type

WordPress predefines five post types, namely Post, Page, Attachment, Revision and Nav Menus. You can define your custom post type in your theme's functions.php file.

```
add_action('init','register_Products');
function register_Products(){
  $labels = ['name' => 'Products',
             'singular_name' => 'Product',
             'add_new' => 'Add New Product',
             'add_new_item' => 'Edit Product',
             'edit_item' => 'Edit Product',
             'new_item' => 'New Product',
             'all_items' => 'All Products',
             'view_item' => 'View Product',
             'search_items' => 'Search Products',
             'not_found' => 'No products found',
             'not_found_in_trash' =>
                             'No products found in Trash',
             'parent_item_colon' => '',
             'menu_name' => 'Products'];
  $args = ['public' => true,
           'has_archive' => true,
           'taxonomies' => ['category'],
           'rewrite' => ['slug'=>'product'],
           'supports' => ['title','editor',
                         'author','thumbnail','comments'],
           'labels' => $labels];
  register_post_type('products',$args);
}
```

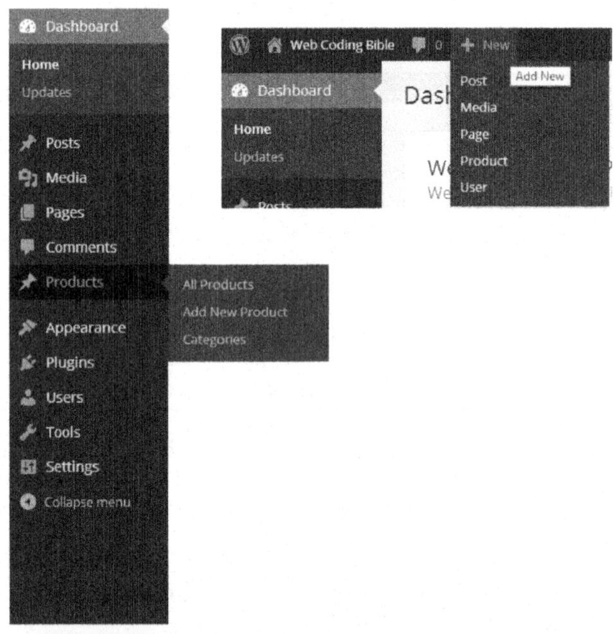

$args in register_post_type()
'public' specifies whether the post type is available on the admin dashboard. The default is false. 'show_ui', 'exclude_from_search', 'publicly_queryable', and 'show_in_nav_menus' inherit their default values here.
'show_ui' sets whether to create a default user interface in the admin dashboard.
'publicly_queryable' sets whether the content can be publicly queried on the front end.
'exclude_from_search' sets whether to exclude post type entries from the WordPress search results.
'show_in_nav_menus' determines if the post type is available for selection in the menu management feature.
'supports' defines what meta boxes appear when creating or editing a new post type entry. The options available are: 'title', 'editor', 'author', 'thumbnail', 'excerpt', 'comments', 'trackbacks', 'custom-fields', 'page-attributes', 'revisions', 'post-formats'.
'labels' sets various labels for your post type in the admin dashboard'.
'hierarchical' defines if the post type is hierarchical.
'has_archive' enables your post type to have an archive page, which displays a list of your post type entries.
'can_export' determines if the post type can be exported using Tools->Export.
'taxonomies' specifies an array of registered taxonomies to attach to the post type. You can pass in 'category' and 'post_tag' to attach the default Categories and Tags taxonomies.
'menu_position' sets the position of the custom post type menu in the admin menu.

'menu_icon' sets an icon for your post type. The default is the posts icon.
'show_in_menu' determines whether to display the admin menu for the post type. A string specifying a top-level page such as edit.php?post_type=page can be passed. You can also set the string to the mnu_slug parameter to add the custom post type as a submenu item to an existing custom menu.
'show_in_admin_bar' sets whether to show the post type in the admin bar.
'capability_type' names a string or an array of capabilities.
'capabilities' specifies an array of custom capabilities required for editing, deleting, viewing, and publishing posts.
'query_var' sets the query variable for posts of the post type.
'rewrite' creates unique permalinks for this post type. The argument can be set to true, false, or an array of values: • 'slug' sets a custom permalink slug. The default is the value for $post_type. • 'with_front' sets whether the post type should use the front base from the permalink settings. • 'pages' sets whether the permalink provides for pagination. The default is true. • 'feeds' sets whether a feed permalink will be built for this post type. The default is the value of 'has_archive'.

To display the contents of a post type, edit the Loop in the theme's index.html. If you use the previous example, you should not use the slug parameter in $args for the following example to work.

```
$args = ['post_per_page' => '-1',
         'post_type' => 'products'];
$myProducts = new WP_Query($args);
while ($myProducts->have_posts()){
  $myProducts->the_post();
  echo "<a href='";
  the_permalink();
  echo "'>";
  the_title();
  echo "</a><br/>";
}
wp_reset_postdata();
```

If the 'has_archive' argument is enabled, you can create an archive template file that will display all of your custom post type entries by default. The file must be named archive-products.php for the post type Products. You can also define a single template for a post type entry. This template will be loaded when you visit a single entry of the post type. This file must be named single-products.php for the post type Products.

To list all custom post types that are publicly available, use the following:

```
$args = ['public'=>true, '_builtin'=>false];
$post_types = get_post_types($args,'names','and');
foreach ($post_types as $post_type){
  echo "<p>".$post_type."</p>";
}
```

To determine the post type of a post:

```
echo get_post_type($post->ID);
```

To determine if a post type exists:

```
echo post_type_exists('products');
```

To add supports for a post type:

```
add_post_type_support('products',
                      ['thumbnail','comments']);
```

To change the post type of a post:

```
set_post_type($post->ID, 'products');
```

17.4.2 Taxonomy

WordPress has three built-in taxonomies:

1. **Category:** hierarchical label for posts
2. **Tag:** non-hierarchical label for posts
3. **Link category:** bucket for similar links

To display all posts along with all taxonomy terms:

```
SELECT wt.name, wp.post_title, wp.post_date
  FROM wp_terms wt
  INNER JOIN wp_term_taxonomy wtt
    ON wt.term_id=wtt.term_id
  INNER JOIN wp_term_relationships wtr
    ON wtt.term_taxonomy_id = wtr.term_taxonomy_id
  INNER JOIN wp_posts wp ON wtr.object_id = wp.ID
  WHERE wp.post_type = 'post'
```

To define a custom taxonomy 'type' for the post type 'products', add to the theme's functions.php:

```
add_action('init','register_Product_Type');
function register_Product_Type(){
  $labels = ['name' => 'Type',
             'singular_name' => 'Types',
             'search_items' => 'Search Types',
             'all_items' => 'All Types',
             'parent_item' => 'Parent Type',
             'parent_item_colon' => 'Parent Type:',
             'edit_item' => 'Edit Type',
             'update_item' => 'Update Type',
             'add_new_item' => 'Add New Type',
             'new_item_name' => 'New Type Name',
             'menu_name' => 'Type'];
  $args = ['labels' => $labels,
           'hierarchical' => true,
           'query_var' => true,
           'rewrite' => true];
  register_taxonomy('type', 'products', $args);
}
```

After you have done this, you will notice that you can define a 'type' taxonomy when you add or edit a 'product'.

$args in register_taxonomy()
'public' specifies whether the taxonomy is publicly available for the admin dashboard. The default is true. 'show_ui' and 'show_in_nav_menus' inherit their default values here.
'show_ui' specifies whether to create a default UI in the admin dashboard for managing this taxonomy.
'show_in_nav_menus' specifies whether the post type is available for selection in the menu management feature.
'show_tagcloud' sets whether to allow the built-in Tag Cloud widget to use this taxonomy. The default is the value in 'show_ui'.
'hierarchical' specifies whether to make the taxonomy hierarchical. The default is false.
'update_count_call_callback' specifies the function name that will be called when a term in your taxonomy gets a count update. The default is none.
'query_var' enables the public query var. Acceptable values are true, false, or a string set to a custom query var value.

'rewrite' specifies the URL parsing rules for permalinks referring to this taxonomy. Acceptable values are true, false, or an array:

- 'slug' sets a custom permalink slug.
- 'with_front' specifies whether to use the front base from your permalink settings.
- 'hierarchical'

'labels' specifies the various labels to be displayed for this taxonomy. Beside those listed in the example, there are other labels (the first three are not meant for hierarchical taxonomies): 'separate_items_with_commas', 'add_or_remove_items', 'choose_from_most_used', and 'popular_items'.

To display a tag cloud showing the taxonomy terms:

```
wp_tag_cloud(['taxonomy'=>'type', 'number'=>10]);
```

To display products for a specific taxonomy term in the Loop:

```
$args = ['post_type' => 'products',
         'tax_query' = [['taxonomy'=>'type',
                         'field' => 'slug',
                         'terms' => 'weapon']]];
$products = new WP_Query($args);
while ($products->have_posts()): $products->the_post();
  echo '<p>'.get_the_title().'</p>';
end while;
wp_reset_postdata();
```

To display the custom taxonomy terms assigned to each post, add this to the loop:

```
echo get_the_term_list($post->ID, 'type' ,'Product Type:',
                       ', ','');
```

To retrieve an array of taxonomy values:

```
print_r(get_terms('type'));
```

17.4.3 Metadata

Also known as Custom Fields, Metadata refers to additional pieces of information attached to a post. All post metadata is stored in the wp_postmeta table in the database.

If the 'supports' argument of a custom post type contains the 'custom-fields' value, when you edit the custom post, a meta box will appear, allowing you to set the metadata.

To manipulate metadata in your code, use the following:

add_post_meta($post_id, $key, $value, $unique)
update_post_meta($post_id, $key, $value, $prev_value)
delete_post_meta($post_id, $key, $value)
get_post_meta($post_id, $key, $single)
get_post_custom($post_id)

```
add_post_meta(24, 'colors', 'orange', false);
add_post_meta(24, 'colors', 'green', false);
update_post_meta(24, 'colors', 'brown', 'green');
$product_colors = get_post_meta(24, 'colors', false);
print_r($product_colors);
echo "<br/>";
print_r(get_post_custom(24)); // array of all metadata
```

17.5 Plugins

Wordpress can be extended by plugins. You can add a plugin written by others by navigating to Plugins->Add New.

To elucidate how to use various plugin features, we break them down into separate plugin files in the codes package that comes along with this book. Note that you can always combine these features within a plugin.

17.5.1 Packaging

All plugin files can be found at *[wordpress]\wp-content\plugins*. You should organise your plugin files and other associated files in directories. Wordpress will walk through the subdirectories, find all of them, and list them as Installed Plugins.

A plugin file is a PHP file that begins with a comment header that looks like:

```
<?php
/*
Plugin Name: Cars: Initialization
Plugin URI: http://example.com/wp-content/plugins/cars
Description: Activation and initialization.
Version: 1.0
Author: Chong Lip Phang
Author URI: https://www.facebook.com/chong.lipphang
License: GPLv2
*/

/* Copyright 2015 Chong Lip Phang
(email : fragment_shader@yahoo.com)
  This program is free software; you can redistribute it and/or
modify it under the terms of the GNU General Public License
as published by the Free Software Foundation; either version
2 of the License, or (at your option) any later version.
  This program is distributed in the hope that it will be useful,
but WITHOUT ANY WARRANTY; without even the implied
warranty of MERCHANTABILITY or FITNESS FOR A
PARTICULAR PURPOSE. See the GNU General Public License
for more details.
  You should have received a copy of the GNU General Public
License along with this program; if not, write to the Free
Software Foundation, Inc., 51 Franklin St, Fifth Floor, Boston,
MA 02110-1301 USA
*/
```

The only required line is the Plugin Name.

Cars: Initialization
Deactivate | Edit
Activation and initialization.
Version 1.0 | By Chong Lip Phang | Visit plugin site

17.5.2 Conversion Functions

Before we implement the core of a plugin, we shall see several special functions that may be used anywhere within a plugin.

Internationalization, sometimes shortened to 'i18n', is the process of making your plugin or theme ready for translation. There are many plugins in the plugins repository that allow you to perform translation on a site. Examples include qTranslate, Polylang, and Multilingual Press.

__(string,textDomain) makes *string* translatable. Note that splitting the string with multitple __() may result in awkward translations.

```
printf(__('I say %1$d is a number.', 'test'), $num);
```

_e(string, textDomain) echoes *string* directly.

```
_e('Hello World', 'test');
```

_n(singularString, pluralString, num, textDomain) can be used to handle plural nouns.

```
printf(_n('There is %d car',
          'There are %d cars',
          $count, 'test'),
       $count);
```

_x(string, context, textDomain) allows you to specify the context information as a comment for the translator.

```
echo _x('Editor', 'person', 'test');
echo _x('Editor', 'program', 'test');
```

After you have prepared your plugin for translation, you must load the localization file to perform the translation using load_plugin_textdomain(textDomain, [DEPRECATED], path), where *path* is the path to your translation files in the /plugins directory.

```
add_action('init','test_init');
function test_init(){
  load_plugin_textdomain('test',false,
     plugin_basename(dirname(__FILE__).
                    '/localization'));
}
```

To make a Wordpress site portable, you should never hard-code any paths.

This returns the full local server path of the current plugin file, eg 'C:\Program Files\Zend\Apache2\htdocs\wordpress\wp-content\plugins\cars'.

```
plugin_dir_path(__FILE__)
```

This returns the full URL of 'images/img.png' relative to the current plugin file, eg. http://binarybehemoth.com/wordpress/wp-content/plugins/cars/smiley.png

```
plugins_url('images/img.png', __FILE__);
```

site_url() returns the site URL such as http://example.com.

home_url() returns the home URL such as http://example.com.

admin_url() returns the admin URL such as http://example.com/wp-admin.

includes_url() returns the includes URL such as http://example.com/wp-include/

content_url() returns the content URL such as http://example.com/wp-content

wp_upload_url() returns an array with location information on the configured upload directory.

Nonces, or 'numbers used once', stop unauthorized access in requests (saving options, form posts, Ajax requests, actions) by generating a secret key.

This generates a hidden form field within the <form> tags. The first parameter is a description of the nonce. The second parameter is a unique name for the field. An error will be generated if the nonce secret key generated by wp_nonce_field() does not match that generated by check_admin_referrer().

```
<form method="post">
  <?php wp_nonce_field('cars_form_save', 'cars_nonce'); ?>
  Enter the car number: <input type="text" name="text"/>
  <input type="submit" name="submit" value="Save"/>
</form>
```

```
function cars_register(){
  if (isset($_POST['submit'])){
    check_admin_referrer('cars_form_save', 'cars_nonce');
    // nonce passed, continue to do other stuff
  }
}
```

Nonces can also be used on links.

```
<a href="
  <?php echo wp_nonce_url($link, 'cars_nonce_url'); ?>
"> Delete </a>
```

```
function cars_register(){
  if (isset($_GET['action'])){
    check_admin_referrer('cars_nonce_url');
    // nonce passed, continue to do other stuff
  }
}
```

Wordpress allows you to validate and sanitize user input with functions that have the form esc_attr_e(). 'attr' specifies the escaping context, and can be 'attr', 'html', 'textarea', 'js', 'sql', 'url', or 'url_raw'. '_e' is an optional suffix that echoes the translated text. If '__' is used in place of '_e', no output will be resulted.

```
<input type="text" name="first_name"
       value="<?php echo esc_attr($text); ?>"/>
```

```
<?php esc_html($text); ?>
```

```
<textarea name="details">
  <?php echo esc_textarea($text); ?>
</textarea>
```

```
<script>
  var v='<?php echo esc_js($text); ?>';
</script>
```

```
<?php esc_sql__($sql); ?>
```

```
<a href="<?php esc_url_e($url); ?>">
```

Use wp_kses() to filter out forbidden tags and attributes.

```
$allowed_tags = array(
  'b' => array(),
  'a' => array(
    'href' => array(),
    'title' => array()
  )
);
echo wp_kses($html, $allowed_tags);
```

There are other functions that allow you to sanitize input such as intval(), absint(), sanitize_text_field(), and sanitize_email(). More information about data validation can be found at http://codex.wordpress.org/Data_Validation.

17.5.3 Hooks

Hooks allow you to execute functions at specific points of time. Action hooks are triggered by events, whereas filter hooks are used to modify content before saving it to the database or displaying it to the screen. There are numerous hooks but only the popular hooks are described here.

Filter hooks:
add_filter($hook, $callback, $priority, $args_num)

$hook can be:

- 'the_content': applied to the content of the post or page before displaying.
- 'the_content_rss': applied to the content of the post or page for RSS inclusion.
- 'the_title': applied to the post or page title before displaying.
- 'comment_text': applied to the comment text before displaying.
- 'wp_title': applied to the page <title> before displaying.
- 'the_permalink': applied to the permalink URL.
- 'default_content': sets the default content when creating a new post or page.

$callback is the function that accepts the content as a parameter and returns the adjusted text.

$priority is an integer that specifies the execution order when multiple hooks are attached to the same filter.

$args_num is the number of arguments the functions accepts.

```
<?php
add_filter('the_content', 'profanity_filter');
function profanity_filter($content){
  $profanities=array('fuck', 'shit');
  $content=str_ireplace($profanities, '[censored]', $content);
  return $content;
}
?>
```

Action hooks:
add_action($hook,$callback,$priority,$args_num)

$hook can be:

- 'publish_post': triggered when a new post is published.
- 'create_category': triggered when a new category is created.
- 'switch_theme': triggered when you switch themes'.
- 'admin_head': triggered in the <head> section of the admin dashboard.
- 'wp_head': triggered in the <head> section of your theme.
- 'wp_footer': triggered in the footer section of your theme usually directly before the </body> tag. An analytic tracking code is often added here.
- 'init': triggered after WordPress has finished loading, but before any headers are sent. Good place to intercept $_GET and $_POST HTML requests.
- 'admin_init': same as 'init' but only runs on admin dashboard pages.
- 'user_register': triggered when a new user is created'.
- 'comment_post': triggered when a new comment is created.

$callback specifies the function to call when a hook is triggered.

$priority is an integer that specifies the execution order when multiple hooks are attached to the same hook.

$args_num is the number of arguments the function accepts.

```
<?php
add_action('wp_head','custom_css');
function custom_css(){
?>
  <style type="text/css">
  a { font-size:16px; }
  </style>
<?php
}
?>
```

Activation hook:
register_activation_hook($file, $callback)

This function is executed when your plugin is activated in Settings.

```
<?php
register_activation_hook(__FILE__, 'cars_activate');
function cars_activate(){
  global $wp_version;
  if (version_compare($wp_version, '3.5', '<')){
    wp_die('This plugin requires Wordpress version 3.5 or
higher.');
  }
}
?>
```

Deactivation hook:
register_deactivation_hook($file, $callback)

Note that deactivation is not the same as uninstallation.

```
<?php
register_deactivation_hook(__FILE__, cars_deactivate');
function cars_deactivate(){
  // deactivate
}
?>
```

Uninstall hook:
register_uninstall_hook($file, $callback);

This deletes the plugin files.

```
<?php
register_uninstall_hook(__FILE__, 'cars_uninstall');
function cars_uninstall(){
  delete_option('car_option');
  // remove options and custom tables
}
?>
```

Alternatively, you can create an uninstall.php file in the root directory of your plugin. It will be executed in preference to the uninstall hook.

```
<?php
if (!defined('ABSPATH')  &&
    !defined('WP_UNINSTALL_PLUGIN')) exit();
delete_option('car_option');
// remove options and custom tables
?>
```

17.5.4 Options

This plugin creates a new post type called Car. Note that you may create options in the process. The first parameter to update_option() and add_option() specifies the option name, which must be unique from all other options, including those from other plugins.

```
<?php
/*
Plugin Name: Cars: Initialization
Plugin URI: http://example.com/wp-content/plugins/cars
Description: Activation and initialization.
Version: 1.0
Author: Chong Lip Phang
Author URI: https://www.facebook.com/chong.lipphang
License: GPLv2
*/

register_activation_hook( __FILE__, 'cars_install' );
function cars_install() {
   $cars_options_arr = array(
      'currency_sign' => '$'
   );
   update_option( 'car_options', $cars_options_arr );
   add_option('car_option_dummy','red');
   delete_option('car_option_dummy');
}

add_action( 'init', 'cars_init' );
function cars_init() {
  $labels = array(
          'name' => __( 'Cars', 'cars-plugin' ),
          'singular_name' => __( 'Car', 'cars-plugin' ),
          'add_new' => __( 'Add New', 'cars-plugin' ),
          'add_new_item' => __( 'Add New Car', 'cars-plugin' ),
          'edit_item' => __( 'Edit Car', 'cars-plugin' ),
          'new_item' => __( 'New Car', 'cars-plugin' ),
          'all_items' => __( 'All Cars', 'cars-plugin' ),
          'view_item' => __( 'View Car', 'cars-plugin' ),
          'search_items' => __( 'Search Cars', 'cars-plugin' ),
          'not_found' => __( 'No cars found', 'cars-plugin' ),
          'not_found_in_trash' => __( 'No cars found in Trash',
                                      'cars-plugin' ),
          'menu_name' => __( 'Cars', 'cars-plugin' )
  );
  $args = array(
          'labels' => $labels,
          'public' => true,
          'publicly_queryable' => true,
          'show_ui' => true,
          'show_in_menu' => true,
          'query_var' => true,
          'rewrite' => true,
          'capability_type' => 'post',
          'has_archive' => true,
          'hierarchical' => false,
          'menu_position' => null,
          'supports' => array( 'title', 'editor', 'thumbnail',
                               'excerpt' )
  );
  register_post_type( 'cars', $args );
}
```

17.5.5 Settings

This adds an item to the Settings menu.

```
<?php
/*
Plugin Name: Cars: Settings
Plugin URI: http://example.com/wp-content/plugins/cars
Description: Adding an item to Settings.
Version: 1.0
Author: Chong Lip Phang
Author URI: https://www.facebook.com/chong.lipphang
License: GPLv2
*/

add_action( 'admin_menu', 'cars_menu' );
function cars_menu() {
  add_options_page( __( 'Cars Settings Page', 'cars-plugin' ),
                    __( 'Cars Settings', 'cars-plugin' ),
                    'manage_options',
                    'cars-settings',
                    'cars_settings_page' );
}
function cars_settings_page() {
  $car_options_arr = get_option( 'car_options' );
  $c_inventory =
           (!empty( $car_options_arr['show_inventory'] ) ) ?
           $car_options_arr['show_inventory'] : '';
  $c_currency_sign = $car_options_arr['currency_sign'];
?>
   <div class="wrap">
   <h2><?php _e( 'Car Options', 'cars-plugin' ) ?></h2>
   <form method="post" action="options.php">
      <?php settings_fields( 'cars-settings-group' ); ?>
      <table class="form-table">
         <tr valign="top">
         <th scope="row">
         <?php _e( 'Show Car Inventory',
                   'cars-plugin' ) ?></th>
         <td><input type="checkbox"
               name="car_options[show_inventory]"
         <?php echo checked( $c_inventory, 'on' ); ?> />
         </td>
         </tr>

         <tr valign="top">
         <th scope="row">
         <?php _e( 'Currency Sign', 'cars-plugin' ) ?></th>
         <td>
         <input type="text"
                name="car_options[currency_sign]"
                value="
                <?php echo esc_attr( $c_currency_sign ); ?>"
                size="1" maxlength="1" /></td>
         </tr>
      </table>

      <p class="submit">
      <input type="submit" class="button-primary"
       value="<?php _e( 'Save Changes', 'cars-plugin' );?>"/>
      </p>
   </form>
   </div>
<?php
}

add_action( 'admin_init', 'cars_register_settings' );
function cars_register_settings() {
  register_setting( 'cars-settings-group',
                    'car_options', 'car_sanitize_options' );
}
function car_sanitize_options( $options ) {
  $options['show_inventory'] =
          (!empty( $options['show_inventory'] ) ) ?
          sanitize_text_field( $options['show_inventory'] ) : '';
  $options['currency_sign'] =
          (!empty( $options['currency_sign'] ) ) ?
          sanitize_text_field( $options['currency_sign'] ) : '';
          return $options;
```

```
}
?>
```

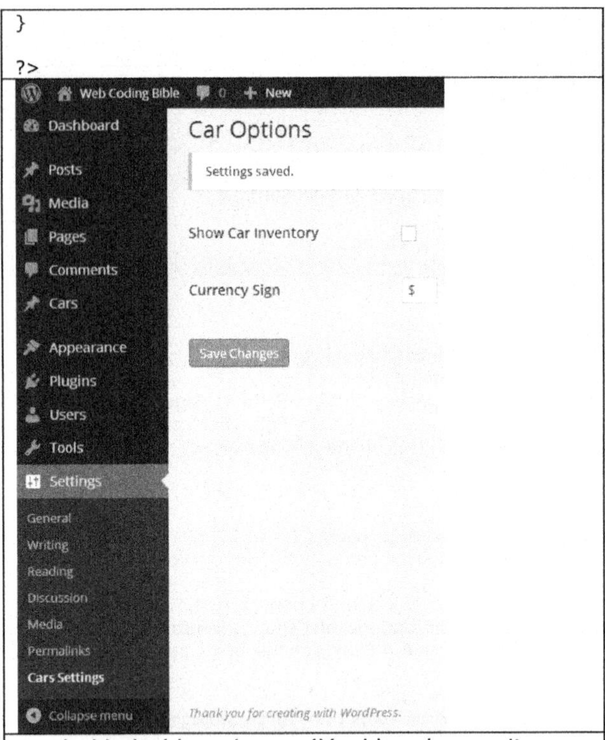

- 'add_dashboard_page()' adds submenu items to the Dashboard menu.
- 'add_posts_page()' adds submenu items to the Posts menu.
- 'add_media_page()' adds submenu items to the Media menu.
- 'add_links_page()' adds submenu items to the Links menu.
- 'add_pages_page()' adds submenu items to the Pages menu.
- 'add_comments_page()' adds submenu items to the Comments menu.
- 'add_plugins_page()' adds submenu items to the Plugins menu.
- 'add_theme_page()' adds submenu items to the Appearance menu.
- 'add_users_page()' adds submenu items to the Users menu.
- 'add_management_page()' adds submenu items to the Tools menu.
- 'add_options_page()' adds submenu items to the Settings menu.

17.5.6 Settings->Readings

This adds setting fields in Settings->Readings.

```
<?php
/*
Plugin Name: Cars: Settings->Reading
Plugin URI: http://example.com/wp-content/plugins/cars
Description: Setting fields in Settings->reading.
Version: 1.0
Author: Chong Lip Phang
Author URI: https://www.facebook.com/chong.lipphang
License: GPLv2
*/

//execute our settings section function
add_action( 'admin_init', 'cars_settings_reading_init' );
function cars_settings_reading_init() {
    add_settings_section( 'cars_id',
                          'About Cars',
                          'fill_cars_reading_section',
                          'reading' );
    add_settings_field( 'cars_enable_id',
                        'Enable Cars Feature?',
                        'fill_cars_enabled',
                        'reading',
                        'cars_id' );
    add_settings_field( 'cars_name_id',
                        'Cars Limit',
                        'fill_cars_limit',
                        'reading',
                        'cars_id' );
    register_setting('reading',
                     'cars_setting_values',
                     'cars_sanitize_settings' );
}
function cars_sanitize_settings( $input ) {
   $input['enabled'] = ( $input['enabled'] == 'on' ) ? 'on' : '';
   $input['name'] = sanitize_text_field( $input['name'] );
   return $input;
}
function fill_cars_reading_section() {
    echo '<p>Configure the Cars plugin options below</p>';
}
function fill_cars_enabled() {
    $car_options = get_option( 'cars_setting_values' );
    echo '<input '.
           checked( $car_options['enabled'], 'on', false ).
           'name="cars_setting_values[enabled]"
            type="checkbox" /> Enabled';
}
function fill_cars_limit() {
    $car_options = get_option( 'cars_setting_values' );
    echo '<input type="text"
            name="cars_setting_values[name]" value="'.
            esc_attr( $car_options['name'] ).'" />';
}
```

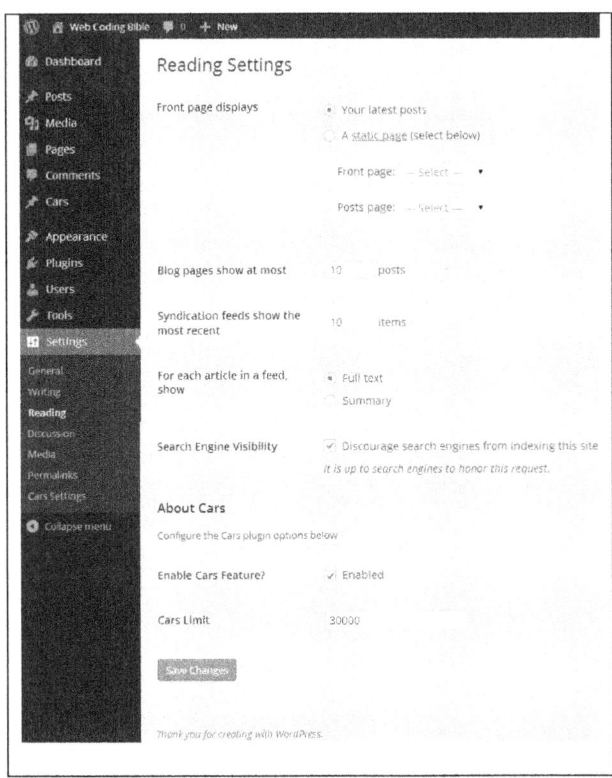

17.5.7 Menus

This adds an item to the Dashboard admin menu.

```
<?php
/*
Plugin Name: Cars: Menu
Plugin URI: http://example.com/wp-content/plugins/cars
Description: Adding an admin menu item.
Version: 1.0
Author: Chong Lip Phang
Author URI: https://www.facebook.com/chong.lipphang
License: GPLv2
*/

add_action( 'admin_menu', 'cars_create_menu' );
function cars_create_menu() {
   add_menu_page( 'Cars Page',
                  'Cars',
                  'manage_options',
                  'cars_main_menu',
                  'cars_settings_page2',
                  plugins_url( 'smiley.png', __FILE__ ) );
   add_action( 'admin_init', 'cars_register_settings2' );
}
function cars_register_settings2() {
   register_setting( 'cars-settings-group',
                     'car_options',
                     'cars_sanitize_options' );
}
function cars_sanitize_options( $input ) {
   $input['option_name'] = sanitize_text_field(
                               $input['option_name'] );
   $input['option_email'] = sanitize_email(
                               $input['option_email'] );
   $input['option_url'] = esc_url( $input['option_url'] );
   return $input;
}
function cars_settings_page2() {
?>
  <div class="wrap">
  <h2>Cars Options</h2>
  <form method="post" action="options.php">
  <?php settings_fields( 'cars-settings-group' ); ?>
  <?php $prowp_options = get_option( 'car_options' ); ?>
  <table class="form-table">
    <tr valign="top">
    <th scope="row">Name</th>
    <td>
    <input type="text" name="car_options[option_name]"
    value="
     <?php echo esc_attr( $car_options['option_name'] ); ?>"
    /></td></tr>

    <tr valign="top">
    <th scope="row">Email</th>
    <td>
    <input type="text" name="car_options[option_email]"
    value="
    <?php echo esc_attr( $car_options['option_email'] ); ?>"
    /></td></tr>

    <tr valign="top">
    <th scope="row">URL</th>
    <td>
     <input type="text" name="car_options[option_url]"
     value="
     <?php echo esc_url( $car_options['option_url'] ); ?>"
     /></td></tr>
  </table>
  <p class="submit">
    <input type="submit" class="button-primary"
      value="Save Changes" />
  </p>
  </form>
  </div>
<?php
}
?>
```

For add_menu_page(), the first two parameters set the page title and the menu title. The third parameter sets the capability level to 'manage_options' so only an admin will see the new menu. The fourth parameter sets the menu slug. The fifth parameter sets the menu function that codes the menu page. The sixth parameter sets the icon.

You may also use add_submenu_page() to add submenus. Refer to Codex for its usage.

17.5.8 Widgets

To implement a widget, you need to extend the WP_Widget class. In the class, form() builds the widget settings form. update() saves the widget settings. widget() handles the display of the widget.

```
<?php
/*
Plugin Name: Cars: Widget
Plugin URI: http://biniarybehemoth.com/wordpress/wp-content/plugins/cars
Description: Using a widget.
Version: 1.0
Author: Chong Lip Phang
Author URI: https://www.facebook.com/chong.lipphang
License: GPLv2
*/

add_action( 'widgets_init', 'cars_register_widgets' );
function cars_register_widgets() {
  register_widget( 'cars_widget' );
}

class cars_widget extends WP_Widget {
   function cars_widget() {
      $widget_ops = array(
                  'classname'   => 'cars-widget-class',
                  'description' =>
                  __( 'Display Car Information','cars-plugin' ) );
      $this->WP_Widget( 'car_widget'
               , __( 'Cars Widget','cars-plugin'), $widget_ops );
   }
   function form( $instance ) {
      $defaults = array(
                      'title' => __( 'Cars', 'cars-plugin' ),
                      'number_cars' => '3' );
      $instance = wp_parse_args( (array) $instance,
                                          $defaults );
      $title = $instance['title'];
      $number_cars = $instance['number_cars'];
?>
   <p><?php _e('Title', 'cars-plugin') ?>:
   <input class="widefat" name="
           <?php echo $this->get_field_name( 'title' ); ?>"
           type="text" value="
           <?php echo esc_attr( $title ); ?>" />
   </p>
   <p><?php _e( 'Number of Cars', 'cars-plugin' ) ?>:
   <input name="
      <?php echo $this->get_field_name( 'number_cars' ); ?>"
      type="text" value="
      <?php echo esc_attr( $number_cars ); ?>" size="2"
      maxlength="2" />
   </p>
<?php
}
   function update( $new_instance, $old_instance ) {
      $instance = $old_instance;
      $instance['title'] =
                   sanitize_text_field( $new_instance['title'] );
      $instance['number_cars'] =
                   absint( $new_instance['number_cars'] );
      return $instance;
   }
   function widget( $args, $instance ) {
      global $post;
      extract( $args );
      echo $before_widget;
      $title = apply_filters( 'widget_title', $instance['title'] );
      $number_cars = $instance['number_cars'];
      if ( ! empty( $title ) ) {
         echo $before_title . esc_html( $title ) . $after_title; };
         $args = array(
                  'post_type'  =>'cars',
                  'posts_per_page'=>absint( $number_cars )
              );
         $dispCars = new WP_Query();
         $dispCars->query( $args );
         while ( $dispCars->have_posts() ) :
           $dispCars->the_post();
           $hween_options_arr = get_option( 'car_options' );
           $hs_price = get_post_meta( $post->ID,
                                   '_car_price', true );
           $hs_inventory = get_post_meta( $post->ID,
                                   '_car_inventory', true );
?>
   <p>
   <a href="<?php the_permalink(); ?>" rel="bookmark"
      title="<?php the_title_attribute(); ?> Car Information">
      <?php the_title(); ?>
   </a>
   </p>
<?php
           echo '<p>' .
                 __( 'Price', 'cars-plugin' ). ': '.
                $hween_options_arr['currency_sign'] .
                $hs_price .'</p>';
           if ( $hween_options_arr['show_inventory'] ) {
              echo '<p>' .__( 'Stock', 'cars-plugin' ). ': ' .
                   $hs_inventory .'</p>';
           }
           echo '<hr>';
         endwhile;
         wp_reset_postdata();
         echo $after_widget;
      }
   }
```

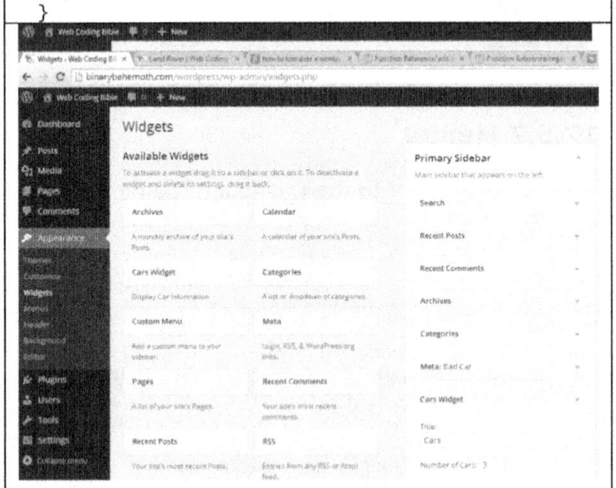

You can add Dashboard Widgets directly to the Dashboard using wp_add_dashboard_widget(). Refer to Codex for more information.

17.5.9 Meta Boxes

You can attach meta boxes to posts or pages to store additional information.

```
<?php
/*
Plugin Name: Cars: Meta Box
Plugin URI: http://example.com/wp-content/plugins/cars
Description: Attaching special information with meta boxes.
Version: 1.0
Author: Chong Lip Phang
Author URI: https://www.facebook.com/chong.lipphang
License: GPLv2
*/

add_action( 'add_meta_boxes', 'cars_meta_box_init' );
function cars_meta_box_init() {
   add_meta_box( 'cars-meta',           // id
                 'Car Information',     // title
                 'cars_meta_box',       // callback
                 'cars',                // page
                 'side',                // context
                 'default' );           // priority
}
function cars_meta_box( $post, $box ) {
   $car_featured = get_post_meta( $post->ID,
                                  '_car_type', true );
   $car_price = get_post_meta( $post->ID,
                               '_car_price', true );
   wp_nonce_field( plugin_basename( __FILE__ ),
                   'cars_save_meta_box' );
   echo '<p>Price: <input type="text" name="car_price"
        value="'.esc_attr( $car_price ).'" size="5" /></p>';
   echo '<p>Type:
        <select name="car_type" id="car_type">
          <option value="0" ' .
           selected( $car_featured, 'normal', false ).
           '>Normal</option>
          <option value="special" ' .
           selected( $car_featured, 'special', false ).
           '>Special</option>
          <option value="featured" ' .
           selected( $car_featured, 'featured', false ).
           '>Featured</option>
          <option value="clearance" ' .
           selected( $car_featured, 'clearance', false ).
           '>Clearance</option>
        </select></p>';
}
add_action( 'save_post', 'cars_save_meta_box' );
function cars_save_meta_box( $post_id ) {
  if( isset( $_POST['car_type'] ) ) {
    if( defined( 'DOING_AUTOSAVE' ) && DOING_AUTOSAVE )
      return;
    check_admin_referer( plugin_basename( __FILE__ ),
                         'cars_save_meta_box' );
    update_post_meta( $post_id, '_car_type',
    sanitize_text_field( $_POST['car_type'] ) );
    update_post_meta( $post_id, '_car_price',
    sanitize_text_field( $_POST['car_price'] ) );
  }
}
```

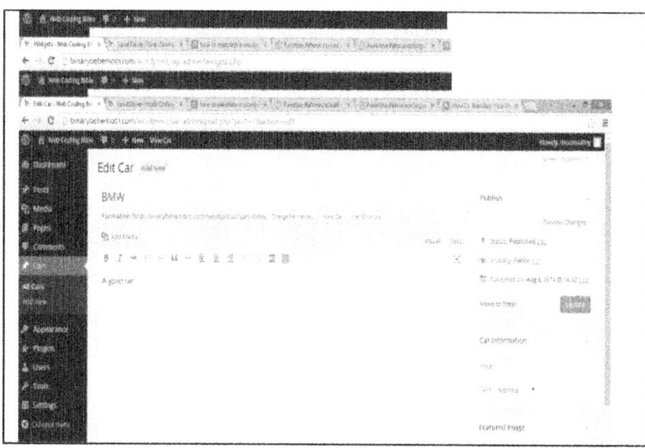

17.5.10 Shortcodes

Shortcodes are macro codes enclosed within [] that can be inserted into a post or a page.

This plugin sets several shortcodes:

- [google] displays a link.
- [smiley] displays a smiley image.
- [car show="price"] displays the metadata 'price'.

```
<?php
/*
Plugin Name: Cars: Short Codes
Plugin URI: http://example.com/wp-content/plugins/cars
Description: Using short codes to obtain information.
Version: 1.0
Author: Chong Lip Phang
Author URI: https://www.facebook.com/chong.lipphang
License: GPLv2
*/

add_shortcode('google', 'google_shortcode');
function google_shortcode(){
  return '<a href="http://google.com">Google</a>';
}

add_shortcode('smiley', 'smiley_shortcode');
function smiley_shortcode(){
  return '<img
          src="'.plugins_url('smiley.png',__FILE__).'"/>';
}

add_shortcode( 'car', 'cars_shortcode' );
function cars_shortcode( $atts, $content = null ) {
   global $post;
   extract( shortcode_atts( array(
      "show" => ''
   ), $atts ) );
   $car_options_arr = get_option( 'car_options' );
   if ( $show == 'type') {
     return get_post_meta( $post->ID, '_car_type', true );
   } elseif ( $show == 'price' ) {
     return $car_options_arr['currency_sign'].
            get_post_meta( $post->ID, '_car_price', true );
   }
}
```

17.5.11 Custom Tables

Although you can store data in simple options, the data stored in that way is unstructured. As the complexity and size of your data increase, sometimes you need to store the data in custom SQL tables.

This demonstrates how to create a custom SQL table in Wordpress. Note that dbDelta() will verify that the table you try to create does not exist. To manipulate SQL data after the table has been created, refer to 17.3.

```
<?php
/*
Plugin Name: Cars: Custom Table
Plugin URI: http://example.com/wp-content/plugins/cars
Description: Adding a custom table.
Version: 1.0
Author: Chong Lip Phang
Author URI: https://www.facebook.com/chong.lipphang
License: GPLv2
*/

register_activation_hook(__FILE__, 'cars_install');
function cars_install(){
  global $wpdb;
  $table_name = $wpdb->prefix . 'cars';
  $sql = "CREATE TABLE $table_name (
           model VARCHAR(20),
           num VARCHAR(10))";
  require_once(ABSPATH . 'wp-admin/includes/upgrade.php');
  dbDelta($sql);
  add_option('cars_version','1.0');
}
```

17.5.12 Publishing

After you have coded a plugin, you can submit it to the Plugin Directory so that other Wordpress users can download and install it.

To publish your plugin, make sure:

- the plugin is compatible with GPLv2 or any later version.
- the plugin is not illegal or morally offensive.
- the Subversion (SVN) repository is used to host the plugin.
- the plugin does not embed external links on the user's site without asking the user's permission.

Follow these steps:

Step 1: Register a new account at http://wordpress.org/support/register.php and log on into it.

Step 2: Submit your plugin at http://wordpress.org/plugins/add/ and wait for approval.

Step 3: Prepare and submit readme.txt. For an example, visit http://wordpress.org/extend/plugins/about/readme.txt. You can access the readme.txt validator at http://wordpress.org/extend/plugins/about/validator/.

Step 4: Set up an SVN client. For Windows, you can use TortoiseSVN which can be downloaded at http://tortoisesvn.net/downloads.html. For other SVN clients, visit http://subversion.apache.org/.

Step 5: Store your plugin files at a directory such as c:\wordpress-plugins.

Step 6: Navigate to your wordpress-plugins directory and create a new directory for your plugin. Right-click this new folder and select SVN Checkout.

Step 7: A dialog box will appear. For 'URL of repository', enter the URL provided to you via email when your plugin was approved. It looks like http://plugins.svn.wordpress.org/cars. For 'Checkout directory', enter the plugin directory such as c:\wordpress-plugins\cars. Make sure Revision is set to HEAD revision. Click OK.

Step 8: Three directories will be created. 'Branches' stores major versions. 'Tags' is expanded every time a new version is released. 'Trunk' is the main development area, containing the code for the next major release. Move your plugin files to the 'trunk' directory. Also place your readme.txt file, any screenshots, includes etc. in the 'trunk' directory.

Step 9: Right-click the 'trunk' folder and select SVN Commit. Fill in the dialog box and click OK. When prompted to enter a username and password, use those created at WordPress.org.

Step 10: Right-click the 'trunk' folder and select TortoiseSVN -> Branch/tag. Fill in the dialog box. The URL should look like http://plugins.svn.wordpress.org /cars/tags/1.1.0.0/.Type in a log message. Verify that 'HEAD revision in the repository' is selected for the Create Copy option. Click OK.

To release a new version of your plugin, follow Step 8 to Step 10, with your new plugin files. A notice will be displayed to all WordPress users that have your plugin installed. They can then use the automatic upgrade process to update the plugin.

17.6 Themes

A theme controls how the content at your website is presented. Starting in 2010, WordPress began shipping a new default theme each year. As of 2014, the three pre-installed themes are Twenty Fourteen, Twenty Thirteen, and Twenty Tweleve. You can find the files in [WordPress]\wp-content\themes.

To use a different theme, go to the admin panel, then navigate along Appearance->Themes. There you will see the installed, customizable themes. Clicking 'Add New' will allow you to install new themes. If you wish to use other themes found outside WordPress.org, you need to download the theme and upload it to your server by clicking 'Upload Theme'. Premium themes can be found via Google and bought online.

17.6.1 Essential Files

style.css and **index.php** are all you need to create a new theme. You should place them in a folder in [wordpress]\wp-content\themes. index.php can be empty and has already been covered in 17.2. WordPress uses style.css to reference your theme. Here is what style.css looks like for Twenty Fourteen:

```
/*
Theme Name: Twenty Fourteen
Theme URI: http://wordpress.org/themes/twentyfourteen
Author: the WordPress team
Author URI: http://wordpress.org/
Description: In 2014, our default theme lets you create a
responsive magazine website with a sleek, modern design.
Feature your favorite homepage content in either a grid or a
slider. Use the three widget areas to customize your website,
and change your content's layout with a full-width page
template and a contributor page to show off your authors.
Creating a magazine website with WordPress has never been
easier.
Version: 1.1
License: GNU General Public License v2 or later
License URI: http://www.gnu.org/licenses/gpl-2.0.html
Tags: black, green, white, light, dark, two-columns, three-
columns, left-sidebar, right-sidebar, fixed-layout, responsive-
layout, custom-background, custom-header, custom-menu,
editor-style, featured-images, flexible-header, full-width-
template, microformats, post-formats, rtl-language-support,
sticky-post, theme-options, translation-ready, accessibility-
ready
Text Domain: twentyfourteen

This theme, like WordPress, is licensed under the GPL.
Use it to make something cool, have fun, and share what
you've learned with others.
*/

(more......)
```

Notice the use of get_template_part() in index.php. This function is similar to PHP's include() and require(). If you use

get_template_part('content', 'index')

WordPress will first look for content-index.php in your theme folder. If it cannot be found, it will settle for content.php.

functions.php is automatically included by WordPress during execution. It contains all the 'library functions'.

Also include a screenshot that is 300px wide by 225px tall and save it as PNG, GIF, or JPG. Internationalization is supported here.

17.6.2 Header, Footer and Sidebar

header.php includes everything at the top of your page, up to the content area. It includes the HTML head, as well as the start of the HTML body. The hook wp_head() must be included in it. To include this file in index.php, call get_header().

footer.php includes everything below the content area and the </body></html> closing tags. Similarly, wp_foot() must be included in it. To include this file in index.php, call get_footer().

sidebar.php includes special content to the right or left of your main content area. To include this file, call get_sidebar(). Calling get_sidebar('right') will get sidebar-right.php.

17.6.3 Other Template Files

As a visitor navigates around your WordPress website, different template files are retrieved in response to different requests. These template files follow a certain order, with index.php being the template file of last resort when all other template files cannot be found in response to a request. The best way to learn how to code these template files is by reading the default theme files.

front-page.php or **home.php** function as your front page.

archive.php shows your older posts by date.

category.php shows your posts from a specific category. To find a category number, hover over the category name in the Edit Category Control Panel and look in the status bar at the bottom of the browser window.

tag.php shows your posts with a specific tag.

single.php shows a single post.

page.php shows a page.

image.php shows an image.

attachment.php shows an attachment.

404.php handles 404 errors that occur when a page cannot be found.

author.php groups all the author's content into one view.

comments.php displays comments.

search.php displays the search engine result page.

searchform.php display the search form.

Visitor Request									
is_search()	is_front_page()	is_page()	is_404()			is_attachment()	is_archive()		
							is_author()	is_category()	is_tag()
	front-page .php	(custom) .php		single-post .php	single-(posttype) .php	(mimetype) .php	author-(nicename) .php	category-(slug) .php	tag-(slug) .php
		page-(slug) .php				attachment .php	author-(id) .php	category-(id) .php	tag-(id) .php
		page-(id) .php					author .php	category .php	tag .php
search.php	home.php	page.php	404.php	single.php			archive.php		
index.php									

(This diagram shows the template hierarchy that dictates which file is preferred in response to a visitor request. The files in an upper row have precedence over those in a lower row. The search template hierarchy is defined in template-loader.php.)

17.6.4 Page Templates

In the admin panel, when you are trying to create or edit a new page in Pages -> All Pages -> (Page), you will notice a small box to your right which is titled Page Attributes:

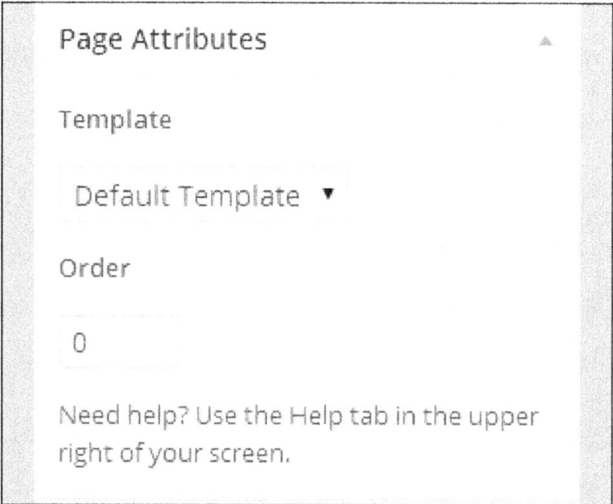

Here you can change the **page template** so that the page appears in a specific way. For Twenty Fourteen, the two other options beside Default Template are Contributor Page and Full Width Page, which are represented by the files in *[wordpress]\wp-content\themes\twentyfourteen\page-templates*. To create your page template, simply create an arbitrarily named PHP file and start it with the following:

```
<?php
/*
Template Name: My Page Template
*/
?>
```

To make life easier, you can copy *page.php* and modify it when creating your page template file.

17.6.5 Menus

If you go to Appearance -> Menus, you will find that you can create menus and assign Pages, Links and Categories to them. A menu is basically a list of shortcut links. The theme Twenty Fourteen comes with two menus, as registered in functions.php:

```
// This theme uses wp_nav_menu() in two locations.
register_nav_menus( array(
'primary'   => __( 'Top primary menu', 'twentyfourteen' ),
'secondary' => __( 'Secondary menu in left sidebar',
                  'twentyfourteen' ),
) );
```

The 'primary' menu is invoked in header.php:

```
wp_nav_menu(
  array( 'theme_location' => 'primary',
         'menu_class' => 'nav-menu' ) );
```

The 'secondary' menu is invoked in sidebar.php and the related files.

```
wp_nav_menu(
  array( 'theme_location' => 'secondary' ) );
```

17.6.6 Widget Areas

Widget areas are similar to menus but can be more dynamic. They are registered in functions.php. For the theme Twenty Fourteen, it looks like:

```
/**
 * Register three Twenty Fourteen widget areas.
 *
 * @since Twenty Fourteen 1.0
 */
function twentyfourteen_widgets_init() {
  require get_template_directory() . '/inc/widgets.php';
  register_widget( 'Twenty_Fourteen_Ephemera_Widget' );

  register_sidebar( array(
      'name' => __( 'Primary Sidebar', 'twentyfourteen' ),
      'id' => 'sidebar-1',
      'description'  =>
                  __( 'Main sidebar that appears on the left.',
                      'twentyfourteen' ),
      'before_widget' =>
                  '<aside id="%1$s" class="widget %2$s">',
      'after_widget'  => '</aside>',
              'before_title'  => '<h1 class="widget-title">',
      'after_title'   => '</h1>',
  ) );
  register_sidebar( array(
      'name' => __( 'Content Sidebar', 'twentyfourteen' ),
      'id' => 'sidebar-2',
      'description'  =>
           __( 'Additional sidebar that appears on the right.',
           'twentyfourteen' ),
      'before_widget' =>
                  '<aside id="%1$s" class="widget %2$s">',
      'after_widget'  => '</aside>',
      'before_title'  => '<h1 class="widget-title">',
      'after_title'   => '</h1>',
  ) );
  register_sidebar( array(
      'name'=> __( 'Footer Widget Area', 'twentyfourteen' ),
      'id' => 'sidebar-3',
      'description'  =>
              __( 'Appears in the footer section of the site.',
                  'twentyfourteen' ),
      'before_widget' =>
                  '<aside id="%1$s" class="widget %2$s">',
      'after_widget'  => '</aside>',
      'before_title'  => '<h1 class="widget-title">',
      'after_title'   => '</h1>',
  ) );
}
add_action( 'widgets_init', 'twentyfourteen_widgets_init' );
```

One of the widget areas is invoked in sidebar.php:

```
<?php if ( is_active_sidebar( 'sidebar-1' ) ) : ?>
  <div id="primary-sidebar"
      class="primary-sidebar widget-area"
      role="complementary">
  <?php dynamic_sidebar( 'sidebar-1' ); ?>
</div><!-- #primary-sidebar -->
```

17.6.7 Post Formats

A post can be displayed in different formats.

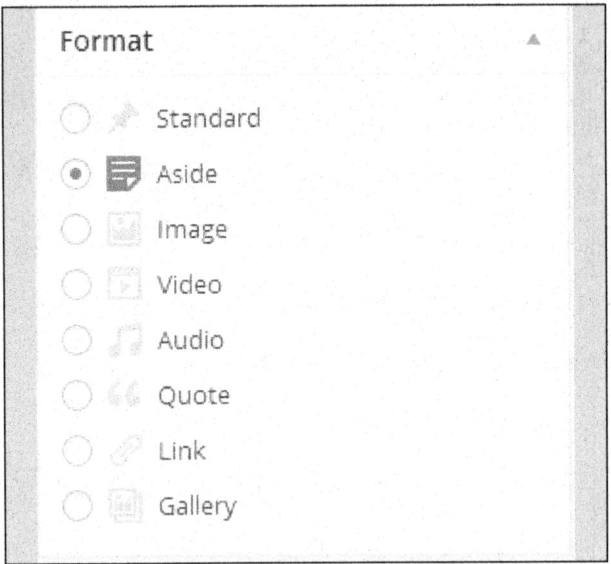

Post formats are enabled in functions.php. For Twenty Fourteen, it looks like:

```
/*
 * Enable support for Post Formats.
 * See http://codex.wordpress.org/Post_Formats
 */
add_theme_support( 'post-formats', array(
'aside', 'image', 'video', 'audio', 'quote', 'link', 'gallery',
) );
```

Post Formats
aside - Typically styled without a title. Similar to a Facebook note update.
gallery - A gallery of images. Post will likely contain a gallery shortcode and will have image attachments.
link - A link to another site. Themes may wish to use the first <a href=""> tag in the post content as the external link for that post. An alternative approach could be if the post consists only of a URL, then that will be the URL and the title (post_title) will be the name attached to the anchor for it.
image - A single image. The first <img /> tag in the post could be considered the image. Alternatively, if the post consists only of a URL, that will be the image URL and the title of the post (post_title) will be the title attribute for the image.
quote - A quotation. Probably will contain a blockquote holding the quote content. Alternatively, the quote may be just the content, with the source/author being the title.
status - A short status update, similar to a Twitter status update.
video - A single video or video playlist. The first <video /> tag or object/embed in the post content could be considered the video. Alternatively, if the post consists only of a URL, that will be the video URL. May also contain the video as an attachment to the post, if video support is enabled on the blog (like via a plugin).
audio - An audio file or playlist. Could be used for Podcasting.
chat - A chat transcript.
(courtesy of http://codex.wordpress.org/Post_Formats)

17.6.8 Child Themes

With child themes, you can inherit and override the functionalities of a parent theme. Note that the parent theme must not be a child theme itself. To create a child theme, add the following line in the header of style.css:

Template: twentyfourteen

where *twentyfourteen* denotes the folder name of the parent theme:

```
/*
Theme Name: Twenty Fourteen Child Theme
Theme URI: example.com
Description: A sample child theme
Author URI: example.com
Tempalte: twentyfourteen
*/

@import url('../twentyfourteen/style.css');

body {
  color: red;
}
......
```

Now you can activate your theme in Appearance -> Themes. Here the property for <body> has been overridden.

As for the template files to use, WordPress first scans your child theme directory for that file. If that file cannot be found, the parent theme directory is scanned.

If you intend to create your own functions.php for your child theme, you should avoid naming conflicts for the functions with those in the parent's functions.php.

To add a theme to WordPress Theme Directory, visit http://wordpress.org/themes/upload/.

17.7 Multisite

A WordPress multisite is a single installation of WordPress with many WordPress websites. Each site is associated with a unique Blog ID in the network. The largest WordPress Multisite network is WordPress.com.

Each site has its own set of registered users. Individual site administrators can enable themes and plugins on their site, but they can't install them. Only Super Admin users have access to the Network Admin section of the multisite, as well as full access to every site in the Multisite network.

17.7.1 Installation

To enable WordPress Multisite, first add the following line in wp-config.php, above the comment /* That's all, stop editing! Happy blogging. */:

define('WP_ALLOW_MULTISITE', true);

Now in the admin panel, Tools -> Network Setup will appear.

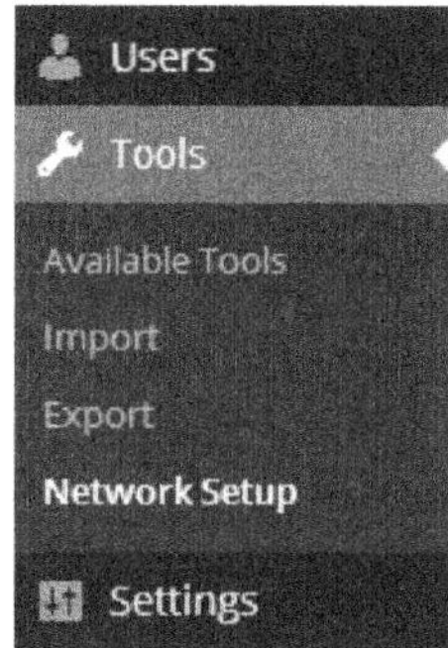

Click it. You will be asked to deactivate all plugins if you have not already done so. After you have deactivated all plugins, in Network Setup, you will be asked to copy some codes to wp-config.php and .htaccess. Follow the instructions. Copy and paste the codes accordingly.

wp-config.php:

```
define('MULTISITE', true);
define('SUBDOMAIN_INSTALL', false);
define('DOMAIN_CURRENT_SITE', 'example.com');
define('PATH_CURRENT_SITE', '/wordpress/');
define('SITE_ID_CURRENT_SITE', 1);
define('BLOG_ID_CURRENT_SITE', 1);
```

.htaccess:

```
RewriteEngine On
RewriteBase /wordpress/
RewriteRule ^index\.php$ - [L]

# add a trailing slash to /wp-admin
RewriteRule ^([_0-9a-zA-Z-]+/)?wp-admin$ $1wp-admin/
[R=301,L]

RewriteCond %{REQUEST_FILENAME} -f [OR]
RewriteCond %{REQUEST_FILENAME} -d
RewriteRule ^ - [L]
RewriteRule ^([_0-9a-zA-Z-]+/)?(wp-
(content|admin|includes).*) $2 [L]
RewriteRule ^([_0-9a-zA-Z-]+/)?(.*\.php)$ $2 [L]
RewriteRule . index.php [L]
```

Log in to you account again. You will notice that a new link, My Sites, has appeared at the top-left corner.

Feel free to adjust various settings in the menu shown above and in Settings -> Network Settings.

A handy plugin at this point is the WordPress MU Domain Mapping available at http://wordpress.org/extend/plugins/wordpress-mu-domain-mapping/. With it, you can assign URLs like http://site1.com to a site in your Multisite network.

17.7.2 Coding Functions

$blog_id is a variable that returns the Blog ID of the site. **is_multisite()** returns true if Multisite is enabled. **get_blog_details($fields, $getall)** returns site-specific information. $fields is the Blog ID, the blog name, or an array of fields to query against. $getall specifies whether to retrieve all details.

```
<?php
  global $blog_id;
  echo 'Current Blog ID: '.$blog_id;
  if (is_multisite()) echo '. Multisite is enabled.<br/>';
  print_r(get_blog_details(1));
?>
```

```
Current Blog ID: 1. Multisite is enabled.
stdClass Object (
  [blog_id] => 1
  [site_id] => 1
  [domain] => binarybehemoth.com
  [path] => /wordpress/
  [registered] => 2014-08-14 13:59:37
  [last_updated] => 0000-00-00 00:00:00
  [public] => 1
  [archived] => 0
  [mature] => 0
  [spam] => 0
  [deleted] => 0
  [lang_id] => 0
  [blogname] => Web Coding Bible
  [siteurl] => http://binarybehemoth.com/wordpress
  [post_count] => )
```

switch_to_blog($blog_id, $validate) switches to the site with Blog ID $blog_id in the network. $validate specifies whether to check if the site exists before proceeding, with the default being false. After this function has been called, **restore_current_blog ()** may be called to restore to the current blog.

To create a new site, call **wpmu_create_blog ($domain, $path, $title, $user_id, $meta, $site_id)**. $user_id is the user ID of the user account which will be the site admin account.

To add menus to Settings -> Network Settings, activate a hook:

The first parameter of add_submenu_page() should be replaced with 'index.php', 'sites.php', 'users.php', 'themes.php', 'plugins.php', 'settings.php', or 'update-core.php', if you wish to insert the submenu into other default, existing menus.

```
<?php
/*
Plugin Name: Network Admin Menus
Plugin URI: http://example/wp-content/plugins/cars
Description: Adding Network Admin Menus to a Multisite
Version: 1.0
Author: Chong Lip Phang
Author URI: https://www.facebook.com/chong.lipphang
License: GPLv2
*/

add_action('network_admin_menu',
           'add_my_network_menu');

function add_my_network_menu(){
  add_menu_page('Menu Page Title',
                'Menu Title',
                'manage_options',
                'menu_slug',
                'my_network_settings_menu');
  add_submenu_page('menu_slug',
                   'Submenu Page Title',
                   'Submenu Title',
                   'manage_options',
                   'submenu_slug',
                   'my_network_settings_submenu');
}
function my_network_settings_menu(){}
function my_network_settings_submenu(){}
```

Site Options
These manage site-specific options in a multisite.
add_blog_option($blog_id, $key, $value)
update_blog_option($blog_id, $key, $value)
get_blog_option($blog_id, $key)
delete_blog_option($blog_id, $key)
Network Options
These manage network-wide options in a multisite.
add_site_option($key, $value)
update_site_option($key, $value)
get_site_option($key)
delete_site_option($key)

is_user_member_of_blog($user_id, $blog_id) returns true if the specified user is a member of the specified blog. To add a member to a blog, call **add_user_to_blog($blog_id, $user_id, $role)**. To remove a member from a blog, call **remove_user_from_blog($user_id, $blog_id)**. To get a list of all sites a user belongs to, call **get_blogs_of_user($user_id)**.

get_super_admins() returns an array of Super Admins' usernames. **is_super_admin($user_id)** returns true if the parameter is the user ID of a Super Admin. **grant_super_admin($user_id)** makes a user a Super Admin. **revoke_super_admin ($user_id)** removes a user from the Super Admin role.

get_blog_count() returns the total number of sites in your network. **get_user_count()** returns the total number of users in your network. **get_sitestats()** retrieves both values at once.

```
$network_stats = get_sitestats();
echo '<p>Total sites: '.$network_stats['blogs'].'</p>';
echo '<p>Total users: '.$network_stats['users'].'</p>';
```

17.7.3 Database Schema

WordPress Multisite uses special tables. These tables are fully described in
http://codex.wordpress.org/Database_Description.

wp_blogs contains each site.

wp_blog_versions contains the current database version of each site.

wp_registration_log contains all users registered and activated.

wp_signups contains users and sites registered using the WordPress registration process.

wp_site contains the primary site's address information.

wp_sitecategories contains global terms and exists only if they have been enabled.

wp_sitemeta contains option data including Super Admin accounts.

wp_users contains all users registered.

wp_usermeta contains all metadata for user accounts.

Assuming the Blog ID is 3, the site-specific tables are:

- **wp_3_commentdata**
- **wp_3_comments**
- **wp_3_links**
- **wp_3_option**
- **wp_3_postmeta**
- **wp_3_posts**
- **wp_3_terms**
- **wp_3_term_relationships**
- **wp_3_term_taxonomy**

17.8 Useful Tools

17.8.1 Visitor's Experience

Thematic (http://wordpress.org/extend/themes/thematic) is a theme framework featuring 13 widget-ready areas, drop-down menus, grid-based layout samples, plugin integration, shortcodes for your footer, & a whole lot more. It is highly extensible and SEO-friendly.

The **P2** theme (http://p2theme.com) combines the best of Twitter, a blog, a discussion forum, and a news site by adding a posting panel, real-time updates, and inline editing right on the homepage.

The **Rich Text Widgets** plugin supports more than plain old text in your widgets or sidebar areas.

The **TinyMCE Advanced** plugin supports tables, more options for lists, Search and Replace in the editor, the ability to set Font Family and Font Size, and many others.

The **pageMash – Page Management** plugin allows your pages to be organized in hierarchical, drop-down menus.

The **Yet Another Related Posts** Plugin (YARPP) displays pages, posts, and custom post types related to the current entry, introducing your readers to other relevant content on your site.

The **Pods - Custom Content Types and Fields** plugin allows you to create new content types beyond post, pages, and custom fields.

bbPress (http://bbpress.org) adds a forum to your site.

cforms (http://www.deliciousdays.com/cforms-plugin/) is a powerful and feature rich form plugin for WordPress, offering convenient deployment of multiple Ajax driven contact forms throughout your blog or even on the same page.

Gravity Forms (http://www.gravityforms.com/) allows you to quickly and easily integrate with a variety of third party services such as PayPal and provides for even deeper integration with WordPress through our collection of optional Add-Ons.

BuddyPress is a plugin that adds a social networking layer to WordPress.

The **Search Everything** plugin extends search to include different content sources in the index, including comments, tags, and categories.

The **Relevanssi - A Better Search** plugin replaces the standard WordPress search with a better search engine, with lots of features and configurable options.

Google Custom Search Engine (https://www.google.com/cse/) add a search box to your homepage to help people find what they need on your website.

The **WPtouch Mobile Plugin** is a mobile plugin for WordPress that automatically enables a simple and elegant mobile theme for mobile visitors of your WordPress website.

The **NextGEN Gallery** plugin allows you to manage image galleries.

17.8.2 External Sites

The **Social Media Widget** plugin allows you to link your WordPress site to your social networking sites.

The **ShareThis** plugin allows visitors to share your WordPress posts to about 120 visitors' social networking channels such as Facebook and Twitter. Facebook Likes and Google g+ are also supported.

The **Tweetily** plugin allows you to construct tweets at your Twitter site from your posts. The **Twitter Tools** plugin allows you to create WordPress posts automatically from tweets from multiple Twitter accounts.

Facebook RSS Graffiti (http://apps.facebook.com/rss-graffiti) allows you to copy content from your WordPress site into Facebook. The **Facebook** plugin integrates various Facebook features.

The **FeedWordPress** plugin takes any RSS or Atom feed and converts it to posts.

With **Google Adsense** (http://www.google.com/adsense/start/) and **Project Wonderful** (https://www.projectwonderful.com/), you can earn money by displaying ads next to your online content.

The **WP eCommerce** plugin integrates payment gateways.

The **OpenID** plugin integrates OpenID. OpenID is an open standard that allows users to authenticate to websites without having to create a new password.

The **Simple LDAP Login** plugin integrates Lightweight Directory Access Protocol (LDAP). LDAP manages centralized identitites.

Trac (http://core.trac.wordpress.org) is the open source bug-tracking and project management software used to develop WordPress.

17.8.3 Efficiency

The **WP-CMS Post Control** plugin simplifies the publishing panel by hiding chosen features.

The **Edit Flow** plugin remixes the admin panel for better editorial workflow. Features include Calendar, Custom Statuses, Dashboard Widgets, Editorial Comments, Editorial Metadata, Story Budget and User Groups.

Firefox's Firebug, **Chrome's Developer Tools**, and **Yahoo's YSlow** improve the network bandwidth of your site.

Ping-O-Matic (http://pingomatic.com) is a service to update different search engines that your blog has updated.

The **Google XML Sitemaps** plugin provides insight into how Google crawler sees your website.

AWStats helps you to monitor your web traffic.

The **JetPack** plugin integrates social media, enhances photo galleries and provides traffic statistics.

WebGrind or **KCacheGrind** analyzes the execution paths of your site to determine bottlenecks in your codes.

APC (Alternative PHP Cache) caches intermediate, compiled PHP code.

The **WP Super Cache** plugin saves your dynamic site as static html files.

The **WP-DB Backup** plugin allows you to easily backup database tables. **HyperDB** (http://codex.wordpress.org/HyperDB) helps you to partition and replicate your WordPress database. **WP-DBManager** schedules regular database maintenance tasks including database backups.

Pound and **F5 BIG-IP** handles load balancing for your site.

17.8.4 Security

The built-in **Akismet** plugin deals with comment spam.

The **Limit Login Attempts** plugin limits the number of a visitor's permissible login attempts.

The **WP-Security Scan**, **WordPress Exploit Scanner**, **WordPress File Monitor**, **WordFence Security** plugins help to improve the security of your WordPress site.

The **Role Scoper** plugin manages the users' access control.

Precautions that you can take to secure your WordPress site include:

- update your version of WordPress regularly.
- hide your WordPress Version. You can add to the bottom of functions.php the following:
  Remove_action('wp_head','wp_generator')
- limit the number of permissible login attempts.
- use good passwords.
- change your table prefix.
- move wp-config.php.
- prevent access to wp-config.php in .htaccess
  <FilesMatch ^wp-config.php$>
  deny from all
  </FilesMatch>
- move the wp-content directory and edit wp-config.php accordingly.
- use secret keys in wp-config.php. You can visit http://api.wordpress.org/secret-key/1.1/salt to get random keys.
- force SSL on logins in wp-config.php:
  define('FORCE_SSL_LOGIN', true);
  define('FORCE_SSL_ADMIN', true);
- adjust the Apache permissions for the files.

18. Search Engine Optimization

The primary goal of SEO is to gain more exposure in search engine results by examining the website, and making both on-site and off-site improvements. By obtaining more exposure in search engine results, you will ultimately get more visitors to your website who are looking for relevant content.

Search Engines in the U.S., Dec 13	
Google	67.3%
Microsoft (Bing)	18.2%
Yahoo	10.8%
Ask Network	2.5%
AOL, Inc,	1.3%
(courtesy of comScore qSearch)	

Search Engines in China, Aug 13	
Baidu	63.16%
360	18.23%
Sogou	10.35%
Soso	3.62%
Google	2.88%
Bing	0.57%
Yahoo	0.48%
Youdao	0.16%
Other	0.09%
(courtesy of http://thenextweb.com/asia/2013/09/17/baidu-still-tops-chinas-search-market-with-63-share-as-merger-shakes-up-chasing-pack/)	

18.1 Introduction

18.1.1 How the Search Engine Operates

The identification of the improvements that are needed for your website requires knowing how the search engines operate. The most basic function of the search engine is to find and correlate all of the internet content, examine the user's phrase or word and quickly convey applicable and authoritative results.

The first important term is **relevance**. Suppose a user wishes to search for 'Website Design Books'. The search engine is tasked with producing a list of results that relate highly to books covering website development. The search engine analyzes all of the web pages and identifies the pages that have content containing website design books.

The search engine decides this by weighing numerous different elements including how the content is written, as well as the number of internet links from other websites that exist.

This is a very complex and highly protected procedure, which eventually produces, the rank of the web pages for 'Website Design Books'. Understanding this concept is very important, as the search engines clearly differentiate the page content that is about 'Website Design Books', from those of content that are relevant for other phrases like 'Website Marketing' or 'Internet Design Techniques'.

In another example, the user types 'queen size mattresses' into the search engine. The search engine immediately knows that pages containing the word 'mattresses' are extremely relevant to the inquiry, but it also figures out that any websites containing content about beds are also relevant. The search engine also knows that websites advertising home furnishing products (such as sheets and quilts), may have some applicability to the inquiry, but in a lesser significance and should be lower down in the search results.

Authority is the other important factor that can influence the exposure of your website. To be blunt, in an unregulated Internet where it is possible for anyone to post anything, is the website that you own a trusted location that the search engines would want to send visitors?

The most crucial method by which the search engines ascertain the authority of a website is to gauge how other independent sites view your domain. This can be evaluated by measuring the number of quality links that are pointing to your website. Basically a link to your site is like a vote of confidence on the Internet. In general, you should try to determine authority websites and acquire a link from them.

In the past, the more links there are, the higher the ranking your pages could achieve. Fortunately this has been addressed by the search engine owners. Today, search engines have been updated to incorporate safeguards to circumvent this type of abuse where a domain builds up meaningless links instead of placing an emphasis on the quality of the link. Google has named this upgrade Penguin and websites have been blacklisted for building up on meaningless links.

A good or trusted link, as seen by a search engine, usually originates from a reputable or industry related site. A link that originates from a website that is new and has no relevance to your content will be marked unfavorably by the search engines. Some links are more effective than others. Therefore those links may be considered to be weighted, are worth more than others and enhance your site's Internet authority.

Understanding how important authority and relevance are to the search engines, will help the person responsible for the website's SEO to recognize how to improve these factors, and ultimately increase both the search engine exposure and the number of visitors to the website.

18.1.2 Interpreting the Results Page

Understanding the results from a search inquiry is very important before changing the website. There are a very large number of search engines around the world, each having their own idiosyncrasies, but their search engine results pages (SERP) all share some common characteristics.

One item that you will always find is paid listings. Paid listings are very different from the conventional organic or natural listings that you have to focus on for the SEO efforts. These paid listings are in fact advertisements.

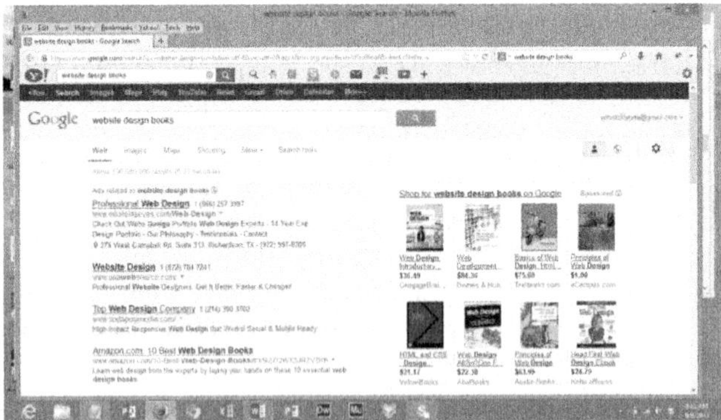

A typical search engine results page will contain pure results that connect out to different relevant web pages. Each result will appear to be different but the main structure of the page contains a headline, a description and a visible URL .

> Amazon.com: 10 Best *Web Design Books*
> www.amazon.com/10-Best-Web-Design-Books/lm/R27QWX3JR2VZK9
> Learn web design from the experts by laying your hands on these 10 essential *web design books.*

It is important to know exactly what these components look like on the results page, as these particular items will be modified and optimized for an individual result.

The Internet has changed drastically since the first appearance of search engines, and subsequently there is a lot of content on the web that isn't just text and web pages. The search engines have done an excellent job of keeping pace with changes, and have also begun returning images, products, videos and even maps on the results page.

The results can contain a group of video clips that match the user's inquiry or show a list of local businesses accompanied by a map showing the business location relative to the users address. It could show a group of prices and images for a particular product. Search engines also use social signals to return more personalized results, such as news articles or postings that your friends have shared.

Basically, your website has a lot of opportunities to have its content be recognized in the search and subsequently appear in the SERP. The more you understand how the search engines decide how to show results, the more you will understand how to make them pick your website.

18.1.3 Business Effects

A reliable and consistent SEO strategy has very real and significant benefits for those websites that are related to a business. Users are divulging their intent by just typing in words or phrases in the search engines, and marketing strategists can measure their results via their SEO efforts. Even though search engines do not charge the individual for the listing of web pages, the planning and implementation of a SEO strategy of a business is not free. To execute the plan you have to spend the time and resources.

Every day more and more content appears on the Internet, and your customers need search engines to make sense of it all. Users have a multitude of questions: where to buy products, book travel, get the latest news, etc. They start looking for answers with a web search. The role of the search engine is to match user inquiries to website pages that match the subject. By creating excellent SEO you are essentially providing your business with the pertinent, targeted traffic that you desire.

The biggest benefit of good SEO is the ability to measure the results in real time. By using website analytics, data can be obtained that shows exactly how the acquisition of search engine users and the associated business goals are being fulfilled.

18.1.4 Setting Goals

SEO requires a lot of time, a lot of patience and a lot of work. In this chapter all of the main aspects of good SEO are covered. SEO has to be approached as a long-term project that builds a long-term value and return. People that state "We can rank you #1 in Google in a week" are scam artists. It takes time to design and implement your strategy, to research keywords, to create new and unique content, to build search engine friendly links, more authority and finally, to resolve all of the technical issues that the website may have.

Search engines also take time to interact with your website. Discovering changes to content, new links to pages and the overall structure of the site is not immediate. Search engines are also liable to change (Google's Penguin for example), and the user has no control over this. The search engine suppliers are always trying to enhance their products to help deliver a better result for the inquiries.

It is important to realize that a successful SEO campaign has two very distinct audiences; the search engine and real people. SEO is a balancing act. By building a website that has authority and creative content that interests people, the search engines will reward the SEO efforts.

18.2 Keywords and Phrases

The main goal of SEO is to optimize the website. Search engines look for a match between the inquiry and your website. These search terms are called keywords or phrases.

Nevertheless, it would be a mistake to think that filling your webpages with keywords will attain top placement for your website. In response to this, search engines penalize websites with exaggerated keyword density.

18.2.1 Keyword Research Plan

Finding the correct keywords or phrases is a challenge. Keywords are items that searchers type into the search engine query point, and that implies that there are as many permutations of keywords as there are search engine users. Data is available from Google, Yahoo and Bing, who all have their search engines go out and retrieve the most relevant results for the search inquiry. The search engine only searches for the information that a user types in and not what they are really after, unless it is spelled out correctly.

An efficient keyword research plan requires a sound and structured method that will allow you to discover usable keywords. In the end, the plan will provide you the data needed to decide which keywords will yield the most return on investment.

18.2.2 The Art of Keyword Research

SEO strategists develop their own approach to find the ultimate keywords that will work in a search engine inquiry. The SEO keyword plan requires taking a step back and taking the place of a person that has an inquiry, suggesting questions and answering them. This will make you look at the primary focus of your website. Make a list of certain aspects of what a client may look for on the search page. Website Design Books means that the potential customer is searching the Internet for a book that will help in the design of a website. Someone that wants a new mattress will use that word. This forces the SEO campaign to examine the potential market segment.

Start by asking 'What services or products does my business offer?" List as many keywords and phrases from a potential customer's perspective. The answers to these questions will give a foundation for the keyword research plan.

SEO strategists have decidedly different ways of explaining websites, products and services. In the Website Design example, the SERP gives 5 million results for the phrase 'Website Design Books'. About 99% of this SERP is trash, so how do you make sure that your website is not buried?

The first stage of the keyword analysis is to examine the results of available tools that help in the identification of the most used keywords and phrases. These tools help to expand and suggest the keywords that can grow the number of visitors.

After establishing a list of keywords and phrases it is beneficial to look at the search engine metrics of the words or phrases. Reports will indicate that a handful of phrases and keywords will get an increase in traffic.

It will be apparent that there are certain words that are searched for hundreds and thousands of times every day. At the same time, there are more that do not get searched for as frequently. These keywords may be more descriptive, or less common variations, but they are still important to the search engine. These are commonly known as long-tailed keywords. Long-tailed keywords are very important to any SEO campaign. They target a bigger audience by targeting a lot of keywords that are not that competitive but are extremely important to your website's business sector.

As an example, consider the person that is looking for dog food. This is in an extremely competitive market and will be difficult to rank in the SERP. You have a website that sells this product but it is organic, so the SEO specialist starts to post content for the keyword phrase 'organic dog food'. This is extremely relevant and it is less competitive which means it is easier to rank. The inquirer types in 'organic dog food' and the site ranks highly.

Once the keywords and phrases have been collected, they have to be organized and designated with some meaning in a file that can be used for reference. Each keyword or phrase should have a topic or theme associated with it. This is known as "Keyword Characterization". The keywords and phrases for organic dog food can be set into several categories. These would include ingredients, the manufacturer and the size of the dog. There is not one correct way to perform this task.

18.2.3 Keyword Research Tools

After an understanding of the basics surrounding how to build a keyword research strategy, the next stage is to examine the tools that are available. There are a lot of tools on the Internet, each promoted by their individual developers. However the tool that gets used the most is the Google Keyword Tool. This tool not only provides a good measure on search volume for keywords and phrases, but it also gives suggestions for keyword improvement. Obtaining access to the tool is simple. The first stage is to set up an Adwords account (even though there is no intent to post any advertisements). From the main panel the tool is accessed from the Tools and Analysis drop down menu option. The tool is called Keywords Planner.

Before a search is performed, it is beneficial to set up some of the filters in the suggestion boxes on the left of the screen: the business or service type, the landing page for the keywords or phrase, and a product category. The keywords that are needed can also be targeted for English language and the USA location. The next stage is to realize that the target device covers all possible search entry devices. You can then press submit.

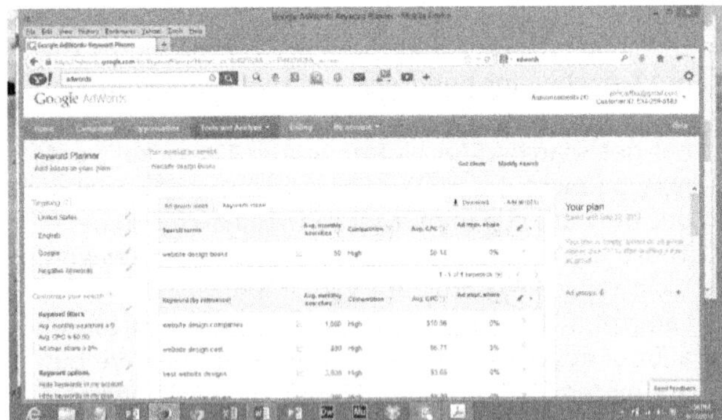

The keywords are listed in terms of relevance and the number of search per month. There is also a column indicating the competition for that word. The higher the competition, the more difficult it is to get a high ranking on the SERP, and subsequently the SEO campaign must be very accurate.

When 'Website Design Books' is typed in, almost 800 other keywords and phrases are listed. The data can be funneled further for a more local search.

Another tool that is available from Google is Google Trends. This tool takes an input for a keyword and shows the search results by location and time. The user can also examine if keywords are being misspelled and what effect that may have on a search.

Beside Google Adwords Keyword Tool, you can also use WordTracker when researching keywords. Firefox plugins like SEO Quake provide much on-page analysis.

Web Content Studio shows the related 'theme words' or 'niche vocabulary' that are listed in the top SERPs for a keyword. Say, the keyword is 'astigmatism'. Some related theme words may be 'vision', 'eye', 'cornea', 'refractive', 'surgery', 'light' and 'focus'. It is said that Google analyses these theme words when ranking a website for a keyword. However, do not over-repeat a theme word or you will be penalized.

18.2.4 Keyword Attributes

There are three points that need to be considered when a keyword is chosen: relevance, search volume and competition.

To examine the relevance of a keyword ask "Does this chosen keyword, accurately describes the nature of the products and services?" If it does, then great! Say the website of the SEO campaign sells used cars. A search of "used cars for sale" is too general. The search would be more specific for "used 2009 red Ford Taurus". If the website has a red Ford Taurus manufactured in 2009 then this is a highly relevant keyword phrase. Relevant keywords are much more likely to drive conversion traffic to the website than generic ones.

Search volume is the second item. This is the number of searches per month for a specific phrase. While the phrase "used 2009 red Ford Taurus" is extremely relevant to the website's business and has a high percentage of being converted into a sale, it will not be seen very often. The results for search volume in the keyword tool is a rolling average over a twelve month period. At this point it is better to use Google Trends, which gives a more precise average.

Competition indicates exactly how difficult it is going to be for your website to be ranked higher in the SERP. Unless the website is introducing a new product or service, there is going to be content on the internet that is similar in construction and content. If the keyword has a very high cost in the paid searches or cost per clicks, then it means the keyword is going to be very difficult to rank from a purely organic search. There are some commercial tools that are available that give an estimation of how difficult it is to rank high in the SERP. These are expensive but can be beneficial if the SEO specialist is running more than a few campaigns. Most are available on a monthly basis ranging from $99 to $499 per month.

18.2.5 Keyword Distribution

The process of assigning your keywords to specific pages within the website is known as keyword distribution. This is a very important phase in the creation of content. After running the keyword research process and having identified the target keywords, it is beneficial to use a spreadsheet to create a mapping structure of the keywords to the pages on the site. This also has the added benefit of recording which pages are targeting which keywords. It has to be understood that for many of the identified target keywords, the webpage will not exist and you will have to create one.

By using a spreadsheet (Microsoft Excel is best), it is easy to see where in the website's architecture you will want to add the new page, and identify some key segments of content before the main content writing begins. Each of the web pages should have its own section. One column can list the targeted keywords. This should be followed by the page's URL, the title tag, the description tag and h1 header (these will be covered in section 18.3).

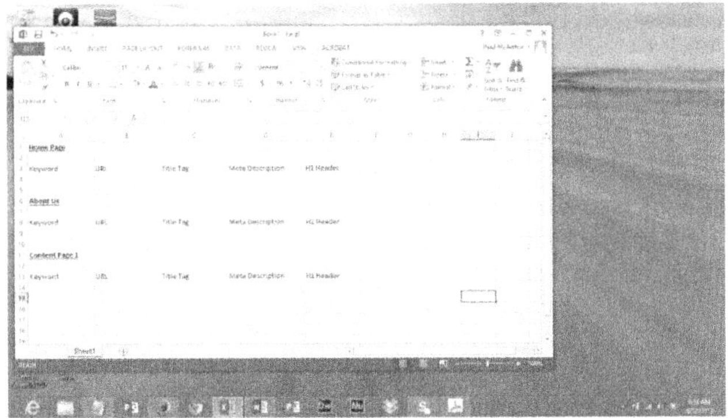

It is very important to remember that the search engines really want to see unique content. Listing these pages out on the spreadsheet will help duplicated content to be identified quickly. Secondly, it is essential to examine all of the keywords from the keyword list, and identify the most relevant pages of the website for each of the keywords. The SEO specialist should ensure that one keyword is distributed per page, which will prevent over-usage. If a keyword is on the list and does not have a matched page on the site, a new page has to be created.

All of the SEO friendly phrases, like the title, description, can be marked out here. Writing the content on the page is easy when the keywords that are being optimized are known upfront. There are a number of on-page analysis tools that can suggest changes that could benefit the page. However the use of a spreadsheet helps in two very distinct ways. It provides a place to organize and document the content of the website. And it helps control the work effort of all of the members in the development team.

18.2.6 Ongoing Keyword Evaluation

By performing an ongoing keyword evaluation, the long-term benefits and success for the SEO campaign are enhanced. Although there is a great abundance of good keyword data, the one factor that you won't have control over, is how the keywords are actually performing.

Once the website starts ranking for keywords that were identified in the research phase and traffic starts to come into the pages as a result, there is a need to see if these keywords are actually yielding conversions and satisfying the business goals. Look at the website that sells used automobiles, in particular the Ford Taurus. When performing an initial research, the phrase 'red 2009 Ford Taurus' is identified as a high-ranking keyword. As it happens the 2009 Ford Taurus was in a recall campaign due to suspected brake problems. Therefore the website will get traffic for people who want their car fixed, and who will not be interested in any of the websites selling cars. The SEO specialist will recognize that and swap in new keywords.

A fast way to perform some testing is through Paid Searches. By using Microsoft's adCenter or Google's Adwords it is possible to buy keywords that need evaluating in a short period of time. Although these paid searches do tend to behave a little different than the generic search, they can yield valuable data that will save the business in the long run.

SEO is a process that has to be continuously maintained over the duration of the website's life. The search engine industry is continually evolving with new algorithms, and keywords that were researched a couple of months ago may not be valid. Stay abreast of changes with new research and focus on how the targeted keywords have a say in the traffic and conversions of the site.

18.3 HTML Tags and Text Markers

When any website is coded there are many HTML tags and text markers that can be used. Some of the tags are descriptive in nature for the search engine (**<title>** for example), and some are more directive for the engine actions (**<meta>).** By using keywords and keyword phrases within the descriptive tags, the search engines are helped to identify the relevancy of the page.

18.3.1 Title Tags

The title tag is one of the most important factors in the SEO strategy. It is weighted very seriously by all of the search engines, particularly Google and Bing, and the content of the tag appears in the SERP. It is imperative to use the most significant keywords and phrases for each page's title tag on the website.

There are good and bad implementations of a title tag. Examining the Website Design Book search, the tag

<title>Welcome**</title>**

is an example of a very bad and useless tag. If a search is performed for *'welcome'*, there are 45 million finds for the SERP and your website will be buried in the lower regions of the search. About 95% of the SERP is useless. A good title tag, that is ranked #1 on Google, would be

<title>Amazon.com: 10 Best Web Design Books**</title>**

where the relevance of the title is self-explanatory.

It is also stipulated in the search engine algorithm that the tag should be no more than 60 characters. If the tag is longer than 60 characters it is truncated on the SERP.

18.3.2 Meta Description

Another tag where the keywords and keyword phrases have to be used is the meta description tag. Keywords and phrases that are contained within the tag will be bolded in the SERP if they are part of the original search inquiry. By looking at the source code of the Amazon site in the Website Design Books search we can see the tag as

<meta name="description" content="Learn web design from the experts by laying your hands on these 10 essential web design books." />

The result from the SERP was

> Amazon.com: 10 Best *Web Design Books*
> www.amazon.com/10-Best-Web-Design-Books/lm/R27QWX3JR2VZK9
> Learn web design from the experts by laying your hands on these 10 essential *web design books.*

and as can be seen the meta description tag is clearly visible. If the inquirer did not type in any of the words in the meta description then the engine would pull a snippet of the text from the page.

The main point to remember about the meta description tag is that it is like the title tag, where you want to use keyword phrases but also want to make a compelling marketing statement.

18.3.3 Header Tags

<h1>, <h2>, <h3> are termed header tags and are used within the content headlines, containing keywords and phrases. It is thought that the search engines give headers extra weighting during the search, but this has never been proven.

An example of a <h1>from the website that was ranked highest in the Website Design Book search is

<h1 style="display:inline;" class="largeTitle">10 Best Web Design Books</h1>

and the high ranking keywords and phrases are included.

18.3.4 Anchor Text

Anchor text is the name for the words that are contained in the clickable part of a link. The words "click here" or "more info" are bad examples of a link anchor text as they are not unique. Anchor text is very important to the overall SEO of the page as it describes to the visitors and search engines what the link is about. It has to be used precisely to describe the page that is being linked to. It is beneficial to use important keywords and phrases within the anchor text.

Search engines put a lot of weight on the anchor text. An example of a piece of good anchor text is from the page describing Website Design Books that was identified during the search. The anchor text for the first link is

Build Your Own Web Site the Right Way Using HTML & CSS, 2nd Edition

and contains several very significant keywords relating to the topic. The link itself goes to a page outlining the reviews for the book. This text should be as descriptive as possible.

18.3.5 'alt' Attribute

Images that reside on the pages can be described using the alt attribute. If the image is being used as a link, the attribute is very important. You want to use the same descriptive text that would be in the anchor text as the alt attribute information. Again from the previous example, the first image on the SERP links directly to a page outlining the attributes of the book. The associated link is shown where all of the details apart from the alt tag have been omitted.

<img width="..." height="..." alt="Build Your Own Web Site The Right Way Using HTML & CSS, 2nd Edition" src="...">

The alt text for the image is exactly the same as the anchor text from the page. This is a very good use of this tag. If the image is not a link, the tag should just describe the image.

18.3.6 Writing Effective Title Tags

After the keyword research has been performed, and the spreadsheet has been constructed it is time to examine the descriptive tags. At this stage there should be some outline of the page's content that is in the basic optimization for the keywords and phrases. From the SEO point the tag needs to be 10 to 12 words, with a maximum of 60 characters. Make sure you use the most important keywords and phrases. Be aware that the search engines do not like duplicate title tags.

The search engine is not case sensitive but does look out for repetition of words. Therefore 'Website Design Books' and 'website design books' are the same, and the search engine ignores the second occurrence. The search engines also ignore any punctuation marks in the title tag.

18.3.7 Writing Meta Description Tags

The meta description tags are designed after the content and the title tags are created. They are given some weight by the search engines and they often show up as a description in the SERP. This makes these tags one of the best ways of controlling the description that the search engine uses. If you do not have a meta description tag, the search engine will pull a snippet from the page.

The first stage is to write out one or two sentences that adequately describe the contents of the page.

This tag is also a good place to insert keywords or phrases that were deemed to be extra for the title tag. The search engine ignores duplicate entries so care must be taken to avoid this pitfall.

Four SEO-related 'name' attributes for the <meta> tags are 'description', 'keywords', 'author' and 'robots'.
<title>Web Coding Bible</title> <meta name="description" content="Web Coding Bible covers all essential technologies about web development."/> <meta name="keywords" content="HTML, CSS, JavaScript, PHP, SQL, XML"/> <meta name="author" content="Chong Lip Phang"/> <meta name="robots" content="all"/>

18.3.8 Search Engine Directive Tags

There are some other tags that can be used to direct the search engines. This is particularly useful when some of the pages are under construction or they are directories where scripts and CSS style sheets are stored.

The tag

<meta name="robots" content="noindex, nofollow">

instructs the search engines not to index the page and not to follow any links on it.

18.4 Content Optimization: What the Search Engines and Users Look For

18.4.1 Understanding Content Optimization

Improving the quality and the relevance of any website's content is termed content optimization. The search engines and users interpret differently what defines good content. However people and search engines expect quality and clarity from the website pages. They both want to know without any uncertainty what the content is about, and more importantly the content is trustworthy. If the page gives the user content that is excellent, discussing all of the keywords, the user and the engine will return to the website. When visitors see content that they like they will share it with other people.

Search engines can see when this content is being shared, and view this favorably from a trust standpoint, rewarding the site with more visibility. When the content writers think about optimization, they have to remember the content is to benefit both users and search engines, focusing both on trust and themes.

Your site should not have irrelevant content. Search engines will view this unfavorably.

18.4.2 Site Structure Optimization

As the writer focuses on keywords and themes for the pages, they will also be developing more content. This has to be structured in a meaningful way to let the search engines operate properly. Search engines need to know how the pages relate to one another.

Take the place of the search engine and the search engine user. A friend recommends a book to you, and you are visiting a library for the first time, looking for that book. The only information that you have is that it is a cookbook and has an author starting with the letter D. Since this is your first visit, the layout is new and the placement of everything is a mystery. Fortunately, the library has some excellent navigation tools to assist you. You look at the library directory and find out where the non-fiction books are located. After you reach this section you look for the subsection covering cookbooks. From there you look at the shelves where the authors beginning with the letter D are located, and there is your book. You are going through this process to learn the library's complete layout. All of the different sections, subsections, shelves, categories and authors are itemized and eventually you know about all of the individual books. This is precisely how a search engine functions. It crawls and navigates the entire website to learn the content, how it is constructed and organized, where the content can be found and what it is about.

Take the role of the librarian instead of the book searcher. All of the information within the library is now stored by you. If a person walks into the library and says they want a cookbook written by an author whose name only begins with the letter D, you can immediately guide the person to the relevant book. You have become the search engine. You give directions when people come to you looking for information.

On the internet the search engines will locate the homepage of the website and start to navigate through it and through all of the links. The method that is adopted to link pages within the website is therefore vitally important and is known as internal linking.

If the website is an online store, the architect will want to have a system of product categories that link to subcategories that hold individual links to products. If the website is informational, it should be organized by topics and then dates of publication. Whatever structure and strategy is used, a clean website will ultimately assist the search engines understand the site, find content and help searchers identify what they are looking for and where to find it on the website.

If the search engine cannot understand the layout and structure of the website, or does not believe that the structure makes sense, or finds missing pages, it will not recommend the website to others. The website's structure should be clear to the owner and should be clear to visitors. Search engines are just trying to imitate the human search process. Therefore, once the website has been designed so that it is logical and easy for the visitor to navigate through, the search engines should understand it as well.

18.4.3 Recognizing Different Content Types

One of the most common forms of content on a web page is text. The visitor sees some text on the homepage that indicates what type of information is available throughout the rest of the site. When the user clicks on the About Us section there is more relevant content presented in a lot of different ways. There are organized headings and subheading along with the paragraphs of body text. All of this diverse content is formatted in different ways so that the visitor and the search engines find it easier to understand the content.

Another form of content is imagery. This is more effective than text when relaying a powerful message. While the accompanying text at the side of an image says the same thing, the image does a better job of communicating the message.

Video is another form of content. The rich sights and sounds of the video can portray a message better than just text and images.

The key is to think about what kind of content will be helpful, effective and useful for the target visitors. While the search engines are the mechanism that brings visitors to the website, once they are there it is up to the content to engage. Using a mix of the most effective content types will accomplish this.

18.4.4 Optimizing Textual Page Elements

The main objective of a search engine is to guide users to content that is relevant to a certain phrase or keyword that was entered as the inquiry. The website page can be fine-tuned for relevance to a certain topic through the process of on-page optimization.

The first element is the URL, as found in the address bar. By thinking of this as being like a file on your computer, you can follow some simple guidelines for the creation of an excellent URL. The length of the URL should be as short as possible, but at the same time contain useable and relevant information about the page. It is important that the keyword phrase that is targeted is included.

The file name for the page on the server has to be updated and the internal links have to be changed. This is worth the exercise as the URL now matches the targeted keyword phrase. The name uses hyphens instead of spaces or underscores. This helps the search engine break up the words properly.

The next element that will be examined and optimized is the title tag. It is very short, descriptive and targeted to the phrase that needs ranked. The tag is not just there for the search engines to identify the theme of the page but is used to entice visitors from the SERP listing. By mentioning the home page of the website in the title may entice the visitor to also navigate to other pages.

The next tag that can be configured is the meta description. Optimizing this tag really has no directly measureable SEO improvement factor, but it can improve the website's click through rate from the SERP. The tag is often used as the text that shows up under the title in the SERP.

The h1 header tag has to be examined. This is typically the main headline that is associated with the page. The main purpose of using this tag is to give the visitor a clear idea of what the content that follows is all about, much like a magazine story. The H1 tag has to be very descriptive and specific to the keyword phrase. There are no limits to the number of characters in the headlines, but it pays to be concise and to the point.

The focus should then be turned to the content itself. The most important thing is that it needs to be optimized for the visitor first and the search engines second. The content has to be written in a manner that it is very engaging to the target audience. The search engines, on the other hand, require no magic formula for good content. The rule that always has to be considered is that the search engines are trying to mimic a human reading the page and then figuring out what it is all about. Search engines are not only looking for the target keyword, but variations of it as well.

Search engines can get very hi-tech trying to relate the semantic and thematic connections between the words on a page, exactly the same as human visitors. Writing the content the way you would for a human is the best way to optimize for the search engine algorithms.

The last element of content is the images. A human will interpret the image from a visual point of view with some significance to the target phrase. The search engine sees the image as a bunch of colorful dots with no way of telling how they are aligned or what they are supposed to spell out. They therefore rely on a few tags to understand what the image really is. In the same manner that the URL filename was changed, the name of the image can be changed to match the target phrase on the page.

While there are many more items on the page that can be optimized focusing on the URL, the title, description, headers, text and images will take care of the on-page optimization. Reevaluation of the website for an ongoing SEO campaign will surprise the owner as to just how much optimization there is to constantly perform.

18.4.5 Optimizing Non-Text Page Elements

Most of the search engines are efficient at analyzing and comprehending the text on website pages. They have a harder time dealing with the other forms of content; videos, images and audio clips. It is therefore important to develop a strategy to optimize these types of content for the targeted keyword phrase.

The simplest is to surround the non-text element with text that describes it exactly. It is very common to have a paragraph of text describing a particular video right next to the actual frame. Images embedded in line with text have text titles under them, and this title is very relevant to the page. Image carousels or slideshows often contain a text title. An audio clip typically has a description and even a complete transcript. Search engines will always analyze the text that is in a close vicinity and it make assumptions that there is correlation between them.

Every home page has a logo. The search engine will look at the image file name and the alt attribute, but will also look at the text that resides nearby. This text should be about the logo. Beside this technique the use of micro formatting (1.7) optimizes the code with some very relevant and specific metadata.

Videos can be made visible to the search engines by optimizing the code that embeds the video. This can be accomplished by adding in some special markup of rich metadata in the tag. This will allow the search engine to really understand the content of the video. For video content it is also beneficial to use a video site map. XML sitemaps are files that use a specific, special syntax to provide search engines with a list of all of the pages and content found on the website. It also includes some of the attributes that describe the content. Google Webmaster Tools has a tremendous support mechanism for this.

18.4.6 Analyzing Content Quality

By using the URL, the title, headers and the overall content of a page we have identified how to optimize the page for any targeted keyword or phrase. To establish how well the content is performing can be done by using one of several commercial tools. These range in cost, and are obviously priced by reputation and results. The most widely used tool is the On-Page Report Card from the SEOmoz Pro and a top free tool is Freegrader.com

The tool of choice will give the page a grade for targeted phrases and keywords. It will also generate a report that will contain a to-do list of fixes and improvements. The required action list to make the site page more optimized is rated easy, moderate and difficult. These tools do provide a benefit by providing a comprehensive list of changes that can be time saving and help increase search engine visibility.

18.4.7 Benefits of User Generated Content

Search engine visibility is increased by the continuous generation of new, unique and quality content. By leveraging the interest and knowledge of the website visitors to create new content is known as user generated content. User generated content is page text that normal visitors can create and given the correct circumstances, this type of content production can be very cost effective. Examples of user generated content are blog comments and forums where allowing people to simply express their views can help generate new, applicable and valuable text or even links. When the website sells products, garnishing reviews from visitors is another means of gathering relevant content.

18.5 Technical Content

18.5.1 The Code behind the Page

When a search engine is crawling through a page, it is trying to determine what a page looks like to the regular human visitor. However the search engine does not see the page in the same way as a human; it sees code that the servers send back to internet browsers. To illustrate this look at the following two screen shots. The first is what a human sees when they visit the website's home page. It is rich and colorful and full of content; text, images, menus and videos. It is very appealing and the visitor is capable of absorbing all of the information

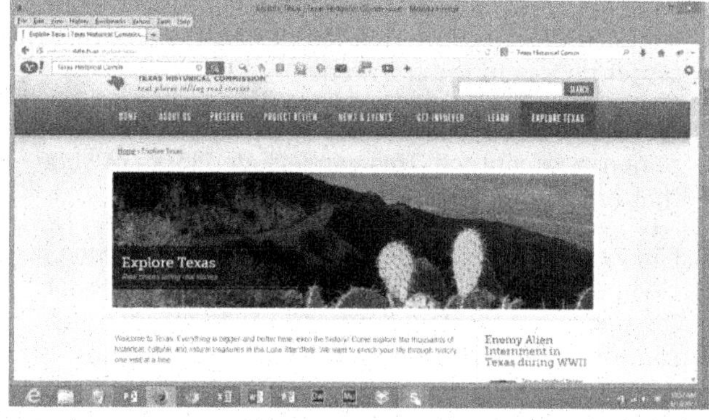

The second shows what the search engine sees.

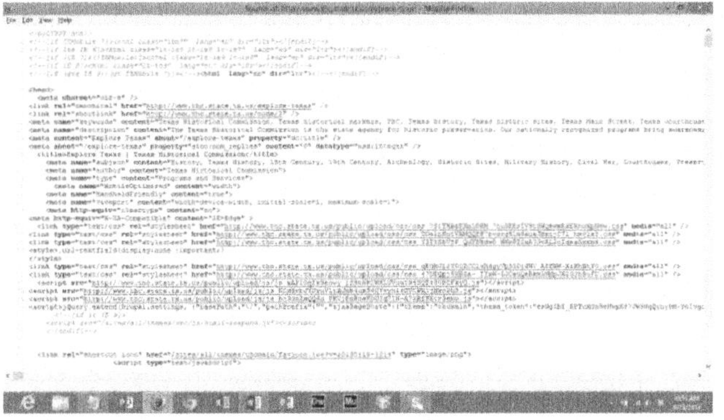

The code is a list of instructions that the browsers can follow in order to render the webpage on the screen. Pages are ultimately created with HTML code and this code helps figure out where to find all of the files that are needed to produce this page. It also controls where links point to within the website and externally.

This code can help the SEO specialist with other opportunities to help the search engines understand the content much more effectively. The HTML is used in the control of the loading of stylesheets, which are extra instructions that help find the visible attributes of a page. Font coloring, content sizing, line spacing, background images, page conventions and all of the rules for the visual depiction of the page are found here. Target phrases can be used for these file locations, increasing the search engine visibility.

HTML is only one of the languages that the browsers and search engines understand. Websites have become more interactive through the use of JavaScript. Using this makes animation, slideshows and dynamic menus possible. Just like the style attribute this code can be inserted into the relevant line, or referenced from different files that contain the target phrase in the file name.

There will also be different codes that provides types of non-text content. This can include blocks of code that are responsible for rendering a video.

Finally, it is important to make sure that the code is clean and free from any errors. This will mean that the pages are displayed properly to the visitor and can be crawled effectively by the search engines.

18.5.2 Links Following

One way that the search engine recognizes new content is by following links. As with the visitor who clicks through links to go from one page to the next, the search engine does exactly the same thing to find and index contents, only they click on every link that they can locate.

18.5.3 XML Sitemaps

Another way is from an XML sitemap. An XML sitemap is really just a listing of the pages' content in a special format that can be easily read through by the search engines. Once the sitemap is generated it can be submitted directly to the search engines thereby giving the owner one more way to let the engines know when content is added or changed.

A sitemap file can only reference files that reside in the directory of the sitemap file or its subdirectories.

```
<?xml version="1.0" encoding="UTF-8"?>
<urlset
  xmlns="http://www.sitemaps.org/schemas/sitemap/0.9">
  <url>
   <loc>http://www.mysite.com/</loc>
   <lastmod>2014-08-22</lastmod>
   <changefreq>daily</changefreq>
   <priority>0.5</priority>
  </url>
  <url>
   <loc>
     http://www.mysite.com/product?id=45&amp
   </loc>
   <changefreq>monthly</changefreq>
  </url>
  <url>
</urlset>
```

<urlset> references the protocol standard.

<url> signifies a URL entry.

<loc> specifies the location.

<lastmod> specifies the date on which the file was last modified. It has the format YYYY-MM-DD.

<changefreq> specifies how frequent the page probably changes. It can be 'always', 'hourly', 'daily', 'weekly', 'monthly', 'yearly', and 'never'.

<priority> specifies the importance of this URL relative to the others of the same site. It ranges from 0.0 to 1.0.

After preparing the sitemap file, you should submit it to the search engines. For instance, you can submit it to Google via GWT. You can also use cURL to submit it.

Each sitemap file must contain no more than 50000 URLs. You can compress it using gzip. The final file size must always be smaller than 10MB. To group multiple sitemap files, use a sitemap index:

```
<?xml version="1.0" encoding="UTF-8"?>
<sitemapindex
    xmlns="http://www.sitemaps.org/schemas/sitemap/0.9">
  <sitemap>
   <loc>http://www.mysite.com/sitemapA.xml.gz</loc>
   <lastmod>2014-08-22T18:30:19+05:00</lastmod>
  </sitemap>
  <sitemap>
   <loc>http://www.mysite.com/sitemapB.xml</loc>
   <lastmod>2014-08-22</lastmod>
  </sitemap>
</sitemapindex>
```

18.5.4 robots.txt

Search engines will always try and crawl a website's links for as much additional information and content. There are a lot of occasions where there are pages that should not be seen. Test pages and members-only areas of your site are examples. To establish how the search engine crawls through the website you can set up rules in the **robots.txt** file.

While XML sitemaps dictate what pages should be indexed, robots.txt tell the search engines what should not be indexed. When the engines see robots.txt they will follow the rules that were set up. These rules can be set for different search engines crawlers and browsers, and the file can specify which area's and pages are off limits.

When placed in the top directory, this robots.txt file prevents all search engines from visiting the three specified directories.
User-agent: * Disallow: /php/ Disallow: /admin/ Disallow: /test/
This allows a single robot. Note that robots *can* ignore your /robots.txt.
User-agent: Google Disallow: Sitemap: http://www.mysite.com/smap-hostA.xml Sitemap: http://www.mysite.com/smap-hostB.xml User-agent: * Disallow: /

As the search engine discovers the content of the website, it will be indexed by the use of URLs. It is important that each page on the site has a single, unique URL enabling the search engines to differentiate that page.

18.5.5 Canonical URLs and Redirects

As the search engines try to index the pages they rely on unique URLs as pointers to each page and unique content. The rule should be that there is a single, unique URL for each page, but often web pages can introduce slightly varied URLs for the same piece of content. This results in duplicate URLs in the search engines index. Duplicate content on a site is always a bad thing. A common reason for this is the URL parameters. These parameters are extra pieces of data that are attached to the end of the URL and can be used to perform a variety of different tasks. They can be used for storing tracking parameters or session identification numbers and while the URL is different, the content seen by the search engine is unaffected. The main problem is that the search engines cannot determine which are important for content, and which for tracking. To solve this use

rel="canonical"

in the <link> tag. This tag is added to the website page, with the other meta tags, and it acts as an instruction for the search engines. It tells the search engines that no matter what URL is showing up in the address bar, make sure to use this URL as the primary index for the content on this page. Another way to clean up the URL parameters is to tell the search engines directly through Big Webmaster Tools and Google Webmaster Tools. There the owner can instruct search engines as to whether or not they can ignore certain URL parameters.

Duplicate content can exist if the content has been moved from one location to another. The search engine could have already indexed that new page. Whenever content is moved around it is important to implement redirect rules. There a few redirect parameters that can be used. The first is known as a temporary or 302 redirect. This should only be used for short-term content moves. An example is when some pages are down due to maintenance. It tells the search engine that the page that it is looking for is not presently there, but will return in the near future, and no re-indexing of the page is required.

If the content move is long term situation it is a permanent or 301 redirect. This tells the search engines that although they may have indexed a previous URL for the content, the old URL is no longer valid. The search engine should take all of the information and indexing concerning the old URL, and apply it to the new one.

If you are using WordPress, associating each post with too many tags will result in duplicate content on your site, something that can be viewed negatively by search engines. You can use the 'Simple Tags' plugin to clean up the spammy tags.

18.5.6 Server Side SEO

As much as links and content affect the website's search engine visibility, the web server also plays a role in how the search engines index the site. The main key is to make sure that the pages are being served up fast and reliably. Before committing to any long-term contract, the website owner must talk to the hosting company to make sure that adequate resources are available and that any possible downtime is minimized. The physical location of the server can also affect the visibility the site receives from the search engines. As visitors navigate the website, the search engines often collect data about how fast all of the elements and content are loaded. If a visitor is in one country and the server is located on the other side of the world, the pages may upload very slowly. This is a concern for the search engine, which will see it as a negative.

18.5.7 Google Webmaster Tools

Google Webmaster Tools are terrific and free. The information Google has collected about the website and a few instructions about how to index pages are available here. To use the tool requires an account and it is as simple as registering an email. Once logged in, Google will prompt for a domain name. To protect the new account Google will verify that the account manager actually has authorization to perform critical tasks and see details of this website.

Once the site is verified, the account holder will have access to a dashboard where there will be a lot of very important options. At this point the account manager will have messages of updates and SEO warnings, such as unnatural inbound links. The Crawl Error report is available to see the problems Google had while crawling and indexing the website.

The Search Query report is very powerful. This generates a portrait of the website's organic search visibility. The report will contain impressions, as well as how many clicks have been performed for different keywords and the average position in the SERP over a period of time. The account manager will also want to examine the optimization section. This is where it is possible to look at the HTML Improvements to identify problems with the site's content that can be addressed immediately.

Also use Google Webmaster Tools or Google Analytics to determine the load speed of the site, which is another important ranking factor as Google dislikes pages that take a long time to load. A great alternative tool for this is GTMetrix.

18.5.8 Bing Webmaster Tools

Another powerful instrument is the Bing Webmaster Tools. It is very similar to Google, allowing you to examine the data that Bing has collected about the website and provides Bing with a few instructions as to indexing. The account manager needs an account and site ownership verification.

When adding the site to the tool, the account manager has to verify the site by clicking on the Verify Now link from the My Sites page. The code should be added to the HTML. The Search Keyword report shows the clicks and impressions for each keyword or phrase as well as the average rankings and click through rates over a given period of time. The Inbound Link report displays a graph showing the count of inbound links to the website's pages and the account manager can click on the page to see where the link is originating.

A third report is the Crawl Information Report. Here the account manager can identify any crawl errors that Bing has found. It will also identify any redirects on the website.

Bing also requires a lot of information about the site and this can be entered in the Configure My Site section. Here the XML sitemap can be managed, configuration of URL rules can be completed, suggestions for the crawler can be made and pages can be blocked. The Tool set also has Keyword research and On-page report card.

18.6 Long Term Content Planning

18.6.1 Overview

Before the start of writing content you have to have a plan. This begins with the writer having an understanding of the target audience and what their specific needs are. It is ideal to think of content as bait, and the audience as the fish. If the wrong type of bait is used, or if the correct bait is thrown in the wrong river, that is a mistake. The target fish will not bite. Understanding where the target audience is, where they congregate and chat online, what they are talking about, will all help the writer to locate the targets and what is important to them. Coupling this with a good keyword research plan, the writer should have a strong grasp of the themes and the kind of topics.

When it is time for the actual creation of the content the writer should realize that not writing new, unique and attractive content will eventually make the website's share of the traffic diminish. Every way that the writer can think of to assist the potential customer in making a decision has to be considered as an opportunity.

The quantity of the content is not as important to the search engine as the relevance and quality of the pages. For SEO purposes, the writer has to remember that it is the page content that attracts visitors, establishes and builds links to other websites and ultimately increases the authority of the page in the mind of the search engine.

Once the content has been written an excellent Content Management System (CMS) will ensure that the writers have an easy mechanism to write, edit, post and maintain the content efficiently and quickly. This helps with workflow and collaboration.

18.6.2 Avoiding Common Mistakes

Every website is different. Visitors operate in different environments, have different needs and organizations have different goals. So everyone's ideal content development strategy will be unique.

First a clear definition of the goals and objectives of the content is needed. By recognizing the keywords and phrases that were researched, what the target audience is searching for, and finally what the desired outcome of the site visit is, you have the foundation of the plan. These goals help the writer with reporting and measurement. The goals can be anything, but have to tie back to the business objectives and bottom line.

Secondly, you have to spend time to really identify and understand the target audience and their needs.

The foundation of a good content strategy is to adequately research the target audience and then figure them out well enough to be able to effectively market to them. Thirdly, it is important for everyone involved with the process to buy into the plan.

The next point is that the webmaster has to ensure that everyone in the business upkeeps a healthy respect for reputation management. It is important that you have a well thought out publishing policy. Ultimately the websites reputation will dictate whether visitors will want to do business.

Lastly, you need to spend time monitoring trends. The only thing that is certain regarding the Internet, is that the online marketing arena is constantly changing. Monitoring trends involves not only examining the industry, but also keywords, content structure, and search engine improvements.

18.6.3 Identifying the Audience, Topics and Style

Understanding and defining the website's target visitor is the first step in writing content. From an SEO point of view attracting just anyone to the website is relatively easy. Attracting the right kind of visitor and offering the right items in the correct tone and style is challenging. There are tools that are available that examine online users and build profiles of demographics, and what content they look at.

Users type keywords into the search engines inquiry box. These keywords are the cornerstone of SEO. So when it comes to choosing topics for the content on a page, it is important to tie them to the keywords of the research, based on search volume, relevance and competition. It is also beneficial to use Google Trends to examine the popularity of the topics and match them to industrial trends.

At this point it is worthwhile to employ the idea of filling in the gaps in already posted content. The odds are fairly high that another website has already written content about your new topic, and the last thing the search engines need is more pages talking about the same thing. You can figure out what is missing for the topic and fill in the holes. Monitoring the competitor's content will establish what they are not writing about.

Next is defining the content angles. This is nothing more than the approach to writing the content tailored to be consistent and appropriate to the audience. Is it the content for a technical website for chemists to read or a series of humorous commentaries on the state of the local sports team? There are very different tones for each and above all, you have to remember that while the content is there to support business goals, there is no visitor that wants to read a blatant sales pitch.

When considering how to position and angle the content, you need to consider two more areas of importance. The first is originality. Take time to make sure that the content is unique and brings something new to the table. The next is style. It is important to state that you may have to write a comparative content comparing product A with product B. It may be informative style content or descriptive. Remember content is not just text, and your other tools can be used to make the page more attractive.

18.6.4 Different Types of Content

The misconception is that content is just text on a page. Content takes many forms including text, images, presentations, infographics and videos. It is important to identify exactly what type of content is out there on the Internet. Other file formats are all forms of the content. Word documents, PDF files and presentation slides are types of content that are used every day and can also be published on the internet. If there is a relevant and unique set of slides that was recently presented, why not publish it in the website and share it with the audience. This builds credibility to the site and if it is posted on a hosting service like SlideShare as well, this provides a very strong link for the website.

Images are evolving quickly as their own content standard. Pinterest and Instagram are the main examples that are completely driven by groups of images arranged and commented on by people all around the globe. Search engines, especially Google, are indexing image content and providing SERP that are only image-based. The image search brings a new way of finding and discovering content in of itself.

Infographics are another new piece of content that has gained in popularity. They represent a concept or a large set of data in a visual manner and can help the visitor absorb and understand a lot of information in a meaningful way that can be understood very quickly. Infographics are just image files in the typical type of use and they are usually found on pages that have plenty of text content around them, enabling indexing by the search engines.

Today, video is everywhere due to advances in technology and video production is now so economical that the return on investment is extremely high. Video content can also be optimized for the search engine. By syndicating the video through popular services and properly choosing the title, description, tags, and categories it can be positioned very highly in a search of the targeted keyword. The videos can also be transcribed into text that can be used for close captioning or subtitles. This is also very relevant to the search engines. It is important to link this to a relevant page on the website.

18.6.5 Getting Ideas for Content

Many people find that getting ideas for content can be tough and struggle with it. The first thing to do is to think of the website in the simple terms of some very broad themes and then think of the unique ways that these themes may be presented.

Content can be categorized in a number of ways and thinking about the style that the page can be written in. Procedural content can be a step by step, this is how you do it, type of article that walks the visitor through a certain process. Educational text can be used to inform the visitors how to accomplish some task. This could also teach them something that they did not know before. Informational content does not have to be ground breaking. By just releasing a page of driving directions to the company's store or office, or a page that tells the background of the executives are both highly relevant content opportunities. News is simply a form of informational page that discusses an event that happened at a specific moment in time.

All of these can be applied to a broad array of themes. While in the process of writing content it might help to have the target keywords in the form of a list. The combination of the specific words and phrases and types of content can often lead to the generation of great ideas that are completely relevant.

The second source of ideas and inspiration can come from your analysis of the competitions content to see if they are missing some vital information. This is easily accomplished by performing a quick search of the targeted keywords in the SEO campaign and click on some of the competitor's pages. The competition can also be analyzed via social media. What information are they tweeting or posting? Do they have exclusive access to an important bit of information?

People that are in close contact to the business are the third source of information. These include customers. Customers are often happy to leave reviews and provide feedback if they are asked. From the search engines perspective this can represent both authority and good content. By asking the customer to write a thorough review, with a skeleton provided by you or holding a contest where the customers write about their experiences, is all content that the search engine likes. The same can be applied to vendors and professional review boards, like the Better Business Bureau, and industry or business contacts.

18.6.6 Using an Editorial Calendar

One of the most important parts of the content strategy is the editorial calendar that allows for the proper planning to establish structure and consistency in the contents posted on the website. The editorial calendar simply charts out the content development process, assigning the necessary resources and dates to the topics of pages, post or other content items. The calendar can be created in a spreadsheet and its structure is dependent on the business or website. It should contain a variety of categories, such as page number, SEO tags, code analysis, on-page report cards, content and responsible persons.

18.6.7 Promoting Content via Social Media

The use of social media is a great mechanism to promote content. Social media is still in its infancy and many businesses have jumped into them without really knowing how to effectively take advantage of the features. If social media is a preferred method of promoting the website's content then the top networks have to be used. These networks are the ones with the largest numbers of active users: Facebook, Twitter, YouTube, LinkedIn and Google+. Every one of these sites offers an excellent opportunity to get the content to a larger audience, attract more links and ensure more sharing of ideas.

Millions of companies and websites use an RSS feed to update visitors with changes. This is a form of active subscription to the content. It is possible to perform the same task using social media by placing the various share buttons for each of the networks on the website's pages, allowing the visitors to quickly pass on the content that they have found interesting to their own network. It is important to keep in mind that most of these Share buttons are configurable. The SEO manager can optimize the default tweet to include the websites Twitter name, to encourage recipients to then follow. On Facebook, you can control the default image to be used in the thumbnail.

As use of social media platforms grows, topics can be identified that can be used to guide conversation on the network. On both Google+ and Twitter, hashtags are used to identify certain conversations, and visitors that are interested in these topics can examine the tweets or posts that contain that specific hashtag. Therefore you can build a useful database by uncovering existing hashtags by searching for targeted keywords on Twitter or Google+, about the website's core business, or by following influencers who tweet regularly.

A good point to remember when planning the content strategy is to pinpoint how the plan will share that content across the social network once it has been published. Answer the questions of which networks will it appear on, what is the message, who is going to monitor it and respond to any activity.

18.6.8 Measuring Content Performance

Measuring the performance of the website's content is critical in determining the success of the SEO campaign. When you evaluate the content's performance it is important to ask these questions

- What content are the visitors looking at?
- What is the most popular content?
- Are the visitor's interacting with the content?
- Is the content being shared by the visitors?
- Are quality business results being generated by the content?

To answer these questions it is important to install a free tool, like Google Analytics, to collect the data that is needed. If you are not familiar with the workings of Google Analytics there are a series of tutorials on Google's website and also training videos on YouTube.

The first thing that needs to be examined is the amount of simple page views. When the dashboard is visible you can move into the Content Reports, and a list of the most popular pages of the website will appear. If you want to discover what the most popular landing pages are, a good indicator of popular working keywords, you can filter into the Landing Pages report. If you are an advanced user it is possible to look at Custom Segments to filter out visits from specific search engines or organic searches.

Writing content is easy, but writing content that provides value, relevance and leaves an impression on visitors is extremely difficult. This is why we need to understand the visitor's engagement. There are three sets of data that are available in Google Analytics that can quickly identify how the visitors are using the content. These are *pages per visit*, *average on-site time* and *bounce rate*.

Visitors are considered to be more engrossed with the site the longer their visits last. This can be measured by both the average on-site time and the number of pages they actually view during the visit. The bounce rate is a measure of how often a visitor lands on the website and then leaves it without examining any other page on the site. In general, the lower the bounce rate the more the visitor is engaged in the content of the landing page, and was then persuaded to dive deeper into the website.

The next issue is to evaluate whether the content is being shared online. Google Analytics can be configured to track interactions that are occurring both on and off the website. The tool can track how many times people are clicking the social media sharing buttons or leaving comments on a blog. It can even retrieve the names of public posts across a network that have shared content from your website.

Perhaps the most important question is whether or not all of the website content that is being produced is actually fulfilling the business objectives. A website analytics tool that is configured properly does not just focus on counting the data of the pages, but also associates all of the data with business outcomes.

18.7 Link Building

18.7.1 The Importance of Links

One of the most important aspects of SEO is links. This has by tradition been the backbone of how any search engine operates. As search engines roam the internet and crawl through all of the pages available throughout the world, they look for, and find, links pointing to other pages. This can be interpreted as a vote of confidence in the website. Some sites are considered to be more authoritative and more trustworthy than others. In this weighted view of websites there are really two things that matter -- the number of inbound links and their quality.

Generally speaking, by increasing the website's link popularity, the visibility to the search engines is improved dramatically. The more quality links that are pointing to the website, the more authoritative it will be to search engines. If there are no other websites pointing to yours, it is very difficult for the search engines to trust your site enough to return in the SERP. The search engines will rather show websites in the SERP that have earned links and therefore authority. The website can have all of the links in the world but it will not matter unless these links are of a high quality.

One of the pointers that a search engine looks at to determine the quality of a link is how relevant the link is to the content on the page. For example if you run a recipe website and you have a link to a natural food blog, the search engine has no hesitation in establishing the strength of the link. Now if you go out and contact someone who owns a fantasy sports site to put a link from their site to yours that will not be justified by the search engines.

The search engines will also look at the text associated with the link, known as the link text. The text that a visitor can click on is known as the anchor text and this text serves as a very good clue as to the content of the destination page. If the anchor text says "nice link" or "click this text" then the search engine will not know much about the link until it visits the page, thereby decreasing the quality.

Another indicator of link quality is freshness and trends. The search engines expect you to naturally obtain a steady amount of links over time. If the website has a bunch of links that existed a couple of years previously and there has been nothing new since then, the website's content will be considered stale.

On the other hand there is a technique affectionately known as "black hat linking". If your website has never had any links during its life cycle or there has been no new ones over a period of time, and then there is a pattern of hundreds of new links showing up, on random websites, the search engines are going to investigate the links. They could find out that someone was hired to buy a bunch of links. These meaningless links are termed "black hat". The search engines look on this as spam and do not like to be tricked by this technique. Google went as far as to redesign their algorithms to combat this.

Search engines are now very aware of just about every illegal trick and there are some very real and strict penalties for getting caught. If a search engine locates an extremely large amount of similar links with the same anchor text, or links that appear to have been paid for, or excessive spamming, it is very easy for them to figure out the intent and penalize the offenders. Penalties can range from dropping in the rankings of the SERP to entirely dropping the website from the entire index, therefore making it completely invisible to the internet.

When a link is established to a social media network this is usually due to the fact that the visitor is encouraged by the content. These links are therefore rated highly.

18.7.2 Building Internal Links

When you are attempting to earn links back to the website from elsewhere it is a challenging task. However there are links that you have complete control over which are nearly as important in the eyes of the search engine -- the links to pages on your own site. Internal linking assists the search engine in learning the structure of the website, the themes and topics of the content and the relative importance of each page. Internal linking can be broken down into two types, Navigation links and Contextual links.

Navigational links are typically links that are located on the top, side and bottom of the website pages. They can be thought of as part of the framework of the website. These links are present on every page of the website, and they are used to help guide visitors as they click around the pages, looking for information. The search engines will analyze the navigational links to determine the hierarchy of the pages that funnel down from the home page, and at the same time see how the content is organized, and how flat or deep the website's structure is designed.

Outside of the navigational structure of the website, there are contextual links. These are links within the content of specific pages that point from one page to another. They can be very useful to the visitor when the content of one page makes a reference to the content of another page. Contextual links help the visitors by cross-referencing other relevant information but they also help the search engine. The search engine can examine the anchor text of the internal link to help it understand the content of the page that it is linking to and can build a picture of the topical relevancy between pages, and the importance of the page by the quality of the internal links pointing to it.

When the initial design and development of the website are being undertaken the developer has to make sure to communicate with the SEO manager to decide on the planning of the navigational elements that should be implemented. Also when the content is being written you have to ensure that the contextual links, with good, appropriate anchor text, to other pages are taken advantage of.

18.7.3 Building External Links

It is well understood that building quality links will increase its overall attractiveness in the eyes of the search engine, improve visibility and SERP ranking. Ask yourself how you can make links point to your website when you have no control over them. External links can come in different forms and be generated by using diverse tactics. Backlinks from webpages that contain related content tend to be viewed more favourably.

There are simple ways to get the links. A very common method of creating external links is to submit the website to different web directories. It pays to be careful about the directories chosen for submission. There are a very large amount of spamming directories, and there are very few that are trusted. Check whether the directory reviews links and accepts only trustworthy websites. The Yahoo! Directory is an extremely good place to start. From there you can submit the website to the respective local business directories. If trusted unique industry specific directories and listing services are available, these should be approached next. Some other authoritative directories are DMOZ, Gimpsy, JoeAnt, and GoGuides.:

Google: http://www.google.com/addurl.html
Yahoo: http://search.yahoo.com/info/submit.html
Bing: http://www.bing.com/webmaster/SubmitSitePage.aspx
Open Directory: http://www.dmoz.org/help/submit.html

A second way of building links is to encourage others to link to your pages. There needs to be quality content that other websites are willing to link to. In a perfect world for search engines, someone reads a piece of content and decides that it is so good and creative that they have to link to it. Sometimes great content attracts links naturally as a consequence of someone discovering it and sharing it around.

Other times you have to outreach to get people to discover the content. When new content has been posted you can leverage social connections to share the fact. Try to find other websites that may have the same audience.

It is not only important to generate links from other websites but it is important to also obtain them from social media sharing. Generally, people are very social and are extremely eager to share information that is interesting with family, friends and colleagues. To the search engine this is a signal that tells them what information people love. Therefore it is important to use the sharing buttons on the content pages.

There are some very bad ways to build links and there are severe penalties for doing this. As a general rule, if it feels like the technique is cheating the search engines, then avoid it. By using the "black hat" techniques it is inevitable that you will get caught and the consequences are catastrophic for the website, and are not easily undone.

Another rule of thumb is to know that if the link building is too easy, it is probably going to lead to trouble. Companies that are offering to sell 100 text links every single month or post whatever you want them to on their blog, all for $20, are predators. Do not trade links with people you do not know that have websites or blogs that have absolutely no relevance to your content or directories whose sole purpose is to get more links.

If possible, try to vary the anchor text of your backlinks. You can also try to backlink your backlinks from quality sites to make them stronger.

18.7.4 Building Authoritative Links

Do try to link to other authority sites if they are related. It is a way to let the theme of your website stand out. Do not use NOFOLLOW links as it says that you don't trust the external site, and that you are trying to hoard Page Rank to your own site.

18.7.5 Finding Link Building Opportunities

To decide if the website's pages are trustworthy and authoritative search engines rely on links. Once a status has been reached it is important to always be on the lookout for new link building opportunities. A simple way to find new opportunities is to analyze the backlinks of other websites' rankings for the targeted keywords and phrases. If a separate website has a high ranking for the target keywords then they must have good backlinks from other sites. By then taking a look at these links, there may be some that would benefit your website's ranking as well.

Be very careful if you ever want to engage in two-way or three-way reciprocal-links schemes, as Google may see this unfavorably.

There are a lot of tools available that are able to perform the backlink research. They all work in the same way. The first thing to do is to choose one of the top ranking URLs from the SERP and enter it into the prompt. At first there will be an initial report with a lot of tabs, but the data that is needed will be in the one labeled Inbound Links. In all of the tools available there will be filters that can be set to narrow down the data to show links from only external sources. This means that data will not include links coming from somewhere else on the same site. The goal is to examine these links and determine if they will be a good fit for your website and what strategy could be used to outreach to the owner.

At this stage it is important to remember that you want to build strong, quality links to your own site. It is a must to focus on backlinks with a high page authority or high domain authority. You should have already submitted the website to many high quality directories, but there is a very high possibility that one or two missed, and that they have shown the competitors' data.

Guest blogging is another common strategy. This is where you can reach out to another website and offer to give it content for their blog. This can be a win-win arrangement where the blog gets content that helps their site and visitors, and in return you can include backlinks to your website within the content that they have produced. This not only assists in the backlink strategy, but it can also enhance professional relationships, provide an outlet for thought development and improve the visible status of the website in the business sector.

It is also important to look for links from non-profit sites. Links from these domains are always considered very trustworthy by the search engines. So you should identify some causes that could be important and relevant to the website, and consider promoting them in the content in exchange for backlinks.

Another technique is to produce some educational content to post on the website for the sole purpose of garnering a backlink. There are many websites in just about every industry sector who have the main purpose of promoting business specific educational content. By creating very high quality, informative content that can fill in the gaps in these educational sites, you will gain a network of people and pages that are happy to link to you. Once again this is a win-win scenario, where the third party website gets the benefit of directing their readers to trustworthy content and your website gets relevant backlinks.

There are of course many more strategies that can be uncovered from competitor backlink analysis, and the key is to spend the time analyzing what opportunities are out there, and how you can take advantage of them.

18.7.6 Link Building Strategy Execution

Executing a link-building plan requires precise organization of the outreach program, and a means to check the progress of the gaining of the new links over time. There are a lot of tools that are available for managing the link building prospects and they are similar in operation. Any Link Manager Tool helps you control the efforts of the outreach endeavors, giving the ability to track the progress from the moment the link is identified, until well after it has been added to the website and been used for ranking in the SERP. This information will be used to monitor the link over time, providing status and link value reporting data.

You can also enter the contact information of the people that are being contacted for a particular link, add any additional details around the process, note conversations and overall progress in the <meta> description tag. As link opportunities start to be identified, and relationships are built with people that make the opportunities a reality, you may find that there is a lot of data to juggle at any given time.

As links are gained over time, the important data that will have to be examined is whether or not these links are increasing the overall authority of the website. Again there are tools available, of course at a cost, which can give you a current snapshot of the value of the links. One such tool is Open Site Explorer. You can try Yahoo! Site Explorer too.

(Note that if 100 out of 100 backlinks use the same anchor text, Google would see this as unnatural.)

To obtain backlink historical data, you can use the Backlink History tool. This gives a strong and insightful trends graph that shows how well the outreach program has been progressing. It also has a feature that allows you to compare the website with up to four of its competitors and view what kind of campaign they are running and how yours stacks up against them.

18.7.7 Understanding Google Penguin

11 Feb 2011	Panda update
24 Apr 2012	Penguin
25 May 2012	Penguin 1.1
5 Oct 2012	Penguin 3
22 May 2013	Penguin 4 / Penguin 2.0
26 Sep 2013	Hummingbird
4 Oct 2013	Penguin 5 / Penguin 2.1
21 May 2014	Panda 4

Early in 2012, Google released a new version of its search algorithm and affectionately named it Penguin. Since that first release there have been several updated versions, each more particular than the last. As linking is the most important aspect of the Penguin updates only this will be discussed here. Penguin can be thought of as Google refining and changing its evaluation of links. This has been in development for years to circumvent the "black hat" technique explosion and is now at a very powerful stage where it can figure out what links to a website are real and which ones are fake.

(Note that one can see a website's Google PageRank by downloading the Google toolbar at http://toolbar.google.com and choosing the Display Google PR option. Mozilla Firefox has a similar plugin called SearchStatus.)

These changes are very specifically related to Google's webmaster guidelines. Google stated that the updates were intended to decrease the rankings for websites that it believed were in violation of Google's quality procedures. These quality procedures state quite clearly that you should not "participate in link schemes designed to increase your site's ranking or PageRank. In particular, avoid links to web spammers or 'bad neighborhoods' on the web, as your own ranking may be affected adversely by those links." By link schemes, Google specifically refers to these types of things.

- Links that are intended to specifically affect the Page Rank.
- Links to spammers or bad Internet neighborhoods.
- Too many reciprocal links and link exchanging between sites.
- Trading links that pass Page Rank. This means Google does not care if you buy or sell nofollow links, but they object to the purchase or selling of follow links.

Another recent development is that Google has been issuing messages through the Webmaster accounts warning people that their incoming links appear to be unnatural or artificial. A spokesman from Google has recently stated that although in the past they would quietly distrust such links (that is, just downgrade the value of the links or ignore them entirely), they are now informing webmasters that these are bad. This is presumably to discourage people from using such links and to force the link networks out of business.

Presently Google has stated that Penguin itself only affects about 3% of internet searches, so that most websites are really not affected. This implies that when a site is damaged, it is really due to egregious on-page problems, like keyword stuffing, garbage anchor text attached to outgoing links and no relationship to incoming links.

There is a lot of debate and speculation in the SEO community, from a linking perspective, about just how Penguin actually deals with links. Unfortunately much of this is exaggerated. Some analysts have examined the things that penalize sites and assume that everything they do must be bad, which in itself is terrible logic.

Google has stated that they actually make it extremely difficult for individuals to hurt other websites, but it does happen every now and then. The developers of the algorithm at Google are very intelligent, so they realize that punishing websites based on incoming links is simply an invitation for more spam, and the less ethical business owner will start attacking their competitors with spam links. This can be in the form of signing the competitor up with a link program that creates thousands of spam links instantaneously.

So the question arises, "Is Google actually penalizing sites for having bad links pointing at them?" Most of the SEO experts say the answer is no, although there are some in the SEO community that have taken Google's statements and turned them into something completely different. As a result the community has seen a couple of things happen.

First of all, some website owners are beginning to threaten other people with legal action if they do not remove links pointing to their websites. Secondly some owners of really bad websites are extorting money from other site owners by refusing to remove the links unless they get paid for the task.

Basically, all of these may be an overreaction to Google's actual statements. As mentioned, most of the experts do not think Google will be penalizing websites based only on linking, except in the really extreme case where the owner of the website is laying games and there are issues with both the links and the on-page factors.

Nonetheless, what is actually going on with Google's linking algorithms and how can you keep the website out of trouble? The first way is obvious. As Google states in its guidelines, it does not like to see links from any website that are to bad neighborhoods or spammers. By this, they essentially mean links to various kinds of link networks, systems that promise you hundreds, if not many thousands of links to your site very quickly and very easily. Secondly, you may use Google Disavow Links Tool to specify inbound links you want blocked and identify them.

Google specifically warns about links from your website to these networks due to the fact that if they see those links they know that the site is involved in bad linking. It is imperative to avoid any kind of program in which you have to provide links to the network in exchange for links from the network. Also avoid programs that create tens of thousands of links or that maybe involved in link manipulation. Excessive reciprocal linking programs should also be avoided and do not sell links pointing from your site to others, unless they are no follow links, as the website will be penalized.

Also you may want to examine and evaluate the website's overall link profile. If the website gets hundreds of links in a few days, that is a major problem. If all of the links are highly keyworded, that could potentially be a problem. You know the significance of keywords in content and links, but if almost all of the links are highly keyworded (if they use only one or two keywords or phrases), that is a problem because it looks unnatural to search engines and to Penguin in particular. Natural linking is likely to include various different phrases with a group of domain links and even "click here" links thrown in sparingly. You need a wide variety of different types of links as well; directories, blogs, websites, forums and social networks. If the links are predominately coming from one type of origin that looks unnatural to Penguin. If Penguin thinks these are unnatural you will get an unnatural linking message from Google. The first thing to do is try to remove them. If this is not possible, reply to Google telling them that the linking site will not remove them and let them deal with it.

Overall, when dealing with Penguin use commonsense. Examine updates and message in the Google Webmaster Tools site and be proactive to any messages that Google may send you.

Be careful when using automated links building tools as they can hurt the ranking of our website. Remember backlinks should come from authoritative sites.

18.8 How to Measure SEO Effectiveness

18.8.1 Measuring SEO Performance

One of the biggest challenges is trying to evaluate whether the SEO campaign is succeeding or failing. SEO measurement not only involves the analysis of metrics like traffic that results from organic search engines and specific targeted keywords, but it also requires a universal approach to measuring business objectives and making adjustments based on the data.

Before you can get any data for the campaign, an analytical package has to be installed. The preferred industry tool is Google Analytics (Yahoo Web Analytics and Adobe Web Analytics are alternatives), and it is free. You will want to invest some time and resources into making sure that the web analytics tracking is implemented and configured properly and recording data accurately.

Ensuring a robust implementation will make the collected data trustworthy enough to use it to make confident, evidence-based decisions. Once you have started collecting the data, the business objectives and the key performance indicators (KPI) that will be used to measure them have to be defined. Remember that there will be a lot of goals for the website, and that means that there will be a lot of KPIs to continually monitor and improve. You will also want to establish some SEO specific KPIs that can help understand how the SEO efforts are paying off. Things like:

- Organic search traffic, or visits to the website from search engines that are not generated by paid search, but organic listings.

- The total organic search traffic compared to a previous timeframe, like month-over-month or year-over-year.
- Non-branded keyword searches, or searches where your brand or your business name was not part of the search term.
- Targeted keyword rankings, or how well the website ranks for each of the targeted keywords.

Although attracting traffic to the website through the SEO campaign is valuable, it should be noted that it is equally important to see what that traffic does when it gets there. When the SEO campaign analyzes traffic that comes from a certain search engine as a result of a certain keyword search, and lands on a certain landing page, you should also start to look at how that traffic converts on the business goals.

It is important to make sure that all of the business goals are being measured so that you can look at the conversions and conversions rates from the traffic the SEO campaign is generating. Ensuring that the correct data is being collected, reporting on your KPIs in a meaningful way, and analyzing the data to really understand what's happening with the SEO strategy, are a solid foundation. Measuring and improving the SEO campaign over time are a continuous cycle of measurement, learning, and taking action. You want to use the data to learn what changes can be made to the strategy, and once those have been made, the campaign will start the cycle over again by measuring whether or not those changes produced an improvement.

18.8.2 Analyzing Keyword Performance

You have to know that keywords are the backbone of search engine optimization, and when the SEO efforts are being measured, analyzing the different keywords that are bringing people to the websites is an excellent place to start. When the user is inside Google Analytics it is very easy to navigate to the Organic Search Traffic report. This report shows all of the targeted keywords that have driven traffic to the pages from the organic search engines.

You should be looking at general site usage metrics. When examining the different keyword rows in the report you can see that a certain targeted keyword keeps visitors on the website much longer than others.

It is not only the SEO goals of the keywords that can be analyzed, but also the online marketing efforts. Once you have set up the goals, they will be able to click on a specific goal and see how the keywords are performing with respect to that business objective. If the analytics are set up for eCommerce you can also look at data regarding transactions for each of the targeted keywords.

When analyzing keyword reports, read only the data for visitors who found the website through a click on your link in the SERP. What that means is that Web Analytics tool is not a very good indicator of what opportunities the business is missing out on. If the site does not rank for a keyword, no one is going to be clicking on a SERP for the site, and no data for those missed opportunities will ever show up here.

It is also possible to link the Google Analytics Tool to the Google Webmaster Toolkit. In the Webmaster Queries report, you can find data on impressions, the average rank position and click through rates. This report is still accurate enough to get some valuable insights based on the trends rather than the raw numbers. One item to look for are keywords that have high impressions, but low click-through rates. This means that the website might be showing up in the SERP, but no one's clicking on the listing. This could mean that there are problems with the title, or maybe the description, and it's worth taking a closer look.

18.8.3 Analyzing Link Performance

Over the course of time, if you are diligently showing quality information, advertising it through a campaign, and utilizing link outreach opportunities, others will link back to the website. The link portfolio can show you exactly how the campaign is faring in the attempt to prove to the search engines how authoritative and trustworthy the website is.

Good tools allow you to analyze the links in any website, not just the one the business owns, and gives the obvious advantage of looking at competitor's backlinks, creating new link opportunities. However, in the process of studying your own backlinks, you will desire metrics that can inform you how your link building endeavour is. By utilizing tools like OpenSite Explorer and Cemper, you can obtain a report on domain and page metrics for any URL. A list of the pages linking back to that website can be seen too. These tools allow you to identify all links pointing to your site and evaluate them from the perspective of website quality and anchor text.

What can also be seen are the total number of links into any page, and the unique number of originating domains. You can also read some public social metrics. What you hope to do here is to make a habit of checking these numbers. The main objective here is consistent progress.

A more authoritative website is more able to influence rankings. A growing link portfolio results in increasing authority scores. Noting only the backlinks from external pages, you can check each link coming back to the website and act on any areas focused.

In any case, knowing the linkers to the website and the way they are doing it, can help you control the link building endeavour. You can also make the process automatic by setting up a campaign to create a history report from the Link Analysis section of the OpenSite Explorer. This will give graphical reports comparing the website to competitors. Alexa.com allows you to measure the fame of websites based on the activity of those using the Alexa toolbar.

Backlink History Reports are available from the Majestic SEO tool. This report shows the number of links that have been obtained on a monthly, cumulative or normalized basis. This can be used to know how the link portfolio has expanded. Besides, you can add up to four competitors' websites to set up a comparison.

18.8.4 Analyzing the Impact of Social Media

SEO experts have been testing social sharing and how search engines may be handling this in their algorithms to rank pages. Google has stated that they do in fact use social media signals to determine rankings. To understand this it is important to examine a few ways to measure how the content is being shared and identify the most sharable content on the website. It is important to look at what has worked in the past, so that you can make improvements in the future. There are lots of tools to measure and manage social media, but one the best to take a look at is called Social Crawlytics.

This tool can be used to audit the pages and see how many shares from a variety of social channels are pointing to the website. Social Crawlytics covers eight social media channels: Facebook, Twitter, YouTube, Delicious, LinkedIn, StumbleUpon, Digg, Google+, and Pinterest. Depending on how deep your site structure goes, you may need to adjust the crawl depth from two to three or four. This tool will only crawl HTML content pages, so keep in mind that if you have other types of files on the website, they will be discarded from the report.

The Summary tells you how many times the website's pages were shared, up to the depth that was specified for the crawl. At this point you can see the number of shares of the number of pages of the website's content that was scanned. The page shares per network bar chart breaks down all of the pages crawled, and shows you which channels were most active.

Having this data to look at, as you continue to create and promote content on the website's pages, can help determine how useful and shareable the content is.

If you want your photo to appear beneath your search result, so that a visitor is more likely to click it, you should sign up for Google Authorship. You can also upload your photo at Gravatar to personalize your comments everywhere etc.

Another technique is called social bookmarking. It involves posting articles to sites like Digg.com, Reddit.com, Delicious, Folkd, Diigo, and StumbleUpon and have the sites linking back to your website. However, you should vary the content of these articles as duplicates can be viewed negatively by search engines. When someone likes a post there, they can share it so that others see it, thereby producing a chain reaction for backlinks.

In addition to social bookmarking sites, there are article directories like WordPress.com, Tumblr.com, Hubpages.com, Livestrong.com, Ask.com, Ezinearticles.com, and Livejournal.com, where you can publicize your sites.

Lastly, you can also try press release sites like Prweb.com and Prnewswire.com.

18.9 SEO for eCommerce

18.9.1 SEO and eCommerce

There are a lot of people who use search engines for shopping research, whether they're in the early stages, or they're ready to buy something. Whatever part of the buying process they're in, the site is going to want to be found, and there are a few different SEO components to consider that are specific to eCommerce websites.

Remember that everything that applies to normal content also applies to eCommerce pages. The best practices around website linking structures, external links, and on-page optimization are very important. As search engines want to explicitly identify content at the most granular level of detail, you will want to make sure that they are very clear that the eCommerce content is exactly that. Beyond the typical HTML code that is found on web pages, you can use very specific metadata to help identify the content as eCommerce and describe the products that are being offered.

You must make sure to analyze the keyword research to determine what intent people have when using certain keywords, and what content they're looking for. If people are searching for comparisons between the website and its competitors, then you might consider building content specific to that need. For inquirers typing in keywords that indicate that they are further down the purchasing process, like "buy product X" or "product Y coupon," you will want to ensure that the content that is being created contains an easy path to the shopping cart.

One more thing that's unique to eCommerce is that the products that the website sells are often being discussed outside the bounds of the website. You can find discussions on forums, social media, or other websites about the products that the website sells, and these can be opportunities to engage in the conversation as a knowledgeable product expert. If someone is posting a review of their experience with your site, you can use tools like Google Alerts or Social Media Monitoring Tools to make sure you are aware of it. Good or bad, it's an opportunity for you to listen and join the conversation.

If people are expressing negative feelings about the website or product, you can reach out to them and resolve the situation in the public eye. On the other hand, if people are saying good things about your products, reach out and say thank you. It could lead to more links in the social media as well as user generated content.

18.9.2 Semantic HTML

eCommerce sites and most other websites are different. eCommerce sites have very specific information on very specific products. To allow search engines to understand these bits of information, the web designer can take advantage of micro-formatting. The eCommerce site will have product pages which should be using the products schema. The designer can describe for a product the name, the description, the image, the brand, the manufacturer, and the model information.

You can also relate your products with offers, which have many properties that you can populate. This could be how much a product is selling for, the current quantity of a product in the stock, the condition of a product, the expiry date, or the rating. This will allow content to be written by customers in the form of reviews.

Besides, the website can display information about the business locations. Micro-formats can be used to define the physical address. You can also show a map, the contact information, and the business description.

18.9.3 Technical Components

Websites that are eCommerce in nature are special because they keep changing due to the product inventory. They are usually big, which can result in more technical issues. When running an eCommerce site, you need to beware of and do certain things..

If the website is not selling a product temporarily, make sure the page is left intact with a correct message. If it is no longer sold permanently, the product URL should return a 'not-found' page, with a status code of 404 and a related message. You should include navigation and search bars so that any visitor landing there can continue to shop at your website.

You should set up a 301 permanent redirect if a product page has moved, possibly to a different section. You should inform search engines of the move and the new destination.

To let search engines discover your new content, you should generate and submit an XML sitemap of all your URLs. Almost all eCommerce platforms can dynamically create these XML sitemaps. Remember to place the **rel="canonical"** <link> tag on each of the pages, so that search engines are indexing only unique URLs. Many eCommerce platforms has such a feature and it can be enabled and configured.

Finally, an eCommerce site often uses paginated content. If there are 30 products for a category, only 10 may be displayed per page. You can use the **rel="next"** or **rel="prev"**, to tell search engines not to view the linked pages as unique pages.

18.9.4 Information Structure

Search engines need to understand how the eCommerce content is organized. By organizing the website with a good content structure, eCommerce pages and the products will be clearly recognizable. Bear in mind that internal linking is important for letting search engines understand the site structure.

As a person walks into a store in the physical world, the person will find it organized into different sections. All eCommerce websites should use links to create that structure.

You can create a hierarchy of categories and subcategories, to let search engines return the most relevant results. Each product should have its different page, and on each of them you will need to include the relevant information. You can associate a product with a name, an image, a description, a color, a size, a price, its availability etc.

Adding special metadata to your code allows the search engines to identify such information even more clearly. Remember to include the categories, the subcategories, and the product pages in the XML sitemaps. You can even tell search engines which pages are more important by assigning weights to the pages.

18.9.5 Producing Content

The content of an eCommerce site should attract the search engines so that the pages can be found. Once the website has been visited, the content needs to encourage people to buy the products and share the information through links and social media.

Most writers want to simply describe a product, but consumers want more. Revisiting Marketing 101, you actually sell solutions to people's problems and requests. Describe beyond the product. Describe its usage, through various media, to let the customers know how an item works. If the competition is not doing fine, then zero-in some very unique information.

The customer has the option of reading through reviews from people just like themselves. As consumers tend to trust these reviews, showing product reviews or service testimonials helps people comprehend the value of the products.

Lastly, remember to add product recommendations. If the eCommerce platform has this feature, use it. If not, consider the product recommendation engines on the market. This can be a great way to cross-sell.

18.9.6 Link Building and Social Media

Create really good content. A site becomes more shareable if it takes the extra step to show how the product will solve problems.

Apart from videos and diagrams, you can create interactive features at your website. Examples include putting together an entire wardrobe and generating a living room. These special features tend to be shared and get blogged about. It is also important to create high quality images, for they can attract links back to your site.

News about free items and discounts can spread like wildfire. Show deals and coupons, run a contest or a sweepstakes, or even offers up a loss leader. Just get people talking about the website.

Make your users produce content in the forms of reviews, follow-up emails, testimonials, or social media integrations. This attracts links and sharing, and helps other customers.

Remember also to add the standard social media sharing and liking buttons!

18.9.7 International Visitors

When the target audience originates from different cultures, you should consider translating and regionalizing the website content. You shouldn't just dump the site into Google Translate and copy and paste the text. You should invest in good translation, as only then the search engines will return relevant content matching the user's language. You should have a different URL for each translated version of the site.

You can help search engines identify the target language and country by providing specific metadata on the pages. This can be done with the **hreflang** link element. You can use these link tags to tell the search engines that these are translations of the same page.

18.10 Local Search

18.10.1 Understanding Local Search

If you have fixed offices and stores, or if you have a local presence, then it is important to note that your potential customers are using search engines to look for local products and services. Search engines are good at giving users exactly what they want, with very specific local types of search results.

If you are in Phoenix with a toothache that needs some immediate attention, you are likely to find an internet connection, then a search engine, preferably Google, and start typing "dentist phoenix". In the SERP you will see a list of businesses in the Phoenix area matching your search. On the SERP there will be some special listings with location markers and a map that shows you where all those businesses are located. When you click on that marker, you end up in a maps interface, showing a map of the area surrounding the business, and information and reviews.

For each business listing that you see, you can either click the link to the website, or head over to the Google+ Local page of that particular business. On the page you can find reviews, photos, and even see who in your social circles has had anything to say about that business. The bottom line is that if you are a dentist in Phoenix and you do not have this kind of local listing on the search engines, your phone isn't likely to be ringing.

How do you position yourself to have your business featured in these special local search results? First of all, there are a few things that you can do. You are going to need to have a Google+ Local page. If you are not on Google+ yet, this is a good time to start, and you can walk through the process of setting up a Google+ account and a Google+ Local page for your business. If you had a Google Places account, it has already been migrated to Google+ Local for you, and you can simply log in and make any updates or changes to leverage the new format. Do not forget to ask your customers for reviews on your Google+ page. The more reviews and the more positive they are, the more likely Google will rank your pages highly.

Next, understand the concept of citations. Each and every mention that search engines find around the web of the name, address, or phone number of your business is regarded as a citation. Getting more citations from quality sources make the search engines trust that this is a business searchers are actively trying to find.

Also, the website is a critical piece of your local marketing strategy. You will want to make sure that you have separate pages on the website for each service or category of products that are on offer, and will want to make sure that the business' name, address, and phone number, are clearly identified on the website. Remember the content strategy that was developed, and make sure that the pages have the relevant keywords to ensure optimal local search performance.

18.10.2 Understanding Google+ Local

Google+ Local, which used to be Google Places, gives you a well-developed online listing for free. When a business listing is created on Google+ Local, you can provide basic information, photos, address etc. Customers can leave reviews, and you can also get to see statistics about your visitors and the searches that they have done to bring them to your page. All of this is only going to be seen if your visitors can find the page. There are essentially three things that determine rankings on Google+ Local: distance, and prominence, relevance.

Relevance is all about how much your listing matches a searcher's term. In most cases, the more complete and accurate a business listing is, the easier it is for Google to properly understand your business and return its listing in the search results.

The second factor is distance. Local searches are tied to a geographic location, and Google uses what it knows about a searcher's location. The search engine then attempts to return the best matches based on the listings there. In many cases, larger metropolitan areas are divided into smaller parts, so you will need to consider how you choose to list your business in Google+ Local. You want to think about how locals will be typing in their inquiries, and mimic that as best you can. If the business is located in multiple locations, you should make individual listings for each, to increase your exposure on the SERP.

The prominence of the listing has an effect on how well it will rank. Prominence is a measure of how famous your business is in the Internet, and much like regular content pages, the search engine looks for evidence around the web that others are talking about you. Important SEO items like links, reviews, articles, blogs, directory listings, and any other mentions about your business are all considered, and generally, the more positive these mentions of your business are, the better.

To maximize your chances of ranking well in local search results, just remember these three things:

- Make sure that your listing is as complete, accurate and relevant to your local searches as possible.
- Make sure that you define your distance from searchers by defining the exact area or areas that your business serves.
- Work on building your brand, customer relationships, and loyalty to earn prominence around the web.

18.10.3 Optimizing Google+ Local

It is important to list your business on Google+ Local so it can appear in the Google Local search results, and the first step is to visit www.google.com/placesforbusiness. When signing up for Google+ Local, it's a good idea to create multiple Google accounts to deal with your listings. This account should really be tied to your corporate domain. Something like local@yourdomain.com will keep your business account tied to the business and separate from your personal account.

After logging in for the first time, you will be prompted to enter your phone number, and Google will tell you if it already knows about the business. If Google does, it will pre-fill whatever information it has found. This is the last chance to provide as much information as you possibly can to Google about the business, so you will want to fill out all the required fields and as many optional ones as is possible.

Start out by entering your company name in the Company/Organization field. Avoid adding keywords here to obtain a higher rank. Remember that consistency across your citations is extremely important to local search rankings, so this can actually hurt you, and it is also against the terms. As consistency in your name, phone number and address is so curcial, it can be helpful to ensure that there is a default that you are using everywhere you can.

The next stage, which is critical, is choosing the categories under which you're going to list your business. Category suggestions will appear as you begin typing, and you will want to choose one of the suggested categories if you can. You can select up to five categories. The Service Areas and Location Settings section asks whether your customers come to you, or you go to your customers. You can also enter your operating Hours and the Payment options that you accept. Generally, you will want to provide as much information as you can throughout your listing. Images and videos are a great way for you to showcase your business to potential customers, and really show them exactly what they will be getting if they choose you.

After you have filled out the form, you need to verify your business listing before it will go live. Google+ Local will send you a PIN verification code, either by mail at your business address, or by a phone, and once you receive your PIN, you will need to enter it into your Google+ Local account to verify that you actually do own the business.

Once your listing is online, you can always come back to edit it or add photos, videos, or anything else that has not already been added to the listing.

18.10.4 Getting More Citations

It is extremely important to have accurate information on the Internet. If your information is incorrect, it can hurt the chances that people will find the business, and that is not good for you. The more a search engine can trust your location information, the more confident it will be in returning your pages to the local searcher, and for this reason, citations are extremely important.

A citation is any display of your business name, address, and phone number on the internet, and this combination of information is often referred to as NAP for short. Beside from having as many as possible on quality sites, citations should also be exactly identical everywhere. You should check how your business looks on lots of directory websites by visiting getlisted.org. GetListed is a site that provides information on local search, and you can use their tool to find out how well your business is listed online by entering your businesses' name and postal code. GetListed will then look up the listing across a host of different popular directories, and give you a listing score that tells you how well you have used the free listings search engines used to collect local search data.

Another wonderful part of GetListed is their studies on local citation sources for each city and category, found in the Learning Center area. These will tell you which local citation sources are the most popular in each city and for each business category, and they can be very helpful in finding specific listing sites that you will want a citation from.

Another tool is the Whitespark Location Citation Finder tool. Here, you can research and manage all of your local citations in one place. You can search by either Keyphrase or a Phone Number, and wait for the tool to generate a list of suggestions on which local directories you could use for this business. You can get a list of lots of potential citation sources you may want to go after.

18.10.5 Getting more Reviews

Online reviews are a major asset, especially for the local search. Recent marketing studies have proven that positive reviews make customers more likely to use a local business, as well as that they trust these reviews as much as personal recommendations. If the business is not getting reviews online you're missing out on a huge opportunity.

A review is a short write-up or a rating, provided by a customer based on their experience with a particular business. Reviews can be found on search engines, local review websites and services, or even blogs. There are basically three ways a user can provide a review of your business: offline, email, or website.

Many businesses communicate with their customers' everyday through phone calls, physical mail, or in-store interactions. Every one of these offline interaction points is an opportunity to ask customers what they thought of their experience. The business can also use negative feedback to help improve the business, and turn the positive feedback into testimonials that can be used on your website or in promotional materials.

If the website is still not collecting email addresses of visitors that want to subscribe to your newsletter or find out more about you, you are missing out on a huge marketing opportunity. Creating, maintaining, and growing a list of your customers and those who are actively interested in becoming your customers give you an extremely useful and valuable asset. Not only can this list be used to inform and market to a very qualified audience, it can also allow you to send out invitations to obtain customer satisfaction surveys, or automate a post-purchase email that asks for, or even provides an incentive to, leave a review for the product or service that the customer has just purchased.

The third way you can get reviews is on websites. And while that might be your own, it is becoming more and more likely that users are going to be using other websites to review you, your products, and your services. The business owned website is where you have the most control over your content, and you should consider creating a section dedicated to testimonials and sharing the experiences of past customers. This is an opportunity to host user-generated content that search engines will rate very high.

Provide an area where users can submit reviews directly on your pages. Whether this is built into the site directly, or you embed one of the many third-party review solutions, you will never get any reviews if you do not ask. Apart from your own pages, there is an ever-growing list of sites out on the internet that cater to collecting user reviews for all kinds of products, services, and businesses. Persuade your happy customers to write reviews on major business listing websites like Google+ Local, Yahoo Local, Yelp, Citysearch, and more.

18.10.6 Website Optimization

When analyzing the pages of your site, Google and other search engines use a number of different signals to decide which pages show, and in what order, when a user types in a search query. When you are optimizing for local search, there are some specific items that you want to focus on.

The first is on-page optimization and content. Every page of your website should be optimized for a specific, well-researched keyword, and you will need to make sure that you are leveraging the important elements from a technical standpoint. At a bare minimum, make sure you spend time optimizing your page title, your meta description, your heading tags, body text, and ALT text on each of your images. At this point in the chapter, this should be nothing new, but now we can talk about some things specific to local search that can help you out.

First, your contact information is going to be especially important, and there are some specific things you need to put on your Contact Us page, in some specific ways. You can find specific schema elements that make sense for your type of business. You have a contact page that shows your name, a description of your business, your address, and your phone number. By adding some tags in the code and explicitly defining these items through the markup defined at schema.org, you'll be telling search engines exactly what type of information each piece of text represents.

Forgetting the human visitors is a huge mistake. You will want to make it easy for them to contact and connect with you through forums and social media. Your business information should always be in the bottom right-hand corner of your footer on every page. This is a very common place that users are conditioned to look for contact information, and it will ensure that they can find your information quickly from any page of your site if they want to contact you.

You have to consider that people are not just searching for you on their desktop PCs anymore, they are also searching with mobile devices when they are not at home or in the office. And much of this on-the-go searching is with local intent. By owning a site that looks good and functions on mobile devices is something that will not only serve you well with the search engines responding to search queries on mobile devices, but will also ensure that your users have a positive experience with you and your site, regardless what device they're using. Google's GoMo program allows you to get a look at how your website looks on a mobile device, and it can scan your site and make recommendations on how you can improve your page's mobile performance. If you have resources or programming expertise, you might choose to address some of these issues by creating a separate site exclusively for your mobile users on a separate domain or sub-domain. Or better yet, you might choose to use a responsive design that adapts to whatever size of screen your website is being rendered on from a single code base. If you are looking for a quick solution and you have a static website, you can take advantage of a partnership that Google has with Duda Mobile to create a quick and dirty mobile version of your pages right from the GoMo site.

The bottom line is that many of your local customers are using mobile devices, and if your site does not provide the information your mobile visitor needs, or if it crashes their browser, you've probably lost a potential customer.

18.10.7 The Future of Local Search

The SEO community knows how people use search engines to find places, things, and businesses in a constant state of change. As technology has improved, local businesses have gained more and more ways to reach their customers, and the pace of change is only going to speed up in the future. The most prominent trends nowadays are social media and mobile devices.

Google+ Local is a great example of social media working with mobile devices to deliver local content. GPS and cell tower signals are used to determine the users' locations. The mobile users can download iPhone or Android apps that connect them to their Google+ account. From there they can find local businesses based on their current location, and read reviews from other users. Visitors can also directions to a local business from wherever you are, by various means of transport.

In addition to Google+, people are using blogging services like Twitter from various devices. They are visiting locations on networks like Foursquare, getting more information about a product, and scanning QR codes to redeem coupons. Each of these means presents an opportunity.

18.11 International SEO

18.11.1 Cultural Aspects

Opening your website to people across the globe is more challenging. Do not forget that people use different search engines in different countries. While US-based searchers generally use Google and Bing, those in other countries use different search engines. Just think of Baidu in China, and Yandex in Russia. Moreover, search engines usually have geography-specific layout, language and content.

For the purpose of international SEO, as a first step, translate and regionalize your website. This will cost some time and resources but it will be a worthwhile investment. There are excellent translation services out there. Equally important is creating new URLs for different languages, and providing navigation allowing users to switch languages.

A language can have varying flavors, dialects, and cultural differences, depending on the geographical locations. After setting up the regionalized pages, you must take a look at the data gathered in your web analytics solution, to see which search engines are driving what kind of traffic to which regionalized sections of your site.

18.11.2 Optimizing Technical Content

Structuring your website is very important for international SEO when you have different languages and localizations of your content, and there are some technical things you can do to your pages to help search engines find, and understand the different internationalized sections of your website.

First, determining where to place your translated content is an important step. Some organizations structure their multilingual websites by placing different translations in different subdomains. For example, you might place your Spanish version of the site on es.yourdomain.com. Other websites will place the content in different subfolders like yourdomain.com/es. Both methods are effective in establishing a different storage site of content dedicated to a certain language, and they both have risks and advantages.

While using different subdomains allows you freedom in implementation, since it can be considered a completely different website, it also brings the risk of not taking advantage of the overall link value of your main domain. Using subfolders to house your multilingual content eliminates this risk, and it brings the full strength of your domain to bear, but it may be challenging to implement different site frameworks this way, depending upon how your ecommerce platform is set up.

Next, make sure to explicitly tell search engines what language and region the content is targeted to by using a hreflang link tags on your pages. These tags will tell a search engine where each internationalized version of the page is located by specifying each of the URLs, along with the language and country targets. You can be more specific by adding country targets as well. If you had one version of the page targeted to French-speaking Canadians for example, you could modify this tag to include both the language and the country code.

Also be sure to use rel="canonical" tags on each language-specific version of your content pages. This can be especially important when you have similar content targeted to different countries within the same languages.

You can avoid duplication problems by explicitly calling out the unique URLs of each piece of content in each language. As long as you determine a scalable structure to house your different international content, and you apply the appropriate location, language, and canonical tags, search engines will have an easy way to determine which languages and countries each of your content pages are intended to serve.

18.11.3 Optimizing Translated Content

When you translate and localize a website's content for different countries and languages, you are essentially creating another website. This means that while you can certainly leverage a lot of the work you have done for your primary language, you will need to go through and create an entire keyword and content strategy from scratch, for each of the different languages.

Starting with the foundation of keyword research, you will want to go through this process in the language you are optimizing for, and come up with language-specific lists of keywords that you can map to the content you are translating. It is possible to start out with translations of some of your top primary language keywords, but remember that many words and phrases do not translate directly between languages.

Once you have done the research and have a solid understanding of your translated keywords, you will be ready to start the translation process. The first step is mapping the pages of your site that you will be translating to the appropriate keywords you will be targeting from your localized research. Once you know what keyword each of your pages will be optimized for, you will need to ensure that whoever is doing the actual translating understands the basic principles of technical, on-page SEO. Titles, headings, and the body are extremely important, and knowing what keywords you are writing or translating for up front will ensure that you are creating content that is optimized for the right target terms, right from the beginning.

Lastly, you will want to evaluate whether or not you need regionalized content within a certain language. Knowing your customers and your business, along with looking at your website analytics data, and consulting people who understand the cultural nuances of each region will help you determine how to write your translated content.

18.11.4 Links for Global Audiences

Search engines do consider regional factors. One way they determine the user's region is by analyzing the back links. In other words, if you hope to optimize your Chinese pages for a Chinese audience, you will be better off creating links from Chinese websites. Focus on websites that operate in the countries you are targeting. It helps to ensure their back links are associated with that target region.

The top 100 search results in one country can vary a lot from the top 100 results in another country. Make sure you are using international versions of the search engines when researching a keyword. If you find difficulties with a foreign language and cultural norms, you should find a resource that has that expertise.

18.11.5 Analyzing International SEO

Google Analytics allows you to filter your reports or make sections to each language-specific sub-domain or subfolder. You can also set up individual profiles for each. This will allow you to configure your international sections differently from one another. You may detect crawl problems affecting one part of the site only.

You can use tools like SEOmoz Campaigns to view ranking data. There you can enter a list of keywords to be tracked on a geo-specific search engine. It will let you see how all your keywords perform for search engines across the world.

18.11.6 International SEO Pitfalls

Although performing International SEO gives you an opportunity to find new foreign markets and engage with people all across the world, it can be a complicated process with pitfalls that can hurt your progress. These are some things to watch out for, and while doing it the right way might take more time and resources upfront, it will be worth the effort in the long run.

You are going to want to steer clear of auto translated content. While auto translation techniques have progressed much, it is still not nearly as good as a competent human translator. An actual person can truly interpret and craft a message that gets the point across in a way that's appropriate to a region and a culture. Auto translated content can be unnatural and awkward, and while some may appreciate the effort, many will view it as a negative, or a clear sign that you're not serious about them.

Watch out for how words and phrases are translated and used in other countries or languages. In the US, an English-speaking American might search the term "car insurance" to get some car insurance quotes. If you were to translate this keyword phrase directly into French, you might end up with "assurance auto". And although it's a valid translation of the phrase, in French-speaking Canada, people will not really recognize it.

And what if you're renting cars? If the English version of your site is talking about car rentals, and you decide to expand to the UK, you better know that in London you can "hire" a car just as easily as "rent" one. These are the nuances that you'll start to find as you do regionalized keyword research, and having someone that understands your target region and language will be invaluable to you as you go through this process.

Next, do not fall into the trap of just translating whatever you can and slapping it up on your pages. While mixing languages on a single page is really confusing to a search engine, even separate pages within an unclear structure can hinder the search engine's ability to find and understand your content. Take the time to plan out your regionalized versions of your website, and develop clear navigation that will help search engines correctly group your content by language and region. You can further help the search engines by using metadata to define language and location targeting, and spending the time and resources to go through these steps will ultimately help your international search engine visibility.

Lastly, make sure that you really internationalize your site for the audience you're targeting. Just as with any business, make sure that you've done the market research to truly understand the international opportunity, as well as how to speak to the specific audience around the needs that your products and services are fulfilling. Your number one priority is to provide your users with the best experience possible, and if you make an effort to create a quality user experience for your differentiated, translated, and regionalized content, it will result in improvements in your global search engine visibility.